New York Yankees

Yankee Stadium, One East 161st Street, Bronx, NY 10451 • (718) 293-4300

2011 NEW YORK YANKEES MEDIA GUIDE AND RECORD BOOK
Official Publication of the New York Yankees

Produced by the Yankees Media Relations Department: Jason Latimer, Michael Margolis, Lauren Moran, Kenny Leandry, Jason Zillo, Alexandra Trochanowski and Germania Dolores Hernandez.

Contributors and Special [...]  [...] ensa, Ken Derry, Kristina Dodge, Elias Sports Bureau,
Ariele Goldman, Tom Hirdt, Ian [...] Morante, National Baseball Hall of Fame and Museum,
James Petrozz [...] [...] Tapper, Nick Tyrell and David Vincent.
Photos throughout book [...] etty Images, Photo File and the Library of Congress.

Layout and Design [...] om, (402) 613-2177; Cover Credit: Ian Johns
[...] (732) 767-1320

Note: The publication date of this guide is February 15, 2011. All individual splits have been omitted in accordance with a league mandate.
Additional or updated information is available through the Yankees Media Relations Department.

Table of Contents

In memory of our friend Bill Shannon (1941-2010)
Official Scorer of approximately 800 Yankees games from 1979-2010

*"Personally, I cannot attend a baseball game without keeping a scorecard.
In my experience, doing so makes the game more meaningful,
because you can observe events within the framework of knowledge."*

–Bill Shannon from his book *Official Scoring in the Big Leagues*

i

George M. Steinbrenner III
1930-2010

New York Yankees Directory

Yankee Stadium, One East 161st Street, Bronx, NY 10451 • (718) 293-4300

Managing General Partner* / Co-Chairperson, New York Yankees .... Harold Z. Steinbrenner
General Partner** / Co-Chairperson, New York Yankees .... Henry G. Steinbrenner
General Partner‡ / Vice Chairperson, New York Yankees .... Jennifer Steinbrenner Swindal
General Partner‡‡ / Vice Chairperson, New York Yankees .... Jessica Steinbrenner
Vice Chairperson, New York Yankees .... Joan Z. Steinbrenner
Executive Vice President / Chief International Officer, New York Yankees.................................... Felix M. Lopez, Jr.
*of Martinique Holdings, Inc.   ** of Bellaire Holdings, Inc.   ‡ of Marsh Harbor Holdings, Inc.   ‡‡ of JJS NYY Holdings, LLC

YANKEES FAMILY
Jerry Cohen, Daniel M. Crown, James S. Crown, Lester Crown, Ike S. Franco, John Freund, Peter Freund, Marvin S. Goldklang, Robert Gorman, Sharon Halper, Jon Hanson, Donald Keogh, Louis A. Lamoriello, David Levinson, Don Marron, Daniel R. McCarthy, Patrick McCarthy, Roberto Mignone, James Murdoch, Thomas Murphy, James Nederlander, James L. Nederlander, Robert E. Nederlander, Mort Olshan, Michael Price, Bill Rose, Edward Rosenthal, Howard Rubenstein, Jerry Speyer, Beth Wilf, Leonard Wilf, Orin Wilf

EXECUTIVE
President .... Randy Levine, Esq.
Chief Operating Officer..................................... Lonn A. Trost, Esq.
Senior Vice President, General Manager..................... Brian Cashman
Senior Vice President, Baseball Operations .... Mark Newman
Vice President, Assistant General Manager .... Jean Afterman, Esq.
Senior Vice President, Strategic Ventures................ Marty Greenspun
Senior Vice President, Chief Security Officer .... Sonny Hight
Senior Vice President, Corporate/Community Relations .... Brian Smith
Senior Vice President, Corporate Sales & Sponsorships .... Michael J. Tusiani
Senior Vice President, Marketing .... Deborah A. Tymon
Senior Vice President, Yankee Global Enterprises CFO... Anthony Bruno
Vice President & CFO, Accounting............................ Robert B. Brown
Deputy General Counsel, Vice President, Legal Affairs........... Alan Chang
Vice President & CFO, Financial Operations................... Scott Krug

BASEBALL OPERATIONS (NEW YORK)
Senior Vice President, Special Advisor....................... Gene Michael
Special Assistant to the General Manager .... Gordon Blakeley
Senior Director, Pro Personnel .... Billy Eppler
Director, Mental Conditioning .... Chad Bohling
Director, Quantitative Analysis .... Michael Fishman
Director, Team Travel & Player Services..................... Ben Tuliebitz
Assistant, Professional Scouting .... Will Kuntz
Assistant, Baseball Operations .... Steve Martone
Systems Architect... Brian Nicosia
Research Assistants, Baseball Operations.... David Grabiner, Jim Logue, Alex Rubin
Special Advisor .... Yogi Berra
Special Advisor .... Reggie Jackson
Special Assistant to the General Manager .... Tino Martinez
Special Assistant to the General Manager .... Stump Merrill
Administrative Assistant...................................... Mary Pellino

FIELD STAFF
Equipment Manager .... Rob Cucuzza
Clubhouse Manager .... Lou Cucuzza Jr.
Assistant Visiting Clubhouse Manager .... Lou Cucuzza Sr.
Advance Scout/Head Video Coordinator .... Charlie Wonsowicz
Video Coordinator .... Anthony Flynn
Bullpen Catcher.. Roman Rodriguez
Baseball Operations Coaching Assistant .... Brett Weber

MEDICAL AND TRAINING STAFF
Team Physician .... Christopher Ahmad, M.D.
Senior Advisor, Orthopedics........................ Stuart Hershon, M.D.
Head Athletic Trainer....................................... Gene Monahan
Assistant Athletic Trainer .... Steve Donohue
Strength & Conditioning Coordinator .... Dana Cavalea
Massage Therapist .... Doug Cecil

ACCOUNTING
Manager, Ticket Accounting .... Jeff Kline
Payroll Administrator....................................... Kathy Bennett
Payroll Clerk .... Maria Jordan
General Ledger Accountant .... David Saltmarsh
Accounts Payable Clerk................................... Raymond Soriano

COMMUNICATIONS & MEDIA RELATIONS DEPARTMENT
Director, Communications & Media Relations .... Jason Zillo
Assistant Director, Media & Player Relations .... Jason Latimer
Assistant Director, Baseball Information & Public Communications... Michael Margolis
Coordinator, Baseball Information .... Lauren Moran
Coordinator, Media Relations and Publicity .... Kenny Leandry
Assistant, Media Relations and Publicity .... Alex Trochanowski
Administrative Assistant.................... Germania Dolores Hernandez

CORPORATE/COMMUNITY RELATIONS
Director, Corporate/Community Relations .... Rocky Halsey
Manager, Fulfillment, Corporate/Community Relations .... Dan Weiss
Executive Assistant, Corporate/Community Relations ...... Jennifer Hansen

CORPORATE SALES & SPONSORSHIPS
Director, Sponsorship Services........................ Nicole Arceneaux
Director, Corporate Sales & Sponsorships .... Bryan Calka
Manager, Corporate Sales & Sponsorships .... Chris Insolera
Manager, Corporate Sales & Sponsorships .... Elizabeth McGuire
Account Manager, Sponsorship Services .... David L. Cohen

Senior Account Representative, Sponsorship Services .... Janine Fortunato
Account Representative, Sponsorship Services .... Jesse Zousmer
Account Executive, Corporate Sales & Sponsorships .... William Beatson
Account Executive, Corporate Sales & Sponsorships .... Jennifer Renzulli
Administrative Assistant, Corporate Sales & Sponsorships ...... Wanda Edwards
Special Advisor, Corporate Opportunities .... Lee Mazzilli

CREATIVE SERVICES
Director, Creative Services .... Kara Mooney

EXECUTIVE DEPARTMENT
Counsel.. Rachel M. Cohen
Director, Financial Operations .... Adam Raiken
Senior Analyst, Financial Operations .... Allison Kluger
Executive Assistant.. Stephanie Fullam
Executive Assistant.. Monica Pisacano
Legal & Financial Assistant............................. Melanie Bernstein
Administrative Assistant.................................... Amy Ficke

HUMAN RESOURCES
Coordinator, Human Resources............................ Alanna Gold

LATINO AFFAIRS
Director, Latino Affairs.............................. Manuel Garcia, Esq.
Senior Coordinator, Latino Affairs................... Vanessa R. Rodriguez

MARKETING, PROMOTIONS & SPECIAL EVENTS
Assistant Director, Promotions, Event Production & Broadcast Marketing .... Craig Cartmell
Assistant Director, Marketing, Events & Fan Development ...... Rob Bernstein
Assistant Director, Marketing and Advertising .... Gregory D. King
Senior Coordinator, Promotions & Special Events.............. Robert Blum
Coordinator, Marketing & Fan Services.................... Elizabeth Molloy

MUSEUM
Museum Curator.. Brian Richards

NON-BASEBALL EVENTS
Director, Non-Baseball Events .... Emily Hamel
Director, Program Development............................ Mark Holtzman
Senior Manager, Non-Baseball Events...................... Gina Chindemi
Manager, Non-Baseball Events............................ Anne Vanderwal
Manager, College Football................................ John Mosley
Assistant Manager, Non-Baseball Events .... Sarah Barker
Coordinator, Non-Baseball Events........................ Greg Marino
Coordinator, Non-Baseball Events....................... Lesley Urivetsky

PREMIUM SALES & SERVICES
Executive Director, Premium Sales & Services .... Troy Tutt
Manager, Premium Services .... Caryn Dolich
Manager, Premium Sales .... Chris Chopey
Manager, Inside Sales .... Dan Rosenthal
Director of Hospitality, Premium Sales & Services .... David Bernstein
Manager, Suite Services .... Samantha Giraud
Manager, Premium Marketing .... Adam Herr
Senior Manager, Premium Sales and Service .... Mark Gennarelli
Account Executives, Premium Sales and Service ....
Rose Barre, Scott Cabaniss, Kyle Hutchinson, Mike Lahaie,
Erin Legg, Jeff Rosenberg, Odette Ross, Yao Williams
Coordinator, Contract Administration...................... Nick Pizzutello
Coordinator, Premium Operations......................... Kate Scanlon
Coordinator, Premium Services........................... Monica Krips
Sales Associates............... Bryan Avolio, David Benoit, Patrick Dempsey,
Michael Ferris, Jordan Gustafson, Kyle Holtsinger,
Reid Mobley, Mario Oliveri, Catherine Ryan, Kelli Sinclair
Coordinator, Luxury Suites .... Beatrice O'Neill

PUBLICATIONS
Director, Publications .... Alfred Santasiere III
Managing Editor, Publications.............................. Ken Derry
Senior Editor, Publications............................ Kristina M. Dodge
Senior Photography Editor, Publications .... Ariele Goldman Hecht
Associate Editor, Publications......................... Nathan Maciborski
Senior Coordinator, Publications........................ Craig Tapper
Writer/Blogger, Yankees Fan Club....................... Jack O'Connell

SCOREBOARD & BROADCASTING
Senior Director, Scoreboard & Broadcasting............... Michael Bonner
Senior Producer, Scoreboard & Video Production....... Nima Ghandforoush
Producer, Scoreboard & Video Production .... Gregory Colello
Manager, Scoreboard & Broadcasting .... Brett Moldoff
Senior Producer, Yankees on Demand...................... Pete Gergely
Producer, Yankees on Demand........................... Brandon Mihm
Public Address Announcer .... Paul Olden
Organists .... Paul Cartier, Ed Alstrom

SECURITY

Executive Director, Team Security.....................Edward Fastook
Executive Director, Stadium/Event Security..............Todd Letcher
Manager, Security Systems Administration.............Matthew Deane
Team Security...Mark Kafalas
Security/Dock Master.................................Robert Gomez
Stadium Security......................................Joe Flannino
Executive Security ....Mike Fitzgerald, James Mennuti,
George Olynyk, George Readding, Robert Schnebly

STADIUM OPERATIONS

Senior Director, Stadium Operations.....................Doug Behar
Stadium Superintendent.................................Pete Pullara
Director, Stadium Development.........................John Palmer
Director, Archives & Records Management...............Tom Barbagallo
Director, Disabled Services & Guest Relations..........Carol Laurenzano
Assistant Director, Stadium Operations.................Robert Passaro
Head Groundskeeper..................................Dan Cunningham
Manager, Stadium Operations.........................Anthony Odierno
Office Manager......................................Debbie Nicolosi
Coordinators, Disabled Services & Guest Relations.....Jamie Colvard, Aaron Pickus
Coordinator, Stadium Operations........................John Papp
Systems Coordinator, Stadium Operations..............Amanda Ivory
Administrative Assistant...............................Josephine Doring
Records Coordinator, Archives & Records Management......Andra McCartney
Mailroom*..David Cervantes, Gerarl Johnson
Reception.............Madeleine Calderon, Danilda Hiraldo, Lena Macchia
*Employed by The Millennium Group, Inc.

TECHNOLOGY

Senior Director, Technology.............................Mike Lane
Systems Administrator...........................Ryan Vilar de Queiros
Systems Engineer...................................Frank Valletutti
Systems Developer..................................Eddie Coblentz
Technical Services Coordinator........................John Klippel

TICKET OPERATIONS

Senior Director, Ticket Operations......................Irfan Kirimca
Executive Director, Ticket Operations..................Kevin Dart
Manager, Season Ticket Sales & Service..............Charles Johnson
Manager, Ticket Operations...........................James Traynor
Assistant Manager, Ticket Operations...................Scott Liller
Business Coordinator, Season Ticket Sales & Service........Valerie Fava
Ticket Office Representatives................Hank Grazioso, Dan Hansbury,
Jessica Holohan, Patrick McLoughlin, Edwin Ruiz
Group Sales Representatives........Frank Costa, Carlos Gomez, Rosa Muniz
Telephone Representatives................Betsy Colon, Simone Moragne,
Stuart Powell, John Terhune
Account Executives, Season Ticket Sales & Service........................
Steven Aprill, Tyson Christensen, Ken Cleary, Seth Conley, Drew Fox,
Nick Fugazy, Jessica Gincel, Joe Leva, John Markiewicz, Adam Skolnick

TOURS & HISTORY

Director, Stadium Tours.................................Tony Morante
Assistant Manager, Stadium Tours.....................Lindsey Spierer
Tour Coordinators.......................Jessica Cerone, Nick True Palmer

---

PLAYER DEVELOPMENT AND SCOUTING
Yankees Complex • 3102 N. Himes Ave. • Tampa, FL 33607
PHONE: (813) 875-7569
FAX: (813) 873-2302

MAJOR LEAGUE SPRING TRAINING FACILITY
George M. Steinbrenner Field
1 Steinbrenner Dr. • Tampa, FL 33614
PHONES: (813) 879-2244 • (800) 96-YANKS
FAX: (813) 879-0247

BASEBALL OPERATIONS (TAMPA)

Vice President, Amateur Scouting....................Damon Oppenheimer
Vice President, Player Personnel.......................Billy Connors
Director, Player Development........................Pat Roessler
Coordinator, International Player Development...........Pat McMahon
Assistant Director, Baseball Operations.................Eric Schmitt
Assistant Director, International Operations.............Alex Cotto
Assistant Director, Amateur Scouting..................John Kremer
Equipment Manager, Player Development..................David Hays
Clubhouse Manager, Player Development.................Chris Root
Clubhouse Assistant, Player Development...............Eddie Rivera
Director of Information Systems........................Rob Owens
Pitching Coordinator................................Nardi Contreras
Hitting Coordinator.................................James Rowson
Defensive Coordinator...............................Torre Tyson
Catching Coordinator................................Julio Mosquera
Special Assistant, Player Development & Scouting..........Jack Hubbard
Video Coordinator..................................Adam Czajkowski
Assistant, Player Development.......................Yunior Tabares
Coordinator, Mental Conditioning....................Chris Passarella
Coordinator, Cultural Development....................Hector Gonzalez
Chinese Interpreter.................................Tim Wei Ting Lin
Administrative Assistant.............................Jackie Williams
Receptionist..Linda Cotney

INTERNATIONAL BASEBALL OPERATIONS

Director, International Scouting......................Donny Rowland
Director, Latin American Scouting.......................Victor Mata
Director, Latin Baseball Academy......................Joel Lithgow
Manager, Latin Baseball Academy....................Aniuska Sanchez
Assistant, Latin Baseball Academy....................Romey Caballero
Latin American Scouting Coordinator...................Ricardo Finol
Clubhouse/Equipment Manager..........................Raudo Baez
Clubhouse Attendants...................Jose Guillen, Ambiorix Ozuna

---

MEDICAL AND TRAINING STAFF (TAMPA)

Team Physician, Tampa...........................Andrew Boyer, M.D.
Team Orthopedic Surgeon, Tampa....................Allen Miller, M.D.
Team Chiropractor, Tampa...........................Scott Hegseth, D.C.
Head Athletic Trainer, Player Development............Mark Littlefield
Strength & Conditioning Coordinator..................Mike Wickland
Asst. Strength & Conditioning Coordinator..............Javier Alvidrez

ADMINISTRATION (TAMPA)

Executive Vice President.............................Philip A. McNiff
Senior Vice President, General Counsel................Norman Stallings
Vice President, Marketing...........................Howard Grosswirth
Vice President, Community Relations...................John Szponar
Vice President, Administration.........................Diann Blanco
Vice President, Operations.............................Dean Holbert
Vice President, Risk Management......................Therese Jenkins
Sr. Security Officer/Special Advisor....................Curtis Lane
Director Security......................................Bill Navarra
Assistant Director, Security......................Nicholas Oppedisano
Stadium Supervisor.................................Ronnie Kaufman
Controller..Derrick Baio
Director, Payroll....................................Newton Linebaugh
Director, Accounting..................................Kevin Adler
Director of Information Technology.....................Rudy Ramirez
Head Groundskeeper................................Ritchie Anderson
Assistant Head Groundskeeper..........................Jeff Eckert
Grounds Supervisor, Player Development...............Chris Connell
Director, Ticket Operations............................Brian Valdez
Assistant Director, Ticket Operations............Jennifer Magliocchetti
Manager, Stadium Services...........................John Sibayan
Director, Florida Operations, General Manager, Tampa Yankees...C. Vance Smith
Assistant General Manager, Tampa Yankees............Matthew Gess
Director, Fantasy Camp.............................Julie Ko Kremer
Community Relations Consultant.......................Ray Negron

TAMPA STAFF

Miguel Amezquita, Steven Ansaldi, Mike Ansotegui, Eric Baio, Gabriel Baker,
Jose Gonzalez Batista, Benjamin Beiro, Brett Boggs, Michael Breden, Kevin
Brown, Aaron Butler, Robert Carbonelli, Christine Carey, John Carredero,
Rolando Chavez, Nicholas Chisolm, Brad Delaosa, Donald DePalma Jr.,
Kimberly Diaz, Richard Di Maio, Luis Duran, Allison Ennis, Matthew Farrar,
Dawn Galuska, Laurie Gaydos, Timothy J. Guidry, Francisco Hernandez,
Juan A. Hernandez, Milagro Hernandez, John Johnson, Holly B. Kelley,
Michael Krautheim, Jessica Lack, Bryant Leonard, Candido Lopez, AmySue
Manzione, Ralph Martinez, Denise Maurer, Joanne Nastal, George Narvaez,
Matthew R. Nixon, Robert Nixon, Gonzalo Noy, Giacomo Parisi, David
Peery, Charles Poole, Doris Recinos, Tom Reynolds, Sylvia Rivera, Josh
Roach, Christian Ruiz, Jenette Sibayan, Joe Sigismondi, Shannon Stein,
Tony Sustaita, Matthew L. Szponar, Robert Testo, Romuald Thibault,
Aquilles Torrealba, Jason Valentin, Jamie Ventura, Jeremy Ventura, Charles
Vissicchio, Robert Vliet, Charles Woodruff, Katie Woytisek, Krystal Woytisek,
Karl Yost, Marilyn Yost.

LEGENDS HOSPITALITY, LLC
Corporate Mailing Address
614 Frelinghuysen Avenue • Newark, NJ • 07114
PHONE: (862)-902-5450 • FAX: (862) 902-5475
Yankee Stadium Mailing Address
Yankee Stadium • One East 161st Street • Bronx, NY 10451

LEGENDS STAFF

Chief Executive Officer..............................Michael Rawlings
Chief Operating Officer..................................Dan Smith
President and Chief Customer Officer................Marty Greenspun
Chief Financial Officer................................David Hammer
Vice President, Finance.............................Jim Sheppard
Vice President, Facilities.............................Jon Muscalo
Vice President & Corporate Controller................Mark Pizzariello
Senior Vice President, Yankee Stadium...............Michael Phillips
Executive Assistant to the Senior VP................Kathleen Kincel
General Manager, Merchandise......................Michael Loparo
Director, Retail Operations...........................Bradley Wilton
Merchandise Warehouse Manager....................Saeed Ramsaroop
Retail Manager, Luxury Suites.......................Anthony Bergamo
General Manager, Concessions.....................Anthony Parnagian
Administrative Assistant, Concessions....................Erin Nargi
Concessions Warehouse Manager.........................Shiv Ally
Assistant Warehouse Manager......................Nathaniel Edelman
Concessions Managers..............Chris Buffa, Joseph Slomski
Vending Manager..................................Leonard Middleton
Utility Manager.......................................Chabbilal Robert
In-Seat Manager.....................................Amanda Robbins
General Manager, Fine Dining.........................Don Muszalski
Executive Chef..Kevin Harry
Executive Sous Chef.................................Matthew Gibson
Suites Chef..Patrick Wood
Manager, Bars......................................Max Resomardono
Manager, Catering & Mohegan Sun Sports Bar...........Jaisun Ihm
Suites Manager......................................Amanda Wood
Manager, Legends In-seat Service & Champions Lounges.......Mia New
Manager, Legends Suite Club....................Margaret Ann Quinlan
Director, Human Resources.........................Kerry-Ann Cowan
Manager, Customer Service........................Kathleen Petrones
Assistant Managers, Human Resources......Jennifer Hayes, Kevin O'Connor
Assistant, Human Resources...........................Austin Mably
Controller..Mark Garramone
Assistant Controller...................................Don Croce
Accounts Payable...................................Kenya Kendricks
Payroll...Michael Zagorski
IT Specialists........................Matthew Block, Joseph Goerlitz
Accountant...Richard DeJesus

September 11, 2001

10th Anniversary

It was 10 years ago that the worst terrorist attacks in our nation's history took place on September 11, 2001. The New York Yankees remember all of the men, women and children who lost their lives or had their lives changed forever by that tragic Tuesday morning.

That evening the Yankees were scheduled to host the Chicago White Sox at 7:05 pm with Roger Clemens going for his 20th win of the season. However the original Yankee Stadium would remain silent after a morning of destruction and terrible loss in New York City, Arlington County, Va., and Shanksville, Penn.

Heroes from all walks of life pulled together that day, with many giving the ultimate sacrifice.

At the urging of President George W. Bush, Americans tried as best they could to return to the normal fabric of their everyday lives. Baseball, the most American of institutions, played a major role. One week after the attacks, the Major Leagues resumed its schedule with the Yankees on the road in Chicago vs. the White Sox.

Yankee Stadium reopened for baseball on September 25 with the Yankees hosting the Tampa Bay Devil Rays. In front of a packed Stadium, the Yankees held a "Tribute to America" prior to first pitch, including a rendition of "Taps," followed by the Harlem Boys Choir performance of "We Shall Overcome." Michael Bolton then sang "Lean on Me," before "God Bless America" was performed. Police, firefighters and emergency workers lined the field with Yankees players as Challenger, the bald eagle, was walked to the mound and Max Von Essen, the son of Fire Commissioner Thomas Von Essen, sang the national anthem. Wearing caps from the NYPD and FDNY, the Yankees lost an emotional game, 4-0, but still managed to clinch the AL East division title that evening thanks to a Boston loss.

A service in honor of the missing and dead was held at Yankee Stadium on September 23, 2001. Hosted by Oprah Winfrey and James Earl Jones, *A Prayer for America* included performances by Placido Domingo ("Ave Maria"), Bette Midler ("The Wind Beneath My Wings"), Lee Greenwood ("God Bless the U.S.A.") and the Harlem Boys Choir ("We Shall Overcome"), as well as remarks from New York City Mayor Rudolph Giuliani.

The drama of the 2001 postseason provided a welcome distraction from the heartache. Though the Yankees would eventually fall in Game 7 of the World Series to Arizona, the club took pride in its role in the nation's healing process.

> *"We play because this is what we do. We play because of the higher purpose that we try to accomplish as a part of society, and we play also because we're grateful that we're alive."*
>
> *– Bernie Williams*

A monument in memory of the victims and heroes of the 9/11 tragedy was erected and dedicated on September 11, 2002 in Yankee Stadium's Monument Park.

A flag from the World Trade Center flew over Yankee Stadium during the 2001 World Series.

> *"This massive attack was intended to break our spirit. It has not done that. It's made us stronger, more determined and more resolved. The bravery of our firefighters, our police officers, our emergency workers and civilians we may never learn of, in saving over 25,000 lives that day, and carrying out the most effective rescue operation in our history, inspires all of us.*
>
> *"New Yorkers are strong and they are resilient. We are unified, and we will not yield to terror. We do not let fear make our decisions for us. We choose to live in freedom."*
>
> *– Rudolph Giuliani, New York City Mayor, 1994-2001*

Yankees™
Everywhere

News, Stats, Scores
Get all the info you need to stay
on top of the Yankees in 2011.

Tickets
Find season ticket packages,
single games, promos,
giveaways and more.

Shop
Buy your favorite
Yankees gear
and collectibles
at the Official
online Shop.

Watch Online
Catch Yankees games online LIVE
or on demand with a subscription
to MLB.TV® or MLB.TV Premium
(blackout restrictions apply).

Mobile
Follow all the action with real-time scores,
LIVE audio, in-game highlights and more on your
smart phone with MLB.com At Bat™ 2011, available
for various mobile devices and on your PC.

yankees.com
™

© 2011 MLB Advanced Media, L.P. Major League Baseball trademarks and copyrights are used with permission of the applicable MLB entities. All rights reserved. Photos: Getty Images.
All screen images simulated. iPhone and iPad are registered trademarks of Apple Inc. All rights reserved.

Harold Z. (Hal) Steinbrenner
Managing General Partner /
Co-Chairperson

Hal Steinbrenner begins his 21st season with the New York Yankees organization in 2011 and his third as Managing General Partner / Co-Chairperson. On November 20, 2008, Major League Baseball formalized Mr. Steinbrenner's role as the New York Yankees' managing partner.

Under Mr. Steinbrenner's leadership, the Yankees have retained and enhanced their global popularity while continuing to field championship-caliber teams. In 2010, the franchise led Baseball in home and road attendance, combining to draw 6,595,941 fans while reaching the postseason for the 15th time in the last 16 seasons (1995-07, '09-10). In his first full year as Managing General Partner in 2009, the Yankees capped their historic inaugural season in Yankee Stadium with their 27th World Championship.

The 42-year-old son of George Steinbrenner was elected General Partner by the New York Yankees Partnership in 1996, and he held that title for 13 seasons. In 2007, Mr. Steinbrenner was also named Chairman of Yankee Global Enterprises, LLC.

Along with General Partner / Co-Chairperson Hank Steinbrenner, his responsibilities include overseeing all areas of the club's business and baseball operations, and directing financial aspects of the New York Yankees, Yankee Global Enterprises and affiliates. In addition, he serves on the Board of Directors for Legends Hospitality, LLC, a concession and merchandising company developed with the Dallas Cowboys, which operates at the Yankees' and Cowboys' new stadiums.

Mr. Steinbrenner is also Chairman and CEO of Steinbrenner Hotel Properties and holds a seat on both the Board of Directors of the Boys & Girls Club of Tampa Bay and the Special Operations Warrior Foundation.

Mr. Steinbrenner attended Culver Military Academy and graduated from Williams College in 1991 with a Bachelor of Arts degree. He earned a Master's degree in Business Administration from the University of Florida in 1994. Mr. Steinbrenner and his wife, Christina, currently reside in Tampa, Fla.

Henry G. (Hank) Steinbrenner
General Partner / Co-Chairperson

Hank Steinbrenner begins his fourth season as General Partner and third season as Co-Chairperson of the New York Yankees. Along with Managing General Partner / Co-Chairperson Hal Steinbrenner, the 53-year-old son of George Steinbrenner is responsible for overseeing all areas of the club's business and baseball operations.

Prior to the 2008 season, Mr. Steinbrenner was directly involved in the delicate negotiations and eventual re-signings of Yankees All-Stars Jorge Posada, Mariano Rivera and Alex Rodriguez, while guiding the managerial search that concluded with the hiring of former Yankees catcher and bench coach Joe Girardi, who led the club to the 2009 World Series title. Mr. Steinbrenner was also part of the collaborative front office effort of the 2008-09 offseason, which led to the signings of free agent first baseman Mark Teixeira and pitchers CC Sabathia and A.J. Burnett, who helped propel the club to the 27th championship in franchise history.

Mr. Steinbrenner has served as Chairman and Director of Minch Transit Company, Vice President and Director of Bay Farms Corporation, Vice President and Director of Mid-Florida Hotels Corporation, and has been a member of the board of the Ocala Breeders Sales Company. In the Tampa Bay community, he has been involved in a number of children's charities.

In 2010, Mr. Steinbrenner sponsored and supervised "Hank's Yanks," an 18-and-under summer league baseball team comprised of teenagers from a variety of socioeconomic backgrounds in the New York community. The team—in their first season—captured the championship of Yaphank, Long Island's "Baseball Heaven" league and also won the inaugural "Boss' Cup" game played at Yankee Stadium.

Mr. Steinbrenner attended Culver Military Academy and Central Methodist College. He is the father of four children and resides in Tampa, Fla.

Hot Ticket

The Yankees drew 3,765,803 fans in their second season of play in Yankee Stadium in 2010, marking the highest home attendance for any Major League team in 2010...the Yankees also led the Majors averaging 46,491 per game, surpassing their home attendance figures for the 2009 regular season (3,719,358 total/45,918 per game)...marked the eighth consecutive season the Yankees led the AL in attendance (2003-10)...the organization also led the Majors in road attendance (2,830,138)...the Yankees' combined draw of 6,595,941 fans topped the American League for the 12th consecutive season. The Yankees currently own five of the six largest single-season attendance totals in professional sports history, including the all-time mark of 7,325,051 fans in 2006. In addition, the Yankees are the only Major League franchise to reach the four-million mark in home attendance in four straight seasons, accomplishing the feat from 2005-08.

HIGHEST SINGLE-SEASON HOME AND ROAD ATTENDANCE

Attendance	Club	Year	Total Attendance (Home, Road)
7,325,051	New York Yankees	2006	(4,243,780 – home; 3,081,271 – road)
7,249,285	New York Yankees	2007	(4,271,083 – home; 2,978,202 – road)
7,178,421	Colorado Rockies	1993	(4,483,350 – home; 2,695,071 – road)
7,149,137	New York Yankees	2008	(4,298,543 – home; 2,850,594 – road)
7,088,291	New York Yankees	2005	(4,090,692 – home; 2,997,599 – road)
7,083,958	New York Yankees	2004	(3,775,292 – home; 3,308,666 – road)

Jennifer Steinbrenner Swindal
General Partner / Vice Chairperson

Jennifer Steinbrenner Swindal begins her third full season in the role of General Partner / Vice Chairperson of the New York Yankees. In 2008, Ms. Steinbrenner held the title of Senior Vice President of New Stadium Public Affairs. The elder daughter of George Steinbrenner previously served in the Yankees Public Affairs Department in 1984-85 prior to spending 23 years actively participating in the philanthropic community.

Her present responsibilities include the implementation and integration of various community programs relating to Yankee Stadium. In addition, she serves in a supervisory role for the New York Yankees and Tampa Yankees Foundations, overseeing numerous local, regional and national outreach efforts.

Ms. Steinbrenner has a distinguished record of contributing to community projects and initiatives, including current commitments on the Florida State Fair Authority (Executive Committee, Agricultural Committee, and Chairwoman of the Marketing Committee), Board of Directors of Mary Lee's House (a child protection and advocacy center in Tampa), Board of Directors and Executive Committee of the H.B. Plant Museum, Board of Directors of the New York Pops, and Advisory Committee for the Tampa Salvation Army. She has also held prior board positions with the Children's Cancer Center of Tampa, Boys & Girls Clubs of Tampa Bay, Florida Orchestra, Red Cross of Tampa and Culver Academies.

A Morehead Scholar and 1981 graduate of the University of North Carolina with a Bachelor of Science degree in business administration, Ms. Steinbrenner continues her commitment to the university, serving on the UNC Board of Visitors and the Parents Council. Her daughter, Haley, received her undergraduate degree from UNC in 2008, and her son, Stephen, is currently a senior there.

Ms. Steinbrenner was born in Cleveland, Ohio, and makes her home in Tampa, Fla.

Jessica Steinbrenner
General Partner / Vice Chairperson

Jessica Steinbrenner begins her third full season as General Partner / Vice Chairperson for the New York Yankees. The younger daughter of George M. Steinbrenner previously served in the role of Senior Vice President for the team in 2008.

In addition, Mrs. Steinbrenner serves as the Chief Executive Officer of Bay Farms Corporation and serves on the board of the Florida Thoroughbred Breeders' and Owners' Association. She has also authored two children's books: *My Sleepy Room* and *My Messy Room*.

She attended Culver Girls Academy and graduated from Sweet Briar College in Virginia. Mrs. Steinbrenner currently resides in Tampa, Fla., with her husband, Felix, and her four children.

Joan Z. Steinbrenner
Vice Chairperson

Joan Steinbrenner holds the position of Vice Chairperson of the New York Yankees. Mrs. Steinbrenner was married to Principal Owner George M. Steinbrenner from 1956 until his passing in 2010.

Mrs. Steinbrenner has participated in many community projects and supported numerous philanthropic organizations. Among her many dignified community roles, she was named State Chairperson for the Florida Special Olympics in 1981 and 1982, and for two years was on the Board of Directors of the National Society to Prevent Blindness. She was also a charter member of Town and Gown, established in 1977 in an effort to form a bond between community supporters in the downtown Tampa area and the University of South Florida.

In addition, Mrs. Steinbrenner was a longtime board member for Children's Home, Inc., and was one of the original members of the H.B. Plant Museum Society. From 1991 to 2000 she served on the Development Council of St. Joseph's Hospital Foundation Board. She currently is a member of the Junior League of Tampa, the Chiselers, and sits on the Board of Directors for the Florida Orchestra.

A graduate of Upper Arlington High School in Columbus, Ohio, and Ohio State University, Mrs. Steinbrenner earned a degree in dental hygiene. She currently resides in Tampa, Fla., with her four children and 13 grandchildren.

Randy Levine
President

Randy Levine begins his 12th season as President of the New York Yankees in 2011. He was named to his position in January 2000, becoming the first person to hold the post with the club since 1986.

Under his supervision and guidance, the franchise constructed the state-of-the art Yankee Stadium, completing the facility on time for the beginning of the 2009 season, which culminated in the franchise's 27th World Championship. Mr. Levine was a principal founder of the YES Network, which was recently named the most-watched regional sports network in the United States for the eighth consecutive year (2003-10).

In 2008, he was instrumental in creating Legends Hospitality, LLC, a new concession and merchandising company with the Dallas Cowboys which currently operates at the Yankees' and Cowboys' new stadiums. In 2004, he helped organize Yankees-Steiner, a leading sports memorabilia company.

Mr. Levine has also played a prominent role in the Yankees' international brand expansion, including the 2007 establishment of a first-of-its-kind working relationship with the Chinese Baseball Association. More recently, he led a 2010 Yankees delegation that visited Tokyo, Beijing and Hong Kong with the 2009 World Series Trophy, marking the first-ever time that the Yankees have brought one of their World Series trophies to Asia. In addition, Mr. Levine helped develop the joint venture agreement in Japan between the Yankees and Yomiuri Shimbun, which is the parent company of the Yomiuri Giants.

In 2007, the Yankees became the first Major League organization to sign players from the Israel Baseball League and also embarked on their first-ever large-scale outreach into Taiwan by holding a clinic for high school players and coaches in Taipei, Taiwan. Mr. Levine is also the Yankees' principal liaison to Major League Baseball and contributes to player negotiations and contract issues.

Mr. Levine has been at the forefront of bringing exciting year-round entertainment and special events to Yankee Stadium. In 2010, he was a driving force that led to a world championship boxing match between Miguel Cotto and Yuri Foreman, a pair of historic concerts featuring JAY-Z and Eminem, a renewed gridiron rivalry between Army and Notre Dame, and college football's newest postseason game—the New Era Pinstripe Bowl.

Mr. Levine's baseball and business vision has also led to record numbers at Yankee Stadium turnstiles. In 2010, the Yankees led Baseball in home attendance for the seventh time in the last eight seasons (2003-08, '10) and have now topped the American League in home attendance in each of the past eight seasons (2003-10). In 2008, his direction helped the club establish the all-time AL single-season attendance record of 4,298,543 to become the only Major League franchise to exceed the 4 million mark at home in four consecutive seasons (2005-08).

Before joining the Yankees, Mr. Levine served as New York City's Deputy Mayor for Economic Development, Planning and Administration. He also served as New York City's Labor Commissioner.

From 1995 through 1997, Mr. Levine was Chief Negotiator for Major League Baseball. In 1996, he negotiated the labor agreement that for the first time included revenue sharing, luxury taxes and Interleague play. Prior to that, Mr. Levine served as Principal Associate Deputy Attorney General and Principal Deputy Attorney General at the United States Department of Justice. He has also served as a special delegate to the United States Department of Labor and was a board member for Hudson River Park. Mr. Levine presently serves on the boards of George Washington University, the ASCPA and the Yogi Berra Museum.

Mr. Levine has served on the Board of Directors of the New Jersey Nets and New Jersey Devils and is a member of the Board of Directors of the YES Network and Legends Hospitality, LLC. He is also an officer of Yankee Global Enterprises, LLC. Mr. Levine serves on the International, Diversity and Labor Policy Committees of Major League Baseball.

Mr. Levine has been a partner in the New York law firm of Proskauer Rose Goetz & Mendelson and is presently Senior Counsel at the law firm of Akin Gump Strauss Hauer & Feld.

Born on February 22, 1955, in Brooklyn, N.Y., Mr. Levine received a Bachelor of Arts degree from George Washington University in 1977, and in 2011 was named as Chair of the school's athletic committee. He received his J.D. from Hofstra University School of Law in 1980. Mr. Levine and his wife, Mindy, reside in Manhattan.

New York Yankees Presidents
(Chief Executive Officers)

Joseph W. Gordon	1903-06
Frank J. Farrell	1907-14
Jacob Ruppert	1915-39
Ed Barrow	1939-45
Lee MacPhail	1945-47
Daniel R. Topping	1947-53
Daniel R. Topping & Del E. Webb	1954-64
Daniel R. Topping	1964-66
Michael Burke	1966-73
Gabe Paul	1973-77
Al Rosen	1978-79
George M. Steinbrenner	1979-80
Lou Saban	1981-82
Eugene McHale	1983-86
RANDY LEVINE	2000-present

New York Yankees president Frank Farrell presents a trophy to Yankees manager Harry Wolverton as Red Sox and Yankees players look on at Hilltop Park on April 11, 1912.

Felix M. Lopez, Jr.
Executive Vice President/Chief International Officer

Felix M. Lopez, Jr. begins his second season as Executive Vice President/Chief International Officer in 2011. From 2005-09, he served as Yankees Senior Vice President. His current responsibilities include overseeing the daily operations of George M. Steinbrenner Field, the Himes Player Development Complex and the Single-A Tampa Yankees. He is also involved with the Yankees' Latin Baseball Academy in Boca Chica, Dominican Republic, as well as player development in Latin America.

Under Mr. Lopez's supervision, the Yankees spring training home in Tampa, Fla., has undergone several structural enhancements and renovations in recent years, including the expansion of field box seating and the redesign of the Yankees' clubhouse facilities.

Fan-friendly amenities have been at the forefront of Mr. Lopez's operational strategy, including the design of the Brighthouse Networks Dugout Club, located underneath the field box seats behind home plate. In addition, Mr. Lopez was instrumental in developing the new Tampa Tribune Deck, which was unveiled in 2008. Located beyond the right field wall, the unique and intimate structure features picnic-style seating for 500 people, private concessions and a full bar.

In January 2010, Mr. Lopez headed a Yankees delegation that took the club's 2009 World Series trophy to the Dominican Republic. The visit included stops at the Presidential Palace, U.S. Embassy, National Police Headquarters and Santo Domingo's Quisqueya Stadium for a Dominican Winter League playoff game.

Mr. Lopez also serves on the boards of Yankee Global Enterprises, LLC, and Legends Hospitality, LLC.

Before joining the Yankees, Mr. Lopez was the president and owner of Architecture Design Construction, Inc., a company specializing in commercial construction in the southeastern United States. Born on April 1, 1954, in Havana, Cuba, Mr. Lopez moved to Tampa, Fla., in 1969 and later graduated from Cam Tech School of Construction. He is a member of the Grand Lodge of Free and Accepted Masons of Florida and Nobles of the Mystic Shrine of North America. He also serves on the board of the Gold Shield Foundation and contributes to the efforts of the Police Athletic League (PAL).

Mr. Lopez and his wife, Jessica, reside in Tampa, Fla.

Lonn A. Trost
Chief Operating Officer

Lonn A. Trost begins his 12th season as Chief Operating Officer of the New York Yankees in 2011. He was named to the position on January 10, 2000, after serving as the club's Executive Vice President and General Counsel from 1997-99.

Mr. Trost is responsible for the overall day-to-day functioning of the Yankees' operations. Under his direction, the Yankees have seen tremendous growth in brand recognition and sponsorship opportunities, while also establishing single-season home attendance records nine times (1998-99; 2002-08). In 2010, the club led Major League Baseball in home attendance, drawing in excess of 16,000 more fans per game than the combined average of the 29 other Major League teams. It also marked the seventh time in the last eight seasons (2003-08, '10) that the Yankees led the Majors in home attendance and the club's eighth straight season topping the American League.

Additionally, Mr. Trost, along with Hal Steinbrenner and Randy Levine, spearheaded the most complex undertaking in New York Yankees history—construction and development of Yankee Stadium, which is the largest privately funded building project in the history of the Bronx. While remaining true to the architectural grandeur of the 1923 original, the current facility is the most technologically advanced stadium in baseball.

Mr. Trost has played a significant role in Yankee Stadium becoming a year-round multi-purpose home to special events. In 2010, his vision and planning came to fruition with a world championship boxing match between Miguel Cotto and Yuri Foreman, a pair of historic concerts featuring JAY-Z and Eminem, a renewed gridiron rivalry between Army and Notre Dame, and college football's newest postseason game—the New Era Pinstripe Bowl.

Before joining the Yankees, Mr. Trost was a partner and member of the Executive Committee of the law firm of Shea and Gould from 1972 to 1994. He was also a partner at the New York law firm of Herrick, Feinstein from 1994 through 1997. While with these firms, he served as outside general counsel for numerous sports franchises, institutions and agents. Among his clients were the New York Yankees and Mets, the New Jersey Nets and Devils, the National Baseball Hall of Fame, Little League Baseball and TCI Cable.

Mr. Trost was instrumental in the creation of the YES Network and is a member of its Board of Directors. He also serves as an officer for Yankee Global Enterprises and Legends Hospitality, LLC, both of which he participated in founding. While he maintains his responsibilities with the New York Yankees Partnership and the Yankees' other affiliates, he is also actively involved with the Tourette Syndrome Association, with whom he is a member of the Corporate and Professional Council.

Born on May 8, 1945, Mr. Trost began his legal career in 1971 with the United States Justice Department, Office of Chief Counsel (Treasury Department). A 1968 graduate of Hunter College in the Bronx, Mr. Trost received his J.D. from Brooklyn Law School in 1971. It's interesting to note that Mr. Trost's initial employment with the Yankees was as a grandstand vendor in the mid-1960s in the original Yankee Stadium. He resides in Monroe Township, N.J., with his wife, Carol. They have two children, Evan and Audra, and one grandchild, Ariella.

Brian Cashman
Senior Vice President, General Manager

Brian McGuire Cashman has literally grown up in the Yankees family. He joined the organization in 1986 as a 19-year-old intern in the Minor League and Scouting Department and now commands one of the most demanding jobs in sports as Yankees Senior Vice President and General Manager.

Over the course of his 24 seasons with the team, he has earned five World Series rings, including four as General Manager, becoming the first GM to win four World Series titles since the Dodgers' Buzzie Bavasi in the 1950s and '60s. Notably, he has won his titles with two different managers — Joe Torre in 1998, 1999 and 2000, and Joe Girardi in 2009.

Mr. Cashman assumed his current post on February 3, 1998. At age 31, he became the second-youngest General Manager in baseball history. In his first season, he became the youngest-ever GM to win a World Series, and with championships in 1999 and 2000, he became the only GM in baseball history to win world titles in each of his first three seasons. A pennant in 2001 gave him four straight League Championships, placing him alongside Hall of Fame Yankees General Managers Ed Barrow (1936-39, four) and George Weiss (1949-53, five) as the only GMs in Baseball history to win four-or-more straight league titles at any point in their careers.

Among his peers, Mr. Cashman has achieved unparalleled success while carrying on the winning tradition of the Yankees. His lifetime winning percentage of .605 (1,272-830-2) is the highest of any General Manager with five seasons of experience since 1950 and marks the best team winning percentage in the Major Leagues during that same stretch. Now in his 14th season, Mr. Cashman has the third-longest tenure among all general managers in baseball and is the longest-serving Yankees GM since Barrow led the team from October 28, 1920 to February 20, 1945.

In all, his clubs have claimed 10 Division titles and six American League championships to go along with four World Series titles. His feat of reaching the playoffs in each of his first 10 seasons (1998-2007) remains unmatched in Baseball history.

In his present role, Mr. Cashman has been involved in dozens of high-profile Major League free-agent signings, including those of A.J. Burnett, Johnny Damon, Orlando Hernandez, Hideki Matsui, Mike Mussina, CC Sabathia, Alfonso Soriano and Mark Teixeira. Mr. Cashman has also executed more than 70 trades involving over 200 players, bringing the talents of Bobby Abreu, Aaron Boone, Curtis Granderson, David Justice, Alex Rodriguez and Nick Swisher to the Bronx.

Recently, Mr. Cashman has focused on rebuilding the Yankees farm system, while still maintaining World Championship talent at the Major League level. The emphasis he and his baseball operations staff have placed on the First-Year Player Draft and international scouting is demonstrated by the organization's homegrown talent, including Manny Banuelos, Dellin Betances, Andrew Brackman, Robinson Cano, Joba Chamberlain, Brett Gardner, Phil Hughes, Jesus Montero, David Robertson and Austin Romine.

There have been three women in Major League history to hold the position of Assistant General Manager, and Mr. Cashman has hired two of them: Jean Afterman, the Yankees' current Vice President and Assistant General Manager; and Kim Ng, who is currently Vice President and Assistant General Manager of the Los Angeles Dodgers.

Various groups have honored the achievements of the Yankees and Mr. Cashman. With the club's recent World Series title, the Yankees were named "2009 Male Team of the Year" by the United States Sports Academy and were nominated as "Team of the Year" in the Laureus World Sports Awards competition. In both 1998 and 2000, the Yankees earned ESPY Awards — presented by ESPN — as "Outstanding Team of the Year," and were named "Organization of the Year" by Baseball America in 1998 and by USA Today in 1999.

Mr. Cashman has been honored as "Executive of the Year" four times: by the Boston Chapter of the BBWAA in 2000 and 2009; and in 1999 and 2003 by the New Jersey Sportswriters' Association. In 2001, he received his third consecutive "40 Under 40" Award presented by Street & Smith's Sports Business Journal to recognize the top 40 people under the age of 40 who have made the greatest impact in the sports business industry. He has since been inducted into the publication's "40 Under 40" Hall of Fame. In 2003, Mr. Cashman was honored by the Latino Sports Writers and Broadcasters Association with their annual "Latino Achievement Award" for his contributions to the Latino media. He was also honored with the 2005 "Ossie Davis Award for Inspirational Leadership," given each year to a key leader in an organization that works to promote opportunity in diversity.

On February 11, 2004, Mr. Cashman was given the honor of ringing the opening bell at the New York Stock Exchange. The market closed at 10,737.70 that day, its highest close since June 13, 2001.

Mr. Cashman remains committed to growing the Yankees brand and increasing the number of people who play and enjoy baseball worldwide. In February 2010, he was part of the Yankees delegation that brought the 2009 World Series trophy to Tokyo, Beijing and Hong Kong. While on the Chinese mainland, the group met with the Chinese Baseball Association to discuss ways the game can be promoted in China. He was also heavily involved in bringing the Yankees to Tokyo for "Opening Series 2004" to honor the 70th anniversary of Major League Baseball's historic tour of Japan, which included Babe Ruth and Lou Gehrig.

His career as a full-time Yankees employee began following his graduation from Catholic University in 1989, when Mr. Cashman became a full-time Assistant in Baseball Operations. He was later promoted and transferred to Tampa, Fla., where he served as Assistant Farm Director from 1990 to 1992. He returned to New York and became Assistant General Manager, Baseball Administration in November 1992 .

Born on July 3, 1967, in Rockville Center, N.Y., Mr. Cashman grew up in Lexington, Ky. He attended Georgetown Prep in Rockville, Md., before attending Catholic University in Washington, D.C., where he majored in history and played intercollegiate baseball. His love for baseball developed when former Brooklyn Dodger Ralph Branca and his wife, Ann, arranged for him to serve as a bat boy for the Los Angeles Dodgers in spring training in 1982.

Mr. Cashman and his wife, Mary, have a daughter, Grace Eva, and a son, Theodore John.

Mark Newman
Senior Vice President, Baseball Operations

Mark Newman begins his 12th season as the Yankees' Senior Vice President of Baseball Operations and his 23rd season with the Yankees. Prior to being named to his current position in 2000, Mr. Newman served as the club's Vice President of Player Development and Scouting from 1997-99.

During his tenure, the Yankees player development system has been recognized for producing homegrown talent including All-Stars Robinson Cano, Phil Hughes, Derek Jeter, Jorge Posada and Mariano Rivera. Under Mr. Newman's supervision over the last decade, the Yankees have drafted and stockpiled talented prospects to evolve into what has been lauded as one of the best player development systems in baseball.

In December 2010, Mr. Newman received the Sheldon "Chief" Bender Award, recognizing his distinguished service to player development.

Over the last five seasons (2006-10), the Yankees' minor league affiliates (from the Dominican Summer League through Triple-A) have produced the most wins and the best winning percentage among all Major League franchises with a combined record of 2,339-1,815 (.563). Over the same stretch, Yankees farm teams captured nine league championships, and in 2008 became the first organization since Houston in 1993 to have its Triple-A and Double-A clubs both win titles in the same season.

In addition to stringing together 15 seasons of Major League postseason play over the last 16 years (1995-2007, '09-10) and winning five World Championships over the stretch, the Yankees are one of only two teams, along with the Cleveland Indians, whose minor league affiliates have combined to post winning records in each of the last 21 seasons since 1990. The Yankees were selected as the "Organization of the Year" by *Baseball America* in 1998 and earned the same honor from *USA Today* in 1999.

Mr. Newman began his career in the Yankees organization in 1989 as Coordinator of Instruction and served in that position until his promotion to Director of Player Development and Scouting in 1996. He was named Vice President of Player Development and Scouting in 1997. In his first role with the club, he oversaw all managers and coaches in the farm system and planned both Major and Minor League spring training.

In 1972, Mr. Newman began his baseball coaching career at 22 years old as the pitching coach for Southern Illinois University. After spending nine successful seasons there—during which he earned his law degree with honors—he was named Head Baseball Coach at Old Dominion University in 1981. Mr. Newman's impressive 321-167-3 record in nine seasons was recognized with his induction into the ODU Hall of Fame in 1997. He was inducted into the SIU Hall of Fame in 2000.

Jean Afterman
Vice President, Assistant General Manager

Jean Afterman enters her 10th season as the Yankees' Assistant General Manager in 2011 (ninth as Vice President). She became only the third female to hold such a position in Major League Baseball history.

Ms. Afterman has been an integral part of the Yankees' efforts to spearhead operations in Asia. In her first year with the Yankees, she was instrumental in developing the club's relationship with the Yomiuri Giants of the Japan Central League and the signing of three-time MVP Hideki Matsui. In 2007, she joined team President Randy Levine and General Manager Brian Cashman on a week-long trip to Asia that concluded with a working agreement with the Chinese Baseball Association. She once again joined Levine and Cashman in 2010, when the Yankees brought the 2009 World Series trophy to Tokyo, Beijing and Hong Kong. While in Hong Kong, Ms. Afterman was given the honor of throwing out one of the ceremonial first pitches at the 2010 Phoenix Cup Tournament, an annual international women's baseball tournament.

Ms. Afterman's contributions and leadership were recognized in 2010, when she was named by WISE (Women in Sports and Events) as one of the "Women of the Year," and was tabbed by *New York Moves Magazine* as a "2010 Power Woman." In 2004, Ms. Afterman was named one of the "Power 100" by the *Sporting News* and was selected as one of the "50 Most Powerful Women in New York" by the *New York Post* in 2003 and 2007. Also in 2007, Ms. Afterman was profiled as one of *Crain's New York Business'* "100 Most Influential Women in New York Business." In 2008, she was profiled by *Forbes Magazine* as one of the top female executives in baseball.

Ms. Afterman joined the Yankees with a diverse business and legal background, focusing on international sports and licensing with an emphasis on US-Japan matters. In 1996, Ms. Afterman was appointed by the U.S. Secretary of Agriculture to a federal advisory committee, the National Organic Standards Board. Prior to joining the Yankees, Ms. Afterman managed her own practice, providing athletic representation and management with a specialization in arbitration proceedings.

From 1994-99, she was General Counsel at KDN Sports, Inc. and handled business and legal affairs for international baseball clients, including Hideo Nomo, Hideki Irabu, Masato Yoshii, Alfonso Soriano and more than 30 other Major and Minor League players.

Ms. Afterman graduated from the University of California at Berkeley in 1979 and was the recipient of the Rosalynn Schneider Eisner Prize and the Mark Goodson Scholarship Grant. She received her J.D. from the University of San Francisco School of Law in 1991. In 2009, she was named the Katherine Delmar Burke School in San Francisco "Alumni of the Year."

Ms. Afterman maintains an active role in the Bronx community, working closely with P.S. 35, an elementary school in walking distance from Yankee Stadium. Over the last three years, she has organized Yankees-sponsored Read-A-Thons and directed a mentoring program that matches Yankees employees with fourth and fifth grade students. Additionally, she has reached out to high school-aged students through New York City's Explorers program, which engages young people through career-orientation programs. Her work with the group was publicly recognized as she was honored with the 2009 "Exploring Leadership Award."

Commitment to Community

The New York Yankees organization takes as much pride in the championship baseball played on the field as it does in its charitable endeavors throughout the community. The Yankees' community efforts reach far beyond the Bronx and the tri-state area, encompassing programs and donations throughout the United States and even spanning into Latin America and Asia.

The Yankees strive to create partnerships with programs that support children's initiatives, education enhancement and health awareness. The club's donations, grants, tickets, promotional items and countless other contributions to such programs exceeded $5.5 million in 2010. Throughout the season, Yankees players and front office personnel make countless visits to various local hospitals, schools and youth groups, and the club makes every effort to recognize community excellence through outreach and during pregame ceremonies.

YANKEES TURN TRIPLE PLAY AGAINST CANCER

The New York Yankees care about their fans' safety and health away from the diamond, and are committed to raising awareness to take the proper steps in cancer awareness, prevention and detection. In September 2010, the Yankees held three cancer awareness events at Yankee Stadium, offering free cancer screenings and a marrow drive to those in attendance at each of three games at Yankee Stadium.

On September 5, prior to the Yankees-Blue Jays game, Dr. Darrell Rigel, M.D., and his team of dermatologists and medical assistants conducted skin cancer screenings. **On September 7**, the Yankees and Ed Randall's Bat For The Cure charity provided free prostate cancer screenings for adult men age 40 and over attending that evening's game vs. Baltimore. Doctors and medical technicians from St. Luke's-Roosevelt Hospital Center assisted with the safe and simple screenings. **On September 22**, the Yankees, New York Blood Center and New York-Presbyterian Hospital teamed up for a bone marrow drive at Yankee Stadium while the Yankees played the Tampa Bay Rays. With a simple swab from the inner cheek, participants were added to the Be The Match Registry, which allows for patients to find a needed marrow match.

CC Sabathia gave free haircuts for neighborhood kids at Jordan's Barber Shop in the Bronx on June 1, 2010.

WOMEN OF YANKEE STADIUM SUPPORT SAME SKY

The women of Yankee Stadium joined forces with Same Sky (www. SameSky.com) for a special event in the H&R Block Lounge on June 2, 2010, to honor the survivors of the 1994 Rwandan genocide, and in particular, HIV positive women artisans who have handcrafted bracelets through the organization's trade-not-aid initiative to effect change in the country.

Asst. GM Jean Afterman (L), Mindy Levine and Nancy Newman supported the Same Sky event at Yankee Stadium.

The bracelets, made of hand-blown glass beads, allow the wearer to become a part of the movement empowering women everywhere under the same sky. All proceeds from the sales of Same Sky bracelets during the exclusive showing went directly toward training and employing more women artisans in Rwanda.

SHARPENING THEIR PENCILS

Beginning in 2009, Yankees front office staff members began a mentoring program with students at P.S. 35 in the Bronx. Under the leadership of Yankees Assistant GM Jean Afterman, mentors from various Yankees front office departments have worked in small groups with students on career awareness and job-readiness projects, such as designing mock advertisements, proposing new product ideas, and evaluating players' statistics. In establishing a "Read-A-Thon" aimed at engaging students in reading and improving their language arts skills, all of the school's 30 classes, comprising more than 700 elementary school students, are participating in a monthly reading competition for Yankees prizes.

YANKEES GO BOWLING IN THE COMMUNITY

The New York Yankees partnered with New York City's Public Schools Athletic League (PSAL) on a series of community initiatives to commemorate the inaugural New Era Pinstripe Bowl in 2010.

In support of the PSAL, the Yankees installed a new all-grass football field at Harry S. Truman High School in the Bronx. The sod was donated by DeLea Sod Farms, which plants the same type of grass at Yankee Stadium. Yankee Stadium also hosted the PSAL Football Championship Game on December 7, marking the first high school football contest in the current Yankee Stadium in which Fort Hamilton H.S defeated Abraham Lincoln H.S., 8-6.

Additionally, the Yankees honored the best scholar-athletes in New York City on December 20 at Yankee Stadium during their first annual "MVP Dinner." The occasion brought together a group of 55 male and female student athletes — 11 from each borough — who have led by example in the community, classroom and in their respective sports. The top graduating high school scholar-athlete from each borough was designated as a "Borough Captain" and also recognized during the New Era Pinstripe Bowl.

The Yankees continued their community outreach during bowl week, as the participating schools (Syracuse and Kansas State) took part in community events, including hosting youth football clinics at the Kips Bay Boys & Girls Club and visiting children at the Memorial Sloan-Kettering Cancer Center.

Robinson Cano and the Yankees players once again greeted fans entering the Great Hall on various days throughout the 2010 season.

WALKING IN A WINTER WONDERLAND

On December 17, 2010, Yankee Stadium's Great Hall transformed into the North Pole for the 2010 Bronx Winter Wonderland event. Approximately 5,000 children from the Bronx were treated to a holiday extravaganza, complete with Christmas decorations and festive holiday music, including caroling from the Bronx-based Renaissance EMS (Education through Music and Sports) program. Complimentary food and beverages were

Yankee Stadium resembled the North Pole during the 2010 Winter Wonderland.

provided by Legends Hospitality and the Hard Rock Cafe.

Additionally, Santa and his helpers set up their workshop in the Great Hall, handing out a toy to each child in attendance, courtesy of the Yankees, who purchased $25,000 in toys, and Mattel, who donated 2,000 toys.

ANNUAL FOOD DRIVES

The Yankees held their 17th Annual Holiday Food Drive at Yankee Stadium on December 16, 2010, presented by White Rose Foods. In conjunction with Bronx clergy, the Yankees distributed the donated food throughout the Bronx to those in need during the holiday season. Fans donating 30 pounds of nonperishable goods received a voucher valid for two tickets to one of 22 designated Yankees games in 2011 (restrictions apply) and a voucher valid for discounted ticket pricing for the 2010 New Era Pinstripe Bowl.

With Yankees Manager Joe Girardi, pitcher Mariano Rivera and Yankees alum Bernie Williams on hand to greet donors, a record-breaking 105,859 lbs. of food and nearly $1,000 was collected. To help kick off the Yankees Food Drive, White Rose Foods – along with their Good Neighbor Brands Kraft, Unilever, Snapple, Masterfoods, Domino, Conagra, New World Pasta, Carolina Rice, Clorox, Campbell's, Nestle, Smuckers and General Mills –donated over 40 pallets of food (approximately 60,000 lbs.).

On November 18, the Yankees and White Rose held their annual Pre-Thanksgiving Food Voucher Giveaway, distributing 750 vouchers to Bronx residents for redemption at a local Met Food market or Pioneer Supermarket.

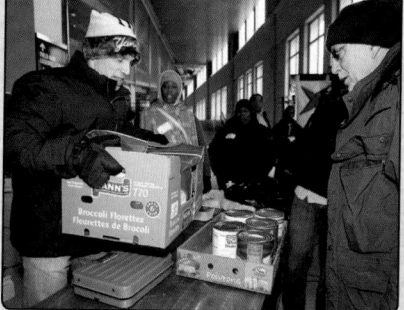

Manager Joe Girardi was on hand to accept donations at the Yankees' annual Holiday Food Drive on December 16, 2010 at Yankee Stadium.

YANKEES PLAYERS HIT COMMUNITY HOME RUNS

Teixeira Steps Up for Harlem RBI

In May 2010, first baseman Mark Teixeira and his wife, Leigh, donated $100,000 to the Harlem RBI Future's Fund for programs supporting programs that guide Harlem RBI's college-bound seniors toward and through higher education. Mark also enlisted as a member of the Harlem RBI Board of Directors and served as a chairperson at the organization's 2010 Bids for Kids Gala.

Additionally, as the Honorary Chair of Harlem RBI's Capital Campaign Committee, Mark will participate in various events to support the organization, including activities with Harlem RBI youth. He will also serve as one of the 2011 Bids for Kids Gala honorees as Harlem RBI celebrates its 20th Anniversary.

Alex Rodriguez played the role of doctor-for-the-day in June with the opening of the pediatric outpatient center in his name at Bronx Lebanon Hospital Center.

A-Rod Donates to Local Hospital

Yankees third baseman Alex Rodriguez saw his dream come to fruition in June 2010, when the Alex Rodriguez Pediatric Outpatient Center was opened at Bronx-Lebanon Hospital Center in the Bronx. Rodriguez contributed $250,000 to help fund construction and completion of the outpatient center, which offers a child-friendly environment ideal for young patients and their families. The state-of-the-art outpatient center offers treatment in a number of specialties, including cardiac illnesses, asthma, diabetes and neurological disorders, among other health problems. Bronx-Lebanon's pediatric-asthma program, part of its outpatient center, is widely recognized as a model program.

Granderson Joins White House Initiative

Yankees outfielder Curtis Granderson teamed up with First Lady Michelle Obama in 2010 as a national spokesman for the anti-obesity campaign Let's Move! The nationwide campaign, which addresses the serious epidemic of childhood obesity, has set a national goal of solving the obesity challenge within a generation, so that America's youngest children reach adulthood at a healthy weight.

CC HONORED FOR COMMUNITY EXCELLENCE

As an active member of the community in the New York metropolitan area as well as in his hometown of Vallejo, Calif., Yankees pitcher CC Sabathia was awarded two special community service awards, recognizing his cross-country charitable endeavors in 2010.

At the January 2011 Baseball Assistance Team Dinner, Sabathia and his wife, Amber, received the Bart Giamatti Award for their many contributions to children, families and communities on both coasts.

In addition, Sabathia was named one of 10 "Dream Team For Public Service" finalists selected for the *Jefferson Awards for Public Service*. The awards, established in 1972 by Jacqueline Kennedy Onassis, U.S. Senator Robert Taft, Jr. and Sam Beard as a Nobel Prize for public service, seek to honor athletes who display an exemplary commitment to service in their community.

Mariano Rivera and the Yankees paid a visit to wounded warriors at Walter Reed Medical Center during their visit to Washington, D.C. in April 2010.

HONORING MILITARY EXCELLENCE

In support of the nation's armed services, the Yankees held their annual "Military Appreciation Day" on June 12, 2010, prior to their game vs. Houston. Paying tribute to the members of the United States Special Operations Command, the Yankees showed an inspirational video dedicated to those helped by the Special Operations Warrior Foundation followed by an on-field recognition of military heroes wounded while in service. The ceremony also featured a donation of $25,000 from Mattel/Fisher-Price to the Warrior Foundation.

In what has become an annual tradition, the U.S. Army Golden Knights parachuted into Yankee Stadium, landing in the outfield. Former U.S. Army Elite Task Force Ranger Keni Thomas, a member of the Army unit that fought in Somalia in 1993 at the Battle of Mogadishu (later depicted in the film *Black Hawk Down*), sang the national anthem, while the West Point Honor Guard presented the colors. Following the anthem, Lt. General Frank Kearney, Deputy Commander of the United States Special Operations Command, threw out the game's ceremonial first pitch.

YANKEES COMMUNITY PARTNERS

44th Clergy Coalition	Kips Bay Boys & Girls Club
161st St. Merchants Association	Knowledge is Power Program
ALS Foundation	Lincoln Medical and Mental
American Latin Association of New York	Health Center
	Make-A-Wish Foundation
American Red Cross	Met Council on Jewish Poverty
ASPCA	Mid-Bronx Senior Citizens Council
Big Brothers/Big Sisters	Montefiore Medical Center
Bronx Arts Cultural Center	Morris High School Robotics
Bronx Central Council	New York City Department of
Bronx Chamber of Commerce	Education
Bronx Children's Psychiatric Center	New York City Parks and Recreation
Bronx Colts Youth Foundation	New York City Sports Commission
Bronx Community College	New York City Urban League
Bronx Dance Theatre	New York Police Foundation
Bronx Lebanon Hospital Center	New York POPS
Bronx Little Leagues	New York Public Library
Bronx Museum	Nos Quidamos
Bronx Neighborhood Cluster	Out 2 Play
Bronx Puerto Rican Day Parade	Police Athletic League
Bronx School for Law, Government and Justice	Public School 35
	Public School 41
Bronx Tourism Council	Public School 114
Bronx Walk for Juvenile Diabetes	Public School Athletic League
Bronx YMCA	Renaissance EMS
Cardinal Hayes High School	Roberto Clemente State Park
Catholic Relief Charities	Rock and Wrap it Up!
The Claremont Center	Salvation Army
The Explorer Program	SCAN New York
The First Tee	Silver Shield Foundation
Fordham University Baseball	South Bronx Concerned Citizens
Grand Concourse Academy	Sports Buddies
Grand Concourse Branch Library	The Sports Foundation
Haven Arts	Sports Professions Program
Harlem RBI	St. Ann's Episcopal Church
Highbridge Community Life Center	Thurgood Marshall Mock Trial Program
Highbridge Voices	United Negro College Fund
Urban Assembly for Careers in Sports	Women's Housing and
Hostos Community College	Economic Development
The Jackie Robinson Foundation	Corporation (WHEDCo)
Junior Achievement	World Vision

Yankees shortstop Derek Jeter was named by *USA Today* as 2010's "Most Caring Athlete."

...the store with more!

Stop In and Start Saving!
Fuel Your Car, Feed Yourself!

* **Gasoline**
* **Fast Food - Made Fresh!**

* **Snacks & Beverages**
* **Great Coffee**

eat Value, Great Service,
Great Selection.

We help keep
Yankee Stadium
'green!'

Our renewable energy certificates
& carbon neutral products contribute to
the green initiatives at Yankee Stadium.

**The Hess Gift Card
Is A Great Way
to Say Thank You!**

1-800-HESS-USA
1-800-437-7872
www.HessEnergy.com

Forward Thinking Energy

2010 Yankees HOPE Week

HOPE WEEK
AUGUST 16-20, 2010
HELPING OTHERS PERSEVERE & EXCEL

The New York Yankees participated in their second annual HOPE Week (Helping Others Persevere & Excel) in 2010, a unique week-long community program bringing to light five remarkable stories intended to inspire individuals into action in their own communities.

Each day from Monday, August 16, through Friday, August 20, the Yankees reached out to an individual, family or organization worthy of recognition and support. Though each day's celebration culminated at Yankee Stadium, outreach often took place away from the Stadium, allowing the Yankees to personally connect with individuals and highlight their success.

Initiated in 2009, HOPE Week is rooted in the fundamental belief that acts of goodwill provide hope and encouragement to more than just the recipient of the gesture.

A unique aspect of HOPE Week is that every player on the roster, Manager Joe Girardi and his coaching staff, General Manager Brian Cashman along with many front office employees, participated in the outreach during the week.

Equally significant during HOPE Week is gaining publicity for the highlighted causes and organizations. The greatest challenge facing many not-for-profits is generating interest, awareness and funding for their missions.

Additionally, the Yankees Foundation made $10,000 donations to non-profit organizations associated with each day's participants.

The Yankees will once again celebrate HOPE Week from July 25-29, 2011. If you know an individual, family or organization that embodies the spirit of HOPE Week, please let the Yankees Media Relations Department know by visiting www.yankees.com, going to the Community dropdown menu, clicking on "HOPE Week," and telling their story in the nomination form.

The Yankees encourage all their fans to get involved…Give HOPE!

During an April 26 White House ceremony honoring the team's 2009 World Series championship, President Barack Obama officially announced the return of HOPE Week in 2010. In conjunction with HOPE Week, the White House's Corporation for National and Community Service awarded honorees "President's Volunteer Service Awards," bestowed by the President to salute volunteers who strengthen the nation's culture of service. At the conclusion of the week, the Yankees were honored with the President's Volunteer Service Award, given "in recognition and appreciation of commitment to strengthening the Nation and for making a difference through volunteer service."

MONDAY, AUGUST 16

The Yankees kicked off HOPE Week by surprising 13-year-old quadruple amputee **Jorge Grajales** of Ridgewood N.J., with a pool party and barbecue, which included generous donations from Stop & Shop and Party City. Mariano Rivera, Nick Swisher and Brett Gardner, along with Yankees coaches Kevin Long and Mike Harkey enjoyed an afternoon with Jorge, his foster parents John and Faye Dyksen, and his family and friends.

Originally born in Panama, Jorge had his hands and feet amputated as an infant due to an infection. Since age 3, the Dyksen family has taken him into their home for three-quarters of the year through a program called Healing the

Nick Swisher and the Yankees kicked off HOPE Week with a pool party for Jorge Grajales.

Children. At that evening's Yankees game, Jorge and the Dyksens were honored during pregame ceremonies and Jorge threw out the first pitch.

TUESDAY, AUGUST 17

The Yankees reached out to Morris Plains, N.J., resident **Jane Lang**, who has been blind since birth. Manager Joe Girardi, players Joba Chamberlain, Chad Gaudin and David Robertson, along with former Yankee Tino Martinez surprised

Joba Chamberlain [R] escorts Jane and Clipper through Herald Square and down to the D train.

Lang at her house and joined her on her normal trek to Yankee Stadium, using public transportation. Once at the Stadium, Jane received a private tour of Monument Park, with former Yankee Paul O'Neill, where she felt some of the monuments and plaques for the first time. She then went on a private tour of the Yankees Museum and felt the 2009 World Championship Trophy as well as one of Babe Ruth's bats. Prior to the game, Jane and her Seeing Eye dog, Clipper, delivered the lineup card to home plate with Joe Girardi, who also escorted Jane around the base paths following the game.

WEDNESDAY, AUGUST 18

The Yankees reached out to Sierra Leone-native, civil war survivor and recent high school graduate **Mohamed Kamara**. CC Sabathia, General Manager Brian Cashman and Hall of Famer Reggie Jackson took Mohamed on a surprise tour of the New York Stock Exchange during the morning bell ringing. The Yankees then escorted Mohamed to City Hall, where the group was joined by Derek Jeter, Marcus Thames and Curtis Granderson before meeting with Mayor Michael Bloomberg. Following their trip to City Hall, the Yankees and Mohamed visited the United Nations where His Excellency Mr. Shekou M. Touray, Permanent Representative of Sierra Leone to the United Nations, spoke with Mohamed and the Yankees in a private meeting and accompanied the group on a tour of the General Assembly Hall.

[L-R] Brian Cashman, Reggie Jackson, Mohamed Kamara and CC Sabathia pause for a moment on the New York Stock Exchange floor during the morning bell ringing ceremony.

THURSDAY, AUGUST 19

The Yankees reached out to children and supporters of "**Beautiful People**." The organization was founded by **Peter Ladka** of Warwick, N.Y., who – though he had two perfectly healthy children of his own – wanted to reach out to children and families with special needs to make them feel more a part of the community. Yankees players and coaches were paired with special-needs children from the Beautiful

People organization in a baseball game on the field at Yankee Stadium following the club's game vs. Detroit. The Yankees, the children and their families also enjoyed an on-field barbecue catered by Hard Rock Cafe and dessert from Dylan's Candy Bar and Turkey Hill.

Jorge Posada and the Yankees buddied up with members of Beautiful People for a baseball game on the Yankee Stadium field.

FRIDAY, AUGUST 20

The Yankees reached out to **Johanna** and **Melida Arias**, sisters who have overcome hardships and homelessness and made their lives better through education and hard work. Two years ago, with their family struggling, Johanna chose to pass up college at Syracuse University in order to work so she could provide for her sister and mother. In the fall of 2010, Melida began her freshman year at Baruch College in Manhattan and hopes to become the first member of her family to graduate college. Yankees players Alex Rodriguez, Robinson Cano, Ramiro Pena, Francisco Cervelli, Sergio Mitre, David Robertson and Bench Coach Tony Pena surprised Melida at her job at Wendy's in the Bronx, and then took both sisters on a surprise shopping spree at DKNY in Manhattan to outfit Melida for

Melida (L) and Johanna (R) pose in items from their new wardrobe at DKNY in Manhattan.

her freshman year of college and Johanna for future professional opportunities.

At that evening's game vs. Seattle, Brian Cashman presented paid internship offers to both girls – Melida with the Yankees and Johanna with Lincoln Hospital in the Bronx. Melida also received a laptop computer courtesy of TekServe and both sisters received gift bags with items donated by Dooney & Bourke, Helen Ficalora and Nike. The girls' mother, Maria, was presented with $1,000 in gift cards from White Rose.

VAN HEUSEN
INSTITUTE OF STYLE

"YOU MAY COME AS SCHLUBS —

BUT YOU WILL LEAVE WITH SWAGGER"

PROF. JERRY RICE   PROF. STEVE YOUNG

Official Sponsor of the
Pro Football Hall of Fame

New York Yankees™

2011 YANKEES

2B **ROBINSON CANO** took home a 2010
Gold Glove Award, Silver Slugger Award
and finished third in American
League MVP voting.

28
JOE GIRARDI

MANAGER • OPENING DAY AGE: 46

FULL NAME
Joseph Elliott Girardi

BIRTHDATE
October 14, 1964

BIRTHPLACE
Peoria, Ill.

RESIDES
Purchase, N.Y.

COLLEGE
Northwestern University

CAREER HIGHLIGHTS
BBWAA
N.L. Manager of the Year
▸ 2006

Sporting News
N.L. Manager of the Year
▸ 2006

N.L. All-Star Team
▸ 2000

STATUS
▸ Re-signed to a three-year contract on October 29, 2010, extending through the 2013 season…was named the 32nd manager in club history on October 30, 2007, becoming the 17th Yankees manager to have played for the club and fourth former Yankees catcher to skipper the team (also Bill Dickey, Ralph Houk and Yogi Berra).

AT THE HELM IN 2010
▸ The 2010 season marked his third as Manager of the New York Yankees, guiding the club to a 95-67 record, their second consecutive postseason appearance and 15th playoff berth in the last 16 years…was the second-best record in the AL behind Tampa Bay (96-66) and the third-best in the Majors, also trailing Philadelphia (97-65)…spent the final 69 days of the season (from 7/18 on) within 2.5 games (either ahead, tied or behind) of Tampa Bay.

> ### FANTASTIC FOUR
> With a 365-283 (.563) career managerial record, only Ken Macha (368-280, .568 with Oakland from 2003-06) recorded a higher winning percentage in the first four years of his managerial career over the past 20 seasons (since 1991).

▸ Led the Yankees to a Major League-high 48 come-from-behind wins, their second straight season leading the category (51 in 2009)…collected six wins when trailing after the end of the eighth inning, one more than their total from 2009.

▸ Did not lose more than four straight games, piloting one of just two Major League teams (also Minnesota) to not record a losing streak of at least five games in 2010…the Yankees were the last team in the Majors to be swept in a series of at least three games (9/10-12 at Texas).

▸ Won 30 series, tied with Tampa Bay for second-most in the AL, behind Minnesota (31).

▸ The Yankees were 52-29 (.642) at home, tying Detroit for the second-highest home winning percentage in the AL behind Minnesota (53-28, .654)…his 109-53 (.673) record in the current Yankee Stadium (2009-10) marks the Majors' most home wins and highest home winning percentage over the stretch.

▸ The Yankees led the Majors with a .988 fielding percentage and committed only 69 errors, setting a franchise record for highest fielding percentage and fewest errors in any season…since taking over in 2008, the Yankees lead the Majors with a .987 fielding percentage.

▸ Earned his 200th win as Yankees Manager on 4/17 vs. Texas…recorded his 300th career managerial win on 5/31 vs. Cleveland.

▸ Was ejected three times in 2010…has been ejected 14 times in his career, 11 times as a Manager (nine as Yankees manager) and 10 times as a Yankee (also 8/6/99 as a player).

▸ At 46 years old, is the third-youngest manager in the Majors, behind Cleveland's Manny Acta (42) and Seattle's Eric Wedge (43).

MANAGING/COACHING CAREER
▸ Led the Yankees to their 27th World Championship in 2009 in his second season, becoming the ninth Yankees manager to win a World Series…in his postseason managerial debut, joined Ralph Houk and Billy Martin as the only three Yankees to play for and manage a Yankees World Championship team…also joined Houk, Bob Lemon and Casey Stengel as the only four Yankees managers to win a World Series in their first postseason as a manager.

▸ Led the club to a Major League-best 103-59 regular season record in 2009, marking the Yankees' most wins since 2002 (103-58)…became the eighth Yankees manager to collect at least 100 wins in a full season, joining Miller Huggins, Joe McCarthy, Casey Stengel, Ralph Houk, Billy Martin, Dick Howser and Joe Torre…joined McCarthy, Houk, Martin and Howser as the only five Yankees skippers to accomplish the feat within their first two full seasons with the team…finished third in AL Manager of the Year voting with 34 total points, including four first-place votes.

GIRARDI'S CAREER MANAGERIAL RECORD					
YEAR	**CLUB**	**W**	**L**	**PCT.**	**POSITION**
2006	Florida	78	84	.481	Fourth
2008	YANKEES	89	73	.549	Third
2009*	YANKEES	103	59	.636	First
2010**	YANKEES	95	67	.586	Second
CAREER TOTALS		**365**	**283**	**.563**	
TOTALS W/ NYY		**287**	**199**	**.591**	
*World Series Winner			**Wild Card		

▸ The Yankees' 114 total wins in 2009 (including postseason) tied their second-most ever in a single year behind the 125 victories of the 1998 squad (also 114W in 1927)…a member of the 1998 Yankees (114-48), became the only active Major League manager at the time to both play for and manage teams that won at least 100 games in a season and won a World Series, according to the *Elias Sports Bureau*…became the only Major League manager in the 2000s to lead a team to 100-or-more regular season wins and a World Series title.

▸ Earned his 200th career managerial win on 6/7/09 vs. Tampa Bay…earned his 100th win as Yankees manager on 4/29/09 at Detroit.

▸ Led the Yankees to a 89-73 record in 2008 in his first season as the club's skipper…was one of only two managers (also the Angels' Mike Scioscia) whose team did not lose more than four consecutive games during the 2008 season…won his Yankees managerial debut on 4/1/08 vs. Toronto (lost his only previous Opening Day as Manager in 2006 with Florida).

WISE BEYOND HIS YEARS

In 2009, Joe Girardi became the youngest manager in Yankees history to win a World Series. He remains the fourth-youngest World Series-winning manager over the last 34 years (1977-2010) behind Minnesota's Tom Kelly (1987 and '91), the White Sox's Ozzie Guillen (2005) and the Mets' Davey Johnson (1986).

▸ Earned his 100th career managerial win on 5/22/08 vs. Baltimore…was ejected by HP umpire Chris Guccione in the bottom of the ninth inning in the game.

▸ Was named the 2006 National League "Manager of the Year" by the Baseball Writers Association of America and the *Sporting News*…guided the Florida Marlins to a 78-84 record in his first season as a Major League manager…with the award, joined the Houston Astros' Hal Lanier (1986) and the San Francisco Giants' Dusty Baker (1993) as the only managers to win the honor in their managerial debuts…at the age of 41, became the youngest manager in Marlins history (previously 47-year-old John Boles in 1996)…was named Marlins manager just two seasons after retiring as a player prior to the 2004 campaign, marking the shortest time between being an active player (2003) and making a managerial debut (2006) since 1987, when both John Wathan (Kansas City) and Larry Bowa (San Diego) became managers after last playing during the 1985 season.

▸ Became the first manager to improve his club's record above .500 after falling at least 20 games below the .500 mark during the same season…the Marlins were a season-low 20 games under .500 on 5/21 (11-31), but then went 62-41 through 9/12 to improve to 73-72…the only other Major League team to return to the .500 mark after falling 20 or more games below was the 1899 Louisville Colonels (managed by Fred Clarke), who were 22 games under at 16-38 and improved to 72-72-3 before finishing with a record of 75-77-3.

▸ Managed Anibal Sanchez's no-hitter on 9/6/06 vs. Arizona…was the fourth no-hitter in Marlins history and the fourth no-hitter that Girardi has been a part of, having caught two (Dwight Gooden's on 5/14/96 and David Cone's perfect game on 7/18/99) and been a teammate in one (David Wells' perfect game on 5/17/98)…according to the *Elias Sports Bureau*, Girardi became the first person since Jeff Torborg to both catch and manage a no-hitter…Torborg managed Wilson Alvarez's no-hitter on 9/11/91 with the White Sox after catching no-hitters by Sandy Koufax (perfect game, 9/9/65), Bill Singer (7/20/70) and Nolan Ryan (5/15/73).

▸ Made his coaching debut in 2005, serving as bench coach and catching instructor on Joe Torre's New York Yankees staff…assisted in guiding the Yankees to a 95-67 (.586) record and the American League East title.

▸ Appeared in 39 career postseason games as a player, most among all current American League managers…among active Major League managers, only Cincinnati's Dusty Baker (40) appeared in more postseason games as a player.

ACTIVE MANAGERS TO WIN WORLD SERIES IN THEIR FIRST POSTSEASON
JOE GIRARDI......................YANKEES, 2009
Ozzie Guillen.......................Chicago-AL, 2005
Terry Francona.........................Boston, 2004
Mike Scioscia.........................Anaheim, 2002

PLAYING CAREER

- Played parts of 15 seasons as a catcher in the Major Leagues with the Chicago Cubs (1989-92 and 2000-02), Colorado Rockies (1993-95), New York Yankees (1996-99) and St. Louis Cardinals (2003)…was a member of three World Series Championship teams in New York (1996, 1998-99) and played in a total of six postseasons with the Cubs (1989), Rockies (1995) and Yankees (1996-99).

- In 1,277 career Major League games, batted .267 (1,100-for-4,127) with 454 runs, 186 doubles, 36HR and 422RBI, finishing with a .991 career fielding percentage while throwing out 27.6% of potential base stealers…batted .184 (21-for-114) with 2 triples and 1RBI in 39 career postseason games.

- Saw his first Major League action in 1989 as the Cubs' Opening Day catcher…was the first rookie catcher to start a season opener for the Cubs since Randy Hundley in 1966…was selected to *Baseball Digest's* All-Rookie Team…played in four games of the 1989 NL Championship Series against San Francisco, recording one hit.

DID YOU KNOW??? Joe Girardi and Yogi Berra are the only Yankees catchers to be behind the plate for two regular season no-hitters. Girardi was the catcher for Dwight Gooden's no-hitter on 5/14/96 vs. Seattle and David Cone's perfect game on 7/18/99 vs. Montreal. Berra caught both of Allie Reynolds' no-hitters in 1951.

- Played his first full big league season in 1990…stole eight bases, the most by a Cubs catcher since Gabby Hartnett's 10 in 1924…ranked second among NL catchers in assists (61) and threw out 33.3% of baserunners attempting to steal (38-of-114).

- On 8/7/91, in his first game back after missing nearly four months with a strained lower back, suffered a broken nose in a home plate collision with the Phillies' John Kruk.

- Was selected by the Rockies with the 19th pick in the Expansion Draft from the Cubs…established career highs with 8HR, 55RBI and 63R in 1995 with the Colorado Rockies.

- Acquired by the Yankees on 11/3/95 from the Rockies in exchange for LHP Mike DeJean…hit a career-high .294 with 2HR and 45RBI for the World Series Champions…stole 13 bases, marking the highest total among big league catchers and a record for a Yankees catcher…stole home on the front end of a double steal on 4/11 vs. Kansas City, becoming the first Yankees catcher to steal home since Jake Gibbs on 7/13/1968…had two triples during the 1996 postseason, including a run-scoring three-base hit off Greg Maddux in Game 6 of the World Series at Yankee Stadium.

- Was the catcher for Dwight Gooden's no-hitter on 5/14/96 vs. Seattle…in his final season as a player with the Yankees, caught David Cone's perfect game on 7/18/99 vs. Montreal…had a career-high 7RBI on 8/23/99 in a 21-3 victory at Texas, going 4-for-6 with 2 doubles and 1 triple.

- Rejoined the Cubs organization in 2000 and earned his first and only trip to an All-Star Game that season in Atlanta as a replacement for the injured Mike Piazza (did not play)…when he homered on 5/2/00 vs. Houston off Jose Lima, it was his first Cubs home run since 5/8/92…only one player, Billy Jurges (nine years, 1938-47), had a longer span between homers with the Cubs.

- Recorded his 1,000th Major League hit on 5/27/01 vs. Milwaukee off Jimmy Haynes – a seventh-inning, game-winning, two-run double.

- Was one of the Cubs' co-captains in 2001 and 2002.

- Played his final career regular season game on 9/28/03 at Arizona with the St. Louis Cardinals…his single in the ninth inning off the Diamondbacks' Edgar Gonzalez gave him 1,100 career hits.

PERSONAL/MISCELLANEOUS

- Graduated high school in 1982 from the Spalding Institute (Ill.), where he was an All-State selection in baseball.

- Graduated from Northwestern University in 1986 with a bachelor's degree in industrial engineering…was a three-time Academic All-American and two-time All-Big 10 selection at catcher…was elected to the College Sports Information Directors Hall of Fame on 7/1/07, becoming the first former Major Leaguer to be enshrined…also received the 2007 Distinguished Alumni Award from the Northwestern University Department of Industrial Engineering and Management Sciences…received the NCAA Silver Anniversary Award on 1/14/10, recognizing the personal achievements of a college graduate 25 years following their collegiate athletic career.

- Established his own charity, Catch 25, which is dedicated to providing support to families and individuals across the country who have been challenged with ALS, Alzheimer's, cancer and fertility issues…Catch 25 provides assistance through scholarships, financial aid and charitable donations and is devoted to serving children and adults that may not otherwise have the financial and emotional support they may need…his father, Jerry, suffers from Alzheimer's…hosts the annual "Remember When, Remember Now" benefit along with Michael Kay in New York City, helping raise funds for his charity and Alzheimer's research.

- Helped assemble 3,000 comfort packs for troops for Veteran's Day, along with Bank of America, on 11/11/10…collected donations at the Yankees' annual holiday food drive in December 2010.

- Received the Community Leadership Award from the New York City Chapter of the Alzheimer's Association at it's annual "Forget-Me-Not" gala on 6/1/09.

- Received the Sweetwater Clifton "City Spirit" Award from the New York Knicks on 11/22/09 for serving as a good Samaritan by stopping to aid a stranded motorist on his way home following the final game of the World Series…was the recipient of the Ben Epstein "Good Guy Award" in 1997, presented annually by the New York chapter of the BBWAA…was honored at the 2007 Lou Gehrig Sports Award Benefit Dinner.

▸ Joined New York City Mayor Michael Bloomberg and Roberto Clemente, Jr. in placing the first "pitch" on 7/29/08 at the Third Annual Gracie Mansion Tee Ball Game…hosted by the Mayor's Office, Little League Baseball and the Roberto Clemente Foundation, the game featured five teams, one from each New York City borough and promoted youth exercise as well as team-building sports…was featured on the special edition Dunkin Donuts "Box o' Joe" in April 2010.

▸ Unveiled a granite sidewalk marker in the Canyon of Heroes on 6/15/10 with the Alliance for Downtown New York, commemorating the Yankees' ticker-tape parade to honor the team's 27th World Series title.

▸ Following his retirement as a player, joined the YES Network as an analyst and won an Emmy Award for hosting YES' *Kids on Deck* series…rejoined YES in 2007, working as an analyst…worked with FOX during the regular season and postseason in '07…was a member of ESPN Radio's team for the 2003 NL Division Series.

▸ He and his wife, Kim, have three children, Serena, Dante and Lena…Kim has hosted several charitable events at Yankee Stadium, including fundraisers for stomach cancer research in which fans could purchase blue hair extensions and mohawks.

Girardi's Major League Playing Career

Year	Club	AVG	G	AB	R	H	2B	3B	HR	RBI	SH	SF	HP	BB	SO	SB	CS	E	OBP	SLG
1989	CHICAGO-NL	.248	59	157	15	39	10	0	1	14	1	1	2	11	26	2	1	7	.304	.331
1990	CHICAGO-NL	.270	133	419	36	113	24	2	1	38	4	4	3	17	50	8	3	11	.300	.344
1991	CHICAGO-NL	.191	21	47	3	9	2	0	0	6	1	0	0	6	6	0	0	3	.283	.234
1992	CHICAGO-NL	.270	91	270	19	73	3	1	1	12	0	1	1	19	38	0	2	4	.320	.300
1993	COLORADO-a	.290	86	310	35	90	14	5	3	31	12	1	3	24	41	6	6	6	.346	.397
1994	COLORADO	.276	93	330	47	91	9	4	4	34	6	2	2	21	48	3	5	5	.321	.364
1995	COLORADO	.262	125	462	63	121	17	2	8	55	12	1	2	29	76	3	3	10	.308	.359
1996	YANKEES-b	.294	124	422	55	124	22	3	2	45	11	3	5	30	55	13	4	3	.346	.374
1997	YANKEES-c	.264	112	398	38	105	23	1	1	50	5	2	2	26	53	2	3	5	.311	.334
1998	YANKEES	.276	78	254	31	70	11	4	3	31	8	1	2	14	36	3	2	4	.317	.386
1999	YANKEES	.239	65	209	23	50	16	1	2	27	8	2	0	10	26	3	1	8	.271	.354
2000	CHICAGO-NL-d	.278	106	363	47	101	15	1	6	40	6	3	3	32	61	1	0	5	.339	.375
2001	CHICAGO-NL	.253	78	229	22	58	10	1	3	25	2	1	0	21	50	0	1	0	.315	.345
2002	CHICAGO-NL	.226	90	234	19	53	10	1	1	13	5	1	0	16	35	1	0	6	.275	.291
2003	ST. LOUIS-e	.130	16	23	1	3	0	0	0	1	0	0	0	3	4	0	0	1	.231	.130
Minor League Totals		**.284**	**323**	**1128**	**152**	**320**	**42**	**13**	**21**	**136**	**7**	**6**	**7**	**88**	**181**	**28**	**10**	**34**	**.339**	**.393**
Major League Totals		**.267**	**1277**	**4127**	**454**	**1100**	**186**	**26**	**36**	**422**	**81**	**23**	**25**	**279**	**607**	**44**	**31**	**77**	**.315**	**.350**
NYY Totals		**.272**	**379**	**1283**	**147**	**349**	**72**	**9**	**8**	**153**	**32**	**8**	**9**	**80**	**172**	**20**	**12**	**19**	**.317**	**.361**

Drafted by the Chicago Cubs in the fifth round of the 1986 First-Year Player Draft.

a- Drafted by the Colorado Rockies from the Cubs as the 19th pick in the 1992 Expansion Draft on November 17, 1992.
b- Traded to New York-AL on November 20, 1995 in exchange for LHP Mike DeJean.
c- Signed by New York-AL as a free agent on December 3, 1996.
d- Signed by Chicago-NL as a free agent on December 15, 1999.
e- Signed by St. Louis as a free agent on December 18, 2002.
f- Signed by New York-AL as a free agent on February 4, 2004.

Girardi's Division Series Record

Year	Club/Opponent	AVG	G	AB	R	H	2B	3B	HR	RBI	BB	SO	SB
1995	COL vs. ATL	.125	4	16	0	2	0	0	0	0	0	2	0
1996	NYY vs. TEX	.222	4	9	1	2	0	0	0	0	4	1	0
1997	NYY vs. CLE	.133	5	15	2	2	0	0	0	0	1	3	0
1998	NYY vs. TEX	.429	2	7	0	3	0	0	0	0	0	1	0
1999	NYY vs. TEX	.000	2	6	0	0	0	0	0	0	0	1	0
Division Series Totals		**.170**	**17**	**53**	**3**	**9**	**0**	**0**	**0**	**0**	**5**	**8**	**0**

Girardi's League Championship Series Record

Year	Club/Opponent	AVG	G	AB	R	H	2B	3B	HR	RBI	BB	SO	SB
1989	CHC vs. SF	.100	4	10	1	1	0	0	0	0	1	2	0
1996	NYY vs. BAL	.250	4	12	1	3	0	1	0	0	1	3	0
1998	NYY vs. CLE	.250	3	8	2	2	0	0	0	0	1	0	0
1999	NYY vs. BOS	.250	3	8	0	2	0	0	0	0	0	2	0
LCS Totals		**.211**	**14**	**38**	**4**	**8**	**0**	**1**	**0**	**0**	**3**	**7**	**0**

Girardi's World Series Record

Year	Club/Opponent	AVG	G	AB	R	H	2B	3B	HR	RBI	BB	SO	SB
1996	NYY vs. ATL	.200	4	10	1	2	0	1	0	1	1	2	0
1998	NYY vs. SD	.000	2	6	0	0	0	0	0	0	0	2	0
1999	NYY vs. ATL	.286	2	7	1	2	0	0	0	0	0	1	0
World Series Totals		**.174**	**8**	**23**	**2**	**4**	**0**	**1**	**0**	**1**	**1**	**5**	**0**
POSTSEASON TOTALS		**.184**	**39**	**114**	**9**	**21**	**0**	**2**	**0**	**1**	**9**	**20**	**0**

Girardi's All-Star Game Record

Year	Club, Site	AVG	G	AB	R	H	2B	3B	HR	RBI	BB	SO	SB
2000	CHC, Atlanta					Did Not Play							

57 — MIKE HARKEY

BULLPEN COACH • OPENING DAY AGE: 44

FULL NAME
Michael Anthony Harkey

BIRTHDATE
October 25, 1966

BIRTHPLACE
San Diego, Calif.

RESIDES
Chino Hills, Calif.

CAREER HIGHLIGHTS
Sporting News
Rookie of the Year
▸ 1990

USA Today
**Minor League Player
of the Year**
▸ 1988

COACHING CAREER
▸ Enters his fourth season as Yankees bullpen coach in 2011…the Yankees have gone 243-4 when leading at the end of the eighth inning since he joined the staff in 2008…Yankees relievers combined for a 3.47 ERA in 2010, third-lowest in the AL, and held opponents to a .230 average, second-lowest in the AL…filled in as pitching coach from 6/4-29/10 during Dave Eiland's leave of absence.

▸ Yankees relievers led the Majors in 2009 with 40 wins and tied for first with 51 saves, ranking second in opponent's batting average (.231) and fifth in strikeouts (483)…allowed 11.64 baserunners/9.0IP, marking the second-lowest ratio in the Majors behind Oakland (11.54)…in 2008, the Yankees' bullpen collected a Major League-high 523K and recorded their lowest ERA (3.78) since 2002 (3.64).

▸ Is his second Major League coaching position, having served as bullpen coach for Joe Girardi with the Florida Marlins in 2006.

▸ Was the pitching coach for the Triple-A Iowa Cubs of the Pacific Coast League in 2007.

▸ Spent six seasons (2000-2005) as a pitching coach in the San Diego organization, making stops at Single-A Rancho Cucamonga (2000), Single-A Fort Wayne (2001, '03), Single-A Lake Elsinore (2002, '04) and Double-A Mobile (2005).

PLAYING CAREER
▸ Appeared in 131 career Major League games (104 starts) over eight seasons with the Cubs (1988-93), Colorado Rockies (1994), Oakland Athletics (1995), California Angels (1995) and Los Angeles Dodgers (1997), going 36-36 with a 4.49 ERA (656.0IP, 327ER).

▸ Was named *Sporting News* 1990 "NL Rookie of the Year" after posting a 12-6 record with a 3.26 ERA in 27 starts for the Cubs…selected as *USA Today* "Minor League Player of the Year" in 1988…made his Major League debut at age 21 on 9/5/88 at Wrigley Field recording a no-decision in Game 2 of a doubleheader vs. the Phillies.

▸ Was a first-round pick by the Cubs in the 1987 First-Year Player Draft (fourth overall)…was originally selected by the San Diego Padres in the 18th round of the 1984 First-Year Player Draft, but chose to attend college.

PERSONAL
▸ Married (Nikki) and has two sons, Tony and Cory, and a daughter, Miani…Tony is a senior infielder for Concordia University and Cory recently completed his junior season as a tight end with UCLA…played baseball at Cal State Fullerton, earning all-American honors as a junior…graduated from Ganesha High School in Pomona, Calif.

Harkey's Career Pitching Record

Year	Club	W-L	ERA	G	GS	CG	SHO	SV	IP	H	R	ER	BB	SO
1987	Peoria	2-3	3.55	12	12	3	0	0	76.0	81	45	30	28	48
	Pittsfield	0-0	0.00	1	0	0	0	0	2.0	1	0	0	0	2
1988	Pittsfield	9-2	1.37	13	13	3	1	0	85.2	66	29	13	35	73
	Iowa	7-2	3.55	12	12	3	1	0	78.2	55	36	31	33	62
	CHICAGO-NL	0-3	2.60	5	5	0	0	0	34.2	33	14	10	15	18
1989	Iowa	2-7	4.43	12	12	0	0	0	63.0	67	37	31	25	37
1990	CHICAGO-NL	12-6	3.26	27	27	2	1	0	173.2	153	71	63	59	94
1991	CHICAGO-NL	0-2	5.30	4	4	0	0	0	18.2	21	11	11	6	15
1992	Peoria	1-0	3.00	2	2	0	0	0	12.0	15	6	4	3	17
	Iowa	0-1	5.56	4	4	0	0	0	22.2	21	15	14	13	6
	Charlotte	0-1	5.63	1	1	1	0	0	8.0	9	5	5	0	5
	CHICAGO-NL	4-0	1.89	7	7	0	0	0	38.0	34	13	8	15	21
1993	CHICAGO-NL	10-10	5.26	28	28	1	0	0	157.1	187	100	92	43	67
	Orlando	0-0	1.69	1	1	0	0	0	5.1	4	1	1	0	5
1994	COLORADO	1-6	5.79	24	13	0	0	0	91.2	125	61	59	35	39
	Colorado Springs	1-1	12.60	2	2	0	0	0	10.0	19	14	14	3	4
1995	OAKLAND	4-6	6.27	14	12	0	0	0	66.0	75	46	46	31	28
	CALIFORNIA	4-3	4.55	12	8	1	0	0	61.1	80	32	31	16	28
1996	Albuquerque	7-11	5.38	49	13	0	0	13	118.2	146	79	71	39	90
1997	LOS ANGELES-NL	1-0	4.30	10	0	0	0	0	14.2	12	8	7	5	6
Minor League Totals		**29-28**	**3.70**	**109**	**72**	**10**	**2**	**13**	**482.0**	**482**	**267**	**214**	**179**	**349**
Major League Totals		**36-36**	**4.49**	**131**	**104**	**4**	**1**	**0**	**656.0**	**720**	**356**	**327**	**225**	**316**

50

MICK KELLEHER

FIRST BASE COACH • OPENING DAY AGE: 63

FULL NAME
Michael Dennis Kelleher

BIRTHDATE
July 25, 1947

BIRTHPLACE
Seattle, Wash.

RESIDES
Solvang, Calif.

COACHING CAREER

▸ Begins his third season as Yankees first base coach in 2011…also serves as infield instructor…the Yankees lead the Majors with a .987 fielding percentage since 2008 when he joined the staff.
▸ In 2010, the Yankees led the Majors with a .988 fielding percentage and committed only 69 errors, setting franchise records for highest fielding percentage and fewest errors for a season…also featured three Gold Glove Award winners (Cano, Jeter, Teixeira), the first time three Yankees infielders won the honor in the same season…the club set a Major League record with 18 consecutive errorless games in 2009.
▸ Is his third tenure on a Major League coaching staff, having served three years as Detroit's first base coach (2003-05) and Pittsburgh's first base coach and infield instructor in 1986.
▸ Spent three years as the Yankees' roving infield instructor (2006-08)…is in his second stint with the Yankees organization, having spent seven seasons (1996-2002) as the Yankees' roving defensive coordinator and one year (1998) as a Major League scout.
▸ Began his coaching career with the San Diego Padres as a roving minor league instructor from 1984-85…joined the Chicago Cubs as a roving minor league infield instructor from 1987-92, taking over as manager of the organization's Triple-A Iowa club in May 1991 for the remainder of the season…also spent two seasons (1994-95) as the roving minor league infield instructor with the Milwaukee Brewers.

PLAYING CAREER

▸ Played 15 seasons of professional baseball, including 11 at the Major League level with the St. Louis Cardinals (1972-73, '75), Houston Astros (1974), Chicago Cubs (1976-80), Detroit Tigers (1981-82) and California Angels (1982)…finished his career with a .974 Major League fielding percentage, appearing in games at second base, third base and shortstop…since retiring in 1982, no position player has accrued as many career plate appearances without a homer (1,202).
▸ Was selected by St. Louis in the third round of the 1969 First-Year Player Draft.
▸ Led shortstops in fielding during four of his minor league seasons and won two Rawlings Silver Glove Awards (1972, '75) as the minors' best fielding SS…established an American Association record for shortstops with a .979 fielding percentage in 1972.
▸ Received his bachelor of science degree in political science from the University of Puget Sound in Tacoma, Wash…was an NCAA Division II All-American in 1969 and was named to the NCAA Division II All-Tournament Team the same season…was also Division II All-Coast in 1968 and '69.

PERSONAL

▸ He and his wife, Renee, have one daughter, Brittney, and two grandchildren…Renee is an accomplished painter, represented at galleries throughout California…is an aficionado of the wine industry and grows his own grapes and olives…in the offseason, works as a ranch hand tending to llamas and cows…also plays in a senior tennis league.

Kelleher's Major League Career Playing Record

Year	Club	AVG.	G	AB	R	H	2B	3B	HR	RBI	BB	SO	SB
1972	ST. LOUIS	.159	23	63	5	10	2	1	0	1	6	15	0
1973	ST. LOUIS	.184	43	38	4	7	2	0	0	2	4	11	0
1974	HOUSTON	.158	19	57	4	9	0	0	0	2	5	10	1
1975	ST. LOUIS	.000	7	4	0	0	0	0	0	0	0	1	0
1976	CHICAGO-NL	.228	124	337	28	77	12	1	0	22	15	32	0
1977	CHICAGO-NL	.230	63	122	14	28	5	2	0	11	9	12	0
1978	CHICAGO-NL	.253	68	95	8	24	1	0	0	6	7	11	4
1979	CHICAGO-NL	.254	73	142	14	36	4	1	0	10	7	9	2
1980	CHICAGO-NL	.146	105	96	12	14	1	1	0	4	9	17	1
1981	DETROIT	.221	61	77	10	17	4	0	0	6	7	10	1
1982	DETROIT	.000	2	1	0	0	0	0	0	0	0	0	0
	CALIFORNIA	.163	34	49	9	8	1	0	0	1	5	5	1
Major League Totals		**.213**	**622**	**1081**	**108**	**230**	**32**	**6**	**0**	**65**	**74**	**133**	**9**

54
KEVIN LONG

HITTING COACH • OPENING DAY AGE: 44

FULL NAME
Kevin Richard Long

BIRTHDATE
December 30, 1966

BIRTHPLACE
Van Nuys, Calif.

RESIDES
Scottsdale, Ariz.

COACHING CAREER

▸ Returns for his fifth season as Yankees hitting coach in 2011…the Yankees have led the Majors in runs scored in three of his four years with the club (2007, '09, and '10).

▸ The 2010 Yankees led the Majors with a .350 on-base percentage and ranked second in in walks (662), third in home runs (201) and eighth in batting average (.267)…had seven players score at least 70 runs, one shy of the franchise record (eight in 1939).

▸ Yankees batters set a franchise record with 244HR in 2009, surpassing the previous mark of 242 (2004)…featured a franchise-record five players with at least 25HR and a franchise-record nine players with at least 65RBI.

▸ The 2008 Yankees ranked third in the AL in OBP (.342), fourth in average (.271) and tied for fourth in HR (180).

▸ Guided a Yankees offense in 2007 that led the Majors in runs (968), hits (1,656), HR (201), RBI (929), team batting average (.290), slugging percentage (.463), OBP (.366) and total bases (2,649)…were the most runs for the franchise since 1937 (979)…the offense also featured the AL MVP (Rodriguez), three Silver Sluggers (Jeter, Posada and Rodriguez) and four of the American League's top-15 batting averages.

▸ Joined the Yankees at the Major League level after serving three years as the hitting coach with the Yankees' Triple-A affiliate in Columbus (2004-06)…before joining the Yankees organization, served as the hitting coach with the Triple-A Omaha Royals (2002-03) and with the Double-A Wichita Wranglers (2000-01)…was named the Northwest League's "co-Manager of the Year" after leading the Spokane Indians to the league title in 1999…made his professional coaching debut at Single-A Wilmington in 1997.

PLAYING CAREER

▸ Was originally selected by the Kansas City Royals in the 31st round of the 1989 First-Year Player Draft and played in their system for eight years from 1989-96 as an outfielder.

▸ Led Class-A Eugene in 1989 in almost all offensive categories, including games played, at-bats, runs scored, hits, doubles and RBI…ranked eighth among all Northwest League hitters with a .312 batting average in his rookie season.

▸ Missed most of the 1994 season after undergoing surgery on his left wrist.

PERSONAL

▸ Named a second-team All-American and first-team PAC-10 in 1989 at the University of Arizona…a three-year letter-winner, Long graduated with the Arizona record for most extra-base hits in a game (five) and ranked in the top 10 in several single-season statistical categories: third in extra-base hits (41), tied for seventh in doubles (23), eighth in multi-hit games (30), ninth in total bases (162) and tied for ninth in runs (80).

▸ Resides in Scottsdale, Ariz., with his wife, Marcey, daughter, Britney, and sons, Tracy and Jaron, a freshman pitcher/outfielder at Chandler-Gilbert Community College.

Long's Career Playing Record

Year	Club	AVG	G	AB	R	H	2B	3B	HR	RBI	BB	SO	SB
1989	Eugene	.312	69	260	54	81	19	1	3	45	36	40	15
1990	Baseball City	.282	85	308	53	87	17	5	5	33	32	28	22
1991	Memphis	.275	106	407	60	112	18	2	3	35	45	63	27
1992	Omaha	.228	88	312	28	71	16	3	1	29	29	41	9
1993	Memphis	.272	79	301	47	82	14	6	1	20	37	56	7
	Omaha	.255	17	51	7	13	2	0	0	4	2	13	3
1994	Memphis	.208	10	24	5	5	3	0	0	1	5	2	2
1995	Omaha	.250	22	64	7	16	3	0	0	1	5	8	1
	Wichita	.292	67	250	38	73	14	1	1	26	41	29	9
1996	Wichita	.273	128	436	62	119	31	3	3	48	56	36	9
Minor League Totals		**.273**	**671**	**2413**	**361**	**659**	**137**	**21**	**17**	**242**	**288**	**316**	**104**

56
TONY PENA

BENCH COACH • OPENING DAY AGE: 53

FULL NAME
Antonio Francisco Pena

BIRTHDATE
June 4, 1957

BIRTHPLACE
Monte Cristi, D.R.

RESIDES
Santiago, D.R.

CAREER HIGHLIGHTS
BBWAA
A.L. Manager of the Year
‣ 2003

N.L. All-Star Team
‣ 1982, 1984, 1985,
  1986, 1989

N.L. Gold Glove Award
‣ 1983, 1984, 1985

A.L. Gold Glove Award
‣ 1991

MANAGERIAL/COACHING CAREER

‣ Enters his third season as Yankees bench coach in 2011…is his sixth season on the Yankees' Major League coaching staff, serving as first base coach from 2006-08 and catching instructor over the entire span…since joining the staff, Yankees catchers have caught a Major League-best 185 potential base stealers.

‣ Previously spent parts of four seasons as manager of the Kansas City Royals from 2002-05.

‣ In his first full season as manager in 2003, led the Royals to an 83-79 record, the sixth-best turnaround in Major League history following a 100-loss season…the 2003 season marked Kansas City's first winning season since 1993, when they went 84-78.

‣ Was selected as the 2003 American League "Manager of the Year" by the Baseball Writers' Association of America, becoming the fourth manager since 1983 to win the award in his first full season as a Major League skipper (also Houston's Hal Lanier, 1986; San Francisco's Dusty Baker, 1993; and San Diego's Bruce Bochy, 1996)… also named the 2003 AL "Manager of the Year" by both *Sporting News* and *Sports Illustrated*.

‣ Became only the third Dominican-born manager in Major League history, joining Felipe Alou and Luis Pujols.

‣ Began his Major League coaching career in 2002 as the bench coach for the Houston Astros…was named Royals manager on 5/15/02.

‣ Also served as manager of Triple-A New Orleans from 1999-2001…began his coaching career as White Sox' Coordinator of Dominican Operations in 1998 and led the Aguilas Dominican team to the Caribbean Series title.

PLAYING CAREER

‣ A five-time National League All-Star catcher, Pena posted a .260 career batting average over an 18-year Major League career, appearing in 1,988 games for the Pittsburgh Pirates (1980-86), St. Louis Cardinals (1987-88), Boston Red Sox (1990-93), Cleveland Indians (1994-96), Chicago White Sox (1997) and Houston Astros (1997).

‣ Ranks fifth all-time among Major League catchers with 1,950 games behind the plate, trailing only Ivan Rodriguez (2,390), Carlton Fisk (2,226), Bob Boone (2,225) and Gary Carter (2,056).

‣ Won four Gold Glove Awards (1983-85, 1991) and recorded a .338 career postseason batting average…was named Topps' Rookie All-Star catcher in 1981 and was selected to the UPI Rookie All-Star Team…originally signed as a non-drafted free agent by the Pittsburgh Pirates on 7/22/75 and made his Major League debut on 9/1/80.

PERSONAL

‣ Married (Amaris) with two sons: Tony, Jr. (who pitched last season in the San Francisco system) and Francisco Antonio (a catcher in the New York Mets system)…also has a daughter, Jennifer Amaris, who won the Miss Dominican Republic-U.S.A. beauty pageant in 2007…his brother, Ramon, pitched with the Detroit Tigers organization.

‣ Tony did not play high school baseball…credits his mother, who was an outstanding softball player, with teaching him how to play the game.

‣ Took part in the Yankees' hurricane relief donation of $35,000 in cash and food to the Dominican Republic in October 2007.

‣ Joined the Yankees delegation and the 2009 World Series trophy on 1/7/10 to meet Dominican Republic President Dr. Leonel Fernandez at the National Palace in Santo Domingo.

Pena's Career Playing Record

Year	Club	AVG	G	AB	R	H	2B	3B	HR	RBI	BB	SO	SB
1976	Bradenton	.209	33	110	10	23	2	2	1	11	4	17	5
	Charleston	.224	14	49	4	11	2	0	1	8	4	7	0
1977	Charleston	.238	29	101	10	24	4	0	3	16	7	21	2
	Salem	.276	84	319	36	88	15	3	7	46	14	60	3
1978	Shreveport	.230	104	348	34	80	14	0	8	42	15	96	3
1979	Buffalo	.313	134	515	89	161	16	4	34	97	39	83	5
1980	Portland	.329	124	450	57	148	23	13	9	77	29	75	5
1980	PITTSBURGH	.429	8	21	1	9	1	1	0	1	0	4	0
1981	PITTSBURGH	.300	66	210	16	63	9	1	2	17	8	23	1
1982	PITTSBURGH	.296	138	497	53	147	28	4	11	63	17	57	2
1983	PITTSBURGH	.301	151	542	51	163	22	3	15	70	31	73	6
1984	PITTSBURGH	.286	147	546	77	156	27	2	15	78	36	79	12
1985	PITTSBURGH	.249	147	546	53	136	27	2	10	59	29	67	12
1986	PITTSBURGH	.288	144	510	56	147	26	2	10	52	53	69	9
1987	ST. LOUIS	.214	116	384	40	82	13	4	5	44	36	54	6
1988	ST. LOUIS	.263	149	505	55	133	23	1	10	51	33	60	6
1989	ST. LOUIS	.259	141	424	36	110	17	2	4	37	35	33	5
1990	BOSTON	.263	143	491	62	129	19	1	7	56	43	71	8
1991	BOSTON	.231	141	464	45	107	23	2	5	48	37	53	8
1992	BOSTON	.241	133	410	39	99	21	1	1	38	24	61	3
1993	BOSTON	.181	126	304	20	55	11	0	4	19	25	46	1
1994	CLEVELAND	.295	40	112	18	33	8	1	2	10	9	11	0
1995	CLEVELAND	.262	91	263	25	69	15	0	5	28	14	44	1
1996	CLEVELAND	.195	67	174	14	34	4	0	1	27	15	25	0
1997	CHICAGO-AL	.164	31	67	4	11	1	0	0	8	8	13	0
	HOUSTON	.211	9	19	2	4	3	0	0	2	2	3	0
Minor League Totals		**.283**	**522**	**1892**	**240**	**535**	**76**	**22**	**63**	**297**	**112**	**359**	**23**
Major League Totals		**.260**	**1988**	**6489**	**667**	**1687**	**298**	**27**	**107**	**708**	**455**	**846**	**80**

Pena's Division Series Record

Year	Club/Opponent	AVG	G	AB	R	H	2B	3B	HR	RBI	BB	SO	SB
1995	CLE vs. BOS	.500	2	2	1	1	0	0	1	1	0	0	0
1996	CLE vs. BAL	.000	1	0	0	0	0	0	0	0	0	0	0
1997	HOU vs. ATL	.000	2	0	0	0	0	0	0	0	0	0	0
Division Series Totals		**.200**	**5**	**2**	**1**	**1**	**0**	**0**	**1**	**1**	**0**	**0**	**0**

Pena's League Championship Series Record

Year	Club/Opponent	AVG	G	AB	R	H	2B	3B	HR	RBI	BB	SO	SB
1987	STL vs. SF	.381	7	21	5	8	0	1	0	0	3	4	1
1990	BOS vs. OAK	.214	4	14	0	3	0	0	0	0	0	0	0
1995	CLE vs. SEA	.333	4	6	1	2	1	0	0	0	1	0	0
LCS TOTALS		**.317**	**15**	**41**	**6**	**13**	**1**	**1**	**0**	**0**	**4**	**4**	**1**

Pena's World Series Record

Year	Club/Opponent	AVG	G	AB	R	H	2B	3B	HR	RBI	BB	SO	SB
1987	STL vs. MIN	.409	7	22	2	9	1	0	0	4	3	2	1
1995	CLE vs. ATL	.167	2	6	0	1	0	0	0	0	0	0	0
World Series Totals		**.357**	**9**	**28**	**2**	**10**	**1**	**0**	**0**	**4**	**3**	**2**	**1**
POSTSEASON TOTALS		**.338**	**29**	**71**	**9**	**24**	**2**	**1**	**1**	**5**	**7**	**6**	**2**

Pena's All-Star Game Record

Year	Club, Site	AVG	G	AB	R	H	2B	3B	HR	RBI	BB	SO	SB
1982	PIT, Montreal	.000	1	1	0	0	0	0	0	0	0	0	1
1984	PIT, San Francisco	.000	1	0	0	0	0	0	0	0	0	0	0
1985	PIT, Minnesota	.000	1	1	0	0	0	0	0	0	0	1	0
1986	PIT, Houston	.000	1	0	0	0	0	0	0	0	0	0	0
1989	STL, Anaheim	.000	1	2	0	0	0	0	0	0	0	0	0
All-Star Game Totals		**.000**	**5**	**4**	**0**	**0**	**0**	**0**	**0**	**0**	**0**	**1**	**1**

PENA'S MANAGERIAL RECORD

Year	Team	W	L	Pct.	Position
2002	KANSAS CITY	49	77	.389	Fourth
2003	KANSAS CITY	83	79	.512	Third
2004	KANSAS CITY	58	104	.358	Fifth
2005	KANSAS CITY	8	25	.242	---
TOTAL		**198**	**285**	**.410**	

58 LARRY ROTHSCHILD

PITCHING COACH • OPENING DAY AGE: 57

FULL NAME
Lawrence Lee Rothschild

BIRTHDATE
March 12, 1954

BIRTHPLACE
Chicago, Ill.

RESIDES
Tampa, Fla.

COACHING CAREER

- Begins his first season as Yankees pitching coach in 2011, marking his 37th season in professional baseball as a player, coach or manager.
- Spent the previous nine seasons (2002-10) as pitching coach for the Chicago Cubs, where the franchise combined to lead the Majors in strikeouts over the stretch (11,604).
- The Cubs led the NL and ranked second in the Majors with 96 quality starts in 2010…Chicago's team ERA ranked in the top five of the NL in three straight seasons from 2007-09, marking the first such stretch in club history since a six-season stretch from 1943-48…Cubs pitchers led the Majors in strikeouts in each of his first seven seasons through 2008, including a still-standing single-season Major League-record of 1,404K in 2003…the '07 Cubs staff posted a 4.04 ERA, second in the NL to San Diego's 3.70 mark.

ROTHSCHILD'S CAREER MANAGERIAL RECORD

Year	Team	W	L	Pct.	Position
1998	Tampa Bay	63	99	.389	Fifth
1999	Tampa Bay	69	93	.426	Fifth
2000	Tampa Bay	69	92	.429	Fifth
2001	Tampa Bay	4	10	.286	---
TOTALS		**205**	**294**	**.411**	

- Was a member of World Series-winning coaching staffs with Cincinnati in 1990 and Florida in 1997.
- Began his coaching career as a roving minor league pitching instructor for the Cincinnati Reds from 1986-89, before joining the Major League staff as bullpen coach from 1990-91 and then pitching coach from 1992-93…served as roving minor league pitching instructor for the Atlanta Braves in 1994…was pitching coach for the Florida Marlins from 1995-97.
- Served as the first manager in Tampa Bay Devil Rays history, getting named to the post on 11/7/97…went 205-294 from 1998 through 4/18/01…increased the franchise's winning percentage in each of his three full seasons with the organization…finished the 2001 season as a consultant in the Marlins organization…was named to Joe Torre's 2000 AL All-Star coaching staff.

PLAYING CAREER

- Had an 11-year career from 1975-85 with the Cincinnati and Detroit organizations…made 387 appearances (80 starts) in the minors, going 66-46 with 50 saves and a 3.96 ERA…signed by the Reds as a non-drafted free agent in 1975.
- Made seven career Major League appearances, all in relief, with the Tigers during the 1981 and '82 seasons, recording a 5.40 ERA with no decisions and one save…made his Major League debut on 9/11/81 vs. Cleveland (0.1IP, 1IBB).

PERSONAL

- Married (Jane) and has three children, Charlotte, Claire and Scott…attended Bradley University and Florida State University, graduating from FSU with a degree in business management…was a member of FSU's 1975 NCAA Regional Championship team.

Rothschild's Career Pitching Record

Year	Club	W-L	ERA	G	GS	CG	SHO	SV	IP	H	R	ER	BB	SO
1975	Billings	0-2	7.88	6	0	0	0	1	8.0	14	11	7	7	12
	Eugene	3-0	2.73	21	0	0	0	6	33.0	17	11	10	21	36
1976	Three Rivers	11-3	2.05	30	12	10	5	5	123.0	96	33	28	29	75
1977	Indianapolis	4-4	4.21	29	14	2	1	1	92.0	93	51	43	34	43
1978	Nashville	0-0	4.50	5	0	0	0	1	12.0	14	7	6	4	9
	Amarillo	5-5	4.17	12	12	5	1	0	82.0	83	42	38	21	57
	Indianapolis	4-0	2.20	8	6	2	0	0	45.0	31	15	11	19	38
1979	Indianapolis	1-6	5.27	33	10	0	0	6	82.0	85	52	48	56	68
1980	Indianapolis	8-7	4.22	33	14	1	0	1	113.0	111	60	53	44	74
1981	Evansville	8-5	3.27	56	0	0	0	15	77.0	62	32	28	29	81
	DETROIT	0-0	1.59	5	0	0	0	1	5.2	4	1	1	6	1
1982	Evansville	6-4	3.65	45	0	0	0	10	69.0	73	34	28	39	45
	DETROIT	0-0	13.50	2	0	0	0	0	2.2	4	4	4	2	0
1983	Las Vegas	9-2	5.09	38	0	0	0	2	74.1	88	43	42	34	39
1984	Denver	6-3	4.02	31	9	1	0	2	109.2	109	58	49	51	71
1985	Iowa	1-5	5.32	40	3	0	0	0	89.2	101	58	53	34	58
Minor League Totals		**66-46**	**3.96**	**387**	**80**	**21**	**8**	**50**	**1009.2**	**977**	**507**	**444**	**413**	**706**
Major League Totals		**0-0**	**5.40**	**7**	**0**	**0**	**0**	**1**	**8.1**	**8**	**5**	**5**	**8**	**1**

59

ROB THOMSON

THIRD BASE COACH • OPENING DAY AGE: 47

FULL NAME
Robert Thomson

BIRTHDATE
August 16, 1963

BIRTHPLACE
Ontario, Canada

RESIDES
Odessa, Fla.

COACHING CAREER

▸ Begins his 22nd season as a member of the Yankees organization in 2011, fourth on the Yankees Major League coaching staff and third as third base coach…served as the club's bench coach for the 2008 season.

▸ Managed the Yankees for three games in 2008, going 1-2, becoming the first Canadian to manage a Major League game since George (Mooney) Gibson, a Londoner, with the Pittsburgh Pirates in 1934…was 0-2 from 4/4-5 vs. Tampa Bay when Joe Girardi missed two games with an upper respiratory infection…won on 5/23 vs. Baltimore while Girardi served a one-game suspension…also guided the Yankees to a "walk-off" victory on 5/22 vs. Baltimore when Joe Girardi was ejected in the sixth inning…went in the books as Girardi's 100th career managerial victory…again took over following a Girardi ejection on 7/5 vs. Boston, also recording a "walk-off" win.

▸ Served as the Yankees' Major League field coordinator in 2007 after spending the previous three seasons as a special assignment instructor…was named to the Yankees' Major League coaching staff on 11/4/03.

▸ Joined the Yankees organization in 1990 as a third-base coach for Single-A Fort Lauderdale.

▸ Coached in the Yankees system for five years before taking over as manager of Single-A Oneonta of the NY-Penn League in 1995.

▸ Served as the third base coach at Triple-A Columbus in 1996 and 1997 before moving to the Yankees front office as a field coordinator in 1998.

▸ Was promoted to director of player development in 2000 and named vice president of minor league development prior to the 2003 season.

PLAYING CAREER

▸ Attended the University of Kansas and was selected in the 32nd round of the 1985 draft by the Detroit Tigers.

▸ Was a catcher and a third baseman in the Tigers system from 1985-88 before joining the Tigers' minor league coaching staff in 1988.

PERSONAL

▸ Resides in Odessa, Fla., with his wife, Michele and their daughters, Jacqueline and Christina.

Thomson's Career Playing Record

Year	Club	AVG	G	AB	R	H	2B	3B	HR	RBI	BB	SO	SB
1985	Bristol	.000	2	5	0	0	0	0	0	0	1	3	0
	Gastonia	.187	39	123	7	23	6	0	0	10	5	17	0
1986	Gastonia	.252	94	298	42	75	11	1	4	38	48	44	1
	Lakeland	.182	8	22	2	4	1	0	1	4	0	2	0
1987	Lakeland	.228	71	206	21	47	12	0	1	22	25	30	2
1988	Lakeland	.000	2	7	0	0	0	0	0	0	0	2	0
Minor League Totals		**.225**	**216**	**661**	**72**	**149**	**30**	**1**	**6**	**74**	**79**	**98**	**3**

Scoring Machine

The Yankees hold the Major League record for consecutive games without being shut out, scoring at least one run in 308 straight contests from 8/3/31-8/2/33…the streak was broken by a 7-0 shutout by Philadelphia's Lefty Grove.

2011 Yankees Field Staff

Gene Monahan
Head Athletic Trainer

The 2011 season will mark his 49th consecutive season with the New York Yankees organization, the last 39 as the Head Athletic Trainer on the Major League level…is the longest-tenured active head trainer in the Major Leagues…in 2009, received the National Athletic Trainers Association "Distinguished Athletic Trainer" Award…was honored with induction into the New York State Athletic Trainers' Association Hall of Fame in 2007…began his athletic-training career with the Yankees' Class-D Ft. Lauderdale affiliate in 1963…had served as a bat boy and clubhouse attendant for the club in 1962 during his senior year at St. Thomas Aquinas High School in Ft. Lauderdale…was promoted to Double-A in 1965 and was head trainer for Columbus (Ga.) and Binghamton (N.Y.) until 1969 when he made the jump to Triple-A Syracuse (1969-72)…served as head trainer for the American League All-Star team for the fourth time in his career in 2008 at Yankee Stadium (also 1977, '86 and '92)…a 1969 graduate of Indiana University, he received a B.S. in physical education (with emphasis on professional athletic training)…was presented with the distinguished service award by the American College of Sports Medicine in 1994…is Chairman of the Professional Baseball Athletic Trainers Society's scholarship committee and a member of the National Athletic Trainers Association's Public Relations Committee…has two daughters, Kelley and Amanda…resides in Hackensack, N.J.

Top Tandem

Gene Monahan and Steve Donohue—whom have been paired together since 1986—were named the "Best Athletic Trainers" in Major League Baseball in 2010 by the Professional Baseball Athletic Trainer Society (PBATS)…the duo was also honored with the Major League Baseball "Athletic Training Staff of the Year" award in 1990.

Steve Donohue
Assistant Athletic Trainer

Begins his 33rd consecutive season in the New York Yankees organization, the last 26 as Assistant Athletic Trainer under Gene Monahan at the Major League level…served as an athletic trainer for the American League squad at the 2006 All-Star Game at Pittsburgh's PNC Park and the 1999 All-Star Game at Fenway Park…began his athletic training career in 1979 at the Yankees' Double-A West Haven affiliate before being promoted to Double-A Nashville (1980-81) and Triple-A Columbus (1982-85)…was promoted to the New York Yankees in 1986…is a 1974 graduate of Cardinal Spellman High School in the Bronx and a 1979 graduate of the University of Louisville…was the trainer for the NCAA Champion University of Louisville basketball team in 1980…is a member of the National Athletic Trainers Association and the Eastern Athletic Trainers Association…also pens the annual Professional Baseball Athletic Trainers Society's *Confidential Directory*…he and his wife, Paula, have two daughters, Shannon and Margaret…was born in Bronxville, N.Y.

Dana Cavalea
Strength and Conditioning Coordinator

Enters his fifth season as the Yankees' strength and conditioning coordinator after taking over the post in May 2007…was appointed as the Yankees' strength and conditioning assistant prior to the start of the 2007 season after serving as a strength and conditioning coach during spring training from 2003-06…also served in the same capacity with the Toronto Blue Jays (2001) and Pittsburgh Pirates (2002)…founded Major League Strength, a sports performance consulting firm that teaches nutrition, injury prevention and performance maximization to coaches around the country…was born on 10/15/82 in New York, N.Y., and attended the University of South Florida in Tampa, where he earned his degree in exercise science in 2004…holds a CSCS certification from the NSCA and PES certification from the NASM…is single and resides in White Plains.

2011 Yankees Field Staff

#87 Charlie Wonsowicz
Advance Scout/Head Video Coordinator

Enters his 19th season in the Yankees organization, third in his current position…is a 1986 graduate of Tottenville High School in Staten Island (N.Y.) where he was a second-team All-American in baseball…from 1987-90, pitched at St. John's University (N.Y.) on a four-year baseball scholarship…coached the Tottenville High varsity baseball team from 1991-92 and coached in the Atlantic Coast Summer Baseball League from 1992-93…was born on 9/5/68 in Staten Island, N.Y.…resides in Waldwick, N.J., with his wife, Leslie, and their three children, Paige Olivia, C.J. and Jake.

#88 Roman Rodriguez
Bullpen Catcher

Begins his 10th year with the Yankees organization as a bullpen catcher…also assists by charting pitches during games…was signed as a non-drafted free agent in 1988 by the Pittsburgh Pirates…spent eight years in the Pirates minor league system…following his playing career, was hired by the Kansas City Royals from 1997-2000 as their bullpen catcher…spent the following season (2001) as the Boston Red Sox bullpen catcher…married his wife, Carminia, on Valentine's Day in 2004 and now resides in Bradenton, Fla, with their daughter, Adriana…was born on 3/30/69 in San Mateo, Venezuela.

Rob Cucuzza
Equipment Manager

Begins his 14th season as home clubhouse manager…was named the 2010 MLB "Home Clubhouse Manager of the Year"—as voted by his peers…has been a member of the Yankees organization since 1984, working as a bat boy (1984-86), assistant visiting clubhouse manager (1987-89) and assistant equipment manager (1990-97)…was born on 1/4/68 in the Bronx, N.Y., and is a 1985 graduate of Mount St. Michael Academy…is single and resides in White Plains, N.Y.

Lou Cucuzza, Jr.
Clubhouse Manager

Is in his 32nd year in the New York Yankees organization, starting as a batboy in 1979…was named the 2010 MLB "Visiting Clubhouse Manager of the Year"—as voted by his peers—earning the title for the second straight season and third time in the last five years (also 2006)…earned a B.A. in public accounting from Iona College…worked five years as an auditor for the accounting firm of KPMG Peat Marwick (1987-91) and five years as budgeting manager for Melville Corporation (1992-96)…was born on 8/5/64 in the Bronx, N.Y.…resides in Yonkers, N.Y., with his wife Joanna and their children, Anthony and Kathryn.

Lou Cucuzza, Sr.
Clubhouse Assistant

Returns for his 35th season in the visiting clubhouse…the patriarch of the Cucuzza baseball family, has 47 years of service in professional baseball, also serving on the Mets clubhouse staff…was born on 11/19/38 in New York, N.Y., and resides in the Bronx with his wife, Joan.

Additional Yankees Support Staff

Chad Bohling, Director, Mental Conditioning
Doug Cecil, Massage Therapist
Anthony Flynn, Video Coordinator
Brett Weber, Coaching Assistant

Clubhouse Assistants:

Cesar Caceres
Chris Cruz
Michael Fosina
Joe Lee
Chris Manzione
Jake Ryan

2011 Yankees Medical Staff

Dr. Christopher Ahmad, M.D.

Team Physician

Dr. Christopher S. Ahmad begins his third season as Yankees Team Physician in 2011…has been an Assistant Attending Orthopaedic Surgeon in the Sports Medicine and Shoulder Service at New York Orthopaedic Hospital since 2001…has also served as an Associate Professor of Orthopedic Surgery at Columbia University since 2007 after having been an Assistant Professor beginning in 2001…trained in sports medicine at the Kerlan-Jobe Orthopaedic Clinic from 2000-01, which included team physician coverage for the Dodgers (MLB), Lakers (NBA), Kings (NHL), Galaxy (MLS) and Fullerton College football…was Administrative Chief Resident of Orthopaedic Surgery from 1999-2000 at Columbia University, where he served his orthopaedic surgery residency from 1996-99…completed the Frank E. Stinchfield Orthopaedic Research Fellowship at Columbia from 1994-95…received his M.D. from the NYU School of Medicine in 1994 and a B.S. in Mechanical Engineering from Columbia University in 1990…is the author of more than 50 peer-reviewed research articles as well as a textbook on minimally invasive shoulder and elbow surgery…has been elected into the American Orthopaedic Society for Sports Medicine and the American Shoulder and Elbow Surgeons Society…his practice specializes in advanced arthroscopic surgical techniques for sports-related injuries of the knee, shoulder and elbow.

Dr. Stuart J. Hershon, M.D., P.C.

Senior Advisor, Orthopedics

Born December 18, 1937, in Brooklyn, N.Y., Hershon enters his 24th season as part of the Yankees' medical staff, serving as the team's head physician from 1988-2008…is an orthopedic surgeon affiliated with Columbia Presbyterian Medical Center, Roosevelt Hospital and North Shore University Hospital, Manhasset, where he is Chief of Sports Medicine…graduated from Harvard University (1959) and New York Medical College (1963) before serving as a medical officer with the U.S. Navy from 1964-66…was a starting tight end for Harvard and their leading receiver in 1958…was also a standout football player at Long Beach (N.Y.) High School and was a *Newsday* "All-Scholastic" end in 1954…has also served as team physician for the New York Arrows of the Major Indoor Soccer League and Nassau Community College…Dr. Hershon and his wife, Judy, reside in Cove Neck, N.Y., and have two children, Joanna and Jordan.

Dr. Andrew G. Boyer, M.D.

Team Physician, Tampa

Enters his 17th season as a Yankees team physician…has been in private practice - Internal Medicine - since 1972…earned his undergraduate degree from Kent State University (Ohio), where he was a team captain for the track team…earned his medical degree from the University of Iowa, Iowa City, and served his internal medicine residency at the Mayo Clinic (Minn.)…was on the faculty of the University of South Florida Medical School, served as the team doctor for the Tampa Bay Rowdies professional soccer team and is presently associated with St. Joseph's Hospital, where he served as Chief of Staff…he is a member of the American Medical Association (AMA), Florida Medical Association (FMA) and the Hillsborough County Medical Association (HCMA)…is married to Ildiko and has two children, Cynthia and Andrew…Cynthia is a radiation oncologist and Andrew is an orthopedic surgeon.

First Home Runs in Franchise History
Courtesy of the *Elias Sports Bureau*

The first home run in franchise history was hit by John Ganzel on May 11, 1903. It was a fifth-inning, inside-the-park, solo homer at the Detroit Tigers' Bennett Park off George Mullin in an 8-2 Highlanders victory.

The first home run hit at home in franchise history was by Ernie Courtney on June 1, 1903. The two-run shot in the bottom of the ninth with one out at Hilltop Park came off Boston's Tom Hughes and accounted for both runs in the 8-2 Highlanders loss.

2011 Yankees Medical Staff

Dr. Allen D. Miller, M.D.

Team Orthopedic Surgeon, Tampa

Begins his 15th season with the New York Yankees…is an orthopedic surgeon affiliated with Orthopedic Associates of Tampa (Fla.), where he has been in practice since 1979…is a graduate of McGill University (1975) in Montreal…also earned an MBA from the University of South Florida in 1995…is a member of both the American Academy of Orthopedic Surgeons and the Florida Orthopedic Society.

Dr. Scott L. Hegseth, D.C.

Team Chiropractor, Tampa

Begins his 25th season as the Yankees' team chiropractor…has been in private practice since 1980…earned his undergraduate degree from Mankato State University (Minn.)–which is now Minnesota State University, Mankato–and graduated from Northwestern College of Chiropractic (Minn.)…is a member of the American Chiropractic Association (ACA), Florida Chiropractic Association (FCA), Hillsborough County Chiropractic Society (HCCS) and is a Diplomat of the National Board of Chiropractic Examiners…is married to Virginia and has three children: Kelsey, Allison and Patrick.

Medical Consultants

Norman Castellano, M.D. - Physician
Adam Cohen, M.D. - Assistant Team Physician
Louis Bigliani, M.D. – Consultant, Orthopedics
Conrad Blum, M.D. – Internist
Scott Levy, DDS – Dentist
Lewis Schneider, M.D. – Consultant, Gastroenterology
George Todd, M.D. – Consultant, Vascular Surgery
Darrell Rigel, M.D. – Dermatologist

Baseball Glossary

HOW TO FIGURE…

Batting Average: (H/AB) Hits divided by at-bats.

ERA: (ERx9/IP) Multiply earned runs by nine and divide the total by innings pitched.

Slugging Percentage: (TB/AB) Total bases (1B=1, 2B=2, 3B=3, HR=4) divided by at-bats.

On-Base Percentage: (H+BB+HBP)/(H+BB+HBP+SF) Add hits, walks, hit by pitch and divide by the total of hits plus walks plus hit-by-pitch plus sacrifice flies.

Fielding Percentage: (PO+A)/(PO+A+E) Total putouts plus assists divided by total chances.

Winning Percentage: The number of games won divided by the total games played.

Magic Number: Determine the number of games yet to be played, add one, then subtract the number of games ahead in the loss column of the standings from the closest opponent.

QUALIFYING RULES

Batting Championship: To qualify for a batting title, a player must make 502 or more plate appearances or 3.1 plate appearances per team game.

Pitching Championship: To qualify for the lowest ERA, a pitcher must throw at least 162.0 innings.

Fielding Championship: To qualify as the top fielder:
  (a) a catcher must have played in at least 81 games.
  (b) an infielder or outfielder must have played in at least 108 games.
  (c) a pitcher must have 162.0 innings pitched.

Rookie: A player shall be considered a rookie unless, during a previous season or seasons, he has (a) exceeded 130 at-bats or 50 innings pitched in the major leagues; or (b) accumulated more than 45 days on the active roster of a major league club or clubs during the period of the 25-player limit.

Save: Credit a pitcher with a save when:
  (1) He is the finishing pitcher in a game won by his club;
  (2) He is not the winning pitcher, and
  (3) He qualifies under one of the following conditions:
    a. He enters the game with a lead of no more than three runs and pitches for at least one inning, or
    b. He enters the game with the potential tying run either on base, at bat or on deck, or
    c. He pitches effectively for at least three innings
  No more than one save may be credited each game.

2011 New York Yankees 40-Man Roster

MANAGER: Joe Girardi (28)
COACHES: Mike Harkey (57, Bullpen), Mick Kelleher (50, First Base), Kevin Long (54, Hitting), Tony Pena (56, Bench), Larry Rothschild (58, Pitching), Rob Thomson (59, Third Base)
HEAD TRAINER: Gene Monahan **ASSISTANT TRAINER:** Steve Donohue **TEAM PHYSICIAN:** Dr. Christopher Ahmad **SPRING TRAINING PHYSICIAN:** Dr. Andrew Boyer
EQUIPMENT MANAGER: Rob Cucuzza **CLUBHOUSE MANAGER:** Lou Cucuzza, Jr. **DIRECTOR OF TEAM TRAVEL:** Ben Tulebitz
DIRECTOR OF COMMUNICATIONS & MEDIA RELATIONS: Jason Zillo

(roster as of 2/15/11)

#	PITCHERS (20)	B-T	HT.	WT.	BORN	BIRTHPLACE	2010 CLUB	W-L	ERA	G	GS	CG	SV	IP	H	R	ER	BB	SO	SVC
72	Betances, Dellin	R-R	6-8	260	3/23/88	New York, NY	Tampa	8-1	1.77	14	14	0	0	71.0	43	18	14	19	88	0.000
							Trenton	0-0	3.77	3	3	0	0	14.1	10	7	6	3	20	
66	Brackman, Andrew	R-R	6-10	232	12/4/85	Cincinnati, OH	Tampa	5-4	5.10	12	12	0	0	60.0	67	38	34	9	56	1.027
							Trenton	5-7	3.01	15	14	0	0	80.2	77	38	27	30	70	
34	Burnett, A.J.	R-R	6-4	230	1/3/77	North Little Rock, AR	YANKEES	10-15	5.26	33	33	1	0	186.2	204	118	109	78	145	11.038
62	Chamberlain, Joba	R-R	6-2	240	9/23/85	Lincoln, NE	YANKEES	3-4	4.40	73	0	0	3	71.2	71	37	35	22	77	3.055
31	Feliciano, Pedro	L-L	5-10	190	8/25/76	Rio Piedras, P.R.	NEW YORK-NL	3-6	3.30	92	0	0	0	62.2	66	24	23	30	56	6.059
79	Fish, Robert	L-L	6-2	230	1/19/88	Montclair, CA	Rancho Cucamonga	2-0	1.13	10	0	0	0	16.0	7	2	2	8	25	0.000
							Arkansas	3-5	8.93	39	0	0	2	42.1	59	50	42	18	48	
82	Garrison, Steve	L-L	6-1	185	9/12/86	Trenton, NJ	Lake Elsinore	1-1	3.14	9	3	0	0	28.2	28	13	10	10	13	0.000
							Portland	1-3	8.87	5	5	0	0	22.1	34	22	22	7	17	
65	Hughes, Phil	R-R	6-5	240	6/24/86	Mission Viejo, CA	YANKEES	18-8	4.19	31	29	0	0	176.1	162	83	82	58	146	3.113
48	Logan, Boone	R-L	6-5	215	8/13/84	San Antonio, TX	Scranton/WB	0-1	2.11	14	0	0	0	21.1	18	5	5	4	23	3.140
							YANKEES	2-0	2.93	51	0	0	0	40.0	34	13	13	20	38	
43	Marte, Damaso	L-L	6-2	213	2/14/75	Santo Domingo, D.R.	YANKEES	0-0	4.08	30	0	0	0	17.2	10	8	8	11	12	9.122
45	Mitre, Sergio	R-R	6-3	225	2/16/81	Los Angeles, CA	YANKEES	0-3	3.33	27	3	0	1	54.0	43	23	20	16	29	5.132
74	Noesi, Hector	R-R	6-2	174	1/26/87	Esperanza, D.R.	Tampa	5-2	2.72	8	8	0	0	43.0	35	14	13	6	53	0.000
							Trenton	8-4	3.10	17	16	2	0	98.2	90	37	34	18	86	
							Scranton/WB	1-1	4.82	3	3	1	0	18.2	23	10	10	4	14	
47	Nova, Ivan	R-R	6-4	225	1/12/87	San Cristobal, D.R	Scranton/WB	12-3	2.86	23	23	0	0	145.0	135	50	46	48	115	0.051
							YANKEES	1-2	4.50	10	7	0	0	42.0	44	22	21	17	26	
80	Pope, Ryan	R-R	6-3	190	5/21/86	Bradenton, FL	Trenton	4-6	4.20	46	7	0	17	94.1	88	48	44	31	85	0.000
42	Rivera, Mariano	R-R	6-2	185	11/29/69	Panama City, Panama	YANKEES	3-3	1.80	61	0	0	33	60.0	39	14	12	11	45	15.105
30	Robertson, David	R-R	5-11	190	4/9/85	Birmingham, AL	YANKEES	4-5	3.82	64	0	0	1	61.1	59	26	26	33	71	2.070
52	Sabathia, CC	L-L	6-7	290	7/21/80	Vallejo, CA	YANKEES	21-7	3.18	34	34	2	0	237.2	209	92	84	74	197	10.000
54	Sanchez, Romulo	R-R	6-5	260	4/28/84	Carora, Venezuela	Scranton/WB	10-8	3.97	31	14	0	0	104.1	88	46	46	59	96	0.117
							YANKEES	0-0	0.00	2	0	0	0	4.1	1	0	0	3	5	
29	Soriano, Rafael	R-R	6-1	220	12/19/79	San Jose, D.R.	TAMPA BAY	3-2	1.73	64	0	0	45	62.1	36	14	12	14	57	8.057
73	Turpen, Daniel	R-R	6-4	230	8/17/86	McMinnville, OR	Richmond	5-5	4.09	37	0	0	1	50.2	55	24	23	19	42	0.000
							Portland	2-1	4.91	8	0	0	0	18.1	18	11	10	9	18	

#	CATCHERS (3)	B-T	HT.	WT.	BORN	BIRTHPLACE	2010 CLUB	AVG	G	AB	R	H	2B	3B	HR	RBI	BB	SO	SB	SVC
7	Cervelli, Francisco	R-R	6-1	210	3/6/86	Valencia, Venezuela	YANKEES	.271	93	266	27	72	11	3	0	38	33	42	1	1.113
55	Martin, Russell	R-R	5-10	215	2/15/83	Ontario, Canada	DODGERS	.248	97	331	45	82	13	0	5	26	48	61	6	4.150
20	Posada, Jorge	S-R	6-2	215	8/17/71	Santurce, P.R.	YANKEES	.248	120	383	49	95	23	1	18	57	59	99	3	14.085

#	INFIELDERS (9)	B-T	HT.	WT.	BORN	BIRTHPLACE	2010 CLUB	AVG	G	AB	R	H	2B	3B	HR	RBI	BB	SO	SB	SVC
24	Cano, Robinson	L-R	6-0	205	10/22/82	San Pedro, D.R.	YANKEES	.319	160	626	103	200	41	3	29	109	57	77	3	5.153
66	Corona, Reegie	S-R	5-11	160	11/7/86	Caracas, Venezuela	Scranton/WB	.238	105	387	46	92	20	5		31	36	58	14	0.000
2	Jeter, Derek	R-R	6-3	195	6/26/74	Pequannock, NJ	YANKEES	.270	157	663	111	179	30	3	10	67	63	106	18	15.043
51	Laird, Brandon	R-R	6-1	215	9/11/87	Cypress, CA	Trenton	.291	107	409	73	119	22	2	23	90	38	84	2	0.000
							Scranton/WB	.246	31	122	13	30	6	0	2	12	4	27	0	
27	Nunez, Eduardo	R-R	6-0	155	6/15/87	Santo Domingo, D.R.	Scranton/WB	.289	118	464	55	134	25	3	4	50	32	60	23	0.046
							YANKEES	.280	30	50	12	14	1	0	1	7	3	7	2	5
19	Pena, Ramiro	S-R	5-11	165	7/18/85	Monterrey, Mexico	YANKEES	.227	85	154	18	35	1	1	0	8	4	23	1	1.137
13	Rodriguez, Alex	R-R	6-3	228	7/27/75	New York, NY	YANKEES	.270	137	522	74	141	29	2	30	125	59	98	4	16.011
3	Russo, Kevin	R-R	5-11	190	9/8/84	West Babylon, NY	Scranton/WB	.259	81	332	41	86	16	2	1	24	28	65	9	0.086
							YANKEES	.184	31	49	5	9	2	0	0	4	3	9	1	
25	Teixeira, Mark	S-R	6-3	220	4/11/80	Annapolis, MD	YANKEES	.256	158	601	113	154	36	0	33	108	93	122	0	8.000

#	OUTFIELDERS (8)	B-T	HT.	WT.	BORN	BIRTHPLACE	2010 CLUB	AVG	G	AB	R	H	2B	3B	HR	RBI	BB	SO	SB	SVC
	Curtis, Colin	L-L	6-1	200	2/1/85	Issaquah, WA	Scranton/WB	.289	66	239	28	69	24	0	5	27	21	38	1	0.069
							YANKEES	.186	31	59	7	11	3	0	1	8	4	15	0	
11	Gardner, Brett	L-L	5-10	183	8/24/83	Holly Hill, SC	YANKEES	.277	150	477	97	132	20	7	5	47	79	101	47	2.072
	Golson, Greg	R-R	6-0	190	9/17/85	Austin, TX	Scranton/WB	.263	116	415	51	109	23	5	10	40	25	99	17	0.077
							YANKEES	.261	24	23	3	6	2	0	0	2	0	5	3	
14	Granderson, Curtis	L-R	6-1	185	3/16/81	Blue Island, IL	YANKEES	.247	136	466	76	115	17	7	24	67	53	116	12	5.077
							Scranton/WB	.250	5	16	0	4	0	0	0	2	2	2	0	
	Jones, Andruw	R-R	6-1	210	4/23/77	Willemstad, Curacao	CHICAGO-AL	.230	107	278	41	64	12	1	19	48	45	73	9	14.047
	Maxwell, Justin	R-R	6-5	235	11/6/83	Olney, MD	Syracuse	.287	66	230	34	66	17	0	6	21	35	75	16	0.108
							WASHINGTON	.144	67	104	16	15	6	0	3	12	25	43	5	
	Mesa, Melky	R-R	6-1	165	1/31/87	Bajos de Haina, D.R.	Tampa	.260	121	446	81	116	21	9	19	74	44	129	31	0.000
	Swisher, Nick	S-L	5-11	210	11/25/80	Columbus, OH	YANKEES	.288	150	566	91	163	33	4	29	89	58	139	1	6.031

2011 Yankees Spring Training Invitees

#	PITCHERS (14)	B-T	HT.	WT.	BORN	BIRTHPLACE	2010 CLUB	W-L	ERA	G	GS	CG	SV	IP	H	R	ER	BB	SO	SVC
39	Anderson, Brian	R-R	6-2	220	3/11/82	Tucson, AZ	AZL Royals	0-0	2.57	6	0	0	0	7.0	4	2	2	1	6	3.053
							Burlington	0-0	3.38	4	0	0	0	5.1	4	3	2	4	5	
							Omaha	0-0	0.00	4	0	0	0	5.0	2	0	0	0	6	
43	Ayala, Luis	R-R	6-2	190	1/12/78	Los Mochis, Mexico	Albuquerque	1-3	4.50	14	0	0	0	14.0	14	8	7	7	10	6.12
							Reno	0-6	7.86	18	0	0	0	26.1	38	23	23	11	17	
							Colorado Springs	1-1	4.91	4	0	0	0	7.1	8	4	4	0	4	
92	Banuelos, Manuel	L-L	5-10	155	3/13/91	Monterrey, Mexico	GCL Yankees	0-0	1.80	2	2	0	0	5.0	1	1	1	3	6	0.00
							Tampa	0-3	2.23	10	10	0	0	44.1	38	16	11	14	62	
							Trenton	0-1	3.52	3	3	0	0	15.1	15	8	6	8	17	
38	Carlyle, Buddy	L-R	6-2	200	12/21/77	Omaha, NE	Hokkaido (Japan)	10-15	4.88	7	0	0	0	27.2	35	18	15	11	14	3.04
40	Colon, Bartolo	R-R	6-0	250	5/24/73	Puerto Plata, D.R.				DID NOT PITCH IN REGULAR SEASON									12.06	
35	Cotts, Neal	L-L	6-3	200	3/25/80	Lebanon, IL				DID NOT PITCH - INJURED									4.08	
36	Garcia, Freddy	R-R	6-4	250	10/6/76	Caracas, Venezuela	CHICAGO-AL	12-6	4.64	28	28	0	0	157.0	171	85	81	45	89	10.06
68	Madrigal, Warner	R-R	6-1	265	3/21/84	San Pedro de Macoris, D.R.	Frisco	1-0	3.72	8	0	0	1	9.2	8	4	4	7	9	1.05
							Oklahoma City	4-2	3.73	27	0	0	2	41.0	33	17	17	7	33	
81	Mitchell, D.J.	R-R	6-0	160	5/13/87	Winston-Salem, N.C.	Trenton	11-4	4.06	23	23	0	0	133.0	128	69	60	57	96	0.00
							Scranton/Wilkes-Barre	2-0	3.57	3	3	0	0	17.2	19	7	7	7	16	
87	Phelps, David	R-R	6-3	190	10/9/86	St. Louis, MO	Trenton	6-0	2.04	14	14	0	0	88.1	63	21	20	23	84	0.00
							Scranton/WB	4-2	3.07	12	11	0	0	70.1	76	31	24	13	57	
22	Prior, Mark	R-R	6-5	225	9/7/80	San Diego, CA	Oklahoma City	0-0	0.00	1	0	0	0	1.0	2	0	0	1	2	6.13
41	Sisco, Andy	L-L	6-10	270	1/13/83	Steamboat Springs, CO	Richmond	4-4	4.32	48	0	0	1	66.2	56	33	32	36	75	3.05
88	Warren, Adam	R-R	6-1	200	8/25/87	New Bern, NC	Tampa	7-5	2.22	15	15	1	0	81.0	72	23	20	17	67	0.00
							Trenton	4-2	3.15	10	10	0	0	54.1	49	26	19	16	59	
89	Wordekemper, Eric	R-R	6-1	200	8/8/83	Storm Lake, IA	Trenton	3-0	2.88	23	0	0	6	34.1	26	12	11	8	35	0.00
							Scranton/WB	2-0	3.13	24	0	0	1	31.2	31	11	11	9	23	

#	CATCHERS (5)	B-T	HT.	WT.	BORN	BIRTHPLACE	2010 CLUB	AVG	G	AB	R	H	2B	3B	HR	RBI	BB	SO	SB	SV
85	Gil, Jose	R-R	6-0	170	9/4/86	Barcelona, Venezuela	Trenton	.236	31	106	19	25	6	1	5	25	9	23	0	0.00
							Tampa	.255	40	141	17	36	4	0	5	19	11	31	4	
53	Molina, Gustavo	R-R	6-1	245	2/24/82	La Guaira, Venezuela	Pawtucket	.241	35	112	12	27	5	0	8	18	7	23	0	0.13
							BOSTON	.143	4	7	1	1	0	0	0	0	0	2	0	
86	Higashioka, Kyle	R-R	6-1	190	4/20/90	Huntington Beach, CA	Charleston	.225	90	320	35	72	18	0	6	24	31	64	0	0.00
83	Montero, Jesus	R-R	6-4	225	11/28/89	Guacara, Venezuela	Scranton/WB	.289	123	453	66	131	34	3	21	75	46	91	0	0.00
84	Romine, Austin	R-R	6-1	195	11/22/88	Lake Forest, CA	Trenton	.268	115	455	61	122	31	0	10	69	37	94	2	0.00

#	INFIELDERS (5)	B-T	HT.	WT.	BORN	BIRTHPLACE	2010 CLUB	AVG	G	AB	R	H	2B	3B	HR	RBI	BB	SO	SB	SV
26	Belliard, Ronnie	R-R	5-10	210	4/7/75	Bronx, NY	LOS ANGELES-NL	.216	82	162	24	35	10	1	2	19	18	35	2	11.14
71	Bernier, Doug	R-R	6-0	185	6/24/80	Santa Maria, CA	Indianapolis	.240	69	200	24	48	14	0	1	15	17	48	6	0.00
12	Chavez, Eric	L-R	6-1	215	12/7/77	Los Angeles, CA	OAKLAND	.234	33	111	10	26	8	0	1	10	8	31	0	12.02
							AZL Athletics	.333	1	3	0	1	0	0	0	0	0	1	0	
93	Suttle, Bradley	S-R	6-2	215	1/24/86	Boerne, TX	Tampa	.272	133	514	61	140	33	4	10	80	53	136	12	0.00
94	Vazquez, Jorge	R-R	6-0	225	3/15/82	Culiacan, Mexico	Trenton	.390	10	41	4	16	4	0	6	6	1	8	0	0.00
							Scranton/WB	.270	76	293	47	79	21	0	18	62	17	95	0	

#	OUTFIELDERS (3)	B-T	HT.	WT.	BORN	BIRTHPLACE	2010 CLUB	AVG	G	AB	R	H	2B	3B	HR	RBI	BB	SO	SB	SV
95	Brewer, Daniel	R-R	6-0	185	7/19/87	Brookfield, IL	Trenton	.270	136	508	83	137	34	3	10	84	53	117	29	0.00
96	Krum, Austin	L-L	6-0	190	1/19/86	Manhattan Beach, CA	Trenton	.229	120	459	77	105	17	1	5	44	64	86	16	0.00
78	Parraz, Jordan	R-R	6-3	215	10/8/84	Henderson, NV	Omaha	.266	123	452	58	115	27	1	11	61	39	78	8	0.00

New York Yankees Numerical Roster & Pronunciation Guide

Numerical Roster

2 Derek Jeter .... INF
11 Brett Gardner .... OF
12 Eric Chavez* .... INF
13 Alex Rodriguez .... INF
14 Curtis Granderson .... OF
17 Francisco Cervelli C
18 Andruw Jones* .... OF
19 Ramiro Pena .... INF
20 Jorge Posada C
22 Mark Prior* .... RHP
24 Robinson Cano .... INF
25 Mark Teixeira .... INF
27 Ronnie Belliard* .... INF
27 Greg Golson .... OF
28 Joe Girardi .... MGR
29 Rafael Soriano .... RHP
30 David Robertson .... RHP
31 Pedro Feliciano* .... LHP
33 Nick Swisher OF/1B
34 A.J. Burnett .... RHP
35 Neal Cotts* .... LHP
36 Freddy Garcia* .... RHP
38 Buddy Carlyle* .... RHP
39 Brian Anderson* .... RHP
40 Bartolo Colon* .... RHP
41 Andy Sisco* .... LHP
42 Mariano Rivera .... RHP
43 Luis Ayala* .... RHP
43 Damaso Marte .... LHP

45 Sergio Mitre .... RHP
47 Ivan Nova .... RHP
48 Boone Logan .... LHP
50 Mick Kelleher .... 1B COACH
52 CC Sabathia .... LHP
53 Gustavo Molina* C
54 Kevin Long .... HITTING COACH
55 Russell Martin C
56 Tony Pena .... BENCH COACH
57 Mike Harkey .... BULLPEN COACH
58 Larry Rothschild ...... PITCHING COACH
59 Rob Thomson .... 3B COACH
60 Kevin Russo .... INF
62 Joba Chamberlain .... RHP
63 Justin Maxwell* .... OF
64 Romulo Sanchez .... RHP
65 Phil Hughes .... RHP
66 Andrew Brackman .... RHP
67 Eduardo Nunez .... INF
68 Warner Madrigal* .... RHP
71 Doug Bernier* .... INF
72 Dellin Betances .... RHP
73 Daniel Turpen* .... RHP
74 Hector Noesi .... RHP
75 Brandon Laird .... INF
76 Reegie Corona .... INF
77 Melky Mesa .... OF
78 Jordan Parraz* .... OF
79 Robert Fish .... LHP

80 Ryan Pope .... RHP
81 D.J. Mitchell* .... RHP
82 Steve Garrison .... LHP
83 Jesus Montero* C
84 Austin Romine* C
85 Jose Gil* C
86 Kyle Higashioka* C
87 David Phelps* .... RHP
88 Adam Warren* .... RHP
89 Eric Wordekemper* .... RHP
92 Manuel Banuelos* .... LHP
93 Bradley Suttle* .... INF
94 Jorge Vazquez* .... INF
95 Daniel Brewer* .... OF
96 Austin Krum* .... OF

*Denotes non-roster invitee

Pronunciation Guide

Dellin Betances ....DELL-in Buh-TAN-s
Robinson Cano ....kuh-NO
Francisco Cervelli ....sir-VEL-le
Derek Jeter ....JEE-te
Damaso Marte ....Duh-MAH-so / MAR-te
Sergio Mitre ....MEE-tra
Hector Noesi ....NO-ess
Jorge Posada ....hor-hay / po-SAH-da
Alex Rodriguez ....rod-REE-ge
Austin Romine ....ROW-ine
CC Sabathia ....sa-BATH-ee
Mark Teixeira ....Tuh-SHARE-u

SearchMercedes.com.

For everything Mercedes-Benz.

Whether you're looking for the nearest authorized Mercedes-Benz dealer, scheduling a service appointment or simply searching for the Certified Pre-Owned Mercedes-Benz of your dreams, SearchMercedes.com is the place to go first. With thousands of vehicle listings, easy service scheduling and detailed dealer maps, SearchMercedes.com is your official one-stop source for everything Mercedes-Benz in the Tri-State area. Log on today.

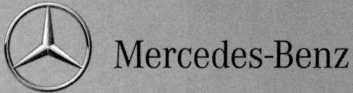

Mercedes-Benz

shown above may have optional equipment.   ©2011 Authorized Mercedes-Benz Dealers   **For more information, call 1-800-FOR-MERCEDES.**

How the Yankees Were Built

FIRST-YEAR PLAYER DRAFT: (12)

Dellin Betances	June 2006, 8th Round
Andrew Brackman	June 2007, 1st Round (30th overall)
Joba Chamberlain	June 2006, Compensation Round A (41st overall)
Colin Curtis	June 2006, 4th Round
Brett Gardner	June 2005, 3rd round
Phil Hughes	June 2004, 1st Round (23rd overall)
Derek Jeter	June 1992, 1st Round (6th overall)
Brandon Laird	June 2007, 27th Round
Ryan Pope	June 2007, 3rd Round
Jorge Posada	June 1990, 24th round
David Robertson	June 2006, 17th Round
Kevin Russo	June 2006, 20th round

SIGNED AS A NON-DRAFTED FREE AGENT: (9)

Robinson Cano	January 5, 2001
Francisco Cervelli	March 1, 2003
Reegie Corona	July 2, 2003
Melky Mesa	July 2, 2003
Hector Noesi	December 3, 2004
Ivan Nova	July 15, 2004
Eduardo Nunez	February 25, 2004
Ramiro Pena	February 18, 2005
Mariano Rivera	February 17, 1990

SIGNED AS A FREE AGENT: (9)

A.J. Burnett	December 18, 2008
Pedro Feliciano	January 5, 2011
Andruw Jones	February 14, 2011
Russell Martin	December 28, 2010
Sergio Mitre	January 14, 2009
Alex Rodriguez	December 13, 2007
CC Sabathia	December 18, 2008
Rafael Soriano	January 18, 2010
Mark Teixeira	January 6, 2009

CLAIMED OFF WAIVERS: (1)

Steve Garrison from San Diego	September 9, 2010

RULE V DRAFT: (2)

Robert Fish from Los Angeles-AL	December 9, 2010
Daniel Turpen from Boston	December 9, 2010

ACQUIRED BY TRADE: (7)

PLAYER	FROM	DATE	FOR
Greg Golson	Texas	January 26, 2010	INF Mitch Hilligoss
Curtis Granderson-a	Detroit	December 9, 2009	Three team, seven player deal
Boone Logan-b	Atlanta	December 21, 2009	OF Melky Cabrera
			LHP Mike Dunn
			RHP Arodys Vizcaino
Damaso Marte-c	Pittsburgh	July 26, 2008	RHP Jeff Karstens
			RHP Dan McCutchen
			RHP Ross Ohlendorf
			OF Jose Tabata
Justin Maxwell	Washington	February 3, 2011	RHP Adam Olbrychowski
Romulo Sanchez	Pittsburgh	May 16, 2009	RHP Eric Hacker
Nick Swisher-d	Chicago (AL)	November 13, 2008	INF Wilson Betemit
			RHP Jeff Marquez
			OF Jhonny Nunez

a – Acquired from the Detroit Tigers in a three-team, seven-player deal in which the Yankees sent LHP Phil Coke and OF Austin Jackson to Detroit and RHP Ian Kennedy to Arizona.

b – Acquired from the Atlanta Braves along with RHP Javier Vazquez in exchange for OF Melky Cabrera, LHP Mike Dunn and RHP Arodys Vizcaino.

c – Acquired from Pittsburgh along with Xavier Nady.

d – Acquired from Chicago-AL along with RHP Kanekoa Texeira.

2011 Yankees Birthdays

January

A.J. Burnett	1/3/1977
Ivan Nova	1/12/1987
Robert Fish	1/19/1988
Hector Noesi	1/26/1987
Melky Mesa	1/31/1987

February

Colin Curtis	2/1/1985
Damaso Marte	2/14/1975
Russell Martin	2/15/1983
Sergio Mitre	2/16/1981

March

Francisco Cervelli	3/6/1986
Larry Rothschild	3/12/1954
Curtis Granderson	3/16/1981
Dellin Betances	3/23/1988

April

David Robertson	4/9/1985
Mark Teixeira	4/11/1980
Andruw Jones	4/23/1977
Romulo Sanchez	4/28/1984

May

Ryan Pope	5/21/1986

June

Tony Pena	6/4/1957
Eduardo Nunez	6/15/1987
Phil Hughes	6/24/1986
Derek Jeter	6/26/1974

July

Kevin Russo	7/8/1984
Ramiro Pena	7/18/1985
CC Sabathia	7/21/1980
Mick Kelleher	7/25/1947
Alex Rodriguez	7/27/1975

August

Boone Logan	8/13/1984
Rob Thomson	8/16/1963
Daniel Turpen	8/17/1986
Jorge Posada	8/17/1971
Brett Gardner	8/24/1983
Pedro Feliciano	8/25/1976

September

Brandon Laird	9/11/1987
Steve Garrison	9/12/1986
Greg Golson	9/17/1985
Joba Chamberlain	9/23/1985

October

Joe Girardi	10/14/1964
Robinson Cano	10/22/1982
Mike Harkey	10/25/1966

November

Justin Maxwell	11/6/1983
Reegie Corona	11/7/1986
Nick Swisher	11/25/1980
Mariano Rivera	11/29/1969

December

Andrew Brackman	12/4/1985
Rafael Soriano	12/19/1979
Kevin Long	12/30/1966

YANKEES
BASEBALL

WATCH IT ON AMERICA'S #1
REGIONAL SPORTS NETWORK

yesnetwork.com

72

DELLIN BETANCES

RIGHT-HANDED PITCHER • 6-8 • 260 • B/T: RIGHT/RIGHT • OPENING DAY AGE: 23

BIRTHDATE
March 23, 1988

BIRTHPLACE
New York, N.Y.

RESIDES
New York, N.Y.

M.L. SERVICE
None
(Rookie)

STATUS
▸ Selected by the Yankees in the eighth round of the 2006 First-Year Player Draft…signed through the 2011 season.

2010
▸ Combined to go 8-1 with a 2.11 ERA (85.1IP, 20ER) in 17 starts with Single-A Tampa and Double-A Trenton.
▸ Began the season on the disabled list recovering from "Tommy John" surgery performed on 8/27/09.
▸ Made his season debut on 6/10 with Tampa…in 14 starts with the Yankees, went 8-1 with a 1.77 ERA (71.0IP, 14ER)…held opponents to 2ER or less in each of his 14 starts and did not allow a run in six of his starts…opponents batted .169 (43-for-254, 1HR); LH .217 (25-for-115, 0HR), RH .129 (18-for-139, 1HR).
▸ Was named the FSL "Pitcher of the Week" for the period from 6/21-28, going 1-0 and tossing 11.0 scoreless innings during the span (3H, 2BB, 1HBP, 14K).
▸ Was promoted to Trenton on 8/23, posting a 3.77 ERA (14.1IP, 6ER) in three starts without recording a decision.
▸ Made two postseason starts for Trenton, going 1-1 with a 3.27 ERA (11.0IP, 4ER) and 15K.
▸ Following the season, was tabbed by *Baseball America* as the third-best prospect (top pitcher) and as having the "Best Fastball" in the Yankees organization.
▸ Was added to the Yankees' 40-man roster on 11/19/10.

2009
▸ Went 2-5 with a 5.48 ERA (44.1IP, 27ER) in 11 starts with Single-A Tampa, recording 44K.
▸ Was placed on the disabled list on 6/25 with elbow inflammation…underwent "Tommy John" surgery on 8/27 and missed the remainder of the season.

2008
▸ Combined to go 9-5 with a 3.92 ERA (121.2IP, 53ER) in 25 appearances (24 starts) with Single-A Charleston and the GCL Yankees…ranked second among Yankees minor league pitchers with 141K. Spent a majority of the season with Charleston, going 9-4 with a 3.67 ERA (115.1IP, 47ER) in 22 starts…led the RiverDogs' staff in wins (90) and strikeouts (135)…tied for fifth in the South Atlantic League, averaging 10.5K/9.0IP…held opponents to a .208 (87-for-419) batting average, eighth-best among all minor league starters.
▸ Was placed on the disabled list on 5/27 with right shoulder inflammation…began a rehab assignment with the GCL Yankees on 6/20, going 0-1 with an 8.53 ERA in three appearances (two starts)…was returned from rehab and reinstated from the disabled list on 7/4.
▸ Struck out a career-high 12 batters in 8/16 win at Lakeland.
▸ Following the season, was ranked by *Baseball America* as the fifth-best prospect in the Yankees organization.

2007
- Was 1-2 with a 3.60 ERA (25.0IP, 10 ER) in six starts with short-season Single-A Staten Island, striking out 29 batters.
- Was placed on the disabled list on 7/21 with right elbow inflammation, missing the remainder of the season.

2006
- Made his professional debut with the GCL Yankees, going 0-1 with a 1.16 ERA (23.1IP, 3ER) in seven starts…held opponents to a .173 batting average (14-for-81).
- Following the season, was ranked as the Yankees' third-best prospect, according to *Baseball America*.

PERSONAL
- As a senior at Grand Street Campus High School in Brooklyn, set a school record with 20K in a single game…became the first player from New York City to be honored as an Aflac All-American in 2005…during the 2005 regular season, posted a 6-0 record with a 0.22 ERA, allowing just 1ER while recording 100K in 41.2IP.

Betances' Career Pitching Record

Year	Club	W	L	ERA	G	GS	CG	SHO	SV	IP	H	R	ER	HR	HP	BB	SO	WP	BK
2006	GCL Yankees	0	1	1.16	7	7	0	0	0	23.1	14	5	3	1	1	7	27	2	1
2007	Staten Island	1	2	3.60	6	6	0	0	0	25.0	24	11	10	0	2	17	29	3	1
2008	Charleston	9	4	3.67	22	22	0	0	0	115.1	87	57	47	9	11	59	135	9	3
	GCL Yankees	0	1	8.53	3	2	0	0	0	6.1	13	7	6	0	0	3	6	2	0
2009	Tampa	2	5	5.48	11	11	0	0	0	44.1	48	29	27	2	2	27	44	3	0
2010	Tampa	8	1	1.77	14	14	0	0	0	71.0	43	18	14	1	3	19	88	3	0
	Trenton	0	0	3.77	3	3	0	0	0	14.1	10	7	6	3	1	3	20	3	0
Minor League Totals		**20**	**14**	**3.39**	**66**	**65**	**0**	**0**	**0**	**299.2**	**239**	**134**	**113**	**16**	**20**	**135**	**349**	**25**	**5**

Selected by the Yankees in the eighth round of the 2006 First-Year Player Draft.

Yankees in Interleague Play

YEAR	OPPONENTS	RECORD
1997	(NYM, ATL, MON, FLA, PHI)	5-10
1998	(NYM, ATL, MON, FLA, PHI)	13-3
1999	(NYM, ATL, MON, FLA, PHI)	9-9
2000	(NYM, ATL, MON, FLA, PHI)	11-6
2001	(NYM, ATL, MON, FLA, PHI)	10-8
2002	(NYM, SF, ARI, CL, SD)	11-7
2003	(NYM, CIN, CHC, HOU, StL)	13-5
2004	(NYM, COL, SD, ARI, LAD)	10-8
2005	(NYM, MIL, StL, PIT, CHC)	11-7
2006	(NYM, WAS, PHI, FLA, ATL)	10-8
2007	(NYM, PIT, ARI, COL, SF)	10-8
2008	(NYM, HOU, SD, CIN, PIT)	10-8
2009	(NYM, PHI, WAS, FLA, ATL)	10-8
2010	(NYM, HOU, ATL, ARI, LAD)	11-7

The Yankees lead the Majors in all-time Interleague wins and winning percentage (.585, 144-102)…went 11-7 vs. the NL in 2010, marking their most Interleague wins since 2005 and collecting their 13th straight non-losing season of Interleague play…SS Derek Jeter has recorded 321 hits and scored 182 runs in Interleague Play, ranking first all time in both categories…3B Alex Rodriguez has 174RBI in Interleague play, most all time…RHP Mariano Rivera ranks first with 63 Interleague saves…Yankees pitchers have batted a combined .105 (30-for-287) all-time in Interleague play with 8 doubles, 11RBI and 31 sacrifice hits…no Yankees pitcher has ever homered in Interleague play.

66 ANDREW BRACKMAN

RIGHT-HANDED PITCHER • 6-10 • 230 • B/T: RIGHT/RIGHT • OPENING DAY AGE: 25

BIRTHDATE
December 4, 1985

BIRTHPLACE
Cincinnati, Ohio

RESIDES
Cincinnati, Ohio

M.L. SERVICE
1 year, 27 days
(Rookie)

COLLEGE
North Carolina
State University

STATUS

‣ Selected by the Yankees in the first round (30th pick overall) of the 2007 First-Year Player Draft…signed a four-year Major League contract on August 16, 2007, with three additional club-option years…contract extends through the 2013 season.

2010

‣ Combined at Single-A Tampa and Double-A Trenton to go 10-11 with a 3.90 ERA in 27 appearances (26 starts), allowing 144H and 61ER in 140.2IP (76R, 39BB, 126K, 8HR)…tied for the fifth-most strikeouts among Yankees minor leaguers.

‣ Began the season with Tampa, going 5-4 with a 5.10 ERA (60.0IP, 34ER) in 12 starts…allowed 20ER over his first four starts (15.2IP), an 11.49 ERA…pitched to a 2.84 ERA (44.1IP, 14ER) over his remaining eight starts with the T-Yanks, including back-to-back scoreless outings on 5/27 at Brevard and 6/2 at Port St. Lucie…struck out a career-high 11 batters in 6/14 win vs. Dunedin (6.0IP).

‣ Was transferred to Trenton on 6/25, where he went 5-7 with a 3.01 ERA in 15 games (14 starts)…limited opponents to 3ER or less in 11 of his starts with the Thunder…went 3-0 with a 0.96 ERA (28.0IP, 3ER) over his final five regular season starts.

‣ Made one postseason start for Trenton, allowing just 1H in 5.0 scoreless innings to earn the win in Game 1 of the Eastern League Championship Series on 9/14 at Altoona (1IBB, 2HBP, 4K).

‣ Joined the Major League staff from Double-A Trenton on 9/23…did not appear in a game.

‣ Following the season, was tabbed by *Baseball America* as the Yankees' fifth-best prospect and as having the organization's "Best Curveball."

2009

‣ Made his regular season professional debut with Single-A Charleston, going 2-12 with a 5.91 ERA in 29 games (19 starts)…struck out 103 batters in 106.2IP…tied for the team lead in starts, ranked second in strikeouts and third in innings pitched…led the South Atlantic League in walks (76) and wild pitches (26).

‣ Opened the season in the rotation, then transitioned to the bullpen on 7/31 for the remainder of the season…went 1-11 with a 6.72 ERA (85.2IP, 64ER) and a .277 opponents batting average as a starter…owned a 1-1 record with a 2.57 ERA (21.0IP, 6ER) and a .218 opponents average in 10 relief appearances.

‣ Lost his first four decisions, remaining winless over his first eight starts of the season…held opponents to 2ER or less in six of the eight outings.

‣ Earned his first professional win on 5/21 vs. Lexington, limiting his opponent to 1ER on 5H in a season-high-tying 8.0IP (1BB, 6K)…walked a season-high 10 batters in his next start on 5/26 vs. Bowling Green…recorded the loss in each of his final seven starts with a 14.27 ERA (23.1IP, 37ER) over the span from 6/17-7/23.

‣ Held his opposition scoreless over his final four outings of the season, tossing 10.0 innings over the stretch with no walks and 9K (6H).

‣ Following the season, was named the organization's 10th-best prospect by *Baseball America*…also noted as having the "Best Fastball" in the organization by the publication.

‣ Made three appearances out of the bullpen during 2009 spring training with the Yankees, allowing 2ER in 3.0IP (3H, 1HR, 1HP).

2008

- Missed the regular season, recovering from "Tommy John" surgery performed in August 2007…following the season, was named the third-best prospect in the organization by *Baseball America*…was also tabbed by the publication as having the organization's "Best Fastball."
- Saw his first professional action, playing with the Waikiki BeachBoys of the Hawaiian Winter Baseball League…made eight starts, going 3-4 with a 5.56 ERA…tied for third in the league with 36K (in 34.0IP)…allowed 3ER or less in six of his starts.

2007

- Missed the professional baseball season after undergoing "Tommy John" surgery on 8/24…surgery was performed by Dr. James Andrews in Birmingham, Ala…ranked by *Baseball America* as the seventh-best overall prospect entering the draft and the third-best junior in the nation…the publication also tabbed him as having the best fastball among college pitchers entering the draft…following the season was named by *Baseball America* as the 10th-best prospect in the Yankees organization.

2006

- Played for the Orleans Cardinals of the Cape Cod League…was 1-0 with a 1.06 ERA in six games (two starts)…was named the No. 2 prospect in the league in a *Baseball America* poll of scouts, managers and coaches…left the Cape Cod League in August to join Team USA…made two appearances (one start) and did not allow an earned run in 4.0IP, pitching in the FISU World Championships in Havana, Cuba…recorded a no-decision in his lone start on 8/10 vs. Mexico (3.0IP, 1H, 1R, 0ER, 2BB, 3K).

COLLEGE CAREER

- Was 11-7 with a 3.80 ERA in 30 career college games (27 starts) at North Carolina State University, recording 149 strikeouts in 149.1IP…made 13 starts as a junior in 2007, going 6-4 with a 3.81 ERA and a .264 opponents batting average…named to the *Baseball America* Preseason All-America team…had his sophomore season cut short due to a stress fracture in his left hip…made just seven appearances (all starts) prior to the injury, posting a 1-3 record and a 6.35 ERA.
- As a freshman in 2005, was 4-0 with a 2.09 ERA, holding opponents to a .216 batting average…allowed just 32H in 43.0IP over 10 games (seven starts) as N.C. State won every game in which he appeared…struck out a career-high 12 batters in 7.0IP on 4/29 vs. seventh-ranked North Carolina…was the most strikeouts by an N.C. State freshman since Preston Woods struck out 13 batters on 4/26/87 vs. Georgia Tech.
- Was a communications major at N.C. State…was a college teammate of Oakland reliever and 2005 first-round pick Joey Devine…also played two seasons (2005-06) on the Wolfpack basketball team, averaging 7.6 points and 3.5 rebounds per game…appeared in all 35 games as a freshman (14 starts), averaging 19 minutes per game.

PERSONAL

- Full name is Andrew Warren Brackman…attended Moeller High School in Cincinnati, Ohio, where he was a two-sport standout in baseball and basketball…his 1.04 career high school ERA was the seventh-best in Ohio's history when he graduated…helped his team win the state championship as a senior, going 7-0 with a 0.60 ERA and 83 strikeouts in 47.1IP… ranked as the 18th-best senior in America by *Team One Baseball* and listed as the No. 4 prospect in the state of Ohio for the 2004 Draft by *Baseball America*…was runner-up Mr. Basketball in Ohio in 2005, as awarded by the Associated Press…shared Ohio's Division 1 "Player of the Year" honors and was named first-team all-state in 2005…averaged 20.2 points and 6.5 rebounds as a senior, leading the conference in scoring and field-goal percentage (.654)…rated as the 42nd-best basketball prospect in the nation by Insiders.com and the 43rd-best basketball prospect by PrepStars following his senior year…enjoys fishing in his free time.

| | | | | | | | | | | Brackman's Career Pitching Record | | | | | | | | |
Year	Club	W	L	ERA	G	GS	CG	SHO	SV	IP	H	R	ER	HR	HP	BB	SO	WP	BK
2009	Charleston	2	12	5.91	29	19	0	0	0	106.2	106	79	70	8	10	76	103	26	0
2010	Tampa	5	4	5.10	12	12	0	0	0	60.0	67	38	34	5	5	9	56	6	0
	Trenton	5	7	3.01	15	14	0	0	0	80.2	77	38	27	3	7	30	70	6	0
Minor League Totals		**12**	**23**	**4.77**	**56**	**45**	**0**	**0**	**0**	**247.1**	**250**	**155**	**131**	**16**	**22**	**115**	**229**	**38**	**0**

34

A.J. BURNETT

RIGHT-HANDED PITCHER • 6-4 • 230 • B/T: RIGHT/RIGHT • OPENING DAY AGE: 34

BIRTHDATE
January 3, 1977

BIRTHPLACE
North Little Rock, Ark.

RESIDES
Monkton, Md.

M.L. SERVICE
11 years, 38 days

CAREER HIGHLIGHTS
No-hitter
‣ 5/12/01
at San Diego

STATUS
‣ Signed as a free agent by the Yankees to a five-year contract on December 18, 2008…contract extends through the 2013 season.

CAREER NOTES
‣ Has recorded six consecutive seasons (2005-10) of 10-or-more wins and eight such seasons in his career (also 2001-02)…has a 61-50 record since joining the American League with Toronto in 2006, ranking fourth in the AL in strikeouts (865) and tied for 10th in the AL in wins over the stretch.

‣ Over the previous decade (2000-09), tied for seventh in the Majors in shutouts (nine) and ranked ninth in lowest opponent's average (.236).

2010
‣ Was 10-15 with a 5.26 ERA (186.2IP, 109ER) in 33 starts with the Yankees…set career highs in losses, runs allowed (118), earned runs, ERA and hit batsmen (19), and tied a career high with 25HR allowed…set the franchise mark for highest single-season ERA among pitchers with at least 30 starts or 180.0IP…opponents batted .285 (204-for-785, 25HR); LH .286 (110-for-385, 11HR) and RH .285 (94-for-330, 14HR)…the Yankees were 13-20 in his starts.

‣ Became one of four Yankees to lose 15-or-more games in a single season in the last 34 years (since 1977), joining Tim Leary (9-19 in 1990), Melido Perez (13-16 in 1992) and Andy Hawkins (15-15 in 1989)…became the first pitcher in franchise history to lose 15-or-more games with an ERA above 5.00 and just the fifth player in Baseball history to post such numbers for a team that made the postseason, joining Tampa Bay's James Shields (13-15, 5.18 ERA in 2010), St. Louis's Jason Marquis (14-16, 6.02 in 2006), Minnesota's Carlos Silva (11-15, 5.94 in 2006) and Baltimore's Dennis Martinez (7-16, 5.53 in 1983), according to the *Elias Sports Bureau*.

‣ Held opponents scoreless six times, tying for the fourth-most such games in the AL…also held opponents without an earned run seven times this season, tying for the sixth-most such starts in the AL in 2010.

‣ Allowed six-or-more runs in a game a Major League-leading 10 times (going 0-10 with a 13.70 ERA in those starts)…marked the most such games by a Yankee since David Cone had 12 in 2000.

‣ Surrendered the first run of the game in 21 of his 33 starts…allowed opponents to bat .345 (48-for-139) with 27 runs scored in the first inning…opponents had a .272 BA (156-for-576) and scored 91 runs from the second inning on.

‣ Threw 16 wild pitches, tied for third in the Majors and second in the AL…owns two of the four highest single-season wild pitch totals in Yankees franchise history (also Tim Leary-23 in 1990; Burnett-17 in 2009; and Jason Grimsley-16 in 2000).

BESTS & STREAKS

Low hit CG
0 - at SD, 5/12/01
IP (start)
9.0 - 16 times
Last: vs. BAL, 5/16/07
IP (relief)
2.0 - at PHI, 10/3/04
Hits
12 - 5 times
Last: vs. SEA, 8/20/10
Runs
9 - 3 times
Last: at CWS, 8/27/10
BB
9 - at SD, 5/12/01
SO
14 - 2 times
Last: vs. MIL, 7/6/05
HR
3 - 8 times
Last: at ARI, 6/21/10
Winning Streak
7g - 7/19-8/19/05
Losing Streak
7g - 8/24/05-4/15/06

- Led the Major Leagues with 19HP, setting a single-season career high (previous was 12HP in 2007 w/ Toronto)...according to baseball-reference.com, marked the Yankees' second-highest single-season total since the franchise was established in New York in 1903 behind Jack Warhop's 26 in 1909.
- Allowed a Major League-leading 37SB...was the highest total allowed by a Yankee since at least 1950, according to baseball-reference.com.
- Started the season 4-0 with a 1.99 ERA over his first six starts, marking the first time he won his first four decisions of a season...his 1.99 ERA was his lowest mark after six starts since 2001, when he posted a 1.71 ERA through his first six starts.

BURNETT'S 2010 PITCHING LINES

Date/Opp	Score	W/L	IP	H	R	ER	HR	BB	K	NP/K	ERA	Left game...
4/6 at BOS*	6-4	ND	5.0	7	4	3	1	1	5	94-58	5.40	Tied 4-4
4/11 at TB	7-3	W	7.0	6	2	2	0	3	1	92-49	3.75	Leading 7-2
4/17 vs. TEX	7-3	W	7.0	6	0	0	0	2	7	111-68	2.37	Leading 7-0
4/23 at LAA*	4-6	ND	6.1	4	4	4	0	2	3	103-59	3.20	Tied 4-4
4/29 at BAL	4-0	W	**8.0**	3	0	0	0	1	4	**116**-77	2.43	Leading 4-0
5/4 vs. BAL	4-1	W	7.1	5	1	0	0	2	**8**	107-68	1.99	Leading 3-1
5/9 at BOS	3-9	L	4.1	9	9	8	1	3	4	97-54	3.40	Trailing 9-2
5/14 at MIN*	8-4	ND	6.2	7	3	2	1	4	4	100-51	3.31	Leading 3-2
5/19 vs. TB*	6-10	L	6.2	9	6	6	1	4	4	116-67	3.86	Trailing 6-2
5/25 at MIN*	1-0	W	5.0	3	0	0	0	2	5	75-46	3.55	Leading 1-0
5/30 vs. CLE*	7-3	W	8.0	5	3	1	0	0	8	115-71	3.28	Leading 7-3
6/4 at TOR	1-6	L	6.0	6	6	6	**3**	1	2	103-59	3.72	Trailing 6-1
6/10 at BAL	3-4	L	6.2	8	4	4	1	1	5	95-60	3.86	Trailing 4-3
6/16 vs. PHI	3-6	L	3.1	6	6	6	2	4	1	87-48	4.33	Trailing 6-0
6/21 at ARI	4-10	L	4.0	9	7	7	**3**	2	4	91-50	4.83	Trailing 7-1
6/26 at LAD	4-9	L	3.0	6	6	6	0	6	5	79-38	5.25	Trailing 6-4
7/2 vs. TOR	1-6	ND	6.2	4	0	0	0	3	6	106-68	4.90	Leading 1-0
7/7 at OAK	6-2	W	7.0	5	2	2	0	2	3	110-67	4.75	Leading 6-2
7/17 vs. TB	5-10	L	2.0	4	4	4	1	0	1	43-25	4.99	Trailing 4-2
7/23 vs. KC	7-1	W	5.0	4	0	0	0	1	3	58-36	4.77	Leading 4-0
7/28 at CLE*	3-4	W	6.1	7	0	0	0	3	7	114-75	4.52	Leading 8-0
8/2 vs. TOR*	6-8	L	4.2	8	8	**8**	2	2	4	95-58	4.93	Trailing 7-2
8/10 at TEX*	3-4 (10)	ND	7.0	6	3	3	1	2	4	112-68	4.87	Trailing 3-2
8/15 at KC	1-0	L	**8.0**	4	1	1	0	3	6	103-64	4.66	Trailing 1-0
8/20 vs. SEA	0-6	L	7.0	**12**	6	6	2	3	4	122-77	4.80	Trailing 6-0
8/27 at CWS*	4-9	L	3.1	8	**9**	**8**	0	3	1	81-47	5.17	Trailing 9-2
9/1 vs. OAK	4-3	W	6.0	6	3	3	1	2	**8**	91-59	5.15	Leading 4-3
9/6 vs. BAL*	3-4	L	7.0	7	4	4	0	4	5	104-63	5.15	Trailing 4-3
9/11 at TEX*	6-7	ND	4.0	4	2	2	0	3	6	88-51	5.13	Tied 2-2
917 at BAL*	4-3	ND	7.0	6	3	3	2	1	5	106-67	5.08	Trailing 3-1
9/22 vs. TB	2-7	L	3.0	2	1	1	0	2	2	51-33	5.05	Trailing 1-0
9/27 at TOR	5-7	L	2.1	7	7	7	2	1	1	48-28	5.23	Trailing 6-0
10/2 at BOS(G2)	6-7(10)	ND	6.0	6	4	2	1	2	5	105-61	5.26	Leading 6-4
Totals		**10-15**	**186.2**	**204**	**118**	**109**	**25**	**78**	**145**		**5.26**	

(*) Denotes start following a team loss   **Bold = season highs**

- Did not allow an earned run in his first 18.1 innings at Yankee Stadium...streak was snapped on 5/14 vs. Minnesota in his third start at home, when he surrendered a fifth-inning solo home run to Joe Mauer.
- Compiled a 21.0-inning stretch without allowing an earned run between 4/23 at Los Angeles-AL and 5/9 at Boston...was his longest such stretch without an earned run surrendered since a 21.1IP streak over three starts from 7/24-8/4/05.
- Made his 250th career start on 5/4 vs. Baltimore, recording the win in a 4-1 Yankees victory...his strikeout of Luke Scott in the fourth inning marked his 1,500th K...came in his 1,621st career IP...among active pitchers at the time, only Kerry Wood (1,303.0IP) and Johan Santana (1,447.0IP) reached 1,500 strikeouts in fewer IP.
- Earned the win on 5/25 at Minnesota in a 1-0 Yankees victory, tossing 5.0 scoreless innings (3H, 2BB, 5K)...game was suspended tied 0-0 prior to the sixth (rain) and resumed the next day...got the win after the Yankees scored in the top of the sixth, despite not pitching the day the game was completed.
- Tossed a season-high-tying 8.0IP in 5/30 win vs. Cleveland (5H, 3R, 1ER, 0BB, 8K, 2HP)...was the fourth time in his career tossing at least 8.0 innings without allowing a walk (first since 6/27/06 w/ Toronto vs. Washington).
- Lost each of his five June starts, going 0-5 with an 11.35 ERA...according to the *Elias Sports Bureau*, became the first Yankee to appear in at least five games and lose them all in a calendar month since Stan Bahnsen in April 1969...*Elias* also notes he became the first Yankee in franchise history to have an ERA above 11.00 in a month with at least 20.0IP...marked the second time in his career he had lost five consecutive starts (also 8/24-9/14/05 w/ Florida).

A TALE OF TWO SEASONS, BURNETT IN 2010

Stat	Thru 6/3	After 6/3
Starts	11	22
Record	6-2	4-13
ERA	3.28	6.48
Innings	71.1	115.1
Hits	69	135
ER	26	83
BB	24	54
K	53	92
HR	4	21

- Rebounded in July to go 3-1 with a 2.00 ERA (27.0IP, 6ER) in five starts during the month…earned the win on 7/7 at Oakland (7.0IP, 2ER), snapping a six-start winless streak.

- Exited his start on 7/17 vs. Tampa Bay after 2.0IP with lacerations on his right hand (4H, 4ER, 0BB, 1K, 1WP, 2HP, 1HR).

- Held opponents scoreless in consecutive starts on 7/28 at Cleveland (6.1 scoreless IP) and 7/23 vs. Kansas City (5.0 scoreless IP before a 1 hour, 25 minute rain delay)…marked the third time in his career holding his opponent scoreless in consecutive starts (also 6/15/02 vs. Tampa Bay and 6/20/02 vs. Cleveland; and 5/29/01 at Pittsburgh and 6/3/01 vs. Mets)

- Won just once over his final 12 starts (beginning 8/2), going 1-7 with a 6.61 ERA (65.1IP, 48ER) in August, September and October.

- Posted an 0-4 record with a 7.80 ERA (30.0IP, 26ER) in five August starts…according to *Elias*, is winless in his last 13 August starts dating to 8/24/08, going 0-9 with a 6.45 ERA (82.1IP, 59ER).

- Recorded his 20th career complete game on 8/15 at Kansas City (8.0IP, 4H, 1ER, 3BB, 6K, 1HP) in a 1-0 Royals victory…was his fourth straight loss when throwing a complete game.

- Went winless over his final six starts from 9/6, going 0-3 with a 5.83 ERA (29.1IP, 19ER) over the stretch.

- Made one postseason start (ALCS Game 4 vs. Texas), suffering the loss (6.0IP, 6H, 5ER, 3BB, 4K, 1HR, 1WP, 1HP).

SINCE 2006
WHEN BURNETT JOINED THE AL

MOST STRIKEOUTS IN AL
1. Felix Hernandez 965
2. Justin Verlander 958
3. CC SABATHIA 898
4. **A.J. BURNETT** **865**
5. Josh Beckett 839

HIGHEST K/9.0IP IN AL
1. Scott Kazmir 8.74
2. **A.J. BURNETT** **8.50**
3. Jon Lester 8.37
4. Zack Greinke 8.27
5. Javier Vazquez 8.23

2009

- Was 13-9 with a 4.04 ERA in 33 starts with the Yankees…his 13 wins and 33 starts were both the second-highest totals of his career (went 18-10 in 34 starts in 2008)…ranked eighth in the American League with 195K…was second in the Majors with 97BB (Arizona's Doug Davis-103BB)…opponents batted .247 (193-for-781, 25HR); LH .217 (91-for-419, 11HR); RH .282 (102-for-362, 14HR)…marked the third-lowest average against left-handed hitters among AL righties and fifth-best in the Majors (min: 200BF)…the Yankees were 21-12 in his starts.

- Tied Felix Hernandez for the Major League lead with 17 wild pitches…marked a personal single-season career high and was the second-highest total in franchise history behind Tim Leary's 23WP in 1990…matched his single-game career-high with 3WP in four games in 2009 (4/19 vs. Cleveland, 5/17 vs. Minnesota, 7/8 at Minnesota and 8/12 vs. Toronto).

- Made his Yankees debut on 4/9 at Baltimore, recording the win in an 11-2 Yankees victory (5.1IP, 7H, 2ER, 1BB, 6K, 1HR)…was the Yankees' first win of the season.

- In his second start on 4/14 at Tampa Bay, retired 18 of his first 19 batters faced and carried a no-hitter through 6.0IP.

- Went winless over seven starts from 4/19-5/22, his longest stretch without a victory in a single season since his last seven starts of the 2005 season w/ Florida.

- Over an 11-start stretch from 5/27-7/27, was 8-2 with a 2.08 ERA (69.1IP, 16ER) and a .209 opponents average (53-for-253), limiting his opponents to 3ER or less in each outing…held his opponents scoreless three times and had one additional start in which he did not allow an earned run (7/27 at Tampa Bay: 1R/0ER).

- Was suspended for six games by MLB on 6/4 for "intentionally throwing a pitch in the head area of Nelson Cruz of the Rangers" during the top of the fifth inning on 6/2…served a reduced five-game suspension from 6/21-26.

- Struck out the side in the third inning in 6/20 loss at Florida on nine pitches (Johnson, Coughlan and Bonifacio – all swinging)…according to *Elias*, became the 40th pitcher all-time to accomplish the feat and just the third Yankee, joining Al Downing (1967) and Ron Guidry (1984).

- Completed the 2009 first half with an 8-4 record (.667), marking his best-ever winning percentage at the All-Star break.

- Picked off Ichiro Suzuki twice in 9/18 loss at Seattle, becoming the first Yankees RHP to record two pickoffs in the same game since Wade Taylor on 8/17/91 vs. the White Sox.

- Won his 100th career game in his final start of the season on 10/4 at Tampa Bay, allowing 2R/1ER in 5.0IP (7H, 1BB, 3K).

- Made his postseason debut, going 1-1 with a 5.27 ERA in five starts…did not draw a decision in first career postseason start on 10/9 in Game 2 of the ALDS vs. Minnesota (6.0IP, 3H, 1ER, 5BB, 6K, 2HP)…marked the

fewest hits allowed by a Yankee making his first career postseason start since Orlando Hernandez (7.0IP, 3H) in ALCS Game 4 at Cleveland on 10/10/98…earned the win in his first World Series start on 10/29 in Game 2, limiting the Phillies to 1ER on 4H in 7.0IP (2BB, 9K)…according to the *Elias Sports Bureau*, entered the 2009 playoffs tied with Brian Moehler for the fourth-most regular season starts among active pitchers without appearing in the postseason, behind only Roy Halladay (287), Randy Wolf (275) and Jamey Wright (246).

2008

- Was 18-10 with a 4.07 ERA in 35 games (34 starts) with 231 strikeouts in 221.1IP for Toronto, recording career highs in wins, innings pitched and strikeouts…opponents batted .249 (211-for-849, 19HR); LH .262 (126-for-481, 11HR), RH .231 (85-for-368, 8HR)…held the opposition to a .203 average (57-for-281) their first time through the order, and then allowed a .271 average (154-for-568) thereafter.
- Led the AL in strikeouts and strikeouts per 9.0IP (9.39), tied for tops in the AL in starts, ranked third in innings pitched and tied for fourth in wins…recorded a career-high six games with 10-or-more strikeouts…became only the third Blue Jays hurler to record at least 200 strikeouts in a season, joining Roy Halladay (2003, '06) and Roger Clemens (1997-98)…also became only the second Blue Jay to lead the league in strikeouts, joining Clemens (1997-98).
- Combined with Roy Halladay for a total of 38 victories, representing the most by any duo in Blue Jays history, surpassing the 37 by Jack Morris (21) and Juan Guzman (16) in 1992.
- Combined to go 5-3 with a 3.09 ERA (75.2IP, 31R, 26ER) in 11 starts against 2008 AL playoff teams…also won his only start against the World Series-champion Phillies on 5/17 at Citizens Bank Park, limiting Philadelphia to 2ER in 6.1IP.
- Opened the season 6-7 with a 5.42 ERA in his first 16 games (15 starts) through 6/19, as the Blue Jays went 7-9…over his final 19 starts, went 12-3 with a 3.12 ERA and 141 strikeouts as the Blue Jays went 13-6…won eight of his last nine decisions.
- Made his lone relief appearance of the season–and fourth of his career–on 4/16 vs. Texas, allowing 2ER in 1.0IP and recording the loss in the 14-inning contest.
- Did not allow an earned run over 17.0 consecutive innings from 9/9-19 facing Chicago-AL and Boston (twice)…was charged with just 4ER total over his final four starts, going 2-0 with a 1.29 ERA.

2007

- Went 10-8 with a 3.75 ERA in 25 starts with the Blue Jays, striking out a team-high 176 batters in 165.2IP…ranked fourth in the AL with 9.56 K/9.0IP…opponents batted .214 (131-for-611, 23HR); LH .200 (66-for-330, 12HR), RH .231 (65-for-281, 11HR)…only Baltimore's Erik Bedard (.212) had a lower opponents average among AL starters…was the lowest batting average allowed by a right-handed pitcher against lefthanders.
- Allowed 11ER in 14.0IP over his first three starts of the season, posting a 7.07 ERA…worked to a 3.44 ERA over the remainder of the year, allowing more than 3ER just five times over his final 22 starts from 4/20 through the end of the season.
- Landed on the 15-day disabled list on 6/13 with a right shoulder strain…reinstated on 6/27 and made one start on 6/28 at Minnesota, allowing 5ER in 4.0IP in a no-decision before returning to the D.L. the next day with the same injury…made one rehab start with Triple-A Syracuse (5.0IP, 3H, 1ER, 1BB, 7K) before being returned from rehab and reinstated from the D.L. on 8/12.
- After returning from the disabled list, posted a 5-2 record with a 3.01 ERA over his final 10 starts…limited opponents to a .202 average over that span (52-for-208)…held opponents to 2ER or less in six of his first seven starts upon returning.

2006

- In his first season with Toronto, went 10-8 with a 3.98 ERA in 21 starts…was limited by two separate stints on the disabled list with scar tissue break-up caused from previous elbow surgery.
- Began the season on the D.L…made two rehab starts with Single-A Dunedin (8.0IP, 3ER) and was reinstated on 4/15…made two starts (0-1, 6.30 ERA) before returning to the D.L. on 4/22…made one rehab start each with Double-A New Hampshire (1-0, 1.50 ERA, 6.0IP, 2ER) and Triple-A Syracuse (1-0, 5.0IP, 0ER) before being returned from rehab and reinstated again on 6/22 for the remainder of the season.
- Earned his first victory as a Blue Jay on 6/27 vs. Washington, throwing his ninth career complete-game shutout (9.0IP, 6H, 7K)…became just the third Toronto pitcher to record a shutout for their first Blue Jays victory, joining Paul Mirabella (4/17/80) and Tom Underwood (5/9/78).
- Went 1-3 with a 4.33 ERA over his first six starts through 7/7…following the All-Star break, posted a 9-5 record with a 3.86 ERA in 15 starts, leading the Toronto staff in second-half wins, starts, innings pitched (100.1) and strikeouts (84).

2005

- Posted a 12-12 record with a 3.44 ERA in 32 starts with Florida…established Marlins career marks for wins (49), losses (50), shutouts (eight), complete games (14), strikeouts (753), games started (131) and innings pitched (847.2)…tied for third in the NL with four complete games.
- Tossed back-to-back complete-game victories on 4/12 vs. Philadelphia and 4/17 at New York-NL, earning NL "Pitcher of the Week" honors…limited Tampa Bay to two hits in a 9.0-inning shutout on 6/26 at Tropicana Field (2BB, 7K)…matched his franchise record with 14 strikeouts on 7/6 vs. Milwaukee.
- Won a career-high seven consecutive starts from 7/19-8/19, recording a 1.71 ERA over the stretch (52.1IP, 7ER)…following the streak, went 0-6 with 5.87 ERA in his final seven starts, marking his longest career losing streak.
- Recorded triples with his first two hits of season, becoming the first pitcher to hit two triples in a season since Mike Hampton hit three with Houston in 1999…of his 10H, five went for extra-base hits…hit third career HR on 7/24 at San Francisco, a solo shot off Kevin Correia.

2004

- Began the season on the disabled list, recovering from "Tommy John" surgery (performed 4/29/03)…was returned from rehab and reinstated on 6/2 and posted a 7-6 record with a 3.68 ERA in 20 games (19 starts)…went 6-0 with a 2.80 ERA and a .188 opponents average in his 11 home games and was 1-6 with a 5.09 ERA and a .291 opponents average in his nine road games (eight starts).
- Established a Marlins club record with 14K over 8.0 innings in 8/29 win vs. Colorado…won each of his final four starts from 8/24-9/12, pitching to a 1.84 ERA over the stretch.
- First pitched on 5/18 in an extended spring training game against the Cardinals then began an official rehab assignment on 5/23…made one start each with Single-A Jupiter (ND, 4.0IP, 2H, 1R, 0ER, 2BB, 4K) and Triple-A Albuquerque (ND, 3.1IP, 7H, 4ER, 2BB, 6K, 1HR, 1HP).

2003

- Made four starts for the eventual World Series-champion Marlins before undergoing season-ending "Tommy John" surgery on 4/29.
- Began the season on the disabled list (retroactive to 3/21) with synovitis in his right elbow…was reinstated from the D.L. on 4/9 and made the start that night vs. the Mets, recording a no-decision in the Marlins victory (7.0IP, 5H, 2ER, 2BB, 4K).
- Went 0-2 with a 4.70 ERA before landing on the disabled list again on 4/26…had surgery to repair the torn elbow ligament performed by Dr. James Andrews in Birmingham, Ala.

2002

- Was named the "Most Improved Marlin" by the South Florida chapter of the Baseball Writers Association of America (BBWAA), going 12-9 with a 3.30 ERA in 31 games (29 starts)…posted the third-highest season strikeout total (203) and the fourth 200-plus strikeout season in franchise history…ranked sixth in the National League and seventh in the Majors in strikeouts…struck out eight or more batters in 15 of his 29 starts (51.7%)…was the third-lowest ERA in club history.
- Opponents batted .209 (153-for-732, 12HR); LH .242 (87-for-359, 5HR), RH .177 (66-for-373, 7HR)…ranked second in the NL and fourth in the Majors in lowest opponents batting average…ranked third in the Majors with a .190 opponents average at home (68-for-358)…led the Majors with five shutouts–all coming at home…tied for third in the Majors with seven complete games, one behind co-leaders Bartolo Colon and Randy Johnson.
- Made his first active Opening Day roster…tossed a four-hit shutout in his third start of the season on 4/14 vs. Atlanta…recorded a three-hit shutout on 6/15 vs. Tampa Bay.
- Was placed on the disabled list from 8/19-9/14 with a right acute bone bruise…made four appearances following his return, including his first two Major League relief appearances.

2001

- Posted an 11-12 record and a 4.05 ERA in 27 starts with the Marlins…opponents batted .231 (145-for-629, 20HR); LH .247 (80-for-320, 5HR), RH .213 (65-for-305, 15HR)…was the fifth-lowest overall opponents average in the NL.
- Began the season on the 15-day disabled list with a stress fracture to the fifth metatarsal in his right foot…made two rehab starts with Single-A Brevard County, allowing 2ER in 9.1IP (1.93 ERA)…was returned from rehab and reinstated on 5/1 and made his season debut on 5/7 at Los Angeles-NL, recording the loss despite allowing only 1ER in 6.0IP.
- Tossed the third no-hitter in Marlins history on 5/12 at San Diego in his second start of the season, striking out seven and walking nine in a 3-0 win (1HP, 1WP)…was the 203rd no-hitter since 1900, the 98th in NL history and the second in the Majors in 2001…became the third Marlins pitcher at the time at the time (also

Al Leiter -5/11/96 vs. Colorado and Kevin Brown-6/10/97 at San Francisco) to accomplish the feat…tied the club record for walks in a game and became the first pitcher in the modern era to issue nine walks in a complete game, nine-inning no-hitter…his 10 baserunners allowed were second only Cincinnati's Jim Maloney who surrendered 12 baserunners in a 10-inning no-hitter at Chicago-NL on 8/9/65…earned NL "Player of the Week" honors.

> **DID YOU KNOW?:** A.J. Burnett's cap and a baseball from his 5/12/01 no-hitter at San Diego are on display at the National Baseball Hall of Fame in Cooperstown, N.Y.

2000

- ▶ Was 3-7 with a 4.79 ERA in 13 starts with the Marlins…made his season debut in the second game of a doubleheader vs. Atlanta on 7/20 after being reinstated from the D.L. earlier that day…recorded his first double-digit strikeout game on 8/28 vs. St. Louis…also hit his first career homer in the same game off Rick Ankiel.
- ▶ Opened the season on the disabled list after suffering a complete rupture of his ulnar collateral ligament in his right thumb during pitcher's fielding practice on 3/14 at spring training in Viera, Fla…underwent surgery on 3/21 at Holy Cross Hospital in Fort Lauderdale, performed by Dr. Brian Fingado.
- ▶ Made three total rehab appearances with Single-A Brevard County and Triple-A Portland, allowing 3ER in 12.1IP (2.19 ERA) with no decisions.

1999

- ▶ Went 4-2 with a 3.48 ERA in seven starts for the Marlins in his first Major League action…made his big league debut on 8/17 at Los Angeles-NL after being recalled to make a spot start for Alex Fernandez, allowing 1ER in 5.2IP with 2BB and 4K…became the first starting pitcher in Marlins history to earn a win in his debut…collected his first hit off Mike Judd in his second AB…was optioned back to Double-A Portland after the game.
- ▶ Recalled a second time on 8/28, making six more starts.
- ▶ Opened the season at Portland, going 6-12 with a 5.52 ERA in 26 games (23 starts)…won his first game out of the bullpen on 8/13 vs. Erie, tossing 3.0 scoreless innings.
- ▶ Selected to pitch for the U.S. team in the inaugural Futures Game…tossed 1.0 scoreless inning in the contest on 7/11 at Fenway Park.

1998

- ▶ In his first season in the Florida organization, was selected as the Marlins' "Pitcher of the Year" after posting a 10-4 record and a 1.97 ERA at Single-A Kane County.
- ▶ Led the organization in strikeouts (186) and ranked second among all hurlers in the Majors or minors…also paced the Florida organization in ERA, ranking second in the Midwest League and third among all minor leaguers…led all minor league starters with 14.07 K/9.0IP and a .179 opponents batting average (74-for-413).
- ▶ Missed the first six weeks of the season (4/9-5/16) after undergoing surgery to repair a broken right hand…named the Marlins' organizational "Player of the Month" for June…earned the Midwest League "Pitcher of the Week" for 6/22-28, going 1-0 in two starts…earned the MWL "Pitcher of the Week" for the second time for the period from 8/30-9/7.
- ▶ Was tabbed by *Baseball America* as the top prospect in the Marlins' organization and the No. 4 prospect in the Midwest League.
- ▶ Was acquired by the Marlins along with LHP Jesus Sanchez, RHP Brandon Villafuerte and a player to be named later (OF Cesar Crespo on 9/14/98) in exchange for LHP Al Leiter and INF Ralph Milliard on 2/6/98.

1997

- ▶ Went 3-2 with a 4.39 ERA in 12 combined appearances (11 starts) with the GCL Mets and short-season Single-A Pittsfield…both teams won their respective league championships…went on the D.L. from 6/17-7/1 with a broken left foot…struck out 63 combined batters in 55.1IP.

1996

- ▶ Was undefeated in 12 starts with rookie-level Kingsport, going 4-0 with a 3.88 ERA…held opponents to a .171 batting average (31-for-181) and struck out 10.55 batters per 9.0IP (68K, 58.0IP), ranking second in the Appalachian League in both categories.

1995

- ▶ Made his professional debut with the GCL Mets, going 2-3 with a 4.28 ERA in nine games (eight starts).

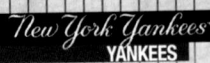
PERSONAL

▸ Full name is Allan James Burnett…is married to Karen with two children, Allan Jr. and Ashton…signed by Larry Chase (Mets)…had his Central Arkansas High School jersey retired on 12/6/02.

▸ Led Yankees in signing and auctioning replica WWE Championship belt to raise over $9,000 for Camp Sundown, a retreat in upstate New York for children suffering from rare genetic disorder called Xeroderma Pigmentosum, and a 2009 HOPE Week participant…accepted award on behalf of the Yankees at National Sportsmanship Awards in November 2009 in St Louis…joined forces with the Adam Walsh Children's Fund and the National Center for Missing and Exploited Children to "Play it Safe," hosting awareness days in 2001 and 2002…also served as the national spokesman for the National Center for Missing and Exploited Children…was an active member of the Marlins' "Adopt-A-Classroom" program, serving as spokesman for Marlins @ School…enjoys fishing and playing instruments.

Burnett's Career Pitching Record

Year	Club	W	L	ERA	G	GS	CG	SHO	SV	IP	H	R	ER	HR	HP	BB	SO	WP	BK
1995	GCL Mets	2	3	4.28	9	8	1	0	0	33.2	27	16	16	2	2	23	26	7	4
1996	Kingsport	4	0	3.88	12	12	0	0	0	58.0	31	26	25	0	7	54	68	16	3
1997	GCL Mets	0	1	3.18	3	2	0	0	0	11.1	8	8	4	0	2	8	15	3	0
	Pittsfield	3	1	4.70	9	9	0	0	0	44.0	28	26	23	2	6	35	48	9	0
1998	Kane County - a	10	4	1.97	20	20	0	0	0	119.0	74	27	26	3	8	45	186	6	2
1999	Portland	6	12	5.52	26	23	0	0	0	120.2	132	91	74	15	5	71	121	16	2
	FLORIDA	4	2	3.48	7	7	0	0	0	41.1	37	23	16	3	0	25	33	0	0
2000	Brevard County	0	0	3.68	2	2	0	0	0	7.1	4	3	3	0	0	6	6	0	2
	Calgary	0	0	0.00	1	1	0	0	0	5.0	0	0	0	0	0	3	6	2	0
	FLORIDA - b	3	7	4.79	13	13	0	0	0	82.2	80	46	44	8	2	44	57	2	0
2001	FLORIDA - c	11	12	4.05	27	27	2	1	0	173.1	145	82	78	20	7	83	128	7	1
	Brevard County	0	0	1.93	2	2	0	0	0	9.1	4	2	2	0	0	4	10	0	0
2002	FLORIDA - d	12	9	3.30	31	29	7	5	0	204.1	153	84	75	12	9	90	203	14	0
2003	FLORIDA - e,f	0	2	4.70	4	4	0	0	0	23.0	18	13	12	2	2	18	21	2	0
2004	Jupiter	0	0	0.00	1	1	0	0	0	4.0	2	1	0	0	0	2	4	2	0
	Albuquerque	0	0	10.80	1	1	0	0	0	3.1	7	4	4	1	1	2	6	1	0
	FLORIDA - g	7	6	3.68	20	19	1	0	0	120.0	102	50	49	9	4	38	113	7	0
2005	FLORIDA - h	12	12	3.44	32	32	4	2	0	209.0	184	97	80	12	7	79	198	12	0
2006	Dunedin	0	0	3.38	2	2	0	0	0	8.0	9	3	3	0	1	2	6	0	0
	New Hampshire	1	0	1.50	1	1	0	0	0	6.0	2	2	1	1	0	3	9	0	0
	Syracuse	1	0	0.00	1	1	0	0	0	5.0	0	0	0	0	1	1	7	1	0
	TORONTO - i, j	10	8	3.98	21	21	2	1	0	135.2	138	67	60	14	8	39	118	6	1
2007	Syracuse	0	0	1.80	1	1	0	0	0	5.0	3	1	1	0	0	1	7	0	0
	TORONTO - k, l	10	8	3.75	25	25	2	0	0	165.2	131	74	69	23	12	66	176	5	0
2008	TORONTO - m	18	10	4.07	35	34	1	0	0	221.1	211	109	100	19	9	86	231	11	2
2009	YANKEES	13	9	4.04	33	33	1	0	0	207.0	193	99	93	25	10	97	195	17	1
2010	YANKEES	10	15	5.26	33	33	1	0	0	186.2	204	118	109	25	19	78	145	16	0
Minor League Totals		**27**	**21**	**3.73**	**91**	**86**	**1**	**0**	**0**	**439.2**	**331**	**210**	**182**	**25**	**33**	**260**	**525**	**63**	**13**
AL Totals		**61**	**50**	**4.23**	**147**	**146**	**7**	**1**	**0**	**916.1**	**877**	**467**	**431**	**106**	**58**	**366**	**865**	**55**	**4**
NL Totals		**49**	**50**	**3.73**	**134**	**131**	**14**	**8**	**0**	**853.2**	**719**	**395**	**354**	**66**	**31**	**377**	**753**	**44**	**1**
Major League Totals		**110**	**100**	**3.99**	**281**	**277**	**21**	**9**	**0**	**1770.0**	**1596**	**862**	**785**	**172**	**89**	**743**	**1618**	**99**	**5**
NYY Total		**23**	**24**	**4.62**	**66**	**66**	**2**	**0**	**0**	**393.2**	**397**	**217**	**202**	**50**	**29**	**175**	**340**	**33**	**1**

Selected by the Mets in the eighth round of the 1995 First-Year Player Draft.

a – Acquired by the Florida Marlins along with LHP Jesus Sanchez, RHP Brandon Villafuerte and a player to be named later (OF Cesar Crespo) in exchange for LHP Al Leiter and INF Ralph Milliard on February 6, 1998.

b – Placed on the 15-day disabled list from March 17 – July 20, 2000 with a ruptured ulnar collateral ligament in his right thumb.

c – Placed on the 15-day disabled list from March 23 – May 7, 2001 with a stress fracture to the fifth metatarsal in his right foot.

d – Placed on the 15-day disabled list from August 19 – September 14, 2002 with a right acute bone bruise.

e – Placed on the 15-day disabled list from March 21 –April 9, 2003 with a sore right elbow.

f – Placed on the 15-day disabled list on April 26, 2003 with a sore right elbow… was transferred to the 60-day disabled list on May 6, 2003 and reinstated on November 19, 2003.

g – Placed on the 15-day disabled list on April 3, 2004 with a sore right elbow… was transferred to the 60-day disabled list on June 2, 2004 and reinstated on June 3, 2004.

h – Signed by Toronto as a free agent on December 6, 2005.

i – Placed on the 15-day disabled list from April 1-14, 2006 with a sore right elbow.

j – Placed on the 15-day disabled list on April 22, 2006 with a sore right elbow… was transferred to the 60-day disabled list on May 29, 2006 and reinstated on June 21, 2006.

k – Placed on the 15-day disabled list from June 13-27, 2007 with a right shoulder strain.

l – Placed on the 15-day disabled list from June 29 – August 28, 2007 with a right shoulder strain.

m – Signed by the Yankees as a free agent on December 18, 2008.

Burnett's Division Series Record

Year	Club vs. Opp.	W	L	ERA	G	GS	CG	SHO	SV	IP	H	R	ER	HR	HP	BB	SO	WP	BK
2009	NYY vs. MIN	0	0	1.50	1	1	0	0	0	6.0	3	1	1	0	2	5	6	0	0
2010	NYY vs. MIN							On Roster - Did Not Appear											
Division Series Totals		**0**	**0**	**1.50**	**1**	**1**	**0**	**0**	**0**	**6.0**	**3**	**1**	**1**	**0**	**2**	**5**	**6**	**0**	**0**

Burnett's League Championship Series Record

Year	Club vs. Opp.	W	L	ERA	G	GS	CG	SHO	SV	IP	H	R	ER	HR	HP	BB	SO	WP	BK
2009	NYY vs. LAA	0	0	5.84	2	2	0	0	0	12.1	11	8	8	0	2	5	7	2	0
2010	NYY vs. TEX	0	1	7.50	1	1	0	0	0	6.0	6	5	5	1	1	3	4	1	0
LCS Totals		**0**	**1**	**6.38**	**3**	**3**	**0**	**0**	**0**	**18.1**	**17**	**13**	**13**	**1**	**3**	**8**	**11**	**3**	**0**

Burnett's World Series Record

Year	Club vs. Opp.	W	L	ERA	G	GS	CG	SHO	SV	IP	H	R	ER	HR	HP	BB	SO	WP	BK
2009	NYY vs. PHI	1	1	7.00	2	2	0	0	0	9.0	8	7	7	1	1	6	11	0	0
World Series Totals		**1**	**1**	**7.00**	**2**	**2**	**0**	**0**	**0**	**9.0**	**8**	**7**	**7**	**1**	**1**	**6**	**11**	**0**	**0**
POSTSEASON TOTALS		**1**	**2**	**5.67**	**6**	**6**	**0**	**0**	**0**	**33.1**	**28**	**21**	**21**	**2**	**6**	**19**	**28**	**3**	**0**

Burnett's Regular Season Batting Record

Year	Team	AVG	G	AB	R	H	2B	3B	HR	RBI	SH	SF	HP	BB	SO	SB	CS
2010	NYY	.000	33	1	0	0	0	0	0	0	2	0	0	0	1	0	0
Major League Totals		**.131**	**281**	**267**	**12**	**35**	**6**	**3**	**3**	**9**	**36**	**0**	**2**	**12**	**127**	**0**	**0**

Burnett's Career Fielding Record

Position	PCT	G	PO	A	E	TC	DP
Pitcher	.918	281	106	195	27	328	11

Home Sweet Home

The Yankees were 52-29 (.642) at Yankee Stadium in 2010, tying Detroit for the second-highest home winning percentage in the AL behind Minnesota (53-28, .654). It marked their 19th consecutive winning season at home (since 1992)…according to the Elias Sports Bureau, it is the longest current streak of any team in the Majors and the longest such streak by any team since a 21-year streak for the Yankees from 1969–89, which included two seasons (1974-75) at Shea Stadium.

The Yankees completed their first two seasons at Yankee Stadium with a 109-53 (.673) record, marking the most wins and highest home winning percentage over the stretch…according to the *Elias Sports Bureau*, their 109 victories were the most by a Major League team in its first two seasons at a particular venue, surpassing the previous mark of 106 shared by the 1909-10 Philadelphia Athletics (Shibe Park) and the 1997-98 Atlanta Braves (Turner Field).

The Yankees own the top two highest single-season home winning percentages all time: .805 (62-15) in 1932 and .802 (65-16) in 1961.

24 ROBINSON CANO

SECOND BASEMAN • 6-0 • 205 • B/T: LEFT/RIGHT • OPENING DAY AGE: 28

BIRTHDATE
October 22, 1982

BIRTHPLACE
San Pedro de Macoris, D.R.

RESIDES
San Pedro de Macoris, D.R.

M.L. SERVICE
5 years, 153 days

CAREER HIGHLIGHTS
A.L. All-Star Team
▸ 2006, 2010

A.L. Gold Glove
▸ 2010

A.L. Silver Slugger
▸ 2006, 2010

MLB All-Star
Futures Game
▸ 2003, 2004

STATUS

▸ Signed as a non-drafted free agent on January 5, 2001…signed a four-year contract with two one-year club options on February 7, 2008…the contract extends through 2011 with options for 2012 and 2013.

CAREER NOTES

▸ Has 1,060 hits as a second baseman since his debut on 5/3/05, most among all Major League second basemen over that span (Philadelphia's Chase Utley ranks second with 962)—credit: *Elias Sports Bureau*.

▸ Recorded 911 hits in the first five years of his Major League career (5/3/05-5/2/10), second-most in franchise history through a player's first five years in the Majors, trailing only Joe DiMaggio (995)—credit: *Elias*.

▸ Recorded his 1,000th career hit with his eighth-inning, two-run double in 7/25/10 win vs. Kansas City…according to the *Elias Sports Bureau*, only two "homegrown" Yankees in the expansion era collected 1,000H in fewer at-bats than Cano (3,232): Derek Jeter (3,112) and Don Mattingly (3,042)…became the sixth second baseman to collect 1,000H with the Yankees, first since Willie Randolph…*Elias* also notes that only six active players reached 1,000H in fewer at-bats than Cano (Ichiro Suzuki, Todd Helton, Albert Pujols, Derek Jeter, Vladimir Guerrero and Matt Holliday)…collected his 500th career hit in 9/25/07 loss at Tampa Bay (came in his 1,600th AB)…according to the *Elias Sports Bureau*, since Joe DiMaggio reached that milestone in 1938 (1,503AB), the only "homegrown" Yankee to collect 500 hits in fewer AB was Mattingly in 1986 (1,549AB).

▸ Owns a .489 career slugging percentage, fifth-highest all-time among Major League second basemen (min. 3,000PA) – credit: *Stats, LLC*.

▸ Is one of just three Yankees second basemen to hit 100HR for the club, joining Tony Lazzeri-169 and Joe Gordon-153 (min. 50.0% of games played at 2B).

▸ In his career, is a .296 (552-for-1,866) batter prior to the All-Star break with 267R, 123 doubles, 11 triples, 51HR and 238RBI in 479 games…in the second half, owns a .324 (523-for-1,615) career average with 242R, 117 doubles, 9 triples, 65HR and 265RBI in 415 games…since 1950, Cano's .337 (221-for-656) career average in September/October regular season games ranks sixth in the Majors (min. 300PA).

▸ Over the last five seasons (2006-10), has posted a .987 fielding percentage, handling a Major League-high 3,722 chances at second base over the span.

▸ Has played in 755 games at second base over the last five seasons (2006-10), most in the AL and second-most in the Majors over the span behind Florida's Dan Uggla (769)…has played more games at second base (886) than any other left-handed batter in franchise history…his 637 games played since the start of the 2007 season are tied for the highest total in the Majors over the span for any one position (also Adrian Gonzalez and Nick Markakis).

▸ Has reached 40 doubles in each of the last two seasons and four times in his career…ties Don Mattingly for the third-most 40-double seasons by a Yankee, behind Lou Gehrig (seven) and Bob Meusel (five).

BESTS & STREAKS

Hits
4 - 17 times
Last: vs. TB, 5/19/10
Runs
4 - at BAL, 4/9/09
2B
3 - 3 times
Last: vat SEA, 9/19/09
3B
1 - 20 times
Last: vs. TB, 7/18/10
HR
2 - 6 times
Last: at BAL, 4/29/10
RBI
6 - vs. SEA, 8/22/10
BB
3 - 4 times
Last: at OAK, 4/20/10
SO
3 - 3 times
Last: at OAK, 8/19/09
SB
1 - 20 times
Last: at BOS, 10/2/10 (G2)
Hit Streak
18g - 2 times
Last: 4/12-5/1/09

▸ Is one of only three second basemen in franchise history to hit at least 25HR in more than one season – also Joe Gordon, 1938-40 and Alfonso Soriano, 2002-03.

2010

▸ Hit .319 (200-for-626) with 103R, 41 doubles, 3 triples, 29HR and 109RBI in 160 games (157 starts at 2B, 2 starts at DH) with the Yankees.

▸ Collected the second-most hits in the Majors, trailing only Ichiro Suzuki (214)…among American Leaguers, ranked fifth in average, tied for sixth in runs, seventh in RBI and slugging pct. (.534), ninth in OBP (.420) and tied for ninth in doubles and home runs…reached safely in 141 of 160 games, starting all but four team games at 2B…led all AL second basemen in average, runs, hits, doubles, HR, RBI, slugging pct. and on-base pct.

SECOND BASEMEN SINCE 1920				
.315, 100R, 200H, 29HR, 100RBI IN A SINGLE SEASON				
Rogers Hornsby	1922	STL	.401 / 141 / 250 / 42 / 152	
Rogers Hornsby	1925	STL	.403 / 133 / 203 / 39 / 143	
Rogers Hornsby	1929	CHC	.380 / 156 / 229 / 39 / 149	
Bret Boone	2001	SEA	.331 / 118 / 206 / 37 / 141	
ROBINSON CANO	**2010**	**NYY**	**.319 / 103 / 200 / 29 / 109**	

▸ Received his first career Gold Glove Award, second Silver Slugger Award (also 2006) and placed third in AL MVP voting…named to the *Sporting News'* 2010 All-Star team…became the seventh second baseman to win the Gold Glove and Silver Slugger in the same season, joining Dustin Pedroia (2008), Placido Polanco (2007), Bret Boone (2003), Roberto Alomar (1992, '96, '99-2000), Chuck Knoblauch (1997), Frank White (1986) and Lou Whitaker (1983-85).

▸ Established single-season career highs with 29HR and 109RBI and tied his career high with 103R…the Yankees were 25-2 in games in which he homered…marked the most RBI by a Yankees second baseman since Joe Gordon (111) in 1939…drew a career-high 57BB (previous high was 39 in 2007).

▸ Finished the season with 200H, reaching the plateau in his final at-bat of the season…became the first-ever Yankees second baseman to record back-to-back 200H seasons, and the first 2B in the Majors to accomplish the feat since Cleveland's Carlos Baerga in 1992-93 (205H and 200H, respectively).

▸ Hit .611 (11-for-18) with 26RBI with the bases loaded, the second-highest such average in the Majors and third-most RBI…batted .322 (55-for-171) with 77RBI with runners in scoring position.

▸ Hit .324 (33-for-102) with 4 doubles, 7HR and 28RBI in 26 games as the No. 4 hitter in the lineup (Yankees went 20-6)…in 28 career games without three-time MVP 3B Alex Rodriguez, has hit .321 (35-for-109) with 28R, 5 doubles, 8HR, 31RBI as the Yankees have gone 21-7.

▸ Hit .285 (61-for-214) with 13HR off left-handed pitching, and .337 (139-for-412) with 16HR against righties…his 13HR and 43RBI off LH pitchers ranked third and first, respectively in the Majors…according to *Elias*, became the first Yankees left-handed batter with at least 10HR off left-handed pitching in two straight seasons since Reggie Jackson in 1979 (10) and '80 (19).

▸ Led AL second basemen in fielding percentage (.996), committing just 3E in 776 total chances (most TC among all Major League second basemen)…was involved in 114 double plays, most for any Major League second baseman…played in 1,393.0 innings, fifth-most among all Major Leaguers…with teammate Derek Jeter's Major League-leading .989 fielding percentage at SS, became the first teammates to finish a season as the fielding leaders at shortstop and second base (in either league) since Omar Vizquel and Roberto Alomar for the 2001 Cleveland Indians and the first Yankees since Phil Rizzuto and Jerry Coleman in 1949.

▸ Established a franchise-record with 81 consecutive errorless games at second base from 4/23-7/26…his error on 7/27 snapped a streak of 37 consecutive errorless games by Yankees middle infielders, the longest such streak in franchise history (credit: *Elias Sports Bureau*).

AMERICAN LEAGUERS TO RECORD A									
.319 AVG., 103R, 200H, 41 DOUBLES, 29HR AND 109RBI									
UNDER THE AGE OF 28 IN LAST 50 YEARS (SINCE 1961)									
Player	Year	Team	Age	Avg	R	H	2B	HR	RBI
ROBINSON CANO	2010	NYY	27	.319	103	200	41	29	109
Alex Rodriguez	1996	SEA	20	.358	141	215	54	36	123
Don Mattingly	1986	NYY	25	.352	117	238	53	31	113
Don Mattingly	1985	NYY	24	.324	107	211	48	35	145
Robin Yount	1982	MIL	26	.331	129	210	46	29	114
Jim Rice	1979	BOS	26	.325	117	201	39	39	130

▸ Was elected to start in his first career All-Star Game (was also selected in 2006 but did not play due to injury)…went 0-for-1 with 1SF before being removed defensively (Ian Kinsler) in the sixth in the National League's 3-1 win…according to *Elias*, Cano and SS Derek Jeter joined Bucky Dent and Willie Randolph as the only Yankees SS/2B combos to start an All-Star game together…also joined Jeter, Joe Mauer and Albert Pujols as the only Major League players to top four million fan votes in 2010.

▸ Made his fifth career Opening Day roster and was named MLB's April American League "Player of the Month," marking his second career monthly award (also September 2006)…finished the month with a Major League-leading .400 (34-for-85) average, 21R, 8HR, 18RBI, 65 total bases, a .765 slugging percentage.

▸ Became just the second American Leaguer to record a .400 average and 8HR in the month of April in the expansion era (since 1961), joining Manny Ramirez w/ Boston in 2001 (.408, 9HR)…became the fourth Yankee to finish April with a .400 batting average or better (min. 50PA) in the expansion era, joining Paul O'Neill in 1994 (.448) and 1996 (.400), Willie Randolph in 1976 (.400) and Clete Boyer in 1962 (.429).

▸ Hit safely in each of the first 10 games of the season (4/4-16)…with Derek Jeter, became the first 2B-SS duo in the Modern Era (since 1900) to each hit safely in nine-or-more of their club's first games of the season—credit: *Elias*…became the first Yankees tandem at any position to each hit safely in each of the team's first 10 games of a season…became the first combo in the Majors to accomplish the feat since Tampa Bay's Carl Crawford and Rocco Baldelli in 2003.

▸ Hit safely in 27 straight April games from 4/12/09-4/16/10…according to the *Elias Sports Bureau*, was the longest such streak in AL history and one shy of the Major League Modern Era record held by the New York Giants' Dan McGann (28 straight April games from 1903-06)…owns a combined .382 (68-for-178) batting average over the last two Aprils, reaching base safely in 42-of-44 contests over the span and hitting safely in 40 of those games.

▸ Hit .400 in April, .336 in May and .333 in June, joining Derek Jeter (1999: .378 in April, .367 in May and .378 in June) as the only Yankees in the last 60 years to hit at least .330 in each of the first three months of the season (min: 50AB each month)—credit: *Elias*.

▸ Collected his fifth career multi-homer game in 4/15 win vs. Los Angeles-AL…both homers came off LHP Scott Kazmir, the first time he hit two homers off a lefthander in the same game.

▸ Was named the AL "Player of the Week" for the period ending 5/30…marked his fourth weekly award, first since the first week of August 2007.

▸ Recorded eight straight multi-hit games from 5/26-6/2, marking the Majors' longest such streak in 2010 and longest by a Yankee since Bernie Williams (10 straight from 8/9-20/02)…had a .576 average, 19H and 14RBI over the span, becoming the first Yankee to reach those totals in hits and RBI over an eight-game stretch since Joe DiMaggio (.528, 19-for-36 with 4HR and 14RBI) over the first eight games of 1941, and the first Yankee with at least 19H, 14RBI and a .576 average over any eight-game stretch since Lou Gehrig in 1936 (6/8-18, .594, 19-for-32, 6HR and 14RBI)—credit: *Elias*…during the multi-hit game stretch, Derek Jeter also collected six straight multi-hit games from 5/27-6/1…according to *Elias*, they became just the second pair of Yankees teammates to each record multiple hits in six straight games, joining Lou Gehrig and Jack Saltzgaver from 7/3-7/34.

▸ Scored at least one run in a career-high eight straight games from 6/8-16, scoring 11 total runs over the span.

▸ Hit his 100th career home run in 6/13 win vs. Houston off Brian Moehler.

▸ Collected his 100th hit of the season on 6/21 at Arizona in the team's 70th game of the season…according to the *Elias Sports Bureau*, since 1936 when Lou Gehrig reached the century mark in the team's 63rd game (the franchise record for the "quickest" to 100 hits), the only Yankees to collect 100 hits within the team's first 70 games of a season are Cano and Derek Jeter (69 games in 1999)…collected his 100th hit of the season in his 274th at-bat…only three players have reached the century mark in hits in fewer at-bats for the Yankees since 1973 (Paul O'Neill in 1994 – 264AB; Dave Winfield in 1984 – 266AB; and Derek Jeter in 1999 – 267AB).

▸ Hit a grand slam and drove in a career-high six runs in 8/22 win vs. Seattle, going 2-for-5…was his fourth career grand slam (second this season, also 5/28 vs. Cleveland).

MAJOR LEAGUE SECOND BASEMEN (2006-10)*

HITS
1. **ROBINSON CANO** 905
2. Chase Utley. .... .828
3. Brandon Phillips .... .808
4. Dan Uggla .... .769
5. Brian Roberts .... .762

RUNS
1. Chase Utley. .... .531
2. Dan Uggla .... .497
3. Ian Kinsler .... .437
4. Brian Roberts .... .431
5. **ROBINSON CANO** **424**
   Dustin Pedroia .... .424

DOUBLES
1. **ROBINSON CANO** 205
2. Brian Roberts .... .196
3. Chase Utley. .... .176
4. Dan Uggla .... .168
5. Dustin Pedroia .... .165

HOME RUNS
1. Dan Uggla .... .154
2. Chase Utley. .... .133
3. Brandon Phillips .... .104
4. **ROBINSON CANO** .... **.99**
5. Ian Kinsler 92

RBI
1. Chase Utley. .... .465
2. Dan Uggla .... .464
3. **ROBINSON CANO** **434**
4. Brandon Phillips .... .400
5. Ian Kinsler. 318

GAMES
1. Dan Uggla .... .769
2. **ROBINSON CANO** **755**
3. Brandon Phillips .... .741
4. Chase Utley. .... .716
5. Orlando Hudson .... .668

BATTING AVERAGE (min. 1,000PA)
1. **ROBINSON CANO** .... **.310 (905-for-2,922)**
2. Placido Polanco .... .307 (698-for-2,278)
3. Dustin Pedroia .... .304 (658-for-2,166)
4. Chase Utley .... .300 (828-for-2,763)
5. Mark Grudzielanek ...... .299 (426-for-1,423)
as a second baseman

▸ Was named AL "co-Player of the Week" with Tampa Bay's Evan Longoria for the week ending 8/22…led the AL with 13RBI and tied for the lead with 4HR while batting .333 (9-for-27) with 7R, a .815 slugging percentage and a .438 OBP…was his fifth career AL weekly award and second of the season.

▸ Went 1-for-4 in the regular season finale on 10/3 at Boston, recording his 200th hit of the season in his final at-bat of the loss.

- Hit .343 (12-for-35) with 8R, 4HR and 6RBI in nine postseason games, leading the team in runs, hits and HR and tying for most RBI...hit all 4HR in the ALCS, becoming the first Yankee to hit 4HR in a single ALCS and fifth to do so in a single postseason series (also Reggie Jackson-5HR in 1977 WS, Hank Bauer-4HR in 1958 WS, Lou Gehrig-4HR in 1928 WS and Babe Ruth-4HR in 1926 WS).

2009

- Hit .320 (204-for-637) with 103R, a team-high 48 doubles, 2 triples, 25HR, 85RBI, 30BB and 5SB in 161 games at 2B with the Yankees...established career highs in runs, hits and doubles...ranked third in the AL in hits, tied for third in doubles and placed fourth in total bases (331)...had 67 multi-hit games, second-most in the Majors behind Ichiro Suzuki's 73...struck out 63 times, tied for the fifth-fewest K's among American Leaguers with at least 600 plate appearances in 2009.

TOP ROAD BATTING AVERAGES, AL, 2006-10 (min. 750PA)		
1.	Joe Mauer	.336 (432-for-1,285)
2.	Ichiro Suzuki	.319 (549-for-1,722)
3.	Vladimir Guerrero	.309 (408-for-1,320)
4.	**ROBINSON CANO**	**.309 (466-for-1,508)**
5.	Carl Crawford	.304 (43-for-1,459)

MOST HITS BY YANKEES 2B, SINGLE SEASON	
1.	Alfonso Soriano, 2002 209
	Bobby Richardson, 1962 209
3.	Steve Sax, 1989 205
	Snuffy Stirnweiss, 1944 205
5.	**ROBINSON CANO, 2009 .... 204**

- Batted .309 (68-for-220) vs. left-handed pitchers and .326 (136-for-417) vs. righties...was the sixth-highest average by a left-handed batter vs. LHP in the AL...his 10HR vs. left-handed pitchers were tied for third-most in the AL among left-handed batters.

- Collected 203H and 25HR as a second baseman, joining Bret Boone (2001) and Alfonso Soriano (2002) as the third second baseman since Rogers Hornsby retired in 1937 to have at least 200H and 25HR in a season as a 2B...over the last 70 years (since 1940), only three other Yankees players have reached those plateaus – Don Mattingly in 1985 and '86, Bernie Williams in 1999 and Soriano in 2002—credit: *Elias Sports Bureau*.

- Became just the third Yankees second baseman to collect 100R and 200H in the same season, joining Alfonso Soriano in 2002 and Snuffy Stirnweiss in 1944.

- Along with Derek Jeter, became the fifth pair of Yankees teammates (sixth time) each to collect at least 200 hits in the same season, joining Lou Gehrig and Earle Combs (1927), Gehrig and Joe DiMaggio (1936, '37), Bernie Williams and Jeter (1999) and Alfonso Soriano and Williams (2002)...according to *Elias*, became the first set of teammates to reach 200 hits in a season at the shortstop and second base position.

- His 48 doubles tied for fourth on the Yankees all-time single-season list and were the second-most all-time among Yankees 2B (Alfonso Soriano, 51 in 2002).

- Received three seventh-place votes for AL MVP and came in second place in AL Gold Glove balloting.

- Hit the first unofficial HR in Yankee Stadium history with a second-inning two-run homer in the Yankees' exhibition win on 4/3 vs. the Cubs.

- Played in the Dominican Republic in the 2009 World Baseball Classic prior to the season, going 3-for-13 (.231) with 2R and 1BB in three games.

- Batted .366 (34-for-93) with 18R, 5 doubles, 5HR, 16RBI, 6BB and 1SB in April after hitting .151 (16-for-106) with 6R, 3 doubles, 2HR, 7RBI and 7BB in 29 games in April 2008...marked the largest April batting average increase (.215) in the Majors (credit: *Elias Sports Bureau*).

- Established a career high with 4R in 4/9 win at Baltimore, marking the most runs scored in a game by a Yankees second baseman since Jose Vizcaino on 7/25/00 at Baltimore.

MOST MULTI-HIT GAMES, 2009-10	
1.	Ichiro Suzuki 142
2.	**ROBINSON CANO................ 126**
3.	Ryan Braun 124
4.	DEREK JETER 119
5.	Miguel Cabrera 108

CONSECUTIVE 200H SEASONS BY 2B, LAST 50 YEARS	
ROBINSON CANO 2009-10	
Carlos Baerga....................... 1992-93
Dave Cash........................... 1974-75
Rod Carew........................... 1973-74
Pete Rose............................ 1965-66

FEWEST TEAM GAMES BY A YANKEE TO REACH 100 HITS IN A SEASON			
Elias Sports Bureau			
	Player	Year	Games
1.	Lou Gehrig	1936	63
2.	Earle Combs	1931	65
3.	Earle Combs	1929	67
4.	Lou Gehrig	1927	68
5.	DEREK JETER	1999	69
T6.	**ROBINSON CANO**	**2010**	**70**
	Lou Gehrig	1934	70
	Lou Gehrig	1930	70
	Earle Combs	1927	70
	Whitey Witt	1923	70

- Hit safely in 33-of-34 games from 9/17/08-5/1/09...according to SABR's Trent McCotter, was one of two Yankees over the last 50 years to record a hit in 33-of-34 games with an official AB, joining Derek Jeter (39-of-40 twice, 4/8-5/25/07 and 8/20/06-4/6/07)...hit .400 (56-for-140) with 30R, 11 doubles, 6HR, 28RBI over the span.

- Compiled a career-high-tying and single-season-best 18-game hitting streak from 4/12-5/1...batted .363 (29-for-80) with 14R, 5 doubles, 4HR and 14RBI during the stretch...according to *Elias*, was the longest single-season hitting streak by a Yankees second baseman since Bobby Richardson hit safely in 19 straight in 1959.

- Recorded his fourth career multi-HR game – and first since 8/30/07 vs. Boston – in 4/25 loss at Boston.

- Went a career-high 54PA without a strikeout from 5/15-28.

- Hit his first career "walk-off" HR in the 10th inning and was 1-for-5 in 8/28 win vs. Chicago-AL...collected his 42nd double of the season in 9/16 win at Toronto, establishing a career high...hit his second career grand slam in 9/28 win vs. Kansas City.

- Batted .193 (11-for-57) with 5R, 1 double, 2 triples and 6RBI in 15 postseason games, reaching base safely in 11 of the contests.

2008

▸ Hit .271 (162-for-597) with 35 doubles, 3 triples, 14HR and 72RBI in 159 games with the Yankees (154 starts at 2B)...batted .292 (50-for-171, 5HR) vs. left-handed pitchers and .263 (112-for-426, 9HR) vs. righties...was the seventh-highest average by a left-handed batter vs. left-handed pitching in the AL.

▸ Ranked fifth among AL second basemen with 13HR while playing the position...all but two of his 14 overall homers were solo.

▸ Struck out 65 times, tied with Ichiro Suzuki for the fourth-fewest K's among American Leaguers with at least 600 plate appearances.

▸ Hit .246 (85-for-346) with 6HR and 38RBI in 93 games prior to the All-Star break...in 66 games following the break, batted .307 (77-for-251) with 8HR and 34RBI.

▸ Batted .347 (114-for-329) with 56R, 27 doubles, 2 triples, 11HR and 54RBI in the 87 Yankees wins he played in...hit just .179 (48-for-268) with 14R, 8 doubles, 1 triple, 3HR and 18RBI in the 72 losses he played in...the Yankees were 34-11 when he recorded a multi-hit game.

▸ Had 800 total chances, most among AL second basemen, recording a .984 fielding percentage (13E).

▸ Hit .151 (16-for-106) in April after batting .306 overall in 2007 and .342 overall in 2006...was the lowest April average among all AL qualifiers (min. 50PA)...hit at a .297 clip (146-for-491) over the remainder of the season.

▸ Hit game-winning, pinch-hit HR in the eighth off Al Reyes in 4/14 win at Tampa Bay...was his second career PH home run (also 6/8/05 at Milwaukee)...according to *Elias*, became the first Yankee to hit a go-ahead, pinch-hit HR since Tino Martinez on 6/25/01 vs. Cleveland.

▸ Batted .373 (28-for-75) with 17RBI and 11 multi-hit contests over a 20-game stretch from 6/15-7/8 as the Yankees went 12-8...led the team in hits, average and RBI over the span, raising his season average 35 points from .220 to .255.

▸ Drove in at least one run in six consecutive games from 6/22-28 (8 total RBI), matching his career-high RBI streak (fifth time)...was part of a stretch in which he recorded at least 1RBI in nine of 11 games from 6/20-7/2 (11RBI total).

▸ Hit safely in eight straight games following the All-Star Break from 7/18-26, going 18-for-35 (.514) with 3 doubles, 3HR and 10RBI and six consecutive games immediately following the break...according to the *Elias Sports Bureau*, became just the fourth player to collect at least 18H and 10RBI in his team's first eight games after the break, joining Cleveland's Earl Averill in 1936 (18H, 12RBI), Detroit's Walt Dropo in 1952 (19, 11) and San Diego's Tony Gwynn in 1988 (18, 10)...also according to *Elias*, became just the second Major Leaguer to produce multi-hit games in each of his team's first six games after the All-Star break and see his team *win* all six games (also Cincinnati's Wally Berger in 1938).

▸ Went a career-high 96 consecutive plate appearances without drawing a walk from 8/20-9/18...according to the *Elias Sports Bureau*, was the longest such streak by a Yankee since Alfonso Soriano in 2002 (132PA)...averaged 24.38 PA/BB in 2008, seventh-highest in the AL.

▸ Appeared in 19 games with Estrellas in the Dominican Winter League, batting .267 with 8 doubles, 1HR and 15RBI.

2007

▸ Hit .306 (189-for-617) with 93R, 41 doubles, 7 triples, 97RBI and 39BB in 160 games with the Yankees...made 157 starts at 2B.

▸ Was tied (with teammate Derek Jeter) for fourth place in the American League with 61 multi-hit games, tied for sixth with 160 games played, ranked seventh with a .329 batting average at night and 10th with 189 hits, 301 total bases and 617 at-bats...drew more walks in 2007 (39 in 160 games) than he did in his previous two seasons combined (34 walks in 254 games).

- Led all AL second basemen with 97RBI…was the second-highest total by a Yankees second baseman over the last 50 years (Alfonso Soriano drove in 101 runs in 2002).
- Batted .328 (63-for-192) against lefties…was the second-highest average in the Major Leagues for a left-handed batter against left-handed pitching, trailing only Seattle's Ichiro Suzuki (.331).
- Hit .274 (90-for-328) with 40R, 24 doubles, 4 triples, 6HR, 40RBI and 15BB in 85 games prior to the All-Star break…in the second half, hit .343 (99-for-289) with 53R, 17 doubles, 3 triples, 13HR, 57RBI and 24BB in 75 games…his 99 second-half hits were tied for fifth-most in the Majors…after hitting 3HR and driving in 33 runs in his first 79G/305AB of the season (from 4/2-7/2), had 16HR and 64RBI in his last 81G/312AB of the season (from 7/3-9/30).
- Recorded 830 total chances, most among Major League second basemen…was involved in 136 double plays, the most in the Majors by a second baseman since Cleveland's Carlos Baerga in 1992 (138)…recorded 11 assists in 9/12 win at Toronto, the most in one game by a Yankees second baseman since Alfonso Soriano had 11 on 7/9/03 at Cleveland, according to the *Elias Sports Bureau*.
- Made his second straight Opening Day start at second base, going 1-for-4 with 1R in 4/2 win vs. Tampa Bay…batted in the leadoff position for the first time in his career in 4/5 loss vs. Tampa Bay, going 3-for-5 with 1R and 1RBI…including the final 13 games of 2006 and the first five games of 2007, hit safely in a career-high 18 consecutive games.
- Committed a career-high three errors in a game in 5/19 loss at the Mets…following 5/19 game, went a career-best 56 consecutive games from 5/20-7/21 without an error…according to the *Elias Sports Bureau*, it was the longest errorless streak by a Yankees second baseman since Steve Sax in 1991 (71 games from 5/11-8/7/91).
- Collected a single-game career-high three doubles and tied a career high with four hits in 5/30 win at Toronto, going 4-for-4 with 1R and 1RBI…each of his first six career four-hit games came on the road.
- Recorded his first career "walk-off" hit with a 10th-inning single on 7/17 vs. Toronto…had five extra-inning hits in 2007, third-most in the American League.
- Led the Majors with a .385 batting average in July…his 42H were tied for most in the Majors for the month and were the most in any calendar month of his Major League career…was named American League "co-Player of the Week" for the period ending 7/22 (.500, 17-for-34, 8R, 2HR, 9RBI)…was also named AL "co-Player of the Week" for the period ending 8/5 (.478, 11-for-23, 9R, 3HR, 9RBI).
- Led the Yankees with a .333 average (5-for-15) in five games during the Division Series vs. Cleveland…also hit a pair of home runs and drove in three runs.

2006

- In his sophomore season, batted .342 (165-for-482) with 41 doubles, 15HR and 78RBI in 122 games with the Yankees (115 starts at 2B, four at DH).
- Earned his first Silver Slugger Award and was selected to his first American League All-Star team (was replaced on roster due to injury)…led the AL with a .364 road batting average and a .363 average versus right-handed pitchers…ranked third in overall batting average (.342) and tied for ninth with 41 doubles…led all Major Leaguers with a .339 average as a second baseman.
- His .342 batting average was the third-highest for a Yankee in his second season in the Majors (minimum: 400AB)…according to the *Elias Sports Bureau*, only Joe DiMaggio (.346 in 1937) and Don Mattingly (.343 in 1984) posted higher marks in the season following their rookie year.
- Went a career-long 160AB without a home run from 4/21-6/8 (a 39-game stretch).
- Was placed on the 15-day disabled list from 6/27-8/8 with a strained left hamstring (missed 35 games)…suffered the injury while running out a double in the sixth inning of 6/25 loss vs. Florida (second game of a day-night doubleheader)…made four rehab-assignment starts (three at 2B, one at DH) for Double-A Trenton (8/3-6) and was 7-for-15 with 1R, 2 doubles, 2RBI and 3BB.
- Drove in at least one run in six straight games from 8/15-20 (13RBI total) and had 16RBI over a nine-game span from 8/12-20…hit third in the lineup for the first time in his career in 9/14 win vs. Tampa Bay, going 2-for-4 with 1R, 2 doubles and 3RBI.
- Hit .373 (41-for-110) in the month of September after posting a .381 average in September 2005 (40-for-105), becoming the first player to post averages of .370-or-higher in consecutive Septembers of at least 100AB since Wade Boggs batted over .400 in three straight Septembers from 1984-86…concluded the season with a 13-game hitting streak…according to the *Elias Sports Bureau*, it was the longest hitting streak by a Yankee to conclude a season also hit safely in 13 straight games to end the 1980 season.
- In his final 53 games of the season after being reinstated from the disabled list on 8/8, hit .365 (77-for-211) with 24 doubles, 11HR and 51RBI…the 24 doubles and 51RBI were the most in the Majors over that span…was named American League "Player of the Month" for September, batting .373 (41-for-110) with 15R, 11 doubles, 7HR, 28RBI and reached base safely in 25 of 28 games…hit .133 (2-for-15) in four Division Series games vs. the Detroit Tigers.

2005

▸ Finished second behind Oakland's Huston Street in American League "Rookie of the Year" voting…hit .297 (155-for-522) with 14HR and 62RBI in 132 games with the Yankees (130 starts at 2B) after his May recall.

▸ Led the AL with a .335 road batting average…led AL rookies in batting average, runs (78), hits, doubles (34), multi-hit games (47) and total bases (239)…ranked second with 52 extra-base hits and a .534 slugging percentage, fourth in RBI and fifth in HR…his 34 doubles ranked second on the team behind Hideki Matsui's 45.

▸ Began the season with Triple-A Columbus and batted .333 (36-for-108) with 8 doubles, 3 triples, 4HR and a club-high 24RBI in 24 games…hit safely in 21 of his contests with the Clippers…was recalled from Triple-A Columbus on 5/3 and made his Major League debut that night at Tampa Bay, starting at 2B and going 0-for-3.

▸ Became the 19th second baseman to start alongside Derek Jeter with the Yankees, recording his first Major League hit with a third-inning single…doubled in five straight games from 5/10-16, the longest such streak by a Yankee since Raul Mondesi did it in five straight games from 4/1-6/03…went 15-for-27 (.556) in eight games after snapping an 0-for-18 stretch with a third-inning single in 5/10 win vs. Seattle.

▸ Established a single-game career high with four hits in 5/15 win at Oakland, going 4-for-5 with 1 double and 1RBI…hit his first career home run—a solo-homer in the eighth—in 5/24 win vs. Detroit…hit two-run, pinch-hit HR in seventh inning of 6/8 win at Milwaukee, the first pinch-hit HR of his career.

▸ Hit in 34 of 36 games from 6/12-7/26, including a season-high 13-game hitting streak from 7/9-26…batted .397 (23-for-58) with 10R, 6 doubles, 3HR and 9RBI during the streak…was the longest hitting streak by an AL rookie in 2005…according to the *Elias Sports Bureau*, it was the longest hitting streak by a Yankees rookie since Derek Jeter hit safely in 17 straight games in 1996.

▸ Had 20-game road hitting streak from 6/27-8/5, the longest such streak in the Majors in 2005 and the longest in the Majors since teammate Derek Jeter hit in 26 straight road games in 2003…was also the longest road hitting streak by a rookie since Ichiro Suzuki hit safely in 25 straight road games in 2001 (credit: *Elias Sports Bureau*).

▸ Established single-game career high with 5RBI in 9/15 win at Tampa Bay, going 3-for-5 with 3R, 1 double, 1 triple and game-tying, sixth-inning grand slam—the first of his Major League career (off Seth McClung)…drove in 12 runs in a three-game span from 9/14-16, going 7-for-15 with 7R, 2 doubles, 1 triple, and 3HR…recorded his first career multi-homer game in 9/16 win at Toronto with three-run HR and two-run HR and equaled single-game career highs with 3R and 5RBI (for second straight game)…homered in consecutive games (9/15-16) for the first time in his career and—according to the *Elias Sports Bureau*—became only the second rookie in the last 40 years to collect at least 5RBI in each of two consecutive games (also Brian Daubach with Boston in 1999).

▸ Was named the AL's "co-Player of the Week" for the period ending 9/18 after batting .429 (12-for-28) with a league-leading 13RBI and 9R…also had eight extra-base hits, including 3HR, 4 doubles and 1 triple while leading the Majors with 27TB…was the first rookie to win the honor since Hideki Matsui (6/29/03).

▸ Was named AL "Rookie of the Month" for September, batting .381 (40-for-105) with 22R, 9 doubles, 2 triples, 5HR and 16RBI…hit safely in 23 of 27 games played in the month.

▸ Hit .263 (5-for-19) in five Division Series games vs. the Angels with a team-leading 5RBI…delivered three-run double in his first postseason at-bat in Game 1.

2004

▸ Split the season between Double-A Trenton and Triple-A Columbus, batting a combined .283 (144-for-508) with 29 doubles, 10 triples, 13HR and 74RBI in 135 games…began the season with Trenton, batting .301 (88-for-292) with 7HR and 44RBI in 74 games…played all but four games at second base for the Thunder…hit "walk-off" homer in 6-4 win over Erie on 4/10…at time of promotion to Columbus, was tied for Eastern League lead in triples (8), ranked third in hits (88), tied for sixth in doubles (20) and was tied for 10th in RBI (44).

▸ Reached base in 22 consecutive games from 4/16-5/9…hit safely in 23 of last 31 games with Trenton…was promoted to Columbus on 6/28 and went 4-for-4 with 1 double and 3RBI in his Clippers debut…in 61 games with the Clippers, hit .259 (56-for-216) with 6HR and 30RBI…went 13-for-32 (.406) with 1HR and 6RBI in first 10 games with Columbus…also went 6-for-11 (.545) with 2RBI in three playoff games…appeared in the 2004 All-Star Futures Game in Houston, going 0-for-2…was ranked the No. 2 prospect in the Yankees organization by *Baseball America*.

2003

▸ Began the season at Single-A Tampa, batting .276 (101-for-366) with 5HR and 50RBI in 90 games…on Opening Day with Tampa, went 5-for-5 with 3R and 3RBI at Lakeland…opened the season with an 11-game hitting streak from 4/3-13…was promoted to Double-A Trenton on 7/19 and hit .280 (46-for-164) with 1HR and 13RBI in 46 games…delivered game-winning RBI single in the 10th inning on 7/21 vs. Reading…was ranked the No. 6 prospect in the Yankees organization by *Baseball America*.

2002

▸ Hit .276 (131-for-474) with 20 doubles, 9 triples, 14HR and 66RBI in 113 games with Single-A Greensboro…led the Bats in hits, RBI and total bases (211)…was named the starting shortstop on the South Atlantic League All-Star team and was tied for second in the league in triples…played in 22 games for short -season Single-A Staten Island, hitting .276 (24-for-87) with 1HR and 15RBI.

2001

▸ Spent the majority of his first professional season with the Gulf Coast League Yankees, hitting .230 (46-for-200) with 3HR and 34RBI in 57 games…also played in two games for Staten Island, going 2-for-8.

PERSONAL

▸ Full name is Robinson Jose Cano…was signed by Carlos Rios…played basketball and baseball at San Pedro Apostol High School in San Pedro de Macoris…father, Jose, was originally signed by the Yankees in 1980 and made his Major League debut with Houston in 1989, pitching in six games.

▸ Received the 2010 "Joe DiMaggio Toast of the Town" Award from the New York Chapter of the BBWAA…was also given the 2010 "Player Citizen of the Year" Award from latinobaseball.com.

▸ Purchased and donated an ambulance for his hometown of San Pedro de Macoris in November 2007…was inspired after a friend perished when he did not receive immediate medical attention from a local ambulance following a motorcycle accident and had to be driven nearly one hour away to Santo Domingo…joined the American Red Cross' National Celebrity Cabinet in 2008…visited with young cancer patients at Hackensack University Medical Center in May 2008…participated in the November 2008 announcement of the alliance formed between MLB, the United States Agency for International Development, the Peace Corps and six Dominican Republic non-profit agencies to use baseball as a catalyst to benefit poorer communities in the D.R.

▸ Participated in CPR training on 6/5/09 at Chelsea Piers as part of National Cardiopulmonary Resuscitation and Automated External Defibrillator Awareness Week…served as "Principal for a Day" at P.S. 55 in the Bronx on 6/16/09…also held a baseball clinic on Randalls Island in June 2009.

▸ Was among 30 finalists for the 2006 Roberto Clemente Award, given annually to the Major League Baseball player who combines outstanding skills on the baseball field with devoted work in the community…on October 23, 2007, received a proclamation from New York City honoring him for his help in the fight against cancer…participated in the Yankees donation of $35,000 in cash, food and supplies to aid in hurricane relief in the Dominican Republic in November 2007…accompanied the Yankees delegation and the World Series trophy on 1/7/10 to meet Dominican Republic President Dr. Leonel Fernandez at the National Palace in Santo Domingo…distributed toys to underprivileged kids in the Dominican Republic in January 2011.

▸ Visited the residence of the U.S. Ambassador to the Dominican Republic on 1/27/11 as part of MLB's "Dominican Baseball Families" initiative to support projects undertaken by the MLB Dominican Development Alliance.

▸ Wears No. 24 to recognize Jackie Robinson (No. 42) whom he was named after.

Cano's Career Playing Record

Year	Club	AVG	G	AB	R	H	2B	3B	HR	RBI	SH	SF	HP	BB	SO	SB	CS	E	OBP	SLG
2001	GCL Yankees	.230	57	200	37	46	14	2	3	34	0	2	3	28	27	11	2	5	.330	.365
	Staten Island	.250	2	8	0	2	0	0	0	2	0	0	0	2	0	0	1		.250	.250
2002	Greensboro	.276	113	474	67	131	20	9	14	66	0	1	3	29	78	2	1	14	.321	.445
	Staten Island	.276	22	87	11	24	5	1	1	15	1	0	0	4	8	6	1	1	.308	.391
2003	Tampa	.276	90	366	50	101	16	3	5	50	0	3	4	17	49	1	1	13	.313	.377
	Trenton	.280	46	164	21	46	9	1	1	13	2	0	6	9	16	0	0	5	.341	.366
2004	Trenton	.301	74	292	43	88	20	8	7	44	0	4	3	24	40	2	4	11	.356	.497
	Columbus	.259	61	216	22	56	9	2	6	30	3	2	1	18	27	0	1	4	.316	.403
2005	Columbus	.333	24	108	19	36	8	3	4	24	0	0	6	13	0	0	4		.368	.574
	YANKEES	.297	132	522	78	155	34	4	14	62	7	3	3	16	68	1	3	17	.320	.458
2006	YANKEES - a	.342	122	482	62	165	41	1	15	78	1	5	2	18	54	5	2	9	.365	.525
	GCL Yankees	.400	1	5	0	2	0	0	0	1	0	0	0	0	0	0	0	0	.400	.400
	Trenton	.500	3	10	1	5	2	0	0	2	0	0	0	3	1	0	0	0	.615	.700
2007	YANKEES	.306	160	617	93	189	41	7	19	97	1	4	8	39	85	4	5	13	.353	.488
2008	YANKEES	.271	159	597	70	162	35	3	14	72	1	5	5	26	65	2	4	13	.305	.410
2009	YANKEES	.320	161	637	103	204	48	2	25	85	0	4	3	30	63	5	7	12	.352	.520
2010	YANKEES	.319	160	626	103	200	41	3	29	109	0	5	8	57	77	3	2	3	.381	.534
Minor League Totals		**.278**	**493**	**1930**	**271**	**537**	**103**	**29**	**41**	**281**	**6**	**12**	**20**	**138**	**261**	**22**	**10**	**90**	**.331**	**.425**
Major League Totals		**.309**	**894**	**3481**	**509**	**1075**	**240**	**20**	**116**	**503**	**10**	**26**	**29**	**186**	**412**	**20**	**23**	**67**	**.347**	**.489**

Signed by the Yankees as a non-drafted free agent on January 5, 2001.

a – Placed on the 15-day disabled list from June 27–August 8, 2006 with a strained left hamstring.

Cano's Division Series Record

Year	Club vs. Opp.	AVG	G	AB	R	H	2B	3B	HR	RBI	SH	SF	HP	BB	SO	SB	CS	E	OBP	SLG
2005	NYY vs. LAA	.263	5	19	3	5	3	0	0	5	0	0	0	2	4	0	1	2	.333	.421
2006	NYY vs. DET	.133	4	15	0	2	0	0	0	0	0	0	0	0	1	0	0	0	.133	.133
2007	NYY vs. CLE	.333	4	15	3	5	1	0	2	3	0	0	0	1	0	0	1	1	.375	.800
2009	NYY vs. MIN	.167	3	12	1	2	0	0	0	1	0	0	0	1	0	0	0	0	.167	.167
2010	NYY vs. MIN	.333	3	12	3	4	0	1	0	1	0	0	0	0	0	0	0	0	.333	.500
Division Series Totals		**.247**	**19**	**73**	**10**	**18**	**4**	**1**	**2**	**10**	**0**	**0**	**0**	**3**	**7**	**0**	**2**	**3**	**.276**	**.411**

Cano's Championship Series Record

Year	Club vs. Opp.	AVG	G	AB	R	H	2B	3B	HR	RBI	SH	SF	HP	BB	SO	SB	CS	E	OBP	SLG
2009	NYY vs. LAA	.261	6	23	4	6	1	2	0	4	0	0	2	4	3	0	0	2	.414	.478
2010	NYY vs. TEX	.348	6	23	5	8	1	0	4	5	0	0	0	1	3	0	0	0	.375	.913
LCS Totals		**.304**	**12**	**46**	**9**	**14**	**2**	**2**	**4**	**9**	**0**	**0**	**2**	**5**	**6**	**0**	**0**	**2**	**.396**	**.696**

Cano's World Series Record

Year	Club vs. Opp.	AVG	G	AB	R	H	2B	3B	HR	RBI	SH	SF	HP	BB	SO	SB	CS	E	OBP	SLG
2009	NYY vs. PHI	.136	6	22	0	3	0	0	0	1	0	1	0	0	5	0	0	0	.130	.136
World Series Totals		**.136**	**6**	**22**	**0**	**3**	**0**	**0**	**0**	**1**	**0**	**1**	**0**	**0**	**5**	**0**	**0**	**0**	**.130**	**.136**
POSTSEASON TOTALS		**.248**	**37**	**141**	**19**	**35**	**6**	**3**	**6**	**20**	**0**	**1**	**2**	**8**	**18**	**0**	**5**		**.296**	**.461**

Cano's All-Star Game Record

Year	Club, Site	AVG	G	AB	R	H	2B	3B	HR	RBI	SH	SF	HP	BB	SO	SB	CS	E	OBP	SLG
2006	NYY, Pittsburgh				Did Not Play - Injured															
2010	NYY, Los Angeles-AL	.000	1	1	0	0	0	0	0	1	0	1	0	0	0	0	0	0	.000	.000
All-Star Game Totals		**.000**	**1**	**1**	**0**	**0**	**0**	**0**	**0**	**1**	**0**	**1**	**0**	**0**	**0**	**0**	**0**	**0**	**.000**	**.000**

Cano's Career Fielding Record

Position	PCT	G	PO	A	E	TC	DP
Second Base	.985	886	1762	2559	67	4388	599

Cano's Career Home Run Chart

MULTI-HOMER GAMES: 6. **TWO-HOMER GAMES:** 6, last on 4/29/10 at Baltimore. **GRAND SLAMS:** 4, last on 8/22/10 vs. Seattle (Luke French). **PINCH-HIT HR:** 2, last on 4/14/08 at Tampa Bay (Al Reyes). **INSIDE-THE-PARK HR:** None. **WALK-OFF HR:** 1, on 8/28/09 vs. Chicago-AL (Randy Williams). **LEADOFF HR:** None.

Gold Caliber

The Yankees led the Majors with a .988 fielding percentage in 2010, committing just 69 errors – the fewest for any Major League team in 2010...marked the Yankees' highest fielding percentage for any season and fewest errors for any non-abbreviated season (previous low was 83E in 2008).

SS Derek Jeter led all Major League shortstops in fielding pct. in 2010 (.989) while 2B Robinson Cano led all AL second basemen with a .996 fielding pct...they became the first teammates to finish a season as the fielding leaders at SS and 2B (in either league) since Omar Vizquel/ Roberto Alomar for Cleveland in 2001, and the first Yankees to accomplish the feat since Phil Rizzuto/Jerry Coleman in 1949 (Credit: *Elias*).

17

FRANCISCO CERVELLI

CATCHER • 6-1 • 210 • B/T: RIGHT/RIGHT • OPENING DAY AGE: 25

BIRTHDATE
March 6, 1986

BIRTHPLACE
Valencia, Venezuela

RESIDES
Valencia, Venezuela

M.L. SERVICE
1 year, 113 days

STATUS
▸ Signed by the Yankees as a non-drafted free agent on March 1, 2003…signed through the 2011 season.

CAREER NOTES
▸ Was named the organization's "Best Defensive Catcher" by *Baseball America* in four straight seasons from 2006-09.

2010
▸ Hit .271 (72-for-266) with 11 doubles, 3 triples and 38RBI in 93 games (80 starts at C) with the Yankees…the Yankees were 44-36 in his starts at catcher…marked the most hits and RBI by a Yankees catcher other than Jorge Posada since Joe Girardi in 1997 (105H and 50RBI)…his 3 triples were the most by a Yankees catcher since Girardi in 1998 (4)…caught 8-of-63 (12.7%) runners attempting to steal.

▸ Hit .545 (6-for-11) with 17RBI with the bases loaded…batted .381 (16-for-42) with 24RBI and a .435 OBP with RISP and two outs, ranking third in the Majors in average in such circumstances (min. 40PA).

▸ Made his first career Opening Day roster…hit safely in each of his first four starts, six of his first seven and 10 of his first 12, batting .360 (9-for-25) in April.

▸ Made his first start—and appearance—of the season, in 4/10 win at Tampa Bay, when CC Sabathia held the Rays hitless through the first 7.2 innings.

▸ Appeared at 3B as eighth-inning defensive replacement in 5/2 win vs. Chicago-AL, marking his first career appearance at a position other than C.

▸ Hit his first career triple, going 3-for-3 with 2R in 5/4 win vs. Baltimore…became the third Yankee in the last 15 years with a triple and bunt single in the same game (also Derek Jeter-1996 and 2009; and Alfonso Soriano-2002)—credit: *Elias*.

▸ Established a career high with 5RBI in 5/8 win at Boston, going 3-for-4 with 1BB…the 5RBI were the most by a Yankees catcher since Jorge Posada on 9/6/06 at Kansas City (6RBI)…were also the most RBI by a Yankees catcher in a game vs. Boston since Yogi Berra had 8RBI on 7/3/57 at Yankee Stadium and the most RBI by a Yankees catcher at Fenway Park since Berra on 5/29/54 (6RBI).

▸ Started 10-of-15 games between 5/20-6/1 when Jorge Posada was on the disabled list, including four straight games from 5/20-23, as the Yankees went 7-5 and starters posted a 3.82 ERA over the stretch.

▸ Went 23 consecutive games without an extra-base hit from 5/20-6/17…snapped the stretch with a seventh-inning double in 6/18 loss vs. the Mets.

▸ Established a career high in hits in 8/29 win at Chicago-AL, going 4-for-4 with 1R and 1 double.

▸ Reached base safely in eight straight plate appearances (two singles, 6BB) over two games from 9/10-11 at Texas…established a career high with 3BB on 9/10 and tied the mark on 9/11.

▸ Appeared in one game during the postseason, starting Game 4 loss of the ALCS vs. Texas (0-for-2).

BESTS & STREAKS

Hits
4 - at CWS, 8/29/10
Runs
3 - 2 times
Last: vs. TB, 9/20/10
2B
2 - vs. TOR, 9/4/10
3B
1 - 3 times
Last: vs. NYM, 6/20/10
HR
1 - at ATL, 6/24/09
RBI
5 - at BOS, 5/8/10
BB
3 - 2 times
Last: at TEX, 9/11/10
SO
2 - 6 times
Last: vs. TB, 9/22/10
SB
1 - vs. TB, 7/17/10
Hit Streak
6g - 6/11-20/10

2009

▸ Hit .298 (28-for-94) with 13R, 4 doubles, 1HR and 11RBI in 42 games (25 starts at C) over two stints with the Yankees (5/5-7/8, 9/1-10/4)…threw out 13-of-21 potential base stealers (61.9%)…at the time of his first start at catcher on 5/8, was the third-youngest active catcher to start a game in the Majors in 2009 (23 years old) behind Pablo Sandoval (Giants, 22) and Lou Marson (Phillies, 22)—credit: *Elias Sports Bureau*…the Yankees were 17-8 when he started behind the plate.

▸ Was recalled from Double-A Trenton on 5/5 when Jorge Posada was placed on the disabled list…made his first appearance in 5/7 loss at Tampa Bay, entering game at catcher in the fifth inning and going 0-for-2.

▸ Made first start and collected his first Major League hit—a fourth-inning single off Jeremy Guthrie—while calling CC Sabathia's CG shutout in 5/8 win at Baltimore, going 1-for-2 with 1R, 1BB and 1SH…according to the *Elias Sports Bureau*, became the second Yankees catcher to call a complete-game shutout in his first start, joining Thurman Munson who did so in his debut on 8/8/69 by catching Al Downing's four-hit shutout vs. the Athletics.

▸ Caught Phil Hughes the next night at Baltimore, becoming the first Yankees battery each under the age of 24 prior to September callups since Steve Kline and Thurman Munson on 6/1/71 (credit: *Elias*).

▸ Hit his first Major League HR in 6/24 win at Atlanta, a solo HR off RHP Kris Medlen.

▸ Was optioned to Triple-A Scranton/Wilkes-Barre on 7/7 when Jose Molina returned from the D.L…returned to the Yankees on 9/1…in 17 September games (two starts at C), was 7-for-16 (.438) with 3R, 1 double and 2RBI…hit game-winning "walk-off" RBI single with one out in the ninth inning of 9/16 win vs. Toronto after entering the game defensively in the eighth at C.

▸ Began the season with Double-A Trenton, batting .190 (11-for-58) with 8R, 1 double, 2HR, 7RBI and 6BB in 16 games at C…in 21 games with Scranton/WB, batted .275 (19-for-69) with 7R, 5 doubles, 1HR, 7RBI and 3BB…was placed on the disabled list from 8/4-25 with a left wrist contusion…made two rehab appearances with the GCL Yankees.

▸ Named to Yankees playoff roster in ALDS and ALCS, appearing in two games and striking out in his only at-bat.

▸ Played with the Lara Cardinals in the Venezuelan Winter League following the season, batting .214 (3-for-14) with 3R and 1 double in six games…participated in the WBC prior to the season, appearing in three games with Team Italy and going 1-for-7 (.143).

2008

▸ Appeared in three games (one start at C) with the Yankees, going hitless in five at-bats as a September call-up in his first Major League action…was recalled from Double-A Trenton prior to 9/15 vs. Chicago-AL…made his Major League debut in 9/18 win vs. Chicago-AL, entering the game as a defensive replacement in the eighth at C (did not bat).

▸ Was one of three Yankees to make their Major League debut in the 9/18 game (also Juan Miranda and Humberto Sanchez)…according to the *Elias Sports Bureau*, was the first time three different Yankees made their ML debut in the same game since 3/31/03 when Hideki Matsui, Jose Contreras and Jason Anderson each debuted in the Yankees' 8-4 win at Toronto.

▸ Made his first Major League start (at catcher) in 9/25 loss at Toronto.

▸ Began the season on the disabled list after suffering a broken right wrist in a home plate collision with Tampa Bay's Elliot Johnson on 3/8 at George M. Steinbrenner Field (then Legends Field)…was taken to St. Joseph's Hospital in Tampa for X-rays and had his wrist casted that night.

▸ Was reinstated from the minor league D.L. on 6/16 and assigned to Single-A Tampa…appeared in three games with Tampa, batting .300 (3-for-10) before suffering a left knee sprain and returning to the D.L.

▸ Returned to action on 7/30, making rehab appearances with the GCL Yankees and Trenton…also appeared in six postseason games for the Eastern League-champion Thunder, batting .200 (4-for-20) with 1 double and 2RBI.

▸ Played winter ball with the Cardenales de Lara of the Venezuelan Baseball League, batting .267 (16-for-60) with 2 doubles, 1HR and 5RBI in 26 games…caught 7-of-19 (36.8%) potential basestealers.

2007

▸ Hit .279 (81-for-290) with 34R, 24 doubles, 2 triples, 2HR, 32RBI and 36BB in 89 games with Single-A Tampa…led all Florida State League catchers with a 41.0% caught stealing rate (41-for-100) and a .997 fielding percentage (2E, 743TC)…ranked second with 667 putouts and 74 assists and tied for fourth with 89 games played…tied for first in doubles, ranked third in runs, hits and walks and placed fourth in RBI among all FSL catchers (min. 40G at C).

▸ Participated in the FSL All-Star Game, entering the game defensively in the seventh at C (was 0-for-1)…was also named to the FSL postseason All-Star team.

- Caught the entire game in a 20-inning loss vs. the Clearwater Threshers on 4/17, recording 24 putouts…fashioned a career-high 10-game hitting streak from 4/27-5/10, batting .500 (16-for-32) with 4 doubles and 4RBI during the span…hit his first career grand slam and recorded a career-high 5RBI in 5/15 win at Dunedin…was placed on the disabled list from 8/10-9/5 with a left knee sprain.
- Played for the Cardenales de Lara of the Venezuelan Baseball League, batting .212 (7-for-33) with 2R, 2 doubles, 10BB and 1SH in 16 games.

2006

- Batted .309 (42-for-306) in 42 games with short season Single-A Staten Island…led the team with a .397 OBP and a .426 slugging percentage and ranked second in batting average…posted a .340 batting average at home (18-for-53) and hit .323 vs. right-handed pitchers (30-for-93)…was named to the American League team for the NY-Penn League All-Star Game…helped lead the team to their second consecutive NYPL Championship.

2005

- Played in 24 games for the GCL Yankees, batting .190 (11-for-58) with 1HR and 9RBI…reached base safely (via hit or walk) in 14 of 21 games with an official plate appearance.

2004

- In his second season, batted .216 (19-for-88) in 40 games with the DSL Yankees.

2003

- Made his professional debut with the Yankees' Dominican Summer League team, batting .239 (37-for-155) in 52 games.

Cervelli's Career Playing Record

Year	Club	AVG	G	AB	R	H	2B	3B	HR	RBI	SH	SF	HB	BB	SO	SB	CS	E	OBP	SLG
2003	DSL Yankees1	.239	52	155	14	37	4	1	0	14	2	0	11	24	25	0	0	-	.379	.277
2004	DSL Yankees1	.216	40	88	14	19	4	0	1	14	4	4	9	19	18	1	2	-	.392	.273
2005	GCL Yankees	.190	24	58	10	11	2	0	1	9	0	2	2	8	13	1	0	2	.300	.276
2006	Staten Island	.309	42	136	21	42	10	0	2	16	1	0	7	13	30	0	0	7	.397	.426
2007	Tampa	.279	89	290	34	81	24	2	2	32	4	2	16	36	59	4	3	2	.387	.397
2008	Tampa	.300	3	10	2	3	0	0	0	1	0	0	1	0	3	0	0	0	.364	.300
	GCL Yankees	.250	3	8	0	2	1	0	0	1	0	0	0	0	1	0	0	0	.250	.375
	Trenton	.315	21	73	8	23	5	0	0	8	0	0	4	11	14	0	0	1	.432	.384
	YANKEES	.000	3	5	0	0	0	0	0	0	0	0	0	0	3	0	0	1	.000	.000
2009	Trenton	.190	16	58	8	11	1	0	2	7	0	0	0	6	13	0	0	5	.266	.310
	YANKEES	.298	42	94	13	28	4	0	1	11	0	1	1	1	13	0	3	0	.309	.372
	Scranton/WB	.275	21	69	7	19	5	0	1	7	1	1	1	3	13	0	0	1	.311	.391
	GCL Yankees	.167	2	6	1	1	0	0	0	0	0	0	0	1	0	0	2	3	.286	.167
2010	YANKEES	.271	93	266	27	72	11	3	0	38	8	4	6	33	42	1	1	13	.359	.335
Minor League Totals		**.262**	**313**	**951**	**119**	**249**	**54**	**3**	**9**	**108**	**12**	**9**	**51**	**121**	**189**	**6**	**7**	**21**	**.372**	**.353**
Major League Totals		**.274**	**138**	**365**	**40**	**100**	**15**	**3**	**1**	**49**	**12**	**5**	**6**	**35**	**56**	**1**	**4**	**14**	**.343**	**.340**

Signed by the Yankees as a non-drafted free agent on March 1, 2003.

Cervelli's Division Series Record

Year	Club vs. Opp.	AVG	G	AB	R	H	2B	3B	HR	RBI	SH	SF	HP	BB	SO	SB	CS	E	OBP	SLG
2009	NYY vs. MIN				On Roster - Did Not Appear															
2010	NYY vs. MIN				On Roster - Did Not Appear															

Cervelli's League Championship Series Record

Year	Club vs. Opp.	AVG	G	AB	R	H	2B	3B	HR	RBI	SH	SF	HP	BB	SO	SB	CS	E	OBP	SLG
2009	NYY vs. LAA	.000	1	1	0	0	0	0	0	0	0	0	0	0	1	0	0	0	.000	.000
2010	NYY vs. TEX	.000	1	2	0	0	0	0	0	0	0	0	0	0	1	0	0	0	.000	.000
LCS Totals		**.000**	**2**	**3**	**0**	**0**	**0**	**0**	**0**	**0**	**0**	**0**	**0**	**0**	**2**	**0**	**0**	**0**	**.000**	**.000**
POSTSEASON TOTALS		**.000**	**3**	**3**	**0**	**0**	**0**	**0**	**0**	**0**	**0**	**0**	**0**	**0**	**2**	**0**	**0**	**0**	**.000**	**.000**

Cervelli's Career Fielding Record

Position	PCT	G	PO	A	E	TC	PB
Catcher	.984	133	797	59	14	870	2
Third Base	1.000	2	1	0	0	1	-

62 JOBA CHAMBERLAIN

RIGHT-HANDED PITCHER • 6-2 • 240 • B/T: RIGHT/RIGHT • OPENING DAY AGE: 25

BIRTHDATE
September 23, 1985

BIRTHPLACE
Lincoln, Neb.

RESIDES
Lincoln, Neb.

M.L. SERVICE
3 years, 55 days

COLLEGE
University of Nebraska

CAREER HIGHLIGHTS
MLB All-Star
  Futures Game
▸ 2007

STATUS

▸ Selected by the Yankees in Compensation Round A (41st overall) of the 2006 First-Year Player Draft…signed through the 2011 season.

CAREER NOTES

▸ Over the last three seasons (2008-10), leads the AL with an average of 8.96K/9.0IP (329.1IP, 328K) among pitchers with at least 300.0IP.

▸ In his career, is 6-6 with a 3.08 ERA in 123 relief appearances (131.2IP, 110H, 45ER, 42BB, 156K, 8HR)…has made 43 career starts, going 12-7 with a 4.18 ERA (221.2IP, 103ER) with 206K.

▸ Owns a 10-3 record with a 3.00 ERA (156.0IP, 52ER) and a .233 (138-for-593) opponents average in 81 career appearances (17 starts) against the AL East…is 8-10 with a 4.38 ERA (197.1IP, 96ER) and a .264 (199-for-754) opponents average against the rest of Baseball.

2010

▸ Was 3-4 with three saves and a 4.40 ERA in a team-leading 73 relief appearances with the Yankees, working exclusively out of the bullpen for the entire season…opponents batted .253 (71-for-281, 6HR); LH .246 (31-for-126, 3HR), RH .258 (40-for-155, 3HR)…retired 48-of-73 first batters faced (65.8%)…prevented 28-of-37 inherited runners from scoring (75.7%)…appeared in consecutive games 18 times…the Yankees were 48-25 in games he appeared in.

▸ Had 56 relief outings of at least 1.0IP (76.7%)…held opponents scoreless in 52 of his appearances.

▸ Made his third consecutive Opening Day roster…held opponents scoreless in 14 of his first 17 outings of the season.

▸ Earned the save in back-to-back games on 5/3 vs. Baltimore and on 5/4 vs. Baltimore—his first save since 9/23/07 vs. Toronto…according to *Elias*, is one of just three Yankees to earn a save in consecutive games since Mariano Rivera became the team's closer in 1997 (also Mike Stanton-4/11-12/98 and Juan Acevedo-4/25-26/03).

▸ Struck out the side in a perfect eighth inning on 5/14 vs. Minnesota (1.0IP, 3K)…was credited with the win despite not being the pitcher of record when the Yankees took the lead.

▸ Allowed a relief-appearance career-high-tying 4ER in 0.1IP on 5/29 vs. Cleveland, recording his first blown save and third loss of the season (4H, 1BB, 1K)…also allowed 4ER in 1.0IP in 7/10 loss at Seattle.

▸ Beginning 7/28, just prior to the acquisition of Kerry Wood on 7/31, through the end of the season, went 2-0 with a 2.15 ERA in 30 relief appearances (29.1IP, 20H, 5BB, 30K)…allowed no more than 2H in any of his outings…three of the seven runs allowed came via solo HRs.

BESTS & STREAKS

Low hit CG
  N/A
IP (start)
  8.0 - 2 times
  Last: at TB, 7/29/09
IP (relief)
  2.0 - 10 times
  Last: at TB, 7/30/10
Hits
  9 - 6 times
  Last: vs. TEX, 8/25/09
Runs
  8 - vs. TOR, 7/5/09
BB
  7 - vs. BOS, 8/6/09
SO
  12 - vs. BOS, 5/5/09
HR
  2 - 4 times
  Last: vs. BOS, 9/25/09
Winning Streak
  5g - 6/24-8/6/09
Losing Streak
  4g - 8/16-9/20/09

- Went nine consecutive appearances without allowing a run from 7/28-8/14 (8.2IP, 2H, 3BB, 6K)…was the second-longest such streak in his career, trailing only an 11-game stretch from 8/7-9/7/07 to begin his Major League career.
- Tossed a season-high 2.0 perfect innings in 7/30 loss at Tampa Bay, striking out three.
- Allowed 1ER in 3.1IP over three relief appearance in the postseason (4H, 2BB, 3K).
- Posted one save and a 10.45 ERA without recording a decision in seven spring training appearances (one start), allowing 13H and 12ER in 10.1IP (8BB, 9K, 1HR)…was selected as a member of the Yankees bullpen on 3/25 when Phil Hughes was named the Yankees' fifth starter.

2009

- Was 9-6 with a 4.75 ERA in 32 appearances (31 starts) with the Yankees…the Yankees were 20-11 in his starts, including 15 come-from-behind victories…were 15-4 in his 19 starts at home…opponents batted .274 (167-for-610, 21HR); LH .266 (85-for-319, 11HR), RH .282 (82-for-291, 10HR)…hit an American League-high 12 batters, matching the most HBP by a Yankees pitcher in the 2000s (Randy Johnson, 2005).

MOST STRIKEOUTS/9.0IP IN THE AL, LAST THREE SEASONS (2008-10), min. 300.0IP		
1.	JOBA CHAMBERLAIN	8.96 (329.1IP, 328K)
2.	Justin Verlander	8.81 (665.1IP, 651K)
3.	Jon Lester	8.72 (621.2IP, 602K)
4.	Francisco Liriano	8.68 (404.1IP, 390K)
5.	Josh Beckett	8.52 (514.1IP, 487K)

- Allowed a total of 21R (19ER) in the first inning of games (30.2IP, 5.58 first-inning ERA)…combined to allow 73R (64ER) over his other 126.2IP (for a 4.55 ERA in the second inning of the game and beyond).
- Was 5-3 with a 4.03 ERA in 13 games (12 starts) on the road…went undefeated in his first nine road starts of the season, going 5-0 with a 2.78 ERA (55.0IP, 17ER)…went 4-3 with a 5.28 ERA (90.1IP, 53ER) in 19 starts at Yankee Stadium…was the second-highest home ERA in the AL behind Scott Kazmir (5.95).
- Did not record a decision in his first three starts of the year and 11 of his first 17 starts of 2009…according to the *Elias Sports Bureau*, Chamberlain's 10 decisions (7-3) through his first 29 career starts were the fewest in Major League history.
- Struck out a career-high 12 batters in 5/5 loss vs. Boston, including nine on called third strikes…were the most strikeouts in a game by a Yankees pitcher since Mike Mussina on 5/7/03 at Seattle (12K)…marked the most by a Yankee in a home game since Mussina on 9/24/02 vs. Tampa Bay (12K)…became the youngest Yankee to strike out 12-or-more batters since Al Downing on 6/21/64 (Game 2) at Chicago-AL (13K)…allowed the first four batters of the game to score and first five to reach, after which he permitted just one infield single, 2BB and 1HP with all 12K…according to the *Elias Sports Bureau*, only two other pitchers since 1900 struck out 12-or-more batters in a game in which they allowed four-or-more first inning runs (Herb Score in 1959 and Nolan Ryan in 1973).
- *Elias* also noted that Chamberlain became one of five pitchers to strike out 12-or-more batters while pitching less than 6.0 innings in a game (also Cole Hamels in 2006, Curt Schilling in 1997, Kevin Appier in 1994 and J.R. Richard in 1978).
- Hit a batter in four consecutive starts from 4/24-5/10, matching the longest such streak for a Yankees pitcher in the last 50 years…also Rick Rhoden (1988), David Cone (1998), Orlando Hernandez (2002) and Randy Johnson (2005)-credit: *Elias*.
- Lost just once over a 17-start stretch from 5/10-8/11…following his defeat on 6/18 vs. Washington, compiled a career-high nine-start undefeated streak from 6/24- 8/11, going 5-0 with a 3.78 ERA (52.1IP, 22ER) over the stretch.
- Won his first four starts immediately following the All-Star break, posting a 2.03 ERA (26.2IP, 6ER) and a .156 (14-for-90) opponent's average from 7/19-8/6…was 3-0 with a 0.83 ERA over three starts from 7/19-29, allowing just 8H and 2ER in 21.2IP (8BB, 2HP, 1WP, 1BK, 1HR)…became the first Yankees pitcher to limit his opposition to 3H or fewer in three straight starts since Randy Johnson in April 2005.
- Recorded his first win at Yankee Stadium on 7/19 vs. Detroit, snapping a nine-start winless stretch at Yankee Stadium to begin the season (0-2, 5.36 ERA)…according to the *Elias Sports Bureau*, it marked the most winless starts at home to begin a season for a Yankees pitcher since 1990 when Andy Hawkins was 0-7 in his first 10 home starts and Tim Leary was 0-6 in his first nine home starts at the original Yankee Stadium.
- Recorded the win on 8/6 vs. Boston despite issuing a career-high 7BB…was the most walks allowed by a Yankees pitcher who also recorded a victory since David Cone walked seven in a 12-3 Yankees win on 4/9/99 vs. Detroit, according to the *Elias Sports Bureau*.
- Lost his first road start of the season on 8/16 at Seattle and had his career-high nine-start undefeated streak snapped, recording the loss (5.0IP, 7H, 4ER, 3BB, 2K)…prior to the loss, had been 8-0 and tied with Pat Darcy (1974-76) as having the most career post-All Star break wins without a defeat since the Midsummer Classic was first played in 1933.
- Set a franchise record by pitching 4.0 innings or less in six consecutive starts from 8/25-9/20, according to the *Elias Sports Bureau*…made his lone relief appearance of the season in the final team game of 2009 on 10/4 at Tampa Bay, tossing 1.0 perfect inning (1K).

▸ Made 10 relief appearances in the 2009 postseason, going 1-0 with a 2.84 ERA (6.1IP, 9H, 2ER, 1BB, 7K)…earned the win in Game 4 of the World Series, allowing the game-tying run on a solo homer and striking out the side in 1.0IP of relief.

2008

▸ Was 4-3 with a 2.60 ERA in 42 appearances (12 starts) with the Yankees…according to the *Elias Sports Bureau*, became the first Yankee since Roy Sherid in 1929 to start his rookie season with at least 10 relief appearances before a mid-season switch resulting in at least 10 starts.

▸ Opponents batted .233 (87-for-373, 5HR); LH .247 (46-for-186, 2HR), RH .219 (41-for-187, 3HR)…was 3-1 with a 2.76 ERA as a starter…the Yankees were 8-4 in his starts…in 30 relief appearances, was 1-2 with a 2.31 ERA…as a reliever, retired 25-of-30 first batters faced (83.3%) and prevented 8-of-10 (80%) inherited runners from scoring.

▸ Began the season in the Yankees bullpen before making the transition to a starter in late May.

▸ Among AL rookies, ranked first in ERA (2.60), second in strikeouts (118), fourth in opponents batting average (.233) and seventh in innings pitched (100.1)…allowed just 5HR, an average of 0.45HR/9.0IP, the second-lowest among all rookie Major Leaguers with at least 75.0IP (behind the Marlins' Chris Volstad, 0.32HR/9.0IP).

**MOST SINGLE-SEASON STRIKEOUTS
BY A YANKEES ROOKIE (LAST 50 YEARS)**

1.	Ron Guidry	176 (1977)
2.	Al Downing	171 (1963)
3.	Stan Bahnsen	162 (1968)
4.	Doc Medich	145 (1973)
5.	Orlando Hernandez	131 (1998)
6.	**JOBA CHAMBERLAIN**	**118 (2008)**
7.	Andy Pettitte	114 (1995)
8.	Dennis Rasmussen	110 (1984)

▸ His strikeout total marked the most by a Yankees rookie in a single season since Orlando Hernandez recorded 131K in 1998…were the third-most in a season by a Yankees pitcher under the age of 23, behind Al Downing's 171 in 1963 and Lefty Gomez's 150 in 1931.

▸ Made his first appearance of the season in 4/1 Opening Day win vs. Toronto, tossing a scoreless eighth inning (1.0IP, 1BB, 2K)…made his first Opening Day roster…was placed on the bereavement list from 4/14-19 to be with his hospitalized father, Harlan, in Nebraska (missed five team games).

▸ Allowed a "walk-off" single to Joe Crede to suffer his first Major League loss on 4/23 at Chicago-AL…was his fourth appearance in five games.

▸ Began the transition from relief pitcher to starter on 5/21 vs. Baltimore, tossing 2.0 scoreless innings (1H, 2BB, 3K)…Manager Joe Girardi announced the move following the game…tossed a relief-appearance career-high 40 pitches on 5/24 vs. Seattle (2.0IP, 1H, 1BB, 2K)…in three "transition" relief appearances, did not allow a run over 5.1IP, holding opponents to 3H and 4BB while striking out eight batters…Girardi announced on 5/30 that Chamberlain would make his first start on 6/3 vs. the Toronto Blue Jays.

▸ Allowed 1ER in 2.1IP (1H, 2R, 4BB, 3K, 1BK) without recording a decision in his first Major League start on 6/3 vs. Toronto…threw 62 pitches overall, facing 12 total batters and marking the first time he faced more than nine batters in a single game…opposed Roy Halladay and, according to *Elias*, joined Greg Cadaret as the only Yankee to make his first Major League start against a former Cy Young Award winner…Cadaret recorded the loss against Roger Clemens on 7/7/89 at Fenway Park after making over 100 relief appearances for the A's and Yankees.

▸ At 22 years old, joined Yankees pitchers Phil Hughes (21) and Ian Kennedy (23), as the first trio all age 23 or younger, to start a game in the same season for the Yankees prior to September callups since 1993 (Sterling Hitchcock, Mark Hutton and Sam Militello)…the last Yankees trio to do it as early in the season (prior to 6/4) was Gil Blanco, Al Downing and Mel Stottlemyre in 1965.

▸ Held opponents to 3ER or less in each of his first 11 Major League starts from 6/3-7/30, becoming the first pitcher to do so since the Marlins' Josh Johnson in 13 straight starts from 2005-06 (credit: *Elias Sports Bureau*)…was the only Yankees pitcher in 2008 to have at least 11 straight starts and allow no more than 3ER in any of them…was the first Yankee to accomplish the feat since Mike Mussina from 4/4-5/31/06 (12 straight starts)…his 2.23 ERA was the lowest for any Yankees pitcher over his first 11 Major League starts since Mel Stottlemyre in 1964 (1.97 ERA).

▸ Earned his first career win as a starter on 6/25 at Pittsburgh, tossing 6.2 scoreless innings…was his first time holding opponents scoreless in a Major League start…tossed a career-high 114 pitches.

- Had 124K at the time he reached 100.0 career IP on 7/25 at Boston, the most for any Yankees pitcher all time through his first 100.0 innings in the Majors…allowed just 24R in his first 100.0IP, the fewest by a Yankee since Dave Righetti allowed 23 in 1981 (credit: *Elias Sports Bureau*).
- Was removed from 8/4 loss at Texas in the fifth inning with right shoulder stiffness after allowing 8H, 5ER and 2HR in 4.2IP…had an MRI performed on 8/5 and was seen by Dr. James Andrews on 8/6…was diagnosed with rotator cuff tendinitis and placed on the 15-day disabled list on 8/6 (missed 24 team games).
- Was reinstated from the 15-day D.L. on 9/2 and returned to the bullpen…made his 21st relief appearance of the season that night at Tampa Bay, allowing 1H and 1BB in 1.1IP.
- Had a 2.38 ERA in 10 relief appearances after returning from the D.L. on 9/2, allowing 11H and 3ER in 11.1IP (14K) without recording a decision.
- Entered the 2008 season ranked by *Baseball America* as the Yankees' top prospect and the top pitching prospect in all of Baseball (third-best overall)…was also rated as having the "Best Fastball," "Best Curveball" and "Best Slider" among all pitchers in the Yankees system.

2007

- Was 2-0 with one save and a 0.38 ERA in 19 relief appearances with the Yankees, allowing only 2R (1ER) in 24.0IP…the Yankees were 17-2 in games he appeared in…opponents batted .145 (12-for-83, 1HR); LH .132 (5-for-38, 0HR), RH .156 (7-for-45, 1HR)…retired 16-of-19 first batters faced (84.2%) holding them to a .111 batting average (2-for-18, 1BB).
- Struck out 34 batters in 24.0IP, averaging 12.75 strikeouts per 9.0IP while issuing just 6BB…was the fourth-highest K/9.0IP ratio among Major League relievers with at least 20.0IP…struck out 24 of the 47 batters he recorded a first-pitch strike against (51.1%).
- Pitched more than 1.0 inning in eight of his 19 appearances…appeared in consecutive games four times…appeared in games on consecutive days just once, on 9/26 and 9/27 at Tampa Bay, tossing 1.0 scoreless inning in each appearance.
- Did not allow a run in his first 15.1 Major League innings…according to the *Elias Sports Bureau*, it was the second longest scoreless-inning streak for any pitcher in Yankees franchise history beginning his Major League career behind Slow Joe Doyle, who went 18.0 innings before allowing his first career run in 1906.
- Made his ML debut in 8/7 win at Toronto, closing out the game with 2.0 scoreless IP (1H, 2BB, 2K)…was signed to a Major League contract and added to the roster from Triple-A Scranton/Wilkes-Barre prior to the game.
- In 8/30 win vs. Boston, allowed 1H and 1BB in 1.1IP before being ejected in the ninth inning by HP Umpire Angel Hernandez…was suspended for two games (8/31-9/1) by Major League Baseball.
- Earned his first Major League win on 9/5 vs. Seattle, tossing a perfect seventh inning (1.0IP)…became the ninth Yankees pitcher to record his first Major League win in 2007, further extending the club record (previous six, done in 1946).
- Allowed one unearned run in 1.2IP on 9/12 at Toronto, snapping his streak of 15.1 scoreless innings to begin his Major League career…allowed solo-HR to Mike Lowell in the eighth on 9/16 at Boston, snapping his streak of 17.0IP without allowing an earned run to begin his Major League career, but still came away with the win.
- Recorded his first career save on 9/23 vs. Toronto, retiring the final four batters (3K) on his 22nd birthday…according to the *Elias Sports Bureau*, he became the third pitcher to earn his first Major League save on his birthday (also Kansas City's D.J. Carrasco and the Mets' Grant Roberts, both in 2003).
- Made two appearances in the Division Series vs. Cleveland, posting a 4.91 ERA with no decisions…made his postseason debut in the seventh inning of Game 2 loss at Cleveland, recording the final two outs of the inning, inheriting two runners (none scored)…while taking the mound for the eighth, small flies known as "midges" descended on the field, congregating mostly above the pitcher's mound…did not allow a hit while completing the inning, but surrendered the tying run on 2BB, 2WP and 1HP…in Game 3 win vs. Cleveland, allowed 1ER in 2.0IP…joined Ross Ohlendorf as the first pair of teammates in Baseball history to pitch in the postseason less than two months after each made their Major League debuts (credit: *Elias Sports Bureau*).
- Combined to make 18 appearances (15 starts) with Single-A Tampa, Double-A Trenton and Scranton/WB, going 9-2 with a 2.45 ERA while registering 135K in 88.1IP…in 15 minor league starts, went 9-2 with a 2.56 ERA…in three relief appearances, tossed 4.0 scoreless innings (1H, 0BB, 10K).
- Was named to the U.S. team for the 2007 Futures Game, played on 7/8 in San Francisco…in the game, allowed 1ER on 1H and 1BB in 1.0IP (1K) in relief.
- Did not allow a run in three appearances (1GS) with Scranton/Wilkes-Barre, going 1-0 with 1BB and 18K in 8.0IP…struck out 10 batters in 5.0 shutout innings in his first and only start for Scranton/WB on 7/25 vs. Louisville.
- Entered the 2007 season ranked by *Baseball America* as the fourth-best prospect in the Yankees organization…also rated as having the "Best Fastball" among all pitchers in the Yankees system.

2006

- Selected by the Yankees in Compensation Round A (41st overall) of the 2006 First-Year Player Draft, becoming the second-highest drafted Native American in baseball history.
- Made professional debut with the West Oahu CaneFires in the Hawaiian Winter League...in nine games (six starts) with West Oahu, was 2-2 with a 2.63 ERA (37.2IP, 28H, 11ER, 3BB, 46K)...ranked second in the league in strikeouts while his ERA was tied for fifth-best in the league.

PERSONAL

- Name is pronounced "Jah-bah"...full name is Justin Louis Chamberlain...the name "Joba" came from a young relative who could not pronounce Justin...signed by Steve Lemke and Tim Kelly...is a decendant of the Winnebago Indian Tribe...has a son, Karter.
- Attended Division II Nebraska-Kearney his freshman year (2004), then transferred to the University of Nebraska the next year...was 10-2 with a 2.81 ERA in 2005, establishing team high in innings pitched (118.2) and strikeouts (130) over 18 starts and helping lead the Cornhuskers to the College World Series...led the Huskers with 102 strikeouts in 2006 and posted a 6-5 record with a 3.93 ERA in 14 starts, allowing 84 hits in 89.1IP...was named a 2006 First-Team Preseason All-American by *Collegiate Baseball* and Second-Team Preseason All-American by the National College Baseball Writers Association...won the 2005 Big 12 "Newcomer Pitcher of the Year" while being named Third-team All-American by *Collegiate Baseball* and First-team All-Big 12.
- Wears No. 62 because the numbers add up to eight as a tribute to Nate Ruan, a childhood friend who died of brain cancer when Joba was 12 and wore No. 8.
- Spent time with area youth at the Kips Bay Boys & Girls Club in the Bronx in August 2007...handed out Christmas gifts to area youngsters from New York City's Police Athletic League in December 2007...also visited the Department of Pediatrics at Memorial Sloan-Kettering Cancer Center in Manhattan on 12/20/07 as part of their "Yankees Universe" initiative...served as spokesman for MSKCC Yankees Universe campaign in 2008.
- Honored by the New York Chapter of the BBWAA with the Joe DiMaggio "Toast of the Town" Award on 1/27/08...received a 2010 Thurman Munson Award for his on-field excellence and community service.
- Has treated a deserving student and their family from Lincoln, Neb., to a trip to Disney World in February in each of the last three years (2008-10)...participated in Health Awareness Day at Kips Bay Boys and Girls Club in New York City in April 2008 where he led the kids—along with Yankees Strength and Conditioning Coordinator Dana Cavelea—in a variety of excercises...honored as the Police Athletic League's 2008 "Athlete of the Year"...visited with children at Memorial Sloan-Kettering Cancer Clinic in September 2009...wrapped gifts on 11/17/09 at the New Yorkers for Children benefit for foster children at Madison Square Garden...passed out gifts to disadvantaged children in Winnebago, Neb., in December 2009.
- Donated himself to the Third Annual "ALS in the Heartland" Bachelor/Bachelorette Charity Auction in Omaha, Neb., on 1/23/09.

Chamberlain's Career Pitching Record

Year	Club	W	L	ERA	G	GS	CG	SHO	SV	IP	H	R	ER	HR	HP	BB	SO	WP	BK
2007	Tampa	4	0	2.03	7	7	0	0	0	40.0	25	10	9	0	1	11	51	2	0
	Trenton	4	2	3.35	8	7	0	0	0	40.1	32	15	15	4	2	15	66	3	0
	Scranton/WB	1	0	0.00	3	1	0	0	0	8.0	5	0	0	0	0	1	18	1	0
	YANKEES	2	0	0.38	19	0	0	0	1	24.0	12	2	1	1	1	6	34	1	0
2008	YANKEES - a	4	3	2.60	42	12	0	0	0	100.1	87	32	29	5	2	39	118	4	2
2009	YANKEES	9	6	4.75	32	31	0	0	0	157.1	167	94	83	21	12	76	133	5	2
2010	YANKEES	3	4	4.40	73	0	0	0	3	71.2	71	37	35	6	1	22	77	5	1
Minor League Totals		9	2	2.45	18	15	0	0	0	88.1	62	25	24	4	3	27	135	6	0
Major League Totals		**18**	**13**	**3.77**	**166**	**43**	**0**	**0**	**4**	**353.1**	**337**	**165**	**148**	**33**	**16**	**143**	**362**	**15**	**5**

Selected by the Yankees in Compensation Round A (41st overall) of the 2006 First-Year Player Draft

a – Placed on the 15-day disabled list from August 6 – September 2, 2008 with right shoulder tendinitis.

Chamberlain's Division Series Pitching Record

Year	Club vs. Opp.	W	L	ERA	G	GS	CG	SHO	SV	IP	H	R	ER	HR	HP	BB	SO	WP	BK
2007	NYY vs. CLE	0	0	4.91	2	0	0	0	0	3.2	3	2	2	0	1	3	4	2	0
2009	NYY vs. MIN	0	0	0.00	3	0	0	0	0	1.2	2	0	0	0	0	0	1	0	0
2010	NYY vs. MIN						On Roster - Did Not Appear												
Division Series Totals		**0**	**0**	**3.38**	**5**	**0**	**0**	**0**	**0**	**5.1**	**5**	**2**	**2**	**0**	**1**	**3**	**5**	**2**	**0**

Chamberlain's League Championship Series Record

Year	Club vs. Opp.	W	L	ERA	G	GS	CG	SHO	SV	IP	H	R	ER	HR	HP	BB	SO	WP	BK
2009	NYY vs. LAA	0	0	5.40	4	0	0	0	0	1.2	5	1	1	0	0	0	2	0	0
2010	NYY vs. TEX	0	0	2.70	3	0	0	0	0	3.1	4	1	1	0	0	2	3	0	0
LCS Totals		**0**	**0**	**3.60**	**7**	**0**	**0**	**0**	**0**	**5.0**	**9**	**2**	**2**	**0**	**0**	**2**	**5**	**0**	**0**

Chamberlain's World Series Record

Year	Club vs. Opp.	W	L	ERA	G	GS	CG	SHO	SV	IP	H	R	ER	HR	HP	BB	SO	WP	BK
2009	NYY vs. PHI	1	0	3.00	3	0	0	0	0	3.0	2	1	1	1	0	1	4	0	0
World Series Totals		**1**	**0**	**3.00**	**3**	**0**	**0**	**0**	**0**	**3.0**	**2**	**1**	**1**	**1**	**0**	**1**	**4**	**0**	**0**
POSTSEASON TOTALS		**1**	**0**	**3.38**	**15**	**0**	**0**	**0**	**0**	**13.1**	**16**	**5**	**5**	**1**	**1**	**6**	**14**	**2**	**0**

Chamberlain's Regular Season Batting Record

Year	Team	AVG	G	AB	R	H	2B	3B	HR	RBI	SH	SF	HP	BB	SO	SB	CS
2010	NYY					Did Not Bat											
Major League Totals		**.000**	**166**	**5**	**0**	**0**	**0**	**0**	**0**	**0**	**2**	**0**	**0**	**1**	**1**	**0**	**0**

Chamberlain's Career Fielding Record

Position	PCT	G	PO	A	E	TC	DP
Pitcher	.968	166	13	48	2	63	6

No Hits For You

DID YOU KNOW??? Former Yankee and Hall of Famer Allie Reynolds (pictured) is one of only four pitchers to record two regular-season no-hitters in the same season, accomplishing the feat in 1951...prior to Reynolds, Cincinnati's Johnny Vander Meer was the only pitcher to hurl two no-hitters in the same season, doing so in back-to-back starts in June 1938...Detroit's Virgil Trucks (1952) and California's Nolan Ryan (1973) are the only other pitchers to match the record.

Reynolds' first no-hitter of the 1951 season came on July 12 vs. Cleveland...his second no-hitter, an 8-0 Yankees victory on September 28 vs. Boston, clinched the American League title for the Yankees.

76

REEGIE CORONA

INFIELDER • 5-11 • 185 • B/T: SWITCH/RIGHT • OPENING DAY AGE: 24

BIRTHDATE
November 7, 1986

BIRTHPLACE
Caracas, Venezuela

RESIDES
Miranda, Venezuela

M.L. SERVICE
None (Rookie)

STATUS
▸ Signed by the Yankees as a non-drafted free agent on July 2, 2003…signed through the 2011 season.

2010
▸ In his first full season at the Triple-A level, batted .238 (92-for-387) with 20 doubles, 5 triples, 5HR and 31RBI in 105G with Scranton/Wilkes-Barre before his season ended on 7/30 when he fractured his right arm…was successful in 14-of-15 stolen base attempts.

▸ Appeared in games at 2B, 3B and SS, combining for a .988 fielding percentage (501TC, 6E)…committed just 1E in 449 total chances over 91 games at second base.

▸ Hit .302 (32-for-106, 0HR) vs. left-handed pitchers and .214 (60-for-281, 5HR) vs. righties…carried a .316 (18-for-57) average with runners in scoring position and two outs.

▸ Suffered a season-ending broken right humerus in 7/30 win vs. Norfolk, colliding with Eric Bruntlett on the game's final play (a pop-up to short right field)…had appeared in 105 of the team's 107G at the time of his injury.

2009
▸ Combined to bat .257 (120-for-467) with 69R, 28 doubles, 6HR, 40RBI and 16SB in 129 games with Double-A Trenton and Triple-A Scranton/Wilkes-Barre…named to the Eastern League midseason All-Star team…appeared in 88 games at SS and 41 games at 2B.

▸ Was promoted to Scranton/WB on 5/14, hitting .147 (10-for-68) with 2 doubles and 1HR before being transferred back to Trenton on 6/4.

▸ Returned to Triple-A on 8/7 and batted .239 (22-for-92) with 5 doubles and 2HR over the final month of the season…had multiple hits in four of his last eight games of the regular season.

▸ Appeared in all seven postseason games for the International League runner-ups, batting .292 (7-for-24) with 3R, 3 doubles and 6BB…started six games at 2B and two games at SS.

▸ Tabbed by *Baseball America* as having the "Best Strikezone Discipline" in the Yankees organization.

▸ Played with Magallanes in the Venezuelan Winter League, batting .317 (44-for-139) with 36R, 17 doubles, 2HR, 18RBI, 28BB and 19K in 44 games, playing primarily 2B…led the league in doubles.

2008
▸ Spent the entire season with Trenton, batting .274 (125-for-457) with 72R, 27 doubles, 3 triples, 3HR, 39RBI and 24SB in 129 games…made 99 starts at 2B and 30 at SS…tied for fourth in the Eastern League and ranked third in the Yankees organization in stolen bases…led all EL second basemen with a .994 fielding percentage (3E, 477TC).

▸ Hit .317 (44-for-139) with 15 extra base hits as a right-handed batter, compared to .255 (81-for-318) from the left side of the plate.

▸ Hit safely in 17 of his final 20 games from 8/12 through the end of the season, batting .387 (29-for-75) to raise his season batting average from .251 to .274…scored 5R in seven playoff games for the Eastern League champions, batting .148 (4-for-27) with 4RBI in the postseason.

2007

▸ Combined to hit .258 with 75R, 23 doubles, 3 triples, 3HR, 43RBI and 29SB in 135 games with Single-A Tampa and Trenton.

▸ Led Tampa in stolen bases (22), getting caught just once in his first 19 attempts…led the FSL in walks (51) and was the top-fielding shortstop in the Florida State League (.942, 27E, 466TC)…was the starting shortstop in the midseason FSL All-Star Game on 6/16 in Daytona.

▸ Was transferred from Tampa to Trenton on 7/30…hit safely in his first nine games at the Double-A level, compiling an 11-game hitting streak from 7/26-8/8 in games with both clubs…batted .290 (9-for-31) with a team-high 6R, 2 doubles, 2RBI and 2SB in eight postseason games for the Eastern League champions as the team's starting shortstop.

▸ Played for the Peoria Javelinas of the Arizona Fall League, batting .188 with 7R, 3 doubles, 1HR and 8RBI in 14 games.

2006

▸ Played in 105 games with Single-A Charleston and Tampa, batting a combined .293 for the fourth-highest average among all Yankees minor leaguers…spent majority of the season with Charleston, batting .292 with 13 doubles, 2 triples, 3HR and 26SB in 96 games (51 at 2B, 25 at SS, 10 at 3B, six in the OF and one at 1B)…ranked third among all South Atlantic League hitters with a strikeout ratio of just one per 8.93 plate appearances (45K)…batted everywhere in the lineup except cleanup.

▸ Homered twice and drove in all three RiverDogs runs in a 3-1 win vs. Savannah on 4/27…marked his first professional home runs…recorded six hits in an 18-inning game vs. Rome on 5/20…was on the disabled list from 5/24-6/14 with a left shoulder strain…returned from the D.L. and posted a .385 (20-for-52) batting average in 14 games during the month of June…was selected to the South Atlantic League midseason All-Star team, but did not play.

▸ Closed out the season with Tampa, hitting safely in eight of his nine games.

2005

▸ Spent majority of the season with short-season Single-A Staten Island, batting .227 with 20RBI in 72 games for the NY-Penn League champions…recorded the game-winning single in the final game of the League Championship Series…posted a 15-game hitting streak from 7/17-31, the longest streak by an SI Yankee in 2005.

▸ Led all NY-Penn League second basemen with a .981 fielding percentage (7E, 369TC)…also paced league second basemen in games (67), total chances, putouts (157), assists (205) and double plays (49).

▸ Appeared in three games for Single-A Tampa before joining Staten Island, going hitless in 12AB.

2004

▸ Spent his first professional season with the Gulf Coast Yankees, batting .261 in 36 games…was 4-for-4 with 3 doubles in his 13th career game on 7/9 vs. the GCL Tigers.

Corona's Career Batting Record

YEAR	CLUB	AVG	G	AB	R	H	2B	3B	HR	RBI	SH	SF	HP	BB	SO	SB	CS	E	OBP	SLG
2004	GCL Yankees	.261	36	92	12	24	5	0	0	4	2	0	0	5	13	8	2	6	.299	.315
2005	Tampa	.000	3	12	1	0	0	0	0	0	0	0	0	2	3	0	0	0	.143	.000
	Staten Island	.227	72	255	32	58	11	0	0	20	4	2	1	27	32	9	3	8	.302	.271
2006	Charleston	.292	96	359	52	105	13	2	3	40	3	5	5	30	45	26	7	20	.351	.365
	Tampa	.297	9	37	5	11	1	0	1	7	0	1	0	1	5	2	0	3	.308	.405
2007	Tampa	.271	100	395	56	107	17	3	3	37	5	5	4	51	65	22	6	27	.356	.352
	Trenton	.221	35	140	19	31	6	0	0	6	1	2	2	18	30	7	2	10	.315	.264
2008	Trenton	.274	129	457	72	125	27	3	3	39	7	4	1	51	78	24	4	12	.345	.365
2009	Trenton-a,b	.287	85	307	56	88	21	2	3	26	3	1	1	56	50	12	4	8	.397	.397
	Scranton/WB	.200	44	160	13	32	7	0	3	14	3	4	1	9	20	4	0	8	.241	.300
2010	Scranton/WB	.238	105	387	46	92	20	5	5	31	3	0	2	36	58	14	1	6	.306	.354
Minor League Totals		**.259**	**714**	**2601**	**364**	**673**	**128**	**15**	**21**	**224**	**31**	**24**	**17**	**286**	**399**	**128**	**29**	**108**	**.333**	**.344**

Signed by the Yankees as a non-drafted free agent on July 2, 2003.

a – Selected by the Mariners in the first round (2nd overall pick) of the 2008 Rule 5 Draft.
b – Returned to the Yankees on April 3, 2009.

61 COLIN CURTIS

OUTFIELDER • 6-1 • 200 • B/T: LEFT/LEFT • OPENING DAY AGE: 26

BIRTHDATE
February 1, 1985

BIRTHPLACE
Issaquah, Wash.

RESIDES
Sammamish, Wash.

M.L. SERVICE
69 days
(Rookie)

COLLEGE
Arizona State University

STATUS
▸ Selected by the Yankees in the fourth round of the 2006 First-Year Player Draft…signed through the 2011 season.

2010
▸ Hit .186 (11-for-59) with 7R, 3 doubles, 1HR and 8RBI in 31 games (nine starts in RF, two in LF and one at DH) over two stints with the Yankees (6/21-7/31 and 9/6-10/3).

▸ Was signed to a Major League contract and selected to the Yankees' 25-man roster from Triple-A Scranton/Wilkes-Barre on 6/21…made his Major League debut that night at Arizona, pinch-hitting for A.J. Burnett in the fifth inning and going 0-for-1 in the Yankees' loss.

▸ Collected his first Major League hit and RBI with a pinch-hit two-run double off Chad Qualls in the eighth inning of 6/22 win at Arizona…drove in the game-tying run with his ninth-inning groundout in 6/27 win at Los Angeles-NL to complete the Yankees' four-run rally in the ninth and send the game to extra innings.

▸ Made his first Major League start—in LF—in 6/30 loss vs. Seattle, going 1-for-3 with 1 double.

▸ Hit the first home run of his Major League career—a pinch-hit, three-run HR—and was 1-for-1 in 7/21 win vs. Los Angeles-AL…entered the game as a pinch-hitter with an 0-2 count after Brett Gardner was ejected…remained in the game in LF…became the first Yankee to hit his first career home run as a pinch-hitter since Andy Phillips on 9/26/04 at Boston.

▸ Was optioned to Scranton/WB on 7/31 when the Yankees acquired OF Austin Kearns from the Cleveland Indians…returned to the Yankees as a September callup on 9/6, playing in nine games and going 0-for-16 with 1BB through the end of the season…finished the year hitless in his final 19AB.

▸ Began the season with Triple-A Scranton/Wilkes-Barre, batting .289 (69-for-239) with 28R, 24 doubles, 5HR and 27RBI in 66 games with Scranton/WB…appeared at all three outfield positions.

▸ Went 4-for-5 with 3RBI and tied a franchise single-game record with 3 doubles in Scranton/WB's 6-3 victory vs. Lehigh Valley on 4/23.

▸ Compiled a 14-game hitting streak from 8/18-9/1, batting .354 (17-for-48) over the stretch…hit safely in 18 of his final 21 games with Scranton/WB, carrying a .450 (27-for-60) average from 8/14 through the end of the Triple-A regular season.

▸ Following the season, played with Escogido in the Dominican Winter League batting .240 (12-for-50) with 3 doubles and 7RBI in 14 games.

▸ Attended spring training with the Yankees as a non-roster invitee for the third straight year, batting .500 (6-for-12) with 2HR and 8RBI in 12 games.

BESTS & STREAKS

Hits
2 - 2 times
Last: at CLE, 7/29/10

Runs
3 - at CLE, 7/29/10

2B
1 - 3 times
Last: at SEA, 7/9/10

3B
NA

HR
1 - vs. LAA, 7/21/10

RBI
3 - vs. LAA, 7/21/10

BB
1 - 4 times
Last: at TB, 9/14/10

SO
2 - 2 times
Last: at TEX, 9/10/10

SB
NA

Hit Streak
3g - 7/20-23/10

2009

- ▶ Combined to bat .250 (116-for-464) with 24 doubles, 7HR and 48RBI in 126 games with Double-A Trenton and Triple-A Scranton/Wilkes-Barre, setting a career high in doubles.
- ▶ Began the season with Trenton, hitting .268 (57-for-213) with 14 doubles, 1HR and 19RBI in 56 games…fashioned a season-high 13-game hitting streak from 4/13-28, batting .408 (20-for-49) with 6R, 7 doubles, 1 triple and 4RBI…collected a career-high five hits on 5/26 at New Britain, going 5-for-5 with 3R and 1BB.
- ▶ Was promoted to Scranton/WB on 6/22, where he batted .235 (59-for-251) with 10 doubles, 6HR and 29RBI in 70 games…recorded his first career multi-homer game on 7/25 vs. Toledo.
- ▶ Following the season, played for Surprise in the Arizona Fall League, batting .397 (31-for-78) with 19R, 7 doubles, 2 triples, 5HR and 18RBI in 20 games and leading the AFL in slugging percentage (.731).

2008

- ▶ Batted .255 (126-for-495) with 20 doubles, 3 triples, 10HR and 71RBI in 132 games with Double-A Trenton, setting career highs in games, runs (68), home runs and RBI…led the league with 9IBB.
- ▶ Hit in 13 straight games from 4/15-30, batting .373 (19-for-51) with 5 doubles over the stretch.

2007

- ▶ Combined to hit .270 (131-for-485) with 69R, 19 doubles and 41RBI in 126 games with Single-A Tampa and Double-A Trenton.
- ▶ Began the season with Tampa, batting .298 (73-for-245) with 37R, 9 doubles, 5HR and 26RBI in 65 games…fashioned a 14-game hitting streak from 5/23-6/7 and hit in 22-of-23 games from 5/23-6/18.
- ▶ Was transferred from Tampa to Trenton on 6/22, where he remained through the end of the season, batting .242 (58-for-240) with 32R, 10 doubles, 3HR and 15RBI in 61 games.

2006

- ▶ Made his professional debut with the GCL Yankees, playing in three games and going 4-for-8 (.500) with 3R, 2 doubles, 1HR and 4RBI before being promoted to short-season Single-A Staten Island on 7/18.
- ▶ With Staten Island, batted .302 (48-for-159) with 25R, 9 doubles, 2 triples, 1HR and 18RBI in 44 games, helping to lead the Yankees to their second straight New York-Penn League Championship.

PERSONAL

- ▶ Full name is Colin Benedict Curtis…graduated from Issaquah High School (Wash.)…was a four-year letter-winner and starter in baseball and a two-year letter-winner in basketball…shared Washington state 3A MVP honors with Washington freshman pitcher Tim Lincecum.
- ▶ Is a cancer survivor after being diagnosed with testicular cancer in 1999…received a signed book by cyclist Lance Armstrong after his diagnosis.
- ▶ Attended Arizona State University where he majored in interdisciplinary studies with an emphasis on business and sociology…earned All-Pac-10 honors in 2006 and All-Pac-10 Honorable Mention in 2004 and 2005…was named to the College World Series All-Tournament Team in 2005…wore No. 9 during college in honor of Roger Maris.
- ▶ Was originally selected by the Cincinnati Reds in the 50th round of the 2003 First-Year Player Draft, but chose to attend college.

Curtis' Career Playing Record

Year	Team	AVG	G	AB	R	H	2B	3B	HR	RBI	SH	SF	HP	BB	SO	SB	CS	E	OBP	SLG
2006	GCL Yankees	.500	3	8	3	4	2	0	1	4	0	0	1	1	0	1	0	0	.600	1.125
	Staten Island	.302	44	159	25	48	9	2	1	18	0	2	4	12	19	4	5	1	.362	.403
2007	Tampa	.298	65	245	37	73	9	2	5	26	3	1	3	29	43	4	4	2	.378	.412
	Trenton	.242	61	240	32	58	10	1	3	15	0	2	3	17	47	1	1	1	.298	.329
2008	Trenton	.255	132	495	68	126	20	3	10	71	2	7	3	55	86	6	3	6	.329	.368
2009	Trenton	.268	56	213	28	57	14	4	1	19	1	1	5	20	37	7	0	1	.343	.385
	Scranton/WB	.235	70	251	29	59	10	0	6	29	1	2	1	24	46	1	2	3	.302	.347
2010	Scranton/WB	.289	66	239	28	69	24	0	5	27	1	2	6	21	38	1	2	0	.452	.358
	YANKEES	.186	31	59	7	11	3	0	1	8	0	0	1	4	15	0	0	0	.250	.288
Minor League Totals		**.267**	**497**	**1850**	**250**	**494**	**98**	**12**	**32**	**209**	**8**	**17**	**26**	**179**	**316**	**25**	**17**	**14**	**.337**	**.385**
Major League Totals		**.186**	**31**	**59**	**7**	**11**	**3**	**0**	**1**	**8**	**0**	**0**	**1**	**4**	**15**	**0**	**0**	**0**	**.250**	**.288**

Selected by the Yankees in the fourth round of the 2006 First-Year Player Draft.

Curtis' Career Fielding Record

Position	PCT	G	PO	A	E	TC
Outfield	1.000	23	22	0	0	22

31 PEDRO FELICIANO

LEFT-HANDED PITCHER • 5-10 • 190 • B/T: LEFT/LEFT • OPENING DAY AGE: 34

BIRTHDATE
August 25, 1976

BIRTHPLACE
Rio Piedras, P.R.

RESIDES
Dorado, P.R.

M.L. SERVICE
6 years, 59 days

STATUS
▸ Signed as a free agent by the Yankees to a two-year contract with a one-year club option on January 3, 2011…contract extends through 2012 with an option for 2013.

CAREER NOTES
▸ Has held left-handed batters to a .214 (146-for-683) batting average with 10HR and 210K in his career…of his 459 career appearances, 398 have been 1.0-inning or less.

▸ Has led the Majors in relief outings in each of the last three seasons (2008-10)…his 266 total appearances over the three-season stretch established a Major League record…has made 344 relief appearances since the start of 2007, also marking an all-time record for most appearances over a four-year stretch.

▸ With 92 appearances in 2010, 88 in 2009 and 86 in 2008, joins Paul Quantrill (2002-04) as the only pitchers in Baseball history to appear in at least 85 games in each of three consecutive seasons (credit: *Elias Sports Bureau*).

▸ Has stranded 229-of-303 inherited runners in his career (75.6%).

▸ In 30 career relief appearances against AL East opponents, is 1-1 with a 2.48 ERA (29.0IP, 8ER) and a .202 (21-for-104) opponents batting average.

▸ Pitched in 459 games with the Mets, trailing only John Franco (695) for second place on the franchise's all-time list.

▸ With his first appearance as a Yankee, will become the 110th player all-time to play in a Major League game with both the Mets and Yankees.

BESTS & STREAKS

Low hit CG
  N/A
IP (start)
  N/A
IP (relief)
  5.0 – at NYY, 6/28/03
Hits
  8 – at HOU, 8/6/03
Runs
  5 – 3 times
  Last: at PHI, 9/3/04
BB
  4 – at NYY, 6/28/03
SO
  5 – 3 times
  Last: at ATL, 9/1/07
HR
  2 – 5 times
  Last: vs. HOU, 8/24/08
Winning Streak
  7g – 7/9/06-4/9/07
Losing Streak
  4g – 6/29-7/28/10

2010
▸ Went 3-6 with a 3.30 ERA (62.2IP, 23ER) in 92 relief appearances with the Mets, surpassing his own franchise record in games pitched (previous record 88 games in 2009).

▸ His 92 appearances tied the Dodgers' Mike Marshall (1973) for fourth place on Baseball's all-time single-season games pitched list, trailing only Marshall (106 games in 1974) and Pittsburgh's Kent Tekulve (94 in 1979) and Salomon Torres (94 in 2006).

▸ Opponents batted .273 (66-for-242, 1HR); LH .211 (26-for-123, 0HR), RH .336 (40-for-119, 1HR)…73 of his 92 appearances were scoreless…held opponents hitless in 44 outings…stranded 41-of-50 inherited runners (82.0%)…appeared in consecutive games 15 times, three straight games six times, four straight games twice and six straight games three times…retired 67-of-92 first batters faced (72.8%).

▸ Each of his three wins (5/4 at Cincinnati, 6/6 vs. Florida and 8/16 at Houston) came in contests in which he recorded just one out.

▸ Went 2-4 with a 2.34 ERA (34.2IP, 9ER) in 49 appearances before the All-Star break…in 43 post-All-Star appearances, was 1-2 with a 4.50 ERA (28.0IP, 14ER).

▸ Allowed a 10th-inning "walk-off" home run to Orlando Cabrera on 5/5 at Cincinnati…was his only home run allowed in 2010…did not allow a homer over his final 49.2IP of the season (76 appearances).

▸ Appeared in his 402nd career game in 6/10 loss vs. San Diego, surpassing Tom Seaver (401) for second place on the Mets' all-time games pitched list…also passed Jerry Koosman (376) and Jesse Orosco (372).

- Appeared in 22 games in September, setting a Major League record for games pitched in a calendar month (previous was 21 games by the Dodgers' Mike Marshall in July 1975 and the Giants' Gary Lavelle in August 1984).

MOST APPEARANCES, LAST THREE SEASONS (2008-10)	
1. **PEDRO FELICIANO**	**266**
2. Carlos Marmol	238
3. Matt Guerrier	229
4. Aaron Heilman	218
5. Francisco Cordero	215

MOST APPEARANCES, SINGLE SEASON ALL TIME		
1. Mike Marshall (LAD)	106	(1974)
2. Kent Tekulve (PIT)	94	(1979)
3. Salomon Torres (PIT)	94	(2006)
4. **PEDRO FELICIANO (NYM)**	**92**	**(2010)**
5. Mike Marshall (LAD)	92	(1973)

2009

- Went 6-4 with a 3.03 ERA (59.1IP, 20ER) with the Mets, leading the Majors with 88 relief appearances.
- Opponents batted .231 (51-for-221, 7HR); LH .215 (32-for-149, 4HR), RH .264 (19-for-72, 3HR)…stranded 44-of-54 (81.5%) inherited runners…retired 67-of-88 first batters faced (76.1%)…opponents hit .183 (19-for-104) with runners on base.
- Recorded a 1.69 ERA (32.0IP, 6ER) in 48 appearances at home, holding opponents without an earned run in his first 33 appearances at Citi Field through 8/3 (25.0IP).
- Held opponents hitless over 22AB with runners on base from 4/8-5/7 vs. Philadelphia…was snapped by a Jayson Werth two-run home run.
- Was named the Mets' "Pitcher of the Month" in September after going 1-0 with a 2.79 ERA (9.2IP, 3ER) and 13K in 17 appearances…did not allow an earned run in 14 of his final 16 outings of the season (7.2IP, 2ER).
- Made four relief appearances for Puerto Rico in the World Baseball Classic prior to the season, allowing 2H in 3.0 scoreless IP (2BB, 3K).

2008

- Was 3-4 with two saves and a 4.05 ERA (53.1IP, 24ER) in a Major League-leading 86 relief appearances with the Mets…opponents batted .281 (57-for-203, 7HR); LH .210 (22-for-105, 2HR); RH .357 (35-for-98, 5HR)…stranded 51-of-71 (71.8%) inherited runners…retired 51-of-86 first batters faced (59.3%).
- Of his 86 relief appearances, 70 were scoreless…opponents hit .179 (5-for-28) with runners in scoring position and two outs.
- Was 2-4 with a 2.34 ERA (34.2IP, 9ER) in 49 appearances prior to the All-Star Game…was 1-2 with a 4.50 ERA (28.0IP, 14ER) after the break.
- Allowed just 1ER in 10.2IP (0.84 ERA) over his first 18 relief outings of the season from 4/2-5/6.
- Held opponents scoreless in 16 of his final 18 appearances of the season from 8/26-9/28 (6.1IP, 3ER).

2007

- Went 2-2 with two saves and a 3.09 ERA (64.0IP, 22ER) in 78 relief appearances with the Mets…opponents batted .200 (47-for-235, 3HR); LH .168 (16-for-95, 1HR), RH .221 (31-for-140, 2HR)…stranded 48-of-60 (80.0%) inherited runners…retired 56-of-78 first batters faced (71.8%)…recorded a career-high 61K in 64.0IP (8.58K/9.0IP).
- Did not allow an earned run over his first 16 outings of the season (14.2IP) prior to allowing 2ER on 5/12 vs. Milwaukee.
- Snapped his career-high seven-game winning streak (7/9/06-4/9/07) with a loss on 6/5 vs. Philadelphia, allowing 2H and 2ER without retiring a batter.
- Earned his first career save on 6/30 at Philadelphia, tossing 2.0 scoreless innings (1H, 2K)…recorded his only other save of the season on 9/1 at Atlanta (2.0IP, 5K)…marked the seventh time in Major League history that a save was recorded with five-or-more strikeouts to end a game.

2006

- Went 7-2 with a 2.09 ERA (60.1IP, 14ER) in 64 relief appearances with the Mets…ranked third among all NL relievers in ERA…tied for fourth among NL relievers in wins…entered the season with just one career Major League win.
- Opponents batted .248 (56-for-226, 4HR); LH .231 (27-for-117, 2HR), RH .266 (29-for-109, 2HR)…stranded 27-of-39 (69.2%) inherited runners…retired 43-of-64 first batters faced (67.2%).
- Did not allow a run over a 16-appearance stretch from 8/8-9/24, going 2-0 and holding opponents to 8H in 14.2 scoreless IP (4BB, 13K).
- Saw his only career postseason action, going 1-0 with a 1.93 ERA (4.2IP, 1ER) in six relief appearances in the NLDS and NLCS…earned his first postseason win in NLDS Game 3 at Los Angeles-NL, retiring Nomar Garciaparra with the bases loaded to end the fifth inning.
- Prior to the season, pitched for Puerto Rico in the inaugural World Baseball Classic, tossing 2.1 scoreless innings over three relief appearances.

2005

- Went 3-2 with a 3.89 ERA (37.0IP, 16ER) and 36K in 37 relief appearances for the Fukuoka Softbank Hawks of the Japanese Pacific League.

2004

- Went 1-1 with a 5.40 ERA (18.1IP, 11ER) in 22 relief appearances over four stints with the Mets (5/25-31, 6/17-19, 7/28-8/12 and 8/14-10/3)…opponents batted .209 (14-for-67, 2HR); LH .128 (5-for-39, 0HR), RH .321 (9-for-28, 2HR)…allowed three-of-nine (33.3%) inherited runners to score…retired 17-of-22 first batters faced (77.3%).
- Earned his first Major League win on 8/4 at Milwaukee, striking out both batters faced and stranding one inherited runner in a 6-5 Mets victory.
- Began the season with Triple-A Norfolk, going 4-3 with two saves and a 5.30 ERA (35.2IP, 21ER) in 32 relief appearances.

2003

- Made 23 relief appearances for the Mets, posting a 3.35 ERA (48.1IP, 18ER) without recording a decision…opponents batted .269 (52-for-193, 5HR); LH .304 (14-for-46, 1HR), RH .259 (38-for-147, 4HR)…stranded 12-of-18 (66.7%) inherited runners…retired 14-of-23 first batters faced (60.9%).
- Was signed to a Major League contract and selected to the Mets' 25-man roster on 5/22 where he remained for the rest of the season.
- Tossed a career-high 5.0 innings on 6/28 at the Yankees, tying the longest relief outing by a Mets pitcher in 2003.
- Began the season with Triple-A Norfolk, going 3-2 with one save and a 3.97 ERA (22.2IP, 10ER) in 15 relief appearances.

2002

- Saw his first Major League action, posting a 7.50 ERA (6.0IP, 5ER) in six relief appearances with the Mets as a September callup…opponents batted .360 (9-for-25, 0HR); LH .444 (4-for-9, 0HR), RH .313 (5-for-16, 0HR)…retired three-of-six first batters faced (50.0%).
- Made his Major League debut in 9/4 win vs. Florida, tossing 2.0 scoreless innings (1BB, 2K)…was signed to a Major League contract and selected to the active roster from Triple-A Norfolk on 9/2.
- Began the season with Double-A Chattanooga, going 2-1 with four saves and a 2.56 ERA (38.2IP, 11ER) in 28 appearances…was transferred to Triple-A Louisville on 6/24, going 1-1 with a 3.04 ERA (26.2IP, 9ER) in 20 outings.
- Was traded from Cincinnati to the Mets along with OF Elvin Andujar and two players to be named later (OF Raul Gonzalez and OF Brady Clark) in exchange for LHP Shawn Estes and cash considerations on 8/15…was assigned to Norfolk where he made five relief appearances, posting a 7.00 ERA (9.0IP, 7ER) with two saves and no decisions.
- Was claimed off waivers by the Detroit Tigers on 10/11…was released on 12/16 and signed by the Mets on 12/20.

2001

- In his final season in the Los Angeles Dodgers organization, combined to go 5-5 with 17 saves and a 2.61 ERA (69.0IP, 20ER) in 60 relief appearances with Double-A Jacksonville and Triple-A Las Vegas.
- Began the season with Jacksonville, going 5-4 with 17 saves and a 1.94 ERA (60.1IP, 13ER) in 54 appearances…was promoted to Las Vegas on 7/3, going 0-1 with a 7.27 ERA (8.2IP, 7ER) in six relief outings before being transferred back to Jacksonville on 7/22.
- Was named to the Southern League All-Star team.
- Was signed by the Cincinnati Reds as a minor league free agent on 11/15.

2000

- Combined to go 4-5 with two saves and a 3.77 ERA (71.2IP, 30ER) in 35 appearances (two starts) with Single-A Vero Beach, Double-A San Antonio and Triple-A Albuquerque.
- Began the season with Vero Beach, going 4-5 with a 3.82 ERA (61.1IP, 26ER) in 25 appearances (two starts)…was transferred to San Antonio on 8/14, posting a 1.93 ERA (9.1IP, 2ER) with two saves and no decisions in nine appearances…promoted to Albuquerque on 9/4, making one appearance and allowing 2ER in 1.0IP.

1999

- Missed the entire season with an impingement in his left shoulder.

1998

- Went 2-5 with two saves and a 4.61 ERA (68.IP, 35ER) in 22 appearances (10 starts) with Single-A Vero Beach.
- Was placed on the disabled list from 5/30-6/27 with a strained left hamstring…was also on the D.L. from 7/31-8/7 with a blister on his left hand.

1997

- Spent the majority of the season with Single-A Savannah, going 3-7 with four saves and a 2.64 ERA (105.2IP, 31ER) in 36 appearances (nine starts).
- Made his final appearance of the season with Single-A Vero Beach on 8/30, allowing 1ER in 2.0IP.

1996

- Went 2-3 with a 5.71 ERA (41.0IP, 26ER) in 22 appearances (one start) with rookie-level Great Falls.

1995

▸ Made six relief appearances with rookie-level Great Falls, posting a 13.50 ERA (6.2IP, 10ER) without recording a decision.

PERSONAL

▸ Full name is Pedro Juan Molina Feliciano…he and his wife, Wanda, have one son, Josker, and one daughter, Josnelly.
▸ Graduated from Jose S. Algeria High School in Dorado, P.R.

Feliciano's Career Pitching Record

Year	Club	W	L	ERA	G	GS	CG	SHO	SV	IP	H	R	ER	HR	HP	BB	SO	WP	BK
1995	Great Falls	0	0	13.50	6	0	0	0	0	6.2	12	12	10	0	0	7	9	4	2
1996	Great Falls	2	3	5.71	22	1	0	0	3	41.0	50	36	26	1	3	26	39	4	3
1997	Savannah	3	7	2.64	36	9	1	0	4	105.2	90	45	31	11	1	39	94	6	4
	Vero Beach	0	0	4.50	1	0	0	0	0	2.0	3	1	1	1	0	0	1	0	0
1998	Vero Beach	2	5	4.61	22	10	0	0	2	68.1	68	44	35	8	2	30	51	2	0
1999								Did Not Pitch - Injured											
2000	Vero Beach	4	5	3.82	25	2	0	0	0	61.1	76	31	26	4	5	24	48	3	0
	San Antonio	0	0	1.93	9	0	0	0	2	9.1	7	2	2	0	1	4	11	0	2
	Albuquerque	0	0	18.00	1	0	0	0	0	1.0	3	3	2	2	0	1	2	0	0
2001	Jacksonville	5	4	1.94	54	0	0	0	17	60.1	41	14	13	3	3	11	55	2	0
	Las Vegas	0	1	7.27	6	0	0	0	0	8.2	16	11	7	2	1	5	5	1	0
2002	Chattanooga – a	2	1	2.56	28	0	0	0	4	38.2	33	14	11	1	3	11	26	0	0
	Louisville	1	1	3.04	20	0	0	0	0	26.2	35	10	9	3	1	4	19	0	0
	Norfolk – b	0	0	7.00	5	0	0	0	2	9.0	14	7	7	1	0	1	11	1	0
	METS	0	0	7.50	6	0	0	0	0	6.0	9	5	5	0	0	1	4	0	0
2003	Norfolk – c, d	3	2	3.97	15	0	0	0	1	22.2	20	10	10	3	0	6	18	0	0
	METS	0	0	3.35	23	0	0	0	0	48.1	52	21	18	5	3	21	43	3	1
2004	Norfolk	4	3	5.30	32	0	0	0	2	35.2	35	25	21	4	4	15	25	3	0
	METS	1	1	5.40	22	0	0	0	0	18.1	14	12	11	2	1	12	14	1	0
2005	Fukuoka – e	3	2	3.89	37	0	0	0	0	37.0	30	17	16	5	6	13	36	0	0
2006	Norfolk – f	0	0	6.23	3	0	0	0	0	4.1	4	3	3	1	0	1	5	0	0
	METS	7	2	2.09	64	0	0	0	0	60.1	56	15	14	4	3	20	54	1	0
2007	METS	2	2	3.09	78	0	0	0	2	64.0	47	26	22	3	5	31	61	1	1
2008	METS	3	4	4.05	*86	0	0	0	2	53.1	57	24	24	7	3	26	50	2	0
2009	METS	6	4	3.03	*88	0	0	0	0	59.1	51	25	20	7	0	18	59	2	1
2010	METS – g	3	6	3.30	*92	0	0	0	0	62.2	66	24	23	1	6	30	56	1	0
Japanese League Totals		**3**	**2**	**3.89**	**37**	**0**	**0**	**0**	**0**	**37.0**	**30**	**17**	**16**	**5**	**6**	**13**	**36**	**0**	**0**
Minor League Totals		**26**	**32**	**3.84**	**285**	**22**	**1**	**0**	**37**	**501.1**	**507**	**268**	**214**	**45**	**24**	**185**	**419**	**26**	**11**
Major League Totals		**22**	**19**	**3.31**	**459**	**0**	**0**	**0**	**4**	**372.1**	**352**	**152**	**137**	**29**	**21**	**159**	**341**	**11**	**3**

*League leader

Selected by the Dodgers in the 31st round of the 1995 First-Year Player Draft.

a – Signed by the Cincinnati Reds as a minor league free agent on December 21, 2001.
b – Acquired by the Mets from Cincinnati along with OF Elvin Andujar and two players to be named later (OF Raul Gonzalez and OF Brady Clark) in exchange for LHP Shawn Estes and cash considerations on August 15, 2002.
c – Claimed off waivers by the Detroit Tigers on October 11, 2002.
d – Signed by the Mets as a free agent on December 16, 2002.
e – Had his contract sold to the Fukuoka Softbank Hawks of the Japanese Pacific League on January 21, 2005.
f – Signed by the Mets as a free agent on December 19, 2005.
g – Signed by the Yankees as a free agent on January 3, 2011.

Feliciano's League Division Series Record

Year	Club vs. Opp.	W	L	ERA	G	GS	CG	SHO	SV	IP	H	R	ER	HR	HP	BB	SO	WP	BK
2006	NYM vs. LAD	1	0	0.00	3	0	0	0	0	1.2	0	0	0	0	0	2	2	0	0
Division Series Totals		**1**	**0**	**0.00**	**3**	**0**	**0**	**0**	**0**	**1.2**	**0**	**0**	**0**	**0**	**0**	**2**	**2**	**0**	**0**

Feliciano's League Championship Series Record

Year	Club vs. Opp.	W	L	ERA	G	GS	CG	SHO	SV	IP	H	R	ER	HR	HP	BB	SO	WP	BK
2006	NYM vs. STL	0	0	3.00	3	0	0	0	0	3.0	2	1	1	1	0	0	1	1	0
LCS Totals		**0**	**0**	**3.00**	**3**	**0**	**0**	**0**	**0**	**3.0**	**2**	**1**	**1**	**1**	**0**	**0**	**1**	**1**	**0**
Postseason Totals		**1**	**0**	**1.93**	**6**	**0**	**0**	**0**	**0**	**4.2**	**2**	**1**	**1**	**1**	**0**	**2**	**3**	**1**	**0**

Feliciano's World Baseball Classic Record

Year	Country, Site	W	L	ERA	G	GS	CG	SHO	SV	IP	H	R	ER	HR	HP	BB	SO	WP	BK
2006	Puerto Rico, P.R.	0	0	0.00	3	0	0	0	0	2.1	0	0	0	0	0	1	1	0	0
2009	Puerto Rico, P.R.	0	0	0.00	4	0	0	0	0	3.0	2	0	0	0	0	2	3	0	0
WBC Totals		**0**	**0**	**0.00**	**7**	**0**	**0**	**0**	**0**	**5.1**	**2**	**0**	**0**	**0**	**0**	**3**	**4**	**0**	**0**

Feliciano's Regular Season Batting Record

Year	Team	AVG	G	AB	R	H	2B	3B	HR	RBI	SH	SF	HP	BB	SO	SB	CS
2010	NYM					Did Not Bat											
Major League Totals		**.000**	**459**	**6**	**0**	**0**	**0**	**0**	**0**	**0**	**1**	**0**	**0**	**2**	**2**	**0**	**0**

Feliciano's Career Fielding Record

Position	PCT	G	PO	A	E	TC	DP
Pitcher	.937	459	27	77	7	111	7

79

ROBERT FISH

LEFT-HANDED PITCHER • 6-2 • 230 • B/T: LEFT/LEFT • OPENING DAY AGE: 23

BIRTHDATE
January 19, 1988

BIRTHPLACE
Montclair, Calif.

RESIDES
San Bernardino, Calif.

M.L. SERVICE
None (Rookie)

STATUS
▸ Selected by the Yankees in the 2010 Rule 5 Draft (first round) from the Los Angeles Angels…signed through the 2011 season.

2010
▸ Combined to go 5-5 with two saves and a 6.79 ERA (58.1IP, 44ER) in 49 relief appearances with Single-A Rancho Cucamonga and Double-A Arkansas in his first full season as a reliever.
▸ Began the season with Rancho Cucamonga, going 2-0 with a 1.13 ERA (16.0IP, 2ER) in 10 relief outings…was promoted to Double-A Arkansas on 5/13.
▸ In 39 relief appearances with Arkansas, went 3-5 with two saves and an 8.93 ERA (42.1IP, 42ER)…led the team in appearances and ranked second among relief pitchers with 48 strikeouts.
▸ Allowed 16ER in 2.1IP over a five-appearance stretch from 7/13-23.
▸ Pitched for Mesa in the Arizona Fall League following the season, going 0-2 with one save and a 10.45 ERA in 11 relief appearances (10.1IP, 12ER).
▸ Was selected by the Yankees from Los Angeles-AL in the first round (28th overall pick) of the Rule 5 Draft on 12/9/10.

2009
▸ Combined to go 1-6 with a 6.07 ERA (75.2IP, 51ER) in 22 appearances (13 starts) with Single-A Rancho Cucamonga, the AZL Angels and Triple-A Salt Lake.
▸ Began the season with Rancho Cucamonga, going 1-6 with a 6.39 ERA (69.0IP, 49ER) in 16 appearances (13 starts).
▸ Was placed on the disabled list from 5/25-6/5 and again from 6/28-8/25 with left shoulder inflammation.
▸ Made five rehab relief appearances with the rookie-level AZL Angels, allowing 2ER in 6.0IP (3.00 ERA) without recording a decision…was reinstated from the D.L. on 8/25 and assigned to Salt Lake…made one relief appearance on 8/26 at Colorado Springs (0.2IP, 1BB) before being optioned back to Rancho Cucamonga on 8/29.
▸ Made three relief appearances with Rancho Cucamonga over the remainder of the season, allowing 1ER in 4.0IP (3H, 2BB, 6K).

2008
▸ Went 10-4 with a 4.85 ERA (143.0IP, 77ER) in 28 starts with Single-A Cedar Rapids.
▸ Led the Midwest League in games started (28) and ranked fifth in strikeouts (138 – most among left-handed pitchers).
▸ Compiled a six-game winning streak during a seven-start stretch from 5/22-6/27.
▸ Was named the Midwest League "Pitcher of the Week" for the period ending 8/11, going 1-0 and tossing 13.0 scoreless innings over two starts during the span (5H, 3BB, 10K).

2007
▸ Combined to go 3-5 with a 3.38 ERA (74.2IP, 28ER) in 17 appearances (16 starts) with Single-A Rancho Cucamonga and rookie-level Orem…made one start with Rancho Cucamonga, taking the loss (3.0IP, 2ER) before being transferred to Orem on 5/13 for the remainder of the season.

- With Orem, went 3-4 with a 3.27 ERA (71.2IP, 26ER) in 16 appearances (15 starts)…earned Pioneer League Postseason All-Star honors after leading the league in strikeouts (77) and ranking second in ERA.
- Was named Pioneer League "Pitcher of the Week" for the period ending 8/20, after tossing 6.0 scoreless, one-hit innings in 8/16 win at Helena (1HP, 5K).

2006

- Made his professional debut with the ASL Angels, going 1-0 with a 3.21 ERA (14.0IP, 5ER) in 10 appearances (one start)…struck out 16 batters in 14.0IP.

PERSONAL

- Full name is Robert Michael Fish…attended AB Miller High School (Fontana, Calif.) where he was first team All-C.B.L., All-CIF and All-San Bernardino County as a senior…also won three consecutive league titles at Miller.

Fish's Career Pitching Record

Year	Club	W	L	ERA	G	GS	CG	SHO	SV	IP	H	R	ER	HR	HP	BB	SO	WP	BK
2006	ASL Angels	1	0	3.21	10	1	0	0	0	14.0	13	5	5	0	1	12	16	2	1
2007	Rancho Cucamonga	0	1	6.00	1	1	0	0	0	3.0	3	2	2	1	0	4	4	0	0
	Orem	3	4	3.27	16	15	0	0	0	71.2	62	33	26	4	10	31	77	3	0
2008	Cedar Rapids	10	4	4.85	28	28	0	0	0	143.0	138	87	77	12	18	68	138	5	1
2009	Rancho Cucamonga	1	6	6.39	16	13	0	0	0	69.0	94	59	49	12	9	28	54	3	0
	AZL Angels	0	0	3.00	5	0	0	0	0	6.0	1	2	2	0	1	1	9	0	0
	Salt Lake	0	0	0.00	1	0	0	0	0	0.2	0	0	0	0	0	1	0	0	0
2010	Rancho Cucamonga	2	0	1.13	10	0	0	0	0	16.0	7	2	2	0	2	8	25	0	0
	Arkansas – a	3	5	8.93	39	0	0	0	2	42.1	69	50	42	9	6	18	48	4	0
Minor League Totals		**20**	**20**	**5.05**	**126**	**58**	**0**	**0**	**2**	**365.2**	**387**	**240**	**205**	**38**	**47**	**171**	**371**	**17**	**2**

Selected by the Angels in the sixth round of the 2006 First-Year Player Draft.

a – Selected by the Yankees with the 28th overall pick in the 2010 Rule 5 Draft on December 9, 2010.

On a Roll

The Yankees have finished with a winning record in each of the last 18 seasons (1993-2010), becoming the only current Major League team to accomplish the feat…it is the longest streak of consecutive seasons with a record above .500 since the Baltimore Orioles reeled off 18 straight winning seasons from 1968-1985…the only team with more than 18 consecutive seasons above .500 is the Yankees, who recorded such a streak was an unprecedented run of 39 straight winning seasons from 1926-1964.

11
BRETT GARDNER

OUTFIELDER • 5-10 • 183 • B/T: LEFT/LEFT • OPENING DAY AGE: 27

BIRTHDATE
August 24, 1983

BIRTHPLACE
Holly Hill, S.C.

RESIDES
Holly Hill, S.C.

M.L. SERVICE
2 years, 72 days

COLLEGE
College of Charleston

STATUS
▸ Selected by the Yankees in the third round of the 2005 First-Year Player Draft…signed through the 2011 season.

CAREER NOTES
▸ Recorded his 50th career stolen base (in 57 career attempts) in 5/1/10 loss vs. Chicago-AL…reached the plateau in his 171st career game, becoming the first Yankee to reach the total in as few games with the club since Rickey Henderson on 8/3/85 (88 games) and the first Yankee to reach 50SB in as few games from the start of his career since Fritz Maisel on 6/21/14 (102 games)—credit: *Elias Sports Bureau.*
▸ His 63SB within two years of his Major League debut (6/30/08-6/29/10) were the most for any Yankee since Snuffy Stirnweiss had 66SB from 4/22/43-4/21/45…stole 30 bases within one year of his Major League debut (6/30/08-6/29/09), marking the most for any Yankee since 1920 (credit: *Elias*).
▸ Has stolen 86 bases in 101 career attempts…his 85.1% success rate ranks fourth among active players with at least 100 stolen base attempts.
▸ Has hit eight home runs in his career, with the Yankees going 8-0 in those contests.

2010
▸ Hit .277 (132-for-477) with 97R, 20 doubles, 7 triples, 5HR, 47RBI and 47SB in 150 games (96 starts in LF, 38 in CF) with the Yankees…stole 47 bases in 56 attempts (83.9%), tied for the fourth-most SB in the Majors.
▸ Led all Major Leaguers with 4.61 pitches seen per plate appearance…swung at only 7.6% of first pitches, the lowest such mark in the Majors…of the 14 times he swung at the first pitch, recorded 8H (.571BA) with 3 doubles and 1 triple…worked the count to 3-2 in 124 of his 569 plate appearances (21.79%), the third-highest percentage among AL qualifiers (credit: *Elias*)…had 75H with two strikes, tied for seventh in the Majors…ranked 10th in the Majors with one walk every 7.20 plate appearances…ranked 10th in the AL with 79BB.
▸ The Yankees were 56-16 when he scored a run and 20-3 when he scored multiple runs.
▸ Hit .290 (27-for-93) with 21R, 6 doubles, 1 triple and 11RBI in 25 games in the leadoff spot in the lineup…batted .342 (40-for-117) when leading off an inning.
▸ Became the seventh Yankee in the last 70 years to reach the 40-steal plateau in a season (also Rickey Henderson, Roberto Kelly, Mickey Rivers, Steve Sax, Alfonso Soriano and Snuffy Stirnweiss)…marked the most steals by a Yankee in a single season since Rickey Henderson in 1988 (93SB).
▸ Recorded 45.6% of the Yankees' 103SB in 2010, marking the highest percentage by a Yankee since Rickey Henderson in 1988 (63.7%, 93-of-147)—credit: *Elias.*
▸ Tied for second in the Majors with 12 outfield assists…his nine assists as a leftfielder trailed only Minnesota's Delmon Young (12) for most in the Majors.
▸ Ranked by *Baseball America* as the AL's third-fastest and third-best baserunner.
▸ Ranked sixth among Major League outfielders with a .997 fielding percentage, committing just 1E in 300 total chances.

BESTS & STREAKS

Hits
5 - at NYM, 6/26/09
Runs
3 - 4 times
Last: vs. TOR, 9/3/10
2B
2 - at TB, 4/14/09
3B
1 - 13 times
Last: vs. TOR, 9/3/10
HR
1 - 8 times
Last: vs. TOR, 7/4/10
RBI
4 - 2 times
Last: vs. TOR, 7/3/10
BB
3 - 2 times
Last: at CLE, 7/29/10
SO
3 - 7 times
Last: at TOR, 8/23/10
SB
3 - 2 times
Last: at BOS, 10/2/10 (G2)
Hit Streak
11g - 2 times
Last: 4/28-5/9/10

- Made his second straight Opening Day roster…stole home on the back end of a double steal in the fourth inning of 4/4 Opening Day loss at Boston…became the first Yankee to steal home since Alex Rodriguez on 7/31/04 vs. Baltimore (also as part of a double steal) and the first Major Leaguer to steal home on Opening Day since Oakland's Mike Bordick on 4/6/92 vs. Kansas City (credit: *Elias*).

- Batted .323 (21-for-65) with 14R in April, his most runs for any calendar month in his career…also stole 10 bases during the month, tied with Oakland's Rajai Davis and Pittsburgh's Andrew McCutchen for most in the Majors…marked the most SB by a Yankee in March/April since Chuck Knoblauch led the AL with 11 in 2001…Rickey Henderson is the only other Yankee to steal double-digit bases in March/April (3x: 1988-20; 1986-15; 1989-14).

HIGHEST SB PERCENTAGE IN AL, 2008-10	
1. Chris Getz	89.1 (41-for-46)
2. Ian Kinsler	85.7 (72-for-84)
3. Johnny Damon	85.2 (52-for-61)
4. BRETT GARDNER	**85.1 (86-for-101)**
5. Coco Crisp	84.4 (65-for-77)

MOST SB BY A YANKEE, SINGLE SEASON, LAST 60 YEARS	
1. Rickey Henderson	93 (1988)
2. Rickey Henderson	87 (1986)
3. Rickey Henderson	80 (1985)
4. BRETT GARDNER	**47 (2010)**

- Had three infield hits—including two to the pitcher—in 4/17 win vs. Texas, marking the most infield hits by a Yankee since Don Mattingly on 8/19/92 vs. Oakland—credit: *Elias*.

- Homered off a left-handed pitcher (Mark Beuhrle) for the first time in his career in 5/2 win vs. Chicago-AL, going 2-for-4 with 2R, 2RBI and 1BB.

- Did not steal a base over a 13-game span from 5/16-29, the second-longest such stretch of his career behind a 14-game span from 5/5-25/09…was caught stealing twice in a game for the first time in his career in 5/31 win vs. Cleveland.

- Hit a team-high .383 (23-for-60) with 13R and a .472OBP in 21 June games, ranking fourth in the Majors in batting average for the month.

- Was removed from 6/8 win at Baltimore for PH (Thames) in the eighth with a sore left thumb and missed the following two games…underwent X-rays on 6/9, the results of which were negative.

- Was hit by a pitch in 6/27 loss at Los Angeles-NL, leaving game in the top of the fourth with a bruised right forearm…was diagnosed with a right wrist contusion after X-rays were negative…missed 6/29-7/1 series at Seattle…hit .233 (56-for-240) over the remainder of the season.

- Hit his first career grand slam and was 2-for-3 with 2R and 1BB in 7/3 win vs. Toronto.

- Hit second career inside-the-park HR (also 5/15/09 vs. Minnesota)—his second homer in as many games—and was 2-for-4 with 2R and 1BB in 7/4 win vs. Toronto…became the first player with multiple inside-the-park HRs as a Yankee since Mickey Rivers (1976-79)—credit: SABR's David Vincent…according to *Elias*, became the first player to hit a grand slam and inside-the-park home run in back-to-back games since Scott Rolen on 7/2-3/99 w/ Philadelphia vs. Chicago-NL.

- Was ejected for the first time in his career in 7/21 win vs. Los Angeles-AL for arguing balls and strikes during his seventh-inning AB.

- Recorded two outfield assists in the same game for the first time in his career in 7/22 win vs. Kansas City…became the first Yankees left fielder with two assist in the same game since Melky Cabrera had two assists on 5/16/06 vs. Texas.

- Recorded at least one walk in 10 straight games from 8/25-9/5, marking the longest streak in the Majors in 2010 and the longest by a Yankee since Jorge Posada's 13-game stretch from 5/9-29/04—credit: *Elias*.

- Played all 20 innings in 10/2 doubleheader at Boston…had 2SB in Game 1 and a career-high-tying 3SB in Game 2, becoming the first player in franchise history to steal five bases in a single day (credit: *Elias*).

- Appeared in all nine postseason games, going 5-for-27 (.185) with 2SB.

- Underwent surgery on 12/8/10 to have inflamed tissue removed from his right wrist…procedure was performed by Dr. Melvin Rosenwasser at New York-Presbyterian Hospital

2009

- Hit .270 (67-for-248) with 48R, 3HR, 23RBI and 26SB in 108 games (63 starts in CF) with the Yankees…went 26-for-31 in stolen base attempts (83.9%), ranking third among all Major League rookies in stolen bases…became the third Yankees rookie over the last 50 years (since 1960) to steal at least 26 bases in a season, joining Alfonso Soriano (43SB in 2001) and Willie Randolph (37SB in 1976).

- Collected a triple and home run in the same game three times in 2009 (5/13 at Toronto, 5/15 vs. Minnesota and 6/26 at the Mets), becoming the first Yankee to accomplish the feat at least three times in a single season since Hank Bauer in 1957 (also three times)—credit: *Elias Sports Bureau*.

- Hit his first Major League home run—a two-run HR in the second inning—and was 2-for-3 with 2R, 1 triple, 3RBI and 1BB in 5/13 win at Toronto…along with Ramiro Pena, became the first pair of Yankees rookies to both hit triples in the same game since 8/31/70, when Thurman Munson and Johnny Ellis did so off Mike Cuellar (credit: *Elias*).

- Hit an inside-the-park solo-HR and was 3-for-3 with 2R and 1 triple on 5/15 vs. Minnesota after entering the game defensively in the fourth in CF when Johnny Damon was ejected…was the first inside-the-park HR by a Yankee since Ricky Ledee on 8/29/99 vs. Seattle…according to *Elias*, became the fifth Yankees rookie since Divisional play began in 1969 to hit an inside-the-park HR (Johnny Ellis-1969, Deion Sanders-1990, Derek Jeter-1996 and Ricky Ledee-1999)…joined Carl Crawford (2005), Brian Giles (2002) and Fred McGriff (1993) as the only players since 1989 to hit an inside-the-park HR and triple in the same contest (credit: *Elias*)…*Elias* also notes that he became just the third Yankee since 1998 to get 3H after entering as a sub (also Lance Johnson, 2000 and Cody Ransom, 2008)

- Missed three games from 5/18-20 with a bruised right shoulder…suffered injury in 5/17 win vs. Minnesota when he was tagged out at the plate by Joe Mauer…upon his return, reached base safely (via hit, walk or HBP) in 22 straight games with an official PA (including 18 starts) from 5/21-6/26, batting .371 (26-for-70) with 14R, 1 double, 2 triples, 1HR, 5RBI and 9BB.
- Stole a career-high three bases in 5/26 loss at Texas, going 3-for-5 with 1R…entered the game in the top of the first in CF, replacing an injured Melky Cabrera…collected three hits in a game that he did not start for the second time in 2009 (also 3-for-3 on 5/15), becoming the first player with two three-hit games off the bench in one season since John Shelby for the 1983 Orioles (credit: *Elias*).
- Hit a solo-HR and was 5-for-6 with 3R, 1 triple, 1HR, 2RBI and 1SB in 6/26 win at the Mets, establishing a career high in hits and tying his career high in runs scored…according to *Elias*, became the first player from either the Yankees or Mets with at least 5H in a Yankees/Mets game during the regular or postseason…*Elias* also notes Gardner became just the third Yankees rookie in franchise history to record at least 5H and 1HR in the same season, joining Joe DiMaggio in 1936 (5H, 1HR) and Shane Spencer in 1998 (5H, 2HR).
- Was placed on the 15-day D.L. on 7/26 with a fractured left thumb…injury occurred while sliding into second base in the first inning in 7/25 loss vs. Oakland…remained in the game and went 1-for-3 with 1 triple…was returned from rehab and reinstated on 9/7 (missed 40 team games).
- Appeared in 14 of the Yankees' postseason games, going 2-for-13 with 3R and 1SB…started the final two games (WS Game 5 and 6) in CF when Melky Cabrera was removed from the roster with a hamstring strain.
- Hit .379 (25-for-66) with 12R, 3HR and 7RBI in 27 spring training games, tying for the team lead in stolen bases (5) and ranking second in hits…won the 2009 James P. Dawson Award, given to the most outstanding rookie in Yankees spring training by the New York chapter of the BBWAA.

2008
- Hit .228 (29-for-117) with 5 doubles, 2 triples, 16RBI and 13SB in 42 games (17 starts in CF, 15 starts in LF) over two stints with the Yankees (6/30-7/25; 8/15-9/28)…the Yankees were 15-3 when he batted ninth.
- Was signed to a Major League contract and selected to the 25-man active roster from Triple-A Scranton/ Wilkes-Barre on 6/30, making his Major League debut that night in a loss vs. Texas and going 0-for-3 with 1SB as the leadoff hitter…according to the *Elias Sports Bureau*, was the first Yankee to make his Major League debut in the leadoff spot since Roberto Kelly on 7/29/87 vs. Kansas City.
- Stole five bases within his first nine games…according to *Elias*, became just the third Yankee since 1938 to accomplish the feat, joining Mickey Rivers (1976) and Bobby Abreu (2006)…was 8-for-8 before being caught for the first time in 9/15 win vs. Chicago-AL…according to *Elias*, was the first Yankee to begin his Major League career with eight straight successful stolen base attempts since Andy Fox went 8-for-8 in 1996.
- Recorded his first Major League hit—a seventh-inning single off Warner Madrigal—and was 1-for-4 with 2R, 1RBI, 1BB and 1SB in 7/2 win vs. Texas, also recording his first run and RBI.
- Notched his first career "walk-off" hit in 7/6 win vs. Boston, going 2-for-5 with 1R, 1RBI and 1SB…singled home Cano from second base in the 10th inning (off Jonathan Papelbon)…according to the *Elias Sports Bureau*, became the first Yankee to record a "walk-off" hit in his sixth career game or earlier since Alfonso Soriano (also in his sixth game) in 1999…*Elias* also noted he was the first Yankees rookie to provide a "walk-off" hit vs. Boston since Derek Jeter had a 10th-inning single off Joe Hudson in a 12-11 Yankees victory on 9/21/96.
- Also had "walk-off" RBI single on 8/16 vs. Kansas City, becoming the first Yankees rookie with two "walk-off" hits in one season since Hideki Matsui in 2003 (credit: *Elias*)…*Elias* also noted that he became the first Major Leaguer to record two game-ending RBI within his first 20 career games since Ted Simmons had two in his first seven ML games spanning from 1968-69.
- Batted .153 (9-for-59) with 8R, 1 double, 7RBI, 1SF, 2SH and 5SB in 17 games (15 starts in LF, one start in CF) in his first stint with the Yankees before being optioned to Scranton/WB on 7/26…recalled on 8/15 and batted .294 (20-for-68) with 4 doubles, 2 triples, 9RBI and 8SB in 25 starts (16 starts in CF) in his second stint.
- In 94 overall games with Scranton/Wilkes-Barre, batted .296 (101-for-341) with 68R, 12 doubles, 11 triples, 3HR, 32RBI, 70BB, 11SH and 37SB, while recording 27 multi-hit games…led all Yankees farmhands in SB and tied for fourth in average…at the time of his first promotion, led all Triple-A players in triples, SB and sacrifice hits and ranked first in the International League in walks, was second in OBP (.412) and fourth in runs scored.
- Hit the first "walk-off" HR in Scranton/WB Yankees history on 4/23 vs. Buffalo, a solo HR in the bottom of the ninth.
- Was tabbed as having the IL's "Best Strike Zone Judgment" and being the IL's "Best Baserunner" by *Baseball America* following the season…was also named to the publication's Triple-A All-Star team…entered the season ranked by *Baseball America* as the eighth-best prospect in the organization and as the "Fastest Baserunner."

2007
- Hit .281 (108-for-384) with 18 doubles, 8 triples, 1HR, 35RBI and 39SB in 99 combined games with Double-A Trenton and Triple-A Scranton/Wilkes-Barre…led all Yankees minor leaguers in stolen bases and tied for the Thunder team-lead with five triples.
- Began the year at Trenton, batting .300 (61-for-203) with 18SB in 54 games…missed a month of action on the disabled list from 5/5-6/8 with a fractured right hand after being hit by an errant pitch on 5/4 at New Britain.
- Was promoted to Scranton/WB on 7/13 where he hit .260 (47-for-181) and successfully stole a base in 21-of-24 attempts…hit his first professional home run on 8/21 vs. Rochester, leading off the game in a 3-1 loss.
- Following the season, played with the Peoria Javelinas, hitting safely in 24-of-26 contests and leading the Arizona Fall League in stolen bases (16) and runs scored (27) while ranking second in hits (37), tying for third in walks (17), and placing fourth in on-base percentage (.433) and fifth in batting average (.343)…was named to the 2007 Arizona Fall League Top Prospects Team.
- Entered the season ranked as the Yankees' 10th-best prospect by *Baseball America*.

2006

- Hit .298 (134-for-449) with 16 doubles, 8 triples, 35RBI and 58SB in 118 combined games with Single-A Tampa and Double-A Trenton…batted .336 (38-for-113) off left-handed pitchers.
- Ranked second among all Yankees prospects in stolen bases and was tied for second in batting average…was selected to the West Division All-Star Team for the Florida State League.
- With Tampa, reached base safely in 23 straight games from 4/17-5/11, batting .410 with 19R during the streak…also recorded 22 multi-hit games, including three four-hit games…in 55 games with Trenton, batted .272 (59-for-217) and reached base safely in 20 straight games from 6/28-7/22…missed a week of action from 8/3-10 while on the D.L. with a left knee contusion…recorded 18 bunt hits with the Thunder.
- Played in 27 games with Peoria in the Arizona Fall League, batting .250 (27-for-108) with 6SB.

2005

- Batted .284 (80-for-282) with 5HR, 32RBI and 19SB in 73 games with short-season Single-A Staten Island…reached base safely in a team-best 24 straight games from 7/17-8/10…ranked second in the league in at-bats (282), second in runs scored (52), fourth in games (73) and fifth in stolen bases (19)…hit .235 (4-for-17) with 1 double and 2RBI in four postseason games for the New York-Penn League Champions.

PERSONAL

- He and his wife, Jessica, have two children, Hunter Thomas and Miller Mack…graduated from the College of Charleston and was the highest-drafted player in the school's history after walking on the baseball team…in his senior year at Charleston, led the Cougars with a .447 batting average (122-for-273)…helped guide the Cougars to a 48-15 regular season record and a berth in the NCAA tournament…played high school football and baseball…gave free haircuts to underprivileged kids at Jordan's Barber Shop in the Bronx on 7/8/08…makes regular visits to ailing children at New York-Presbyterian Morgan Stanley Children's Hospital.
- Was the Yankees nominee for the 2010 "Heart and Hustle Award," presented annually by the MLB Players Alumni Association.

Gardner's Career Playing Record

Year	Club	AVG	G	AB	R	H	2B	3B	HR	RBI	SH	SF	HP	BB	SO	SB	CS	E	OBP	SLG
2005	Staten Island	.284	73	282	62	80	9	1	5	32	3	5	6	39	49	19	3	0	.376	.377
2006	Tampa	.323	63	232	46	75	12	5	0	22	1	0	2	43	51	30	7	0	.418	.433
	Trenton	.272	55	217	41	59	4	3	0	13	1	4	2	27	39	28	5	0	.318	.352
2007	Trenton	.300	54	203	43	61	14	5	0	17	1	4	0	33	32	18	4	1	.419	.392
	Scranton/WB	.260	45	181	37	47	4	3	1	9	3	0	2	21	43	21	3	2	.331	.343
2008	Scranton/WB	.296	94	341	68	101	12	11	3	32	11	3	1	70	76	37	9	0	.414	.422
	YANKEES	.228	42	127	18	29	5	2	0	16	3	1	2	8	30	13	1	0	.283	.299
2009	YANKEES - a	.270	108	248	48	67	6	6	3	23	6	1	3	26	40	26	5	2	.345	.379
	Scranton/WB	.091	4	11	3	1	0	0	0	0	0	0	0	5	1	3	0	0	.375	.091
2010	YANKEES	.277	150	477	97	132	20	7	5	47	5	3	5	79	101	47	9	1	.383	.379
Minor League Totals		**.289**	**386**	**1467**	**300**	**424**	**55**	**28**	**9**	**125**	**20**	**16**	**13**	**238**	**291**	**156**	**31**	**3**	**.389**	**.383**
Major League Totals		**.268**	**300**	**852**	**163**	**228**	**31**	**15**	**8**	**86**	**14**	**5**	**10**	**113**	**171**	**86**	**15**	**3**	**.358**	**.367**

Selected by the Yankees in the third round of the 2005 First-Year Player Draft.

a – Placed on the 15-day disabled list from July 26– September 7, 2009 with a left thumb fracture.

Gardner's Division Series Record

Year	Club vs. Opp.	AVG	G	AB	R	H	2B	3B	HR	RBI	SH	SF	HP	BB	SO	SB	CS	E	OBP	SLG
2009	NYY vs. MIN	---	3	0	0	0	0	0	0	0	0	0	0	0	0	1	0	0	---	---
2010	NYY vs. MIN	.200	3	10	1	2	0	0	0	1	0	1	0	1	3	1	0	0	.250	.200
Division Series Totals		**.200**	**6**	**10**	**1**	**2**	**0**	**0**	**0**	**1**	**0**	**1**	**0**	**1**	**3**	**2**	**0**	**0**	**.250**	**.200**

Gardner's Championship Series Record

Year	Club vs. Opp.	AVG	G	AB	R	H	2B	3B	HR	RBI	SH	SF	HP	BB	SO	SB	CS	E	OBP	SLG
2009	NYY vs. LAA	.667	6	3	2	2	0	0	0	1	0	0	0	0	0	2	0	0	.667	.667
2010	NYY vs. TEX	.176	6	17	1	3	0	0	0	1	1	0	0	2	5	1	0	0	.263	.176
LCS Totals		**.250**	**12**	**20**	**3**	**5**	**0**	**0**	**0**	**1**	**2**	**0**	**0**	**2**	**5**	**1**	**2**	**0**	**.318**	**.250**

Gardner's World Series Record

Year	Club vs. Opp.	AVG	G	AB	R	H	2B	3B	HR	RBI	SH	SF	HP	BB	SO	SB	CS	E	OBP	SLG
2009	NYY vs. PHI	.000	5	10	1	0	0	0	0	0	0	0	0	0	4	0	0	0	.000	.000
World Series Totals		**.000**	**5**	**10**	**1**	**0**	**0**	**0**	**0**	**0**	**0**	**0**	**0**	**0**	**4**	**0**	**0**	**0**	**.000**	**.000**
POSTSEASON TOTALS		**.175**	**23**	**40**	**5**	**7**	**0**	**0**	**0**	**2**	**2**	**1**	**0**	**3**	**12**	**3**	**2**	**0**	**.227**	**.175**

Gardner's Career Fielding Record

Position	PCT	G	PO	A	E	TC
Outfield	.995	283	551	20	3	574

Gardner's Career Home Run Chart

MULTI-HOMER GAMES: None. **TWO-HOMER GAMES:** None. **GRAND SLAMS:** 1, 7/3/10 vs. Toronto (Ricky Romero). **PINCH-HIT HR:** None. **INSIDE-THE-PARK HR:** 2, last on 7/4/10 vs. Toronto (Brandon Morrow). **WALK-OFF HR:** None. **LEADOFF HR:** None.

82

STEVE GARRISON

LEFT-HANDED PITCHER • 6-1 • 195 • B/T: SWITCH/LEFT • OPENING DAY AGE: 24

BIRTHDATE
September 12, 1986

BIRTHPLACE
Trenton, N.J.

RESIDES
Ewing, N.J.

M.L. SERVICE
None (Rookie)

STATUS
▸ Claimed off waivers by the Yankees from the San Diego Padres on September 9, 2010…contract extends through the 2011 season.

2010
▸ Was limited to 17 combined appearances (11 starts) with Single-A Lake Elsinore, Triple-A Portland and the rookie-level Arizona Padres, going 2-4 with a 5.37 ERA (57.0IP, 34ER).
▸ Opened the season on the disabled list recovering from surgery to repair a torn ACL in his right knee…joined Lake Elsinore on 5/31.
▸ Promoted to Portland on 6/21 for his first Triple-A action…made five starts before returning to the disabled list on 7/20 with a left ankle sprain suffered in the first inning of his start on 7/18 vs. Colorado Springs.
▸ Had a three-start rehab assignment with the AZL Padres (0-0, 3.00 ERA) from 8/14-19 before resuming his season with Lake Elsinore…surrendered just 2ER over his final six outings—all in relief—allowing just 2H in 12.2IP.
▸ Was designated for assignment on 9/6 and claimed off waivers by the Yankees on 9/9…reported to Tampa to continue rehabbing his ankle.

2009
▸ Combined at three different levels to go 1-2 with a 5.56 ERA (34.0IP, 21ER) in 13 appearances (12 starts) with Single-A Lake Elsinore, Double-A San Antonio and the AZL Padres.
▸ Began the season on the disabled list recovering from surgery to repair a partially torn rotator cuff…rehabbed with the Arizona Padres from 6/25-7/24, going 0-2 with a 6.20 ERA (20.1IP, 14ER) in nine starts (9BB, 22K).
▸ Following the season, made six starts with Peoria in the Arizona Fall League, going 2-2 with a 3.86 ERA…suffered a torn ACL in his right knee fielding a bunt on 11/14…underwent surgery to repair the tear on 11/25.

2008
▸ Spent the entire season at Double-A San Antonio, posting a 7-7 record with a 3.82 ERA (129.2IP, 55ER) in 24 starts…ranked seventh in the Texas League—and ninth among Padres farmhands—in ERA…among league starters, allowed the second-fewest baserunners/9.0IP (11.24), had the fourth-highest K/9.0IP ratio (7.50) and had the fifth-lowest opponents batting average (.249).
▸ Was the starting pitcher in three of the Missions' shutouts…tossed 7.0 hitless innings in his start on 4/12 vs. Arkansas…named the TL "Pitcher of the Week" on 6/23.
▸ Season was cut short on 8/22 when he went on the disabled list for the rest of the year with left shoulder soreness.
▸ Following the season, was ranked by *Baseball America* as the sixth-best prospect in the San Diego organization.

2007

▸ Split the season between the Milwaukee and San Diego organizations following a 7/25 trade to the Padres in exchange for RHP Scott Linebrink.

▸ Combined at Single-A Brevard County and Single-A Lake Elsinore to go 10-7 with a 3.25 ERA (146.2IP, 53ER) in 27 starts.

▸ Won his final four starts with Brevard County, allowing just 2ER over the stretch (26.2IP).

▸ Tossed at least 7.0IP in each of his first four starts with Lake Elsinore…held opponents to a .205 (32-for-156) batting average over his seven total starts with the team…went 1-0 with a 3.27 ERA (11.0IP, 4ER, 1BB, 10K) in two postseason starts with the California League runners up.

2006

▸ Spent the entire season at Single-A West Virginia, joining the team at the end of May…posted a 7-6 record with a 3.45 ERA (88.2IP, 34ER) in 17 games (16 starts)…tied for third-most starts on the team.

2005

▸ Spent his first professional season with the rookie-level Arizona Brewers, going 2-2 with two saves and a 2.86 ERA (34.2IP, 11ER) in 11 games (four starts)…struck out 28 batters with only 5BB.

PERSONAL

▸ Full name is Stevenson Garrison…graduated from the Hun School in Princeton, N.J.

Garrison's Career Pitching Record

Year	Club	W	L	ERA	G	GS	CG	SHO	SV	IP	H	R	ER	HR	HP	BB	SO	WP	BK
2005	AZL Brewers	2	2	2.86	11	4	0	0	2	34.2	39	13	11	0	0	5	28	5	0
2006	West Virginia	7	6	3.45	17	16	0	0	0	88.2	86	38	34	10	3	22	77	1	1
2007	Brevard County	8	4	3.44	20	20	1	1	0	104.2	105	58	40	6	1	28	74	2	0
	Lake Elsinore – a	2	3	2.79	7	7	0	0	0	42.0	32	15	13	2	1	6	28	1	1
2008	San Antonio	7	7	3.82	24	24	0	0	0	129.2	123	59	55	13	2	37	108	5	0
2009	Lake Elsinore	0	0	1.17	2	1	0	0	1	7.2	5	2	1	0	1	2	7	0	0
	San Antonio	1	0	9.00	2	2	0	0	0	6.0	9	6	6	2	0	1	3	0	0
	AZL Padres	0	2	6.20	9	9	0	0	0	20.1	22	14	14	1	2	5	22	3	0
2010	Lake Elsinore	1	1	3.14	9	3	0	0	0	28.2	28	13	10	1	1	10	13	0	1
	Portland	1	3	8.87	5	5	0	0	0	22.1	34	22	22	5	1	7	17	0	0
	AZL Padres – b	0	0	3.00	3	3	0	0	0	6.0	5	2	2	0	0	1	8	0	0
Minor League Totals		**29**	**28**	**3.82**	**109**	**94**	**1**	**1**	**3**	**490.2**	**488**	**242**	**208**	**40**	**12**	**124**	**385**	**17**	**3**

Selected by the Milwaukee Brewers in the 10th round of the 2005 First-Year Player Draft.

a – Acquired by the San Diego Padres along with LHP Joe Thatcher and RHP Will Inman from the Brewers in exchange for RHP Scott Linebrink on July 25, 2007.

b – Claimed by the Yankees off waivers from the Padres on September 9, 2010.

Highest Single-Season Road Attendance, Major League History

ATTENDANCE	CLUB	YEAR
3,308,666	**New York Yankees**	**2004**
3,130,043	Boston Red Sox	2007
3,107,743	Boston Red Sox	2008
3,080,268	**New York Yankees**	**2006**
3,056,535	Boston Red Sox	2005
3,016,074	Cincinnati Reds	2000
2,997,599	**New York Yankees**	**2005**
2,978,206	**New York Yankees**	**2007**
2,953,637	Chicago Cubs	2005
2,940,048	**New York Yankees**	**2002**

27

GREG GOLSON

OUTFIELDER • 6-0 • 190 • B/T: RIGHT/RIGHT • OPENING DAY AGE: 25

BIRTHDATE
September 17, 1985

BIRTHPLACE
Austin, Texas

RESIDES
Austin, Texas

M.L. SERVICE
77 days
(Rookie)

STATUS
▸ Acquired by the Yankees from the Texas Rangers in exchange for minor league infielder Mitch Hilligoss on January 26, 2010…is signed through the 2011 season.

2010
▸ Hit .261 (6-for-23) with 3R, 2 doubles and 2RBI in 24 games (four starts in RF, one in CF and one in LF) over three stints with the Yankees (also 5/4-7, 5/12-18, 9/1-10/3).
▸ Was recalled from Triple-A Scranton/Wilkes-Barre on 5/4 and made his Yankees debut in that night's win vs. Baltimore, entering the game defensively in the eighth in CF (did not bat)…did not appear in another game before being optioned back to Scranton/WB on 5/7.
▸ Recalled for a second time on 5/12, appearing in five games (one start in RF in 5/13 loss at Detroit).
▸ Collected his first Major League hit in 5/12 Game 2 win at Detroit, entering game in the seventh in CF and singling off Phil Coke in the ninth.
▸ Joined the Yankees a third time as a September callup on 9/1…played in 18 games over the final month of the season, batting .222 (4-for-18) with 3R, 2 doubles and 2RBI.
▸ Entered 9/14 win at Tampa Bay defensively in the ninth in RF…threw out Carl Crawford at third base on a fly ball out to complete a double play and end the game…according to the *Elias Sports Bureau*, marked the Yankees first extra-inning win to end on an outfield assist since 8/16/03 when Karim Garcia started a 9-4-5-2-5 putout of Baltimore's Jack Cust in the 12th inning to preserve a 5-4 win.
▸ Began the season with Triple-A Scranton/Wilkes-Barre, batting .263 (109-for-415) with 51R, 23 doubles, 5 triples, 10HR and 40RBI in 116 games…hit safely in each of his last nine games with Scranton/WB, batting .382 (13-for-34) with 7R, 5 doubles, 1 triple, 1HR and 2RBI over the stretch.
▸ Hit an inside-the-park home run in the third inning of 4/30 win vs. Louisville off the Bats' Matt Maloney.

2009
▸ In his lone season with the Texas organization, spent the bulk of his time with Triple-A Oklahoma City, batting .258 with 46R, 17 doubles, 8 triples, 2HR, and 40RBI in 123 games…was 20-for-24 in stolen base attempts…led the team in triples and ranked second in games played.
▸ Appeared in one game during his one stint with Texas from 5/4-9…lone appearance came in 5/7 loss at Oakland, replacing Marlon Byrd defensively in CF in the bottom of the eighth, then striking out looking in his only Rangers at-bat to lead off the ninth inning…was optioned back to Oklahoma City on 5/9 when Joaquin Arias was added to the roster.
▸ Was labeled by *Baseball America* as the Texas organization's "Best Athlete," "Fastest Baserunner" and "Best Outfield Arm" entering the season.

BESTS & STREAKS

Hits
2 - vs. TB, 9/23/10
Runs
1 - 5 times
Last: at TOR, 9/28/10
2B
1 - 2 times
Last: vs. TB, 9/23/10
3B
NA
HR
NA
RBI
1 - 2 times
Last: at TOR, 9/29/10
BB
NA
SO
3 - vs. WAS, 9/28/08
SB
1 - at WAS, 9/3/08
Hit Streak
2 - 5/14-9/5/10

2008

▸ Saw his first Major League action as a September call up with the World Champion Phillies, going hitless in 6AB with 2R and 1SB...was selected from Double-A Reading and signed to a Major League contract on 9/1...made his Major League debut as a pinch-runner on 9/3 at Washington, stealing one base...struck out in his first big league at-bat on 9/7 at New York-NL.

▸ Began the season with Double-A Reading, batting .282 with 64R, 18 doubles, 13HR, and 60RBI in 106 games...went 23-for-28 in SB attempts (81.2%)...set career-highs in walks (34) and slugging pct. (.434) and tied for sixth in the league in stolen bases...named to the Eastern League's midseason All-Star team.

▸ Was on the disabled list from 6/18-7/10 with a sprained left wrist, suffered while swinging on 6/13...had a .329 (70-for-213) average through the end of May...in his final 44 games after the injury, batted .257 (45-for-175).

▸ Played for the U.S. squad in the 2008 MLB Futures Game on 7/13 at the original Yankee Stadium, going 0-for-2 after pinch-hitting and remaining in the game in LF.

▸ Was acquired by the Rangers on 11/20/08 in exchange for 2005 first-round pick OF John Mayberry, Jr.

2007

▸ Appeared in 136 combined games with Single-A Clearwater and Double-A Reading, batting .273 (156-for-571) with 86R, 32 doubles, a career-high 15HR and 68RBI...also stole 30 bases in 38 attempts.

▸ Began the year at Clearwater, where he led the club in doubles (27) and stolen bases (25), finishing eighth in the Florida State League in steals...was promoted on 7/26 to Reading where he finished out the season.

▸ Played for the Peoria Saguaros in Arizona Fall League following the season.

2006

▸ Combined to hit .233 (127-for-546) with 87R, 26 doubles, 13HR, 48RBI and 30SB in 133 games with Single-A Lakewood and Single-A Clearwater.

▸ Named the organization's June "Player of the Month" before being promoted to Clearwater on 7/20...hit for the cycle on 8/28 vs. Ft. Myers.

▸ Following the season, tabbed by *Baseball America* as the Phillies' 10th-best prospect.

2005

▸ Batted .264 with 51R, 19 doubles, 8 triples, 4HR and 27RBI in 89 games with Single-A Lakewood...also stole a team-high 25 bases (in 34 attempts)...tied for fourth in the South Atlantic League in triples.

2004

▸ Made his professional debut with the GCL Phillies, batting .295 with 34R, 8 doubles, 5 triples, 1HR and 22RBI in 47 games...tied for second in the league in triples and tied for sixth in average...led the team in average, AB (183), runs, hits (54), triples, and SB (12)...ranked as the Phillies' fourth-best prospect by *Baseball America*.

PERSONAL

▸ Full name is Gregory Joseph Golson...graduated in 2004 from John B. Connally High School in Austin, Tex...named to the *USA Today* All-USA High School Baseball Team in 2004.

Golson's Career Batting Record

Year	Club	AVG	G	AB	R	H	2B	3B	HR	RBI	SH	SF	HP	BB	SO	SB	CS	E	OBP	SLG
2004	GCL Phillies	.295	47	183	34	54	8	5	1	22	1	2	5	10	54	12	2	1	.345	.410
2005	Lakewood	.264	89	375	51	99	19	8	4	27	2	0	6	26	106	25	9	2	.322	.389
2006	Lakewood	.220	93	387	56	85	15	4	7	31	8	3	2	19	107	23	7	3	.258	.333
	Clearwater	.264	40	159	31	42	11	2	6	17	1	0	3	11	53	7	3	1	.324	.472
2007	Clearwater	.285	99	418	66	119	27	3	12	52	2	4	4	21	124	25	8	7	.322	.450
	Reading	.242	37	153	20	37	5	2	3	16	1	1	1	2	49	5	0	0	.255	.359
2008	Reading	.282	106	426	64	120	18	4	13	60	4	5	1	34	130	23	5	8	.333	.434
	PHILADELPHIA	.000	6	6	2	0	0	0	0	0	0	0	0	0	4	1	0	1	.000	.000
2009	Oklahoma City – a	.258	123	457	46	118	17	8	2	40	8	6	0	29	114	20	4	4	.299	.344
	TEXAS – b	.000	1	1	0	0	0	0	0	0	0	0	0	0	1	0	0	0	.000	.000
2010	Scranton/WB	.263	116	415	51	109	23	5	10	40	6	2	6	25	99	17	4	5	.313	.414
	YANKEES	.261	24	23	3	6	2	0	0	2	0	0	0	0	3	0	2	0	.261	.348
Minor League Totals		**.263**	750	2973	419	783	143	41	58	305	33	23	28	177	836	157	42	31	.309	.398
Major League Totals		**.200**	31	30	5	6	2	0	0	2	0	0	0	0	8	1	2	1	.200	.267

Selected by Philadelphia in the first round (21st overall) of the 2004 First-Year Player Draft.

a – Acquired by Texas in exchange for OF John Mayberry Jr. on November 20, 2008.
b – Acquired by the Yankees in exchange for INF Mitch Hilligoss on January 26, 2010.

Golson's Career Fielding Record

Position	PCT	G	PO	A	E	TC
Outfield	.967	27	28	1	1	30

14

CURTIS GRANDERSON

OUTFIELDER • 6-1 • 185 • B/T: LEFT/RIGHT • OPENING DAY AGE: 30

BIRTHDATE
March 16, 1981

BIRTHPLACE
Blue Island, Ill.

RESIDES
Chicago, Ill.

M.L. SERVICE
5 years, 77 days

COLLEGE
University of Illinois

CAREER HIGHLIGHTS
A.L. All-Star Team
▸ 2009

STATUS
▸ Acquired by the Yankees from the Detroit Tigers in a three-team, seven-player deal in which the Yankees sent LHP Phil Coke and OF Austin Jackson to Detroit and RHP Ian Kennedy to Arizona on December 9, 2009…enters the fourth year of a five-year contract that extends through 2012 with a club option for 2013.

CAREER HIGHLIGHTS
▸ Owns 24 career lead-off home runs, tying Derek Jeter for the seventh-most among all active players behind Alfonso Soriano (54), Jimmy Rollins (33), Ichiro Suzuki (30), Johnny Damon (26), Rafael Furcal (25) and Hanley Ramirez (25).
▸ Over the last five seasons (since 2006), ranks third in the Majors with 56 triples…since 2007, is tied with Boston's David Ortiz for the most extra-base hits (206) among American Leaguers.
▸ In 2010, became the first player in Major League history to be acquired during the offseason by defending World Series champions after coming off a 30-homer season (hit 30HR in 2009 w/ Detroit)—credit: *Elias*.
▸ Was the only Major Leaguer to score 100-or-more runs, collect 20-or-more doubles, 10-or-more triples, 20-or-more home runs and 10-or-more stolen bases in both 2007 and 2008.
▸ In his career, has hit .287 (650-for-2,268) with 57HR vs. right-handed pitchers…owns a .215 (167-for-777) batting average with 20HR off lefties.
▸ Among Major League outfielders since 2005, ranks second with 2,068 total chances behind only Ichiro (2,279)…has committed just 15 errors over the six-year span, ranking fifth among AL outfielders in fielding percentage (.993).

BESTS & STREAKS

Hits
5 - 2 times
Last: at CLE, 7/30/08
Runs
4 - at KC, 7/21/08
2B
2 - 8 times
Last: at BOS, 9/14/10
3B
2 - 5 times
Last: vs. LAA, 4/15/10
HR
2 - 7 times
Last:vs. TB, 9/20/10
RBI
5 - 3 times
Last: vs. TB, 9/20/10
BB
3 - 3 times
Last: vs. OAK, 5/17/09
SO
4 - 4 times
Last: vs. TOR, 7/4/10
SB
3 - at CWS, 9/30/07
Hit Streak
15g - 6/10-27/08

2010
▸ Batted .247 (115-for-466) with 76R, 17 doubles, 7 triples, 24HR, 67RBI and 12SB in 136 games (134 starts in CF) with the Yankees…started at five different spots in the batting order (No. 2 and 6-9)…the Yankees were 36-8 when he drove in a run.
▸ From 8/12 through the end of the season, hit .286 (16-for-56) with 3HR vs. lefthanded pitching…batted just .206 (21-for-102) off lefties through 8/11 and had hit only 3HR against LH pitchers from Opening Day 2009 through 8/11/10…overall in 2010, hit .234 (37-for-158) with 4HR vs. left-handed pitchers and .253 (78-for-308) with 20HR against righties.
▸ Hit a team-high 14HR in 157AB over his final 46 games of the season (from 8/14) after hitting just 10HR in 309AB over his first 90 games of the season…hit 9HR over his last 23 home games of the season.
▸ Committed just two errors in 323 total chances, a .994 fielding percentage, eighth-best among AL outfielders.
▸ Made his fourth career Opening Day roster…hit solo HR in his first plate appearance as a Yankee in the second inning of 4/4 Opening Day loss at Boston, going 1-for-4 with 1BB…was his second straight year with an Opening Day homer…was the

first Yankee to homer in his first at-bat as a Yankee on Opening Day since Jimmy Wynn on 4/7/77 vs. Milwaukee…became the fourth player to homer in his first AB or PA as a Yankee coming at Fenway Park (also John Miller-1966, Graig Nettles-1973 and Andy Phillips-2004)—credit: *Elias*…was the second of back-to-back homers with Jorge Posada, becoming the first pair of Yankees to hit back-to-back home runs on Opening Day since Dave Winfield and Steve Kemp on 4/5/83 at Seattle (credit: *Elias*).

▸ Was 1-for-4 with 1R in 4/6 win at Boston, batting ninth in the starting batting order for the first time since 6/30/08 at Minnesota and 11th time in his career…marked the first time in franchise history the Yankees batted a 30-or-more HR hitter from the previous season in the ninth spot (credit: *Elias*).

▸ Hit a game-winning solo HR in the 10th inning of 4/7 win at Boston off Jonathan Papelbon…marked his second career go-ahead HR in the ninth inning or later (also 9/26/05 vs. Chicago-AL off Cliff Politte).

▸ Was 2-for-4 with 1R, 2 triples and 1RBI in 4/15 win vs. Los Angeles-AL…tripled twice in the same game for the fifth time in his career and first since 8/18/08 at Texas…became the first Yankee to triple twice in the same contest since Bobby Abreu on 5/30/08 at Minnesota and the first Yankee to do so at home since Enrique Wilson on 7/3/02 vs. Cleveland…became the first Yankee to triple in consecutive at-bats in the same game since Clay Bellinger on 8/26/00 at Oakland.

▸ Went hitless in 17 consecutive at-bats from 4/21-27…was the second-longest hitless stretch of his career behind a 21AB hitless streak from 8/15-23/06.

▸ Was placed on the 15-day disabled list with a Grade 2 strain of the left groin from 5/2-28…suffered the injury while running the bases in 5/1 loss vs. Chicago-AL…was taken to New York-Presbyterian Hospital for an MRI following the game…rehabbed with Triple-A Scranton/Wilkes-Barre, going 4-for-16 (.250) with 2RBI and 2BB/1IBB in 5G (3GS in CF, 2GS at DH).

▸ Was reinstated from the 15-day disabled list prior to 5/28 win vs. Cleveland and batted second in the starting lineup for just the third time in his career (also 7/23/05 Game 2 vs. Minnesota and 9/30/07 at Chicago-AL)—credit: *Elias*.

▸ Hit a solo HR off Brian Matusz in 6/1 win vs. Baltimore, marking his first homer since 4/7 at Boston and his first home run off a left-hander since 4/22/09 at Los Angeles-AL off Joe Saunders.

▸ Hit a grand slam and was 2-for-5 with 2R, 4RBI and 1SB in 6/8 win at Baltimore…was his second career grand slam (also 4/4/07 vs. Toronto) and his most RBI in a game since 9/28/08 vs. Tampa Bay (also 4RBI).

▸ Hit a game-winning solo-HR in the 10th and was 3-for-5 with 2R, 1 double and 1SB in 6/23 win at Arizona…was his third career extra-inning HR and second this season (also 10th inning of 4/7 win at Boston off Jonathan Papelbon).

▸ Was 3-for-3 with 1 double and 1BB in 8/16 loss vs. Detroit…was caught stealing in the fifth, marking his first CS since 7/31/09 at Cleveland to snap a streak of 13 straight successful stolen base attempts.

▸ Collected 9HR and 23RBI in September, each marking highs for any calendar month in his career.

▸ Went 2-for-3, with his second multi-HR game this season in 9/2 win vs. Oakland, entering the game defensively in the second in CF when Swisher left with a left knee injury…became the third player in franchise history to collect a multi-homer game despite not being in the starting lineup, joining Steve Balboni (5/23/90 at Minnesota) and Cody Ransom (9/26/08 at Boston)–credit: *Elias Sports Bureau*.

MOST LEADOFF HR, ACTIVE PLAYERS		
1.	Alfonso Soriano	54
2.	Jimmy Rollins	35
3.	Ichiro Suzuki	32
4.	Johnny Damon	26
	Rafael Furcal	26
6.	Hanley Ramirez	25
7.	**CURTIS GRANDERSON**	**24**
	DEREK JETER	24
9.	Rickie Weeks	21
	Grady Sizemore	21

▸ Collected his seventh career multi-HR game and third this season in 9/20 win vs. Tampa Bay…tied his career high with 5RBI in the contest.

▸ Hit 4HR with 9RBI in seven games over the Yankees' final homestand of the season (9/20-26)…overall, homered seven times in his final 16 games from 9/15 through the end of the season, collecting 19RBI over the stretch.

▸ Hit a team-high .357 (10-for-28) with 2 doubles, 1 triple, 1HR, a team-high-tying 6RBI and a team-high 8BB in nine postseason games…the Yankees were 5-1 in the playoffs when he hit safely.

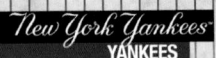
2009

▸ Batted .249 (157-for-631) with 91R, 23 doubles, 8 triples, 30HR, 71RBI and 20SB in 160 games with the Tigers…set a career high in home runs…was tied for fifth in the American League in triples and ranked ninth with 141K…led the Majors by grounding into a double play in just 0.9 percent of GDP situations in 2009 (1 GDP in 106 GDP).

▸ Was one of three American Leaguers to record 30HR and 20SB, joining Texas' Ian Kinsler and Nelson Cruz…marked his second straight season with at least 20HR and 20SB, becoming one of just three Tigers players to reach the totals in multiple seasons, joining Kirk Gibson (four times) and Alan Trammell (three times).

▸ Hit .275 (124-for-451) with 28HR vs. right-handed pitchers and .183 (33-for-180) with 2HR against left-handed pitchers…batted .267 (86-for-322) in 81 games on the road, tying for fourth in the AL with 20 road homers…hit .230 (71-for-309) with 10HR in 79 games at home.

▸ Connected for seven leadoff homers, matching his own 2007 Tigers club record.

▸ Was selected to the American League All-Star team for the first time in his career…tripled in his only AB (off Heath Bell) and scored the game-winning run in the eighth inning of the 4-3 AL win at St. Louis.

▸ Made 155 starts in CF, committing just 3E in 407 total chances (.993 fielding percentage)…ranked fifth in fielding percentage among AL outfielders with at least 125 games…did not commit an error in his first 96 games of the season from 4/6-7/26, a total of 221 errorless chances.

▸ Connected for three two-homer games in 2009 (4/21 at Los Angeles-AL, 6/17 at St. Louis and 7/29 at Texas).

▸ Hit his 100th career home run on 9/27 at Chicago's U.S. Cellular Field, a solo homer off Daniel Hudson in the first inning.

▸ Following the season was tabbed the third-best defensive outfielder in the American League by *Baseball America*.

2008

▸ Hit .280 (155-for-553) with 112R, 26 doubles, 13 triples, 22HR, 66RBI and 12SB…led the American League in triples, becoming the first Tigers player to lead the league in triples in consecutive seasons since Ty Cobb in 1917 (24) and 1918 (14)…became the fourth player in Detroit history to post double-digit totals in a single-season in doubles, triples, homers and RBI, joining Bobby Veach (1920-21), Ty Cobb (1921, 1925) and Charlie Gehringer (1929-30).

▸ Ranked second in the AL in runs scored, becoming the first Tigers player to score 100-or-more runs in back-to-back seasons since Tony Phillips in 1992-93…was the ninth-hardest player to double up, grounding into a double play once every 79.0AB.

▸ Led off a game with a home run four times (4/24 vs. Texas, 5/4 at Minnesota, 6/20 at San Diego and 8/27 vs. Cleveland).

▸ Began the season on the 15-day disabled list with a non-displaced fracture of the third metacarpal in his right hand…reinstated from the D.L. on 4/23, and hit safely in six of his first seven games back.

▸ Established a career high with a 15-game hitting streak from 6/10-27, batting .443 (27-for-61) with 4 doubles, 3 triples, 1HR and 7RBI…scored a career-high 4R in 7/21 win at Kansas City.

▸ Equaled a career high five hits on 7/30 at Cleveland, going 5-for-7 with 3R and 2RBI in the Tigers' 13-inning win.

▸ Prior to the season, agreed to terms on a five-year contract with a club option for 2013 on 2/4.

2007

▸ Hit .302 (185-for-612) with 122R, 38 doubles, 23 triples, 23HR, 74RBI and 26SB in 158 games for the Tigers, recording career-highs in runs, hits, doubles, triples, RBI and stolen bases…led the AL in triples, ranked third in runs scored and extra-base hits (84), fourth in total bases (338), sixth in slugging percentage (.552), seventh in strikeouts (141) and tied for ninth in multi-hit games (57).

▸ Became the third player in Major League history to collect at least 30 doubles, 20 triples, 20HR and 20SB in a single season, joining the Cubs' Wildfire Schulte (1911) and Philadelphia's Jimmy Rollins (also in 2007)…became the 13th player in Tigers history to post double-digits in doubles, triples, home runs and stolen bases…joined teammate Gary Sheffield as one of seven Tigers all-time to collect at least 20HR and 20SB in a single season.

TWENTY GRAND

In 2007, Curtis Granderson became one of four players in Major League history to collect at least 20 doubles, 20 triples, 20HR and 20SB in the same season:

Player	Year	2B	3B	HR	SB
Wildfire Schulte, CHC	1911	30	21	21	23
Willie Mays, NYG	1957	26	20	35	38
CURTIS GRANDERSON, DET	**2007**	**38**	**23**	**23**	**26**
Jimmy Rollins, PHI	2007	38	20	30	41

▸ His 23 triples were the most by a Tiger since Ty Cobb finished with 24 triples in 1917, while his 122 runs were the most by a Tigers player since Ron LeFlore scored 126 runs in 1978.

- Was successful in 96.3 percent of his stolen base attempts (26-for-27), marking the best single-season stolen base percentage by a Tigers player since it became an official statistic in 1920.
- Hit .337 (166-for-493) with 20HR against right-handed pitchers, ranking fourth in the AL with a .621 slugging percentage and sixth in batting average against righties…batted .160 (19-for-119) with 3HR vs. lefthanders, recording the lowest batting average in the league against left-handed pitchers among qualifiers.
- Led all Major League outfielders with 428 putouts, tying for eighth in the AL with 10 assists…tied for the third-most putouts by a Tigers outfielder in franchise history with Barney McCosky (1939).
- Set a Detroit franchise record with seven leadoff homers (4/24 at Los Angeles-AL, 5/9 vs. Seattle, 7/14 at Seattle, 7/23 at Chicago-AL, 8/26 vs. New York-AL, 9/16 at Minnesota and 9/22 vs. Kansas City).
- Hit his first career grand slam in 4/4 win vs. Toronto, connecting in the third inning off Shaun Marcum…matched his career high with 5RBI (second time).
- Named the AL "Player of the Week" for 7/9-15 after hitting .500 (8-for-16) with 7R in four games.
- Batted .283 (96-for-339) with 62R, 24 doubles, 15 triples, 12HR and 43RBI in 85 games prior to the All-Star break, tying for the AL lead with 51 extra-base hits…became the ninth Major League player since 1957 to post double-digit totals in doubles, triples and home runs prior to the All-Star break…hit .326 (89-for-273) with 60R, 14 doubles, 8 triples, 11HR and 31RBI in 73 games following the break.
- Collected his second career inside-the-park home run off Phil Hughes in 8/26 win vs. the Yankees…stole a career-high three bases in 9/30 win at Chicago-AL in the final game of the season.

2006

- In his first full season at the Major League level, batted .260 (155-for-596) with 31 doubles, 9 triples, 19HR, 68RBI and 8SB in 159 games (153 starts in CF)…led all AL outfielders with a .997 fielding percentage, ranking second with 389 total chances and 385 putouts…was the best fielding percentage by a Tigers centerfielder since Mickey Stanley posted a 1.000 fielding percentage in 1970.
- Led the American League with 174K, marking the third-highest single-season strikeout total in Detroit club history.
- Batted .274 (123-for-449, 15HR) against right-handed pitchers and .218 (32-for-147, 4HR) vs. lefties…hit .278 (92-for-331) with 11HR in 87 games prior to the All-Star break…in 72 games following the All-Star break, batted .238 (63-for-265) with 8HR.
- Established a career high with 5RBI and was 2-for-5 with 1 triple in 5/26 win vs. Cleveland.
- Collected his first career lead off home run in 6/18 win Chicago-AL (off Mark Prior), going 2-for-5 with 2R and 1RBI…hit six lead-off homers during the season (also 6/23 vs. St. Louis, 8/27 at Cleveland, 9/7 at Minnesota, 9/23 at Kansas City and 9/29 vs. Kansas City).
- Committed the first error of his Major League career on 7/25 at Cleveland, snapping a 150-game errorless streak…marked the longest errorless streak to begin a Major League career by a non-pitcher since Dave Roberts went his first 205 career games without an error from 8/7/99-4/20/03, and the longest such streak ever by a Tigers outfielder.
- Homered and tripled in the first inning in 9/23 win at Kansas City, going 2-for-6 with 2R and 4RBI…became just the fifth Major Leaguer since 1987 to accomplish the feat in the same inning, joining Detroit's Tony Phillips (1991), Arizona's Steve Finley (1999), Detroit's Brandon Inge (2004) and Tampa Bay's Carl Crawford (2005).
- Recorded his first career multi-homer game in 9/29 loss vs. Kansas City.
- Saw his first postseason action for the American League champions, batting .226 (12-for-53) with 3 doubles, 1 triple, 3HR, 7RBI and 2SB…went 3-for-5 with 1HR and 1RBI in his first career playoff game in Game 1 of the ALDS on 10/3 at the original Yankee Stadium.

2005

- Batted .272 (44-for-162) with 6 doubles, 3 triples, 8HR and 20RBI in 47 games over two stints with the Tigers (7/22-27; 8/15-10/2)…named the Tigers "Rookie of the Year" by the Detroit Sports Broadcasters' Association.
- Hit .318 (7-for-22) over his first five-day stay with the club, collecting 2 triples, 2HR and 4RBI in six games…hit his first Major League homer on 7/23 vs. Minnesota, a solo shot off Carlos Silva…became the first player to hit two triples and 2HR in his first four games of a season since Milwaukee's Pedro Garcia in 1974.
- Re-joined the Tigers on 8/15 for the remainder of the season…recorded his first career inside-the-park home run on 9/15 at Los Angeles-AL…went 5-for-5 with 1 double in 9/18 loss at Los Angeles-AL…hit his first career "walk-off" home run on 9/26 vs. Chicago-AL in the ninth inning off Cliff Politte.
- Opened the season with Triple-A Toledo and batted .290 (129-for-445) with 29 doubles, 13 triples, 15HR, 65RBI and 22SB, ranking second in the International League in triples…led all league outfielders with 15 assists.
- Named to the International League's postseason all-star squad…tabbed as the 19th-best prospect in the International League following the season by *Baseball America*.
- Played in 21 games with Licey in the Dominican Winter League, hitting .194 (14-for-72) with 9R, 1 double, 1HR and 8RBI.

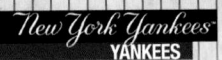
2004

▸ Saw his first Major League action, appearing in nine games as a September callup with the Tigers, batting .240 (6-for-25) with 1 double and 1 triple.

▸ Was signed to a Major League contract and added to Detroit's active roster on 9/12…made his Major League debut the next night vs. Minnesota, starting in center field and going hitless in four at-bats in the Tigers loss…threw out Jacques Jones at third base in the fifth inning for his first career assist…collected his first hit on 9/19 at Chicago-AL, singling as a pinch-hitter in the eighth inning off Freddy Garcia.

▸ Began the season at Double-A Erie, batting .301 (139-for-462) with 19 doubles, 8 triples, 21HR, 94RBI and 14SB, earning the Tigers' Minor League "Player of the Year" award…ranked second in the Eastern League with a .405 on-base percentage, tied for third with 89R and 8 triples, tied for fourth in RBI, ninth with 139H and tied for ninth in batting average…selected to the Eastern League's post-season All-Star team and *Baseball America*'s Double-A All-Star team.

▸ Reached base safely in 33 straight games from 5/28-7/16…named Tigers Minor League "Player of the Month" for July…homered in five consecutive games from 7/30-8/3 (6HR total).

▸ Appeared in three games during the EL playoffs, batting .182 (2-for-11) with 1 double and 1RBI.

▸ Following the season, *Baseball America* named him the top prospect in the Tigers organization, the seventh-best prospect in the Eastern League, the 16th-best outfield prospect in baseball, the "Best Hitter for Average" and the "Best Strike-Zone Discipline" in the Tigers organization.

▸ Hit .321 (27-for-84) with 16 runs scored, 4 doubles, 1HR and 15RBI in 23 games for Grand Canyon in the Arizona Fall League following the season…named one of six nominees for the MLB.com Arizona Fall League Dernell Stenson Sportsmanship Award.

2003

▸ In 127 games with Single-A Lakeland, batted .286 (136-for-476) with 29 doubles, 10 triples, 11HR, 51RBI and 10SB, leading the Florida State League in triples, tying for second with 218 total bases, ranking fourth with 71R, 136H and a .458 slugging percentage, fifth with 50 extra-base hits and eighth in batting average…also tied for the lead among league outfielders with 15 assists.

▸ Selected to the FSL mid-season All-Star team…named the eighth-best prospect in the Tigers organization by *Baseball America* following the season.

2002

▸ Named the New York-Penn League's "Most Valuable Player," batting .344 (73-for-212) with 15 doubles, 4 triples, 3HR, 34RBI and 9SB in 52 games with Single-A Oneonta…was selected to the league's postseason All-Star squad and *Baseball America*'s short-season All-Star team…received the NYPL Stedler Award, given to the league player deemed likely to go the farthest in professional baseball.

▸ Named to *Baseball America*'s College Draft All-Star squad and rated by the publication as the fifth-best pure hitter and having the fifth-best debut among college players in the draft…named the 10th-best prospect in the New York-Penn League and 18th-best prospect in the Tigers organization following the season by *Baseball America*.

▸ Reached base safely via a hit or walk in 21 straight games from 7/10-8/1, batting .400 (38-for-95) with 20R, 8 doubles, 3 triples, 2HR and 6BB.

PERSONAL

▸ Graduated from Thornton Fractional South High School in Illinois…was selected SICA Central All-Conference, as well as receiving *Illinois Times*, *Daily Southtown* and *Star Newspaper* All-Area recognition.

▸ Graduated from the University of Illinois-Chicago with a business degree, completing his final two years of school while playing in the Tigers organization…as a junior, was named Horizon League "Player of the Year" and earned All-Horizon League honors…also selected as a Second-Team All-American by *Baseball America* and *USA Today's Baseball Weekly* and a Third-Team Louisville Slugger NCAA Division I All-American…ranked second among all NCAA Division I players with a .483 batting average as a junior and established single-season records at UIC in batting average, runs (76) and hits (100)…concluded his college career as the school's all-time leader with 178R, placing second on the all-time list with 41 doubles and 24HR, third with 9 triples, fourth with 220H and 624AB, tied for fourth with 125RBI, fifth with 107BB and tied for fifth with a .350 average…inducted into the University of Illinois-Chicago Athletics Hall of Fame on 1/18/08.

▸ Represented Major League Baseball as an ambassador in a January 2011 trip to New Zealand, participating in clinics and taking part in the Oceanic 16 and Under Tournament…also went as an MLB ambassador to Europe following the 2006 season, South Africa following the 2007 season and China following the 2008 season.

- Received the Pop Lloyd Award from the Negro Leagues Baseball Museum on 1/10/09 for his baseball and community leadership.

- In 2008, established the Grand Kids Foundation to focus on improving opportunities for inner-city youth in the areas of education and youth baseball…released a children's book, *All You Can Be*, which encourages children to chase their dreams and included illustrations from fourth graders all across the state of Michigan…donated a copy of the book to each public elementary school library in Michigan…organized Team Granderson for the 2010 NYC Marathon, raising money for the foundation.

- Was named the Yankees' 2010 Roberto Clemente Award nominee, the third such time he has received the honor (also 2007 and 2009 w/ Detroit)…received the 2009 Marvin Miller Award (as voted by MLB players) for his work on and off the field that inspires others to higher levels of achievement, and for displaying as much passion to give back to others as he shows between the lines on the baseball diamond…received a 2009 Jefferson Award for Public Service from All Stars Helping Kids as a top athlete who has given back to the community…has twice (2008, '09) been nominated for the Branch Rickey Award, given by the Rotary Club of Denver to recognize professionals in Major League baseball for exceptional community service…visited with children at PS114X in the Bronx in June 2010…honored at the 2011 "Heroes for Hope" ALS fundraiser held by Northport (NY) High School.

- Is an official spokesman for the White House's anti-obesity campaign, joining First Lady Michelle Obama as MLB's representative for the official announcement on 2/8/10 at the White House…is also a captain for MLBPA Action Teams, which teams with Volunteers of America to encourage youth to volunteer within their communities.

- While with the Tigers, was an active participant in Play Baseball Detroit, Tigers Dreams Come True and the Detroit Tigers Autographed Memorabilia Donation Program…served as a spokesman for Gloves for Kids, reading to students in association with the Detroit Newspapers in Education, sponsored youth baseball teams during the annual Negro Leagues Weekend…judged entries in the annual Detroit Tigers Jackie Robinson Essay, Art and Poetry Contest, and attended the Rockin' Rooftop fundraising event to benefit the Coalition on Temporary Shelter (COTS).

- Was a studio analyst for TBS during Major League Baseball playoff broadcasts in both 2007 and 2008 and served the same role with ESPN in 2007.

- Took part in the Detroit Action Team, a national youth volunteer initiative administered by the Major League Baseball Players Trust and Volunteers of America that is actively recruiting the next generation of volunteers.

Granderson's Career Batting Record

Year	Club	AVG	G	AB	R	H	2B	3B	HR	RBI	SH	SF	HP	BB	SO	SB	CS	E	OBP	SLG
2002	Oneonta	.344	52	212	45	73	15	4	3	34	0	1	7	20	35	9	2	1	.417	.495
2003	Lakeland	.286	127	476	71	136	29	10	11	51	5	3	12	49	91	10	7	5	.365	.458
2004	Erie	.303	123	462	89	140	19	8	21	93	3	4	4	80	95	14	8	3	.407	.515
	DETROIT - a	.240	9	25	2	6	1	1	0	0	0	0	0	3	8	0	0	0	.321	.360
2005	Toledo	.290	111	445	79	129	29	13	15	65	2	5	3	48	129	22	6	4	.359	.515
	DETROIT	.272	47	162	18	44	6	3	8	20	2	0	0	10	43	1	1	0	.314	.494
2006	DETROIT	.260	159	596	90	155	31	9	19	68	7	6	4	66	174	8	5	1	.335	.438
2007	DETROIT	.302	158	612	122	185	38	23	23	74	5	2	5	52	141	26	1	5	.361	.552
2008	Toledo	.333	2	9	1	3	1	0	0	0	0	0	0	0	1	0	0	0	.333	.444
	West Michigan	.364	3	11	1	4	0	2	0	1	0	0	0	1	2	0	0	0	.417	.727
	DETROIT - b	.280	141	553	112	155	26	13	22	66	1	1	3	71	111	12	4	4	.365	.494
2009	DETROIT - c	.249	160	631	91	157	23	8	30	71	3	2	2	72	141	20	6	3	.327	.453
2010	YANKEES - d	.247	136	466	76	115	17	7	24	67	4	3	2	53	116	12	2	2	.324	.468
	Scranton/WB	.250	5	16	0	4	0	0	0	2	0	0	0	2	2	0	0	0	.333	.250
Minor League Totals		**.300**	**423**	**1631**	**286**	**489**	**93**	**37**	**50**	**246**	**10**	**13**	**26**	**200**	**355**	**55**	**23**	**13**	**.382**	**.494**
Major League Totals		**.268**	**810**	**3045**	**511**	**817**	**142**	**64**	**126**	**366**	**22**	**14**	**16**	**327**	**734**	**79**	**19**	**15**	**.341**	**.481**

Selected by the Detroit Tigers in the third round of the 2002 First-Year Player Draft.

a – Placed on the disabled list from June 21-July 3, 2004 with a left ankle sprain.
b – Placed on the disabled list from March 23-April 23, 2008 with a non-displaced fracture of the third metacarpal in his right hand.
c – Acquired by the Yankees from the Detroit Tigers in a three-team, seven-player deal in which the Yankees sent LHP Phil Coke and OF Austin Jackson to Detroit and RHP Ian Kennedy to the Arizona Diamondbacks on December 9, 2009.
d – Placed on the 15-day disabled list from May 2-27, 2010 with a grade 2 left groin strain.

Granderson's Division Series Record

Year	Club vs. Opp.	AVG	G	AB	R	H	2B	3B	HR	RBI	SH	SF	HP	BB	SO	SB	CS	E	OBP	SLG
2006	DET vs. NYY	.294	4	17	3	5	0	1	2	5	0	1	0	0	1	1	0	0	.278	.765
2010	NYY vs. MIN	.455	3	11	2	5	1	1	0	3	1	0	0	1	1	1	0	0	.500	.727
Division Series Totals		**.357**	**7**	**28**	**5**	**10**	**1**	**2**	**2**	**8**	**1**	**1**	**0**	**1**	**2**	**2**	**0**	**0**	**.367**	**.750**

Granderson's Championship Series Record

Year	Club vs. Opp.	AVG	G	AB	R	H	2B	3B	HR	RBI	SH	SF	HP	BB	SO	SB	CS	E	OBP	SLG
2006	DET vs. OAK	.333	4	15	4	5	2	0	1	2	0	0	0	4	2	1	0	0	.474	.667
2010	NYY vs. TEX	.294	6	17	1	5	1	0	1	3	0	0	1	7	4	0	1	0	.520	.529
LCS Totals		**.313**	**10**	**32**	**5**	**10**	**3**	**0**	**2**	**5**	**0**	**0**	**1**	**11**	**6**	**1**	**1**	**0**	**.500**	**.594**

Granderson's World Series Record

Year	Club vs. Opp.	AVG	G	AB	R	H	2B	3B	HR	RBI	SH	SF	HP	BB	SO	SB	CS	E	OBP	SLG
2006	DET vs. STL	.095	5	21	1	2	1	0	0	0	0	0	0	1	7	0	0	0	.136	.143
World Series Totals		**.095**	**5**	**21**	**1**	**2**	**1**	**0**	**0**	**0**	**0**	**0**	**0**	**1**	**7**	**0**	**0**	**0**	**.136**	**.143**
POSTSEASON TOTALS		**.272**	**22**	**81**	**11**	**22**	**5**	**2**	**4**	**13**	**1**	**1**	**1**	**13**	**15**	**3**	**1**	**0**	**.375**	**.531**

Granderson's All-Star Game Record

Year	Club, Site	AVG	G	AB	R	H	2B	3B	HR	RBI	SH	SF	HP	BB	SO	SB	CS	E	OBP	SLG
2009	DET, St. Louis	1.000	1	1	1	1	0	1	0	0	0	0	0	0	0	0	0	0	1.000	3.000
All-Star Game Totals		**1.000**	**1**	**1**	**1**	**1**	**0**	**1**	**0**	**0**	**0**	**0**	**0**	**0**	**0**	**0**	**0**	**0**	**1.000**	**3.000**

Granderson's World Baseball Classic Record

Year	Country, Site	AVG	G	AB	R	H	2B	3B	HR	RBI	SH	SF	HP	BB	SO	SB	CS	E	OBP	SLG
2009	USA, USA	.235	7	17	1	4	0	0	0	2	0	0	0	2	5	0	0	0	.316	.235
WBC Totals		**.235**	**7**	**17**	**1**	**4**	**0**	**0**	**0**	**2**	**0**	**0**	**0**	**2**	**5**	**0**	**0**	**0**	**.316**	**.235**

Granderson's Career Fielding Record

Position	PCT	G	PO	A	E	TC
Outfield	.993	667	1724	25	13	1762

Granderson's Career Home Run Chart

MULTI-HOMER GAMES: 7. **TWO-HOMER GAMES:** 7, last on 9/20/10 vs. Tampa Bay. **GRAND SLAMS:** 2, on 6/8/10 at Baltimore (Kevin Millwood). **PINCH-HIT HR:** None. **INSIDE-THE-PARK HR:** 2, last on 8/26/07 vs. New York-AL (Phil Hughes). **WALK-OFF HR:** 1, on 9/26/05 vs. Chicago-AL (Cliff Politte). **LEADOFF HR:** 15, last on 9/27/09 at Chicago-AL (Daniel Hudson).

Home Runs in First At-Bat with the Yankees
Since 1961 (expansion era)

John A. Miller.........................9/11/1966
Graig Nettles 4/6/1973*
Jimmy Wynn 4/7/1977
Barry Foote............................4/28/1981
Glenallen Hill...........................7/24/2000
Ron Coomer............................4/6/2002
Marcus Thames.......................6/10/2002
Todd Zeile...............................4/2/2003
Bubba Crosby 4/9/2004
Andy Phillips.........................9/26/2004
Nick Green 7/2/2006*
Wilson Betemit........................8/2/2007
Cody Ransom.........................8/17/2008**
CURTIS GRANDERSON....4/4/10 (Opening Day)

*All players except Nettles and Green homered in their first plate appearance as a Yankee.
**Ransom also homered in his second plate appearance (and AB) with the Yankees, becoming the first Yankee ever to accomplish the feat.*

65

PHIL HUGHES

RIGHT-HANDED PITCHER • 6-5 • 240 • B/T: RIGHT/RIGHT • OPENING DAY AGE: 24

BIRTHDATE
June 24, 1986

BIRTHPLACE
Mission Viejo, Calif.

RESIDES
Tampa, Fla.

M.L. SERVICE
3 years, 113 days

CAREER HIGHLIGHTS
A.L. All-Star Team
‣ 2010

All-Star Futures Game
‣ 2006

Kevin Lawn Award
Yankees "Minor
League Pitcher
of the Year"
‣ 2006

STATUS
‣ Selected by the Yankees in the first round (23rd overall) of the 2004 First-Year Player Draft…signed through the 2011 season.

CAREER NOTES
‣ According to the *Elias Sports Bureau*, Hughes' 31 career wins are the most victories by a player the Yankees selected in the first round of the First-Year Player Draft, surpassing the six career wins of Bill Burbach (Yankees 1965 first-round pick).

‣ Was 23-11 prior to turning 24 on 6/24/10, marking the most wins by a Yankee under 24 since 1965, when Mel Stottlemyre (29 wins) and Al Downing (32 wins) each celebrated their 24th birthday.

‣ Is 25-17 with a 4.68 ERA (315.2IP, 164ER) in 57 career starts…is 6-1 with a 1.35 ERA (53.1IP, 8ER) in 46 career relief appearances.

‣ Is 9-0 in his last 12 starts immediately following a Yankees loss (since May 2009).

‣ Is 9-2 with a 3.27 ERA (85.1IP, 31ER) in 29G/11GS in day games over the last two years (2009-10), including relief appearances.

BESTS & STREAKS

Low hit CG
  N/A
IP (start)
  8.0 - 2 times
  Last: at TEX, 5/25/09
IP (relief)
  3.2 - at BOS, 6/10/09
Hits
  10 - vs. SEA, 6/29/10
Runs
  8 - at BAL, 5/9/09
BB
  5 - 4 times
  Last: vs. OAK, 8/31/10
SO
  10 - at OAK, 4/21/10
HR
  3 - 3 times
  Last: vs. TOR, 9/5/10
Winning Streak
  9g - 8/14/09-5/12/10
Losing Streak
  4g - 4/8-29/08

2010
‣ Went 18-8 with a 4.19 ERA (176.1IP, 82ER) and 146K in 31G/29GS with the Yankees, setting career highs in wins, losses, IP and strikeouts…was tied for fourth in the AL and tied for seventh in the Majors in wins…was tied for fifth in the AL and tied for sixth in the Majors with a .692 winning percentage…lasted at least 5.0IP in 28 of his 29 starts (only exception on 8/25 at Toronto, 3.2IP)…opponents batted .244 (162-for-665, 25HR); LH .235 (81-for-345, 17HR) and RH .253 (81-for-320, 8HR)…the Yankees went 20-9 in his starts.

‣ Became the second Yankees pitcher age 24 or younger in the last 45 years to win at least 18 games in a season (also Andy Pettitte in 1996, 21 wins)…was the youngest Yankees righthander to win at least 18 games in a season since 23-year old Mel Stottlemyre won 20 games in 1965.

‣ Joined CC Sabathia (21-7) as the first set of Yankees teammates with at least 18 wins each since 2002 (Mike Mussina 18-10 and Davis Wells 19-7)…was the first time a pair of 18-game winning Yankees were 30 years old or younger since 1978 (Ron Guidry 25-3 and Ed Figueroa 20-9).

‣ Allowed 20HR at home (including each of his first 15 total HR allowed), tying Scott Sanderson (20 in 1992) for the most HRs allowed at home in a single season in franchise history, according to the *Elias Sports Bureau*…tied Baltimore's Kevin Millwood and the Dodgers' Ted Lilly for most homers allowed at home in the Majors in 2010…according to *Elias*, became the first pitcher to allow his first 15HR at home since Seattle's Gaylord Perry in 1982…allowed just 5HR in 70.0 road IP.

‣ Did not hit a batter, becoming the first Yankee since Ron Guidry in 1985 to throw at least 175.0IP in a season and not hit anyone.

- Received 7.49R/9.0IP of support in his starts, the highest mark among qualifying Major League pitchers.

- Appeared on his first All-Star roster, receiving his selection via the player ballot...according to the *Elias Sports Bureau*, became the third-youngest pitcher to represent the Yankees in an All-Star Game (1956-Johnny Kucks age 22; and 1965-Mel Stottlemyre age 23)...was charged with the loss in the 3-1 NL victory (0.1IP, 2H, 2ER), becoming the first Yankee to take the loss in the Midsummer Classic since Tommy John in 1980...faced three batters in the seventh inning, retiring Cincinnati's Joey Votto before allowing back-to-back singles to Cincinnati's Scott Rolen and St. Louis' Matt Holliday (who would both come around to score after he left).

HUGHES' 2010 STARTING PITCHING LINES

Date/Opp	Score	W/L	IP	H	R	ER	HR	BB	K	NP/K	ERA	Left game
4/15 vs. LAA*	6-2	W	5.0	3	2	2	1	**5**	6	108-66	3.60	Leading 6-1
4/21 at OAK	3-1	W	**7.1**	1	1	1	0	2	**10**	101-70	2.19	Leading 2-0
4/27 at BAL*	4-5	ND	5.2	2	1	1	0	4	2	109-68	2.00	Leading 2-1
5/2 vs. CWS	12-3	W	7.0	4	0	0	0	1	6	99-69	1.44	Leading 12-0
5/7 at BOS	10-3	W	7.0	7	2	2	0	1	7	101-70	1.69	Leading 10-2
5/12 at DET (G2)*	8-0	W	7.0	5	0	0	0	1	8	101-71	1.38	Leading 2-0
5/17 vs. BOS*	11-9	ND	5.0	6	5	5	2	1	3	104-71	2.25	Leading 6-5
5/22 at NYM	3-5	L	5.2	8	4	4	0	3	7	**117**-88	2.72	Trailing 4-1
5/28 vs. CLE*	8-2	W	7.0	5	2	2	1	1	8	109-76	2.70	Leading 8-2
6/2 vs. BAL	9-1	W	7.0	6	1	1	0	1	7	101-72	2.54	Leading 8-1
6/8 at BAL	12-7	W	6.0	9	3	3	0	0	5	102-70	2.71	Leading 12-3
6/13 vs. HOU	9-5	W	5.2	7	5	5	1	2	6	110-73	3.11	Leading 5-7
6/19 vs. NYM*	5-3	W	7.0	5	3	3	2	3	4	99-62	3.17	Leading 5-3
6/29 vs. SEA	4-7	L	5.2	**10**	**7**	**6**	1	2	3	94-63	3.58	Trailing 1-7
7/4 vs. TOR	7-6 (10)	ND	6.0	6	5	5	**3**	2	5	101-66	3.83	Tied 5-5
7/9 at SEA	6-1	W	7.0	6	1	1	0	0	5	109-79	3.65	Leading 5-1
7/20 vs. LAA	2-10	L	5.0	9	6	**6**	2	3	2	98-57	3.99	Trailing 6-2
7/25 vs. KC	12-6	W	5.1	6	3	3	2	0	3	95-61	4.04	Leading 5-3
7/30 at TB	2-3	L	6.0	4	3	3	1	2	6	104-61	4.07	Trailing 3-2
8/4 vs. TOR*	5-1	W	5.1	4	1	1	0	2	5	99-60	3.96	Leading 5-1
8/9 vs. BOS	1-2	L	6.0	6	2	2	0	1	5	114-74	3.92	Trailing 2-0
8/14 at KC*	8-3	W	6.0	9	3	3	1	1	0	99-71	3.94	Leading 4-3
8/19 vs. DET	11-5	W	6.0	4	2	2	1	0	6	84-61	3.90	Leading 11-2
8/25 at TOR	3-6	L	3.2	6	5	5	1	**5**	6	102-66	4.12	Trailing 5-2
8/31 vs. OAK	9-3	W	5.0	4	2	2	0	**5**	1	98-46	4.10	Leading 9-3
9/5 vs. TOR	3-7	L	6.0	7	6	**6**	**3**	1	5	100-69	4.29	Trailing 6-2
9/10 at TEX	5-6 (13)	ND	1.0	0	0	0	0	0	1	11-7	4.26	Tied 5-5
9/15 at TB	3-4	L	6.2	6	4	4	2	0	5	106-65	4.31	Trailing 4-3
9/21 vs. TB	8-3	W	6.1	4	3	3	1	**5**	6	112-67	4.31	Leading 5-2
9/26 vs. BOS*	4-3 (10)	ND	6.0	3	1	1	0	4	4	105-67	4.21	Trailing 1-0
10/2 at BOS (G1)	*6-5 (10)*	*W*	*1.0*	*0*	*0*	*0*	*0*	*0*	*2*	*14-9*	*4.19*	*Leading 6-5*
Totals		18-8	176.1	162	83	82	25	58	146	--	4.19	

*start came after a Yankees loss – **Bold**-season high – *italics*-relief appearance

- Was named the Yankees' fifth starter to open the season by Manager Joe Girardi on 3/25...following spring training, made two starts in extended spring training while remaining on the Yankees' 25-man active roster.

- Made his season debut in 4/15 win vs. Los Angeles-AL, recording the victory...was his first start since 5/31/09...struck out four of his first seven batters faced.

- Allowed just 10 combined hits in his first four starts of the season (25.0IP) and 17 combined hits in his first five starts (32.0IP) of 2010...according to the *Elias Sports Bureau*, became the first Major League pitcher since the Yankees' David Cone in 1999 to limit his opposition to as few hits with as many IP over his first four and first five starts of a season.

- Carried a no-hitter through 7.0 innings on 4/21 at Oakland, recording the win in a 3-1 Yankees victory (7.1IP, 1H, 1ER, 2BB, 10K)...marked his first double-digit strikeout game, recording eight swinging Ks.

- Retired 25 consecutive RH batters over three starts from 4/27-5/7 – including all 13 faced on 5/2 vs. Chicago-AL.

- Won each of his first five decisions to start the season, becoming the youngest Yankees starter to begin a season 5-0 since Whitey Ford in 1950 (9-0)...according to *Elias*, with a 1.38 ERA after his first six starts, became the first Yankee with at least five wins and a sub-1.50 ERA through his first six starts since Bob Turley in 1958 (6-0, 0.83 ERA), and the first Major Leaguer since the Angels' Jered Weaver in 2006 (6-0, 1.12 ERA).

- Joined Andy Pettitte at 5-0 to start the season, marking just the fourth time in the last 50 years that two Yankees starters each won their first five decisions in the same season...also occurred in 2004 (Kevin Brown and Orlando Hernandez), 2003 (Mike Mussina and David Wells) and 1980 (Ron Guidry and Tommy John), according to *Elias*.

- Had his 11-start undefeated streak and a nine-game overall winning streak (including starts and relief apps.) snapped in 5/22 loss at Citi Field...tossed a career-high 117 pitches in his first loss since 8/2/09.

- Faced off against Mike Pelfrey (who entered 9-1) on 6/19 vs. the Mets and recorded his 10th win in a 5-3 Yankees victory (7.0IP, 5H, 3ER, 3BB, 4K, 2HR)...according to the *Elias Sports Bureau*, the game was only the second time in Major League history in which both starting pitchers came into the game with at least nine wins and a winning percentage of .900 or higher (also 6/22/1900 at Baker Bowl when Brooklyn's Joe McGinnity at 12-1 faced the Phillies' Bill Bernhard also at 12-1).

▸ Had 10-1 record and a 3.17 ERA through 6/19, becoming the 12th Yankees pitcher to win at least 10 of his first 11 decisions (all as a starter) to start a season…was the first such Yankee with an ERA at or below 3.17 since Jimmy Key in 1994 (10-1, 2.99 ERA).

▸ Took the loss on 6/29 vs. Seattle, snapping a 10-game winning streak at home that dated back to 5/20/09…had been tied for the longest home winning streak in the Majors with teammate CC Sabathia.

▸ Made his 50th career start on 8/14 at Kansas City, recording the win (6.0IP, 9H, 3ER, 1BB, 0K, 1HR) in an 8-3 Yankees victory…became the youngest Yankee to at the time of his 50th start since Al Downing (at 24 years, 51 days) in 1964, according to the *Elias Sports Bureau*.

▸ Recorded his 16th win of the season on 8/31 vs. Oakland…joined CC Sabathia (18-5) to give the Yankees two pitchers each with 16 wins prior to September 1 for the first time since 1998 (David Cone-18 and David Wells-16).

YANKEES TEAMMATES WITH 18 OR MORE WINS EACH OVER THE LAST 50 YEARS (since 1961)

2010	Phil Hughes (18) and CC Sabathia (21)
2002	Mike Mussina (18) and David Wells (19)
1998	David Cone (20) and David Wells (18)
1979	Ron Guidry (18) and Tommy John (21)
1978	Ed Figueroa (20) and Ron Guidry (25)
1974	Pat Dobson (19) and Doc Medich (19)
1963	Jim Bouton (21) and Whitey Ford (24)

▸ Was skipped in the rotation from 9/6-14, going nine days without a start…made his first of two relief appearances of the season on 9/10 at Texas, tossing 1.0 perfect inning of relief (1K) in the Yankees' 6-5, 13-inning loss…also tossed 1.0 scoreless inning of relief in his final appearance of the season on 10/2 at Boston in the Game 1 win of a doubleheader.

▸ Made three postseason starts, going 1-2 with a 6.32 ERA (15.2IP, 11ER)…threw 7.0 scoreless innings in his first career postseason start in Game 3 of the ALDS on 10/9/10 vs. Minnesota, recording the win in the 6-1 victory to complete the series sweep…became the third Yankee to toss at least 7.0 scoreless IP in his first career postseason start, joining Orlando Hernandez (Gm 4, ALCS 10/10/98 at Cleveland - 7.0IP) and Waite Hoyt (Gm 2, WS 10/6/21 vs. NY Giants - 9.0IP)…became the first Yankee under the age of 25 to win a postseason start since Dave Righetti on 10/15/81 in Game 3 of the ALCS vs. Oakland…started and took the loss in Game 2 and Game 6 of the ALCS at Texas (8.2IP, 11ER)…at 24 years, 114 days, became the youngest Yankee to start either Game 1 or 2 of a playoff series since Andy Pettitte started Game 2 of the 1996 ALDS at 24 years, 109 days.

2009

▸ Was 8-3 with three saves and a 3.03 ERA in 51 appearances (seven starts) with the Yankees…opponents batted .217 (68-for-314, 8HR); LH .257 (36-for-140, 3HR), RH .184 (32-for-174, 5HR).

▸ In 44 relief appearances, was 5-1 with three saves and a 1.40 ERA, leading all qualifying Major League relievers in ERA…struck out 33.7% of his batters faced as a reliever (65K, 193BF), the second-highest mark in the Majors…opponents batted .172 (31-for-180, 2HR)…37 of his 44 appearances were scoreless…held opponents hitless in 24 outings…stranded 15-of-16 inherited runners (93.8%)…retired 35-of-44 first batters faced (79.5%)…appeared in consecutive games 11 times and three straight games once (8/2-5).

▸ The Yankees were 35-9 in his relief appearances, including a 27-4 mark following the All-Star break…the Yankees won 18 consecutive games Hughes appeared in from 8/2-9/16…allowed just 3H in 33AB with runners in scoring position as a reliever (credit: *Elias Sports Bureau*)…held opponents hitless in 26 consecutive AB with RISP from 6/14-9/22.

▸ Recorded the American League's lowest post-All-Star break ERA (1.64)…averaged 12.55 K/9.0IP after the All-Star break, ranking fourth in the Majors over the span.

▸ After stepping into the primary setup role on 7/3, the Yankees went 58-26, including a 31-5 mark in games Hughes appeared in…following his first relief appearance on 6/8, the Yankees bullpen went 27-7 with a 3.37 ERA and 37 saves in 105 games, allowing 277H and 127ER in 339.2IP (138R, 120BB, 326K, 37HR) while holding opponents to a .219 batting average…in 54 games prior to Hughes joining the bullpen, Yankees relievers were 13-10 with a 4.88 ERA, 14 saves and a .251 opponents average (175.1IP, 168H, 103R, 95ER, 78BB, 157K, 35HR).

▸ In seven starts, went 3-2 with a 5.45 ERA, allowing 37H and 21ER in 34.2IP (15BB, 31K, 6HR)…held his opponents to 3ER or less in five of his seven starts.

▸ Was recalled from Triple-A Scranton/Wilkes-Barre on 4/28 and made the start that night at Detroit, recording the win in an 11-0 Yankees victory…threw 6.0 scoreless innings and struck out six batters (2H, 2BB), snapping a personal four-game losing streak.

▸ Allowed a career-high 8ER on 8H in 1.2IP on 5/9 at Baltimore, recording the loss in a 12-5 Orioles victory…marked his shortest career start (2BB, 0K, 1HR)…tossed a scoreless first inning then allowed nine of his next 11 batters faced to reach.

▸ Went undefeated over his final four starts from 5/15-31 (2-0, 3.91 ERA, 23.0IP, 10ER)…tossed 8.0 shutout innings (3H, 1BB, 6K) and recorded the win in an 11-1 Yankees victory on 5/25 at Texas…matched his career high in innings pitched (also 9/24/08 at Toronto).

▸ Made his first career regular season relief appearance in 6/8 win vs. Tampa Bay, tossing a perfect seventh inning (1.0IP, 1K).

▸ Did not allow a run over 16 consecutive outings from 6/14-7/26, tossing 21.0 shutout innings over the stretch (11H, 4BB/1IBB, 25K)…compiled a 23.1-inning scoreless stretch dating back to 6/10 at Boston, marking the longest single-season scoreless stretch for a Yankees reliever since Mariano Rivera's 30.2-inning scoreless stretch to finish the 1999 regular season (credit: *Elias*)…was also the fifth-longest by a Yankees pitcher, starter or reliever, in the last 25 seasons (1985-2009), behind Rivera, Lee Gutterman (30.2 in 1989), Steve Farr (27.0 in 1991) and Rivera (26.0 in 1996)…had his scoreless streak broken on 7/30 at Chicago-AL, when he was charged with 1ER in 2.0IP (2H, 1K)…exited with the score tied 2-2 and two runners on base before Phil Coke allowed a "walk-off" RBI single.

▸ Earned his first regular-season win as a reliever on 7/17 vs. Detroit, tossing 2.0 scoreless IP while striking out six-of-nine batters faced (3H, 1BK)…according to the *Elias Sports Bureau*, became just the third pitcher in Yankees history to record at least 6K in a game with all his outs being recorded via strikeout (also Joe Page, 6K vs. Detroit on 9/13/47 and Goose Gossage, 6K vs. Kansas City on 9/1/79).

▸ Earned his first career save in 7/23 win vs. Oakland, tossing 2.0 perfect innings…according to *Elias*, became the youngest Yankees pitcher to earn a save of at least six outs since 18-year-old Jose Rijo notched a 3.0-inning save on 4/18/84 at Cleveland.

▸ Opened the year with Scranton/WB, going 3-0 with a 1.86 ERA (19.1IP, 4ER) in three starts…allowed only 3BB while striking out 19 batters 19.1IP…opponents were batting .233 (17-for-73) at the time of his recall.

▸ Made nine postseason appearances in 2009, going 0-1 with an 8.53 ERA (6.1IP, 11H, 6ER, 4BB, 7K, 1HR)…pitched in all three Division Series wins vs. Minnesota.

2008

▸ Was 0-4 with a 6.62 ERA in eight starts over two stints with the Yankees (3/31-7/30 and 9/13-28)…the Yankees were 3-5 in his starts…opponents batted .314 (43-for-137, 3HR); LH .333 (20-for-60, 1HR), RH .299 (23-for-77, 2HR)…his eight starts were the third-most all time by a Yankees pitcher in a winless season behind Steve Trout (9, 1987) and Ian Kennedy (9, 2008).

▸ Leadoff batters hit at a .412 clip (14-for-34)…according to the *Elias Sports Bureau*, opponents scored in 12 of the 17 innings the leadoff batter reached, but only two of 20 innings in which he retired the first batter.

▸ Opened the season as the youngest pitcher in the Majors and the second youngest player in the Majors behind Arizona's Justin Upton (20 years old, born 8/25/87)…according to the *Elias Sports Bureau*, was the youngest pitcher to begin a season in the Yankees rotation since Bill Burbach in 1969 (Opening Day age of 21 years, 232 days).

▸ Turned 22 on 6/24…made 19 starts with a 5-7 record and 71 career strikeouts before the age of 22…were the most starts, wins and strikeouts by a Yankees starting pitcher prior to his 22nd birthday since Bill Burbach went 6-8 with 76K in 24 starts prior to turning 22 years old on 8/22/69.

▸ At 21 years old, joined Yankees pitchers Joba Chamberlain (22) and Ian Kennedy (23) as the first trio—each under age 24—to start a game in the same season for the Yankees prior to September callups since 1993 (Sterling Hitchcock, Mark Hutton and Sam Militello)…the last Yankees trio to do it prior to June 4 of a season was Gil Blanco, Al Downing and Mel Stottlemyre in 1965.

▸ With his first start of the season on 4/3 vs. Toronto in the Yankees' third game, became the youngest Yankees pitcher to start one of the team's first three games since Waite Hoyt (21 years, 217 days) took the mound for the club's second game in 1921.

▸ Was 21 years old at the start of the season, and—with Ian Kennedy (age 23)—became the fourth pair of pitchers, each under the age of 24, to start for the Yankees within the team's first four games of a season (also Dave Righetti-23 and Mike Morgan-22 in 1982; Hippo Vaughn-23, Ray Fisher-23 and Ray Caldwell-22 in 1911; and Mel Stottlemyre-23 and Al Downing-23 in 1965)—credit: *Elias Sports Bureau*.

▸ Underwent an MRI on 5/1 that revealed a stress fracture in his ninth right rib and was placed on the 15-day disabled list that day…was transferred to the 60-day disabled list on 7/18 when the Yankees signed 1B Richie Sexson…was returned from rehab, reinstated from the 60-day D.L. and optioned to Charleston on 7/30…did not allow a run in two relief appearances with Charleston, going 2-0 (6.2IP, 3H, 2BB, 6K)…was promoted to Triple-A Scranton/Wilkes-Barre on 8/6 where he went 1-0 with a 5.90 ERA in six starts…in two postseason starts with Scranton/WB, was 1-0 with a 0.69 ERA, allowing 1ER in 13.0IP and striking out 23 batters (8H, 4BB)…recorded the series-clinching win in Game 4 of the Governor's Cup Series on 9/12 at Durham, allowing just 1ER in 5.0IP and striking out 12 (4H, 4BB) to establish a Scranton/WB single-game playoff strikeout record…his 23K also set a franchise-postseason record.

▸ Was recalled from Scranton/WB prior to 9/13 doubleheader vs. Tampa Bay and joined the Yankees the following day…made start on 9/17 vs. Chicago-AL, allowing 1ER in 4.0IP (4H, 2BB, 4K)…allowed three combined earned runs over his final two starts of the season (12.0IP), walking two and striking out 10.

▸ Established a career-high with 8.0IP in his final start of the season on 9/24 at Toronto…limited the Blue Jays to 2ER with 0BB and 6K…did not record a decision after the Yankees won in 10th on Bobby Abreu's grand slam.

▸ Pitched for the Peoria Javelinas of the Arizona Fall League following the season, making seven starts and going 2-0 with a 3.00 ERA (30.0IP, 10ER).

2007

▸ Was 5-3 with a 4.46 ERA in 13 starts for the Yankees in his first Major League action…at 21 years old, was the youngest member of the Yankees rotation in 2007…the Yankees were 8-5 in games he started…opponents batted .235 (64-for-272, 8HR); LH .264 (34-for-129, 6HR), RH .210 (30-for-143, 2HR)…held opponents to 3ER or less in eight of his 13 Major League starts…opponents batted just .194 (19-for-98) the first time through the order and hit .259 after that (45-for-174).

▸ Had contract purchased from Triple-A Scranton/Wilkes-Barre on 4/25 and made his Major League debut the next night vs. Toronto, recording the loss in a 6-0 Blue Jays victory…was the youngest Yankees pitcher (20 years, 306 days old) to debut since Jose Rijo on 5/8/84 (18 years, 328 days)…since Rijo's first appearance, the only other Yankees to make their Major League debuts under the age of 21 were Derek Jeter (20 years, 337 days), Dioner Navarro (20 years, 211 days) and Melky Cabrera (20 years, 330 days).

▸ According to the *Elias Sports Bureau*, was the youngest Yankees draftee to debut with the Bombers since the amateur draft began in 1965…was the youngest Yankee to debut as a starter since Gene Nelson on 5/4/81 (20 years, 152 days)…became the Yankees' first top draft choice to pitch for the club since Bill Burbach, who was chosen in 1965 (the inaugural year of the First-Year Player Draft).

▸ Earned his first Major League win in his second start on 5/1 at Texas…tossed 6.1 hitless innings (3BB, 6K) in the Yankees' 10-1 victory before being removed in the seventh inning with a strained left hamstring…according to the *Elias Sports Bureau*, it was the furthest into a game that a Yankees starter had been removed with a no-hitter still intact since David Cone on 9/2/96, when he threw 7.0 no-hit innings in his first start after returning from aneurysm surgery (5-0 win at Oakland).

▸ Was placed on the 15-day disabled list with a strained left hamstring from 5/3-8/4 (retroactive to 5/2), missing 85 team games…was transferred to the 60-day D.L. on 6/9…endured a setback on 5/25 when he suffered a sprained left ankle while participating in agility drills in Tampa…made five rehab starts from 7/9-29 with Single-A Tampa, Double-A Trenton and Triple-A Scranton/WB, going 2-0 with a 0.42 ERA.

▸ Participated in the Triple-A All-Star Game on 7/11 at Isotopes Park in Albuquerque, pitching in relief and allowing 2H and 3ER in 0.2IP (1BB, 1K, 1HR) in a 7-5 International League win…was named International League "Pitcher of the Week" for the period from 7/23-29 (2-0, 0.00 ERA, 12.2IP, 5H, 4BB, 11K, .122 opp. avg.).

▸ Was returned from rehab and reinstated from the 60-day D.L. on 8/4 and started that day vs. Kansas City, recording a no-decision (4.2IP, 6ER)…surrendered his first Major League home run to David DeJesus in the fifth inning…was the first home run he allowed in either the Majors or minors in 2007, snapping a streak of 52.2 homerless innings (15.0IP Major Leagues, 37.2IP minor leagues).

▸ Recorded the win on 8/10 at Cleveland, allowing 4H and 1ER in 6.0IP… at 21 years, 48 days old, combined with RHP Joba Chamberlain (21 years, 322 days old) to become the youngest pair of Yankees pitchers to appear in the same game since 19-year-old Mike Jurewicz and 19-year-old Gil Blanco pitched in relief on 9/7/65 vs. Baltimore (Game 2).

▸ Was 3-0 in September and led Yankees starters with a 2.73 ERA (29.2IP, 9ER) for the month (ninth-best in the AL)…the Yankees won each of his final five starts (9/5-27) as he held opponents to 3ER or less in each outing.

▸ Appeared in two Division Series games vs. Cleveland, allowing only 1ER in 5.2IP of relief (1.59 ERA, 3H, 0BB, 6K)…tossed 2.0 innings in Game 1 loss at Jacobs Field, allowing a Ryan Garko solo-HR…at 21 years, 102 days old, became the youngest Yankees pitcher to appear in a postseason game since Bill Stafford (21 years, 58 days) in Game 5 of the 1960 World Series vs. Pittsburgh.

- Tossed 3.2 scoreless innings to earn the win in ALDS Game 3…at 21 years, 105 days old, surpassed Whitey Ford (21 years, 351 days old in 1950 World Series Game 4) as the youngest pitcher in franchise history to earn a postseason victory.
- Entered the 2007 season ranked as the top right-handed pitching prospect throughout all of Baseball by *Baseball America*…also ranked as the Yankees' No. 1 prospect for the second straight year and was rated as having the "Best Curveball" and "Best Control" among all Yankees farmhands.

2006

- Earned the 2006 "Kevin Lawn Minor League Pitcher of the Year" Award, given annually to the top pitching prospect in the Yankees organization, after posting a combined record of 12-6 with a 2.16 ERA in 26 starts with Class-A Tampa and Double-A Trenton…led all Eastern League pitchers with a 2.25 ERA and ranked fourth in the league with 138 strikeouts.
- Began the season in Tampa and went 2-3 with a 1.80 ERA, holding opponents to a .178 batting average and recording 30 strikeouts in 30.0IP…was promoted to Trenton on 4/30…in 21 starts with Trenton, went 10-3 with a Thunder franchise-record 2.25 ERA and 138 strikeouts in 116.0 innings…limited opposing batters to a .179 batting average and held left-handed hitters to just .161 (27-for-168)…was selected to participate in the Eastern League All-Star Game and was named to the U.S. team for the All-Star Futures Game at PNC Park in Pittsburgh.
- Did not allow a run in four consecutive starts from 6/23-7/17 (22.2IP, 7H, 6BB, 31K)…was named the Eastern League "Pitcher of the Week" from 8/7-13 after going 2-0 with a 0.90 ERA and 15K in 10.0IP…set a record for most strikeouts by a Thunder pitcher in a postseason game when he recorded 13K in 6.0IP on 9/6 vs. Portland in Game 1 of the Division Series.
- Following the season was named by *Baseball America* to the 2006 Minor League All-Star team as well as the Double-A All-Star squad.

2005

- In his sophomore campaign, fought through two stints on the disabled list with right shoulder inflammation to go 9-1 with a 2.19 ERA and 93 strikeouts in 17 combined appearances (16 starts) with Single-A Charleston and Single-A Tampa.
- Went 7-1 with a 1.97 ERA in 12 starts for Charleston, striking out 72 batters in 68.2IP with only 16 walks…opponents batted just .192 and right-handed hitters were held to a .172 average…struck out eight batters and allowed only two hits in 5.0 shutout innings on 4/26 at Augusta…was credited with his first career complete game in a 6/1 win vs. Greensboro (game 1), limiting the Grasshoppers to 1ER on 2H in 7.0IP for the win…was scheduled to start the South Atlantic League All-Star Game on 6/28 but was scratched after being placed on the D.L. with mild inflammation in his shoulder…went 2-0 with a 3.06 ERA in five games (four starts) for the Tampa Yankees.

2004

- Made only three starts for the Yankees' Gulf Coast League squad in his first professional season, holding opponents scoreless over 5.1IP without recording a decision (4H, 0BB, 8K)…missed most of the season with a fractured toe on his left foot.

PERSONAL

- Graduated from Foothill High School in Santa Ana, Calif., where he owns the school record for most career wins (23) and ranks third in school history with 182 strikeouts…also spent time playing third base and first base…was named the 2004 Most Valuable Player with a 9-1 record and a 0.69 ERA…was honored as a preseason All-American prior to his junior year and set school single-season records with 12 wins and a 0.64 ERA that season…tossed a perfect game on 4/8/04 in a 9-0 win over Laguna Hills…named to the *Los Angeles Times'* 2004 All-Star team…prior to being drafted, was named by *Baseball America* as the top right-handed pitcher in the Orange County region…was primarily a third baseman until his sophomore year of high school…was signed by Jeff Patterson.
- Received the 2010 Ben Epstein-Dan Castellano "Good Guy" Award from the New York chapter of the BBWAA.
- Visited children at Memorial Sloan-Kettering Cancer Center in New York in September 2009.

Hughes' Career Pitching Record

YEAR	CLUB	W	L	ERA	G	GS	CG	SHO	SV	IP	H	R	ER	HR	HB	BB	SO	WP	BK
2004	GCL Yankees	0	0	0.00	3	3	0	0	0	5.0	4	0	0	0	0	0	8	0	0
2005	Charleston	7	1	1.97	12	12	1	0	0	68.2	46	19	15	1	3	16	72	3	0
	Tampa	2	0	3.06	5	4	0	0	0	17.2	8	6	6	0	3	4	21	0	0
2006	Tampa	2	3	1.80	5	5	0	0	0	30.0	19	7	6	0	1	2	30	0	0
	Trenton	10	3	2.25	21	21	0	0	0	116.0	73	30	29	5	2	32	138	5	0
2007	Tampa	0	0	0.00	1	1	0	0	0	2.0	1	0	0	0	0	2	3	0	0
	Trenton	0	0	1.29	2	2	0	0	0	7.0	5	1	1	0	0	2	11	0	0
	Scranton/WB	4	1	2.20	5	5	0	0	0	28.2	16	7	7	0	1	8	28	2	0
	YANKEES - a	5	3	4.46	13	13	0	0	0	72.2	64	39	36	8	2	29	58	4	0
2008	YANKEES - b	0	4	6.62	8	8	0	0	0	34.0	43	26	25	3	1	15	23	2	0
	Charleston	2	0	0.00	2	2	0	0	0	6.2	3	0	0	0	0	2	6	2	0
	Scranton/WB	1	0	5.90	6	6	0	0	0	29.0	34	19	19	2	2	9	31	0	0
2009	Scranton/WB	3	0	1.86	3	3	0	0	0	19.1	17	4	4	2	0	3	19	0	0
	YANKEES	8	3	3.03	51	7	0	0	3	86.0	68	31	29	8	5	28	96	4	2
2010	YANKEES	18	8	4.19	31	29	0	0	0	176.1	162	83	82	25	0	58	146	9	1
Minor League Totals		**31**	**8**	**2.37**	**65**	**62**	**1**	**0**	**0**	**330.0**	**225**	**94**	**87**	**10**	**12**	**80**	**367**	**12**	**0**
Major League Totals		**31**	**18**	**4.20**	**103**	**29**	**0**	**0**	**3**	**369.0**	**337**	**83**	**172**	**44**	**8**	**130**	**323**	**19**	**3**

Selected by the Yankees in the first round (23rd overall) of the 2004 First-Year Player Draft.

a – Placed on the 15-day disabled list from May 3-August 4, 2007 with a strained left hamstring (transferred to 60-day D.L. on June 9).

b – Placed on the 15-day disabled list from May 1 – July 30, 2008 with a stress fracture in his ninth right rib (transferred to 60-day D.L. on July 18).

Hughes' Division Series Record

Year	Club vs. Opp.	W	L	ERA	G	GS	CG	SHO	SV	IP	H	R	ER	HR	HP	BB	SO	WP	BK
2007	NYY vs. CLE	1	0	1.59	2	0	0	0	0	5.2	3	1	1	1	0	0	6	1	0
2009	NYY vs. MIN	0	0	9.00	3	0	0	0	0	2.0	5	2	2	0	0	1	3	0	0
2010	NYY vs. MIN	1	0	0.00	1	1	0	0	0	7.0	4	0	0	0	0	1	6	0	0
Division Series Totals		**2**	**0**	**1.84**	**6**	**1**	**0**	**0**	**0**	**14.2**	**12**	**3**	**3**	**1**	**0**	**2**	**15**	**1**	**0**

Hughes' League Championship Series Record

Year	Club vs. Opp.	W	L	ERA	G	GS	CG	SHO	SV	IP	H	R	ER	HR	HP	BB	SO	WP	BK
2009	NYY vs. LAA	0	1	3.38	3	0	0	0	0	2.2	4	1	1	0	0	1	3	0	0
2010	NYY vs. TEX	0	2	11.42	2	2	0	0	0	8.2	14	11	11	1	0	7	6	2	0
LCS Totals		**0**	**3**	**9.53**	**5**	**2**	**0**	**0**	**0**	**11.1**	**18**	**12**	**12**	**1**	**0**	**8**	**9**	**2**	**0**

Hughes' World Series Record

Year	Club vs. Opp.	W	L	ERA	G	GS	CG	SHO	SV	IP	H	R	ER	HR	HP	BB	SO	WP	BK
2009	NYY vs. PHI	0	0	16.20	3	0	0	0	0	1.2	2	3	3	1	0	2	1	0	0
World Series Totals		**0**	**0**	**16.20**	**3**	**0**	**0**	**0**	**0**	**1.2**	**2**	**3**	**3**	**1**	**0**	**2**	**1**	**0**	**0**
POSTSEASON TOTALS		**2**	**3**	**5.86**	**14**	**3**	**0**	**0**	**0**	**27.2**	**32**	**18**	**18**	**3**	**0**	**12**	**25**	**3**	**0**

Hughes' All-Star Game Record

Year	Club, Site	W	L	ERA	G	GS	CG	SHO	SV	IP	H	R	ER	HR	HP	BB	SO	WP	BK
2010	NYY, Los Angeles-AL	0	1	54.00	1	0	0	0	0	0.1	2	2	2	0	0	0	0	0	0
All-Star Game Totals		**0**	**1**	**54.00**	**1**	**0**	**0**	**0**	**0**	**0.1**	**2**	**2**	**2**	**0**	**0**	**0**	**0**	**0**	**0**

Hughes' Career Fielding Record

Position	PCT	G	PO	A	E	TC	DP
Pitcher	.979	103	17	30	1	48	2

Hughes' Regular Season Batting Record

Year	Team	AVG	G	AB	R	H	2B	3B	HR	RBI	SH	SF	HP	BB	SO	SB	CS
2010	NYY	.000	31	1	0	0	0	0	0	0	1	0	0	0	0	0	0
Major League Totals		**.000**	**103**	**1**	**0**	**0**	**0**	**0**	**0**	**0**	**1**	**0**	**0**	**0**	**0**	**0**	**0**

2

DEREK JETER

SHORTSTOP • 6-3 • 195 • B/T: RIGHT/RIGHT • OPENING DAY AGE: 36

BIRTHDATE
June 26, 1974

BIRTHPLACE
Pequannock, N.J.

RESIDES
Tampa, Fla.

M.L. SERVICE
15 years, 43 days

CAREER HIGHLIGHTS
World Series MVP
‣ 2000

All-Star Game MVP
‣ 2000

A.L. All-Star Team
‣ 1998, 1999, 2000,
2001, 2002, 2004,
2006, 2007, 2008,
2009, 2010

A.L. Gold Glove
‣ 2004, 2005, 2006,
2009, 2010

A.L. Silver Slugger
‣ 2006, 2007, 2008,
2009

A.L. Rookie of the Year
‣ 1996

Sports Illustrated
Sportsman of the Year
‣ 2009

Roberto Clemente Award
‣ 2009

Hank Aaron Award
‣ 2006, 2009

STATUS
‣ Selected in the first round (sixth pick overall) of the 1992 First-Year Player Draft…re-signed to a three-year contract on December 7, 2010…contract extends through the 2013 season with a one-year player option for 2014.

CAREER NOTES
‣ Leads all active Major Leaguers with 2,926 career hits…according to the *Elias Sports Bureau*, is the first Yankee to hold that distinction since Johnny Mize in 1952.

‣ Is one of just 10 players in Baseball history with at least 1,500R, 2,500H, 200HR and 300SB (also teammate Alex Rodriguez, Roberto Alomar, Craig Biggio, Barry Bonds, Johnny Damon, Rickey Henderson, Willie Mays, Paul Molitor and Joe Morgan).

‣ Over the last 10 seasons, (2001-10), ranks second in the Majors in hits (1,918), third in runs scored (1,080), fourth in at-bats (6,192) and ninth in games played (1,509).

‣ His 1,602 runs and 2,807 hits from 5/29/95-5/28/10 were the most for any player in Major League history through his first 15 years in the Majors…is one of four players since 1920 with at least 2,600H, 200HR and 1,000RBI within his first 15 seasons (also Hank Aaron, Stan Musial and Al Simmons)—credit: *Elias Sports Bureau*.

‣ Has reached the 200-hit plateau seven times in his career, one shy of Lou Gehrig's club record, marking the most 200H seasons by a shortstop…also owns 10 seasons with at least 190 hits, tying Stan Musial for third-most 190H seasons behind Pete Rose (13) and Ty Cobb (12)—credit: *Elias Sports Bureau*.

‣ Has 15 consecutive seasons with at least 150 hits (since 1996), extending both the longest such streak among active players and the longest in franchise history.

‣ Has at least 150 hits against 11 Major League teams (every American League opponent except the White Sox and Twins)…among players who have debuted over the last 25 years, joins only Craig Biggio (12), Barry Bonds (11), Rafael Palmeiro (11) and Mark Grace (11) as the only players to have 150-or-more hits against at least 11 franchises—credit: *Elias*.

‣ Has recorded 11 seasons with at least a .300 average, the third-most such seasons in club history behind Lou Gehrig (12 seasons) and Babe Ruth (13 seasons), according to the *Elias Sports Bureau*.

‣ Has 42 career hitting streaks of at least 10 games, the most among active players and most ever by a Yankee in franchise history…according to *Elias*, is tied for the fifth-highest total in Baseball since 1903, trailing Ty Cobb (66), Hank Aaron (48), Tris Speaker (47) and Al Simmons (44)…his 13 career 40-hit months are the most in club history since Joe DiMaggio (17).

‣ According to the *Elias Sports Bureau*, has 11 single-season hitting streaks of at least 15 games during his career, trailing Ichiro Suzuki (14) for the most among active Major League players…has hitting streaks of more than 15 games in seven different seasons (1996, '99, 2002, '04, '06, '07 and '09), most among active players…has six career single-season hitting streaks of at least 17 games (17, 19 and 20 games in 2007, 25 in 2006 and 17-game streaks in 1996 and 2004), matching Suzuki for the most such single-season hitting streaks among active players.

BESTS & STREAKS

Hits
5 - 2 times
Last: vs. TB, 6/21/05
Runs
5 - vs. TB, 6/21/05
2B
3 - at TOR, 5/28/99
3B
2 - at DET, 9/10/96
HR
2 - 9 times
Last: vs. HOU, 6/12/10
RBI
5 - 3 times
Last: vs. CHC, 6/18/05
BB
3 - 21 times
Last: vs. TOR, 7/3/10
SO
4 - 2 times
Last: at PHI, 9/1/97
SB
3 - 2 times
Last: vs. BOS, 5/11/06
Hit Streak
25g - 8/20-9/16/06

- Has reached the 100-run plateau 13 times in his career, tied with Lou Gehrig for most 100R seasons in franchise history…according to *Elias*, is tied with Gehrig, Rickey Henderson and teammate Alex Rodriguez for the second-most 100-run seasons in Major League history behind Hank Aaron (15).

- Has reached double digits in home runs in 15 consecutive seasons (since 1996)…is one of only five active players to record double-digit home run totals over 15 consecutive seasons at some point in their career, joining teammate Alex Rodriguez, Chipper Jones, Manny Ramirez and Ivan Rodriguez (credit: *Elias Sports Bureau*)…has collected at least 10HR and 10SB in each of his last 15 seasons (since 1996), the second-longest streak all time behind only Barry Bonds (16 straight from 1986-2001)—credit: *Elias*.

> **DID YOU KNOW???** Of the 2,295 career regular season games Derek Jeter has played in, there has been just one in which the Yankees had already been mathematically eliminated from postseason play (9/26/08).

- Owns 24 career leadoff home runs (17 at home, seven on the road), tied with Rickey Henderson (24) for most in franchise history…11 have come in the month of August.

- Owns the most hits in Major League history from the shortstop position, surpassing Luis Aparicio (2,673) on 8/16/09 at Seattle…according to the *Elias Sports Bureau*, is one of four players all time to record 1,500R and 1,500 games played at shortstop (also Bill Dahlen, Honus Wagner and Cal Ripken, Jr.).

- Has played 2,275 games at shortstop for the Yankees…according to the *Elias Sports Bureau*, is second on Baseball's all-time list in games at shortstop for one club, trailing the Orioles' Cal Ripken (2,302)…marks the third-most among players who never played a game at any other fielding position, trailing only Luis Aparicio (2,583) and Ozzie Smith (2,511)—credit: *Elias Sports Bureau*.

- Among the Yankees' all-time leaders, ranks first in hits (2,926) and at-bats (9,322), second in games played (2,295), doubles (468) and stolen bases (323), third in runs (1,685), fifth in batting average (.314), sixth in walks (948) and extra-base hits (763), ninth in RBI (1,135) and 10th in home runs (234)…is the franchise leader in singles (2,163) and hit by pitches (152)…is one of three players who hold their current franchise's all-time hits record (also Colorado's Todd Helton and Texas' Michael Young).

- According to the *Elias Sports Bureau*, at 1,379-914-2, has the highest personal winning percentage (.601) among active players (min. 1,000G)…*Elias* also notes he has played in 1,379 regular season victories, surpassing Mickey Mantle (1,376) for the most in franchise history…the only active player who has played in as many wins as Jeter is Omar Vizquel (1,482)…*Elias* also notes that only five players who made their Major League debuts since 1929 played in more winning games than Jeter (1,197) before reaching the 2000-game mark: Yogi Berra (1,221), Pee Wee Reese (1,221), Paul Blair (1,207), Mickey Mantle (1,206) and Gil Hodges (1,200).

- Leads all active players with 252 career games of three-or-more hits (credit: *Elias Sports Bureau*)…posted at least a dozen games with three-or-more hits in 14 consecutive seasons from 1996-2009, matching Tony Gwynn (1984-97) for the second-longest streak of its kind for any player during the expansion era (since 1961) behind Pete Rose's 19 consecutive seasons from 1963-81 (credit: *Elias Sports Bureau*)…since the start of the 1996 season, has a Major League-best 860 multi-hit games.

- Along with Jorge Posada and Mariano Rivera, have become the first trio of teammates in MLB, NBA, NFL and NHL history to appear in a game together in each of 16 straight seasons (credit: *Elias Sports Bureau*).

- Finished with 1,274 career hits at the original Yankee Stadium…surpassed Lou Gehrig (1,269) for the most hits all-time at the Stadium in 9/16/08 loss vs. Chicago-AL…according to the *Elias Sports Bureau*, recorded 120 career games of three-or-more hits at Yankee Stadium, most all-time ahead of second-place Gehrig (109)…his 18 career four-hit games at Yankee Stadium rank second all-time to Gehrig's 19.

- Is one of five players to play in at least 1,000 games at the original Yankee Stadium (also Mantle, Gehrig, Berra and B. Williams)…according to the *Elias Sports Bureau*, only the Angels' Garrett Anderson (1,021 at Angel Stadium) appeared in more games in a single stadium among active players.

- Earned his 11th trip to the All-Star Game in 2010, including his sixth fan-selected start (fifth consecutive start)…went 1-for-2 with 1BB before being removed for PR (Elvis Andrus) in the sixth in the 3-1 National League win on 7/13…according to the *Elias Sports Bureau*, Jeter and 2B Robinson Cano joined Bucky Dent and Willie Randolph as the only Yankees SS/2B combos to start an All-Star game together…also joined Cano, Joe Mauer and Albert Pujols as the only Major League players to top four million fan votes, finishing second behind Mauer…his 11 All-Star Game selections are tied with Bill Dickey and Mariano Rivera for the fifth-most in club history, trailing Mickey Mantle (20), Yogi Berra (19), Joe DiMaggio (13) and Elston Howard (12)…joins teammate Mariano Rivera as the only players to be named to the All-Star team with their current team at least 11 times, according to *Elias*.

- Ranks first on Major League Baseball's all-time postseason lists with 185 career hits, 101 runs, 147 games played, 54 extra-base hits…also ranks third in home runs (20), with 12 of the homers tying the game or giving the Yankees the lead…owns three career leadoff home runs in postseason play (2009 ALCS Game 3 at Los Angeles-AL, 2004 ALDS Game 2 vs. Minnesota and 2000 World Series Game 4 at the Mets)…is the only player ever with a leadoff homer in each the three rounds of the playoffs…owns a .397 (58-for-146) career average against LH pitching in postseason play.

- Is the all-time Division Series leader in hits (78), runs (37), singles (56) and games played (56)…ranks first all time with 53 Championship Series games played, is tied for first in doubles (10), ranks second in hits (57), is fifth in RBI (24) and tied for sixth in home runs (seven)…has scored 32 runs in the World Series, fourth-most all time, while ranking fifth with 50 World Series hits…has carried at least a .300 average in five World Series (1998- 2000, '03 and '09), matching Babe Ruth and Yogi Berra for the most such Series all-time.

2010

- Hit .270 (179-for-663) with 111R, 30 doubles, 3 triples, 10HR and 67RBI in 157 games (150 starts at SS, five at DH) with the Yankees…his 111R were his most since 2006 (118)…six of his 10HR tied the game or gave the Yankees the lead.

- Ranked second among Major League leadoff hitters with 104R and 60RBI when batting first in the lineup…ranked fifth with 167H as the leadoff batter.

- With 2B Robinson Cano (103R), and 1B Mark Teixeira (113R), became the fourth trio of infield teammates to each score at least 100R in consecutive seasons – also 1999-2000 Cleveland Indians (R. Alomar, J. Thome, O. Vizquel), 1936-38 Yankees (F. Crosetti, L. Gehrig, R. Rolfe) and 1929-30 Philadelphia A's (M. Bishop, M. Cochrane, J. Foxx).

- Earned his fifth career Gold Glove Award…became the sixth shortstop since 1958 (when Gold Glove Awards were first awarded in each league) to win the honor at least five times, and joined Don Mattingly (nine-time winner), Dave Winfield (five), Ron Guidry (five) and Bobby Richardson (five) as the only Yankees to win the award at least five times…recorded a career-best .989 fielding percentage at SS and made just six errors, the lowest full-season total of his career and the fewest among all Major League shortstops in 2010 (min. 110G at SS)…compiled a career-long 52-game errorless stretch from 6/12-8/15.

- Led the Majors in fielding percentage at SS…with teammate Robinson Cano leading the American League with a .996 fielding percentage at second base, became the first teammates to finish a season as the fielding leaders at shortstop and second base (in either league) since Omar Vizquel and Roberto Alomar for the 2001 Cleveland Indians and the first Yankees to accomplish the feat since Phil Rizzuto and Jerry Coleman in 1949 (credit: *Elias*).

- Made his 14th Opening Day start at SS for the Yankees on 4/4 at Boston, the most Opening Day starts by a Yankee at shortstop in franchise history…became the oldest shortstop (35 years, 282 days) to start for the Yankees in a season opener since Phil Rizzuto in 1955 (37 years, 200 days)—credit: *Elias*.

- According to *Elias*, is the only active player to make 14 Opening Day starts, all for the same team, at any single position…is the first shortstop to do so since Barry Larkin started 17 Opening Day games for the Reds (1987-2004)…was his sixth Opening Day start at SS with Alex Rodriguez at 3B, matching Bucky Dent/Graig Nettles (six) and Frank Crosetti/Red Rolfe (six) for most such starts in franchise history.

- Batted .330 (31-for-94) with 18RBI in April…marked his most RBI in a calendar month since May 2007 (20RBI)…recorded at least 30H in April for the seventh time in his career, one shy of Tony Gwynn's Major League record (credit: *Elias*)…hit 4HR in April for the second straight year after going homerless in April 2008.

- Hit safely in each of his first 11 games (4/4-17), the longest hitting streak to start a season of his career…according to *Elias*, with Robinson Cano, became the first 2B-SS duo in the Modern Era (since 1900) to each hit safely in nine-or-more of their club's first games of the season…became the first Yankees tandem at any position to each hit safely in each of the team's first 10 games of a season.

- Hit solo-HR and was 2-for-5 with 2RBI in 4/13 home opening win vs. Los Angeles-AL…has hit safely in nine straight home openers (since 2002), marking the second-longest streak in franchise history, trailing Lou Gehrig (12 straight from 1926-37)—credit: *Elias*.

- Appeared in his 2,165th game on 5/7 at Boston, surpassing Lou Gehrig (2,164) for sole possession of second place on the Yankees' all-time list.

MOST HITS IN FRANCHISE HISTORY

1.	**DEREK JETER**	**2,926**
2.	Lou Gehrig	2,721
3.	Babe Ruth	2,518
4.	Mickey Mantle	2,415
5.	Bernie Williams	2,336

MOST 200-HIT SEASONS, ALL-TIME

1.	Pete Rose	10
	Ichiro Suzuki	10
3.	Ty Cobb	9
4.	Paul Waner	8
	Lou Gehrig	8
6.	**DEREK JETER**	**7**
	Wade Boggs	7
	Charlie Gehringer	7
	Rogers Hornsby	7
10.	Six others tied	6

ALL-TIME AMERICAN LEAGUE CAREER HITS LIST

Player	Team	AL Hits
1. Cal Ripken, Jr.	Baltimore	3,184
2. Robin Yount	Milwaukee	3,142
3. **DEREK JETER**	New York-AL	2,926

AMONG ACTIVE MAJOR LEAGUE PLAYERS

MOST RUNS SCORED

1.	ALEX RODRIGUEZ	1,757
2.	**DEREK JETER**	**1,685**
3.	Johnny Damon	1,564
4.	Manny Ramirez	1,544
5.	Jim Thome	1,534

MOST HITS

1.	**DEREK JETER**	**2,926**
2.	Ivan Rodriguez	2,817
3.	Omar Vizquel	2,799
4.	ALEX RODRIGUEZ	2,672
5.	Manny Ramirez	2,573

- Hit game-winning solo-HR in the sixth inning to lead off the resumption 5/25 suspended-game win at Minnesota…was his first career RBI in a 1-0 Yankees win…became the first Yankee to homer in a 1-0 Yankees victory since Melky Cabrera on 4/28/07 at Cleveland.

- Recorded six straight multi-hit games from 5/27-6/1, one shy of his career high…overlapping the six-game multi-hit contest stretch, Robinson Cano collected eight straight multi-hit games (5/26-6/2)…according to *Elias*, became the second pair of Yankees teammates to collect at least two hits apiece in each of six straight games, joining Lou Gehrig and Jack Saltzgaver from 7/3-7/34.

- Hit leadoff HR and three-run HR and was 2-for-4 with 3R, 1BB and 1SB in 6/12 win vs. Houston…was his ninth career multi-homer game and first since 8/27/06 at Los Angeles-AL…was his first multi-homer game at home since 6/18/05 vs. the Cubs…hit his 24th career leadoff HR, tying Rickey Henderson for most such homers in franchise history.

- Did not drive in a run in a career-high 19 consecutive games from 6/13-7/5 (previous high was 13G from 7/16-30/04)—credit: *Elias*.

- Collected 2,834 career hits prior to his 36th birthday on 6/26…since 1961, the only players to accumulate more hits prior to turning 36 years old were Hank Aaron (2,956) and Robin Yount (2,868)—credit: *Elias Sports Bureau*.

- Hit inside-the-park HR and was 2-for-5 with 2R in 7/22 win vs. Kansas City…was his second career inside-the-park home run (also 8/2/96 at Kansas City off Jeff Montgomery, with Joe Girardi scoring on the play)…at 36 years, 26 days old, became the oldest Yankee to hit an inside-the-park home run since Earle Combs on 6/28/35 (36 years, 45 days)—credit: *Elias*…according to SABR's David Vincent, only three other players had a longer stretch between inside-the-park homers: Luke Appling (16-plus years, 5/26/33-5/13/49); Nick Altrock (14-plus years, 5/26/1904-9/2/1918) and Tony Fernandez (14-plus years, 8/10/84-9/22/98).

- Surpassed Babe Ruth (2,873) for sole possession of 39th place on Baseball's all-time hits list with a second-inning single in 8/8 win vs. Boston.

- Collected his 2,877th career hit with a first-inning single in 8/11 win at Texas, surpassing Mel Ott for 38th place on Baseball's all-time list…also surpassed Ott—who played his entire career with the New York Giants—for the most hits by a player while playing for a New York team (credit: *Elias*).

- Over his final 20 games of the season (9/10-10/3), batted .326 (28-for-86) with 15R and a .416OBP, hitting safely in 19 of those contests.

- Scored his 1,678th career run in the sixth inning of 9/22 loss vs. Tampa Bay, surpassing Mickey Mantle (1,677) for sole possession of third place on the Yankees' all-time list…tied Mantle in 9/20 win vs. Tampa Bay.

- Played in his 1,377th regular season victory on 9/26 vs. Boston, surpassing Mickey Mantle (1,376) for the most in franchise history.

- Hit .250 (10-for-40) with 3 doubles, 1 triple and 2RBI in nine postseason games, hitting safely in seven of the contests…had his 11-game postseason hitting streak snapped in ALCS Game 3 loss vs. Texas on 10/18/10.

MOST CAREER POSTSEASON HITS, ALL-TIME

1.	**DEREK JETER**	185
2.	Bernie Williams	128
3.	Manny Ramirez	117
4.	Kenny Lofton	97
	JORGE POSADA	97

MOST CAREER POSTSEASON RUNS, ALL-TIME

1.	**DEREK JETER**	101
2.	Bernie Williams	83
3.	Manny Ramirez	67
4.	Kenny Lofton	65
5.	Chipper Jones	58

HIGHEST CAREER AVERAGES, WORLD SERIES HISTORY (min. 100 AB)

Player	AVG.
1. Lou Gehrig	.361 (43-for-119)
2. Eddie Collins	.328 (42-for-128)
3. Babe Ruth	.326 (42-for-129)
4. **DEREK JETER**	**.321 (50-for-156)**
5. Steve Garvey	.319 (36-for-113)

> *"[You are] Major League Baseball's foremost champion and ambassador. You embody all the best of Major League Baseball…you have represented the sport magnificently throughout your Hall of Fame career. On and off the field, you are a man of great integrity, and you have my admiration."*
>
> **-Commissioner Bud Selig, in a letter to Derek Jeter on March 3, 2009**

2009

- Hit .334 (212-for-634) with 107R, 27 doubles, 1 triple, 18HR, 66RBI and 30SB in 153 games with the Yankees (147 starts at SS, five starts at DH)…was named the "Sportsman of the Year" by *Sports Illustrated*, becoming the first Yankee to win the honor in its 56-year history…also earned his fourth Silver Slugger Award, fourth Gold Glove Award (led all SS with a .986 fielding pct.) and second Hank Aaron Award (as the AL's top offensive player voted on by fans)…named to the *Sporting News* AL All-Star team and finished third in AL MVP voting (193 points)…played in a total of 193 games in 2009, including spring training, World Baseball Classic, regular season, All-Star Game and postseason.

▸ Ranked second in the Majors in hits and fourth in batting average…ranked third in the AL in on-base percentage (.406) and tied with teammate Johnny Damon for fourth in the AL in runs scored…ranked third in the Majors with 66 multi-hit games. and third in the AL in road average (.337)…his 107R were the most among regular shortstop in the Majors…ranked third in the Majors with a .395 (70-for-177) average vs. left-handed pitchers in 2009…led the Majors with a .409 OBP as the No. 1 batter in the lineup, while his .336 average (205-for-611) ranked third among Major League leadoff men…recorded 21 three-hit games, the highest such total of his career and third-most in the Majors behind Florida's Hanley Ramirez (24) and Minnesota's Joe Mauer (23)…were the most home runs by an AL shortstop.

▸ According to *Elias*, became the oldest player to post a 200-hit season for the Yankees and became the oldest regular shortstop to ever record 200H in a season (previous was Honus Wagner-201H at age 34 in 1908)…became the seventh player in Major League history to collect 200 hits in a season both before age 25 and after turning 34, joining Nap Lajoie, Ty Cobb, Tris Speaker, Paul Waner, Pete Rose and Tony Gwynn…marked the second-highest batting average by a shortstop at age 35 or older in the last 100 years behind Honus Wagner who hit .339 at age 35.

▸ Became the oldest player in the last 84 years and one of three players in the modern era (since 1900) to bat .334 and steal 30 bases at age 35-or-older, joining Hall-of-Famers Max Carey (1925), Eddie Collins (1923-24) and Honus Wagner (1909).

▸ Surpassed Lou Gehrig (2,721) for most hits in franchise history with his third-inning single to right-field off Orioles starter Chris Tillman in 9/11 loss vs. Baltimore…according to *Elias*, became the sixth different player to hold the Yankees hit record at the conclusion of a season, joining Willie Keeler (1903-11), Hal Chase (1911-22), Wally Pipp (1922-29), Babe Ruth (1929-37) and Gehrig (1937-2009)…was voted as the MLB.com "Moment of the Year"…tied Gehrig with a seventh-inning single to right field off Rays starter Jeff Niemann in 9/9 win vs. Tampa Bay, going 3-for-4 with 1 double, 1BB and 1SB.

According to the *Elias Sports Bureau*, prior to Jeter setting the all-time franchise hits record on 9/11/09, Lou Gehrig had held the mark since 9/6/37, when he surpassed Babe Ruth (2,518H)…Willie Keeler led the Highlanders in hits in 1903, their first season in New York, and he remained the all-time leader for New York until Hal Chase passed him in August 1911…Chase led the franchise until September 1922, when he was followed by Wally Pipp (1922–1929), then Ruth (1929–1937).

DID YOU KNOW??? Derek Jeter hit safely in 92 of 100 games from 7/21/06-5/16/07 (G1), becoming the first player in modern Major League history (since 1900) to accomplish the feat…according to the Society for American Baseball Research, the last player prior to Jeter to accomplish the feat was Wee Willie Keeler, who hit in 93 of 100 games over a stretch from 1898 to 1899.

▸ Along with Robinson Cano (204H), became just the fifth pair of Yankees teammates (sixth time) to each collect at least 200 hits in the same season…also Lou Gehrig and Earle Combs (1927), Gehrig and Joe DiMaggio (1936, '37), Bernie Williams and Jeter (1999) and Alfonso Soriano and Williams (2002)…also joined Cano as the first pair of teammates in Baseball history to reach 200 hits in a season at the shortstop and second base position (credit: *Elias Sports Bureau*).

▸ Stole 30 bases in 35 attempts (85.7%), more SB than his totals from '07 and '08 combined (26)…marked his third season with at least 200H and 30SB, the most such seasons for any shortstop.

▸ Was the AL's top overall All-Star vote-getter for the first time in his career, garnering 4,851,889 fan votes to earn his 10th career All-Star selection and sixth as the AL's starting shortstop…went 0-for-2 with 2R and 1HBP in the 4-3 American League win in St. Louis on 7/14, playing five innings as the AL's starting SS.

▸ Recorded the first unofficial hit by a Yankee at Yankee Stadium with a first-inning double on 4/3 vs. the Cubs in an exhibition game…played for Team USA in the World Baseball Classic, batting .276 (8-for-29) with 2 doubles in eight games (four starts at SS, three at DH).

▸ Made his 13th Opening Day start at SS for the Yankees, going 3-for-5 in 4/6 Opening Day loss at Baltimore…were his most hits on Opening Day since 1999 (3-for-3)…are the most Opening Day starts by a Yankees shortstop in franchise history.

- Recorded the first at-bat by a Yankee in Yankee Stadium in 4/16 loss vs. Cleveland…prior to his first-inning plate appearance, the bat used by Babe Ruth to hit the first home run in the first game at the original Yankee Stadium on 4/18/1923 was placed across the plate in a symbolic nod to the original Stadium.

- Played in his 2,000th career game and hit a solo-HR, in 4/22 win vs. Oakland…struck out in his 8,103rd career at-bat in 4/27 loss at Detroit, surpassing Mickey Mantle for sole possession of first place on the Yankees' all-time at-bats list.

- Committed his first error of the year in 5/2 loss vs. Los Angeles-AL (sixth-inning throwing error)…according to the *Elias Sports Bureau*, his 23-game errorless stretch was his longest to start a season of his career.

- Scored the 1,500th run of his career in the fourth inning of 6/2 win vs. Texas…became the fourth Yankee (also Babe Ruth, Lou Gehrig and Mickey Mantle) to reach the 1,500R plateau…reached the milestone in his 2,035th career game…according to the *Elias Sports Bureau*, only Rickey Henderson (1,891), Alex Rodriguez (1,903), Mickey Mantle (1,949) and Willie Mays (2,009) did so in fewer games than Jeter in the expansion era (since 1961).

- Batted at a .358 (122-for-341) clip from 7/1 through the end of the season, leading the Majors in hits and batting average over the stretch.

- His third-inning RBI double on 8/16 at Seattle was his 2,674th career hit as a shortstop (also has 13 hits as a DH), surpassing Luis Aparicio (2,673) for the most hits in Major League history from the shortstop position (credit: *Elias*).

- Was 2-for-3 with 1 double and 2BB in 8/25 loss vs. Texas…his first-inning walk snapped a career-long 113 plate appearance stretch (7/28-8/23) without a base-on-balls (previous long was 68 PA in 2000).

PLAYERS TO MATCH JETER'S 2009 TOTALS*
(.334, 107R, 212H, 18HR, 30SB)
1. George Sisler-STL, 1920 .407, 137R, 257H, 19HR, 42SB
2. Kiki Cuyler-PIT, 1925 .357, 144R, 220H, 18HR, 41SB
* *According to Baseball-Reference.com*

JETER'S CAREER BATTING AVERAGE BY POSITION
No. 1 .313 . . . . (732G, 961-for-3069, 83HR, 3377RBI)
No. 2 .314 . . . . (1270G, 1627-for-5188, 133HR, 656RBI)
No. 3 .339 . . . . (128G, 171-for-505, 9HR, 66RBI)
No. 4 .000 . . . . (1G, 0-for-4)
No. 5 --- . . . . (1G, 0-for-0)
No. 6 .000 . . . . (1G, 0-for-1)
No. 7 .251 . . . . (45G, 43-for-171, 2HR, 20RBI)
No. 8 .311 . . . . (26G, 23-for-74, 1HR, 12RBI)
No. 9 .326 . . . . (91G, 101-for-310, 6HR, 44RBI)

MOST HITS BEFORE THE AGE OF 37, DURING EXPANSION ERA (Since 1961)
1. Hank Aaron 3,100
2. Robin Yount 3,006
3. Pete Rose 2,976
4. DEREK JETER. 2,926*
*turns 37 on June 26, 2011

- Stole his 300th career base in the first inning on 9/9, making him one of two players to steal 300 bases with the Yankees (also Rickey Henderson–326).

- Batted .344 (22-for-64) with 14R, 5 doubles, 3HR and 6RBI in 15 postseason games, leading the team in hits (22)…reached base safely in all 15 contests, trailing only Barry Bonds (17 straight in 2002) and Gary Sheffield (16 straight in 1997) for the longest streak of reaching base in a single postseason…reached base four times in ALDS Game 1 win (single, HR, 2BB)…collected his third career postseason leadoff HR in the ALCS Game 3 loss at Los Angeles-AL, the first leadoff HR by a Yankee in ALCS history…batted .407 (11-for-27) in the World Series, hitting safely in all six games and marking his most hits in any postseason series…became the oldest starting shortstop on a World Series-winning team since Pee Wee Reese in 1955…donated his bat from Game 6 of the World Series to the Baseball Hall of Fame.

2008

- Hit .300 (179-for-596) with 88R, 25 doubles, 3 triples, 11HR and 69RBI in 150 games with the Yankees (147 starts at SS, two starts at DH).

- Struck out 85 times, the fewest for any full season in his Major League career (previous low was 88K in 2003).

- Committed 12 errors, marking his fewest miscues since 1998 (nine) while his .979 fielding percentage was his highest since 2005 (also .979)…was the second-fewest errors among AL shortstops with at least 100 games played at the position, trailing only Texas' Michael Young (10)…went 31 consecutive games without an error from 7/8-8/15.

- Was selected to his ninth All-Star Game…finished second in the AL with 3,737,437 votes (behind teammate Alex Rodriguez)…was 1-for-3 (first-inning infield single) with 1SB in the All-Star Game on 7/15 at Yankee Stadium…following the season, was named to the 2008 *Sporting News* AL All-Star team, which was selected by a panel of 41 general managers and assistant general managers from both leagues…also earned his third consecutive Silver Slugger Award.

- Was 1-for-4 in 4/1 Opening Day win vs. Toronto…was his 12th Opening Day start at SS for the Yankees, surpassing Phil Rizzuto (11) for the most Opening Day starts by a Yankees shortstop in franchise history…started his fifth straight Opening Day at shortstop with Alex Rodriguez at third base, becoming the first pair of Yankees to start on the left side of the infield in five consecutive years since Graig Nettles and Bucky Dent started six consecutive season openers from 1977-82.

- Missed six games from 4/8-13 with a strained left quadriceps…was the longest stretch of consecutive DNPs in his career, not counting times he's been on the D.L. (credit: *Elias Sports Bureau*)…upon returning, hit in seven straight games from 4/14-20, going 12-for-31 (.387) with 4R, 2 doubles, 1 triple, 10RBI and 2BB…did not score a run in nine straight games from 4/18-27, the longest such stretch of his career (credit: *Elias*).

- Hit his first home run of the season and was 2-for-5 with 2R in 5/10 win at Detroit, snapping a 128AB homerless stretch, the longest streak to begin a season of his career (credit: *Elias*).

- Recorded his first stolen base of the season in his 38th game played (5/18 loss vs. the Mets)…his 37-game streak without a steal was his longest in a single season since going 49 straight games without a steal from 6/4-7/26/96 (credit: *Elias*)…was just his second stolen base attempt of 2008 (also 4/1 vs. Toronto)…the streak of 36 games without a steal attempt was the longest of his career (previous high was 30 games in 1996).

- Went hitless in five straight games (0-for-18), his longest such streak since going hitless in seven straight from 4/21-28/04…was picked off second base in the top of the sixth inning by Dennis Sarfate in 5/27 loss at Baltimore…according to *Elias*, it was the first time he had been picked off any base since 9/2/98.

- Turned 34 years old on 6/26…his 2,438 career hits were the most by a Yankee before turning 34 years old (17 more than Lou Gehrig when he turned 34)…was the most among all active players prior to their 34th birthday…in AL history, only Ty Cobb and Robin Yount accumulated more hits than Jeter before turning 34.

- In 7/12 win at Toronto, hit his 19th career leadoff homer and first since 9/27/05 at Baltimore…was also his 200th home run as a Yankee…the *Elias Sports Bureau* notes that with Jason Giambi (8/9) and Alex Rodriguez (8/12) also hitting their 200th Yankees homers in 2008, they became the first teammates on any club to reach the 200HR plateau together in the same season.

- Became the 88th player all time—and the sixth active Major Leaguer—to reach the 2,500-hit plateau with his first-inning single in 8/22 win vs. Baltimore…also became the third player in Yankees franchise history to tally 2,500 hits with the club, joining Lou Gehrig (2,721) and Babe Ruth (2,518)…according to the *Elias Sports Bureau*, only two players in the last 65 years were younger than Jeter (34 years, 57 days) at the time of their 2,500th hit (Hank Aaron in 1967 and Robin Yount in 1989).

- In 9/7 loss at Seattle, hit solo-HR to mark his 1,000th career RBI…had a third-inning single to tie Babe Ruth (2,518) for second place on the all-time Yankees hit list…collected his 2,519th career hit with a first-inning single off the Angels' Ervin Santana on 9/9 at Los Angeles, surpassing Ruth…marked the first time since 6/22/33 that someone other than Ruth or Gehrig occupied first or second place on the Yankees' all-time hits list (credit: *Elias Sports Bureau*).

**DEREK JETER'S FAREWELL SPEECH FOLLOWING FINAL GAME
AT THE ORIGINAL YANKEE STADIUM (9/21/08)**

"For all of us up here, it's a huge honor to put this uniform on every day and come out here and play. Every member of this organization, past and present, has been calling this place home for 85 years. There's a lot of tradition, a lot of history, and a lot of memories. Now, the great thing about memories, is you're able to pass [them] along from generation to generation. And although things are going to change next year – we're going to move across the street – there are a few things with the New York Yankees that never change. That's pride, it's tradition, and most of all, we have the greatest fans in the world.

"We're relying on you to take the memories from this Stadium, add them to the new memories that come at the new Yankee Stadium and continue to pass them on from generation to generation. So, on behalf of the entire organization, we just want to take this moment to salute you, the greatest fans in the world."

- Went 6-for-7 in 9/13 doubleheader vs. Tampa Bay, going 3-for-4 in Game 1 loss and 3-for-3 in Game 2 win…according to the *Elias Sports Bureau*, became the first Yankee to record 3H in each game of a doubleheader in remodeled Yankee Stadium (since 1976) and only the sixth Yankee over the last 40 years to accomplish the feat at any park (Johnny Damon in 2006, Willie Randolph in 1987, Dave Winfield in 1983, Matty Alou in 1973 and Roy White in 1972)…also recorded 3H in the series finale on 9/14, finishing the series 9-for-11 and reaching base in 11 of his 13 plate appearances (1BB, 1HBP)…according to the *Elias Sports Bureau*, became the fifth player (and second Yankee) to record at least three hits in every game of a series of three games or more at Yankee Stadium joining Boston's Edgar Renteria (2005), the Yankees' Ken Griffey Sr. (1982), Oakland's Reggie Jackson (1973), and Boston's Dom DiMaggio (1949).

- Tied Lou Gehrig's all-time record of 1,269 career hits at the original Yankee Stadium in 9/14 win vs. Tampa Bay with a fifth-inning solo-HR off David Price, going 3-for-4…in 9/15 win vs. Chicago-AL, tied Gehrig (8,001) for second place on the Yankees' all-time at-bats list (according to the *Elias Sports Bureau*, Gehrig had held sole possession of first place on the franchise's all-time list since 9/6/37).

- With a first-inning single off Gavin Floyd in 9/16 loss vs. Chicago-AL, passed Lou Gehrig (1,269) as all-time hits at the original Yankee Stadium…in the same at-bat, gained sole possession of second place on the Yankees' all-time at-bats list, passing Gehrig (8,001AB)…following the game, his spikes were sent to the National Baseball Hall of Fame.

- Was 0-for-5 in the final game at the original Yankee Stadium on 9/21 vs. Baltimore, making the last Yankees out on a groundout (third base to first base)…gave a speech to the Stadium crowd following the game…the bat he used during the final homestand was sent to the National Baseball Hall of Fame…his final game speech was voted by fans as the MLB.com "Moment of the Year."

- Was scratched from the lineup prior to 9/23 win at Toronto (sore left hand)…entered the game at SS in the ninth…originally suffered the injury on 9/20 vs. Baltimore when he was hit by a Jim Miller pitch in his final at-bat of the game…left 9/26 win at Boston in the third inning with a sore wrist…missed final two games of the season.

CAREER GAMES AT THE ORIGINAL YANKEE STADIUM

1.	Mickey Mantle	1,213
2.	Lou Gehrig	1,080
3.	Yogi Berra	1,068
4.	Bernie Williams	1,039
5.	**DEREK JETER**	**1,004**

(Credit: *Elias Sports Bureau*)

FIVE-TIME GOLD GLOVE WINNERS AT SS

Ozzie Smith	13
Omar Vizquel	11
Luis Aparicio	9
Mark Belanger	8
Dave Concepcion	5
DEREK JETER	**5**

2007

- Hit .322 (206-for-639) with 102R, 39 doubles, 12HR, 73RBI and 15SB in 156 games (153 starts at SS)…ranked third in the American League with 206 hits, tied for fourth with 61 multi-hit games and 639 at-bats, ranked seventh with 14HBP, eighth with a .334 home average, tied for eighth with a .354 average with RISP and ninth with a .322 batting average…batted .418 (28-for-67) with runners in scoring position and two outs, the third-highest average in the Majors…was elected to the AL All-Star team, the eighth All-Star selection of his career (1998-2002; '04, '06-07)…started at shortstop and was 1-for-3 in the AL's 5-4 win on 7/10 at AT&T Park in San Francisco…also earned a Silver Slugger Award, his second straight.

- Recorded his sixth 200-hit season…also recorded his 11th career season with 100-or-more runs scored (1996-2002; 2004-07), tying Babe Ruth for second-most such seaosns behind only Lou Gehrig (13) in franchise history.

- Fashioned 17-game, 19-game and 20-game hit streaks in the first 72 games of the season…according to the *Elias Sports Bureau*, became the first player since 1950 to record three separate hitting streaks of at least 17 games in the same season and the only player to record three hitting streaks of at least 15 games in his team's first 70 games of a season…collected four separate hitting streaks of at least 15 games in 2007, becoming the first Major Leaguer since 1941 to accomplish the feat (credit: *Elias Sports Bureau*).

- Was 1-for-4 with 2RBI and 1HP in 4/2 Opening Day win vs. Tampa Bay…was his 11th Opening Day start at SS for the Yankees, tying Phil Rizzuto's franchise record for most starts by a Yankee at SS on Opening Day.

- Hit safely in 20 straight games from 4/8-5/3 and 23 of his 24 games played with an official at-bat to begin the season…during the 20-game streak, hit .364 (32-for-88) with 17R…including the final 37 games of 2006, hit safely in 59 of 61 regular season games (since 8/20/06)…also reached base safely in each of his 25 games played to begin 2007 and 66-of-67 games dating back to the previous season (since 8/17/06)…became only the third player in Yankees history to have at least two separate single-season hitting streaks of 20 or more games (also 25 games, 8/20-9/16/06)…Joe DiMaggio had four of them (streaks of 21 and 22 in 1937, 23 in 1940 and 56 in 1941); Don Mattingly had a pair (20 games in 1985 and 24 in 1986).

▸ Hit safely in 25 consecutive Interleague games from 6/25/06-6/23/07, batting .396 (40-for-101) with 18R, 11 doubles, 2HR, 11RBI, 13BB and 4SB…according to the *Elias Sports Bureau*, was the second-longest hit streak in the history of Interleague play (Matt Lawton hit in 37 straight Interleague games from 6/5/99-7/12/01).

▸ Reached his 33rd birthday on 6/26 with 2,250 career hits, the most since Robin Yount had 2,391 at that juncture of his career (credit: *Elias Sports Bureau*)…was 83 more hits than Pete Rose (2,167)—Baseball's all-time hits leader—had at the time of his 33rd birthday.

▸ Hit safely in the final 15 games of the regular season, batting .386 (27-for-70), 13R, 7 doubles, 1 triple, 3HR and 11RBI during the streak…according to the *Elias Sports Bureau*, it was the longest hitting streak by a Yankee to close out a season since Bobby Murcer in 1971 (also 15 games).

▸ Batted .176 (3-for-17) with 1RBI in four Division Series games vs. Cleveland.

2006

▸ Finished second in American League Most Valuable Player voting while earning his first Silver Slugger Award and third consecutive Gold Glove Award…hit .343 (214-for-623) with 118R, 39 doubles, 14HR, 97RBI and a career-high 34SB in 154 games (149 starts at SS, five starts at DH)…became just the third player to reach those totals in average, runs, home runs, RBI and stolen bases in a single season, joining Kiki Cuyler with Pittsburgh in 1925 and George Sisler with St. Louis in 1920…received the Hank Aaron Award, recognizing the most outstanding offensive performer.

▸ Ranked second in the AL in batting average, runs, average with runners in scoring position (.381) and average vs. left-handed pitchers (.390), ranked third with a .354 home batting average, tied for third with 214H, fourth with a .417 on-base percentage, tied for fifth with 12HBP, seventh with 34SB and ninth with 623AB.

▸ According to the *Elias Sports Bureau*, became only the fifth player since 1932 to hit .340-or-higher, drive in at least 90 runs and steal 30-or-more bases in the same season, joining Larry Walker (1997), Ellis Burks (1996), Willie Mays (1958) and Jackie Robinson (1949)…was elected to the 2006 AL All-Star team, the seventh All-Star selection of his career…started at SS and was 0-for-3 in the AL's 3-2 win on 7/11 at Pittsburgh's PNC Park.

▸ In 4/3 win at Oakland, made his 10th Opening Day start at SS for the Yankees…batted a career-best .398 (35-for-88) in April, hitting safely in 20 of the 23 games played.

▸ Became the eighth Yankee to reach the 2,000-hit plateau with a fourth-inning infield single in 5/26 loss vs. Kansas City, joining Lou Gehrig (2,721), Babe Ruth (2,518), Mickey Mantle (2,415), Bernie Williams (2,336), Joe DiMaggio (2,214), Don Mattingly (2,153) and Yogi Berra (2,148)…according to the *Elias Sports Bureau*, only one of the seven other Yankees with 2,000 hits reached the milestone in fewer games than Jeter's 1,571 (DiMaggio in 1,537 games)…in the expansion era (since 1961), only four players reached the 2,000-hit mark in fewer games than Jeter (also according to the *Elias Sports Bureau*): Wade Boggs (in 1,515 games), Kirby Puckett (1,542), Tony Gwynn (1,560) and Rod Carew (1,562).

▸ Missed three games (5/30-6/1) with a sprained right hand…was removed from 5/29 win at Detroit in the fifth inning after suffering the injury in a slide at second base in the third inning…on 6/2 at Baltimore, batted third for first time since 9/28/03 (vs. Baltimore)…left 6/4 loss at Baltimore with a bruised right thumb after being hit by a Rodrigo Lopez pitch in the top of the sixth inning and missed next three games (6/5-7 vs. Boston)…started following three games at DH (6/9-11).

MILESTONE HITS

Hit No.	Date/Opp.
1	5/30/95 at SEA (Tim Belcher)
100	7/17/96 at BOS (Joe Hudson)
1,000	9/25/00 vs. DET (Steve Sparks)
2,000	5/26/06 vs. KC (Scott Elarton)
2,416*	6/4/08 vs. TOR (Jesse Litsch)
2,519**	9/9/08 at LAA (Ervin Santana)
2,722***	9/11/09 vs. BAL (Chris Tillman)

* Surpassed Mickey Mantle for sole possession of third place on the Yankees' all-time list

** Surpassed Babe Ruth for sole possession of second place on the Yankees' all-time list

*** Surpassed Lou Gehrig for sole possession of first place on the Yankees' all-time list

- Hit .412 (42-for-102) in the month of July, the third time in his career that he has batted .400 or better for a calendar month.

- Was successful in 14 consecutive stolen-base attempts from 6/13-8/4, including nine straight successful steals of third base…played in the 1,648th game of his career at shortstop on 9/4 at Kansas City, surpassing Phil Rizzuto (1,647) for the most games played at shortstop in franchise history.

- Hit in a career-high 25 straight games from 8/20-9/16, batting .377 (40-for-106) with 21R, 3HR and 21RBI during the streak…was the longest hitting streak by a Yankee since Joe Gordon hit in 29 straight games in 1942…also reached base safely in 30 consecutive games, the longest such streak by a Yankee in 2006…was 3-for-3 with 3R, 1BB and 1SB in 9/30 loss vs. Toronto…recorded his 2,149th career hit, surpassing Yogi Berra (2,148) for seventh place on the club's all-time list.

- Hit safely in 36 of the last 37 games to end the season, batting .368 (57-for-155) with 33R, 4HR and 22RBI during the stretch…reached base safely in 41 of his final 42 games.

- Batted .500 (8-for-16) in four Division Series games vs. Detroit, leading the team with 4R and 4 doubles…tied the Major League record for hits in a single postseason game with five in Game 1 of the ALDS (sixth time, including Hideki Matsui in Game 3 of the 2004 ALCS at Boston), but became only the second player to go 5-for-5 (Atlanta's Marquis Grissom went 5-for-5 in Game 4 of the 1995 NLDS vs. Colorado).

2005

- Hit .309 (202-for-654) with 122R, 19HR, 70RBI and 14SB in 159 games (158 starts at SS), while earning his second consecutive Gold Glove Award…led the American League with a .354 home batting average, ranked second with 122 runs and 62 multi-hit games, third with 202H, tied for third with 654AB, sixth with a .309 batting average and a .389 on-base percentage, and ninth with 77BB…made his ninth Opening Day start at SS on 4/3 vs. Boston.

- Played in the 1,400th game of his career on 5/10 vs. Seattle and had 1,775 career hits, the most by any player through 1,400 games since Kirby Puckett had 1,830…had a leadoff single in five straight games from 5/11-16, the longest such streak of his career…hit 13th career leadoff home run–and first since 4/29/04 vs. Oakland–in 5/29 loss vs. Boston…did not play on 6/3 or 6/4 at Minnesota (chest cold), missing his first two games of the season.

- Hit grand slam and solo-HR and was 2-for-5 in 6/18 win vs. Chicago-NL…was his first career grand slam in his 136th career at-bat with the bases loaded…had 156 career home runs before the grand slam, the most home runs by any active player without a grand slam as well as the most by any player in Yankee history…was his first multi-home run game of the season and the seventh of his career (last hit 2HR in a game on 6/27/04 vs. Mets)…the 5RBI tied his career-high (third time)…was 5-for-6 with 5R, 1 double and a solo-HR in 6/21 win vs. Tampa Bay…established a career high with his five runs and tied a career high with 5H (second time, also on 5/23/01 vs. Boston).

- Hit game-winning solo home runs in consecutive games on 8/11 and 8/12 vs. Texas…made second career start at DH in 8/15 win at Tampa Bay (also 7/7/02 vs. Detroit) and was 1-for-5 with 1R…did not play in 8/22 win vs. Toronto (jammed right thumb)…in the month of August, was tied for the AL lead with 40 hits.

- Played in the 1,500th game of his career on 9/6 vs. Tampa Bay…over that span, amassed 1,906H and 1,140R…marked the most hits and runs by a Major Leaguer in his first 1,500 games since Joe DiMaggio (1,965H and 1,211R).

- Drove in at least one run in six straight games from 9/23-28, the longest streak in the Majors in 2005 from the leadoff position in the batting order…according to the *Elias Sports Bureau*, no player had a longer streak from that spot in the order since Matt Lawton had an eight-game RBI streak for Cleveland in 2002…hit leadoff HR in 9/27 loss at Baltimore, his fifth leadoff HR of the season (also 9/23 vs. Toronto, 9/4 at Oakland, 6/24 vs. NY Mets and 5/29 vs. Boston) and 17th of his career.

- Batted .333 (7-for-21) with 2HR and 5RBI in four Division Series games vs. the Angels…reached base safely in a Division Series-record 21 straight games (dating back to Game 4 of the 2000 ALDS vs. Oakland) before going 0-for-5 in Game 2.

2004

- Emerged from an early-season slump to hit .292 (188-for-643) with a career-high 44 doubles, 23HR, 78RBI and 23SB in 154 games (154 starts at SS)…committed only 13 errors and earned his first career Gold Glove…ranked second in the American League with 16 sacrifice hits, tied for fourth with 44 doubles and 14HBP, was sixth with 111R and 23SB, seventh with 188H and tied for eighth with 68 extra-base hits…was elected to the 2004 American League All-Star team, the sixth All-Star selection of his career…was the first Yankees' shortstop to be elected to start the All-Star Game since Bucky Dent in 1981…started at SS in the 7/13 AL win, going 3-for-3 with 1R.

- Was batting .189 on 5/25, going 36-for-190 in his first 43 games of the season with 17R, 8 doubles, 3HR and 17RBI…in his final 111 games, beginning on 5/26, hit .336 (152-for-453) with 94R, 36 doubles, 20HR and 61RBI.

- Made his eighth Opening Day start at SS on 3/30 at Tampa Bay in Tokyo, Japan…hit 12th lead-off home run of his career in 4/29 win vs. Oakland—and first since 8/5/03 vs. Texas—to snap an 0-for-32 stretch (longest such stretch of his career)…recorded three straight three-hit games from 5/26-28, marking the second time in his career (also in June 2000)…drove in at least one run in nine straight games from 5/23-6/2…was the longest RBI streak by a Yankee since Don Mattingly drove in at least one run in nine straight games in 1987…missed three games (6/5-8) with tightness in the left groin.

- Had his 21-game hitting streak at Camden Yards snapped on 6/23, going 0-for-4 (batted .351, 34-for-97, during that span which began on 4/4/02)…hit .396 in 23 games in June (36-for-91) with 24R, 9HR and 17RBI…set a calendar-month career high with 9HR and his .396 average was his highest monthly average since he hit .425 in July 2003.

- Was 1-for-4 with 1HBP in 7/1 win vs. Boston before being removed from the game in the bottom of the 12th inning after suffering a laceration of the chin, a bruised right cheek and a bruised right shoulder…suffered the injuries after catching a fly ball by Trot Nixon and diving into the stands to end the top of the 12th…was taken to Columbia Presbyterian where precautionary X-rays of his right cheek were negative…started at SS the following night…did not play in two straight games from 7/21-22 because of a small, non-displaced fracture of the fifth metacarpal of his right hand…sustained injury after being hit by a pitch in the sixth inning of 7/20 win at Tampa Bay.

- Before fifth-inning throwing error in 8/8 win vs. Toronto, had gone a career-high 46 consecutive games without committing an error.

- Had 17-game hitting streak from 7/30-8/17, batting .338 (25-for-74) with 12R, 1HR and 5RBI over the span…was also the longest hitting streak by a Yankee since Bernie Williams hit safely in 19 straight games from 8/7-28/02…reached the 1,000-run plateau with a solo-HR on 8/24 at Cleveland in his 1,331st game, becoming only the fifth player in the expansion era (since 1961) to accomplish the feat in fewer than 1,400 games…according to the *Elias Sports Bureau*, he joined Rickey Henderson (1,252 games), Alex Rodriguez (1,261), Kenny Lofton (1,305) and Chuck Knoblauch (1,379).

- Scored at least one run in 11 straight games from 9/5-15, the longest such streak of his career…it is the longest such streak by a Yankee since Bernie Williams scored in a career-high 13 straight games in 2000…was named the AL's "Player of the Week" for the week of 9/6-12…was the second weekly award of his career (also 8/5/01)…batted in the leadoff position in the batting order in his final 25 games of the season, hitting .388 (40-for-103) with 28R, 11 doubles, 5HR and 18RBI.

- In 11 postseason games, batted .245 (12-for-49) with 1HR and 9RBI…hit solo-HR to lead off the bottom of the first inning of ALDS Game 2 vs. Minnesota and became the 19th player to homer into the black batters-eye section of the remodeled Yankee Stadium, the third in postseason play (also Reggie Jackson in Game 6 of the 1977 World Series and Seattle's Jay Buhner in Game 3 of the 2001 ALCS)…was his second career leadoff home run in postseason play (also 10/25/00 in Game 4 of the World Series at the New York Mets).

2003

- Rebounded from an early-season injury to hit .324 (156-for-482) with 10HR, 52RBI and 11SB in 119 games (118 starts at SS)…ranked third in the AL in average and 10th in the league with a .393 on-base percentage…was placed on the 15-day disabled list on 4/1 after suffering a dislocated left shoulder in third inning of 3/31 Opening Day win at Toronto…was reinstated from the 15-day D.L. on 5/13 after missing 36 games…hit leadoff-HR in 5/27 win vs. Boston, the 10th leadoff HR of his career and first since 6/1/01 vs. Seattle…was named the 11th team captain in Yankees history by Principal Owner George Steinbrenner on 6/3.

- Was 37-for-87 (.425) in the month of July (with 17R, 8 doubles, 1HR, 12RBI, and 12BB), the second-highest batting average in the Majors during the month behind only the White Sox' Magglio Ordonez…left 7/7 win vs. Boston in third inning after being hit by pitch on right hand in the first inning…did not start the next day at Cleveland after suffering a bone bruise on his right hand…recorded a season-high four hits in 7/9 win at Cleveland, going 4-for-5 with 1R and a two-run double.

- Hit leadoff HR and two-run HR and was 2-for-4 on 8/5 vs. Texas…was his second leadoff-HR of the season and 11th of his career…was his first multi-HR game of the season and fourth of his career (last on 9/19/01 at Chicago-AL)…recorded his 1,500th career hit with a third-inning single and was 1-for-6 in 8/16 win at Baltimore…missed five games (9/1-6) after suffering strained rib-cage muscle in 8/31 win at Boston.

- Hit .314 (22-for-70) with 10R, 2HR and 5RBI in 17 postseason games.

2002

- Batted .297 (191-for-644) with 18HR, 75RBI and 32SB in 157 games (156 starts at SS, one at DH)…ranked third in the American League with 124R and 32SB, fifth in multi-hit games (58), and seventh in hits (191)…became only the fourth player since 1900 to score at least 100 runs in each of seven straight seasons starting with his rookie year…Earle Combs (1925-32) and Ted Williams (1939-49) both did it in each of their first eight seasons; Johnny Pesky did it in each of his first six (1942-50)…with Bernie Williams, were only the second set of teammates to score at least 100 runs in seven consecutive seasons (1996-2002), joining the Yankees' Earle Combs, Babe Ruth and Lou Gehrig (1926-32)…was selected by Manager Joe Torre to participate in his fifth consecutive All-Star Game on 7/9 at Miller Park in Milwaukee…pinch-hit and was 0-for-1.

- In Opening Day loss at Baltimore, hit his 100th career home run with two-run HR in the eighth inning…collected his 500th career RBI with a first-inning double in 4/19 win vs. Toronto…had season-high and team-high 16-game hitting streak from 5/9-25, batting .348 (24-for-69) with 3HR and 6RBI over the stretch.

- Hit leadoff home run in the first inning and was 1-for-2 with 2R, 2RBI, 1BB, 1SF and 1HBP in 6/1 win vs. Boston…was his ninth career leadoff home run…played in his 1,000th career game and hit a solo-HR in 6/10 win vs. Arizona…was 2-for-4 with 1R, 1RBI, 1BB and a career-high 3SB in 6/28 win at New York-NL…left 7/4 game vs. Cleveland in the top of the third inning after being slid into at second base by John McDonald…missed the following two games with a sprained knee and bruised lower leg…made his first career start at DH in 7/7 win vs. Toronto and hit two-run HR while going 1-for-4 with 2R and 1BB.

- Recorded season-high four hits in 8/14 win at Kansas City, going 4-for-7…hit in the final five games of the season, going 9-for-21 to raise his average from .292 to .297.

- Hit .500 (8-for-16) with 6R, 2HR and 3RBI in four Division Series games versus the Angels…collected his 100th career postseason hit in Game 4 at Anaheim on 10/5 (first-inning single off Jarrod Washburn).

2001

- Batted .311 (191-for-614) with 110R, 21HR and 74RBI in 150 games (150 starts at SS)…hit .324 (34-for-105) with 17R, 5HR and 11RBI in 26 games as a leadoff hitter and had nine first-inning hits (seven for extra bases) in 24AB…appeared in only five spring training games, going 3-for-15 with 1RBI…missed first nine games of spring training with inflammation in his right shoulder and final 14 games with a strained right quadriceps…was placed on the 15-day D.L. (retroactive to 3/23) with strained right quad to begin the season…snapped a stretch of five straight Opening Day starts at SS.

- Was activated from the 15-day D.L. prior to 4/7 game and made first appearance of the season that day vs. Toronto, going 1-for-5…his steal of home in the third inning of 5/5 win at Baltimore was the first by a Yankee since he did it on 6/18/99 at the Angels…established a career high with 5H, hit a solo-HR and was 5-for-5 with 3R and 1 double in 5/23 win vs. Boston…became first Yankee SS to have a five-hit game since Tony Kubek in 1962.

- Was selected to his fourth consecutive All-Star Game, hitting his first All-Star home run (solo shot in the sixth) in the AL's 4-1 win on 7/10 in Seattle…was the first homer by a Yankee in an All-Star Game since Yogi Berra in 1959…led the AL with 40 hits in July…was named AL "Player of the Week" for 7/30-8/5, batting .524 (11-for-21) in six games with 2HR and 5RBI (his first such award)…hit leadoff HR and was 4-for-5 with 2R and 1RBI in 8/11 loss at Oakland…was his fifth career leadoff HR and first since 8/20/97 at Anaheim…in his next start as leadoff hitter in 8/18 loss vs. Seattle, hit his second straight leadoff home run and fourth in a six-start stretch from the leadoff spot.

- His seventh-inning throwing error on 8/22 at Texas snapped his 36-game errorless streak…collected 43 hits in August (third-most in AL), marking the eighth time in his career he reached the 40-hit plateau in one month…among active players, only Tony Gwynn had more 40-hit months (19) at that time…missed four games (9/5-9) with a strained left hamstring sustained while running to first base in the second inning on 9/4 at Toronto…in 9/19 win at Chicago-AL, recorded the third multi-HR game of his career and first since 9/9/98 at Boston…in his last 82 games of the season (since 6/24), batted .334 (111-for-332) with 68R, 16HR and 39RBI.

- Batted .226 (14-for-62) in 17 postseason games…in five Division Series games vs. Oakland, batted .444 (8-for-18)…made famous "flip play" on 10/13/01 in Game 3 at Oakland, relaying Shane Spencer's errant throw to Jorge Posada in time to nail Jeremy Giambi at the plate in the seventh inning…was 2-for-3 in Game 5 of the ALDS and established a Major League record for most career postseason hits with 87 (in 66 games), surpassing Pete Rose's 86 hits (in 67 games)…had his 12-game postseason hitting streak snapped in Game 3 of the ALDS…had his 14-game World Series hitting streak snapped in Game 1 of the World Series…his streak tied Roberto Clemente for the third-longest streak of all time (behind only Hank Bauer, Yankees, 17 straight games, 1956-58; and Marquis Grissom, Atlanta-Cleveland, 15, 1995-97).

2000

- Was a member of his fourth World Series championship team, becoming the first player in Major League history to be named MVP of the Fall Classic and All-Star Game in the same season…the only other player to win both awards in his career is Frank Robinson, World Series MVP in 1966 and All-Star MVP in 1971…at 26 years old, only Joe DiMaggio and Mickey Mantle (at 24) and Billy Martin (25) earned four World Championships at a younger age…hit .339 with 15HR and 73RBI in 148 games (148 starts at SS).

- Recorded his third straight 200-hit season, becoming only the third Yankee to compile three consecutive 200-hit seasons (joining Lou Gehrig, 1927-29 and Don Mattingly, 1984-86)…joined Bernie Williams in reaching the 100-run plateau for the fifth straight season…was only the third time since 1900 that teammates have each scored 100 or more runs in at least five consecutive seasons…the Yankees' Babe Ruth, Lou Gehrig and Earle Combs accomplished the feat in seven consecutive seasons (1926-32) and Cincinnati's Joe Morgan and Pete Rose broke the 100-run plateau in five straight seasons (1972-76).

- Reached his 26th birthday on 6/26 with 887 career hits…only two Yankees had more hits at age 26 (Mickey Mantle, 1,080 and Joe DiMaggio, 970)…only three active players at the time had more hits before turning 26 (Roberto Alomar, 1054; Ken Griffey, Jr., 1039 and Ivan Rodriguez, 948)…was selected to his third All-Star Game by Manager Joe Torre…went 3-for-3 with 1R and 2RBI in his first start and was named Most Valuable Player of the 71st All-Star Game in Atlanta…became the first player in Yankees history to be named MVP of the All-Star Game and the fourth shortstop to take home the honor.

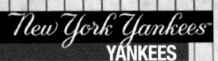

- Made fifth straight Opening Day start at SS…reached base safely in 26 of the first 28 games of the season (4/3-5/6)–including 23 straight from 4/7-5/3…scored his 500th career run on 4/23 at Toronto, becoming only the fourth Yankee to reach the 500-run plateau before his 26th birthday (joining Gehrig, DiMaggio and Mantle)…was hitless in four straight games (5/7-9, 5/11) for the first time since 4/26-29/97…left game in third inning on 5/11 vs. Tampa Bay and missed five games (5/12-17) with an abdominal strain…was placed on the 15-day disabled list from 5/19-27.

- Compiled a streak of 10 consecutive games with at least one walk from 8/14-23, (14BB total)…was the longest such streak by a Yankee since Jesse Barfield also walked in 10 straight games from 8/9-19/90…reached the 1,000-hit plateau with a fifth-inning single and was 3-for-4 on 9/25 vs. Detroit…at 26, became the second-youngest Yankee to reach 1,000 hits (behind only Mickey Mantle, who was 25 when he collected his 1,000th hit in 1957).

- Hit .317 (20-for-63) and led the Yankees with 13R and 4HR in the postseason…had his 17-game postseason hitting streak snapped in Game 1 of the Division Series at Oakland, going 0-for-3…was the World Series MVP, hitting .409 (9-for-22) with two doubles, one triple, 2HR and 2RBI in five games…set a five-game World Series record with 19 total bases and tied five-game records with 9H and 6R…also became the eighth player to lead off a World Series game with a home run in Game 4.

- Became the third shortstop to ever win the World Series MVP Award, joining the Yankees' Bucky Dent in 1978 and Detroit's Alan Trammell in 1984…hit safely in all five World Series games, extending his hitting streak in the Series to 14 games.

1999

- Won his third World Championship in his first four full seasons…only two other Yankee players (Mickey Mantle, 21 years old and Joe DiMaggio, 23 years old) won three championships at a younger age than Jeter (25)…hit .349 with 37 doubles, 24HR and 102RBI in 158 games (all at SS)…set career highs in nearly every offensive category, including batting average, runs (134), hits (219), triples (9), home runs, RBI, and walks (91)…was named to his second All-Star team by Yankees manager Joe Torre (was 0-for-1).

- Was among the AL leaders in multi-hit games (first-67), hits (first), batting average (second), runs (second), triples (tied for second), on-base percentage (third-.438) and total bases (tied for fourth-346)…his 102RBI were the second-most ever by a Yankees shortstop in a single season behind only Lyn Lary's 107 in 1931…led the Yankees in hits for the fourth straight season and became the first player since Ernie Banks (1954-57) to lead his team in hits in each of his first four full seasons…his 219 hits were the fourth-highest single-season total by a Yankee and most since 1986 (Don Mattingly, 238)…joined centerfielder Bernie Williams as the first pair of Yankee teammates to record 200 or more hits in the same season since DiMaggio and Lou Gehrig accomplished the feat in 1939…became the first player to score at least 100 runs in four straight seasons starting with his rookie year since Jim Gilliam did it for the Brooklyn Dodgers from 1953-56.

- Reached base safely in each of the first 53 games of the season, the longest streak in the Majors in 1999 and the longest by a Yankee in the post-expansion era (since 1961)…the streak ended in a 7-2 loss on 6/6 vs. New York-NL…had six hitting streaks of at least 10 games, including a season-high 16-game streak from 5/4-22.

- Tied his career high with 5RBI in a 10-1 win on 5/7 vs. Seattle…posted seven consecutive multi-hit games from 6/7-14, the most by a Yankee since Dave Winfield in 1988…batted third for the first time in his career on 6/18 vs. Anaheim and went 2-for-3 with 2R, 1RBI and 1HBP…also stole home on the front end of a double steal with Chili Davis…hit in the third position from 6/18-7/1, batting .395 (17-for-43) and hitting safely in each of the 11 games…batted fourth for the first time ever on 7/10 at New York-NL…was 0-for-4 with 1IBB.

- Snapped an 0-for-17 skid with the game-winning two-run home run off David Wells in the eighth inning of a 3-1 victory on 8/2 vs. Toronto…the home run was his 20th of the season, making him the first Yankees shortstop ever to hit 20HR in a season.

- Hit .375 (18-for-48) and led the Yankees with 10R in the postseason…hit safely in all 12 games and 17 consecutive postseason games dating back to 1998, tying Hank Bauer for the all-time record.

1998

- Batted .324 with 19HR and 84RBI in 149 games (148 starts at SS)…finished third in the American League MVP voting behind Juan Gonzalez and Nomar Garciaparra…was among the American League leaders in runs (first-127), multi-hit games (tied for second), hits (third-203), triples (tied for fourth-8), batting average (fifth) and at-bats (sixth-626)…broke the single-season home run record for Yankees shortstops (previously held by Roy Smalley in 1982 with 16)…with 203 hits, joined Phil Rizzuto as the second Yankees shortstop to collect 200 or more hits in a season (Rizzuto had 200 in 1950).

- Set a Major League record for most runs scored by a shortstop in his first three full seasons with 352, surpassing the previous mark of 343 held by Detroit's Donie Bush from 1908-11…joined Frank Crosetti as the only Yankees shortstops to score 100 or more runs in three or more consecutive seasons (Crosetti did it in four straight seasons from 1936-39)…combined with 2B Chuck Knoblauch to become the first pair of Yankees middle infielders to each hit 15 or more home runs in the same season (Knoblauch had 17)…they also became the third pair of middle-infield teammates in AL history to record at least 30 stolen bases each in a single season (also SS Jack Barry and 2B Eddie Collins of the 1911 Philadelphia Athletics and SS Bert Campaneris and 2B Phil Garner of the 1976 Oakland Athletics)…was named to his first All-Star team by Cleveland manager Mike Hargrove and went 0-for-1 in the game.

- Drove in a career-high five runs on 5/6 at Texas…had a season-high 15-game hitting streak from 5/2-20, batting .456 (31-for-68) with 4HR and 19RBI during the streak…was placed on the disabled list for the first time in his career on 6/4 with a strained abdominal muscle sustained on a check swing on 6/3 vs. Tampa Bay (missed 12 team games)…was named the American League's "Player of the Month" for August, batting .382 (50-for-131) with 30R, 9 doubles, 4HR and 22RBI in 32 games.
- With 50 hits in August, he became the first Yankee to collect 50 hits in a month since Joe DiMaggio had 53 in July 1941…joined Alex Rodriguez (54 hits in August 1996) as the only players to reach 50 hits in a month in the 1990s.
- Started every game of the postseason, batting .235 (12-for-51) with 7R and 3RBI…hit .353 (6-for-17) vs. San Diego in the World Series.

1997
- In his sophomore campaign, batted .291 with 10HR and 70RBI in 159 games (all starts at SS)…led the American League with 748 plate appearances and tied for first with 142 singles…ranked third in at-bats (654) and hits (190) and tied for fourth in games played (159)…also ranked fourth in runs scored (116), tied for fifth in triples (7) and ninth in stolen bases (23).
- Had a team-leading 57 multi-hit games, tying him for third in the American League…scored at least 100 runs in each of his first two seasons, making him only the second Yankee to accomplish the feat (Joe DiMaggio 1936-37)…became only the fifth Yankee to play 140 or more games in each of their first two seasons seasons (also Earle Combs, Tony Lazzeri, Tom Tresh and Alvaro Espinoza)…in 102 games in the leadoff spot, hit .321 (137-for-427) with 6HR and 45RBI.
- Collected a hit in a career-high seven consecutive PA from 4/6-8…snapped a career-high 75-game homerless drought with a leadoff homer on 8/7 at Texas…had his first career multi-homer game with 2HR and 4RBI on 8/20 at Anaheim (G2).
- Started all five games of the Division Series vs. Cleveland at SS, hitting .333 (7-for-21) with 2HR and 2RBI…hit the second of three consecutive home runs in the sixth inning of Game 1 (between Tim Raines and Paul O'Neill), marking the first time three consecutive home runs have ever been hit in postseason play.

1996
- Hit .314 with 10HR and 78RBI, winning the American League "Rookie of the Year" Award…was the fifth time a Yankee had won the award and the first since Thurman Munson in 1970…became the club's first Opening Day rookie shortstop since Tom Tresh in 1962…hit his first Major League home run on Opening Day on 4/2 at Cleveland, a solo shot off Dennis Martinez…led the Yankees with 183H and 156 games started (all at SS) and tied with Tino Martinez for the team lead in multi-hit games with 49.
- Played the most games of any AL rookie (157) and had a stretch of 105 consecutive starts before sitting out the second game of a doubleheader on 9/25 vs. Milwaukee…had a season-high 17-game hitting streak from 9/7-25, the longest by a Yankees rookie since Joe DiMaggio's streak of 18 games in 1936…his 77RBI were the most by a rookie shortstop since Julio Franco drove in 80 in 1980…hit an inside-the-park home run on 8/2 at Kansas City, the first by a Yankee since Alvaro Espinoza on 7/21/90 at Minnesota.
- Hit .361 with 12R, 1HR and 3RBI in the postseason…scored the game-winning run in the bottom of the 12th inning in Game 2 of the Division Series vs. Texas after 3B Dean Palmer overthrew first base on a Charlie Hayes bunt…hit controversial game-tying home run off Armando Benitez in the eighth inning of Game 1 of the ALCS when a young fan reached over the wall and deflected the ball (Yankees would win 5-4 in 11 innings).

1995
- Saw his first Major League action, batting .250 (12-for-48) with 4 doubles and 7RBI in 15 games across two stints with the Yankees…contract was purchased on 5/29 after Tony Fernandez was placed on the disabled list with a strained rib cage muscle…made 13 starts and batted .234 with 0HR and 6RBI before he was optioned back to Columbus on 6/11…was recalled on 9/3, appearing in two games and raising his average to .250…was named to the International League All-Star team…his .317 batting average led all Yankees minor leaguers and ranked third among Triple-A shortstops…ranked third among Triple-A players with 96R, tied for fifth with 9 triples and was seventh with 154 hits.

1994
- Was named Minor League "Player of the Year" by *Baseball America*, *Sporting News*, *USA Today Baseball Weekly* and Topps/NAPBL after hitting .344 with 5HR, 68RBI and 50SB combined at Triple-A Columbus, Double-A Albany and Single-A Tampa…became the first Yankees prospect to win the *Baseball America* and *USA Today* awards…was also named MVP of the Florida State League…his .344 average led all minor league shortstops and ranked 10th in the minors overall…also ranked among all minor leaguers with 186H (second), 103R (10th) and 50SB (tied for 14th)…was named the Yankees "Minor League Player of the Year" after leading the organization in batting average, stolen bases, runs, hits and triples…was named the organization's "Player of the Month" for May after hitting .391 and leading the organization with 31R…earned a June promotion to Albany after hitting .367 in his last 49 games at Tampa.

▶ Was the Florida State League's "Player of the Month" for June…had a five-hit game on 6/10 at Sarasota…hit .420 in July at Albany and was named Topps' Eastern League "Player of the Month"…was promoted to Columbus on 8/1…hit safely in 28-of-35 games with the Clippers and did not go hitless in consecutive games…finished the season with a five-game hitting streak, batting .579 (11-for-19), including a 4-for-4 performance on 8/31 vs. Toledo…Yankees affiliates combined for a .621 winning percentage (87-53) with Jeter on the roster and a .502 winning percentage without him (138-137)…committed 25 errors in 616 chances at shortstop…played for Chandler in the Arizona Fall League and hit .278 with 9RBI, 2SB and 11 errors in 16 games before he was sidelined with mild inflammation in his right shoulder.

1993

▶ Was voted the "Most Outstanding Major League Prospect" by South Atlantic League managers after hitting .295 with 5HR, 71RBI and 18SB at Class-A Greensboro…was named to the All-Star team after finishing second in the league in triples (11), third in hits (152) and 11th in batting average…ranked fifth in the organization in batting average…committed 56 errors in 126 games at shortstop, ranking second in the league in errors by a shortstop…was voted by *Baseball America* as the South Atlantic League's "Best Defensive Shortstop," "Most Exciting Player" and "Best Infield Arm."

1992

▶ Was the Yankees' first-round selection and the sixth pick overall in the June 1992 First-Year Player Draft…was the first high school player chosen in the draft…became the third shortstop in Yankees history selected with a first-round pick, joining Rex Hudler (1978) and Dennis Sherrill (1974)…combined to hit .210 with 4HR and 29RBI in 58 games at Single-A Tampa and Single-A Greensboro…had 12 errors in 211 chances at Tampa and nine errors in 48 chances at Greensboro.

PERSONAL

▶ Full name is Derek Sanderson Jeter…was signed by Dick Groch…graduated in 1992 from Kalamazoo Central High School (Mich.), where he hit .508 (30-for-59) with 4HR, 23RBI, 21BB and 1K in 23 games as a senior…was 12-for-12 in stolen base attempts, had an .831 slugging percentage and a .637 on-base percentage…hit .557 with 7HR as a junior…was named 1992 High School "Player of the Year" by the American Baseball Coaches Association…was elected into the Kalamazoo High School Hall of Fame in December 2007.

▶ Was the recipient of the Joan Payson Award for community service in 1997, presented annually by the New York chapter of the BBWAA…received the New York Press Photographers' annual "Good Guy" Award for 1998…also received the Babe Ruth Award from the New York Chapter of the BBWAA in 2000, awarded annually to the Postseason MVP…was one of three finalists for the 2008 "Marvin Miller Man of the Year" Award given annually by the MLB Players' Association to the player in either league whose on-field performance and contributions to his community inspire others to higher levels of achievement…was the recipient of the Joe DiMaggio "Toast of the Town" Award New York Chapter of the BBWAA for the third time in 2009 (also 1999 and 2000)…also honored along with teammates Andy Pettitte, Jorge Posada and Mariano Rivera with the "Willie, Mickey and the Duke" Award from the New York BBWAA in 2009.

▶ Selected as the 2009 "Roberto Clemente Award" winner, given annually to the Major League Baseball player who combines a dedication to giving back to the community with outstanding skills on the baseball field…hosted Saturday Night Live on 12/1/01…was honored with the *Sporting News* "Good Guy in Sports" Award in 2002 and also received an ESPY for the Best Play Award that same year for his "flip play" in Game 3 of the 2001 ALDS at Oakland.

▶ Named the No. 1 sports celebrity in WFAN's (660AM) Top 20 New York Athletes of the Last 20 Years in December 2007…selected as a member of *Time Out New York's* "Top 40 under 40" in 2008.

▶ Since 1996, his Turn 2 Foundation has enjoyed 15 years of supporting various programs and activities designed to motivate youth to "Turn 2" a healthy lifestyle, academic achievement and leadership development and "turn away" from drugs and alcohol…the Foundation has awarded more than $10 million to support signature programs in Tampa, where Derek resides, New York, where he works, and West Michigan, where he grew up…along with his "Jeter's Leaders," hosted a leadership conference at the University of Texas at Arlington in August 2008, that brought together high school student leaders from New York, West Michigan, Louisville and Chicago…held his annual Holiday Express on 12/3/10 in New York City…treated students from the Turn 2 Us Program at P.S. 128 and P.S. 4 in Washington Heights to a private screening of "Megamind," at the Coliseum Theater, then joined children involved in the Turn 2 After School Programs for a private carnival themed holiday event at Lost Battalion Hall Recreation Center in Queens…also hosted separate holiday parties at the Air Zoo in Portage, Mich., and Tampa, Fla., later in the month….hosted the eighth Annual Derek Jeter Celebrity Golf Classic in Tampa, Fla., in January 2011…the sold-out event brought together celebrities from MLB, the NBA and the NFL as well as musicians and actors, raising nearly $1 million…hosts annual baseball clinics in Michigan, New York City and Tampa, as well as an annual fundraising dinner in New York City.

- Donated $500,000 to launch the "Derek Jeter Center at Phoenix House" in Tampa, an outpatient counseling center for troubled teens combining individual and family substance abuse treatment…attended ribbon-cutting on 10/2/09.
- Selected by *USA Today* as their 2010 "Most Caring Athlete," gracing the publication's cover on the June 27, 2010, weekend edition.

Jeter's Career Batting Record

Year	Club	AVG	G	AB	R	H	2B	3B	HR	RBI	SH	SF	HP	BB	SO	SB	CS	E	OBP	SLG
1992	GCL Yankees	.202	47	173	19	35	10	0	3	25	0	2	5	19	36	2	2	9	.296	.312
	Greensboro	.243	11	37	4	9	0	0	1	4	0	0	1	7	16	0	1	12	.378	.324
1993	Greensboro	.295	128	515	85	152	14	11	5	71	2	4	11	58	95	18	9	56	.376	.394
1994	Tampa	.329	69	292	61	96	13	8	0	39	3	3	3	23	30	28	2	6	.380	.428
	Albany	.377	34	122	17	46	7	2	2	13	3	1	1	15	16	12	2	12	.446	.516
	Columbus	.349	35	126	25	44	7	1	3	16	3	1	1	20	15	10	4	7	.439	.492
1995	Columbus	.317	123	486	96	154	27	9	2	45	2	5	4	61	56	20	12	29	.394	.422
	YANKEES	.250	15	48	5	12	4	1	0	7	0	0	0	3	11	0	0	2	.294	.375
1996	YANKEES	.314	157	582	104	183	25	6	10	78	6	9	9	48	102	14	7	22	.370	.430
1997	YANKEES	.291	159	654	116	190	31	7	10	70	8	2	10	74	125	23	12	18	.370	.405
1998	YANKEES - a	.324	149	626	*127	203	25	8	19	84	3	3	5	57	119	30	6	9	.384	.481
	Columbus	.400	1	5	2	2	2	0	0	0	0	0	0	0	2	0	0	1	.400	.800
1999	YANKEES - b	.349	158	627	134	*219	37	9	24	102	3	6	12	91	116	19	8	14	.438	.552
2000	YANKEES - b	.339	148	593	119	201	31	4	15	73	3	3	12	68	99	22	4	24	.416	.481
	Tampa	.667	1	3	2	2	1	0	0	0	0	0	0	0	0	0	0	0	.667	1.000
2001	YANKEES - c	.311	150	614	110	191	35	3	21	74	5	1	10	56	99	27	3	15	.377	.480
2002	YANKEES	.297	157	644	124	191	26	0	18	75	3	3	7	73	114	32	3	14	.373	.421
2003	YANKEES - d	.324	119	482	87	156	25	3	10	52	3	1	13	43	88	11	5	14	.393	.450
	Trenton	.444	5	18	2	8	1	1	0	5	0	0	1	3	0	0	0	1	.545	.611
2004	YANKEES	.292	154	643	111	188	44	1	23	78	16	2	14	46	99	23	4	13	.352	.471
2005	YANKEES	.309	159	654	122	202	25	5	19	70	7	3	11	77	117	14	5	15	.389	.450
2006	YANKEES	.343	154	623	118	214	39	3	14	97	7	4	12	69	102	34	5	15	.417	.483
2007	YANKEES	.322	156	639	102	206	39	4	12	73	3	2	14	56	100	15	8	18	.388	.452
2008	YANKEES	.300	150	596	88	179	25	3	11	69	7	4	9	52	85	11	5	12	.363	.408
2009	YANKEES	.334	153	634	107	212	27	1	18	66	4	1	5	72	90	30	5	8	.406	.465
2010	YANKEES	.270	157	663	111	179	30	3	10	67	1	3	9	63	106	18	5	6	.340	.370
Minor League Totals		**.308**	**454**	**1777**	**313**	**548**	**82**	**32**	**16**	**218**	**13**	**16**	**27**	**206**	**266**	**90**	**32**	**133**	**.385**	**.418**
Major League Totals		**.314**	**2926**	**9322**	**1685**	**2926**	**468**	**61**	**234**	**1135**	**79**	**47**	**152**	**948**	**1572**	**323**	**85**	**219**	**.385**	**.452**

* denotes league leader

Selected by the Yankees in the first round (sixth pick overall) of the 1992 First-Year Player Draft.

a - Placed on the 15-day disabled list on June 6, 1998 with a strained abdominal muscle.
b - Placed on the 15-day disabled list from May 19-27, 2000 (retroactive to May 12) with a strained abdominal muscle.
c - Placed on the 15-day disabled list from March 31 - April 7, 2001 (retroactive to March 23) with a strained right quad.
d - Placed on the 15-day disabled list from April 1 - May 13, 2003 with a dislocated left shoulder.

Jeter's Division Series Record

Year	Club vs. Opp.	AVG	G	AB	R	H	2B	3B	HR	RBI	SH	SF	HP	BB	SO	SB	CS	E	OBP	SLG
1996	NYY vs. TEX	.412	4	17	2	7	1	0	0	1	0	0	0	0	2	0	0	2	.412	.471
1997	NYY vs. CLE	.333	5	21	6	7	1	0	2	2	0	0	0	3	5	1	0	0	.417	.667
1998	NYY vs. TEX	.111	3	9	0	1	0	0	0	0	1	0	0	2	2	0	0	0	.273	.111
1999	NYY vs. TEX	.455	3	11	3	5	1	1	0	0	0	0	0	2	3	0	0	0	.538	.727
2000	NYY vs. OAK	.211	5	19	1	4	0	0	0	2	0	0	1	2	3	0	1	0	.318	.211
2001	NYY vs. OAK	.444	5	18	2	8	1	0	0	1	0	1	1	1	0	0	1	0	.476	.500
2002	NYY vs. ANA	.500	4	16	6	8	0	0	2	3	0	1	0	2	3	0	0	1	.526	.875
2003	NYY vs. MIN	.429	4	14	2	6	0	0	1	1	0	0	0	4	2	1	0	1	.556	.643
2004	NYY vs. MIN	.316	4	19	3	6	1	0	1	4	1	0	0	1	4	1	0	1	.350	.526
2005	NYY vs. LAA	.333	5	21	4	7	0	0	2	5	0	1	0	1	5	1	0	0	.348	.619
2006	NYY vs. DET	.500	4	16	4	8	4	0	1	1	0	0	0	1	2	0	1	1	.529	.938
2007	NYY vs. CLE	.176	4	17	0	3	0	0	0	1	0	0	0	0	4	0	0	0	.176	.176
2009	NYY vs. MIN	.400	3	10	4	4	2	0	1	2	0	0	0	3	0	0	0	0	.538	.900
2010	NYY vs. MIN	.286	3	14	0	4	0	0	0	1	0	0	0	0	3	1	0	0	.286	.286
Division Series Totals		**.351**	**56**	**222**	**37**	**78**	**11**	**1**	**10**	**24**	**2**	**3**	**2**	**22**	**38**	**5**	**3**	**6**	**.410**	**.545**

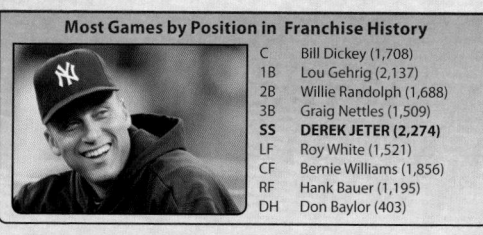

Most Games by Position in Franchise History

C	Bill Dickey (1,708)
1B	Lou Gehrig (2,137)
2B	Willie Randolph (1,688)
3B	Graig Nettles (1,509)
SS	**DEREK JETER (2,274)**
LF	Roy White (1,521)
CF	Bernie Williams (1,856)
RF	Hank Bauer (1,195)
DH	Don Baylor (403)

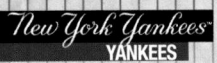

Jeter's League Championship Series Record

Year	Club vs. Opp.	AVG	G	AB	R	H	2B	3B	HR	RBI	SH	SF	HP	BB	SO	SB	CS	E	OBP	SLG
1996	NYY vs. BAL	.417	5	24	5	10	2	0	1	1	0	0	0	0	5	2	0	0	.417	.625
1998	NYY vs. CLE	.200	6	25	3	5	1	1	0	2	2	0	0	2	5	3	0	0	.259	.320
1999	NYY vs. BOS	.350	5	20	3	7	1	0	1	3	0	0	0	2	3	0	0	2	.409	.550
2000	NYY vs. SEA	.318	6	22	6	7	0	0	2	5	0	0	0	6	7	1	0	0	.464	.591
2001	NYY vs. SEA	.118	5	17	0	2	0	0	0	2	1	1	0	2	2	0	0	0	.200	.118
2003	NYY vs. BOS	.233	7	30	3	7	2	0	1	2	0	0	0	2	4	1	0	0	.281	.400
2004	NYY vs. BOS	.200	7	30	5	6	1	0	0	5	2	0	0	6	2	1	0	2	.333	.233
2009	NYY vs. LAA	.259	6	27	5	7	0	0	2	3	0	0	0	6	5	0	1	1	.394	.481
2010	NYY vs. TEX	.231	6	26	2	6	3	1	0	1	0	0	0	2	7	0	0	0	.286	.423
LCS Totals		**.258**	**53**	**221**	**32**	**57**	**10**	**2**	**7**	**24**	**5**	**1**	**0**	**28**	**40**	**8**	**1**	**5**	**.340**	**.416**

Jeter's World Series Record

Year	Club vs. Opp.	AVG	G	AB	R	H	2B	3B	HR	RBI	SH	SF	HP	BB	SO	SB	CS	E	OBP	SLG
1996	NYY vs. ATL	.250	6	20	5	5	0	0	0	1	1	0	1	4	6	1	0	2	.400	.250
1998	NYY vs. SD	.353	4	17	4	6	0	0	0	1	0	0	0	3	3	0	0	0	.450	.353
1999	NYY vs. ATL	.353	4	17	4	6	1	0	0	1	0	0	0	1	3	3	1	0	.389	.412
2000	NYY vs. NYM	.409	5	22	6	9	2	1	2	2	0	0	0	3	8	0	0	0	.480	.864
2001	NYY vs. ARI	.148	7	27	3	4	0	0	1	1	0	0	1	0	6	0	0	0	.179	.259
2003	NYY vs. FLA	.346	6	26	5	9	3	0	0	2	0	0	1	1	7	0	0	1	.393	.462
2009	NYY VS. PHI	.407	6	27	5	11	3	0	0	1	0	0	0	1	6	0	0	0	.429	.519
World Series Totals		**.321**	**38**	**156**	**32**	**50**	**9**	**1**	**3**	**9**	**1**	**0**	**3**	**13**	**39**	**4**	**1**	**3**	**.384**	**.449**
POSTSEASON TOTALS		**.309**	**147**	**599**	**101**	**185**	**30**	**4**	**20**	**57**	**8**	**4**	**5**	**63**	**117**	**17**	**5**	**14**	**.377**	**.472**

Jeter's All-Star Game Record

Year	Club, Site	AVG	G	AB	R	H	2B	3B	HR	RBI	SH	SF	HP	BB	SO	SB	CS	E	OBP	SLG
1998	NYY, Colorado	.000	1	1	0	0	0	0	0	0	0	0	0	0	1	0	0	0	.000	.000
1999	NYY, Boston	.000	1	1	0	0	0	0	0	0	0	0	0	0	1	0	0	0	.000	.000
2000	NYY, Atlanta	1.000	1	3	1	3	1	0	0	2	0	0	0	0	0	0	0	0	1.000	1.333
2001	NYY, Seattle	1.000	1	1	1	1	0	0	1	1	0	0	0	0	0	0	0	0	1.000	4.000
2002	NYY, Milwaukee	.000	1	1	0	0	0	0	0	0	0	0	0	0	1	0	0	0	.000	.000
2004	NYY, Houston	1.000	1	3	1	3	0	0	0	0	0	0	0	0	0	0	0	0	1.000	1.000
2006	NYY, Pittsburgh	.000	1	3	0	0	0	0	0	0	0	0	0	0	2	0	0	0	.000	.000
2007	NYY, San Francisco	.333	1	3	0	1	0	0	0	0	0	0	0	0	0	0	0	0	.333	.333
2008	NYY, New York-AL	.333	1	3	0	1	0	0	0	0	0	0	0	0	0	1	0	0	.333	.333
2009	NYY, St. Louis	.000	1	2	2	0	0	0	0	0	0	0	1	0	0	0	0	0	.333	.000
2010	NYY, Los Angeles-AL	.500	1	2	0	1	0	0	0	0	0	0	0	1	1	0	0	0	.667	.500
All-Star Game Totals		**.435**	**11**	**23**	**5**	**10**	**1**	**0**	**1**	**3**	**0**	**0**	**1**	**1**	**6**	**1**	**0**	**0**	**.480**	**.609**

Jeter's World Baseball Classic Record

Year	Country, Site	AVG	G	AB	R	H	2B	3B	HR	RBI	SH	SF	HP	BB	SO	SB	CS	E	OBP	SLG
2006	USA, USA	.450	6	20	5	9	0	1	0	1	1	0	1	2	1	0	0	2	.522	.550
2009	USA, USA	.276	8	29	2	8	2	0	0	0	0	0	1	4	1	0	1	1	.382	.345
WBC Totals		**.347**	**14**	**49**	**7**	**17**	**2**	**1**	**0**	**1**	**1**	**0**	**2**	**6**	**2**	**0**	**1**	**3**	**.439**	**.429**

Jeter's Career Fielding Record

Position	PCT	G	PO	A	E	TC	DP
Shortstop	.976	2295	3341	5718	219	9278	1227

Jeter's Career Home Run Chart

MULTI-HOMER GAMES: 9. **TWO HOMER GAMES:** 9, last on 6/12/10 vs. Houston. **GRAND SLAMS:** 1, 6/18/06 vs. Chicago-NL (Joe Borowski). **PINCH-HIT HR:** None. **INSIDE-THE-PARK HR:** 2, last on 7/22/10 vs. Kansas City (Bruce Chen). **WALK-OFF HR:** 1, on 4/5/05 vs. Boston (Keith Foulke). **LEADOFF HR:** 24, last on 6/12/10 vs. Houston (Wandy Rodriguez).

Sheppard Honored by Congress

On November 16, 2010, Congresswoman Carolyn McCarthy (NY-04) issued the following statement in support of House Resolution 1529, commending Bob Sheppard – the Voice of Yankee Stadium – for his respected career as the public-address announcer for the New York Yankees and the New York Giants. The resolution was voice-voted and there was no opposition.

18

ANDRUW JONES

OUTFIELDER • 6-1 • 210 • B/T: RIGHT/RIGHT • OPENING DAY AGE: 33

BIRTHDATE
April 23, 1977

BIRTHPLACE
Willemstad, Curacao

RESIDES
Duluth, Ga.

M.L. SERVICE
14 years, 47 days

CAREER HIGHLIGHTS:
N.L. Gold Glove Award
▸ 1998, 1999, 2000, 2001, 2002, 2003, 2004, 2005, 2006, 2007

Silver Slugger Award
▸ 2005

N.L. All-Star Game
▸ 2000, 2002, 2003, 2005, 2006

Hank Aaron Award
▸ 2005

***Sporting News* Player of the Year**
▸ 2005

MLBPA Players Choice Player of the Year
▸ 2005

***Baseball America* Minor League Player of the Year**
▸ 1995, 1996

***USA Today* Minor League Player of the Year**
▸ 1995, 1996

Topps Minor League Player of the Year
▸ 1996

STATUS
▸ Signed by the Yankees as a free agent to a one-year contract on February 14, 2011.

CAREER
▸ Has hit 407 career home runs, tied for 46th all-time with Duke Snider and ranking ninth among active players...his 1,222RBI rank 14th among active players.

▸ Is one of four players all time with at least 400 career home runs and 10 Gold Glove Awards, joining Ken Griffey Jr., Willie Mays and Mike Schmidt.

▸ Hit 342 home runs before turning 30, tying Mel Ott and Hank Aaron for sixth-most HR at that age in Major League history.

▸ Has seven seasons of at least 30HR, five seasons of at least 100RBI and four seasons of at least 100R...hit at least 25HR in 10 straight seasons from 1998-2007, tied for the sixth-most such seasons among active players.

▸ Won 10 consecutive Gold Glove Awards from 1998-2007...is one of just five outfielders in Major League history to win the honor at least 10 times, joining Roberto Clemente (12), Willie Mays (12), Ken Griffey Jr. (10) and Al Kaline (10), and is one of 15 players all-time with at least 10 Gold Gloves.

▸ Owns a .992 (39 E/4,597 TC) fielding percentage in 1,724 career games in center field.

▸ Is a five-time National League All-Star and has appeared in four Midsummer Classics with a .500 (4-for-8) career batting average, 2HR and 6RBI.

▸ Reached the postseason in 10 straight seasons with Atlanta from 1996-2005, and is a career .273 (65-for-238) batter in the playoffs with 8 doubles, 10HR and 33RBI in 75 games...has twice appeared in the World Series in 1996 and 1999 with Atlanta...in his first career World Series contest (Game 1 in 1996), went 3-for-4 with 3R, 2HR and 5RBI at the original Yankee Stadium, homering in each of his first two World Series at-bats to join Oakland's Gene Tenance (1972) as the only players all time to accomplish the feat.

BESTS & STREAKS

Hits
5 – 2 times
Last: at STL, 7/18/06
Runs
4 – 2 times
Last: vs. BAL, 4/15/09
2B
3 – at MON, 7/14/02
3B
2 – at MIL, 6/2/98
HR
3 – 2 times
Last: at LAA, 7/8/09
RBI
6 – 2 times
Last: at STL, 7/18/06
BB
3 – 13 times
Last: vs. WAS, 8/26/06
SO
5 – 2 times
Last: vs. FLA, 7/12/08
SB
3 – at CHC, 5/21/99
Hit Streak
14 games, 8/13-27/99

2010
▸ Hit .230 (64-for-208) with 12 doubles, 19HR and 48RBI in 107 games (41 starts in RF, 13 in CF, 12 in LF and 10 at DH) in his lone season with Chicago-AL...marked his highest average, on-base percentage (.341) and slugging percentage (.486) since 2006.

▸ Finished the season with 407 career home runs, passing the following players in 2010: Johnny Bench, Graig Nettles, Joe Carter, Dale Murphy, Andres Galarraga and Al Kaline...averaged 1HR/14.63AB.

▸ Batted .256 (22-for-86) with 8HR vs. left-handers and .219 (42-for-192) with 11HR vs. righties...hit .337 (28-for-83) during the day and .185 (36-for-195) at night...was 9-for-11 in stolen base attempts, his most steals since 2001 (11).

▸ Made his White Sox debut in Opening Day win on 4/5 vs. Cleveland (0-for-1)...drove in the winning run with a pinch-hit single on 4/11 vs. Minnesota.

- Hit 2HR on 4/23 vs. Seattle on his 33rd birthday, including his seventh career "walk-off" homer…became the first player since Alex Rodriguez on 7/27/02 (w/Texas vs. Oakland) to hit two or more homers, including a "walk-off," on his birthday.
- Recorded his 40th career multi-homer game on 5/1 at the Yankees, becoming the first opposing player to hit two or more home runs in a single game at the original and current Yankee Stadiums.
- Stole his 150th career base on 7/5 vs. Los Angeles-AL…appeared in his 2,000th career game on 8/15 vs. Detroit…hit his fifth career grand slam on 9/12 vs. Kansas City and first as a pinch hitter.
- Hit his 400th career HR in 7/11 win vs. Kansas City, a three-run homer off Andy Lerew in the third inning.
- Closed out the season with 14 hits in his last 34 at-bats (.412) and batted .375 (18-for-48) after 8/15.

2009

- Joined Texas for his first season in the American League, batting .214 (60-for-281) with 43R, 18 doubles, 17HR and 43RBI in 82 games…made a team-high 53 starts at DH, 12 in LF, five in RF and four at 1B.
- Hit all 17 home runs in his first 58 games, going homerless in his final 24 contests.
- Made his first career appearance at 1B on 4/23 at Toronto…had made 1,743 Major League starts, all in the outfield, prior that game.
- Led the AL with 8HR in July…recorded his second career three-homer game in 7/8 win at Los Angeles-AL.

2008

- Was limited to 75 games in his lone season with Los Angeles-NL, batting .158 (33-for-209) with 3HR and 14RBI…endured three separate stints on the disabled list with right knee injuries, marking his first career trips to the D.L.
- Went on the 15-day disabled list on 5/25 with torn cartilage in his right knee and underwent surgery on 5/27…was reinstated on 7/4 and played in 31 games (.153, 11-for-72) before returning to the 15-day disabled list on 8/10 with patellar tendinitis in the knee…was activated on 9/1 and played in one game (9/9 at San Diego) before going on the 60-day disabled list on 9/13.
- Following the season, played in five games for Aguilas in the Dominican Winter League.

2007

- In his final season with Atlanta, hit .222 (127-for-572) with 83R, 27 doubles, 26HR and 94RBI…finished second on the club in home runs and third in RBI.
- Won his 10th straight Gold Glove Award, becoming the fifth outfielder in Major League history to win at least 10 times.
- Scored his 1,000th career run on 7/4 vs. Los Angeles-NL.

2006

- Appeared in 156 games with Atlanta, batting .262 (148-for-565) with 107R, 29 doubles, 41HR and a career-high 129RBI…ranked fourth in the NL in RBI and tied for fifth in home runs…finished 11th in the NL Most Valuable Player voting…was named to the NL All-Star team, but did not play.
- Received his ninth consecutive Gold Glove Award…collected his 1,500th hit on 7/14 at San Diego…was NL "Co-Player of the Week" for 9/18-24…played for the Netherlands in the inaugural World Baseball Classic.

MOST SEASONS 30HR AND 100RBI, ACTIVE OUTFIELDERS

1.	Manny Ramirez	11
2.	Vladimir Guerrero	8
3.	ANDRUW JONES	5
4.	5 tied	4

ACTIVE HR LEADERS

1.	ALEX RODRIGUEZ	613
2.	Jim Thome	589
3.	Manny Ramirez	555
4.	Vladimir Guerrero	436
5.	Chipper Jones	436
6.	Jason Giambi	415
7.	Albert Pujols	408
8.	ANDRUW JONES	407

MOST HOMERS BY A CENTER FIELDER IN ONE SEASON

No.	Name	Team, Year
56	Ken Griffey, Jr.	Seattle, 1998
56	Hack Wilson	Chicago-NL, 1930
54	Mickey Mantle	New York-AL, 1961
54	Ken Griffey, Jr.	Seattle, 1997
52	Mickey Mantle	New York-AL, 1956
51	Willie Mays	New York-NL, 1955
51	Willie Mays	San Francisco, 1965
51	Brady Anderson	Baltimore, 1996
51	ANDRUW JONES	Atlanta, 2005

MOST GAMES OF THREE-OR-MORE HITS IN POSTSEASON PLAY, ALL-TIME

1.	DEREK JETER	12
2.	Bernie Williams	11
3.	Roberto Alomar	9
4.	ANDRUW JONES	8
	Kenny Lofton	8
	Manny Ramirez	8

MOST ASSISTS BY CF SINCE 1996

1.	Carlos Beltran	109
	Jim Edmonds	109
3.	ANDRUW JONES	102
4.	Kenny Lofton	87
5.	Steve Finley	79
	Torii Hunter	79

MOST CAREER HR AT TIME ACQUIRED BY THE YANKEES

1.	Jose Canseco (2000)	440
2.	ANDRUW JONES (2011)	407
3.	Gary Sheffield (2003)	379
4.	Rocky Colavito (1968)	369
5.	ALEX RODRIGUEZ (2004)	345

2005

▸ Finished second in NL MVP voting, batting .263 (154-for-586) with 95R, 24 doubles, 51HR and 128RBI in 160 games with the Braves…led the Majors in homers and topped the NL in RBI…garnered 351 points in MVP voting, 27 behind Albert Pujols.

▸ His 51HR tied for the sixth-highest total by a centerfielder…became the first player in Atlanta Braves history to record back-to-back 40-homer seasons and the first to lead the NL in that department since Dale Murphy in 1985…also ranked among the NL leaders in total bases (fourth, 337), extra-base hits (tied for fourth, 78) and slugging percentage (fifth, .575).

▸ Was selected as "Player of the Year" in player voting by the *Sporting News* and in the MLBPA Players Choice Awards…also earned his first career Silver Slugger Award and his eighth straight Gold Glove Award.

▸ Named to his fourth career All-Star Game, homering off Kenny Rogers in the contest.

▸ Was named NL "Player of the Month" for June (13HR, 26RBI) and August (11HR, 29RBI)…also honored as NL "Player of the Week" for 6/20-26 and 9/5-11.

▸ Hit his 300th career home run in 9/14 loss at Philadelphia, becoming the fourth-youngest Major Leaguer to reach the milestone (28 years, 144 days), and youngest ever in the NL.

▸ Led the team with a .471 (8-for-17) average in the NLDS loss vs. Houston, with 5R, 3 doubles, 1HR and 5RBI in four games.

2004

▸ Batted .261 (149-for-570) with 85R, 34 doubles, 29HR and 91RBI in 154 games with the Braves…ranked third on the team in home runs and RBI.

▸ Won his seventh consecutive Gold Glove Award.

▸ Hit his 250th career HR in 9/24 win vs. Florida off Ismael Valdez.

▸ Hit safely in all five postseason games in Atlanta's NLDS loss vs. Houston, batting .526 (10-for-19) with 2HR and 5RBI.

2003

▸ Hit .277 (165-for-595) with 101R, 28 doubles, 36HR and 116RBI in 156 games with the Braves…ranked seventh in the NL in RBI and tied for 10th in home runs.

▸ Was named to his third NL All-Star Team and went 2-2 with 2R, 1 double, 1HR (Mark Mulder) and 3RBI…won his sixth consecutive Gold Glove Award.

▸ Reached base safely in 34 consecutive games from 4/20-5/27…set a franchise record with at least 1RBI in nine straight games from 4/29-5/8.

▸ Collected his 1,000th career hit on 5/30 at the Mets…hit his 200th career HR in 6/7 win vs. Pittsburgh, becoming the seventh-youngest player in history to reach the milestone (26 years, 45 days).

▸ Had 1H in 17AB (.059) in Atlanta's NLDS loss vs. Chicago, drawing a team-high 4BB.

2002

▸ Hit .264 (148-for-560) with 91R, 34 doubles, 35HR and 94RBI in 154 games with the Braves…ranked ninth in the NL in homers…won his fifth consecutive Gold Glove Award…earned his second All-Star team selection.

▸ Was named NL "Player of the Week" for 6/3-9…homered in four consecutive at-bats from 9/7-10, tying a Major League record, the 33rd time the feat was accomplished…recorded his first career three-homer game in 9/25 win at Philadelphia.

▸ Missed consecutive starts on 8/3-4 vs. St. Louis with right shoulder tendinitis, missing action for the first time since 9/27-28/97.

▸ Batted .316 (6-for-19) in the Braves' NLDS loss vs. eventual NL-champion San Francisco.

2001

▸ Appeared in 161 games with the Braves, batting .251 (157-for-625) with 104R, 25 doubles, 34HR, 104RBI and 11SB…led the Braves in RBI and was second in home runs…tied for fourth in the NL in games played and was sixth in at-bats.

▸ Won his fourth straight Gold Glove Award…became the fourth outfielder in Braves history with 100-plus RBI in back-to-back seasons, joining Wally Berger (1933-35), Hank Aaron (1961-62) and Dale Murphy (1982-85)…played in every inning until sitting out last three frames on 8/28.

▸ Combined to hit .310 (9-for-29) with 6R, 2HR and 2RBI in the postseason, appearing in all eight games…hit safely in five consecutive AB over NLDS Games 1 and 2 and finished the series sweep with a .500 average (6-for-12).

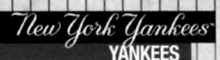

2000

- Hit .303 (199-for-656) with 122R, 36 doubles, 6 triples, 36HR, 104RBI and 21SB in 161 games with the Braves, setting career highs in average, runs, hits and doubles…led the NL in at-bats and ranked third in hits and multi-hit games (59), tied for fourth in games played, and was fifth in runs scored and total bases (355).
- Won his third straight Gold Glove Award and was named to his first career All-Star team…joined Hank Aaron as the only Braves with 20HR and 20SB in at least three straight seasons…had his streak of 301 consecutive games played snapped on 8/27 (sore legs).
- Went 1-for-9 (.111) with 3R and 1HR in the NLDS as the Braves were swept by the Cardinals.

1999

- Played in all 162 games with the Braves, batting .275 (163-for-592) with 97R, 35 doubles, 5 triples, 26HR, 84RBI and 24SB.
- Won his second straight Gold Glove Award…tied for sixth in the NL with 13 outfield assists.
- With 26HR and 24SB, joined Chipper Jones (45HR/25SB) as the first-ever Braves teammates with 20-or-more homers and steals in the same season.
- Combined to hit .185 (10-for-54) with 7R, 1 doubles and 3RBI in 14 postseason games…drew bases-loaded "walk-off" walk in NLCS Game 6 vs. the Mets to give Braves 10-9 win in 11 innings and the NL pennant.

1998

- Hit .271 (158-for-582) with 89R, 33 doubles, 8 triples, 31HR, 90RBI and 27SB in 159 games with the Braves…tied for fifth in the NL in triples and tied for sixth in stolen bases…became the sixth-youngest player in Major League history to hit at least 30HR in a season…also became the youngest player in history to record 20HR/20SB in season.
- Won the first of his 10 consecutive Gold Glove Awards as a center fielder…recorded a career-high 20 assists, tying Florida's Mark Kotsay for the NL lead.
- Hit his 50th career home run on 9/6 at the Mets, becoming the third-youngest player in history to reach that milestone (21 years and four months and 14 days) behind Mel Ott and Tony Conigliaro.
- Hit .194 (6-for-31) with 5R, 1HR and 3RBI in nine postseason games…went hitless (0-for-9) in the NLDS vs. Chicago, then rebounded to hit .273 (6-for-22) in the NLCS loss vs. San Diego.

1997

- In his first full Major League season, batted .231 (92-for-399) with 60R, 18 doubles, 18HR and 70RBI in 153 games…tied for third in the NL with 14 outfield assists…recorded three game-winning hits in extra innings.
- Was named to the Topps Rookie All-Star Team and finished fifth in the NL "Rookie of the Year" Award voting.
- Appeared in eight postseason games (three starts in RF), batting .286 (4-for-15) with 1R and 2RBI…went 0-for-5 in the NLDS win vs. Houston.

1996

- The *Baseball America, Baseball Weekly, USA Today* and TOPPS "Minor League Player of the Year" saw his first Major League action after being recalled on 8/14…hit .217 (23-for-106) with 5HR and 13RBI in 31 games.
- Made his Major League debut in 8/15 win at Philadelphia, and at 19 years, 3 months and 23 days old became the fourth-youngest player in Braves history…went 1-for-5 with a ninth-inning RBI single off Toby Borland for his first hit…homered the following day vs. Pittsburgh off Denny Neagle, becoming the youngest NL player to hit a HR since Houston's Larry Dierker in 1965.
- Recorded his first career multi-homer game in 8/22 loss vs. Cincinnati, homering twice to become the youngest player to accomplish that feat since the Cubs' Danny Murphy in 1961.
- Combined to hit .339 (151-for-445) with 34HR, 92 RBI and 30SB in 116 games with Single-A Durham, Double-A Greenville and Triple-A Richmond prior to recall…with Durham, ranked second in the Carolina League in home runs (17) and RBI (43) when he was promoted to Greenville on 6/19…was named to the Carolina League All-Star Team…played in just 12 games at the Triple-A level, hitting .378 (17-for-45), before joining the Major League squad.
- Hit .345 (10-for-29) with 7R, 1 doubles, 3HR, 9RBI and 7BB in 14 postseason games…appeared in all three NLDS games vs. Los Angeles with no at-bats…went 2-for-9 in NLCS win vs. St. Louis, with both hits coming in Game 7 win…singled in the second inning for his first career playoff hit, and homered in sixth off Mark Petkovsek becoming the youngest player ever to hit a HR in the postseason (surpassing Mickey Mantle)
- Homered in each of his first two World Series at-bats against the Yankees, becoming the second player ever to accomplish the feat (also Gene Tenace w/ Oakland in 1972) and youngest player ever to homer in the WS…his 5RBI in the Game 1 win tied the NL single-game WS record…hit .400 (8-for-20) with 4R, 1 double, 2HR and 6RBI overall in the Series.

1995

▸ Named the "Minor League Player of the Year" by *Baseball America* and *USA Today* after hitting .277 (149-for-537) with 41 doubles, 25HR, 100RBI and 50SB with Single-A Macon…led all minor-leaguers in extra-base hits, ranked third in runs, tied for fourth in doubles and seventh in steals…was the first minor leaguer since Don Zimmer in 1950 with at least 20HR, 100RBI and 50SB…led the South Atlantic League in runs scored (104), extra-base hits (71) and SB and was second in doubles, third in homers and fourth in RBI.

1994

▸ In his first professional action, combined to hit .290 (69-for-238) with 21SB with the GCL Braves and Single-A Danville.

PERSONAL

▸ Married to Nicole…has two children, Druw and Madison…attended St. Paulus T.C. School in Willemstad, Curacao…upon his debut on 8/15/96, became the third player born in Curacao to reach the Major Leagues, joining Yankees outfielder Hensley Meulens and Florida infielder Ralph Milliard.

▸ Donated $50,000 to the Atlanta chapter of Jaden's Ladder, a charity that aids abused women, in 2006…was the Atlanta Braves' nominee for the 2005 Marvin Miller Man of the Year Award…is an annual sponsor of Curacao's Little League All-Star Team, which won the World Series in 2004.

Jones' Career Batting Record

Year	Club	AVG	G	AB	R	H	2B	3B	HR	RBI	SH	SF	HP	BB	SO	SB	CS	E	OBP	SLG
1994	GCL Braves	.221	27	95	22	21	5	1	2	10	0	0	2	16	19	5	2	3	.345	.358
	Danville	.336	36	143	20	48	9	2	1	16	0	1	3	9	25	16	9	2	.385	.448
1995	Macon	.277	*139	537	*104	149	41	5	25	100	0	9	16	70	122	56	11	4	.372	.512
1996	Durham	.313	66	243	65	76	14	3	17	43	0	1	3	42	54	16	4	7	.419	.605
	Greenville	.369	38	157	39	58	10	1	12	37	0	1	1	17	34	12	4	1	.432	.675
	Richmond	.378	12	45	11	17	3	1	5	12	0	0	0	1	9	2	2	1	.391	.822
	ATLANTA	.217	31	106	11	23	7	1	5	13	0	0	0	7	29	3	0	2	.265	.443
1997	ATLANTA	.231	153	399	60	92	18	1	18	70	5	3	4	56	107	20	11	7	.329	.416
1998	ATLANTA	.271	159	582	89	158	33	8	31	90	1	4	4	40	129	27	4	2	.321	.515
1999	ATLANTA	.275	*162	592	97	163	35	5	26	84	0	2	9	76	103	24	12	10	.365	.483
2000	ATLANTA	.303	161	*656	122	199	36	6	36	104	0	5	9	59	100	21	6	2	.366	.541
2001	ATLANTA	.251	161	625	104	157	25	2	34	104	0	9	3	56	142	11	4	6	.312	.461
2002	ATLANTA	.264	154	560	91	148	34	0	35	94	0	6	10	83	135	8	3	3	.366	.513
2003	ATLANTA	.277	156	595	101	165	28	2	36	116	0	6	5	53	125	4	3	3	.338	.513
2004	ATLANTA	.261	154	570	85	149	34	4	29	91	0	2	3	71	147	6	6	3	.345	.488
2005	ATLANTA	.263	160	586	95	154	24	3	*51	*128	0	7	15	64	112	5	3	2	.347	.575
2006	ATLANTA	.262	156	565	107	148	29	0	41	129	0	9	13	82	127	4	1	2	.363	.531
2007	ATLANTA	.222	154	572	83	127	27	2	26	94	0	9	8	70	138	5	2	2	.311	.413
2008	LOS ANGELES-NL+	.158	75	209	21	33	8	1	3	14	0	1	1	27	76	0	1	1	.256	.249
	Las Vegas	.323	11	31	7	10	0	0	4	11	0	2	0	3	5	2	0	0	.361	.710
2009	TEXAS – e, f	.214	82	281	43	60	18	0	17	43	0	3	2	45	72	5	1	0	.323	.459
	Frisco	.222	3	9	0	2	0	0	0	0	0	0	0	3	1	1	0	0	.417	.222
2010	CHICAGO-AL – g	.230	107	278	41	64	12	1	19	48	0	2	3	45	73	9	2	3	.341	.486
Minor League Totals		**.302**	**332**	**1260**	**268**	**381**	**82**	**13**	**66**	**229**	**0**	**14**	**25**	**161**	**269**	**110**	**32**	**18**	**.388**	**.545**
AL Totals		**.222**	**189**	**559**	**84**	**124**	**30**	**1**	**36**	**91**	**0**	**5**	**5**	**90**	**145**	**14**	**3**	**3**	**.332**	**.472**
NL Totals		**.259**	**1836**	**6617**	**1066**	**1716**	**338**	**35**	**371**	**1131**	**6**	**63**	**84**	**744**	**1470**	**138**	**56**	**45**	**.339**	**.489**
Major League Totals		**.256**	**2025**	**7176**	**1150**	**1840**	**368**	**36**	**407**	**1222**	**6**	**68**	**89**	**834**	**1615**	**152**	**59**	**48**	**.338**	**.488**

* League Leader

Signed as a free agent by the Atlanta Braves on July 2, 1993.

+ – Transactions a through d

a – Signed by Los Angeles-NL as a free agent on December 12, 2007.

b – Placed on the 15-day disabled list with a right knee meniscus tear from May 24 - July 4, 2008.

c – Placed on the 15-day disabled list with left knee patella tendinitis from August 12 - September 1, 2008.

d – Placed on the 60-day DL with a sore right knee from September 13 - November 4, 2008.

e – Signed by Texas as a minor league free agent on February 11, 2009.

f – Placed on the 15-day disabled list with a strained left hamstring form August 24 - September 8, 2009.

g – Signed by Chicago-AL as a free agent on November 25. 2009.

h – Signed by the Yankees as a free agent on February 14, 2011.

Jones' Division Series Record

Year	Club vs. Opp	AVG	G	AB	R	H	2B	3B	HR	RBI	SH	SF	HP	BB	SO	SB	CS	E	OBP	SLG
1996	ATL vs. LAD	.000	3	0	0	0	0	0	0	0	0	0	0	1	0	0	0	0	1.000	.000
1997	ATL vs. HOU	.000	3	5	1	0	0	0	0	1	0	0	0	1	1	0	0	0	.167	.000
1998	ATL vs. CHC	.000	3	9	2	0	0	0	0	1	0	1	0	3	2	2	0	0	.231	.000
1999	ATL vs. HOU	.222	4	18	1	4	1	0	0	2	0	0	0	1	3	0	0	0	.263	.278
2000	ATL vs. STL	.111	3	9	3	1	0	0	0	1	0	0	0	4	1	0	1	0	.385	.444
2001	ATL vs. HOU	.500	3	12	2	6	0	0	1	1	0	0	0	0	3	0	0	0	.500	.750
2002	ATL vs. SF	.316	5	19	4	6	1	0	0	2	0	0	0	2	3	0	0	0	.381	.368
2003	ATL vs. CHC	.059	5	17	1	1	0	0	0	1	0	0	0	4	7	0	0	1	.238	.059
2004	ATL vs. HOU	.526	5	19	4	10	2	0	0	5	0	0	0	2	3	1	0	0	.571	.947
2005	ATL vs. HOU	.471	4	17	5	8	3	0	1	5	0	1	0	2	3	0	0	0	.524	.824
Division Series Totals		**.288**	**38**	**125**	**23**	**36**	**7**	**0**	**5**	**19**	**0**	**2**	**1**	**20**	**26**	**3**	**1**	**1**	**.385**	**.464**

Jones' Championship Series Record

Year	Club vs. Opp	AVG	G	AB	R	H	2B	3B	HR	RBI	SH	SF	HP	BB	SO	SB	CS	E	OBP	SLG
1996	ATL vs. STL	.222	5	9	3	2	0	0	1	3	0	0	0	3	2	0	0	0	.417	.556
1997	ATL vs. FLA	.444	5	9	0	4	0	0	0	1	0	0	0	1	1	0	0	0	.500	.444
1998	ATL vs. SD	.273	6	22	3	6	0	0	1	2	0	1	0	1	4	1	0	0	.292	.409
1999	ATL vs. NYM	.217	6	23	5	5	0	0	0	1	1	0	0	4	3	0	1	0	.333	.217
2001	ATL vs. ARI	.176	5	17	4	3	0	0	1	1	0	0	0	1	5	0	0	1	.222	.353
LCS Totals		**.250**	**27**	**80**	**15**	**20**	**0**	**0**	**3**	**8**	**1**	**1**	**0**	**10**	**15**	**1**	**1**	**0**	**.330**	**.363**

Jones' World Series Record

Year	Club vs. Opp	AVG	G	AB	R	H	2B	3B	HR	RBI	SH	S	HP	BB	SO	SB	CS	E	OBP	SLG
1996	ATL vs. NYY	.400	6	20	4	8	1	0	2	6	0	0	1	3	6	1	2	0	.500	.750
1999	ATL vs. NYY	.077	4	13	1	1	0	0	0	0	0	0	0	1	3	0	0	0	.143	.077
World Series Totals		**.273**	**10**	**33**	**5**	**9**	**1**	**0**	**2**	**6**	**0**	**0**	**1**	**16**	**9**	**1**	**2**	**0**	**.368**	**.485**
POSTSEASON TOTALS		**.273**	**75**	**238**	**43**	**65**	**8**	**0**	**10**	**33**	**1**	**3**	**2**	**34**	**50**	**5**	**5**	**1**	**.365**	**.433**

Jones' All-Star Game Record

Year	Club, Site	AVG	G	AB	R	H	2B	3B	HR	RBI	SH	SF	HP	BB	SO	SB	CS	E	OBP	SLG
2000	ATL, Atlanta	.500	1	2	0	1	0	0	0	1	0	0	0	0	1	0	0	0	.500	.500
2002	ATL, Milwaukee	.000	1	3	0	0	0	0	0	0	0	0	0	0	2	0	0	0	.000	.000
2003	ATL, Chicago - AL	1.000	1	2	2	2	1	0	1	3	0	0	0	0	0	0	0	0	1.000	3.000
2005	ATL, Detroit	1.000	1	1	2	1	0	0	1	2	0	0	0	1	0	0	0	0	1.000	4.000
2006	ATL, Pittsburgh					Did Not Play														
All-Star Game Totals		**.500**	**4**	**8**	**4**	**4**	**1**	**0**	**2**	**6**	**0**	**0**	**0**	**1**	**3**	**0**	**0**	**0**	**.556**	**1.375**

Jones' World Baseball Classic Record

Year	Club, Site	AVG	G	AB	R	H	2B	3B	HR	RBI	SH	SF	HP	BB	SO	SB	CS	E	OBP	SLG
2006	Netherlands, P.R.	.000	2	6	0	0	0	0	0	0	0	0	0	2	2	0	0	0	.250	.000

Jones' Career Fielding Record

Position	Pct.	G	PO	A	E	TC
Outfield	.990	1920	4785	120	48	4953
First Base	1.000	8	32	1	0	33

Jones' Career Home Run Chart

MULTI-HOMER GAMES: 40; **TWO-HOMER GAMES:** 38, last on 5/1/10 at New York-AL; **THREE-HOMER GAMES:** 2, last on 7/8/09 at Los Angeles-AL; **GRAND SLAMS:** 5, last on 9/12/10 vs. Kansas City (Blake Wood as PH); **PINCH-HIT HR:** 3, last on 9/12/10 vs. Kansas City (Blake Wood-grand slam); **INSIDE-THE-PARK HR:** None; **WALK-OFF HR:** 7, last on 4/23/10 vs. Seattle (Mark Lowe); **LEADOFF HR:** None.

Yankees to Homer in Their First Career World Series At-Bat
According to *Elias Sports Bureau* Record Book

Chick Fewster	10/11/21 in Game 6 loss vs. the New York Giants off Jesse Barnes (second inning, 1 on)*
George Selkirk	9/30/36 in Game 1 loss at the New York Giants off Carl Hubbell (third inning, solo)
Elston Howard	9/28/55 in Game 1 win vs. Brooklyn off Don Newcombe (second inning, 1 on)
Roger Maris	10/5/60 in Game 1 loss at Pittsburgh off Vern Law (first inning, solo)
Jim Mason	10/19/76 in Game 3 loss vs. Cincinnati off Pat Zachry (seventh inning, solo) – pinch-hit homer was his only career World Series plate appearance.
Bob Watson	10/20/81 in Game 1 win vs. Los Angeles (NL) off Jerry Reuss (first inning, 2 on)

All but Fewster homered in their first plate appearance.

75 BRANDON LAIRD

INFIELDER • 6-1 • 215 • B/T: RIGHT/RIGHT • OPENING DAY AGE: 23

BIRTHDATE
September 11, 1987

BIRTHPLACE
Cypress, Calif.

RESIDES
Garden Grove, Calif.

M.L. SERVICE
None
(Rookie)

COLLEGE
Cypress College

STATUS
▸ Selected by the Yankees in the 27th round of the 2007 First-Year Player Draft…signed through the 2011 season.

CAREER NOTES
▸ Over the last three seasons (2008-10), has compiled 393H, 79 doubles, 61HR and 263RBI…is one of just five minor league players to reach those totals since 2008, joining Chris Carter (Oakland Athletics), John Lindsey (Los Angeles Dodgers), Mike Moustakas (Kansas City Royals) and Mark Trumbo (Los Angeles Angels).

2010
▸ Combined to bat .281 (149-for-531) with 86R, 28 doubles, 25HR and 102RBI in 138 games with Double-A Trenton and Triple-A Scranton/Wilkes-Barre, setting career highs in runs scored, home runs, RBI and games played…tied for 10th among all minor leaguers in RBI…led all Yankees minor leaguers in home runs and RBI and ranked ninth in batting average, collecting the most RBI by a Yankees farmhand since Cody Ehlers (106) in 2006…appeared in 128 games at 3B, six games at 1B and four games at DH.

▸ Began the season with Double-A Trenton and was named the Eastern League's "Most Valuable Player" and "Rookie of the Year" after batting .291 (119-for-409) with 73R, 22 doubles, 23HR and 90RBI in 107 games…ranked fifth in the Eastern League in home runs (23) and RBI (90)…had 1HR/17.78AB, fourth-best in the EL…was named to the Eastern League's midseason and postseason All-Star teams.

▸ With Trenton, batted .391 (45-for-115) with 73RBI with runners in scoring position and .390 (23-for-59) with 43RBI with RISP and two outs.

▸ Named the Eastern League "Player of the Month" in May, batting .339 (39-for-115) with 25R, 9 doubles, 1 triple, 6HR, 33RBI, a .591 slugging percentage and a .374 on-base percentage in 29 games…had 12 multi-hit games and 10 games with at least 2RBI…his 33RBI in May set a franchise-record and led all Eastern League players…also led the EL in total bases (68) and tied for the lead in runs scored…became just the second Trenton Thunder player to win an EL "Player of the Month" Award since the award began in 1997 (also David Eckstein in May 1999).

▸ Drove in a franchise-record and career-high 7RBI on 5/16 vs. Binghamton and 6/24 at Erie, going 3-for-5 and hitting a grand slam and three-run home run in each contest.

▸ Was named the Eastern League "Player of the Week" for the period ending 5/30, batting .341 (14-for-41) with 8R, 3 doubles, 1 triple, 2HR and 12RBI in 10 games…hit for the cycle with a ninth-inning, two-run "walk-off" home run vs. Erie SeaWolves on 5/26.

▸ Was promoted to Triple-A Scranton/Wilkes-Barre on 8/2, batting .246 (30-for-122) with 6 doubles, 2HR and 12RBI in 31 games…hit .370 (10-for-27) over his final seven games with Scranton/WB, raising his average from .211 to .246…was hitless in 15AB over four postseason games with Scranton/WB.

▸ Played for the Phoenix Desert Dogs in the Arizona Fall League after the season, batting .236 (26-for-110) with 10 doubles and 22RBI in 27 games…appeared in LF (22 games), DH (four games) and 1B (one game)…named to the AFL Rising Stars team.

▸ Attended spring training with the Yankees as a non-roster invitee, batting .267 (8-for-30) in 13 games.

▸ Following the season, was rated by Baseball America as the 10th-best prospect in the Yankees organization…was also named to the *Sporting News* "All-Minor League Team" at third base.

▸ Was added to the Yankees' 40-man roster on 11/19/10.

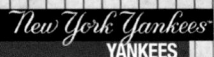
2009

▸ Batted .266 (120-for-451) with 20 doubles, 13HR and 75RBI in 124 games with Single-A Tampa…tied for third among all Yankees minor leaguers and led the Florida State League in RBI…was named to the FSL postseason All-Star team.

▸ Led the team with 8RBI in seven playoff games for the FSL-champion Yankees.

▸ Following the season, played for Surprise in the Arizona Fall League, batting .333 (30-for-90) with 18R, 9 doubles, 6HR and 24RBI in 22 games and was named to the AFL top prospects team.

2008

▸ Hit .273 (124-for-454) with 71R, 31 doubles, 23HR and 86RBI in 122 games with Single-A Charleston…led all Yankees farmhands in homers and ranked second in RBI…hit .333 (20-for-60) with 4HR and 26RBI with RISP and two outs.

▸ Split time between first base and third base, batting .310 (98-for-316) with 60R, 23 doubles, 20HR and 73RBI as a first baseman and .171 (22-for-129) with 9R, 6 doubles, 3HR and 11RBI as a third baseman.

▸ Batted .324 (34-for-105) with 24R, 7 doubles, 11HR and 37RBI during the month of August.

2007

▸ Made his professional debut with the GCL Yankees, hitting .339 (57-for-168) with 27R, 14 doubles, 8HR and 29RBI in 45 games…ranked third among all Yankees farmhands in batting average…was named to the GCL postseason All-Star team.

PERSONAL

▸ Is the younger brother of St. Louis Cardinals catcher Gerald Laird.

▸ Was a two-year starter at Cypress College in California…played in 106-of-107 games combined over both seasons…in 2007, led his team in almost every major offensive category (average, runs, hits, doubles, home runs and RBI).

▸ Was named Orange County "Player of the Year" as a senior at La Quinta High School where he helped his team win the CIF Championship, playing games at Angel Stadium of Anaheim…was named to the *Los Angeles Times'* 2005 All-Star team…played on USA Baseball's junior national team in the summer of 2005.

▸ Was selected by Cleveland in the 27th round of the 2005 First-Year Player Draft but did not sign, opting to attend school…participated in the Gene Autry R.B.I. (Reviving Baseball in Inner Cities) program.

Laird's Career Playing Record

Year	Club	AVG	G	AB	R	H	2B	3B	HR	RBI	SH	SF	HP	BB	SO	SB	CS	E	OBP	SLG
2007	GCL Yankees	.339	45	168	27	57	14	1	8	29	1	1	2	6	26	0	0	7	.367	.577
2008	Charleston	.273	122	454	71	124	31	1	23	86	0	7	5	40	86	1	0	12	.334	.498
2009	Tampa	.266	124	451	53	120	20	4	13	75	0	5	6	39	75	1	1	16	.329	.415
2010	Trenton	.291	107	409	73	119	22	2	23	90	0	3	4	38	84	2	2	20	.355	.523
	Scranton/WB	.246	31	122	13	30	6	0	2	12	0	1	0	4	27	0	0	2	.268	.344
Minor League Totals		**.281**	**429**	**1604**	**237**	**450**	**93**	**8**	**69**	**292**	**1**	**17**	**17**	**127**	**298**	**4**	**3**	**57**	**.337**	**.478**

Selected by the Yankees in the 27th round of the 2007 First-Year Player Draft.

Two Great Sports Brands Unite

On October 20, 2008, the New York Yankees and Dallas Cowboys, along with Goldman Sachs and Cic Partners, announced the founding of Legends Hospitality Management, LLC. Offering a broad range of sports business services, Legends will have the exclusive right to operate concessions, catering and merchandising services at the new, state-of-the-art Yankees and Cowboys stadiums. Legends will place an initial focus on operating catering, concessions, retail merchandising and other facility management enterprises for major sports and entertainment facilities with the intent to expand beyond the two anchor teams to provide its services to professional and college sports teams and other event facilities worldwide.

Led by Michael Rawlings, former President of Pizza Hut, Inc., Legends is headquartered in Newark, New Jersey, and will offer differentiated solutions to create innovative, high-quality stadium experiences for fans. For more information, please visit Legends' website at www.legendshm.com.

LEGENDS

48

BOONE LOGAN

LEFT-HANDED PITCHER • 6-5 • 223 • B/T: RIGHT/LEFT • OPENING DAY AGE: 26

BIRTHDATE
August 13, 1984

BIRTHPLACE
San Antonio, Texas

RESIDES
Helotes, Texas

M.L. SERVICE
3 years, 140 days

COLLEGE
Temple College (Tex.)

STATUS

▸ Acquired by the Yankees along with RHP Javier Vazquez from Atlanta in exchange for OF Melky Cabrera, LHP Mike Dunn and RHP Arodys Vizcaino on December 22, 2009…signed through the 2011 season.

2010

▸ Was 2-0 with a 2.93 ERA in 51 relief appearances over three stints with the Yankees (4/16-5/26, 6/15-7/2, 7/17-10/3)…opponents batted .231 (34-for-147, 3HR); LH .190 (15-for-79, 0HR), RH .279 (19-for-68, 3HR)…retired 38-of-51 first batters faced (74.5%)…prevented 24-of-31 inherited runners from scoring (77.4%)…appeared in consecutive games nine times and three straight games three times.

▸ Tossed less than 1.0 inning in 31 of his 51 relief outings (60.8%)…held opponents scoreless in 39 of the appearances…faced just one batter 13 times.

▸ Began the season allowing 22H and 9ER in 20.0IP (4.05 ERA) over his first 18 relief appearances (4/20-7/18)…over his final 33 outings (beginning 7/19), had a 1.80 ERA (20.0IP, 4ER), after taking over as the primary lefthander in the bullpen when Damaso Marte went on the disabled list.

▸ Was recalled from Triple-A Scranton/Wilkes-Barre prior to 4/16 win vs. Texas when RHP Chan Ho Park was placed on the 15-day disabled list.

▸ Made his Yankees debut in 4/20 win at Oakland, tossing 1.1 scoreless innings (2H, 1BB, 1K)…was optioned back to Scranton/WB on 5/26.

▸ Recalled for a second time on 6/15 when Sergio Mitre was placed on the 15-day disabled list…allowed 2ER in four outings (7.2IP) before being optioned again to Scranton/WB on 7/2.

▸ Tossed 2.2 scoreless innings (1BB, 3K) in 6/16 loss vs. Philadelphia…was his longest outing since 4/25/07 w/ Chicago-AL vs. Detroit (3.0IP) and the longest scoreless outing of his career.

▸ Recalled for a third time on 7/17 when Marte went on the D.L., remaining with the Yankees for the rest of the season…limited left-handed hitters to a .148 average (8-for-54) over the stretch…held left-handers hitless in 20 consecutive at-bats against him from 6/29-8/14.

▸ Compiled a streak of 25 consecutive scoreless outings from 7/21-9/13…was the second-longest streak by a Yankees hurler since 1920, trailing only a 28-game scoreless stretch for Mariano Rivera from 7/22-10/2/99…had the streak snapped after surrendering a three-run pinch-hit HR to Willy Aybar in 9/14 win at Tampa Bay…during the stretch, allowed just 8H and 6BB with 18K in 15.1IP…held opponents hitless in 11 straight outings from 7/25-8/13.

▸ Tossed a perfect seventh inning for his first win as a Yankee on 8/21 vs. Seattle (1.0IP).

▸ Held opposing left-handed batters to 3H in their final 17AB against him.

BESTS & STREAKS

Low hit CG
N/A
IP (start)
N/A
IP (relief)
3.0 - 2 times
Last: vs. DET, 4/25/07
Hits
6 - at TB, 5/16/06
Runs
5 - 2 times
Last: vs. MIN, 7/6/07
BB
2 - 15 times
Last: at LAD, 6/26/10
SO
5 - at CLE, 5/2/06
HR
2 - 2 times
Last: at MIN 9/23/08
Winning Streak
2g - 2 times
Last: 8/21-9/26/10
Losing Streak
2g - 7/13-8/9/08

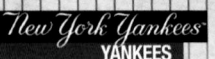

- Began the season with Scranton/WB, going 0-1 with a 2.11 ERA in 14 relief appearances (21.1IP, 5ER)…held left-handed batters to a .162 (6-for-37) batting average.
- Made his postseason debut, appearing in five games and allowing 2ER in 1.2IP (3H, 1BB, 1K).

2009

- In his first season with the Atlanta organization, split the year between the Braves and Triple-A Gwinnett…went 1-1 with a 5.19 ERA in 20 relief appearances with the Braves…opponents batted .292 (21-for-72, 1HR); LH .231 (9-for-39, 0HR), RH .364 (12-for-33, 1HR)…retired 16-of-20 first batters faced (80.0%)…stranded 11-of-13 inherited runners (84.6%)…eight of his appearances were less than 1.0IP…appeared in consecutive games once and three straight once (8/17-19).
- Was recalled from Gwinnett on 6/25 and made his Braves debut that night vs. the Yankees, allowing 2ER on 1H and 2BB in 1.1IP…did not allow an earned run over his next nine appearances from 6/30-7/29 (7.2IP).
- Went 22 days between outings from 8/27-9/17.
- Began the season with Gwinnett, going 4-2 with two saves and a 3.28 ERA in 29 relief appearances…held opponents scoreless in 19 of his outings and did not allow an earned run 21 times.

2008

- Made his second Opening Day roster and spent the majority of the season with the White Sox, going 2-3 with a 5.95 ERA in 55 relief appearances…established a career high with 42K and averaged 8.9K/9.0IP…30 of his outings were less than 1.0IP.
- Opponents batted .317 (57-for-180, 7HR); LH .291 (30-for-103, 5HR), RH .351 (27-for-77, 2HR)…marked the third-highest opponents batting average among AL relievers…retired 41-of-55 first batters faced (74.5%)…stranded 32-of-44 inherited runners (72.7%)…appeared in consecutive games nine times, three straight games twice and four straight once (4/20-24).
- Went 2-1 with a 1.95 ERA (32.1IP, 7ER) through his first 36 appearances of the season (through 7/9) with opponents batting .223 (27-for-121, 2HR)…posted an 0-2 record and an 18.90 ERA (10.0IP, 21ER) over his remaining 19 appearances from 7/10 until the end of the season as opponents batted .508 (30-for-59, 5HR).
- Made 17 straight scoreless outings from 4/29-6/14 (14.2 P) and held the opposition hitless in six consecutive games from 5/24-6/4 (20AB)…did not allow a run in 10 relief appearances in May (7.2IP).
- Was optioned to Triple-A Charlotte on 8/10 and recalled on 8/31…went 0-1 with a 6.00 ERA in five games with the Knights…worked to an 18.00 ERA (2.0IP, 4ER) in seven games following his return to the Sox.

2007

- Went 2-1 with a 4.97 ERA in 68 relief appearances in his first full season with the White Sox…tied for sixth in appearances among AL lefthanders and tied for 10th-most games on the club's all-time list by a lefthander…opponents batted .298 (59-for-198, 7HR); LH .221 (19-for-86, 1HR), RH .357 (40-for-112, 6HR)…tied Milwaukee's Brian Shouse for the Major League lead with 78 inherited runners, stranding 56 (71.8%)…retired 46-of-68 first batters faced (67.6%)…appeared in consecutive games 10 times, three consecutive games seven times and four straight games once (8/5-9).
- Of his 68 appearances, 48 were scoreless…40 of his outings were less than 1.0IP…posted a 2.88 ERA (25.0IP, 8ER) on the road, compared to a 7.01 mark (25.2IP, 20ER) at home.
- Matched his career high (second time) with 3.0IP in 4/25 loss vs. Detroit, allowing 2ER in 3.0 innings of relief (4H).
- Began the season with Triple-A Charlotte, going 0-1 with a 2.16 ERA and one save in four games with the Knights…was recalled from Charlotte on 4/17…earned his first Major League win on 4/24 at Kansas City (0.2IP, 1BB, 2K)…made eight straight scoreless appearances from 7/31-8/14 (8.0IP).

2006

- Saw his first Major League action, making the White Sox' Opening Day roster after not having appeared above Single-A in his professional career…became the first Sox player to jump from Single-A to the Majors in consecutive seasons since Mike Caruso in 1997 and 1998.
- Posted an 8.31 ERA with one save and no decisions in 21 relief appearances with the White Sox…opponents hit .288 (21-for-73, 2HR), including a .357 (10-for-28, 1HR) mark by lefthanders…first-batters faced were just 1-for-14 (.071)…appeared in inconsecutive games four times and three straight once (9/8-10).
- Made his Major League debut in 4/4 loss vs. Cleveland, tossing 2.0 scoreless innings…recorded his first career save on 4/25 at Seattle, allowing 1ER over a career-high 3.0IP…was optioned to Triple-A Charlotte on 5/16, going 3-1 with a 3.38 ERA and 11 saves in 38 relief appearances before being recalled on 9/1…compiled a 15.43 ERA (4.2IP, 8ER) in his second stint with the White Sox.
- Pitched in five games for LaGuaira in the Venezuelan Winter League, recording a 2.08 ERA (4.1IP, 1ER).

2005

▸ Combined to go 1-1 with a 3.54 ERA and two saves in 25 relief appearances between rookie-level Great Falls and Single-A Winston-Salem, working exclusively out of the bullpen the entire season…lowered the arm angle in his delivery prior to the season.

2004

▸ Spent his second full season at Great Falls…went 2-5 with a 6.26 ERA (41.2IP, 29 ER) in nine starts and 1-2 with a 4.37 ERA (22.2IP, 11ER) and one save in nine relief appearances…earned his first professional save on 8/18 vs. Provo (3.0IP).

2003

▸ Made his professional debut at Great Falls, going 3-3 with a 6.58 ERA in 16 games (14 starts).

PERSONAL

▸ Was selected to the San Antonio All-Star Team at O'Connor High School…lost a pregame, on-field cow-milking contest to the Angels' Brandon Wood on 5/4/07 at Angel Stadium.

Logan's Career Pitching Record

Year	Team	W	L	ERA	G	GS	CG	SHO	SV	IP	H	R	ER	HR	HP	BB	SO	WP	BK
2003	Great Falls	3	3	6.58	16	14	0	0	0	67.0	76	60	49	4	11	31	48	8	1
2004	Great Falls	3	7	5.6	18	9	0	0	1	64.1	74	48	40	7	4	31	48	8	2
2005	Great Falls	1	1	3.31	21	0	0	0	2	35.1	34	15	13	1	3	4	29	4	0
	Winston-Salem	0	0	5.06	4	0	0	0	0	5.1	7	3	3	2	0	4	5	0	0
2006	Charlotte	3	1	3.38	38	0	0	0	11	42.2	35	18	16	1	9	12	57	3	0
	CHICAGO-AL	0	0	8.31	21	0	0	0	1	17.1	21	18	16	2	3	15	15	1	0
2007	Charlotte	0	1	2.16	4	0	0	0	0	8.1	8	2	2	1	0	4	11	0	0
	CHICAGO-AL	2	1	4.97	68	0	0	0	0	50.2	59	30	28	7	0	20	35	2	0
2008	CHICAGO-AL	2	3	5.95	55	0	0	0	0	42.1	57	31	28	7	1	14	42	1	0
	Charlotte	0	1	6.00	5	0	0	0	0	9.0	10	8	6	2	3	6	7	1	0
2009	Gwinnett - a	4	2	3.28	29	0	0	0	2	35.2	26	15	13	2	6	17	39	4	0
2009	ATLANTA - b	1	1	5.19	20	0	0	0	0	17.1	21	12	10	1	1	9	10	0	0
2010	YANKEES	2	0	2.93	51	0	0	0	0	40.0	34	13	13	3	1	20	38	1	0
	Scranton/WB	0	1	2.11	14	0	0	0	0	21.1	18	5	5	1	2	4	23	1	0
Minor League Totals		**14**	**17**	**4.58**	**149**	**23**	**0**	**0**	**17**	**289.0**	**288**	**174**	**147**	**21**	**38**	**113**	**267**	**29**	**3**
AL Totals		**6**	**4**	**5.11**	**194**	**0**	**0**	**0**	**1**	**149.2**	**171**	**92**	**85**	**19**	**5**	**69**	**129**	**5**	**0**
NL Totals		**1**	**1**	**5.19**	**20**	**0**	**0**	**0**	**0**	**17.1**	**21**	**12**	**10**	**1**	**1**	**9**	**10**	**0**	**0**
Major League Totals		**7**	**5**	**5.10**	**215**	**0**	**0**	**0**	**1**	**167.2**	**192**	**104**	**95**	**20**	**6**	**78**	**139**	**5**	**0**

Selected by the Chicago White Sox in the 20th round of the 2002 First-Year Player Draft.

a – Acquired by the Atlanta Braves along with RHP Javier Vazquez from the White Sox in exchange for INFs Jon Gilmore and Brent Lillibridge, C Tyler Flowers and LHP Santos Rodriguez on December 4, 2008.

b – Acquired by the Yankees along with RHP Javier Vazquez from the Braves in exchange for OF Melky Cabrera, LHP Mike Dunn and RHP Arodys Vizcaino on December 22, 2009.

Logan's Division Series Record

Year	Club vs. Opp.	W	L	ERA	G	GS	CG	SHO	SV	IP	H	R	ER	HR	HP	BB	SO	WP	BK
2010	NYY vs. MIN	0	0	0.00	2	0	0	0	0	1.0	1	0	0	0	0	0	0	0	0
Division Series Totals		**0**	**0**	**0.00**	**2**	**0**	**0**	**0**	**0**	**1.0**	**1**	**0**	**0**	**0**	**0**	**0**	**0**	**0**	**0**

Logan's League Championship Series Record

Year	Club vs. Opp.	W	L	ERA	G	GS	CG	SHO	SV	IP	H	R	ER	HR	HP	BB	SO	WP	BK
2010	NYY vs. TEX	0	0	27.00	3	0	0	0	0	0.2	2	2	2	1	0	1	1	0	0
LCS Totals		**0**	**0**	**27.00**	**3**	**0**	**0**	**0**	**0**	**0.2**	**2**	**2**	**2**	**1**	**0**	**1**	**1**	**0**	**0**
POSTSEASON TOTALS		**0**	**0**	**10.80**	**5**	**0**	**0**	**0**	**0**	**1.2**	**3**	**2**	**2**	**1**	**0**	**1**	**1**	**0**	**0**

Logan's Regular Season Batting Record

Year	Team	AVG	G	AB	R	H	2B	3B	HR	RBI	SH	SF	HP	BB	SO	SB	CS
2010	NYY					Did Not Bat											
Major League Totals		**-**	**215**	**-**	**-**	**-**	**-**	**-**	**-**	**-**	**-**	**-**	**-**	**-**	**-**	**-**	**-**

Logan's Career Fielding Record

Position	PCT	G	PO	A	E	TC	DP
Pitcher	.900	215	10	17	3	30	1

43

DAMASO MARTE

LEFT-HANDED PITCHER • 6-2 • 213 • B/T: LEFT/LEFT • OPENING DAY AGE: 36

BIRTHDATE
February 14, 1975

BIRTHPLACE
Santo Domingo, D.R.

RESIDES
Santo Domingo, D.R.

M.L. SERVICE
9 years, 122 days

STATUS

▸ Acquired by the Yankees along with OF Xavier Nady from the Pittsburgh Pirates in exchange for OF Jose Tabata and RHPs Ross Ohlendorf, Jeff Karstens and Daniel McCutchen…signed to a three-year contract with a one-year option on November 12, 2008…contract extends through 2011 with a team option for 2012.

CAREER NOTES

▸ Among left-handed pitchers in the Majors since 2002, ranks second in appearances (542)…among lefty relievers since '02, has the fourth-most strikeouts (461).

▸ Owns a career record of 3-4 with a 2.19 ERA (90.1 IP, 22ER) in 93 appearances vs. the AL East.

▸ Reached the 50-appearance plateau in seven consecutive seasons from 2002-08, one of only seven pitchers to accomplish the feat over the span.

2010

▸ Was 0-0 with a 4.08 ERA in 30 relief appearances with the Yankees…opponents batted .161 (10-for-62, 2HR); LH .146 (6-for-41, 1HR), RH .190 (4-for-21, 1HR)…retired 23-of-30 first batters faced (76.7%)…prevented 16-of-22 inherited runners from scoring (72.7%)…appeared in consecutive games six times.

▸ Tossed less than 1.0 inning in 22 of his 30 outings…held opponents scoreless in his first seven appearances and 21 of his first 23 games through 6/13…included was nine straight scoreless outings from 5/15-6/13 (4.1IP).

▸ Made his ninth career Opening Day roster in 2010, second with the Yankees.

▸ Tossed 1.2IP in 5/17 win at Boston, marking his longest outing since throwing 2.0 innings of relief on 6/20/08 vs. Toronto.

▸ Threw 29 pitches in 6/17 loss vs. Philadelphia, allowing 1ER in 0.2IP (2BB)…marked his most pitches since 8/10/08 at Los Angeles-AL (also 29 pitches).

▸ Retired 23 of his final 25 left-handed batters faced from 5/15-7/7 (1H, 1BB).

▸ Held opponents hitless in 17 straight at-bats from 5/17-6/30 prior to Chone Figgins' single in 6/30 loss vs. Seattle, marking his longest such streak as a Yankee…also allowed a Russell Branyan home run in the game, snapping an 0-for-19 stretch by left-handed batters (dating back to a double by Minnesota's Justin Morneau on 5/14 at Yankee Stadium)—credit: *Elias*.

▸ Was placed on the 15-day disabled list prior to 7/17 game with left shoulder inflammation (retroactive to 7/8)…was transferred to the 60-day disabled list on 9/1, missing the remainder of the season (78 games).

2009

▸ Was 1-3 with a 9.45 ERA in 21 relief appearances with the Yankees…opponents batted .278 (15-for-54, 3HR); LH .120 (3-for-25, 1HR), RH .414 (12-for-29, 2HR)…15 of his 21 appearances were scoreless…stranded 17-of-21 inherited runners (81.0%)…retired 16-of-21 first batters faced (76.2%)…appeared in consecutive games once and three straight games twice (4/22-25 and 9/22-25).

BESTS & STREAKS

Low hit CG
  N/A
IP (start)
  N/A
IP (relief)
  4.0 - vs. ARI, 7/20/99
Hits
  10 - vs. ARI, 7/20/99
Runs
  6 - 2 times
  Last: vs. CLE, 4/16/09
BB
  4 - 2 times
  Last: vs. MIL, 8/16/06
SO
  5 - 3 times
  Last: at FLA, 6/17/04
HR
  2 - 5 times
  Last: vs. CLE, 4/16/09
Single-Season Winning Streak
  4g - 4/23-5/25/08
Winning Streak
  7g - 8/22/06-5/25/08
Single-Season Losing Streak
  7g - 4/5-8/16/06
Losing Streak
  8g - 9/9/05-8/16/06

- Made his eighth career Opening Day roster…allowed 1H in 0.1IP in the Yankees' Opening Day loss at Baltimore on 4/6…surrendered a career-high-tying 6R/6ER (second time, also 1999) in 4/16 loss vs. Cleveland, throwing 1.0 inning of relief in the first regular season game at Yankee Stadium (3H, 1BB, 1HP, 2HR)…on 4/24 at Boston, allowed "walk-off" solo-HR to Kevin Youkilis in the bottom of the 11th to suffer his first loss (1.1IP, 1H, 1ER, 3K).

- Was placed on the 15-day disabled list on 5/3 (retroactive to 4/26) with left shoulder inflammation…began throwing program in Tampa on 5/23…was transferred to the 60-day D.L. on 8/8…made 12 rehab appearances, combining to go 0-1 with a 3.00 ERA (12.0IP, 10H, 4ER, 4BB, 10K, 2HR) with Scranton/WB and the GCL Yankees.

- Was returned from rehab on 8/14 and excused for personal reasons…was reinstated from the disabled list on 8/21, prior to the Yankees' 20-11 win at Fenway Park…retired both of his batters faced (0.2IP, 1K) that night in the Yankees victory, entering with the bases loaded in the seventh inning in first appearance since 4/25.

- Held opponents scoreless in 12 of his 14 outings after returning from the disabled list…four of his five runs allowed came over the span in 9/11 loss vs. Baltimore, in which he was tagged with the loss…snapped a 14-game winning streak by the Yankees bullpen, dating back to 8/5.

- Did not allow a run in eight postseason appearances, holding opponents to 2H with 0BB and 5K in 4.0IP…after allowing singles to his first two hitters faced in the ALDS, retired his final 12 batters of the postseason…tied eight other pitchers for the fifth-most appearances in a single postseason without allowing any runs.

- Faced eight batters in four World Series appearances vs. Philadelphia, recording 5K (Utley twice, Howard twice and Werth)…faced Ryan Howard in all four outings, retiring him each time.

- Made two scoreless relief appearances with the Dominican Republic in the World Baseball Classic prior to the season (2.0IP, 1H, 2K)…missed a little over a week upon return from the WBC with left shoulder inflammation.

2008

- Was 5-3 with a 4.02 ERA in 72 combined relief appearances between the Yankees and Pirates…was acquired by the Yankees along with OF Xavier Nady on 7/26 in exchange for OF Jose Tabata and RHPs Ross Ohlendorf, Jeff Karstens and Daniel McCutchen.

- Opponents batted .214 (52-for-243, 5HR); LH .247 (21-for-85, 1HR), RH .196 (31-for-158, 4HR)…appeared in consecutive games 16 times, three straight once (5/24-27) and four straight once (8/27-30)…stranded 37-of-46 inherited runners (80.4%)…retired 55-of-72 first-batters faced (76.4%)…tossed more than 1.0 inning 13 times, including a season-high 2.0 innings four times…was called upon to face one batter seven times, including five times with the Yankees.

- In 25 games with the Yankees, went 1-3 with a 5.40 ERA…while with the Yankees, retired 15-of-25 first batters faced (60.0%)…stranded 11-of-15 inherited runners (73.3%)…opponents batted .206 (14-for-68, 1HR); LH .233 (7-for-30, 0HR); RH .184 (7-for-38, 1HR).

- Made his Yankees debut in 7/26 win at Boston, striking out only batter faced (Ortiz) with two on and one out in the seventh (0.1IP, 1K)…arrived at Fenway Park less than two hours before first pitch following the trade.

- Suffered first loss of the season on 8/4 at Texas, allowing "walk-off" grand slam in the bottom of the ninth to Marlon Byrd…according to the Elias Sports Bureau, became the fourth Yankee since 1960 to allow a game-ending grand slam, joining Lindy McDaniel (7/7/70 at Baltimore, Brooks Robinson), Cecilio Guante (6/21/88 at Detroit, Alan Trammell) and Mariano Rivera (7/14/02 at Cleveland, Bill Selby).

- Recorded his first win as a Yankee in 9/13 Game 2 victory vs. Tampa Bay, tossing a perfect seventh (2K) after the Yankees rallied from 4-1 deficit.

- Was 4-0 with five saves and a 3.47 ERA in 47 relief appearances with the Pirates, striking out 47 batters in 46.2 innings pitched (16BB) before being acquired by the Yankees…at the time of the trade, opponents were batting .217 (38-for-175, 4HR); LH .255 (14-for-55, 1HR), RH .200 (24-for-120, 3HR)…was a member of Pittsburgh's Opening Day roster for the third straight year.

- Walked two of three batters faced and allowed two runs in 0.1IP on 3/31 Opening Day in Atlanta…was charged with 4ER in his next outing on 4/2 at Atlanta, combining for an 81.00 ERA over his first two appearances of the season (0.2IP, 4H, 6ER, 2BB, 1K, 1HR)…over his next 45 outings from 4/5-7/23, posted a 2.35 ERA (46.0IP, 12ER) before being acquired by the Yankees.

- Picked up his first career NL save on 6/12 vs. Washington and his first save since 8/27/05 (w/ Chicago-AL)…became the Pirates' full-time closer on 7/2 when Matt Capps was placed on the disabled list…converted each of his five save opportunities from 7/2-23.

2007

- Spent second straight full season with Pittsburgh, going 2-0 with a 2.38 ERA in 65 appearances…opponents batted .200 (32-for-160, 2HR); LH .094 (6-for-64, 0HR), RH .271 (26-for-96, 2HR)…prevented 45-of-56 inherited runners from scoring (80.4%)…retired 45-of-65 first batters faced (69.0%)…both of his home runs allowed were to switch hitters who were batting right-handed – Tony Clark at Arizona on 8/9 and Lance Berkman at Houston on 9/14…pitched 1.0 inning or less in 58 of his 65 appearances.

- Held opponents without an earned run in his first 21G at PNC Park from 4/9-8/14 (17.2IP, 6H, 1R, 5BB, 23K).

- Did not allow an earned run in his first eight outings (6.1IP, 1R)…allowed his first earned run in 4/21 loss at Los Angeles (NL)…following that outing, made 13 consecutive scoreless appearances from 4/22-5/26 (10.2IP)…was scored upon once in 12 outings during May and held opponents to a .118 average (4-for-34) for the month.

▸ Held left-handed batters hitless in 32 consecutive at-bats from 5/18-8/9, marking the longest such streak in the Majors in 2007…streak was snapped on 8/11 at San Francisco when Ryan Klesko's fly ball to left was lost in the sun by Jason Bay and ruled a double…held left-handed hitters to just two hits in their final 44AB (.045) from 5/18 through the remainder of the season.

▸ Had 13 consecutive scoreless appearances from 6/27-8/2 (11.2IP), throwing 10.1 shutout innings in July (10 appearances).

2006

▸ Was 1-7 with a 3.70 ERA in a career-high 75 appearances with Pittsburgh…was three games shy of the club record for a left-handed pitcher (Scott Sauerbeck with 78 in 2002)…worked 1.0 inning or less in 66 of his 75 outings…averaged 9.7 K/9.0IP (58.1IP, 63K)…opponents batted .244 (51-for-209, 5HR); LH .225 (20-for-89, 2HR), RH .258 (31-for-120, 3HR)…retired 48-of-75 first batters faced (64.0%)…prevented 29-of-40 inherited runners from scoring (72.5%).

▸ Lost his first seven decisions from 4/5-8/16, marking a career high losing streak.

▸ Suffered a blown save on Opening Day loss at Milwaukee…was scored upon just three times in his first 19 games through 5/17 (12.0IP, 3ER, 2.25 ERA)…retired only batter faced on 8/22 at Atlanta to pick up lone victory of the season…was scored upon just once in final 10 appearances (10.0IP, 2ER).

▸ Made two appearances in Dominican Winter League (3.2IP, 0R).

▸ Went 0-1 with a 20.25 ERA (1.1IP, 3ER) in three relief appearances for the Dominican Republic in the inaugural World Baseball Classic…returned to Bradenton, Fla., prior to the end of the WBC with left shoulder irritation…was limited to one game in spring training while battling left shoulder irritation and a stiff neck.

2005

▸ Was 3-4 with four saves and a 3.77 ERA in 66 games for the World Series-champion Chicago White Sox…averaged 10.7K/9.0IP (45.1IP, 54K), his best mark since 2002 (also 10.7).

▸ Opponents batted .256 (45-for-176, 5HR); LH .267 (24-for-90, 1HR), RH .244 (21-for-86, 4HR)…converted 4-of-8 save chances…was scored upon in just 16-of-66 appearances…stranded 28-of-37 inherited runners (75.7%)…retired 31-of-52 first batters faced (59.6%), holding them to a .173 (9-for-52) average, the seventh-lowest mark in the AL…threw a season-high 2.0 innings twice (both scoreless)…57 of his outings were 1.0 inning or less.

▸ Had 14 consecutive scoreless outings on the road from 5/6-7/30 (10.2IP, 8H, 6BB, 10K).

▸ Did not pitch from 6/8-13 due to a sore left bicep…was placed on the 15-day disabled list from 6/27-7/14 with an inflamed left trapezius…made one rehab appearance with Triple-A Charlotte on 7/10 at Louisville (1.2IP, 4H, 1ER, 1BB, 2K)…was returned from rehab and reinstated from the D.L. on 7/14, throwing 1.0 scoreless inning in that night's win at Cleveland.

▸ Made one appearance in the AL Division Series against Boston, walking two batters and allowing one hit in Game 3 win on 10/7 at Boston…was not on the ALCS roster vs. the Angels…was the winning pitcher in Game 3 of the World Series, tossing 1.2 scoreless innings in Chicago's 7-5, 14-inning victory at Houston.

2004

▸ Was 6-5 with six saves and a 3.42 ERA in 74 appearances with the White Sox…ranked seventh in the American League in appearances, recording the eighth-highest total in White Sox history and fifth-highest among club lefthanders at the time…also established a career high in wins.

▸ Opponents batted .217 (56-for-258, 10HR); LH .143 (14-for-98, 2HR), RH .263 (42-for-160, 8HR)…prevented 30-of-40 inherited runners from scoring (75.0%)…retired 55-of-75 first batters faced (73.3%)…converted 6-of-12 save opportunities.

▸ Posted a 2.45 ERA (40.1IP, 11ER) prior to the All-Star break and a 4.59 ERA (33.1IP, 17ER) in the second half.

▸ Suffered a blown save and recorded the loss on Opening Day at Kansas City, surrendering a game-tying, three-run homer to Mendy Lopez and a game-winning, two-run shot to Carlos Beltran without recording an out…compiled a 1.69 ERA (42.2IP, 8ER) over his next 38 games from 4/11-7/24…matched his career high with 5K in 6/17 loss at Florida (2.0IP).

2003

▸ Was 4-2 with 11 saves and a 1.58 ERA in 71 appearances with the White Sox…established career highs in saves, innings pitched (79.2) and strikeouts (87)…ranked fourth among AL relievers in ERA, recording the second-lowest mark by a Sox reliever since Ed Farmer in 1979 (1.07)…also ranked among AL relief leaders in strikeouts (fifth).

▸ Converted 11-of-18 save opportunities, including each of his final seven chances…was scored upon in just 11 of his 71 total appearances.

▸ Opponents batted .185 (50-for-271, 3HR); LH .168 (21-for-125, 1HR), RH .199 (29-for-146, 2HR)…was the third-lowest average against left-handers among AL relievers…prevented 37-of-53 inherited runners from scoring (69.8%)…retired 49-of-71 first batters faced (69.0%).

- Made 18 straight scoreless outings from 4/20-6/10, allowing just 8H and 5BB, while striking out 20 batters over the stretch…the streak came to an end on 6/12 vs. San Francisco when he gave up game-winning grand slam to Rich Aurilia after inheriting bases-loaded jam…matched his career high with 5K in 8/20 win vs. Anaheim…compiled a 1.09 ERA (49.2IP, 6ER) over his final 39 outings and a 0.84 ERA (21.1IP, 2ER) over his final 16.
- Pitched in five games for Estrellas in the Dominican Winter League, going 1-0 with a 0.00 ERA (6.1IP).

2002

- Spent first full season in the Majors with Chicago-AL after being acquired from Pittsburgh in exchange for RHP Matt Guerrier on 3/27.
- Was 1-1 with a 2.83 ERA in 68 appearances with the White Sox, striking out 72 batters in 60.1IP…led the staff in appearances and the bullpen in ERA and strikeouts…his average of 10.74K/9.0IP ranked second among relievers in Sox history behind Roberto Hernandez (12.67 in 1995).
- Opponents batted .204 (44-for-216, 5HR); LH .149 (15-for-101, 2HR), RH .252 (29-for-115, 3HR)…was the lowest mark in the AL and lowest figure by a Sox pitcher since Kevin Hickey in 1981 (.146)…prevented 36-of-50 inherited runners from scoring (72.0%)…retired 45-of-68 first batters faced (66.1%).
- Earned his first Major League win on 4/16 vs. Cleveland (1.2IP, 1H, 1ER, 1BB, 4K).
- Compiled a 1.92 ERA (51.2IP, 11ER) in 57 appearances from 5/1 through the end of the season…earned first Major League save on 7/6 vs. Cleveland, recording 1.2 scoreless innings (1BB)…converted all 10 saves chances over the remainder of the season.
- Pitched for Estrellas in the Dominican Winter League, going 0-1 with a 3.97 ERA (11.1IP, 5ER) and 14K in 12 appearances…went 3-0 with a 1.69 ERA (10.2IP, 2ER) and 17K in the playoffs.

2001

- Was 0-1 with a 4.71 ERA in 23 games with Pittsburgh…was acquired by the Pirates from the Yankees in exchange for INF Enrique Wilson on 6/13 and was assigned to Triple-A Nashville.
- Had his contract purchased by Pittsburgh on 6/23 and made his National League debut the next day, tossing 3.0 scoreless innings in 6/24 loss vs. Montreal (1H, 1BB, 1K)…made four straight scoreless outings (6.0IP) before giving up three runs in 0.2IP in 7/5 loss at Cincinnati…surrendered just 1ER over eight outings from 7/24-8/22 (14.0IP), lowering his ERA from 6.75 to 2.61…established a career high with five strikeouts in 8/31 loss at Cincinnati.
- Began season with the Yankees' Double-A affiliate Norwich, going 3-1 with a 3.50 ERA in 23 games…held lefthanders to a .194 average (6-for-31)…went 2-0 with a 1.20 ERA (15.0IP, 3R, 2ER) in nine games during the month of April…notched first professional save on 5/6 at New Haven (3.0IP, 5H, 1ER, 1K).
- Appeared in four games with Nashville before joining Major League club, posting a 3.38 ERA with no decisions.

2000

- Opened season on the disabled list from 4/7-8/22 with a left elbow strain…made two rehab starts for the Peoria Mariners of the Arizona Rookie League, surrendering just 1H with 6K in 5.0IP…was transferred to Double-A New Haven on 8/22…did not record a decision in his four Double-A outings.

1999

- Was 0-1 with a 9.35 ERA in five appearances with Seattle in his first Major League action…was recalled from Triple-A Tacoma on 6/30 and made his Major League debut that night at Oakland (1.0IP, 2H, 3ER, 1BB)…threw a career-high 4.0 innings in 7/20 loss vs. Arizona in his final outing before being optioned back to Tacoma on 7/22.
- Posted a 3-3 record with a 5.13 ERA in 31 games (11 starts) at Triple-A Tacoma…went 1-2 with a 5.94 ERA as a starter (47.0, 31ER) with opponents batting .287 (54-for-188)…in 20 relief appearances, was 2-1 with a 3.71 ERA (26.2IP, 11ER) and a .243 opponents average (25-for-103).

1998

- In his first action at the Double-A level, was 7-6 with a 5.27 ERA with Orlando…ranked second on the staff in strikeouts (99) and third in innings pitched (121.1)…began season on D.L. with a left elbow strain…was reinstated on 5/2 and tossed 5.0 innings that night in a 9-1 win vs. Knoxville…tossed 6.2 scoreless innings in a 13-0 win vs. West Tenn on 8/15…returned to D.L. from 9/2-22 with a left forearm strain…made two appearances with Escogido in the Dominican Winter League.

1997

- Was 8-8 with a 4.13 ERA in 25 starts with Single-A Lancaster…was on the D.L. with tendinitis in his left elbow from 4/3-17…set minor league career high in strikeouts (127)…won eight of his 10 decisions from 6/19-8/26, including four straight wins from 6/29-7/30…named California League "Pitcher of the Week" on 8/16 after going 2-0 with a 0.56 ERA (16.0IP, 1ER) in two starts…tossed four-hit shutout at Stockton on 8/15 (11K)…pitched with Escogido in the Dominican Winter League following the season.

1996

▸ Was 8-6 with a 4.49 ERA in 26 starts with Single-A Wisconsin…led club in strikeouts (115) and ranked second in starts and innings pitched (142.1)…established a minor league career high in innings pitched…pitched four-hit shutout vs. South Bend on 7/6.

1995

▸ Was 2-2 with a 2.21 ERA in 11 games (five starts) with Single-A Everett…held opposing batters to a .195 average (25-for-128).

1993-94

▸ Went 7-0 with a 3.86 ERA (65.1IP, 28ER) in 17 games (13 starts) for Santo Domingo in the Dominican Summer League in 1994.

▸ Made professional debut with Santo Domingo in the Dominican Summer League in 1993, going 2-5 with a 6.55 ERA in 17 games (15 starts).

PERSONAL

▸ Damaso Savinon Marte ("DAH-mah-so" "MAR-tay")…signed his first professional contract at the age of 16.

▸ Visited with kids at P.S. 55 in the Bronx for National Literacy Day in September 2008.

Marte's Career Pitching Record

Year	Club	W	L	ERA	G	GS	CG	SHO	SV	IP	H	R	ER	HR	HB	BB	SO	WP	BK
1993	DSL Mariners	2	5	6.55	17	15	2	0	0	56.1	62	48	41	5	7	50	29	4	4
1994	DSL Mariners	7	0	3.86	17	13	0	0	0	65.1	53	41	28	5	0	48	80	12	1
1995	Everett	2	2	2.21	11	5	0	0	0	36.2	25	11	9	2	1	10	39	3	0
1996	Wisconsin	8	6	4.49	26	26	2	1	0	142.1	134	82	71	8	6	75	115	4	3
1997	Lancaster	8	8	4.13	25	25	2	1	0	139.1	144	75	64	15	8	62	127	8	4
1998	Orlando	7	6	5.27	22	20	0	0	0	121.1	136	82	71	14	2	47	99	6	2
1999	Tacoma	3	3	5.13	31	11	0	0	0	73.2	79	43	42	13	2	40	59	1	2
	SEATTLE	0	1	9.35	5	0	0	0	0	8.2	16	9	9	3	0	6	3	0	0
2000	Peoria	0	0	0.00	2	2	0	0	0	5.0	1	0	0	0	1	0	6	0	0
	New Haven - a	0	0	1.59	4	0	0	0	0	5.2	6	1	1	1	0	2	4	0	1
2001	Norwich - b	3	1	3.50	23	0	0	0	0	36.1	34	21	19	5	3	12	39	1	0
	Nashville	0	0	3.58	4	0	0	0	0	5.1	3	2	2	2	0	4	0	0	0
	PITTSBURGH	0	1	4.71	23	0	0	0	0	36.1	34	21	19	5	3	12	39	1	0
2002	CHICAGO-AL - c	1	1	2.83	68	0	0	0	10	60.1	44	19	19	5	4	18	72	3	1
2003	CHICAGO-AL	4	2	1.58	71	0	0	0	11	79.2	50	16	14	3	3	34	87	1	0
2004	CHICAGO-AL	6	5	3.42	74	0	0	0	6	73.2	56	28	28	10	3	34	68	3	0
2005	Charlotte-d	0	0	5.40	1	0	0	0	0	1.2	4	1	1	0	0	1	2	1	0
	CHICAGO-AL - e	3	4	3.77	66	0	0	0	4	45.1	45	21	19	5	3	33	54	1	1
2006	PITTSBURGH	1	7	3.70	75	0	0	0	0	58.1	51	30	24	5	4	31	63	3	1
2007	PITTSBURGH	2	0	2.38	65	0	0	0	0	45.1	32	14	12	2	2	18	51	0	1
2008	PITTSBURGH - f	4	0	3.47	47	0	0	0	5	46.2	38	18	18	4	1	16	47	1	0
	YANKEES	1	3	5.40	25	0	0	0	0	18.1	14	11	11	1	1	10	24	0	0
2009	YANKEES - g	1	3	9.45	21	0	0	0	0	13.1	15	14	14	3	1	6	13	0	0
	GCL Yankees	0	0	4.50	2	2	0	0	0	2.0	2	1	1	0	0	0	2	0	0
	Scranton/WB	0	1	2.45	11	0	0	0	0	11.0	10	3	3	2	0	4	9	0	1
2010	YANKEES - h	0	0	4.08	30	0	0	0	0	17.2	10	8	8	2	1	11	12	2	1
Minor League Totals		**40**	**32**	**4.46**	**196**	**119**	**6**	**2**	**1**	**701.2**	**688**	**406**	**348**	**70**	**29**	**346**	**611**	**39**	**19**
AL Totals		**16**	**19**	**3.46**	**360**	**0**	**0**	**0**	**31**	**317.0**	**250**	**126**	**122**	**32**	**16**	**152**	**333**	**10**	**3**
NL Totals		**7**	**8**	**3.52**	**210**	**0**	**0**	**0**	**5**	**186.2**	**155**	**83**	**73**	**16**	**10**	**77**	**200**	**5**	**2**
Major League Totals		**23**	**27**	**3.48**	**570**	**0**	**0**	**0**	**36**	**503.2**	**405**	**209**	**195**	**48**	**26**	**229**	**533**	**15**	**5**
NYY Totals		**2**	**6**	**6.02**	**76**	**0**	**0**	**0**	**0**	**49.1**	**39**	**33**	**33**	**6**	**3**	**27**	**49**	**2**	**1**

Signed by Seattle as a non-drafted free agent on November 6, 1992.

a – Signed by the Yankees as a minor league free agent on November 16, 2000
b – Acquired by Pittsburgh for the Yankees in exchange for INF Enrique Wilson on June 13, 2001.
c – Acquired by Chicago-AL from Pittsburgh in exchange for RHP Matt Guerrier on March 27, 2002.
d – Placed on the 15-day disabled list from June 27 – July 14, 2005 with an inflamed left trapezius.
e – Acquired by Pittsburgh from Chicago-AL in exchange for INF/OF Rob Mackowiak on December 13, 2005.
f – Acquired by the Yankees from Pittsburgh with OF Xavier Nady in exchange for RHPs Jeff Karstens, Dan McCutchen and Ross Ohlendorf and OF Jose Tabata on July 26, 2008.
g – Placed on the 15-day disabled list from May 3 (retroactive to April 26) – August 19, 2009 with left shoulder inflammation (transferred to 60-day disabled list on August 8).
h – Placed on the 15-day disabled list on July 17 (retroactive to July 8) with left shoulder inflammation and was transferred to the 60-day disabled list on September 1, missing the remainder of the season.

Marte's Division Series Record

Year	Club vs. Opp.	W	L	ERA	G	GS	CG	SHO	SV	IP	H	R	ER	HR	HP	BB	SO	WP	BK
2005	CWS vs. BOS	0	0	---	1	0	0	0	0	0.0	1	0	0	0	0	2	0	0	0
2009	NYY vs. MIN	0	0	---	1	0	0	0	0	0.0	2	0	0	0	0	0	0	0	0
Division Series Totals		**0**	**0**	**---**	**2**	**0**	**0**	**0**	**0**	**0.0**	**3**	**0**	**0**	**0**	**0**	**2**	**0**	**0**	**0**

Marte's League Championship Series Record

Year	Club vs. Opp.	W	L	ERA	G	GS	CG	SHO	SV	IP	H	R	ER	HR	HP	BB	SO	WP	BK
2005	CWS vs. LAA						Did Not Pitch - Not on Roster												
2009	NYY vs. LAA	0	0	0.00	3	0	0	0	0	1.1	0	0	0	0	0	0	0	0	0
LCS Totals		**0**	**0**	**0.00**	**3**	**0**	**0**	**0**	**0**	**1.1**	**0**	**0**	**0**	**0**	**0**	**0**	**0**	**0**	**0**

Marte's World Series Record

Year	Club vs. Opp.	W	L	ERA	G	GS	CG	SHO	SV	IP	H	R	ER	HR	HP	BB	SO	WP	BK
2005	CWS vs. HOU	1	0	0.00	1	0	0	0	0	1.2	0	0	0	0	0	2	3	0	0
2009	NYY vs. PHI	0	0	0.00	4	0	0	0	0	2.2	0	0	0	0	0	0	5	0	0
World Series Totals		**1**	**0**	**0.00**	**5**	**0**	**0**	**0**	**0**	**4.1**	**0**	**0**	**0**	**0**	**0**	**2**	**8**	**0**	**0**
POSTSEASON TOTALS		**1**	**0**	**0.00**	**10**	**0**	**0**	**0**	**0**	**5.2**	**3**	**0**	**0**	**0**	**0**	**4**	**8**	**0**	**0**

Marte's World Baseball Classic Record

Year	Country, Site	W	L	ERA	G	GS	CG	SHO	SV	IP	H	R	ER	HR	HP	BB	SO	WP	BK
2006	D.R., USA	0	1	20.25	3	0	0	0	1	1.1	4	4	3	0	0	1	2	0	0
2009	D.R., Puerto Rico	0	0	0.00	2	0	0	0	0	2.0	1	0	0	0	0	0	2	0	0
WBC Totals		**0**	**1**	**8.10**	**5**	**0**	**0**	**0**	**1**	**3.1**	**5**	**4**	**3**	**0**	**0**	**1**	**4**	**0**	**0**

Marte's Regular Season Batting Record

Year	Team	AVG	G	AB	R	H	2B	3B	HR	RBI	SH	SF	HP	BB	SO	SB	CS
2010	NYY					Did Not Bat											
Major League Totals		**.000**	**540**	**9**	**0**	**0**	**0**	**0**	**0**	**0**	**0**	**0**	**0**	**0**	**3**	**0**	**0**

Marte's Career Fielding Record

Position	PCT	G	PO	A	E	TC	DP
Pitcher	.973	570	14	59	2	75	3

Milestone Wins in Franchise History

1 – 4/23/1903 at Washington, 7-2
100 – 6/19/1904 at St. Louis (G1), 4-3
500 – 8/31/1909 at Cleveland (G1), 4-1
1,000 – 9/9/1916 at Philadelphia (G1), 4-1
2,000 – 6/2/1928 at Detroit, 5-2 (10 innings)
3,000 – 8/27/1938 vs. Cleveland (G1), 8-7
4,000 – 6/30/1949 at Boston, 6-3
5,000 – 9/11/1959 vs. Detroit, 9-3
6,000 – 5/8/1971 at Chicago (AL), 2-1 (11 innings)
7,000 – 8/4/1982 vs. Chicago (AL), 6-2
8,000 – 7/21/1994 at California, 11-7
9,000 – 5/17/2005 at Seattle, 6-0

*The Yankees currently have 9,552 all-time wins.

The Yankees celebrate Mark Teixeira's grand slam in their 4-0 win – and 9,500th victory in franchise history – vs. the Mets on 6/20/10.

55
RUSSELL MARTIN

CATCHER • 5-10 • 215 • B/T: RIGHT/RIGHT • OPENING DAY AGE: 28

BIRTHDATE
February 15, 1983

BIRTHPLACE
East York, Ontario, Canada

RESIDES
Chelsea, Quebec, Canada

M.L. SERVICE
4 years, 150 days

COLLEGE
Chipola Junior College (Fla.)

CAREER HIGHLIGHTS
N.L. All-Star Team
▸ 2007, 2008

N.L. Gold Glove
▸ 2007

N.L. Silver Slugger
▸ 2007

STATUS
▸ Signed by the Yankees as a free agent on December 16, 2010…signed through the 2011 season.

CAREER NOTES
▸ Has caught 119-of-459 (25.9%) of potential base stealers since making his Major League debut in 2006, totaling the second-most runners caught stealing in the Majors over the stretch behind only the Cardinals' Gerald Laird (142)…leads all Major League catchers with a 3.76 catchers ERA (min. 240G) over the same span.

▸ Over the last four seasons (since 2007), ranks second in the Majors with 4,484.1 innings caught and ranks third with 503 starts at catcher.

▸ Joins Carlton Fisk and Ivan Rodriguez as one of just three catchers in Major League history to have at least 10HR, 60RBI and 10SB in a single season three times (2006-08).

▸ Hit at least 10HR in each of his first three Major League seasons (2006-08), joining Andre Ethier (also 2006-08) as the first Dodgers players to accomplish the feat since Jackie Robinson (1947-49).

▸ Collected 66SB with Los Angeles-NL, setting a Dodgers franchise record for a catcher.

2010
▸ Batted .248 (82-for-331) with 45R, 13 doubles, 5HR and 26RBI in 97 games with the Dodgers…hit in seven different spots in the lineup (one through three and six through nine)…batted .361 (26-for-72) with 5HR in the eighth spot in the order.

▸ Caught 19-of-62 potential basestealers (30.6%)…picked off four baserunners over a 13-game stretch from 6/4-22.

▸ Made his fourth consecutive Opening Day start at catcher for the Dodgers…recorded at least 1BB in each of his first eight games of the season.

▸ Hit 13th-inning, game-winning RBI single on 4/24 at Washington…drove in game-winning run with eighth-inning RBI double on 7/25 vs. New York-NL.

▸ Hit safely in a career-high 15 straight games from 5/5-20, batting .305 (18-for-59) over the stretch.

▸ Suffered a season-ending right hip fracture and torn labrum while trying to score from third base on a sacrifice fly on 8/3 vs. San Diego…was placed on the 15-day disabled list on 8/4 and transferred to the 60-day D.L. on 9/6…was his first career appearance on the disabled list.

▸ Appeared in just five games during spring training with the Dodgers, batting .286 (4-for-14) with 2R and 1RBI…missed time after straining his groin on 3/6.

BESTS & STREAKS

Hits
4 – 3 times
Last: at NYM, 5/30/08
Runs
3 – 14 times
Last: at MIL, 7/10/09
2B
2 – 4 times
Last: vs. STL, 8/18/09
3B
1 – 7 times
Last: at SF, 9/9/07
HR
2 – vs. HOU, 8/15/07
RBI
4 – 7 times
Last: vs. CHC, 8/20/09
BB
4 – at PHI, 8/23/07
SO
3 – 8 times
Last: vs. NYY, 6/27/10
SB
2 – 4 times
Last: at SF, 6/29/10
Hitting Streak
15g – 5/5-20/10

2009

▸ Batted .250 (126-for-505) with 63R, 19 doubles, 7HR and 53RBI in 143 games (133 starts at C) with the Dodgers…recorded 11SB, leading all Major League catchers in the category for the third straight season.

▸ Ranked second in the Majors in starts at catcher, trailing only Yadier Molina (136)…his 1,201.0 innings at catcher led the Majors…caught 25-of-99 (25.3%) potential base stealers…only Detroit's Gerald Laird (39) caught more base runners trying to steal.

CATCHERS TO WIN NL SILVER SLUGGER AND NL GOLD GLOVE AWARDS IN SAME SEASON	
PLAYER / TEAM	YEARS
RUSSELL MARTIN / DODGERS 2007	
Benito Santiago / San Diego . . . . 1988, '90	
Gary Carter / Montreal 1981-82	

▸ Made his only appearance at 3B on 8/12 loss at San Francisco, moving defensively from catcher in the 10th inning.

▸ Hit his second career grand slam on 8/20 vs. Chicago-NL off Angel Guzman (also a "walk-off" grand slam on 4/21/07 vs. Pittsburgh).

▸ Stole his 60th career base on 10/3 vs. Colorado, establishing a Dodgers franchise record for catchers, surpassing Johnny Roseboro (59).

▸ Went 5-for-25 (.200) with 1 double and 3RBI in eight postseason games.

▸ Played for Canada in the World Baseball Classic prior to the season, batting .222 (2-for-9) in two games.

2008

▸ Hit .280 (155-for-553) with 87R, 25 doubles, 13HR and 69RBI in 155 games (138 starts at C, eight at 3B) with the Dodgers…walked more times (90) than he struck out (83)…batted in every spot in the lineup except ninth.

▸ Tied for the Major League lead in games caught (149), breaking Mike Piazza's Dodgers single-season franchise record (146, 1993 and '96)…ranked second in the Majors with 138 starts at catcher and 1,238.0 innings caught…posted a 3.62 catcher's ERA, the best mark in the NL and second-best in the Majors behind Toronto's Rod Barajas (3.32).

▸ Made 11 appearances (eight starts) at third base, marking his first ever Major League action at the position.

▸ Was selected to the NL All-Star team for the second straight season, getting voted in on the player ballot…became the first Dodgers position player to make back-to-back All-Star appearances since Paul Lo Duca in 2003-04…caught 10-of-15 innings in the game.

▸ Hit .356 (36-for-101) in May, his highest average and most hits ever in a calendar month during his career.

▸ Batted leadoff for the first time in his career on 8/29 at Arizona, going 1-for-5…hit leadoff in 18 of the Dodgers' final 26 games of the season and 28 times overall…the Dodgers went 14-4 when he batted leadoff.

2007

▸ Batted .293 (158-for-540) with 87R, 32 doubles, 19HR and 87RBI in 151 games (143 starts at C) with the Dodgers…his 21 stolen bases led all Major League catchers and set the single-season Dodgers franchise record by a catcher, surpassing Con Daily's 18SB in 1892…became the first Major League catcher with at least 15HR and 20SB in a single season since Ivan Rodriguez w/ Texas in 1999.

▸ Earned the Silver Slugger Award and Gold Glove Award, joining Dusty Baker in 1981 as the only Dodgers players to ever win both honors in the same season…along with Gary Carter (1981-82) and Benito Santiago (1988, '90), is one of just three NL catchers to win both awards in the same season.

▸ Was named the Tip O'Neill Award winner as the top Canadian Major League player…was also named to the *Sporting News* National League All-Star team.

▸ Became just the sixth catcher in Dodgers history to collect at least 80RBI in a season, joining Roy Campanella (six times), Mike Piazza (five), Paul Lo Duca (one), Joe Ferguson (one) and Bruce Edwards (one).

▸ Hit .357 (46-for-129) with a .458 on-base percentage against left-handed pitching, marking the second-highest single-season OBP vs. left-handers by a Dodger since 1974, trailing only Jimmy Wynn (.488OBP in 1975).

▸ Led all ML catchers with 145 games and 1,254.0 innings caught…his 3.95 catcher's ERA was fourth in the NL.

▸ Was named to his first All-Star team, going 0-for-3 after being elected as the league's starting catcher…was the first Dodgers catcher to start the Midsummer Classic since Mike Piazza in 1997…became the first Canadian catcher in All-Star history and just the third Canadian Dodger to make an All-Star team, joining Eric Gagne and Grady Rosen, who was selected in 1945, but did not play…was the third Canadian player to start an All-Star Game, joining Larry Walker (1997-99) and Jason Bay (2006)…the shoes he wore during the game were sent to the Canadian Baseball Hall of Fame.

▸ Hit his first career grand slam on 4/21 vs. Pittsburgh, a 10th-inning "walk-off" home run off Shawn Chacon…was the 11th "walk-off" grand slam and the sixth extra-inning grand slam in Dodgers history.

▸ Caught each of the 17 innings in 4/29 win at San Diego, collecting 2H in a career-high 8AB.

▸ Recorded his first career multi-homer game in 8/15 win at Houston.

▸ Hit .308 (4-for-13) with 3 doubles, 1HR and 5RBI in the NLDS against the Cubs, including a key, three-run double that sparked the club's Game 2 victory in Chicago…batted . 118 (2-for-17) in the NLCS loss vs. Philadelphia.

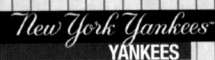

2006

- In his first Major League action, hit .282 (117-for-415) with 65R, 26 doubles, 10HR, 65RBI and 10SB in 121 games (114 starts at C) with the Dodgers...joined John Roseboro and Benito Santiago as the only rookie catchers in Baseball history with at least 10HR and 10SB in their first Major League season...marked the most SB by a Dodgers catcher since Roseboro in 1962 (10SB)...named to the Topps Major League Rookie All-Star team.
- Was just the sixth Dodgers catcher since 1900 to steal at least 10 bases in a single season, joining Lew Ritter (1904-05), Otto Miller (1912), Al Lopez (1933), Mickey Owen (1942) and Roseboro (1958, '62).
- Threw out 25-of-96 potential basestealers (26.0%)...recorded a 3.93 catcher's ERA, third-best in the NL...did not make an error over his first 47 games (5/5-7/2) and committed just 6E overall.
- Made his Major League debut on 5/5 vs. Milwaukee, collecting his first career hit with a two-run double off Chris Capuano...was recalled from Triple-A Las Vegas prior to the game when Dioner Navarro was placed on the 15-day D.L. with a fractured right wrist...hit first Major League HR on 5/7 vs. Milwaukee off Dave Bush.
- Hit 10th-inning "walk-off" home run on 8/13 vs. San Francisco, driving in the game's only run...was the first extra-inning, "walk-off" home run in a 1-0 win in the Majors since the Dodgers' Paul Lo Duca in 2002.
- Hit the third of four consecutive home runs in the bottom of the ninth inning of 9/18 win vs. San Diego...was part of the third time in Major League history a team hit four consecutive home runs.
- Began the season with Triple-A Las Vegas, batting .297 (22-for-74) with 14R, 9 doubles, and 9RBI in 23 games.
- Went 4-for-12 (.333) with 2R in the three NLDS games vs. New York-NL.

2005

- Hit .311 (127-for-409) with 83R, 17 doubles, 9HR and 61RBI in 129 games with Double-A Jacksonville...ranked second in the Southern League with a .430 on-base pct., and was named to the SL postseason All-Star team
- Was selected to play for the World Team in the All-Star Futures Game on 7/10, going 0-for-1 with 1BB after entering the game as a pinch-hitter in the fifth inning and remaining in the game at C.
- Following the season, was ranked as the Dodgers' fourth-best prospect, according to *Baseball America*, which also tabbed him as having the "Best Strike-Zone Judgment" and as the "Best Defensive Catcher" in the Southern League and entire Dodgers' minor league system.

2004

- Hit .250 (104-for-416) with 74R, 24 doubles, 15HR and 64RBI in 122 games with Single-A Vero Beach...led the Florida State League with 72BB.
- Was selected to play in the FSL All-Star Game and named to the FSL postseason All-Star team.
- Played for Scottsdale in the Arizona Fall League after the season, batting .296 (16-for-54) with 9RBI in 17 games...was rated by *Baseball America* as the eighth-best prospect in the AFL.
- Following the season, was named the sixth-best prospect in the Dodgers organization by *Baseball America*.

2003

- Combined to bat .276 (79-for-286) with 40R, 17 doubles, 9HR and 50RBI in 77 games with Single-A South Georgia and rookie-level Ogden, converting from third baseman to catcher at the beginning of the season.
- Began the season with South Georgia, batting .286 (28-for-98) in 25 games...was transferred to Ogden on 6/12 where he hit .271 (51-for-188) in 52 games.

2002

- Hit .286 (36-for-126) with 22R, 3 doubles, 3 triples and 10RBI in 41 games for the GCL Dodgers in his first professional season.

PERSONAL

- Full name is Russell Nathan Jeanson Coltrane Martin Jr...in 2009, added the letter "J" on the back of his uniform in addition to Martin as a tribute to his mother's side of the family, whose last name is Jeanson.
- On 6/18/09, announced a donation of $600,000 over the next 10 years to the ONE DROP Foundation, whose mission is to fight poverty by supporting access to clean water...the foundation also seeks to raise awareness of water-related issues and the need to get involved to ensure good quality water is accessible to all in sufficient quantity, today and tomorrow...launched his official Web site, www.russellmartin55.com the same day.
- Took part in the 2006-09 Dodger Caravans...made visits to the Center for Cancer and Blood Diseases.
- Earned the Heart & Hustle Award in 2007, which is chosen by the MLB Players Alumni Association...was also awarded the annual Roy Campanella Award in 2007 as the "Most Inspirational Dodger," which is voted upon by his teammates and coaches.

▸ Won a fan vote at dodgers.com to have his likeness depicted on "Bobblehead Night" on 8/2/07, marking the first time fans decided which player would appear on a Los Angeles Dodgers promotional giveaway.

▸ Was selected to play for the Canadian team in the 2000 World Junior Championships…also chosen as a member of Canada's qualifying team for the 2004 Olympic Games.

▸ Is a graduate of Polyvalente Edouard-Montpetit High School in Montreal, the same high school attended by Eric Gagne…played third base at Chipola Junior College in Marianna, Fla…was slated to attend North Carolina State University before being drafted by the Dodgers…lived in Paris from ages 8-10.

▸ His father, Russell Sr., is an accomplished saxophone player and played the National Anthem on his saxophone before a Dodgers/Pirates game on 9/20/06 at Dodger Stadium…his middle name (Coltrane) is a nod to jazz musician John Coltrane.

Martin's Career Playing Record

Year	Club	AVG	G	AB	R	H	2B	3B	HR	RBI	SH	SF	HP	BB	SO	SB	CS	E	OBP	SLG
2002	GCL Dodgers	.286	41	126	22	36	3	3	0	10	2	0	4	23	18	7	1	9	.412	.357
2003	South Georgia	.286	25	98	15	28	4	1	3	14	1	1	0	9	11	5	2	5	.343	.439
	Ogden	.271	52	188	25	51	13	0	6	36	2	2	4	26	26	3	1	13	.368	.436
2004	Vero Beach	.250	122	416	74	104	24	1	15	64	0	8	10	72	54	9	5	10	.368	.421
2005	Jacksonville	.311	129	409	83	127	17	1	9	61	5	3	10	78	69	15	7	11	.430	.423
2006	Las Vegas	.297	23	74	14	22	9	0	0	9	1	3	0	13	11	0	2	2	.389	.419
	LOS ANGELES-NL	.282	121	415	65	117	26	4	10	65	1	3	4	45	57	10	5	6	.355	.436
2007	LOS ANGELES-NL	.293	151	540	87	158	32	3	19	87	0	6	7	67	89	21	9	14	.374	.469
2008	LOS ANGELES-NL	.280	155	553	87	155	25	0	13	69	0	2	5	90	83	18	6	14	.385	.396
2009	LOS ANGELES-NL	.250	143	505	63	126	19	0	7	53	2	1	11	69	80	11	6	7	.352	.329
2010	LOS ANGELES-NL –a,b	.248	97	331	45	82	13	0	5	26	1	3	4	48	61	6	2	10	.347	.332
Minor League Totals		**.281**	**392**	**1311**	**233**	**368**	**70**	**6**	**33**	**194**	**11**	**17**	**28**	**221**	**189**	**39**	**18**	**50**	**.391**	**.419**
Major League Totals		**.272**	**667**	**2344**	**347**	**638**	**115**	**7**	**54**	**300**	**4**	**15**	**31**	**319**	**370**	**66**	**28**	**51**	**.365**	**.396**

Selected by the Dodgers in the 17th round of the 2002 First-Year Player Draft.

a – Placed on the 15-day disabled list on August 4, 2010 for the rest of the season…transferred to the 60-day D.L. on September 6, 2010.
b – Signed by the Yankees as a free agent on December 16, 2010.

Martin's Division Series Record

Year	Country, Site	AVG	G	AB	R	H	2B	3B	HR	RBI	SH	SF	HP	BB	SO	SB	CS	E	OBP	SLG
2006	LAD vs. NYM	.333	3	12	2	4	0	0	0	0	0	0	0	1	2	0	0	0	.385	.333
2008	LAD vs. CHC	.308	3	13	2	4	3	0	1	5	0	0	0	1	3	0	0	0	.357	.769
2009	LAD vs. STL	.111	3	9	0	1	0	0	0	1	0	0	1	3	1	0	0	0	.385	.111
Division Series Totals		**.265**	**9**	**34**	**4**	**9**	**3**	**0**	**1**	**6**	**0**	**0**	**1**	**5**	**6**	**0**	**0**	**0**	**.375**	**.441**

Martin's League Championship Series Record

Year	Country, Site	AVG	G	AB	R	H	2B	3B	HR	RBI	SH	SF	HP	BB	SO	SB	CS	E	OBP	SLG
2008	LAD vs. PHI	.118	5	17	3	2	0	0	0	1	0	0	2	3	7	1	0	0	.318	.118
2009	LAD vs. PHI	.250	5	16	2	4	1	0	0	2	0	0	1	1	3	0	0	0	.333	.313
LCS Totals		**.182**	**10**	**33**	**5**	**6**	**1**	**0**	**0**	**3**	**0**	**0**	**3**	**4**	**10**	**1**	**0**	**0**	**.325**	**.212**
POSTSEASON TOTALS		**.224**	**19**	**67**	**9**	**15**	**4**	**0**	**1**	**9**	**0**	**0**	**4**	**9**	**16**	**1**	**0**	**0**	**.350**	**.328**

Martin's All-Star Game Record

Year	Country, Site	AVG	G	AB	R	H	2B	3B	HR	RBI	SH	SF	HP	BB	SO	SB	CS	E	OBP	SLG
2007	LAD, San Francisco	.000	1	3	0	0	0	0	0	0	0	0	0	0	1	0	0	0	.000	.000
2008	LAD, New York-AL	.000	1	3	0	1	0	0	0	0	1	0	0	0	0	0	0	0	.333	.333
All-Star Game Totals		**.000**	**2**	**6**	**0**	**1**	**0**	**0**	**0**	**0**	**1**	**0**	**0**	**0**	**1**	**0**	**0**	**0**	**.167**	**.167**

Martin's World Baseball Classic Record

Year	Country, Site	AVG	G	AB	R	H	2B	3B	HR	RBI	SH	SF	HP	BB	SO	SB	CS	E	OBP	SLG
2009	Canada, USA	.222	2	9	3	2	1	0	1	1	0	0	1	1	2	0	0	0	.300	.667
WBC Totals		**.222**	**2**	**9**	**3**	**2**	**1**	**0**	**1**	**1**	**0**	**0**	**1**	**1**	**2**	**0**	**0**	**0**	**.300**	**.667**

Martin's Career Fielding Record

Position	PCT	G	PO	A	E	TC	PB
Catcher	.990	641	4615	358	48	5021	24
Third Base	.885	12	2	21	3	26	---

Martin's Career Home Run Chart

MULTI-HOMER GAMES: 1; **TWO-HOMER GAMES:** 1, on 8/15/07 vs. Houston (Jason Jennings); **GRAND SLAMS:** 2, last on 8/20/09 vs. Chicago-NL (Angel Guzman); **PINCH-HIT HR:** 1, on 9/26/08 at San Francisco (Brian Wilson); **INSIDE-THE-PARK HR:** None; **WALK-OFF HR:** 2, last on 4/21/07 vs. Pittsburgh (Shawn Chacon); **LEADOFF HR:** None.

63

JUSTIN MAXWELL

OUTFIELDER • 6-5 • 235 • B/T: R/R • OPENING DAY AGE: 27

BIRTHDATE
November 6, 1983

BIRTHPLACE
Bethesda, Md.

RESIDES
Union Bridge, Md.

M.L. SERVICE
1 year, 38 days

COLLEGE
University of Maryland

STATUS

▸ Acquired by the Yankees from Washington in exchange for RHP Adam Olbrychowski on February 2, 2011…signed through the 2011 season.

CAREER NOTES

▸ Has six career plate appearances with the bases loaded, going 3-for-5 with three grand slams, 13RBI and 1BB…his three grand slams include a pinch-hit slam on 9/11/07 at Florida for his first big league hit, a "walk-off" slam on 9/30/09 vs. the Mets and a game-winning slam on 9/15/10 at Atlanta…hit all three grand slams within his first four career at-bats with the bases loaded, joining the Yankees' Shane Spencer (1998) as the only two players in Major League history to accomplish the feat.

2010

▸ Batted .144 (15-for-104) with 6 doubles, 3HR, 12RBI and 5SB in 67 games (13 starts in CF, 10 in RF and three in LF) over four stints (4/15-5/7; 5/23-28; 7/10-19 and 8/2-10/3) with the Nationals.

▸ Drew 25BB in 131 plate appearances, a ratio of 5.24PA per walk…marked the second-highest such ratio in the Majors among players with a minimum of 100PA, trailing only Cleveland's Carlos Santana (5.19PA/BB).

▸ Hit his third career grand slam off Mike Minor in the second inning on 9/15 at Atlanta, accounting for all four Nationals runs in a 4-2 victory.

▸ Hit .287 (66-for-230) with 17 doubles, 6HR, 21RBI, 16SB and 35BB in 66 games with AAA Syracuse…recorded a .348 (23-for-66) average against left-handers with the Chiefs.

▸ Underwent "Tommy John" surgery on his left elbow on 10/13 after suffering the injury while diving for a ball on 10/2.

2009

▸ Hit .247 (22-for-89) with 4 doubles, 4HR, 9RBI and 6SB in 40 games over three stints (4/19-27; 5/20-29 and 9/1-10/4) with the Nationals…averaged one walk every 8.5 plate appearances.

▸ Batted .292 (19-for-65) with all 4HR in 27 games following his September callup…recorded his first career multi-homer game in 9/12 loss at Florida…hit "walk-off" grand slam off Francisco Rodriguez, on a 3-2 count (trailing 4-3) in 9/30 win vs. the Mets…hit second "walk-off" homer of the season three days later in 10/3 win at Atlanta with a two-run opposite field homer off Manny Acosta.

▸ In 111 games with Triple-A Syracuse, hit .242 (93-for-384) with 68R, 10 doubles, 13HR, 42RBI and 35 SB (in 43 attempts)…ranked fourth in the International League in stolen bases…also led the team in walks (54) and runs scored, and tied for tops on the team with 5 triples.

BESTS & STREAKS

Hits:
3 – vs. PHI, 9/9/09
Runs
2 – 3 times
Last: at FLA, 9/1/10
2B
2 – at FLA, 9/1/10
3B
1 – at ATL, 10/2/09
HR
2 – at FLA, 9/12/09
RBI
4 – 3 times
Last: at ATL, 9/15/10
BB
3 – at ATL, 10/4/09
SO
4 – 2 times
Last: at LAD, 8/6/10
SB
2 – at NYM, 4/26/09
Hit Streak
5 games, 9/28-10/3/09

2008

- Opened the year at Double-A Harrisburg, appearing in just 43 games before having his season cut short with a fractured right wrist sustained on 5/19 at New Britain...hit .233 (34-for-146) with 6 doubles, 7HR, 28RBI, 13SB and 31BB prior to the injury.
- Following the season, played winter ball for Caguas of the Puerto Rican Winter League.

2007

- Began the season with Single-A Hagerstown, rising all the way to the Majors as a September callup with the Nationals...in his first Major League action, hit .269 (7-for-26) with 2HR and 5RBI in 15 games.
- Was signed to a Major League contract and selected from Single-A Potomac on 9/4, appearing with the Major League team despite not ever playing a game at the Double-A or Triple-A levels...made his Major League debut as a pinch-hitter in 9/5 win vs. Florida (fly out).
- Collected his first big league hit—a pinch hit grand slam off Chris Seddon—in 9/11 loss at Florida...came in his third ML at-bat, becoming the first player in Montreal/Washington franchise history to hit a grand slam as his first homer since Scott Sanderson on 9/11/82 at Chicago-NL.
- Selected as the Nationals' "Minor League Player of the Year" after combining to hit .281 (123-for-437) with 25 doubles, 27HR, 83RBI and 35SB with Hagerstown and Potomac...led Nationals farmhands in homers, ranking second in both RBI and stolen bases...twice earned Topps Player of the Month honors (May in the South Atlantic League and August in the Carolina League).
- Was one of six players to tally at least 25 doubles, 25HR and 25SB—combined at any level—joining Cincinnati's Brandon Phillips (26-30-32), Florida's Hanley Ramirez (48-29-51), Philadelphia's Jimmy Rollins (38-30-41), the Mets' David Wright (42-30-34) and Arizona's Chris Young (29-32-27).
- Following the season, played in 30 games with the Peoria Javelinas in the Arizona Fall League.

2006

- In his professional debut, combined at Single-A Savannah and short-season Single-A Vermont to bat .252 (83-for-329) with 13 doubles, 5 triples, 5HR and 40RBI in 91 games...spent majority of season at Vermont, where he led the New York-Penn League in games (74) and ranked fifth in stolen bases (20).

PERSONAL

- Full name is Justin Austin Maxwell...compiled a 4.0 GPA at Sherwood (MD) High School and chose to attend Maryland over Harvard...while at Sherwood, lettered twice in both baseball and basketball...was named second-team All-Met by the *Washington Post*.
- In three seasons at Maryland, hit .299 with 20 doubles, 16HR, 71RBI and 24SB in 103 games...named a 2005 preseason All-America, and was rated as the "Best Athlete" and "Top Defensive Outfielder" in the ACC entering the 2005 season by *Baseball America*...played in Cape Cod League in 2004, batting .263 with 4 doubles, 1HR and 9SB.

Maxwell's Career Batting Record

Year	Team	AVG	G	AB	R	H	2B	3B	HR	RBI	SH	SF	HP	BB	SO	SB	CS	E	OBP	SLG
2006	Savannah	.172	17	58	8	10	2	2	1	7	0	0	2	8	23	1	0	0	.294	.328
	Vermont	.269	74	271	36	73	11	3	4	33	0	2	6	27	61	20	5	5	.346	.376
2007	Hagerstown	.301	56	209	51	63	12	2	14	40	0	1	6	26	57	14	3	1	.389	.579
	Potomac	.263	58	228	35	60	13	0	13	43	0	4	4	24	65	21	5	2	.338	.491
	WASHINGTON	.269	15	26	5	7	0	0	2	5	0	0	0	1	8	0	0	0	.296	.500
2008	Harrisburg	.233	43	146	35	34	6	3	7	28	0	2	1	31	28	13	4	3	.367	.459
2009	Syracuse	.242	111	384	68	93	10	5	13	42	3	1	6	54	136	35	8	2	.344	.396
	WASHINGTON	.247	40	89	13	22	4	1	4	9	0	0	1	12	32	6	1	0	.343	.449
2010	Syracuse	.287	66	230	34	66	17	0	6	21	3	0	4	35	75	16	7	6	.390	.439
	WASHINGTON	.144	67	104	16	15	6	0	3	12	0	2	0	25	43	5	1	2	.305	.288
Minor League Totals		**.261**	**425**	**1526**	**267**	**399**	**71**	**15**	**58**	**214**	**6**	**12**	**29**	**205**	**445**	**120**	**32**	**19**	**.357**	**.442**
Major League Totals		**.201**	**122**	**219**	**34**	**44**	**10**	**1**	**9**	**26**	**0**	**2**	**1**	**38**	**83**	**11**	**2**	**2**	**.319**	**.379**

Selected by Washington in the fourth round of the 2005 First-Year Player Draft.

Maxwell's Career Fielding Record

Position	Pct.	G	PO	A	E	TC	DP
Outfield	.987	93	150	5	2	157	2

Maxwell's Career Home Run Chart

MULTI-HOMER GAMES: 1; **TWO-HOMER GAMES:** 1, on 9/12/09 at Florida; **GRAND SLAMS:** 3, last on 9/15/10 at Atlanta (Mike Minor); **PINCH-HIT HR:** 1, on 9/11/07 at Florida (Chris Seddon-GS); **INSIDE-THE-PARK HR:** None; **WALK-OFF HR:** 1, on 9/30/09 vs. New York-NL (off Francisco Rodriguez-GS); **LEADOFF HR:** None.

77 MELKY MESA

OUTFIELDER • 6-1 • 189 • B/T: RIGHT/RIGHT • OPENING DAY AGE: 24

BIRTHDATE
January 31, 1987

BIRTHPLACE
Bajos de Haina, D.R.

RESIDES
Bajos de Haina, D.R.

M.L. SERVICE
None
 (Rookie)

STATUS

▸ Signed by the Yankees as a non-drafted free agent on July 2, 2003…signed through the 2011 season.

2010

▸ Was named the Florida State League's "Player of the Year" after hitting .260 (116-for-446) with 81R, 21 doubles, 9 triples, 19HR and 74RBI in 121 games with Single-A Tampa…set career highs in runs, hits and triples and tied his career high in RBI…was named to the FSL postseason All-Star team.

▸ Ranked third among all Yankees minor leaguers in home runs (19) and stolen bases (31) and fifth in RBI (74)…ranked second in the FSL in slugging percentage (.475), third in HR, triples (9) and extra-base hits (49) and fifth in runs (81)…ranked second in the league with 1HR every 23.47AB.

▸ Hit two grand slams (6/7 vs. Jupiter and 7/7 at Daytona) and hit .286 (2-for-7) with 10RBI with the bases loaded.

▸ Was named the FSL "Player of the Week" for the period from 8/2-9, batting .406 (13-for-32) with 5R, 3 doubles, 2HR and 9RBI in seven games…recorded two four-hit games during the span (8/3 at Ft. Myers and 8/5 vs. St. Lucie)…hit an 11th-inning "walk-off" RBI single on 8/5.

▸ Following the season, was rated by *Baseball America* as the "Best Athlete" and as having the "Best Outfield Arm" in the Yankees organization.

▸ Was added to the Yankees' 40-man roster on 11/1/10.

2009

▸ Hit .225 (112-for-497) with 24 doubles, 7 triples, 74RBI and a career-high 20HR in 133 games with Single-A Charleston…finished the season tied for fourth in the South Atlantic League in home runs and ranked fifth in runs (76)…hit all 20HR in his first 93 games of the season (from 4/9-7/23), going homerless in his final 40 contests of the year (7/24-9/7).

▸ Was the only RiverDogs player to be selected to both the South Atlantic League's midseason and postseason All-Star teams…hit 2HR in a game three times (4/15 vs. Augusta, 4/22 at Augusta and 6/25 at Savannah).

▸ Was named the SAL's "Player of the Week" from 6/23-29, batting .550 (11-for-20) with 3R, 1 triple, 2HR, 5RBI and 2BB in five games over the stretch.

▸ Was tabbed by *Baseball America* as the "Fastest Baserunner," "Best Athlete" and as having the "Best Outfield Arm" in the Yankees organization.

2004-08

▸ Made his professional debut in 2004, batting .146 (21-for-144) with 3HR and 10RBI in 49 games for the Yankees' DSL 2 squad.

▸ In 2005, appeared in eight games with the DSL Yankees 1, batting .304 (7-for-23).

▸ Batted .207 (30-for-145) in 40 games with the GCL Yankees, appearing in 39 games in the outfield in 2006.

▸ Hit .235 (36-for-153) with 27R, 10 doubles, 3HR and 13RBI in 49 games with the GCL Yankees in 2007.

▸ In 2008, batted .221 (27-for-122) with 19R, 5 doubles, 2 triples, 7HR and 23RBI in 46 games with short-season Single-A Staten Island…led the team in homers…over half (14) of his 27 hits went for extra bases.

PERSONAL

▸ Full name is Melquisedec Mesa.

Mesa's Career Playing Record

Year	Club	AVG	G	AB	R	H	2B	3B	HR	RBI	SH	SF	HP	BB	SO	SB	CS	E	OBP	SLG
2004	DSL Yankees 2	.146	49	144	13	21	5	0	3	10	0	1	15	12	67	2	2	-	.279	.243
2005	DSL Yankees 1	.304	8	23	3	7	2	0	2	6	0	0	1	3	7	1	0	-	.407	.652
2006	GCL Yankees	.207	40	145	20	30	7	2	3	22	1	1	1	11	45	3	3	4	.266	.345
2007	GCL Yankees	.235	49	153	27	36	10	2	3	13	2	1	4	9	55	5	3	8	.293	.386
2008	Staten Island	.221	46	122	19	27	5	2	7	23	1	0	1	4	38	4	1	2	.252	.467
2009	Charleston	.225	133	497	76	112	24	7	20	74	0	5	11	51	168	18	6	14	.309	.423
2010	Tampa	.260	121	446	81	116	21	9	19	74	1	5	11	44	129	31	9	4	.338	.475
Minor League Totals		**.228**	**446**	**1530**	**239**	**349**	**74**	**22**	**57**	**222**	**5**	**13**	**44**	**134**	**509**	**64**	**24**	**32**	**.306**	**.417**

Signed by the Yankees as a non-drafted free agent on July 2, 2003.

Steinbrenner High Opens

Named after the Yankees Principal Owner, George M. Steinbrenner High School opened in August 2009 on Lutz Lake Fern Road just north of Tampa.

"Over the years, Mr. Steinbrenner has been deeply involved in the community, particularly with the schools and the school system," said Steven Ayers, director of community relations for Hillsborough County public schools. "He's been very involved and very philanthropic. He's probably donated in tens of millions over the length of time. He's had a significant amount of money and significant amount of involvement in the community."

In addition to regular classroom curriculum, the school also offers classes for students preparing for a career in sports with sports marketing, sports medicine and the business of sports (BOSS). The school's mascot is the Warriors, featuring navy and gold coloring.

45 SERGIO MITRE

RIGHT-HANDED PITCHER • 6-3 • 225 • B/T: RIGHT/RIGHT • OPENING DAY AGE: 30

BIRTHDATE
February 16, 1981

BIRTHPLACE
Los Angeles, Calif.

RESIDES
Chula Vista, Calif.

M.L. SERVICE
5 years, 132 days

COLLEGE
San Diego City College

STATUS
▸ Signed to a one-year contract on December 2, 2010…signed through the 2011 season.

2010
▸ Was 0-3 with one save and a 3.33 ERA in 27 appearances (three starts) with the Yankees…opponents batted .223 (43-for-193, 7HR); LH .226 (24-for-106, 3HR), RH .218 (19-for-87, 4HR)…retired 17-of-24 first batters faced (70.8%)…prevented five-of-nine inherited runners from scoring (55.6%)…appeared in consecutive games four times.
▸ Went 0-1 with a 2.45 ERA in 24 relief appearances…11 of his 24 relief outings were at least 2.0IP…17 of his 24 outings were scoreless.
▸ In three starts, was 0-2 with a 5.93 ERA (13.2IP, 9ER), throwing no more than 5.0 innings each start.
▸ Made his third career Opening Day roster in 2010, first with the Yankees…began the season in the bullpen, holding opponents scoreless in three of his first six outings (2.79 ERA, 9.2IP, 3ER).
▸ Made consecutive starts on 5/10 at Detroit (loss) and 5/16 vs. Minnesota (no-decision), replacing Javier Vazquez in the rotation.
▸ Returned to the bullpen from 5/22-6/4, allowing just 2H and 1ER in 6.0IP over five outings (2BB, 5K, 1HBP)…appeared on consecutive days in 5/22 and 5/23 losses at the Mets, marking the first time in his career pitching on back-to-back days.
▸ Was placed on the 15-day disabled list from 6/15-7/24 with a strained left oblique (suffered during batting practice), missing 32 team games.
▸ Made five rehab appearances (four starts), combining to go 0-2 with a 4.61 ERA (13.2IP, 11H, 7ER, 2BB, 1HR, 16K) with Single-A Tampa, the GCL Yankees and Triple-A Scranton/Wilkes-Barre.
▸ Was returned from rehab and reinstated from the D.L. on 7/24…made his third-and final-start of the sease that night vs. Kansas City, allowing 7H and 5ER in 4.1IP to record his second loss (7R, 1BB, 1K, 1HR, 1HBP).
▸ Returned to the bullpen on 7/28 for the remainder of the year, going 0-1 with a 2.55 ERA (24.2IP, 7ER)…earned his first career save in 8/19 win vs. Detroit, pitching the final 3.0 innings of the Yankees' victory (6H, 3ER, 1BB, 3K, 1HR).
▸ Tossed 4.2 scoreless innings in 8/28 loss at Chicago-AL (1H, 1BB), tying for the longest outing by a Yankees reliever in 2010.
▸ Suffered his third loss of the season on 9/13 at Tampa Bay, throwing one pitch and allowing a "walk-off" home run to Reid Brignac in the bottom of the 11th inning of a 1-0 Yankees loss…was the first game-ending homer allowed in his career…became the first Yankee to surrender a "walk-off" homer in an extra-inning, 1-0 loss since Paul Quantrill on 5/18/04 at the Angels (Adam Riggs 11th-inning RBI single).
▸ Did not allow a run over his last four outings (4.2IP), holding opponents hitless over his final three appearances (0-for-8).
▸ Made his postseason debut, appearing in three games and surrendering 3ER in 2.2IP.

BESTS & STREAKS
Low hit CG
  5 - vs. FLA, 6/14/05
IP (start)
  9.0 - vs. FLA, 6/14/05
IP (relief)
  5.0 - at SEA, 9/20/09
Hits
  12 - at KC, 6/15/07
Runs
  11 - at TOR, 9/6/09
BB
  4 - 5 times
  Last: at COL, 9/15/07
SO
  8 - vs. NYM, 5/25/07
HR
  4 - vs. TOR, 9/15/09
Winning Streak
  2g - 4 times
  Last: 8/15-29/09
Losing Streak
  7g - 4/11/06-4/11/07

2009

- Was 3-3 with a 6.79 ERA in 12 appearances (nine starts) with the Yankees…did not record a decision in his three relief outings, posting a 4.70 ERA…went 3-3 with a 7.16 ERA as a starter, allowing 65H in 44.0IP…opponents batted .321 (71-for-221, 10HR); LH .421 (40-for-95, 6HR); RH .246 (31-for-126, 4HR).
- Allowed at least one run in the first inning of six of his nine starts, compiling an 8.00 first-inning ERA (9.0IP, 8ER)…had a 6.94 ERA (35.0IP, 27ER) from the second inning onward.
- Was signed to a Major League contract and selected to the Yankees' 25-man roster from Triple-A Scranton/Wilkes-Barre on 7/21…started and recorded the win that night vs. Baltimore at Yankee Stadium, allowing 3ER and 8H in 5.2IP (4R, 1BB, 4K)…was his first Major League start since 9/15/07 w/ Florida at Colorado and his first Major League win since 7/29/07 w/ Florida at San Francisco.
- Moved to the bullpen for the final two weeks of the season and made two relief appearances…tossed 5.0 scoreless innings in 9/20 loss at Seattle (1H, 1BB, 5K)…was the longest relief outing of his career (previous was 3.0IP) and longest by a Yankees reliever in 2009.
- Opened the year on the disabled list, recovering from "Tommy John" surgery…also served a 50-game suspension at the start of the season for violating Major League Baseball's Drug Prevention and Treatment Program…made nine combined starts with Single-A Tampa and Triple-A Scranton/Wilkes-Barre, going 4-1 with a 2.32 ERA…named the International League "Pitcher of the Week" with Scranton/Wilkes-Barre for the period from 7/6-12.

2008

- Underwent "Tommy John" surgery on 7/15 and did not pitch the entire season…opened the year on the disabled list with a right elbow strain.

2007

- Went 5-8 with a 4.65 ERA in 27 starts with the Marlins, setting career highs in wins, games, starts, IP (149.0) and strikeouts (80)…began the season with a 1.59 ERA (56.2IP, 10ER) through his first 10 starts.
- Left his third start on 4/17 at Houston with a blister on his right middle finger and was placed on the 15-day disabled list from 4/18-5/5…did not allow an earned run in 24.2 consecutive innings over five starts from 5/20-6/15…was winless over his final eight starts from 8/4-9/15 (0-3, 7.96 ERA).

2006

- Went 1-5 with 5.71 ERA in 15 games (seven starts) in his first season with the Florida Marlins…was 1-4 with a 4.89 ERA in seven starts, and 0-1 with a 10.50 ERA in eight relief outings…was placed on the 15-day disabled list with right shoulder inflammation on 5/15 and transferred to the 60-day D.L. on 5/26…was reinstated on 8/8 and pitched out of the bullpen for the remainder of the season…was shut down in September.

2005

- Appeared in 21 games over three stints (5/10-12; 5/24-8/5; 9/4-9/30) with Chicago-NL, making seven starts and going 2-5 with a 5.37 ERA.
- Recorded his first Major League shutout and first complete game with 14-0 win vs. Florida on 6/14, allowing just 5H and striking out three in 9.0IP…was the second of back-to-back starts without allowing a run (also 6/8 vs. Toronto – 7.0IP, 2H).
- Pitched for Hermosillo in the Mexican Winter League, going 0-1 with 4.15 ERA in three starts…was acquired by the Marlins following the season in a trade for OF Juan Pierre.

2004

- Made his first career Opening Day roster and went 2-4 with a 6.62 ERA in 12 appearances (nine starts) over two stints with the Cubs…earned his first Major League win in his start on 4/21 at Pittsburgh, allowing only 4H over 6.0 scoreless innings in a 12-1 victory.
- While with Triple-A Iowa, went 6-3 with a 2.98 ERA in 18 games (15 starts)…collected his first professional save on 7/6 vs. Albuquerque, tossing the final 4.0 innings of the game (1H, 1ER, 1BB, 5K, 1HR)…tossed a 9.0-inning one-hit shutout on 8/13 vs. Albuquerque with 1BB and 9K.

2003

- Saw his first Major League action, going 0-1 with an 8.31 ERA in three games (two starts) over three stints…was signed to a Major League contract and added to the Cubs' 40-man roster on 7/21 in place of the injured Mark Prior…made his debut on 7/22 at Atlanta in an emergency start, recording the loss in an 8-4 Braves victory (3.2IP, 10H, 8ER, 3BB, 0K, 1HR).
- Made 25 appearances (24 starts) with Double-A West Tenn, going 7-9 with a 3.34 ERA…held his opponents to 1ER or less in 13 starts, including eight of his final 10 outings.

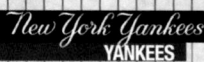
2002

▶ Spent the season at Single-A Lansing, where he went 8-10 with a 2.83 ERA in 27 starts…ranked fourth in the Midwest League in innings pitched (168.2) and sixth in ERA…walked just 27 batters.

2001

▶ Made his professional debut with short-season Single-A Boise, going 8-4 with a 3.07 ERA…ranked second in the Northwest League in wins, innings pitched (91.0) and starts (15) and 10th in ERA…threw the first shutout of his pro career on 7/24 at Tri-City, allowing just 3H in a 9-0 victory.

PERSONAL

▶ Full name is Sergio Armando Mitre (MEE-tray)…originally selected by Chicago-NL in the seventh round of the 2001 First-Year Player Draft…graduated from Montgomery High School (Calif.) in 1999…attended San Diego City College…he and his wife, Tonya, have one son, Sam.

Mitre's Career Pitching Record

Year	Club	W	L	ERA	G	GS	CG	SHO	SV	IP	H	R	ER	HR	HB	BB	SO	WP	BK
2001	Boise	8	4	3.07	15	15	1	1	0	91.0	85	37	31	2	3	18	71	3	3
2002	Lansing	8	10	2.83	27	27	2	0	0	168.2	166	72	53	7	10	27	96	10	0
2003	West Tenn	7	9	3.34	25	24	0	0	0	145.2	162	75	54	6	12	41	128	6	0
	CHICAGO-NL	0	1	8.31	3	2	0	0	0	8.2	15	8	8	1	0	4	3	0	0
2004	Iowa	6	3	2.98	18	15	1	1	1	102.2	97	38	34	9	6	39	95	7	1
	CHICAGO-NL	2	4	6.62	12	9	0	0	0	51.2	71	38	38	6	4	20	37	5	1
2005	Iowa	5	6	4.33	13	13	1	0	0	70.2	72	34	34	5	1	22	55	4	2
	CHICAGO-NL - a	2	5	5.37	21	7	1	1	0	60.1	62	37	36	11	3	23	37	5	0
2006	FLORIDA - b	1	5	5.71	15	7	0	0	0	41.0	44	28	26	7	6	20	31	1	0
	GCL Marlins	0	0	0.00	1	1	0	0	0	1.0	0	0	0	0	1	0	0	0	0
2007	FLORIDA - c	5	8	4.65	27	27	0	0	0	149.0	180	88	77	9	10	41	80	6	0
	Jupiter	2	0	1.00	2	1	0	0	0	9.0	5	1	1	0	0	0	4	0	0
2008								Injured - Did Not Pitch - d											
2009	Tampa - e, f	1	0	1.93	2	2	0	0	0	9.1	10	6	2	0	1	2	8	1	0
	Scranton/WB	3	1	2.40	7	7	0	0	0	45.0	40	13	12	3	3	5	35	1	0
	YANKEES - f	3	3	6.79	12	9	0	0	0	51.2	71	45	39	10	3	13	32	3	0
2010	YANKEES - g	0	3	3.33	27	3	0	0	1	54.0	43	23	20	7	2	16	29	1	0
Minor League Totals		**40**	**33**	**3.09**	**110**	**105**	**5**	**2**	**1**	**643.0**	**637**	**276**	**221**	**32**	**36**	**155**	**492**	**32**	**6**
AL Totals		**3**	**6**	**5.07**	**38**	**12**	**0**	**0**	**1**	**104.2**	**114**	**68**	**59**	**17**	**5**	**29**	**61**	**4**	**0**
NL Totals		**10**	**23**	**5.36**	**78**	**52**	**1**	**1**	**0**	**310.2**	**372**	**199**	**185**	**34**	**23**	**108**	**188**	**17**	**1**
Major League Totals		**13**	**29**	**5.27**	**117**	**64**	**1**	**1**	**1**	**416.1**	**486**	**267**	**244**	**51**	**28**	**137**	**249**	**21**	**1**
NYY Totals		**3**	**6**	**5.07**	**38**	**12**	**0**	**0**	**1**	**104.2**	**114**	**68**	**59**	**17**	**5**	**29**	**61**	**4**	**0**

Selected by Chicago-NL in the seventh round of the 2001 First-Year Player Draft.

a – Traded to Florida from Chicago-NL with RHP Carlos Nolasco and LHP Renyel Pinto in exchange for OF Juan Pierre on December 7, 2005.
b – Placed on the 15-day disabled list from May 13 - August 9, 2006 with right shoulder tendinitis (transferred to the 60-day disabled list on May 26).
c – Placed on the 15-day disabled list from April 18 - May 5, 2007 with a blister on his right middle finger.
d – Placed on the 15-day disabled list on March 21, 2008 with a right elbow strain (transferred to the 60-day disabled list on April 18)…was released on September 29, 2008.
e – Signed by New York-AL as a free agent on November 16, 2008.
f – Served a 50-game suspension from April 9 - June 1, 2009 for violating Major League Baseball's Drug Prevention and Treatment Program.
g – Placed on the 15-day disabled list from June 15-July 23, 2010 with a strained left oblique.

Mitre's Division Series Record

Year	Club vs. Opp.	W	L	ERA	G	GS	CG	SHO	SV	IP	H	R	ER	HR	HP	BB	SO	WP	BK
2010	NYY vs. MIN							On Roster - Did Not Appear											

Mitre's League Championship Series Record

Year	Club vs. Opp.	W	L	ERA	G	GS	CG	SHO	SV	IP	H	R	ER	HR	HP	BB	SO	WP	BK
2010	NYY vs. TEX	0	0	10.13	3	0	0	0	0	2.2	3	3	3	2	0	3	1	1	0
LCS Totals		**0**	**0**	**10.13**	**3**	**0**	**0**	**0**	**0**	**2.2**	**3**	**3**	**3**	**2**	**0**	**3**	**1**	**1**	**0**
POSTSEASON TOTALS		**0**	**0**	**10.13**	**3**	**0**	**0**	**0**	**0**	**2.2**	**3**	**3**	**3**	**2**	**0**	**3**	**1**	**1**	**0**

Mitre's Regular Season Batting Record

Year	Team	AVG	G	AB	R	H	2B	3B	HR	RBI	SH	SF	HP	BB	SO	SB	CS
2010	Yankees					Did Not Bat											
Major League Totals		**.141**	**117**	**78**	**5**	**11**	**4**	**0**	**0**	**2**	**13**	**0**	**0**	**3**	**33**	**0**	**0**

Mitre's Career Fielding Record

Position	PCT	G	PO	A	E	TC	DP
Pitcher	.953	117	43	80	6	129	3

74

HECTOR NOESI

RIGHT-HANDED PITCHER • 6-3 • 200 • B/T: RIGHT/RIGHT •OPENING DAY AGE: 24

BIRTHDATE
January 26, 1987

BIRTHPLACE
Esperanza, D.R.

RESIDES
Mao, D.R.

M.L. SERVICE
None (Rookie)

STATUS
▸ Signed by the Yankees as a non-drafted free agent on December 3, 2004…signed through the 2011 season.

MINOR LEAGUE CAREER
▸ Has averaged 8.56K and just 1.56BB per 9.0 innings pitched in his career with a 5.49 BB/K ratio (384K, 70BB).

2010
▸ Combined to go 14-7 with a 3.20 ERA in 28 games (27 starts) with Single-A Tampa, Double-A Trenton and Triple-A Scranton/Wilkes-Barre…walked just 28 batters while striking out 153…held left-handed hitters to a .220 combined average (63-for-286, 2HR).
▸ Led all Yankees minor leaguers in wins and strikeouts (153), and ranked seventh in ERA.
▸ Opened the season with Tampa, winning his first three starts and five of his first six…struck out a career-high 13 batters in 6.0 scoreless innings on 4/29 vs. Dunedin…was named a Florida State League All-Star just prior to his promotion and earned league "Pitcher of the Week" honors for 4/8-19.
▸ Joined Trenton on 5/16 where he spent the majority of his season…held opponents to 2R or less in 12 of his 16 starts with the Thunder…collected his first career complete game on 6/13 vs. Binghamton, tossing a career-high 9.0IP (9H, 2R, 1ER, 1HR, 1BB, 6K, 1WP)…recorded his first career shutout two weeks later on 6/29 at New Brunswick, tossing 7.0 scoreless innings in Game 1 of a doubleheader (5H, 0BB, 4K)…earned Eastern League "Pitcher of the Week" honors for the week ending 6/7.
▸ Was selected to the World Team roster for the 2010 All-Star Futures' Game at Angel Stadium in Anaheim, tossing 1.0 scoreless inning of relief (1H).
▸ Made his final three starts with Scranton/WB, winning his Triple-A debut on 8/27 vs. Lehigh Valley (6.0IP, 7H, 4ER, 1BB, 1K).
▸ Attended his first Major League spring training, making two relief appearances (2.0IP, 3ER).
▸ Following the season, was named the seventh-best prospect in the Yankees organization and having the "Best Control" by *Baseball America*.

2009
▸ Appeared in 26 combined games (20 starts) with Single-A Charleston and Tampa, going 6-4 with a 2.92 ERA and 118 strikeouts in 117.0 IP…combined to hold opponents to a .220 batting average (96-for-436) with only 15 walks…struck out at least seven batters in nine of his starts.
▸ Began the season with 27.1 consecutive scoreless innings over his first nine appearances (three starts), striking out 35 batters with only three walks over the stretch…was named a midseason All-Star with Charleston.
▸ Went on the disabled list from 7/19-8/2 with right shoulder tendinitis.
▸ Made two postseason relief appearances for the FSL Champion Tampa squad, allowing 4ER in 7.0IP…earned the win in Game 1 of the Championship Series at Port Charlotte.

2008

▶ Combined to go 3-2 with a 3.33 ERA in 14 appearances (seven starts) with the GCL Yankees and short-season Single-A Staten Island…began the season with the GCL Yankees, going 2-1 with a 3.65 ERA in nine appearances (two starts)…was promoted to Staten Island on 8/10 and went 1-1 with a 3.00 ERA in five starts.

2007

▶ Suffered a season-ending right elbow strain on 6/23 that limited him to only five starts with Single-A Charleston, going 1-1 with a 4.50 ERA…began the season serving a 50-day suspension for violating the Minor League Drug Prevention and Treatment Program.

2006

▶ Was limited to just five relief appearances with the Yankees' Gulf Coast League team, beginning the season on the disabled list with a strained right shoulder (6/18-7/31)…walked only one batter while recording 11 strikeouts in 7.0IP.

2005

▶ Made his professional debut with the Yankees' Dominican Summer League team, going 5-3 with a 1.60 ERA in 13 games (10 starts).

Noesi's Career Pitching Record

YEAR	CLUB	W	L	ERA	G	GS	CG	SHO	SV	IP	H	R	ER	HR	HB	BB	SO	WP	BK
2005	DSL Yankees 1	5	3	1.60	13	10	0	0	0	50.2	34	19	9	2	5	8	36	2	1
2006	GCL Yankees	0	0	1.29	5	0	0	0	1	7.0	5	1	1	0	0	1	11	0	0
2007	Charleston	1	1	4.50	5	5	0	0	0	20.0	25	10	10	2	0	8	11	2	0
2008	GCL Yankees	2	1	3.65	9	2	0	0	0	24.2	23	11	10	2	1	3	24	1	0
	Staten Island	1	1	3.00	5	5	0	0	0	24.0	20	12	8	5	1	7	31	3	1
2009	Charleston	3	4	2.38	17	11	0	0	0	75.2	62	24	20	3	0	11	78	0	1
	Tampa	3	0	3.92	9	9	0	0	0	41.1	34	18	18	3	1	4	40	2	0
2010	Tampa	5	2	2.72	8	8	0	0	0	43.0	35	14	13	3	2	6	53	5	1
	Trenton	8	4	3.10	17	16	2	1	0	98.2	90	37	34	7	2	18	86	5	0
	Scranton/WB	1	1	4.82	3	3	1	0	0	18.2	23	10	10	1	1	4	14	1	0
Minor League Totals		**29**	**17**	**2.97**	**91**	**69**	**3**	**1**	**1**	**403.2**	**351**	**156**	**133**	**28**	**13**	**70**	**384**	**21**	**4**

Signed by the Yankees as a non-drafted free agent on December 3, 2004.

Futures Game History

Major League Baseball, in conjunction with the 30 Major League Clubs, MLB.com and Baseball America, select the 25-man rosters for the U.S. Team and the World Team. Players from all full-season Minor Leagues are eligible to participate.

Five players currently on the Yankees' 40-man roster (**bolded below**) have appeared in at least one Future's Game while in the Yankees' minor league system.

Yankees prospects Ramiro Pena [L] and Jesus Montero participated in the 2008 XM All-Star Futures Game at Yankee Stadium.

YEAR	PLAYER, PO. (TEAM)	YEAR	PLAYER, PO. (TEAM)
2010	Austin Romine, C (US)	2003	**Robinson Cano, INF (World)**
	Hector Noesi, RHP (World)		Chien-Ming Wang, P (World)
2009	Manny Banuelos, LHP (World)	2002	Drew Henson, 3B (US)
2008	Jesus Montero, C (World)	2001	Nick Johnson, INF (US)
	Ramiro Pena, INF (World)		Juan Rivera, OF (World)
2007	**Joba Chamberlain, P (US)**	2000	Drew Henson, 3B (US)
2006	**Phil Hughes, P (US)**		Jackson Melian, OF (World)
	Jose Tabata, CF (World)	1999	Nick Johnson, INF (US)
2005	Melky Cabrera, OF (World)		*Alfonso Soriano, INF (World)
2004	**Robinson Cano, INF (World)**	*Most Valuable Player	
	Dioner Navarro, C (World)		

47
IVAN NOVA

RIGHT-HANDED PITCHER • 6-4 • 225 • B/T: RIGHT/RIGHT: OPENING DAY AGE: 24

BIRTHDATE
January 12, 1987

BIRTHPLACE
San Cristobal, D.R.

RESIDES
San Cristobal, D.R.

M.L. SERVICE
51 days (Rookie)

STATUS
▸ Signed by the Yankees as a non-drafted free agent on July 15, 2004…signed through the 2011 season.

2010
▸ Was 1-2 with a 4.50 ERA in 10 games (seven starts) with the Yankees in his first Major League action…opponents batted .268 (44-for-164, 4HR)…LH .276 (27-for-98, 3HR), RH .258 (17-for-98, 7HR)…went 0-1 with a 1.69 ERA (5.1IP, 1ER) in his three relief outings…posted a 1-1 record with a 4.91 ERA in his seven starts.

▸ Opposing batters hit .230 (17-for-74) with two extra-base hits their first time through the order, .262 (17-for-65) with eight extra-base hits their second pass and .400 (10-for-25) with two extra-base hits the third time through.

▸ Was recalled from Triple-A Scranton/Wilkes-Barre on 5/10…made his Major League debut in 5/13 loss at Detroit, tossing 2.0 scoreless innings (2H, 1K) of relief…made one additional relief appearance (5/16 vs. Minnesota) before being optioned back to Scranton/WB on 5/17 when Chan Ho Park was reinstated from the 15-day D.L.

▸ Was recalled a second time on 8/22, joining the starting rotation…completed 6.0 innings just once (9/8 vs. Baltimore)…was removed with a lead in four of his seven starts.

▸ Made his first Major League start against Toronto at Rogers Centre on 8/23, recording a no-decision, (5.1IP, 6H, 2ER, 1BB, 3K, 1HR)…pitched out of a bases-loaded, no-out jam in the first inning…both runs allowed came on a two-run HR by Jose Bautista in the third.

▸ Recorded his first Major League win in his second start on 8/29 at Chicago-AL, allowing 1ER in 5.2IP (5H, 1BB, 7K)…became the first Yankees rookie starter to earn a win since Alfredo Aceves on 9/9/08 (credit: *Elias*) as the Yankees became the last Major League team in 2010 to have a rookie earn a win.

▸ Suffered his first loss on 9/25 vs. Boston in his ninth appearance, seventh start (4.2IP, 4H, 4ER, 3BB, 2K, 1HP)…according to the *Elias Sports Bureau*, became one of two Yankees since 1980 to go undefeated in his first six career starts, joining Joba Chamberlain (first 7GS in 2008).

▸ Went 12-3 with a 2.86 ERA in 23 starts at Triple-A Scranton/WB (145.0IP, 135H, 50R, 46ER, 48BB, 115K, 10HR, .250 opp. BA)…led the staff in wins, ERA, inning pitched (145.0) and strikeouts (115)…ranked second in the International League in ERA, trailing only *Baseball America* "Player of the Year" Jeremy Hellickson…tied for first in winning percentage and ranked third in wins…among Yankees farmhands, tied for third in wins and ranked fifth in ERA.

▸ Made 17 "quality starts" (at least 6.0IP, 3ER or fewer) with SWB, lasting 7.0 or more innings in seven of his outings and recording a season-high-tying 8.0IP twice.

▸ Lost just one of his final 14 starts with SWB, going 10-1 with a 2.19 ERA (94.2IP, 23ER) over his final 14 starts from 6/5-8/18.

▸ Did not record a decision in three spring training relief appearances with the Yankees, allowing 1ER in 4.0IP (2.25 ERA, 4H, 2BB, 3K, 1HR).

▸ Made three relief appearances in his first spring training, limiting opponents to 1ER in 4.0IP.

BESTS & STREAKS

Low hit CG
NA
IP (start)
6.0 - vs. BAL, 9/8/10
IP (relief)
2.1 - at BOS, 10/2/10 (G2)
Hits
6 - 4 times
Last: at TB, 9/14/10
Runs
6 - at TB, 9/14/10
BB
3 - 3 times
Last: at BOS, 10/2/10
SO
7 - at CWS, 8/29/10
HR
1 - 4 times
Last: at TB, 9/14/10
Winning Streak
1g - 8/29/10
Losing Streak
2g - 9/25/10-present

2009

▸ Made 24 combined starts with Double-A Trenton and Triple-A Scranton/Wilkes-Barre, going 6-8 with a 3.68 ERA (139.1IP, 57ER).

▸ Held opponents to 2ER or less in 10 of his 12 starts with Trenton, including each of his final seven outings…left-handers batted just .188 (25-for-133, 1HR) against him at the Double-A level.

▸ Tossed 5.2 scoreless innings and allowed just 1H in his Triple-A debut on 6/29 vs. Rochester, earning the win in a 5-0 SWB victory (3BB, 5K)…was credited with his first career complete game on 7/30 vs. Durham, throwing all 7.0 innings and recording the loss in Game 1 of a doubleheader (6H, 6R, 5ER, 3BB, 2K, 1HR).

▸ Made two postseason starts for Scranton/WB, going 1-0 with a 1.93 ERA, allowing just three earned runs in 14.0IP and striking out 10 batters.

▸ Following the season, appeared in five games (four starts) with Escogido in the Dominican Winter League, going 1-0 with a 1.05 ERA (25.2IP, 17H, 3ER, 4BB, 17K).

▸ Was selected by the San Diego Padres in the second round of the 2008 Rule 5 Draft…attended Major League Spring Training with the Padres, allowing 11R (8ER) on 13H in 8.2IP over eight relief appearances…was returned to the Yankees on 3/29/09.

2008

▸ Made 26 appearances (24 starts) with Single-A Tampa, going 8-13 with a 4.36 ERA and striking out 109 batters…ranked second among Florida State League pitchers with 148.2IP…led the team in starts, tied for most wins and ranked second in strikeouts.

2007

▸ Was 6-8 with a 4.98 ERA in 21 starts with Single-A Charleston…was placed on the disabled list from 7/7-14 with a left hip strain.

▸ Made one relief appearance for Leones del Escogido of the Dominican Winter League, throwing 1.2 scoreless innings and earning the win (1BB, 1K).

2006

▸ Posted a 3-0 record with a 2.72 ERA in 10 games (five starts) with the Gulf Coast League Yankees…ranked second in the league with 5HR allowed.

2005

▸ Made professional debut with the Yankees' Dominican Summer League squad, going 0-1 with a 2.29 ERA in 11 games (seven starts).

Nova's Career Pitching Record

YEAR	CLUB	W	L	ERA	G	GS	CG	SHO	SV	IP	H	R	ER	HR	HB	BB	SO	WP	BK
2005	DSL Yankees 1	0	1	2.29	11	7	0	0	0	39.1	29	11	10	2	3	11	38	5	0
2006	GCL Yankees	3	0	2.72	10	5	0	0	1	43.0	36	13	13	5	3	7	36	3	0
2007	Charleston	6	8	4.98	21	21	0	0	0	99.1	121	64	55	8	6	31	54	4	0
2008	Tampa-a	8	13	4.36	26	24	0	0	0	148.2	168	81	72	6	9	46	109	12	1
2009	Trenton-b	5	4	2.36	12	12	0	0	0	72.1	65	27	19	3	2	31	47	5	3
	Scranton/WB	1	4	5.10	12	12	1	0	0	67.0	72	39	38	4	3	28	43	4	0
2010	Scranton/WB	12	3	2.86	23	23	0	0	0	145.0	135	50	46	10	2	48	115	4	1
	YANKEES	1	2	4.50	10	7	0	0	0	42.0	44	22	21	4	1	17	26	2	0
Minor League Totals		35	33	3.70	115	104	1	0	1	614.2	626	285	253	38	28	202	442	37	5
Major League Totals		1	2	4.50	10	7	0	0	0	42.0	44	22	21	4	1	17	26	2	0

Signed by the Yankees as a non-drafted free agent on July 15, 2004.

a – Selected by the San Diego Padres in the Rule 5 Draft on December 11, 2008.
b – Returned to the Yankees on March 29, 2009.

Nova's Career Fielding Record

Position	PCT	G	PO	A	E	TC
Pitcher	.909	10	5	5	1	11

Home Runs by Yankee Pitchers

Fifty-eight Yankees pitchers have combined to hit 154 home runs in the franchise's 106-year history. The top five: Red Ruffing, 30; Tommy Byrne, 10; Spud Chandler, 9; Don Larsen, 8; Mel Stottlemyre, 7...the first home run hit by a Yankee pitcher was by Clark Griffith on July 14, 1903...the last was hit by Lindy McDaniel on September 28, 1972 off Mickey Lolich at Detroit…no Yankee pitcher has ever homered in a postseason game. Two current Yankees pitchers – A.J. Burnett (three times) and CC Sabathia (three times) – have homered in a Major League game.

67

EDUARDO NUNEZ

INFIELDER • 6-0 • 155 • B/T: RIGHT/RIGHT • OPENING DAY AGE: 23

BIRTHDATE
June 15, 1987

BIRTHPLACE
Santo Domingo, D.R.

RESIDES
Azua, D.R.

M.L. SERVICE
46 days
(Rookie)

STATUS
▸ Signed by the Yankees as a non-drafted free agent on February 25, 2004…signed through the 2011 season.

2010
▸ Hit .280 (14-for-50) with 12R, 1 double, 1HR and 7RBI in 30 games (10 starts at 3B and three at SS) with the Yankees…stole five bases without being caught…struck out just twice in 53 plate appearances.

▸ Was recalled from Triple-A Scranton/WB on 8/19 when Lance Berkman went on the 15-day D.L.…made his Major League debut in that night's win vs. Detroit, entering the game defensively in the seventh at SS and going 0-for-1.

▸ Made his first Major League start (at 3B) in 8/21 win vs. Seattle, going 1-for-3 with 1R and 1RBI…collected his first hit with a go-ahead RBI-single off Jason Vargas in the seventh inning.

▸ Made 11 starts from 8/21-9/4 (nine at 3B and two at SS) while Alex Rodriguez was on the disabled list…hit .293 (12-for-41) over the stretch, committing just one error in 27 chances.

▸ Hit two-run HR—the first of his Major League career—and was 3-for-4 with 2R, 4RBI, 1BB and 1SB in 8/29 win at Chicago-AL…marked the most RBI in a game by a Yankees rookie since Brett Gardner on 9/26/08 at Boston (also 4RBI)…became the first Yankee to drive in at least four runs in a game within his first 10 Major League contests since Shelley Duncan in 2007 (4RBI vs. Tampa Bay) and just the fifth to do so in the last 44 years (since 1967), joining Andy Phillips (4RBI on 4/24/05 vs. Texas), Hideki Matsui (4RBI on 4/8/03 vs. Minnesota) and Brian Dayett (4RBI on 9/18/83 Game 2 at Cleveland)…according to *Elias*, became just the fifth Yankee in franchise history to hit his first Major League HR and steal his first base in the same game, joining Willie Randolph (1976), Roy White (1966), Gil McDougald (1951) and Wally Pipp (1915).

▸ Began the season with Triple-A Scranton/Wilkes-Barre, batting .289 (134-for-464) with 55R, 25 doubles, 3 triples, 4HR, 50RBI and 23SB in 118 games…recorded the third-highest average among all Yankees farmhands and led all Scranton/WB batters in hits, doubles and stolen bases…at the time of his recall, was leading the International League in hits…was named to the International League postseason All-Star team as the league's top shortstop…also selected to the IL midseason All-Star team, starting at SS and going 0-for-2 in the IL's 2-1 victory.

▸ Following the season, was named by *Baseball America* as the eighth-best prospect in the Yankees organization…also selected by the publication as the "Best Defensive Infielder" and possessing the "Best Infield Arm" among Yankees farmhands.

▸ Batted .348 (8-for-23) with 2RBI in seven games with the Toros del Este in the Dominican Winter League following the season…missed time after a ball he bunted ricocheted off his face.

▸ Appeared in 17 official spring training games with the Yankees, batting .231 (6-for-17) with 5R, 3 doubles and 4RBI.

BESTS & STREAKS

Hits
3 - at CWS, 8/28/10
Runs
2 - at CWS, 8/28/10
2B
1 - vs. SEA, 8/22/10
3B
None
HR
1 - at CWS, 8/28/10
RBI
4 - at CWS, 8/28/10
BB
1 - 3 times
Last: at BOS, 10/2/10
SO
1 - 2 times
Last: at TOR, 8/24/10
SB
1 - 5 times
Last: vs. BOS, 9/26/10
Hit Streak
3g - 2 times
Last: 9/1-3/10

2009

▸ Batted .322 (160-for-497) with 9HR, 55RBI and 19SB in 123 games with Double-A Trenton in 2009, making 120 starts at shortstop…set career highs in hits, doubles and home runs in his first season at the Double-A level…ranked second in the Eastern League in hits and third in batting average…committed 33 errors, most among Eastern League players.

▸ Was named the top shortstop in the EL, earning a spot on the postseason All-Star team…was also the starting shortstop for the North Division in the Eastern League midseason All-Star Game, the lone Thunder player to earn both midseason and postseason All-Star honors in 2009.

▸ Compiled five hitting streaks of eight-or-more games, including a career-high-tying 11-game hitting streak from 4/30-5/11, in which he batted .378 (17-for-45) over the stretch with just 5K.

▸ Appeared in four games with Toros del Este in the Dominican Winter League, going 2-for-10 (.200)

2008

▸ Spent the entire season with Single-A Tampa, batting .271 with 18 doubles, 6HR and 42RBI in 94 games…appeared in 92 games at shortstop…batted .269 (28-for-104, 1HR) against left-handed pitchers and .271 (73-for-269, 5HR) off righties.

▸ Opened the season on the disabled list with a sprained right thumb and was activated on 4/20…returned to the D.L. from 5/12-6/3 with a sprained left thumb.

▸ Recorded a career-high five consecutive multi-hit games from 6/8-12 (all two-hit games).

2007

▸ Combined to hit .251 with 15 doubles, 2HR and 41RBI in 121 games with Single-A Charleston and Tampa…went more than two straight games without a hit just twice.

▸ Began the season with the RiverDogs and was named the starting shortstop for the North Division in the South Atlantic League All-Star Game.

▸ Promoted to Tampa on 7/30…recorded multiple hits in 13 of his 30 games with Tampa.

2006

▸ Combined to hit .214 in 127 games with Tampa and Charleston, seeing time at 2B, 3B and SS…began the season with Tampa and batted .184 in 37 games before being transferred to Charleston on 5/18…in 90 games with the RiverDogs, hit .227 with 16SB.

2005

▸ Batted .313 with 11 doubles, 3HR and 46RBI in 73 games with short-season Single-A Staten Island…was selected to participate in the NY-Penn League All-Star Game and was 1-for-3 with 1R and 1RBI in the contest…ranked third in the NYPL in hits (88), tied for third in triples (6), fourth in games played (73), fourth in at-bats (281) and ninth in average (.313)…following the season, was named the sixth-best prospect in the Yankees organization by *Baseball America*.

2004

▸ Played in 63 games with the DSL Yankees 1, batting .249 with 7 doubles and 33RBI.

Nunez's Career Batting Record

YEAR	CLUB	AVG	G	AB	R	H	2B	3B	HR	RBI	SH	SF	HP	BB	SO	SB	CS	E	OBP	SLG
2004	DSL Yankees 1	.249	63	229	27	57	7	1	0	33	1	2	5	13	23	5	4	—	.301	.288
2005	Staten Island	.313	73	281	37	88	11	6	3	46	6	0	3	20	43	6	3	28	.365	.427
2006	Tampa	.184	37	147	17	27	5	3	4	26	4	2	0	8	28	16	5	14	.223	.340
	Charleston	.227	90	344	36	78	11	3	2	40	0	2	2	23	48	16	5	26	.278	.294
2007	Charleston	.238	91	328	36	78	10	2	1	28	2	3	2	25	42	20	8	27	.293	.290
	Tampa	.285	30	123	16	35	5	0	1	13	0	1	3	7	18	9	0	6	.336	.350
2008	Tampa	.271	94	373	45	101	18	3	6	42	5	4	1	19	48	14	10	19	.305	.383
2009	Trenton	.322	123	497	70	160	26	1	9	55	4	4	1	22	63	19	7	33	.349	.433
2010	Scranton/WB	.289	118	464	55	134	25	3	4	50	3	2	5	32	60	23	5	14	.340	.381
	YANKEES	.280	30	50	12	14	1	0	1	7	0	0	0	3	2	5	0	1	.321	.360
Minor League Totals		**.270**	**713**	**2748**	**341**	**742**	**120**	**26**	**33**	**320**	**26**	**18**	**21**	**183**	**391**	**129**	**45**	**167**	**.319**	**.369**
Major League Totals		**.280**	**30**	**50**	**12**	**14**	**1**	**0**	**1**	**7**	**0**	**0**	**0**	**3**	**2**	**5**	**0**	**1**	**.321**	**.360**

Signed by the Yankees as a non-drafted free agent on February 25, 2004.

Nunez's Career Fielding Record

Position	PCT	G	PO	A	E	TC	DP
Second Base	—	1	0	0	0	0	0
Third Base	.944	15	3	14	1	18	1
Shortstop	1.000	11	7	16	0	23	4

19
RAMIRO PENA

INFIELDER • 5-11 • 175 • B/T: SWITCH/RIGHT • OPENING DAY AGE: 25

BIRTHDATE
July 18, 1985

BIRTHPLACE
Monterrey, Mexico

RESIDES
San Nicolas de los Garza, Mexico

M.L. SERVICE
1 year, 137 days

STATUS
▸ Signed as a non-drafted free agent on February 18, 2005…signed through the 2011 season.

2010
▸ Hit .227 (35-for-154) with 18R, 1 double, 1 triple and 18RBI in 85 games (27 starts at 3B, nine at SS and five at 2B) with the Yankees…combined for a .970 fielding percentage at 2B, SS, 3B and RF (5E, 165TC)…made his second career Opening Day roster.
▸ Hit .264 (19-for-72) in 44 games following the All-Star break…in 41 games before the break, hit just .195 (16-for-82).
▸ Had 3H in 7AB with the bases loaded (.429 average), driving in seven runs…batted .333 (17-for- 51) in 34 games against the AL East.
▸ Entered the game as a pinch-runner 14 times, scoring four times and stealing two bases.
▸ Made his first career appearance in the outfield in 5/16 loss vs. Minnesota, starting at SS and moving to RF in the ninth.
▸ Hit safely in 12 of his 19 starts from 8/1 through the end of the season, batting .250 (15-for-60) with 6RBI and five multi-hit games over the stretch.
▸ Hit safely in a career-high seven straight games from 8/22-9/5, batting .476 (10-for-21) during the streak.
▸ Appeared on the ALDS and ALCS rosters but did not appear in a game.

2009
▸ Batted .287 (33-for-115) with 17R, 6 doubles, 1HR and 10RBI in 69 games (14 starts at 3B, 11 at SS, three at 2B) over three stints with the Yankees (4/4-7/1; 8/7-21 and 9/1-10/4) in his first Major League action.
▸ Made his first Opening Day roster…was signed to a Major League contract and selected to the Yankees' 25-man roster on 4/4…became the first Yankee without experience above the Double-A level to make the club's Opening Day active Major League roster since RHP Jose Contreras in 2003 and the first such position player since 3B Scott Seabol in 2001.
▸ Made his Major League debut in 4/6 Opening Day loss at Baltimore, entering the game as a pinch-runner in the eighth inning and remaining in the game at 3B…batted .267 (23-for-86) with 5 doubles, 1 triple and 7RBI in 46 games during his first stint with the Yankees…played in 24G/14GS at 3B, the majority of which came while Alex Rodriguez was on the D.L.
▸ Collected his first Major League hit—in his first PA—in 4/9 win at Baltimore, singling to center off Chris Ray in the ninth and scoring…became the first Yankee to record a hit in his first Major League plate appearance since Andy Cannizaro on 9/8/06, according to Elias, was only the second Yankee since 1963 to do so during the first week of a season (also Hideki Matsui in 2003).
▸ Both he and Brett Gardner tripled on 5/13 at Toronto, becoming the first pair of Yankees rookies to hit triples in the same game since 8/31/70, when Thurman Munson and Johnny Ellis did so off Mike Cuellar (credit: Elias Sports Bureau).

BESTS & STREAKS

Hits
3 - 2 times
Last: at NYM, 6/26/09
Runs
2 - 3 times
Last: vs. CLE, 5/31/10
2B
2 - at NYM, 6/26/09
3B
1 - 2 times
Last: vs. DET, 8/18/10
HR
1 - vs. KC, 9/28/09
RBI
2 - 8 times
Last: vs. BOS, 8/7/10
BB
1 - 11 times
Last: vs. TOR, 9/4/10
SO
2 - 5 times
Last: at SEA, 7/10/10
SB
1 - 11 times
Last: at BOS, 10/2/10 (G1)
Hit Streak
7g - 8/22-9/5/10

- Was optioned to Triple-A Scranton/Wilkes-Barre on 7/1, recalled by the Yankees on 8/7 and optioned back to Scranton/WB on 8/21…was recalled for a third time on 9/1 for the remainder of the season.
- Recorded the Yankees' only hit of the game off Roy Halladay in 9/4 loss at Toronto, going 1-for-3 with 1 double…hit solo-HR off Luke Hochevar—the first of his career and sixth of his professional career—and was 2-for-4 with 2R, 2RBI and 1SB in 9/28 win vs. Kansas City.
- Was added to the Yankees' World Series roster prior to Game 5 when Melky Cabrera sustained an injury (did not appear).
- In 43 games with Scranton/WB, batted .231 (36-for-156) with 9 doubles, 2HR, 9RBI and 5SB, appearing in games at SS (22 games), 2B (11), CF (seven) and 3B (three)…marked his first career action in the outfield.
- Following the season, appeared in 26 games with Culiacan in the Mexican Winter League, batting .247 (21-for-85) with 10R, 3 doubles, 4RBI and 11BB.

2008
- Played the entire season at Double-A Trenton, batting .266 with 20 doubles, 7 triples, 2HR and 45RBI in 111 games (all at shortstop)…set career highs in nearly every offensive category.
- Appeared on the World Team at the 2008 Futures Game during All-Star weekend at the original Yankee Stadium, going 0-for-1 with 1BB.
- Batted .345 (10-for-29) with 6R and 2SB in seven postseason games for the Eastern League champions…following the season, was tabbed as the "Best Defensive Infielder" in the Yankees organization and Eastern League by *Baseball America*…played winter ball with Culiacan in the Mexican Winter League.

2007
- Was limited to 52 games with Double-A Trenton due to injuries, batting .252 with 7 doubles, 1 triple and 10RBI.
- Went on the disabled list from 5/24-6/1 with a groin strain…returned on 6/2 and played in 11 more games before his season was cut short on 6/14 with a dislocated right shoulder…suffered the injury on 6/13 vs. Connecticut, sliding into second base in the seventh inning.

2006
- Endured three stints on the disabled list and batted .257 in 80 combined games with Double-A Trenton and Single-A Tampa.
- Began the season with Trenton and batted .198 in 26 games…was placed on the disabled list on 5/11 after suffering a right knee contusion on 5/10 at Portland…was reinstated from the D.L. on 5/24 and transferred to Tampa…played in 51 games before suffering a sprained right ankle on 7/20 vs. Palm Beach…was placed on the D.L. the next day and missed a week of action…was reinstated on 7/28 and played in three games before being placed on the D.L. for a third time for the rest of the season, this time with a left thumb injury.
- Played in 33 games with Culiacan of the Mexican Winter League, batting .221 (15-for-68).

2005
- In his first professional season, played in 91 combined games with Single-A Tampa and Double-A Trenton…began the season with Tampa, batting .247 in 23 games before being promoted to Trenton on 6/14…in 68 games with the Thunder, batted .250 with 5 doubles and 12RBI.

Pena's Career Batting Record

YEAR	CLUB	AVG	G	AB	R	H	2B	3B	HR	RBI	SH	SF	HP	BB	SO	SB	CS	E	OBP	SLG
2005	Tampa	.247	23	73	11	18	4	1	1	6	2	2	0	9	12	1	0	4	.321	.370
	Trenton	.250	68	236	28	59	5	2	0	12	8	1	0	10	48	4	1	15	.279	.288
2006	Trenton	.198	26	86	6	17	2	0	0	6	5	1	1	5	19	0	1	2	.247	.221
	Tampa	.280	54	218	31	661	4	2	0	23	4	4	4	16	26	8	4	12	.335	.317
2007	Trenton	.252	52	202	23	51	7	1	0	10	7	0	2	22	33	7	3	4	.332	.297
2008	Trenton	.266	111	443	57	118	20	7	2	45	12	6	4	41	86	8	6	21	.330	.357
2009	YANKEES	.287	69	115	17	33	6	1	1	10	1	0	0	5	20	4	1	5	.317	.383
	Scranton/WB	.231	43	156	18	36	9	0	2	9	6	0	0	18	28	5	1	2	.310	.327
2010	YANKEES	.227	85	154	18	35	1	1	0	18	4	2	1	6	27	7	1	5	.258	.247
Minor League Totals		**.255**	**377**	**1414**	**174**	**360**	**51**	**13**	**5**	**111**	**44**	**14**	**11**	**121**	**252**	**33**	**16**	**60**	**.315**	**.320**
Major League Totals		**.253**	**154**	**269**	**35**	**68**	**7**	**2**	**1**	**28**	**5**	**2**	**1**	**11**	**47**	**11**	**2**	**10**	**.283**	**.305**

Signed by the Yankees as a non-drafted free agent on February 18, 2005.

Pena's Career Fielding Record

Position	PCT	G	PO	A	E	TC	DP
Shortstop	.964	57	43	64	4	111	16
Third Base	.961	75	27	97	5	129	10
Second Base	.979	16	19	27	1	47	8
Outfield	1.000	2	1	0	0	1	0

80

RYAN POPE

RIGHT-HANDED PITCHER • 6-3 • 210 • B/T: RIGHT/RIGHT • OPENING DAY AGE: 24

BIRTHDATE
May 21, 1986

BIRTHPLACE
Bradenton, Fla.

RESIDES
Bradenton, Fla.

M.L. SERVICE
None (Rookie)

COLLEGE
Savannah College of
  Art and Design

STATUS
▶ Selected by the Yankees in the third round of the 2007 First-Year Player Draft…signed through the 2011 season.

2010
▶ Went 4-6 with 17 saves and a 4.20 ERA in 46 appearances (seven starts) with Double-A Trenton…ranked third among all Yankees minor leaguers—and tied for third in the Eastern League—in saves…walked just 12 batters in 57.1IP (1.88BB/9.0IP), the third-best ratio in the EL…allowed 67 baserunners in 57.1IP (10.52/9.0IP), the fifth-best ratio among all Eastern League players.

▶ Began the season in the Thunder's starting rotation, going 1-3 with a 5.11 ERA (37.0IP, 21ER) in seven starts.

▶ Made his first relief appearance on 5/16 vs. Binghamton…remained in the bullpen for the remainder of the season, going 3-3 with 17 saves and a 3.61 ERA (57.1IP, 23ER) in 39 appearances…had made just two prior relief outings in his professional career.

▶ Made two postseason relief appearances for Trenton, recording one save while tossing 2.0 scoreless innings (3H, 2K).

▶ Following the season, pitched for the Phoenix Desert Dogs in the Arizona Fall League, going 0-1 with one save and a 3.18 ERA in nine relief appearances (11.1IP, 14H, 5R, 4ER, 4BB, 10K, 2HR).

▶ Made three spring training relief appearances for the Yankees, recording one save and allowing 1H in 3.0 scoreless IP (3K).

▶ Was added to the Yankees' 40-man roster on 11/19/10.

2009
▶ Spent the season with Trenton, going 5-12 with a 4.78 ERA (141.1IP, 75ER) in 26 appearances (25 starts)…recorded 106K with only 34BB.

▶ Made his only relief appearance of the season—the second of his career—on 6/13 vs. Binghamton, allowing 9H and 4ER in 4.2IP (1K, 1HR).

2008
▶ Spent the majority of the season with Tampa, going 7-7 with a 4.15 ERA (104.0IP, 48ER) in 20 starts…was named to the Florida State League's midseason All-Star team.

▶ Missed over a month on the disabled list from 5/25-7/2 with a right groin strain…made two rehab appearances (one start) with the GCL Yankees (6.43 ERA, 7.0IP, 5ER).

▶ Went 4-4 with a 2.81 ERA prior to the injury and 3-3 with a 5.47 ERA after returning to Tampa's starting rotation.

▶ Tossed his first career complete game on 7/18 at Jupiter, earning the win in Game 1 of a doubleheader (7.0IP, 4H, 2ER, 0BB, 8K).

2007
▶ Made his professional debut, going 3-0 with a 2.49 ERA (43.1IP, 12ER) and 46K in 10 starts for short-season Single-A Staten Island…held opponents to 2ER or less in nine starts and did not allow an earned run in four of his starts…tossed 3.0 scoreless innings in his debut vs. Vermont on 7/14.

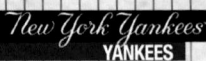
PERSONAL

▸ Full name is Ryan Joseph Pope…became the first player ever drafted out of the Savannah College of Art and Design…set a school single-season record in 2007 with a 1.15 ERA, ranking third among all NAIA pitchers…also ranked third among NAIA hurlers in opponents batting average (.162) and 11th in strikeouts per 9.0IP (10.76)…threw the school's second no-hitter on 1/27/07 in the season opener against Tennessee Temple University…holds school career records in complete games (32) and ERA (2.36), while tying for the lead in strikeouts in a single season (122 in 2007)…was named the 2007 "Player of the Year" for the Florida Sun Conference and the NAIA Region XIV and earned the SCAD "Male Athlete of the Year" Award in 2006 and '07…was named to the 2007 NAIA All-American first team as well as the Rawlings NAIA Gold Glove team.

Pope's Career Pitching Record

Year	Club	W	L	ERA	G	GS	CG	SHO	SV	IP	H	R	ER	HR	HP	BB	SO	WP	BK
2007	Staten Island	3	0	2.49	10	10	0	0	0	43.1	41	16	12	2	1	10	46	1	0
2008	Tampa	7	7	4.15	20	20	1	0	0	104.0	114	57	48	8	4	22	72	2	0
	GCL Yankees	0	0	6.43	2	1	0	0	0	7.0	7	5	5	1	1	1	4	0	0
2009	Trenton	5	12	4.78	26	25	0	0	0	141.1	155	91	75	7	8	34	106	4	1
2010	Trenton	4	6	4.20	46	7	0	0	17	94.1	88	48	44	10	7	31	85	7	0
Minor League Totals		**19**	**25**	**4.25**	**104**	**63**	**1**	**0**	**17**	**390.0**	**405**	**217**	**184**	**28**	**21**	**98**	**313**	**14**	**1**

Selected by the Yankees in the third round of the 2007 First-Year Player Draft.

James P. Dawson Award Winners

The James P. Dawson Award is presented annually to the top rookie in the Yankees' spring training camp. The award is named in honor of Dawson (1896-1953), who began a 45-year career with the *New York Times* as a copy boy in 1908 before becoming editor of boxing eight years later and covering boxing and baseball until his death during spring training in 1953.

2010 – Jon Weber, OF	1991 – Hensley Meullens, OF	1972 – Rusty Torres, OF
2009 – Brett Gardner, OF	1990 – Alan Mills, RHP	1971 – None selected
2008 – Shelley Duncan, INF/OF	1989 – None selected	1970 – John Ellis, 1B/C
2007 – Kei Igawa, LHP	1988 – Al Leiter, LHP	1969 – Jerry Kenney, OF and
2006 – Eric Duncan, INF	1987 – Kevin Hughes, OF	Bill Burbach, RHP
2005 – Andy Phillips, INF	1986 – Bob Tewksberry, RHP	1968 – Mike Ferraro, 3B
2004 – Bubba Crosby, OF	1985 – Scott Bradey, C	1967 – Bill Robinson, OF
2003 – Hideki Matsui, OF	1984 – Jose Rijo, RHP	1966 – Roy White, OF
2002 – Nick Johnson, 1B	1983 – Don Mattingly, 1B	1965 – Arturo Lopez, OF
2001 – Alfonso Soriano, 2B	1982 – Andre Robertson, SS	1964 – Pete Mikkelsen, RHP
2000 – None selected	1981 – Gene Nelson, RHP	1963 – Pedro Gonzalez, 2B
1999 – None selected	1980 – Mike Griffin, RHP	1962 – Tom Tresh, SS
1998 – Homer Bush, INF	1979 – Paul Mirabella, LHP	1961 – Rollie Sheldon, RHP
1997 – Jorge Posada, C	1978 – Jim Beattie, RHP	1960 – Johnny James, RHP
1996 – Mark Hutton, RHP	1977 – George Zeber, INF	1959 – Gordon Windhorn, OF
1995 – None selected	1976 – Willie Randolph, 2B	1958 – Johnny Blanchard, C
1994 – Sterling Hitchcock, LHP	1975 – Tippy Martinez, LHP	1957 – Tony Kubek, SS
1993 – Mike Humphreys, OF	1974 – Tom Buskey, RHP	1956 – Norm Siebern, OF
1992 – Gerald Williams, OF	1973 – Otto Velez, OF	

20 JORGE POSADA

CATCHER/DH • 6-2 • 215 • B/T: SWITCH/RIGHT • OPENING DAY AGE: 39

BIRTHDATE
August 17, 1971

BIRTHPLACE
Santurce, P.R.

RESIDES
Miami, Fla.

M.L. SERVICE
14 years, 85 days

COLLEGE
Calhoun Community College

CAREER HIGHLIGHTS
A.L. All-Star Team
▸ 2000, 2001, 2002, 2003, 2007

A.L. Silver Slugger Award
▸ 2000, 2001, 2002, 2003 2007

STATUS
▸ Selected in the 24th round of the 1990 First-Year Player Draft…signed a four-year contract on November 29, 2007…contract extends through the 2011 season.

CAREER NOTES
▸ Ranks seventh on the Yankees' all-time list with 365 doubles, eighth with 261HR and 897BB, and 11th with 1,021RBI… his 246HR as a catcher rank second on the Yankees' all-time list behind only Yogi Berra (306).

▸ Among active Major League catchers, ranks second in home runs and RBI, third in runs scored (866), hits (1,583) and doubles and fourth in games played (1,714).

▸ Has caught 1,573 games for the Yankees…only Bill Dickey (1,708) and Yogi Berra (1,695) have caught more games in pinstripes.

▸ Is the first Major Leaguer to catch at least one game with the same team in 16 straight seasons since Cincinnati's Johnny Bench (17 consecutive seasons, 1967-83)—credit: *Elias Sports Bureau*.

▸ Owns a .275 career batting average, 261HR and 1,021RBI…of the 13 former Major League catchers in the Hall of Fame (Johnny Bench, Yogi Berra, Roger Bresnahan, Roy Campanella, Gary Carter, Mickey Cochrane, Bill Dickey, Buck Ewing, Rick Ferrell, Carlton Fisk, Gabby Hartnett, Ernie Lombardi and Ray Schalk), only Berra (.285BA, 358HR, 1,430RBI) has better numbers in all three categories…is eighth all-time in HR among players who played at least 50.0% of their games at catcher.

▸ Is one of five players all time to record at least 1,500H, 350 doubles, 250HR and 1,000RBI while playing at least 50.0% of his games at catcher (also the Nationals' Ivan Rodriguez and Hall of Famers Johnny Bench, Gary Carter and Carlton Fisk).

▸ Is one of six catchers all-time to hit at least 20HR in eight seasons, joining Mike Piazza (11), Johnny Bench (11), Yogi Berra (10), Gary Carter (9) and Carlton Fisk (8)—credit: *Elias*…is one of eight players to hit at least 250 home runs for his current team, joining Todd Helton, Ryan Howard, Chipper Jones, Paul Konerko, Albert Pujols, David Ortiz and teammate Alex Rodriguez—credit: *Elias Sports Bureau*.

▸ According to *Elias*, has homered in more ballparks (28) than any player in Yankees history.

▸ Along with Derek Jeter and Mariano Rivera, have become the first trio of teammates in MLB, NBA, NFL and NHL history to appear in a game together in each of 16 straight seasons (credit: *Elias Sports Bureau*).

▸ Started 68 consecutive postseason games from 10/27/99 (World Series Game 4)-10/5/05 (Division Series Game 2)…his 46 Division Series games are the third-most on Baseball's all-time list…is third on Baseball's all-time list with 120 career postseason games played…his 119 postseason contests at catcher are the most all-time (Yogi Berra is second with 63)…has 23 postseason doubles, third-most all time.

▸ Has caught at least one game in six different World Series, tied for third-most all time with Elston Howard and Wally Schang, trailing Yogi Berra (12) and Bill Dickey (8).

BESTS & STREAKS

Hits
4 - 17 times
Last: at TOR, 8/24/10
Runs
4 - 3 times
Last: vs. SEA, 9/4/07
2B
3 - at CWS, 4/23/08
3B
1 - 10 times
Last: vs. OAK, 8/31/10
HR
2 - 16 times
Last: at BAL, 9/1/09
RBI
7 - vs. DET, 9/10/03
BB
4 - 2 times
Last: at CLE, 7/9/03
SO
4 - 5 times
Last: at ATL, 6/23/09
SB
1 - 20 times
Last: vs. DET, 8/17/10
Hit Streak
15g - 5/3-20/07

2010

▸ Hit .248 (95-for-383) with 49R, 23 doubles, 1 triple, 18HR and 57RBI in 120 games (78 starts at C, 28 at DH) with the Yankees...the Yankees were 49-29 in his starts at catcher...caught 10-of-78 (11.4%) potential base stealers.

▸ Had 3SB, tying his career high (also 3SB in 2006)...all 3SB came in a nine-game stretch from 8/7-17 after having just 1SB in his previous 297G (7/15/07-8/6/10).

▸ Made his 11th career Opening Day start at catcher (since 2000), surpasing Thurman Munson (10) and trailing only Bill Dickey (14, 1930-43) for most consecutive starts behind the plate for the Yankees on Opening Day in franchise history...became the oldest catcher (38 years, 230 days) to start an opener for the Yankees since Dickey in 1946 (38 years, 314 days).

▸ Hit solo HR in his first AB of the season in the second inning of 4/4 Opening Day loss at Boston, going 3-for-4 with 2RBI and 1BB...was his fourth career Opening Day home run, tied with Mickey Mantle and Yogi Berra for second-most Opening Day home runs in franchise history behind Babe Ruth (five)...was the first of back-to-back homers with Curtis Granderson, becoming the first pair of Yankees to hit back-to-back home runs on Opening Day since Dave Winfield and Steve Kemp on 4/5/83 at Seattle (credit: *Elias*).

▸ Hit his 345th career double in the seventh inning of 4/13 home opening win vs. Los Angeles-AL, surpassing Mickey Mantle (344) for sole possession of seventh place in franchise history...is a .444 (16-for-36) hitter in 11 career home openers with 8R, 6 doubles, 4HR, 7RBI and 9BB.

▸ Recorded his 1,500th career hit in 4/17 win vs. Texas...became the 19th overall Yankee and fourth Yankee whose primary position was catcher to reach the plateau (also Yogi Berra, Bill Dickey and Thurman Munson).

▸ Left 4/28 win at Baltimore in the bottom of the second inning after being hit by a pitch by Baltimore starter Jeremy Guthrie in the top of the inning...suffered a right knee contusion and missed 4/29 game with the injury...missed four games with a strained right calf from 5/4-8.

▸ Was placed on the 15-day disabled list on 5/20 (retroactive to 5/17) with a hairline fracture of the bottom of his right foot...was reinstated from the D.L. on 6/2 (missed 15 team games).

▸ Hit grand slams in consecutive games on 6/12 and 6/13 vs. Houston, becoming the first Yankee to hit a grand slam in back-to-back games since Bill Dickey on 8/3 (G2) and 8/4/37...according to *Elias*, the only other Yankee to accomplish the feat was Babe Ruth in 1927 and 1929...prior to his grand slam on 6/12, had hit 102HR since his last slam on 7/26/04 at Toronto (off Sean Douglass)...his grand slam on 6/13 was the 251st HR of his career, surpassing Graig Nettles for sole possession of seventh place on the Yankees' all-time list.

▸ Drove in at least one run in a career-high eight straight games (10RBI total) from 7/11-24...was the longest such streak by a Yankee since Jason Giambi drove in a run in eight straight from 8/27-9/3/08 and tied for the second-longest streak in the Majors in 2010, trailing only Florida's Jorge Cantu (10 straight from 4/5-15).

▸ In 7/20 loss vs. Los Angeles-AL, caught Bobby Abreu stealing 2B in the fifth and the seventh innings, the first time he caught the same runner stealing twice in the same game since 7/29/04 vs. Baltimore (Jerry Hairston, Jr.).

▸ Collected his 1,000th career RBI with his run-scoring double in the first inning of 7/23 win vs. Kansas City, going 2-for-3 with 1R, 1 double, 2RBI and 1BB...became the 12th overall

MAJOR LEAGUE CATCHERS
(SINCE 2000*)

MOST HITS
1. Jason Kendall........................ 1,628
2. Ivan Rodriguez 1,431
3. A.J. Pierzynski 1,351
4. **JORGE POSADA** **1,246**
5. Bengie Molina........................ 1,243

MOST HOME RUNS
1. **JORGE POSADA** **212**
2. Ivan Rodriguez 160
3. Mike Piazza............................ 159
4. Jason Varitek 153
5. Ramon Hernandez...................... 141

MOST RBI
1. **JORGE POSADA** **816**
2. Ivan Rodriguez 669
3. Bengie Molina.......................... 667
4. Ramon Hernandez...................... 635
5. Jason Varitek 598

MOST GAMES STARTED
1. Jason Kendall........................1,517
2. A.J. Pierzynski 1,235
3. Ivan Rodriguez 1,216
4. **JORGE POSADA** **1,213**
5. Bengie Molina........................ 1,204

WALKS
1. **JORGE POSADA** **695**
2. Jason Kendall.......................... 538
3. Jason Varitek 518
4. Brad Ausmus 384
5. Joe Mauer 366

DOUBLES
1. **JORGE POSADA** **292**
2. Ivan Rodriguez 288
3. A.J. Pierzynski 279
4. Jason Kendall.......................... 275
5. Jason Varitek 238
*as a catcher

MOST GAMES CAUGHT IN YANKEES FRANCHISE HISTORY
1. Bill Dickey 1,708
2. Yogi Berra 1,695
3. **JORGE POSADA** **1,573**
4. Thurman Munson 1,278
5. Elston Howard........................ 1,030

Yankee and 11th player in Major League history whose primary position was catcher to reach the plateau.

▸ Collected his 10th career triple in the first inning of 8/31 win vs. Oakland…became the oldest Yankee to triple since Chili Davis on 9/1/99 at age 39.

▸ Was ejected on 9/1 vs. Oakland by HP Umpire Dana DeMuth for arguing balls and strikes…was his sixth career ejection, first since 9/15/09 vs. Toronto.

▸ Suffered a mild concussion after being hit with foul tip while catching on 9/7 vs. Baltimore and did not start the Yankees' first two games at Texas on 9/10 and 9/11.

▸ Hit game-winning, pinch-hit HR in the 10th inning on 9/14 at Tampa Bay…was his fifth career pinch-hit home run…had been hitless in his previous 10AB as a pinch-hitter in 2010.

▸ Played in all nine postseason games, making eight starts at C…hit .267 (8-for-30) with 3R, 2 doubles and 3RBI…Yankees were 3-0 when he scored a run.

▸ Underwent arthroscopic surgery on 11/10/10 to correct a small meniscus tear in his left knee…the procedure was performed by Dr. Lee Kaplan in Miami.

2009

▸ Hit .285 (109-for-383) with 55R, 25 doubles, 22HR and 81RBI in 111 games (88 starts at C and nine at DH) with the Yankees…batted .290 (36-for-124, 5HR) vs. left-handed pitchers and .282 (73-for-259, 17HR) vs. righties.

DID YOU KNOW??? JORGE POSADA has caught at least one game for 16 straight years. The last man to accomplish that with the same team was Johnny Bench with the Reds from 1967-83 (17 consecutive seasons). Credit: *Elias Sports Bureau.*

▸ Played in 100 games at catcher in a season in which he turned 38 years old, the most games ever for a Yankees catcher in a season at that age and the most by any catcher since Benito Santiago in 2003 w/ San Francisco…among all-time Major League catchers, only Carlton Fisk (130G, 37HR and 107RBI in 1985 with Chicago-AL) reached Posada's totals in games, home runs and RBI in a season in which they entered at 37 years of age or older.

▸ Among Major League catchers, ranked fourth in HR, fifth in RBI and tied for seventh in doubles…ranked seventh in the Majors with a 4.73AB/RBI ratio (383AB, 81RBI)…had the most RBI for any player with fewer than 400 at-bats.

▸ Made his 10th straight Opening Day start at catcher (2000-09)…hit solo-HR and was 1-for-3 with 1BB in 4/6 Opening Day loss at Baltimore, his third career Opening Day homer.

▸ Hit the first HR in Yankee Stadium history in the fifth inning in the Yankees' 4/16 home opening loss vs. Cleveland.

▸ Hit go-ahead, two-run, pinch-hit HR in the seventh and was 1-for-2 in 4/19 win vs. Cleveland…was his third career pinch-hit home run and first since 8/29/04 at Toronto…the home run was reviewed via replay, becoming the first HR to go under umpire review in Yankee Stadium.

▸ Caught all 14 innings in 4/22 win vs. Oakland…marked the seventh time in his career he caught at least 14.0 innings and the first since catching 17.0 innings on 6/1/03 at Detroit.

▸ Was placed on the 15-day disabled list from 5/5-29 with a Grade 2 right hamstring strain (missed 22 team games).

▸ Hit solo-HR and game-winning "walk-off" single in the 12th inning on 7/4 vs. Toronto, going 2-for-6…according to the *Elias Sports Bureau*, the 12th-inning RBI single—in his 1,533rd Major League game—was his first career "walk-off" RBI in extra innings…the last player whose first extra-inning "walk-off" RBI came as far into his career as Posada's was Tony Fernandez, who accomplished the feat in his 2,123rd game in 2001 w/ Toronto.

▸ Was suspended for three games by MLB for his actions during eighth-inning altercation in 9/15 loss vs. Toronto…served his suspension from 9/16-19.

▸ Was selected by Joe Girardi to "manage" the Yankees' final regular season game, guiding the team to a 10-2 win on 10/4 at Tampa Bay.

▸ Appeared in all 15 Yankees postseason games (10 starts), batting .260 (13-for-50) with 5R, 2 doubles, 2HR and 8RBI…reached base in 14 of the contests…hit go-ahead solo home run in the seventh inning in Game 3 clincher of ALDS at Minnesota.

2008

▸ Hit .268 (45-for-168) with 13 doubles, 3HR and 22RBI in 51 games with the Yankees before being placed on the disabled list from 7/21 through the conclusion of the season with a right shoulder strain…made 28 starts at C, 15 at DH, three at 1B…marked his most starts at 1B since 2000 (8GS).

▸ Was placed on the 15-day D.L. on 7/21 (retroactive to 7/20)…underwent season-ending arthroscopic surgery on his right shoulder on 7/30 at the Hospital for Special Surgery in New York…the procedure was performed by Dr. David Altcheck (missed 63 team games).

▸ Was his second stint on the D.L. in 2008…was also on the 15-day D.L. from 4/28-6/3 with a right shoulder strain that was later diagnosed as right rotator cuff tendinitis (missed 32 team games)…had never spent time on the disabled list prior to the 2008 season…according to the *Elias Sports Bureau*, at the time of his injury, Posada was one of six current players with at least 10 years of service that had never been placed on the disabled list along with Brad Ausmus, Johnny Damon, Andruw Jones, Derek Lowe and Livan Hernandez…prior to 4/28/08, the Yankees' last game without Posada on the active roster had been 9/1/96 at California (Jim Leyritz started at C).

▸ Had started at least 120 games behind the plate in each of his previous eight seasons (2000-07), a streak equaled only by Jason Kendall…caught three of 37 potential base stealers (8.1%).

▸ Made his ninth straight Opening Day start at catcher (2000-2008) in 4/1 win vs. Toronto…was 0-for-2 with 1BB in 4/1 Opening Day win vs. Toronto, allowing three stolen bases…missed the next two games from 4/2-3 with a strained right shoulder.

▸ Established a career high with three doubles and tied a career best with four hits in 4/23 win at Chicago-AL, going 4-for-5 with 2RBI…according to the *Elias Sports Bureau*, became the first Yankees catcher to collect three doubles in a game since Buddy Rosar on 4/20/41.

▸ Made first appearance on the D.L. on 4/28…was returned from rehab and reinstated from the disabled list on 6/4…started at C and was 1-for-3 with 1BB in 6/5 win vs. Toronto in his first game back…hit safely in eight of his first 11 games following his return from D.L.

2007

▸ Hit a career-high .338 (171-for-506) while establishing career highs in hits, doubles (42) and slugging percentage (.543)…also hit 20HR and drove in 90 runs in 144 games with the Yankees (125 starts at C, five at DH and one at 1B).

▸ Ranked fourth in the American League in average, becoming the first Yankees catcher to finish a season in the top 10 in the league in batting average since Thurman Munson finished 10th in 1978 with a .297 average…also became the only player in Major League history to bat at least .330 with 40 doubles, 20HR and 90RBI in a year in which he caught in at least half of his games played (credit: *Elias Sports Bureau*)…led the AL with a .344 road average, ranked third with a .426 overall on-base percentage, eighth with a .543 slugging percentage and tied for eighth in doubles.

▸ Won his fifth career Silver Slugger Award and was named the starting catcher on both the *Baseball America* and the *Sporting News* Major League All-Star teams.

▸ His .338 batting average was 61 points higher than in 2006 (.277), the largest increase for any Major Leaguer who qualified for the batting title in 2006 and 2007…according to the *Elias Sports Bureau*, from 1939-2008, the only other Yankee to improve his batting average by 60 or more points from one season to the next was Bobby Murcer who hit .331 in 1971 after posting a .251 average in 1970 (an 80 point increase)…from 1940-2007, only four players appearing primarily at catcher recorded a higher single-season batting average: St. Louis' Joe Torre (.363 in 1971), the Dodgers' Mike Piazza (.362 in 1997 and .346 in 1995) and Minnesota's Joe Mauer (.347 in 2006).

▸ His average never went below .311 (on 4/29) and he never went more than three games without hitting safely…his longest hitless streak of the season was 11AB.

▸ His 42 doubles established a franchise record for a catcher, surpassing his own record of 40 set in 2002…joined Ivan Rodriguez (47 in 1996 and 40 in 1998) as the only two catchers in Major League history to have two seasons of 40 or more doubles (credit: *Elias*)…became only the 17th player in Major League history to collect at least 300 career doubles while appearing in at least 1,000 games at catcher.

▸ Was selected to the 2007 American League All-Star team, his fifth career All-Star selection and first since 2003…went 1-for-3 with 1 double in 7/10 AL win, pinch-hitting for Josh Beckett in the fifth inning and remaining in game at C.

▸ Combined with Alex Rodriguez for a .325 batting average, 74HR and 246RBI…according to *Elias*, no Yankees teammates had combined for numbers that high in each of those categories since 1937, when Joe DiMaggio and Lou Gehrig had a .349BA, 83HR and 326RBI between them.

▸ Hit solo-HR—his second career Opening Day HR and the 199th of his career—and was 2-for-4 with 2R in 4/2 win vs. Tampa Bay…hit his 200th career home run in 4/17 win vs. Cleveland.

▸ Compiled a career-high 15-game hitting streak from 5/3-20, batting .448 (26-for-58) with 13R, 7 doubles, 3HR and 8RBI…was the longest hitting streak for a Yankees catcher since Bob Geren hit safely in 15 straight games in 1989.

▸ Hit solo home runs from each side of the plate and tied career highs with 4H and 4R in 9/4 win vs. Seattle, going 4-for-4 with 1BB…was the second time in 2007 (also 8/1 vs. Chicago-AL) and the eighth time in his career he hit homers from both sides of the plate in the same game, tying Bernie Williams for the second most in team history and marking the most single-game switch-hit HR by a catcher all-time.

▸ Recorded his 300th career double and was 2-for-3 with a solo-HR, 3R and 2BB in 9/11 win at Toronto…according to the *Elias Sports Bureau*, became only the 17th player to reach the 300-double plateau while appearing in at least 1,000 games at catcher.

▸ Went a career-high 37 plate appearances without a strikeout from 8/31-9/12 (previous high was 33PA in 1997).

- Hit a team-best .395 in September (30-for-76), fifth-highest in the AL for the month…according to the *Elias Sports Bureau*, only two players had a higher September average than Posada in a year in which they caught at least 130 games: the Dodgers' Mike Piazza in 1997 (.406) and Pittsburgh's Jason Kendall in 2004 (.400)…named honorary Yankees Manager for the regular season finale on 10/1 at Baltimore.

- Batted .133 (2-for-15) in four Division Series games vs. Cleveland.

2006

- Batted .277 (129-for-465) with 23HR and 93RBI in 143 games (121 starts at C, two at DH)…was the sixth time in a seven-year span (2000-06) he hit at least 20HR and drove in at least 80 runs…ranked 10th in the American League with 1RBI every 5.0AB.

- In 4/3 win at Oakland, made his seventh straight Opening Day start at catcher (2000-06)…hit two-run "walk-off" home run and was 2-for-3 with 2R, 2RBI, 1BB and 2SF in 5/16 win vs. Texas…was his second career "walk-off" HR (also on 5/5/00 vs. Baltimore).

- Missed two games (5/20-21) with tightness in his upper back…suffered tear in his hamstring tendon behind his left knee on 5/23 at Boston and

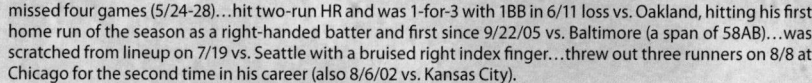

missed four games (5/24-28)…hit two-run HR and was 1-for-3 with 1BB in 6/11 loss vs. Oakland, hitting his first home run of the season as a right-handed batter and first since 9/22/05 vs. Baltimore (a span of 58AB)…was scratched from lineup on 7/19 vs. Seattle with a bruised right index finger…threw out three runners on 8/8 at Chicago for the second time in his career (also 8/6/02 vs. Kansas City).

- Snapped career-high 0-for-25 stretch with a second-inning single in 8/14 win vs. the Angels…hit two three-run HRs in back-to-back at-bats in the sixth and eighth innings and was 2-for-3 with 3R and a season-high 6RBI and 1BB in 9/6 win at Kansas City…was his second multi-home-run game of the season (also 4/9 at Los Angeles-AL) and the 13th of his career (all 2HR games).

- Hit .500 (7-for-14) with 1HR and 2RBI in four Division Series games vs. Detroit.

2005

- Hit .262 (124-for-474) with 19HR and 71RBI in 142 games (122 starts at C, three starts at DH)…threw out 39-of-129 potential base stealers (30.2%)…homered from both sides of the plate in 5/24 win vs. Detroit, hitting solo-HR in the fourth and three-run HR in the fifth.

- Did not strike out in 32 straight plate appearances before fanning in third inning of 6/3 loss at Minnesota…recorded his 1,000th career hit with a seventh-inning double in 8/20 win at Chicago-AL, going 1-for-2 with 2R and 2BB…did not play in 9/10 loss vs. Boston (jammed right shoulder)…hit solo-HR and three-run HR in 9/22 win vs. Baltimore…was his second multi-HR game of the season (also 5/24 vs. Detroit) and the 11th of his career.

- Hit .231 (3-for-13) with 1HR, 2RBI and 6BB in five games vs. the Angels in the Division Series…had his streak of 68 consecutive postseason starts snapped in Game 3 of the ALDS (had started each of the Yankees' postseason games since Game 4 of the 1999 World Series).

2004

- Batted .272 (122-for-449) with 21HR and 81RBI in 137 games (126 starts at C)…led the American League in games caught for the second time in his career, becoming the first Yankee to lead the league in games caught more than once since Thurman Munson in 1970, 1972 and 1973…was tied for third in the AL with 88BB and ranked fourth with a .400 on-base percentage.

- Homered from both sides of the plate (three-run homers in the fifth and seventh innings) and was 2-for-5 with 6RBI in 3/31 win vs. Tampa Bay at Tokyo Dome…accomplished the feat for the fifth time in his career, tying Roy White for third place on the club's all-time list.
- Missed four games after suffering a broken nose in 5/12 game vs. Anaheim (was hit in the nose by a ball thrown by Angels shortstop Alfredo Amezaga in a double-play attempt in bottom of the second inning)…was taken to Columbia Presbyterian Hospital where he was seen by ear, nose and throat specialist, Dr. Hector Rodriguez and surgery was performed to set the fracture.
- Drew at least one walk in a career-high 13 straight games from 5/9-29…hit solo-HR and was 2-for-2 with 2RBI in 7/11 win vs. Tampa Bay before being removed in the third with a sprained right ankle (precautionary X-rays were negative)…hit first-inning grand slam in 7/26 win at Toronto, the seventh of his career to tie Charlie Keller for ninth place on the club's all-time list…missed three games from 8/6-8 with a bruised right thumb…missed two games on 8/14-15, suffering from a low-grade viral infection.
- Hit pinch-hit solo-HR off Jason Frasor in the ninth inning of 8/29 loss at Toronto…was his second career pinch-hit HR (also on 6/16/01 vs. Baltimore off Mike Trombley).
- Hit .244 (11-for-45) with 2RBI in 11 postseason games…caught every inning of the postseason for the Yankees.

2003

- Ranked third in American League Most Valuable Player voting behind Texas' Alex Rodriguez and Toronto's Carlos Delgado…batted .281 (135-for-481) and established career highs with 30HR and 101RBI in 142 games (131 starts at C, two at DH)…his 30HR tied the Yankees' single-season record for home runs by a catcher (Yogi Berra hit 30 in 1952 and 1956).
- Earned his fourth consecutive Silver Slugger Award…ranked fifth in the American League with a .405 on-base percentage and sixth with 93 walks.
- Was elected to start the 2003 All-Star Game at catcher for second straight season, his fourth consecutive All-Star selection (was 0-for-2 at U.S. Cellular Field)…made fourth straight Opening Day start at catcher on 3/31 at Toronto…hit two-run HR in 4/1 win at Toronto, snapping the longest HR drought of his career (140AB/37G since previous HR on 8/17/02)…with seven home runs in April, tied his highest HR total for any single month (also hit 7HR in April 2000 and May 2002)…was ejected in the eighth inning of 5/24 loss vs. Toronto by 2B umpire Fieldin Culbreth for arguing interference call.
- Tied his career high with four walks in 7/9 win at Cleveland, going 0-for-2 with 1R (also 4BB on 5/30/00 vs. Oakland)…missed two games (8/8-9) vs. Seattle with a stiff neck…tied his career high with four hits (ninth time) in 8/12 win at Kansas City, going 4-for-5 with 2R, 1 double and 2RBI…hit two home runs and was 2-for-5 with 2R and 3RBI in 8/30 win at Boston, snapping an 0-for-17 stretch…was the eighth multi-home-run game of his career and first since 6/28/02 vs. New York-NL.
- Hit grand slam and was 3-for-4 with 2R, a career-high 7RBI and 1BB in 9/10 win vs. Detroit…the 7RBI were the most by a Yankee since Bernie Williams also collected 7RBI on 6/17/00 vs. Chicago-AL…was his sixth career grand slam.
- Batted .222 (14-for-63) with 1HR and 7RBI in 17 postseason games.

2002

- Batted .268 (137-for-511) with 40 doubles, 20HR and 99RBI in 143 games (131 starts at C, five at DH and one at 1B)…the 40 doubles were the most by a catcher since Texas' Ivan Rodriguez had 45 in 1996…his 99RBI were the most by any catcher in the Majors in 2002 and his 266RBI from 2000-02 trailed only Mike Piazza (279) for most RBI by a catcher over that span.
- Earned his third Silver Slugger Award…was elected to his third career All-Star Game on 7/9 at Miller Park in Milwaukee…started at catcher and was 0-for-3…made third straight Opening Day start (and appearance) at catcher on 4/1 at Baltimore…tied a career high with 4R and was 3-for-6 with 1 double and 1RBI in 6/19 win at Colorado.
- Homered from both sides of the plate for fourth time in his career in 6/28 win vs. New York-NL…hit three-run homer from the left side in the third and hit two-run shot in the fifth from the right side…hit grand slam and was 1-for-3 with 1BB in 7/2 win vs. Cleveland…was his first grand slam of the season and fourth of his career…hit two-run HR, the 100th HR of his career, and was 1-for-3 with 1BB in 7/5 win vs. Toronto…hit second grand slam of the season—and fifth of his career—and was 3-for-5 with 2R, 1 double and 6RBI in 7/13 win at Cleveland.
- Missed 7/15 game at Toronto to be with wife, Laura, for birth of their second child, Paulina, born that morning in New York…was 1-for-2 in 7/23 loss at Cleveland before being removed from game in fifth with laceration of the left ear (missed 7/24 game at Cleveland)…did not homer in the season's last 40 regular season games (134AB) after 8/17 at Seattle.
- Hit .235 (4-for-17) with 1HR and 3RBI in four Division Series games vs. the Angels.

2001

- Batted .277 with 22HR and 95RBI in 138 games (126 starts at C, six at DH, one at 1B)…hit a three-run HR—his first on Opening Day—and was 3-for-4 with 1R, 1 double and 4RBI in 4/2 win vs. Kansas City…was his second straight Opening Day start for the Yankees at catcher…hit first career grand slam in 4/8 win vs. Toronto.

- Homered in career-high three straight games from 4/7-9…did not appear at catcher for seven games (6/4-10) because of a sprained ligament in his left thumb (3-DH; 3-DNP; 1-PH).
- Pinch-hit for Todd Greene in the eighth and hit game-winning grand slam in 6/6 win vs. Baltimore…was his second career grand slam and second of the season (also 4/8 vs. Toronto)…was his first career pinch-hit home run and the first by a Yankee in 2001…was the 21st pinch-hit grand-slam in Yankees history and first since Glenallen Hill on 7/28/00 at Minnesota.
- Was selected to his second All-Star Game, going 1-for-1 in the American League's 4-1 win on 7/10 in Seattle…missed three straight games (7/31-8/2) with a stomach illness…was ejected from 9/3 win by HP Umpire Andy Fletcher in the ninth after being called out on strikes for second time…appealed six-game suspension by MLB and had sentence reduced by one game (served five-game suspension from 9/26-10/1)…hit third grand slam of the season (and career) and tied a season high with 5RBI in 9/18 win at Chicago.
- Struck out in 12 straight games from 8/30-9/19, the longest such streak by a Yankee since Jim Leyritz also fanned in 12 straight games in 1995.
- Batted .273 (15-for-55) with 2HR and 3RBI in 17 postseason games…in Game 3 of the ALDS on 10/13 at Oakland, became only the 10th player in postseason history—and second Yankee—to hit a home run in a 1-0 game (also Tommy Henrich in Game 1 of the 1949 World Series vs. Brooklyn at Yankee Stadium).

2000

- Batted .287 with 28HR and 86RBI in 151 games (136 starts at C, eight at 1B and three at DH)…drew 107BB, including 95 while appearing in games at catcher, breaking the club record for most walks in a single season by a catcher (Wally Schang, 1921 and Bill Dickey, 1939 each drew 77BB at catcher).
- With 26HR as a catcher, fell four shy of tying Yogi Berra for the most home runs in a single season by a Yankees catcher (Berra hit 30 home runs in 1952 and '56)…threw out 34-of-104 potential base stealers (32.7%)…was selected to his first All-Star Game by Manager Joe Torre and went 0-for-2…in 13 games batting from the second spot in the order, hit .364 (20-for-55) with 12R, 3HR and 10RBI.
- Homered from both sides of the plate for the third time in his career on 4/23 at Toronto, going 3-for-5 with 2R and 3RBI…along with OF Bernie Williams, became the first pair of players in Major League history to hit switch-hit home runs in the same game.
- Hit three-run "walk-off" home run in the ninth and was 4-for-5 with 4RBI in 5/5 win vs. Baltimore…set a career high with 4BB on 5/30 vs. Oakland.
- Established a career high with 4R, in 6/19 win at Boston…was ejected on 7/1 at Tampa Bay for fighting and served a one-game suspension on 7/17 vs. Philadelphia…batted second for the first time in his career on 8/4 vs. Seattle and tied a career high with 4H (sixth time), going 4-for-5 with 2R, 2 doubles and 4RBI.
- Hit .204 (11-for-54) in 16 postseason games with four doubles and 5RBI.

1999

- Batted .245 with 12HR and 57RBI in 112 games (98 starts at C, one at DH and one at 1B)…threw out 20-of-95 potential stealers (21.1%)…team posted a 4.20 ERA in games he caught…did not play in the three-game series at Detroit (4/16-18) after being scratched from the lineup before 4/16 game with a sore right calf (suffered when he was doubled off first base in sixth inning in 4/15 loss vs. Baltimore)…on 4/28 at Texas hit upper-deck home run to snap an 0-for-25 streak from the left side of the plate to begin the season.
- Collected his first career triple on 6/23 at Tampa Bay…was 1-for-3 with an RBI double on 6/25 at Baltimore before leaving the game in the seventh inning with a mild contusion of his left thumb (missed two games, 6/26-27).
- Hit two home runs and was 2-for-5 on 7/10 at Shea Stadium–the third multi-HR game of his career…became only the second catcher in Baseball history to have switch-hit homers in two separate games (Todd Hundley also five times)…established a career-high with 4H (4-for-6) and had 3R and 3RBI on 7/24 vs. Cleveland…was a single shy of hitting for the cycle on 8/22 at Minnesota.
- Batted .182 with 1HR and 3RBI in six postseason games (five starts at C)…hit two-run home run in pennant-clinching win at Boston on 10/18 in ALCS Game 5.

1998

- In first season as the Yankees' primary catcher, batted .268 with 17HR and 63RBI in 111 games…made 91 starts (85 at C, five at DH and one at 1B)…threw out 29-of-76 potential base stealers (38.1%)…team posted a 3.83 ERA in games he caught (792.0IP, 337ER)…hit the Yankees' first home run of the season in his first start of the season on 4/5 at Oakland (was 3-for-5 with 2R and 2RBI in the 9-7 win).
- Caught David Wells' perfect game on 5/17 vs. Minnesota…made his first career start at first base on 6/26 at New York-NL…had the first multi-homer game of his career in 5-2 win on 7/31 at Seattle (two solo HRs)…became only the sixth Yankee ever to homer from both sides of the plate in recording the second multi-home run game of his career (and season) on 8/23 at Texas.

▸ Batted .227 with 2HR and 4RBI in nine postseason games, six starts at C…belted his first career postseason home run in the Yankees' 7-2 victory in Game 6 of the ALCS vs. Cleveland (a solo shot off Chad Ogea)…batted .333 (3-for-9) with 1HR and 2RBI in the World Series vs. San Diego…hit his first career World Series home run in the Yankees' 9-3 victory in Game 2 at Yankee Stadium (a two-run homer off ex-Yankee Brian Boehringer).

1997
▸ Hit .250 with 6HR and 25RBI in his first full season in the Majors…played 60 games, making 52 starts (all at C)…team posted a 4.71 ERA in games he caught (479.1IP, 251ER)…threw out 9-of-48 potential base stealers (18.8%)…was the only rookie on the Yankees' 25-man Opening Day roster…won the James P. Dawson Award, given annually to the Yankees' top rookie in spring training (.357, 2HR, 11RBI)…became the Yankees' second switch-hitting catcher to appear in at least two games in the last 50 years (also Butch Wynegar, 1982-86).

▸ Hit his first Major League home run on 5/4 at Kansas City, a solo HR off Jim Converse.

▸ Appeared in two games of the Division Series vs. Cleveland, going 0-for-2…hit .224 (17-for-76) with 2HR and 13RBI for Santurce of the Puerto Rican Winter League.

1996
▸ Hit .071 (1-for-14) in eight games with the Yankees over four stints in the Majors (4/3-5/11, 5/22-24, 6/29-7/6 and 9/2-9/29)…batted .271 with 11HR and 62RBI at Triple-A Columbus…caught a team-high 94 games…led the International League with 79 walks…was the International League's "Player of the Week" from 5/6-12…was named to the International League All-Star team for the second straight season.

1995
▸ Spent most of the season at Triple-A Columbus, batting .255 with 8HR and 51RBI in 108 games…started 93 games behind the plate…was named to the International League All-Star team…homered from each side of the plate on 5/1 at Ottawa (off Dennis Gray and Tim Crabtree)…was the International League's "Player of the Week" from 8/13-19, batting .391 with 1HR and 10RBI…was on the disabled list from 5/3-12 with a sore back…was third in the International League with 32 doubles before being promoted on 8/31…appeared in one game for the Yankees, making his Major League debut on 9/4 vs. Seattle (caught the ninth inning).

▸ Appeared in one game of the Division Series vs. Seattle, pinch-running for Wade Boggs in the bottom of the 12th inning of Game 2…scored the tying run, making it 5-5 (Yankees won 7-5 in 15 innings).

1994
▸ Hit .240 with 11HR and 48RBI in 92 games at Triple-A Columbus…caught 79 games…hit .188 with 5HR vs. LHP and .277 with 6HR vs. RHP…tied for the International League lead in errors by a catcher (11)…threw out 18-of-83 potential base stealers (21.7%)…season was cut short on 7/25 vs. Norfolk when he suffered a fractured left fibula and a dislocated left ankle after a collision at home plate with Pat Howell…hit .429 in four games prior to the injury and had 16 hits in his last 50 at-bats (.320 BA)…was added to the Yankees' 40-man roster on 11/18.

1993
▸ Combined to hit .260 in 118 games at Single-A Prince William and seven games at Double-A Albany…was named to the Carolina League All-Star team after hitting .259 with 17HR, 61RBI and 17SB at Prince William…ranked second on the team in HR and RBI behind Tate Seefried (21HR, 89RBI)…hit a grand slam on 7/16 off Lynchburg's Joel Bennett…committed 15 errors in 107 games at catcher and one at third base…played for Ponce of the Puerto Rican Winter League, batting .234 with 6HR and 25RBI.

1992
▸ Made the transition from second base to catcher and hit .277 with 12HR and 58RBI in 101 games at Single-A Greensboro…had a 15-game hitting streak from 4/25-5/25…played 41 games at catcher and five at third base.

1991
▸ Batted .235 with 4HR and 33RBI in 71 games, playing his first professional season at Short-A Oneonta…led New York-Penn League second basemen in double plays turned (42).

PERSONAL
▸ Full name is Jorge Rafael de Posada, Jr…first name pronounced HOR-hay…he and his wife, Laura, have a son, Jorge Jr., and a daughter, Paulina.

▸ Selected as a finalist for the 2010 "Marvin Miller Man of the Year" Award…was honored as a recipient of a 2010 "Father of the Year" Award at the National Father's Day Committee annual luncheon on 6/17/10.

- Received the Ted Williams Community Award from the Ted Williams Museum and Hitters Hall of Fame on 3/20/09…honored by the New York BBWAA along with Derek Jeter, Andy Pettitte and Mariano Rivera as the "Willie, Mickey and the Duke" Award winner at the 2010 annual dinner.

- Selected as the Yankees' recipient of the 2007 Roberto Clemente Award, given annually to recognize players who combine outstanding skills on the baseball field with devoted work in the community…was his second nomination (also 2005)…also received the Kids in Distressed SitUations' 2007 Mentor Award and the Bart Giamatti Award at the 2007 Baseball Assistance Team (B.A.T.) dinner, presented annually to the individual associated with the baseball community who best exemplifies the compassion demonstrated by the late Baseball commissioner…received the 2004 "Good Guy" Award by the New York Press Photographers Association…given the 2001 Milton Richman "You Gotta' Have Heart" Award by the New York Chapter of the BBWAA…received the 2001 Thurman Munson Award for his baseball accomplishments and philanthropic work in New York.

- In the fall of 2000, initiated the Jorge Posada Foundation, part of the Giving Back Fund family of charities…proceeds support families of children who suffer from craniosynostosis and provide athletic programs for children in New York City and Puerto Rico…held the Foundation's third Family Day in San Juan, Puerto Rico, in July 2008…the event included games, rides, food and live entertainment…held the foundation's Annual Heroes for Hope Gala in June 2009 in NYC…hosted the fourth annual BaseBowl charity event at Chelsea Piers in New York in November 2010, raising funds for his foundation…co-authored the book *The Beauty of Love* with his wife, Laura, .

- He and Laura teamed with Nike to design "Hip, Hip, Jorge" T-shirts in 2010 in honor of reaching 1,000 career RBI, with 100% of the net proceeds going to the foundation…held a fundraising event to introduce the shirts on 9/7/10 at Yankee Stadium.

- Was honored at the first annual Puerto Rican Yankees Festival in 2007 at the Puerto Rican Sports Museum in Guaynabo…the festival was established to raise money for underprivileged children in Puerto Rico…Jorge Posada, Sr. presented his son with a plaque that commemorated the 30 Puerto Ricans who have played for the Yankees during the team's history…wife, Laura, received the 2007 "Commitment to Family" Award from Boys and Girls Town of New York and was honored as an "Inspiring Woman" by *Siempre Mujer* in 2008.

- Teamed up with Charity Wines to make "Jorge Cabernet" in 2008 with proceeds going to the Jorge Posada Foundation…the wine, from the Clos LaChance Winery and Estate Vineyard in San Martin, Calif. (Napa Valley), is available across the Tri-State area and retails for $13.

- Was signed by Leon Wurth…uncle, Leo Posada, was an instructor for the Dodgers…father, Jorge, is a scout for the Rockies…was a baseball All-Star in 1988-89 at Colegio Alejandrino High School…also participated in basketball, volleyball and track…in 1991, he received an Associate's degree from Calhoun Community College in Decatur, Ala…at Calhoun, he was voted best hitter in 1990 and was a co-captain and all-conference selection in 1991…in 2006, was elected to the Alabama Community College Athletic Hall of Fame…inducted into the Hall of Fame at Pfitzner Stadium on 8/25/07, having played there during the 1993 season with Single-A Prince William…became the seventh member of their Hall of Fame, joining Barry Bonds (2004), Bernie Williams (2004), Andy Pettitte (2004), Art Silber (2005), Bobby Bonilla (2005) and Albert Pujols (2006).

Posada's Career Hitting Record

Year	Team	AVG	G	AB	R	H	2B	3B	HR	RBI	SH	SF	HP	BB	SO	SB	CS	E	OBP	SLG
1991	Oneonta	.235	71	217	34	51	5	5	4	33	7	1	4	51	51	6	5	21	.388	.359
1992	Greensboro	.277	101	339	60	94	22	4	12	58	0	3	6	58	87	11	6	11	.389	.472
1993	Prince William	.259	118	410	71	106	27	2	17	61	1	6	6	67	90	17	5	15	.366	.459
	Albany	.280	7	25	3	7	0	0	0	0	0	0	0	2	7	0	0	2	.333	.280
1994	Columbus	.240	92	313	46	75	13	3	11	48	4	5	1	32	81	5	5	11	.308	.406
1995	Columbus	.255	108	368	60	94	32	5	8	51	6	3	1	54	101	4	4	4	.350	.435
	YANKEES	.000	1	0	0	0	0	0	0	0	0	0	0	0	0	0	0	0	.000	.000
1996	Columbus	.271	106	354	76	96	22	6	11	62	1	3	3	79	86	3	3	10	.405	.460
	YANKEES	.071	8	14	1	1	0	0	0	0	0	0	0	1	6	0	0	0	.133	.071
1997	YANKEES	.250	60	188	29	47	12	0	6	25	1	2	3	30	33	1	2	3	.359	.410
1998	YANKEES	.268	111	358	56	96	23	0	17	63	0	4	0	47	92	0	1	4	.350	.475
1999	YANKEES	.245	112	379	50	93	19	2	12	57	0	2	3	53	91	1	0	5	.341	.401
2000	YANKEES	.287	151	505	92	145	35	1	28	86	0	4	8	107	151	2	2	8	.417	.527
2001	YANKEES	.277	138	484	59	134	28	1	22	95	0	5	6	62	132	2	6	11	.363	.475
2002	YANKEES	.268	143	511	79	137	40	1	20	99	0	3	3	81	143	1	0	12	.370	.468
2003	YANKEES	.281	142	481	83	135	24	0	30	101	0	4	10	93	110	2	4	6	.405	.518
2004	YANKEES	.272	137	449	72	122	31	0	21	81	0	1	9	88	92	1	3	9	.400	.481
2005	YANKEES	.262	142	474	67	124	23	0	19	71	0	4	2	66	94	1	0	3	.352	.430
2006	YANKEES	.277	143	465	65	129	27	2	23	93	0	5	11	64	97	3	0	9	.374	.492
2007	YANKEES	.338	144	506	91	171	42	1	20	90	0	3	6	74	98	2	0	5	.426	.543
2008	YANKEES - a, b	.268	51	168	18	45	13	1	3	22	0	1	2	24	38	0	0	1	.364	.411
2009	YANKEES - c	.285	111	383	55	109	25	0	22	81	0	5	2	48	101	1	0	7	.363	.522
2010	YANKEES - d	.248	120	383	49	95	23	1	18	57	0	2	9	52	99	3	1	8	.357	.454
Minor League Totals		**.258**	**603**	**2026**	**350**	**523**	**121**	**25**	**63**	**313**	**19**	**21**	**21**	**343**	**503**	**46**	**28**	**74**	**.368**	**.436**
Major League Totals		**.275**	**1714**	**5748**	**866**	**1583**	**365**	**10**	**261**	**1021**	**1**	**45**	**72**	**897**	**1377**	**20**	**19**	**91**	**.377**	**.479**

Selected by the Yankees in the 24th round of the 1990 First-Year Player Draft.

a – Placed on the 15-day disabled list from April 28 – June 3, 2008 with a right shoulder strain.
b – Placed on the 15-day disabled list from July 21 – September 28, 2008 with a right shoulder strain.
c – Placed on the 15-day disabled list from May 5-27, 2009 with a Grade 2 right hamstring strain.
d – Placed on the 15-day disabled list from May 20 (retroactive to May 17) - June 1, 2010 with a fractured right foot.

Posada's Division Series Record

Year	Club vs. Opp.	AVG	G	AB	R	H	2B	3B	HR	RBI	SH	SF	HP	BB	SO	SB	CS	E	OBP	SLG
1995	NYY vs. SEA	---	1	0	1	0	0	0	0	0	0	0	0	0	0	0	0	0	---	---
1997	NYY vs. CLE	.000	2	2	0	0	0	0	0	0	0	0	0	1	0	0	0	0	.000	.000
1998	NYY vs. TEX	.000	1	2	1	0	0	0	0	0	0	0	0	1	2	0	0	0	.333	.000
1999	NYY vs. TEX	.250	1	4	0	1	1	0	0	0	0	0	0	0	0	0	0	0	.250	.500
2000	NYY vs. OAK	.235	5	17	2	4	2	0	0	1	0	0	0	3	5	0	0	0	.350	.353
2001	NYY vs. OAK	.444	5	18	3	8	1	0	1	2	0	0	0	2	2	1	0	0	.500	.667
2002	NYY vs. ANA	.235	4	17	2	4	0	0	0	3	0	1	0	3	0	0	1	.222	.412
2003	NYY vs. MIN	.176	4	17	1	3	1	0	0	0	0	0	0	6	0	0	0	0	.176	.235
2004	NYY vs. MIN	.222	4	18	2	4	0	0	0	0	0	0	0	6	0	0	0	0	.222	.222
2005	NYY vs. LAA	.231	5	13	3	3	1	0	1	2	0	0	0	6	2	0	0	0	.474	.538
2006	NYY vs. DET	.500	4	14	2	7	1	0	1	2	0	0	0	2	2	0	0	0	.563	.786
2007	NYY vs. CLE	.133	4	15	1	2	1	0	0	0	0	0	0	2	3	0	0	0	.235	.200
2009	NYY vs. MIN	.364	3	11	1	4	0	0	1	2	0	0	0	2	0	0	0	0	.364	.636
2010	NYY vs. MIN	.273	3	11	2	3	0	0	0	2	0	0	0	1	4	0	0	0	.333	.273
Division Series Totals		**.270**	**46**	**159**	**21**	**43**	**8**	**0**	**5**	**14**	**0**	**1**	**0**	**17**	**38**	**1**	**0**	**1**	**.339**	**.415**

Posada's League Championship Series Record

Year	Club vs. Opp.	AVG	G	AB	R	H	2B	3B	HR	RBI	SH	SF	HP	BB	SO	SB	CS	E	OBP	SLG
1998	NYY vs. CLE	.182	5	11	1	2	0	0	1	2	0	0	0	4	2	0	1	0	.400	.455
1999	NYY vs. BOS	.100	3	10	1	1	0	0	1	2	0	0	0	1	2	0	0	1	.182	.400
2000	NYY vs. SEA	.158	6	19	2	3	1	0	0	3	0	0	1	5	5	0	1	0	.360	.211
2001	NYY vs. SEA	.214	5	14	4	3	1	0	0	0	0	0	0	6	7	0	0	0	.450	.286
2003	NYY vs. BOS	.296	7	27	5	8	4	0	1	6	0	0	0	3	4	0	0	0	.367	.556
2004	NYY vs. BOS	.259	7	27	4	7	1	0	0	2	0	1	1	7	1	0	0	0	.417	.296
2009	NYY vs. LAA	.200	6	20	3	4	1	0	1	1	0	0	0	5	5	1	0	0	.360	.400
2010	NYY vs. TEX	.263	6	19	1	5	2	0	0	1	0	0	0	1	8	0	0	0	.300	.368
LCS Totals		**.224**	**45**	**147**	**21**	**33**	**10**	**0**	**4**	**17**	**0**	**1**	**2**	**32**	**34**	**1**	**2**	**1**	**.368**	**.374**

Posada's World Series Record

Year	Club vs. Opp.	AVG	G	AB	R	H	2B	3B	HR	RBI	SH	SF	HP	BB	SO	SB	CS	E	OBP	SLG
1998	NYY vs. SD	.333	3	9	2	3	0	0	1	2	0	0	0	2	2	0	0	0	.455	.667
1999	NYY vs. ATL	.250	2	8	0	2	1	0	0	1	0	0	0	3	0	0	0	0	.250	.375
2000	NYY vs. NYM	.222	5	18	2	4	1	0	0	1	0	0	0	5	4	0	0	0	.391	.278
2001	NYY vs. AZ	.174	7	23	2	4	1	0	1	1	0	0	0	3	8	0	0	1	.269	.348
2003	NYY vs. FLA	.158	6	19	0	3	1	0	0	1	0	0	0	5	7	1	1	0	.333	.211
2009	NYY vs. PHI	.263	6	19	1	5	1	0	0	5	0	1	0	2	7	0	0	1	.318	.316
World Series Totals		**.219**	**29**	**96**	**7**	**21**	**5**	**0**	**2**	**11**	**0**	**1**	**0**	**17**	**31**	**1**	**1**	**2**	**.333**	**.333**
POSTSEASON TOTALS		**.241**	**120**	**402**	**49**	**97**	**23**	**0**	**11**	**42**	**0**	**3**	**2**	**66**	**103**	**3**	**3**	**4**	**.349**	**.381**

Posada's All-Star Game Record

Year	Club, Site	AVG	G	AB	R	H	2B	3B	HR	RBI	SH	SF	HP	BB	SO	SB	CS	E	OBP	SLG
2000	NYY, Atlanta	.000	1	2	0	0	0	0	0	0	0	0	0	0	1	0	0	0	.000	.000
2001	NYY, Seattle	1.000	1	1	0	1	1	0	0	0	0	0	0	0	0	0	0	0	1.000	2.000
2002	NYY, Milwaukee	.000	1	3	0	0	0	0	0	0	0	0	0	0	2	0	0	0	.000	.000
2003	NYY, Chicago-AL	.000	1	2	0	0	0	0	0	0	0	0	0	0	2	0	0	0	.000	.000
2007	NYY, San Francisco	.333	1	3	0	1	1	0	0	0	0	0	0	0	0	0	0	0	.333	.333
All-Star Game Totals		**.182**	**5**	**11**	**0**	**2**	**2**	**0**	**0**	**0**	**0**	**0**	**0**	**0**	**5**	**0**	**0**	**0**	**.182**	**.364**

Posada's Career Fielding Record

Position	PCT	G	PO	A	E	TC	PB
Catcher	.992	1573	10009	694	90	10793	142
First Base	.992	28	117	12	1	130	---

Posada's Career Home Run Chart

MULTI-HOMER GAMES: 16. **TWO-HOMER GAMES:** 16, last 9/1/09 at Baltimore. **GRAND SLAMS:** 9, last on 6/13/10 vs. Houston (Casey Daigle). **PINCH-HIT HR:** 5, last on 9/14/10 at Tampa Bay (Dan Wheeler). **INSIDE-THE-PARK HR:** None. **WALK-OFF HR:** 2, last on 5/16/06 vs. Texas (Akinori Otsuka). **LEADOFF HR:** None.

Long Shot

The Yankees set a franchise record with 244HR in 2009, surpassing the previous mark of 242 set in 2004…according to the *Elias Sports Bureau*, they finished the season with the outright Major League lead in HR for the first time since 1961, homering in 127 of their 162 games (78.4%), including 73 of their 81 games at home…the Yankees have reached the 200HR plateau 10 times since 2000 (2000-07, '09-10).

42 MARIANO RIVERA

RIGHT-HANDED PITCHER • 6-2 • 185 • B/T: RIGHT/RIGHT • OPENING DAY AGE: 41

BIRTHDATE
November 29, 1969

BIRTHPLACE
Panama City, Panama

RESIDES
Purchase, NY

M.L. SERVICE
15 years, 105 days

CAREER HIGHLIGHTS
A.L. All-Star Team
▸ 1997, 1999, 2000, 2001, 2002, 2004, 2005, 2006, 2008, 2009, 2010

League Championship Series MVP
▸ 2003

World Series MVP
▸ 1999

Sporting News **Pro Athlete of the Year**
▸ 2009

Sporting News **A.L. Reliver of the Year**
▸ 1997, 1999, 2009

A.L. Rolaids Relief Man Award
▸ 1999, 2001, 2004, 2005, 2006, 2009

MLB Delivery Man of the Year
▸ 2005, 2006, 2009

STATUS
▸ Signed as a non-drafted free agent on February 17, 1990…signed a two-year contract on December 14, 2010 that extends through the 2012 season.

CAREER NOTES
▸ Owns 559 career saves, the most in AL history and second-most all time behind Trevor Hoffman (601)…has an 89.3% career conversion rate in 626 save opportunities.

▸ Has a career ERA of 2.23, the second-lowest all time among pitchers with at least 1,000.0IP behind only Eddie Cicotte (2.20) since earned runs became an official statistic in the National League (in 1912) and American League (in 1913) - credit: *Elias Sports Bureau*.

▸ Has recorded at least one save in 15 consecutive seasons (since 1996)…according to the *Elias Sports Bureau*, is tied with Tom Burgmeier for the longest streak in AL history and sixth-longest all time.

▸ Has recorded at least 25 saves in 14 consecutive seasons (since 1997), marking the longest such streak since saves became an official statistic in 1969…has reached the 30-save plateau 13 times in his career, one shy of Trevor Hoffman's record (14)…his eight straight seasons of at least 30 saves (since 2003) matches Hoffman (1995-2002) for the longest streak all time… has saved at least 35 games in a season 10 times in his career, ranking second all time to Hoffman's 12…has reached the 40-save mark seven times in his career, second-most all time behind Hoffman (nine).

▸ Over the last 10 years (2001-10) leads the Majors with 394 saves and 646 appearances.

▸ Has made 60 appearances 13 times in his career, tied with Mike Stanton for the most all time…has made at least 60 outings with a sub-2.00 ERA in seven of his last eight seasons, including each of his last three seasons (2008-10), becoming the only pitcher in Baseball history to record three such consecutive seasons after the age of 35.

▸ His 978 career appearances ranks 17th on Baseball's all-time list, most among active players.

▸ Has the most saves in Yankees franchise history…his 978 appearances are the most in club history (456 more than second-place Dave Righetti's 522)…ranks ninth in club history with 1,051K…owns eight of the 10 highest single-season save totals in franchise history (1. 53 in 2004; 2. 50 in 2001; 4. 45 in 1999; 5. 44 in 2009; T6. 43 in 1997 and 2005; 9. 40 in 2003; 10. 39 in 2008)…Dave Righetti's 46 saves in 1986 ranks third and John Wetteland's 43 saves in 1996 is tied for sixth.

▸ Owns 115 career saves when recording more than three outs and 11 saves when tossing at least 2.0 innings.

▸ Converted 51 straight saves at home from 8/18/07-4/30/10, tied with Eric Gagne (51 straight from 8/28/02-7/1/04) for the longest such streak all time (credit: *Elias*).

▸ Is the all-time leader in Interleague saves with 63…since blowing a save on 7/14/01 at Florida, has converted 38 of his last 39 save chances in Interleague play, including each of his last 19 since 6/20/06 (credit: *Elias*).

BESTS & STREAKS

Low-hit CG
NA
IP (start)
8.0 - at CWS, 7/4/95
IP (relief)
5.1 - at SEA, 8/25/95
Hits
8 - at CAL, 5/23/95
Runs (start)
7 - vs. OAK, 6/6/95
Runs (relief)
6 - at CLE, 7/14/02
BB
4 - 2 times
Last: at SEA, 8/23/97
SO
11 - at CWS, 7/4/95
HR
2 - 4 times
Last: vs. TB, 5/7/09
Winning Streak
5g - 3 times
Last: 5/28-7/25/03
Losing Streak
3g - 3 times
Last: 4/15-5/7/07
Consecutive Saves
36 - 4/30-9/14/09

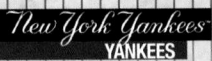

- Recorded his 1,000th strikeout on 9/18/09 at Seattle, at which time he had walked just 255 batters in his career…according to *Elias*, only three pitchers since 1900 (Shane Reynolds-233; Ben Sheets-247; and Billy Wagner-255) had as many or fewer walks at the time of their 1,000th strikeout.
- Has been selected to 11 All-Star teams, joining teammate Derek Jeter as the only players to be named to the All-Star team with their current team at least 10 times, according to *Elias Sports Bureau*…is tied for the third-most All-Star selections by a pitcher all time.
- Along with Derek Jeter and Jorge Posada, have become the first trio of teammates in each of the four major sports (MLB, NBA, NFL, NHL) to play together in each of 16 straight seasons.
- According to the *Elias Sports Bureau*, his 230 saves at the original Yankee Stadium are the most by any one pitcher in any one ballpark.
- Has 42 career postseason saves—including 11 in the World Series—both Major League records…his 24 World Series appearances are the most all time…owns a 0.71 ERA (139.2IP, 11ER) in 94 postseason games, the lowest ERA all-time (min. 30.0IP) and the most postseason appearances for any pitcher in Major League history…owns 14 career 2.0-inning saves in the postseason.

2010

- Was 3-3 with 33 saves (in 38 chances) and a 1.80 ERA in 61 relief appearances with the Yankees…opponents batted .183 (39-for-213, 2HR); LH .214 (22-for-103, 2HR), RH .155 (17-for-110, 0HR)…retired 49-of-61 first batters faced (80.3%)…prevented 13-of-16 inherited runners from scoring (81.3%)…appeared in consecutive games 15 times and three straight games once…his five blown saves were his most since 2003 (six).
- Just five of his 61 relief outings—and one of his 33 saves—were more than 1.0IP…51 of his 61 outings were scoreless.
- Named to his 11th All-Star Game in 2010, tying Derek Jeter and Bill Dickey for the fifth-most selections in franchise history…did not attend the game to rest a sore right knee and left side…named to *Sporting News'* 2010 Top 50 Baseball Players list (No. 11).
- Made his 15th career Opening Day roster in 2010, most among all current Yankees.
- Did not allow a run in his first 11.0IP of the season…according to *Elias*, matched his second-longest scoreless streak to begin a season (also 11.0IP in 1998 and 16.0 in 2008).
- With his save on 4/6 at Boston, became the second pitcher in franchise history to record a save after turning 40 (40 years, 129 days), joining Jim Kaat, who earned two saves as a 40-year-old in 1979 (40 years, 312 days when he notched the second such save)—credit: *Elias Sports Bureau*.
- Went 11 days between appearances from 4/30-5/11…was the second-longest gap between appearances in his 15 seasons as a reliever (not including D.L. stints)…went 21 days between outings from 8/31-9/22/06.
- In 5/16 loss vs. Minnesota, registered first blown save since 9/18/09 at Seattle after entering the game with the bases loaded and two outs in the eighth inning…walked in a run and allowed a grand slam to his next batter (Kubel) before recording his first and only out…was his fourth career grand slam surrendered and third as a reliever (first since Bill Selby "walk-off" GS on 7/14/02 at Cleveland)…was the fourth bases-loaded walk issued in his career and first since 5/6/05 vs. Oakland (Keith Ginter).
- Recorded two saves in the same day for the sixth time in his career on 5/26 at Minnesota (also 5/3/07 at Texas; 9/16/97 vs. Boston, 7/8/00 in a split-stadium DH vs. the Mets; 9/13/03 vs. Tampa Bay and 9/29/04 vs. Minnesota)…the first of the two saves came in the completion of 5/25 win at Minnesota and was credited to that day.
- Did not allow a run over a 16-appearance stretch from 5/25-7/2, holding opponents to just 5H and 3BB (1IBB) in 18.0IP while converting each of his 10 save opportunities (1HP, 20K)…allowed just 1ER over a 27-appearance stretch (27.2IP) from 5/25-8/8.

LOWEST ERAs ALL-TIME, MIN. 1000.0IP
(Since becoming an official statistic in NL-1912 and AL-1913 / credit: *Elias*)

1.	Eddie Cicotte	2.20
2.	**MARIANO RIVERA**	**2.23**
3.	Jim Scott	2.26
4.	Babe Ruth	2.28

ALL-TIME SAVES LEADERS

1.	Trevor Hoffman	601
2.	**MARIANO RIVERA**	**559**
3.	Lee Smith	478
4.	John Franco	424
5.	Billy Wagner	422

MOST SAVES, LAST 10 YEARS

1.	**MARIANO RIVERA**	**394**
2.	Trevor Hoffman	330
3.	Billy Wagner	315
4.	Francisco Cordero	290
5.	Francisco Rodriguez	268

BEST CAREER SAVE PERCENTAGE
Since 1969 (min. 200 save opps.)

1.	Eric Gagne	91.7 (187-for-204)
2.	Joe Nathan	89.5 (247-for-276)
3.	**MARIANO RIVERA**	**89.3 (559-for-626)**
4.	Trevor Hoffman	88.8 (601-for-677)
5.	Jonathan Papelbon	87.9 (188-for-214)

MOST CAREER POSTSEASON SAVES

1.	**MARIANO RIVERA**	**42**
2.	Brad Lidge	18
3.	Dennis Eckersley	15
4.	Jason Isringhausen	11
	Rob Nenn	11

MOST GAMES PITCHED, ACTIVE PLAYERS

1.	**MARIANO RIVERA**	**978**
2.	Billy Wagner	853
3.	Arthur Rhodes	849
4.	LaTroy Hawkins	771
5.	Bob Howry	769

- Was voted as the winner of June's "Clutch Performer of the Month Award Presented by Pepsi"...went 2-0 in 11 games, converting each of his seven save chances without allowing a run in 13.0IP (4H, 2BB, 16K).

- Held opponents hitless in 25 straight AB between a Luke Scott single on 6/1 at Baltimore and Stephen Drew's single on 6/23 at Arizona...also held right-handed batters hitless in 21 consecutive AB prior to Justin Upton's double on 6/23 at Arizona (streak started after Jason Bay double on 5/21 at New York-NL).

MARIANO RIVERA SAVES BREAKDOWN		
Category .... 2010..Career		
0.1IP...................1 ....22 (last, 4/15/10 vs. Los Angeles-AL)		
0.2IP...................1 ....14 (last, 4/13/10 Los Angeles-AL)		
1.0IP...................30 ....408 (last, 10/2/10 at Boston)		
1.1IP...................1 ....70 (last, 8/21/10 vs. Seattle)		
1.2IP...................0 .... 34 (last, 8/29/08 vs. Toronto)		
2.0IP...................0 ....10 (last, 7/16/06 vs. Chicago-AL)		
2.1IP...................0 ....1 (8/23/96 vs. Oakland)		
Three consecutive games.......................28 times (last 7/17-19/09)		
Four consecutive games.................. 2 times (6/1-4/04; 6/23-27/97)		
Three consecutive days.........................21 times (last 7/17-19/09)		
Four consecutive days.................................. 1 time (6/1-4/04)		

- Tossed 2.0 scoreless innings to earn his first win on 6/23 at Arizona...pitched out of a bases-loaded, no out situation in the bottom of the 10th...also had his third career at-bat (and fourth plate appearance) in the game, grounding out to first in the 10th inning.

- Made his second 2.0-inning outing in a five-day span on 6/27 at Los Angeles-NL, recording the win in both games...marked the first time he tossed at least 2.0IP twice in a five-day stretch since 7/6-8/08 vs. Boston and 7/9/08 vs. Tampa Bay, when he also recorded the win in both games.

- Had three blown saves in September, his most in a calendar month since August 2003 (four)—credit: Elias.

- Suffered his third loss and third blown save of the season on 9/11 at Texas, marking his first blown save on the road since 9/18/09 at Seattle.

- Suffered his fifth blown save of the season in 9/26 win vs. Boston, allowing 2H and 2ER in 1.1IP...was his first blown save at home against Boston since back-to-back blown saves on 4/5 and 4/6/05...allowed four stolen bases in the ninth inning, marking the first time a Yankees reliever allowed 4SB in a single inning since Lindy McDaniel in 1969—credit: Elias.

- Appeared in six postseason games, tossing 6.1 scoreless IP and converting all three save chances...earned the 600th save of his Major League career (regular and postseason) in 10/7 ALDS Game 2 win at Minnesota.

2009

- Was 3-3 with a 1.76 ERA and 44 saves in 66 relief appearances for the Yankees...ranked second in the Majors with a 95.7% (44-for-46) save percentage and third in saves...placed fifth in the American League with 55 games finished...tabbed as Sporting News' "Pro Athlete of the Year," becoming the second Yankees pitcher to receive the honor (also Ron Guidry in 1978)...also earned the MLB "Delivery Man of the Year" Award, "Closer of the Year" by MLB.com and Sporting News "Reliever of the Year"...named co-winner of the 2009 "Rolaids Relief Man" Award, joining Dan Quisenberry (1980, '82-85) as the only five-time winners of the award...received four votes for AL MVP (17 points).

- Made appearances in consecutive games 14 times, three-straight games twice (6/28-7/1; 7/17-19) and four straight games twice (4/19-24 and 6/4-8)...recorded saves in two consecutive games 10 times, on two consecutive days 10 times, in three straight games twice and three straight days once (7/17-19 in Detroit)...recorded seven saves of more than 1.0IP, including a season-high 2.0IP in 5/16 win vs. Minnesota...retired 47-of-66 first batters faced (71.2%)...prevented 15-of-20 inherited runners from scoring (75.0%)...opponents batted .197 (48-for-244, 7HR); LH .182 (22-for-121, 3HR), RH .211 (26-for-123, 4HR).

- In his final 40 appearances of the season (from 6/16), went 2-1 with a 0.68 ERA and converted 30-of-31 save opportunities (39.2IP, 21H, 3ER, 9BB, 40K, 2HR)...over his first 26 appearances (from 4/9-6/12), went 1-2 with a 3.38 ERA while going 14-of-15 in save opportunities (26.2IP, 27H, 10ER, 3BB, 32K, 5HR).

- Converted a career-high 36 straight save opportunities from 4/30-9/14...went 2-2 with a 1.44 ERA over the stretch (50.0IP, 30H, 9R, 8ER, 11BB, 53K, 4HR), allowing just 2ER in save situations.

- Was named to his 10th All-Star team...earned the save in the American League win in St. Louis on 7/14, tossing a perfect ninth inning (1.0IP, 1K)...was his fourth career All-Star save, surpassing Dennis Eckersley for most all time.

- Made his 14th Opening Day roster...in 4/17 win vs. Cleveland, tossed a scoreless ninth inning to earn the first save in Yankee Stadium history (1.0IP, 2H, 2K).

- Allowed back-to-back solo-HR in the ninth (Carl Crawford and Evan Longoria) to suffer the loss (0.2IP, 2H, 2ER, 1K) on 5/7 vs. Tampa Bay...surrendered consecutive home runs for the first time in his career, and allowed two HR in an appearance for only the fourth time in his career (first since 7/18/98 at Toronto—Stanley and Sprague).

MOST WIN-SAVE COMBINATIONS, ALL-TIME	
1. Andy Pettitte/**MARIANO RIVERA (NYY)**........................ 68	
2. Bob Welch/Dennis Eckersley (OAK) 57	
3. Mike Mussina/**MARIANO RIVERA (NYY)**......................49	
4. Dave Stewart/Dennis Eckersley (OAK).........................43	
T5. Jimmy Key/ Tom Henke (TOR)..................................37	
Kevin Tapani/Rick Aguilera (MIN) 37	

▸ In 5/29 win at Cleveland, tossed a scoreless ninth for his 10th save (1.0IP, 1H, 2K)…was his 58th save in a game in which Andy Pettitte was the winning pitcher, surpassing Bob Welch and Dennis Eckersley (57) for the highest total for any pair of pitchers since saves became an official statistic in 1969 (credit: *Elias*).

▸ Did not allow a run over 21 straight appearances from 6/16-8/9, compiling a 22.1-inning scoreless stretch dating back to the ninth inning on 6/12…according to the *Elias Sports Bureau*, was the fourth-longest scoreless stretch of his career (behind 30.2IP in 1999, 26.0IP in 1996 and 23.0IP in 2005)…did not allow a run in a save situation over 25 save chances from 5/20-8/9, a 25.1-inning scoreless span.

▸ In 6/24 win at Atlanta, struck out all four batters faced to earn his 16th save (1.1IP)…was the first time in his career he faced at least four batters and retired each of them via strikeout…also made second career regular season plate appearance in the game, lining out to CF in the ninth.

▸ Earned his 500th career save (18th of the season) in 6/28 win at the Mets, tossing 1.1 scoreless innings (1H, 2K)…also recorded his first career RBI with a bases-loaded walk off Francisco Rodriguez in the ninth inning…according to *Elias*, was the first AL pitcher to record both a save and RBI in the same game since Detroit's Chad Durbin at Atlanta on 6/25/07.

▸ Was named the AL "co-Player of the Week" for the period ending 6/28…was his second career weekly award (also 6/9/08).

▸ On 6/30 vs. Seattle, threw out the ceremonial first pitch in recognition of earning his 500th career save and tossed a perfect ninth for his 19th save (1.0IP, 1K).

▸ Was named the winner of the "MLB Delivery Man of the Month" Award in July for the second time in his career (also April 2008)…was 10-for-10 in save opportunities without allowing a run…marked just the second time in his career he earned at least 10 saves in a single month without allowing a run (also August 1999).

▸ Allowed a two-run "walk-off" home run to Ichiro Suzuki with two outs in the bottom of the ninth on 9/19 at Seattle…marked just the fifth "walk-off" homer allowed by Rivera in his career (first since Cleveland's Bill Selby-7/14/02)…snapped a career-high streak of 36 straight converted save chances…his strikeout of Mike Carp in the ninth was the 1,000th K of his career.

▸ Was a part of his fifth World Championship team, making 12 postseason appearances in 2009, recording five saves (in five opportunities) and allowing just 1ER in 16.0IP (0.56 ERA)…six of the outings were more than 1.0 inning, including two 2.0-inning saves (Game 6 of ALCS and Game 2 of WS)…was on the mound for the clinching game in each of the three rounds for the fourth time in his career…made his 23rd career World Series appearance in Game 4 on 11/1 at Philadelphia, surpassing Whitey Ford (22) for most all time…with two World Series saves, became the second-oldest pitcher to earn a save in a World Series game behind Baltimore's Dick Hall (age 40 in 1971)…tossed a World Series career-high 41 pitches in Game 6 on 11/4 at Yankee Stadium…has been the Yankees final pitcher in each of their last four World Series wins (1998, '99, 2000 and '09)…donated his postseason cap to the Baseball Hall of Fame.

2008

▸ Was 6-5 with 39 saves (in 40 chances) and a 1.40 ERA in a team-high 64 appearances with the Yankees…were his most wins and saves and his lowest ERA since 2005 (7, 43, 1.38)…established a career high with a 97.5% save percentage, the highest mark by an AL closer since Boston's Tom Gordon in 1998 (97.9%, 46-for-47)…finished fifth in AL Cy Young Award voting.

▸ Opponents batted .165 (41-for-249, 4HR); LH .147 (19-for-129, 2HR), RH .183 (22-for-120, 2HR)…was the lowest opponents average among qualifying AL relievers, trailing only the Cubs' Carlos Marmol (.135) among all Major League relievers…stranded 16-of-20 inherited runners (80.0%)…retired 47-of-64 first batters faced (73.4%)…pitched consecutive games nine times, three straight three times and four straight three times…appeared in four straight games four times combined over his previous four years (2004-07)…saved consecutive games five times and earned the save in three straight games three times.

▸ Had the Majors' lowest ERA among all pitchers with at least 70.0IP…ranked third among AL relievers in strikeouts and was tied with Joe Nathan for fifth in the AL in saves.

▸ According to the *Elias Sports Bureau*, Rivera's 12.83-to-1 strikeouts-to-walk ratio (77K, 6BB) was the third highest in modern Major League history (min. 50.0IP), behind Dennis Eckersley's 1989 (18.33-to-1) and 1990 (18.25-for-1) campaigns.

▸ Converted his first 28 save opportunities to start the season, marking a career best (converted first 12 chances in 2004)…was not charged with a run in any of his first 22 save opportunities, becoming the first pitcher since 1975 (when the current save rules came into effect) to accomplish the feat (credit: *Elias*).

▸ Was selected to his ninth All-Star Game…tossed 1.2 scoreless innings in the 15.0-inning AL victory on 7/15 at the original Yankee Stadium, entering with one out and one on in the ninth…donated his jersey as well as dirt from the mound to the Baseball Hall of Fame.

▸ Recorded his second career Opening Day save—the most in franchise history—tossing a perfect ninth inning (1.0IP, 1K) in 4/1 win vs. Toronto…made his 13th career Opening Day roster…did not allow a run or walk in his first 14 appearances (4/1-5/10), recording 10 saves and striking out 12 batters in 15.0IP (6H)…was the longest scoreless streak to begin a season in his career…named the April winner of the "DHL Presents the Major League Baseball Delivery Man of the Month" Award.

▸ On 5/13 at Tampa Bay, in his 15th appearance of the year, allowed "walk-off" RBI single in the 11th to suffer the loss (1.0IP, 3H, 1ER, 1K)…was his first run allowed of the season, marking the latest into a season he had gone without allowing a run…previous best was in 1998 when he first allowed a run in his 11th appearance on 5/14/98 vs. Texas.

▸ Was named AL "Player of the Week" for the period ending 6/1, earning his first career weekly award…in 6/7 win vs. Kansas City, recorded his second win of the season despite allowing a home run to David DeJesus, his first batter faced, on his first pitch (1.0IP, 1H, 1ER, 1K, 1HR)…was his first HR allowed since 8/15/07 vs. Baltimore (Aubrey Huff) and marked the first time he had allowed a HR on his first pitch after entering a game since 8/23/97 at Seattle to Roberto Kelly (credit: *Elias*).

▸ Allowed his first run of the season in a save opportunity in 7/5 win vs. Boston…allowed 1ER and loaded the bases with no outs (2HP) before retiring the final three batters of the game to earn his 23rd save…according to the *Elias Sports Bureau*, it was the first time Rivera escaped a bases-full-none-out jam with the tying run on third in the game's final inning.

▸ In 7/29 loss vs. Baltimore, pitched the ninth to surpass the 1000.0IP plateau…on 8/1 at Los Angeles-AL, allowed one-out ninth-inning "walk-off" RBI-single to Chone Figgins on his first and only pitch of the game as the Angels won 1-0…was the second time he threw just one pitch (also 8/7/05 at Toronto – earned the save).

▸ In 8/12 win at Minnesota, allowed game-tying three-run HR to Delmon Young in the eighth for his first and only blown save of the season (1.2IP, 2H, 1ER)…in 8/15 loss vs. Kansas City, allowed the go-ahead run to score on a wild pitch…was just the second time in his career he allowed a run on a wild pitch (also 6/24/00 at Chicago-AL) and his first time allowing the go-ahead run on a WP (credit: *Elias*).

▸ Saved all three games of the Yankees' series at Baltimore from 8/22-24, marking the sixth time in his career he has saved all of the games in a series of three or more games (previous 6/1-3/04 vs. Baltimore)…was also the 19th time in his career he recorded a save on three or more consecutive days…the only other Yankees pitchers to earn a save in each game of a series (of at least three games) are Dave Righetti (1986), Steve Howe (1994) and John Wetteland (twice in 1996).

YANKEES ALL-TIME SAVES

1.	**MARIANO RIVERA**	**559**
2.	Dave Righetti	224
3.	Goose Gossage	151
4.	Sparky Lyle	141

MOST GAMES PITCHED, YANKEES, ALL-TIME

1.	**MARIANO RIVERA**	**978**
2.	Dave Righetti	522
3.	Whitey Ford	498
4.	Mike Stanton	456
5.	Red Ruffing	426

MOST SAVES, SINGLE SEASON (since 2000)

1.	Francisco Rodriguez-2008-LAA	62
2.	Eric Gagne, 2003-LAD	55
	John Smoltz, 2002-ATL	55
4.	**MARIANO RIVERA, 2004-NYY**	**53**
5.	Eric Gagne, 2002-LAD	52
6.	**MARIANO RIVERA, 2001-NYY**	**50**
7.	Francisco Cordero, 2004-TEX	49

LOWEST CAREER AVERAGE AGAINST LEFT-HANDERS AMONG ACTIVE MAJOR LEAGUE RIGHT-HANDED PITCHERS

1.	**MARIANO RIVERA**	**.205 (449-for-2189)**
2.	Francisco Rodriguez	.208 (215-for-1034)
3.	Joe Nathan	.214 (243-for-1134)
4.	Scot Shields	.215 (273-for-1271)
5.	Joaquin Benoit	.218 (262-for-1200)

MOST CONSECUTIVE SEASONS WITH AT LEAST ONE SAVE (ALL TIME)
List courtesy of the *Elias Sports Bureau*

1.	John Franco (1984-2001)	18
2.	Lee Smith (1981-1997)	17
T3.	Gene Garber (1973-1988)	16
	Goose Gossage (1974-1989)	16
	Jeff Reardon (1979-1994)	16
T6.	**MARIANO RIVERA (1996-2010)**	**15**
	Tom Burgmeier (1970-1984)	15
	Doug Jones (1986-2000)	15
	Kent Tekulve (1975-1989)	15

▸ Recorded his 479th career save in 9/15 win vs. Chicago-AL, surpassing Lee Smith (478) for sole possession of second place on Baseball's all-time saves list.

▸ Threw 1.0 scoreless inning in the final game at Yankee Stadium on 9/21 vs. Baltimore, inducing a Brian Roberts groundout to 1B Cody Ransom with the game's final pitch to secure the Yankees victory.

▸ Returned to New York during the season's final road trip to undergo an MRI on his shoulder that revealed calcification in the AC joint in his right shoulder.

▸ Collected his 39th and final save of the season in 9/28 Game 1 win at Boston…tossed 1.1 scoreless innings to save Mike Mussina's 20th win of the season…was the second time he recorded a save in a pitcher's 20th win (also Roger Clemens in 2001).

▸ Underwent surgery on the AC Joint in his right shoulder on 10/7…procedure was done by Dr. David Altchek at the Hospital for Special Surgery in New York.

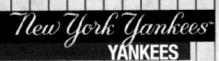
2007

▸ Was 3-4 with a 3.15 ERA and 30 saves in 67 relief appearances for the Yankees…ranked fourth in the American League with 59 games finished and tied for eighth with 30 saves…opponents batted .248 (68-for-274, 4HR); LH .255 (35-for-137, 1HR), RH .241 (33-for-137, 3HR)…converted 30-of-34 save opportunities (88.2%).

▸ Saved consecutive games five times and earned the save in three consecutive games once, from 7/14-16…made appearances in consecutive games 11 times and three straight games once…recorded 11 saves of more than 1.0IP…tossed a season-high 2.0IP twice…retired 43-of-67 first batters faced (64.2%)…prevented 19-of-26 inherited runners from scoring (73.1%).

▸ In his final 59 appearances of the season (from 4/28), went 2-2 with a 2.23 ERA and converted 30-of-32 save opportunities (64.2IP, 58H, 16ER, 9BB, 66K)…in his first eight games (4/2-27), went 1-2 with a 12.15 ERA while blowing both of his save opportunities (6.2IP, 10H, 9ER, 3BB, 8K).

▸ Allowed three-run "walk-off" home run to Marco Scutaro with two strikes and two outs in the ninth inning on 4/15 at Oakland, suffering the loss and blown save…was the first time in his career that he blew a multiple-run lead against a team that was down to its last out with the bases empty (credit: *Elias Sports Bureau*)…according to *Elias*, it was Rivera's first home run allowed on an 0-2 pitch since Marquis Grissom hit a 10th-inning game-winner on 7/14/97 vs. Cleveland…was the fourth "walk-off" home run allowed in his career in the regular season and first since 7/20/06 at Toronto (Vernon Wells)…was also the 14th time that Rivera was on the mound for a "walk-off" loss in a regular season game.

▸ Blew his second save chance on 4/20 at Boston, allowing 3H and 2ER in 0.2IP (1K)…following the consecutive setbacks, converted 19 consecutive save opportunities from 4/28-8/12, allowing just 3ER in 22.2IP (1.19 ERA) with no walks and 24K.

▸ Recorded saves in both games of a doubleheader on 5/3 at Texas…according to the *Elias Sports Bureau*, was the fifth time in his career that he has recorded two saves on the same day (in either official doubleheaders or split day/night games), becoming one of only three pitchers in Major League history to accomplish the feat, joining Sparky Lyle and Jose Mesa.

▸ Notched his fourth save of the season in 5/30 win at Toronto, his first save and save opportunity since 5/3 at Texas (a span of 27 days)…was the longest gap between save opportunities since becoming the Yankees closer in 1997.

▸ Appeared in three games (no save opportunites) in the Division Series vs. Cleveland, throwing 4.2 scoreless innings with 1BB and 6K.

2006

▸ Went 5-5 with a 1.80 ERA and 34 saves in 63 relief appearances for the Yankees, winning his second consecutive "DHL Delivery Man of the Year" Award and third straight "Rolaids Relief Man of the Year" Award…ranked second in the American League with 59 games finished and ninth with 34 saves.

▸ Converted 34-of-37 save opportunities (91.9%)…saved consecutive games four times…made appearances in consecutive games nine times, three straight games three times and four consecutive games once…recorded at least six outs in eight appearances (tossed 2.0 innings seven times and 3.0 innings once)…retired 48-of-63 first batters faced (76.2%)…prevented 11-of-18 inherited runners from scoring (61.1%)…opponents batted .223 (61-for-274, 3HR); LH .194 (25-for-129, 1HR), RH .248 (36-for-145, 2HR).

▸ Was selected to the American League All-Star team, his eighth career selection…tossed a scoreless ninth to earn the save in the American League's 3-2 victory on 7/11 at PNC Field in Pittsburgh…was his third career All-Star save, tying Dennis Eckersley for most saves in All-Star history.

▸ Tossed 3.0 scoreless innings on 5/30 at Detroit to earn the win, marking his longest outing in the regular season since 9/6/96 vs. Toronto when he also went 3.0 innings…in 6/6 win vs. Boston, tossed a perfect ninth for his 12th save of the season and the 391st of his career, surpassing Dennis Eckersley for fourth place on Baseball's all-time list.

▸ On 7/20 at Toronto, allowed 11th-inning "walk-off" home run to Vernon Wells to record fifth loss (1.1IP, 2H, 1ER)…was the third "walk-off" home run allowed in his career in the regular season and the first since 7/24/04 at Boston (Bill Mueller)…had gone 51.0 innings without allowing a home run in 2006 and had gone 73.0 innings since he had last allowed a home run (Eduardo Perez on 8/16/05 at Tampa Bay), marking the longest such streak by a Yankees pitcher since Andy Pettitte in 2002 (also 73.0 innings)…missed 22 games from 9/1-20 with a strained right forearm.

▸ Made one relief appearance in the Division Series vs. Detroit, allowing 1H in 1.0IP in Game 1 win on 10/13.

2005

▸ Was 7-4 with a career-low 1.38 ERA and 43 saves in 71 relief appearances…won his second straight "Rolaids Relief Man of the Year" Award…also was named "DHL Delivery Man of the Year"…became only the third pitcher in Major League history to save at least 40 games with a sub-1.50 ERA while working 75.0 innings or more (also John Wetteland in 1993 and Eric Gagne in 2003)…led the American League with 67 games finished, was tied for third with 43 saves and was tied for eighth with 71 games…led all American League relievers in ERA and opponent's batting average (.177)…was tied for seventh with 78.1IP…allowed more than one earned run in an appearance only once (2ER in 2.0IP on 8/13 vs. Texas)…allowed only 1ER on the road in 34 appearances (35.0IP) the entire season (0.26 ERA).

▸ Converted 43-of-47 save opportunities (91.5%)…saved consecutive games five times…saved three consecutive games three times…made appearances in consecutive games 13 times and three straight games six times…retired 58-of-71 first batters faced (81.7%)…prevented 16-of-18 inherited runners from scoring (88.9%)…opponents batted .177 (50-for-283, 2HR); LH .177 (25-for-141, 1HR), RH .176 (25-for-142, 1HR).

▸ Was selected to the 2005 American League All-Star team, his seventh career All-Star selection…retired the final batter of the All-Star Game at Detroit to record his second career All-Star save.

▸ Blew his first two save chances of the season on consecutive days, 4/5 and 4/6 vs. Boston, the first time he blew consecutive save opportunities in the regular season since 7/24/04 at Boston and 7/26/04 at Toronto (he had never blown saves on consecutive days)…following the back-to-back setbacks, converted 31 straight save opportunities from 4/9-8/11, the longest such streak of his career, allowing only 1ER in 31.2IP (0.28 ERA) while limiting batters to a .140 batting average (15-for-107, 3BB, 33K)…allowed only 4ER in his 46 overall appearances during that same span (51.2IP, 0.70ERA).

▸ Did not allow a run in 22 appearances from 5/9-7/4 (23.0IP, 8H, 5BB, 23K)…the longest single-season scoreless innings streak by a Yankees pitcher since Mike Mussina threw 23.0 straight scoreless innings in 2001…was the longest such streak by any Yankees reliever since 1999, when Rivera finished the regular season with 30.2 shutout innings, the longest streak of his career.

▸ On 8/16 at Tampa Bay, allowed game-tying ninth-inning home run (Eduardo Perez) to record fourth blown save of the season and second in span of three opportunities…prior to blowing the save, had recorded 33 consecutive saves vs. the Devil Rays, the most saves—without a blown save—by a pitcher against one particular opponent in AL history.

▸ Recorded saves in each of his two appearances versus the Angels in the Division Series (3.0IP, 1H, 1ER, 1BB, 1K)…recorded the 15th Division Series save of his career in Game 4 vs. the Angels, tossing 2.0 perfect innings for his first two-inning postseason save since Game 5 of the 2003 ALCS at Boston…it also was his Major League-leading 34th career postseason save (in 39 opportunities).

2004

▸ Was 4-2 with a 1.94 ERA and a single-season franchise-record 53 saves in career-high 74 relief appearances…led the Major Leagues in saves and was tied for fourth in the American League in appearances…his 53 saves tied Randy Myers (Chicago Cubs, 1993) and Trevor Hoffman (San Diego Padres, 1998) for fourth place on Baseball's single-season all-time list…joined Eric Gagne as the only relievers in Major League history to record two 50-save seasons…earned his third "Rolaids Relief Man of the Year" Award…converted 53-of-57 save opportunities (93.0%)…saved two consecutive games seven times…saved three consecutive games four times, and saved four straight games once…made appearances in consecutive games 13 times, three straight games seven times, and four straight games once…retired 53-of-74 first batters faced (71.6%)…prevented 11-of-17 inherited runners from scoring (64.7%)…opponents batted .225 (65-for-289, 3HR); LH .234 (36-for-154, 2HR), RH .215 (29-for-135, 1HR)…was selected to the 2004 American League All-Star team, his sixth career All-Star selection…pitched a perfect ninth inning in the American League's 9-4 win on 7/13.

▸ In 5/11 win vs. Anaheim, allowed 2ER in 1.0IP to suffer his first blown save of the season, snapping a stretch of 28 consecutive save conversions…in 5/19 win at Anaheim, tossed perfect ninth to record league-leading 15th save in the Yankees' 39th game of the season…became the first Yankees reliever to reach 15 saves in fewer than 50 games into any season…became the 17th pitcher in Major League history—and first Yankee—to reach the 300-save plateau in 5/28 win at Tampa Bay…became the fifth-youngest pitcher to reach 300 saves—at 34 years, 181 days—behind Robb Nen (32 years, 251 days), Lee Smith (33/264), John Wetteland (33/265) and Trevor Hoffman (33/306)…with 11 saves in June, tied his career high for any calendar month.

▸ In 7/8 win vs. Tampa Bay, pitched a perfect 1.2 innings (1K) to earn his 30th save…tied the then-American League record for fewest team games in a season to reach the 30-save plateau, joining Bobby Thigpen of the Chicago White Sox (1990) and Boston's Lee Smith (1993), who also reached 30 saves in their team's 83rd game…record later surpassed by the Angels' Francisco Rodriguez in 2008 (76 games)…established an AL record with 32 saves before the All-Star break (two shy of the mark of 34 set by Atlanta's John Smoltz in 2003)…surrendered "walk-off," two-run home run to Bill Mueller in the bottom of the ninth in 7/24 loss at Boston.

▸ Recorded save No. 40 in 8/14 win at Seattle (Game 116), becoming the quickest to the 40-save plateau and breaking Bobby Thigpen's record of 118 games set with the Chicago White Sox in 1990…record later broken by the Angels' Francisco Rodriguez in 2008 (98 games)…earned his 45th save of the season in the Yankees' 18-6 win on 8/28 at Toronto, retiring last four batters of the game (entered the game with a 9-6 lead and two runners on base)…became the first Yankee to earn a save in a game in which the Yankees won by at least 12 runs was Ed Figueroa, who earned a save in a 16-3 Yankees win on 5/14/80 vs. Kansas City.

▸ Was 1-0 with two saves and a 0.71 ERA in nine postseason appearances…earned his 10th career LCS save in Game 2 vs. Boston…recorded back-to-back blown saves for the first time in his postseason career in Games 4 and 5 of the ALCS at Boston.

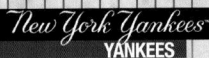
2003

- Was 5-2 with a 1.66 ERA and 40 saves in 64 relief appearances with the Yankees…ranked third in the American League with 40 saves despite missing the first 25 games of the season and having only four saves through the Yankees' 59th game…had 36 saves in the final 104 games of the season…converted 40-of-46 save opportunities (87.0%)…saved two consecutive games eight times and three consecutive games twice (6/24-26 and 6/28-30)…retired 44-of-64 first batters faced (68.8%)…prevented 18-of-35 inherited runners from scoring (51.4%)…opponents batted .235 (61-for-260, 3HR); LH .197 (29-for-147, 1HR), RH .281 (32-for-113, 2HR)…made appearances in consecutive games 11 times, three straight games five times and four straight games once.

- Began the season on the 15-day D.L. (retroactive to 3/25) with a strained right groin…suffered the injury on the last pitch of his 3/24 spring training outing vs. Detroit…was reinstated from the D.L. on 4/29 (missed first 25 games of the season)…made his 2003 debut in 4/30 win vs. Seattle andrecorded his first save of the season in 5/1 win vs. Seattle…in 6/13 win vs. St. Louis, pitched a perfect ninth to save Roger Clemens' 300th victory.

- Did not allow a run in his final 15 appearances of the season (16.1IP, 10H, 3BB, 16K) and saved all 16 of his opportunities from 8/19 through the conclusion of the regular season.

- Was 1-0 with a 0.56 ERA and five saves in eight postseason relief appearances…also struck out 14 batters without allowing a walk in postseason play…was named American League Championship Series Most Valuable Player, going 1-0 with a 1.13 ERA and two saves in four appearances vs. Boston…earned the win in Game 7, pitching 3.0 scoreless innings–his first three-inning stint since 9/6/96 vs. Toronto.

DID YOU KNOW? MARIANO RIVERA has saved wins for five former Cy Young Award winners (Dwight Gooden, David Cone, Roger Clemens, Randy Johnson and CC Sabathia)…only two pitchers have saved wins for six former Cy Young winners: *Goose Gossage*-Ron Guidry, LaMarr Hoyt, Catfish Hunter, Sparky Lyle, Gaylord Perry and Rick Sutcliffe and *John Franco*-John Denny, Dwight Gooden, Orel Hershiser, Bret Saberhagen, Tom Glavine and Frank Viola. Credit: *Elias Sports Bureau*

2002

- Battled through three stints on the disabled list to go 1-4 with a 2.74 ERA and 28 saves in 45 games…in 5/9 win at Tampa Bay, recorded the 225th save of his career to surpass Dave Righetti (224) as the club's all-time saves leader…converted 28-of-32 save opportunities (87.5%)…had to record more than three outs in four of his 28 saves…saved two consecutive games five times and three consecutive twice…retired 35-of-45 first batters faced (77.8%)…prevented 11-of-20 inherited runners from scoring (55.0%)…made appearances in consecutive games 12 times and three straight games twice…opponents batted .203 (35-for-172, 3HR); LH .181 (15-for-83, 1HR), RH .225 (20-for-89, 2HR)…was selected to his fifth All-Star Game by Manager Joe Torre and pitched a scoreless ninth inning (1H) on 7/9 at Miller Park in Milwaukee, as the game ended tied in the 13th inning.

- Was placed on the 15-day disabled list three separate times in 2002 (entering the season had been placed on the disabled list once in his eight-year Major League career)…was placed on the 15-day D.L. from 6/9-25 with a strained right groin…on 6/26 at Baltimore, struck out the side in first appearance since reinstatement, pitching in the seventh inning for first time since 10/1/00 at Baltimore…was removed from 7/20 win vs. Boston—after six pitches—with tightness in his right shoulder (1H, 1ER in 0.1IP)…was placed on the 15-day disabled list for a second time from 7/26 (retroactive to 7/21) to 8/8 with a mild muscle strain of the right shoulder…was placed on 15-day D.L. for a third time from 8/19 (retroactive to 8/16) to 9/21 with a muscle strain of the right shoulder.

- Converted 17 consecutive save opportunities from 4/23-7/11 without allowing a run (17.0IP, 8H)…on 7/14 at Cleveland, allowed "walk-off" grand slam by Bill Selby in the ninth inning to suffer his second consecutive blown save and fourth loss on the season (0.2IP, 5H, 6ER, 1IBB, 1K)…was his second game-winning home run allowed in 2002 (also Shea Hillenbrand on 4/13 at Boston) and fourth of his career…6ER were the most allowed in a relief appearance in his career.

- Made one appearance in the Division Series vs. the Angels, saving Game 1 (1.0IP, 1H).

2001

- Went 4-6 with a 2.34 ERA and 50 saves in 71 games…became only the sixth player in Major League history to reach the 50-save plateau in a single season…saved at least 30 games for the fifth straight season, surpassing Dave Righetti for most 30-save seasons by a Yankee.

- Converted 50-of-57 save opportunities (87.7%)…had to record more than three outs in 13 of his 50 saves…saved two consecutive games nine times and three consecutive games three times (4/27-29; 6/14-16; 7/16-18)…retired 57-of-71 first batters faced (80.3%) and prevented 20-of-25 inherited runners from scoring (80.0%)…made appearances in consecutive games 13 times, three straight games six times and pitched in four straight games once…opponents batted .209 (61-for-292, 5HR); LH .187 (26-for-139, 0HR), RH .229 (35-for-153, 5HR)…was selected to participate in the All-Star Game, but did not attend to rest an injured right ankle.

- Saved all three games a series vs. Oakland from 4/27-29…in 8/1 win vs. Texas, recorded his 200th career save, pitching 2.0 scoreless innings (2K).
- Was 2-1 with a 1.13 ERA and five saves in 11 postseason relief appearances…allowed two runs in the bottom of the ninth in Game 7 of the World Series at Arizona and recorded the loss…was his first career blown save in World Series play (had been 8-for-8 in save opportunities)…had converted 23 consecutive saves in postseason play (last blown save was Game 4 of 1997 ALDS at Cleveland).

2000

- Was 7-4, with a 2.85 ERA and 36 saves in 66 appearances…converted 36-of-41 save opportunities (87.8%)…saved two consecutive games three times and three consecutive games twice…was asked to record more than three outs in 13 of his 36 saves…retired 51-of-66 first batters faced (77.3%)…prevented 14-of-24 inherited runners from scoring (58.3%)…opponents batted .208 (58-for-279, 4HR); LH .210 (28-for-143, 1HR), RH .206 (28-for-136, 3HR).
- Made his first Opening Day appearance on 4/3 at Anaheim and recorded the save, allowing 1ER in 1.0IP…tossed 2.2IP to record his second win of the season on 4/19 at Texas, his longest outing since tossing 3.0IP and earning the win on 9/6/96 vs. Toronto…recorded his first loss and second blown save of season on 5/7 vs. Baltimore, allowing 4H and 3ER in the ninth inning…was the first time he received the loss when leading by two or more runs in the ninth inning or later since 8/2/96 at Kansas City when he allowed 4ER in 0.2IP.
- Saved both games of 7/8 doubleheader vs. the Mets (Game 1 at Shea Stadium and Game 2 at Yankee Stadium), pitching scoreless ninth innings.
- Was 0-0 with a 1.72 ERA and six saves in a team-high 10 postseason relief appearances…with his save in Game 5 of the Division Series at Oakland on 10/8, Rivera established the Major League record for most saves in postseason play with 16 (surpassing Dennis Eckersley-15)…had his postseason record scoreless streak end at 33.1IP in Game 6 of the ALCS on 10/17 vs. Seattle, allowing 1ER in 2.0IP…streak had covered 23 appearances, dating back to Sandy Alomar's solo-HR in Game 4 of the 1997 Division Series at Cleveland…surpassed Whitey Ford's 33.0 consecutive scoreless innings from 1960-62…had his World Series scoreless streak snapped at 14.1 innings when he allowed 2ER in the ninth inning of Game 2 vs. the Mets on 10/22…saved Games 4 and 5 of the World Series to bring his career Series saves total to seven, the most all-time, surpassing Rollie Fingers' six.

1999

- Made 66 appearances out of the Yankees bullpen, going 4-3 with a 1.83 ERA and 45 saves…converted 45-of-49 save opportunities (91.8%)…led the American League in saves, save percentage and relief ERA…became the first Yankees pitcher to have two 40-save seasons (also had 43 saves in 1997)…retired 60-of-66 first batters faced (90.9%)…prevented 22-of-27 inherited runners from scoring (81.5%)…opponents batted .176 (43-for-245, 2HR); LH .143 (20-for-140, 1HR), RH .219 (23-for-105, 1HR).
- Appeared in a career-high six consecutive games from 4/20-27, recording four saves over the stretch…was selected to participate in his second All-Star Game, but did not attend because of personal matters in his native country of Panama…was named AL "Pitcher of the Month" in August…saved a league-leading 11 games in the month and did not allow a run in 13 appearances (14.2IP, 15K).
- Did not allow a run in his final 28 appearances of the season (30.2IP), converting his last 22 save opportunities.
- Tossed 12.1 scoreless innings in eight postseason appearances and was 6-for-6 in save opportunities…pitched 4.2 scoreless innings with a win and two saves in three games in the World Series vs. the Atlanta Braves and was selected as the Most Valuable Player…became only the third reliever to be named World Series MVP, joining Oakland's Rollie Fingers in 1974 and former Yankee John Wetteland in 1996…including postseason play, did not allow a run in his final 43.0IP of the season over a span of 36 appearances.

1998

- Posted 36 saves and was 3-0 with a 1.91 ERA in 54 relief appearances…converted 36-of-41 save opportunities (87.8%)…retired 41-of-54 first-batters faced (75.9%)…prevented 20-of-24 inherited runners from scoring (83.3%)…opponents batted .215 (48-for-223, 3HR); LH .235 (27-for-115, 0HR), RH .194 (21-for-108, 3HR).
- Threw 1.1IP in his season debut on 4/5 at Oakland, leaving the game with a strained right groin…was placed on the 15-day disabled list the next day (missed 13 games)…returned on 4/24 and did not allow a run in his next nine appearances (9.2IP), going 7-for-7 in save opportunites…in a 6/1 blown save vs. Chicago-AL, was asked to record as many as six outs for the save for the first time in his career…entered in the eighth with no outs and a 4-2 lead, but allowed two inherited runners to score (Yankees won 5-4 in 10 innings)…following that game, converted 22 consecutive save opportunities before blowing a save on 8/18 at Kansas City (Yankees won 3-2).
- Tossed 13.1 scoreless innings in 10 postseason appearances and was 6-for-6 in save opportunities…saved three of the Yankees' four wins vs. San Diego in the World Series…earned his first career World Series save in the Yankees' 9-6 victory in Game 1 at Yankee Stadium…completed the Yankees' sweep with a save in Game 4 at San Diego, retiring Mark Sweeney on a ground ball to third base for the final out.

1997

- Took over as the Yankees' full-time closer, going 6-4 with a 1.88 ERA and 43 saves in 66 relief appearances…ranked second among American League relievers in ERA and saves…also led the AL in save opportunities (52), ranked sixth in games finished (56) and batting average with runners in scoring position (.151, 11-for-73) and seventh in save percentage (82.7%, 43-for-52)…opponents batted .237 (65-for-274, 5HR); LH .243 (37-for-152, 1HR), RH .230 (28-for-122, 4HR).
- Recorded saves in four straight games from 6/23-27, becoming only the third Yankees pitcher to save four consecutive games during the regular season…John Wetteland accomplished the feat twice in 1996 and Sparky Lyle did it in 1973…his 27 saves at the All-Star break were the sixth-highest total since the inception of the save rule…became the first Yankee to earn a save in the All-Star Game, tossing a perfect ninth on 7/8 at Jacobs Field in his All-Star debut…became only the sixth Yankees reliever to record 30 saves in a season with his save on 7/17 at Chicago-AL…saved both games of a doubleheader on 9/16 vs. Boston.
- Was 0-0 with a 4.50 ERA and one save in two games vs. Cleveland in the Division Series…earned his first career postseason save in the Yankees' 8-6 victory in Game 1 at Yankee Stadium…suffered a blown save in the Yankees' 3-2 loss in Game 4 at Cleveland, surrendering the game-tying home run to Sandy Alomar, Jr. in the bottom of the eighth inning.

1996

- Was 8-3 with a 2.09 ERA and five saves in 61 appearances in his first season of full-time relief…led all Yankees pitchers in ERA and led all Yankees relievers in wins, tying for most relief wins in the American League…was the most wins by a Yankees reliever since Lee Guetterman recorded 11 victories in 1990…opponents batted just .189 (73-for-386, 1HR); LH .215 (46-for-214, 1HR), RH .157 (27-for-172, 0HR)…struck out the side (facing only three batters) four times…had at least one strikeout in 54 of his 61 appearances…first batters were 5-for-56 (.089) with 27K, 4BB and 1HBP…recorded 130 strikeouts in 107.2 innings, the most ever by a Yankees reliever (Gossage had 122 in 1978)…permitted only one home run (Baltimore's Rafael Palmeiro on 6/28 at Yankee Stadium).
- Had a 26.0-inning scoreless streak from 4/19-5/21, the most by a Yankee since Steve Farr went 27.0 innings without allowing a run from 5/29-8/4/91…picked up wins vs. Minnesota on 4/26 and 4/28, tossing three no-hit innings in each game…had a streak of 15.0 consecutive hitless innings over six appearances snapped on 5/5 vs. Chicago-AL…recorded six strikeouts in three innings on 9/6 vs. Toronto, the most by a Yankees reliever in 1996.
- Was 1-0 with a 0.63 ERA in the postseason (14.1IP, 1ER)…picked up his second career postseason victory in the Yankees' 5-4, 11-inning victory in Game 1 of the ALCS vs. Baltimore.

1995

- Saw his first Major League action, going 5-3 with a 5.54 ERA in 19 appearances (nine starts) with the Yankees…was 3-3 with a 5.94 ERA as a starter and 2-0 with a 4.32 ERA as a reliever…opponents batted .266 (71-for-267, 11HR); LH .246 (35-for-142, 6HR), RH .288 (36-for-1125, 5HR).
- Was recalled from Triple-A Columbus on 5/16 and made his Major League debut on 5/23 at California, losing a 10-0 decision (3.1IP, 8H, 5ER, 3BB, 5K)…became the first Yankees rookie to lose his starting debut since Jeff Johnson in 1991…earned his first ML victory in a 4-1 win on 5/28 at Oakland (5.1IP, 7H, 1ER, 3BB, 1K)…allowed two home runs for the first time in his career, including a grand slam to Geronimo Berroa, in an 8-6 loss on 6/6 vs. Oakland…was optioned back to Columbus on 6/11 and made just one start with the Clippers because of a sore right shoulder…in that start (on 6/26), pitched a five-inning, rain-shortened no-hitter.
- Was recalled on 7/4 and started that night at Chicago-AL, recording 11K in 8.0 shutout innings (both career highs) as the Yankees won 4-1…his 11K were the most by a Yankees rookie since Al Leiter, who also struck out 11 on 4/14/88 at Toronto…made his first Major League relief appearance on 8/1 vs. Milwaukee, picking up the win despite blowing his first save opportunity…was optioned back to Columbus between games of an 8/10 doubleheader vs. Cleveland…started Game 1 and did not receive a decision…tossed a career-high 5.1 innings of relief on 8/25 at Seattle, allowing 1ER on 2Hin a 7-4 loss (2BB, 5K, 1HR)…allowed his second career grand slam (Bobby Bonilla) in an 8-1 loss on 9/15 at Baltimore.
- Overall with Columbus, was 2-2 with a 2.10 ERA in seven starts.
- Was 1-0 with a 0.00 ERA in three appearances vs. Seattle in the Division Series (5.1IP, 8K)…won his postseason debut, tossing 3.1 scoreless innings of relief in a 7-5, 15-inning victory in Game 2 at Yankee Stadium (2H, 5K).

1994

- Combined to go 10-2 with a 3.09 ERA in 22 starts at Triple-A Columbus, Double-A Albany and Single-A Tampa…began the season at Tampa, was promoted to Albany on 6/5 and promoted to Columbus on 7/22…ranked sixth in the organization in ERA…in 131.0IP, allowed just 126 hits and 30 walks while striking out 89…combined to go 6-0 with a 2.25 ERA in 16 starts at Albany and Tampa…was on Tampa's disabled list from 4/23-5/9 with a strained right shoulder…went 4-2 with a 5.81 ERA in six starts at Columbus…was on the Clippers' disabled list from 8/4-14 with a strained left hamstring.

1993

▸ Went 1-1 with a 2.08 ERA in 12 starts combined at Single-A Greensboro and Single-A Tampa…opponents batted just .208…combined on a shutout with Sandi Santiago, Bruce Pool and Billy Coleman on 7/4 vs. Hickory.

1992

▸ Suffered through an injury-plagued season at Single-A Ft. Lauderdale…went 5-3 with a 2.28 ERA in 10 starts…allowed just 40 hits and five walks in 59.1IP…averaged less than a walk for every 9.0IP…had a strikeout/ walk ratio of 8.4…season was cut short due to surgery on his right elbow…surgery was performed by Dr. Frank Jobe on 8/27…was rated the ninth-best prospect in the Yankees' system by *Baseball America*.

1991

▸ Went 4-9 with a 2.75 ERA in 29 games (15 starts) at Single-A Greensboro…struck out 123 batters in 114.2IP, averaging 9.7 strikeouts per nine innings…allowed 103 hits and 36 walks.

1990

▸ Spent his first season of professional ball with the Gulf Coast Yankees, going 5-1 with a league-leading 0.17 ERA in 22 appearances (one start)…allowed just one earned run in 52.0IP, surrendering only 17 hits and seven walks while striking out 58…was named Gulf Coast League "Star of Stars"…threw a seven-inning no-hitter in his lone start on 8/31 vs. Bradenton.

PERSONAL

▸ He and his wife, Clara have three sons, Mariano Jr., Jafet, and Jaziel…was signed by Herb Raybourn…received the Buck Canel Award by the BBWAA as the top Latin American player in 1996…donated his 2001 Rolaids Relief Man Award to the FDNY…received the 2003 Thurman Munson Award for his accomplishments on the field and his philanthropic work within the community…along with Bobby Abreu, delivered Christmas gifts to the Kips Bay Boys and Girls Club in the Bronx in December 2007…sponsored a youth baseball tournament at Franz Siegel Park in the Bronx in September 2008…delivered holiday gifts to kids at Harlem's Gregorio Luperon High School in December 2008…served as a spokesman for President Obama's United We Serve campaign in 2009…was honored along with teammates Derek Jeter, Andy Pettitte and Jorge Posada with the 2009 "Willie, Mickey and the Duke" Award from the New York Baseball Writer's Association of America.

▸ In 2004, helped open two Intel Computer Clubhouses in Panama City as part of an after-school program that provides area youth with access to computers and adult mentors in order to develop self-confidence and learning skills…spends time in the off-season in his native Panama, where he provides Christmas gifts for many local children…helped finance the construction of a new elementary school and a new church building in Puerto Caimito, Panama…is the first cousin of former Yankee, Ruben Rivera…is the only active player currently wearing uniform No. 42.

▸ Joined with jeweler Michael C. Fina and *Hearts on Fire* to announce Yankee Stadium's "Final Engagement" via the in-stadium Diamond Vision scoreboard during the 9/18/08 game vs. Chicago-AL…registrations were $1 with all proceeds going to the Mariano Rivera Foundation…helped collect canned goods at the Yankees' annual holiday food drive in December 2010.

▸ Is a four-time recipient of the LatinoMVP "American League Reliever of the Year" Award (2003-06)…was also honored with the Citizen Award from latinobaseball.com for his commitment to the well-being of children throughout the United States and Latin America…participates in annual baseball clinics in the Dominican Republic during the offseason…received the prestigious Manuel Amador Guerrero Order during Panama's Independence Day parade on 11/3/99 in Panama City.

▸ Named the No. 7 sports celebrity on WFAN's (660 AM) Top 20 New York Athletes of the Last 20 Years in December 2007.

Most Seasons with the Yankees
(as player only)

PLAYER	SEASONS
Yogi Berra	18 (1946-63)
Mickey Mantle	18 (1951-68)
Frank Crosetti	17 (1932-48)
Bill Dickey	17 (1928-43, '46)
Lou Gehrig	17 (1923-39)
DEREK JETER	16 (1995-2010)
JORGE POSADA	16 (1995-2010)
MARIANO RIVERA	**16 (1995-2010)**
Whitey Ford	16 (1950, '53-67)
Bernie Williams	16 (1991-2006)
Babe Ruth	15 (1920-34)

Rivera's Career Pitching Record

Year	Club	W	L	ERA	G	GS	CG	SHO	SV	IP	H	R	ER	HR	HP	BB	SO	WP	BK
1990	GCL Yankees	5	1	0.17	22	1	1	1	1	52.0	17	3	1	0	2	7	58	2	0
1991	Greensboro	4	9	2.75	29	15	1	0	0	114.2	103	48	35	2	3	36	123	3	0
1992	Ft. Lauderdale	5	3	2.28	10	10	3	1	0	59.1	40	17	15	5	0	5	42	0	0
1993	GCL Yankees	0	1	2.25	2	2	0	0	0	4.0	2	1	1	0	0	1	6	1	0
	Greensboro	1	0	2.06	10	10	0	0	0	39.1	31	12	9	0	0	15	32	2	0
1994	Tampa	3	0	2.21	7	7	0	0	0	36.2	34	12	9	2	2	12	27	0	0
	Albany	3	0	2.27	9	9	0	0	0	63.1	58	20	16	5	0	8	39	1	0
	Columbus	4	2	5.81	6	6	1	0	0	31.0	34	22	20	5	0	10	23	0	1
1995	Columbus	2	2	2.1	7	7	1	1	0	30.0	25	10	7	2	0	3	30	0	1
	YANKEES	5	3	5.51	19	10	0	0	0	67.0	71	43	41	11	2	30	51	0	1
1996	YANKEES	8	3	2.09	61	0	0	0	5	107.2	73	25	25	1	2	34	130	1	0
1997	YANKEES	6	4	1.88	66	0	0	0	43	71.2	65	17	15	5	0	20	68	2	0
1998	YANKEES - a	3	0	1.91	54	0	0	0	36	61.1	48	13	13	3	1	17	36	0	0
1999	YANKEES	4	3	1.83	66	0	0	0	45	69.0	43	15	14	2	3	18	52	2	1
2000	YANKEES	7	4	2.85	66	0	0	0	36	75.2	58	26	24	4	0	25	58	2	0
2001	YANKEES	4	6	2.34	71	0	0	0	50	80.2	61	24	21	5	1	12	83	1	0
2002	YANKEES - b, c, d	1	4	2.74	45	0	0	0	28	46.0	35	16	14	3	2	11	41	1	1
	GCL Yankees	0	0	0.00	1	1	0	0	0	2.0	2	0	0	0	0	1	2	0	0
2003	YANKEES - e	5	2	1.66	64	0	0	0	40	70.2	61	15	13	3	4	10	63	0	0
2004	YANKEES	4	2	1.94	74	0	0	0	53	78.2	65	17	17	3	5	20	66	0	0
2005	YANKEES	7	4	1.38	71	0	0	0	43	78.1	50	18	12	2	4	18	80	0	0
2006	YANKEES	5	5	1.80	63	0	0	0	34	75.0	61	16	15	3	5	11	55	0	0
2007	YANKEES	3	4	3.15	67	0	0	0	30	71.1	68	25	25	4	6	12	74	1	0
2008	YANKEES	6	5	1.40	64	0	0	0	39	70.2	41	11	11	4	2	6	77	1	0
2009	YANKEES	3	3	1.76	66	0	0	0	44	66.1	48	14	13	7	1	12	72	1	0
2010	YANKEES	3	3	1.80	61	0	0	0	33	60.0	39	14	12	2	5	11	45	0	0
Minor League Totals		27	18	2.35	103	68	7	3	1	432.1	346	145	113	21	7	98	382	9	2
Major League Totals		74	55	2.23	978	10	0	0	559	1150.0	887	309	285	62	43	267	1051	12	3

*Denotes league leader

Signed by the Yankees as a non-drafted free agent on February 17, 1990.

a – Was placed on the 15-day disabled list with a strained right groin on April 6 - 24, 1998.
b – Was placed on the 15-day disabled list with a strained groin from June 9 - 25, 2002.
c – Was placed on the 15-day disabled list with a right shoulder muscle strain from July 21 - August 8, 2002
d – Was placed on the 15-day disabled list with a right shoulder muscle strain from August 19 - September 21, 2002.
e – Was placed on the 15-day disabled list from March 30 - April 29, 2003 with a strained right groin.

Rivera's Division Series Record

Year	Club vs. Opp.	W	L	ERA	G	GS	CG	SHO	SV	IP	H	R	ER	HR	HP	BB	SO	WP	BK
1995	NYY vs. SEA	1	0	0.00	3	0	0	0	0	5.1	3	0	0	0	0	1	8	0	0
1996	NYY vs. TEX	0	0	0.00	2	0	0	0	0	4.2	0	0	0	0	0	1	0	0	0
1997	NYY vs. CLE	0	0	4.50	2	0	0	0	1	2.0	2	1	1	1	0	0	1	0	0
1998	NYY vs. TEX	0	0	0.00	3	0	0	0	2	3.1	1	0	0	0	0	1	2	0	0
1999	NYY vs. TEX	0	0	0.00	3	0	0	0	2	3.0	1	0	0	0	0	0	3	1	0
2000	NYY vs. OAK	0	0	0.00	3	0	0	0	3	5.0	2	0	0	0	0	0	2	0	0
2001	NYY vs. OAK	0	0	0.00	3	0	0	0	2	5.0	4	1	0	0	0	0	4	0	0
2002	NYY vs. ANA	0	0	0.00	1	0	0	0	1	1.0	1	0	0	0	0	0	0	0	0
2003	NYY vs. MIN	0	0	0.00	2	0	0	0	2	4.0	0	0	0	0	0	0	4	0	0
2004	NYY vs. MIN	1	0	0.00	4	0	0	0	2	5.2	2	0	0	0	0	0	2	0	0
2005	NYY vs. LAA	0	0	3.00	2	0	0	0	2	3.0	1	1	1	0	0	1	2	0	0
2006	NYY vs. DET	0	0	0.00	1	0	0	0	0	1.0	0	0	0	0	0	0	0	0	0
2007	NYY vs. CLE	0	0	0.00	3	0	0	0	0	4.2	2	0	0	0	1	1	6	0	0
2009	NYY vs. MIN	0	0	0.00	3	0	0	0	1	3.2	4	0	0	0	0	1	7	0	0
2010	NYY vs. MIN	0	0	0.00	3	0	0	0	2	3.1	2	0	0	0	0	1	1	0	0
Division Series Totals		2	0	0.33	37	0	0	0	18	54.2	26	3	2	1	1	6	43	1	0

Rivera's League Championship Series Record

Year	Club vs. Opp.	W	L	ERA	G	GS	CG	SHO	SV	IP	H	R	ER	HR	HP	BB	SO	WP	BK
1996	NYY vs. BAL	1	0	0.00	2	0	0	0	0	4.0	6	0	0	0	0	1	5	0	0
1998	NYY vs. CLE	0	0	0.00	4	0	0	0	1	5.2	0	0	0	0	0	1	5	0	0
1999	NYY vs. BOS	1	0	0.00	3	0	0	0	2	4.2	5	0	0	0	0	0	4	0	0
2000	NYY vs. SEA	0	0	1.93	3	0	0	0	1	4.2	4	1	1	0	0	0	1	0	0
2001	NYY vs. SEA	1	0	1.93	4	0	0	0	2	4.2	2	1	1	0	0	1	3	2	0
2003	NYY vs. BOS	1	0	1.13	4	0	0	0	2	8.0	5	1	1	0	0	0	6	0	0
2004	NYY vs. BOS	0	0	1.29	5	0	0	0	2	7.0	6	1	1	0	0	2	6	0	0
2009	NYY vs. LAA	0	0	1.29	5	0	0	0	2	7.0	3	1	1	0	0	2	4	0	0
2010	NYY vs. TEX	0	0	0.00	3	0	0	0	1	3.0	2	0	0	0	0	0	1	0	0
LCS Totals		4	0	0.92	33	0	0	0	13	48.2	33	5	5	0	0	7	34	2	0

Rivera's World Series Record

Year	Club vs. Opp.	W	L	ERA	G	GS	CG	SHO	SV	IP	H	R	ER	HR	HP	BB	SO	WP	BK
1996	NYY vs. ATL	0	0	1.59	4	0	0	0	0	5.2	4	1	1	0	0	3	4	0	0
1998	NYY vs. SD	0	0	0.00	3	0	0	0	3	4.1	5	0	0	0	0	0	4	0	0
1999	NYY vs. ATL	1	0	0.00	3	0	0	0	2	4.2	3	0	0	0	0	1	3	0	0
2000	NYY vs. NYM	0	0	3.00	4	0	0	0	2	6.0	4	2	2	1	1	1	7	0	0
2001	NYY vs. ARI	1	1	1.42	4	0	0	0	1	6.1	6	2	1	0	1	1	7	0	0
2003	NYY vs. FLA	0	0	0.00	2	0	0	0	1	4.0	2	0	0	0	0	0	4	0	0
2009	NYY vs. PHI	0	0	0.00	4	0	0	0	2	5.1	3	0	0	0	0	2	3	0	0
World Series Totals		**2**	**1**	**0.99**	**24**	**0**	**0**	**0**	**11**	**36.1**	**27**	**5**	**4**	**1**	**2**	**8**	**32**	**0**	**0**
POSTSEASON TOTALS		**8**	**1**	**0.71**	**94**	**0**	**0**	**0**	**42**	**139.2**	**86**	**13**	**11**	**2**	**3**	**21**	**109**	**3**	**0**

Rivera's All-Star Game Record

Year	Club, Site	W	L	ERA	G	GS	CG	SHO	SV	IP	H	R	ER	HR	HP	BB	SO	WP	BK
1997	NYY, Cleveland	0	0	0.00	1	0	0	0	1	1.0	0	0	0	0	0	0	1	0	0
1999	NYY, Boston								Selected - Did Not Pitch											
2000	NYY, Atlanta	0	0	0.00	1	0	0	0	0	1.0	2	1	0	0	0	0	0	0	0
2001	NYY, Seattle								Selected - Did Not Pitch											
2002	NYY, Milwaukee	0	0	0.00	1	0	0	0	0	1.0	1	0	0	0	0	0	0	0	0
2004	NYY, Houston	0	0	0.00	1	0	0	0	0	1.0	0	0	0	0	0	0	0	0	0
2005	NYY, Detroit	0	0	0.00	1	0	0	0	1	0.1	0	0	0	0	0	0	1	0	0
2006	NYY, Pittsburgh	0	0	0.00	1	0	0	0	1	1.0	0	0	0	0	0	0	0	0	0
2008	NYY, New York-AL	0	0	0.00	1	0	0	0	0	1.2	2	0	0	0	0	0	2	0	0
2009	NYY, St. Louis	0	0	0.00	1	0	0	0	1	1.0	0	0	0	0	0	0	1	0	0
2010	NYY, Los Angeles-AL								Selected - Did Not Pitch											
All-Star Game Totals		**0**	**0**	**0.00**	**8**	**0**	**0**	**0**	**4**	**8.0**	**5**	**1**	**0**	**0**	**0**	**0**	**5**	**0**	**0**

Rivera's Regular Season Batting Record

Year	Team	AVG	G	AB	R	H	2B	3B	HR	RBI	SH	SF	HP	BB	SO	SB	CS
2010	NYY	.000	61	1	0	0	0	0	0	0	0	0	0	1	0	0	0
Major League Totals		**.000**	**978**	**3**	**0**	**0**	**0**	**0**	**0**	**1**	**0**	**0**	**0**	**1**	**1**	**0**	**0**

Rivera's Career Fielding Record

Position	PCT	G	PO	A	E	TC	DP
Pitcher	.982	978	103	232	6	341	11

Most Seasons With Same Team, Active Players

1. Chipper Jones . . . . Atlanta 18 (1993-2010)
2. DEREK JETER . . . . YANKEES 16 (1995-2010)
   JORGE POSADA . . . . YANKEES 16 (1995-2010)
   MARIANO RIVERA . . . . YANKEES 16 (1995-2010)

According to the *Elias Sports Bureau*, Jeter, Posada and Rivera have become the first trio of teammates in MLB, NBA, NFL and NHL history to appear in at least one game together in each of 16 consecutive seasons…the second-longest trios in Yankees franchise history played 13 years together (Bill Dickey, Lefty Gomez and Red Ruffing from 1930-42; and Whitey Ford, Elston Howard and Mickey Mantle from 1955-67).

The first game in which Derek Jeter, Jorge Posada and Mariano Rivera appeared together was September 28, 1996 at Boston's Fenway Park. Posada pinch-hit and struck out, Jeter started and went 0-for-4. LHP Andy Pettitte also appeared in his first career game with the trio that day, starting and going two innings. Ramiro Mendoza went the next four and picked up the win. Rivera pitched one inning and earned the hold and John Wetteland earned his 43rd save. The Yankees won 4-2 and the losing pitcher was Roger Clemens.

30 DAVID ROBERTSON

RIGHT-HANDED PITCHER • 5-11 • 195 • B/T: RIGHT/RIGHT • OPENING DAY AGE: 25

BIRTHDATE
April 9, 1985

BIRTHPLACE
Birmingham, Ala.

RESIDES
Tampa, Fla.

M.L. SERVICE
2 years, 70 days

COLLEGE
University of Alabama

STATUS

▸ Selected in the 17th round of the 2006 First-Year Player Draft…signed through the 2011 season.

2010

▸ Was 4-5 with one save and a 3.82 ERA in 64 relief appearances with the Yankees, striking out 71 batters in 61.1IP…opponents batted .258 (59-for-229, 5HR); LH .268 (26-for-97, 2HR), RH .250 (33-for-132, 3HR)…retired 43-of-64 first batters faced (67.2%)…prevented 23-of-33 inherited runners from scoring (69.7%)…appeared in consecutive games 10 times and three straight games twice.

▸ Of his 64 relief outings, 48 were 1.0 inning or less (75.0%)…50 of his 64 outings were scoreless.

▸ Ranked seventh among all AL relievers with 10.42K/9.0IP.

▸ Allowed 11ER over his first 10 appearances of the season from 4/4-5/7 (7.1IP)…in 54 appearances from 5/8 through the end of the season, posted a 2.50 ERA (54.0IP, 15ER)…held opponents scoreless in 45 of those 54 outings.

▸ Tossed a season-high 2.0 scoreless IP (2BB, 2K, 1BK) in 5/16 loss vs. Minnesota…faced three batters before being removed from 5/29 loss vs. Cleveland with a mild lower back strain (0.1IP, 1H, 2ER, 1HBP)…did not pitch for six days.

▸ Surrendered a season-high-tying 4ER and was charged with the loss on 7/2 vs. Toronto, allowing all 4R in the 11th inning…following that outing, pitched to a 2.06 ERA (35.0IP, 8ER) over the remainder of the season.

▸ Earned his first win of the season on 7/4 vs. Toronto, tossing a scoreless 10th inning (1.0IP, 1H, 1BB, 1IBB, 1K)…was the first of 19 consecutive scoreless appearances from 7/4-8/21 (18.1IP, 9H, 8BB, 24K)…according to *Elias*, held opponents hitless in 23 consecutive at-bats prior to Willie Bloomquist's ninth-inning double on 8/12 at Kansas City, the longest such streak of his career.

▸ Pitched to a 2.27 ERA (31.2IP, 8ER) in 33 appearances after the All-Star break with 39 strikeouts.

▸ Earned his second career save in 8/12 win at Kansas City (also 7/27/09 at Tampa Bay), recording the final out of the game.

▸ Appeared in six postseason games, allowing 6ER in 3.1IP…surrendered 5ER in 10/18 ALCS Game 3 loss at Texas.

2009

▸ Was 2-1 with one save and a 3.30 ERA (43.2IP, 16ER) in 45 relief appearances over three stints with the Yankees (4/16; 4/24-5/9; 5/26-10/4)…opponents batted .216 (36-for-167, 4HR); LH .189 (14-for-74, 2HR), RH .237 (22-for-93, 2HR)…stranded 16-of-25 inherited runners (64.0%)…retired 34-of-45 first batters faced (75.6%)…appeared in consecutive games eight times…threw less than 1.0 inning 12 times.

BESTS & STREAKS

Low hit CG
N/A
IP (start)
N/A
IP (relief)
2.0 - 10 times
Last: vs. TB, 5/20/10
Hits
4 - 4 times
Last: vs. LAA, 4/13/10
Runs
5 - vs. BAL, 7/28/08
BB
3 - 3 times
Last: vs. TOR, 9/3/10
SO
4 - 3 times
Last: vs. TB, 5/20/10
HR
2 - vs. BAL, 5/5/10
Winning Streak
5g - 7/19/08-6/4/09
Losing Streak
3g - 4/27-7/2/10

- Had a 12.98K/9.0IP ratio (43.2IP, 63K)…among pitchers with at least 40.0IP, marked the second-best K/9.0IP ratio in the Majors behind the Dodgers' Jonathan Broxton (13.50).

- Was recalled from Triple-A Scranton/Wilkes-Barre prior to the Yankees' first-ever regular season game at Yankee Stadium on 4/16…made his first appearance of the season in the loss that day vs. Cleveland, striking out three batters in 2.0 scoreless innings (2H)…was optioned back to Scranton/WB the next day…recalled a second time on 4/24 when RHP Chien-Ming Wang was placed on the D.L…appeared in four games (2.2IP, 2H, 3R, 2ER, 4BB, 4K) before being optioned back to Scranton/WB.

- Was recalled a third time on 5/26 and pitched out of the Yankees bullpen for the remainder of the season…did not allow a run in any of his first seven appearances following his third recall (5.0IP, 2H, 2BB, 6K).

- Threw one pitch (Elvis Andrus flyout to LF) to earn his first win of the season on 6/4 vs. Texas…was his second career one-pitch win (also 7/22/08 vs. Minnesota).

- Held opposing left-handed batters hitless in 18 consecutive at-bats from 4/25-6/18.

- Struck out three batters in 0.2IP in 8/6 win vs. Boston, becoming the first Yankee to record at least three strikeouts without completing a full inning of work since Ron Davis on 9/17/80 vs. Toronto (0.2IP, 3K).

- Was shut down for three weeks from 9/6-28 with elbow stiffness…had an MRI on 9/7 and was seen by Dr. James Andrews in Pensacola, Fla., on 9/10.

- Did not allow a run in five appearances during the 2009 playoffs, tossing 5.1 scoreless innings (4H, 3BB, 3K)…earned the win in each of his first two postseason appearances (Game 2 of ALDS vs. Minnesota and Game 2 of ALCS vs. Los Angeles-AL), as the Yankees recorded "walk-off" wins in each contest.

- In eight relief appearances with Scranton/WB, went 0-3 with two saves and a 1.84 ERA (14.2IP, 10H, 7R, 3ER, 6BB, 25K).

2008

- Was 4-0 with a 5.34 ERA in 25 relief appearances over two stints with the Yankees (6/28-8/28; 9/13-28)…opponents batted .257 (29-for-113, 3HR); LH .259 (14-for-54, 0HR), RH .254 (15-for-59, 3HR)…retired 16-of-25 first batters faced (64.0%)…prevented 6-of-14 inherited runners from scoring (42.9%)…pitched in three consecutive games twice (7/13-18 and 8/24-27)…tossed a season-high 2.0 innings on six occasions.

- Was signed to a Major League contract and selected to the Yankees' 25-man roster on 6/28…made his ML debut in 6/29 loss at the Mets, allowing 1ER in 2.0IP (4H, 1K)…struck out his first batter faced (Oliver Perez).

- Held left-handed batters hitless over 16AB from 6/29-7/21 (9G) before Luke Scott's leadoff single in the sixth on 7/28 vs. Baltimore.

- Pitched a scoreless 12th inning and recorded his first Major League victory on 7/19 vs. Oakland (1.0IP, 1H, 1BB, 1K) after Jose Molina was hit by a pitch with the bases loaded, bringing in the game-winning run.

- Recorded his second Major League victory (within a four-game span) on 7/22 vs. Minnesota, stranding two inherited runners and getting the final out in the sixth on one pitch.

- In 7/28 loss vs. Baltimore, allowed a grand slam to Adam Jones and set a career high with 5ER…was his first HR allowed as a professional after 148.1 career IP (minors-136.0IP from 2007-08 and Majors-12.1IP).

- Allowed 16ER over 10 outings (13.1IP) from 7/28-8/27 and was optioned to Scranton/WB on 8/28.

- Was recalled from Scranton/WB on 9/13…did not allow a run over four appearances in his second stint (4.2IP, 2H, 3BB, 7K).

- In 53.2 combined minor league innings with Scranton/WB and Double-A Trenton, went 4-0 with three saves and a 1.67 ERA over 30 relief appearances (28H, 13R, 10ER, 23BB, 77K).

- Made three postseason relief outings with IL-champion SWB, allowing 3ER in 4.1IP (6.23 ERA, 2H, 4BB, 6K).

- Named the International League's "Best Reliever" in *Baseball America*'s 2008 Best Tools survey.

2007

- In his first professional season, pitched at Single-A Charleston, Single-A Tampa and Double-A Trenton, combining to go 8-3 with four saves and a 0.96 ERA in 44 relief appearances (32BB, 113K).

- Ranked third among minor league relievers, with a .154 opponents batting average…was named to the South Atlantic League's midseason All-Star team (w/ Charleston)…39 of his 44 outings were 2.0 innings and all but two were more than 1.0 inning…held opponents scoreless in 35 of his appearances and did not allow a hit in 16 of his games…converted on four of five save opportunities.

- Was 5-2 with three saves and a 0.77 ERA (47.0IP, 4ER) in 24 appearances with Charleston…began his career with 10 consecutive scoreless outings from 4/3-5/3, allowing just 7H in 18.1IP (6BB, 27K).

- Went 3-1 with one save and a 1.08 ERA with Tampa…did not allow an earned run in nine appearances at home (17.1IP, 8H, 2R, 9BB, 12K).

- Made two regular season appearances with Trenton, allowing 1ER in 4.0IP (2.25 ERA)…appeared in two postseason games for the Eastern League champion Thunder, surrendering 2ER in 5.0IP (3.60 ERA) and striking out five batters.

PERSONAL

▸ Full name is David Alan Roberston…married Erin in January 2009…older brother, Connor, was drafted by Oakland in 2004.

▸ Was drafted by the Yankees out of the University of Alabama…ranked among all-time school career leaders in strikeouts, appearances and saves…was named to the 2005 Louisville Slugger Freshmen All-America team as well as the 2005 Freshman All-SEC team as selected by the league's head coaches…named a freshman All-America by *Baseball America* and *Collegiate Baseball Magazine*…was also a Freshman All-SEC selection by SEBaseball.com and a Third-Team All-SEC pick by SEBaseball.com after leading the team in games (32) wins (seven), ERA (2.92) and saves (eight) and setting the single-season rookie record for most strikeouts (105) and overall highest average of strikeouts per nine innings pitched (12.8)…also led the SEC in lowest opponents average (.105)…became the fifth former Alabama player to wear pinstripes, joining Joe Sewell, Ken Sears, Butch Hobson and Andy Phillips.

▸ Is a 2004 graduate of Paul W. Bryant High School, where he played baseball and led the Stampede to the Class 6A state playoffs in the school's first year of existence.

▸ Appeared at local Bronx schools during the 2010 season, reading to school kids with the "Story Pirates."

Robertson's Career Pitching Record

YEAR	Club	W	L	ERA	G	GS	CG	SHO	SV	IP	H	R	ER	HR	HB	BB	SO	WP	BK
2007	Charleston	5	2	0.77	24	0	0	0	3	47.0	25	5	4	0	0	15	67	5	0
	Tampa	3	1	1.08	18	0	0	0	1	33.1	18	6	4	0	0	15	37	2	0
	Trenton	0	0	2.25	2	0	0	0	0	4.0	2	1	1	0	0	2	9	1	0
2008	Trenton	0	0	0.96	9	0	0	0	2	18.2	8	2	2	0	1	6	26	1	0
	Scranton/WB	4	0	2.06	21	0	0	0	1	35.0	20	11	8	1	1	17	51	1	0
	YANKEES	4	0	5.34	25	0	0	0	0	30.1	29	18	18	3	0	15	36	6	0
2009	Scranton/WB	0	3	1.84	8	0	0	0	2	14.2	10	7	3	0	0	6	25	0	0
	YANKEES	2	1	3.30	45	0	0	0	1	43.2	36	19	16	4	1	23	63	6	0
2010	YANKEES	4	5	3.82	64	0	0	0	1	61.1	59	26	26	5	3	33	71	7	2
Minor League Totals		12	6	1.30	82	0	0	0	9	152.2	83	32	22	1	2	61	215	10	0
Major League Totals		10	6	3.99	134	0	0	0	2	135.1	124	63	60	12	4	71	170	19	2

Selected by the Yankees in the 17th round of the 2006 First-Year Player Draft.

Robertson's Division Series Record

Year	Club vs. Opp.	W	L	ERA	G	GS	CG	SHO	SV	IP	H	R	ER	HR	HP	BB	SO	WP	BK
2009	NYY vs. MIN	1	0	0.00	1	0	0	0	0	1.0	1	0	0	0	0	0	0	0	0
2010	NYY vs. MIN	0	0	0.00	2	0	0	0	0	0.2	0	0	0	0	0	1	1	0	0
Division Series Totals		1	0	0.00	3	0	0	0	0	1.2	1	0	0	0	0	1	1	0	0

Robertson's League Championship Series Record

Year	Club vs. Opp.	W	L	ERA	G	GS	CG	SHO	SV	IP	H	R	ER	HR	HP	BB	SO	WP	BK
2009	NYY vs. LAA	1	0	0.00	2	0	0	0	0	2.0	1	0	0	0	0	2	1	0	0
2010	NYY vs. TEX	0	0	20.25	4	0	0	0	0	2.2	8	6	6	1	0	1	4	1	0
LCS Totals		1	0	11.57	6	0	0	0	0	4.2	9	6	6	1	0	3	5	1	0

Robertson's World Series Record

Year	Club vs. Opp.	W	L	ERA	G	GS	CG	SHO	SV	IP	H	R	ER	HR	HP	BB	SO	WP	BK
2009	NYY vs. PHI	0	0	0.00	2	0	0	0	0	2.1	2	0	0	0	0	1	2	0	0
World Series Totals		0	0	0.00	2	0	0	0	0	2.1	2	0	0	0	0	1	2	0	0
POSTSEASON TOTALS		2	0	6.23	11	0	0	0	0	8.2	12	6	6	1	0	5	8	1	0

Robertson's Regular Season Batting Record

Year	Team	AVG	G	AB	R	H	2B	3B	HR	RBI	SH	SF	HP	BB	SO	SB	CS
2010	NYY					Did Not Bat											
Major League Totals		-	134	-	-	-	-	-	-	-	-	-	-	-	-	-	-

Robertson's Career Fielding Record

Position	PCT	G	PO	A	E	TC	DP
Pitcher	1.000	134	1	11	0	12	0

Comeback Kids

The Yankees led the Majors with 48 come-from-behind wins in 2010, seven of which were by more than three runs…also led the Majors with 51 comeback victories in 2009, including a franchise-record 36 comeback wins at home (previous record was 34 in 1932) — credit: *Elias Sports Bureau.*

13 ALEX RODRIGUEZ

THIRD BASEMAN • 6-3 • 228 • B/T: RIGHT/RIGHT • OPENING DAY AGE: 35

BIRTHDATE
July 27, 1975

BIRTHPLACE
New York, N.Y.

RESIDES
Miami, Fla.

M.L. SERVICE
16 years, 11 days

CAREER HIGHLIGHTS
A.L. Most Valuable Player
‣ 2003, 2005, 2007

A.L. All-Star Team
‣ 1996, 1997, 1998, 2000, 2001, 2002, 2003, 2004, 2005, 2006, 2007, 2008, 2010

A.L. Silver Slugger Award
‣ 1996, 1998, 1999, 2000, 2001, 2002, 2003, 2005, 2007, 2008

A.L. Gold Glove Award
‣ 2002, 2003

Baseball America Player of the Year
‣ 2000, 2002, 2007

Sporting News Player of the Year
‣ 1996, 2002, 2007

STATUS
‣ Acquired from the Texas Rangers with cash in exchange for 2B Alfonso Soriano and a player to be named later (INF Joaquin Arias) on February 16, 2004…signed a seven-year contract with player options for three additional years on December 11, 2000…opted out of the contract on October 28, 2007…re-signed by the Yankees to a 10-year contract on December 17, 2007…contract extends through the 2017 season.

CAREER NOTES
‣ Ranks sixth on Baseball's all-time list with 613 career home runs…in 2010, surpassed Hall of Famer Frank Robinson (586), Mark McGwire (583) and Sammy Sosa (609)…ranks seventh on the Yankees' all-time list with 268 HR.

‣ Is the only player in Baseball history to collect at least 30HR and 100RBI at least 14 times in his career…has accomplished the feat in each of the last 13 seasons (1998-2010), surpassing Jimmie Foxx (12) for the longest such streak all time.

‣ Has reached 30HR in 13 consecutive seasons and 14 times in his career…only one player has hit at least 30HR in as many consecutive seasons: Barry Bonds (13)…is tied with Bonds (14) for second-most 30-homer seasons all-time behind Hank Aaron (15)…his 13 consecutive seasons with at least 25HR are tied with Willie Mays (13) for third-longest in Major League history behind Babe Ruth and Barry Bonds (each 15 straight)…his 14 overall seasons with at least 25HR are tied with Jim Thome for most among active players…his 15 consecutive seasons of at least 20HR are tied with Bonds for the third-longest streak in Major League history behind Hank Aaron (20) and Babe Ruth (16)—credit: *Elias Sports Bureau*.

‣ Owns eight seasons of at least 40HR, tying Barry Bonds, Hank Aaron and Harmon Killebrew for second-most all-time behind Babe Ruth (11)…compiled six straight seasons with 40-or-more home runs from 1998-2003, matching Sammy Sosa (1998-2003) for the second-longest streak of 40-homer seasons in Major League history behind Babe Ruth (7, 1926-32).

‣ Has hit at least 50HR in three separate seasons (54-2007; 57-2002; 52-2001), becoming the fourth player in Major League history to have more than two seasons with at least 50HR: Babe Ruth, Mark McGwire and Sammy Sosa each did it four times (credit: *Elias Sports Bureau*)…is one of only three players to hit 50-or-more home runs in a season with more than one club, joining Jimmie Foxx (58HR w/ Philadelphia in 1932; 50 w/ Boston in 1938) and Mark McGwire (52 w/ Oakland in 1996; 70 w/ St. Louis in 1998 and 65 w/ St. Louis in 1999), according to SABR'S David Vincent.

‣ Owns 58 career multi-homer games (four in 2010), marking the seventh-most multi-homer games all-time.

BESTS & STREAKS

Hits
5 - 5 times
Last: at TEX, 5/25/09
Runs
5 - 2 times
Last: vs. TB, 4/18/05
2B
3 - vs. SEA, 4/7/01
3B
1 - 29 times
Last: at OAK, 4/21/10
HR
3 - 4 times
Last: at KC, 8/14/10
RBI
10 - vs. LAA, 4/26/05
BB
5 - vs. KC, 4/23/00
SO
4 - 4 times
Last: at KC, 4/8/08
SB
3 - 2 times
Last: vs. BOS, 9/25/09
Single-Season Hit Streak
20g - 8/16-9/4/96
Hit Streak
23g - 9/25/06-4/23/07

▸ According to the *Elias Sports Bureau*, his 599HR were the most for any player prior to turning 35 years old (on 7/27/10)…collected the most hits (2,629) and games played (2,259) for any player prior to turning 35 since Robin Yount (2,733H and 2,436G)…recorded the third-most RBI (1,787) for any player prior to turning 35 behind only Lou Gehrig (1,910) and Jimmie Foxx (1,884)–credit: *Elias*.

▸ Has hit 21 career grand slams, tying Manny Ramirez (21) for second place all-time behind Lou Gehrig (23)…is one of three players in Major League history to have three career "walk-off" grand slams, joining Vern Stephens (1946 w/ St. Louis-AL, '49 and '50 with Boston-AL) and the Philadelphia Phillies' Cy Williams (one in 1924 and two in 1926)…owns six career "walk-off" homers as a Yankee, the most since Graig Nettles had six from 1973-81.

▸ Owns 21 career home runs in the ninth inning or later that have tied the game or given his team the lead…has nine "walk-off" home runs in his career, tied with Vladimir Guerrero for third-most among active players behind Jim Thome (12) and David Ortiz (10).

▸ Since the start of 2009, has been involved in driving in the game-winning or tying run in seven of the Yankees' 20 "walk-off" innings (two game-ending HRs, two game-tying HRs, two game-winning runs scored and hit the pop-up resulting in a two-run "walk-off" error vs. the Mets).

▸ Has collected 100RBI in 13 consecutive seasons and 14 times in his career…marks the most 100RBI seasons all time…his current streak of 13 straight seasons with at least 100RBI matches Lou Gehrig (1926-38) and Jimmie Foxx (1929-41) for the longest such stretch all time.

▸ Is one of six players all time to collect at least 600HR and 2,500H (also Hank Aaron, Barry Bonds, Ken Griffey Jr., Willie Mays and Babe Ruth).

▸ Is one of three players all time with 400 doubles, 600HR and 300SB, joining Barry Bonds (601/762/514) and Willie Mays (523/660/338).

▸ Over the last 10 seasons (2001-10), leads the Majors in home runs (424) and RBI (1,236).

▸ Had his streak of consecutive 100R seasons snapped at 13 in 2009, remaining tied with Hank Aaron (13, 1955-67) and Gehrig (13, 1926-38) as the only players in Baseball history to accomplish the feat…reached the 100RBI and 100R plateaus in 11 consecutive seasons from 1998-2008, trailing only Lou Gehrig for the longest such streak all time (13 straight seasons from 1926-38).

▸ Has hit 268HR with the Yankees after hitting 189HR with Seattle and 156HR with Texas…according to the *Elias Sports Bureau*, joins Paul Konerko as the only active players with at least 300HR for teams other than the one for which they made their Major League debut…is the only player in Major League history to hit at least 150HR with three different teams.

▸ Is one of eight players to hit at least 250 HR for his current team, joining teammate Jorge Posada, Chipper Jones, Albert Pujols, Paul Konerko, Todd Helton, David Ortiz and Ryan Howard—credit: *Elias Sports Bureau*.

MOST GRAND SLAMS, ALL TIME

1.	Lou Gehrig	23
2.	Manny Ramirez	21
	ALEX RODRIGUEZ	**21**
4.	Eddie Murray	19
5.	Willie McCovey	18
	Robin Ventura	18

MOST "WALK-OFF" HOME RUNS AMONG ACTIVE PLAYERS
credit: *Elias Sports Bureau*

1.	Jim Thome	12
2.	David Ortiz	10
3.	**ALEX RODRIGUEZ**	**9**
	Vladimir Guerrero	9

MOST HOME RUNS, ALL-TIME

1.	Barry Bonds	762
2.	Hank Aaron	755
3.	Babe Ruth	714
4.	Willie Mays	660
5.	Ken Griffey, Jr.	630
6.	**ALEX RODRIGUEZ**	**613**
7.	Sammy Sosa	609
8.	Jim Thome	589
9.	Frank Robinson	586
10.	Mark McGwire	583

▸ Compiled 344HR as a shortstop, one shy of the all-time record held by Cal Ripken Jr., who played in 2,303 games with 8,934 at-bats at shortstop…his eight consecutive 20-homer seasons as a shortstop (1996-2003) is the second-longest such streak, two behind Cal Ripken Jr. (1982-91).

▸ Has compiled over 3,000AB with the Yankees and Mariners, joining Manny Ramirez (Indians and Red Sox) as the only current Major Leaguers with at least 3,000AB for each of two different teams…joins Dave Winfield (3,997AB with San Diego) as the only players to accumulate 3,000 at-bats with the Yankees and at least that many for another team (credit: *Elias*).

▸ Is the all-time leader with 174 Interleague RBI and ranks second in Interleague hits (267) and third in runs (161).

▸ Played in 431 career games at the original Yankee Stadium, marking the fifth-highest total among New York City-born players, behind Lou Gehrig (1,080), Phil Rizzuto (825), Joe Pepitone (525) and Snuffy Stirnweiss (442), according to the *Elias Sports Bureau*.

- Was selected to his 13th All-Star team in 2010—the most among active Major League players—by American League All-Star Manager Joe Girardi (did not play).

- Owns a .290 (67-for-231) career postseason batting average with 41R, 16 doubles, 13HR and 38RBI in 63 games…is tied for fourth among active Major Leaguers in postseason home runs, ranks sixth in runs scored, and eighth in RBI and on-base percentage (.396).

2010

- Hit .270 (141-for-522) with 74R, 29 doubles, 30HR and 125RBI in 137 games (122 starts at 3B, 12 at DH) with the Yankees…ranked second in the Majors in RBI…had 16 game-winning RBI, tied with Chicago-AL's Paul Konerko and Toronto's Vernon Wells for most such RBI in the AL…led the Majors with 4.18 AB/RBI…13 of his 30HR (43.3%) tied the game or gave the Yankees the lead…58 of his 125RBI (46.4%) either tied the game or gave the Yankees the lead.

> ### Century City
> **Alex Rodriguez** has driven in at least 100 runs while playing fewer than 140 games in each of the last three seasons (2008-10)…the only other players ever to have three such consecutive seasons were Joe DiMaggio (1939-41) and Chick Hafey (1928- 30)…joins DiMaggio as the only players to also have at least 30HR in each of those three seasons—credit: *Elias*.

- Had a Major League-leading 48RBI in the seventh inning or later, 20 of which tied the game or put the team ahead…hit four go-ahead home runs in the seventh inning or later and has nine such homers since the start of 2009.

- Played in 137 games and drove in 125 runs…since RBI became an official statistic in 1920, only nine players (12 occasions) have recorded more RBI while playing 137G or fewer, including just two Yankees–Babe Ruth in 1929 (154RBI) and '32 (137) and Joe DiMaggio in 1939 (126) and '40 (133).

- Matched his career high with 11 sacrifice flies (also 2000 w/Seattle).

- Was 9-for-20 (.450) with 3HR and a Major League-leading 34RBI with the bases loaded…tied for most grand slams in the Majors in 2010 and marked the fourth time in his career he hit at least three grand slams in a season (also 1996, '99 and 2007)…according to *Elias*, matches Jimmie Foxx (1932, '34, '38 and '40) as the only players with at least four seasons with three-or-more grand slams…became the third Yankee to hit three grand slams before the All-Star break (also Lou Gehrig – four in 1934; and Don Mattingly – three in 1987).

- Committed just two errors over his final 81 games (80 starts) at 3B beginning on 5/27…made 5E in his first 43 games of the season (4/4-5/26)…went 45 straight games (44 starts) at third base without making an error from 7/17-9/28, marking the third-longest errorless stretch at 3B in his career (46 games from 5/30-7/23/07 and 61 games from 6/23-9/1/05)…ranked fourth among all Major League third basemen with a .976 fielding percentage…only Jhonny Peralta (5E) and Placido Polanco (5E) committed fewer errors than Rodriguez (7E) among Major Leaguers with at least 100G at 3B.

- Made his 14th career Opening Day roster…was his sixth Opening Day start at 3B after making eight Opening Day starts at SS…joined Manny Ramirez (seven Opening Day starts in RF and eight in LF) as the only active players to make at least six Opening Day starts at two different positions in their career…the last player to do so at both SS and 3B was Cal Ripken Jr. (credit: *Elias Sports Bureau*)…also made his sixth Opening Day start at 3B with Derek Jeter at SS, matching Bucky Dent and Graig Nettles (six) and Frank Crosetti and Red Rolfe (six) for most such starts in franchise history.

MAN ON
According to STATS Inc., **Alex Rodriguez** has had the hitter before him intentionally walked to load the bases 17 times in his career and he has hit three home runs in those situations…according to STATS Inc., Rodriguez is 5-for-7 with 1BB, 3HR, 1SF and 18RBI in nine plate appearances after Mark Teixeira has been intentionally walked to load the bases in front of him (including postseason).

- Hit just 2HR in April, his lowest home run total of his career for a calendar month (min. 70AB).

- Reached the 1,000-hit plateau as a Yankee with his second-inning single off Wade Davis in 4/10 win at Tampa Bay…became the 39th player to reach the plateau with the Yankees and first since Jorge Posada on 8/20/05 at the White Sox…had 966H with Seattle (1994-2000) and 569 with Texas (2001-03), becoming the second player to have 1,000H with other team(s) prior to getting 1,000 with the Yankees, joining Dave Winfield (1,134 w/ San Diego from 1973-80; and 1,300 w/ the Yankees from 1981-88, '90)—credit: *Elias*.

- Hit his 584th career home run in 4/17 win vs. Texas, surpassing Mark McGwire for sole possession of eighth place on Baseball's all-time list…the home run also snapped a 41AB homerless stretch to begin the season, his longest such stretch to begin a campaign since 1995 when he homered in his 49th at-bat and third-longest of his career (did not homer in 54AB in 1994 rookie season).

- Snapped an 0-for-19 stretch with a first-inning double in 4/30 win vs. Chicago-AL, his longest hitless stretch since a career-high-tying 0-for-21 from 7/25-8/2/07.

- Did not record an RBI over a seven-game stretch from 5/20-27, marking his longest drought without driving in a run since a nine-game span from 5/9-18/07.

- Did not play in four games from 6/11-15 (hip flexor tendinitis).

- Hit game-winning two-run HR in the eighth in 7/1 win vs. Seattle…was his 250th as a Yankee in his 963rd game with the Yankees…according to *Elias*, the only player to reach the 250-homer plateau with the Yankees in fewer games was Babe Ruth (774th game).

- Had 70RBI prior to the All-Star break for the seventh time in his career, tying Ted Williams for the most such seasons in Major League history…no other player has done it six times (credit: *Elias*).

- Collected a Major League-best 31RBI in July, marking his most RBI in a calendar month since September 2007 (also 31RBI)…was his fourth 30RBI month as a Yankee (also April and June 2007-both 34RBI), the most such months by a Yankee since Mickey Mantle (July 1952, May 1956, June 1957 and June 1961).

- Hit first-inning, two-run HR—the 600th HR of his career—in 8/4 win vs. Toronto, becoming the seventh player in Major League history to reach the plateau…at 35 years, 8 days old, became the youngest player ever to hit his 600th career HR, surpassing Babe Ruth (36 years, 196 days)…the home run came in his 2,267th career game, trailing only Ruth (2,044) for fewest games needed to reach the mark…joined Ruth (600th HR on 8/21/31 at St. Louis) as the only players to hit his 600th career homer as a Yankee…came exactly three years to the day after he hit his 500th home run (8/4/07 vs. Kansas City, off Kyle Davies)…snapped a 46AB homerless stretch and an 0-for-17 stretch overall with the homer…hit .196 (9-for-46) with 3 doubles and 8RBI between his 599th and 600th home runs (7/22-8/3).

- Stole his 300th career base in the sixth inning of 8/8 win at Boston.

- Hit three home runs (solo-HR and two two-run HRs) in 8/14 win at Kansas City, going 4-for-5…hit the three homers in consecutive plate appearances off three different pitchers (a span of five pitches)…was his fourth career three-homer game and first since 4/26/05 vs. Los Angeles-AL.

- Missed three games from 8/17-19 with tightness in his left calf and was placed on the 15-day disabled from 8/21-9/5 with the injury (missed 14 team games).

AMONG ACTIVE PLAYERS

GAMES PLAYED
1. Omar Vizquel.........................2,850
2. Ivan Rodriguez 2,499
3. Jim Thome 2,391
4. **ALEX RODRIGUEZ 2,303**
5. Manny Ramirez.........................2,297

RUNS SCORED
1. **ALEX RODRIGUEZ 1,757**
2. DEREK JETER 1,685
3. Johnny Damon 1,564
4. Manny Ramirez.........................1,544
5. Jim Thome 1,534

HITS
1. DEREK JETER 2,926
2. Ivan Rodriguez 2,817
3. Omar Vizquel.........................2,799
4. **ALEX RODRIGUEZ 2,672**
5. Manny Ramirez.........................2,573

RBI
1. **ALEX RODRIGUEZ 1,831**
2. Manny Ramirez.........................1,830
3. Jim Thome 1,624
4. Chipper Jones 1,491
5. Vladimir Guerrero 1,433

- Hit 9HR with 28RBI in 25 games over the remainder of the season after being reinstated from the disabled list on 9/5, ranking third in the Majors in home runs and second in RBI over the stretch.

- Was named the MLB "AL Player of the Month" for September (.309, 25-for-81, 15R, 9HR and 26RBI in 22 games).

- Hit solo HR in the sixth and two-run HR in the seventh and was 2-for-4 with 1BB in 9/24 loss vs. Boston…were his 609th and 610th career home runs, tying and surpassing Sammy Sosa (609) for sole possession of sixth place all-time…was his 58th career multi-HR game (54th two-homer game) and fourth in 2010.

- Appeared in all nine postseason games, reaching base in eight of the contests (.219, 7-for-32, 5R, 2 doubles, 3RBI and 4BB).

600 HOME RUN CLUB

Player	Team	Date	Pitcher	Opp.	Age	AB
Babe Ruth	Yankees	8/21/31	George Blaeholder	at St. Louis	36 yrs, 196 days	6,921
Willie Mays	Giants	9/22/69	Mike Corkins	at San Diego	38 yrs, 139 days	9,514
Hank Aaron	Braves	4/27/71	Gaylord Perry	vs. San Francisco	37 yrs, 81 days	10,014
Barry Bonds	Giants	8/9/02	Kip Wells	vs. Pittsburgh	38 yrs, 16 days	8,211
Sammy Sosa	Rangers	6/20/07	Jason Marquis	vs. Chicago-NL	38 yrs, 220 days	8,637
Ken Griffey, Jr.	Reds	6/9/08	Mark Hendrickson	at Florida	38 yrs, 201 days	9,042
ALEX RODRIGUEZ	**Yankees**	**8/4/10**	**Shaun Marcum**	**vs. Toronto**	**35 yrs, 8 days**	**8,688**

2009

- Hit .286 (127-for-444) with 17 doubles, 1 triple, 30HR, 100RBI and 14SB in 124 games (113 starts at 3B, nine at DH) with the Yankees…missed 28 team games at the beginning of the season due to injury…became the 12th player all time to reach 30HR and 100RBI in a season in which he played fewer than 125G, first since Manny Ramirez in 2002.

- The Yankees went 90-44 (.672) following his return from the disabled list on 5/8, marking the best winning percentage in the Majors over the stretch…ranked second in the American League in RBI and tied for second in the AL in home runs after coming off the D.L., trailing only teammate Mark Teixeira.

- Was involved in scoring or driving in the game-winning or tying run in six of the Yankees' 15 "walk-off" innings in 2009 (two game-ending home runs, one game-tying home run, two game-winning runs scored and hit a pop-up resulting in a two-run "walk-off" error vs. the Mets)…batted .310 (18-for-58) with 8HR and 21RBI in "close and late" situations, tying for second-most HR in the Majors in such situations.

- According to Elias, 15 of his 30HR either tied the game or put the team ahead…had 12HR in the seventh inning or later, seven of which tied the game or put the Yankees ahead…51 of his 100RBI tied the game or put the team ahead, tying for second in the AL with 29 go-ahead RBI…had 33RBI in the seventh inning or later, 15 of which tied the game or put the team ahead.

- Became the third Yankee to reach the 100RBI plateau in fewer than 125 games in a season (also Joe DiMaggio in 1939 and Bill Dickey in 1936).

- Was placed on the 15-day D.L. from 4/4–5/8 (retroactive to 3/27)…missed 28 team games…underwent arthroscopic surgery on 3/9 to repair his right hip labrum, remove an impingement in the joint and drain a cyst in the hip…the procedure was performed by Dr. Marc Philippon at the Vail Valley Surgery Center in Vail, Colo…the cyst and tear were discovered during an MRI taken on 2/28…cyst was originally drained on 3/5.

- In 44 plate appearances during rehab assignment from 4/30-5/7, was 7-for-36 (.194) with 3HR, 8BB and 8K…reported to Tampa on 4/13 to continue his rehab program…was selected to participate in the World Baseball Classic with the Dominican Republic, but was unable to play (hip surgery).

MOST RBI, SINGLE POSTSEASON, ALL TIME

1.	Sandy Alomar, Jr.	19 (1997, CLE)
	David Ortiz	19 (2004, BOS)
	Scott Spiezio	19 (2002, ANA)
4.	**ALEX RODRIGUEZ**	**18 (2009, NYY)**

MOST GAME-WINNING RBI, LAST FIVE YEARS (2006-10)

1.	**ALEX RODRIGUEZ**	**74**
2.	Miguel Cabrera	67
3.	David Ortiz	66
4.	Justin Morneau	65
5.	Torii Hunter	62

FEWEST AB/RBI IN AL, LAST TWO YEARS (2009-10)

1.	**ALEX RODRIGUEZ**	**4.29**
2.	Miguel Cabrera	5.06
3.	Carlos Pena	5.19
4.	MARK TEIXEIRA	5.26
5.	David Ortiz	5.27

- Missed the Opening Day active roster for the first time since 1995, snapping a stretch of 13 straight Opening Day starts.

- Hit three-run HR on his first pitch seen of the season and was 1-for-4 in 5/8 win at Baltimore…became the first Yankee to homer on the first pitch of his first plate appearance of a season since Andy Phillips on 9/26/04 at Boston, in the first PA of his Major League career…was the second time that Rodriguez hit a HR in his first AB of a season (also 2006).

- Seven of his first 10 hits after returning from the disabled list on 5/8 were home runs…according to the Elias Sports Bureau, was the first Yankee in franchise history to collect 7HR within his first 10H of the season.

- Homered on four straight days from 5/16-19, marking the eighth time in his career he homered in at least four consecutive games…according to Elias, his five streaks of four straight games with a HR as a Yankee tie him with Babe Ruth, Lou Gehrig and Yogi Berra for the most in franchise history.

- Hit 6HR on the Yankees' 10-game homestand from 5/15-24, matching his most HR hit during any homestand in his Major League career (third time).

- Reached the 14-year anniversary of his first HR (Tom Gordon on 6/12/95 w/ Seattle vs. Kansas City) with 561 homers…according to the Elias Sports Bureau, his career total of within 14 years of hitting his first were most all time…the next-highest home run totals as of the 14th anniversary of their first were Mark McGwire (552) and Sammy Sosa (539).

- Hit two-run HR—the 564th of his career to surpass Reggie Jackson for 11th place on Baseball's all-time list—in 6/26 win at the Mets.

- Hit two-run "walk-off" HR in the 15th inning of 8/7 win vs. Boston, becoming the fifth player in Baseball history to hit a "walk-off" HR in the 15th inning or later to break a scoreless tie, joining Old Hoss Radbourn in 1882 w/ Providence (18th inning), Earl Averill in 1935 w/ Cleveland (15th inning), Willie Mays in 1963 w/ San Francisco (16th inning) and Adrian Garrett in 1975 w/ Chicago-NL (16th inning)—credit: *Elias Sports Bureau*…was his ninth career extra-inning HR.

- The homer snapped a single-season career-high 72AB homerless stretch dating back to 7/19 (third-longest of career).

- Two games later, hit the go-ahead solo-HR in the seventh in 8/9 win vs. Boston…according to the *Elias Sports Bureau*, became the first player in Major League history to snap scoreless ties by hitting home runs in the seventh inning or later twice in one series.

- Recorded his 2,500th hit with a fifth-inning single in 9/2 win at Baltimore, becoming the 78th player all time to reach the hit total…according to the *Elias Sports Bureau* - at the age of 34 years, 37 days old – became the third-youngest player to reach the 2,500H plateau in the Expansion era, behind Hank Aaron (33 years, 127 days) and Robin Yount (33 years, 289 days)…among active players, only teammate Derek Jeter (1,999G) collected his 2,500th hit in fewer games than him (2,141G).

- Was ejected for the fifth time in 9/13 win vs. Baltimore in the middle of the fifth by Marty Foster for arguing balls and strikes.

- Homered twice in the sixth inning of the Yankees' regular season finale win at Tampa Bay on 10/4, with a three-run home run and a grand slam…the 7RBI marked the most in a single inning by an American Leaguer…became the second player in the modern era (since 1900) to drive in seven-or-more runs in an inning (also Fernando Tatis—8RBI on 4/23/99 vs. Los Angeles-NL)…became just the third player in the last 55 years (since 1955) to collect at least 7RBI in a season finale, joining Philadelphia's Dick Allen (7RBI in 1968) and Minnesota's Kirby Puckett (7RBI in 1994 on the day before the strike took effect)…became the 10th player since 1900 to hit two home runs in one inning, one of which was a grand slam…was the second time in his career he has homered twice in the same inning (also 9/5/07 vs. Seattle), marking the sixth time a Yankee has homered twice in the same frame and becoming the first Yankee to accomplish the feat twice in pinstripes.

- Hit .365 (19-for-52) with 15R, 5 doubles, 6HR and 18RBI in the postseason, leading the team in average, runs, home runs, RBI and tying for tops in doubles…hit three game-tying HR in the seventh inning or later in the 2009 postseason, the most such HR ever for a player in their postseason career (credit: *Elias*)…hit ninth-inning, two-run home run (off Joe Nathan) to tie game in Game 2 win of ALDS vs. Minnesota and solo HR (off Carl Pavano) to tie game in seventh inning of Game 3 ALDS clincher at Minnesota…tied the game with a solo HR (off Brian Fuentes) in the 11th inning of ALCS Game 2 win vs. Los Angeles-AL…matched Bernie Williams (6HR in 1996) for the most HR in a single postseason in franchise history, and was 1HR shy of tying the AL record (7-ANA Troy Glaus-2002 and TB B.J. Upton-2008)…his solo HR on 10/31/09 in Game 4 of World Series at Philadelphia became the first playoff homer to be reviewed by video replay.

- Drove in a run in 11 games and set a franchise record with 18RBI, falling one RBI shy of the all-time postseason record shared by Sandy Alomar, Jr. (1997, CLE), Scott Spiezio (2002, ANA) and David Ortiz (2004, BOS)…eight of his RBI tied the game or put the Yankees ahead…drove in at least one run in eight straight playoff games from 10/8/07 (ALDS Game 4)-10/20/09 (ALCS Game 4), matching the all-time record, (also Lou Gehrig and Ryan Howard)…joined Boston's David Ortiz (2004) as the only two players to record three game-tying or go-ahead RBI hits in the ninth inning or later in a single postseason.

- Collected 11 extra-base hits in the 2009 playoffs, tying six others – including teammate Hideki Matsui (2004) – for most in a single postseason (credit: *Elias*)…was hit by a pitch three times in the World Series, tying Pittsburgh's Max Carey (1925) and teammate Mark Teixeira (2009) for the all-time record.

- Won the Babe Ruth Award from the New York Chapter of the Baseball Writers Association of America as the postseason MVP.

LAST 10 SEASONS, MAJORS (2001-2010)

MOST HOME RUNS

1.	**ALEX RODRIGUEZ**	**424**
2.	Albert Pujols	408
3.	Jim Thome	356
4.	Adam Dunn	354
5.	David Ortiz	329

MOST RUNS SCORED

1.	Albert Pujols	1,186
2.	**ALEX RODRIGUEZ**	**1,130**
3.	DEREK JETER	1,080
4.	Johnny Damon	1,060
5.	Ichiro Suzuki	1,047

MOST RBI

1.	**ALEX RODRIGUEZ**	**1,236**
2.	Albert Pujols	1,230
3.	David Ortiz	1,055
4.	Vladimir Guerrero	1,029
5.	Manny Ramirez	1,026

2008

- Hit .302 (154-for-510) with 104R, 33 doubles, 35HR, 103RBI and 18SB in 138 games with the Yankees (131 starts at 3B, seven at DH).
- Led the American League with a .573 slugging percentage, ranked third with 35HR and a 14.6 AB/HR ratio, fourth with 14HBP, tied for fifth with 104R, fifth with a .392 on-base percentage, seventh with a .316 average vs. right-handed pitchers and a .339 day batting average, tied for eighth with 103RBI, ninth with a 5.0 AB/RBI ratio and 10th with a .324 home batting average…finished eighth in AL MVP voting.
- According to the *Elias Sports Bureau*, recorded his fourth consecutive season (2005-08) of hitting 20-or-more home runs at the original Yankee Stadium…only Babe Ruth (six straight seasons) had a longer such stretch in original Yankee Stadium history (1926-31)…batted .324 (60-for-185) with 17HR and 47RBI in his last 50 games at the original Yankee Stadium beginning 6/7.
- Was named to his 12th All-Star team, marking his 11th selection via the fan vote and fifth overall selection as a third baseman…tallied the most votes in the Majors (3,934,518) for the second straight season, becoming the first back-to-back leader since Ichiro Suzuki (three seasons, 2001-03)…was 0-for-2 in the 15-inning AL victory on 7/15 at Yankee Stadium, starting at 3B.
- Following the season, was named to the 2008 *Sporting News* AL All-Star team, which was selected by a panel of 41 general managers and assistant general managers from both leagues…also earned his 10th career Silver Slugger Award.
- Made his fifth straight Opening Day start at 3B for the Yankees—the 13th OD start of his career—and was 2-for-3 with 1R, 1 double, 1RBI and 1BB in 4/1 win vs. Toronto…started his fifth straight Opening Day at third base with Derek Jeter at shortstop, becoming the first pair of Yankees to start on the left side of the infield in five consecutive years since Graig Nettles and Bucky Dent started six consecutive from 1977-82.
- Was 0-for-4 in 4/8 loss at Kansas City, striking out a career-high-tying four times for the fourth time in his career (third as a Yankee, first since 8/25/06 at Los Angeles-AL).
- Was placed on the 15-day D.L. from 4/30-5/20 with a strained right quadriceps (missed 16 team games, Yankees were 6-10)…was his first stint on the disabled list since 7/8-24/00 (w/ Seattle) when he missed 15 games with a right knee strain…originally injured his quad running out a ground ball on 4/20 at Baltimore…missed three games from 4/22-24 (spent three days from 4/21-23 in Miami, Fla., welcoming the birth of his second daughter, Ella Alexander, on 4/21)…returned to the lineup on 4/25 and played in four games before being removed for PH (Damon) in the eighth inning of 4/28 win at Cleveland (left game with discomfort in his right quad).
- In his final 114 games of the season after returning from the D.L. on 5/20, hit .305 (128-for-419) with 90R, 26 doubles, 31HR, 92RBI, 59BB and 17SB…the Yankees were 68-46 (.596) over the stretch as he led the AL in home runs and ranked third in runs and RBI…was the third-highest winning percentage in the AL following his return.
- Hit two-run HR on 5/20 vs. Baltimore and solo-HR on 5/21 vs. Baltimore, becoming the first player to homer in each of his first two games after spending at least three weeks on the D.L. since Chris Richard from 7/31-8/1/02 with Baltimore (credit: *Elias Sports Bureau*).

MOST HOME RUNS BY A YANKEE IN A SINGLE SEASON

No.	Player	Year
61	Roger Maris	1961
60	Babe Ruth	1927
59	Babe Ruth	1921
54	**ALEX RODRIGUEZ**	**2007**
54	Mickey Mantle	1961
54	Babe Ruth	1928
54	Babe Ruth	1920

50 OR MORE HOME RUNS, THREE DIFFERENT SEASONS

No.	Player	Years
4	Babe Ruth	1920-21, '27-28
	Mark McGwire	1996-99
	Sammy Sosa	1998-2001
3	**ALEX RODRIGUEZ**	**2001-02, '07**

SEASONS WITH 35-OR-MORE HOME RUNS (ALL-TIME)

1.	Babe Ruth	12
	ALEX RODRIGUEZ	**12**
3.	Hank Aaron	11
	Mike Schmidt	11

140 RUNS, 50 HOME RUNS, 150 RBI IN ONE SEASON

Year	Player	Team	(R-HR-RBI)
1921	Babe Ruth	New York-AL	177-59-171
1927	Babe Ruth	New York-AL	158-60-164
1930	Hack Wilson	Chicago-NL	146-56-191
1932	Jimmie Foxx	Philadelphia-AL	151-58-169
2001	Sammy Sosa	Chicago-NL	146-64-160
2007	**ALEX RODRIGUEZ**	**New York-AL**	**143-54-156**

‣ Hit game-winning solo-HR in the 12th—his 200th homer as a Yankee—and was 1-for-6 on 8/12 at Minnesota…became the 15th player in franchise history to reach 200 home runs with the Yankees, including two others who did it within the previous month: Derek Jeter (7/12) and Jason Giambi (8/9)…according to the *Elias Sports Bureau*, it marked the first time that any set of teammates on one club accomplished the feat in the same season…*Elias* also notes that Rodriguez became the second-fastest Yankee to reach 200HR, doing so in 729 games with the club (Babe Ruth reached 200HR with the Yankees in 586 games).

MOST GAME-ENDING HR BY A YANKEE	
1. Mickey Mantle	12
2. Babe Ruth	11
3. Yogi Berra	7
4. Graig Nettles	6
ALEX RODRIGUEZ	**6**

‣ Grounded into 11 double plays in the month of August, the most in a single month in franchise history since GDPs were first recorded in the American League in 1939 (credit: *Elias Sports Bureau*).

‣ His solo-HR on 9/2 at Tampa Bay was the 1,000th extra-base hit of his career, coming at the age of 33 years, 37 days…according to the *Elias Sports Bureau*, only Jimmie Foxx (32 years, 294 days on 8/13/40) reached the milestone at a younger age.

‣ Hit grand-slam-HR in the first inning and was 2-for-4 with 2R and 1 double in 9/14 win vs. Tampa Bay…according to *Elias*, became the first Yankees cleanup hitter to hit a grand slam after the first three batters of the game reached base since Mel Hall on 6/24/89 at Kansas City and the first such Yankee at Yankee Stadium since Dave Winfield on 7/16/84 vs. Texas.

2007

‣ Won his third career American League MVP Award and his second in four seasons with the Yankees, hitting .314 (183-for-583) with 143R, 54HR, 156RBI and 24SB in 158 games (154 starts at 3B, four starts at DH)…established career highs in runs and RBI…received 26-of-28 first-place votes in BBWAA MVP voting (382 total points)…became the ninth player in Major League history to win at least three MVP Awards and fifth AL player…became the sixth player to win multiple MVP's with the Yankees, joining Lou Gehrig (two), Joe DiMaggio (three), Mickey Mantle (three), Yogi Berra (three) and Roger Maris (two)…became just the fourth player to win the MVP Award three times within a five-year span, joining Roy Campanella, Berra and Barry Bonds.

‣ Was elected to the 2007 AL All-Star team, the 11th All-Star selection of his career (1996-98; 2000-07)…was the first time he led the Majors in All-Star balloting (3,890,515 votes)…started at 3B and went 1-for-3 in the 7/10 American League win…also named "Major League Player of the Year" by *Baseball America* and the *Sporting News* and was named starting 3B on each publication's All-Star team…became just the third player in the 72-year history of the *Sporting News* Award to win at least three times, joining Ted Williams (five) and Barry Bonds (three)…received his ninth career Silver Slugger Award, fourth career Hank Aaron Award, the Oscar Charleston Legacy Award and Josh Gibson Award presented by the Negro Leagues Baseball Museum, and was named the MLB.com "Clutch Performer of the Year," This Week in Baseball's "Hitter of the Year" and the Latinosports.com "2007 LatinoMVP Player of the Year"…was also named the Sid Mercer "Player of the Year" by the New York chapter of the BBWAA and was selected by his peers as the Players Choice 2007 "Player of the Year" and the American League's "Outstanding Player"…was named American League "Player of the Week" three times in 2007 (4/2-9, 6/4-10 and 9/3-9).

Most MVPs by Franchise*	
YANKEES	**22**
Cardinals	20
Athletics	13
Giants	13
Reds	12

Yankees MVPs*	
Berra	3
DiMaggio	3
Mantle	3
Gehrig	2
Maris	2
RODRIGUEZ	**2**
Chandler	1
Gordon	1
Howard	1
Mattingly	1
Munson	1
Rizzuto	1
Ruth	1

*Lists include winners of the Chalmers Award (1911-14), League Awards (1922-29) and BBWAA MVP Awards (1931-present).

‣ Led the Majors in runs, home runs and RBI…since RBI became an official statistic in 1920, became only the fourth player (and the first in the past 50 years) to finish a season with the outright Major League lead in each of those categories, according to the *Elias Sports Bureau*: Babe Ruth (three times: 1920-21, 1926), Ted Williams (1942-also won Triple Crown) and Mickey Mantle (1956-also won Triple Crown)…also led the Major Leagues with a .645 slugging percentage and an average of 1RBI every 3.7 at-bats…tied for the lead with three grand slams.

‣ Led the American League with 376 total bases, ranked second with 85 extra-base hits, 21HBP and 1HR/10.8AB, fourth with a .422 on-base percentage, tied for fourth with nine sacrifice flies, seventh with a .326 road batting average and a .340 day average, tied for seventh with 95BB and eighth with a .327 average vs. right-handed pitching.

‣ Hit .463 (19-for-41) with 8HR, 21RBI, 9BB and 7K in the ninth inning of games, leading the Majors in ninth-inning homers…tied Philadelphia's Ryan Howard and Houston's Lance Berkman for the Major League lead with 22HR that tied the game or put his team ahead (credit: *Elias Sports Bureau*).

‣ Became the fifth player in Major League history to have 140R, 50HR and 150RBI in a season, joining Sammy Sosa (2001), Jimmie Foxx (1932), Hack Wilson (1930) and Babe Ruth (1921, '27) and the first to also record 20SB …according to the *Elias Sports Bureau*, is only the fourth player to post two seasons of at least 50HR, 130R and 130RBI (2001, '07)…Babe Ruth accomplished the feat four times; Jimmie Foxx and Sammy Sosa both did it twice.

▸ With 54HR, established the Yankees franchise record for most home runs in a single season by a right-handed batter…were the most by any Yankees player since Roger Maris (61HR in 1961) and were tied for the fourth-highest single-season total in franchise history…the Yankees were 35-11 in games in which he homered.

▸ Established the Major League record for most home runs in a single season by a third baseman with 52 homers (hit two as DH), surpassing Mike Schmidt (48 with Philadelphia in 1980) and Adrian Beltre (48 with Los Angeles-NL in 2004).

MOST HOME RUNS IN A SINGLE SEASON BY A RIGHT HANDED BATTER IN YANKEES HISTORY	
1. ALEX RODRIGUEZ, 2007	**54**
2. ALEX RODRIGUEZ, 2005	**48**
3. Joe DiMaggio, 1937	46
4. Joe DiMaggio, 1948	39
Alfonso Soriano, 2002	39

▸ Finished with 26HR at home, tying his own record (established in 2005) for the most home runs in a single season at Yankee Stadium by a right-handed batter…Yankees were 21-2 in games in which he homered at Yankee Stadium…hit 28HR on the road…only four Yankees have hit more road homers in a single-season: Babe Ruth in 1927 (32), Roger Maris in 1961 (31), Mickey Mantle in 1961 (30) and Jason Giambi in 2003 (29).

▸ His 156RBI were the most by a Yankee in a single season since 1937 when Joe DiMaggio had 167 and Lou Gehrig had 159…was the second-highest single-season total by a right-handed hitter in franchise history behind only DiMaggio's 167 in 1937…the total also ranks 10th on the Yankees' all-time single-season list and were the most in the American League since Manny Ramirez in 1999 with Cleveland (165RBI)…drove in 111 runs in his final 105 games of the season…became the first Yankee to record multiple seasons of at least 130RBI (2005, '07) since Joe DiMaggio accomplished the feat in 1937, '38, '40 and '48 (credit: *Elias Sports Bureau*).

▸ His 143 runs scored were the highest single-season total in the American League since the Yankees' Rickey Henderson scored 146 runs in 1985 and was the second-highest single-season total by a Yankee in the last 70 years (since 1938).

▸ Drove in 100 runs through the club's first 99 games of the season…according to the *Elias Sports Bureau*, became the first Yankee to reach the 100-RBI mark in fewer than 100 "team games" into a season since 1937, when both Joe DiMaggio (91 games) and Lou Gehrig (96 games) did so.

▸ His 24 stolen bases were the most for any player from the cleanup spot in the batting order since Preston Wilson stole 36 bases from that spot for the 2000 Marlins…became just the fourth player all-time to record at least 50HR and at least 20SB in a single season, joining Willie Mays (1955, New York Giants), Brady Anderson (1996, Baltimore) and Ken Griffey, Jr. (1998, Seattle).

▸ Hit two-run HR—his third career Opening Day home run and second as a Yankee—and was 2-for-5 with 2R and 1SB in 4/2 win vs. Tampa Bay…was his fourth straight Opening Day start at 3B for the Yankees and 12th Opening Day start of his career.

▸ Hit two-run HR and "walk-off" grand slam in the ninth inning in 4/7 win vs. Baltimore, and was 3-for-4 with 4R, 1 double and 1BB…according to the *Elias Sports Bureau*, became the third player in franchise history to hit a game-ending grand slam with the Yankees trailing when they came to the plate: also Jason Giambi on 5/27/02 vs. Minnesota and Babe Ruth in 1925…marked only the eighth time in franchise history that the Yankees won a game with a "walk-off" grand slam and the first since Giambi in 2002…was his third career "walk-off" grand slam (also on 7/27/02 w/ Texas vs. Oakland and 7/31/03 w/ Texas vs. Boston).

▸ According to the *Elias Sports Bureau*, became only the second player in AL history to hit six home runs through his team's first seven games, joining Ken Griffey, Jr. (1997)…became the first player in Yankees franchise history to hit 7HR in the team's first 10 games of the season and 8HR in the first 12 games…hit 12HR in the first 15 games of the season, joining Mike Schmidt (12HR in the first 15 games of 1976) as the fastest players in Major League history to reach 12 home runs…drove in 31 runs in the first 16 games of the season, the most of any Major Leaguer over any 16-game span since Sammy Sosa had 32 in May/June 1998.

▸ Drove in 16 runs in his first eight games of the season (4/2-11), the most RBI for any AL player through his club's first eight games of a season since Minnesota's Brant Alyea in 1970 (credit: *Elias Sports Bureau*).

▸ According to the *Elias Sports Bureau*, became the first player in Yankees history (and the only Major Leaguer since 1958) to collect an extra-base hit in each of his team's first eight games of a season…his streak of 11 straight regular season games with an extra base hit (dating back to 2006) was the longest for any player in franchise history, breaking the mark of 10 straight shared by Don Mattingly (1987) and Paul O'Neill (2001).

▸ Hit three-run "walk-off" HR in the ninth inning—his third home run in a three-game span—and was 1-for-5 in 4/19 win vs. Cleveland…was his second "walk-off" home run of the season (also 4/7 vs. Baltimore) and seventh of his career (fourth as a Yankee)…according to *Elias*, became the fourth player in Major League history to hit two "walk-off" home runs so early in the season (through his team's first 14 games), joining Pat Burrell (nine games in 2002), Robin Yount (12 games in 1991) and Tommy Henrich (12 games in 1949)…is only the third player in Yankees history to hit a pair of "walk-off" homers within a span of five home games at any point in a season, joining Babe Ruth (August 1922) and Claudell Washington (September 1988) who each hit two "walk-off" home runs in three-game spans.

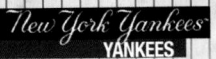
- In his 18th game, on 4/23 at Tampa Bay, became the fastest player in Major League history to reach 14HR to begin a season (previous record was held by Albert Pujols, who hit 14HR in the first 24 games of 2006)…according to the *Elias Sports Bureau*, only two players hit more than 14HR over an 18-game span for their team at any point during a season: Sammy Sosa in 1998 (16) and Barry Bonds in 2001 (15)…three others also hit 14 over a period of 18 games (Rudy York, 1937 Tigers; Albert Belle, 1995 Indians; and Mark McGwire, 1998 Cardinals).

- Began the season with an 18-game hitting streak, the longest hitting streak by an American Leaguer to start a season since George Brett hit safely in his first 19 games of the 1983 season…dating back to 2006, hit safely in a career-high 23 straight games.

- Was named the AL "Player of the Month" for April, hitting .355 (33-for-93) and leading the Majors with 14HR, 34RBI and 27R in 23 games…tied the mark for most home runs hit in April (also Albert Pujols in 2006) and finished 1RBI shy of Juan Gonzalez's Major League record for April (35) set in 1998 with Texas…with 14HR, fell 1HR shy of tying a career high for any calendar month (15HR with Texas in August 2003)…established a single-month career high with 34RBI (previous high was 31RBI with Texas in August 2003)…according to the *Elias Sports Bureau*, became the first player in Major League history to record at least 14HR and 34RBI by the end of April.

- Became the first Yankee with at least 14HR and 34RBI in any calendar month since Roger Maris in June 1961 (15HR, 35RBI)…according to the *Elias Sports Bureau*, the only other Yankees with more home runs in a calendar month were Babe Ruth, who did it four times (17 in September 1927; 15 in May 1928, August 1929 and June 1930), Joe DiMaggio (15 in July 1937) and Mickey Mantle (16 in May 1956)…only Harmon Killebrew (15 with the Washington Senators in May 1959) has hit more home runs in any calendar month all time among Major League third basemen.

- Went 47 consecutive games without committing an error from 5/30-7/23, the longest errorless streak by a Yankees third baseman since he went 61 straight games without an error from 6/23-9/1/05.

- Hit game-winning solo-HR in the ninth and was 2-for-5 with 2RBI in 6/3 win at Boston…was his second ninth-inning, game-winning home run at Fenway Park since joining the Yankees (also 7/14/05 off Curt Schilling)…over the last 20 years, only two other Yankees have hit a game-winning homer in the ninth inning at Fenway: Bernie Williams and Alfonso Soriano (one each in 2001)…hit grand slam in the ninth—his third ninth-inning homer of the road trip—and was 2-for-4 with 1BB in 6/7 win at Chicago-AL…according to the *Elias Sports Bureau*, became the second player in Yankees history to hit two grand slams in the ninth inning or later in the same season, joining Darryl Strawberry who hit two pinch-hit grand slams in 1998.

- Was named the AL "Player of the Month" for June, his second "Player of the Month" Award in 2007, fifth as a Yankee and ninth of his career—the most among American Leaguers…led the AL with 28R, 9HR, 34RBI, a .773 slugging percentage and a .496 on-base percentage, while ranking fourth with a .402 batting average…his 34RBI tied his personal best for any calendar month of his career, which he set in April, and were the most by any Yankee in June since Roger Maris (35RBI) in 1961…no Yankee had posted as high of calendar-month numbers in average, home runs and RBI in over 50 years since Mickey Mantle batted .414 with 16HR and 35RBI in May 1956.

- Missed his first game of the season in 7/5 win vs. Minnesota (strained left hamstring)…was the only Yankee to start each of the first 81 games of 2007.

- Set personal highs for home runs (30) and RBI (86) before the All-Star break…according to the *Elias Sports Bureau*, Lou Gehrig (90 in 1934) is the only player in franchise history to have as many RBI at the break…was the first Yankee to lead the Majors in home runs at the All-Star break since Roger Maris in 1961 (33HR)…led the Major Leagues in runs (79), HR (30) and RBI (86) at the All-Star break, becoming the first player in the Majors to accomplish the feat since the Yankees' Mickey Mantle in 1956 (credit: *Elias Sports Bureau*)…also reached the All-Star break with 20HR for the Major League-record seventh consecutive season.

- Hit three-run HR in the first inning—the 500th of his career—and was 3-for-4 with 3R, 1BB and 1SB in 8/4 win vs. Kansas City…became the 22nd player in Major League history to reach the 500-HR plateau…according to the *Elias Sports Bureau*, became the youngest player to hit 500 career home runs (32 years, 8 days), surpassing Jimmie Foxx (32 years, 338 days)…became the third player to hit his 500th home run as a Yankee (also Babe Ruth and Mickey Mantle) and only the second to hit his 500th at Yankee Stadium (Mantle on 5/14/67 off Baltimore's Stu Miller)…according to the *Elias Sports Bureau*, is one of only two players with at least 500 career HR to have hit 100 or more with three different teams (Seattle-189; Yankees-208: Texas-156), joining Reggie Jackson (Oakland-269; Yankees-144; California-123)…went 28AB between home runs #499 and #500…according to the *Elias Sports Bureau*, that tied Mickey Mantle for the third-longest homerless streak between #499 and #500 (Jimmie Foxx-61AB, Harmon Killebrew-43AB).

- His 44HR were the most for a Yankee through the end of August since 1961, when Roger Maris and Mickey Mantle began September with 51 and 48 home runs, respectively (credit: *Elias Sports Bureau*)…hit solo-HR and two-run HR in the seventh inning and was 2-for-3 with 1BB in 9/5 win vs. Seattle…hit two home runs in the same inning for the first time in his career becoming the fourth Yankee to accomplish the feat (first since Cliff Johnson in the eighth inning on 6/30/77 at Toronto).

- Hit two-run HR and was 2-for-5 with 2R in 9/9 win at Kansas City, homering in his fifth consecutive game (7HR overall) from 9/4-9/9, tying a career high (also 8/11-16/99 and 8/17-21/03)…was the first Yankee to homer in five straight games since Tino Martinez did so from 5/7-11/05…joined Albert Pujols as the only Major Leaguers to homer in at least five straight games in 2007.

- On 9/28 at Baltimore, became the second player in Major League history (since RBI became an official statistic in 1920) to reach 1,500 career runs and 1,500 career RBI in the same game…according to the *Elias Sports Bureau*, Houston's Jeff Bagwell reached both milestones on 9/18/04 vs. Milwaukee…became the third-youngest player to reach 1,500 career RBI, behind Jimmie Foxx and Lou Gehrig (credit: *Elias Sports Bureau*)…hit his 54th and final home run of the season in the game, going 3-for-5…came in his 1,903rd career game, marking the fourth-fewest games needed to reach the plateaus since 1920 (when RBIs became an official statistic) behind Lou Gehrig (1,715 games), Ted Williams (1,761) and Jimmie Foxx (1,850).
- Batted .267 (4-for-15) in four Division Series games vs. Cleveland with 1HR and 1RBI.

2006

- In his third season with the Yankees, hit .290 (166-for-572) with 113R, 35HR, 121RBI and 15SB in 154 games (148 starts at 3B, three at DH)…ranked fourth in the American League in RBI, fifth in runs scored and a .340 average vs. lefthanders, seventh with 139 strikeouts, eighth with 90BB, tied for eighth in home runs and ninth with 1RBI every 4.7 at bats…was elected to the 2006 American League All-Star team, the 10th All-Star selection of his career (1996-98; 2000-06)…started at 3B and was 0-for-2 in the American League's 3-2 victory on 7/11.
- In 4/3 Opening Day win at Oakland, hit the 12th grand slam of his career…was the fourth grand slam by a Yankee on Opening Day (also Russ Derry on 4/17/45 vs. Boston; Bobby Murcer on 4/9/81 vs. Texas; and Alfonso Soriano on 3/31/03 at Toronto)…became the 56th Yankee to hit a home run on Opening Day…made his third straight Opening Day start at 3B for the Yankees and the 11th of his career…hit two-run HR and solo-HR and scored a season-high four runs in 5/27 win vs. Kansas City.
- Was named AL "Player of the Month" for May…reached base safely in 25 of 28 games during the month, batting .330 (36-for-109) with 8HR while tying Boston's David Ortiz and Cleveland's Travis Hafner for the AL lead with 28RBI…finished the month with a nine-game hitting streak…was his seventh career "Player of the Month" Award, third as a Yankee, and marked the second consecutive year he won the award for the month of May.
- Missed two games (6/2-3) at Baltimore with a stomach virus…hit two-run "walk-off" home run (#16) in the 12th inning and was 2-for-5 with 3RBI and 1BB in 6/28 win vs. Atlanta…was the fifth "walk-off" home run of his career and first since 8/4/04 vs. Oakland…was also the first by a Yankee to end an extra-inning game when trailing since 5/17/02 when Jason Giambi hit a 14th-inning grand slam to give the Yankees a 13-12 win vs. Minnesota…the home run was the 100th of his career as a Yankee, making him the third player in Major League history to record at least 100 home runs with three different teams (also 189HR with Seattle, 156 with Texas)…according to the *Elias Sports Bureau*, Reggie Jackson (269 with KC/Oakland A's, 144 with the Yankees and 123 with California) and Darrell Evans (131 with Atlanta, 142 with San Francisco and 141 with Detroit) also accomplished the feat.
- In 7/17 win vs. Seattle, committed three errors in a single game for the first time in his career…hit a three-run home run in 7/21 loss at Toronto, six days shy of his 31st birthday, becoming only the eighth player in Major League history to accumulate 2,000 hits before age 31, according to the *Elias Sports Bureau*…joined Ty Cobb (29), Rogers Hornsby (29), Met Ott (30), Hank Aaron (30), Joe Medwick (30), Jimmie Foxx (30) and Robin Yount (30)…was also his 450th career home run and at 30 years, 359 days old, became the youngest player in Major League history to reach the 450 mark, surpassing Ken Griffey Jr. who was 31 years, 261 days old when he hit his 450th career home run on 8/9/01.
- Was named the AL "Player of the Week" for the week of 8/28-9/3…hit solo-HR and three-run HR and was 3-for-5 with 5RBI in 9/3 win vs. Minnesota…was his fourth multi-home run game of the season and second in a three-game span (also 9/1 vs. Minnesota)…missed two games (9/9-10 at Baltimore) with a stomach virus…made only two errors in his final 34 games at third base (8/19-9/30)… hit .071 (1-for-14) in four Division Series games vs. Detroit.

2005

- Captured his second career American League Most Valuable Player Award, hitting .321 (194-for-605) and leading the American League with 124R and 48HR while driving in 130 runs in 162 games with the Yankees (161 starts at 3B, one start at DH)…became the first Yankee to win the AL home run title since Reggie Jackson (41) in 1980.
- Led the AL with a .610 slugging percentage, tied for the lead with 162 games played, ranked second with a .321 batting average, .351 home batting average, .421 on-base percentage and 369 total bases, third with 91 walks, 139 strikeouts and a .327 average vs. right-handed pitching, fourth with 130RBI and 78 extra-base hits, tied for fifth with 16HBP, tied for sixth with 194H, and tied for eighth with 53 multi-hit games…joined Willie Mays (New York Giants, 1955), Barry Bonds (San Francisco Giants, 1993) and Larry Walker (Colorado Rockies, 1997) as the only players to bat .300, hit 45 or more home runs and steal 20 or more bases in a single season.
- Was elected to the 2005 American League All-Star team, the ninth All-Star selection of his career (1996-98; 2000-05)…started at 3B and was 1-for-2 with 1R and 1BB…also earned his eighth career Louisville Slugger "Silver Slugger" Award.

▸ Established the franchise record for most home runs in a single season by a right-handed batter (later passed with 54HR in 2007), breaking Joe DiMaggio's mark of 46 set in 1937…his 48 home runs were the most by any Yankee since Roger Maris hit 61 and Mickey Mantle hit 54 in 1961…hit 26 home runs at Yankee Stadium in 2005, establishing the single-season club record for right-handed batters (previous record was 19HR by Joe DiMaggio in 1937 and Gary Sheffield in 2004)…with Hideki Matsui, became the first pair of Yankees to each play in every game in the same season since 1945, when Nick Etten and Snuffy Stirnweiss accomplished the feat for the second straight year (credit: *Elias Sports Bureau*)…committed 12 errors in his second season at third base and only two over his last 91 games of the season…among third basemen with 400 or more chances, only the Rangers' Hank Blalock (11) had fewer errors.

▸ On 4/5 vs. Boston, became only the second player to hit a HR into the black "batter's-eye" section of remodeled original Yankee Stadium both as a Yankee and as an opponent (also 8/17/96 w/ Seattle), joining Tony Clark.

▸ Hit a three-run HR in the first inning, a two-run HR in the third and a grand slam in the fourth and was 4-for-5 with a career-high 10RBI in 4/26 win vs. the Angels (all HR off Bartolo Colon)…was the 38th multi-homer game of his career and his second of the season (was his third three-home run game and first since 8/17/02 with Texas vs. Toronto)…became the 19th Yankee to hit three home runs in a single regular season game and the first since Tony Clark on 8/28/04 at Toronto (24th time overall)…his 10RBI were the most by a Yankee since Tony Lazzeri established the franchise- and American League record with 11 in a 25-2 win at Philadelphia on 5/24/36 (the Major League record for RBI in a single game is 12 by the Cardinals' Jim Bottomley on 9/16/24 and the Cardinals' Mark Whiten on 9/7/93)…became the 11th player in Major League history to drive in at least 10 runs in a game and the first since Boston's Nomar Garciaparra on 5/10/99 vs. Seattle…became the first and only player ever to accomplish the feat at the original Yankee Stadium.

▸ Became the first player to hit eight home runs at Yankee Stadium in April (in a single season)…the previous record was five (by Lou Gehrig in 1933 and Paul O'Neill in 2001)…was named co-winner of the AL's "Player of the Week" award (with White Sox pitcher Jon Garland) for the week ending 5/1…was his ninth career "Player of the Week" Award…was named the AL "Player of the Month" for May…reached base safely in 10 straight plate appearances from 5/26-29.

▸ Had his fourth multi-home-run game of the season in 6/8 win at Milwaukee, the 40th of his career (37th 2HR game)…the two home runs were the 399th and 400th home runs of his career…at 29 years, 316 days old, became the youngest player in Major League history to reach the 400 mark…became the sixth player to hit his 400th career home run as a Yankee, joining Babe Ruth (on 9/2/27 at Philadelphia), Lou Gehrig (on 7/10/36 vs. Cleveland), Mickey Mantle (on 9/10/62 at Detroit), Reggie Jackson (on 8/11/80 vs. Chicago) and Gary Sheffield (on 7/27/04 at Toronto).

▸ Hit a solo-HR—his second in as many games—and was 1-for-3 with 1HP in 8/26 win vs. Kansas City…his home run was his second "batter's eye" home run of the season (also 4/5 vs. Boston) and the third of his career (also on 8/17/96 with Seattle), tying Danny Tartabull and Bernie Williams for the most by any player.

▸ Named AL "Player of the Month" for August…went 61 consecutive games without committing an error from 6/23-9/2…was the longest such streak by an AL third baseman since Boston's John Valentin in 1998 (65 games)…hit solo-HR and was 4-for-5 with 2R and 1 double in AL East-clinching win on 10/1 at Boston…hit six home runs against the Red Sox in 2005, the most by any Yankee since Mickey Mantle hit six in 1964…hit .133 (2-for-15) with 6BB in five Division Series games vs. Los Angeles-AL.

2004

▸ In his first season with the Yankees, batted .286 (172-for-601) with 112R, 36HR, 106RBI and a team-high 28SB in 155 games (155 starts at 3B)…ranked fifth in the American League in runs and stolen bases, was tied for sixth in home runs, was ninth with 80BB and ranked 10th with 308TB…was elected to the 2004 American League All-Star team, the eighth All-Star selection of his career (1996-98; 2000-04)…started at 3B and was 1-for-3 with an RBI triple in the American League's 9-4 win on 7/13 at Houston's Minute Maid Park.

▸ With three-run HR in 5/4 win at Oakland, became the 70th player to reach 350 career home runs and, at 28 years, 282 days old, also became the youngest player ever to reach the 350 mark (previous youngest to reach 350 home runs was Ken Griffey, Jr., who was 28 years, 308 days old)…with his 4RBI on 5/4, he reached 1,001 in his career to become the third-youngest player ever to reach the 1,000 RBI plateau (behind only Mel Ott, 27 years, 94 days; and Jimmie Foxx, 27 years, 236 days)…reached base safely in a career-high 53 consecutive games from 4/18–6/18 (longest previous such streak was 37 straight games from 4/6-6/22/99 w/ Seattle)…was the longest such streak in the Major Leagues in 2004 and the longest by a Yankee within a single season since Derek Jeter reached base safely in the first 53 games of the 1999 season.

▸ Hit three-run HR and two-run HR and collected a season-high 5RBI in 6/22 win at Baltimore, his second multi-home-run game of the season (also 5/15 vs. Seattle) and the 35th of his career…was successful in 17 straight stolen-base attempts from 4/20-6/29, the longest such streak of his career…hit two solo home runs in 7/15 win at Detroit, his third multi-homer game of the season and the 36th of his career…was 0-for-1 with 1R and 1HBP before being ejected (fighting) in the top of the third inning of 7/24 loss at Boston.

▸ Had 369 career home runs before his 29th birthday, the most of any Major League player…hit two-run "walk-off" HR (#29) in the 11th inning on 8/4 vs. Oakland…was his fourth career "walk-off" HR and first since 7/31/03 (w/ Texas) vs. Boston.

▸ Did not play in 8/13 win at Seattle, missing his first game of the season with a viral infection…in 9/6 win vs. Tampa Bay, batted second in the lineup for the first time since 10/2/99 (w/ Seattle vs. Oakland) and was 2-for-4 with two doubles, 3RBI and 1BB…remained second in the lineup for the remainder of the season, batting .301 (28-for-93) with 19R, 3HR and 25RBI in 24 games.

▸ Hit .320 (16-for-50) with 11R, 3HR and 8RBI in 11 postseason games…went 4-for-6 with 3RBI in Game 2 of the Division Series, driving in the game-tying run with a 12th-inning double…with five runs scored in Game 3 of the ALCS, matched the single-game postseason record for runs scored (also Hideki Matsui in the same game)…homered in back-to-back games in the ALCS, driving in game-tying run in Game 3 and go-ahead run in Game 4.

2003

▸ Earned his first American League MVP Award, batting .298 (181-for-607) with 47HR and 118RBI in 161 games with Texas (158 starts at SS, one at DH)…was tied for the Major League lead in home runs and led the AL in HR, runs (124) and slugging precentage (.600)…ranked second in the league in RBI and total bases (364), placed third in extra base hits (83) and was eighth in walks (87) and on-base percentage (.396)…became the third player in the last 71 years to win three consecutive AL home run titles and the fifth since 1954 to top the league in homers, runs and slugging percentage in the same year…was second in the AL in go-ahead RBI (30) and tied for third in game-winning RBI (16), including three consecutive games, 8/17-19.

▸ Won his second consecutive Rawlings Gold Glove Award, leading all Major League shortstops with a .989 fielding percentage (8E/699TC), the highest figure in Rangers history and a career best…were the fewest errors ever for a Texas shortstop (among qualifiers) and the fewest of his career…led AL shortstops in double plays (111), tied for second in games (158), and placed third in putouts (227), assists (464) and total chances…longest errorless streak was 33 games from 6/1-7/9…won the AL Silver Slugger Award (SS) for the fifth consecutive year and seventh time overall…won third consecutive AL Hank Aaron Award as league's top offensive player and the latinosports.com LatinoMVP American League Award.

▸ Was elected as starting shortstop for seventh time on the AL All-Star team…went 1-for-3 with 1R on 7/15 at Chicago's U.S. Cellular Field…won Players' Choice Award as the American League's Outstanding Player…won the Negro Leagues Baseball Museum Oscar Charleston Legacy Award (AL MVP) and his third consecutive Josh Gibson Legacy Award (AL Home Run Leader).

▸ Tied Philadelphia's Jim Thome for the most home runs in the Majors, becoming the first player to lead Majors in home runs in consecutive seasons since Mark McGwire in 1998-99 and the second Ranger to accomplish the feat (Juan Gonzalez in 1992-93)…homered once every 12.9 at-bats, the AL's top ratio…had three two-homer games (4/16 vs. Anaheim, 8/28 at Kansas City and 9/20 vs. Anaheim)…connected for 10th career grand slam to win the game in the bottom of 11th inning on 7/31 vs. Boston, becoming the 11th player ever with at least two "walk-off" grand slams…tied the club record at the time with home runs in five consecutive games from 8/17-21…had 25 homers in his last 62 games beginning 7/23…led the Majors and tied the club mark for homers in a month with a career-high 15HR in August…of that total, 14 came while playing shortstop, the highest monthly total ever for a player at that position…established team mark for homers vs. an opponent with 11 against Anaheim.

▸ Connected for his 300th career home run off Ramon Ortiz on 4/2 at Anaheim at the age of 27 years, 249 days, becoming the youngest player in history to reach the milestone (79 days younger than Jimmie Foxx)…had 322 homers before turning 28, also the most ever by that age…homered as the DH on 8/31/03 vs. Minnesota…drove in 53 runs in last 54 games beginning 7/31…tied for the Major League lead with 31RBI in August.

▸ Had appeared in 546 consecutive games—the 25th longest streak in Major League history at the time—before sitting out on 9/24 at Oakland…was first missed contest since 7/23/00 with starts in 542 of those games…had played in all 482 games since joining the Rangers, a club record for consecutive contests…became the 35th player in history to appear in 500 consecutive contests on 8/5 at New York…did not start due to bruised left knee on 6/7-8 vs. Montreal in San Juan, Puerto Rico, but pinch-hit in both games…hit safely in 25 of 26 games from 7/27-8/22 with streaks of 12 (7/27-8/8) and 13 (8/10-22) games, the latter the longest by a Ranger in 2003…selected as the AL and Texas Rangers' "Player of the Month" for August.

▸ Tied club record and career-high with five hits on 4/27 vs. New York-AL and followed with 4H on 4/29 in Toronto, the first Ranger ever with nine hits in consecutive games…became the second youngest player ever to score 1,000 career runs at 28 years, 47 days on 9/12 vs. Oakland, topped only by the New York Giants' Mel Ott (27 years, 104 days in 1936).

2002

▸ Led the Major Leagues with 57HR, 142RBI and 389TB, the first player to lead the Majors in all three categories since Boston's Tony Armas in 1984…batted .300 (187-for-624) and finished among American League leaders in games (tied for first, 162), runs (second, 125), slugging (third, .623), extra base hits (tied for third, 86), multi-hit games (tied for sixth, 57), intentional walks (seventh, 12), on-base percentage (eighth, .392), hits (ninth), walks (ninth, 87), and at-bats (10th)…started 160 games at shortstop while setting career bests for homers, RBI, and intentional walks…selected as the Major League "Player of the Year" by the *Sporting News*.

▸ Had the sixth-most home runs in AL history, the most since Roger Maris' AL-record 61 in 1961, and the most ever for a shortstop for the second consecutive year…his 57 homers were tied for the 12th most ever in Major League history and were the most ever in a season for a Major League infielder other than a first baseman…was one shy of the AL record for homers in a season by a right-handed batter, shared by Jimmie Foxx in 1932 and Hank Greenberg in 1938…became just the fifth player in Major League history to post consecutive 50-homer seasons, tying the AL record for consecutive 50-homer campaigns with Babe Ruth (1920-21; 1927-28) and Ken Griffey, Jr. (1997-98).

▸ Became the first player to lead the Majors in homers and RBI since Detroit's Cecil Fielder in 1991…was just the third time a shortstop has ever led the Majors in homers, joining the Cubs' Ernie Banks in 1958 (47) and 1960 (41)…the only other times a shortstop has led his league in homers were both in the AL: Vern Stephens of the St. Louis Browns in 1945 (24) and Rodriguez in 2001 (52)…was the first shortstop to lead the Majors in RBI since Banks in both 1958 and 1959 and the sixth all-time, also joining Pittsburgh's Honus Wagner in 1908 and Vern Stephens, then with the Boston Red Sox in 1949 and 1950 (tied both years)…Stephens (three times, also with the Browns in 1944) is the only other shortstop to top the AL in RBI…became first shortstop to lead Majors in total bases since Ripken (368) in 1991…led the AL in total bases for the second consecutive year, the first player to do so since Belle in 1994 and 1995…his 109 homers in 2001-02 are the most ever by an American League player in consecutive seasons.

▸ His postseason honors included his first Rawlings Gold Glove and his second consecutive Rangers "Player of the Year" Award…named Major League "Player of the Year" by players in MLBPA Players Choice Award voting and by *Baseball America*…won second consecutive AL Hank Aaron Award as league's top offensive player as well as his second consecutive Josh Gibson Legacy Award from the Negro Leagues Baseball Museum (NLBM) for winning the AL home run crown…finished second in BBWAA AL MVP voting to Oakland's Miguel Tejada (21 first place votes and 356 points) with five first place votes and 254 points.

▸ Selected to AL Silver Slugger team for fifth consecutive year and sixth time overall…named as shortstop on *Baseball America* Major League All-Star team and AL All-Star squad selected by the *Sporting News*.

▸ Hit 250th career home run on 4/30 at Toronto at 26 years, 277 days of age, the second youngest ever to reach the figure behind Foxx (26 yrs., 269 days)…had Texas-record 10 multi-homer games, one shy of the Major League mark shared by Hank Greenberg (1938) and Sammy Sosa (1998)…tied club record with three homers on 8/17 vs. Toronto, the 11th time that had been done in Rangers history…joined Ernie Banks, Nomar Garciaparra and Miguel Tejada as only shortstops with two three-homer contests.

▸ Was the AL "Player of the Month" for both July (.349, 12 HR, 27 RBI) and August (.339, 12 HR, 27 RBI), the first player to win that honor in consecutive months since Cleveland's Albert Belle in August and September, 1995…named the AL "Player of the Week" for 7/11-14 and 8/12-18 (shared with Bernie Williams).

2001

▸ In his first season with Texas, batted .318 (201-for-632) with 52HR and 135RBI in 162 games…led the American League in homers, runs (133) and total bases (393)…tied for the league lead in games and extra-base hits (87), ranked third in RBI, slugging percentage (.622), tied for third in hit by pitches (16), and was also among the AL leaders in hits (fourth), at-bats (sixth), multi-hit games (sixth, 55), sacrifice flies (tied for sixth, 9), average (seventh) and on-base percentage (eighth, .399)…established Rangers club records for homers, runs, total bases and hit by pitches, had the second most extra-base hits, and the fourth-highest RBI total…became the fourth player, first since 1932, with 50 homers and 200 hits in a season.

▸ Was named the Rangers' "Player of the Year" and finished sixth in BBWAA AL MVP voting…named as shortstop on *Baseball America* Major League All-Star team and AL All-Star squad as selected by the *Sporting News*…named the Rangers' "Player of the Month" for May and a was a two-time selection as AL "Player of the Week," 4/9-15 and 9/17-23…his .318 average was the second highest of his career since his .358 in 1996…led the AL with a .361 (113-for-313) home average, ranked sixth with a .323 (162-for-501) mark vs. right-handers, and was seventh with a .329 (48-146) average in day games…tied club record with three doubles on 4/7 vs. Seattle…singled for 1,000th hit on 5/5 vs. Chicago-AL.

2000

▸ Batted .316 (175-for-554) with a career-high 134R, 41HR and 132RBI in 148 games (148 starts at SS) in his final season with the Mariners…was second in the AL in runs scored and ranked among the league leaders in homers (tied for fourth), sacrifice flies (tied for fourth, 11), slugging percentage (fifth, .606), RBI (sixth), extra-base hits (sixth, 77), total bases (tied for sixth, 336), on-base percentage (seventh, .420), walks (10th, 100) and average (15th)…led Seattle in runs, total bases, homers, and sacrifice flies…had AL's third-highest road average at .356 (103-for-289) and .370 (34-for-92) mark vs. left-handers was fourth-best…set a career-high with 100BB…joined Edgar Martinez (three consecutive years from 1995-97) as the only Mariners to have a .300 average with 100R, 100RBI and 100BB in one season.

▸ Selected as the Major League "Player of the Year" by *Baseball America*, finished third in AL MVP voting and was named Seattle's MVP by local BBWAA chapter…selected as shortstop on the Major League All-Star teams of the Associated Press and *Baseball America*, as well as the *Sporting News'* AL All-Star squad…named the AL "Player of the Week" for the week of 4/10-16…sustained a concussion while trying to break up a double play on 7/7 vs. Los Angeles-AL…also strained his right knee in the collision and was placed on 15-day disabled list on 7/14 (retroactive to 7/8)…missed 13 games with the injury…activated on 7/24…walked a club-record five times on 4/23 vs. Kansas City and tied team mark with five runs scored on 4/16 at Texas, establishing career-highs in both categories.

1999

▸ Despite missing 32 games while on the disabled list with a left knee injury, batted .285 (143-for-502) with 42HR and 111RBI in 129 games at SS with Seattle…joined Ernie Banks as the only shortstops in Major League history to hit 40 or more home runs more than once…teamed with David Bell (21) to hit more home runs than any middle-infield combo in Major League history (62)…ranked second on club in runs (110), total bases (294), homers, and RBI…ranked fifth in the AL in homers and sixth in slugging percentage (.586).

▸ Won AL Silver Slugger Award…played in just two games before going on D.L. on 4/7…had surgery the following day to repair torn cartilage in his left knee…activated on 5/14 and homered in his first at-bat that night vs. Kansas City…missed 32 games with injury…homered in five straight games from 8/11-16 to become only the fourth Seattle player to homer in five straight games…was at .315 at end of August before hitting .173 in September…scored 15 runs in a six-game span from 5/23-29…recorded his 100th career stolen base on 6/1 vs. Baltimore.

1998

▸ Batted .310 with 42HR, 124RBI and 46SB in 161 games with Seattle, joining Jose Canseco (1988) and Barry Bonds (1996) as the only players in history with 40 or more homers and 40 or more steals in a single season…led the AL in at-bats (686), hits (213), and multi-hit games (64) and ranked among the league leaders in runs (third, 123), total bases (third, 384), extra-base hits (tied for fourth, 82), RBI (fifth), and homers (seventh)…became the first Mariner ever with at least 30 homers and 30 steals in a season…tied AL record with eight extra base hits over three games from 4/18-20.

▸ Was selected as Players Choice AL "Player of the Year" and was Seattle's co-MVP with Ken Griffey, Jr.…finished ninth in AL MVP balloting…named to Associated Press Major League All-Star Team and AL All-Star Club picked by the *Sporting News*…won second Silver Slugger Award…batted leadoff for first time in career from 5/10-14…voted starting shortstop for the second straight All-Star Game (third overall selection).

1997

▸ Batted .300 with 23HR and 84RBI in 141 games (140 starts at SS) with the Mariners…tied for the team lead in doubles (40) and ranked third in hits (176) and total bases (291)…had three hitting streaks of at least 10 games, including a 16-game streak from 6/1-7/3…hit for the cycle on 6/5 at Detroit, with a homer in the first inning, single in the fourth, triple in the eighth and double in the ninth…was the second Mariner ever to accomplish the feat and at 21 years, 10 months, was fifth-youngest in Baseball history to hit for the cycle.

▸ Suffered a deep bruise of his chest wall in a collision with Roger Clemens on 6/11 at Toronto…was placed on the 15-day disabled list and missed 14 games…ejected for the first time in his career on 8/9 at Chicago-AL…became the first AL shortstop other than Cal Ripken to start an All-Star Game since 1983 (Milwaukee's Robin Yount).

1996

▸ In his first full Major League season, batted .358 (215-for-601) with 36HR and 123RBI in 146 games and was selected by both the *Sporting News* and Associated Press as the Major League "Player of the Year"…finished three points behind Juan Gonzalez in AL MVP voting, matching the second-closest AL MVP voting in history…was the AL batting champ with a .358 average, highest for an AL right-handed batter since Joe DiMaggio (.381) in 1939…at 21 years, one month, was the AL's third youngest batting leader ever behind Al Kaline (20, in 1955) and Ty Cobb (20, in 1907)…was the first Major League shortstop to win a batting title since Pittsburgh's Dick Groat in 1960 (.325) and the first in the AL since Cleveland's Lou Boudreau (.327) in 1944…was the third-highest single-season batting average ever for a shortstop.

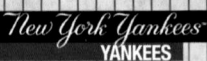
▸ Was a postseason All-Star shortstop and won first AL Silver Slugger Award…led the AL in runs (141), total bases (379) and doubles (54) and ranked among the league leaders in hits (second, 215), extra-base hits (second, 91), multi-hit games (third, 65), slugging percentage (fourth, .631), RBI (eighth, 123), and on-base percentage (eighth, .414)…posted then-records for a shortstop in runs, hits, doubles, extra-base hits and slugging percentage…established Seattle club records for average, runs, hits, doubles and total bases…named the AL "Player of the Month" for August and won league "Player of the Week" awards for weeks ending 8/19 and 9/1…hit in a single-season career-high 20 consecutive games from 8/16-9/4…was on the D.L. with pulled left hamstring from 4/22-5/7.

1995

▸ Batted .232 (33-for-142) with 5HR and 19RBI in 48 games over four stints with Seattle (5/6-27; 6/8-23; 7/20-8/15; and 8/31-10/2), starting 38 games at SS…connected for first Major League HR off Tom Gordon on 6/12 vs. Kansas City…despite playing in just 54 games at Triple-A Tacoma, batted .360 and was named to *Baseball America's* Triple-A All-Star team…also selected by the publication as the Pacific Coast League's "Most Exciting Player."

1994

▸ Advanced from Single-A Appleton to Seattle in his first pro season at age 19…hit a combined .300 (144-for-480) with 21HR and 86RBI in 131 games…joined Seattle on 7/7 and made his Major League debut as

18-YEAR-OLD SHORTSTOPS, SINCE 1900	
ALEX RODRIGUEZ, Seattle Mariners	**1994**
Robin Yount, Milwaukee Brewers	1974
Tony LaRussa, Kansas City Athletics.............................	1963

the starting shortstop on 7/8 at Boston at 18 years, 11 months and 11 days of age, just the Majors' third 18-year-old shortstop since 1900 (Kansas City's Tony LaRussa in 1963 and Milwaukee's Robin Yount in 1974)…became the Majors' first 18-year-old player since Yankees pitcher Jose Rijo in 1984…was the youngest position player in Seattle history with pitcher Edwin Nunez (18 yrs, 10 months, 11 days in 1982) the only younger player…singled off Boston's Sergio Valdez for first hit on 7/9 at Fenway Park (2-for-4, 1SB)…started 17 games at SS before being optioned to Triple-A Calgary for rest of season on 8/2.

▸ Started the season at Appleton, hitting .319 in 65 games…went 2-for-4 in pro debut on 4/8 at Quad City and hit first homer on 4/24 vs. Fort Wayne…selected to play in Midwest League All-Star Game on 6/20 but was promoted to Double-A Jacksonville on 6/16…named to Southern League's postseason All-Star squad…homered in first Double-A at-bat on 6/16 against Port City…played in 17 games before joining Seattle…played with Escogido in Dominican Winter League.

PERSONAL

▸ Full name is Alexander Enmanuel Rodriguez…has two daughters, Natasha and Ella…signed by Fernando Arguelles…had outstanding three-year career at Westminster Christian High School in Miami, Fla. (graduated in 1993)…batted .419 with 17HR, 70RBI and 90SB in 100 games as team went 86-13-1…was first team prep All-American as a senior, hitting .505 with 9HR, 36RBI and 35SB (in 35 attempts) in 33 games…selected as the USA Baseball Junior "Player of the Year" and as Gatorade's "National Baseball Student Athlete of the Year"…was the first high school player to try out for Team USA in 1993 and also play with U.S. Junior National Squad that summer…participated in Little League and American Legion programs…also played basketball and football in high school…hobbies include basketball, golf and boating…favorite players growing up were Keith Hernandez, Dale Murphy and Cal Ripken, Jr.

▸ Joined the Boys & Girls Club of Miami-Dade in 1982 at the age of 7 and remained a member until the day he was drafted in 1993…since reaching the Major Leagues, has worked extensively with the Boys & Girls Club of Miami-Dade, dedicating time, effort and resources toward its continued development…created the Alex Rodriguez Evening with the All-Stars in 1998…five benefits have since been hosted, raising over $500,000 for the Club …has also served as a national spokespersons for the Boys & Girls Clubs of America…championed Campaign 3 p.m., which is the Boys & Girls Clubs national initiative to enroll every child in America in an after-school program…hosted a two-hour clinic at the Boys & Girls Club in November 2007 for approximately 85 youngsters between the ages of 9 and 14 on a field named after him.

▸ In 2007, personally donated $500,000 to the Alex Rodriguez Learning Center at the Boys & Girls Club of Miami-Dade which opened in January 2010…the 8,000 square foot educational facility for the advancement of literacy, computer study and math, includes three separate classrooms, a computer technology lab and a research technology lab with 25 computers…an additional wing houses the teen center with a study hall with computers and a teen lounge with games, a big screen television and books.

▸ In January of 2003, donated $3.9 million to the University of Miami…the money was directed to construction costs for the remodeling of the baseball stadium, as well as scholarship money for the Boys & Girls Clubs of Miami-Dade…one student from the Club will be awarded a four-year scholarship to the University each year…the scholarship will be awarded in perpetuity, so an unlimited number of children benefit from this donation…in 2005, donated $200,000 to the Children's Aid Society, a New York City-based children's advocacy and charity group…his donation supported the placement of therapists into schools located in Washington Heights—the neighborhood in which Alex was born…the donation will fund the project for an entire school year.

▸ Also in 2005, Alex donated $50,000 to the Dominican Republic branch of UNICEF…this donation fully funded five day-care centers outside of Santo Domingo…these five centers were able to purchase enough school supplies, food and personal hygiene products for one full year, with over 1,500 students benefiting from his contribution.

▸ Is dedicated to positively impacting families in distress by supporting programs focusing on improved quality of life, education and mental health…teamed up with hip-hop icon Jay-Z on 11/15/06 to host a celebrity poker tournament with over $500,000 in proceeds going to charitable endeavors of both men…co-hosted Family Fun Day at the Miami Seaquarium in January 2007 with the Ronald McDonald House Charities of South Florida…authored a children's picture book in February 2007, "Out of the Ballpark," published in English and Spanish…hosted a book signing at FAO Schwartz in Manhattan on 7/20/07 and read to a group of 9 year olds…participated in a Q & A session with Michael Kay for 500 kids from local community groups at Niketown in New York on 8/1/07.

▸ Received a 2007 Thurman Munson Award for his accomplishments on the field and his philanthropic work within the community…was also honored with the 2008 Sid Mercer Award, presented by the New York chapter of the BBWAA to their "Player of the Year"…was presented the Key to the City by New York City Mayor Michael Bloomberg on 8/16/07 during an on-field, pregame ceremony in recognition of his 500th home run.

▸ Was presented with a plaque by the United Youth Baseball League on 4/4/08 after donating $10,000 to the league to help pay for field fees, insurance and uniforms for the kids…spoke to 2,000 local Bronx kids about the importance of education and practice in life at Macombs Dam Park, adjacent to Yankee Stadium in July 2008…held a hitting clinic at a youth sports complex in Mexico City in November 2008.

▸ Donated $250,000 towards the completion of the new Pediatric Outpatient Unit at Bronx-Lebanon Hospital in New York City in 2008, aimed at providing quality medical attention for local children who are not covered by insurance…participated in the opening ceremony of the Alex Rodriguez Pediatric Outpatient Center on 6/30/10…also pledged another $250,000 over the next five years to fund the Community DentCare Network from the Columbia University College of Dentistry, sponsoring mobile vans in the Bronx and Washington Heights areas that provide dental care and education to those who cannot otherwise afford it.

▸ Joined actor Richard Gere as coaches for an All-Star Little League game at Franz Sigel Park in the Bronx on 6/6/09…served as "Chef-for-a-Day" each of the last two seasons at El Nuevo Caridad Restaurant in Washington Heights, feeding nearly 50 neighborhood kids…played in community stickball game across the street from Yankee Stadium on 8/29/09.

▸ Collected donations from fans at the Yankees' 16th Annual Holiday Food Drive on 12/17/09 at Yankee Stadium…hosted six high-achieving students from the Bronx Preparatory Charter School ("Bronx Prep") for a private lunch at Yankee Stadium on 8/8/10.

Rodriguez's Career Playing Record

Year	Club	AVG	G	AB	R	H	2B	3B	HR	RBI	SH	SF	HP	BB	SO	SB	CS	E	OBP	SLG
1994	Appleton	.319	65	248	49	79	17	6	14	55	1	3	2	24	44	16	5	19	.379	.605
	Jacksonville	.288	17	59	7	17	4	1	1	8	0	0	0	10	13	2	1	3	.391	.441
	SEATTLE	.204	17	54	4	11	0	0	0	2	1	1	0	3	20	3	0	6	.241	.204
	Calgary	.311	32	119	22	37	7	4	6	21	0	0	1	8	25	2	4	3	.359	.588
1995	Tacoma	.360	54	214	37	77	12	3	15	45	1	2	2	18	44	2	4	10	.411	.654
	SEATTLE	.232	48	142	15	33	6	2	5	19	1	0	0	6	42	4	2	8	.264	.408
1996	SEATTLE - a	.358	146	601	141	215	54	1	36	123	6	7	4	59	104	15	4	15	.414	.631
	Tacoma	.200	2	5	0	1	0	0	0	0	0	0	0	2	1	0	0	1	.429	.200
1997	SEATTLE - b	.300	141	587	100	176	40	3	23	84	4	1	5	41	99	29	6	24	.350	.496
1998	SEATTLE	.310	161	686	123	213	35	5	42	124	3	4	10	45	121	46	13	18	.360	.560
1999	SEATTLE - c	.285	129	502	110	143	25	0	42	111	1	8	5	56	109	21	7	14	.357	.586
2000	SEATTLE - d	.316	148	554	134	175	34	2	41	132	0	11	7	100	121	15	4	10	.420	.606
2001	TEXAS - e	.318	162	632	133	201	34	1	52	135	0	9	16	75	131	18	3	18	.399	.622
2002	TEXAS	.300	162	624	125	187	27	2	57	142	0	4	10	87	122	9	4	10	.392	.623
2003	TEXAS	.298	161	607	124	181	30	6	47	118	0	6	15	87	126	17	3	8	.396	.600
2004	YANKEES - f	.286	155	601	112	172	24	2	36	106	0	7	10	80	131	28	4	13	.375	.512
2005	YANKEES	.321	162	605	124	194	29	1	48	130	0	3	16	91	139	21	6	12	.421	.610
2006	YANKEES	.290	154	572	113	166	26	1	35	121	0	4	8	90	139	15	4	24	.392	.523
2007	YANKEES	.314	158	583	143	183	31	0	54	156	0	9	21	95	120	24	4	13	.422	.645
2008	YANKEES - g	.302	138	510	104	154	33	0	35	103	0	5	14	65	117	18	3	10	.392	.573
2009	YANKEES - h	.286	124	444	78	127	17	1	30	100	0	3	8	80	97	14	2	9	.402	.532
2010	YANKEES - i	.270	137	522	74	141	29	2	30	125	0	11	3	59	98	4	3	7	.341	.506
Minor League Totals		**.327**	**170**	**645**	**115**	**211**	**40**	**14**	**36**	**129**	**2**	**5**	**5**	**62**	**127**	**22**	**14**	**36**	**.388**	**.600**
Major League Totals		**.303**	**2303**	**8826**	**1757**	**2672**	**474**	**29**	**613**	**1831**	**16**	**93**	**152**	**1119**	**1836**	**301**	**72**	**219**	**.387**	**.571**
NYY Total		**.296**	**1027**	**3833**	**748**	**1136**	**189**	**7**	**268**	**840**	**0**	**42**	**80**	**559**	**839**	**124**	**26**	**88**	**.393**	**.559**

* League leader   # Tied for league lead

Selected by Seattle in the first round (first pick overall) of the 1993 First-Year Player Draft.

a – Placed on the 15-day disabled list from April 22 - May 7, 1996 with a pulled left hamstring.
b – Placed on the 15-day disabled list from June 12-27, 1997 with a deep chest bruise.
c – Placed on the 15-day disabled list from April 7 - May 14, 1999 with torn cartilage in his left knee.
d – Placed on the 15-day disabled list from July 8-24, 2000 with a right knee strain.
e – Signed by Texas as a free agent on December 11, 2000.
f – Traded to New York (AL) on February 16, 2004 with cash in exchange for 2B Alfonso Soriano and player to be named later (INF Joaquin Arias).
g – Placed on the 15-day disabled list from April 30 - May 20, 2008 with a strained right quadriceps.
h – Placed on the 15-day disabled list on April 4 (retroactive to March 27) – May 8, 2009 with a right hip labral tear.
i – Placed on the 15-day disabled list from August 21-September 4, 2010 with a strained left calf.

Rodriguez's Division Series Record

YEAR	TEAM	AVG	G	AB	R	H	2B	3B	HR	RBI	SH	SF	HP	BB	SO	SB	CS	E	OBP	SLG
1995	SEA vs. NYY	.000	1	1	1	0	0	0	0	0	0	0	0	0	0	0	0	0	.000	.000
1997	SEA vs. BAL	.313	4	16	1	5	1	0	1	1	0	0	0	0	5	0	0	0	.313	.563
2000	SEA vs. CWS	.308	3	13	0	4	0	0	0	2	1	0	0	0	2	0	1	0	.308	.308
2004	NYY vs. MIN	.421	4	19	3	8	3	0	1	3	0	0	0	2	1	2	1	0	.476	.737
2005	NYY vs. LAA	.133	5	15	2	2	1	0	0	0	0	0	2	6	5	1	1	1	.435	.200
2006	NYY vs. DET	.071	4	14	0	1	0	0	0	0	0	0	1	0	4	0	0	1	.133	.071
2007	NYY vs. CLE	.267	4	15	2	4	0	0	1	1	0	0	0	2	6	0	0	0	.353	.467
2009	NYY vs. MIN	.455	3	11	4	5	0	0	2	6	0	0	0	1	2	0	0	0	.500	1.000
2010	NYY vs. MIN	.273	3	11	1	3	0	0	0	1	0	1	0	1	2	1	0	0	.308	.273
Division Series Totals		**.278**	**31**	**115**	**14**	**32**	**5**	**0**	**5**	**14**	**1**	**1**	**3**	**12**	**27**	**4**	**3**	**2**	**.359**	**.452**

Rodriguez's League Championship Series Record

Year	Club vs. Opp.	AVG	G	AB	R	H	2B	3B	HR	RBI	SH	SF	HP	BB	SO	SB	CS	E	OBP	SLG
1995	SEA vs. CLE	.000	1	1	0	0	0	0	0	0	0	0	0	0	1	0	0	0	.000	.000
2000	SEA vs. NYY	.409	6	22	4	9	2	0	2	5	0	0	0	3	8	1	0	0	.480	.773
2004	NYY vs. BOS	.258	7	31	8	8	2	0	2	5	0	0	2	4	6	0	0	0	.378	.516
2009	NYY vs. LAA	.429	6	21	6	9	2	0	3	6	0	0	1	8	3	1	0	0	.567	.952
2010	NYY vs. TEX	.190	6	21	4	4	2	0	0	2	0	1	0	3	4	1	0	1	.320	.286
LCS Totals		**.313**	**26**	**96**	**22**	**30**	**8**	**0**	**7**	**18**	**0**	**1**	**3**	**18**	**22**	**3**	**0**	**1**	**.432**	**.615**

Rodriguez's World Series Record

Year	Club vs. Opp.	AVG	G	AB	R	H	2B	3B	HR	RBI	SH	SF	HP	BB	SO	SB	CS	E	OBP	SLG
2009	NYY vs. PHI	.250	6	20	5	5	3	0	1	6	0	0	3	3	8	1	0	0	.423	.550
World Series Totals		**.250**	**6**	**20**	**5**	**5**	**3**	**0**	**1**	**6**	**0**	**0**	**3**	**3**	**8**	**1**	**0**	**0**	**.423**	**.550**
POSTSEASON TOTALS		**.290**	**63**	**231**	**41**	**67**	**16**	**0**	**13**	**38**	**1**	**2**	**9**	**33**	**57**	**8**	**3**	**4**	**.396**	**.528**

Rodriguez's All-Star Game Record

Year	Club, Site	AVG	G	AB	R	H	2B	3B	HR	RBI	SH	SF	HP	BB	SO	SB	CS	E	OBP	SLG
1996	SEA, Philadelphia	.000	1	1	0	0	0	0	0	0	0	0	0	0	0	0	0	0	.000	.000
1997	SEA, Cleveland	.333	1	3	0	1	0	0	0	0	0	0	0	0	2	0	0	0	.333	.333
1998	SEA, Colorado	.667	1	3	2	2	0	0	1	0	0	0	0	0	1	0	0	0	.667	1.667
2000	SEA, Atlanta								Injured - Did Not Play											
2001	TEX, Seattle	.000	1	2	0	0	0	0	0	0	0	0	0	0	2	0	0	0	.000	.000
2002	TEX, Milwaukee	.000	1	2	0	0	0	0	0	0	0	0	0	0	2	0	0	0	.000	.000
2003	TEX, Chicago-AL	.333	1	3	1	1	0	0	0	0	0	0	0	0	1	0	0	0	.333	.333
2004	NYY, Houston	.333	1	3	0	1	0	1	0	1	0	0	0	0	1	0	0	0	.333	1.000
2005	NYY, Detroit	.500	1	2	1	1	0	0	0	0	0	0	1	0	0	0	0	0	.667	.500
2006	NYY, Pittsburgh	.000	1	2	0	0	0	0	0	0	0	0	0	0	0	0	0	0	.000	.000
2007	NYY, San Francisco	.333	1	3	0	1	0	0	0	0	0	0	0	0	0	0	0	0	.333	.333
2008	NYY, New York-AL	.000	1	2	0	0	0	0	0	0	0	0	0	0	0	0	0	0	.000	.000
2010	NYY, Los Angeles-AL								Selected - Did Not Play											
All-Star Game Totals		**.269**	**11**	**26**	**4**	**7**	**0**	**1**	**1**	**2**	**0**	**0**	**0**	**1**	**10**	**1**	**0**	**0**	**.296**	**.462**

Rodriguez's World Baseball Classic Record

Year	Country, Site	AVG	G	AB	R	H	2B	3B	HR	RBI	SH	SF	HP	BB	SO	SB	CS	E	OBP	SLG
2006	USA, USA	.333	6	21	3	7	1	0	0	3	0	0	0	2	7	0	0	0	.391	.381

Rodriguez's Career Fielding Record

Position	PCT	G	PO	A	E	TC
Third Base	.964	992	617	1738	88	2443
Shortstop	.977	1272	2014	3605	131	5750

Rodriguez's Home Run Chart

MULTI-HOMER GAMES: 58. **TWO-HOMER GAMES:** 54, last on 9/26/10 vs. Boston. **THREE-HOMER GAMES:** 4, last on 8/14/10 at Kansas City. **GRAND SLAMS:** 21, last on 7/6/10 at Oakland (Trevor Cahill). **PINCH-HIT HR:** None. **INSIDE-THE-PARK HR:** None. **WALK-OFF HR:** 9 (six as a Yankee), last on 8/7/09 vs. Boston (Junichi Tazawa). **LEADOFF HR:** None.

Triple Your Pleasure

The Yankees turned a triple play in the sixth inning of their April 22, 2010 loss at Oakland (5-4-3 – Alex Rodriguez to Robinson Cano to Nick Johnson on a ground ball hit by Kurt Suzuki), marking the team's first since June 3, 1968 vs. Minnesota, when the Twins' Johnny Roseboro hit into a 1-5-3 (Dooley Womack to Bobby Cox to Mickey Mantle). The Yankees had gone 6,632 regular season games between turning triple plays, during which every other Major League team had made at least one triple play and the Yankees themselves had hit into nine triple plays.

KEVIN RUSSO

INFIELDER • 5-11 • 190 •B/T: RIGHT/RIGHT: OPENING DAY AGE: 26

BIRTHDATE
July 8, 1984

BIRTHPLACE
West Babylon, N.Y.

RESIDES
Boulder, Colo.

M.L. SERVICE
86 days

COLLEGE
Baylor University

STATUS
- Selected by the Yankees in the 20th round of the 2006 First-Year Player Draft…signed through the 2011 season.

2010
- Hit .184 (9-for-49) with 5R, 2 doubles and 4RBI in 31 games (10 starts in LF, three at 3B) over three stints with the Yankees (5/8-13, 5/20-7/16, 9/12-10/3)…also appeared defensively at 2B in two games.
- Was recalled from Triple-A Scranton/Wilkes-Barre on 5/8 and made his Major League debut that day at Boston, entering the game in the eighth at 2B and going 0-for-1…was 0-for-2 in four games before being optioned back to Scranton/WB on 5/13 when Juan Miranda was recalled.
- Was recalled from Scranton/WB for a second time on 5/20 when C Jorge Posada went on the disabled list.
- Made his first Major League start in 5/21 win at the Mets, driving in both Yankees runs in the 2-1 win…recorded his first Major League hit—a third-inning single off Hisanori Takahashi—going 2-for-3 with 2RBI before being removed defensively in the seventh…recorded his first career RBI with a game-winning two-run double in the seventh.
- According to the *Elias Sports Bureau*, became the first Major Leaguer to drive in all of his team's runs in a victory in his first Major League start since Montreal's Shane Andrews in a 2-1 win at Pittsburgh on 4/27/95…*Elias* also notes that no Yankee had accomplished that feat in the Expansion Era (since 1961) and Archie Moore was the last Yankee to drive in all of his club's runs in his first Major League start (in a 2-1 Yankees loss on 10/4/64 vs. Cleveland).
- Was optioned to Scranton/WB on 7/16 when Juan Miranda was recalled…returned to the Yankees a third time as a September recall on 9/12…appeared in two games following his recall, going 0-for-1.
- In 81 games with Triple-A Scranton/Wilkes-Barre, hit .259 (86-for-332) with 41R, 16 doubles, 1HR and 24RBI…saw time at 2B, 3B, SS, LF, CF, RF and DH…combined for a .966 fielding percentage (9E, 256TC).
- Hit safely in a season-high 12 straight games from 4/28-5/16, batting .380 (19-for-50) with 9R, 3 doubles, 1 triple, 1HR and 9RBI…had three 3H games during the stretch (4/29 vs. Louisville, 5/2 at Norfolk and 5/6 at Durham).
- In four postseason games for Scranton/WB, hit .143 (2-for-14) with 2R, 1 triple, 1RBI, 3BB and 1SB.

2009
- Played the entire season with Triple-A Scranton/Wilkes-Barre, batting .326 (115-for-353) with 51R, 18 doubles, 5HR, 31RBI and 13SB in 90 games…led all Yankees minor leaguers in batting average…ranked third in the International League in batting average and fourth in the IL with a team-high .397 on-base percentage…had 34 multi-hit games.

BESTS & STREAKS

Hits
2 - 2 times
Last: at MIN, 5/26/10
Runs
1 - 5 times
Last: vs. HOU, 6/11/10
2B
1 - 2 times
Last: at MIN, 5/26/10
3B
N/A
HR
N/A
RBI
2 - at NYM, 5/21/10
BB
1 - 3 times
Last: vs. HOU, 6/11/10
SO
1 - 9 times
Last: at TB, 9/23/10
SB
1 - vs. HOU, 6/11/10
Hit Streak
2g - 2 times
Last: 6/12-16/10

- Was named to the International League's 2009 postseason All-Star team as the league's top second baseman and the Topps Triple-A All-Star Team as the top 2B…also appeared in games at shortstop and third base.
- Batted primarily in the leadoff position, hitting .329 (112-for-340) as the No. 1 batter…owned a .407 batting average in the first inning (33-for-81).
- Hit safely in his first six games of the season and 12 of the first 13…had two stints on the disabled list with a strained right hamstring, from 4/16-5/3 and 5/12-6/6…batted .600 (9-for-15) in four games between stints.
- Appeared in all seven postseason games for the IL Champion SWB Yankees, batting .125 (4-for-32) with 4RBI.

2008

- Hit .307 with 17 doubles, 3 triples, 2HR and 33RBI in 71 games with Double-A Trenton, appearing in games at 2B, 3B and the outfield.
- Missed nearly two months from 6/14-7/30 on the disabled list after fracturing his left cheekbone when he was hit by a batting practice grounder prior to 6/6 game.
- Started all seven postseason games at 3B for the Eastern League champions, batting .174 (4-for-23).
- Appeared in 30 games with the Peoria Javelinas of the Arizona Fall League following the season, batting .309 with 16R, 8 doubles, 3HR and 16RBI, leading Yankees winter leaguers with 34H.

2007

- With Single-A Tampa, hit .281 with 22 doubles, 3 triples, 2HR and 45RBI in 109 games…was successful in 19-of-25 stolen base attempts, including 10 of his first 11 tries.
- Named by *Baseball America* as the best defensive second baseman in the Florida State League…started at 2B in the FSL midseason All-Star Game…appeared in 104 games at 2B, recording a .977 fielding percentage (13E, 559TC)…was involved in 81 double plays, second-most among FSL second basemen.
- Hit safely in 19 of 20 games from 4/26-5/22, including a career-high 12 straight games from 4/26-5/12 (.426, 20-for-47)…batted .338 in July (25-for-74).

2006

- Made professional debut with the Yankees' Gulf Coast League team, batting .273 in 45 games (36 at 2B, 11 at 3B)…was among the most difficult batters in the league to strike out, ranking third in K/PA ratio (1/10.06)…ranked fifth in the league with a .383 on-base percentage.
- Led all GCL second basemen with a .986 fielding percentage, committing only two errors in 142 total chances.

PERSONAL

- Was drafted out of Baylor University, where he was named to the 2006 Preseason All-Big 12 Conference team by *Baseball America*, received a 2005 All-Big 12 Conference Honorable Mention and was a three-time member of the Big 12 Conference Commissioner's Honor Roll…was one of four players to start every game in 2005, establishing a school record…at San Jacinto JC in 2004, earned Junior College World Series all-tournament honors…graduated from Fairview High School in Boulder, Colo., where he was a first-team all-state honoree as a senior and a two-time first-team All-Centennial League and first-team all-region selection.

Russo's Career Batting Record

Year Club		AVG	G	AB	R	H	2B	3B	HR	RBI	SH	SF	HP	BB	SO	SB	CS	E	OBP	SLG
2006	GCL Yankees	.273	45	150	23	41	10	0	3	23	1	2	8	20	18	6	2	4	.383	.400
2007	Tampa	.281	109	385	47	108	22	3	2	45	3	6	5	15	66	19	6	14	.311	.369
2008	Trenton	.307	71	267	46	82	17	3	2	33	3	3	2	23	42	8	3	9	.363	.416
2009	Scranton/WB	.326	90	353	51	115	18	2	5	31	3	5	3	42	55	13	7	12	.397	.431
2010	Scranton/WB	.259	81	332	41	86	16	2	1	24	1	0	9	28	65	9	4	9	.333	.328
	YANKEES	.184	31	49	5	9	2	0	0	4	1	0	1	3	9	1	0	1	.245	.224
Minor League Totals		**.291**	**396**	**1487**	**208**	**432**	**83**	**10**	**13**	**156**	**11**	**16**	**27**	**128**	**246**	**55**	**22**	**48**	**.354**	**.386**
Major League Totals		**.184**	**31**	**49**	**5**	**9**	**2**	**0**	**0**	**4**	**1**	**0**	**1**	**3**	**9**	**1**	**0**	**1**	**.245**	**.224**

Selected by the Yankees in the 20th round of the 2006 First-Year Player Draft.

Russo's Career Fielding Record

Position	PCT	G	PO	A	E	TC	DP
Second Base	1.000	2	2	1	0	3	0
Third Base	1.000	16	4	6	0	10	1
Outfield	.933	11	14	0	1	15	0

52
CC SABATHIA

LEFT-HANDED PITCHER • 6-7 • 290 • B/T: LEFT/LEFT • OPENING DAY AGE: 30

BIRTHDATE
July 21, 1980

BIRTHPLACE
Vallejo, Calif.

RESIDES
Alpine, N.J.

M.L. SERVICE
10 years

CAREER HIGHLIGHTS
A.L. Cy Young Award
‣ 2007

A.L. All-Star Team
‣ 2003, 2004, 2007,
2010

ALCS MVP
‣ 2009

STATUS
‣ Signed as a free agent to a seven-year contract on December 18, 2008…contract extends through the 2015 season.

CAREER NOTES
‣ Since his debut in 2001, has a 157-88 (.641) record, marking the most wins in the Majors…is second in shutouts (11), third in complete games (30) and IP (2127.0), and fourth in strikeouts (1,787) and starts (322) over the span…owns the fifth-highest winning percentage among active pitchers.

‣ Has gone 88-43 (.672) over the last five seasons (2006-10), leading the Majors in strikeouts, ranking second in wins, innings pitched (1154.1) and shutouts (9), and tying for fourth in starts (165) over the stretch.

‣ Among active Major League lefthanders (min 1,000.0IP), ranks second in ERA (3.57) and winning percentage (.641), third in wins (157), fourth in strikeouts (1,787), and sixth in IP (2127.0) and starts (322).

‣ Recorded 40 wins from 2009-10, marking the most by a Yankee over a two-season stretch since Tommy John's 43 wins in 1979 (21-9) and 1980 (22-9)…also became the first Yankee with at least 230.0IP in two consecutive seasons since John (1979-276.1IP and 1980-265.1IP)…according to the *Elias Sports Bureau*, is one of three Yankees since 1923 to win at least 19 games in each of his first two seasons with the club, joining Tommy John (1979-80) and Herb Pennock (19-6 in 1923 and 21-9 in 1924).

‣ Became the first pitcher to win least 17 games in four consecutive years (2010: 21-7 w/ NYY; 2009: 19-8 w/ NYY; 2008: 17-10 w/ Cleveland and Milwaukee; and 2007: 19-7 w/ Cleveland), since Randy Johnson accomplished the feat in six straight seasons from 1997-2002 (credit: *Elias*)…*Elias* also notes he is the first pitcher to start at least 34 games in four consecutive years (2007-10) since San Francisco's Barry Zito accomplished the feat over a six-season stretch from 2001-06.

‣ Has recorded at least 11 wins in each of his first 10 seasons to begin his Major League career, marking the longest such current streak among active pitchers.

‣ His .641 career winning percentage is ninth-best all time among lefthanders (min: 150 decisions).

‣ Leads all active Major League pitchers under the age of 31 in career wins (157), strikeouts (1,787) and innings pitched (2127.0)…the last Major Leaguer to compile as many wins prior to his 31st birthday was Greg Maddux, who won 166 games before turning 31.

‣ Has participated in the postseason in each of the last four seasons with three different clubs (2009 and '10 w/ the Yankees, 2008 w/ Milwaukee and 2007 w/ Cleveland).

‣ Named to *Sporting News'* 2010 list of the 50 greatest players in baseball today (No. 13), as selected by a panel of 125 Hall of Famers, major award winners and other baseball experts.

BESTS & STREAKS

Low hit CG
1 - at PIT, 8/31/08
IP (start)
9.0 - 23 times
Last: at BAL, 5/8/09
IP (relief)
N/A
Hits
13 - at MIN, 7/15/06
Runs
9 - 5 times
Last: at TB, 10/2/09
BB
6 - 3 times
Last: at OAK, 4/22/10
SO
13 - vs. KC, 9/14/07
HR
3 - 6 times
Last: at DET, 7/5/07
Winning Streak
12g - 6/10-8/31/08
Losing Streak
5g - 7/6-30/05

2010

▸ Was 21-7 (.750) with a 3.18 ERA (237.2IP, 84ER) and 197K in 34 starts with the Yankees, marking his first career 20-win season…opponents batted .239 (209-for-876, 20HR); LH .261 (53-for-203, 4HR) and RH .232 (156-for-673, 16HR)…the Yankees went 23-11 in his starts…finished third in AL Cy Young Award voting and garnered six votes in AL MVP voting (two eighth place, three ninth place and one 10th place).

▸ Became the first American Leaguer to win 21 games since Cleveland's Cliff Lee in 2008 and just the second Yankee in the last 25 years (since 1986) to reach the total (Andy Pettitte, 21-8 in 2003 and 1996).

▸ Ranked among the leaders in wins (first in AL, tied for first in Majors), IP (second in AL, third in Majors), winning percentage

SABATHIA'S 2010 PITCHING LINES

Date/Opp	Score	W/L	IP	H	R	ER	HR	BB	K	NP/K	ERA	Left game
4/4 at BOS	7-9	ND	5.1	6	5	5	0	2	4	104-58	8.44	Leading 5-4
4/10 at TB	10-0	W	7.2	1	0	0	0	2	5	111-69	3.46	Leading 8-0
4/16 vs. TEX	5-1	W	6.0^	3	1	1	0	0	9	73-58	2.84	Leading 5-1
4/22 at OAK	2-4	L	8.0^	4	4	3	1	6	5	97-51	3.00	Trailing 4-2
4/28 at BAL*	8-3	W	7.2	11	3	3	1	2	5	111-72	3.12	Leading 8-3
5/3 vs. BAL	4-1	W	8.0	6	1	1	1	2	2	106-67	2.74	Leading 4-1
5/8 at BOS	14-3	ND	4.2	4	3	3	2	2	4	89-52	3.04	Leading 6-3
5/13 at DET	0-6	L	6.0	9	6	6	2	0	4	79-55	3.71	Trailing 6-0
5/18 vs. BOS	6-7	ND	7.0	4	1	1	1	3	5	112-66	3.43	Leading 5-1
5/23 at NYM*	4-6	L	5.0	10	6	5	2	2	6	93-61	3.86	Trailing 6-0
5/29 vs. CLE	11-13	ND	6.0	7	5	5	0	2	5	113-78	4.16	Leading 10-5
6/3 vs. BAL	6-3	W	7.0	3	3	3	2	1	7	94-60	4.14	Leading 6-3
6/9 at BAL	4-2	W	7.0	9	2	2	0	3	8	114-72	4.01	Leading 4-2
6/15 vs. PHI	8-3	W	7.0	5	3	3	0	3	7	113-68	4.00	Leading 8-3
6/20 vs. NYM	4-0	W	8.0	4	0	0	0	2	6	100-66	3.68	Leading 4-0
6/25 at LAD	2-1	W	8.0	4	1	1	0	3	7	115-75	3.49	Leading 2-1
7/1 vs. SEA*	4-2	W	8.0	5	2	1	0	2	4	117-71	3.33	Leading 4-2
7/6 at OAK	6-1	W	7.2	7	1	1	0	3	10	118-74	3.19	Leading 6-1
7/11 at SEA	8-1	W	7.0	6	1	1	0	1	9	96-61	3.09	Leading 8-1
7/16 vs. TB	5-4	ND	7.0	8	4	3	0	4	6	113-66	3.13	Trailing 4-3
7/22 vs. KC	10-4	W	6.1	11	4	3	0	4	9	120-78	3.18	Leading 5-4
7/27 at CLE	4-1	L	7.0	9	4	2	0	3	5	123-79	3.15	Trailing 4-0
8/1 at TB	0-3	L	6.2	8	3	3	0	3	3	112-67	3.19	Trailing 3-0
8/7 vs. BOS*	5-2	W	8.0	6	2	2	1	1	4	101-62	3.14	Leading 5-2
8/12 at KC	4-3	W	8.2	10	3	3	0	2	3	110-67	3.14	Leading 4-1
8/17 vs. DET*	6-2	W	7.0	5	2	2	3	3	9	115-71	3.12	Leading 6-2
8/22 vs. SEA	10-0	W	6.0	3	0	0	0	0	8	76-54	3.02	Leading 8-0
8/28 at CWS	12-9	W	7.0	9	5	5	2	1	9	113-78	3.14	Leading 10-5
9/2 vs. OAK	5-0	W	8.0	1	0	0	0	3	5	95-58	3.02	Leading 5-0
9/7 vs. BAL	2-6	L	6.1	9	6	5	1	1	5	109-74	3.14	Trailing 6-2
9/13 at TB*	0-1 (11)	ND	8.0	2	0	0	0	2	9	119-77	3.03	Tied 0-0
9/18 at BAL	11-3	W	7.0	7	3	3	1	1	4	104-68	3.05	Leading 8-3
9/23 vs. TB*	3-10	L	5.1	10	7	7	0	3	6	111-71	3.26	Trailing 4-3
9/28 at TOR*	6-1	W	8.1	3	1	1	1	2	8	111-67	3.18	Leading 6-1
Totals	**21-7**		237.2	209	92	84	20	74	197	–	3.18	

(*) Denotes start following a team loss – **Bold indicates season highs** – ^ Denotes complete game

(third in Majors and AL), starts (tied for first in AL, tied for third in Majors), strikeouts (sixth in AL) and ERA (seventh in AL)…became the first Yankee in franchise history to have at least a share of the American League lead in wins in consecutive seasons (also tied for the AL lead with 19 wins in 2009).

▸ Became the 34th different Yankee to record a 20-win season, marking the 59th 20-win season in franchise history…became the ninth Yankees lefthander all time to collect at least 20 wins in a season…marked the most single-season wins by an African-American pitcher in Yankees franchise history…was the Majors' first African-American 20-game winner since Florida's Dontrelle Willis in 2005 (22-10) and the AL's first since Oakland's Dave Stewart in 1990 (21-12).

▸ Became the 26th different Yankee to record a 21-win season (eighth lefty), marking the 43rd 21-win season in franchise history.

▸ Went 11-2 with a 3.00 ERA (111.0IP, 37ER) at Yankee Stadium, beginning the season 11-0 at home…became the first Yankee to win his first 11 home decisions to begin a season since David Cone and David Wells in 1998 (credit: *Elias Sports Bureau*).

▸ Compiled 22 starts in which he held his opponent to 3ER or less and threw at least 7.0IP, the third-highest total in the Majors behind Felix Hernandez (25) and Roy Halladay (23)…went at least 8.0IP in 10 starts.

▸ Did not allow a HR over a career-long 80.2IP stretch between Luke Scott's HR on 6/3 vs. Baltimore and Victor Martinez's second-inning HR on 8/7 vs. Boston.

▸ In his final 22 starts of the season (beginning on 6/3), went 17-4 with a 2.76 ERA (166.1IP, 144H, 51ER, 51BB, 143K), leading the Majors in wins over the stretch.

▸ Was named to his fourth career All-Star team in 2010 (also 2003-04, '07 w/ Cleveland) and was in uniform for the contest in Anaheim, Calif…was not allowed to participate in the game due to the MLB rule barring starting pitchers who pitched on the Sunday prior to the ASG from participating.

- Made his seventh career Opening Day start, second with the Yankees, on 4/4 at Boston, recording a no-decision in the 9-7 Red Sox victory (5.1IP, 6H, 5ER, 2BB, 4K)...became the 22nd pitcher in franchise history to make multiple Opening Day starts, first since Randy Johnson in 2005 and 2006.

- Carried a no-hitter through two outs in the eighth inning of a 10-0 win on 4/10 at Tampa Bay until Kelly Shoppach singled to left field (7.2IP, 1H, 2BB, 5K, 111/69)...was removed immediately following the single...was the furthest he had ever gone in a game without allowing a hit...was the deepest a Yankee had taken a no-hitter since Mike Mussina took a perfect game 8.2IP on 9/2/01 at Boston (Carl Everett single).

- Recorded complete games in two straight starts, despite not throwing 9.0 innings in either start (6.0IP win on 4/16 vs. Texas and 8.0IP loss on 4/22 at Oakland)...became the first Yankee credited with back-to-back complete games since David Wells in September 1998.

- Struck out six straight batters on 4/16 vs. Texas in a rain-shortened complete-game win...marked the most consecutive K's in a game by a Yankee since 8/8/99 when David Cone fanned six in-a-row at Seattle–credit: *Elias*.

- Won a career-high eight consecutive starts from 6/3-7/11, compiling a 1.81 ERA (59.2IP, 43H, 12ER, 18BB, 50K, 2HR)...became the first Yankee to win eight straight starts since Roger Clemens won eight in-a-row from 5/26-7/4/01.

- Made his 300th career start on 6/3 vs. Baltimore, recording the win in a 6-3 Yankees victory...allowed a seventh-inning HR to Luke Scott, the only regular season HR he has surrendered to a left-handed batter at the current Yankee Stadium...snapped a streak of 37 consecutive home starts without allowing a HR to a lefty, dating back to 4/5/08.

- Became the youngest pitcher at the time of his 300th start since Dwight Gooden (age 29 yrs, 205 days on 6/9/94) and the youngest lefty since Fernando Valenzuela (age 29 yrs, 226 days on 6/15/90)–credit: *Elias*...became the eighth pitcher to make his 300th career start with the Yankees since 1955, just the second such pitcher to win (also Jimmy Key in 1994)–credit: *Elias*...his career .627 (141-84) winning pct. was the third-highest among active pitchers through their first 300 career starts behind Tim Hudson (.655, 144-76) and teammate Andy Pettitte (.642, 156-87).

- Allowed 1ER or less in a career-high five straight starts from 6/20-7/11...according to the *Elias Sports Bureau*, it marked the longest such stretch by a Yankee since David Cone in 1999.

SABATHIA ON THE MAJOR LEAGUE AND AL LEADERBOARD IN 2010

Statistic		AL Rank	ML Rank
Wins	21	1	T1
Win Pct	.750	3	3
Innings	237.2	2	3
Starts	34	T1	T3
Strikeouts	197	6	T17
ERA	3.18	7	22

YANKEES 20-GAME WINNERS
(Last 25 years – since 1986)

Player	Record	Year
CC SABATHIA	(21-7)	2010
Mike Mussina	(20-9)	2008
*Andy Pettitte	(21-8)	2003
Roger Clemens	(20-3)	2001
David Cone	(20-7)	1998
*Andy Pettitte	(21-8)	1996
*Left-handed pitcher		

YANKEES LEFTHANDED 20-GAME WINNERS (All time)

Player	No. (Years)
Lefty Gomez	4 (1931-32, '34, '37)
Ron Guidry	3 (1978, '83, '85)
Andy Pettitte	2 (1996, 2003)
Tommy John	2 (1979-80)
Whitey Ford	2 (1961, '63)
Herb Pennock	2 (1924, '26)
CC SABATHIA	1 (2010)
Fritz Peterson	1 (1970)
Ed Lopat	1 (1951)

ADDITIONAL YANKEES 20-WIN NOTES
* Sabathia is the Yankees first 20-game winner since Mike Mussina (20-9 in 2008).
* 34 different Yankees have had a total of 59 20-win seasons since the franchise was established in New York in 1903.
* Red Ruffing, Lefty Gomez and Bob Shawkey have had the most 20-win seasons by a Yankee (four each).
* The Yanks' first 20-win season was 1903, when Jack Chesboro set the still-standing, modern era (since 1900) single-season win mark, going 41-12.

- Made his 50th start as a Yankee on 6/25 at Los Angeles-NL, recording the win to improve his record to 28-11 with 286K as a Yankee...according to the *Elias Sports Bureau*, only two other pitchers posted as many wins and Ks over their first 50 starts with the Yankees: Ron Guidry (31-10, 347K) and David Cone (28-10, 374K).

- Surpassed 2,000.0 career IP in 7/1 win vs. Seattle, becoming the youngest pitcher to reach the mark since Greg Maddux in 1995 and the youngest lefthander since Fernando Valenzuela in 1990.

- Reached the All-Star break with a 12-3 record and a 3.09 ERA, recording the most pre-All-Star break wins by a Yankee since Mike Mussina went 12-3 in the first half of 2002...matched his most wins prior to the All-Star Break (also 12-3 pre-ASG in 2007).

- Was undefeated in 11 starts from 5/29-7/22, going 9-0 with two no-decisions and a 2.62 ERA (79.0IP, 69H, 23ER, 28BB, 70K, 2HR).

- Recorded his 150th career victory on 8/7 vs. Boston...reached the plateau with just 86 losses (a .636 winning pct.)...according to the *Elias Sports Bureau*, only three active pitchers at the time reached the plateau with fewer losses (Roy Halladay was 150-76, Tim Hudson was 150-79, and Andy Pettitte was 150-79).

- Suffered the loss on 9/7 vs. Baltimore, his first loss at Yankee Stadium since 7/2/09, snapping a 21-start undefeated streak at home…over the stretch, went 16-0 with a 2.05 ERA (149.0IP, 34ER) as the Yankees went 19-2 in those starts…according to the *Elias Sports Bureau*, the streak tied Whitey Ford (8/8/64-8/18/65 at the original Yankee Stadium) for the longest undefeated streak of starts by a Yankee at any Stadium (home or away)…it was the longest undefeated streak of starts by any pitcher at any stadium since Johan Santana's 24-start undefeated streak at the Metrodome from 8/6/05-4/2/07…*Elias* also notes that Sabathia's 16-game home winning streak matched Johnny Allen (1932-33) and Ron Guidry (1985-86) for the longest in franchise history.

- Recorded his 20th win on 9/18 at Baltimore in an 11-3 Yankees victory (7.0IP, 7H, 3ER, 1BB, 4K, 1HR)…won his 21st game on 9/28 at Toronto, limiting the Jays to 3H and 1ER in 8.1IP (2BB, 8K, 1HR).

- Went 2-0 with a 5.63 ERA in three postseason starts…started ADS Game 1 and ALCS Game 1 - his sixth and seventh career Game 1 starts, putting him in a four-way tie for the fourth-most all time, trailing only Greg Maddux (11), Whitey Ford (8) and Roger Clemens (8).

2009

- Was 19-8 with a 3.37 ERA and two complete games in 34 starts with the Yankees, tying for the Major League lead in wins with Seattle's Felix Hernandez, Detroit's Justin Verlander and St. Louis' Adam Wainwright…was third in the American League with a .232 opponents batting average against (197-for-849, 18HR), and fourth in both IP (230.0) and ERA (3.37)…left-handed batters hit just .198 (39-for-197, 3HR) against him, while righties batted .242 (158-for-652, 15HR)…the Yankees were 22-12 in his starts.

- With 19 wins, surpassed Dock Ellis' (17-8 in 1976) record for most single-season victories by an African-American pitcher…marked the most wins by a Yankee in his first season with the franchise since Tommy John in 1979 (21-9).

- Began the season 1-3 with a 4.85 ERA (39.0IP, 21ER) in his first six starts, then posted an 18-5 record with a 3.06 ERA (191.0IP, 65ER) in 28 starts from 5/8 through the end of the season.

- Led the Majors in wins after the All-Star break, compiling an 11-2 record with a 2.74 ERA in 15 starts…the Yankees went 13-2 in his post-All-Star break starts, which included an 11-start undefeated stretch from 8/2-9/26 in which he went 9-0 with a 2.04 ERA (79.1IP, 56H, 18ER, 19BB, 85K, 6HR).

- Compiled a 12-6 record with a 3.53 ERA on the road, tying Texas' Scott Feldman and St. Louis' Adam Wainwright for the most road wins among all Major League pitchers…marked the most road wins by a Yankee since Ron Guidry went 13-2 away from the original Yankee Stadium in 1978.

- Tossed at least 7.0IP in 24 of his 34 starts, the most such starts in a season by a Yankee since Melido Perez (27) in 1992 and the most while also allowing 3ER or less (20) since Mike Mussina in 2001 (21).

- Selected as the recipient of the "Warren Spahn Award" as the season's top left-handed pitcher for the third straight year (given by the Oklahoma Sports Museum)…placed fourth in AL Cy Young Award voting and received one eighth-place vote for AL MVP.

- Made his sixth career Opening Day start on 4/6 at Baltimore, recording the loss in a 10-5 Orioles victory (4.1IP, 8H, 6ER, 5BB, 0K)…marked just the fifth time in his career that he failed to strike out a batter and first since 7/25/05 at Oakland (w/ Cleveland)…according to *Elias*, he became the first Yankees starter to not record a strikeout in an Opening Day assignment since George Mogridge in 1918…was the Yankees' first African-American Opening Day starter.

LAST 10 YEARS (2001-10)

WINS
1. CC SABATHIA 157
2. Roy Halladay 156
3. Roy Oswalt 150
4. Mark Buehrle 144
5. Derek Lowe 142

INNINGS PITCHED
1. Mark Beuhrle 2220.0
2. Livan Hernandez 2173.0
3. CC SABATHIA 2127.0
4. Barry Zito 2105.2
5. Javier Vazquez 2102.2

STRIKEOUTS
1. Javier Vazquez 1,926
2. Randy Johnson 1,835
3. Johan Santana 1,813
4. CC SABATHIA 1,787
5. Roy Oswalt 1,666

COMPLETE GAMES
1. Roy Halladay 56
2. Livan Hernandez 33
3. CC SABATHIA 30
4. Mark Buehrle 27
5. Mark Mulder 25

MOST RBI, ALL-TIME IN INTERLEAGUE PLAY BY AL PITCHER (1997-2010)
1. CC SABATHIA 8
2. Josh Beckett 5
   Felix Hernandez 5
   Mike Mussina 5
5. Jon Garland 4
   Jarrod Washburn 4

HIGHEST CAREER WINNING PERCENTAGE, ACTIVE LHP (min. 150 dec.)
1. Johan Santana .... .658 (133-69)
2. CC SABATHIA .... .641 (157-88)
3. Andy Pettitte .... .635 (240-138)
4. Cliff Lee .... .626 (102-61)
5. Mark Buehrle .... .574 (148-110)

BEST HOME WINNING PERCENTAGE IN MAJORS, LAST TWO SEASONS (2009-10)
1. CC SABATHIA .... .818 (18-4)
2. Justin Verlander .... .815 (22-5)
3. Tommy Hunter .... .813 (13-3)
4. Kevon Slowey .... .800 (16-4)
5. David Price .... .773 (17-5)

- Started the first-ever regular season game in Yankee Stadium on 4/16 vs. Cleveland, leaving without a decision in a 10-2 Indians victory.

- Recorded a 4-0 complete-game shutout victory on 5/8 at Baltimore…marked the first CG-shutout by a Yankee since Chien Ming Wang on 7/28/06 vs. Tampa Bay (2H, 2BB, 1K), snapping a franchise-record 414-game stretch without a Yankees pitcher recording a shutout (credit: *Elias*).

- Exited his start on 6/21 at Florida after 1.1IP with a sore left biceps muscle…did not miss a start.

- Recorded his 1,500th career strikeout on 7/28 at Tampa Bay (Carl Crawford).

- Struck out at least seven batters in a career-high seven straight starts from 8/8-9/7, matching Mike Mussina (4/2-5/7/03 – 7GS) and Ron Guidry (7/14-8/15/78 – 7GS) as the only three Yankees pitchers since 1954 to post seven such consecutive games.

- Made five postseason starts, going 3-1 with a 1.98 ERA (36.1IP, 28H, 9R, 8ER, 9BB, 32K, 4HR, 1HP), limiting opponents to 3ER or less in each outing…started Game 1 in all three rounds, making his two other starts on three-days' rest…earned ALCS MVP after winning both starts with a 1.13 ERA (16.0IP, 2ER)…won his Yankees postseason debut on 10/7 in Game 1 of the ALDS vs. Minnesota (6.2IP, 8H, 2R, 1ER, 0BB, 8K, 1HP), marking just the fifth time in postseason franchise history a Yankees pitcher recorded at least 8K without walking a batter…became the third African-American Yankees pitcher to start a World Series game, joining Dock Ellis and Al Downing…became the seventh Yankee to record three-or-more wins in a single postseason, joining David Wells (1998), Andy Pettitte (2003 and '09), Mike Stanton (2000), Orlando Hernandez (1999 and 2000), Dave Righetti (1981) and Sparky Lyle (1977).

MAJOR LEAGUE LEADERS
(since 2007)

WINS

1.	CC SABATHIA	76
2.	Roy Halladay	74
3.	Justin Verlander	66
4.	Adam Wainwright	64
5.	Dan Haren	57
	Derek Lowe	57

STRIKEOUTS

1.	Tim Lincecum	907
2.	CC SABATHIA	854
3.	Dan Haren	837
4.	Justin Verlander	834
5.	Felix Hernandez	789

INNINGS PITCHED

1.	CC SABATHIA	961.2
2.	Roy Halladay	961.0
3.	Dan Haren	903.0
4.	Felix Hernandez	879.1
5.	Justin Verlander	867.0

2008

- Went 17-10 with a 2.70 ERA in 35 combined starts with Cleveland and Milwaukee…led the Majors in innings pitched (253.0), complete games (10) and shutouts (five), ranked second in strikeouts (251) and fourth in ERA…despite midseason trade, finished fifth in National League Cy Young Award voting and sixth in NL MVP voting.

- Opponents batted .237 (223-for-942, 19HR); LH .205 (48-for-234, 5HR), RH .247 (175-for-708, 14HR)…his five shutouts were the most in a single season since Randy Johnson's six in 1998 and his 10CG were the most since Johnson's 12 in 1999)…marked the most innings pitched by any Major League pitcher since Montreal's Livan Hernandez in 2004 (255.0).

- Lost his first three decisions (0-3, 4GS, 13.50 ERA)…over his remaining 31 starts (beginning 4/22), posted a 17-7 record and a 1.88 ERA, leading the Majors in ERA over the span.

- Opened the year at Cleveland, going 6-8 with a 3.83 ERA in 18 starts before being acquired by Milwaukee on 7/7…finished with 106 wins as an Indian, ranking second all time among club lefthanders behind Sam McDowell (122).

- Won a career-high 12 straight decisions over 16 starts from 6/10-8/31, pitching to a 1.55 ERA over the stretch and striking out 126 batters in 128.0IP with only 28 walks.

- Was acquired by Milwaukee on 7/7 in exchange for OF Matt LaPorta, LHP Zach Johnson, RHP Rob Bryson and a player to be named later (OF Michael Brantley)…became the fifth defending Cy Young Award winner to be traded before the end of the following season, joining Frank Viola, David Cone, Pedro Martinez and Roger Clemens…was leading the AL with 123K at the time of the trade.

- Went 11-2 with a 1.65 ERA in 17 starts as a Brewer, tossing seven complete games and three shutouts…the Brewers went 14-3 in his starts…opponents batted .222 (106-for-478, 6HR)…after joining the Brewers, led the Majors in ERA, tied Cliff Lee for most wins and ranked second in strikeouts (128)…the Brewers went 41-32 (.562) from 7/8 (Sabathia's first start) through the remainder of the year, recording the fifth-best winning percentage in the NL over the span.

- Won his first nine decisions over his first 13 starts after joining Milwaukee, winning the NL "Player of the Month" Award in July (4-0, 2.27 ERA) and August (5-0, 1.12).

- Became the second pitcher in the last 90 years to win his first nine decisions following a midseason change of teams, joining Doyle Alexander who went 9-0 after going from the Braves to the Tigers in 1987.

- Tossed a one-hit shutout on 8/31 at Pittsburgh in a 7-0 win for his ninth career shutout...lone hit was an Andy LaRoche check-swing dribbler back to Sabathia in the fifth inning.
- Made each of his final three starts of the season on three-days' rest, going 2-1 with a 0.83 ERA...included was a complete-game, 3-1 win on 9/28 vs. the Cubs to clinch the Brewers' Wild Card berth (9.0IP, 4H, 1R, 0ER, 1BB, 7K) on the final day of the season.
- Recorded the loss in his only postseason start on 10/2 at Philadelphia in Game 2 of the NLDS, allowing 5ER in 3.2IP.

YOUNGEST TO REACH 100 WINS SINCE			
By a...	Name	Since Date	Years+Days
	CC SABATHIA (CLE)	9/28/07	27+069
P	G. Maddux (ATL)	5/31/93	27+047
AL P	B. Saberhagen (KC)	5/10/91	27+029
LHP	F. Valenzuela (LAD)	4/12/87	26+162
AL LHP	V. Blue (OAK)	7/23/76	26+361
		Courtesy: BASEBALL REFERENCE	

YOUNGEST TO REACH 1,000 STRIKEOUTS SINCE...			
By a...	Name	Since Date	Years+Days
	CC SABATHIA (CLE)	5/21/07	26+304
P	K. Wood (CHC)	8/11/03	26+056
AL P	R. Clemens (BOS)	4/31/89	26+252
LHP	F. Valenzuela (LAD)	8/31/85	24+303
AL LHP	F. Tanana (DET)	6/20/78	24+325
		Courtesy: BASEBALL REFERENCE	

2007

- Won the American League Cy Young Award after compiling a 19-7 record with a 3.21 ERA and 209K...set career highs in wins, starts (34) and innings pitched (241.0)...became just the second Indian to win the award, joining Gaylord Perry (1972)...marked the most wins by a Cleveland left-hander since Sam McDowell (20) in 1970.
- Became the first Cleveland left-hander to lead the Majors in innings pitched, the first Indian since Early Wynn in 1954 to lead the AL in innings pitched and the first Indian since Bob Feller in 1947 to lead the Majors in innings pitched...were the most IP by an Indian since Charles Nagy in 1992.
- Bested Boston's Josh Beckett (119 points to 86) to become the first African-American Cy Young Award winner since Dwight Gooden in 1985 and the first in the AL since Vida Blue in 1971...also placed 14th in AL MVP voting...was named AL "Pitcher of the Year" by the MLBPA and the *Sporting News* and was named Indians "Man of the Year" by the Cleveland chapter of the BBWAA.
- Tied for first in the AL in starts, tied for second in wins, ranked second in complete games (four), third in pitches thrown (3,582), tied for third in winning percentage (.731), placed fifth in strikeouts and tied for ninth in GIDPs induced (23)...along with teammate Fausto Carmona (19 wins), became the first set of Tribe teammates since 1956 to each win at least 19 games...allowed 2ER or less in 20 of 34 starts and lasted 6.0IP in 32 starts.
- Reached double-digit wins for the seventh straight season to begin his career, becoming the second pitcher (and only LHP) in club history to accomplish the feat, joining RHP Addie Joss (1902-09)...no other Indians lefty had won 10+ games in seven straight years at any point in his career.
- Collected the most strikeouts by an Indian since Bartolo Colon (201) in 2001 and the most by an Indians lefthander since Sam McDowell in 1970 (304)...recorded the second-highest K/BB ratio (MLB-best 5.65) by a LHP in MLB history and the highest K/BB ratio ever by an AL lefty...finished second in the AL to Paul Byrd, averaging just 1.38 BB/9.0IP.
- Became the first pitcher to beat Johan Santana three times in the same season (8/3, 8/29 and 9/3).
- Made his fourth career Opening Day start and won at Chicago-AL on 4/2 (6.0IP, 8H, 3R/ER)...began the year 5-0 for the first time in his career, winning nine of his first 10 decisions and 12 of his first 14.
- Went 16 consecutive starts without walking more than one batter from 4/20-7/5, the longest such streak in the Majors in 2007 and longest such stretch by a Cleveland pitcher since 1957.
- Notched his 1,000th career strikeout in 5/21 win vs. Seattle (Ichiro Suzuki in the fifth inning)...collected his fifth career complete-game shutout on 6/5 vs. Kansas City, then tossed 9.0 shutout innings (ND) in his next start on 6/10 at Cincinnati, a 12-inning 1-0 loss to the Reds...stretched his scoreless innings streak to 22.0 in his 6/15 start vs. Atlanta, but lost a 5-4 decision...was named AL "Player of the Week" for 6/25-7/1 (2-0, 2.25 ERA, 16.0IP, 15H, 4ER, 0BB, 16K).
- Did not allow a homer over a 41.0-inning stretch from 7/19-8/19...struck out a career-high 13 batters on 9/14 vs. Kansas City.
- Collected his 19th win of the season and 100th career win in his final start at Kansas City on 9/28 (7.0IP, 8H, 3ER)...became the youngest Major League pitcher (27 years, 70 days) since Greg Maddux in 1993 to win 100 games...of the 16 pitchers to win 300 games from 1900-2007, only three (Christy Mathewson, Maddux and Walter Johnson) were younger than Sabathia at the time of their 100th win...became the youngest Indians lefty ever to win 100 games and youngest overall pitcher since Bob Feller in 1941.
- Went 1-2 with an 8.80 ERA in three playoff starts (15.1IP, 21H, 15ER, 13BB, 14K).

2006

- In a career-low 28 starts, went 12-11 with a 3.22 ERA…was his sixth straight season to begin his career with double-digit wins, becoming just the second pitcher in club history to accomplish the feat, joining Hall of Famer Addie Joss (first eight seasons 1902-09)…became the only lefty in club history with six straight seasons of 10+ wins at any point in a career.
- Opponents batted .247 (182-for-738, 17HR); LH .271 (29-for-107, 3HR), RH .242 (153-for-631, 14HR).
- Led the Majors with six complete games, the most by an Indians LHP since Greg Swindell tossed seven in 1991…had the lowest road ERA (2.90) in the AL and the second-lowest day ERA (2.33) in the AL…ranked third in the AL in ERA, sixth in K/9.0IP (8.03) and opponents' average, and tied for eighth in strikeouts (172).
- Made his third career Opening Day start on 4/2 at Chicago-AL and left the game in the third inning with a strained right oblique muscle (2.1IP, 3H, 3ER, 1BB, 3K)…was placed on the 15-day disabled list the following day…made a rehab assignment on 4/27 for Triple-A Buffalo vs. Syracuse (5.0IP, 6H, 2R, 1ER, 1BB, 5K)…was his second career stint on the D.L.…was activated prior to his 5/2 start vs. Chicago-AL, earning his first win of the season.
- Named AL "Pitcher of the Month" for May, going 5-1 with a 1.20 ERA in six starts after coming off the D.L. on 5/2…tossed his third career shutout on 5/24 at Minnesota (9.0IP, 6H, 0R, 0BB, 8K)…tossed his seventh career complete game while allowing only 3H in 5/19 win vs. Pittsburgh (9.0IP, 1R/ER, 1BB, 9K).
- Underwent arthroscopic surgery on his right knee on 9/29 at the Cleveland Clinic to remove torn cartilage.

2005

- Went 15-10 with a 4.03 ERA in 31 starts…ranked sixth in the AL in K/9.0IP (7.37), seventh in strikeouts, tied for eighth in wins and placed 10th in opponents' average…opponents batted .248 (185-for-745, 19HR); LH .248 (27-for-109, 4HR), RH .248 (158-for-636, 15HR).
- Began the season on the 15-day D.L. (placed on D.L. officially on 3/25; activated on 4/16) after straining his right oblique muscle warming up prior to his first spring start on 3/6 vs. Detroit…was his first trip to the Major League disabled list in his career.
- Hit his first career homer on 5/25 in Cincinnati in the fourth inning off Elizardo Ramirez…had 4RBI on the year (most by an Indians pitcher since 1972).
- Lost a career-high five straight starts from 7/6-7/30, then won seven straight starts from 8/5-9/7, recording the longest winning streak for an Indians pitcher since Ken Schrom in June/July of 1986.
- Tossed a four-hit complete game on 9/7 at Detroit, retiring his last 21 batters faced.
- Had his 2006 club option exercised by Cleveland and was then signed to a two-year extension through 2008 on 4/27.

2004

- Posted an 11-10 record with a 4.12 ERA in 30 starts…was selected to his second consecutive All-Star team, pitching 1.0 inning in the AL win at Houston…had six potential wins blown by the Cleveland bullpen.
- Made his second consecutive Opening Day start on 4/5 at Minnesota (7.0IP, 2H, 0R, 4BB, 9K)…was scratched from his start on 4/22 vs. Kansas City due to an irritated left biceps tendon and did not start from 4/17-30.
- Made his 100th career start on 5/1 vs. Baltimore, earning the win…became only the second Indian to make 100 career starts before age 24, joining Hall of Famer Bob Feller (175GS).
- Left his start on 6/26 vs. Colorado after 1.0 inning with irritation in his left shoulder…after MRI results in Cleveland were negative, traveled for a second opinion to Birmingham, Ala., on 6/28 to visit Dr. James Andrews, who cleared him to return…was 3-0 with a 2.57 ERA in six June starts (35.0IP, 27H, 10ER, 11BB, 26K).
- Notched his 50th career win on 7/27 vs. Detroit at the age of 24 years, 6 days, becoming the youngest pitcher to reach 50 career wins since Atlanta's Steve Avery (10/1/93 at 23 years, 170 days)…according to *Elias*, was the youngest active pitcher at the time to reach 50 career wins
- Tossed the second complete-game shutout of his Major League career on 9/6 at Seattle (9.0IP, 5H, 0R, 1BB, 8K) as he allowed just two runners to second base…sat out last two weeks of season due to a strained right hamstring.

2003

- Was 13-9 with a 3.60 ERA in 30 starts, earning his first career All-Star selection…did not appear in the Midsummer Classic, and at 22 years, 352 days, became the youngest Indians All-Star since RHP Dennis Eckersley in 1977 and the first Tribe All-Star LHP since Greg Swindell in 1989.
- Ranked sixth among AL pitchers with a 3.09 home ERA, eighth with a 3.38 night ERA and 10th in overall ERA…threw at least 5.0 innings in 29 of his 30 starts as the Indians averaged just 3.8 runs per game during his starts (the fifth worst run support among AL starting pitchers).

- Made his first career Opening Day start on 3/31 at Baltimore (ND, 7.0IP, 8H, 2ER, Riske BS) and was the youngest Opening Day starting pitcher (22 years, 252 days) in the Major Leagues since Dwight Gooden (22 years, 143 days) started for the New York Mets on 4/8/86 at Pittsburgh...was also the youngest Indians pitcher to start on Opening Day since Eckersley (21 years old) on 4/10/76 vs. Detroit.
- Tossed his first career complete-game shutout on 8/15 vs. Tampa Bay in a 1-0 win (9.0IP, 4H, 0R, 3BB, 9K)...was the first complete game, 1-0 shutout by a Tribe hurler since Bud Black in 1990 and the Tribe's first 1-0 win since 1997...collected a pinch-hit single off Mike Williams in 15.0-inning game on 6/20 at Pittsburgh in the 11th inning, becoming first Cleveland pitcher with a pinch-hit base hit since Dick Donovan on 7/28/63.

2002

- Went 13-11 with a 4.37 ERA in 33 starts, leading Cleveland pitchers in wins, IP (210.0), starts and strikeouts (149)...was tied for fourth in the AL with a 2.48 day ERA, tied for sixth with 24 induced GIDP, ranked seventh with 0.73 HR allowed per 9.0IP (17HR, 210.0IP), ninth with 3,379 pitches thrown and 10th in strikeouts.
- Became the fifth pitcher since 1987 to win 30 games over his first two seasons in the Majors.
- Took a no-hitter into the eighth inning of his second start at Detroit on 4/7 before yielding a lead-off single to Randall Simon...collected his first Major League hit on 6/15 at Colorado, a single off Dennys Reyes...tossed his first career complete game in 8/18 loss at Anaheim (8.0IP, 8H, 4ER, 3BB, 4K).
- Signed a four-year contract through 2005 with a club option for 2006 on 2/23.

2001

- Saw his first Major League action as a 20-year-old, going 17-5 with a 4.39 ERA in 33 starts, leading all rookie pitchers in wins, starts (33) and strikeouts (171)...became the first Indians rookie since Gene Bearden (20-7) in 1948 to win 17-or-more games in his rookie season...finished second to Seattle's Ichiro Suzuki in the AL BBWAA "Rookie of the Year" voting with 73 points...was the youngest active player in the big leagues all season...led AL rookie pitchers in innings (180.1) and ERA.
- Overall among AL pitchers, ranked third in winning percentage (.773) tied for sixth in wins and ranked seventh in strikeouts...his .228 average against (149-for-654) was the second-lowest mark among AL starters...led the AL with 13 road wins...also paced the AL, allowing a league-low 7.44 H/9.0IP.
- Became the first player to finish a season under 22 years of age with at least 17 wins since Atlanta's Steve Avery (18-8) in 1991 and the first AL pitcher to accomplish the feat since Chicago's Britt Burns in 1980 (19-13)...was the most wins by a left-handed rookie pitcher since Seattle's Dave Fleming in 1992 (17-10).
- After the season, was named the *Sporting News'* AL "Rookie Pitcher of the Year" and was selected to the *Baseball Digest* & Topps Major League All-Rookie Teams.
- Was a member of the Opening Day roster and made his Major League debut on 4/8 vs. Baltimore, drawing a no-decision in Cleveland's 4-3 win (5.2IP, 3H, 3ER, 2BB, 3K, 1HR)...was the youngest pitcher to start and appear in a game for Cleveland since Julian Tavarez in August 1993...registered his first Major League win in his second start on 4/13 at Detroit (5.0IP, 5H, 4R/ER, 2BB, 2K) in a 9-8 Indians victory.
- Won the AL "Rookie of the Month" Award in July, going 3-0 with a 2.83 ERA as the Indians went 6-0 in his starts.
- Won his first postseason start in Game 3 of the ALDS vs. Seattle (6.0IP, 6H, 2ER, 5BB, 5K), becoming the second-youngest pitcher to win a Division Series game behind only the Dodgers' Fernando Valenzuela (defeated Houston in 1981)...also became the youngest Indians pitcher to start a Division Series game and the third-youngest pitcher in Division Series history (youngest in ALDS history) to start a game behind Valenzuela (1981, 20 years, 339 days) and St. Louis' Rick Ankiel (2000, 21 years, 77 days).

2000

- Split the season between Single-A Kinston and Double-A Akron, posting a combined 3.57 ERA (146.1IP, 58ER) in 27 starts over the two stops while striking out an organization-high 159 batters.
- Began the year at Kinston and went 3-2 with a 3.54 ERA in 10 starts, which included a 9.0-inning, two-hit, complete game shutout in his final start there on 5/23 at Myrtle Beach...was promoted to Akron on 5/27, throwing 5.0 or more innings in 23 of his 27 starts with the Aeros.
- Started the Hall of Fame Game for Cleveland against the Arizona Diamondbacks on 7/24 in Cooperstown, N.Y...did not record a decision in the outing (3.0IP, 3H, 3ER, 2BB, 4K, HR)...also pitched in the Futures Game in Atlanta, Ga. for Team USA on 7/10.
- Tabbed as the top prospect in the organization and the No. 2 prospect in the Eastern League by *Baseball America* after the season.

1999

▸ Missed the first two and half months of the season with a bone bruise in his left pitching elbow…was activated off the D.L. on 6/20 and assigned to short-season Single-A Mahoning Valley…made six starts with the Scrappers, which increased by 1.0-inning increments, before being promoted to Single-A Columbus of the South Atlantic League on 7/17…was promoted to Single-A Kinston of the Carolina League on 8/2 where he spent the remainder of the season…combined on the year between his three minor league stops to go 5-3 with a 3.29 ERA in 16 starts (68.1IP, 47H, 25ER, 36BB, 76K)…overall, minor league hitters hit .198 (47-for-237) off him with 4HR.

1998

▸ Signed on 6/29 and was assigned to rookie-level Burlington, where he made five starts and struck out 35 batters in 18.0IP (17.50K/9.0IP)…was ranked by *Baseball America* as Cleveland's second-best prospect, the fourth-best prospect in the Appalachian League and was tabbed as having the best fastball in the organization.

PERSONAL

▸ Full name is Carsten Charles Sabathia…he and his wife, Amber, have two sons, Carsten Charles III and Carter Charles, and two daughters, Jaden Arie and Cyia Cathleen…attended Vallejo Senior High School where he compiled a mark of 6-0 with a 0.77 ERA (46.2IP, 14H, 4ER, 14BB, 82K) during his senior season…was the top high school prospect coming out of Northern California according to *Baseball America*…was also an all-conference tight end in football at Vallejo…had scholarship offers to play college football and had signed a letter of intent at Hawaii…was selected to the 2000 United States Olympic Team Roster and appeared in one pre-Olympic tournament game in Sydney, Australia, but was not on the official 24-man, Gold Medal-winning roster.

▸ In 2009, officially established the CC Sabathia Family Foundation's "PitCCh In" along with his wife, Amber…the foundation is committed to the care and needs of inner-city children while helping to raise self-esteem through sports activities and education.

▸ Through "PitCCh In," the Sabathias have provided backpacks filled with back-to-school essentials and an autographed photo each of the last two years at his elementary school, Loma Vista School in Vallejo, Calif…replicated the charitable endeavor, along with his wife Amber, on 9/8/10 at P.S. 152 in the Bronx…for Thanksgiving 2009, joined Safeway to deliver 500 dinners to Vallejo families in need…played secret Santa for 22 Vallejo teenagers in foster care for Christmas 2009, taking the kids on a shopping spree…provided holiday gifts to children in need through "Toys for Tots" for the fourth straight year…also provided sports equipment to the Madison Square Boys & Girls Club in New York City in 2009.

▸ Renovated Thurmon Field, his former Little League field, in Vallejo, Calif…threw out the first pitch at the field's Spring Classic on 4/19/10…held clinics at the field in January 2010 and 2011, and hosted the Vallejo High Baseball Bash on 1/22/11 to raise funds for his former school…refurbished the Omega Boys & Girls Club in Vallejo in 2010.

▸ Took part in Payless ShoeSource's *Payless Gives Shoes 4 Kids* event on 12/9/10, joining children selected by the PitCCh In Foundation and the Madison Square Boys & Girls Club in a group shoe-shopping trip in New York City.

▸ Hosted a Christmas Caravan in 2010 with Amber, creating four consecutive days of community events in Vallejo focused on infant, youth , teen and adult programs…refurbished a foster home nursery, held a holiday party at the Kaiser Vallejo Pediatric Ward, hosted a shopping excursion for troubled teens who have overcome challenges and refurbished, redecorated and landscaped the Rosewood Women's Home.

▸ Received the Bart Giamatti Award for compassion and community service at the 2011 Baseball Assistance Team (B.A.T.) Dinner…also named a finalist for the 2010 Jefferson Award for Public Service by an athlete…served as Yankees representative for the Pepsi Refresh Project, supporting Out2Play…was honored at the Vallejo Mayor's Community Recognition Dinner on 11/28/09 where he received the Mayor's Achievement Awards.

▸ Joined Carl Crawford at Tropicana Field on 7/29/09 and Orlando Hudson on 5/14/10 at Yankee Stadium to speak to African-American youth and encourage them to get involved with baseball…also served as an MLB spokesman for RBI (Reviving Baseball in Inner Cities)…gave free haircuts to Bronx neighborhood kids at Jordan's Barber Shop on 6/3/09 and 6/1/10.

- Purchased 500 tickets to a Golden State Warriors basketball game in 2009 and distributed them to children from the Boys & Girls Clubs in Oakland and Vallejo…assisted in funding two programs for inner-city children at Tony La Russa's Animal Rescue Foundation in 2009…purchased lights for the 2008 Macy's Holiday Tree as part of a fundraising benefit for the University of California-San Francisco Children's Hospital.

- Was a regular participant in the Indians' Winter Press Caravan and was involved in numerous community endeavors during his tenure with Cleveland, including: OfficeMax Parent-Child Clinics, the Larry Doby RBI Program, Red Cross' "Fire Prevention Week", the Cleveland Scholarship Program, Grand Slam Summer Literacy, High Achievers and the Giant Eagle week-long baseball camps…was also a regular visitor to area hospitals as part of the "Tribe Loving Care" program…co-chaired the Swim for Diabetes and participated in the Dick's Sporting Goods "Shop with a Pro" in 2006-07…danced in the Oakland Ballet's "Nutcracker" in 2005 along with Barry Zito and Tony La Russa for charity…organized the Sabathia Baseball Clinic in his hometown of Vallejo in 2003.

- Since 2005, has teamed with Barry Zito's foundation "Strikeouts For Troops," a national program which provides "comforts of home" to wounded troops being treated in military hospitals nationwide and assists their families…has personally contributed $100 for each strikeout since 2005…participated in adopting 25 military families and providing Thanksgiving and Christmas dinner as well as Christmas gifts for the children from 2007-09.

Sabathia's Career Pitching Record

Year	Club	W	L	ERA	G	GS	CG	SHO	SV	IP	H	R	ER	HR	HP	BB	SO	WP	BK
1998	Burlington	1	0	4.50	5	5	0	0	0	18.0	20	14	9	1	1	8	35	1	1
1999	Mahoning Valley	0	0	1.83	6	6	0	0	0	19.2	9	5	4	0	0	12	27	0	0
	Columbus	2	0	1.08	3	3	0	0	0	16.2	8	2	2	1	1	5	20	1	0
	Kinston	3	3	5.34	7	7	0	0	0	32.0	30	22	19	3	1	19	29	6	0
2000	Kinston	3	2	3.54	10	10	2	2	0	56.0	48	23	22	4	2	24	69	2	1
	Akron	3	7	3.59	17	17	0	0	0	90.1	75	41	36	6	7	48	90	2	1
2001	CLEVELAND	17	5	4.39	33	33	0	0	0	180.1	149	93	88	19	7	95	171	7	3
2002	CLEVELAND	13	11	4.37	33	33	2	0	0	210.0	198	109	102	17	1	88	149	6	*3
2003	CLEVELAND	13	9	3.60	30	30	2	1	0	197.2	190	85	79	19	6	66	141	4	2
2004	CLEVELAND	11	10	4.12	30	30	1	1	0	188.0	176	90	86	20	7	72	139	1	1
2005	Akron	0	1	1.00	2	2	0	0	0	9.0	4	3	1	0	1	2	9	1	0
	CLEVELAND - a	15	10	4.03	31	31	1	0	0	196.2	185	92	88	19	7	62	161	7	0
2006	CLEVELAND - b	12	11	3.22	28	28	*6	*2	0	192.2	182	83	69	17	7	44	172	3	0
	Buffalo	1	0	1.80	1	1	0	0	0	5.0	6	2	1	0	0	1	5	1	0
2007	CLEVELAND	19	7	3.21	34	*34	4	1	0	*241.0	238	94	86	20	8	37	209	1	0
2008	CLEVELAND	6	8	3.83	18	18	3	2	0	122.1	117	54	52	13	3	34	123	1	2
	MILWAUKEE - c	11	2	1.65	17	17	*7	#3	0	130.2	106	31	24	6	4	25	128	1	0
2009	YANKEES - d	#19	8	3.37	34	34	2	1	0	230.0	197	96	86	18	9	67	197	5	0
2010	YANKEES	*21	7	3.18	34	#34	2	0	0	237.2	209	92	84	20	7	74	197	8	1
Minor League Totals		13	13	3.43	51	51	2	2	0	246.2	200	112	94	15	13	119	284	14	3
AL Totals		146	86	3.70	305	305	23	8	0	1996.1	1841	888	820	182	62	639	1659	43	12
NL Totals		11	2	1.65	17	17	7	3	0	130.2	106	31	24	6	4	25	128	1	4
Major League Totals		157	88	3.57	322	322	30	11	0	2127.0	1947	919	844	188	66	664	1787	44	12
NYY Total		40	15	3.27	68	68	4	1	0	467.2	406	188	170	38	16	141	394	13	1

* League leader # Tied for league lead

Selected by Cleveland in the first round (20th overall) of the 1998 First-Year Player Draft.

a – Placed on the 15-day disabled list from March 25 – April 15, 2005 with a right oblique strain.

b – Placed on the 15-day disabled list from April 3 – May 2, 2006 with a right oblique strain.

c – Acquired by Milwaukee from Cleveland on July 7, 2008 in exchange for OF Matt LaPorta, LHP Zach Jackson, RHP Rob Bryson and a player to be named later.

d – Signed by the Yankees as a free agent on December 18, 2008.

Sabathia's Division Series Record

Year	Club vs. Opp.	W	L	ERA	G	GS	CG	SHO	SV	IP	H	R	ER	HR	HP	BB	SO	WP	BK
2001	CLE vs. SEA	1	0	3.00	1	1	0	0	0	6.0	6	2	2	0	0	5	5	0	0
2007	CLE vs. NYY	1	0	5.40	1	1	0	0	0	5.0	4	3	3	2	0	6	5	0	0
2008	MIL vs. PHI	0	1	12.27	1	1	0	0	0	3.2	6	5	5	1	0	4	5	0	0
2009	NYY vs. MIN	1	0	1.35	1	1	0	0	0	6.2	8	2	1	0	1	0	8	1	0
2010	NYY vs. MIN	1	0	4.50	1	1	0	0	0	6.0	5	4	3	1	1	3	5	0	0
Division Series Totals		**4**	**1**	**4.61**	**5**	**5**	**0**	**0**	**0**	**27.1**	**29**	**16**	**14**	**4**	**2**	**18**	**28**	**1**	**0**

Sabathia's League Championship Series Record

Year	Club vs. Opp.	W	L	ERA	G	GS	CG	SHO	SV	IP	H	R	ER	HR	HP	BB	SO	WP	BK
2007	CLE vs. BOS	0	2	10.45	2	2	0	0	0	10.1	17	12	12	1	3	7	9	1	0
2009	NYY vs. LAA	2	0	1.13	2	2	0	0	0	16.0	9	2	2	1	0	3	12	0	0
2010	NYY vs. TEX	1	0	6.30	2	2	0	0	0	10.0	17	7	7	2	0	4	10	1	1
LCS Totals		**3**	**2**	**5.20**	**6**	**6**	**0**	**0**	**0**	**36.1**	**43**	**21**	**21**	**4**	**3**	**14**	**31**	**2**	**1**

Sabathia's World Series Record

Year	Club vs. Opp.	W	L	ERA	G	GS	CG	SHO	SV	IP	H	R	ER	HR	HP	BB	SO	WP	BK
2009	NYY vs. PHI	0	1	3.29	2	2	0	0	0	13.2	11	5	5	3	0	6	12	0	0
World Series Totals		**0**	**1**	**3.29**	**2**	**2**	**0**	**0**	**0**	**13.2**	**11**	**5**	**5**	**3**	**0**	**6**	**12**	**0**	**0**
POSTSEASON TOTALS		**7**	**4**	**4.66**	**13**	**13**	**0**	**0**	**0**	**77.1**	**83**	**42**	**40**	**11**	**5**	**38**	**71**	**3**	**1**

Sabathia's All-Star Game Record

Year	Club, Site	W	L	ERA	G	GS	CG	SHO	SV	IP	H	R	ER	HR	HP	BB	SO	WP	BK
2003	CLE, Chicago-AL				Selected - Did Not Pitch														
2004	CLE, Houston	0	0	27.00	1	0	0	0	0	1.0	4	3	3	0	0	0	0	0	0
2007	CLE, San Francisco	0	0	0.00	1	0	0	0	0	1.0	1	0	0	0	0	0	0	0	0
2010	NYY, Los Angeles-AL				Selected - Did Not Pitch														
All-Star Game Totals		**0**	**0**	**13.50**	**2**	**0**	**0**	**0**	**0**	**2.0**	**5**	**3**	**3**	**0**	**0**	**0**	**0**	**0**	**0**

Sabathia's Regular Season Batting Record

Year	Team	AVG	G	AB	R	H	2B	3B	HR	RBI	SH	SF	HP	BB	SO	SB	CS
2010	NYY	.200	34	5	0	1	0	0	0	0	0	0	0	0	3	0	0
Major League Totals		**.258**	***323**	**92**	**7**	**25**	**3**	**0**	**3**	**14**	**3**	**0**	**0**	**1**	**26**	**0**	**0**

*one game as pinch-hitter

Sabathia's Career Fielding Record

Position	PCT	G	PO	A	E	TC	DP
Pitcher	.955	322	33	218	12	265	17

Most Championships in the Four Major Sports

MLB – NEW YORK YANKEES . . . . (27)
NHL – Montreal Canadiens . . . . (24)
NBA – Boston Celtics . . . .(17)
NFL – Green Bay Packers . . . . (13)
*as of 2/7/11

Closer John Wetteland celebrates with teammates after Game 6 of the 1996 World Series vs. the Atlanta Braves at Yankee Stadium.

64 ROMULO SANCHEZ

RIGHT-HANDED PITCHER • 6-5 • 270 • B/T: RIGHT/RIGHT • OPENING DAY AGE: 26

BIRTHDATE
April 28, 1984

BIRTHPLACE
Carora, Venezuela

RESIDES
Carora, Venezuela

M.L. SERVICE
117 days (Rookie)

STATUS
▸ Acquired by the Yankees from the Pittsburgh Pirates in exchange for minor league RHP Eric Hacker on May 16, 2009…signed through the 2011 season.

2010
▸ Allowed 1H in 4.1IP in two scoreless relief appearances over two stints with the Yankees (5/7-10 and 9/17-10/3).
▸ Was recalled from Triple-A Scranton/Wilkes-Barre on 5/7…made one relief appearance in 5/9 loss at Boston, allowing 1H in 3.2 scoreless IP (1BB, 3K)…was optioned back to Scranton/WB on 5/10.
▸ Returned to the Yankees as a September call-up on 9/17…made his second—and final—appearance in 9/25 loss vs. Boston, tossing 0.2 scoreless IP (2BB, 2K).
▸ Went 10-8 with a 3.97 ERA in 31 games (14 starts) with Scranton/WB, holding opponents to a .232 batting average (88-for-380).
▸ Worked exclusively as a reliever from 7/5 through the end of the season, allowing just 5ER in 25.0IP (1.80 ERA)…overall as a reliever with SWB, went 7-1 with a 1.69 ERA, striking out 37 batters in 32.0IP…posted a 3-7 record with a 4.98 ERA as a starter.
▸ Following the season, pitched with Lara in the Venezuelan Winter League, going 1-2 with one save and a 6.89 ERA (15.2IP, 12ER) in 19 relief appearances.
▸ Did not record a decision in three spring training relief appearances with the Yankees, allowing 1ER in 4.0IP (2.25 ERA, 4H, 2BB, 3K, 1HR).

BESTS & STREAKS

Low hit CG
N/A
IP (start)
N/A
IP (relief)
3.2 - at BOS, 5/9/10
Hits
4 - vs. ARI, 9/27/07
Runs
3 - 2 times
Last: vs. ARI, 9/27/07
BB
3 - vs. NYM, 8/16/08
SO
3 - 2 times
Last: at BOS, 5/9/10
HR
1 - 2 times
Last: at CHC, 9/23/07
Winning Streak
1g - 9/14/07
Losing Streak
N/A

2009
▸ Spent the year at the Triple-A level, combining to go 6-5 with a 4.09 ERA and 79K in 29 games (13 starts) with Indianapolis (PIT) and Scranton/Wilkes-Barre (NYY)…was acquired by the Yankees on 5/16 in exchange for minor league RHP Eric Hacker.
▸ Went 5-5 with a 4.04 ERA in 19 games (13 starts) with Scranton/WB…struck out 55 batters in 55.1IP as a starter, posting a 4-5 record and a 3.90 ERA…went 1-0 with a 4.82 ERA as a reliever…became a permanent fixture in the rotation on 7/20, making his final nine appearances as a starter…tossed 7.0 scoreless innings and earned the win on 8/27 vs. Syracuse, limiting the Chiefs to 2H with 9K (2BB, 2HP).
▸ Made two postseason starts for the IL North Division champs, going 1-1 with a 2.70 ERA and 17 strikeouts in 10.0IP…earned the win in his postseason debut, tossing 5.0 scoreless innings on 9/9 at Gwinnett (5H, 3BB, 9K).
▸ Made 10 relief appearances with Indianapolis prior to being traded, going 1-0 with a 4.38 ERA…held opponents scoreless in seven outings…struck out four of his eight batters faced on 4/22 at Toledo (2.0IP, 1H, 2BB).
▸ Pitched with both Lara and Caracas in the Venezuelan Winter League, going 6-4 with one save and a 3.82 ERA in 26 relief appearances…struck out 47 batters in 33.0IP.

2008
▸ Made 10 relief appearances, posting a 4.05 ERA with no decisions over three stints with the Pirates (6/29-7/13; 8/5-23 and 9/2-28)…earned his first Major League save in his first outing of the season on 7/1 at Cincinnati (1.0IP, 2H, 1ER, 1BB)…tossed 2.1 scoreless innings (1H, 1HP) on 8/20 at St. Louis, prior to being optioned back to the minors a second time…collected three straight scoreless appearances from 9/7-14 (2.2IP) when recalled a third time.

- Spent majority of the season with Triple-A Indianapolis, going 5-1 with a 3.46 ERA in 33 total relief appearances...allowed runs in just two of his eight April outings, going 2-0 with one save...tossed five straight scoreless outings from 7/18-8/1 in between recalls (10.1IP, 5H, 2BB, 5K).
- Pitched with Caracas in the Venezuelan Winter League, going 2-2 with an 11.70 ERA in 12 relief appearances.

2007

- Went 1-0 with a 5.00 ERA (18.0IP, 10ER) in 16 relief appearances with the Pirates in his first Major League action...was recalled by Pittsburgh on 8/25 and made his Major League debut the following night at Houston, tossing 0.2 scoreless innings of relief...struck out in his first career plate appearance on 9/1 at Milwaukee.
- Led Pirates pitchers with 14 relief appearances in September...held opponents scoreless in nine of his first 11 outings...pitched a career-high 3.0IP in his third career outing on 9/1 at Milwaukee (3H, 1ER, 1BB, 1K) earned his first win on 9/14 at Houston, striking out his only batter faced...allowed a run in three of his final five outings (5.1IP, 8ER).
- Opened the year with Double-A Altoona, going 6-3 with a 2.81 ERA in 40 relief appearances...struck out 52 batters with just 17 walks and held opponents to a .204 batting average (43-for-211)...right-handers hit just .155 (18-for-116, 4HR)...did not allow an earned run over 12 consecutive outings from 4/24-5/21 (11.1IP, 2H, 1R, 4BB, 10K)...earned his lone save on 5/27 at Bowie (1.0P, 1H, 1BB).
- Pitched with Caracas in the Venezuelan Winter League, going 1-2 with a 4.30 ERA in 14 relief appearances.

2006

- Appeared in 37 combined games (three starts) with Single-A Hickory, Single-A Lynchburg and Double-A Altoona, going 0-3 with a 5.86 ERA.
- Opened the year in Hickory...converted back-to-back save chances on 7/1 and 7/3 at Lakewood...was promoted to Lynchburg on 7/13, holding opponents scoreless in seven of his eight outings there and allowing only 12 baserunners (7H, 4BB, 1HP)...closed the season with Altoona after a promotion on 8/6...made 10 relief appearances with Caracas in the Venezuelan Winter League, posting a 4.66 ERA with no decisions.

2005

- Played at three levels, combining to go 5-3 with a 4.15 ERA with the GCL Pirates, Double-A Altoona and Single-A Hickory...won his Double-A debut on 7/5 vs. Erie, allowing just 1ER in 5.0IP (6H)...pitched for Caracas of the Venezuelan Winter League, advancing to the Caribbean World Series.

2004

- Signed with the Pirates organization on 5/7 after being released by the Dodgers on 3/12...spent the entire season pitching for Pittsburgh's Venezuelan Summer League entry...led the team in appearances (21) and saves (6)...tossed a 9.0-inning no-hitter on 8/3 vs. Ciudad Alienza, striking out 12 batters, in his final start of the season.

2002-03

- Opened his career in the Dodgers organization, playing his first two seasons with the Dominican League Dodgers.

Sanchez's Career Pitching Record

YEAR	CLUB	W	L	ERA	G	GS	CG	SHO	SV	IP	H	R	ER	HR	HB	BB	SO	WP	BK
2002	DSL Dodgers	1	4	4.44	15	0	0	0	1	24.1	24	16	12	4	6	10	22	4	0
2003	DSL Dodgers	2	3	4.46	9	0	0	0	0	38.1	40	25	19	1	4	10	21	7	0
2004	VSL Pirates-a	4	2	1.03	21	2	1	1	6	43.2	33	9	5	0	7	7	49	3	0
2005	GCL Pirates	1	0	1.80	2	1	0	0	0	10.0	7	2	2	1	0	4	7	0	0
	Altoona	1	0	3.60	2	2	0	0	0	10.0	11	4	4	2	0	4	5	1	0
	Hickory	3	3	4.70	10	10	0	0	0	53.2	59	34	28	5	10	19	24	4	1
2006	Hickory	0	3	7.08	21	3	0	0	4	40.2	51	36	32	4	6	18	28	6	1
	Lynchburg	0	0	1.04	8	0	0	0	1	8.2	7	1	1	0	1	4	6	0	0
	Altoona	0	0	5.00	8	0	0	0	0	9.0	8	5	5	1	0	8	5	0	0
2007	Altoona	6	3	2.81	40	0	0	0	1	57.2	43	24	18	8	3	17	52	5	1
	PITTSBURGH	1	0	5.00	16	0	0	0	0	18.0	16	10	10	2	1	8	11	1	0
2008	Indianapolis	5	1	3.46	33	0	0	0	4	54.2	50	27	21	5	3	19	32	2	0
	PITTSBURGH	0	0	4.05	10	0	0	0	0	13.1	14	6	6	0	1	6	3	4	0
2009	Indianapolis	1	0	4.38	10	0	0	0	0	12.1	11	6	6	1	1	5	15	0	0
	Scranton/WB-b	5	5	4.04	19	13	0	0	0	64.2	66	31	29	3	5	34	64	8	2
2010	Scranton/WB	10	8	3.97	31	14	0	0	0	104.1	88	50	46	8	1	59	96	6	1
	YANKEES	0	0	0.00	2	0	0	0	0	4.1	1	0	0	0	0	3	5	0	0
Minor League Totals		39	32	3.86	229	54	1	1	17	532.0	498	270	228	43	47	218	426	46	6
NL Totals		1	0	4.60	26	0	0	0	1	31.1	30	16	16	2	2	14	14	5	0
AL Totals		0	0	0.00	2	0	0	0	0	4.1	1	0	0	0	0	3	5	0	0
Major League Totals		1	0	4.04	28	0	0	0	1	35.2	31	16	16	2	2	17	19	5	0

Signed by the Los Angeles Dodgers as a non-drafted free agent on March 8, 2002.

a – Signed by the Pittsburgh Pirates as a minor league free agent on May 7, 2004.
b – Acquired by the Yankees from the Pirates in exchange for minor league RHP Eric Hacker on May 16, 2009.

Sanchez's Career Fielding Record

Position	PCT	G	PO	A	E	TC
Pitcher	1.000	28	4	4	0	8

29

RAFAEL SORIANO

RIGHT-HANDED PITCHER • 6-1 • 230 • B/T: RIGHT/RIGHT • OPENING DAY AGE: 31

BIRTHDATE
December 19, 1979

BIRTHPLACE
San Jose, D.R.

RESIDES
Andres Boca Chica, D.R.

M.L. SERVICE
8 years, 57 days

CAREER HIGHLIGHTS
Sporting News AL Rookie Pitcher of the Year
▸ 2003

A.L. All-Star Team
▸ 2010

STATUS
▸ Signed by the Yankees as a free agent to a three-year contract on January 18, 2011…contract extends through the 2013 season.

CAREER
▸ Has limited opponents to a .185 batting average in his career as a reliever, the second-lowest mark among all active Major League relievers with at least 200.0IP behind only Carlos Marmol (.158).

▸ Has held right-handed batters to a .162 (124-for-767) batting average in his career, marking the lowest such average among all active pitchers (min. 500 batters faced).

▸ Over the last two seasons (in which he served primarily as a closer), has allowed the seventh-lowest opponents batting average (.180), the seventh-fewest baserunners/9.0IP (8.61) and struck out the ninth-most batters (159) among all Major League relievers.

▸ Was a perfect 22-for-22 in save opportunities at home in 2010 and has converted 38 consecutive saves at home dating back to 2007 (last blown save came 7/22/07 w/ Atlanta vs. St. Louis), the longest such active streak and sixth-longest all time.

▸ Began his career as an outfielder in the Mariners organization, before converting to pitcher prior to the 1999 season…in eight career Major League starts, is 0-3 with a 5.10 ERA (42.1IP, 24ER)…in 334 career relief appearances, has gone 11-17 with 88 saves and a 2.45 ERA (352.2IP, 96ER).

BESTS & STREAKS

IP (start)
7.0 - 2 times
Last: vs. CHC, 6/9/02
IP (relief)
4.0 - vs. TEX, 7/25/03
Hits
8 - at SD, 6/15/02
Runs
5 - vs. CHC, 6/9/02
BB
3 - 2 times
Last: vs. OAK, 6/27/02
SO
7 - vs. CHC, 6/9/02
HR
2 - 2 times
Last: vs. CHC, 6/9/02
Winning Streak
3g - 7/5/03-4/7/04
Losing Streak
6g - 6/11/09-10/1/09

2010
▸ Went 3-2 with an American League-leading 45 saves (in 48 opportunities) and a 1.73 ERA in 64 relief appearances in his lone season with the Rays, setting a club record and a career high in saves…struck out 57 batters in 62.1IP with only 14BB…appeared in consecutive games 11 times, three straight three times and a season-high four in-a-row three times (4/30-5/4, 7/3-6 and 9/12-15).

▸ Held opponents to a .163 (36-for-221, 4HR) batting average; RH (.196, 21-for-107, 2HR), LH .132 (15-for-114, 2HR)…marked the lowest batting average against RHH in the Majors (min. 100 BF)…first batters hit just .115 (7-for-61) against him.

▸ Became only the fourth pitcher in Major League history to reach his totals for saves, ERA and opponents average in a single season, joining Oakland's Dennis Eckersley in 1990, Los Angeles-NL's Eric Gagne in 2003 and Florida's Armando Benitez in 2004.

▸ Converted 45-of-48 save opportunities (93.8%), leading the AL and ranking second in the Majors behind San Diego's Heath Bell (94.0%, 47-for-50)…ranked third in the Majors in saves behind San Francisco's Brian Wilson (48) and Bell (47)…among AL relievers, ranked second in opponents average and third in ERA.

▸ Earned his first career All-Star appearance, replacing the injured Mariano Rivera on the AL roster…threw a perfect eighth inning on only eight pitches, retiring San Diego's Adrian Gonzalez, and Cincinnati's Joey Votto and Scott Rolen on three fly balls…named to the *Sporting News* AL All-Star team as the league's top reliever, and won the 2010 Rolaids Relief Man of the Year Award in the AL.

- Named "DHL Delivery Man of the Month" for May, July and August…since the award was founded in 2005, no pitcher had won it twice in the same season…also received consideration for the AL Cy Young Award, placing eighth in the voting–the highest finish by a reliever in 2010 AL balloting.

- Converted each of his first 16 save chances to begin the season, suffering his first blown save in 6/19 win vs. Florida in his only appearance of the season in which he entered the game prior to the ninth inning.

- Held opponents scoreless in 19 of his final 22 appearances of the season beginning 8/1, converting 16-of-17 save chances and holding opponents to a .125 batting average (9-for-72).

- Struck out the side on nine pitches in 8/23 win at Los Angeles-AL, the only pitcher to do so in 2010 and the first to accomplish the feat while recording a save since Chicago-NL's LaTroy Hawkins on 9/11/04 vs. Florida.

- Recorded his 40th save in 9/1 win vs. Toronto, joining the Angels' Francisco Rodriguez (62 saves) in 2008 as the only AL pitchers to collect at least 40 saves by September 1.

- Appeared in three Division Series games with the Rays, allowing 3ER in 3.0IP and converting his only save chance.

LOWEST OPPONENTS' BATTING AVERAGE IN RELIEF, CAREER, ACTIVE ML PITCHERS (min. 200.0IP)

1.	Carlos Marmol	.158 (174-for-1101)
2.	**RAFAEL SORIANO**	**.185 (234-for-1264)**
3.	Joe Nathan	.186 (346-for-1861)
4.	Billy Wagner	.187 (601-for-3220)
5.	Francisco Rodriguez	.194 (401-for-2072)

MOST SAVES, AL, 2010

1.	**RAFAEL SORIANO, TB**	**45**
2.	Joakim Soria, KC	43
3.	Neftali Feliz, TEX	40
4.	Jonathan Papelbon, BOS	37
	Kevin Gregg, TOR	37

LOWEST ERA, AL RELIEVERS, 2010

1.	Joaquin Benoit, TB	1.34
2.	Chris Perez, CLE	1.71
3.	**RAFAEL SORIANO, TB**	**1.73**
4.	Joakim Soria, KC	1.78
5.	MARIANO RIVERA, NYY	1.80

MOST CONSECUTIVE SAVES AT HOME

1.	MARIANO RIVERA	51, 8/18/07-4/30/10
	Eric Gagne	51, 8/28/02-7/1/04
3.	Trevor Hoffman	49, 8/4/98-7/15/00
4.	John Smoltz	47, 6/3/02-4/8/04
5.	Robb Nen	39, 7/17/97-6/18/99
6.	**RAFAEL SORIANO**	**38, 9/18/07-present**

2009

- Went 1-6 with 27 saves (in 31 chances), a 2.97 ERA and 102K in 77 relief appearances with the Braves…in his first season as the team's primary closer, established career bests in innings pitched (75.2), appearances and strikeouts…opponents batted .194 (53-for-273, 6HR); RH .258 (33-for-128, 4HR), LH .138 (20-for-145, 2HR).

- Among Major League relievers, tied for second in strikeouts (behind Los Angeles-NL's Jonathan Broxton-114), third with 12.13 K/9.0IP and 10th in games…his 27 saves tied for 10th in the NL…led all ML relievers in opponents average against right-handed hitters and ranked fourth with a .153 (17-for-111) opponents average with runners on base (min. 100 AB).

- Was 1-1 with a 1.48 ERA and a .158 (23-for-146, 1HR) opponents batting average prior to the All-Star break…went 0-5 with a 4.91 ERA and a .236 (30-for-127, 5HR) opponents batting average over the second half.

2008

- Was limited to 14 relief appearances with Atlanta (0-1, 2.57 ERA), enduring three stints on the disabled list with right elbow injuries.

- Made his fourth career Opening Day roster and allowed just 1ER in four games (4.0IP) before going on the 15-day disabled list from 4/7-5/28 with right elbow tendinitis…landed on the 15-day D.L. again from 6/6-7/21 with right elbow inflammation.

- Returned to the disabled list a third time on 8/3 with right elbow inflammation for the remainder of the season…underwent ulnar nerve transposition surgery on 8/28 and had a bone spur removed by Dr. James Andrews in Birmingham, Ala.

2007

- In his first season in the National League, went 3-3 with nine saves and a 3.00 ERA in 71 appearances with Atlanta…struck out 70 batters with only 15BB…held opponents to a .181 batting average (47-for-259, 12HR), fifth-lowest among NL relievers, and a .232 on-base percentage, second-lowest among NL relievers…allowed 8.00 base runners/9.0IP, second-fewest among NL relievers.

- Compiled a 15.2-inning scoreless stretch over 15 appearances from 4/22-5/28, allowing just 2H and converting all four save chances over the span with 18K and 4BB.

- Allowed just 1ER over his final 17 outings of the season, going 1-0 and holding opponents to 8H in 19.1IP.

2006

- Spent the entire season in the Majors with Seattle, going 1-2 with two saves and a 2.25 ERA in 53 relief appearances.

- Allowed just 1R over his first 11 outings (13.0IP)…was placed on the 15-day disabled list on 7/29 (retroactive to 7/20), with right shoulder fatigue.

- Did not pitch the final month of the season due to a concussion…was hit on the right side of the head by a line drive from the Angels' Vladimir Guerrero in 8/29 win vs. Los Angeles-AL…never lost consciousness, and was released from Harborview Medical Center the next day.

- Following the season, was acquired by Atlanta in exchange for LHP Horacio Ramirez.

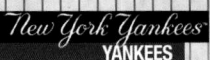

2005
▶ Spent most of the season on the disabled list recovering from "Tommy John" surgery.
▶ Made rehab appearances with short-season Single-A Everett, Single-A Inland Empire, Double-A San Antonio and Triple-A Tacoma before being reinstated from the 60-day disabled list and recalled on 9/5.
▶ Made seven relief appearances in September, allowing 2ER in 7.1IP (2.45 ERA) with no decisions.

2004
▶ Was limited to six Major League games (0-3, 13.50 ERA), undergoing "Tommy John" surgery on his right elbow on 8/17 in Los Angeles…surgery was performed by Dr. Lewis Yocum.
▶ Made his first Opening Day roster and appeared in three games before being optioned to the minors on 4/14…pitched with Single-A Inland Empire and Double-A San Antonio before returning the Major League club on 5/4…made three additional appearances before going on the 15-day DL with a right elbow sprain on 5/12…made a rehab assignment with Triple-A Tacoma (7/28– 8/2) before elbow pain returned and he underwent surgery…was limited to four spring training games by a strained oblique muscle.

2003
▶ Went 3-0 with a 1.53 ERA in 40 relief appearances over two stints with Seattle (4/24-5/8, 6/16-9/28)…struck out 68 batters in 53.0IP and held opponents to a .163 (30-for-185, 2HR) batting average.
▶ Named *Sporting News* "AL Rookie Pitcher of the Year."
▶ Recalled from Triple-A Tacoma on 4/24 and appeared in three games (4.0IP, 1ER) before being optioned…recalled a second time on 6/16 for the remainder of the season.
▶ Earned his first ML win on 7/5 at Texas with 1.0 scoreless inning of relief…pitched the final 4.0 innings in 7/25 win vs. Texas to earn the save…struck out seven straight batters over two games, fanning his final batter faced in 7/28 loss vs. Texas and all six batters faced in 7/30 win vs. Detroit.
▶ Named AL "Rookie of the Month" for August after going 2-0 with a 1.62 ERA (16.2IP, 3ER) in 12 outings.
▶ Following the season, pitched for Escogido in the Dominican Winter League and set a league record with a 0.21 ERA (42.1IP, 2ER).

2002
▶ Made his Major League debut with Seattle, going 0-3 with a 4.56 ERA in 10 games (eight starts).
▶ Was signed to a Major League contract and selected from Double-A San Antonio on 5/8…made his Major League debut in relief in 5/10 win vs. Boston and earned the save with 3.0 scoreless IP (2H, 1K).
▶ Made his first ML start on 5/25 at Baltimore and suffered the loss in the 3-2 defeat (5.2IP, 4H, 3ER, 3BB, 2K)…allowed three runs or fewer in six of his eight starts but was 0-2 with four no-decisions in those six outings.
▶ Was placed on the 15-day disabled list on 7/10 with a right shoulder strain…reinstated 8/2 and optioned to San Antonio, where he remained through the remainder of the season.
▶ Overall with San Antonio, went 2-3 with a 2.31 ERA in 10 games (eight starts), striking out 52 batters in 46.2IP…made three postseason starts for the Missions, including a 14K performance (7.0IP, 2H, 1ER) in a 4-1 win over Tulsa (Rangers) to clinch the Texas League championship.

2001
▶ Split the 2001 season between Single-A San Bernardino and Double-A San Antonio, going 8-5 with a 2.82 ERA in 23 starts…combined to strike out 151 batters in 137.1IP with a .174 opponents average (83-for-476, 9HR).
▶ Began season on the disabled list with a right elbow sprain…was reinstated and assigned to San Bernardino on 5/5 before being promoted to San Antonio on 6/28.
▶ Following the season, pitched for Escogido in the Dominican Winter League.

2000
▶ In his first full-season action, went 8-4 with a 2.87 ERA in 21 starts with Single-A Wisconsin, leading the team in ERA.

1999
▶ Converted to pitcher prior to the season and made 14 starts with short-season Single-A Everett, going 5-4 with a 3.11 ERA and 83K in 75.1IP…ranked second in the Northwest League in ERA and strikeouts and third in walks allowed (49).

1998
▶ In his final season as a position player, hit .167 (18-for-108) in 32 games with the AZL Mariners.

1997
▶ Made his professional debut with the AZL Mariners, batting .269 (32-for-119) with 12RBI in 38 games (21 games at 1B, 17 in the OF).

PERSONAL

▸ Is married to Maria…has six children: daughters Loidys, Rafaela and Aracelis, and sons Rafael Jr., Rafael Alberto and Raul…is an avid chef, cooking meals native to the Dominican Republic.

Soriano's Career Pitching Record

Year	Club	W	L	ERA	G	GS	CG	SHO	SV	IP	H	R	ER	HR	HP	BB	SO	WP	BK
1999	Everett	5	4	3.11	14	14	0	0	0	75.1	56	34	26	8	4	49	83	2	0
2000	Wisconsin	8	4	2.87	21	21	1	0	0	122.1	97	41	39	3	12	50	90	5	2
2001	San Bernardino	6	3	2.53	15	15	2	1	0	89.0	49	28	25	4	4	39	98	2	0
	San Antonio	2	2	3.35	8	8	0	0	0	48.1	34	18	18	5	2	14	53	2	1
2002	San Antonio	2	3	2.31	10	8	0	0	0	46.2	32	13	12	6	1	15	52	0	0
	SEATTLE - a	0	3	4.56	10	8	0	0	1	47.1	45	25	24	8	0	16	32	2	0
2003	Tacoma	4	3	3.19	11	10	0	0	0	62.0	43	24	22	2	4	12	63	0	1
	SEATTLE	3	0	1.53	40	0	0	0	1	53.0	30	9	9	2	3	12	68	0	0
2004	SEATTLE - b	0	3	13.50	6	0	0	0	0	3.1	9	6	5	0	0	3	3	0	0
	Inland Empire	0	0	2.25	2	2	0	0	0	8.0	7	3	2	1	0	1	9	0	0
	San Antonio	1	0	1.13	2	1	0	0	0	8.0	4	1	1	1	0	0	10	0	0
	Tacoma	0	0	2.45	3	3	0	0	0	3.2	2	1	1	1	0	2	5	0	0
2005	Everett	0	0	3.00	4	4	0	0	0	6.0	6	3	2	0	1	2	8	0	1
	Inland Empire	0	0	0.00	3	3	0	0	0	4.0	2	0	0	0	0	0	5	0	0
	San Antonio	0	0	0.00	1	1	0	0	0	1.0	0	0	0	0	1	0	0	0	0
	Tacoma	1	0	0.00	5	0	0	0	0	5.1	3	0	0	0	0	1	11	0	0
	SEATTLE - c	0	0	2.45	7	0	0	0	0	7.1	6	2	2	0	1	1	9	0	0
2006	SEATTLE - d	1	2	2.25	53	0	0	0	2	60.0	44	15	15	6	2	21	65	2	0
2007	ATLANTA - e	3	3	3.00	71	0	0	0	9	72.0	47	26	24	12	2	15	70	0	0
2008	ATLANTA - f,g,h	0	1	2.57	14	0	0	0	3	14.0	7	5	4	1	1	9	16	1	0
	Mississippi	0	0	0.00	2	1	0	0	0	2.0	1	0	0	0	0	1	2	0	0
	DSL Braves	0	1	0.00	2	2	0	0	0	2.0	3	1	0	0	0	0	2	1	0
2009	ATLANTA	1	6	2.97	77	0	0	0	27	75.2	53	25	25	6	1	27	102	0	0
2010	TAMPA BAY - i	3	2	1.73	64	0	0	0	*45	62.1	36	14	12	4	1	14	57	0	0
Minor League Totals		**29**	**20**	**2.75**	**103**	**93**	**3**	**1**	**0**	**483.2**	**339**	**167**	**148**	**31**	**29**	**186**	**491**	**12**	**5**
AL Totals		**7**	**10**	**2.73**	**180**	**8**	**0**	**0**	**49**	**233.1**	**170**	**71**	**67**	**20**	**7**	**67**	**234**	**4**	**0**
NL Totals		**4**	**10**	**2.95**	**162**	**0**	**0**	**0**	**39**	**161.2**	**107**	**56**	**53**	**19**	**4**	**51**	**188**	**1**	**0**
Major League Totals		**11**	**20**	**2.73**	**342**	**8**	**0**	**0**	**88**	**395.0**	**277**	**127**	**120**	**39**	**11**	**118**	**422**	**5**	**0**

*Denotes league leader

Signed by Seattle as a non-drafted free agent, August 30, 1996…signed by Ramon de los Santos

a – Placed on the 15-day disabled list with a right shoulder strain from July 10 - August 2, 2002
b – Placed on the 15-day disabled list for right elbow surgery on May 11, 2004 through the end of the season…transferred to the 60-day disabled list on September 1, 2004.
c – Placed on the 60-day disabled list to recover from right elbow surgery from April 1 - September 1, 2005.
d – Placed on the 15-day disabled list with right shoulder fatigue from July 29 - August 4, 2006.
e – Acquired by the Atlanta Braves from the Seattle Mariners in exchange for LHP Horacio Rameriez, December, 7, 2006.
f – Placed on the 15-day disabled list for right elbow tendinitis from April 9 - May 28, 2008.
g – Placed on the 15-day disabled list with right elbow inflammation from June 6 - July 21, 2008.
h – Placed on the 15-day disabled list with right elbow inflammation on August 4, 2008…transferred to the 60-day disabled list from September 2 - November 3, 2008 with right elbow inflammation.
i – Acquired by the Tampa Bay Rays from the Atlanta Braves in exchange for RHP Jesse Chavez, December 11, 2009.
j – Signed by the Yankees as a free agent on January 18, 2011.

Soriano's Career Batting Record

Year	Club	AVG	G	AB	R	H	2B	3B	HR	RBI	BB	SO	SB	CS	SF	SAC	HBP
2010	TAMPA BAY					Did Not Bat											
Major League Totals		**.000**	**342**	**4**	**0**	**0**	**0**	**0**	**0**	**0**	**0**	**1**	**0**	**0**	**0**	**0**	**0**

Soriano's Division Series Record

Year	Club vs. Opp.	W	L	ERA	G	GS	CG	SHO	SV	IP	H	R	ER	HR	HP	BB	SO	WP	BK
2010	TB vs. TEX	0	0	9.00	3	3	0	0	1	3.0	4	3	3	2	0	0	1	0	0
Division Series Totals		**0**	**0**	**9.00**	**3**	**3**	**0**	**0**	**1**	**3.0**	**4**	**3**	**3**	**2**	**0**	**0**	**1**	**0**	**0**

Soriano's All-Star Game Record

All-Star Game		W	L	ERA	G	GS	CG	SHO	SV	IP	H	R	ER	HR	HP	BB	SO	WP	BK
2010	TB, Los Angeles-AL	0	0	0.00	1	0	0	0	0	1.0	0	0	0	0	0	0	0	0	0
All-Star Game Totals		**0**	**0**	**0.00**	**1**	**0**	**0**	**0**	**0**	**1.0**	**0**	**0**	**0**	**0**	**0**	**0**	**0**	**0**	**0**

Soriano's Career Fielding Record

Position	PCT	G	PO	A	E	TC	DP
Pitcher	.902	342	15	22	4	41	0

33 NICK SWISHER

OUTFIELDER/INFIELDER • 5-11 • 210 • B/T: SWITCH/LEFT • OPENING DAY AGE: 30

BIRTHDATE
November 25, 1980

BIRTHPLACE
Columbus, Ohio

RESIDES
Tampa, Fla.

M.L. SERVICE
6 years, 31 days

COLLEGE
Ohio State University

CAREER HIGHLIGHTS
A.L. All-Star Team
▸ 2010

STATUS
▸ Acquired by the Yankees along with RHP Kanekoa Texeira from the Chicago White Sox on November 13, 2008, in exchange for INF Wilson Betemit and RHPs Jeff Marquez and Jhonny Nunez…signed a five-year contract with a one-year club option on May 11, 2007 (w/ Oakland)…contract extends through the 2011 season, with a one-year club option for 2012.

CAREER NOTES
▸ Is one of four American Leaguers to hit at least 20HR in each of the last six seasons (2005-10), joining Paul Konerko, David Ortiz and teammate Alex Rodriguez.
▸ His 139HR since 2006 are the third-most among Major League switch-hitters over the last five seasons, trailing only Mark Teixeira (168) and Lance Berkman (147).
▸ Has homered from both sides of the plate 10 times in his career…according to SABR's David Vincent, the 10 career switch-hit homers are tied with teammate Mark Teixeira for the most among active players and tied with Teixeira, Ken Caminiti, Tony Clark and Mickey Mantle for the second-most all-time behind Chili Davis and Eddie Murray (11 each).
▸ Was the only player to hit 15 or more home runs with three different franchises from 2007-09 (22 w/ Oakland in 2007, 24 w/ Chicago-AL in 2008 and 29 w/ the Yankees in 2009)…according to *Elias*, the only other player to cap such a three-year streak with the Yankees was Reggie Jackson (36HR for the 1975 Athletics, 27HR for the 1976 Orioles and 32 for the 1977 Yankees).

2010
▸ Hit .288 (163-for-566) with 91R, 33 doubles, 3 triples, 29HR and 89RBI in 150 games (131 starts in RF, 11 at DH) with the Yankees, setting career highs in batting average, at-bats, hits and triples…made his sixth career Opening Day roster, second as a Yankee…hit .286 (110-for-384) with 25HR as a lefthanded batter and .291 (53-for-182) with 4HR from the right side…17 of his 29 homers tied the game or gave the Yankees the lead.
▸ Among Major League switch-hitters, ranked second in runs scored (91), home runs (29) and RBI (89), trailing only teammate Mark Teixeira in each of the three categories (113R, 33HR and 108RBI)…ranked third in batting average (.288).
▸ Hit .345 (88-for-255) with 15 doubles, 3 triples, 13HR, 73RBI and 29BB with runners on base, marking the fourth-best average in the AL.
▸ Batted in seven different spots in the starting lineup (two through eight), homering in five of those spots (two, four, five, six and eight).
▸ Had at least three hits in a game 14 times, the most such games in any season in his career (previous was 10 in 2007)…only Robinson Cano (19) had more three-hit games among Yankees in 2010.
▸ Collected 10 outfield assists, eight more than his total from 2009 (two) and surpassing his previous career high (six in 2005 w/ Oakland).

BESTS & STREAKS

Hits
4 - 2 times
Last: at SEA, 7/8/10
Runs
3 - 17 times
Last: at DET, 4/28/09
2B
2 - 14 times
Last: vs. OAK, 8/30/10
3B
1 - 9 times
Last: at ARI, 6/21/10
HR
2 - 16 times
Last: vs. TOR, 8/2/10
RBI
5 - 4 times
Last: at BAL, 6/8/10
BB
3 - 18 times
Last: vs. LAA, 4/13/10
SO
5 - 5 times
Last: at SD, 6/29/06
SB
1 - 8 times
Last: vs. TOR, 7/2/10
Hit Streak
11g - 4/30-5/11/06

- Won the 2010 All-Star Final Vote, earning the final spot on the AL's All-Star roster...pinch hit for Ty Wigginton in the seventh (0-for-1)...with his dad, Steve, a 1976 NL All-Star for the Chicago Cubs, the Swishers became the 12th family to have both a father and son named to an MLB All-Star team.

- Hit safely in each of his first six games of the season with an official at-bat for the second time in his career (first nine games in 2009).

- Batted .374 (34-for-91) with 7HR and 17RBI in May, marking his most hits in any calendar month of his career (previous best was 32H in May 2007 and May 2006)...hit three home runs in a four-game stretch from 5/5-9 and five HR in an eight-game span from 5/1-9.

- Missed four games with a sore left biceps (5/13 and 5/17-19)...underwent an MRI at New York-Presbyterian Hospital on 5/14 and was diagnosed with a slight strain of the left biceps.

- Recorded two outfield assists in 6/23 win at Arizona, both coming in the first inning (Johnson at home, Montero at third)...marked his first career multi-assist game as an outfielder.

- Recorded his 15th career multi-HR game in 6/29 loss vs. Seattle, homering twice off LHP Cliff Lee...was his first multi-HR game since 9/8/09 vs. Tampa Bay...marked the second time in his career he hit 2HR off left-handed pitching in the same game (also 5/11/06 w/ Oakland at Toronto – both off Ted Lilly).

- Was 4-for-4 with 1R, 2 doubles and 1BB, reaching base five times in 7/8 win at Seattle...tied his career high in hits (also 9/8/06 w/ Oakland at Tampa Bay).

- Scored at least one run in 10 consecutive starts from 7/10-26, tying a career high (also 9/5-15/07) and marking the longest such streak in the AL in 2010.

MOST WALKS IN THE AL, 2005-10	
1. David Ortiz	558
2. NICK SWISHER	**489**
3. ALEX RODRIGUEZ	480
4. Joe Mauer	422
Jim Thome	422

MOST HOME RUNS BY MAJOR LEAGUE SWITCH-HITTERS, 2005-10	
1. MARK TEIXEIRA	211
2. Lance Berkman	171
3. NICK SWISHER	**160**
4. Carlos Beltran	134
5. Chipper Jones	126

MOST GAMES WITH HOMERS FROM BOTH SIDES OF THE PLATE	
1. Chili Davis	11
Eddie Murray	11
3. Ken Caminiti	10
Tony Clark	10
Mickey Mantle	10
NICK SWISHER	10
MARK TEIXEIRA	10

- Hit ninth-inning "walk-off" RBI single and was 3-for-5 with 1R, 1HR and 3RBI in 7/16 win vs. Tampa Bay...was his third career "walk-off" hit, second with the Yankees.

- Collected his 16th career multi-HR game (also 6/29 vs. Seattle) and second of 2010 in 8/2 loss vs. Toronto, going 2-for-5 with a two-run HR and solo HR...moved to CF at the start of the ninth inning, playing the position for the first time since 9/1/08 w/ Chicago-AL at Cleveland.

- Fouled a ball off his left knee in 8/24 win at Toronto and was removed from the game with a 2-2 count in the seventh...missed the next game on 8/25 at Toronto with soreness in the knee...also missed two games (9/3-4) with left knee stiffness.

- Hit ninth-inning, two-run "walk-off" HR and was 2-for-4 in 9/8 win vs. Baltimore...was his fourth career "walk-off" hit and third such HR...came one year to the day after his last "walk-off" homer (9/8/09 vs. Tampa Bay off Dan Wheeler)...became the fourth player in Baseball history ever to hit "walk-off" home runs exactly a year apart and first since the Giants' Jack Clark on 9/4/81 and 9/4/82—credit: *Elias*.

- Started all nine Yankees postseason games, batting .176 (6-for-34) with 6R, 3 doubles and 2HR...the Yankees were 4-0 when he scored a run.

2009

- Hit .249 (124-for-498) with 84R, 35 doubles, 29HR and 82RBI in 150 games (126 starts in RF, 10 at 1B, four in LF, one at DH) in his first season with the Yankees...batted .250 (84-for-336, 20HR) as a left-handed batter and .247 (40-for-162, 9HR) as a right-handed batter.

- Ranked third among Major League switch-hitters in home runs, tied for third with 97BB and ranked sixth in RBI...ranked second overall in the AL in walks, marking the most free passes by a Yankees switch-hitter since Jorge Posada in 2000 (107)...ranked second in the AL and seventh in the Majors with 4.26 pitches seen per plate appearance...led the AL with a .585 slugging percentage on the road.

- Homered from both sides of the plate three times (4/29 at Detroit, 7/27 at Tampa Bay and 9/8 vs. Tampa Bay)...according to the *Elias Sports Bureau*, his three sets of switch-hit homers tied his high for any season (also 2007) and tied the AL single-season mark, also shared by Tony Clark (1998 with Detroit) and teammate Mark Teixeira, who joined Swisher in accomplishing the feat in 2009.

- Homered from seven different spots in the batting order (two through eight), becoming the first player to accomplish the feat in one season for the Yankees since Dan Pasqua in 1987—credit: *Elias*...became the first player in franchise history to hit 21 of his first 24HR of the season on the road.

- He and teammate Mark Teixeira became the third set of Yankees teammates over the last 50 years to each hit at least 25HR in their first full season in pinstripes (also Alex Rodriguez/Gary Sheffield in 2004 and Jason Giambi/Robin Ventura in 2002).

- Made his Yankees debut in Opening Day loss at Baltimore on 4/6, going 1-for-1 with a pinch-hit double…was his fifth career Opening Day roster.
- Started his first game of the season on 4/9 at Baltimore in the Yankees first win of the season, going 3-for-5 with 2R, 1 double, 1HR and a career-high-tying 5RBI…according to the *Elias Sports Bureau*, became the first player to drive in four-or-more runs in his first career start with the Yankees since Roger Maris on 4/19/60 at Boston, when he went 4-for-5 with 2HR and 4RBI…*Elias* also noted that Swisher became just the second Yankee in franchise history (since RBI became an official statistic in 1920) to record five-or-more RBI in a single game within his first three contests with the club (also Bob Tillman on 8/13/67 at Cleveland, third game w/ NYY, 2-for-5, 1HR, 6RBI).
- Recorded a hit in each of his first nine games with an official at-bat, the longest hitting streak to begin a season of his career…according to the *Elias Sports Bureau*, set a franchise record with nine extra-base hits (4 doubles, 1 triple, 4HR) in his first eight games with the Yankees, surpassing Roger Maris, who had seven in 1960…*Elias* also notes his 11RBI tied the franchise record for most RBI in a player's first eight games with the club, matching Maris in 1960 and Robin Ventura in 2002.
- Reached base safely in each of his first 17 games, becoming the first Yankee to accomplish the feat since Matty Alou reached in his first 19 games in 1973 (credit: *Elias*).
- Pitched a scoreless eighth inning (1.0IP, 1H, 1BB, 1K) in 4/13 loss at Tampa Bay, becoming the Yankees' first position player to pitch in a game since Wade Boggs on 8/19/97 at Anaheim…went 1-for-3 with a solo HR, becoming the first Yankee to homer and strike out a batter in the same game since Lindy McDaniel on 9/28/72 at Detroit.
- Led the team with 7HR and 19RBI in April, becoming the first offseason acquisition to lead the Yankees in March/April RBI in his first year with the club since Dave Winfield tied Bucky Dent for the team lead with nine April RBI in 1981…also became the first to hold the outright lead in both categories since Bobby Bonds in 1975 (4HR, 15RBI).
- Hit each of his first 8HR on the road…according to *Elias*, became the first Yankee to hit each of his first 8HR of a season on the road since Bernie Williams in 2003 (first 9HR on the road).
- Reached base safely in 30 consecutive games from 7/17-8/22, the longest such streak by a Yankee in 2009 and the second-longest streak of his career (36 games in 2006 w/ Oakland).
- Hit solo-HR in the second and "walk-off" solo-HR in the ninth and was 2-for-3 with 1BB in 9/8 win vs. Tampa Bay…was his second career "walk-off" hit and home run…was his third multi-HR game in 2009 and 14th of his career…marked the eighth time in Baseball history a player homered from both sides of the plate in the same game with one of those home runs being a "walk-off" (also Yankees Mickey Mantle in 1956, Roy White in 1976 and Melky Cabrera on 4/22/09, Donnie Scott in 1985, Kevin Bass in 1987 and 1989 and Carlos Guillen in 2006)—credit: *Elias Sports Bureau*.
- Appeared in 14 of the Yankees' 15 postseason games in 2009, batting .128 (6-for-47) with 5R, 2 doubles, 1HR, 2RBI and 7BB…hit his first career postseason homer in Game 3 of the World Series at Philadelphia.

2008

- Hit .219 (109-for-497) with 21 doubles, 24HR and 69RBI in 153 games in his only season with the White Sox (69 starts in CF, 47 at 1B, 16 in LF and 11 in RF)…was his fourth consecutive season with 20-or-more home runs.
- Led all AL switch-hitters in home runs and finished second in RBI to Texas' Milton Bradley…batted .227 (83-for-365) with 18HR as a left-handed batter and .197 (26-for-132) with 6HR from the right side…hit in eight different spots in the lineup.
- Led the AL with 4.51 pitches seen per plate appearance and tied for eighth with 82BB…owned the third-lowest batting average among AL qualifiers, ahead of only Oakland's Daric Barton (.214) and Jack Hannahan (.216)…hit .247 (64-for-259) with 19HR at U.S. Cellular Field, while batting .189 (45-for-238) with 5HR on the road…batted .385 (5-for-13) with 2HR and 19RBI with the bases loaded.
- Made just two errors in 481 chances at 1B (.996 fielding pct.), while making 5E in 202TC as an outfielder (.975).
- Made his fourth career Opening Day roster and start in 3/31 loss at Cleveland, going 2-for-4 with 2R.
- Walked in six consecutive plate appearances from 4/4-5 at Detroit, becoming the first player to walk six straight times since Ivan Rodriguez in 2003 and the first White Sox player to do so since Chet Lemon in 1980.
- Hit his first career leadoff home run off Justin Verlander on 4/6 at Detroit…hit his first career "walk-off" home run on 8/5 vs. Detroit, a 14th-inning, three-run shot off Joel Zumaya…homered in a career-high four straight games from 8/18-21…included was his 100th career home run on 8/20 vs. Seattle.
- Snapped a career-high 0-for-19 stretch with an eighth-inning double on 9/2 at Cleveland.
- Went 1-for-4 (.250) with 1R and 2BB in three ALDS games vs. Tampa Bay.
- Was traded to Chicago-AL from Oakland on 1/3/08 in exchange for RHP Fautino De Los Santos, LHP Giovany Gonzalez and OF Ryan Sweeney.

2007

- Hit .262 (141-for-539) with 36 doubles, 22HR, 78RBI and 100BB in 150 games with Oakland (57 starts in CF, 46 in RF, 39 at 1B, and five at DH)…set career highs in average, doubles, walks and on-base percentage (.381).
- Ranked sixth in the American League in walks, seventh in pitches per plate appearance (4.25) and 10th in strikeouts (131)…also ranked among the AL leaders in sacrifice flies (tied for fourth, nine), intentional walks (tied for fifth, 12) and percent of pitches taken (seventh, 62.8).

- His 22HR ranked second among AL switch-hitters behind Cleveland's Victor Martinez (25) and tied for the third-highest total in Athletics history for a switch-hitter…of his 22 homers, 15 were solo shots and 10 either tied the game or gave the A's the lead…had three multi-HR games, homering from both sides of the plate each time (4/23 at Baltimore, 7/26 at Seattle and 9/9 at Texas).

- Became the third player in Oakland history to start at least 30 games at three different positions, joining Jay Payton (2006) and Jason Giambi (1996)…had a .993 fielding percentage at 1B (3E), .986 in CF (2E) and 1.000 in RF (0E).

- Hit .291 (44-for-151) with 6HR, 22RBI and a .458 on-base percentage vs. left-handed pitchers and .250 (97-for-388) with 16HR, 56RBI and a .348OBP vs. righties.

- Established a career high with 5RBI on 5/21 at Chicago-AL, becoming the eighth player in Oakland history to drive in five runs without a home run.

- Committed his first error of the season on 8/2 vs. Los Angeles-AL in his 98th game…also snapped a career-high 103-game errorless stretch dating back to 9/24/06.

- Scored a run in 10 consecutive games from 9/5-15 (15R overall).

- Served a three-game suspension from 9/18-21 after being ejected on 9/16 vs. Texas for charging the mound when he was hit by a Vicente Padilla pitch in his first at-bat…marked his third straight game of being hit by a pitch (also 9/14 and 9/15 vs. Texas)…also homered in each of those games.

2006

- Batted .254 (141-for-556) with 106R, 35HR, 95RBI and 97BB in 157 games with Oakland (80 starts at 1B, 71 in LF)…led the team in games played, runs scored, walks, extra-base hits (61), total bases (254), intentional walks (seven) and strikeouts…led all AL switch-hitters and ranked eighth in the AL in home runs…became just the 23rd switch-hitter in Major League history to homer at least 30 times in a season…ranked sixth in the AL in walks and eighth in runs scored…tied for fourth in the AL with 152K, the highest total by an A's player since Jose Canseco also had 152 in 1991.

- Hit .291 (41-for-141) with 8HR vs. left-handed pitchers and .241 (100-for-415) with 27HR vs. right-handers…hit .412 (7-for-17) with 2HR and 20RBI with the bases loaded.

- Became the first player in Oakland history to start at least 70 games at two different positions and was the first to do so in the Majors since Cleveland's Carlos Baerga in 1991…started 63-of-88 games in LF before the All-Star break and 59-of-74 at 1B after the break.

- Reached base safely in 36 consecutive games from 4/7-5/19, going 41-for-131 (.313) with 12HR, 33RBI and 35R…hit his first career grand slam on 4/22 vs. Los Angeles-AL off Jeff Weaver.

- Compiled a career-high 11-game hitting streak from 4/30-5/11, batting .341 (14-for-41) with 12R, 6 doubles, 3HR, 10RBI and 8BB during the stretch.

- Started all seven postseason games at 1B for the Athletics (three vs. Minnesota-ALDS and four vs. Detroit-ALCS), batting .200 (4-for-20) with 1RBI and 7BB.

2005

- Hit .236 (109-for-462) with 32 doubles, 21HR and 74RBI in 131 games with Oakland (115 starts in RF, 13 at 1B)…ranked fourth among AL switch hitters in RBI and tied for fourth in home runs…ranked eighth in the AL with an average of 4.13 pitches per plate appearance.

- Finished sixth in the AL "Rookie of the Year" balloting after leading all Major League rookies in walks (55) and extra-base hits (62)…among American League rookies, led in RBI, tied for the lead in home runs, ranked third in doubles and total bases (206), fourth in runs (66) and slugging percentage (.446), fifth in multi-hit games (26) and sixth in hits.

- Batted .203 (25-for-123) with 3HR vs. left-handed pitchers and .248 (84-for-339) with 18HR vs. right-handers.

- Was placed on the 15-day disabled list on 5/2 with a right AC joint sprain after running into the wall on a Jeremy Reed fly ball on 5/1 vs. Seattle…was reinstated from the D.L. on 5/25…missed 19 team games.

- Had a 34-game, 119AB homerless stretch from 4/13-6/16, the longest such streaks of his career.

- Homered from both sides of the plate for the first time in his career on 6/26 vs. San Francisco, becoming the second player in Oakland history—and third in Athletics history—to accomplish the feat.

- Drew a bases-loaded, "walk-off" walk on 9/7 vs. Seattle—the fifth run scored in the inning by the A's—capping the largest ninth-inning comeback in Oakland history.

2004

- Hit .250 (15-for-60) with 11R, 4 doubles, 2HR and 8RBI in 20 games with Oakland (11 starts in LF, three in RF, two at 1B and two at DH).

- Was recalled by the Athletics from Triple-A Sacramento on 9/3, making his Major League debut that day at Toronto and going 1-for-3 with 2R, 1 double and 2BB…walked in his first plate appearance and doubled off Ted Lilly in the fourth inning for his first Major League hit…hit his first career home run on 9/5 at Toronto off Sean Douglass…started 13 of the A's first 14 games after his recall, replacing an injured Jermaine Dye.

▸ Began the season with Sacramento, batting .269 (119-for-443) with 109R, 29HR, 92RBI and 103BB in 125 games…led all minor leaguers in walks and tied for fourth in runs scored…topped the Pacific Coast League in walks and runs and ranked eighth in on-base percentage (.406)…tied Dan Johnson for the most homers among A's farmhands…reached base safely in 26 straight games from 6/11-7/7…recorded 2HR and 6RBI on 7/24 at Las Vegas…hit 20HR in his last 69 games after homering just nine times in his first 56 contests.

2003
▸ Split the season between Single-A Modesto and Double-A Midland, combining to hit .256 (122-for-476) with 15HR and 86RBI in 127 games…his 11SF tied for fifth in the minors.

▸ Began the season at Modesto, batting .296 (56-for-189) with 10HR and 43RBI in 51 games…was named California League "Player of the Week" for the period from 4/28-5/4…reached base safely in 31 consecutive games from 4/17-5/24 and 47 of his 51 games overall…was promoted to Midland on 6/8 where he hit .230 (66-for-287) with 36R, 24 doubles and 43RBI in 76 games.

2002
▸ Combined to hit .242 (55-for-227) with 6HR and 35RBI in 62 games with Single-A Vancouver and Single-A Visalia…began his career at Vancouver, but was promoted to Visalia after just 13 games.

PERSONAL
▸ Full name is Nicholas Thomas Swisher…married Joanna Garcia following the 2010 season…was signed by Rich Sparks (Athletics)…was selected by the Athletics with Boston's first-round pick in 2002 as compensation for the loss of free agent Johnny Damon.

▸ Established the Nick Swisher Foundation "Swish's Wishes" in 2007 to assist children with life-threatening illnesses and to help lift the spirits of kids going through difficult times…in 2009, provided Christmas dinner for the families of children battling cancer at the Ronald McDonald House in New York and was the co-Ambassador to the Entertainment Industry Foundation's Lee Denim Day to help raise money for breast cancer research…continued his practice of hosting "Swish's Wishes Days" at Yankee Stadium, inviting children to his home ballpark throughout the year as he did in Oakland and Chicago…made a $10,000 donation to the United Way Alliance of the Mid-Ohio Valley in November 2009…also purchased uniforms for the football team at his junior high school.

▸ Received a 2011 Thurman Munson Award for his on-field excellence and community service.

▸ Is a regular visitor at children's hospitals…supports Lynn Sage Cancer Center in Chicago…in the past, has dyed his goatee pink on Mother's Day to raise awareness for breast cancer and blue on Father's Day to raise awareness for prostate cancer…grew and shaved a mustahce in November 2010 as part of Movember to raise awareness for cancer…provides holiday gifts and a party for mentally challenged children at Janet Pomeroy School in San Francisco…supports UCSF Medical Center in San Francisco, where he served as the honorary chairman for the 2007 Macy's Tree Lighting Ceremony…has also funded programs at the Children's Hospital & Research Center in Oakland and frequently reads books to children in the hospital…teamed with Columbia Pictures in 2007 to host a private screening of the movie *Water Horse: Legend of the Deep* for 400 sick and low-income Bay Area children.

▸ Participates in Strikeouts For Troops, a non-profit organization that provides assistance to wounded war veterans and their children by providing "comforts of home" while they recover in military hospitals nationwide…toured U.S. bases in Spain, Greece and Italy on a goodwill mission to visit American soldiers and their families stationed abroad in January 2007…helped fund two programs for low-income children in need at Tony La Russa's Animal Rescue Foundation…participated in adopting 25 military families in need and provided Thanksgiving and Christmas dinner as well as Christmas gifts for the children in 2007, 2008 and 2009.

▸ Threw out the first pitch to eight-year-old Adam Bender on 7/1/08 vs. Cleveland…Bender lost his leg to cancer at the age of 1 and was flown from Kentucky to Chicago with his parents, older brother and younger sister by Swisher's foundation to celebrate the one-year anniversary of "Swish's Wishes"…Bender played catcher for his Little League team in Lexington, Ky…Swisher provided Bender with a personalized White Sox jersey and a bat autographed by the team.

▸ In honor of his grandmother, Betty, who lost her battle with cancer in 2005, Nick joined as an ambassador to the EIF Foundation and the Women's Cancer Research Fund…went without a haircut for nearly one year in 2007 as part of the non-profit Pantene Beautiful Lengths program that encourages people to grow, cut and donate their hair to create live hair wigs for women who have lost their hair due to cancer treatments…his father, Steve, made the "kindest cut of all" on the field in Oakland on 5/19/07, cutting Nick's hair to be donated to the program…also supports childhood diabetes, prostate and breast cancer, and the Special Olympics…was the Athletics' 2007 Roberto Clemente Award nominee.

▸ Appeared as himself in an episode of the television show *How I Met Your Mother* in February 2010 and *Better With You* in 2011…also appeared as himself in the television show *The Game* in 2007 and 2008.

▸ Attended Ohio State University where he was named Big Ten "Freshman of the Year" in 2000 after hitting .299 with 10HR and 48RBI…was All-Big Ten at first base as a sophomore in 2001 after hitting .322 with a league-best 15HR and 56RBI…also earned All-Conference honors as an outfielder in 2002 when he batted .348 with 10HR and 52RBI…graduated from Parkersburg (W. Va.) High School.

▸ Is the son of Steve Swisher, who batted .216 (305-for-1,414) in 509 Major League games with Chicago-NL (1974-77), St. Louis (1978-80) and San Diego (1981-82)…Steve was selected by the White Sox in the first round (21st overall) of the 1973 draft.

Swisher's Career Playing Record

Year	Club	AVG	G	AB	R	H	2B	3B	HR	RBI	SH	SF	HP	BB	SO	SB	CS	E	OBP	SLG
2002	Vancouver	.250	13	44	10	11	3	0	2	12	0	1	2	13	11	3	0	0	.433	.455
	Visalia	.240	49	183	22	44	13	2	4	23	2	1	2	26	48	3	1	4	.340	.399
2003	Modesto	.296	51	189	38	56	14	2	10	43	0	5	2	41	49	0	2	4	.418	.550
	Midland	.230	76	287	36	66	24	2	5	43	0	6	6	37	76	0	1	5	.324	.380
2004	Sacramento	.269	125	443	109	119	28	2	29	92	0	5	3	103	109	3	3	7	.406	.537
	OAKLAND	.250	20	60	11	15	4	0	2	8	0	1	2	8	11	0	0	3	.352	.417
2005	OAKLAND - a	.236	131	462	66	109	32	1	21	74	0	1	4	55	110	0	1	2	.322	.446
	Sacramento	.391	6	23	4	9	3	0	1	0	0	0	1	2	7	0	1	0	.462	.522
2006	OAKLAND	.254	157	556	106	141	24	2	35	95	2	6	11	97	152	1	2	8	.372	.493
2007	OAKLAND	.262	150	539	84	141	36	1	22	78	1	9	10	100	131	3	2	5	.381	.455
2008	CHICAGO-AL - b	.219	153	497	86	109	21	1	24	69	1	4	4	82	135	3	3	7	.332	.410
2009	YANKEES - c	.249	150	498	84	124	35	1	29	82	3	6	3	97	126	0	0	6	.371	.498
2010	YANKEES	.288	150	566	91	163	33	3	29	89	3	2	6	58	139	1	2	4	.359	.511
Minor League Totals		**.261**	**320**	**1169**	**219**	**305**	**85**	**8**	**50**	**214**	**2**	**18**	**16**	**222**	**300**	**9**	**8**	**20**	**.381**	**.476**
Major League Totals		**.252**	**911**	**3178**	**528**	**802**	**185**	**9**	**162**	**495**	**10**	**29**	**40**	**497**	**804**	**8**	**10**	**35**	**.358**	**.469**
NYY Totals		**.270**	**300**	**1064**	**175**	**287**	**68**	**4**	**58**	**171**	**6**	**8**	**9**	**155**	**265**	**1**	**2**	**10**	**.365**	**.505**

Selected by Oakland in the first round (16th overall) of the 2002 First-Year Player Draft.

a – Placed on the 15-day disabled list from May 2-25,2005 with a right shoulder sprain.
b – Acquired by Chicago-AL on January 3, 2008 in exchange for RHP Fautino De Los Santos, LHP Giovany Gonzalez and OF Ryan Sweeney.
c – Acquired by the Yankees along with RHP Kanekoa Texeira on November 13, 2008 in exchange for INF Wilson Betemit and RHPs Jeff Marquez and Jhonny Nunez.

Swisher's Division Series Record

Year	Club vs. Opp.	AVG	G	AB	R	H	2B	3B	HR	RBI	SH	SF	HP	BB	SO	SB	CS	E	OBP	SLG
2006	OAK vs. MIN	.300	3	10	3	3	2	0	0	1	0	0	0	2	2	0	0	0	.417	.500
2008	CWS vs. TB	.250	3	4	1	1	0	0	0	0	0	0	0	2	1	0	0	0	.500	.250
2009	NYY vs. MIN	.083	3	12	0	1	1	0	0	1	0	0	0	4	0	0	0	0	.083	.167
2010	NYY vs. MIN	.333	3	12	3	4	2	0	1	1	0	0	0	1	1	0	0	0	.385	.750
Division Series Totals		**.237**	**12**	**38**	**7**	**9**	**5**	**0**	**1**	**3**	**0**	**0**	**0**	**5**	**8**	**0**	**0**	**0**	**.326**	**.447**

Swisher's Championship Series Record

Year	Club vs. Opp.	AVG	G	AB	R	H	2B	3B	HR	RBI	SH	SF	HP	BB	SO	SB	CS	E	OBP	SLG
2006	OAK vs. DET	.100	4	10	0	1	0	0	0	0	0	0	0	5	5	0	0	0	.400	.100
2009	NYY vs. LAA	.150	6	20	2	3	0	0	1	0	1	0	1	3	7	0	0	0	.292	.150
2010	NYY vs. TEX	.091	6	22	3	2	1	0	1	1	0	0	0	3	7	0	0	0	.200	.273
LCS Totals		**.115**	**16**	**52**	**5**	**6**	**1**	**0**	**1**	**1**	**1**	**0**	**1**	**11**	**19**	**0**	**0**	**0**	**.281**	**.192**

Swisher's World Series Record

Year	Club vs. Opp.	AVG	G	AB	R	H	2B	3B	HR	RBI	SH	SF	HP	BB	SO	SB	CS	E	OBP	SLG
2009	NYY vs. PHI	.133	5	15	3	2	1	0	1	1	0	0	0	4	4	0	0	0	.316	.400
World Series Totals		**.133**	**5**	**15**	**3**	**2**	**1**	**0**	**1**	**1**	**0**	**0**	**0**	**4**	**4**	**0**	**0**	**0**	**.316**	**.400**
POSTSEASON TOTALS		**.162**	**33**	**105**	**15**	**17**	**7**	**0**	**3**	**5**	**1**	**0**	**1**	**20**	**31**	**0**	**0**	**0**	**.302**	**.314**

Swisher's All-Star Game Record

Year	Club, Site	AVG	G	AB	R	H	2B	3B	HR	RBI	SH	SF	HP	BB	SO	SB	CS	E	OBP	SLG
2010	NYY,Los Angeles-AL	.000	1	1	0	0	0	0	0	0	0	0	0	0	1	0	0	0	.000	.000
All-Star Game Totals		**.000**	**1**	**1**	**0**	**0**	**0**	**0**	**0**	**0**	**0**	**0**	**0**	**0**	**1**	**0**	**0**	**0**	**.000**	**.000**

Swisher's Career Fielding Record

Position	PCT	G	PO	A	E	TC	DP
Outfield	.983	687	1348	29	24	1401	7
First Base	.994	255	1740	116	11	1867	161
Pitcher	-	1	0	0	0	0	0

Swisher's Career Home Run Chart

MULTI-HOMER GAMES: 16. **TWO-HOMER GAMES:** 16, last on 8/2/10 vs. Toronto. **GRAND SLAMS:** 4, last on 6/30/08 vs. Cleveland (Jeremy Sowers). **PINCH-HIT HR:** None. **INSIDE-THE-PARK HR:** 1, on 6/11/06 at New York-AL (Shawn Chacon). **WALK-OFF HR:** 3, last on 9/9/10 vs. Baltimore (Koji Uehara). **LEADOFF HR:** 1, on 4/6/08 at Detroit (Justin Verlander).

25 MARK TEIXEIRA

FIRST BASEMAN • 6-3 • 220 • B/T: SWITCH/RIGHT • OPENING DAY AGE: 30

BIRTHDATE
April 11, 1980

BIRTHPLACE
Annapolis, Md.

RESIDES
Greenwich, Conn.

M.L. SERVICE
8 years

COLLEGE
Georgia Tech

CAREER HIGHLIGHTS

A.L. All-Star Team
▸ 2005, 2009

A.L. Gold Glove
▸ 2005, 2006, 2009, 2010

A.L. Silver Slugger
▸ 2004, 2005, 2009

STATUS

▸ Signed as a free agent to an eight-year contract on January 6, 2009…contract extends through the 2016 season.

CAREER NOTES

▸ Is one of only three Major Leaguers to reach 30HR and 100RBI in each of the last seven seasons (2004-10), joining Albert Pujols and teammate Alex Rodriguez…according to *Elias*, is one of three first basemen all time to surpass 30HR and 100RBI in seven straight years by age 30 (also Jimmie Foxx and Pujols).

▸ Is one of just three Yankees first basemen in franchise history to record at least 100R, 30HR and 100RBI in multiple seasons with the club, joining Lou Gehrig (10 times, 1927 and '29-37) and Don Mattingly (twice, 1985-86)…is the only player to accomplish the feat in his first two seasons with the club.

▸ Is the sixth Yankee all time to hit at least 30HR in each of his first two seasons with the club (also Babe Ruth, Roger Maris, Jason Giambi, Alex Rodriguez and Gary Sheffield).

▸ Has reached the 25HR plateau in each of his first eight Major League seasons…according to *Elias*, became just the fourth player in Baseball history to accomplish the feat, joining Eddie Mathews (11 seasons), Albert Pujols (10) and Darryl Strawberry (nine).

▸ Is one of 13 players all-time to hit at least 250 home runs within the first eight years of their Major League career and one of just four active players to accomplish the feat, joining Albert Pujols (319 from 2001-08), Adam Dunn (278 from 2001-08) and Todd Helton (251 from 1997-2004)…his 275 career home runs are the most ever by a switch-hitter in his first eight seasons.

▸ Has homered from both sides of the plate in the same game 10 times in his career (tied with teammate Nick Swisher for most among actives)…is tied with Swisher, Ken Caminiti, Tony Clark and Mickey Mantle for the second-most such games all-time behind Chili Davis and Eddie Murray (11 each).

▸ Since returning to the AL on 7/29/08 when he was acquired by Los Angeles-AL from Atlanta, ranks second in RBI (273) and home runs (85) among American Leaguers.

▸ Leads all active first basemen with a .99643 career fielding percentage at 1B.

BESTS & STREAKS

Hits
4 - 21 times
Last: at TOR, 8/24/10
Runs
4 - 2 times
Last: at CIN, 8/20/07
2B
3 - at NYY, 5/10/07
3B
1 - 16 times
Last at SEA, 9/19/09
HR
3 - 3 times
Last: at BOS, 5/8/10
RBI
7 - 2 times
Last: at BAL, 7/13/06
BB
5 - 2 times
Last: at BOS, 4/25/09
SO
5 - 2 times
Last: at TOR, 6/5/10
SB
1 - 15 times
Last: at CWS, 8/2/10
Hit Streak
14g - 5/18-6/1/09

2010

▸ Hit .256 (154-for-601) with 113R, 36 doubles, 33HR and 108RBI in 158 games (148 starts at 1B, nine at DH) with the Yankees…was one of nine Major Leaguers in 2010 with at least 100R and 100RBI…led the AL and ranked second in the Majors in runs scored, trailing only the Cardinals' Albert Pujols (115).

- Was awarded his fourth Gold Glove Award, becoming the Yankees' first repeat winner at first base since Don Mattingly won four straight awards from 1991-94...committed just 3E in 1,310 chances, a .998 fielding percentage...marked the second-fewest errors and second-highest fielding percentage among qualifying Major League first basemen, behind only Seattle's Casey Kotchman...recorded 54 putouts on foul balls, the most for any fielder in 2010—credit: *Elias*.

- Hit .245 (102-for-417) with 23HR as a left-handed batter and .283 (52-for-184) with 10HR as a righthanded batter...owned a .533 batting average (8-for-15) with 1 double, 1HR and 22RBI with the bases loaded.

- Over his final 101 games of the season (from 6/8), batted .283 (107-for-378) with 25HR and 74RBI...ranked second in the AL in HRs and tied for fourth in RBI over the stretch...began the season batting just .211 (47-for-223) with 8HR and 34RBI over his first 57 games.

- Made his eighth career Opening Day roster (second as a Yankee) and seventh Opening Day start at 1B.

- Was hitless in his first 17 at-bats to start the season, the longest hitless streak to begin a season of his career...snapped streak with a fifth-inning RBI double in 4/10 win at Tampa Bay...was 3-for-4 with 2R, 1 double, 1RBI and 1BB in the game...following the 4/10 game, again went hitless in his next 17AB before snapping the stretch with a second-inning single in 4/17 win vs. Texas.

MOST HOME RUNS AMONG ACTIVE PLAYERS IN FIRST EIGHT MLB SEASONS

1.	Albert Pujols	.319 (2001-08)
2.	Adam Dunn	278 (2001-08)
2.	**MARK TEIXEIRA**	**275 (2003-10)**
4.	Ryan Howard	.253 (2004-10)
5.	Todd Helton	251 (1997-2004)

MAJOR LEAGUE LEADERS SINCE 2004

HOME RUNS

1.	Albert Pujols	.294
2.	Adam Dunn	.282
3.	ALEX RODRIGUEZ	.268
4.	David Ortiz	.260
5.	Ryan Howard	.253
6.	**MARK TEIXEIRA**	**249**

RBI

1.	Albert Pujols	.849
2.	ALEX RODRIGUEZ	.841
3.	David Ortiz	.831
4.	**MARK TEIXEIRA**	**822**
5.	Miguel Cabrera	.817

EXTRA-BASE HITS

1.	Albert Pujols	.590
2.	David Ortiz	.539
3.	**MARK TEIXEIRA**	**533**
4.	Miguel Cabrera	.522
5.	Adam Dunn	.496

- Hit his first HR in 4/18 win vs. Texas, snapping a 40AB homerless stretch to start the season...marked the second-longest such stretch of his career behind a 76AB homerless span to start the 2007 season.

- Collected 33H and 25RBI in 29 games in May after having 11H and 9RBI in 22 games in April.

- Recorded his 26th career multi-HR game and third three-homer game in 5/8 win at Boston...became the fourth player in Major League history to have a 3HR game with three different teams, (also Johnny Mize-Cardinals, Giants, Yankees; Dave Kingman- Mets, Cubs, Athletics; and Alex Rodriguez-Mariners, Rangers, Yankees)...became just the second Yankee in franchise history to hit 3HR in a game vs. Boston (also Lou Gehrig on 6/23/27 at Boston).

- Went 10 games without an RBI from 5/18-28, one game shy of a career-high 11-game span without driving in a run from 5/7-21/04.

- Hit his 250th career home run in 5/31 win vs. Cleveland, snapping a 56AB homerless stretch.

- Was removed from 6/1 win vs. Baltimore in the top of the fourth inning with a bruised left foot, suffered on a foul ball in his first-inning at-bat...did not miss a game.

- Struck out five times in 6/5 loss at Toronto, tying his career high (second time, also 8/18/03 at Detroit)...became the sixth Yankee to strike out five times in a game and first since Melky Cabrera in July 2007.

- Reached base safely (via hit, walk or hit-by-pitch) in a career-high 42 straight games from 6/6-7/26...marked the longest such streak by a Yankee since Alex Rodriguez reached safely in 53 straight from 4/18-6/17/04.

- Made his first error of the season—and first since 10/2/09—in 6/13 win vs. Houston, snapping a 64-game errorless stretch.

- Hit his fifth career grand slam and was 1-for-3 with 1BB in 6/20 win vs. the Mets...was his first grand slam since 8/3/08 w/ Los Angeles-AL at Yankee Stadium (off Edwar Ramirez).

- Hit safely in a season-high 12 straight games from 6/18-7/1, batting .292 (14-for-48) with 8R, 3HR and 11RBI.

- Batted .344 (33-for-96) with 26RBI and 20BB in 26 games in July, collecting 11 multi-hit contests...18 of his 33H (54.5%) went for extra bases (10 doubles, 8HR).

- Homered from both sides of the plate for the 10th time in his career—and second in 2010—in 7/9 win at Seattle...homered six times in a nine-game stretch from 7/31-8/9.

- Missed two-game series in Texas on 8/10 and 8/11 for the birth of his son, William Charles...played the final month with a broken right pinky toe suffered on 8/31 (hit by pitch).

- Was named AL "Player of the Week" for the period ending 9/5...hit .476 (10-for-21) with 3 doubles, 2HR and 8RBI during the week...marked his fifth career weekly award and first since 2007 with Texas.

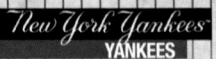
- Became the first player to record both 100R and 100RBI in 2010, reaching the totals in 9/10 loss at Texas.
- Appeared in seven postseason games (.148, 4-for-27)…hit game-winning homer in ALDS Game 1 at Minnesota in the seventh inning…suffered a torn right hamstring in the ninth inning (running to first base) of the Yankees' ALCS Game 4 loss vs. Texas and missed the Yankees' final two playoff contests.

2009

- Batted .292 (178-for-609) with 103R, 43 doubles, 39HR and 122RBI in 156 games (150 starts at 1B, five at DH) in his first season with the Yankees…hit .282 (122-for-432) with 30HR as a left-handed batter and .316 (56-for-177) with 9HR as a right-handed batter…earned his third Gold Glove Award and third Silver Slugger Award.

- From 5/8 (when Alex Rodriguez returned to the lineup) through the end of the season, batted .310 (159-for-513) with 89R, 39 doubles, 34HR, 107RBI and 62BB in 131G (the Yankees were 88-43 in those games)…led the AL in home runs and RBI over the span…prior to Rodriguez's return, Teixeira hit .198 (19-for-96) with 14R, 4 doubles, 5HR, 15RBI and 19BB in 25G.

- Led the American League in RBI and tied Tampa Bay's Carlos Pena for the lead in home runs…led the Majors in home runs (24) and RBI (71) at home…led the AL in go-ahead RBI (31) and ranked second in go-ahead home runs (13).

- With 103R, 43 doubles and 39HR, was one of only two players in the Majors to collect at least 100R, 40 doubles and 35HR, joining St. Louis' Albert Pujols (124R, 45 doubles, 47HR).

- Became just the second player ever to lead or tie for the AL lead in home runs in his first season with the Yankees, joining Babe Ruth in 1920 (54HR)-credit: Elias Sports Bureau…Elias also noted Teixeira was one of three Yankees to lead the AL in RBI in their first season with the club, joining Ruth (136RBI) and Roger Maris (112 in 1960)…became one of just three players to reach 39HR and 122RBI in their first season with the Yankees, joining Babe Ruth in 1920 (54HR, 136RBI) and Jason Giambi in 2002 (41HR, 122RBI)—credit: Elias.

TOP OFFENSIVE MONTHS BY A YANKEE SINCE 1954 (min. .330 Avg. / 13HR / 34RBI)		
Mickey Mantle	May 1956	.414 / 16 / 35
Roger Maris	June 1960	.331 / 14 / 34
ALEX RODRIGUEZ	April 2007	.355 / 14 / 34
MARK TEIXEIRA	**May 2009**	**.330 / 13 / 34**

MOST BACK-TO-BACK HOME RUNS IN A SINGLE SEASON BY THE SAME YANKEES TANDEM (Credit: *Elias*)

1.	Johnny Damon/**MARK TEIXEIRA**	6 (2009)
2.	Gary Sheffield/ALEX RODRIGUEZ	5 (2005)
	Lou Gehrig/Joe DiMaggio	5 (1936)
	Lou Gehrig/Babe Ruth	5 (1927)

- According to the *Elias Sports Bureau*, became the eighth player to hit at least 30HR in his first season with the Yankees (did so in his 112th game of the season), joining Babe Ruth (1920), Roger Maris (1960), Bobby Bonds (1975), Reggie Jackson (1977), Jason Giambi (2002), Alex Rodriguez (2004) and Gary Sheffield (2004)…only two of those players hit their 30th homer fewer games into the season than Teixeira (Maris in 82 games and Ruth in 88 games).

- Became the fifth Yankee to reach 100R, 40 doubles, 35HR and 100RBI in a season (also Babe Ruth-1921 and '23; Lou Gehrig-1927, '30 and '34; Don Mattingly-1985 and Alfonso Soriano-2002)…is the only player to do so in his first season with the club.

- Homered from both sides of the plate three times in 2009 (5/4 vs. Boston, 5/18 vs. Minnesota and 9/19 at Seattle)…became the 11th Yankee all time to accomplish the feat and one of three in 2009 (also Melky Cabrera and Nick Swisher)…along with Swisher (2007 and 2009), tied Tony Clark (1998 w/ Detroit) for the most switch-hit homers in a single season.

- His 43 doubles were the most by a Yankees first baseman in a season since Don Mattingly had 53 in 1986…85 of his 178 hits (47.8%) went for extra bases (43 doubles, 3 triples and 39HR).

- Was voted as the AL's starting first baseman in the 2009 All-Star Game…went 0-for-3 in the AL's 4-3 win in St. Louis on 7/14, playing five innings at 1B…was named the starting AL All-Star at 1B for the second time in his career (also 2005)…was the first Yankee 1B to start an All-Star Game since Jason Giambi in 2004.

- Batted .200 (14-for-70) with 3HR and 10RBI in April…hit at a .304 (164-for-539) clip over the remainder of the season.

- Collected the 1,000th hit of his career with a third-inning infield single in 4/24 loss at Boston.

- Tied a career high with 5BB in 4/25 loss at Boston…also walked five times on 9/23/04 w/ Texas vs. Oakland…is the only current Major Leaguer to walk five times in two games (credit: Elias)…Elias also noted he became the first player to draw 5BB in two nine-inning contests since Mel Ott who had three (1929, 1943 and 1944)…were the most walks drawn by a Yankee since Roger Maris drew 5BB in a 12-inning game against the Angels on 5/22/62…were the most walks by a Yankee in a nine-inning game since Russ Derry drew 5BB in Game 1 of a doubleheader on 9/6/45 vs. Detroit.

- Hit 13HR in May, tying a career-high for his most HRs in any calendar month (also July 2004))...were the most by a Yankee since Alex Rodriguez hit 14HR in April 2007...led the Majors in HR and RBI (34) during May and, according to *Elias*, matched the most RBI for a Yankees player in a calendar month over the past 20 years: Tino Martinez (April 1997), Bernie Williams (August 1999) and Alex Rodriguez (April 2007 and June 2007).

- Both he and Alex Rodriguez each hit 4HR over a four-game span from 5/16-19, becoming the first pair of Yankees teammates since 1977 (Reggie Jackson and Bucky Dent) to accomplish the feat (credit: *Elias*).

- Hit safely in a career-high 14 straight games from 5/18-6/1...during the stretch, hit .397 (23-for-58) with 14R, 5 doubles, 8HR and 20RBI.

- Had 47RBI through his first 50 games with the Yankees, matching Harry Rice, Joe Gordon and Roger Maris for the third-most for any player in franchise history over his first 50 games with the team since 1920 when RBI became an official statistic...only Babe Ruth (57) and Joe DiMaggio (56) had more through their first 50 games (credit: *Elias*).

- Made ninth-inning throwing error in 7/2 loss vs. Seattle, snapping a 72-game stretch at 1B to start the season without committing an error...had been the longest errorless streak in one season for a Yankees first baseman since Tino Martinez went 82 straight games without an error in 1996 (credit: *Elias*)...also snapped a 106-game errorless stretch at 1B overall, dating back to 8/20/08.

- Snapped a career-long 95AB homerless stretch with solo-HR in 7/9 win at Minnesota.

- Played in his 1,000th career Major League game in 7/28/09 loss at Tampa Bay, going 1-for-4 with 1R and 1 double...the double was the 250th of his career—and with 228HR—became only the second active player to accumulate at least 250 doubles and 225HR through his first 1,000 games (also Albert Pujols – 273 doubles, 266 HR)—credit: *Elias Sports Bureau*.

- Drove in his 100th run of the season with a three-run home run in 8/30 win vs. Chicago-AL in his 126th game of the season...according to *Elias*, only four players reached the 100RBI milestone fewer games into their Yankees career than Teixeira: Babe Ruth in 1920 (97 games), Joe DiMaggio in 1936 (102), Roger Maris in 1960 (118) and Tony Lazzeri in 1926 (125).

- Batted .180 (11-for-61) with 2 doubles, 2HR and 8RBI in the postseason...hit "walk-off" solo home run off Jose Mijares in 11th inning in Game 2 of ALDS vs. Minnesota, marking his first career postseason home run and first career "walk-off" HR (regular and postseason)...was the Yankees' second "walk-off" homer in ALDS play (also Jim Leyritz in 1995 vs. Seattle)...scored a run in five of the six World Series games...was hit by a pitch three times in the WS, joining Alex Rodriguez (also 2009) and Pittsburgh's Max Carey (1925) as the only players to get plunked three times in a single Series.

2008

- In 157 combined games with Atlanta and Los Angeles-AL, batted .308 (177-for-574) with 41 doubles, 33HR and 121RBI...ranked sixth in the Majors in RBI.

- Hit 20 home runs for the Braves and 13 with the Angels in 2008, a year after hitting 13 homers for the Rangers and 17 for the Braves...according to *Elias*, he became the first player in history to hit at least 30 home runs in each of back-to-back seasons while playing for more than one team in both years.

- Batted .366 (83-for-227) with 18 doubles, 16HR and 52RBI in 64 games after the All-Star break, ranking third in the Majors in batting average behind Manny Ramirez (.388) and Albert Pujols (.368)...hit .271 (94-for-347) with 23 doubles, 17HR and 69RBI in 93 games prior to the break.

- Opened the season with Atlanta, hitting .283 (108-for-381) with 27 doubles, 20HR and 78RBI in 103 games prior to being dealt...at the time of the trade, ranked fifth in the NL in walks (65) and tied for 10th in doubles (27).

- Compiled 134RBI in 157 games with the Braves over 2007-08...according to the *Elias Sports Bureau*, only one Major League player had as many RBI in so few career games for one team – Juan Gonzalez, who had 140RBI for the Indians in 141 games (140 games in 2001 and one game in 2005).

- Recorded his second career three-homer game in 6/22 win vs. Seattle, homering from each side of the plate for the fifth time in his career...became the first Brave with a three-homer game at Turner Field.

- Was acquired by the Angels on 7/29 in exchange for 1B Casey Kotchman and RHP Steve Marek...hit .358 (122-for-393) with 14 doubles, 13HR and 43RBI in 54 games with Los Angeles-AL, reaching base safely in 49 of those contests...recorded the highest average, on-base percentage (.449) and slugging percentage (.632) in the AL following the trade, the sixth-most RBI, tied for the sixth-most home runs and tied for the ninth-most hits and extra-base hits.

- Collected 66H in his first 50 games with Angels, tallying the fourth-most base hits by an Angel in their first 50 contests with the club behind Johnny Ray (79), Alex Johnson (71) and Vladimir Guerrero (70).

- Hit .386 (39-for-101) in August, ranking fifth in the AL and marking his highest average for any month in his career...hit his first homer as an Angel in 8/3 loss at Yankee Stadium, an eighth-inning grand slam...was just the third player in club history whose first homer as an Angel was a slam.

- Saw his first career postseason action, batting .467 (7-for-15) with 4R, 1RBI and 4BB in four Division Series games against Boston.

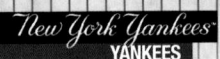
2007

▸ Combined with Texas and Atlanta to hit .306 (151-for-494) with 86R, 33 doubles, 30HR and 105RBI in 132 games…was acquired by the Braves at the 7/31 trade deadline in a seven-player deal.

▸ Was one of just eight players to record a .300 average with 30HR and 100RBI in 2007, doing so in the fewest at-bats (494) and games (132)…Boston's David Ortiz needed the second-fewest at-bats (549) and games (149) to reach the plateaus.

▸ Batted .357 (55-for-154) with 6HR off left-handed pitching, and .282 (96-for-340) with 24HR against right-handers…his .405 (53-for-131) average with runners in scoring position ranked third in the Majors (min. 100AB)…was a .382 (50-for-131) hitter during the day and .278 (101-for-363) hitter at night.

▸ Opened the year with Texas and batted .297 with 24 doubles, 13HR and 49RBI in 78 games with the Rangers prior to the trade.

▸ Tied for second in the AL in May with 27RBI and 19 extra-base hits while hitting .348 with 7HR for the month…his 38 hits were a career high for any month.

▸ Was on the 15-day disabled list from 6/9-7/13 with a strained left quadriceps (missed 27 games)…snapped his consecutive games played streak at 507 games.

▸ Batted .317 with 17HR and 56RBI in 54 games with Atlanta, hitting safely in 33 of his last 38 games and in 43 of 54 games overall with the Braves…also drove in a run in 32 of his 54 Braves games…had 21 multi-hit games and 14 multi-RBI games, including three contests with four-or-more RBI.

▸ Homered in each of his first three games with Atlanta from 8/1-4, becoming the first Brave to accomplish the feat since Gary Sheffield from 4/1-4/02…went 1-for-4 with a three-run homer and 4RBI in his Atlanta debut on 8/1 vs. Houston…walked with the bases loaded in the first inning for his 500th career RBI.

	SWITCH-HITTING RECORD				
Year		AVG	AB	H	HR	RBI
2003	Left	.244	353	86	15	52
	Right	.290	176	51	11	32
2004	Left	.266	376	100	27	77
	Right	.314	169	53	11	35
2005	Left	.304	470	143	37	115
	Right	.293	174	51	6	29
2006	Left	.276	457	126	21	78
	Right	.298	171	51	12	32
2007	Left	.284	335	95	24	69
	Right	.352	159	56	6	36
2008	Left	.311	379	118	26	80
	Right	.303	195	59	7	41
2009	Left	.282	432	122	30	91
	Right	.316	177	56	9	31
2010	Left	.245	417	102	23	68
	Right	.283	184	52	10	40
Totals	Left	.277	3219	892	203	630
	Right	.305	1405	429	72	276

▸ Earned the NL "Player of the Month" award in August, hitting .315 (35-for-111) with 32RBI and 10HR…marked the most RBI in the Majors in August and tied for the most homers…named NL "co-Player of the Week" (with Jason Isringhausen) for 8/20-26, hitting .414 (12-for-29) with 8R, 3HR and 11RBI over the stretch.

▸ Homered twice in back-to-back games on 8/19 (vs. Arizona) and 8/20 (at Cincinnati) to become the fourth player in Atlanta history with consecutive multi-homer games and first since Chipper Jones in July 2003.

▸ Drove in the "walk-off" run in the 11th inning on 9/22 vs. Milwaukee with an RBI single…homered in three straight games from 9/25-27.

2006

▸ Played in all 162 games for Texas, batting .282 (177-for-628) with 45 doubles, 33HR and 110RBI…won his second straight AL Gold Glove at first base, becoming the first Rangers first baseman to win the award twice.

▸ Became the first Ranger since Pete Incaviglia (1986-90) to record 20-or-more homers in each of his first four Major League seasons and the fourth player in club history to record three consecutive seasons of at least 30 home runs.

▸ Led the AL in game-winning RBI (19), ranked third in extra-base hits (79), fifth in doubles, sixth in at-bats (628), seventh in total bases (323), eighth in intentional walks (12) and ninth in walks (89).

▸ Collected his third consecutive 100-RBI season, becoming the fourth player in Texas history to accomplish the feat…also became the fourth Ranger to notch 30HR and 100RBI in consecutive seasons…was second on the club with 26 go-ahead RBI as well as 40 two-out RBI.

▸ Ranked by *Baseball America* as the best defensive first baseman in a survey of AL managers…posted a .997 fielding percentage (4E, 1572 TC), ranking second among all Major League first baseman behind Tampa Bay's Travis Lee (.998) for the second consecutive season.

▸ Hit .302 (51-for-169) off lefties and .275 (126-for-459) against right-handed pitching…totaled 21HR from the left side of the plate and 12HR from the right.

▸ Batted .275 (97-for-353) with 9HR and 49RBI prior to the All-Star break…following the break, hit .291 (80-for-275) with 24HR and 61RBI in the second half, ranking first in the Majors in homers, tied for second in RBI, placed fourth in walks (42) and slugging percentage (.604) and eighth in runs scored (51).

▸ Named Rangers' July "Player of the Month," batting .316 (15-for-37) with seven home runs and 18RBI.

- Tied a club record with a career-high 3HR on 7/13 at Baltimore in the first game after the All-Star break, and also tied career high with 7RBI…was the third time he homered from both sides in the same game…according to the *Elias Sports Bureau*, he became the first player to hit three-or-more home runs in his team's first game after the All-Star break.

- Reached base safely in 36 consecutive games from 7/3-8/13 (.352, 44-for-125, 27R, 10HR, 26RBI, 22BB), matching the second-longest streak in the Majors in 2006 behind Orlando Cabrera's 63-game run.

- Participated in the inaugural World Baseball Classic for the United States, going hitless in four games.

2005

- Hit .301 with 41 doubles, 43HR and 144RBI in 162 games with Texas…set club records for home runs and RBI as a first baseman…established a Major League record for RBI by a switch hitter in a single season, surpassing the previous mark of 136 by the New York Giants' George Davis in 1896…finished seventh in AL Most Valuable Player voting.

- Led the AL in total bases (370), ranked second in extra-base hits (87), tied for second in RBI (144), placed fourth in home runs (43) and multi-hit games (59), fifth in slugging percentage (.575), tied for sixth in hits (194) and at-bats (644), ranked seventh in doubles (41), tied for seventh in runs (112) and finished 10th in on-base percentage (.379)…batted .366 (59-for-161) with runners in scoring position, placing second in the AL…hit .334 (104-for-311) with 30HR and 88RBI in 81 games at home, recording the fourth-best home average in the AL.

- Batted .292 (50-171) with 6HR and 29 RBI against left-handers and .304 (144-for-473) with 37HR and 115RBI against right-handers…hit his first 27 home runs from the left side of the plate, the most ever by a switch-hitter from one side of the plate to begin a season.

- Of his 43HR, 40 came as a first baseman…was the fourth-highest HR total in Major League history by a switch-hitter…became the fourth player in Texas history to record a 40-homer season, joining Juan Gonzalez, Rafael Palmeiro and Alex Rodriguez…became the 30th player all time with 20-or-more home runs in each of his first full Major League campaigns…averaged one HR every 15.0 at-bats, the eighth-best ratio in the AL.

- Registered 133RBI as a first baseman, leading all Major Leaguers and breaking his own club record of 112RBI as a first baseman, set in 2004…became just the fifth player in Texas history to record consecutive 100-RBI seasons…had the AL's third-best RBI ratio, averaging one every 4.5 at-bats.

- Earned his first career All-Star nod, receiving 2,187,115 fan votes and becoming the first Texas first baseman elected to start an All-Star game…started at 1B in the AL win on 7/12 at Detroit, going 1-for-3 with a sixth inning HR off Florida's Dontrelle Willis…the homer came from the right side, his first right-handed HR in any game (including spring training) in 2005…participated in the Home Run Derby on 7/11 and homered twice.

- Received his first career Rawlings Gold Glove Award, joining Rafael Palmeiro (1999) as the only Texas first basemen to claim the honor…made 154 starts at first base and led all qualifying AL first basemen with a .998 fielding percentage (3E, 1483TC), trailing only Cincinnati's Sean Casey among all Major League first basemen…was the eighth-best fielding percentage by a first baseman since 1986…led AL first basemen in total chances (1,483), putouts (1,378) and innings played at the position (1,358.0), and ranked second in assists (102).

- Earned an AL Silver Slugger Award for the second consecutive year.

- Named AL "Player of the Week" for the periods of 5/16-22 and 8/29-9/4.

- Hit his 100th career home run on 9/6 at Minnesota, joining Ralph Kiner, Albert Pujols, Eddie Mathews and Joe DiMaggio as the fifth player in Major League history to reach 100HR in their first three seasons…hit his 100th homer in his 430th career game, becoming one of four then-active Major Leaguers to reach 100 career home runs in 430-or-fewer games (also Albert Pujols-415 games, Mike Piazza-422 and Juan Gonzalez-423).

- Batted .356 (37-for-104) with 9HR and a Major League-best 35RBI in 27 games in September…marked the highest September RBI total for a Major Leaguer since Don Mattingly had 37RBI in September 1985…matched Carlton Fisk (1977) for the second-highest September RBI total since Divisional play began in 1969.

2004

- In his sophomore campaign, batted .281 (153-for-545) with 101R, 34 doubles, 38HR and 112RBI in 145 games with the Rangers…ranked fifth in the American League in home runs and extra base hits (74), tied for fifth in intentional walks (12), placed sixth in slugging percentage (.560), seventh in RBI and was the eighth hardest to double up, averaging 90.8 at-bats per GIDP…led the team in each of those categories as well as on-base percentage (.370)…received his first AL Silver Slugger Award.

- Had a .313 (51-for-163) batting average with 11HR from the right side and hit .267 (102-for-382) with 27HR from the left side…hit .314 (43-for-137) with runners in scoring position.

- Recorded the highest home run total in Major League history by a switch-hitter 24 years old or younger, surpassing Mickey Mantle's 37HR in 1955 at age 23…led the AL with 33HR after 6/1…became the 12th player in club history to record a 30-homer season, joining Ruben Sierra (1987) and Mickey Tettleton (1995) as the only switch-hitters to do so…averaged a home run every 14.3 at-bats, the fifth-best ratio in the AL.

- All 112 of his RBI came as a first baseman, surpassing the club record set by Rafael Palmeiro (105) in 1993.

- Made 138 starts at 1B, four in RF and two as DH…led AL first basemen in assists (98) and ranked second in total chances…had just one error in his final 35 games (311 chances) in the field.

- Named AL "Player of the Month" and Rangers "Player of the Month" for July, batting .300 (30-for-100) with 27R, 13HR and 30RBI and becoming the first Texas player other than Alex Rodriguez to win the monthly

HITTING FOR THE CYCLE

On August 17, 2004 vs. Cleveland, Teixeira became the second Rangers player in franchise history to hit for the cycle, joining Oddibe McDowell (July 23, 1985 vs. Cleveland). Was the 245th cycle in Baseball history, 223rd since 1900 and 110th in the American League. Teixeira became the 14th switch-hitter to hit for the cycle and just the sixth American League switch-hitter to accomplish the feat. Was the fifth player to hit for the cycle in 2004 and the first switch-hitter, since 1970, to complete the cycle with a single. Became the first player to hit for the cycle in Rangers Ballpark (formerly Ameriquest Field) and the third player to do it in the city of Arlington, joining McDowell and Baltimore's Cal Ripken, Jr. (May 6, 1984) who both accomplished the feat at Arlington Stadium.

First AB: .... Strikeout vs. Cliff Lee (first inning)
Second AB: .... Double off Lee (third inning)
Third AB: .... Home run off Rick White (fourth inning)
Fourth AB: .... Triple off White (fifth inning)
Fifth AB: .... Single off Cliff Bartosh (seventh inning)

award since 1999…tied for the Major League lead in homers, RBI and runs scored for the month…was the fourth-highest home run total in club history for a single month…homered 12 times in a span of 18 games from 6/28-7/19, including home runs in five consecutive games from 7/11-19 (5HR) to match a club record…also matched the second-longest home run streak ever by a switch-hitter.

- Homered from both sides of the plate for the first time in his career in 7/4 win at Houston, including a grand slam…named AL "Player of the Week" for the period ending 7/4…also connected for a grand slam in 7/18 win at Toronto.

- Recorded his first career four-hit game in 8/17 win vs. Cleveland, hitting for the cycle (third-inning double, fourth-inning homer, fifth-inning triple, seventh-inning single)…became the second player in Rangers history to hit for the cycle in a game, joining Oddibe McDowell who accomplished the feat on 7/23/85 vs. Cleveland…recorded 7RBI in the game, the most in a cycle game since Boston's Rich Gedman on 9/18/85…at the time, became the 14th switch-hitter to hit for the cycle, and first since Jose Valentin on 4/27/00…was the sixth switch-hitter with a cycle in AL history…recorded two hits from each side of the plate in the cycle, becoming just the third known switch-hitter to accomplish the feat (also Mickey Mantle and Wes Parker).

2003

- In his first Major League season, hit .259 (137-for-529) with 29 doubles, 5 triples, 26HR and 84RBI in 146 games with Texas…led all rookies in homers and extra base hits (60), ranked second in RBI and walks (44), third in slugging percentage (.480), fourth in hits, total bases (254) and triples, and fifth in runs (66) and doubles…were the second-most homers ever for a Texas first-year player behind Pete Incaviglia (30) in 1986…the total also tied for the third-most ever by a rookie switch-hitter.

- Selected as the first baseman on the *Baseball Digest* and Topps Major League All-Star Rookie teams…named Rangers "Rookie of the Year" by local BBWAA chapter.

- Started 104 games at 1B and was also in the starting lineup at 3B (11), LF (10), RF (8) and DH (5)…had never played 1B prior to the 2003 season…ranked fifth among AL first basemen with a .996 fielding percentage (4E, 1006TC)…did not commit an error in his final 36 games at 1B beginning 8/20.

- Made his first Opening Day roster having played in just 86 professional games, the fewest for a Ranger since Incaviglia went directly from college to the Majors in 1986.

- Started at DH in his Major League debut on 4/1 at Anaheim, going 1-for-3 with 1BB…went hitless in his first 16AB before doubling off Mark Mulder on 4/9 vs. Oakland…connected for his first homer off Ted Lilly the next day vs. Oakland…hit his first grand slam off Baltimore's Rick Helling on 5/25, marking the first slam for a Texas rookie since Mike Stanley on 7/3/87 at the Yankees.

- Set a Texas club record for spring training homers (8).

2002

- Combined to bat .318 (102-for-321) with 19HR and 69RBI in 86 games at Single-A Charlotte and Double-A Tulsa in his first professional season…despite missing the first two months of the season, was selected as the third baseman on the *Baseball America* overall Minor League All-Star team as well as the Rangers' "Minor League Player of the Year."

- Opened season on the D.L. after rupturing a tendon in his left elbow and forearm while attempting to catch a foul pop in March...activated on 6/1 and hit safely in his first 12 games at a .354 (17-for-48) clip...named the Topps Florida State League "Player of the Month" for June.

- Promoted to Tulsa on 7/12 and hit .316 with 10HR and 28RBI in 47 starts at third base and one as the DH...had a .243 (9-for-37) average with 1HR and 4RBI in 10 Texas League playoff games.

- Selected as the top prospect in the both the Texas League and Florida State League by *Baseball America*...played for Peoria in Arizona Fall League, batting .333 (33-for-99) with 7HR and 23RBI in 27 games...ranked among the league leaders in slugging (second, .616), homers (tied for third), RBI (tied for fourth) and average (fifth) despite missing the last two weeks of the season with a strained abdominal muscle.

2001

- Was the fifth overall pick by the Rangers in the 2001 First-Year Player Draft, Texas' highest selection since 1989...signed a four-year contract through 2006 on 8/22 and participated in the Rangers' Florida Instructional League program, batting .246 with a team-high 13RBI in 20 games.

PERSONAL

- Full name is Mark Charles Teixeira...he and his wife, Leigh, have two sons, Jack and William and daughter Addison...met his wife, an industrial-design Major, as a freshman at Georgia Tech...signed by Zackary Hoyrst (Rangers)...is an avid golfer...his favorite team growing up was the Baltimore Orioles and his favorite player was Don Mattingly...is a natural right-handed hitter...decided to become a dedicated switch hitter at the age of 13...is of Portugese decent...his father, John, is a former Navy pilot who played high school baseball with Bucky Dent...his uncle, Pete, played in the Braves minor league system.

- In 2006, Mark and his wife established the Mark Teixeira Charitable Fund that supported six $5,000 scholarships at three high schools in the Dallas/Ft. Worth area...in 2007, he increased the number of scholarships to 12...following the 2007 season, he held the first Tex's Holiday Hold 'Em poker tournament that raised over $55,000 for his foundation...other community groups that have been helped by the Teixeiras include Cook Children's Medical Center, the Arlington Boys & Girls Club and the Arlington Police Department, where they worked to start a local Police Athletic League (PAL) for the youth of Arlington...won the 2006 "Harold McKinney Good Guy Award" as voted on by the Dallas/Ft. Worth chapter of the BBWAA.

- Teamed up with Coppertone's "Help Strike Out Sun Damage" program in 2009 as a spokesman for the National Foundation for Cancer Research.

- In May 2010, Mark and Leigh partnered up with Harlem RBI, making a $100,000 donation to the Harlem RBI Futures Fund to support Harlem RBI's college-bound seniors...in addition, Mark signed up as a member of the Harlem RBI Board of Directors and serves as an Honorary Chair of Harlem RBI's Capital Campaign.

- Batted .409 (216-528) with 36HR and 165RBI in 140 games in three seasons at Georgia Tech...became just the second player in Atlantic Coast Conference history to have a career .400 average, joining Wake Forest's Bill Merrifield (.400 from 1981-83)...batted .419 (26-for-62) with 5HR and 20RBI in 16 games for the Yellow Jackets as a senior in 2001...fractured right ankle in season's seventh game on 2/23 vs. Elon...won the Dick Howser Trophy as the "National Collegiate Player of the Year" in 2000, hitting .427 (103-for-241) with 18HR and 80RBI in 66 games...selected as "National Player of the Year" by *Baseball America* and the Sporting News, was the ACC "Player of the Year" and was a consensus first-team All-American...led the ACC in batting average, runs (school-record 104), homers, walks (67), slugging percentage (.772) and on-base percentage (.547)...was a three-time ACC "Player of the Week"...named to all-tournament team in NCAA regional in Atlanta with 2HR and 7RBI...hit .387 (87-for-225) with 13HR and 65RBI in 58 games in 1999...named ACC Rookie of the Year and was first-team all-conference selection...picked as "National Freshman of the Year" by *Collegiate Baseball*...set Georgia Tech freshman records for hits and RBI and tied the doubles mark (18)...led Tech in batting, becoming the first freshman to do so since 1978...spent summer of 2000 with USA Baseball National Team, leading the club in batting (.385), runs (26), hits (46), RBI (23) and total bases (70)...hit .289 with 7HR and 26RBI for Orleans in the Cape Cod League in the summer of 1999...earned team MVP in league All-Star Game and received Robert A. McNeese Award as Cape League's most outstanding pro prospect.

- Makes an annual donation to the Georgia Tech baseball scholarship, including a $500,000 pledge in February 2009.

- Played baseball, basketball and soccer at Mt. St. Joseph's High School in Baltimore (graduated 1998)...set Maryland state records for career homers (29), RBI (105) and runs (128)...in 1998, earned first-team High School All-American honors from *Baseball America*, *USA Today/Sports Weekly*, *Collegiate Baseball*, and the American Baseball Coaches Association, hitting .548 with 12 homers and 36 RBI...was named Maryland "Player of the Year" in 1997 and 1998...also played in the Babe Ruth League and American Legion programs...endowed a scholarship at Mt. St. Joseph in the name of his friend Nick Liberatore who was killed in a car accident while the two were in school.

Teixeira's Career Hitting Record

Year	Team	AVG	G	AB	R	H	2B	3B	HR	RBI	SH	SF	HP	BB	SO	SB	CS	E	OBP	SLG
2002	Charlotte	.320	38	150	32	48	10	2	9	41	0	1	3	21	24	2	0	9	.411	.593
	Tulsa	.316	48	171	31	54	11	3	10	28	0	0	4	25	36	3	2	12	.415	.591
2003	TEXAS	.259	146	529	66	137	29	5	26	84	0	2	14	44	120	1	2	4	.331	.480
2004	TEXAS - a	.281	145	545	101	153	34	2	38	112	0	2	10	68	117	4	1	10	.370	.560
	Frisco	.000	1	3	0	0	0	0	0	0	0	0	0	1	0	1	0	0	.250	.000
2005	TEXAS	.301	#162	644	112	194	41	3	43	144	0	3	11	72	124	4	0	3	.379	.575
2006	TEXAS	.282	#162	628	99	177	45	1	33	110	0	6	4	89	128	2	0	4	.371	.514
2007	TEXAS - b	.297	78	286	48	85	24	1	13	49	0	1	3	45	66	0	0	1	.397	.524
	Frisco	.000	1	2	0	0	0	0	0	0	0	0	0	2	0	0	0	0	.500	.000
	ATLANTA - c	.317	54	208	38	66	9	1	17	56	0	1	4	27	46	0	0	4	.404	.615
2008	ATLANTA	.283	103	381	63	108	27	0	20	78	0	2	3	65	70	0	0	4	.390	.512
	LOS ANGELES-AL - d	.358	54	193	39	69	14	0	13	43	0	5	4	32	23	2	0	3	.449	.632
2009	YANKEES - e	.292	156	609	103	178	43	3	#39	*122	0	5	12	81	114	2	0	4	.383	.565
2010	YANKEES	.256	158	601	*113	154	36	0	33	108	0	5	13	93	122	0	1	3	.365	.481
Minor League Totals		**.313**	**88**	**326**	**63**	**102**	**21**	**5**	**19**	**69**	**0**	**1**	**8**	**48**	**61**	**5**	**2**	**21**	**.413**	**.583**
AL Totals		**.284**	**1061**	**4035**	**681**	**1147**	**266**	**15**	**238**	**772**	**0**	**29**	**71**	**524**	**814**	**15**	**4**	**40**	**.374**	**.535**
NL Totals		**.295**	**157**	**589**	**101**	**174**	**36**	**1**	**37**	**134**	**0**	**3**	**7**	**92**	**116**	**0**	**0**	**6**	**.395**	**.548**
Major League Totals		**.286**	**1218**	**4624**	**782**	**1321**	**302**	**16**	**275**	**906**	**0**	**32**	**78**	**616**	**930**	**15**	**4**	**46**	**.377**	**.536**
NYY Total		**.274**	**314**	**1210**	**216**	**332**	**79**	**3**	**72**	**230**	**0**	**10**	**25**	**174**	**236**	**2**	**1**	**7**	**.374**	**.523**

*Denotes league leader   #Tied for league lead

Selected by Boston in the ninth round of the 1998 First-Year Player Draft but did not sign.
Selected by Texas in the first round (fifth pick overall) of the 2001 First-Year Player Draft.

a – Placed on the 15-day disabled list from April 13-29, 2004 with a strained left oblique.
b – Placed on the 15-day disabled list from June 9 – July 13, 2007 with a strained left quadriceps.
c – Traded to the Atlanta Braves along with LHP Ron Mahay from the Texas Rangers in exchange for C Jarrod Saltalamacchia, INF Elvis Andrus, RHP Neftali Perez and LHPs Matt Harrison and Beau Jones on July 31, 2007.
d – Traded to the Los Angeles Angels from the Atlanta Braves in exchange for INF Casey Kotchman and RHP Steve Marek on July 29, 2008.
e – Signed as a free agent by the Yankees to an eight-year contract on January 6, 2009.

Teixeira's Division Series Record

Year	Club vs. Opp.	AVG	G	AB	R	H	2B	3B	HR	RBI	SH	SF	HP	BB	SO	SB	CS	E	OBP	SLG
2008	LAA vs. BOS	.467	4	15	4	7	0	0	0	1	0	1	0	4	3	0	0	0	.550	.467
2009	NYY vs. MIN	.167	3	12	3	2	0	0	1	1	0	0	0	1	1	0	0	0	.231	.417
2010	NYY vs. MIN	.308	3	13	2	4	1	0	1	3	0	0	0	1	2	0	0	0	.357	.615
Division Series Totals		**.325**	**10**	**40**	**9**	**13**	**1**	**0**	**2**	**5**	**0**	**1**	**0**	**6**	**6**	**0**	**0**	**0**	**.404**	**.500**

Teixeira's League Championship Series Record

Year	Club vs. Opp.	AVG	G	AB	R	H	2B	3B	HR	RBI	SH	SF	HP	BB	SO	SB	CS	E	OBP	SLG
2009	NYY vs. LAA	.222	6	27	2	6	1	0	0	4	0	1	0	3	8	0	0	0	.290	.259
2010	NYY vs. TEX	.000	4	14	1	0	0	0	0	0	0	0	0	3	4	0	0	0	.176	.000
LCS Totals		**.146**	**10**	**41**	**3**	**6**	**1**	**0**	**0**	**4**	**0**	**1**	**0**	**6**	**12**	**0**	**0**	**0**	**.250**	**.171**

Teixeira's World Series Record

Year	Club vs. Opp.	AVG	G	AB	R	H	2B	3B	HR	RBI	SH	SF	HP	BB	SO	SB	CS	E	OBP	SLG
2009	NYY vs. PHI	.136	6	22	5	3	1	0	1	3	0	0	3	2	8	0	0	0	.296	.318
World Series Totals		**.136**	**6**	**22**	**5**	**3**	**1**	**0**	**1**	**3**	**0**	**0**	**3**	**2**	**8**	**0**	**0**	**0**	**.296**	**.318**
POSTSEASON TOTALS		**.214**	**26**	**103**	**17**	**22**	**3**	**0**	**3**	**12**	**0**	**2**	**3**	**14**	**26**	**0**	**0**	**0**	**.320**	**.330**

Teixeira's All-Star Game Record

Year	Club, Site	AVG	G	AB	R	H	2B	3B	HR	RBI	SH	SF	HP	BB	SO	SB	CS	E	OBP	SLG
2005	TEX, Detroit	.333	1	3	1	1	0	0	1	2	0	0	0	0	0	0	0	0	.333	1.333
2009	NYY, St. Louis	.000	1	3	0	0	0	0	0	0	0	0	0	0	0	0	0	0	.000	.000
All-Star Game Totals		**.167**	**2**	**6**	**1**	**1**	**0**	**0**	**1**	**2**	**0**	**0**	**0**	**0**	**0**	**0**	**0**	**0**	**.167**	**.667**

Teixeira's World Baseball Classic Record

Year	Country, Site	AVG	G	AB	R	H	2B	3B	HR	RBI	SH	SF	HP	BB	SO	SB	CS	E	OBP	SLG
2006	USA, USA	0	4	15	0	0	0	0	0	0	0	0	0	0	4	1	0	0	.000	.000

Teixeira's Career Fielding Record

Position	PCT	G	PO	A	E	TC	DP
First Base	.996	1154	9949	663	38	10650	990
Outfield	.974	32	37	0	1	38	0
Third Base	.811	15	10	20	7	37	0

Teixeira's Career Home Run Chart

MULTI-HOMER GAMES: 29. **TWO-HOMER GAMES:** 26, last on 9/24/10 vs. Boston. **THREE-HOMER GAMES:** 3, last on 5/8/09 at Boston. **GRAND SLAMS:** 5, last on 6/20/10 vs. New York-NL (Johan Santana). **PINCH-HIT HR:** None. **INSIDE-THE-PARK HR:** None. **WALK-OFF HR:** None. **LEADOFF HR:** None.

73

DANIEL TURPEN

RIGHT-HANDED PITCHER • 6-4 • 245 • B/T: RIGHT/RIGHT • OPENING DAY AGE: 24

BIRTHDATE
August 17, 1986

BIRTHPLACE
McMinnville, Ore.

RESIDES
McMinnville, Ore.

M.L. SERVICE
None (Rookie)

COLLEGE
Oregon State University

STATUS
▸ Selected by the Yankees in the 2010 Rule 5 Draft (second round) from Boston…contract extends through the 2011 season.

2010
▸ Split the season between the San Francisco and Boston organizations, combining to go 7-6 with four saves and a 4.30 ERA (69.0IP, 33ER) in 49 relief appearances with Double-A Richmond and Double-A Portland…ranked fifth in the Eastern League in games pitched…held opponents to a .175 (7-for-40) batting average with runners in scoring position and two outs.

▸ Began the season with Richmond, going 5-5 with one save and a 4.09 ERA (50.2IP, 23ER) in 37 relief outings…tossed more than 1.0 inning in 20 of his 37 appearances and at least 2.0 innings in 12 of those outings.

▸ Was acquired by the Boston Red Sox on 7/31 in exchange for RHP Ramon Ramirez and assigned to Double-A Portland…went 2-1 with three saves and a 4.91 ERA (18.1IP, 10ER) in 12 relief appearances with the Sea Dogs.

▸ Pitched for Peoria in the Arizona Fall League following the season, going 0-1 with one save and a 5.40 ERA in 10 relief appearances (11.2IP, 7ER).

▸ Attended his first spring training as a non-roster invitee with the Giants, making three relief outings (2.1IP, 3ER).

▸ Was selected by the Yankees from Boston in the Rule 5 Draft (second round) on 12/9/10.

2009
▸ Spent the majority of the season with Single-A San Jose, going 4-2 with seven saves and a 1.24 ERA in 46 relief appearances (65.1IP, 9ER)…led the team in innings pitched.

▸ Went 1-1 with four saves and a 0.72 ERA with San Jose following the All-Star break, including a 0.64 ERA (14.0IP, 1ER) with 17K in 11 combined appearances in August and September.

▸ Appeared in four postseason games for the California League champions, tossing 6.0 scoreless innings and recording two saves.

▸ Made one appearance for Triple-A Fresno on 8/3, allowing 2H and 1R in 2.1IP (0ER).

▸ Following the season, pitched for Scottsdale in the Arizona Fall League, going 1-0 with a 3.94 ERA (16.0IP, 7ER) in 11 relief outings.

2008
▸ Combined to go 5-4 with five saves and a 3.66 ERA (73.2IP, 30ER) in 46 relief appearances for Single-A Augusta and Single-A San Jose.

▸ Began the season with Augusta, going 5-4 with five saves and a 3.45 ERA (62.2IP, 24ER) in 40 relief outings…over his final 12 games with the GreenJackets, went 1-0 with a 1.53 ERA (17.2IP, 3ER).

▸ Was promoted to San Jose on 8/10, allowing 6ER in 11.0IP (4.91 ERA) in 11 appearances.

2007
▸ Made his professional debut with the AZL Giants and short-season Single-A Salem-Keizer, combining to allow 4ER in 28.2IP (1.26 ERA) over 14 relief appearances.

▸ Started the season with the AZL Giants, making four relief appearances and allowing just 1R in 9.1IP (0ER)...was promoted to Salem-Keizer on 7/28, making 10 appearances and allowing 4ER in 19.1IP (1.86 ERA) with 19K...held right-handed hitters to a .171 (7-for-41) batting average, allowing just two extra-base hits (one double and 1HR).

PERSONAL

▸ Graduated from McMinnville High School (Ore.), where Yankee alum Scott Brosius served as a part-time coach...attended Oregon State University and was a member of the 2006 NCAA Champion Beavers...signed by Matt Woodward (Giants).

Turpen's Career Pitching Record

Year	Club	W	L	ERA	G	GS	CG	SHO	SV	IP	H	R	ER	HR	HP	BB	SO	WP	BK
2007	AZL Giants	0	0	0.00	4	0	0	0	1	9.1	10	1	0	0	0	3	5	1	0
	Salem-Keizer	0	0	1.86	10	0	0	0	0	19.1	15	6	4	1	2	7	18	3	0
2008	Augusta	5	4	3.45	40	0	0	0	5	62.2	67	26	24	2	3	13	48	9	0
	San Jose	0	0	4.91	6	0	0	0	0	11.0	11	7	6	0	1	6	11	0	0
2009	San Jose	4	2	1.24	46	0	0	0	7	65.1	56	15	9	1	4	22	55	3	0
	Fresno	0	0	0.00	1	0	0	0	0	2.1	1	2	0	0	0	2	1	0	0
2010	Richmond	5	5	4.09	37	0	0	0	1	50.2	55	24	23	4	1	19	42	2	0
	Portland – a, b	2	1	4.91	12	0	0	0	3	18.1	18	11	10	0	2	9	18	1	0
Minor League Totals		**16**	**12**	**2.86**	**156**	**0**	**0**	**0**	**17**	**239.0**	**233**	**92**	**76**	**8**	**13**	**81**	**198**	**19**	**0**

Selected by San Francisco in the eighth round of the 2007 First-Year Player Draft.

a – Acquired by the Boston Red Sox from the San Francisco Giants on 7/31 in exchange for RHP Ramon Ramirez.
b – Selected by the Yankees in the 2010 Rule 5 Draft.

Consecutive World Championships

NEW YORK YANKEES (5)	1949-1953
NEW YORK YANKEES (4)	1936-1939
Oakland A's (3)	1972-1974
NEW YORK YANKEES (3)	1998-2000
Chicago Cubs (2)	1907-1908
Philadelphia A's (2)	1910-1911
Boston Red Sox (2)	1915-1916
New York Giants (2)	1921-1922
NEW YORK YANKEES (2)	1927-1928
Philadelphia A's (2)	1929-1930
NEW YORK YANKEES (2)	1961-1962
Cincinnati Reds (2)	1975-1976
NEW YORK YANKEES (2)	1977-1978
Toronto Blue Jays (2)	1992-1993

Celebrating
50 Years in the Greater New York Area!

At Banco Popular we care about our customers and our communities. Today we stand committed to helping you reach your financial goals while we continue working to strengthen the social and economic well-being of the communities we serve.

To learn more about Banco Popular, call **1-800-377-0800** or visit: **mypopularbanking.com**

BANCO POPULAR®

Celebrating 50 years 1961-2011 in NEW YORK

2011 Banco Popular North America. **Member FDIC.**

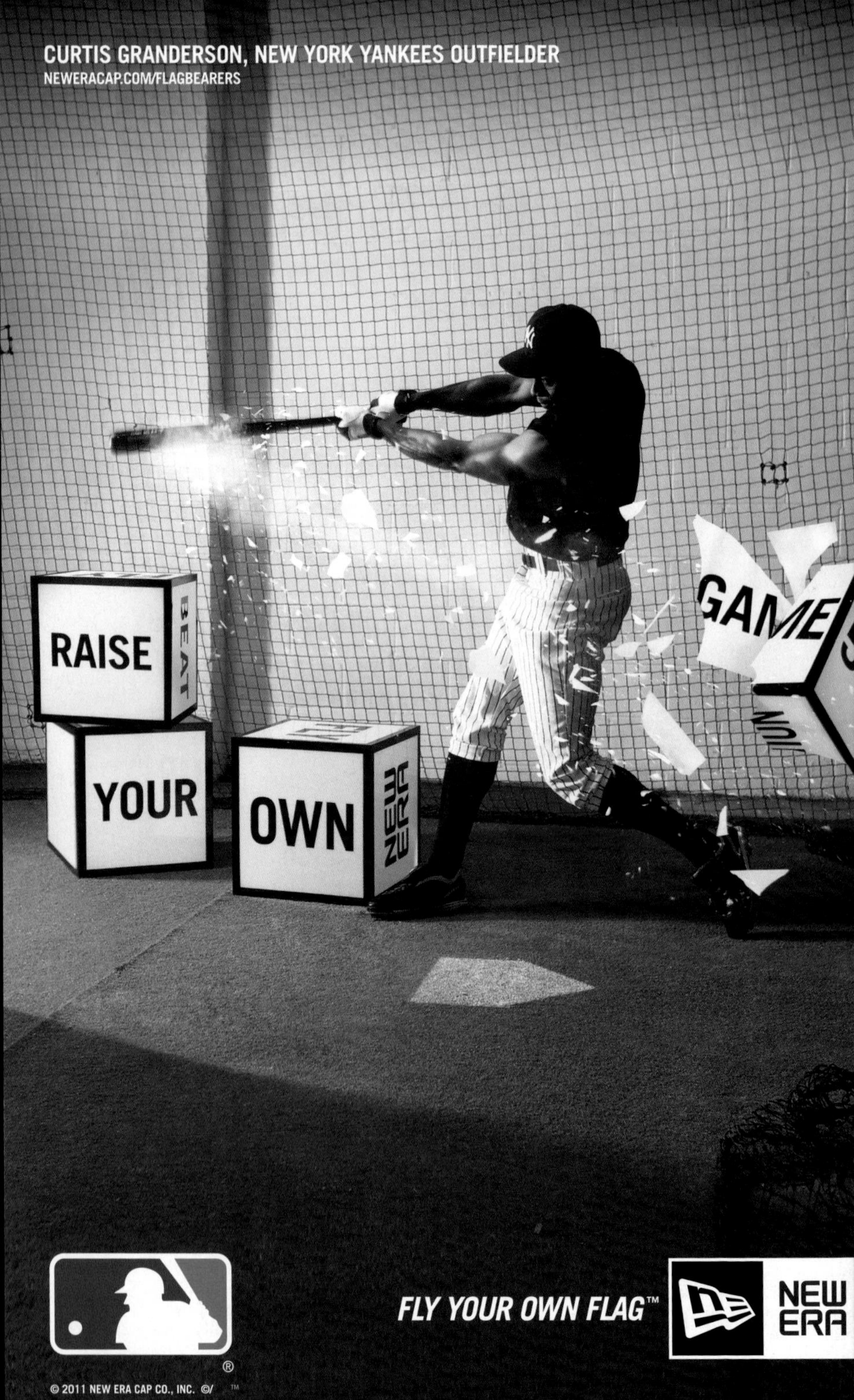

CURTIS GRANDERSON, NEW YORK YANKEES OUTFIELDER
NEWERACAP.COM/FLAGBEARERS

RAISE

YOUR

OWN

GAME

FLY YOUR OWN FLAG™

NEW ERA

© 2011 NEW ERA CAP CO., INC. ©/   ™

2010 REVIEW

3B ALEX RODRIGUEZ became the seventh player – and youngest – all time to reach the 600-homer plateau on August 4, 2010.

2010 Postseason Summary

ALDS RECAP

New York Yankees	**3**
Minnesota Twins	**0**

The Yankees swept the Minnesota Twins (three-games-to-none) for the second straight year in the 2010 ALDS, marking their fourth ALDS sweep all time (also 1998 and '99 vs. Texas), fifth "best-of-five" series sweep all time (also 1981 ALCS vs. Oakland) and 13th postseason series sweep overall…marked the first time the Yankees won an ALDS series after making the postseason as a "Wild Card" entry (losses in 1995 vs. Seattle, and 1997 and 2007 vs. Cleveland)…outscored the Twins 17-7 in the three-game series…Yankees relievers combined to allow just 1ER in 7.0IP (1.29 ERA).

GAME 1 – October 6 at Target Field

	1 2 3	4 5 6	7 8 9	-	R	H	E
NYY	0 0 0	0 0 4	2 0 0	-	6	9	0
MIN	0 2 1	0 0 1	0 0 0	-	4	8	0

WP: CC Sabathia   **LP:** Jesse Crain   **SV:** Mariano Rivera
HR: NYY, M. Teixeira (inning: 7, 1 out, 1 on) off J. Crain; MIN, M. Cuddyer (inning: 2, 0 out, 1 on) off C. Sabathia

In the first-ever postseason contest at Target Field, the Yankees defeated Minnesota in Game 1, 6-4…the Yankees came back from a 3-0 deficit, scoring four runs in the sixth inning, capped by a go-ahead two-run triple from **CF Curtis Granderson**…**LHP CC Sabathia** (6.0IP, 5H, 4R, 3ER, 3BB, 5K, 1HR) earned his fourth career Game 1 win…**1B Mark Teixeira** (2-for-5) hit a game-winning two-run HR in the seventh, the third straight postseason game vs. the Twins in which the Yankees hit a go-ahead HR in the seventh inning or later.

GAME 2 – October 7 at Target Field

	1 2 3	4 5 6	7 8 9	-	R	H	E
NYY	0 0 0	1 1 0	2 0 1	-	5	12	0
MIN	0 1 0	0 0 1	0 0 0	-	2	6	0

WP: Andy Pettitte   **LP:** Carl Pavano   **SV:** Mariano Rivera
HR: NYY, L. Berkman (inning: 5, 1 out, 0 on) off C. Pavano; MIN, O. Hudson (inning: 6, 1 out, 0 on) off A. Pettitte

The Yankees defeated the Twins, 5-2, in Game 2…was the eighth straight postseason game vs. Minnesota in which the Yankees came from behind, the longest such winning streak in postseason history (credit: *Elias*)…**LHP Andy Pettitte** (7.0IP, 5H, 2ER, 1BB, 4K, 1HR) extended his all-time record with his 19th career postseason win…retired 15 of his final 17 batters faced…**DH Lance Berkman** homered in the fifth and doubled home the go-ahead run in the seventh…became the ninth player since 1981 to collect a home run as his first postseason hit as a Yankee, first since Melky Cabrera in 2007 (credit: *Elias*)…**RHP Mariano Rivera** (1.0IP, 1H) collected his 600th career save (regular and postseason combined) and his 11th postseason save of an Andy Pettitte win.

GAME 3 – October 9 at Yankee Stadium

	1 2 3	4 5 6	7 8 9	-	R	H	E
MIN	0 0 0	0 0 0	0 1 0	-	1	7	1
NYY	0 1 1	3 0 0	1 0 x	-	6	12	0

WP: Phil Hughes   **LP:** Brian Duensing   **SV:** ---
HR: NYY, M. Thames (inning: 4, 0 out, 1 on) off B. Duensing; N.Swisher (inning: 7, 0 out, 0 on) off S. Baker

The Yankees completed the series sweep with a 6-1 win at Yankee Stadium…**RHP Phil Hughes** made his first career postseason start, holding the Twins to 4H in 7.0 scoreless innings (1BB, 6K)…was perfect his first time through the order and retired 12 of his first 13 batters faced…became the first Yankee under the age of 25 since Dave Righetti in 1981 to win a postseason start…was just the third Yankee ever to throw at least 7.0 scoreless innings in his first career postseason start, joining Orlando Hernandez (1998 ALCS Game 4 at Cleveland – 7.0IP, 3H, 0R) and Waite Hoyt (1921 WS Game 2 vs. N.Y. Giants – 9.0IP, 2H, 0R)…**DH Marcus Thames** hit his first career postseason home run…**RHP Mariano Rivera** tossed 1.0 scoreless IP and recorded the final out of the series…the sellout attendance of 50,840 was the largest for a baseball game in Yankee Stadium history (including regular season and postseason games).

MINNY STREAK
The Yankees have won nine straight postseason games against Minnesota, dating to Game 2 of the 2004 ALDS on 10/6/04, marking the fourth-longest winning streak by one team over one opponent in postseason history.

ALCS RECAP
Texas Rangers 4
New York Yankees 2

The Yankees were defeated by the Texas Rangers in six games, losing the series four-games-to-two…was just their third ALCS defeat in 14 trips…marked their first-ever postseason series loss to the Rangers after winning three-games-to-one in the '96 ALDS and sweeping them in the 1998 and '99 ALDS…the Yankees were outscored 38-19 in the series, and outhit 63-38.

GAME 1 – October 15 at Rangers Ballpark

	1	2	3	4	5	6	7	8	9	-	R	H	E
NYY	0	0	0	0	0	0	1	5	0	-	6	10	1
TEX	3	0	0	2	0	0	0	0	0	-	5	7	1

WP: CC Sabathia   **LP:** Darren O'Day   **SV:** Mariano Rivera
HR: NYY, R. Cano (inning: 7, 0 out, 0 on) off C. Wilson; TEX, J. Hamilton (inning: 1, 0 out, 2 on) off C. Sabathia

The Yankees opened the 2010 ALCS with a 6-5 win at Rangers Ballpark…trailed 5-0 after six innings…scored five runs in the eighth (all with nobody out) when sending 10 men to the plate…**RHP Dustin Moseley** tossed 2.0 scoreless innings of relief for the win in his Yankees postseason debut…Yankees relievers allowed just 1H over 5.0 combined IP…**2B Robinson Cano** scored the Yankees' first run with a seventh-inning HR…**SS Derek Jeter** doubled twice and scored his 100th career postseason run, becoming the first player ever to reach the mark…**LHP CC Sabathia** (4.0IP, 6H, 5ER, 4BB, 3K, 1HR, 1WP, 1BK) did not record a decision, allowing three first-inning runs in his shortest outing of 2010.

GAME 2 – October 16 at Rangers Ballpark

	1	2	3	4	5	6	7	8	9	-	R	H	E
NYY	0	0	0	1	0	1	0	0	0	-	2	7	0
TEX	1	2	2	0	2	0	0	0	x	-	7	12	0

WP: Colby Lewis   **LP:** Phil Hughes   **SV:** ---
HR: NYY, R. Cano (inning: 6, 1 out, 0 on) off C. Lewis; TEX, D. Murphy (inning: 2, 1 out, 0 on) off P. Hughes

The Yankees suffered their first postseason defeat in 2010, losing, 7-2, at Rangers Ballpark…snapped their 10-game playoff winning streak vs. Texas…was their first-ever postseason loss at Rangers Ballpark…allowed 12H, seven of which went for extra bases…**SS Derek Jeter** singled to reached base safely (via hit or walk) in his 21st consecutive postseason game (since 2007 ALDS Game 4 vs. Cleveland)…**2B Robinson Cano** scored both Yankees runs and recorded the Yankees' only multi-hit game with a double and his second HR in as many games…**RHP Phil Hughes** started and suffered the loss, allowing 7ER on 10H in 4.0IP (3BB, 3K, 1HR, 1WP)…tied for the third-most runs ever allowed by a Yankees starter in a postseason game.

TEXAS 10-STEP

The Yankees won 10 straight postseason games against Texas from 1996 ALDS Game 2 (10/2/96) through 2010 ALDS Game 1 (10/15/10), tying for the second-longest winning streak by one team over one opponent in postseason history (Boston defeated Los Angeles-AL: 11 straight games from 10/12/86-10/3/08; and Oakland defeated Boston: 10 straight games from 10/5/88-10/2/03).

GAME 3 – October 18 at Yankee Stadium

	1	2	3	4	5	6	7	8	9	-	R	H	E
TEX	2	0	0	0	0	0	0	0	6	-	8	11	0
NYY	0	0	0	0	0	0	0	0	0	-	0	2	0

WP: Cliff Lee   **LP:** Andy Pettitte   **SV:** ---
HR: TEX, J. Hamilton (inning: 2, 1 out, 1 on) off A. Pettitte

The Yankees suffered their worst ever postseason shutout loss all time, falling 8-0, vs. Texas…Yankees batters recorded just 2H and struck out 15 times…marked the third time the Yankees were held to two or fewer hits in the playoffs (also 1958 WS Game 4 loss vs. Milwaukee and 2001 ALDS Game 3 win at Oakland)…matched the Yankees' most strikeouts in a nine-inning postseason game (also 10/2/63 in Game 1 of the WS vs. the Dodgers)…**LHP Andy Pettitte** suffered the loss, allowing 2ER in 7.0IP (5H, 0BB, 5K, 1HR)…snapped his stretch of nine straight undefeated postseason starts…both of his runs allowed came on a Josh Hamilton first-inning homer…retired 20 of his final 23 batters after the HR…**C Jorge Posada** and **LF Brett Gardner** accounted for both Yankees hits…**1B Mark Teixeira** (0-for-3) walked in the fourth, marking the Yankees' only other baserunner.

GAME 4 – October 19 at Yankee Stadium

	1	2	3	4	5	6	7	8	9	-	R	H	E
TEX	0	0	2	0	0	3	2	0	3	-	10	13	0
NYY	0	1	1	1	0	0	0	0	0	-	3	7	0

WP: Derek Holland   **LP:** A.J. Burnett   **SV:** Darren Oliver
HR: NYY, R. Cano (inning: 2, 1 out, 0 on) off T. Hunter; TEX, B. Molina (inning: 6, 2 out, 2 on) off A. Burnett, J. Hamilton (inning: 7, 2 out, 0 on) off B. Logan, J. Hamilton (inning: 9, 0 out, 0 on) off S. Mitre, N. Cruz (inning: 9, 0 out, 1 on) off S. Mitre

The Yankees lost their third straight game, falling 10-3 vs. Texas…allowed 4HR, matching their most ever surrendered in a postseason game (seventh time, fourth time at home)…**RHP A.J. Burnett** recorded the loss in his only postseason start of 2010, allowing 5ER on 6H in 6.0IP (3BB, 4K, 1HR, 1WP, 1HP)…allowed just 2H (both singles) through his first 16 batters faced…**2B Robinson Cano** collected his fourth multi-hit game of the 2010 playoffs and homered for the third time in the series…**SS Derek Jeter** (2-for-5) doubled and tripled for the Yankees' only other extra-base hits in the game.

GAME 5 – October 20 at Yankee Stadium

	1	2	3	4	5	6	7	8	9	-	R	H	E
TEX	0	0	0	0	1	1	0	0	0	-	2	13	1
NYY	0	3	2	0	1	0	1	x		-	7	9	0

WP: CC Sabathia   **LP:** C.J. Wilson   **SV:** ---
HR: NYY, N. Swisher (inning: 3, 0 out, 0 on) off C. Wilson, R. Cano (inning: 3, 0 out, 0 on) off C. Wilson, C. Granderson (inning: 8, 1 out, 0 on) off A. Ogando; TEX, M. Treanor (inning: 5, 0 out, 0 on) off C. Sabathia

The Yankees snapped their three-game losing streak with a 7-2 win vs. Texas at Yankee Stadium…**LHP CC Sabathia** (6.0IP, 11H, 2ER, 0BB, 7K, 1HR) became the sixth starting pitcher all time in postseason play to allow at least 11H and surrender two or fewer runs, the first since Boston's Bruce Hurst in Game 2 of the 1986 ALCS vs. the Angels…six different Yankees scored at least one run…the Yankees hit 3HR, matching their total from the first four games of the series…**CF Curtis Granderson** (3-for-4) doubled and homered…**C Jorge Posada** (2-for-4) had a second-inning RBI, marking the 42nd of his postseason career to tie Jim Edmonds for eighth all time.

GAME 6 – October 22 at Rangers Ballpark

	1	2	3	4	5	6	7	8	9	-	R	H	E
NYY	0	0	0	0	1	0	0	0	0	-	1	3	0
TEX	1	0	0	4	0	1	0	x		-	6	7	0

WP: Colby Lewis   **LP:** Phil Hughes   **SV:** ---
HR: TEX, N. Cruz (inning: 5, 2 out, 1 on) off D. Robertson

The Yankees were eliminated from postseason play with a 6-1 loss at Rangers Ballpark…the Yankees did not record a hit until the fifth inning (Rodriguez double) and were held to just 3H overall…**RHP Phil Hughes** started and recorded his second loss of the ALCS, allowing 4ER in 4.2IP (4H, 4BB, 3K)…**RHP Mariano Rivera** (1.0IP) had his sixth scoreless outing of the 2010 postseason.

2010 Transactions

Jan. 7	Signed **RHP Sergio Mitre** to a one-year contract, avoiding arbitration.
Jan. 18	Signed **RHP Chad Gaudin** and **LHP Boone Logan** to one-year contracts, avoiding arbitration.
Jan. 26	Acquired **OF Greg Golson** from the Texas Rangers in exchange for minor league INF Mitch Hilligoss.
Feb. 8	Signed **OF Randy Winn** to a one-year contract.
	Invited 20 non-roster players to spring training: **LHP Wilkins Arias, LHP Jeremy Bleich, OF Colin Curtis, RHP Grant Duff, OF Reid Gorecki, C Kyle Higashioka, RHP Jason Hirsh, LHP Kei Igawa, RHP Zach McAllister, C Jesus Montero, C P.J. Pilittere, LHP Royce Ring, C Mike Rivera, C Austin Romine, RHP Amaury Sanit, RHP Zack Segovia, OF Marcus Thames, RHP Kevin Whelan** and **OF David Winfree**.
Feb. 16	Invited **RHPs D.J. Mitchell** and **Justin Pope** and **INFs Brandon Laird** and **Jorge Vazquez** to spring training; signed **RHP Dustin Moseley** as a free agent.
Feb. 19	Invited **C Jose Gil** to spring training.
Feb. 28	Signed **RHP Chan Ho Park** to a one-year contract; designated **RHP Edwar Ramirez** for assignment.
Mar. 9	Traded **RHP Edwar Ramirez** to the Texas Rangers for cash considerations.
Mar. 13	Optioned **LHP Wilkin De La Rosa** to Triple-A Scranton/Wilkes-Barre, optioned **RHP Christian Garcia** to Double-A Trenton, optioned **RHP Andrew Brackman** to Single-A Tampa and reassigned **LHP Wilkins Arias, LHP Jeremy Bleich, RHP Grant Duff, C Jose Gil, C Kyle Higashioka, LHP Kei Igawa, RHP D.J. Mitchell** and **RHP Kevin Whelan** to minor league camp.
Mar. 14	Reassigned **RHP Zach McAllister** to minor league camp.
Mar. 15	Optioned **RHP Ivan Nova** to Triple-A Scranton/Wilkes-Barre and optioned **RHP Hector Noesi** to Single-A Tampa.
Mar. 19	Optioned **RHP Romulo Sanchez** to Triple-A Scranton/Wilkes-Barre; reassigned **RHP Jason Hirsh** and **RHP Ryan Pope** to minor league camp.
Mar. 20	Reassigned **RHP Dustin Moseley** to minor league camp.
Mar. 21	Reassigned **OF Colin Curtis, OF Reid Gorecki, C Jesus Montero, C Austin Romine** to minor league camp.
Mar. 22	**OF Jamie Hoffmann** was returned to the Los Angeles Dodgers after the Yankees selected him in the 2009 Rule 5 Draft; optioned **INF Reegie Corona** and **INF Eduardo Nunez** to Triple-A Scranton/Wilkes-Barre; reassigned **INF Brandon Laird** and **INF Jorge Vazquez** to minor league camp.
Mar. 24	Optioned **RHP Jonathan Albaladejo, OF Greg Golson, RHP Mark Melancon, 1B Juan Miranda,** and **INF Kevin Russo** to Triple-A Scranton/Wilkes-Barre.
Mar. 25	Released **RHP Chad Gaudin.**
Mar. 26	Reassigned **RHP Amaury Sanit** to minor league camp.
Mar. 30	Reassigned **OFs Jon Weber** and **David Winfree** to minor league camp.
Apr. 1	Reassigned **RHP Zack Segovia** to minor league camp.
Apr. 2	Reassigned **LHP Royce Ring** to minor league camp.
Apr. 3	Signed **OF Marcus Thames** to a Major League contract and selected him to the 25-man roster; optioned **LHP Boone Logan** to Triple-A Scranton/Wilkes-Barre; reassigned **C P.J. Piliterre** to minor league camp; and gave **C Mike Rivera** his outright release.
Apr. 7	Acquired **OF Chad Huffman** off waivers from San Diego and added him to the 40-man roster.
Apr. 16	Placed **RHP Chan Ho Park** on the 15-day disabled list with a right hamstring strain; recalled **LHP Boone Logan** from Triple-A Scranton/Wilkes-Barre.
May 2	Placed **CF Curtis Granderson** on the 15-day disabled list with a Grade 2 left groin strain; recalled **RHP Mark Melancon** from Triple-A Scanton/Wilkes-Barre.
May 5	Recalled **OF Greg Golson** from Triple-A Scranton/Wilkes-Barre; optioned **RHP Mark Melancon** to Scranton/WB.
May 7	Recalled **RHP Romulo Sanchez** from Triple-A Scranton/Wilkes-Barre; optioned **OF Greg Golson** to Scranton/WB.
May 8	Placed **DH/1B Nick Johnson** on the 15-day disabled list with an inflamed right wrist tendon; recalled **INF Kevin Russo** from Triple-A Scranton/Wilkes-Barre.
May 10	Recalled **RHP Ivan Nova** from Triple-A Scranton/Wilkes-Barre; optioned **RHP Romulo Sanchez** to Scranton/WB.
May 12	Placed **RHP Alfredo Aceves** on the 15-day disabled list with a strained lower back; recalled **OF Greg Golson** from Triple-A Scranton/Wilkes-Barre.
May 13	Recalled **INF Juan Miranda** from Triple-A Scranton/Wilkes-Barre; optioned **INF Kevin Russo** to Scranton/WB.
May 14	Claimed **RHP Shane Lindsay** off waivers from the Colorado Rockies and assigned him to Single-A Tampa; released **RHP Christian Garcia.**
May 17	Returned from rehab and reinstated **RHP Chan Ho Park** from the 15-day disabled list; optioned **RHP Ivan Nova** to Triple-A Scranton/Wilkes-Barre.
May 18	Recalled **RHP Mark Melancon** from Triple-A Scranton/Wilkes-Barre; optioned **OF Greg Golson** to Scranton/WB.
May 20	Placed **C Jorge Posada** on the 15-day disabled list with a fractured right foot; signed **C Chad Moeller** to a Major League contract and selected him to the 25-man roster; recalled **INF Kevin Russo** from Triple-A Scranton/Wilkes-Barre; transferred **DH Nick Johnson** from the 15-day disabled list to the 60-day disabled list; optioned **RHP Mark Melancon** to Triple-A Scranton/WB.
May 26	Signed **RHP Chad Gaudin** to a Major League contract and selected him to the 25-man roster; optioned **LHP Boone Logan** to Triple-A Scranton/Wilkes-Barre; designated **RHP Shane Lindsay** for assignment.
May 28	Returned from rehab and reinstated **OF Curtis Granderson** from the 15-day disabled list; designated **OF Randy Winn** for assignment.
June 1	**RHP Shane Lindsay** was claimed off waivers by the Cleveland Indians.
June 2	Reinstated **C Jorge Posada** from the 15-day disabled list; optioned **INF Juan Miranda** to Triple-A Scranton/Wilkes-Barre.
June 4	Released **OF Randy Winn.**
June 13	Placed **OF Marcus Thames** on the 15-day disabled list with strained right hamstring; recalled **OF Chad Huffman** from Triple-A Scranton/Wilkes-Barre.
June 15	Placed **RHP Sergio Mitre** on the 15-day diabled list with strained left oblique; recalled **LHP Boone Logan** from Triple-A Scranton/Wilkes-Barre.
June 21	Designated **C Chad Moeller** for assignment; signed **OF Colin Curtis** to a Major League contract and selected him to the 25-man roster.

2010 Transactions

June 26	**C Chad Moeller** cleared waivers and was outrighted to Triple-A Scranton/WB.
July 2	Signed **RHP Dustin Moseley** to a Major League contract and selected him to the 25-man roster from Triple-A Scranton/Wilkes-Barre; optioned **LHP Boone Logan** to Triple-A Scranton/Wilkes-Barre.
July 4	Returned from rehab and reinstated **OF Marcus Thames** from the 15-day disabled list; optioned **OF Chad Huffman** to Triple-A Scranton/Wilkes-Barre.
July 16	Recalled **1B Juan Miranda** from Triple-A Scranton/Wilkes-Barre; optioned **INF Kevin Russo** to Scranton/WB; returned **RHP Sergio Mitre** from rehab.
July 17	Placed **LHP Damaso Marte** on the 15-day disabled list with left shoulder inflammation; recalled **LHP Boone Logan** from Triple-A Scranton/Wilkes-Barre.
July 20	Placed **LHP Andy Pettitte** on the 15-day disabled list with a Grade 1 left groin strain; recalled **RHP Jonathan Albaladejo** from Triple-A Scranton/Wilkes-Barre.
July 24	Returned from rehab and reinstated **RHP Sergio Mitre** from the 15-day disabled list; optioned **RHP Jonathan Albaladejo** to Triple-A Scranton/Wilkes-Barre.
July 30	Acquired **OF Austin Kearns** from the Cleveland Indians for a player to be named later (RHP Zach McAllister).
July 31	Acquired **1B/DH Lance Berkman** and cash from the Houston Astros in exchange for RHP Mark Melancon and minor league INF Jimmy Paredes; acquired **RHP Kerry Wood** and cash from the Cleveland Indians for a player to be named later or cash considerations; optioned **OF Colin Curtis** and **1B/DH Juan Miranda** to Triple-A Scranton/Wilkes-Barre; designated **RHP Chan Ho Park** for assignment.
Aug. 4	**RHP Chan Ho Park** was claimed off waivers by the Pittsburgh Pirates.
Aug 19	Placed **1B/DH Lance Berkman** on the 15-day disabled list with a right ankle sprain (retroactive to 8/16); recalled **INF Eduardo Nunez** from Triple-A Scranton/Wilkes-Barre.
Aug. 21	Placed **3B Alex Rodriguez** on the 15-day disabled list with a strained left calf.
Aug. 22	Recalled **RHP Ivan Nova** from Triple-A Scranton/Wilkes-Barre.
Sept. 1	Recalled **RHP Jonathan Albaladejo** and **OF Greg Golson** from Triple-A Scranton/Wilkes-Barre; signed **C Chad Moeller** to a Major League contract and added him to the 40-man roster; returned from rehab and reinstated **DH/1B Lance Berkman** from the 15-day disabled list; transferred **LHP Damaso Marte** to the 60-day D.L.
Sept. 5	Reinstated **3B Alex Rodriguez** from the 15-day disabled list.
Sept. 6	Recalled **OF Colin Curtis** from Triple-A Scranton/Wilkes-Barre.
Sept. 9	Claimed **LHP Steve Garrison** off waivers from the San Diego Padres; designated **LHP Wilkin De La Rosa** for assignment.
Sept. 12	Recalled **1B Juan Miranda** and **INF Kevin Russo** from Triple-A Scranton/Wilkes-Barre; outrighted **LHP Wilkin De La Rosa** to Double-A Trenton.
Sept. 15	Signed **LHP Royce Ring** to a Major League contract and added him to the active roster; designated **OF Chad Huffman** for assignment.
Sept. 17	Recalled **RHP Romulo Sanchez** from Triple-A Scranton/Wilkes-Barre; **OF Chad Huffman** was claimed off waivers by Cleveland.
Sept. 19	Returned from rehab and reinstated **LHP Andy Pettitte** from the 15-day disabled list.
Sept. 24	Recalled **RHP Andrew Brackman** from Double-A Trenton.
Nov. 18	Acquired **RHP Scott Allen** from the Arizona Diamondbacks in exchange for 1B Juan Miranda.
Nov. 19	Released **RHP Jonathan Alabaladejo** to sign a contract in Japan; acquired minor league **OF Cody Johnson** from the Atlanta Braves in exchange for cash considerations; added **RHP Dellin Betances**, **INF Brandon Laird** and **RHP Ryan Pope** to the 40-man roster.
Dec. 2	Signed **RHP Sergio Mitre** to a one-year contract; did not tender contracts to **RHPs Alfredo Aceves** and **Dustin Moseley**.
Dec. 7	Re-signed **SS Derek Jeter** to a three-year contract through 2013, with a one-year player option for 2014.
Dec. 9	Selected **LHP Robert Fish** (first round) from Los Angeles-AL and **RHP Daniel Turpen** (second round) from Boston in the Rule 5 Draft.
Dec. 14	Re-signed **RHP Mariano Rivera** to a two-year contract through the 2012 season.
Dec. 15	Signed **RHPs Brian Anderson, Buddy Carlyle** and **Mark Prior**, **LHPs Neal Cotts** and **Andrew Sisco**, **INF Doug Bernier** and **C Gustavo Molina** to minor league contracts with an invitation to Major League Spring Training.
Dec. 16	Signed **C Russell Martin** to a one-year contract.

2011

Jan. 3	Signed **LHP Pedro Feliciano** to a two-year contract, extending through 2012 with a club option for 2013.
Jan. 5	Claimed **RHP Brian Schlitter** off waivers from the Chicago Cubs.
Jan. 18	Signed **RHP Rafael Soriano** to a three-year contract; signed **RHPs Joba Chamberlain** and **Phil Hughes** and **LHP Boone Logan** to one-year contracts, avoiding arbitration.
Feb. 2	Acquired **OF Justin Maxwell** from the Washington Nationals in exchange for **RHP Adam Olbrychowski**; designated **OF Jordan Parraz** for assignment.
Feb. 11	Signed **RHPs Luis Ayala, Bartolo Colon, Freddy Garcia** and **Warner Madrigal** and **INFs Ronnie Belliard** and **Eric Chavez** to minor league contracts with an invitation to Major League spring training; **OF Jordan Parraz** cleared waivers and was assigned to Triple-A Scranton/Wilkes-Barre; invited **LHP Manuel Banuelos**, **OF Daniel Brewer**, **C Jose Gil**, **C Kyle Higashioka**, **OF Austin Krum**, **RHP D.J. Mitchell**, **C Jesus Montero**, **OF Jordan Parraz**, **RHP David Phelps**, **C Austin Romine**, **INF Bradley Suttle**, **INF Jorge Vazquez**, **RHP Adam Warren** and **RHP Eric Wordekemper** to spring training.
Feb. 14	Signed **OF Andruw Jones** to a one-year contract; designated **RHP Brian Schlitter** for assignment.
Feb. 15	**RHP Brian Schlitter** was claimed off waivers by Philadelphia.

2010 Day-by-Day

Gm	Date	Opponent	W/L	Score	Winning Pitcher	Losing Pitcher	Save	Rec.	Pos.	GA/GB	Att.
1	4/4	at Boston	L	7-9	Okajima (1-0)	Park (0-1)	Papelbon (1)	0-1	5th	-1.0	*37,440
	4/5		OFF DAY						T4th	-1.0	
2	4/6	at Boston	W	6-4	Aceves (1-0)	Okajima (1-1)	Rivera (1)	1-1	T2nd	-0.5	*38,000
3	4/7	at Boston	W	3-1 (10)	Park (1-1)	Papelbon (0-1)	Rivera (2)	2-1	2nd	-0.5	*38,238
	4/8		OFF DAY						T1st	---	
4	4/9	at Tampa Bay	L	3-9	Price (1-0)	Vazquez (0-1)	-	2-2	3rd	-1.0	33,221
5	4/10	at Tampa Bay	W	10-0	Sabathia (1-0)	Davis (0-1)	-	3-2	T2nd	-1.0	29,892
6	4/11	at Tampa Bay	W	7-3	Burnett (1-0)	Choate (0-1)	-	4-2	2nd	-1.0	31,253
	4/12		OFF DAY						2nd	-0.5	
7	4/13	Los Angeles-AL	W	7-5	Pettitte (1-0)	Santana (0-2)	Rivera (3)	5-2	2nd	-0.5	*49,293 (1)
8	4/14	Los Angeles-AL	L	3-5	Pineiro (1-1)	Vazquez (0-2)	Rodney (1)	5-3	3rd	-0.5	42,372
9	4/15	Los Angeles-AL	W	6-2	Hughes (1-0)	Kazmir (0-1)	Rivera (4)	6-3	T2nd	-0.5	44,722
10	4/16	Texas	W	5-1 (6)	**Sabathia (2-0)**	**Wilson (0-1)**	-	7-3	T1st	---	42,145
11	4/17	Texas	W	7-3	Burnett (2-0)	Feldman (1-1)	-	8-3	T1st	---	44,963
12	4/18	Texas	W	5-2	Pettitte (2-0)	Harden (0-1)	Rivera (5)	9-3	T1st	---	44,121
	4/19		OFF DAY						2nd	-0.5	
13	4/20	at Oakland	W	7-3	Vazquez (1-2)	Gonzalez (1-1)	-	10-3	1st	+0.5	19,849
14	4/21	at Oakland	W	3-1	Hughes (2-0)	Sheets (1-1)	Rivera (6)	11-3	1st	+0.5	30,211
15	4/22	at Oakland	L	2-4	Braden (3-0)	**Sabathia (2-1)**	Bailey (2)	11-4	2nd	-0.5	21,986
16	4/23	at Los Angeles-AL	W	4-6	Rodney (2-0)	Chamberlain (0-1)	Fuentes (2)	11-5	2nd	-0.5	44,002
17	4/24	at Los Angeles-AL	W	7-1	Pettitte (3-0)	Pineiro (2-2)	-	12-5	2nd	-0.5	43,390
18	4/25	at Los Angeles-AL	L	4-8	Kazmir (2-1)	Vazquez (1-3)	-	12-6	2nd	-1.5	42,284
	4/26		OFF DAY						2nd	-1.5	
19	4/27	at Baltimore	L	4-5	Castillo (1-0)	Robertson (0-1)	Simon (1)	12-7	2nd	-2.5	20,536
20	4/28	at Baltimore	W	8-3	Sabathia (3-1)	Guthrie (0-3)	-	13-7	2nd	-2.5	17,248
21	4/29	at Baltimore	W	4-0	Burnett (3-0)	Matusz (2-1)	-	14-7	2nd	-2.5	26,439
22	4/30	Chicago-AL	W	6-4	Aceves (2-0)	Thornton (2-2)	Rivera (7)	15-7	2nd	-1.5	44,783
23	5/1	Chicago-AL	L	6-7	Linebrink (1-0)	Robertson (0-2)	Jenks (5)	15-8	2nd	-1.5	45,465
24	5/2	Chicago-AL	W	12-3	Hughes (3-0)	Buehrle (2-4)	-	16-8	2nd	-1.5	45,303
25	5/3	Baltimore	W	4-1	Sabathia (4-1)	Guthrie (0-4)	Chamberlain (1)	17-8	2nd	-1.0	41,571
26	5/4	Baltimore	W	4-1	Burnett (4-0)	Matusz (2-2)	Chamberlain (2)	18-8	2nd	-1.0	43,260
27	5/5	Baltimore	W	7-5	Pettitte (4-0)	Hernandez (0-4)	Aceves (1)	19-8	2nd	-1.0	43,425
	5/6		OFF DAY						2nd	-1.5	
28	5/7	at Boston	W	10-3	Hughes (4-0)	Beckett (1-1)	-	20-8	2nd	-1.5	*37,898
29	5/8	at Boston	W	14-3	Aceves (3-0)	Buchholz (3-3)	-	21-8	2nd	-0.5	*37,138
30	5/9	at Boston	L	3-9	Lester (3-2)	Burnett (4-1)	-	21-9	2nd	-0.5	*37,618
31	5/10	at Detroit	L	4-5	Bonine (3-0)	Mitre (0-1)	Valverde (9)	21-10	2nd	-0.5	34,365
	5/11	at Detroit	Ppd., rain						2nd	-1.0	
32	5/12	at Detroit	L	0-2	Porcello (3-3)	Vazquez (1-4)	Valverde (10)	21-11	2nd	-1.5	27,376
33	5/12	at Detroit	W	8-0	Hughes (5-0)	Bonderman (1-2)	-	22-11	2nd	-1.5	28,514
34	5/13	at Detroit	L	0-6	Verlander (4-2)	Sabathia (4-2)	-	22-12	2nd	-2.0	31,130
35	5/14	Minnesota	W	8-4	Chamberlain (1-1)	Baker (4-3)	-	23-12	2nd	-1.0	45,195
36	5/15	Minnesota	W	7-1	Pettitte (5-0)	Liriano (5-2)	-	24-12	2nd	-1.0	46,347
37	5/16	Minnesota	L	3-6	Blackburn (4-1)	Chamberlain (1-2)	Rauch (10)	24-13	2nd	-2.0	46,628
38	5/17	Boston	W	11-9	Vazquez (2-4)	Papelbon (1-3)	-	25-13	2nd	-2.0	48,271
39	5/18	Boston	L	6-7	Bard (1-1)	Rivera (0-1)	Papelbon (10)	25-14	2nd	-3.0	47,734
40	5/19	Tampa Bay	L	6-10	Davis (1-4)	Burnett (4-2)	Benoit (1)	25-15	2nd	-4.0	43,283
41	5/20	Tampa Bay	L	6-8	Shields (5-1)	Pettitte (5-1)	Soriano (11)	25-16	2nd	-5.0	45,483
42	5/21	at New York-NL	W	2-1	Vazquez (3-4)	Dessens (0-1)	Rivera (8)	26-16	2nd	-4.0	*41,382
43	5/22	at New York-NL	L	3-5	Pelfrey (6-1)	Hughes (5-1)	Rodriguez (7)	26-17	2nd	-5.0	*41,343
44	5/23	at New York-NL	L	4-6	Santana (4-2)	Sabathia (4-3)	Rodriguez (8)	26-18	2nd	-6.0	*41,422
	5/24		OFF DAY						2nd	-5.5	
45	5/25	at Minnesota	W	1-0	Burnett (5-2)	Duensing (2-1)	Rivera (9)	27-18	2nd	-4.5	*38,962
46	5/26	at Minnesota	W	3-2	Pettitte (6-1)	Rauch (1-1)	Rivera (10)	28-18	2nd	-3.5	*39.353
47	5/27	at Minnesota	L	2-8	Blackburn (6-1)	Vazquez (3-5)	-	28-19	2nd	-4.5	*39,087
48	5/28	Cleveland	W	8-2	Hughes (6-1)	Carmona (4-3)	-	29-19	2nd	-3.5	44,634
49	5/29	Cleveland	L	11-13	Perez, R. (1-0)	Chamberlain (1-3)	Wood (2)	29-20	2nd	-4.5	46,599
50	5/30	Cleveland	W	7-3	Burnett (6-2)	Sipp (0-1)	-	30-20	2nd	-3.5	45,706
51	5/31	Cleveland	W	11-2	Pettitte (7-1)	Talbot (6-4)	-	31-20	2nd	-2.5	44,976
52	6/1	Baltimore	W	3-1	Vazquez (4-5)	Matusz (2-6)	Rivera (11)	32-20	2nd	-2.5	43,059
53	6/2	Baltimore	W	9-1	Hughes (7-1)	Bergesen (3-4)	-	33-20	2nd	-2.5	44,465
54	6/3	Baltimore	W	6-3	Sabathia (5-3)	Millwood (0-6)	Rivera (12)	34-20	2nd	-2.0	44,927

2010 Day-by-Day

Gm	Date	Opponent	W/L	Score	Winning Pitcher	Losing Pitcher	Save	Rec.	Pos.	GA/GB	Att.
55	6/4	at Toronto	L	1-6	Cecil (6-2)	Burnett (6-3)	-	34-21	2nd	-2.0	30,089
56	6/5	at Toronto	L	2-3 (14)	Janssen (4-0)	Gaudin (0-3)	-	34-22	2nd	-2.0	37,165
57	6/6	at Toronto	W	4-3	Vazquez (5-5)	Downs (1-5)	Rivera (13)	35-22	2nd	-2.0	33,622
	6/7		OFF DAY						2nd	-2.0	
58	6/8	at Baltimore	W	12-7	Hughes (8-1)	Millwood (0-7)	-	36-22	2nd	-2.0	23,171
59	6/9	at Baltimore	W	4-2	Sabathia (6-3)	Tillman (0-2)	Rivera (14)	37-22	2nd	-2.0	16,451
60	6/10	at Baltimore	L	3-4	Arrieta (1-0)	Burnett (6-4)	Hernandez (1)	37-23	2nd	-2.0	27,064
61	6/11	Houston	W	4-3	Pettitte (8-1)	Myers (4-4)	Rivera (15)	38-23	2nd	-1.0	46,883
62	6/12	Houston	W	9-3	Vazquez (6-5)	Rodriguez (3-9)	-	39-23	2nd	-1.0	46,159
63	6/13	Houston	W	9-5	Hughes (9-1)	Moehler (0-3)	-	40-23	T1st	---	46,832
	6/14		OFF DAY						T1st	---	
64	6/15	Philadelphia	W	8-3	Sabathia (7-3)	Halladay (8-5)	-	41-23	T1st	---	47,135
65	6/16	Philadelphia	L	3-6	Moyer (7-6)	Burnett (6-5)	-	41-24	T1st	---	47,414
66	6/17	Philadelphia	L	1-7	Kendrick (4-2)	Pettitte (8-2)	-	41-25	T1st	---	47,204
67	6/18	New York-NL	L	0-4	Takahashi (6-2)	Vazquez (6-6)	Rodriguez (16)	41-26	T1st	---	*49,220 (2)
68	6/19	New York-NL	W	5-3	Hughes (10-1)	Pelfrey (9-2)	Rivera (16)	42-26	T1st	---	*49,073 (3)
69	6/20	New York-NL	W	4-0	Sabathia (8-3)	Santana (5-4)	-	43-26	1st	+1.0	*49,240 (4)
70	6/21	at Arizona	L	4-10	Lopez (3-6)	Burnett (6-6)	-	43-27	1st	+0.5	47,229
71	6/22	at Arizona	W	9-3	Pettitte (9-2)	Haren (7-6)	-	44-27	1st	+1.5	45,776
72	6/23	at Arizona	W	6-5 (10)	Rivera (1-1)	Rosa (0-2)	-	45-27	1st	+2.5	46,325
	6/24		OFF DAY						1st	+2.0	
73	6/25	at Los Angeles-NL	W	2-1	Sabathia (9-3)	Padilla (1-2)	Rivera (17)	46-27	1st	+3.0	*56,000
74	6/26	at Los Angeles-NL	L	4-9	Kuroda (7-5)	Burnett (6-7)	-	46-28	1st	+2.0	*56,000
75	6/27	at Los Angeles-NL	W	8-6 (10)	Rivera (2-1)	Troncoso (1-2)	-	47-28	1st	+2.0	*56,000
	6/28		OFF DAY						1st	+2.0	
76	6/29	Seattle	L	4-7	Lee (7-3)	Hughes (10-2)	-	47-29	1st	+1.0	45,780
77	6/30	Seattle	L	0-7	Hernandez (6-5)	Vazquez (6-7)	-	47-30	1st	+1.0	46,309
78	7/1	Seattle	W	4-2	Sabathia (10-3)	Aardsma (0-5)	Rivera (18)	48-30	1st	+1.5	45,591
79	7/2	Toronto	L	1-6 (11)	Frasor (3-1)	Robertson (0-3)	-	48-31	1st	+0.5	45,792
80	7/3	Toronto	W	11-3	Pettitte (10-2)	Romero (6-5)	-	49-31	1st	+0.5	46,364
81	7/4	Toronto	W	7-6 (10)	Robertson (1-3)	Purcey (0-1)	-	50-31	1st	+1.5	46,810
82	7/5	at Oakland	W	3-1	Vazquez (7-7)	Sheets (3-8)	Rivera (19)	51-31	1st	+2.0	27,405
83	7/6	at Oakland	W	6-1	Sabathia (11-3)	Cahill (8-3)	-	52-31	1st	+2.0	20,473
84	7/7	at Oakland	W	6-2	Burnett (7-7)	Gonzalez (7-6)	-	53-31	1st	+2.0	31,518
85	7/8	at Seattle	W	3-1	Pettitte (11-2)	Aardsma (0-6)	Rivera (20)	54-31	1st	+2.0	37,432
86	7/9	at Seattle	W	6-1	Hughes (11-2)	Pauley (0-1)	-	55-31	1st	+3.0	39,645
87	7/10	at Seattle	L	1-4	Hernandez (7-5)	Chamberlain (1-4)	-	55-32	1st	+2.0	42,558
88	7/11	at Seattle	W	8-2	Sabathia (12-3)	Rowland-Smith (1-9)	-	56-32	1st	+2.0	42,069
	7/12 – 7/15				(81st All-Star Game on 7/13 at Angel Stadium of Anaheim)						
89	7/16	Tampa Bay	W	5-4	Rivera (3-1)	Choate (2-3)	-	57-32	1st	+3.0	47,524
90	7/17	Tampa Bay	L	5-10	Niemann (8-2)	Burnett (7-8)	-	57-33	1st	+2.0	*48,957 (5)
91	7/18	Tampa Bay	W	9-5	Park (2-1)	Price (12-5)	-	58-33	1st	+2.0	46,969
	7/19		OFF DAY						1st	+2.5	
92	7/20	Los Angeles-AL	L	2-10	O'Sullivan (1-0)	Hughes (11-3)	-	58-34	1st	+2.5	47,775
93	7/21	Los Angeles-AL	W	10-6	Vazquez (8-7)	Pineiro (10-7)	-	59-34	1st	+2.5	47,521
94	7/22	Kansas City	W	10-4	Sabathia (13-3)	Chen (5-4)	-	60-34	1st	+3.0	47,484
95	7/23	Kansas City	W	7-1	Burnett (8-8)	Bannister (7-9)	-	61-34	1st	+4.0	46,801
96	7/24	Kansas City	L	4-7	Davies (5-6)	Mitre (0-2)	Soria (27)	61-35	1st	+3.0	*48,138 (6)
97	7/25	Kansas City	W	12-6	Hughes (12-3)	O'Sullivan (1-1)	-	62-35	1st	+3.0	47,890
98	7/26	at Cleveland	W	3-2	Vazquez (9-7)	Westbrook (6-7)	Rivera (21)	63-35	1st	+3.0	27,224
99	7/27	at Cleveland	L	1-4	Tomlin (1-0)	Sabathia (13-4)	Perez (10)	63-36	1st	+2.0	27,416
100	7/28	at Cleveland	W	8-0	Burnett (9-8)	Carmona (10-8)	-	64-36	1st	+2.0	22,965
101	7/29	at Cleveland	W	11-4	Moseley (1-0)	Herrmann (0-1)	-	65-36	1st	+2.0	34,455
102	7/30	at Tampa Bay	L	2-3	Hughes (12-4)	Davis (9-9)	Soriano (29)	65-37	1st	+1.0	*36,973
103	7/31	at Tampa Bay	W	5-4	Robertson (2-3)	Soriano (22)	Rivera (22)	66-37	1st	+1.0	*36,973
104	8/1	at Tampa Bay	L	0-3	Shields (10-9)	Sabathia (13-5)	Soriano (30)	66-38	1st	+1.0	*36,973
105	8/2	Toronto	L	6-8	Morrow (8-6)	Burnett (9-9)	Gregg (24)	66-39	T1st	---	47,034
106	8/3	Toronto	L	2-8	Romero (9-7)	Moseley (1-1)	-	66-40	2nd	-1.0	46,480
107	8/4	Toronto	W	5-1	Hughes (13-4)	Marcum (10-5)	-	67-40	T1st	---	47,659
	8/5		OFF DAY						1st	+0.5	

2010 Day-by-Day

Gm	Date	Opponent	W/L	Score	Winning Pitcher	Losing Pitcher	Save	Rec.	Pos.	GA/GB	Att.
108	8/6	Boston	L	3-6	Buchholz (12-5)	Vazquez (9-8)	Papelbon (27)	67-41	1st	+0.5	*49,555 (7)
109	8/7	Boston	W	5-2	Sabathia (14-5)	Lackey (10-7)	Rivera (23)	68-41	1st	+1.5	*49,716 (8)
110	8/8	Boston	W	7-2	Moseley (2-1)	Beckett (3-2)	-	69-41	1st	+2.5	*49,096 (9)
111	8/9	Boston	L	1-2	Lester (12-7)	Hughes (13-5)	Papelbon (28)	69-42	1st	+1.5	*49,476 (10)
112	8/10	at Texas	L	3-4 (10)	Feliz (3-2)	Rivera (3-2)	-	69-43	1st	+0.5	46,121
113	8/11	at Texas	W	7-6	Wood (2-4)	Feliz (3-3)	Rivera (24)	70-43	1st	+1.5	*48,676
114	8/12	at Kansas City	W	4-3	Sabathia (15-5)	Chen (7-6)	Robertson (1)	71-43	1st	+2.0	23,337
115	8/13	at Kansas City	L	3-4	Davies (6-7)	Moseley (2-2)	Soria (32)	71-44	1st	+2.0	30,680
116	8/14	at Kansas City	W	8-3	Hughes (14-5)	O'Sullivan (1-4)	-	72-44	1st	+2.0	34,206
117	8/15	at Kansas City	L	0-1	Bullington (1-2)	**Burnett** (9-10)	Soria (33)	72-45	1st	+1.0	26,012
118	8/16	Detroit	L	1-3	Scherzer (8-9)	Vazquez (9-9)	Valverde (23)	72-46	T1st	---	46,098
119	8/17	Detroit	W	6-2	Sabathia (16-5)	Verlander (13-8)	-	73-46	T1st	---	46,906
120	8/18	Detroit	W	9-5	Moseley (3-2)	Bonderman (6-9)	-	74-46	1st	---	46,479
121	8/19	Detroit	W	11-5	Hughes (15-5)	Porcello (5-11)	Mitre (1)	75-46	1st	+1.0	*48,143 (11)
122	8/20	Seattle	L	0-6	Hernandez (9-10)	Burnett (9-11)	-	75-47	1st	+1.0	46,493
123	8/21	Seattle	W	9-5	Logan (1-0)	Vargas (9-6)	Rivera (25)	76-47	1st	+1.0	*48,158 (12)
124	8/22	Seattle	W	10-0	Sabathia (17-5)	French (2-4)	-	77-47	1st	+1.0	46,778
125	8/23	at Toronto	L	2-3	Downs (5-5)	Robertson (2-4)	Gregg (28)	77-48	T1st	---	29,198
126	8/24	at Toronto	W	11-5	Moseley (4-2)	Rzepczynski (1-2)	-	78-48	T1st	---	30,567
127	8/25	at Toronto	L	3-6	Cecil (11-6)	Hughes (15-6)	Gregg (29)	78-49	T1st	---	31,449
	8/26		OFF DAY					78-49	T1st		
128	8/27	at Chicago-AL	L	4-9	Garcia (11-5)	Burnett (9-12)	-	78-50	T1st	---	*38,596
129	8/28	at Chicago-AL	W	12-9	Sabathia (18-5)	Danks (12-9)	Rivera (26)	79-50	T1st	---	*38,811
130	8/29	at Chicago-AL	W	2-1	Nova (1-0)	Floyd (9-11)	Rivera (27)	80-50	T1st	---	*39,433
131	8/30	Oakland	W	11-5	Vazquez (10-9)	Cahill (14-6)	-	81-50	T1st	---	46,356
132	8/31	Oakland	W	9-3	Hughes (16-6)	Mazzaro (6-7)	-	82-50	1st	+1.0	44,575
133	9/1	Oakland	W	4-3	Burnett (10-12)	Anderson (3-6)	Rivera (28)	83-50	1st	+1.0	45,222
134	9/2	Oakland	W	5-0	Sabathia (19-5)	Braden (9-10)	-	84-50	1st	+1.5	44,644
135	9/3	Toronto	W	7-3	Wood (3-4)	Morrow (10-7)	-	85-50	1st	+1.5	44,739
136	9/4	Toronto	W	7-5	Chamberlain (2-4)	Frasor (3-4)	Rivera (29)	86-50	1st	+2.5	47,478
137	9/5	Toronto	L	3-7	Cecil (12-7)	Hughes (16-7)	-	86-51	1st	+2.5	47,737
138	9/6	Baltimore	L	3-4	Matusz (8-12)	Burnett (10-13)	Uehara (7)	86-52	1st	+2.5	46,103
139	9/7	Baltimore	L	2-6	Arrieta (5-6)	Sabathia (19-6)	-	86-53	1st	+1.5	46,432
140	9/8	Baltimore	W	3-2	Chamberlain (3-4)	Uehara (1-1)	-	87-53	1st	+2.5	44,163
	9/9		OFF DAY					87-53	1st	+2.5	
141	9/10	at Texas	L	5-6 (13)	Feldman (7-10)	Gaudin (0-4)	-	87-54	1st	+1.5	46,179
142	9/11	at Texas	L	6-7	Ogando (4-1)	Rivera (3-3)	-	87-55	1st	+0.5	*49,210
143	9/12	at Texas	L	1-4	Lee (11-8)	Moseley (4-3)	Feliz (36)	87-56	1st	+0.5	42,007
144	9/13	at Tampa Bay	L	0-1 (11)	Balfour (2-1)	Mitre (0-3)	-	87-57	2nd	-0.5	26,907
145	9/14	at Tampa Bay	W	8-7 (10)	Robertson (3-4)	Wheeler (2-3)	Rivera (30)	88-57	1st	+0.5	28,713
146	9/15	at Tampa Bay	L	3-4	Qualls (1-0)	Hughes (16-8)	Soriano (43)	88-58	2nd	-0.5	29,733
	9/16		OFF DAY					88-58	2nd	-0.5	
147	9/17	at Baltimore	W	4-3	Robertson (4-4)	Uehara (1-2)	Rivera (31)	89-58	1st	+0.5	32,874
148	9/18	at Baltimore	W	11-3	Sabathia (20-6)	Guthrie (10-14)	-	90-58	1st	+0.5	*48,775
149	9/19	at Baltimore	L	3-4 (11)	Gonzalez (1-3)	Robertson (4-5)	-	90-59	1st	+0.5	39,537
150	9/20	Tampa Bay	W	8-6	Gaudin (1-4)	Garza (14-9)	Rivera (32)	91-59	1st	+1.5	47,437
151	9/21	Tampa Bay	W	8-3	Hughes (17-8)	Shields (13-13)	Chamberlain (3)	92-59	1st	+2.5	46,609
152	9/22	Tampa Bay	L	2-7	Hellickson (4-0)	Burnett (10-14)	-	92-60	1st	+1.5	46,986
153	9/23	Tampa Bay	L	3-10	Price (18-6)	Sabathia (20-7)	-	92-61	1st	+0.5	47,646
154	9/24	Boston	L	8-10	Beckett (6-5)	Hughes (11-3)	Papelbon (37)	92-62	2nd	-0.5	*49,457 (13)
155	9/25	Boston	L	3-7	Lester (19-8)	Nova (1-1)	-	92-63	2nd	-1.5	*49,588 (14)
156	9/26	Boston	W	4-3 (10)	Logan (2-0)	Okajima (4-4)	Save	93-63	2nd	-0.5	*49,199 (15)
157	9/27	at Toronto	L	5-7	Rzepczynski (3-4)	Burnett (10-15)	-	93-64	2nd	-0.5	16,004
158	9/28	at Toronto	W	6-1	Sabathia (21-7)	Drabek (0-3)	-	94-64	2nd	-0.5	18,193
159	9/29	at Toronto	L	4-8	Cecil (15-7)	Vazquez (10-10)	-	94-65	2nd	-0.5	33,143
	9/30		OFF DAY						T1st	---	
	10/1	at Boston	Ppd., rain						1st	+0.5	
160	10/2	at Boston	W	6-5 (10)	Hughes (18-8)	Papelbon (5-7)	Rivera (33)	95-65	1st	+1.0	*37,467
161	10/2	at Boston	L	6-7 (10)	Manuel (1-0)	Nova (1-2)	-	95-66	T1st	---	*37,589
162	10/3	at Boston	L	4-8	Lackey (14-11)	Moseley (4-4)	-	95-67	2nd	-1.0	*37,453

BOLD (Complete Game)   *Denotes Sellout (#Home Sellouts)

2010 Major League Standings

AMERICAN LEAGUE

AL EAST	WON	LOST	PCT.	GB
*TAMPA BAY	96	66	.593	--
#NEW YORK	95	67	.586	1.0
BOSTON	89	73	.549	7.0
TORONTO	85	77	.525	11.0
BALTIMORE	66	96	.407	30.0

AL CENTRAL	WON	LOST	PCT.	GB
*MINNESOTA	94	68	.580	--
CHICAGO	88	74	.543	6.0
DETROIT	81	81	.500	13.0
CLEVELAND	69	93	.426	25.0
KANSAS CITY	67	95	.414	27.0

AL WEST	WON	LOST	PCT.	GB
*TEXAS	90	72	.556	--
OAKLAND	81	81	.500	9.0
LOS ANGELES	80	82	.494	10.0
SEATTLE	61	101	.377	29.0

* - DIVISION WINNER
\# - WILD CARD WINNER

NATIONAL LEAGUE

NL EAST	WON	LOST	PCT.	GB
*PHILADELPHIA	97	65	.599	--
#ATLANTA	91	71	.562	6.0
FLORIDA	80	82	.494	17.0
NEW YORK	79	83	.488	18.0
WASHINGTON	69	93	.426	28.0

NL CENTRAL	WON	LOST	PCT.	GB
*CINCINNATI	91	71	.562	--
ST. LOUIS	86	76	.531	5.0
MILWAUKEE	77	85	.475	14.0
HOUSTON	76	86	.469	15.0
CHICAGO	75	87	.463	16.0
PITTSBURGH	57	105	.352	34.0

NL WEST	WON	LOST	PCT.	GB
*SAN FRANCISCO	92	70	.568	--
SAN DIEGO	90	72	.556	2.0
COLORADO	83	79	.512	9.0
LOS ANGELES	80	82	.494	12.0
ARIZONA	65	97	.401	27.0

2010 Yankees Club Statistics

	HOME W	HOME L	ROAD W	ROAD L	TOTALS W	TOTALS L
VS. BALTIMORE	7	2	6	3	13	5
VS. BOSTON	4	5	5	4	9	9
VS. TAMPA BAY	4	5	4	5	8	10
VS. TORONTO	5	4	3	6	8	10
TOTALS VS. EAST	20	16	18	18	38	34

	HOME W	HOME L	ROAD W	ROAD L	TOTALS W	TOTALS L
VS. CLEVELAND	3	1	3	1	6	2
VS. CHICAGO	2	1	2	1	4	2
VS. DETROIT	3	1	1	3	4	4
VS. KANSAS CITY	3	1	2	2	5	3
VS. MINNESOTA	2	1	2	1	4	2
TOTALS VS. CENTRAL	13	5	10	8	23	13

	HOME W	HOME L	ROAD W	ROAD L	TOTALS W	TOTALS L
VS. LOS ANGELES	3	2	1	2	4	4
VS. OAKLAND	4	0	5	1	9	1
VS. SEATTLE	3	3	3	1	6	4
VS. TEXAS	3	0	1	4	4	4
TOTALS VS. WEST	13	5	10	8	23	13

	HOME W	HOME L	ROAD W	ROAD L	TOTALS W	TOTALS L
TOTALS VS. AL	46	26	38	34	84	60

	HOME W	HOME L	ROAD W	ROAD L	TOTALS W	TOTALS L
VS. ARIZONA	0	0	2	1	2	1
VS. HOUSTON	3	0	0	0	3	0
VS. LOS ANGELES	0	0	2	1	2	1
VS. NEW YORK	2	1	1	2	3	3
VS. PHILADELPHIA	1	2	0	0	1	2
TOTALS VS. NL	6	3	5	4	11	7

	HOME W	HOME L	ROAD W	ROAD L	TOTALS W	TOTALS L
OVERALL TOTALS	52	29	43	38	95	67

	HOME W	HOME L	ROAD W	ROAD L	TOTALS W	TOTALS L
SHUTOUTS	3	3	5	5	8	8
SHO – INDIVIDUAL	0	1	0	0	0	1
EXTRA INNINGS	2	1	5	6	7	7
ONE-RUN DECISIONS	6	4	14	15	20	19
TWO-RUN DECISIONS	9	6	7	7	16	13
VS. LH STARTERS	17	12	14	15	31	27
VS. RH STARTERS	35	17	29	23	64	40
GRASS FIELDS	52	29	36	27	88	56
ARTIFICIAL FIELDS	0	0	7	11	7	11
DAY GAMES	28	11	8	11	36	22
NIGHT GAMES	24	18	35	27	59	45

	NYY	OPP
DOUBLE PLAYS	161	143
TRIPLE PLAYS	1	0
LEFT ON BASE	1228	1082
GRAND SLAM HR	10	3
HOME RUNS – HOME	115	108
HOME RUNS – ROAD	86	71

	WON	LOST	SPLIT
DOUBLEHEADERS (HOME)	WON 0	LOST 0	SPLIT 0
DOUBLEHEADERS (ROAD)	WON 0	LOST 0	SPLIT 2

	WON	LOST
STARTERS	72	50
RELIEVERS	23	17
STREAKS	8	4

ATTENDANCE			
HOME	3,765,803	(81 DATES)	46,491 AVG
ROAD	2,830,138	(81 DATES)	34,940 AVG

2010 Final Yankees Statistics

PLAYER	AVG	G	AB	R	H	TB	2B	3B	HR	RBI	SH	SF	HP	BB	IBB	SO	SB	CS	DP	E	SLG	OBP
Berkman	.255	37	106	9	27	37	7	0	1	9	0	0	0	17	3	15	0	0	6	1	.349	.358
Burnett	.000	33	1	0	0	0	0	0	0	0	2	0	0	0	0	1	0	0	0	4	.000	.000
Cano	.319	160	626	103	200	334	41	3	29	109	0	5	8	57	14	77	3	2	19	3	.534	.381
Cervelli	.271	93	266	27	72	89	11	3	0	38	8	4	6	33	1	42	1	1	7	13	.335	.359
Curtis	.186	31	59	7	11	17	3	0	1	8	0	0	1	4	0	15	0	0	0	0	.288	.250
Gardner	.277	150	477	97	132	181	20	7	5	47	5	3	5	79	1	101	47	9	6	1	.379	.383
Golson	.261	24	23	3	6	8	2	0	0	2	0	0	0	0	0	3	0	2	0	0	.348	.261
Granderson	.247	136	466	76	115	218	17	7	24	67	4	3	2	53	3	116	12	2	3	2	.468	.324
Huffman	.167	9	18	1	3	3	0	0	0	2	0	0	1	2	0	5	0	0	1	0	.167	.286
Hughes	.000	31	1	0	0	0	0	0	0	0	0	0	0	0	0	0	0	0	0	0	.000	.000
Jeter	.270	157	663	111	179	245	30	3	10	67	1	3	9	63	4	106	18	5	22	6	.370	.340
Johnson	.167	24	72	12	12	22	4	0	2	8	0	0	2	24	0	23	0	1	2	0	.306	.388
Kearns	.235	36	102	13	24	33	3	0	2	7	0	0	5	12	0	38	0	0	4	0	.324	.345
Miranda	.219	33	64	7	14	27	2	1	3	10	0	0	0	7	0	12	0	0	1	0	.422	.296
Moeller	.214	9	14	2	3	6	3	0	0	0	0	0	0	1	0	4	0	0	0	0	.429	.267
Nunez	.280	30	50	12	14	18	1	0	1	7	0	0	0	3	0	2	5	0	4	1	.360	.321
Pena	.227	85	154	18	35	38	1	1	0	18	4	2	1	6	0	27	7	1	4	5	.247	.258
Pettitte	.250	21	4	0	1	1	0	0	0	0	0	0	0	0	0	3	0	0	0	3	.250	.250
Posada	.248	120	383	49	95	174	23	1	18	57	0	2	4	59	3	99	3	1	6	8	.454	.357
Rivera	.000	61	1	0	0	0	0	0	0	0	0	0	0	0	0	0	0	0	0	0	.000	.000
Rodriguez	.270	137	522	74	141	264	29	2	30	125	0	11	3	59	1	98	4	3	7	1	.506	.341
Russo	.184	31	49	5	9	11	2	0	0	4	1	0	1	3	0	9	1	0	0	1	.224	.245
Sabathia	.200	34	5	0	1	1	0	0	0	0	0	0	0	0	0	3	0	0	0	1	.200	.200
Swisher	.288	150	566	91	163	289	33	3	29	89	3	2	6	58	0	139	1	2	13	4	.511	.359
Teixeira	.256	158	601	113	154	289	36	0	33	108	0	5	13	93	6	122	0	1	15	3	.481	.365
Thames	.288	82	212	22	61	104	7	0	12	33	0	3	3	19	0	61	0	0	3	0	.491	.350
Vazquez	.000	31	1	0	0	0	0	0	0	0	0	2	0	0	0	2	0	0	0	0	.000	.667
Winn	.213	29	61	7	13	18	0	1	1	8	1	1	0	8	0	15	1	0	1	0	.295	.300
YANKEES	**.267**	**162**	**5567**	**859**	**1485**	**2427**	**275**	**32**	**201**	**823**	**33**	**44**	**73**	**662**	**36**	**1136**	**103**	**30**	**124**	**69**	**.436**	**.350**
OPPONENTS	**.249**	**162**	**5411**	**693**	**1349**	**2160**	**246**	**14**	**179**	**662**	**36**	**52**	**62**	**540**	**37**	**1154**	**132**	**23**	**137**	**96**	**.399**	**.322**

PITCHER	W	L	ERA	G	GS	CG	GF	SHO	SV	IP	H	R	ER	HR	HB	BB	IBB	SO	WP	BK	AVG
Aceves	3	0	3.00	10	0	0	2	0	1	12.0	10	5	4	1	1	4	1	2	0	0	.208
Albaladejo	0	0	3.97	10	0	0	5	0	0	11.1	9	5	5	1	2	8	1	8	0	0	.231
Burnett	10	15	5.26	33	33	1	0	0	0	186.2	204	118	109	25	19	78	2	145	16	0	.285
Chamberlain	3	4	4.40	73	0	0	18	0	3	71.2	71	37	35	6	1	22	2	77	5	1	.253
Gaudin	1	2	4.50	30	0	0	17	0	0	48.0	46	27	24	11	5	20	0	33	3	0	.254
Hughes	18	8	4.19	31	29	0	0	0	0	176.1	162	83	82	25	0	58	1	146	9	1	.244
Logan	2	0	2.93	51	0	0	8	0	0	40.0	34	13	13	3	1	20	3	38	1	0	.231
Marte	0	0	4.08	30	0	0	3	0	0	17.2	10	8	8	2	1	11	1	12	2	1	.161
Melancon	0	0	9.00	2	0	0	2	0	0	4.0	7	5	4	1	0	0	0	3	0	0	.389
Mitre	0	3	3.33	27	3	0	13	0	1	54.0	43	23	20	7	2	16	0	29	1	0	.223
Moseley	4	4	4.96	16	9	0	2	0	0	65.1	66	36	36	13	2	27	0	33	0	0	.269
Nova	1	2	4.50	10	7	0	3	0	0	42.0	44	22	21	4	1	17	2	26	2	0	.268
Park	2	1	5.60	27	0	0	15	0	0	35.1	40	25	22	7	1	12	0	29	2	0	.280
Pettitte	11	3	3.28	21	21	0	0	0	0	129.0	123	52	47	13	3	41	3	101	2	0	.257
Ring	0	0	15.43	5	0	0	0	0	0	2.1	3	4	4	0	0	2	0	0	0	0	.300
Rivera	3	3	1.80	61	0	0	55	0	33	60.0	39	14	12	2	5	11	3	45	0	0	.183
Robertson	4	5	3.82	64	0	0	10	0	1	61.1	59	26	26	5	3	33	6	71	7	2	.258
Sabathia	21	7	3.18	34	34	2	0	0	0	237.2	209	92	84	20	7	74	6	197	8	1	.239
Sanchez	0	0	0.00	2	0	0	1	0	0	4.1	1	0	0	0	0	3	0	5	0	0	.071
Vazquez	10	10	5.32	31	26	0	4	0	0	157.1	155	96	93	32	7	65	4	121	8	0	.267
Wood	2	0	0.69	24	0	0	0	0	0	26.0	14	2	2	1	1	18	2	31	3	0	.161
YANKEES	**95**	**67**	**4.06**	**162**	**162**	**3**	**159**	**8**	**39**	**1442.1**	**1349**	**693**	**651**	**179**	**62**	**540**	**37**	**1154**	**69**	**6**	**.249**
OPPONENTS	**67**	**95**	**5.10**	**162**	**162**	**5**	**157**	**8**	**34**	**1430.2**	**1485**	**859**	**811**	**201**	**73**	**662**	**36**	**1136**	**73**	**4**	**.267**

2010 Yankees Fielding Statistics

PITCHERS	PCT	G	GS	PO	A	E	TC	DP	TP
Aceves	1.000	10	0	0	2	0	2	0	0
Albaladejo	1.000	10	0	0	2	0	2	0	0
Burnett	.862	33	33	9	16	4	29	1	0
Chamberlain	1.000	73	0	2	6	0	8	1	0
Gaudin	.750	30	0	1	2	1	4	0	0
Hughes	1.000	31	29	7	13	0	20	1	0
Logan	1.000	51	0	1	3	0	4	0	0
Marte	.500	30	0	0	1	1	2	0	0
Melancon	.000	2	0	0	0	0	0	0	0
Mitre	1.000	27	3	5	7	0	12	0	0
Moseley	1.000	16	9	7	10	0	17	1	0
Nova	.909	10	7	5	5	1	11	0	0
Park	1.000	27	0	3	3	0	6	0	0
Pettitte	.857	21	21	3	15	3	21	1	0
Ring	.000	5	0	0	0	0	0	0	0
Rivera	1.000	61	0	2	16	0	18	0	0
Robertson	1.000	64	0	0	5	0	5	0	0
Sabathia	.971	34	34	4	30	1	35	0	0
Sanchez	.000	2	0	0	0	0	0	0	0
Vazquez	1.000	31	26	14	23	0	37	2	0
Wood	1.000	24	0	3	3	0	6	0	0

FIRST BASE	PCT	G	GS	PO	A	E	TC	DP	TP
Berkman	.982	8	7	54	2	1	57	8	0
Huffman	.000	1	0	0	0	0	0	0	0
Johnson	1.000	2	2	18	0	0	18	1	1
Miranda	1.000	13	4	53	5	0	58	5	0
Posada	.000	1	0	0	0	0	0	0	0
Swisher	1.000	6	1	19	2	0	21	2	0
Teixeira	.998	149	148	1227	80	3	1310	137	0

SECOND BASE	PCT	G	GS	PO	A	E	TC	DP	TP
Cano	.996	158	157	341	432	3	776	114	1
Nunez	.000	1	0	0	0	0	0	0	0
Pena	.967	8	5	12	17	1	30	6	0
Russo	1.000	2	0	2	1	0	3	0	0

THIRD BASE	PCT	G	GS	PO	A	E	TC	DP	TP
Cervelli	1.000	2	0	1	0	0	1	0	0
Nunez	.944	15	10	3	14	1	18	1	0
Pena	.966	48	27	17	67	3	87	5	0
Rodriguez	.976	124	122	61	224	7	292	25	1
Russo	1.000	16	3	4	6	0	10	1	0
Thames	.000	1	0	0	0	0	1	0	0

SHORTSTOP	PCT	G	GS	PO	A	E	TC	DP	TP
Jeter	.989	151	150	182	365	6	553	94	0
Nunez	1.000	11	3	7	16	0	23	4	0
Pena	.979	23	9	22	24	1	47	7	0

OUTFIELDERS	PCT	G	GS	PO	A	E	TC	DP	TP
Curtis	1.000	23	11	22	0	0	22	0	0
Gardner	.997	146	134	287	12	1	300	2	0
Golson	1.000	23	6	25	1	0	26	0	0
Granderson	.994	134	123	316	5	2	323	2	0
Huffman	1.000	7	4	14	0	0	14	0	0
Kearns	1.000	34	28	55	1	0	56	1	0
Pena	1.000	2	0	1	0	0	1	0	0
Russo	.933	11	10	14	0	1	15	0	0
Swisher	.986	134	131	265	10	4	279	1	0
Thames	.947	32	23	34	2	2	38	1	0
Winn	1.000	27	16	31	1	0	32	0	0

CATCHERS	PCT	G	GS	PO	A	E	TC	DP	TP	PB
Cervelli	.980	90	80	579	45	13	637	2	0	2
Moeller	1.000	9	4	33	6	0	39	0	0	2
Posada	.986	83	78	562	22	8	592	2	0	8

Robinson Cano led the Yankees with 159 games started in 2010.

2010 STARTS BY POSITION

PLAYER	C	1B	2B	3B	SS	LF	CF	RF	DH
Berkman	--	7	--	--	--	--	--	--	21
Cano	--	--	157	--	--	--	--	--	2
Cervelli	80	--	--	--	--	--	--	--	--
Curtis	--	--	--	--	--	2	--	9	1
Gardner	--	--	--	--	--	96	38	--	--
Golson	--	--	--	--	--	1	1	4	--
Granderson	--	--	--	--	--	--	123	--	--
Huffman	--	--	--	--	--	2	--	2	--
Jeter	--	--	--	--	150	--	--	--	5
Johnson	--	2	--	--	--	--	--	--	19
Kearns	--	--	--	--	--	20	--	8	1
Miranda	--	4	--	--	--	--	--	--	10
Moeller	4	--	--	--	--	--	--	--	--
Nunez	--	--	--	10	3	--	--	--	--
Pena	--	--	5	27	9	--	--	--	--
Posada	78	--	--	--	--	--	--	--	28
Rodriguez	--	--	--	122	--	--	--	--	12
Russo	--	--	--	3	10	--	--	--	--
Swisher	--	1	--	--	--	--	--	131	11
Teixeira	--	148	--	--	--	--	--	--	9
Thames	--	--	--	--	--	17	--	6	34
Winn	--	--	--	--	--	14	--	2	--

2010 STARTS BY BATTING ORDER

PLAYER	1	2	3	4	5	6	7	8	9
Berkman	--	2	2	--	--	13	10	1	--
Cano	--	1	--	26	132	--	--	--	--
Cervelli	--	--	--	--	--	4	13	42	21
Curtis	--	--	--	--	--	--	1	5	6
Gardner	25	17	--	--	--	8	28	56	--
Golson	--	--	--	--	--	--	--	1	5
Granderson	--	21	--	--	--	4	63	32	3
Huffman	--	--	--	--	--	--	4	--	--
Jeter	137	18	--	--	--	--	--	--	--
Johnson	--	21	--	--	--	--	--	--	--
Kearns	--	--	--	1	1	20	7	--	--
Miranda	--	--	--	--	--	2	7	5	--
Moeller	--	--	--	--	--	--	--	--	4
Nunez	--	--	--	--	--	--	1	5	7
Pena	--	--	--	--	--	--	7	34	--
Posada	--	--	--	5	93	8	--	--	--
Rodriguez	--	--	134	--	--	--	--	--	--
Russo	--	--	--	--	--	--	--	5	8
Swisher	--	82	1	1	13	30	6	10	--
Teixeira	--	157	--	--	--	--	--	--	--
Thames	--	--	2	1	11	15	24	4	--
Winn	--	--	--	--	--	--	1	6	9

2010 Yankees Starters

STARTERS	W	L	PCT	ERA	G	GS	CG	IP	H	TBF	R	ER	HR	SH	SF	HB	BB	IBB	SO	WP	BK	AVG
Burnett	10	15	.400	5.26	33	33	1	186.2	204	829	118	109	25	7	10	19	78	2	145	16	0	.285
Hughes	17	8	.680	4.23	29	29	0	174.1	162	724	83	82	25	2	5	0	58	1	143	9	1	.246
Mitre	0	2	.000	5.93	3	3	0	13.2	16	62	12	9	3	1	1	1	4	0	8	0	0	.291
Moseley	4	4	.500	5.29	9	9	0	51.0	52	218	30	30	10	0	3	2	22	0	26	0	0	.272
Nova	1	1	.500	4.91	7	7	0	36.2	36	159	21	20	4	0	1	1	14	2	24	2	0	.254
Pettitte	11	3	.786	3.28	21	21	0	129.0	123	536	52	47	13	8	5	3	41	3	101	2	0	.257
Sabathia	21	7	.750	3.18	34	34	2	237.2	209	970	92	84	20	5	8	7	74	6	197	8	1	.239
Vazquez	8	10	.444	5.56	26	26	0	144.0	147	628	92	89	31	2	6	4	61	4	109	7	0	.265
TOTALS	72	50	.590	4.35	162	162	3	973.0	949	4126	500	470	131	25	39	37	352	18	753	44	2	.258

2010 Yankees Relievers

RELIEVERS	W	L	PCT	ERA	APP	GF	SV	IP	H	TBF	R	ER	HR	SH	SF	HB	BB	IBB	SO	WP	BK	AVG
Aceves	3	0	1.000	3.00	10	2	1	12.0	10	53	5	4	1	0	0	1	4	1	2	0	0	.208
Albaladejo	0	0	.000	3.97	10	5	0	11.1	9	50	5	5	1	0	1	2	8	1	8	0	0	.231
Chamberlain	3	4	.429	4.40	73	18	3	71.2	71	305	37	35	6	0	1	1	22	2	77	5	1	.253
Gaudin	1	2	.333	4.50	30	17	0	48.0	46	209	27	24	11	2	1	5	20	0	33	3	0	.254
Hughes	1	0	1.000	0.00	2	0	0	2.0	0	6	0	0	0	0	0	0	0	0	3	0	0	.000
Logan	2	0	1.000	2.93	51	8	0	40.0	34	169	13	13	3	0	1	1	20	3	38	1	0	.231
Marte	0	0	.000	4.08	30	3	0	17.2	10	76	8	8	2	0	2	1	11	1	12	2	1	.161
Melancon	0	0	.000	9.00	2	2	0	4.0	7	19	5	4	1	0	1	0	0	0	3	0	0	.389
Mitre	0	1	.000	2.45	24	13	1	40.1	27	151	11	11	4	0	0	1	12	0	21	1	0	.196
Moseley	0	0	.000	3.77	7	2	0	14.1	14	60	6	6	3	0	1	0	5	0	7	0	0	.259
Nova	0	1	.000	1.69	3	3	0	5.1	8	26	1	1	0	0	1	0	3	2	0	0	0	.364
Park	2	1	.667	5.60	27	15	0	35.1	40	157	25	22	7	1	0	1	12	0	29	2	0	.280
Ring	0	0	.000	15.43	5	0	0	2.1	3	12	4	4	0	0	0	0	2	0	2	0	0	.300
Rivera	3	3	.500	1.80	61	55	33	60.0	39	230	14	12	2	0	1	5	11	3	45	0	0	.183
Robertson	4	5	.444	3.82	64	10	1	61.1	59	273	26	26	5	5	3	3	33	6	71	7	2	.258
Sanchez	0	0	.000	0.00	2	1	0	4.1	1	17	0	0	0	0	0	0	3	0	5	0	0	.071
Vazquez	2	0	1.000	2.70	5	4	0	13.1	8	55	4	4	1	0	1	3	4	0	12	3	0	.170
Wood	2	0	1.000	0.69	24	1	0	26.0	14	108	2	2	1	1	2	0	18	2	31	3	0	.161
TOTALS	23	17	.575	3.47	430	159	39	469.1	400	1976	193	181	48	11	13	25	188	19	401	25	4	.230

Yankees Pinch Hitters

BATTER	AVG	APP	AB	R	H	TB	2B	3B	HR	RBI	SH	SF	HP	BB	IBB	SO	SB	CS	GDP	SLG	OBP
Berkman	.286	9	7	0	2	3	1	0	0	0	0	0	0	2	0	2	0	0	0	.429	.444
Cano	.000	1	1	0	0	0	0	0	0	0	0	0	0	0	0	0	0	0	0	.000	.000
Cervelli	.000	4	4	0	0	0	0	0	0	0	0	0	0	0	0	2	0	0	0	.000	.000
Curtis	.364	12	11	1	4	8	1	0	1	7	0	0	0	1	0	3	0	0	0	.727	.417
Gardner	.000	3	3	1	0	0	0	0	0	0	0	0	0	0	0	0	0	0	0	.000	.000
Granderson	.000	8	7	1	0	0	0	0	0	0	0	0	0	1	0	4	0	0	0	.000	.125
Huffman	.000	2	2	0	0	0	0	0	0	0	0	0	0	0	0	0	0	0	0	.000	.000
Jeter	.500	2	2	0	1	1	0	0	0	0	0	0	0	0	0	0	0	0	0	.500	.500
Johnson	.000	3	1	0	0	0	0	0	0	0	0	0	0	2	0	0	0	0	0	.000	.667
Kearns	.000	6	5	0	0	0	0	0	0	0	0	0	0	1	0	4	0	0	0	.000	.167
Miranda	.222	11	9	1	2	2	0	0	0	2	0	0	0	2	0	4	0	0	1	.222	.364
Pena	.250	5	4	0	1	1	0	0	0	1	1	0	0	0	0	1	0	0	0	.250	.250
Posada	.077	14	13	1	1	4	0	0	1	1	0	0	0	1	0	5	0	0	1	.308	.143
Rodriguez	.000	3	2	0	0	0	0	0	0	0	0	0	0	1	0	1	0	0	0	.000	.333
Swisher	.000	7	6	0	0	0	0	0	0	0	0	0	0	1	1	0	0	0	0	.000	1.000
Teixeira	.000	1	0	0	0	0	0	0	0	0	0	0	0	1	0	0	0	0	0	.000	.000
Thames	.211	24	19	0	4	4	0	0	0	1	0	0	0	3	0	6	0	0	0	.211	.318
Winn	.000	1	1	0	0	0	0	0	0	0	0	0	0	0	1	0	0	0	0	.000	.000
TOTALS	.155		97	5	15	23	2	0	2	12	1	0	1	14	1	34	0	0	2	.237	.268

2010 Yankees Highs & Lows

CLUB

MOST RUNS, GAME -

14	NEW YORK AT BOSTON	5/08/10
12	NEW YORK VS KANSAS CITY	7/25/10
12	NEW YORK VS CHICAGO	5/02/10
12	NEW YORK AT CHICAGO	8/28/10
12	NEW YORK AT BALTIMORE	6/08/10

MOST RUNS, GAME, BOTH CLUBS -

24	CLEVELAND (13) AT NEW YORK (11)	5/29/10
21	NEW YORK (12) AT CHICAGO (9)	8/28/10

MOST RUNS, INNING -

11	NEW YORK VS TORONTO	7/03/10 (INNING 3)
9	NEW YORK VS DETROIT	8/19/10 (INNING 6)

MOST HITS, GAME -

18	NEW YORK VS CLEVELAND	5/31/10
17	NEW YORK AT TORONTO	8/24/10
17	NEW YORK AT BOSTON	5/08/10

MOST HITS, GAME, BOTH CLUBS -

30	LOS ANGELES (15) AT NEW YORK (15)	7/21/10
30	NEW YORK (14) AT CHICAGO (16)	8/28/10
30	NEW YORK (15) AT BALTIMORE (15)	6/08/10
28	KANSAS CITY (14) AT NEW YORK (14)	7/22/10

MOST TOTAL BASES, GAME -

33	NEW YORK AT TORONTO	8/24/10
31	NEW YORK AT KANSAS CITY	8/14/10

MOST DOUBLES, GAME -

5	NEW YORK AT SEATTLE	7/11/10
5	NEW YORK VS TAMPA BAY	9/21/10
5	NEW YORK VS KANSAS CITY	7/22/10
5	NEW YORK VS MINNESOTA	5/14/10
4	15 GAMES/CLUBS TIED	
4	NEW YORK AT TAMPA BAY	9/14/10 (10 INN.)
4	NEW YORK AT BOSTON	10/02/10 -G1 (10 INN.)

MOST TRIPLES, GAME -

2	NEW YORK AT OAKLAND	4/21/10
2	NEW YORK VS LOS ANGELES	4/15/10
1	27 GAMES/CLUBS TIED	
1	NEW YORK AT BOSTON	10/02/10 - G1 (10 INN.)

MOST HOME RUNS, GAME -

6	NEW YORK VS BOSTON	9/24/10
5	NEW YORK AT TORONTO	8/24/10
5	NEW YORK AT KANSAS CITY	8/14/10

MOST HOME RUNS, GAME, BOTH CLUBS -

8	BOSTON (2) AT NEW YORK (6)	9/24/10
7	BOSTON (5) AT NEW YORK (2)	5/17/10
7	NEW YORK (4) AT CHICAGO (3)	8/28/10

MOST EXTRA BASE HITS, GAME -

8	NEW YORK VS DETROIT	8/18/10
8	NEW YORK VS MINNESOTA	5/14/10
8	NEW YORK VS LOS ANGELES	4/15/10
7	NEW YORK VS KANSAS CITY	7/22/10
7	NEW YORK VS LOS ANGELES	7/21/10
7	NEW YORK VS CHICAGO	5/02/10
7	NEW YORK AT KANSAS CITY	8/14/10
7	NEW YORK AT CHICAGO	8/28/10
7	NEW YORK AT TAMPA BAY	9/14/10 (10 INN.)

MOST WALKS, GAME -

12	NEW YORK AT CLEVELAND	7/29/10
10	NEW YORK AT OAKLAND	4/20/10
10	NEW YORK VS HOUSTON	6/13/10
10	NEW YORK AT BOSTON	5/08/10
13	NEW YORK AT ARIZONA	6/23/10 (10 INN.)
10	NEW YORK AT BOSTON	10/02/10 - G2 (10 INN.)

MOST WALKS, GAME, BOTH CLUBS -

17	NEW YORK (12) AT CLEVELAND (5)	7/29/10
16	NEW YORK (9) AT TEXAS (7)	9/11/10
19	NEW YORK (13) AT ARIZONA (6)	6/23/10 (10 INN.)
16	NEW YORK (10) AT BOSTON (6)	10/02/10 - G2 (10 INN.)

MOST STRIKEOUTS, GAME -

17	NEW YORK AT TEXAS	8/11/10
15	NEW YORK AT TORONTO	8/23/10
15	NEW YORK AT TEXAS	9/10/10 (13 INN.)

MOST STRIKEOUTS, GAME, BOTH CLUBS -

22	NEW YORK (15) AT TORONTO (7)	8/23/10
21	NEW YORK (11) AT TORONTO (10)	6/06/10
21	NEW YORK (17) AT TEXAS (4)	8/11/10
21	NEW YORK (10) AT OAKLAND (11)	4/20/10
21	TORONTO (9) AT NEW YORK (12)	8/02/10
32	NEW YORK (14) AT BOSTON (18)	10/02/10 - G2 (10 INN.)
30	NEW YORK (14) AT TORONTO (16)	6/05/10 (14 INN.)
22	TORONTO (10) AT NEW YORK (12)	7/04/10 (10 INN.)

MOST STOLEN BASES, GAME -

4	NEW YORK VS TEXAS	4/18/10
3	NEW YORK VS OAKLAND	8/31/10
3	NEW YORK VS DETROIT	8/17/10
3	NEW YORK VS BOSTON	8/07/10
3	NEW YORK VS KANSAS CITY	7/25/10
3	NEW YORK AT KANSAS CITY	4/20/10
4	NEW YORK AT BOSTON	10/02/10 - G1 (10 INN.)
4	NEW YORK AT BOSTON	10/02/10 - G2 (10 INN.)

MOST STOLEN BASES, GAME, BOTH CLUBS -

7	BOSTON (6) AT NEW YORK (1)	8/09/10
6	TAMPA BAY (6) AT NEW YORK	5/19/10
6	NEW YORK (2) AT KANSAS CITY (4)	8/13/10
6	BOSTON (5) AT NEW YORK (1)	9/26/10 (10 INN.)

MOST DOUBLE PLAYS, GAME -

4	NEW YORK VS BALTIMORE	5/05/10
3	NEW YORK AT TAMPA BAY	4/11/10
3	NEW YORK AT OAKLAND	4/20/10
3	NEW YORK VS KANSAS CITY	7/23/10
3	NEW YORK AT MINNESOTA	5/26/10
3	NEW YORK AT KANSAS CITY	8/15/10
3	NEW YORK AT CLEVELAND	7/27/10

MOST DOUBLE PLAYS, GAME, BOTH CLUBS -

4	10 GAMES/CLUBS TIED	
6	NEW YORK (1) AT ARIZONA (5)	6/23/10 (10 INN.)
4	NEW YORK (2) AT TORONTO (2)	6/05/10 (14 INN.)
4	NEW YORK (1) AT BALTIMORE (3)	9/19/10 (11 INN.)

MOST ERRORS, GAME -

3	NEW YORK AT KANSAS CITY	8/15/10
3	NEW YORK AT BOSTON	4/06/10
2	NEW YORK VS KANSAS CITY	7/25/10
2	NEW YORK VS TAMPA BAY	7/16/10
2	NEW YORK VS SEATTLE	6/29/10
2	NEW YORK VS BOSTON	5/18/10
2	NEW YORK AT CLEVELAND	7/27/10
2	NEW YORK AT BALTIMORE	4/27/10
2	NEW YORK AT BOSTON	10/02/10 - G2 (10 INN.)
2	NEW YORK AT LOS ANGELES	6/27/10 (10 INN.)

MOST ERRORS, GAME, BOTH CLUBS -

4	SEATTLE (3) AT NEW YORK (1)	8/22/10
4	KANSAS CITY (2) AT NEW YORK (2)	7/25/10
4	BOSTON (2) AT NEW YORK (2)	5/18/10
4	NEW YORK (3) AT BOSTON (1)	4/06/10
4	NEW YORK (2) AT BALTIMORE (2)	4/27/10
3	10 GAMES/CLUBS TIED	
6	NEW YORK (4) AT BOSTON (2)	10/02/10 - G2 (10 INN.)
3	NEW YORK AT TEXAS (3)	8/10/10 (10 INN.)

MOST LEFT ON BASE, GAME -

14	NEW YORK AT TEXAS	9/11/10
14	NEW YORK AT CLEVELAND	7/29/10
13	NEW YORK AT NEW YORK	5/22/10
18	NEW YORK AT TEXAS	9/10/10 (13 INN.)
15	NEW YORK AT BOSTON	10/02/10 - G2 (10 INN.)

MOST LEFT ON BASE, GAME, BOTH CLUBS -

27	NEW YORK (14) AT TEXAS (13)	9/11/10
21	NEW YORK (13) AT NEW YORK (8)	5/22/10
21	DETROIT (12) AT NEW YORK (9)	8/16/10
21	KANSAS CITY (14) AT NEW YORK (7)	7/22/10
21	NEW YORK (11) AT BALTIMORE (10)	6/09/10
26	NEW YORK (18) AT TEXAS (8)	9/10/10 (13 INN.)
26	NEW YORK (15) AT BOSTON (11)	10/02/10 - G2 (10 INN.)
24	NEW YORK (12) AT BOSTON (12)	10/02/10 - G1 (10 INN.)
22	NEW YORK (9) AT TORONTO (13)	6/05/10 (14 INN.)
21	TORONTO (13) AT NEW YORK (8)	7/02/10 (11 INN.)

2010 Yankees Highs & Lows

MOST INN., GAME -

14.0	TORONTO VS NEW YORK	6/05/10
13.0	TEXAS VS NEW YORK	9/10/10

LONGEST TIME, GAME -

4:22	NEW YORK VS CLEVELAND	5/29/10
4:16	TEXAS VS NEW YORK	9/11/10
5:12	TEXAS VS NEW YORK	9/10/10 (13 INN.)
4:18	BOSTON VS NEW YORK	10/02/10 - G1 (10 INN.)

SHORTEST TIME, GAME -

1:58	NEW YORK VS TEXAS	4/16/10 (6 INN.)
2:07	OAKLAND VS NEW YORK	4/22/10
2:07	KANSAS CITY VS NEW YORK	8/15/10

HIGHEST ATTENDANCE, GAME -

49,716	NEW YORK VS BOSTON	8/07/10
49,558	NEW YORK VS BOSTON	9/25/10

LONGEST WINNING STREAK -

8	NEW YORK	8/28/10 THRU 9/04/10
7	NEW YORK	7/03/10 THRU 7/09/10

LONGEST LOSING STREAK -

4	NEW YORK	9/10/10 THRU 9/13/10
4	NEW YORK	9/22/10 THRU 9/25/10

INDIVIDUAL BATTING

LONGEST HITTING STREAK -

17	Cano	NEW YORK	5/17/10 THRU 6/03/10
14	Jeter	NEW YORK	9/10/10 THRU 9/25/10

MOST RUNS, GAME -

3	Rodriguez	NEW YORK AT LOS ANGELES	6/27/10 9 INN.
3	Jeter	NEW YORK AT ARIZONA	6/23/10 9 INN.
3	27 PLAYERS TIED		

MOST HITS, GAME -

4	12 PLAYERS TIED

MOST TOTAL BASES, GAME -

13	Rodriguez	NEW YORK AT KANSAS CITY	8/14/10
13	Teixeira	NEW YORK AT BOSTON	5/08/10
10	Cano	NEW YORK AT BALTIMORE	4/29/10

MOST DOUBLES, GAME -

2	18 PLAYERS TIED		
2	Cano	NEW YORK AT BOSTON	10/02/10 - G1 (10 INN.)
2	Granderson	NEW YORK AT TAMPA BAY	9/14/10 (10 INN.)
2	Teixeira	NEW YORK VS TORONTO	7/04/10 (10 INN.)

MOST TRIPLES, GAME -

2	Granderson	NEW YORK VS LOS ANGELES 4/15/10
1	29 PLAYERS TIED	
1	Granderson	NEW YORK AT BOSTON	10/02/10 - G1 (10 INN.)

MOST HOME RUNS, GAME -

3	Rodriguez	NEW YORK AT KANSAS CITY	8/14/10
3	Teixeira	NEW YORK AT BOSTON	5/08/10
2	15 PLAYERS TIED		

MOST EXTRA BASES, GAME -

3	Rodriguez	NEW YORK AT KANSAS CITY	8/14/10
3	Cano	NEW YORK AT TAMPA BAY	7/31/10
3	Rodriguez	NEW YORK VS KANSAS CITY	7/22/10
3	Teixeira	NEW YORK AT BOSTON	5/08/10
3	Cano	NEW YORK AT BALTIMORE	4/29/10
2	52 PLAYERS TIED		
3	Cano	NEW YORK AT BOSTON	10/02/10 - G1 (10 INN.)
2	5 PLAYERS TIED		

MOST RUNS BATTED IN, GAME -

6	Cano	NEW YORK VS SEATTLE	8/22/10
6	Rodriguez	NEW YORK VS CLEVELAND	5/31/10
5	Granderson	NEW YORK VS TAMPA BAY	9/20/10
5	Rodriguez	NEW YORK AT KANSAS CITY	8/14/10
5	Rodriguez	NEW YORK AT OAKLAND	7/06/10
5	Swisher	NEW YORK AT BALTIMORE	6/08/10
5	Cervelli	NEW YORK AT BOSTON	5/08/10
5	Teixeira	NEW YORK AT BOSTON	5/08/10

MOST STOLEN BASES, GAME -

2	Gardner	NEW YORK VS OAKLAND	8/31/10
2	Gardner	NEW YORK VS TEXAS	4/18/10
1	80 PLAYERS TIED		
3	Gardner	NEW YORK AT BOSTON	10/02/10 - G2 (10 INN.)
2	Gardner	NEW YORK AT BOSTON	10/02/10 - G1 (10 INN.)

INDIVIDUAL PITCHING

MOST STRIKEOUTS GAME (STARTER) -

10	Sabathia	NEW YORK AT OAKLAND	7/06/10
10	Hughes	NEW YORK AT OAKLAND	4/21/10
9	6 PLAYERS TIED		
10	Pettitte	NEW YORK AT TAMPA BAY	6/05/10 (14 INN.)
9	Sabathia	NEW YORK AT TAMPA BAY	9/13/10 (11 INN.)

MOST STRIKEOUTS GAME (RELIEVER) -

6	Vazquez	NEW YORK VS OAKLAND	8/30/10
5	Gaudin	NEW YORK VS TAMPA BAY	7/17/10

MOST INN., GAME (STARTER) -

8.2	Sabathia	NEW YORK AT KANSAS CITY	8/12/10
8.1	Sabathia	NEW YORK AT TORONTO	9/28/10

MOST INN., GAME (RELIEVER) -

4.2	Vazquez	NEW YORK VS OAKLAND	8/30/10
4.2	Mitre	NEW YORK AT CHICAGO	8/27/10
4.2	Moseley	NEW YORK VS KANSAS CITY	7/24/10
4.1	Vazquez	NEW YORK AT TORONTO	8/25/10

MOST HOME RUNS ALLOWED, GAME -

3	Vazquez	NEW YORK AT TORONTO	9/29/10
3	Hughes	NEW YORK VS SEATTLE	9/05/10
3	Vazquez	NEW YORK VS SEATTLE	8/21/10
3	Moseley	NEW YORK VS DETROIT	8/18/10
3	Burnett	NEW YORK AT ARIZONA	6/21/10
3	Burnett	NEW YORK AT TORONTO	6/04/10
3	Pettitte	NEW YORK VS TAMPA BAY	5/20/10
3	Vazquez	NEW YORK VS CHICAGO	5/01/10
2	30 PLAYERS TIED		
3	Hughes	NEW YORK VS TORONTO	7/04/10 (10 INN.)
2	Pettitte	NEW YORK AT TORONTO	6/05/10 (14 INN.)

LONGEST WINNING STREAK -

9	Sabathia	NEW YORK	6/03/10 THRU 7/22/10
6	Sabathia	NEW YORK	8/07/10 THRU 9/02/10

LONGEST LOSING STREAK -

5	Burnett	NEW YORK	6/04/10 THRU 6/26/10
4	Burnett	NEW YORK	8/02/10 THRU 8/27/10

MOST CONSECUTIVE SCORELESS INN. -

23.1	Wood	NEW YORK	8/03/10 THRU 10/02/10
18.1	Robertson	NEW YORK	7/02/10 THRU 8/23/10

YANKEES BY THE NUMBERS, 2010

Pre-All-Star Break	56-32
Post-All-Star Break	39-24
vs. LH starters	31-27
vs. RH starters	64-40
Yankees Score First	55-20
Opponents Score First	40-47
Yankees Score 4 Runs or More	83-25
Yankees Score 3 Runs or Fewer	12-42
Yankees Outhit Opp.	69-9
Opp. Outhits Yankees:	15-44
Hit Totals Are Even:	11-13
One-Run Games:	20-19
Leading After 6:	74-9
Trailing After 6:	12-51
Tied After 6:	9-7
Leading After 7:	80-7
Trailing After 7:	9-56
Tied After 7:	5-4
Leading After 8:	81-2
Trailing After 8:	6-58
Tied After 8:	6-8
Extra-Inning Games:	7-7
On Grass	88-56
On Turf	7-11
Day	36-22
Night	59-45
Series Record:	30-16-6
Series Record, home:	16-6-4
Series Record, road:	14-10-2
Series Openers:	27-25
Series Finales	30-22
vs. AL East	38-34
vs. AL Central	23-13
vs. AL West	23-13
vs. NL	11-7

Foundations made of stone, not sand

Quality, honesty, integrity and trust are important elements of doing business, because when you have them, you can begin to build real value.

Through our global network of firms with more than 161,000 people in 154 countries, we provide assurance, tax and advisory services to many of the world's most successful companies. To discover how we can help create value for you, visit pwc.com

© 2011 PricewaterhouseCoopers. All rights reserved. "PricewaterhouseCoopers" and "PwC" refer to the network of member firms of PricewaterhouseCoopers International Limited (PwCIL). Each member firm is a separate legal entity and does not act as agent of PwCIL or any other member firm. This document is for general information purposes only, and should not be used as a substitute for consultation with professional advisors.

JMKSAAB.com

INTRODUCING
OUR
ALL-STAR TEAM!

NEW 2011
SAAB 9-5
MVP

NEW 2011
SAAB 9-3
CONVERTIBLE
ALL-STAR

NEW 2011
SAAB 9-4x
ROOKIE OF THE YEAR
COMING SOON

SAAB
move your mind

JMK·SAAB

f JOIN US TODAY ON FACEBOOK!

RT. 22 EAST
SPRINGFIELD, NJ

Enjoy your flight!

ONLINE AT JMKSAAB.COM
866.HOT.SAAB
866.468.7222

SALES: Mon.-Fri 8:30am-7:00pm, Sat 9:00am-5:00pm

SERVICE: Mon.-Fri 7:30am-5:30pm, Closed Saturda

New York Yankees™

OPPONENTS

[L-R] **JACKIE ROBINSON, SID GORDON** and **JOE DIMAGGIO** pose for a photo prior to a three-way New York charity game between the Dodgers, Giants and Yankees on July 11, 1949

Baltimore Orioles

Oriole Park at Camden Yards, 333 W. Camden St., Baltimore, MD 21201
(410) 685-9800 • (410) 547-6272 - Fax
Capacity: 45,971
Dimensions: 330 LF, 400 CF, 318 RF

President, Baseball Operations: Andy MacPhail
Manager: Buck Showalter

2010 Record, Finish . . . . 66-96, 5th in AL East (-30.0 games)

Yankees vs. Baltimore
2010 vs. BAL 13-5
2010 at New York 7-2
2010 at BAL 6-3

All-Time vs. BAL 510-419-3
All-Time at New York . . . 264-203-1
All-Time at BAL 246-216-2

at original Yankee Stadium .241-190-1
at current Stadium 14-4
at Camden Yards 94-52-1

Longest Winning Streaks
by NYY . . . . .10 games
(5/10-9/2/2009; 4/21-6/29/1955)
by BAL . . . . .9 games
(8/15/67-5/22/1968)

Series Sweeps at New York
by NYY
3-game 6/1-3/10
4-game 9/19-22/05

by BAL
3-game 6/6-8/86
4-game 9/21-23/76

Series Sweeps at Baltimore
by NYY
3-game 8/31-9/2/09
4-game 8/14-17/03

by BAL
3-game 4/15-17/05
4-game 9/5-7/66

Series Results, Last 10 Years

Year	Home	Road	Total
2010	7-2	6-3	13-5
2009	7-2	6-3	13-5
2008	6-3	5-4	11-7
2007	5-4	4-5	9-9
2006	5-4	7-3	12-7
2005	7-2	4-5	11-7
2004	7-3	7-2	14-5
2003	6-4	7-2	13-6
2002	7-3	6-3	13-6
2001	5-3	8-2	13-5
TOTAL	**62-30**	**60-32**	**122-62**

2011 Schedule
at New York:
April 12-14, July 29-31, Sept. 5-7
at Baltimore:
April 22-24, May 18-19, Aug. 26-29

Boston Red Sox

Fenway Park, 4 Yawkey Way, Boston, MA 02215
(617) 267-9440 • (617) 375-0944 - Fax
Capacity: 37,402 (night); 36,974 (day)
Dimensions: 310 LF, 420 CF, 380 RF

Executive Vice President/General Manager: Theo Epstein
Manager: Terry Francona

2010 Record, Finish . . . . 89-73, 3rd in AL East (-7.0 games)

Yankees vs. Boston
2010 vs. BOS 9-9
2010 at New York 4-5
2010 at BOS 5-4

All-Time vs. BOS 1113-916-14
All-Time at New York 601-409-7
All-Time at BOS 512-507-7

at original Yankee Stadium . .484-285-4
at current Yankee Stadium 11-7
at Fenway Park 463-446-4

Longest Winning Streaks
by NYY . . . . .12 games
(8/16/1952-4/23/1953;
5/27-8/23/1936)
by BOS . . . . .17 games
(10/3/1911-7/1/1912)

Series Sweeps at New York
by NYY
3-game 9/25-27/09
4-game 8/6-9/09
5-game *9/28-30/51

by BOS
3-game 4/23-25/04
4-game . . . . .none
5-game *7/9-13/39

Series Sweeps at Boston
by NYY
3-game 8/31-9/2/01
4-game 10/2-5/86
5-game **8/18-21/06

by BOS
3-game 6/09-11/09
4-game 6/4-7/90
5-game . . . . .none
* includes two doubleheaders
** includes one doubleheader

Series Results, Last 10 Years

Year	Home	Road	Total
2010	4-5	5-4	9-9
2009	7-2	2-7	9-9
2008	4-5	5-4	9-9
2007	6-3	4-5	10-8
2006	4-6	7-2	11-8
2005	5-4	5-5	10-9
2004	5-4	3-7	8-11
2003	5-5	5-4	10-9
2002	5-4	5-5	10-9
2001	8-1	5-4	13-5
TOTAL	**53-39**	**46-47**	**99-86**

2011 Schedule
at New York:
May 13-15, June 7-9, Sept. 23-25
at Boston:
April 8-10, Aug. 5-7, Aug. 30-Sept. 1

Chicago White Sox

U.S. Cellular Field, 333 West 35th St., Chicago, IL 60616
(312) 674-5300 • (312) 674-5116 - Fax
Capacity: 40,615
Dimensions: 330 LF, 400 CF, 335 RF

Senior Vice President/General Manager: Ken Williams
Manager: Ozzie Guillen

2010 Record, Finish . . . . .88-74, 2nd in AL Central (-6.0 games)

Yankees vs. Chicago
2010 vs. CWS 4-2
2010 at New York 2-1
2010 at CWS 2-1

All-Time vs. CWS 1035-800-14
All-Time at New York . . . 552-363-5
All-Time at CWS 483-437-9

at original Yankee Stadium . . .428-255-3
at current Yankee Stadium 5-1
at U.S. Cellular Field: 47-42

Longest Winning Streaks
by NYY . . . . .10 games
(4/22-6/22/1964;
8/14/1944-5/26/1945)
by CWS . . . . 8 games
(3x, 9/3/1972-7/10/1973;
6/10-8/22/1967; 7/16-8/22/1906)

Series Sweeps at New York
by NYY
3-game 8/28-30/09
4-game 6/6-8/69

by CWS
3-game 9/14-16/92
4-game 6/15-18/00

Series Sweeps at Chicago
by NYY
3-game 5/27-29/02
4-game 6/17-20/76

by CWS
3-game 8/6-8/91
4-game 8/17-20/64

Series Results, Last 10 Years
Year	Home	Road	Total
2010	2-1	2-1	4-2
2009	3-0	1-3	4-3
2008	3-1	2-1	5-2
2007	2-1	4-3	6-4
2006	3-0	1-2	4-2
2005	1-2	2-1	3-3
2004	2-2	2-1	4-3
2003	1-2	1-2	2-4
2002	1-2	3-0	4-2
2001	3-0	2-1	5-1
TOTAL	**21-11**	**20-15**	**41-26**

2011 Schedule
at New York:
April 25-28
at Chicago:
Aug. 1-4

Cleveland Indians

Progressive Field, 2401 Ontario St., Cleveland, OH 44115
(216) 420-4200 • Fax: (216) 420-4396
Capacity: 43,441
Dimensions: 325 LF, 405 CF, 325 RF

Executive Vice President, General Manager: Chris Antonetti
Manager: Manny Acta

2010 Record, Finish . . . . 69-93, 4th in AL Central (-25.0 games)

Yankees vs. Indians
2010 vs. CLE 6-2
2010 at New York 3-1
2010 at CLE 3-1

All-Time vs. CLE 1071-846-12
All-Time at New York . . . 581-379-5
All-Time at CLE 490-467-7

at original Yankee Stadium . . 456-262-1
at Current Yankee Stadium 5-3
at Progressive Field: 47-26

Longest Winning Streaks
by NYY . . . . .13 games
(7/2/1976-7/7/1977)
by CLE . . . . .13 games
(7/13-9/23/1908)

Series Sweeps at New York
by NYY
3-game 4/17-19/07
4-game 7/17-20/03

by CLE
3-game 4/7-9/89
4-game . . . . .none

Series Sweeps at Cleveland
by NYY
3-game 8/10-12/07
4-game 6/21-23/96

by CLE
3-game 9/11-13/70
4-game *6/15-17/62
includes one doubleheader

Series Results, Last 10 Years
Year	Home	Road	Total
2010	3-1	3-1	6-2
2009	2-2	3-1	5-3
2008	1-2	2-2	3-4
2007	3-0	3-0	6-0
2006	2-1	2-2	4-3
2005	3-1	1-2	4-3
2004	2-1	2-1	4-2
2003	4-0	1-2	5-2
2002	3-0	3-3	6-3
2001	3-3	2-1	5-4
TOTAL	**26-11**	**22-15**	**48-26**

2011 Schedule
at New York:
June 10-13
at Cleveland:
July 4-6

Detroit Tigers

Comerica Park, 2100 Woodward Avenue, Detroit, MI 48201
(313) 471-2000 • (313) 471-2138 - Fax
Capacity: 41,255
Dimensions: 345 LF, 420 CF, 330 RF

President/CEO/General Manager: Dave Dombrowski
Manager: Jim Leyland

2010 Record, Finish . . . . 81-81, 3rd in AL Central (-13.0 games)

Yankees vs. Detroit

2010 vs. DET 4-4
2010 at New York 3-1
2010 at DET. 1-3

All-Time vs. DET 1020-903-10
All-Time at New York . . . 557-405-4
All-Time at DET. 463-498-6

at original Yankee Stadium 433-288-2
at current Yankee Stadium. 6-1
at Comerica Park 21-22

Longest Winning Streaks

by NYY . . . . .11 games
(7/12-9/17/1942)
by DET. . . . . .12 games
(6/10-8/18/1908)

Series Sweeps at New York
by NYY

3-game 7/17-19/09
4-game 9/8-11/88

by DET

3-game 4/29-5/1/08
4-game 6/13-15/58

Series Sweeps at Detroit
by NYY

3-game 9/20-22/02
4-game 6/8-11/26

by DET

3-game 5/12-14/00
4-game *8/12-13/45
includes two doubleheaders

Series Results, Last 10 Years

Year	Home	Road	Total
2010	3-1	1-3	4-4
2009	3-0	2-1	5-1
2008	0-3	2-1	2-4
2007	3-1	1-3	4-4
2006	2-1	3-1	5-2
2005	3-0	2-1	5-1
2004	1-2	2-2	3-4
2003	3-0	2-1	5-1
2002	5-1	3-0	8-1
2001	3-0	2-4	5-4
TOTAL	**26-9**	**20-17**	**46-26**

2011 Schedule

at New York:
March 31-April 3
at Detroit:
May 2-5

Kansas City Royals

Kauffman Stadium, One Royal Way, Kansas City, MO 64129
(816) 921-8000 • (816) 921-5775 - Fax
Capacity: 37,840
Dimensions: 330 LF, 400 CF, 330 RF

Senior VP & General Manager – Baseball Operations: Dayton Moore
Manager: Ned Yost

2010 Record, Finish . . . . 67-95, 5th in AL Central (-27.0 games)

Yankees vs. Kansas City

2010 vs. KC 5-3
2010 at New York 3-1
2010 at KC 2-2

All-Time vs. KC 261-177-1
All-Time at New York 146-74
All-Time at KC 115-103-1

at original Yankee Stadium . . 134-67
at current Yankee Stadium. 5-2
at Kauffman Stadium 102-92

Longest Winning Streaks

by NYY . . . . .12 games
(8/13/1997-8/18/1998)
by KC . . . . .5 games
(5/26-7/4/1990; 5/14-7/24/1978)

Series Sweeps at New York
by NYY

3-game 8/3-5/07
4-game *8/7-9/98
5-game 7/12-15/84

by KC

3-game 6/3-5/94
4-game .none
5-game .none

Series Sweeps at Kansas City
by NYY

3-game 9/7-9/07
4-game .none

by KC

3-game 5/31-6/2/05
4-game .none
includes one doubleheader

Series Results, Last 10 Years

Year	Home	Road	Total
2010	3-1	2-2	5-3
2009	2-1	2-1	4-2
2008	4-3	1-2	5-5
2007	3-0	6-1	9-1
2006	5-1	2-1	7-2
2005	3-0	0-3	3-3
2004	3-0	2-1	5-1
2003	3-0	1-2	4-2
2002	2-1	3-0	5-1
2001	3-0	3-0	6-0
TOTAL	**31-7**	**22-13**	**53-20**

2011 Schedule

at New York:
May 10-12
at Kansas City:
Aug.15-17

Los Angeles Angels

Angel Stadium of Anaheim, 2000 Gene Autry Way, Anaheim, CA 92806
(714) 940-2000 • (714) 940-2205 - Fax
Capacity: 45,285
Dimensions: 365 LF, 400 CF, 365 RF

Vice President & General Manager: Tony Reagins
Manager: Mike Scioscia

2010 Record, Finish . . . . 80-82, 3rd in AL West (-10.0 games)

Yankees vs. Los Angeles
2010 vs. LAA 4-4
2010 at New York 3-2
2010 at LAA. 1-2

All-Time vs. LAA 326-275
All-Time at New York 181-116
All-Time at LAA 145-159

at original Yankee Stadium . . . 166-109
at current Yankee Stadium. 6-3
at Angel Stadium 121-138

Longest Winning Streaks
by NYY . . . . 7 games
       (8/23/1980-5/4/1981)
by LAA. . . . . 5 games
       (4x, last 4/27-7/23/2005)

Series Sweeps at New York
by NYY
3-game 8/29-31/95
4-game 7/22-25/93

by LAA
3-game 5/25-27/07
4-game . . . . none

Series Sweeps at Los Angeles
by NYY
3-game 7/29-31/03
4-game 7/21-24/94

by LAA
3-game 7/10-12/09
4-game . . . . none

Series Results, Last 10 Years
Year	Home	Road	Total
2010	3-2	1-2	4-4
2009	3-1	2-4	5-5
2008	2-2	1-5	3-7
2007	2-4	1-2	3-6
2006	2-2	2-4	4-6
2005	3-3	1-3	4-6
2004	2-4	2-1	4-5
2003	1-2	5-1	6-3
2002	2-1	2-2	4-3
2001	2-2	1-2	3-4
TOTAL	**22-23**	**18-26**	**40-49**

2011 Schedule
<u>at New York</u>:
Aug. 9-11
<u>at Los Angeles</u>:
June 3-5, Sept. 9-11

Minnesota Twins

Target Field, 1 Twins Way, Minneapolis, MN 55403
(612) 659-3400 • (612) 659-4029 - Fax
Capacity: 39,800
Dimensions: 339 LF, 404 CF, 328 RF

Senior Vice President, General Manager: Bill Smith
Manager: Ron Gardenhire

2010 Record, Finish . . . . 94-68, 1st in AL Central (+6.0 games)

Yankees vs. Minnesota
2010 vs. MIN 4-2
2010 at New York 2-1
2010 at MIN. 2-1

All-Time vs. MIN 328-242-1
All-Time at New York . . . 172-108-1
All-Time at MIN 156-134

at original Yankee Stadium . . . 159-103-1
at Yankee Stadium 6-1
All-Time at Metrodome 77-64

Longest Winning Streaks
by NYY . . . . 13 games
       (5/10/2002-4/21/2003)
by MIN. . . . . 6 games
       (3x, last 5/24-6/4/1969)

Series Sweeps at New York
by NYY
3-game 7/21-23/08
4-game 5/15-18/09

by MIN
3-game 8/9-11/68
4-game . . . . none

Series Sweeps at Minnesota
by NYY
3-game 7/7-9/09
4-game 4/18-21/03

by MIN
3-game 9/6-8/91
4-game 7/3-5/67

Series Results, Last 10 Years
Year	Home	Road	Total
2010	2-1	2-1	4-2
2009	4-0	3-0	7-0
2008	3-0	3-4	6-4
2007	3-1	2-1	5-2
2006	2-1	1-2	3-3
2005	2-1	1-2	3-3
2004	3-0	1-2	4-2
2003	3-0	4-0	7-0
2002	3-0	3-0	6-0
2001	1-2	1-2	2-4
TOTAL	**26-6**	**21-14**	**47-20**

2011 Schedule
<u>at New York</u>:
April 4-7
<u>at Minnesota</u>:
Aug. 18-21

Oakland Athletics

Oakland Alameda-County Coliseum, 7000 Coliseum Way • Oakland, CA 94621
(510) 638-4900 • (510) 562-1633 - Fax
Capacity: 34,077
Dimensions: 330 LF, 400 CF, 330 RF

Vice President and General Manager: Billy Beane
Manager: Bob Geren

2010 Record, Finish . . . . 81-81, 2nd in AL West (-9.0 games)

Yankees vs. Oakland

2010 vs. OAK. 9-1
2010 at New York 4-0
2010 at OAK 5-1

All-Time vs. OAK. 255-218
All-Time at New York 140-98
All-Time at OAK 115-120

at original Yankee Stadium . . . 124-92
at Yankee Stadium 9-1
at County Coliseum 115-120

Longest Winning Streaks
by NYY . . . . .8 games
        (3x, last 6/12/2008-7/24/2009)
by OAK . . . . .16 games
            (9/9/1989-5/1/1991)

Series Sweeps at New York
by NYY
3-game 7/18-20/08
4-game 8/30-9/2/10

by OAK
3-game 6/9-11/06
4-game 7/14-16/72

Series Sweeps at Oakland
by NYY
3-game 7/5-7/10
4-game 7/6-8/79

by OAK
3-game 8/10-12/01
4-game . . . . none

Series Results, Last 10 Years

Year	Home	Road	Total
2010	4-0	5-1	9-1
2009	5-1	2-1	7-2
2008	3-0	2-1	5-1
2007	1-2	1-2	2-4
2006	2-4	1-2	3-6
2005	2-1	5-1	7-2
2004	5-1	2-1	7-2
2003	1-2	2-4	3-6
2002	3-3	2-1	5-4
2001	3-0	0-6	3-6
TOTAL	**29-14**	**22-20**	**51-34**

2011 Schedule
at New York:
July 22-24, Aug. 23-25
at Oakland:
May 30-June 1

Seattle Mariners

Safeco Field, 1250 First Ave. South, Seattle, WA 98134
(206) 346-4000 • (206) 346-4400 - Fax
Capacity: 47,447
Dimensions: 331 LF, 405 CF, 326 RF

Executive Vice President & General Manager: Jack Zduriencik
Manager: Eric Wedge

2010 Record, Finish . . . . 61-101, 4th in AL West (-29.0 games)

Yankees vs. Seattle

2010 vs. SEA 6-4
2010 at New York 3-3
2010 at SEA 3-1

All-Time vs. SEA 203-161
All-Time at New York 103-77
All-Time at SEA. 100-84

at original Yankee Stadium . . . 98-73
at Yankee Stadium 5-4
at Safeco Field 33-22

Longest Winning Streaks
by NYY . . . . .8 games
    (9/4/2007-5/25/2008; 5/9-8/29/1999)
by SEA. . . . . .5 games
        (3x, last 5/29-6/10/1995)

Series Sweeps at New York
by NYY
3-game 5/23-25/08
4-game . . . . none

by SEA
3-game 5/3-5/02
4-game . . . . none

Series Sweeps at Seattle
by NYY
3-game 5/9-11/05
4-game 8/5-8/99

by SEA
3-game 8/26-28/96
4-game . . . . none

Series Results, Last 10 Years

Year	Home	Road	Total
2010	3-3	3-1	6-4
2009	2-1	4-3	6-4
2008	6-0	1-2	7-2
2007	4-3	1-2	5-5
2006	2-1	1-2	3-3
2005	3-0	4-3	7-3
2004	2-1	4-2	6-3
2003	3-3	2-1	5-4
2002	0-3	4-2	4-5
2001	1-5	2-1	3-6
TOTAL	**26-20**	**26-19**	**52-39**

2011 Schedule
at New York:
July 25-27
at Seattle:
May 27-29, Sept. 12-14

Tampa Bay Rays

Tropicana Field, One Tropicana Drive, St. Petersburg, FL 33705
(727) 825-3137 • (727) 825-3111 - Fax
Capacity: 36,973
Dimensions: 315 LF, 404 CF, 320 RF

Executive Vice President, Baseball Operations: Andrew Friedman
Manager: Joe Maddon

2010 Record, Finish . . . . .96-66, 1st in AL East (+1.0 game)

Yankees vs. Tampa Bay
2010 vs. TB. 8-10
2010 at New York 4-5
2010 at TB 4-5

All-Time vs. TB *141-79
All-Time at New York 75-34
All-Time at TB 65-44

at original Yankee Stadium 65-26
at current Yankee Stadium. 10-8
at Tropicana Field 65-44
  *includes 2 games at Tokyo from
  3/30-31/04*

Longest Winning Streaks
by NYY . . . . .11 games
  (9/17/1998-9/24/1999)
by TB . . . . .4 games
  (5/3-6/20/2005)

Series Sweeps at New York
by NYY
3-game 9/12-14/06
4-game *9/7-9/09
  includes one doubleheader

by TB
3-game .none
4-game .none

Series Sweeps at Tampa Bay
by NYY
3-game 9/13-15/05
4-game 7/9-12/98

by TB
3-game 9/26-28/00
4-game .none

Series Results, Last 10 Years
Year	Home	Road	Total
2010	4-5	4-5	8-10
2009	6-3	5-4	11-7
2008	6-3	5-4	11-7
2007	5-4	5-4	10-8
2006	7-2	6-3	13-5
2005	3-6	5-5	8-11
2004	10-0	5-4	15-4
2003	6-3	8-2	14-5
2002	7-2	6-3	13-5
2001	8-1	5-5	13-6
TOTAL	**62-29**	**54-39**	**116-68**

2011 Schedule
at New York:
July 7-10, Aug. 12-14, Sept. 20-21
at Tampa Bay:
May 16-17, July 18-21, Sept. 26-28

Texas Rangers

Ballpark in Arlington, 1000 Ballpark Way, Suite #400, Arlington, TX 76011
(817) 273-5222 • (817) 273-5110 - Fax
Capacity: 48,911
Dimensions: 332 LF, 400 CF, 325 RF

General Manager: Jon Daniels
Manager: Ron Washington

2010 Record, Finish . . . . 90-72, 1st in AL West (+9.0 games)

Yankees vs. Texas
2010 vs. TEX 4-4
2010 at New York 3-0
2010 at TEX 1-4

All-Time vs. TEX 236-174
All-Time at New York 134-73
All-Time at TEX 102-101

at original Yankee Stadium . . 120-66
at current Yankee Stadium. 6-3
at Rangers Ballpark. 44-32

Longest Winning Streaks
by NYY . . . . .8 games
  (7/24/2006-5/9/2007;
  7/20/2005-5/7/2006)
by TEX . . . . .7 games
  (4/20-9/10/1990)

Series Sweeps at New York
by NYY
3-game 4/16-18/10
4-game 8/11-14/05

by TEX
3-game 5/16-18/03
4-game .none

Series Sweeps at Texas
by NYY
3-game 5/1-3/07*
4-game .none

by TEX
3-game 9/10-12/10
4-game 7/20-23/89
  includes one doubleheader

Series Results, Last 10 Years
Year	Home	Road	Total
2010	3-0	1-4	4-4
2009	3-3	2-1	5-4
2008	1-2	2-2	3-4
2007	2-1	3-0	5-1
2006	2-2	6-0	8-2
2005	5-2	2-1	7-3
2004	2-1	3-3	5-4
2003	2-4	2-1	4-5
2002	2-2	2-1	4-3
2001	1-2	2-2	3-4
TOTAL	**23-19**	**25-15**	**48-34**

2011 Schedule
at New York:
April 15-17, June 14-16
at Texas:
May 6-8

Toronto Blue Jays

Rogers Centre, 1 Blue Jays Way, Suite 3200 • Toronto, Ontario M5V 1J1
(416) 341-1000 • (416) 341-1250 - Fax
Capacity: 49,160
Dimensions: 328 LF, 400 CF, 328 RF

Senior VP, Baseball Operations and GM: Alex Anthopoulos
Manager: John Farrell

2010 Record, Finish . . . . 85-77, 4th in AL East (-11.0 games)

Yankees vs. Toronto
2010 vs. TOR 8-10
2010 at New York 5-4
2010 at TOR 3-6

All-Time vs. TOR 267-215
All-Time at New York 135-107
All-Time at TOR 132-108

at original Yankee Stadium . . . 124-100
at current Yankee Stadium 11-7
at Rogers Centre: 84-77

Longest Winning Streaks
by NYY . . . . .13 games
(5/10/1995-6/4/1996)
by TOR . . . . .10 games
(4/14-9/25/1992)

**Series Sweeps at New York
by NYY**
3-game 8/1-3/06
4-game 9/18-21/95

by TOR
3-game 7/31-8/2/92
4-game 5/22-25/03

**Series Sweeps at Toronto
by NYY**
3-game 3/31-4/2/03
4-game . . . . none

by TOR
3-game 9/19-21/00
4-game . . . . none

Series Results, Last 10 Years

Year	Home	Road	Total
2010	5-4	3-6	8-10
2009	6-3	6-3	12-6
2008	5-4	4-5	9-9
2007	5-4	5-4	10-8
2006	6-3	4-5	10-8
2005	6-4	6-2	12-6
2004	6-3	6-4	12-7
2003	4-6	6-3	10-9
2002	6-3	4-6	10-9
2001	5-5	6-3	11-8
TOTAL	**54-39**	**50-41**	**104-80**

2011 Schedule
at New York:
April 29-May 1, May 23-25, Sept. 2-4
at Toronto:
April 19-20, July 14-17, Sept. 16-18

Chicago Cubs

Wrigley Field, 1060 W. Addison, Chicago, IL 60613
(773) 404-2827 • (773) 404-4129 - Fax
Capacity: 41,210
Dimensions: 355 LF, 400 CF, 353 RF

Vice President & General Manager: Jim Hendry
Manager: Mike Quade

2010 Record, Finish . . . . 75-87, 5th in NL Central (-16.0 games)

Yankees vs. Chicago
2010 vs. CHC . . . . NA
2010 at New York . . . . NA
2010 at CHC . . . . NA

All-Time vs. CHC 4-2
All-Time at New York 3-0
All-Time at CHC 1-2

at original Yankee Stadium 3-0
at Wrigley Field 1-2

**Series Sweeps at New York
by NYY**
3-game 6/17-19/05
4-game . . . . none

by CHC
3-game . . . . none
4-game . . . . none

**Series Sweeps at Chicago
by NYY**
3-game . . . . none
4-game . . . . none

by CHC
3-game . . . . none
4-game . . . . none

Series Results, All-Time*

Year	Home	Road	Total
2005	3-0	-	3-0
2003	-	1-2	1-2
TOTAL	**3-0**	**1-2**	**4-2**

*The Yankees swept the Cubs, 4-games-
to-none, in the 1932 and 1938 World
Series.

2011 Schedule
at Chicago:
June 17-19

Cincinnati Reds

Great American Ball Park, 100 Joe Nuxhall Way, Cincinnati, OH 45202
(513) 765-7800 • (513) 765-7180 - Fax
Capacity: 42,319
Dimensions: 328 LF, 404 CF, 325 RF

President, Baseball Operations & General Manager: Walt Jocketty
Manager: Dusty Baker

2010 Record, Finish . . . . 91-71, 1st in NL Central (+5.0 games)

Yankees vs. Cincinnati
2010 vs. CIN. . . . . NA
2010 at New York . . . . NA
2010 at CIN . . . . NA

All-Time vs. CIN 2-4
All-Time at New York 1-2
All-Time at CIN 1-2

at original Yankee Stadium 1-2
at Great American Ball Park. . . . 1-2

Series Sweeps at New York
by NYY
3-game . . . . none
4-game . . . . none

by CIN
3-game . . . . none
4-game . . . . none

Series Sweeps at Cincinnati
by NYY
3-game . . . . none
4-game . . . . none

by CIN
3-game . . . . none
4-game . . . . none

Series Results, All-Time*

Year	Home	Road	Total
2008	1-2	-	1-2
2003	-	1-2	1-2
TOTAL	**1-2**	**1-2**	**2-4**

The Yankees and Reds have met three times in the World Series with the Yankees prevailing twice. The Yankees swept Cincinnati in four games in 1939 and won 4-games-to-1 in 1961. In 1976, the Reds swept the Yankees in four games, marking just the third time in Yankees franchise history that they had been held winless in a World Series (also 1922 vs. Giants and '63 vs. Dodgers).

2011 Schedule
at Cincinnati:
June 20-22

Colorado Rockies

Coors Field, 2001 Blake Street, Denver, CO 80205
(303) 292-0200 • (303) 312-2319 - Fax
Capacity: 50,490
Dimensions: 347 LF, 415 CF, 350 RF

Executive Vice President & General Manager: Dan O'Dowd
Manager: Jim Tracy

2010 Record, Finish . . . . 83-79, 3rd in NL West (-9.0 games)

Yankees vs. Colorado
2010 vs. COL . . . . NA
2010 at New York . . . . NA
2010 at COL. . . . . NA

All-Time vs. COL. 5-4
All-Time at New York 3-0
All-Time at COL 2-4

at original Yankee Stadium 3-0
at Coors Field 2-4

Series Sweeps at New York
by NYY
3-game 6/8-10/04
4-game . . . . none

by COL
3-game . . . . none
4-game . . . . none

Series Sweeps at Colorado
by NYY
3-game . . . . none
4-game . . . . none

by COL
3-game 6/19-21/07
4-game . . . . none

Series Results, All-Time

Year	Home	Road	Total
2007	-	0-3	0-3
2004	3-0	-	3-0
2002	-	2-1	2-1
TOTAL	**3-0**	**2-4**	**5-4**

2011 Schedule
at New York:
June 24-26

Milwaukee Brewers

Miller Park, One Brewers Way, Milwaukee, WI 53214
(414) 902-4400 • (414) 902-4053 - Fax
Capacity: 41,900
Dimensions: 344 LF, 400 CF, 345 RF

Executive Vice President & General Manager: Doug Melvin
Manager: Ron Roenicke

2010 Record, Finish . . . . 77-85, 3rd in NL Central (-14.0 games)

Yankees vs. Milwaukee
2010 vs. MIL . . . . NA
2010 at New York . . . . NA
2010 at MIL . . . . NA

All-Time vs. MIL *208-182-1
All-Time at New York 120-72
All-Time at MIL 84-108-1
* includes 7-5 mark against Seattle
Pilots in 1969.

at original Yankee Stadium 109-65
at Miller Park 1-2

Longest Winning Streaks
by NYY . . . . .7 games
(7/16/71-4/19/72)
by MIL . . . . .7 games
(9/19/72-4/22/73)

Series Sweeps at New York
by NYY
3-game 6/6-8/97
4-game 7/30-8/2/84

by MIL
3-game 10/2-4/72
4-game . . . . none

Series Sweeps at Milwaukee
by NYY
3-game 8/1-3/94
4-game 7/23-25/71

by MIL
3-game 8/14-16/89
4-game . . . . none

Series Results, Last 10 Years*

Year	Home	Road	Total
2005	-	1-2	1-2
TOTAL	**-**	**1-2**	**1-2**

The Yankees defeated Milwaukee, 3-games-to-2, in the Division Series of the strike-shortened 1981 season, when the Brewers played in the American League.

2011 Schedule
at New York Yankees:
June 28-30

New York Mets

Citi Field, 126th Street, Flushing, NY 11368
(718) 507-6387 • (718) 639-3619 - Fax
Capacity: 41,800
Dimensions: 335 LF, 408 CF, 330 RF

Executive VP/General Manager: Sandy Alderson
Manager: Terry Collins

2010 Record, Finish . . . . .79-83, 4th in NL East (-18.0 games)

Yankees vs. Mets
2010 vs. NYM 3-3
2010 at New York-AL 2-1
2010 at NYM 1-2

All-Time vs. NYM 45-33
All-Time at New York-AL 24-15
All-Time at NYM 21-18

at original Yankee Stadium 20-13
at current Yankee Stadium 4-2
at Citi Field 4-2

Longest Winning Streaks
by NYY . . . . .7 games
(6/30/02-6/29/03)
by NYM . . . . .3 games
(3x, last 5/17-6/27/08)

Series Sweeps at Yankees
by NYY
3-game 6/27-29/03
4-game . . . . none

by NYM
3-game . . . . none
4-game . . . . none

Series Sweeps at Mets
by NYY
3-game 6/26-28/09
4-game . . . . none

by NYM
3-game 7/2-4/04
4-game . . . . none

Series Results, All Time*

Year	Home	Road	Total
2010	2-1	1-2	3-3
2009	2-1	3-0	5-1
2008	0-3	2-1	2-4
2007	2-1	1-2	3-3
2006	2-1	1-2	3-3
2005	1-2	2-1	3-3
2004	2-1	0-3	2-4
2003	3-0	3-0	6-0
2002	2-1	1-2	3-3
2001	2-1	2-1	4-2
2000	2-1	2-1	4-2
1999	2-1	1-2	3-3
1998	0-0	2-1	2-1
1997	2-1	0-0	2-1
TOTAL	**24-15**	**21-18**	**45-33**

The Yankees have faced the Mets once in the postseason, winning the 2000 World Series, 4-games-to-1.

2011 Schedule
at NYY: May 20-22
at NYM: July 1-3

All-Time Series Results by Year

YEAR	BAL	BOS	CWS	CLE	DET	KC	LAA	MIL	MIN	OAK	SEA	TB	TEX	TOR
2010	13-5	9-9	4-2	6-2	4-4	5-3	4-4	--	4-2	9-1	6-4	8-10	4-4	8-10
2009	13-5	9-9	4-3	5-3	5-1	4-2	5-5	–	7-0	7-2	6-4	11-7	5-4	12-6
2008	11-7	9-9	5-2	3-4	2-4	5-5	3-7	–	6-4	5-1	7-2	11-7	3-4	9-9
2007	9-9	10-8	6-4	6-0	4-4	9-1	3-6	–	5-2	2-4	5-5	10-8	5-1	10-8
2006	12-7	11-8	4-2	4-3	5-2	7-2	4-6	–	3-3	3-6	3-3	13-5	8-2	10-8
2005	11-7	10-9	3-3	4-3	5-1	3-3	4-6	1-2	3-3	7-2	7-3	8-11	7-3	12-6
2004	14-5	8-11	4-3	4-2	3-4	5-1	4-5	–	4-2	7-2	6-3	15-4	5-4	12-7
2003	13-6	10-9	2-4	5-2	5-1	4-2	6-3	–	7-0	3-6	5-4	14-5	4-5	10-9
2002	13-6	10-9	4-2	6-3	8-1	5-1	4-3	–	6-0	5-4	4-5	13-5	4-3	10-9
2001	13-5	13-5	5-1	5-4	5-4	6-0	3-4	–	2-4	3-6	3-6	13-6	3-4	11-8
2000	7-5	7-6	4-8	5-5	4-8	8-2	5-5	–	5-5	6-3	4-6	6-6	10-2	5-7
1999	9-4	4-8	7-5	7-3	7-5	4-5	4-6	–	6-4	6-4	9-1	8-4	8-4	10-2
1998	9-3	7-5	7-4	7-4	8-3	10-0	5-6	–	7-4	8-3	8-3	11-1	8-3	6-6
1997	4-8	8-4	9-2	6-5	10-2	8-3	7-4	7-4	8-3	6-5	4-7	–	7-4	7-5
1996	10-3	6-7	7-6	9-3	8-5	8-4	6-7	6-6	7-5	9-3	3-9	–	5-7	8-5
1995	7-6	8-5	2-3	6-6	8-5	7-3	5-7	6-5	4-3	4-9	4-9	–	6-3	12-1
1994	6-4	7-3	2-4	9-0	3-3	2-4	8-4	7-2	5-4	7-5	8-4	–	3-2	3-4
1993	7-6	7-6	8-4	7-6	9-4	6-6	6-6	9-4	8-4	6-6	7-5	–	3-9	5-8
1992	8-5	6-7	4-8	6-7	8-5	7-5	5-7	7-6	5-7	6-6	6-6	–	6-6	2-11
1991	8-5	7-6	4-8	7-6	5-8	5-7	6-6	7-6	2-10	6-6	3-9	–	5-7	6-7
1990	7-6	4-9	2-10	8-5	6-7	4-8	6-6	7-6	6-6	0-12	9-3	–	3-9	5-8
1989	5-8	6-7	6-5	4-9	7-6	6-6	6-6	5-8	6-6	3-9	8-4	–	5-7	7-6
1988	10-3	4-9	9-3	7-6	5-8	6-6	6-6	7-6	9-3	6-6	5-7	–	5-6	6-7
1987	10-3	6-7	7-5	7-6	8-5	7-5	9-3	6-7	6-6	5-7	7-5	–	5-7	6-7
1986	8-5	8-5	6-6	8-5	7-6	8-4	5-7	5-8	8-4	5-7	8-4	–	7-5	7-6
1985	12-1	8-5	6-6	7-6	3-9	7-5	9-3	6-7	9-3	7-5	8-4	–	8-4	6-7
1984	8-5	6-7	5-7	11-2	6-7	7-5	4-8	7-6	4-8	8-4	7-5	–	6-6	8-5
1983	7-6	6-7	4-8	7-6	8-5	6-6	7-5	9-4	8-4	8-4	7-5	–	7-5	7-6
1982	2-11	6-7	4-8	9-4	5-8	7-5	5-7	5-8	10-2	7-5	6-6	–	7-5	6-7
1981	6-7	3-3	7-5	5-7	7-3	10-2	2-2	3-3	3-3	4-3	2-3	–	5-4	2-3
1980	6-7	10-3	7-5	8-5	8-5	4-8	10-2	8-5	8-4	8-4	9-3	–	7-5	10-3
1979	6-5	8-5	8-4	8-5	6-7	7-5	5-7	4-9	5-7	9-3	6-6	–	8-4	9-4
1978	9-6	9-7	9-1	9-6	11-4	5-6	5-5	5-10	7-3	8-2	6-5	–	6-4	11-4
1977	7-8	7-8	7-3	12-3	9-6	5-5	7-4	7-8	8-2	9-2	6-4	–	7-3	9-6
1976	5-13	11-7	11-1	12-4	8-9	5-7	7-5	13-5	10-2	6-6	–	–	9-3	–
1975	10-8	5-11	6-6	9-9	12-6	5-7	5-7	9-9	8-4	6-6	–	–	8-4	–
1974	7-11	7-11	8-4	11-7	7-11	8-4	9-3	9-9	8-4	7-5	–	–	8-4	–
1973	9-9	4-14	4-8	11-7	11-7	6-6	6-6	8-10	9-3	4-8	–	–	8-4	–
1972	6-7	9-9	5-7	11-7	9-7	5-7	8-4	9-9	6-6	3-9	–	–	8-4	–
1971	7-11	11-7	7-5	10-8	8-10	7-5	6-6	10-2	4-8	5-7	–	–	7-11	–
1970	7-11	8-10	7-5	10-8	11-7	11-1	7-5	9-3	7-5	6-6	–	–	10-8	–
1969	7-11	7-11	9-3	8-9	8-10	7-5	9-3	7-5	2-10	6-6	–	–	10-8	–
1968	5-13	8-10	12-6	8-10	8-10	–	12-6	–	6-12	10-8	–	–	14-4	–
1967	5-13	6-12	6-12	9-9	8-10	–	9-9	–	6-12	11-7	–	–	12-6	–
1966	3-15	10-8	9-9	6-12	7-11	–	7-11	–	10-8	13-5	–	–	5-10	–
1965	5-13	9-9	10-8	6-12	8-10	–	12-6	–	5-13	11-7	–	–	11-7	–
1964	8-10	9-9	12-6	15-3	10-8	–	11-7	–	10-8	12-6	–	–	12-6	–
1963	11-7	12-6	10-8	11-7	10-8	–	13-5	–	11-6	12-6	–	–	14-4	–
1962	7-11	12-6	10-8	7-11	11-7	–	10-8	–	11-7	13-5	–	–	15-3	–
1961	9-9	13-5	12-6	14-4	10-8	–	12-6	–	14-4	14-4	–	–	11-7	–
1960	13-9	15-7	12-10	16-6	14-8	–	–	–	12-10	15-7	–	–	–	–
1959	10-12	9-13	9-13	11-11	8-14	–	–	–	15-7	17-5	–	–	–	–
1958	14-8	13-9	15-7	15-7	10-12	–	–	–	12-10	13-9	–	–	–	–
1957	13-9	14-8	14-8	13-9	12-10	–	–	–	13-9	19-3	–	–	–	–
1956	13-9	14-8	13-9	12-10	10-12	–	–	–	17-5	18-4	–	–	–	–
1955	19-3	14-8	11-11	9-13	12-10	–	–	–	16-6	15-7	–	–	–	–
1954	17-5	13-9	15-7	11-11	16-6	–	–	–	13-9	18-4	–	–	–	–
1953	17-5	11-10	13-9	11-11	16-6	–	–	–	14-6	17-5	–	–	–	–
1952	14-8	14-8	14-8	12-10	13-9	–	–	–	15-7	13-9	–	–	–	–
1951	17-5	11-11	14-8	15-7	12-10	–	–	–	16-6	13-9	–	–	–	–
1950	17-5	13-9	14-8	14-8	11-11	–	–	–	14-8	15-7	–	–	–	–
1949	17-5	13-9	15-7	12-10	11-11	–	–	–	15-7	14-8	–	–	–	–
1948	16-6	8-14	16-6	12-10	13-9	–	–	–	17-5	12-10	–	–	–	–
1947	15-7	13-9	12-10	15-7	14-8	–	–	–	15-7	13-9	–	–	–	–
1946	14-8	8-14	14-8	12-10	9-13	–	–	–	14-8	16-6	–	–	–	–
1945	7-15	16-6	12-9	9-12	7-15	–	–	–	14-8	16-6	–	–	–	–
1944	10-12	11-11	12-10	14-8	8-14	–	–	–	15-7	13-9	–	–	–	–
1943	17-5	17-5	12-10	13-9	12-10	–	–	–	11-11	16-6	–	–	–	–
1942	15-7	10-12	15-7	15-7	15-7	–	–	–	17-5	16-6	–	–	–	–
1941	18-4	13-9	14-8	15-7	11-11	–	–	–	16-6	14-8	–	–	–	–
1940	14-8	13-9	11-11	12-10	8-14	–	–	–	17-5	13-9	–	–	–	–
1939	19-3	8-11	18-4	15-7	13-9	–	–	–	15-7	13-9	–	–	–	–
1938	15-7	11-11	14-8	13-8	14-8	–	–	–	16-6	16-5	–	–	–	–
1937	16-6	15-7	13-9	15-7	13-9	–	–	–	16-6	14-8	–	–	–	–
1936	14-8	15-7	14-7	16-6	14-8	–	–	–	13-9	16-6	–	–	–	–

All-Time Series Results by Year

YEAR	BAL	BOS	CWS	CLE	DET	KC	LAA	MIL	MIN	OAK	SEA	TB	TEX	TOR
1935	12-10	12-9	11-9	14-8	11-11	–	–	–	15-7	14-6	–	–	–	–
1934	17-5	12-10	17-5	11-11	10-12	–	–	–	12-10	15-7	–	–	–	–
1933	14-7	14-8	15-7	13-7	15-7	–	–	–	8-14	12-9	–	–	–	–
1932	16-6	17-5	17-5	15-7	17-5	–	–	–	11-11	14-8	–	–	–	–
1931	16-6	16-6	15-6	9-13	14-8	–	–	–	13-9	11-11	–	–	–	–
1930	16-6	16-6	14-8	12-10	13-9	–	–	–	5-17	10-12	–	–	–	–
1929	14-8	17-5	16-6	8-14	13-9	–	–	–	12-10	8-14	–	–	–	–
1928	12-10	16-6	13-9	16-6	15-7	–	–	–	13-9	16-6	–	–	–	–
1927	21-1	18-4	17-5	12-10	14-8	–	–	–	14-8	14-8	–	–	–	–
1926	16-6	17-5	14-8	11-11	12-10	–	–	–	12-10	9-13	–	–	–	–
1925	11-11	13-9	9-13	12-10	8-14	–	–	–	7-15	9-13	–	–	–	–
1924	12-10	17-5	16-6	14-8	9-13	–	–	–	9-13	12-8	–	–	–	–
1923	15-5	14-8	15-7	10-12	12-10	–	–	–	16-6	16-6	–	–	–	–
1922	14-8	9-13	13-9	15-7	11-11	–	–	–	15-7	17-5	–	–	–	–
1921	13-9	15-7	9-13	14-8	17-5	–	–	–	13-8	17-5	–	–	–	–
1920	12-10	13-9	12-10	13-9	15-7	–	–	–	11-11	19-3	–	–	–	–
1919	12-8	9-12	8-12	7-13	12-8	–	–	–	14-6	18-2	–	–	–	–
1918	10-10	11-6	6-12	7-11	10-9	–	–	–	8-11	8-4	–	–	–	–
1917	13-9	9-13	10-12	7-15	9-13	–	–	–	8-13	15-7	–	–	–	–
1916	9-13	11-11	10-12	10-12	8-14	–	–	–	15-7	15-7	–	–	–	–
1915	12-10	12-10	7-15	13-9	5-17	–	–	–	9-13	11-9	–	–	–	–
1914	11-11	11-11	10-12	14-8	9-13	–	–	–	7-15	8-14	–	–	–	–
1913	11-11	6-14	10-11	8-14	11-11	–	–	–	6-16	5-17	–	–	–	–
1912	13-9	2-19	9-13	8-13	6-16	–	–	–	7-15	5-17	–	–	–	–
1911	16-5	10-12	9-13	8-14	15-7	–	–	–	12-10	6-15	–	–	–	–
1910	16-6	13-8	9-13	8-13	9-13	–	–	–	15-7	9-12	–	–	–	–
1909	13-8	9-13	8-14	14-8	8-14	–	–	–	14-6	8-14	–	–	–	–
1908	5-17	10-12	6-16	6-16	7-15	–	–	–	9-13	8-14	–	–	–	–
1907	8-14	12-8	10-12	7-15	8-13	–	–	–	15-7	10-9	–	–	–	–
1906	13-8	17-5	10-12	11-10	11-11	–	–	–	15-7	13-8	–	–	–	–
1905	15-7	8-13	10-12	12-10	13-9	–	–	–	15-7	8-11	–	–	–	–
1904	16-6	10-12	10-12	11-9	15-7	–	–	–	18-4	12-9	–	–	–	–
1903	15-5	7-13	11-7	6-14	9-10	–	–	–	14-5	10-8	–	–	–	–
Totals	1221-818	1113-917	1035-800	1071-846	1020-903	261-177	326-275	208-182	1083-749	1103-788	203-161	141-79	357-248	267-215

Orioles include St. Louis Browns, 1903-1953 (711-399). Brewers include Seattle Pilots, 1969 (7-5). Twins include original Washington Senators, 1903-1960 (755-507). A's include Philadelphia A's, 1903-1954 (665-445) and Kansas City A's 1955-1967 (183-75). Rangers include Washington Senators, 1961-1971 (121-74).

Most Recent Trades with Each Team

AMERICAN LEAGUE EAST

Baltimore (Nov. 12, 2006): Yankees acquire RHP Chris Britton for RHP Jaret Wright.

Boston (Aug. 13, 1997): Yankees acquire 1B/DH Mike Stanley and minor league INF Randy Brown for RHP Tony Armas and a player to be named later.

Tampa Bay (May 25, 2006): Yankees acquire INF Nick Green for cash considerations.

Toronto (July 1, 2002): Yankees acquire OF Raul Mondesi for RHP Scott Wiggins.

AMERICAN LEAGUE CENTRAL

Chicago (Nov. 13, 2008): Yankees acquire INF/OF Nick Swisher and RHP Kanekoa Texeira for INF Wilson Betemit and RHPs Jeff Marquez and Jhonny Nunez.

Cleveland (July 31, 2010): Yankees acquire RHP Kerry Wood in exchange for player(s) to be named later (RHP Andrew Shive and RHP Matt Cusick).

Detroit (Dec. 9, 2009): Yankees acquire OF Curtis Granderson for LHP Phil Coke and OF Austin Jackson in a three-team, seven-player trade (also sent RHP Ian Kennedy to Arizona).

Kansas City (Aug. 11, 2000): Yankees acquire INF Nick Ortiz for INF Wilson Delgado.

Minnesota (Sept. 3, 2003): Yankees acquire RHP Juan Padilla as player to be named following 8/31/03 trade for LHP Jesse Orosco.

AMERICAN LEAGUE WEST

Los Angeles (July 21, 2007) Yankees acquire C Jose Molina for RHP Jeff Kennard.

Oakland (July 5, 2002): Yankees acquire RHP Jeff Weaver (from Detroit) in a three-team trade, sending LHP Ted Lilly, RHP Jason Arnold and OF John-Ford Griffin to Oakland.

Seattle (Aug. 6, 2003): Yankees acquire RHP Jeff Nelson for RHP Armando Benitez and cash considerations.

Texas (March 9, 2010): Yankees trade RHP Edwar Ramirez for cash considerations.

NATIONAL LEAGUE EAST

Atlanta (Dec. 22, 2009): Yankees acquire RHP Javier Vazquez and LHP Boone Logan for OF Melky Cabrera, RHP Arodys Vizcaino and LHP Mike Dunn.

Florida (Dec. 16, 2005): Yankees acquire LHP Ron Villone for LHP Ben Julianel.

Washington (Feb. 3, 2011): Yankees acquire OF Justin Maxwell for RHP Adam Olbrychowski.

New York (Dec. 3, 2004): Yankees acquire LHP Mike Stanton for LHP Felix Heredia.

Philadelphia (July 30, 2006): Yankees acquire OF Bobby Abreu and RHP Cory Lidle for INF C.J. Henry, C Jesus Sanchez, RHP Carlos Monasterios and LHP Matt Smith.

NATIONAL LEAGUE CENTRAL

Chicago (Aug. 27, 2005): Yankees acquire OF Matt Lawton for RHP Justin Berg.

Cincinnati (July 31, 2009): Yankees acquire INF/OF Jerry Hairston, Jr. for C Chase Weems.

Houston (July 31, 2010): Yankees acquire 1B/DH Lance Berkman and cash for RHP Mark Melancon and INF Jimmy Paredes.

Milwaukee (Feb. 4, 2009): Yankees acquire OF/C Eric Fryer for LHP Chase Wright.

Pittsburgh (June 30, 2009): Yankees acquire INF/OF Eric Hinske and cash considerations for OF Eric Fryer and RHP Casey Erickson.

St. Louis (Aug. 22, 2003): Yankees acquire RHP Justin Pope and LHP Ben Julianel for LHP Sterling Hitchcock.

NATIONAL LEAGUE WEST

Arizona (Nov. 18, 2010): Yankees acquire RHP Scott Allen for 1B Juan Miranda.

Colorado (July 29, 2009): Yankees acquire RHP Jason Hirsh for cash considerations.

Los Angeles (July 31, 2007): Yankees acquire INF Wilson Betemit for RHP Scott Proctor.

San Diego (Aug. 6, 2009): Yankees acquire RHP Chad Gaudin for cash considerations.

San Francisco (Dec. 13, 2001): Yankees acquire OF John Vander Wal for RHP Jay Witasick.

Home Record vs. AL Opponents, 1976-2010

YEAR	BAL	BOS	CWS	CLE	DET	KC	LAA	MIL	MIN	OAK	SEA	TB	TEX	TOR	TOTAL
2010	7-2	4-5	2-1	3-1	3-1	3-1	3-2	---	2-1	4-0	3-3	4-5	3-0	5-4	46-26
2009	7-2	7-2	3-0	2-2	3-0	2-1	3-1	---	4-0	5-1	2-1	6-3	3-3	6-3	53-19
2008	6-3	4-5	3-1	1-2	0-3	4-3	2-2	---	3-0	3-0	6-0	6-3	1-2	5-4	48-33
2007	5-4	6-3	2-1	3-0	3-1	3-0	2-4	---	3-1	1-2	4-3	5-4	2-1	5-4	44-28
2006	5-4	4-6	3-0	2-1	2-1	5-1	2-2	---	2-1	2-4	2-1	7-2	2-2	6-3	44-28
2005	7-2	5-4	1-2	3-1	3-0	3-0	3-3	---	2-1	2-1	3-0	3-6	5-2	6-4	46-26
2004	7-3	5-4	2-2	2-1	1-2	3-0	2-4	---	3-0	5-1	2-1	10-0	2-1	6-3	50-22
2003	6-4	5-5	1-2	4-0	3-0	3-0	1-2	---	3-0	1-2	3-3	6-3	2-4	4-6	42-31
2002	7-3	5-4	1-2	3-0	5-1	2-1	2-1	---	3-0	3-3	0-3	7-2	2-2	6-3	52-28
2001	5-3	8-1	3-0	3-3	3-0	3-0	2-2	---	1-2	3-0	1-5	8-1	1-2	5-5	46-24
2000	4-2	2-4	1-5	1-3	3-3	5-1	2-2	---	3-3	4-2	1-3	4-2	5-1	4-2	39-33
1999	4-3	2-4	4-2	4-2	5-1	1-2	2-4	---	2-2	2-2	5-1	3-3	4-2	5-1	43-29
1998	6-0	3-3	4-1	4-1	5-1	5-0	3-3	---	5-1	4-1	4-1	6-0	4-2	2-4	55-18
1997	1-5	4-2	4-1	3-2	4-2	4-2	2-2	5-0	3-2	4-2	2-4	---	4-1	3-3	43-28
1996	4-3	4-2	5-2	3-3	4-3	5-1	3-3	5-1	3-2	4-2	2-4	---	4-2	3-3	49-31
1995	4-2	6-1	0-2	2-4	4-2	3-1	4-2	3-3	2-2	3-4	3-3	---	5-0	7-0	46-26
1994	3-3	4-2	1-2	7-0	1-2	0-3	3-3	1-2	3-0	3-3	3-3	---	2-0	2-1	33-24
1993	4-3	4-3	4-2	4-2	5-1	4-2	4-2	4-2	4-2	4-2	4-2	---	2-4	3-4	50-31
1992	3-3	4-2	1-5	3-4	4-3	4-2	4-2	5-2	2-4	4-2	3-3	---	3-3	1-5	41-40
1991	5-2	3-4	3-3	4-2	3-3	2-4	2-4	3-3	2-4	3-3	2-4	---	4-2	3-4	39-42
1990	3-3	4-2	1-5	4-3	3-4	3-3	3-3	3-4	3-3	0-6	4-2	---	3-3	3-3	37-44
1989	2-5	4-3	4-2	1-5	5-1	3-3	5-1	3-3	3-3	1-5	3-3	---	4-2	3-4	41-40
1988	5-1	2-4	5-1	4-3	5-2	2-4	3-3	6-1	4-2	4-2	2-4	---	3-2	1-5	46-34
1987	6-1	4-3	4-2	4-2	5-1	6-0	4-2	3-3	4-2	3-3	3-3	---	3-3	2-5	51-30
1986	2-4	2-4	2-4	5-2	4-3	4-2	3-3	4-3	3-3	3-3	3-2	---	4-2	2-4	41-39
1985	7-0	5-2	4-2	3-3	2-3	5-1	5-1	3-3	6-0	5-1	5-1	---	6-0	2-5	58-22
1984	4-2	2-4	3-3	7-0	3-3	6-0	2-4	5-2	3-3	5-1	2-4	---	3-3	5-1	50-30
1983	4-3	4-3	2-4	5-2	3-3	3-3	5-1	6-0	5-1	4-2	3-3	---	3-3	5-2	52-30
1982	2-4	3-3	1-5	3-4	3-4	3-3	3-3	4-3	5-1	4-2	3-3	---	4-2	4-2	42-39
1981	5-2	2-1	4-2	2-4	3-0	5-1	0-0	2-1	1-2	2-1	1-1	---	4-2	1-2	32-19
1980	3-3	3-3	3-3	5-2	5-2	2-4	6-0	3-4	4-2	5-1	5-1	---	4-2	5-1	53-28
1979	4-3	3-3	6-0	3-3	3-3	4-2	4-3	2-4	3-3	4-2	5-1	---	5-1	5-2	51-30
1978	3-4	4-1	6-2	6-2	3-3	3-2	3-4	5-3	3-2	5-0	4-1	---	4-1	6-1	55-26
1977	6-2	4-1	6-1	3-4	4-1	4-1	4-4	3-4	4-1	5-1	5-0	---	3-2	4-4	55-26
1976	9-2	5-1	5-3	4-5	2-4	2-4	1-8	8-1	5-1	2-4	---	---	4-2	---	47-35

Road Record vs. AL Opponents, 1976-2010

YEAR	BAL	BOS	CWS	CLE	DET	KC	LAA	MIL	MIN	OAK	SEA	TB	TEX	TOR	TOTAL
2010	6-3	5-4	2-1	3-1	1-3	2-2	1-2	---	2-1	5-1	3-1	4-5	1-4	3-6	38-34
2009	6-3	2-7	1-3	3-1	2-1	2-1	2-4	---	3-0	2-1	4-3	5-4	2-1	6-3	40-32
2008	5-4	5-4	2-1	2-2	2-1	1-2	1-5	---	3-4	2-1	1-2	5-4	2-2	4-5	41-40
2007	4-5	4-5	4-3	3-0	1-3	6-1	1-2	---	2-1	1-2	5-4	3-0	5-4	5-4	40-32
2006	7-3	7-2	1-2	2-2	3-1	2-1	2-4	---	1-2	1-2	1-2	6-3	6-0	4-5	43-29
2005	4-5	5-5	2-1	1-2	2-1	0-3	1-3	---	1-2	5-1	4-3	5-5	2-1	6-2	38-34
2004	7-2	3-7	2-1	2-1	2-2	2-1	2-1	---	1-2	2-1	4-2	5-4	3-3	6-4	41-31
2003	7-2	5-4	1-2	1-2	1-2	1-2	5-1	---	4-0	2-4	2-1	8-2	2-1	6-3	46-25
2002	6-3	5-5	3-0	3-3	3-0	3-0	2-2	---	3-0	2-1	4-2	6-3	2-1	4-6	51-30
2001	8-2	5-4	2-1	2-1	2-4	3-0	1-2	---	1-2	0-6	2-1	5-5	2-2	6-3	39-33
2000	3-3	5-2	3-3	4-2	1-5	3-1	3-3	---	2-2	2-1	3-3	2-4	5-1	1-5	37-35
1999	5-1	2-4	3-3	3-1	2-4	3-3	2-2	---	4-2	4-2	4-0	5-1	4-2	5-1	46-26
1998	3-3	4-2	3-3	3-3	3-2	5-0	2-3	---	2-3	4-2	4-2	5-1	4-1	4-2	46-27
1997	3-3	4-2	5-1	3-3	6-0	4-1	5-2	2-4	5-1	2-3	2-3	---	3-3	4-2	48-28
1996	6-0	2-5	2-4	6-0	4-2	3-3	3-4	1-5	4-3	5-1	1-5	---	1-5	5-2	43-39
1995	3-4	2-4	2-1	4-2	4-3	4-2	1-5	3-2	2-1	1-5	1-6	---	1-3	5-1	33-39
1994	3-1	3-1	1-2	2-0	2-1	2-1	5-1	6-0	2-4	4-2	5-1	---	1-2	1-3	37-19
1993	3-3	3-3	4-2	3-4	4-3	2-4	2-4	5-2	4-2	2-4	3-3	---	1-5	2-4	38-43
1992	4-2	2-5	3-3	3-3	4-2	3-3	1-5	2-4	3-3	2-4	3-3	---	3-3	1-6	35-46
1991	3-3	4-2	1-5	3-4	2-5	3-3	4-2	4-3	0-6	3-3	1-5	---	1-5	3-3	32-49
1990	4-3	0-7	1-5	4-2	3-3	1-5	3-3	4-2	3-3	0-6	5-1	---	0-6	2-5	30-51
1989	3-3	2-4	2-3	3-4	2-5	3-3	1-5	2-5	3-3	2-4	5-1	---	1-5	4-2	33-47
1988	5-2	2-5	4-2	3-3	0-6	4-2	3-3	1-5	5-1	2-4	3-3	---	2-4	5-2	39-42
1987	4-2	2-4	3-3	3-4	3-4	1-5	5-1	3-4	2-4	2-4	4-2	---	2-4	5-2	38-43
1986	6-1	6-1	4-2	3-3	3-3	2-4	2-4	1-5	5-1	2-4	5-2	---	3-3	5-2	49-33
1985	5-1	3-3	2-4	4-3	1-6	2-4	4-2	3-4	3-3	2-4	4-2	---	2-4	4-2	39-42
1984	4-3	3-3	2-4	4-2	3-4	1-5	2-4	2-4	1-5	3-3	5-1	---	3-3	3-4	37-45
1983	3-3	2-4	2-4	2-4	5-2	3-3	2-4	4-3	3-3	4-2	4-2	---	4-2	2-4	39-41
1982	0-7	3-4	3-3	6-0	2-4	4-2	2-4	1-5	5-1	3-3	3-3	---	3-3	2-5	37-44
1981	1-5	1-2	3-3	3-3	4-3	5-1	2-2	1-2	2-1	2-2	1-2	---	1-2	1-1	27-29
1980	3-4	7-0	4-2	3-3	3-3	2-4	4-2	5-1	4-2	3-3	4-2	---	3-3	5-2	50-31
1979	4-2	5-1	2-5	3-4	4-2	1-5	2-2	2-5	2-4	5-1	1-5	---	3-3	4-2	38-41
1978	6-3	5-0	3-4	5-2	2-3	2-3	6-2	0-7	4-1	3-2	2-4	---	2-3	5-3	45-37
1977	1-6	3-2	6-2	6-2	1-4	3-3	3-4	4-4	4-1	4-1	1-4	---	4-1	5-2	45-36
1976	4-5	6-0	7-1	4-4	3-3	5-1	4-5	5-4	5-1	4-2	---	---	5-1	---	52-27

QUALITY IS ALL WE THINK ABOUT. THAT AND QUALITY.

THINK ABOUT IT.

First, we pioneered the 10-year/100,000-mile warranty. Then, we led the way with Hyundai Assurance. And now, we continue to receive accolades for quality. To us, these achievements represent important milestones. But they also serve as a reminder for us to stay focused on whatever lies ahead. For more about Hyundai, visit Hyundai.com.

©2011 Hyundai Motor America

New York Yankees™

HISTORY

This year marks the 50th anniversary of **ROGER MARIS'** record-setting 1961 season, when he surpassed Babe Ruth's single-season home run mark.

History
of the
New York
Yankees

The Yankees are Baseball's most storied franchise. With 27 World Championships and 40 American League pennants to its name, the Yankees stand alone in both categories.

The team's glorious history has surprisingly humble origins at the start of the previous century, when the upstart American League declared itself a Major League following the 1900 season. At that time, the league sought to place a team in New York for the 1901 campaign. But due to the political strength of the National League's New York Giants, the American League instead put a team in Baltimore, calling it the Orioles, with the intent to move it to New York as soon as possible.

Managed by John McGraw, the 1901 Orioles finished 68-65 and failed to draw substantial crowds. The following season, McGraw, fearing the team would relocate to New York without him in 1903, precipitated a midseason release from his contract. He immediately teamed with Giants owner Andrew Freedman and Cincinnati Reds owner John T. Brush, helping them acquire a majority interest in the Orioles. With control of Baltimore's players, the pair of owners decimated the squad, divvying up the players between them. On July 17, 1902, the Baltimore Orioles were left with five players on their roster and were forced to forfeit their game against the St. Louis Browns. The American League quickly stepped in and lent Baltimore players from other teams so they could finish the season.

Prior to the 1903 campaign, the two leagues reached a truce, part of which involved the National League agreeing to allow an American League team in New York City. Racehorse owner Frank Farrell and ex-New York chief of police Bill Devery purchased the remnants of the Baltimore franchise for $18,000 and reestablished it in upper Manhattan.

The New York Americans, as they were formally named, were New York City's third Major League team, joining the Giants and Brooklyn Dodgers of the National League. They played home games at American League Park, a hastily constructed all-wooden structure at 168th Street and Broadway. Because the site was one of the highest spots in Manhattan, the team was commonly called the "Hilltoppers" or "Highlanders" and their home field "Hilltop Park." The club played its inaugural game on April 22, 1903, at Washington, losing 3-1 to the Senators. The next day, they defeated the Senators, 7-2, recording the very first win in franchise history.

Led by future Hall of Famers Jack Chesboro, Clark Griffith and Wee Willie Keeler, the Highlanders finished with a 72-62 record, 17.0 games out of first place. They nearly captured the American League pennant in 1904—finishing 1.5 games behind the Boston Pilgrims—as Chesboro went 41-12 with a 1.82 ERA in 454.2 innings pitched, setting a modern-era (since 1900) record with his win total. That season marked the first of three second-place finishes for the club between 1904 and 1910.

After a spectacular fire severely damaged the Polo Grounds in 1911, the Highlanders' owners invited the Giants to share Hilltop Park until their home could be rebuilt. Two years later, the Giants returned the favor and allowed the Highlanders to become tenants in their rebuilt and vastly superior facility. With the move in 1913, the

The 1927 Yankees were known as "Murderers' Row."

Highlanders officially changed their name to "Yankees," by which they had actually been known for most of their history.

From 1911 to 1919, the Yankees won as many as 80 games in a season only twice. But three key moves—the January 11, 1915, purchase of the ballclub by Colonel Jacob Ruppert and Colonel Tillinghast L'Hommedieu Huston, the 1918 hiring of Manager Miller Huggins by Ruppert (without Huston's blessing) and the 1919 midseason trade for right-handed pitcher Carl Mays (26 wins in 1920 and 27 wins in 1921)—set the stage for the most course-altering transaction in baseball history.

On January 3, 1920, the Yankees purchased the contract of George Herman "Babe" Ruth from the Boston Red Sox for $125,000 and a $350,000 loan against the mortgage on Fenway Park.

Ruth's impact was immediate. The Yankees won 95 games in 1920, their highest victory total up to that point, then captured their first American League pennant a year later. With the Babe hitting 54 home runs in 1920—more than any other *team* in the American League—Yankees attendance at the Polo Grounds doubled to 1,289,422. In 1921, the Giants, being outdrawn in their own park, asked the Yankees to vacate the Polo Grounds as soon as possible. Now bitter rivals, the two teams squared off in the World Series in 1921 and 1922 with the Giants winning on both occasions.

Though he came up on the wrong end in both Series, Yankees pitcher—and 1969 Hall of Fame inductee—Waite Hoyt allowed just one earned run over 35.0 combined innings over the two Fall Classics. Remarkably, he went 2-2 in his five appearances (four starts), including a 1-0, Series-clinching loss (on an unearned run) in Game 8 of the 1921 best-of-nine championship.

With their departure from the Polo Grounds inevitable, the Yankees' owners set out to build a ballpark of their own. Designed to be baseball's first triple-decked structure with an advertised capacity of 70,000, it would also be the first baseball facility to be labeled a "stadium."

Construction began on May 5, 1922, and in only 284 working days, Yankee Stadium was ready for its inaugural game on April 18, 1923 vs. the Boston Red Sox. An announced crowd of 74,200 fans packed Yankee Stadium for a glimpse of Baseball's grandest facility while thousands milled around outside after the fire department finally ordered the gates closed. Appropriately, Ruth christened his new home with a three-run homer to cap a four-run third inning as the Yankees won, 4-1.

Playing in their new stadium, the Yankees won the American League by 16.0 games in 1923, using just eight pitchers all season. Each of their five starters—Bob Shawkey, Joe Bush, Waite Hoyt, Sam Jones and Herb Pennock—won at least 16 games. Yet it was Ruth's tremendous power that people were coming to see, and Yankee Stadium quickly became known as "The House That Ruth Built." Later that season, the Stadium hosted the first of 37 World Series at the structure, and the Yankees won their first World Championship over their former landlord, the Giants.

On June 1, 1925, in a 5-3 loss vs. Washington, Huggins inserted a 21-year-old rookie first baseman as a pinch-hitter for light-hitting shortstop Paul "Pee Wee" Wanninger. No one could have imagined at the time that this appearance would be the first of 2,130 consecutive games played by Lou Gehrig, who, with Ruth and later Joe DiMaggio, anchored some of the greatest ballclubs of all time.

After a tough loss to the St. Louis Cardinals in the 1926 World Series, the Yankees rolled to World Championships in both 1927 and 1928, sweeping Pittsburgh and St. Louis, respectively. The 1927 club, the second Yankees team to be labeled "Murderers' Row" (the first was the 1919 squad), is often used as the yardstick by which team greatness is measured. During that season, Ruth broke his own single-season home run record (previously 59 in 1921) with his 60th on September 30, 1927, off Washington's Tom Zachary. Gehrig also added 47 homers and 175 RBI.

In his 15 seasons in pinstripes, Ruth helped build a winning tradition with seven American League pennants and four World Championships (also 1932). He finished his unparalleled career with 714 home runs (including 49 with the Red Sox from 1914-19 and six with the Boston Braves in 1935), 12 American League home run titles and six RBI crowns, including five seasons with more than 150 RBI. A charter member of Baseball's Hall of Fame, he remains widely regarded as the greatest player of all time.

Throughout Ruth's time in pinstripes, he often overshadowed the soft-spoken, Manhattan-born Gehrig. Yet the "Iron Horse" posted incredible numbers in his own right. From 1926 through 1938, Gehrig drove in at least 112 runs each season. A member of six World Championship clubs (1927-28, 1932, 1936-38), he finished with a .340 lifetime batting average and 493 career home runs in just 8,001 at-bats. He was the AL's starting first baseman in each of the first five Major League Baseball All-Star Games, and in 1934, he became the first of two Yankees in franchise history (also Mickey Mantle in 1956) to win the Triple Crown, hitting .363 with a career-best 49 homers and 165 RBI. He also still holds the American League record for RBI in a single season with 184 in 1931.

Lou Gehrig

After the 1934 season, Ruth's last in New York, the Yankees purchased the contract of a budding star named Joe DiMaggio from the San Francisco Seals

Joe DiMaggio

of the Pacific Coast League. Two years later, DiMaggio made his debut in pinstripes and helped the Yankees to an incredible string of four consecutive World Championships under Manager Joe McCarthy from 1936 through 1939. The 1930s also produced one of the game's greatest lefty-righty pitching combinations in future Hall of Famers Lefty Gomez and Red Ruffing. A four-time 20-game winner—including 24-7 in 1932 and 26-5 in 1934—Gomez posted a 6-0 record over five World Series. Ruffing, who was acquired in May 1930 from the Boston Red Sox for outfielder Cedric Durst and $50,000, had been 39-96 with the Red Sox since his 1924 rookie season. After coming to the Yankees, however, he forged a legacy worthy of Cooperstown, going 231-124 in pinstripes while posting 20, 20, 21 and 21 wins on the four World Championship clubs from 1936 through 1939. He was also an exceptionally good hitter for a pitcher, totaling 36 career home runs and a .269 lifetime batting average.

From 1931 through part of the 1946 season, the Yankees were led by McCarthy, who compiled a Yankees-record 1,460 wins in his time at the helm. Having also spent time leading the Chicago Cubs (1926-1930) and the Boston Red Sox (1948-50), he stands at eighth place on the all-time managerial wins list with 2,125 victories. With the Yankees, he reached eight World Series (1932, 1936-39, 1941-43), winning a World Championship in all but one—the 1942 Fall Classic against St. Louis.

Sadly, in 1939, Gehrig was diagnosed with a crippling disease, eventually determined to be amyotrophic lateral sclerosis (ALS), and his streak of playing in 2,130 consecutive games came to an end on May 2, when he took himself out of the lineup prior to the Yankees' 22-2 win at Detroit. He never played in a Major League game again.

On July 4 of the same year, the Yankees honored their captain with an emotional Lou Gehrig Appreciation Day at Yankee Stadium, and his uniform No. 4 became the first in Baseball to be retired. He died on June 2, 1941.

With Gehrig's retirement, DiMaggio became the pillar of the next generation of Yankees champions. In his 13 seasons in pinstripes (1936-42 and '46-51), DiMaggio made the AL All-Star team every year, and his club played in the World Series in all but three years (1940, '46, '48), winning nine World Series titles. Along the way, he tallied three AL MVP Awards (1939, '41, '47) and batted .324 over his career, marking the third-highest average in franchise history. The legendary "Yankee Clipper" compiled one of the game's most remarkable—and perhaps unbreakable—records in 1941, when he hit safely in an all-time-best 56 consecutive games.

DiMaggio's retirement after the 1951 season at the age of 37 was made easier by the emergence of Mickey Mantle, who played side-by-side with DiMaggio in the outfield in the Yankee Clipper's final campaign. With contributions from future Hall of Famers Yogi Berra, Whitey Ford and Phil Rizzuto, the Yankees were nearly unstoppable from the late 1940s through the early 1960s. Manager Casey Stengel sublimely handled the Yankee juggernaut following his surprising appointment prior to the 1949 season as the club marched to an all-time record five consecutive World Series titles from 1949 through 1953.

His emphasis on platooning players (often to their chagrin) allowed him to exploit matchups in a way not emphasized in his era. Nicknamed "The Old Perfessor," with a vernacular called "Stengelese," he remains one of the most colorful personalities in the game's history.

In 12 seasons as manager of the Yankees, he brought his club to the World Series 10 times, winning on seven occasions (also 1956 and 1958).

Mantle would achieve greatness despite suffering from osteomyelitis (a painful inflammatory bone disease) and numerous other injuries. The powerful switch-hitter belted 536 home runs, collected 2,415 hits and batted .300 or higher 10 times in an 18-year career. In his first 14 seasons in pinstripes (1951-64), the Yankees missed the World Series only twice (1954 and 1959) and won the Fall Classic seven times. With his .353 batting average, 52 homers and 130 RBI in 1956, he remains the last Yankees player to win the Triple Crown.

Ford, who played his whole career in pinstripes, is the Yankees' all-time wins leader. His lifetime record of 236-106 gives him the second-best career winning percentage (.690) of any modern-era (since 1900) pitcher with 100 or more decisions, trailing only career-Yankee Spud Chandler (.717, 109-43). Ford paced the American League in victories

Lefty Gomez

three times and in ERA and shutouts twice. He still holds many World Series records, including those for wins (10), consecutive scoreless innings (33.0) and strikeouts (94).

The heart of the Yankees for 18 seasons, Berra played on an incredible 14 pennant winners and 10 World Championship teams—a record number for any individual player in Baseball history. He is one of only 10 players in Major League history to win three MVP Awards, and he was selected to the All-Star team in every season from 1948 through 1962.

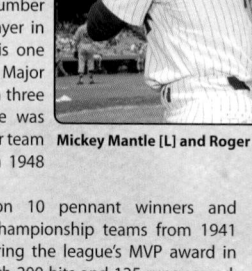

Mickey Mantle [L] and Roger Maris

Rizzuto played on 10 pennant winners and eight World Series championship teams from 1941 through 1956, capturing the league's MVP award in 1950, batting .324 with 200 hits and 125 runs scored. Eventually elected to the Baseball Hall of Fame in 1994, he gave one of the most memorable induction speeches in the history of the ceremony.

Not every notable Yankee was a future Hall of Famer. In Game 5 of the 1956 World Series vs. the Brooklyn Dodgers at Yankee Stadium, right-hander Don Larsen authored one of the game's greatest pitching performances when he retired all 27 Dodger batters for the only perfect game in World Series history.

The Yankees opened the 1960s winning pennants in the first five seasons (1960-64) and World Series titles in 1961 and 1962. Incredibly, in the 29 seasons from 1936 to 1964, the Yankees won 22 pennants and 16 World Championships. The 1961 club is still regarded as one of the best teams in Baseball history. With Mantle and Roger Maris embroiled in a season-long race to break Ruth's single-season home run record, the Yankees rolled to 109 wins en route to a World Championship. Maris broke Ruth's record when he belted his 61st home run on October 1 off Boston's Tracy Stallard at Yankee Stadium in the last game of the season.

Age finally caught up with the ballclub after a seven-game Series loss to the St. Louis Cardinals in 1964. The Yankees would finish above fourth place just once in the next nine seasons and actually fell to last place in 1966 for the first time in 53 years.

The team's fall from grace ended on January 2, 1973, when it was sold by CBS to a group headed by George M. Steinbrenner III. With the addition of Catfish Hunter, Baseball's first marquee free agent, shrewd trades that brought Ed Figueroa, Mickey Rivers, Chris Chambliss and Willie Randolph to the club, and a strong nucleus that included Thurman Munson, Graig Nettles, Roy White and Sparky Lyle, the Yankees returned to the postseason in 1976, ending an 11-year drought (1965-1975) by winning their first American League East title. Then on October 14, 1976, in the deciding Game 5 of the AL Championship Series vs. Kansas City, Chambliss launched a ninth-inning, pennant-winning home run

to put the Yankees back in the World Series.

This newfound success took place in a remodeled Yankee Stadium. The 1974 and '75 Yankees played in Shea Stadium for two years while vast improvements were made to the original Yankee Stadium (for more details, see "History of Original Yankee Stadium").

After a disheartening four-game sweep by the Cincinnati Reds in the 1976 World Series, the Yankees introduced Reggie Jackson—the most prolific slugger of his era—as the club's newest free-agent acquisition. Jackson capped an exciting 1977 season with one of baseball's greatest individual performances. In the Game 6 World Series-clinching win vs. Los Angeles at Yankee Stadium, "Mr. October" belted three home runs on three swings of the bat to join Babe Ruth as the only players to hit three home runs in a single World Series game.

In 1978, the Yankees overcame a 14.0-game deficit in the American League East to force a one-game playoff with the Boston Red Sox at Fenway Park to decide the American League pennant. Shortstop Bucky Dent erased a 2-0, seventh-inning Red Sox lead with a dramatic three-run homer, and the Yankees went on to a 5-4 win en route to a second straight World Championship over the Dodgers.

The 1978 season also saw the emergence of Ron Guidry as one the franchise's greatest pitchers. A four-time American League All-Star, Guidry compiled one

Reggie Jackson hit three home runs in Game 6 of the 1977 World Series.

Bucky Dent hits his famous three-run home run in the one-game AL East playoff contest on Oct. 2, 1978 at Fenway Park.

of the most dominating seasons in baseball history while becoming known as "Louisiana Lightning." He went 25-3 with a 1.74 ERA in leading the Yankees to their dramatic comeback, compiling a club-record 248 strikeouts and nine shutouts en route to a unanimous selection as the AL Cy Young Award recipient. On June 17, 1978 vs. the California Angels at Yankee Stadium, Guidry set a club record by striking out 18 batters. A five-time Gold Glove Award winner, Guidry also racked up 20-win seasons in 1983 (21-9) and 1985 (22-6).

The 1970s ended with tragedy. Thurman Munson, the Yankees' first captain since Gehrig, was killed when his private jet crashed on August 2, 1979. Only 32 years old at the time of his death, Munson was the undisputed leader of the clubs that won three consecutive pennants and two World Championships. After the captain's death, the Yankees would make only one more World Series appearance (1981) in the next 17 years despite compiling the best record in the Major Leagues during the 1980s.

During this period, Don Mattingly became one of the most popular players in franchise history, batting .307 in a 14-year career (1982-95) played en-

Thurman Munson, Goose Gossage

tirely in pinstripes. He compiled an incredible six-year stretch from 1984 through 1989, in which he batted .327 and topped 100 RBI five times, including a career-high 145 in 1985, when he captured the AL MVP Award. A year earlier, he out-dueled teammate Dave Winfield for the 1984 AL batting crown (.343 to .340), going 4-for-5 on the final day of the season. His performance and loyalty were recognized when he was named the 10th captain in Yankees history from 1991-95.

Winfield, who came to the Yankees as the game's most sought-after free agent in 1981, compiled Hall of Fame credentials in his eight-plus seasons in pinstripes (1981-90). With the Yankees, he belted 205 home runs with 818 RBI and won five Gold Glove Awards.

After a 13-year absence (1982-94), the Yankees returned to postseason play in 1995 as the American League's first-ever "Wild Card" entry. A heart-wrenching five-game loss to the Seattle Mariners in the Division Series marked the start of a 13-year run of consecutive postseason appearances (1995-2007), a record topped only by the Atlanta Braves' 14-season streak (1991-93, 1995-2005).

In 1996 under new skipper Joe Torre, the Yankees returned to the World Series against Atlanta, coming back from an 0-2 deficit to win four straight games, including Games 3, 4 and 5 in Atlanta. Following a Division Series exit in 1997, the Yankees won three straight World titles from 1998 through 2000, giving them four championships in five years. Their 114 victories in 1998 shattered the 44-year-old American League mark of 111 wins set by the 1954 Cleveland Indians (since broken by Seattle in 2001) and their 125 total victories, including 11 postseason wins, remains the highest single-season total in baseball history.

In the last two decades since the signing of non-drafted free agent Bernie Williams in 1991, the Yankees

Rudy Giuliani, George Steinbrenner and Joe Torre

farm system has produced All-Stars Robinson Cano, Derek Jeter, Andy Pettitte, Phil Hughes, Jorge Posada and Mariano Rivera. In addition, trades and free-agent acquisitions have brought such All-Stars as Wade Boggs, Scott Brosius, David Cone, Jimmy Key, Tino Martinez, Hideki Matsui and Mike Mussina to the Bronx. Another of those players, Paul O'Neill, acquired in a November 3, 1992, trade with Cincinnati, became adored by Yankees fans for his intense and gritty approach. Winner of the 1994 batting title (.359) and often described as a "warrior," he is typically thought of as the heart and soul of the club's turn-of-the-century success.

In 2001, the Yankees fell just shy of becoming the second team in history to win four consecutive World Series titles, but they nevertheless captured the hearts of the nation in the aftermath of the terrorist attacks of September 11. The Yankees dropped the first two games of the Series at the Arizona Diamondbacks' Bank One Ballpark but rallied to win the next three at Yankee Stadium behind dramatic ninth-inning comebacks in both Games 4 and 5. On consecutive nights, Martinez and Brosius erased two-run, ninth-inning Diamondbacks leads with home runs, and the Yankees won both games in extra innings. It was in Game 4 that Jeter earned his "Mr. November" nickname with a 10th-inning "walk-off" home run. The victories marked the first time in World Series history that a team won two games in the same Series when trailing by at least two runs in the ninth inning.

Scott Brosius hits a two-run, ninth-inning, game-tying homer in Game 5 of the 2001 World Series vs. Arizona.

Former Yankees catcher Joe Girardi was named the 32nd manager in franchise history on October 30, 2007, heading into the final year of the original Yankee Stadium. The 2008 season was full of nostalgia, and notable events included the third Papal Mass in Stadium history on April 20 and a 15-inning, 4-3 American League victory in the All-Star Game on July 15. Though the Yankees played their last-ever home game in the original Stadium on September 21, defeating the Baltimore Orioles, 7-3, the drama of the season didn't end until its final day as Mike Mussina earned a win in the first game of a doubleheader over Boston at Fenway Park to become the oldest first-time 20-game winner in baseball history.

The 2009 season proved nothing short of storybook material as the club finished the inaugural season in the newly-constructed Yankee Stadium with the best regular season record in the Majors (103-59) and a six-game World Series win over the Phillies. The 2009 season featured 15 "walk-off" wins along with an all-time Major League-record 18-consecutive errorless games from May 14 through June 1. Free-agent acquisitions CC Sabathia (19 wins), A.J. Burnett (13 wins) and Mark Teixeira (second in AL MVP voting, 39 homers, 122 RBI) each played major roles in the club's success.

The most recent season, 2010, will be sadly remembered for the passings of Principal Owner George M. Steinbrenner III and longtime public address announcer Bob Sheppard.

On the field, the season marked the 15th time in the last 16 years (since 1995) that the Yankees had made the postseason. Looking forward, the Yankees will continue to concentrate on procuring and nurturing young talent. Pitcher Phil Hughes and second baseman Robinson Cano are illustrative of the team's commitment to youth and international scouting. With the 2011 season at hand, the Yankees will strive toward the singular goal of bringing a 28th championship back to the Bronx. ⚜

No one personifies the Yankees' success since 1996 more than Jeter, who was a rookie on that squad. Heading into the 2011 season, his 2,926 hits make him Baseball's active hit leader, and his personal career winning percentage of .601 (1,379-914-2) is the best among active Major League players who have played in a minimum of 1,000 games. In 2009, he further cemented his legacy by becoming the Yankees' all-time hits leader (2,747), passing Lou Gehrig (2,721), who had held the mark since 1937. Jeter has also recorded seven 200-hit seasons and is one of two players in franchise history along with Gehrig (eight) with as many as four. In fact, according to the *Elias Sports Bureau*, no other player has had as many as four 200-hit seasons while playing at least 100 games at shortstop per year.

Posada and Rivera have crafted special places for themselves in the annals of the franchise. Posada, a 24th-round selection in the 1990 First-Year Player Draft, is one of six catchers in Major League history to hit at least 20 home runs in eight seasons while playing a minimum of 50 percent of his games behind the plate. Known for his toughness and durability, the Puerto Rico-born backstop started at least 120 games in eight consecutive seasons from 2000-07. Rivera, with 559 career saves going into 2011, ranks second on Baseball's all-time list behind only Trevor Hoffman (601). His reputation has been cemented by postseason excellence, which includes an 8-1 record and 0.71 ERA in 94 career postseason games (139.2 innings pitched). His Major League-leading 42 career postseason saves is almost as many as the totals of the second, third and fourth place pitchers on the list combined (44). Additionally, his 2.23 career ERA is the second-lowest all time among pitchers with at least 1.000.0IP since ERA was made an official statistic in 1912 in NL and 1913 in AL (Eddie Cicotte 2.20).

In 2004, the organization acquired Alex Rodriguez in a trade from the Texas Rangers. Since his arrival in the Bronx, the now 13-time All-Star transitioned to a new position at third base and was voted the AL MVP in 2005 and 2007, while becoming the seventh—and youngest—player in baseball history reach the 600-home run plateau in 2007.

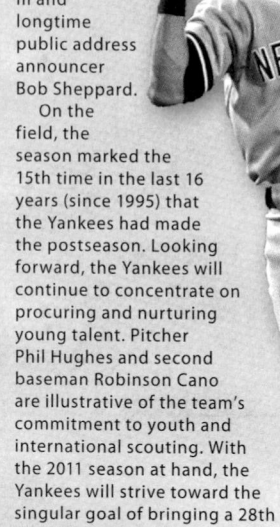

Derek Jeter

History of the Yankees Uniform

When the Yankees (then "Highlanders") first took the field for their inaugural season in 1903, their uniforms did not resemble the iconic style for which they are known today. A large ornate "N" decorated one breast and a large ornate "Y" the other. Two years later for the 1905 season, the "N" and "Y" were merged side by side into a monogram on the left breast, creating a forerunner of the now legendary emblem.

It wasn't until 1909 that the most recognizable insignia in sports—the interlocking "NY"—made its first appearance on the caps and left sleeves of Highlanders uniforms. The design was created in 1877 by Tiffany & Co. for a medal to be given by the New York City Police Department to Officer John McDowell, the first NYC policeman shot in the line of duty. Perhaps because one of the club's owners, Bill Devery, was a former NYC police chief, the design was adopted by the organization. The familiar "NY" eventually migrated from the left sleeve to the left breast of home uniforms from 1912-16, albeit in a larger version than is currently worn today.

In 1912, their final season at Hilltop Park, the Yankees (as they were commonly known by then) made a fashionable debut at their April 11 home opener by wearing pinstripes for the first

Jack Chesbro models the franchise's earliest "NY" design in 1903.

time in their history. The club was not the first team to wear pinstripes (eight of Baseball's other 15 teams had already worn them at some point), and they would actually abandon the look in the following two seasons (1913-14). By 1915, though, home pinstripes were back for good.

In 1917, the Yankees removed the "NY" monogram from the jersey and went with a plain, pinstripes-only look. The "NY" remained off the uniform—except for the cap—for the next 20 years until it was reinstated in 1936. Babe Ruth, whose Yankees career spanned 1920-1934, played his entire Yankees career without ever wearing the club's now-legendary insignia on his jersey.

The Yankees utilized numerous cap designs from 1903 until 1921—including pinstripes in 1915, '16, '19 and '21—until they finally settled on a solid navy cap with the interlocking "NY" insignia in 1922.

The club's road uniforms have remained relatively unchanged since 1918—solid grey with "NEW YORK" in block letters across the chest. The notable exception was from 1927-30, when "NEW YORK" was replaced by "YANKEES." In 1973, with the introduction of more breathable double-knit uniforms, Yankees road jerseys added navy-and-white banded trim to the cuffs of the sleeves as well as white shadowing behind the jersey lettering.

Babe Ruth sports the pinstriped-cap look of 1921.

The home uniform remains the Yankees' signature look. With the exception of minor alterations—including bolder pinstripes in the 1940s—it has remained mostly unchanged for more than 70 years.

For the 2008 season, the Yankees wore an All-Star Game patch on their left sleeve and a Yankee Stadium Final Season tribute patch on their right sleeve. In 2009, the club wore a patch on their left sleeve and one on the back

Lou Gehrig and Tony Lazzeri display the pre-1936 home uniform without insignia.

of their cap, each to commemorate the inaugural season of Yankee Stadium. And most recently, in 2010, the club wore a "GMS" patch above the NY logo on their jersey front to honor the passing of Principal Owner George M. Steinbrenner III, as well as a patch on their left sleeve as a tribute to the passing of Bob Sheppard. They also wore a black armband on the left sleeve to remember the passing of Ralph Houk. ※

Origin of Numbered Uniforms

Numbers first appeared on Major League uniforms on June 26, 1916, when the Cleveland Indians wore large numerals on their left sleeves in an experiment that lasted just a few weeks. Another brief trial by Cleveland the next season and a similar sleeve trial by the St. Louis Cardinals in 1923 both proved temporary. It wasn't until the 1929 season that another attempt was made, as both Cleveland and the New York Yankees began their seasons with numbers as a permanent part of their respective uniforms. Though the Yankees are typically credited as being the team with the longest-standing such policy, it should be noted that the Indians began their season two days earlier than the Bombers, as the Yankees' April 16 Opening Day contest was rained out.

The initial distribution of numbers to the Yankees roster was made according to the player's position in the batting order. Therefore, in 1929, leadoff hitter Earle Combs wore No. 1, Mark Koenig No. 2, Babe Ruth No. 3, Lou Gehrig No. 4, Bob Meusel No. 5, Tony Lazzeri No. 6, Leo Durocher No. 7, Johnny Grabowski No. 8, Benny Bengough No. 9 and Bill Dickey No. 10 (Grabowski, Bengough and Dickey shared the catching duties). By the mid-1930s, other teams adopted the idea, and uniform numbers became the standard for all teams.

Important Dates in Yankees History

Hilltop Park, first home of the Yankees

Jan. 9, 1903 - Frank Farrell and Bill Devery purchase the defunct Baltimore franchise of the American League for $18,000, then move the team to Manhattan.

March 12, 1903 - The New York franchise is approved as a member of the American League. The team will play in a hastily constructed, wooden ballpark at 168th Street and Broadway. Because the site is one of the highest spots in Manhattan, their home field is referred to as "Hilltop Park."

April 22, 1903 - The Highlanders (as the Yankees were commonly known then) play their first game, a 3-1 loss at Washington.

April 23, 1903 - Pitcher Harry Howell records the first victory in franchise history, a 7-2 win at Washington.

April 30, 1903 - The Highlanders notch a 6-2 win vs. Washington in their inaugural home opener at Hilltop Park.

April 11, 1912 - Pinstripes first appear on Highlanders uniforms, creating a look that would become the most famous uniform design in sports.

April 1913 - The Highlanders are officially renamed "Yankees" after moving to the Polo Grounds, home of the National League's New York Giants.

Jan. 11, 1915 - Col. Jacob Ruppert and Col. Tillinghast L'Hommedieu Huston purchase the Yankees for $465,000.

April 24, 1917 - George Mogridge becomes the first Yankee to throw a no-hitter in a 2-1 win at Fenway Park.

Jan. 3, 1920 - The Yankees purchase the contract of Babe Ruth from the Boston Red Sox for $125,000 and a $350,000 loan against the mortgage on Fenway Park.

Oct. 5, 1921 - The Yankees play the first postseason game in franchise history, as Carl Mays tosses a complete game shutout to defeat the New York Giants at the Polo Grounds in Game 1 of the World Series.

May 5, 1922 - Construction begins on Yankee Stadium.

May 21, 1922 - Col. Ruppert buys out Col. Huston for $1.5 million.

April 18, 1923 - Yankee Stadium opens with a 4-1 win over the Boston Red Sox before an announced crowd of 74,200. Babe Ruth hits the Stadium's first home run.

Oct. 15, 1923 - The Yankees defeat the New York Giants, 6-4, at the Polo Grounds in Game 6 of the World Series, clinching the first World Championship in franchise history.

June 1, 1925 - Lou Gehrig begins his record streak of 2,130 consecutive games played, pinch-hitting for "Pee Wee" Wanniger in a 5-3 loss to Washington at Yankee Stadium.

Oct. 6, 1926 - Babe Ruth becomes the first player to hit three home runs in a single World Series game in Game 4 at St. Louis.

June 23, 1927 - In an 11-4 Yankees win at Fenway Park, Lou Gehrig become the first (of two) players in franchise history to hit 3HR in a single game against the Red Sox (also see May 8, 2010).

Sept. 30, 1927 - Babe Ruth breaks his own single-season Major League record by hitting his 60th home run (off Tom Zachary) in a 4-2 win over Washington at Yankee Stadium.

April 20, 1928 - Yankee Stadium's left field stands are enlarged to three decks.

Oct. 9, 1928 - In Game 4 of the World Series vs. the Cardinals at St. Louis' Sportsman's Park, Babe Ruth hits three home runs, marking his second three-homer World Series game.

April 18, 1929 - The Yankees wear numbered uniforms for the first time in their history, two days after the Cleveland Indians permanently adopt them as well (Numbers would become standard for all teams by 1932).

Sept. 24, 1929 - The Yankees celebrate Babe Ruth Day at Fenway Park by winning, 5-3, over Boston. Ruth goes 2-for-3 with a double and Tom Zachary (pitching for the Yankees) records his final decision of the season, improving to 12-0, still a Major League record for most wins in a season without a loss.

Origin of the Names "Highlanders" and "Yankees"

When the American League moved the Baltimore Orioles to New York for the 1903 season, the club made its home at 168th Street and Broadway, one of the highest spots in Manhattan. As a result, the team became known as the "Hilltoppers" and their field "Hilltop Park," even though their formal team name was "New York Americans" and formal ballpark name "American League Park."

The name "Highlanders," as the team of that era is most-popularly remembered today, also started in the club's formative years. It originated not only as a nod to their elevated Manhattan perch, but also as a reference to club president Joseph W. Gordon, whose last name conjured up thoughts of the famous British army unit, the Gordon Highlanders.

Other nicknames for the team were "Porch Climbers," "Burglars," and "Invaders"—all three usually reserved for writers sympathetic to the New York Giants, who held lingering animosity at having American League competition in such close proximity.

As early as 1904, however, the name "Yankees" became common in the press. The earliest known use was in an April 7, 1904, article in the *New York Evening Journal* that bore the headline "YANKEES WILL START HOME FROM SOUTH TODAY," which was published following a successful spring training spent in the Southern U.S. A week later, the same newspaper's coverage of Opening Day was headlined "YANKEES BEAT BOSTON," and the term also appeared in the article's lead sentence.

"Yankees" was a natural fit given the club's formal name, but likely owes its success to newspaper typesetters and editors grateful for a team name with fewer letters than "Highlanders" or "Hilltoppers." When the franchise moved from Hilltop Park to the Polo Grounds in 1913, it officially changed its name to "New York Yankees."

Sept. 25, 1929 - Manager Miller Huggins, who guided the Yankees to their first six AL pennants and three World Championships, dies of blood poisoning.

June 3, 1932 - Lou Gehrig becomes the first player to hit four home runs in a single game in the Yankees' 20-13 win at Philadelphia. The news is overshadowed by the retirement announcement of New York Giants Manager John McGraw. Gehrig remains the only Yankee to hit four home runs in one game.

Aug. 13, 1932 - Red Ruffing throws a complete game shutout and hits a 10th-inning solo home run off Washington Senators pitcher Al Thomas, giving the Yankees a 1-0 victory at Griffith Stadium. Though not the first to do so, no Major League pitcher has since thrown a complete game shutout and hit a home run in a 1-0 game.

Oct. 1, 1932 - In the fifth inning of the Yankees' 7-5 victory over the Chicago Cubs at Wrigley Field in Game 3 of the World Series, Babe Ruth gestures toward the bleachers before hitting his second home run of the game. Though Lou Gehrig also hits two homers that day, the game will be remembered for Ruth's much-debated "called shot."

June 6, 1934 - Myril Hoag goes 6-for-6 in a 15-3, nine-inning win in Game 1 of a doubleheader at Boston, becoming the first of only two Yankees to go 6-for-6 in a single game (see June 7, 2008 - Johnny Damon).

Joe DiMaggio

Nov. 21, 1934 - The Yankees purchase Joe DiMaggio from the San Francisco Seals of the Pacific Coast League for $50,000.

May 24, 1936 - Tony Lazzeri hits three home runs (including two grand slams) and a triple, setting a still-standing AL record with 11 RBI in a single game in a 25-2 win at Philadelphia.

April 20, 1937 - The Yankees' 15th season at Yankee Stadium opens with the right-field stands enlarged to three decks. Wooden bleachers are replaced by a concrete structure, and the distance to center field drops from 490 feet to 461 feet.

May 30, 1938 - A franchise-record crowd of 81,841 attends a doubleheader sweep of the Boston Red Sox at Yankee Stadium.

Aug. 27, 1938 - Monte Pearson authors the first Yankee Stadium no-hitter by a Yankee, defeating Cleveland, 13-0, in Game 2 of a doubleheader.

May 2, 1939 - Lou Gehrig's playing streak of 2,130 consecutive games ends when he does not make an appearance in a 22-2 Yankees win at Detroit. Babe Dahlgren plays first base for the Yankees and contributes a double and a home run.

July 4, 1939 - "Lou Gehrig Appreciation Day" is held at Yankee Stadium in between games of a doubleheader vs. Washington. His uniform No. 4 is the first to be retired in Major League Baseball. Gehrig makes his famous "luckiest man on the face of the earth" speech.

May 15, 1941 - Joe DiMaggio's 56-game hitting streak begins with a single off Edgar Smith in a 13-1 loss vs. Chicago at Yankee Stadium.

June 2, 1941 - Lou Gehrig dies of Amyotrophic Lateral Sclerosis at the age of 37 in the Riverdale section of the Bronx.

July 17, 1941 - Joe DiMaggio's consecutive-game hitting streak ends at 56 when he goes 0-for-3 in a 4-3 Yankees win at Cleveland. Indians third baseman Ken Keltner twice robs DiMaggio of hits with great fielding plays. DiMaggio hits safely in his next 16 games, giving him hits in 72 of 73 games.

Jan. 25, 1945 - Dan Topping, Del Webb and Larry MacPhail purchase the Yankees for $2.8 million from the estate of the late Col. Jacob Ruppert. MacPhail replaces Ed Barrow as President and General Manager.

May 28, 1946 - The first night game is played at Yankee Stadium, a 2-1 loss vs. Washington before 49,917 fans.

April 27, 1947 - "Babe Ruth Day" is celebrated at Yankee Stadium and throughout Major League Baseball.

June 13, 1948 - Babe Ruth's uniform No. 3 is retired at Yankee Stadium's 25th Anniversary celebration. The visit marks the Babe's final Stadium appearance.

Aug. 16, 1948 - Babe Ruth dies of throat cancer in New York at age 53.

Oct. 12, 1948 - The Yankees announce that Casey Stengel will replace Bucky Harris as manager.

Oct. 1-2, 1949 - The Yankees come back from a one-game deficit with two games to play, defeating the Boston Red Sox in the final two games of the season at Yankee Stadium, 5-4 and 5-3, respectively, marking the first of five consecutive American League pennants.

Oct. 5, 1949 - In Game 1 of the World Series vs. Brooklyn at Yankee Stadium, Tommy Henrich breaks up a scoreless pitchers' duel between the Yankees' Allie Reynolds and the Dodgers' Don Newcombe, hitting a game-winning solo home run in the bottom of the ninth.

April 17, 1951 - Mickey Mantle makes his Major League debut, going 1-for-4 in a 5-0 win vs. Boston at Yankee Stadium. The game also marks Bob Sheppard's first as Yankees public-address announcer. Boston's Dom DiMaggio is the first hitter announced.

Sept. 28, 1951 - In an 8-0 Game 1 win in a doubleheader vs. Boston at Yankee Stadium, Allie Reynolds becomes the second of four players in Baseball history to toss two no-hitters in the same season (also Johnny Vander Meer in 1938, Virgil Trucks in 1952 and Nolan Ryan in 1973). Reynolds had previously no-hit the Indians at Cleveland's Municipal Stadium on July 12 in a 1-0 win.

Dec. 12, 1951 - Joe DiMaggio officially announces his retirement.

April 17, 1953 - Exactly two years after his Yankees debut, Mickey Mantle hits what is recognized as the game's first "tape-measure" home run, a 565-foot shot off the Senators' Chuck Stobbs at Washington's Griffith Stadium.

Oct. 5, 1953 - Billy Martin singles home the winning run in the ninth inning of a 4-3, Game 6 victory over the Brooklyn Dodgers at Yankee Stadium. The win clinches the Yankees' fifth-consecutive World Championship.

Oct. 4, 1955 - Brooklyn's Johnny Podres outduels Yankees starter Tommy Byrne and two relievers, 2-0, clinching the Dodgers' first World Series Championship. The World Series loss snaps the Yankees' string of seven consecutive team appearances in the Fall Classic without losing a Series (1943, '47, '49-53). It also marks the Yankees' first World Series loss to Brooklyn after wins in 1941, '47, '49, '52 and '53.

May 30, 1956 - Batting against Pedro Ramos in Game 1 of a doubleheader vs. Washington, Mickey Mantle nearly hits a home run out of Yankee Stadium, with the ball striking the upper deck frieze in right field.

Oct. 8, 1956 - Don Larsen hurls the only perfect game in World Series history, a 2-0 win over Brooklyn in Game 5 at Yankee Stadium.

Oct. 10, 1956 - Johnny Kucks pitches a complete game shutout, defeating the Brooklyn Dodgers at Ebbets Field, 9-0, to win Game 7 of the World Series.

April 22, 1959 - Whitey Ford pitches a 1-0, 14-inning complete game shutout at Washington, allowing just seven hits and striking out 15.

Oct. 8, 1960 - Second baseman Bobby Richardson sets an all-time World Series record (since tied by Hideki Matsui on 11/4/09 in Game 6 vs. Philadelphia) with 6RBI in Game 3 of the World Series vs. Pittsburgh, hitting a grand slam in the first inning and two-run single in the fourth inning of a 10-0 Yankees win.

Oct. 1, 1961 - Roger Maris hits his 61st home run in the season's final game, establishing a then-Major League record and still-standing AL record.

June 24, 1962 - Jack Reed's two-run, 22nd-inning home run ends the longest game in Yankees history, a 9-7 win at Detroit.

Oct. 16, 1962 - In Game 7 of the World Series, superb fielding from outfielder Roger Maris holds Matty Alou at third base after a two-out, ninth-inning Willie Mays double. Bobby Richardson then snares a screaming line drive off the bat of Willie McCovey for the game's final out, securing a 1-0, Series-clinching victory over the San Francisco Giants at Candlestick Park. New York scores the game's only run when Tony Kubek grounds into a fifth-inning double play. It would be the last championship for the Yankees for 15 seasons.

May 22, 1963 - In an 8-7, 11-inning win vs. the Kansas City A's, Mickey Mantle hits the upper deck frieze in right field for the second time in his career, this time off righthander Bill Fischer.

Nov. 2, 1964 - CBS purchases 80 percent of the Yankees for $11.2 million. The network later buys the remaining 20 percent.

May 14, 1967 - Mickey Mantle becomes only the sixth player—and second Yankee—to reach the 500 home run plateau, when he connects off Baltimore's Stu Miller at Yankee Stadium.

June 8, 1969 - "Mickey Mantle Day" is celebrated at Yankee Stadium and his uniform No. 7 is retired.

June 24, 1970 - Bobby Murcer hits home runs in four consecutive at-bats over two games of a doubleheader vs. Cleveland at Yankee Stadium.

Aug. 8, 1972 - The Yankees sign a 30-year lease to play in a remodeled Yankee Stadium. Completion is scheduled for 1976.

Jan. 3, 1973 - A limited partnership, headed by George M. Steinbrenner III as its managing general partner, purchases the Yankees for a net price of $8.7 million from CBS.

April 6, 1974 - The Yankees begin the first of two seasons at Shea Stadium as Yankee Stadium is remodeled. The Yankees will go 90-69 at Shea over the two seasons (1974-75).

Dec. 31, 1974 - Free agent Catfish Hunter signs a then-record five-year contract.

Aug. 1, 1975 - Billy Martin replaces Bill Virdon for his first of five stints as manager.

April 15, 1976 - Remodeled Yankee Stadium opens with an 11-4 win over the Minnesota Twins. The Twins' Dan Ford hits the first home run.

Jim "Catfish" Hunter

April 17, 1976 - Thurman Munson hits the first homer by a Yankee in remodeled Yankee Stadium in a 10-0 win vs. the Minnesota Twins (off Jim Hughes).

Oct. 14, 1976 - Chris Chambliss' ninth-inning home run off Mark Littell in Game 5 of the ALCS vs. Kansas City at Yankee Stadium gives the Yankees their 30th AL pennant and first trip to the World Series since 1964.

Nov. 29, 1976 - Free agent Reggie Jackson signs a five-year contract.

Oct. 9, 1977 - The Yankees rally for one run in the eighth inning and three runs in the ninth for a 5-3, series-clinching win in the decisive Game 5 of the 1977 ALCS at Kansas City. Sparky Lyle earns the win for the second consecutive night, finishing the game with 1.1 scoreless innings on no rest following his scoreless 5.1-inning relief appearance at Kauffman Stadium in Game 4.

Sparky Lyle

Oct. 18, 1977 - Reggie Jackson hits three home runs (on three consecutive pitches) in Game 6 of the World Series vs. the Los Angeles Dodgers at Yankee Stadium. He joins Babe Ruth as the only players to hit three home runs in a single World Series game.

June 17, 1978 - Ron Guidry establishes a franchise record by striking out 18 batters in the Yankees' 4-0 win vs. California.

July 24, 1978 - Billy Martin resigns as manager.

July 25, 1978 - Bob Lemon is named manager, replacing Billy Martin.

July 29, 1978 - On Old-Timers' Day, the Yankees announce that Billy Martin will return as Yankees manager in 1980 and Bob Lemon will become General Manager (also see June 18, 1979).

Oct. 2, 1978 - The Yankees, 14.0 games behind Boston as late as July 19, defeat the Red Sox, 5-4, at Fenway Park in only the second one-game playoff in AL history. Bucky Dent's three-run, seventh-inning home run becomes one of the most memorable in Baseball history.

June 18, 1979 - Billy Martin is rehired as Yankees manager, replacing Bob Lemon.

Aug. 2, 1979 - Yankees Captain Thurman Munson dies in a plane crash in Canton, Ohio, at age 32. His No. 15 is immediately retired.

Aug. 6, 1979 - After delivering a eulogy at Thurman Munson's funeral earlier that morning in Canton, Ohio, Bobby Murcer hits a three-run seventh inning homer and a two-run ninth-inning single, accounting for all five of the Yankees' runs in an emotional 5-4 comeback win vs. Baltimore at Yankee Stadium.

Dec. 15, 1980 - Free agent Dave Winfield signs a then-record 10-year contract.

Sept. 6, 1981 - Bob Lemon is named manager for a second time, replacing Gene Michael.

April 26, 1982 - Gene Michael becomes manager for a second time, replacing Bob Lemon.

Aug. 3, 1982 - Clyde King is named Yankees manager, replacing Gene Michael.

July 4, 1983 - Dave Righetti pitches the sixth regular season no-hitter in franchise history and the first since 1951 in a 4-0 win vs. Boston at Yankee Stadium. Righetti strikes out Wade Boggs for the final out.

July 24, 1983 - The Yankees and Kansas City play the infamous "Pine Tar" game at Yankee Stadium. George Brett hits a two-out, ninth-inning home run off Goose Gossage to give the Royals an apparent 5-4 lead. Manager Billy Martin points out that the pine tar on Brett's bat is above the allowable 18 inches and Brett is subsequently called out for using an illegal bat. The Yankees (temporarily) win 4-3 (see Aug. 18, 1983).

"The Pine Tar Game"

Aug. 18, 1983 - Kansas City's protest is upheld and play is resumed at Yankee Stadium from the point immediately after Brett's home run. Yankees pitcher Ron Guidry plays center field while lefthanded first baseman Don Mattingly plays second base. Royals' reliever Dan Quisenberry retires the Yankees in order in the bottom of the ninth for a 5-4 Royals win.

April 28, 1985 - Billy Martin is named manager for the fourth time, replacing Yogi Berra.

Aug. 4, 1985 - The Yankees celebrate "Phil Rizzuto Day" at Yankee Stadium, dedicating a plaque in his honor and retiring his No. 10. The Yankees lose their scheduled game to the Chicago White Sox, 4-1, as Tom Seaver wins his 300th career game.

Oct. 6, 1985 - Phil Niekro tosses a four-hit complete game shutout in an 8-0 victory at Toronto's Exhibition Stadium for his 300th career win.

Oct. 17, 1985 - Lou Piniella is named manager, replacing Billy Martin.

July 18, 1987 - Don Mattingly homers off Texas' Jose Guzman to tie Dale Long's Major League record of hitting a home run in eight consecutive games (Mattingly hits 10 HR during the streak).

Sept. 29, 1987 - Don Mattingly hits a grand slam off Boston's Bruce Hurst, setting a Major League record (tied by Travis Hafner in 2008) with six grand slams in a season.

June 23, 1988 - Billy Martin is replaced as manager of the Yankees for the fifth and final time. Lou Piniella is named manager for the second time.

Dec. 9, 1988 - The Yankees sign a 12-year television contract with the Madison Square Garden Network.

Dec. 25, 1989 - Billy Martin dies in an automobile accident near Binghamton, N.Y. at age 61.

Sept. 4, 1993 - Jim Abbott tosses a 4-0, no-hit win vs. Cleveland at Yankee Stadium.

Aug. 13, 1995 - Mickey Mantle dies of cancer at age 63 in Dallas, Tex.

Sept. 6, 1995 - Lou Gehrig's Major League record of 2,130 consecutive games played is broken when Baltimore's Cal Ripken, Jr. plays in his 2,131st.

Oct. 4, 1995 - The Yankees play the longest postseason game in their history, a 15-inning, 7-5 win over Seattle at Yankee Stadium, giving them a 2-0 series lead. The contest was the final Yankee Stadium game for Don Mattingly.

Nov. 2, 1995 - Joe Torre is named the Yankees' 31st manager.

Mar. 1, 1996 - The Yankees defeat the Cleveland Indians, 5-2, in the first ever game at Legends Field (renamed George M. Steinbrenner Field in 2008), the club's new spring training home.

May 14, 1996 - Dwight Gooden hurls the eighth regular season no-hitter in Yankees history, a 2-0 blanking of the Seattle Mariners at Yankee Stadium.

June 16, 1996 - Mel Allen, the legendary "Voice of the Yankees" from 1939-64, dies at age 83 in Greenwich, Connecticut.

Aug. 25, 1996 - A monument in honor of Mickey Mantle is unveiled in Yankee Stadium's Monument Park.

Oct. 23, 1996 - In Game 4 of the World Series at Atlanta's Fulton County Stadium, Jim Leyritz hits a three-run eighth inning homer off the Braves' Mark Wohlers, knotting the game at 6-6. The Yankees went on to win, 8-6, in 10 innings.

Oct 24, 1996 - The Yankees' Andy Pettitte (8.1IP) outduels Atlanta's John Smoltz (8.0IP), 1-0, in Game 5 in Atlanta, giving the Yankees a 3-games-to-2 World Series lead.

Oct. 26, 1996 - In Game 6 of the World Series at Yankee Stadium, John Wetteland closes out a 3-2 win vs. Atlanta, giving the Yankees their first World Championship in 18 years.

May 17, 1998 - David Wells tosses the first regular-season perfect game by a Yankee, the 14th in Baseball history.

David Wells' perfect game

Sept. 25, 1998 - The Yankees establish an American League record with their 112th win of the season (a 6-1 win vs. Tampa Bay at Yankee Stadium), breaking the mark of 111 by the 1954 Cleveland Indians (they complete the season with a then AL-record 114th victory on September 27 vs. Tampa Bay).

Oct. 21, 1998 - The Yankees complete an incredible season with a four-game World Series sweep of the San Diego Padres to capture the franchise's 24th World Championship. The 3-0 win gives the club a 125-50 record over the entire season (114-48 in the regular season, 11-2 in postseason).

March 8, 1999 - Joe DiMaggio dies at age 84 in Hollywood, Fla.

April 25, 1999 - A monument in honor of Joe DiMaggio is unveiled in Yankee Stadium's Monument Park in front of a sold out Stadium and many of DiMaggio's former teammates. Paul Simon sings "Mrs. Robinson" while standing in center field.

July 18, 1999 - On "Yogi Berra Day," David Cone tosses the 15th regular season perfect game in Baseball history, one season after David Wells accomplishes the feat. Amazingly, Don Larsen—who tossed a perfect game in the 1956 World Series—throws out the ceremonial first pitch.

Oct. 27, 1999 - The Yankees play Baseball's last game of the century and complete a four-game sweep of the Atlanta Braves, capturing their 25th World Championship.

July 8, 2000 - The Yankees and Mets play their first-ever dual stadium day/night doubleheader: Game 1 is a 4-2 Yankees win at Shea Stadium and Game 2 is another 4-2 Yankees win at Yankee Stadium.

Oct. 21, 2000 - The Yankees' World Series Game 1 win vs. the Mets at Yankee Stadium marks their 13th consecutive victory in World Series play, breaking the 12-game record of the 1927, 1928 and 1932 Yankees.

Oct. 26, 2000 - The Yankees win World Series Game 5 over the Mets at Shea Stadium, clinching their third consecutive World Championship in the first "Subway Series" since 1956. It marks the first time a club has won three consecutive World Series titles since the 1972-74 Oakland Athletics.

Oct. 13, 2001 - With a 1-0 lead and two-out in the bottom of the seventh of Game 3 of the ALDS in Oakland, Derek Jeter picks up Shane Spencer's errant throw from the outfield and "flips" the ball in a backhand motion to Jorge Posada, who tags Jeremy Giambi for the final out of the inning. The Yankees go on to win the game, 1-0, and the series 3 games to 2. The play will be known as the "Flip Play."

Oct. 30, 2001 - President George W. Bush throws out the first pitch prior to the Yankees' 2-1 World Series Game 3 win vs. Arizona at Yankee Stadium.

Oct. 31, 2001 - In Game 4 of the World Series vs. Arizona at Yankee Stadium, Tino Martinez's two-out, bottom-of-the-ninth, two-run home run off Byung-Hyun Kim sends the game into extra innings. Shortly after the stroke of midnight, Derek Jeter wins the game with a "walk-off" solo home run in the 10th, earning him the nickname "Mr. November."

Nov. 1, 2001 - In the late innings of Game 5 of the World Series vs. Arizona at Yankee Stadium, fans serenade Paul O'Neill, who is playing in his last game at Yankee Stadium. Scott Brosius' two-out, bottom-of-the-ninth, two-run home run off Byung-Hyun Kim sends the game into extra innings, and Alfonso Soriano singles in the winning run in the 12th.

May 17, 2002 - Jason Giambi becomes only the 21st player—and second Yankee—to hit a "walk-off" grand slam with his team trailing by three runs (Babe Ruth did it on 9/24/25). His 14th-inning slam off Minnesota's Mike Trombley erases a 12-9 Twins lead, giving the Yankees a 13-12 win.

June 13, 2003 - In a 5-2 win vs. the St. Louis Cardinals at Yankee Stadium, Roger Clemens records both his 300th career win and 4,000 career strikeout (Edgar Renteria).

Oct. 16, 2003 – In Game 7 of the ALCS vs. Boston at Yankee Stadium, Aaron Boone becomes only the fifth player—and second Yankee—to end a postseason series with a "walk-off" home run (also Chris Chambliss, 1976 ALCS vs. Kansas City), when his 11th-inning leadoff solo shot off Tim Wakefield clinches the Yankees' 39th pennant.

July 1, 2004 - Derek Jeter makes his most famous catch, diving into Yankee Stadium's third base stands to nab a 12th-inning popup off the bat of Boston's Trot Nixon. John Flaherty wins the game with a 13th-inning RBI single.

April 26, 2005 - Alex Rodriguez hits three home runs (all off Bartolo Colon) and becomes just the second Yankee in franchise history to record at least 10 RBI in a game (also Tony Lazzeri, 11 on 5/24/36) in a 12-4 win vs. the Angels at Yankee Stadium.

June 15, 2005 – The Yankees announce plans for a new Yankee Stadium to be constructed in Macombs Dam and John Mullaly Parks, which are located on the north side of 161st Street (adjacent to the original Stadium's longtime site).

Sept. 25, 2005 – The Yankees conclude their 81-game home schedule at Yankee Stadium with a season attendance of 4,090,696, establishing a single-season American League record. They become only the third franchise in sports history to reach the 4 million mark, joining the Toronto Blue Jays (1991-93) and Colorado Rockies (1993). The Yankees will subsequently break their home attendance mark in each of the next three seasons (2006-08).

May 16, 2006 - The Yankees tie a franchise record by overcoming a nine-run deficit to beat Texas to win, 14-13, in nine innings. Jorge Posada hits a two-run "walk-off" home run off Akinori Otsuka.

Aug. 16, 2006 – The Yankees break ground for a new Yankee Stadium, scheduled to be ready for Opening Day 2009.

Groundbreaking ceremony for the current Yankee Stadium

Aug. 4, 2007 - Alex Rodriguez becomes the 22nd and youngest (32 years, 8 days) player in Baseball history to reach the 500-home run mark in a 16-8 win vs. Kansas City at Yankee Stadium. He is the third player to hit his 500th career homer as a Yankee, joining Babe Ruth and Mickey Mantle.

Sept. 5, 2007 - Bob Sheppard works his final game as Yankees Public Address Announcer, a 3-2 win over Seattle.

Oct. 30, 2007 - Joe Girardi is named the 32nd manager in Yankees franchise history.

March 27, 2008 - Prior to the Yankees' final home exhibition game of spring training, Legends Field is renamed George M. Steinbrenner Field.

June 7, 2008 - Johnny Damon goes 6-for-6 in the Yankees' 12-11 win vs. Kansas City, matching the franchise record for hits in a nine-inning game (see June 6, 1934 - Myril Hoag) and becoming the only Yankee in original Yankee Stadium history to record six hits in a game of any length. His final hit is a "walk-off" single.

Sept. 16, 2008 - Derek Jeter singles off Chicago's Gavin Floyd in the first inning for his 1,270th career hit at Yankee Stadium, surpassing Lou Gehrig for the most all-time hits at the ballpark. Jeter finishes the game 2-for-3 in the 6-2 loss.

Sept. 21, 2008 - The Yankees play their last ever game in the original Yankee Stadium. Julia Ruth Stevens, daughter of Babe Ruth, throws out the ceremonial first pitch, and Jose Molina hits the park's final home run in the fourth inning. Following the Yankees' 7-3 win over Baltimore, Derek Jeter thanks the fans over the Stadium public address system.

Sept. 28, 2008 - On the final day of the season in the first game of a doubleheader at Boston's Fenway Park, Mike Mussina records his 20th win of the year, becoming the oldest pitcher in Major League history to win 20 games for the first time.

Nov. 8, 2008 - Local Bronx high school youth groups are joined by Scott Brosius, David Cone, Jeff Nelson and Paul O'Neill of the Yankees' 1998 World Championship team and Yankees General Partner and Vice Chairperson Jennifer Steinbrenner Swindal in removing home plate, the pitcher's rubber and pails of dirt from the original Yankee Stadium, then installing them in the current Yankee Stadium.

April 3-4, 2009 – The Yankees play their first exhibition games in Yankee Stadium, defeating the Chicago Cubs, 7-4 and 10-1, respectively. Chien-Ming Wang tosses the first pitch in the April 3 contest.

April 16, 2009 – The Yankees play the first regular season game in Yankee Stadium history, falling to Cleveland, 10-2. CC Sabathia tosses the Stadium's first official pitch, Johnny Damon records the first hit (first-inning single off Cliff Lee) and Jorge Posada hits the first home run (fifth-inning off Lee).

May 14 – June 1, 2009 – The Yankees set an all-time Major League mark with 18 consecutive errorless games, safely handling 660 chances over the stretch.

Sept. 11, 2009 – Derek Jeter breaks Lou Gehrig's all-time franchise mark of 2,721 hits with a single off Baltimore's Chris Tillman at Yankee Stadium. Gehrig had held the mark since 9/6/37.

Oct. 4, 2009 – Alex Rodriguez hits a three-run home run and a grand slam in the sixth-inning of the season finale at Tampa Bay in a 10-2 Yankees victory, setting an all-time AL mark with 7RBI in an inning.

Nov. 4, 2009 – The Yankees win their 27th World Championship, defeating Philadelphia in Game 6 of the World Series, 7-3. Hideki Matsui ties Bobby Richardson's all-time World Series mark (1960 Game 3 vs. Pittsburgh) with 6RBI. Andy Pettitte records the win, becoming the first pitcher to start and record the win in the clinching game in all three rounds of a single postseason. Manager Joe Girardi joins Billy Martin and Ralph Houk as the only individuals in franchise history to win a World Series with the Yankees as a player and as a manager.

2009 World Champions

May 8, 2010 – Mark Teixeira becomes the second Yankee in franchise history to hit 3HR in a single game against the Red Sox (also see June 23, 1927), homering in the fifth, seventh and ninth innings of a 14-3 Yankees win at Fenway Park.

June 12-13, 2010 – Jorge Posada becomes the first Yankee since Bill Dickey (June 3, Game 2 - June 4, 1937) to hit grand slams in back-to-back games as he accomplishes the feat in 9-3 and 9-5 wins vs. Houston.

July 11, 2010 – Longtime Yankees Public Address Announcer Bob Sheppard passes away at his home in Baldwin, Long Island, at age 99.

July 13, 2010 – Yankees Principal Owner George M. Steinbrenner III passes away in Tampa, Fla. at age 80.

Aug. 4, 2010 – Alex Rodriguez becomes the seventh (and youngest) player in Major League history to hit his 600th HR, accomplishing the feat at 35 years, 8 days old in a 5-1 win vs. Toronto off pitcher Shaun Marcum.

Sept. 20, 2010 - The Yankees dedicate a monument to Principal Owner George M. Steinbrenner III in Monument Park.

George M. Steinbrenner III (1930-2010)

From 1973 until his passing on July 13, 2010, George M. Steinbrenner III created a legacy of winning unmatched by his peers. His foresight, drive and commitment permanently transformed not only the Yankees organization, but the game of Baseball.

On January 3, 1973, a group of businessmen formed and led by Mr. Steinbrenner purchased the New York Yankees from CBS for a net price of $8.7 million. It took just five years for his aggressive leadership to turn the organization back into World Champions. In his time as Principal Owner of the club, the Yankees won more pennants (11) and World Series (7) than any other team in baseball, while posting a Major League-best .566 winning percentage (3,364-2,583-3 record) over the stretch.

In addition to the team's on-field success under the direction of Mr. Steinbrenner, the New York Yankees consistently shattered franchise and league attendance records at home and on the road. In 2009, they drew 3,719,358 fans in their first season of play in the current Yankee Stadium, topping the American League in attendance for the seventh straight season (2003-09). The Yankees remain the only franchise in Baseball history to draw more than 4 million fans at home in four consecutive seasons (2005-08).

Most recently, Mr. Steinbrenner's foresight into both sports and business continued to build the value and prominence of the franchise, positioning it for the future. In 2002, *Sporting News* named him the No. 1 "Most Powerful Man in Sports," and *Forbes* magazine has continued to list the Yankees as the most valuable franchise in all of Baseball.

Mr. Steinbrenner's vision led to the creation of YankeeNets, which owned the New Jersey Nets and New Jersey Devils and ultimately led to the launch of the YES Network, a trailblazing enterprise that has been the nation's most watched regional sports network since 2003. Additionally, Mr. Steinbrenner teamed with long-time friend and Dallas Cowboys owner Jerry Jones, creating Legends Hospitality, LLC, a new concession and merchandising company which currently operates at the Yankees' and Cowboys' new stadiums.

In 2006, his participation in the groundbreaking ceremony for the new Yankee Stadium underscored his role as the principal impetus in moving the much-anticipated facility towards its opening in 2009.

Mr. Steinbrenner's tenure of over 37 years exceeded that of any other New York Yankees owner by 13 years (Colonel Jacob Ruppert purchased the Yankees with Tillinghast L'Hommedieu Huston in January 1915, bought out Huston in 1922, and maintained sole ownership in the club until his death in January 1939—a total of 24 years). During Mr. Steinbrenner's time as the sole Principal Owner of the Yankees, the other 29 Major League clubs had over 100 owners or ownership groups.

Mr. Steinbrenner's success in the sports world began at an early age. He was a multi-sport athlete at Culver Military Academy (where he is in the Athletic Hall of Fame) and at Williams

College. He began his successful coaching career as an assistant football coach at two Big Ten universities, Northwestern and Purdue. Then he assembled championship basketball teams in the National Industrial and American Basketball Leagues. In 2002, he was honored with the prestigious Gold Medal Award from the National Football Foundation and College Hall of Fame for a lifetime of "outstanding commitment, dedication and dynamic leadership in his business, as well as his personal life."

Mr. Steinbrenner devoted as much time and effort to the U.S. Olympic Committee (USOC) as he did to his many other sporting endeavors. He was on the U.S. Olympic Foundation Board from 1986-2002 and served as Chairman over the last six years of his tenure. He also was Chairman of the 1989 Olympic Overview Commission, which was created to evaluate the structure and efforts of the U.S. Olympic program, and served as Vice President of the USOC from 1989 to 1992. As a result of his distinguished service, he was presented with the General Douglas MacArthur USOC Foremost Award and the F. Don Miller United States Olympic Award. In 2005, the U.S. Olympic Foundation created the George M. Steinbrenner Sports Leadership Award in his honor, which celebrates a member of the U.S. Olympic family who has made outstanding contributions to sport.

Additionally, Mr. Steinbrenner was a member of the Baseball Hall of Fame's Board of Directors and served on the NCAA Foundation Board of Trustees beginning in 1990.

Most of Mr. Steinbrenner's philanthropic endeavors were performed without fanfare. However, he was repeatedly recognized by the communities in which he immersed himself. In 1993, he earned the Tampa Civitan Club's "Outstanding Citizen" Award, and in 1998, Tampa Law Enforcement named him "Citizen of the Year" for founding a scholarship fund for the children of slain law enforcement officers. Mr. Steinbrenner was also honored as an "Outstanding New Yorker" by the New York Society of Association Executives in 1997 and credited in 2009 by the Museum of the City of New York as one of the "New York City 400," recognizing "people who have helped create the world's greatest city since its founding in 1609."

In February 2008, the Tampa City Council and the Board of the Hillsborough County Commissioner's Office both passed resolutions endorsing the renaming of Legends Field in Tampa after Mr. Steinbrenner to pay tribute to his numerous contributions to the area. On March 27, 2008, Mr. Steinbrenner—joined by his family—pulled down a curtain draped above the outfield scoreboard to unveil the new name for the Yankees' spring training home: George M. Steinbrenner Field.

On September 20, 2010, prior to the team's game vs. Tampa Bay, the Yankees unveiled a monument in Mr. Steinbrenner's honor in Monument Park, reflecting the special connection, appreciation and responsibility that he felt toward Yankees fans.

GEORGE M. STEINBRENNER III
JULY 4, 1930 – JULY 13, 2010

New York Yankees Principal Owner
"The Boss"
1973 - 2010

Purchased the New York Yankees on January 3, 1973.
A true visionary who changed the game of baseball forever, he was considered the most influential owner in all of sports.
In his 37 years as Principal Owner, the Yankees posted a Major League-best .566 winning percentage, while winning 11 American League pennants and seven World Series titles, becoming the most recognizable sports brand in the world.
A devoted sportsman, he was Vice President of the United States Olympic Committee, a member of the Baseball Hall of Fame's Board of Directors and a member of the NCAA Foundation Board of Trustees.
A great philanthropist whose charitable efforts were mostly performed without fanfare, he followed a personal motto of the greatest form of charity is anonymity.

Dedicated by the New York Yankees
September 20, 2010

In the fall of 2009, George M. Steinbrenner High School opened in Lutz, Fla. The school was named after Mr. Steinbrenner by the Hillsborough County School Board in recognition of his philanthropic involvement in the community, particularly with the school system.

Mr. Steinbrenner was dually honored in January 2011, winning the Joan Payson Community Service Award from the New York chapter of the BBWAA and having his legacy of charitable work recognized at the 22nd annual Baseball Assistance Team (B.A.T.) Dinner.

He is survived by his wife, Joan; sisters Susan Norpell and Judy Kamm, children, Hank, Hal, Jennifer and Jessica; and his grandchildren.

Chronology of Yankees Ownership

January 9, 1903:	Frank Ferrell and Bill Devery purchase the Baltimore franchise of the American League for $18,000 and move the team to New York.
January 11, 1915:	Col. Jacob Ruppert and Col. Tillinghast L'Hommedieu Huston purchase the Yankees for $460,000.
May 21, 1922:	Col. Ruppert buys out Col. Huston for $1,500,000.
January 13, 1939:	Col. Ruppert dies.
January 25, 1945:	Dan Topping, Del Webb and Larry MacPhail purchase the Yankees for $2,800,000 from the estate of the late Col. Ruppert.
November 2, 1964:	CBS purchases 80 percent of the Yankees for $11,200,000, later buys the remaining 20 percent.
January 3, 1973:	A limited partnership, headed by George M. Steinbrenner as its Managing General Partner, purchases the Yankees from CBS for a net price of $8.7 million.

Lou Gehrig Appreciation Day - July 4, 1939

Prior to the Yankees' May 2, 1939, game at Detroit's Briggs Stadium, captain Lou Gehrig gave the umpires his team's lineup card—which did not have his name on it. He watched the entire game from the bench, marking the end of his 2,130-consecutive-games-played streak. "The Iron Horse" was suffering the effects of amyotrophic lateral sclerosis (ALS), a disease known since as Lou Gehrig's Disease. He would never play again.

Just over two months later, on July 4, 1939, Lou Gehrig Appreciation Day was held in front of approximately 62,000 fans in Yankee Stadium. Ceremonies took place between games of a doubleheader against the Washington Senators. Gehrig and his teammates were joined by members of the 1927 Yankees. After speeches by Mayor Fiorello La Guardia and Postmaster James A. Farley, Manager Joe McCarthy said his public goodbye to Gehrig: "Lou, what can I say except that it was a sad day in the life of everybody who knew you when you came to my hotel room that day in Detroit and told me you were quitting as a ballplayer because you felt yourself a hindrance to the team. My God, man, you were never that."

Various gifts were presented to Gehrig from club employees and the rival New York Giants. His teammates gave him a trophy, which was inscribed with a poem by *New York Times* writer John Kiernan. As the crowd chanted, "We want Lou; We want Lou…," Gehrig stepped to the microphone to deliver one of the most oft-quoted speeches in American history.

"Fans, for the past two weeks you have been reading about the bad break I got. Yet today I consider myself the luckiest man on the face of the Earth. I have been in ballparks for 17 years and have never received anything but kindness and encouragement from you fans.

"Look at these grand men. Which of you wouldn't consider it the highlight of his career just to associate with them for even one day? Sure, I'm lucky. Who wouldn't consider it an honor to have known Jacob Ruppert? Also, the builder of

baseball's greatest empire, Ed Barrow? To have spent six years with that wonderful little fellow, Miller Huggins? Then to have spent the next nine years with that outstanding leader, that smart student of psychology, the best manager in baseball today, Joe McCarthy? Sure, I'm lucky.

"When the New York Giants, a team you would give your right arm to beat, and vice versa, sends you a gift—that's something. When everybody down to the groundskeepers and those boys in white coats remember you with trophies—that's something. When you have a wonderful mother-in-law who takes sides with you in squabbles with her own daughter—that's something. When you have a father and a mother who work all their lives so you can have an education and build your body—it's a blessing. When you have a wife who has been a tower of strength and shown more courage than you dreamed existed—that's the finest I know.

"So I close in saying that I might have been given a bad break, but I've got an awful lot to live for."

During the ceremony, Gehrig had his No. 4 retired by the Yankees, becoming the first person in sports to be given such an honor. To this day he remains the only Yankee ever to wear the number.

Gehrig died on June 2, 1941, at his home in the Riverdale section of the Bronx. He was 37.

Babe Ruth Day - April 27, 1947

On April 27, 1947, Babe Ruth Day was celebrated throughout Major League Baseball, as the Babe said goodbye in an on-field ceremony at Yankee Stadium. Dressed in a topcoat and hat, Ruth, weakened by throat cancer, made the following remarks:

"Thank you very much, ladies and gentlemen. You know how bad my voice sounds—well it feels just as bad.

"You know this baseball game of ours comes up from the youth. That means the boys. And after you're a boy and grow up to know how to play ball, then you come to the boys you see representing themselves today in your national pastime. The only real game—I think—in the world is baseball.

"As a rule, some people think if you give them a football, or a baseball, or something like that—naturally they're athletes right away. But you can't do that in baseball. You've gotta start from way down [at] the bottom, when you're 6 or 7 years of age. You can't wait until you're 15 or 16. You gotta let it grow up with you. And if you're successful, and you try hard enough, you're bound to come out on top—just like these boys have come to the top now.

"There has been so many lovely things said about me, and I'm glad that I've had the opportunity to thank everybody. Thank you."

Ruth returned to Yankee Stadium once more, on June 13, 1948, to celebrate the 25th anniversary of Yankee Stadium and have his uniform No. 3 retired.

He died on Aug. 16, 1948, at Memorial Hospital in New York at age 53. His body lay in state at the entrance of Yankee Stadium on Aug. 17 and 18, before his funeral on Aug. 19 at New York's St. Patrick's Cathedral.

The 1961 Yankees and Roger Maris' 61-Home Run Season

50TH ANNIVERSARY

This year marks the 50th anniversary of the historic 1961 season that saw Roger Maris break Babe Ruth's all-time single-season home run mark and the Yankees power their way to a World Series championship, cementing their reputation as one of the best teams of all time.

The Yankees finished the regular season with a 109-53 (.673) record, eight games ahead of the 101-61 (.623) Detroit Tigers. The clubs were just 1.5 games apart in the standings heading into the final full month of the season before the Yankees reeled off a 13-game winning streak from Sept. 1-12 to vault an insurmountable 11.5 games in front. Their massive win total was fueled by a 65-16 mark at Yankee Stadium, the best single-season home record in Major League history.

The club, assembled by General Manager George Weiss, had sluggers up and down the lineup, including Moose Skowron (28 HR), Yogi Berra (22 HR), Elston Howard (21 HR) and "Super-sub" Johnny Blanchard, who hit 21 homers in just 243 at-bats. Of the 240 home runs the Yankees hit, 10 were pinch-hit homers, setting a still-standing single-season franchise mark.

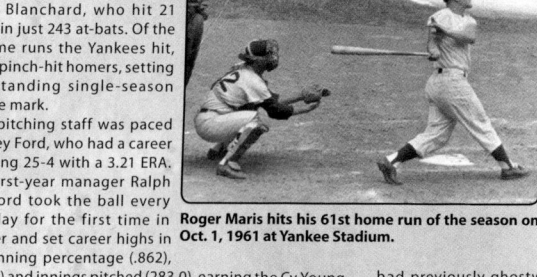

The pitching staff was paced by Whitey Ford, who had a career year, going 25-4 with a 3.21 ERA. Under first-year manager Ralph Houk, Ford took the ball every fourth day for the first time in his career and set career highs in wins, winning percentage (.862), starts (39) and innings pitched (283.0), earning the Cy Young Award as the best pitcher in both leagues. Bill Stafford (14-9, 2.68 ERA), Ralph Terry (16-3, 3.15 ERA) and Rollie Sheldon (11-5, 3.60 ERA) were the Yankees' other top starters, and Luis Arroyo picked up 15 wins in relief, the highest total by a reliever in franchise history.

In the World Series, the Yankees triumphed over Cincinnati, 4-games-to-1, as Ford tossed 14.0 combined scoreless innings, earning wins in Game 1 and 4. With the Series knotted at one game apiece, Game 3 proved pivotal. Down, 2-1, heading into the eighth, Blanchard tied the game with a solo homer before Maris hit a game-winning solo shot in the ninth. The Yankees then outscored the Reds 20-5 over the final two contests to win the first of two consecutive World Series titles.

Much of the season's drama centered on the chase by the M&M Boys – Roger Maris and Mickey Mantle – to break Ruth's seemingly untouchable single-season record of 60 home runs, which he set with the 1927 Murderers' Row Yankees. Maris, the American League MVP in 1960 and 1961, was joined in his pursuit by Mantle, who topped out at 54 home runs after sitting out seven of the club's final 10 games with an abscess in his right hip.

Maris tied Ruth's mark on Sept. 26 at Yankee Stadium with a home run off Baltimore's Jack Fisher in the team's 159th game of the season. Needing one homer to break the record with four games to go (the Yankees had played a tie earlier in the year), Maris was given a full game off prior to going homerless in the first two games of a three-game series against Boston at Yankee Stadium.

In the season's final game on Oct. 1, Maris connected in the fourth inning off Tracy Stallard, hitting a line-drive into the right-field stands for his 61st home run, which turned out to be the only run in a 1-0 Yankees victory. The quiet and humble Maris had to be pushed back onto the field by his teammates for his curtain call.

The chase was not without controversy as writers and fans loyal to Ruth clamored that the record should receive a special notation given that the American League was playing a 162-game schedule in 1961 due to the addition of two expansion teams. With the exceptions of 1901-03 and 1918-19, the AL had always played a 154-game format.

Ford Frick, a former sportswriter and New York City sportscaster who had previously ghostwritten Ruth's 1928 autobiography *Babe Ruth's Own Book of Baseball*, was the commissioner of baseball at the time. In the middle of the season, he issued the directive that baseball's official record book, *The Little Red Book of Major League Baseball*, compiled by the *Elias Sports Bureau*, should show two records — one for a 154-game schedule and another for a 162-game schedule. Contrary to popular lore, an asterisk was never used for the notation, and separate designations remained in the official record book until 1991, when Major League Baseball finally rescinded the distinction.

Maris' 61 in '61 remains the highest single-season home run total in American League history and the seventh-highest single-season total all time, behind those of Barry Bonds (73), Mark McGwire (70, 65) and Sammy Sosa (66, 64 and 63). ⚕

Roger Maris hits his 61st home run of the season on Oct. 1, 1961 at Yankee Stadium.

Front Row: Whitey Ford, Bill Skowron, Hal Reniff, Jim Hegan, Frank Crosetti, Ralph Houk, John Sain, Wally Moses, Earl Torgeson, Clete Boyer, Yogi Berra, Mickey Mantle. **Middle Row:** Gus Mauch (Trainer), Billy Gardner, Bob Hale, Joe DeMaestri, Tony Kubek, Tex Clevenger, Ralph Terry, Hector Lopez, Bob Cerv, Elston Howard, Roger Maris, Bob Turley, Joe Soares (Trainer). **Top Row:** Bobby Richardson, Al Downing, Luis Arroyo, John Blanchard, Bill Stafford, Rollie Sheldon, Jim Coates, Spud Murray (Batting Practice Pitcher), Bud Daley, Bruce Henry (Traveling Secretary). **Seated on Ground:** Batboys Frank Prudenti, Fred Bengis.

Bob Sheppard "The Voice of Yankee Stadium"

Bob Sheppard will forever be the "The Voice of Yankee Stadium." With his instantly recognizable elocution — in which each syllable was given meticulous attention — Sheppard provided a soundtrack of irreproachable dignity to Yankee Stadium for 57 years.

Sadly, he passed away on July 11, 2010, at his home in Baldwin, N.Y., with his wife, Mary, by his side. He was 99 years old.

Born in Ridgewood, Queens, Sheppard began his tenure as Yankees public address announcer on April 17, 1951—Opening Day of Joe DiMaggio's final season and the day of Mickey Mantle's Major League debut. Among the approximately 4,500 baseball games he worked over his tenure with the Yankees were 121 consecutive postseason contests from 1951 to 2006, including 62 games in 22 World Series.

Sheppard's incredible career behind the microphone started when he volunteered his services for a charity football game in Freeport, Long Island, in the late 1940s. An executive from the Brooklyn Dodgers football team of the All-America Conference was at the game. He liked Sheppard's style ("clear, concise and correct") and hired him. The football Dodgers folded after just one season at Ebbets Field (1948), but one of their opponents—the New York football Yankees— heard Sheppard's booming voice and offered him their PA job at Yankee Stadium. Baseball's Yankees discovered him as a result and offered him their PA role for the 1950 season. Though he turned down their offer due to conflicts with his teaching schedule, he changed his mind the following year.

In addition to his baseball duties, Sheppard was the public address voice for the New York football Giants for 50 seasons—from their move to Yankee Stadium in 1956 until his retirement after the 2005 season. Sheppard also served the New York Titans of the American Football League at the Polo Grounds, the New York Stars of the World Football League at Downing Stadium, the New York Cosmos soccer team, and St. John's University's basketball and football teams. Sheppard also handled PA duties for five Army-Navy football games in Philadelphia.

Some of the events he listed as the most memorable of his incredible career were: Don Larsen's perfect game in Game 5 of the 1956 World Series on October 8, 1956; Roger Maris' 61st home run on October 1, 1961; Reggie Jackson's three home runs in Game 6 of the World Series on October 18, 1977; and the Giants-Colts overtime NFL Championship Game on December 28, 1958.

Sheppard attended St. John's College, which eventually became St. John's University. Always a talented athlete, he received a full athletic scholarship to the school,

playing quarterback on the football team all four years. He later enrolled at Columbia University, where he received his master's degree in speech and worked his way up from teacher-in-training to substitute teacher to permanent teacher to department chairman. In order to supplement his teaching salary, Sheppard played semiprofessional football on Sundays in Long Island with the Valley Stream Red Riders and the Hempstead Monitors, earning $25 a game.

In 1998, Sheppard was presented with the prestigious William J. Slocum "Long and Meritorious Service" Award by the New York chapter of the BBWAA as well as the "Pride of the Yankees" award by the ballclub.

On May 7, 2000, a plaque was dedicated to Sheppard in Monument Park of the original Yankee Stadium to commemorate his 50th anniversary season. Additionally, the Yankee Stadium media dining room was named "Sheppard's Place" prior to the 2009 season to commemorate his legacy.

The native New Yorker was elected to the St. John's University Sports Hall of Fame, the Long Island Sports Hall of Fame and the New York Sports Hall of Fame. He was awarded honorary doctorates from St. John's University (Pedagogy) and Fordham University (Rhetoric), and in 2007, received St. John's' Medal of Honor, the highest award that the university can confer on a graduate.

Sheppard also made cameo appearances in numerous motion pictures and television shows, including *61**, *It's My Turn*, *It Could Happen to You*, *Anger Management*, *Seinfeld* and *Mad About You*.

Sheppard announced his final game at Yankee Stadium on September 5, 2007, a 3-2 Yankees victory over the Seattle Mariners.

On September 21, 2008, Sheppard provided a valedictory in the bottom of the seventh inning of the final game at the original Yankee Stadium. Unable to say goodbye in person as he continued to recover from an illness that had kept him away from the Stadium since the final weeks of the 2007 season, Sheppard gave his tribute through a taped segment played on the video board. He recited, "Farewell, old Yankee Stadium, farewell / What a wonderful story you can tell / DiMaggio, Mantle, Gehrig and Ruth / A baseball cathedral in truth."

BOB SHEPPARD'S FIRST LINEUP CARD	
April 17, 1951	
Boston Red Sox	**New York Yankees**
Dom DiMaggio, CF	Jackie Jensen, LF
Billy Goodman, RF	Phil Rizzuto, SS
Ted Williams, LF	Mickey Mantle, RF
Vern Stephens, 3B	Joe DiMaggio, CF
Walt Dropo, 1B	Yogi Berra, C
Bobby Doerr, 2B	Johnny Mize, 1B
Lou Boudreau, SS	Billy Johnson, 3B
Buddy Rosar, C	Jerry Coleman, 2B
Billy Wright, P	Vic Raschi, P

Voices Before Sheppard

Hard to believe, but Bob Sheppard was not the only Public Address Announcer in the original Yankee Stadium's fabled history. But no one—not even Sheppard himself—could remember who immediately preceded the current Stadium P.A. announcer behind the microphone. After all, the last game by this mystery man would likely have been the fourth and final game of the 1950 World Series between the Yankees and Philadelphia's "Whiz Kids" Phillies.

But, after years of search and research, the answer may have turned up in the transcript of an interview conducted in 1991 by writer Paul Doherty with Don Carney, the producer-director of Yankees telecasts for more than three decades.

Extolling Sheppard's longevity, Carney told Doherty that "Bob's been around forever. He followed Red Patterson, who was the club's Public Relations Director and also did the P.A."

Red Patterson: The man who preceded Sheppard

Carney's words give not only the answer but may also explain the mystery. Sheppard's predecessor was widely but anonymously quoted in the newspapers for an infamous gaffe he made during a Yankees-Philadelphia Athletics game on May 31, 1946. "Will the spectators in the front row please remove their clothing…" he began, with the rest of his announcement: "from the front railing," drowned out by the crowd's laughter.

The story got into the papers, but the identity of the speaker did not. Of course, it didn't. The writers didn't want to embarrass their main conduit for information about the club!

Additional research shows that Yankee Stadium was the last ballpark in the Majors to install a public-address system. It debuted in Game 3 of the 1936 World Series and was manned by Jack Lenz and George Levy, two veterans of the time when information was still relayed to the crowd by megaphone.

The careers of Lenz and Levy began in 1915 when the Yankees and Giants shared the Polo Grounds. When the Yankees hopped across the Harlem River in 1923, Levy stayed with the Giants while Lenz took the Yankee post. "I grabbed the offer," Lenz said. "Who wouldn't, with the old Bambino holding forth at the Stadium?"

To do his job, Lenz sat in a box alongside the Yankees dugout (then on the third-base side of Yankee Stadium) and shouted the batting orders and batteries (each team's pitcher and catcher) as well as the changes throughout the game. Unlike today, players were not announced each time they came to bat and Lenz was called upon only when a change was made.

Jack Lenz: "The little man with the big voice."

According to a feature article which appeared in the *New York Evening News* in the early 1930s to celebrate a career of more than 2,000 consecutive games, Lenz—the "mild-mannered megaphone man"—would receive the lineups and batting orders from both managers approximately 15 minutes before the start of the game (3:15 p.m. in those days). After telephoning the press box with the "necessary dope," Lenz would pick up his megaphone and shout the batting orders and batteries. He directed his voice first toward the bleachers, then to the upper tiers of the grandstand and again to the lower stands.

Due to the vast size of their new ballpark, the Yankees actually began the 1927 season with two public address announcers to service Yankee Stadium. After the idea proved successful before a crowd of more than 65,000 on Opening Day, the "two-ply announcer system" of Lenz and Levy was used again for the second game when the crowd was only about 7,000. The experiment was likely short lived.

Research for "The Voices Before Sheppard" by Keith Olbermann.

Yankees in Cooperstown

There are 47 members of the Baseball Hall of Fame who have played, managed, coached, owned or been a general manager for the New York Yankees at one time or another. The Yankees' first inductee was Babe Ruth, who entered the Hall in its inaugural 1936 class along with Ty Cobb, Walter Johnson, Christy Mathewson and Honus Wagner. The Yankees' most recent inductees are Joe Gordon and Rickey Henderson, who were formally enshrined in Cooperstown on July 26, 2009.

In addition to the 47 individuals below, at least three Hall of Famers worked for the Yankees in other capacities, including Joe Kelley (HOF in 1971 / Yankees Scout from 1915-25), Dick Williams (HOF in 2008 / NYY adviser from 1995-2001) and Pat Gillick (HOF in 2011 / NYY scouting director from 1974-76).

Currently, the choice of which insignia appears on the cap of each Hall of Famer's plaque belongs to the Hall of Fame itself. The decision is based on the "historical accomplishments" of the player and "where that player makes his most indelible mark" (though the wishes of the inductee are always considered). It is important to remember that caps have not always had insignias and some players' images are cast as profiles without visible insignias.

* Information listed below each photo includes name of Hall of Famer, primary career position, year inducted, years with Yankees, number of games played with Yankees and insignia on Hall of Fame cap.

Frank "Home Run" Baker
3B (1955)
1916-22, 676 games
Cap: No insignia (A's style)

Ed Barrow
Executive (1953)
1920-45
No Cap

Yogi Berra
C (1972)
1946-63 (player), 2,116 games
1964, 1984-85 (Mgr), 340 games
Cap turned, insignia unseen

Wade Boggs
3B (2005)
1993-97, 602 games
Cap: Boston Red Sox

Frank Chance
1B/Manager (1946)
1913-14 (1B), 12 games
1913-14 (Mgr), 285 games
Cap: Chicago Cubs

Jack Chesbro
RHP (1946)
1903-09, 269 games
Cap: Head turned, insignia unseen

Earle Combs
CF (1970)
1924-35, 1,454 games
Cap: New York Yankees

Stan Coveleski
RHP (1969)
1928, 12 games
Cap: Cleveland Indians

Bill Dickey
C (1954)
1928-46 (Player), 1,789 games
1946 (Mgr), 105 games
Cap: New York Yankees

Joe DiMaggio
CF (1955)
1936-51, 1,736 games
Cap: New York Yankees

Leo Durocher
Manager (1994)
1925, 28-29 (INF), 210 games
Cap: Brooklyn Dodgers

Whitey Ford
LHP (1974)
1950-67, 498 games
Cap: New York Yankees

Lou Gehrig
1B (1939)
1923-39, 2,164 games
Cap: New York Yankees

Lefty Gomez
LHP (1972)
1930-42, 367 games
Cap: New York Yankees

Joe Gordon
2B (2009)
1938-43, '46, 1000 games
Cap: New York Yankees

Rich "Goose" Gossage
RHP (2008)
1978-83, 89, 319 games
Cap: New York Yankees

Clark Griffith
Player, Manager, Executive (1946)
1903-07 (RHP), 87 games
1903-08 (Mgr), 789 games
Cap: No insignia

Burleigh Grimes
RHP (1964)
1934, 10 games
Cap: Brooklyn Dodgers

Bucky Harris
Manager (1975)
1947-48, 308 games
Cap: Washington Senators

Rickey Henderson
CF/LF (2009)
1985-89, 596 games
Cap: Oakland A's

Waite Hoyt
RHP (1969)
1921-30, 365 games
Cap: New York Yankees

Miller Huggins
Manager (1964)
1918-29, 1,786 games
Cap: New York Yankees

Jim "Catfish" Hunter
RHP (1987)
1975-79, 137 games
Cap: No insignia

Reggie Jackson
RF (1993)
1977-81, 653 games
Cap: New York Yankees

Willie Keeler
RF (1939)
1903-09, 873 games
Cap: Brooklyn Dodgers

Tony Lazzeri
2B (1991)
1926-37, 1,658 games
Cap: New York Yankees

Bob Lemon
RHP (1976)
1978-79, 81-82 (Mgr), 172 games
Cap: Cleveland Indians

Larry MacPhail
Executive (1978)
1945-47
No Cap

Lee MacPhail
Executive (1998)
1949-58, 1966-73
No Cap

Mickey Mantle
CF (1974)
1951-68, 2,401 games
Cap: New York Yankees

Joe McCarthy
Manager (1957)
1931-46, 2,327 games
Cap: New York Yankees

Bill McKechnie
Manager (1962)
1913 (INF), 44 games
Cap: Cincinnati Reds

Johnny Mize
1B (1981)
1949-53, 375 games
Cap: No insignia

Phil Niekro
RHP (1997)
1984-85, 65 games
Cap: Atlanta Braves

Herb Pennock
LHP (1948)
1923-33, 346 games
Cap: No insignia

Gaylord Perry
RHP (1991)
1980, 10 games
Cap: San Francisco Giants

Branch Rickey
Executive (1967)
1907 (OF, C, 1B), 52 games
No Cap

Phil Rizzuto
SS (1994)
1941-42, 46-56, 1,661 games
Cap: New York Yankees

Red Ruffing
RHP (1967)
1930-42, 45-46, 426 games
Cap: New York Yankees

Babe Ruth
OF (1936)
1920-34, 2,084 games
Cap: New York Yankees

Joe Sewell
SS (1977)
1931-33, 389 games
Cap: Cleveland Indians

Enos Slaughter
OF (1985)
1954-55, 56-59, 350 games
Cap: St. Louis Cardinals

Phil Rizzuto gives his Hall of Fame Induction speech in 1994.

Casey Stengel
Manager (1966)
1949-60, 1,845 games
Cap: New York Yankees

Dazzy Vance
RHP (1955)
1915, 1918, 10 games
Cap: Brooklyn Dodgers

Paul Waner
RF (1952)
1944-45, 10 games
Cap: Pittsburgh Pirates

George Weiss
Executive (1971)
1932-60
No Cap

Goose Gossage and Dick Williams at the 2008 Baseball Hall of Fame induction ceremony.

Dave Winfield
RF (2001)
1981-90, 1,172 games
Cap: San Diego Padres

NATIONAL BASEBALL HALL OF FAME AND MUSEUM

25 Main Street, Cooperstown, New York 13326
Phone: (607) 547-7200 **Fax:** (607) 547-2044
Public Relations: (607) 547-0215
e-mail address: info@baseballhalloffame.org
Web site: baseballhall.org
Summer Hours: Memorial Day Weekend - Labor Day Weekend: 9 a.m. to 9 p.m.
Regular Hours: 9 a.m. to 5 p.m.
Holiday Closings: Thanksgiving Day, Christmas Day, and New Year's Day.

DIRECTORY: Jane Forbes Clark (Chairman), Joe Morgan (Vice Chairman), Jeff Idelson (President), Bill Haase (Senior Vice President), Sean Gahagan (Vice President, Retail Marketing & Licensing), Erik Strohl (Senior Director of Exhibitions and Collections), Ken Meifert (Senior Director, Development), Brad Horn (Senior Director, Communications & Education), Jim Gates (Librarian), Tim Wiles (Research Director)
COMMUNICATIONS CONTACTS: Craig Muder (Comm. Director), Jackie Brown (Comm. Associate)

HALL OF FAME WEEKEND 2011: July 22-25
Inductees: Roberto Alomar, Bert Blyleven & Pat Gillick
Awards: Sat. July 23, 4:30 p.m. ET, Doubleday Field
Induction: Sun. July 24, 1:30 p.m. ET, Clark Sports Center

HALL OF FAME CLASSIC 2011: June 18-19
Golf tournament & other events all weekend
Game: Sun. June 19, 2 p.m., Doubleday Field;
For more information, visit **baseballhall.org**

YANKEES IN THE HALL OF FAME
A total of 47 members of the Hall of Fame have either played, managed, coached, owned or been a general manager for the New York Yankees, including the club's most recent 2009 Inductees Rickey Henderson (1985-1989) and Joe Gordon (1938-1943, 1946). For a complete list of New York Yankees in the Hall of Fame, visit the "Hall of Famers" team pages at **www.baseballhall.org.**

HALL OF FAME ARTIFACTS FROM 2009 WORLD CHAMPIONSHIP
Bat used by World Series MVP Hideki Matsui during Game 6.
Bat used by Derek Jeter and spikes worn by Alex Rodriguez during Game 6.
Scorecard from Game 6 used by Suzyn Waldman, the first female World Series broadcaster.
Spikes worn by Johnny Damon during Game 4, when he stole two bases.
Caps worn by Andy Pettitte and Mariano Rivera during the World Series.

2009 World Series artifacts

OTHER NOTABLE YANKEES ARTIFACTS IN COOPERSTOWN
Bat used by Nick Swisher to hit game-winning walk-off single on July 16, 2010, the team's first game following the death of George Steinbrenner.
Spikes worn by Alex Rodriguez on Aug. 4, 2010 to hit his 600th career home run, becoming the youngest player in history to reach the coveted mark.
Batting gloves worn by Derek Jeter on Sept. 11, 2009, when he passed Lou Gehrig on the Yankees' all-time hits list with his 2,722nd hit.
Ball and Andy Pettitte cap from May 30, 2009, when Pettitte and Mariano Rivera set record for combined win-saves (58).
Spikes worn by starting pitcher CC Sabathia on April 16, 2009, and a ticket from the home opener at new Yankee Stadium.
Ticket to last game and spikes worn by Jose Molina to record final home run in old Yankee Stadium on Sept. 21, 2008.
Bat used by Aaron Boone to end Game Seven of the 2003 ALCS against the Boston Red Sox.
Batting helmet worn by World Series MVP Derek Jeter in the 2000 World Series.
Cap, ball, ticket and beanie baby giveaway from David Wells' perfect game on May 17, 1998.
Bat used by Mickey Mantle to hit his 500th career home run on May 14, 1967.
Ticket to Lou Gehrig Day on July 4, 1939, when he made the "Luckiest Man" speech.
Bats used by Hall of Famer Babe Ruth to hit his 57th, 58th, and 60th home runs in 1927.
Ball thrown by New York Governor Al Smith at Yankee Stadium dedication ceremony, April 18, 1923.

LOOK AHEAD TO 2012
Ballots for the 2012 Hall of Fame/BBWAA election will be distributed in early December with results from the voting scheduled to be announced in January 2012. A partial list of first-year candidates for election include: David Bell, Jeromy Burnitz, Vinny Castilla, Scott Erickson, Javy Lopez, Bill Mueller, Terry Mulholland, Brad Radke, Tim Salmon, Ruben Sierra and Bernie Williams. Historical voting data from all past BBWAA elections can be accessed at **www.baseballhall.org** or by contacting the Hall of Fame Public Relations department.

CONNECT TO COOPERSTOWN
For up-to-the-minute news from Cooperstown, visit at **www.baseballhall.org**. Stay up-to-date on all the activity at the Hall of Fame's official site and through social networking on Facebook, LinkedIn, Twitter and YouTube.
If you would like to receive interesting stories and timely news items direct from the Hall of Fame and get the inside track on the latest happenings in Cooperstown, sign up for *Inside Pitch*. There's no cost to receive our weekly electronic newsletter in your e-mail box at home or work and it's easy to enroll: Just log on to **www.hofclubhouse.com.**
If you have an interest in receiving *Around The Horn*, the Hall's monthly media newsletter, please send an e-mail to **info@baseballhalloffame.org**. Be sure to include your name, name of organization and e-mail address.

RESEARCH ASSISTANCE
The Hall of Fame is pleased to provide assistance in baseball research and members of the media are encouraged to utilize its valuable baseball resource whenever necessary by calling the Public Relations department at (607) 547-0215, or the Library Reference desk at (607) 547-0330.

Yankees Retired Uniform Numbers

Beginning with Lou Gehrig's No. 4 in 1939, the Yankees have retired 15 uniform numbers to honor 16 players and managers.

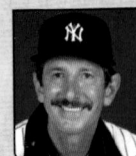

1 Billy Martin (Number retired in 1986)
Born: May 16, 1928 in Berkeley, Calif. • **Died:** Dec. 25, 1989 in Binghamton, N.Y.
Height: 5-11 • **Weight:** 165 • **B/T:** R/R

Had as much "Yankee Pride" as any player or manager to wear pinstripes, and he implanted his own fierce desire to win in his teams. Played an integral part in four World Series in the 1950s as a player, and added another ring managing the Yankees in 1977. His .333 lifetime series batting average is sixth with at least 75 AB on the all-time series list. Combative and daring, Martin was a brilliant baseball strategist and a legend in Yankees history.

3 Babe Ruth (Number retired in 1948)
Born: Feb. 6, 1895 in Baltimore, Md. • **Died:** Aug. 16, 1948 in New York, N.Y.
Height: 6-2 • **Weight:** 215 • **B/T:** L/L

Baseball's greatest slugger and the most colorful figure in the game's history. Debuted as a pitcher for the Boston Red Sox, winning 89 games over six seasons before being converted to the outfield because of his tremendous power. Was sold to the Yankees in 1920 and his 54 home runs that year were more than any other American League team. En route to 714 career home runs, won 12 home run titles, hitting 60 in 1927. Added 15 home runs in World Series competition as he led the Yankees to seven Series appearances and four World Championships. A member of the inaugural class of Hall of Fame inductees in 1936.

4 Lou Gehrig (Number retired in 1939)
Born: June 19, 1903 in New York, N.Y. • **Died:** June 2, 1941 in Riverdale, N.Y.
Height: 6-1 • **Weight:** 212 • **B/T:** L/L

Durable, powerhitting first baseman who played in an amazing 2,130 consecutive games between 1925 and 1939. Drove in at least 100 runs for 13 straight seasons (1926-38) and established an American League record with 184 RBI in 1931. Compiled a .340 lifetime batting average and belted 493 home runs in a career shortened by terminal illness. Was honored at Yankee Stadium on July 4, 1939, and made memorable, "Today, I consider myself the luckiest man on the face of the earth" speech. Life was immortalized in classic 1942 motion picture, *The Pride of the Yankees*, starring Gary Cooper. Elected to the Hall of Fame in 1939.

5 Joe DiMaggio (Number retired in 1952)
Born: Nov. 25, 1914 in Martinez, Calif. • **Died:** March 8, 1999 in Hollywood, Fla.
Height: 6-2 • **Weight:** 193 • **B/T:** R/R

The "Yankee Clipper" is considered by many experts as the best all-around baseball player in history. Was a sensational hitter for average and power, and a splendid, graceful, ball-hawking center fielder. Owned a powerful and accurate arm, and was a daring and alert baserunner. Compiled a .325 lifetime batting average from 1936 to 1951. A two-time batting champion and three-time MVP, he powered the Yankees to the first of four consecutive World Championships in his 1936 rookie season. Many rate his 56-consecutive-game batting streak in 1941 as the top baseball feat of all time. Elected to the Hall of Fame in 1955.

7 Mickey Mantle (Number retired in 1969)
Born: Oct. 20, 1931 in Spavinaw, Okla. • **Died:** Aug. 14, 1995 in Dallas, Tex.
Height: 6-0 • **Weight:** 201 • **B/T:** S/R

"The Mick" was the most feared hitter on some of the most successful teams in history. Could run like the wind and hit tape measure homers, like his famous 565-footer in Washington in 1953. In the 14 seasons between 1951 and 1964, he led the Yanks to 12 Fall Classics and seven World Championships. He still owns records for most homers, RBI, runs and walks in World Series play. In 1956, Mantle had one of the greatest seasons ever at the plate, hitting 52 homers with 130 RBI and a .353 average to win the Triple Crown. Elected to the Hall of Fame in 1974.

8 Yogi Berra (Number retired in 1972)
Born: May 12, 1925 in St. Louis, Mo.
Height: 5-8 • **Weight:** 191 • **B/T:** L/R

A mainstay behind the plate for some of the most dominating teams in history from the end of World War II until the early 1960s. Although he never led the league in a single major offensive category, he was just the third man to win three Most Valuable Player Awards. Was selected to play in the All-Star Game in 15 successive seasons (1948-62). Played on 14 pennant winners and 10 World Champions, more than anyone in history. Led the Yankees to the 1964 pennant as manager. Elected to the Hall of Fame in 1972.

Yankees Retired Uniform Numbers

8 **Bill Dickey** (Number retired in 1972)
Born: June 6, 1907 in Bastrop, La. • **Died:** Nov. 12, 1993 in Little Rock, Ark.
Height: 6-1 • **Weight:** 185 • **B/T:** L/R

Regarded as one of the greatest catchers of all-time. A durable and tireless worker, he caught more than 100 games in 13 consecutive seasons (1929-41), an American League record. In 1931, he did not allow a single passed ball in 125 games behind the plate, another AL record. Dickey also excelled at the plate, batting over .300 in 10 of his first 11 full seasons, while hitting 202 homers during his career. He handled Yankees pitching staffs on eight World Series teams, winning seven championships.

9 **Roger Maris** (Number retired in 1984)
Born: Sept. 10, 1934 in Hibbing, Minn. • **Died:** Dec. 14, 1985 in Houston, Tex.
Height: 6-0 • **Weight:** 197 • **B/T:** L/R

In one of the most dramatic assaults on a baseball record, Maris caught, then surpassed Babe Ruth's famous home run record of 60. Maris hit 61 home runs in 1961, a Major League record which stood until 1998 and is still the American League mark. The two-time American League MVP (1960-61) is also considered one of the best-fielding right fielders in Yankees history.

10 **Phil Rizzuto** (Number retired in 1985)
Born: Sept. 25, 1917 in New York, N.Y. • **Died:** Aug. 13, 2007 in West Orange, N.J.
Height: 5-6 • **Weight:** 150 • **B/T:** R/R

Playing 13 years for the Yankees, "Scooter" went to nine World Series. That stat may best explain why the diminutive shortstop is regarded as a true Yankees legend. He was durable, a skilled bunter and an enthusiastic baserunner with a solid .273 career batting average. In 1950, Rizzuto earned the AL MVP Award, batting .324 with 200 hits, 92 walks and 125 runs scored. He batted .320 in the 1951 World Series and was named Series MVP. He also spent 40 years as a Yankees broadcaster (1957-96) and was elected to the Hall of Fame in 1994.

15 **Thurman Munson** (Number retired in 1979)
Born: June 7, 1947 in Akron, Ohio • **Died:** Aug. 2, 1979 in Canton, Ohio
Height: 5-11 • **Weight:** 190 • **B/T:** R/R

Was the undisputed leader and most respected man on Yankees teams that won three consecutive AL pennants (1976-78) and two World Championships. Munson was a tremendous defensive catcher, winning the Gold Glove Award in three consecutive seasons (1973-75). From 1975-77, Thurman drove in more than 100 runs and hit better than .300 in each season. He hit the first Yankees home run in remodeled Yankee Stadium. There is no more tragic date in Yankees history than August 2, 1979, when Munson passed away in a plane crash at age 32.

16 **Whitey Ford** (Number retired in 1974)
Born: Oct. 21, 1928 in New York, N.Y.
Height: 5-10 • **Weight:** 181 • **B/T:** L/L

"The Chairman of the Board" was the ace pitcher on great Yankees teams of the 1950s and early '60s. The wily southpaw's lifetime record of 236-106 gives him the best winning percentage (.690) of any left-handed pitcher in the 20th century with 100 or more wins. He paced the American League in victories three times, and in ERA and shutouts twice. The 1961 Cy Young Award winner still holds many World Series records, including 10 wins, 33 consecutive scoreless innings and 94 strikeouts. Elected to the Hall of Fame in 1974.

23 **Don Mattingly** (Number retired in 1997)
Born: April 20, 1961 in Evansville, Ind.
Height: 6-0 • **Weight:** 185 • **B/T:** L/L

"Donnie Baseball" was only the 10th captain to be named by the Yankees in their storied history. The premier first baseman of his era, Mattingly was a nine-time Gold Glove winner. The 1985 American League MVP set records for most grand slams in a season (6–since tied) and most home runs in seven consecutive games (9) and eight consecutive games (10). A humble man of grace and dignity, Mattingly carried on the legacy of the pinstripe tradition and dedicated his career to the pursuit of excellence.

Yankees Retired Uniform Numbers

32 Elston Howard (Number retired in 1984)
Born: Feb. 23, 1929 in St. Louis, Mo. • **Died:** Dec. 14, 1980 in New York, N.Y.
Height: 6-2 • **Weight:** 196 • **B/T:** R/R

Became the first black player in Yankees history when he made the club in the spring of 1955. The versatile two-time Gold Glove catcher was an important member of AL pennant-winning Yankees teams in nine of his first 10 seasons with the club. The 1963 American League MVP, Howard was a clubhouse leader who was respected as both a player and a man. Howard's dignified manner off the field and competitive spirit on the field set a powerful example for his teammates.

37 Casey Stengel (Number retired in 1970)
Born: July 30, 1890 in Kansas City, Mo. • **Died:** Sept. 29, 1975 in Glendale, Calif.
Height: 5-11 • **Weight:** 175 • **B/T:** L/L

In a distinguished 54-year professional career, "The Old Perfessor" emerged as one of the game's greatest managers. His feat of guiding the Yankees to 10 pennants and seven world titles in a 12-year span ranks as one of the top managerial accomplishments of all time. Simply put, Casey Stengel was one of the best things to ever happen to the game of Baseball. He was an authentic baseball ambassador, making the game fun for millions of Americans. Elected to the Hall of Fame in 1966.

44 Reggie Jackson (Number retired in 1993)
Born: May 18, 1946 in Wyncote, Pa.
Height: 5-10 • **Weight:** 181 • **B/T:** L/L

One of the game's premier power hitters, "Mr. October" blasted 563 career home runs, good for 13th place on Baseball's all-time list. In Game 6 of the 1977 World Series, Jackson hit three home runs, all on the first pitch, as the Yankees beat the Dodgers to wrap up the club's first World Championship since 1962. Jackson was an exciting clutch player and an intimidating clean-up hitter with a .490 career slugging percentage. The 1973 American League MVP once said, "Some people call October a time of pressure. I call it a time of character." He was elected to the Hall of Fame in 1993.

49 Ron Guidry (Number retired in 2003)
Born: Aug. 28, 1950 in Lafayette, La.
Height: 5-11 • **Weight:** 165 • **B/T:** L/L

Known as "Louisiana Lightning," Ron Guidry was a four-time American League All-Star and three-time 20-game winner. He compiled one of the most dominating seasons in Baseball history in 1978, going 25-3 with a 1.74 ERA. He led the Yankees to a dramatic comeback from 14.0 games behind the Boston Red Sox to capture their second straight World Championship. That season, he also compiled a club-record 248 strikeouts and nine shutouts en route to a unanimous selection as the American League's Cy Young Award winner. On June 17, 1978 vs. California at Yankee Stadium, Guidry struck out 18 Angels, breaking the club's single-game record. With Willie Randolph, he served as the Yankees' co-captain from 1986 through his retirement in 1989. He remains in the Top 10 on the Yankees' all-time list in games pitched (368), innings pitched (2392.0), wins (170), winning percentage (.651), strikeouts (1778) and shutouts (26).

Yankees retired numbers are immortalized in Yankee Stadium's Monument Park.

All-Time Roster

In the Yankees' 108 seasons in the American League, 1,475 players have appeared in at least one game.

*Deceased

A (41)

Jim Abbott 1993-94
Harry Ables* 1911
Bobby Abreu 2006-08
Juan Acevedo 2003
Alfredo Aceves 2008-10
Spencer Adams* 1926
Doc Adkins* 1903
Steve Adkins 1990
Luis Aguayo 1988
Jack Aker 1969-72
Jonathan Albaladejo 2008-10
Mike Aldrete 1996
Doyle Alexander ... 1976, 1982-83
Walt Alexander* 1915-17
Bernie Allen 1972-73
Johnny Allen* 1932-35
Neil Allen 1985, 1987-88
Carlos Almanzar 2001
Erick Almonte 2001, 2003
Sandy Alomar 1974-76
Felipe Alou 1971-73
Matty Alou 1973
Dell Alston 1977-78
Ruben Amaro 1966-68
Jason Anderson 2003, 2005
John Anderson* 1904-05
Rick Anderson* 1979
Ivy Andrews* ... 1931-32, 1937-38
Pete Appleton* 1933
Angel Aragon* 1914, 1916-17
Alex Arias 2002
Rugger Ardizoia 1947
Mike Armstrong 1984-86
Brad Arnsberg 1986-87
Luis Arroyo 1960-63
Tucker Ashford 1981
Paul Assenmacher 1993
Joe Ausanio 1994-95
Jimmy Austin* 1909-10
Chick Autry* 1924
Oscar Azocar* 1990

Yogi Berra

B (137)

Loren Babe* 1952-53
Stan Bahnsen 1966, 1968-71
Bill Bailey* 1911
Frank Baker* 1916-19, 1921-22
Frank Baker 1970-71
Steve Balboni ... 1981-83, 1989-90
Neal Ball* 1907-09
Scott Bankhead 1995
Willie Banks 1997-98
Steve Barber* 1967-68
Jesse Barfield 1989-92
Cy Barger* 1906-07
Ray Barker 1965-67
Frank Barnes* 1930
Honey Barnes* 1926
Ed Barney* 1915
Chris Basak 2007
George Batten* 1912
Hank Bauer* 1948-59
Paddy Baumann* 1915-17
Don Baylor 1983-85
Walter Beall* 1924-27
T.J. Beam 2006
Colter Bean 2005-07
Jim Beattie 1978-79
Rich Beck 1965
Zinn Beck* 1918
Fred Beene 1972-74
Joe Beggs* 1938
John Bell* 1907
Zeke Bella 1957
Mark Bellhorn 2005
Clay Bellinger 1999-2001
Benny Bengough* 1923-30
Juan Beniquez 1979
Armando Benitez 2003
Lou Berberet* 1954-55
Dave Bergman 1975, 1977
Lance Berkman 2010
Juan Bernhardt 1976
Walter Bernhardt* 1918
Dale Berra 1985-86
Yogi Berra 1946-63
Angel Berroa 2009
Wilson Betemit 2007-08
Bill Bevens* 1944-47
Monte Beville* 1903-04
Harry Billiard* 1908
Doug Bird 1980-81
Ewell Blackwell* 1952-53
Rick Bladt 1975
Paul Blair 1977-80
Walter Blair* 1907-11
Johnny Blanchard* . 1955, 1959-65
Gil Blanco 1965
Wade Blasingame 1972
Steve Blateric 1972
Gary Blaylock 1959
Curt Blefary* 1970-71
Elmer Bliss* 1903
Ron Blomberg 1969, 1971-76
Mike Blowers 1989-91
Eddie Bockman 1946
Ping Bodie* 1918-21
Len Boehmer 1969, 1971
Brian Boehringer ... 1995-97, 2001
Wade Boggs 1993-97
Don Bollweg* 1953
Bobby Bonds* 1975
Ricky Bones 1996
Ernie Bonham* 1940-46
Juan Bonilla 1985, 1987
Aaron Boone 2003
Luke Boone* 1913-16
Frenchy Bordagaray* 1941
Rich Bordi 1985, 1987
Joe Borowski 1997-98
Hank Borowy* 1942-45
Babe Borton* 1913
Daryl Boston 1994
Jim Bouton 1962-68
Clete Boyer* 1959-66
Ryan Bradley 1998
Scott Bradley 1984-85
Neal Brady* 1915, 1917
Darren Bragg 2001
Ralph Branca 1954
Norm Branch* 1941-42
Marshall Brant 1980
Garland Braxton* 1925-26
Don Brennan* 1933
Jim Brenneman* 1965
Ken Brett* 1976
Marv Breuer* 1939-43
Billy Brewer 1996
Fritzie Brickell* 1958-59
Jim Brideweser* 1951-53
Marshall Bridges* 1962-63
Harry Bright* 1963-64
Ed Brinkman* 1975
Chris Britton 2007-08
Johnny Broaca* 1934-37
Lew Brockett* 1907, 1909, 1911
Jim Bronstad 1959
Tom Brookens 1989
Scott Brosius 1998-2001
Bob Brower 1989
Jim Brower 2007
Boardwalk Brown* 1914-15

Wade Boggs

Dr. Bobby Brown ... 1946-52, 1954
Bobby Brown 1979-81
Curt Brown 1984
Hal Brown 1962
Jumbo Brown* .. 1932-33, 1935-36
Kevin Brown 2004-05
Brian Bruney 2006-09
Jim Bruske 1998
Billy Bryan 1966-67
Jess Buckles* 1916
Mike Buddie 1998-99
Jay Buhner 1987-88
Bill Burbach 1969-71
Lew Burdette* 1950
Tim Burke 1992
A.J. Burnett 2009-10
George Burns* 1928-29
Alex Burr* 1914
Ray Burris 1979
Homer Bush 1997-98, 2004
Joe Bush* 1922-24
Tom Buskey* 1973-74
Ralph Buxton* 1949
Joe Buzas* 1945
Harry Byrd* 1954
Sammy Byrd* 1929-34
Tommy Byrne* ... 1943, 46-51, 54-57
Marty Bystrom 1984-85

Chris Chambliss

C (119)

Melky Cabrera 2005-09
Greg Cadaret 1989-92
Miguel Cairo 2004, 2006-07
Charlie Caldwell* 1925
Ray Caldwell* 1910-18
Johnny Callison* 1972-73
Howie Camp* 1917
Bert Campaneris 1983
Archie Campbell* 1928
John Candelaria 1988-89
Andy Cannizaro 2006
Robinson Cano 2005-10
Jose Canseco 2000
Mike Cantwell* 1916
Andy Carey 1952-60
Roy Carlyle* 1926
Duke Carmel 1965
Dick Carroll* 1909
Ownie Carroll* 1930
Tommy Carroll 1955-56
Chuck Cary 1989-91
Hugh Casey* 1949
Kevin Cash 2009
Alberto Castillo 2002
Roy Castleton* 1907
Bill Castro 1981
Danny Cater 1970-71
Rick Cerone ... 1980-84, 1987, 1990
Bob Cerv 1951-56, 1960-62
Francisco Cervelli 2008-10
Shawn Chacon 2005-06
Joba Chamberlain 2007-10
Chris Chambliss 1974-79, 1988
Frank Chance* 1913-14
Spud Chandler* 1937-47
Les Channell* 1910, 1914
Darrin Chapin 1991
Ben Chapman* 1930-36
Mike Chartak* 1940, 1942
Hal Chase* 1905-13
Jack Chesbro* 1903-09
Randy Choate 2000-03
Justin Christian 2008
Clay Christiansen 1984
Al Cicotte* 1957
Anthony Claggett 2009
Allie Clark 1947
George Clark* 1913
Jack Clark 1988
Tony Clark 2004
Horace Clarke 1965-74
Walter Clarkson* 1904-07
Brandon Claussen 2003
Ken Clay 1977-79
Roger Clemens ... 1999-2003, 2007
Pat Clements 1987-88
Tex Clevenger 1961-62
Lu Clinton* 1966-67
Tyler Clippard 2007
Al Closter 1971-72
Andy Coakley* 1911
Jim Coates 1956, 1959-62
Jim Cockman* 1905
Rich Coggins 1975-76
Phil Coke 2008-09
Rocky Colavito 1968
King Cole* 1914-15
Curt Coleman* 1912
Jerry Coleman 1949-57
Michael Coleman 2001
Rip Coleman* 1955-56
Bob Collins* 1944
Dave Collins 1982
Joe Collins* 1948-57
Orth Collins* 1904
Pat Collins* 1926-28
Rip Collins* 1920-21
Frank Colman* 1946-47
Loyd Colson 1970
Earle Combs* 1924-35
David Cone 1995-2000
Tom Connelly* 1920-21
Joe Connor* 1905
Wid Conroy* 1903-08
Jose Contreras 2003-04
Andy Cook 1993
Doc Cook* 1913-16
Dusty Cooke* 1930-32
Ron Coomer 2002
Johnny Cooney* 1944
Phil Cooney* 1905
Don Cooper 1985
Guy Cooper* 1914
Dan Costello* 1913
Henry Cotto 1985-87
Ensign Cottrell* 1915
Clint Courtney* 1951
Ernie Courtney* 1903
Stan Coveleski* 1928
Billy Cowan 1969
Joe Cowley 1984-85
Bobby Cox 1968-69
Casey Cox 1972-73

Birdie Cree*............ 1908-15
Lou Criger*...............1910
Herb Crompton*..........1945
Bubba Crosby......... 2004-06
Frank Crosetti*....... 1932-48
Ivan Cruz 1997
Jose Cruz 1988
Jack Cullen........ 1962, 1965-66
Roy Cullenbine*...........1942
Nick A. Cullop*........ 1916-17
Nick Cullop* 1926
John Cumberland 1968-70
Jim Curry* 1911
Chad Curtis 1997-99
Colin Curtis 2010
Fred Curtis*..............1905

Ryne Duren

D (66)

Babe Dahlgren*..... 1937-40
Bud Daley 1961-64
Tom Daley* 1914-15
Johnny Damon 2006-09
Bert Daniels*......... 1910-13
Bobby Davidson 1989
Chili Davis 1998-99
George Davis* 1912
Kiddo Davis* 1926
Lefty Davis*.............1903
Ron Davis 1978-81
Russ Davis 1994-95
Brian Dayett 1983-84
John Deering*............1903
Jim Deidel 1974
Ivan DeJesus.............1986
Frank Delahanty* .. 1905-06, 1908
Wilson Delgado 2000
Bobby Del Greco 1957-58
David Dellucci 2003
Jim Delsing* 1949-50
Joe DeMaestri 1960-61
Ray Demmitt*............1909
Rick Dempsey 1973-76
Bucky Dent 1977-82
Jorge DePaula 2003-05
Claud Derrick*...........1913
Russ Derry* 1944-45
Matt DeSalvo 2007
Jim Deshaies............1984
Jimmie Deshong* 1934-35
Orestes Destrade........1987
Charlie Devens* 1932-34
Al DeVormer* 1921-22
Bill Dickey* 1928-43, 1946
Murry Dickson*...........1958
Joe DiMaggio*.. 1936-42, 1946-51
Kerry Dineen.......... 1975-76
Craig Dingman...........2000
Art Ditmar 1957-61
Sonny Dixon 1956
Pat Dobson* 1973-75
Cozy Dolan* 1911-12
Atley Donald 1938-45
Mike Donovan*...........1908
Wild Bill Donovan*... 1915-16
Brian Dorsett 1989-90
Octavio Dotel ....
Richard Dotson 1988-89
Patsy Dougherty* 1904-06

John Dowd* 1912
Al Downing* 1961-69
Brian Doyle 1978-80
Jack Doyle* 1905
Slow Joe Doyle*....... 1906-10
Doug Drabek 1986
Bill Drescher 1944-46
Karl Drews* 1946-48
Monk Dubiel* 1944-45
Joe Dugan* 1922-28
Mariano Duncan 1996-97
Shelley Duncan 2007-09
Michael Dunn............2009
Ryne Duren 1958-61
Leo Durocher* 1925, 1928-29
Cedric Durst* 1927-30

E (26)

Mike Easler 1986-87
Rawly Eastwick...........1978
Doc Edwards............1965
Foster Edwards*..........1930
Robert Eenhoorn 1994-96
Dave Eiland 1988-91, 1995
Darrell Einertson 2000
Kid Elberfeld* 1903-09
Gene Elliott* 1911
Dock Ellis 1976-77
John Ellis 1969-72
Kevin Elster 1994-95
Alan Embree 2005
Red Embree*.............1948
Clyde Engle* 1909-10
Jack Enright*............1917
Morgan Ensberg 2008
Todd Erdos 1998-2000
Roger Erickson 1982-83
Scott Erickson 2006
Juan Espino 1982-83, 1985-86
Felix Escalona 2004-05
Alvaro Espinoza 1988-91
Bobby Estalella...........2001
Nick Etten* 1943-46
Barry Evans 1982

F (44)

Charles Fallon*...........1905
Kyle Farnsworth 2006-08
Steve Farr 1991-93
Doc Farrell* 1932-33
Sal Fasano 2006
Alex Ferguson* ... 1918, 1921, 1925
Frank Fernandez 1967-69
Tony Fernandez 1995
Mike Ferraro 1966, 1968
Wes Ferrell* 1938-39
Tom Ferrick* 1950-51
Chick Fewster* 1917-22
Cecil Fielder 1996-97
Mike Figga 1997-99
Ed Figueroa 1976-80
Pete Filson 1987
Happy Finneran*..........1918
Mike Fischlin 1986
Brian Fisher 1985-86
Gus Fisher* 1912
Ray Fisher* 1910-17
Mike Fitzgerald* 1911
John Flaherty 2003-05
Tim Foli 1984
Ray Fontenot 1983-84
Barry Foote 1981-82
Ben Ford 2000
Russ Ford* 1909-13
Whitey Ford....... 1950, 1953-67
Tony Fossas 1999
Eddie Foster* 1910
Jack Fournier* 1918
Andy Fox 1996-97
Ray Francis*.............1925
Wayne Franklin 2005
George Frazier 1981-83
Mark Freeman* 1959
Ray French* 1920
Lonny Frey* 1947-48
Bob Friend 1966
John Frill*...............1910
Bill Fulton 1987
Dave Fultz* 1903-05
Liz Funk* 1929

G (75)

John Gabler* 1959-60
Joe Gallagher*...........1939
Mike Gallego 1992-94
Oscar Gamble ... 1976, 1979-84
John Ganzel* 1903-04
Mike Garbark* 1944-45
Damaso Garcia 1978-79
Karim Garcia 2002, 2003
Billy Gardner 1961-62
Brett Gardner 2008-10
Earle Gardner 1908-12
Rob Gardner 1970-72
Ned Garvin* 1904
Milt Gaston* 1924
Chad Gaudin 2009-10
Mike Gazella* 1923, 1926-28
Joe Gedeon 1916-17
Lou Gehrig*........... 1923-39
Bob Geren 1988-91
Al Gettel* 1945-46
Jason Giambi 2002-08
Joe Giard* 1927
Jake Gibbs 1962-71
Paul Gibson 1993-94, 1996
Sam Gibson*.............1930
Dan Giese 2008
Frank Gilhooley* 1913-18
Charles Gipson 2003
Joe Girardi 1996-99
Fred Glade* 1908
Frank Gleich* 1919-20
Joe Glenn* 1932-33, 1935-38
Greg Golson 2010
Lefty Gomez* 1930-42
Jessie Gonder* 1960-61
Alberto Gonzalez 2007-08
Fernando Gonzalez 1974
Pedro Gonzalez 1963-65
Wilbur Good* 1905
Dwight Gooden ... 1996-97, 2000
Art Goodwin* 1905
Joe Gordon* 1938-43, 1946
Tom Gordon 2004-05
Tom Gorman* 1952-54
Rich Gossage 1978-83, 1989
Dick Gossett* 1913-14
Larry Gowell 1972
Johnny Grabowski* ... 1927-29
Alex Graman 2004-05
Curtis Granderson........2010
Wayne Granger 1973
Ted Gray* 1955
Eli Grba 1959-60
Nick Green 2006
Paddy Greene* 1903
Todd Greene 2001
Ken Griffey* 1982-86
Mike Griffin 1979-81
Clark Griffith* 1903-07
Bob Grim* 1954-58
Burleigh Grimes*.........1934
Oscar Grimes* 1943-46
Jason Grimsley 1999-2000
Lee Grissom* 1940
Buddy Groom 2005
Cecilio Guante 1987-88
Lee Guetterman 1988-92
Ron Guidry 1975-88
Aaron Guiel 2006
Brad Gulden 1979-80
Don Gullett 1977-78
Bill Gullickson...........1987
Randy Gumpert* 1946-48
Larry Gura 1974-75
Freddy Guzman 2009

H (112)

John Habyan* 1990-93
Bump Hadley* 1936-40
Kent Hadley*............1960
Ed Hahn* 1905-06
Noodles Hahn* 1906
Hinkey Haines* 1923
Jerry Hairston, Jr.........2009
George Halas*............1919
Bob Hale 1961
Jimmie Hall 1969
Mel Hall 1989-92
Brad Halsey 2004
Roger Hambright 1971
Steve Hamilton* 1963-70
Chris Hammond 2003
Mike Handiboe* 1911
Jim Hanley* 1913
Truck Hannah* 1918-20
Ron Hansen........... 1970-71
Harry Hanson* 1913
Jim Hardin* 1971
Bubbles Hargrave* 1930
Harry Harper* 1921
Toby Harrah.............1984
Greg Harris 1994
Joe Harris* 1914
Jim Ray Hart 1973-74
Roy Hartzell*......... 1911-16
Buddy Hassett* 1942
Ron Hassey 1985-86
Andy Hawkins 1989-91
LaTroy Hawkins..........2008
Chicken Hawks*..........1921
Charlie Hayes 1992, 1996-97
Fran Healy 1976-78
Mike Heath 1978
Neal Heaton 1993
Don Heffner* 1934-37
Mike Hegan .. 1964, '66-67, '73-74
Fred Heimach* 1928-29
Woodie Held* 1954, 1957
Charlie Hemphill* 1908-11
Rollie Hemsley* 1942-44
Bill Henderson* 1930
Rickey Henderson 1985-89
Harvey Hendrick* 1923-24
Elrod Hendricks* 1976-77
Tim Hendryx* 1915-17
Sean Henn 2005-07
Tommy Henrich* 1937-42, 1946-50
Bill Henry 1966
Drew Henson 2002-03
Felix Heredia 2003-04
Adrian Hernandez 2001-02
Leo Hernandez 1986
Michel Hernandez 2003
Orlando Hernandez 1998-2002, '04
Xavier Hernandez 1994
Ed Herrmann.............1975
Hugh High* 1915-18
Oral Hildebrand* 1939-40
Glenallen Hill 2000
Jesse Hill* 1935
Shawn Hillegas 1992
Frank Hiller* 1946, 1948-49
Mack Hillis* 1924
Eric Hinske 2009
Rich Hinton 1972
Sterling Hitchcock .. 1992-95, '01-03
Myril Hoag* 1931-32, 1934-38
Butch Hobson 1982

Rickey Henderson

Red Hoff* 1911-13
Danny Hoffman* 1906-07
Solly Hofman* 1916
Fred Hofmann* 1919-25
Bill Hogg* 1905-08
Bobby Hogue* 1951-52
Ken Holcombe* 1945
Bill Holden* 1913-14
Al Holland 1986-87
Ken Holloway* 1930
Darren Holmes 1998
Fred Holmes* 1903
Roger Holt 1980
Ken Holtzman 1976-78
Rick Honeycutt 1995
Don Hood 1979
Wally Hood* 1949
Johnny Hopp* 1950-52
Shags Horan* 1924
Ralph Houk* 1947-54
Elston Howard* 1955-67
Matt Howard 1996
Steve Howe* 1991-96
Harry Howell* 1903
Jay Howell 1982-84
Dick Howser* 1967-68
Waite Hoyt* 1921-30

Waite Hoyt

Rex Hudler 1984-85
Charlie Hudson 1987-88
Chad Huffman 2010
Keith Hughes 1987
Phil Hughes 2007-10
Long Tom Hughes* 1904
Tom Hughes* . . . 1906-07, 1909-10
John Hummel 1918
Mike Humphreys 1991-93
Ken Hunt* 1959-60
Billy Hunter 1955-56
Catfish Hunter* 1975-79
Mark Hutton 1993-94, 1996
Ham Hyatt* 1918

I (3)
Pete Incaviglia 1997
Kei Igawa 2007-08
Hideki Irabu 1997-99

J (44)
Fred Jacklitsch* 1905
Grant Jackson 1976
Reggie Jackson 1977-81
Dion James 1992-93, 95-96
Johnny James* . . . 1958, 1960-61
Stan Javier 1984
Domingo Jean 1993
Stanley Jefferson 1989
Jackie Jensen* 1950-52
Mike Jerzembeck 1998
Derek Jeter 1995-2010
D'Angelo Jimenez 1999

Elvio Jimenez 1964
Brett Jodie 2001
Tommy John . . . 1979-82, 1986-89
Alex Johnson 1974-75
Billy Johnson* 1943, 1946-51
Cliff Johnson 1977-79
Darrell Johnson* 1957-58
Deron Johnson* 1960-61
Don Johnson 1947, 1950
Ernie Johnson* 1923-25
Hank Johnson* . . 1925-26, '28-32
Jeff Johnson 1991-93
Johnny Johnson* 1944
Ken Johnson 1969
Lance Johnson 2000
Nick Johnson . . . . . . 2001-03, '10
Otis Johnson* 1911
Randy Johnson 2005-06
Roy Johnson* 1936-37
Russ Johnson 2005
Jay Johnstone 1978-79
Darryl Jones 1979
Gary Jones 1970-71
Jimmy Jones 1989-90
Ruppert Jones 1980
Sad Sam Jones* 1922-26
Tim Jordan* 1903

Art Jorgens* 1929-39
Felix Jose 2000
Jeff Juden 1999
Mike Jurewicz 1965
David Justice 2000-01

K (53)
Jim Kaat 1979-80
Scott Kamieniecki 1991-96
Bob Kammeyer 1978-79
Frank Kane* 1919
Bill Karlon* 1930
Herb Karpel* 1946
Steve Karsay 2002-05
Jeff Karstens 2006-07
Benny Kauff* 1912
Curt Kaufman 1982-83
Austin Kearns 2010
Eddie Kearse* 1942
Ray Keating* 1912-16, 1918
Bob Keefe* 1907
Willie Keeler* 1903-09
Randy Keisler 2000-01
Mike Kekich 1969-73
Charlie Keller* . . . 1939-43, '45-49, '52
Pat Kelly 1991-97
Roberto Kelly 1987-92, 2000
Steve Kemp 1983-84
Ian Kennedy 2007-09
John Kennedy 1967
Jerry Kenney 1967, 1969-72
Matt Keough 1983
Jimmy Key 1993-96

Steve Kiefer 1989
Dave Kingman 1977
Harry Kingman* 1914
Fred Kipp 1960
Frank Kitson* 1907
Ron Kittle 1986-87
Ted Kleinhans* 1936
Red Kleinow* 1904-10
Ed Klepfer* 1911, 1913
Ron Klimkowski* . . . 1969-70, 1972
Steve Kline 1970-74
Mickey Klutts 1976-78
Bill Knickerbocker* 1938-40
Brandon Knight 2001-02
John Knight* 1909-11, 1913
Chuck Knoblauch 1998-2001
Mark Koenig* 1925-30
Jim Konstanty* 1954-56
Andy Kosco 1968
Steve Kraly* 1953
Jack Kramer* 1951
Ernie Krueger* 1915
Dick Kryhoski* 1949
Tony Kubek* 1957-65
Johnny Kucks* 1955-59
Bill Kunkel* 1963
Bob Kuzava 1951-54

L (64)
Joe Lake* 1908-09
Bill Lamar* 1917-19
Hal Lanier 1972-73
Dave Lapoint 1989-90
Frank LaPorte* 1905-10
Dave LaRoche 1981-83
Don Larsen 1955-59
Lyn Lary* 1929-34
Chris Latham 2003
Marcus Lawton 1989
Matt Lawton 2005
Gene Layden* 1915
Tony Lazzeri* 1926-37
Tim Leary 1990-92
Ricky Ledee 1998-00
Travis Lee 2004
Joe Lefebvre 1980
Al Leiter 1987-89, 2005
Mark Leiter 1990
Frank Leja* 1954-55
Jack Lelivelt* 1912-13
Eddie Leon* 1975
Louis LeRoy* 1905-06
Ed Levy* 1942, 1944
Duffy Lewis* 1919-20
Jim Lewis 1982
Terry Ley* 1971
Jim Leyritz . . . 1990-96, 1999-2000
Cory Lidle* 2006
Jon Lieber 2004
Ted Lilly 2000-02
Paul Lindblad* 1978
Johnny Lindell* 1941-50
Phil Linz 1962-65
Bryan Little 1986
Jack Little* 1912
Clem Llewellyn* 1922
Graeme Lloyd 1996-98
Esteban Loaiza 2004
Gene Locklear 1976-77
Kenny Lofton 2004
Boone Logan 2010
Sherm Lollar* 1947-48
Tim Lollar 1980
Phil Lombardi 1986-87
Dale Long* 1960, 1962-63
Herman Long* 1903
Terrence Long 2000
Ed Lopat* 1948-55
Art Lopez* 1965
Hector Lopez 1959-66
Baldy Louden* 1907
Slim Love* 1916-18
Torey Lovullo 1991
Mike Lowell 1998
Johnny Lucadello* 1947
Joe Lucey* 1920
Roy Luebbe* 1925
Matt Luke 1996
Jerry Lumpe 1956-59
Scott Lusader 1991
Sparky Lyle 1972-78
Al Lyons* 1944, 1946-47
Jim Lyttle 1969-71

M (152)
Duke Maas* 1958-61
Kevin Maas 1990-93
Bob MacDonald 1995
Danny MacFayden* 1932-34
Ray Mack* 1947
Tommy Madden* 1910
Elliott Maddox 1974-76
Dave Madison* 1950
Lee Magee* 1916-17
Sal Maglie* 1957-58
Stubby Magner* 1911
Jim Magnuson* 1973
Fritz Maisel* 1913-17
Hank Majeski* 1946
Frank Makosky* 1937
Pat Malone* 1935-37
Pat Maloney* 1912
Al Mamaux* 1924
Rube Manning* 1907-10
Mickey Mantle* 1951-68
Jeff Manto 1999
Josias Manzanillo 1995
Cliff Mapes* 1948-51
Roger Maris* 1960-66
Cliff Markle* 1915-16, 1924
Jim Marquis* 1925
Armando Marsans* 1917-18
Cuddles Marshall* . . 1946, 1948-49
Sam Marsonek 2004
Damaso Marte 2008-10
Billy Martin* 1950-53, 1955-57
Hersh Martin* 1944-45
Jack Martin* 1912
Tino Martinez . . . 1996-2001, 2005
Tippy Martinez 1974-76
Jim Mason 1974-76
Vic Mata 1984-85
Hideki Matsui 2003-09
Don Mattingly 1982-95
Carlos May 1976-77
Darrell May 2005
Rudy May 1974-76, 1980-83
John Mayberry 1982
Carl Mays* 1919-23
Lee Mazzilli 1982
Larry McCall 1977-78
Joe McCarthy* 1905
Pat McCauley* 1903
Larry McClure* 1910
George McConnell* . . 1909, '12-13
Mike McCormick 1970
Lance McCullers 1989-90
Lindy McDaniel 1968-73
Mickey McDermott* 1956
Danny McDevitt* 1961
Dave McDonald 1969
Donzell McDonald 2001
Jim McDonald 1952-54
Gil McDougald* 1951-60
Jack McDowell 1995
Sam McDowell 1973-74
Lou McEvoy* 1930-31
Herm McFarland* 1903
Andy McGaffigan 1981
Lynn McGlothen* 1982
Bob McGraw* 1917-20
Deacon McGuire* 1904-07
Marty McHale* 1913-15
Irish McIlveen* 1908-09
Tim McIntosh 1996
Bill McKechnie* 1913
Rich McKinney 1972
Frank McManus* 1904
Norm McMillan* 1922
Tommy McMillan* 1912
Mike McNally* 1921-24
Herb McQuaid* 1926
George McQuinn* 1947-48
Bobby Meacham 1983-88
Charlie Meara* 1914
Jim Mecir 1996-97
George Medich 1972-75
Mark Melancon 2009-10
Bob Melvin 1994

Ramiro Mendoza*..1996-2002, 2005
Fred Merkle*.............1925-26
Andy Messersmith..........1978
Tom Metcalf................1963
Bud Metheny*...........1943-46
Hensley Meulens*.......1989-93
Bob Meusel*.............1920-29
Bob Meyer..................1964
Danny Miceli...............2003
Gene Michael............1968-74
Ezra Midkiff*...........1912-13
Doug Mientkiewicz*........2007
Pete Mikkelsen*........1964-65
Larry Milbourne........1981-83
Sam Militello...........1992-93
Bill Miller*...........1952-54
Elmer Miller*.... 1915-18, 1921-22
John Miller................1966
Alan Mills..............1990-91
Buster Mills*..............1940
Mike Milosevich*.......1944-45
Paul Mirabella.............1979
Juan Miranda...........2008-10
Willie Miranda*........1953-54
Bobby Mitchell.............1970
Fred Mitchell*.............1910
Johnny Mitchell*.......1921-22
Sergio Mitre...........2009-10
Johnny Mize*...........1949-53
Keven Mmahat...............1989
Chad Moeller..........2008, '10
George Mogridge*.......1915-20
Dale Mohorcic..........1988-89
Fenton Mole................1949
Jose Molina............2007-09
Bill Monbouquette*.....1967-68
Raul Mondesi...........2002-03
Ed Monroe*.............1917-18
Zack Monroe............1958-59
John Montefusco........1983-86
Rich Monteleone........1990-93
Archie Moore...........1964-65
Earl Moore*................1907
Wilcy Moore*... 1927-29, 1932-33
Ray Morehart*..............1927
Omar Moreno............1983-85
Mike Morgan................1982
Tom Morgan*... 1951-52, 1954-56
George Moriarty*.......1906-08
Jeff Moronko*..............1987
Hal Morris.............1988-89
Ross Moschitto........1965, 1967
Dustin Moseley.............2010
Jerry Moses................1973
Terry Mulholland...........1994
Charlie Mullen*........1914-16
Jerry Mumphrey.........1981-83
Bob Muncrief*..............1951
Bobby Munoz...............1993
Thurman Munson*........1969-79

Bobby Murcer

Bobby Murcer* 1965-66, '69-74, '79-83
Johnny Murphy*...1932,'34-43,'46
Rob Murphy................1994
Dale Murray............1983-85
George Murray*............1922
Larry Murray...........1974-76
Mike Mussina...........2001-08
Mike Myers.............2006-07

N (30)

Xavier Nady........... 2008-09
Jerry Narron...............1979
Dan Naulty.................1999
Dioner Navarro.............2004
Denny Neagle...............2000
Bots Nekola*...............1929
Gene Nelson................1981
Jeff Nelson...1996-2000, 2003
Luke Nelson*...............1919
Graig Nettles*.........1973-83
Tex Neuer*.................1907
Ernie Nevel*...........1950-51
Floyd Newkirk*.............1934
Bobo Newsom*...............1947
Doc Newton*............1905-09
Gus Niarhos*....1946, 1948-50
Joe Niekro*............1985-87
Phil Niekro*...........1984-85
Jerry Nielsen..............1992
Scott Nielsen......1986, 1988-89
Wil Nieves.............2005-07
Harry Niles*...............1908
C. J. Nitkowski*...........2004
Otis Nixon.................1983
Matt Nokes*............1990-94
Irv Noren*.............1952-56
Don Nottebart*.............1969
Ivan Nova..................2010
Les Nunamaker*.........1914-17
Eduardo Nunez..............2010

O (27)

Johnny Oates*.......... 1980-81
Mike O'Berry*..............1984
Andy O'Connor*.............1908
Jack O'Connor*.............1903
Paddy O'Connor*............1918
Heinie Odom*...............1925
Lefty O'Doul*.... 1919-20, 1922
Rowland Office.............1983
Ross Ohlendorf*.......2007-08
Bob Ojeda..................1994
Rube Oldring*.......1905, 1916
John Olerud................2004
Bob Oliver.................1975
Joe Oliver.................2001
Nate Oliver................1969
Paul O'Neill..........1993-2001
Steve O'Neill*.............1925
Jesse Orosco...............2003
Queenie O'Rourke*..........1908
Al Orth*..............1904-09
Donovan Osborne............2004
Champ Osteen*..............1904
Joe Ostrowski*........1950-52
Antonio Osuna..............2003
Bill Otis*.................1912
Stubby Overmire*...........1951
Spike Owen.................1993

Q (5)

Paul Quantrill......... 2004-05
Mel Queen*...1942, 1944, 1946-47
Ed Ouick*..................1903
Jack Ouinn*... 1909-12, 1919-21
Jamie Quirk................1989

R (83)

Tim Raines........... 1996-98
Dave Rajsich...............1978
Edwar Ramirez........ 2007-09
Bobby Ramos................1982
Domingo Ramos..............1978
John Ramos.................1991
Pedro Ramos............1964-66
Lenny Randle...............1979
Willie Randolph........1976-88
Cody Ransom........... 2008-09
Vic Raschi*...........1946-53
Dennis Rasmussen.......1984-87
Darrell Rasner........ 2006-08
Shane Rawley...........1982-84
Jeff Reardon...............1994
Tim Redding................2005
Jack Reed..............1961-63
Kevin Reese........... 2005-06
Jimmie Reese*..........1930-31
Hal Reniff*............1961-67
Bill Renna*................1953
Tony Rensa*................1933
Roger Repoz............1964-66

Chan Ho Park...............2010
Christian Parker...........2001
Clay Parker............1989-90
Ben Paschal*...........1924-29
Dan Pasqua.............1985-87
Gil Patterson..............1977
Jeff Patterson.............1995
Mike Patterson.........1981-82
Scott Patterson............2008
Carl Pavano... 2005, 2007-08
Dave Pavlas............1995-96
Monte Pearson*.........1936-40
Roger Peckinpaugh*.... 1913-21
Steve Peek*................1941
Hipolito Pena..............1988
Ramiro Pena............2009-10
Herb Pennock*.........1923-33
Joe Pepitone...........1962-69
Marty Perez................1977
Melido Perez...........1992-95
Pascual Perez..........1990-91
Robert Perez...............2001
Cecil Perkins..............1967
Cy Perkins*................1931
Gaylord Perry*.............1980
Fritz Peterson.........1966-74
Andy Pettitte...1995-2003, 2007-10
Josh Phelps................2007
Ken Phelps.............1988-89
Andy Phillips..........2004-07
Eddie Phillips*............1932
Jack Phillips..........1947-49
Cy Pieh*..............1913-15
Bill Piercy*.......1917, 1921
Duane Pillette.........1949-50
Lou Piniella...........1974-84
George Pipgras* 1923-24, 1927-33
Wally Pipp*............1915-25
Jim Pisoni*............1959-60
Eric Plunk.............1989-91
Dale Polley................1996
Luis Polonia...1989-90, '94-95, '00
Sidney Ponson....... 2006, 2008
Bob Porterfield*.......1948-51
Jorge Posada.........1995-2010
Scott Pose.................1997
Jack Powell*..........1904-05
Jake Powell*..........1936-40
Mike Powers*...............1905
Del Pratt*............1918-20
Jerry Priddy*.........1941-42
Curtis Pride...............2003
Johnny Priest*........1911-12
Bret Prinz.............2003-04
Scott Proctor.........2004-07
Alfonso Pulido.............1986
Ambrose Puttmann*..... 1903-05

Allie Reynolds

Rick Reuschel.............1981
Dave Revering.........1981-82
Al Reyes...................2003
Allie Reynolds*.......1947-54
Bill Reynolds*........1913-14
Rick Rhoden...........1987-88
Gordon Rhodes*........1929-32
Harry Rice*................1930
Bobby Richardson......1955-66
Nolen Richardson*..........1935
Branch Rickey*.............1907
Dave Righetti... 1979, 1981-90
Jose Rijo..................1984
Royce Ring.................2010
Danny Rios.................1997
Juan Rivera........... 2001-03
Mariano Rivera.......1995-2010
Ruben Rivera.......... 1995-96
Mickey Rivers......... 1976-79
Phil Rizzuto*...1941-42, 1946-56
Roxey Roach*..........1910-11
Dale Roberts*..............1967
Andre Robertson....... 1981-85
David Robertson....... 2008-10
Gene Robertson*.......1928-29
Aaron Robinson*... 1943, 1945-47
Bill Robinson.........1967-69
Bruce Robinson........1979-80
Eddie Robinson........1954-56
Hank Robinson*.............1918
Jeff Robinson..............1990
Alex Rodriguez........ 2004-10
Aurelio Rodriguez*.... 1980-81
Carlos Rodriguez...........1991
Edwin Rodriguez............1982
Ellie Rodriguez............1968
Felix Rodriguez............2005
Henry Rodriguez............2001
Ivan Rodriguez.............2008
Gary Roenicke..............1986
Oscar Roettger*.......1923-24
Jay Rogers*................1914
Kenny Rogers.......... 1996-97
Tom Rogers*................1921
Jim Roland*................1972
Red Rolfe*...... 1931, 1934-42
Buddy Rosar*..........1939-42
Larry Rosenthal*...........1944
Steve Roser*.......... 1944-46
Braggo Roth*...............1921
Jerry Royster..............1987
Muddy Ruel*...........1917-20
Dutch Ruether*........1926-27
Red Ruffing*... 1930-42, 1945-46
Allen Russell*........1915-19
Kevin Russo................2010
Marius Russo*..... 1939-43, 1946
Babe Ruth*............1920-34
Blondy Ryan*...............1935
Rosy Ryan*.................1928

P (64)

John Pacella...............1982
Del Paddock*...............1912
Juan Padilla...............2004
Dave Pagan............1973-76
Joe Page*.............1944-50
Mike Pagliarulo........1984-89
Donn Pall..................1994

S (143)

CC Sabathia........... 2009-10
Johnny Sain*..........1951-55
Lenn Sakata................1987
Mark Salas.................1987
Jack Saltzgaver*... 1932, 1934-37
Billy Sample...............1985
Celerino Sanchez*..... 1972-73
Humberto Sanchez..........2008

Rey Sanchez 1997, 2005
Romulo Sanchez 2010
Deion Sanders 1989-90
Roy Sanders* 1918
Scott Sanderson 1991-92
Charlie Sands 1967
Fred Sanford 1949-51
Rafael Santana 1988
Bronson Sardinha 2007
Don Savage* 1944-45
Rick Sawyer 1974-75
Steve Sax 1989-91
Ray Scarborough* 1952-53
Germany Schaefer* 1916
Harry Schaeffer* 1952
Roy Schalk* 1932
Art Schallock 1951-55
Wally Schang* 1921-25
Bob Schmidt 1965
Butch Schmidt* 1909
Johnny Schmitz 1952-53
Pete Schneider* 1919
Dick Schofield 1966
Paul Schreiber* 1945
Art Schult 1953
Al Schulz* 1912-14
Don Schulze 1989
Pius Schwert* 1914-15
Everett Scott* 1922-25
George Scott 1979
Rodney Scott 1982
Rod Scurry* 1985-86
Scott Seabol 2001
Ken Sears* 1943
Bob Seeds* 1936
Kal Segrist 1952
Fernando Seguignol 2003
George Selkirk* 1934-42
Ted Sepkowski* 1947
Hank Severeid* 1926
Joe Sewell* 1931-33
Richie Sexson 2008
Howard Shanks* 1925
Billy Shantz* 1960
Bobby Shantz 1957-60
Bob Shawkey* 1915-27
Spec Shea* 1947-49, 1951
Al Shealy* 1928
George Shears* 1912
Tom Sheehan* 1921
Gary Sheffield 2004-06
Rollie Sheldon . . . . 1961-62, '64-65
Skeeter Shelton* 1915
Roy Sherid* 1929-31
Pat Sheridan 1991
Dennis Sherrill 1978, 1980
Ben Shields* 1924-25
Steve Shields 1988
Bob Shirley 1983-87
Urban Shocker* . . .1916-17, 1925-28
Tom Shopay 1967, 1969
Ernie Shore* 1919-20
Bill Short 1960
Norm Siebern 1956, 1958-59
Ruben Sierra 1995-96, 2003-05
Charlie Silvera 1948-56
Dave Silvestri 1992-95
Ken Silvestri* 1941, 1946-47
Hack Simmons* 1912
Dick Simpson 1969
Harry Simpson* 1957-58
Duke Sims 1973-74
Bill Skiff* 1926
Camp Skinner* 1922
Joel Skinner 1986-88
Lou Skizas 1956
Bill Skowron 1954-62
Roger Slagle 1979
Don Slaught 1988-89
Enos Slaughter* . 1954-55, 1956-59
Aaron Small 2005-06
Roy Smalley 1982-84
Walt Smallwood* 1917, 1919
Charley Smith* 1967-68
Elmer Smith* 1922-23
Joe Smith* 1913
Keith Smith 1984-85
Klondike Smith* 1912

Lee Smith 1993
Matt Smith 2006
Harry Smythe* 1934
J.T. Snow 1992
Eric Soderholm 1980
Luis Sojo . . 1996-99, 2000-01, 2003
Tony Solaita* 1968
Alfonso Soriano 1999-2003
Steve Souchock* 1946, 1948
Jim Spencer* 1978-81
Shane Spencer 1998-2002
Charlie Spikes* 1972
Russ Springer 1992
Bill Stafford* 1960-65
Jake Stahl* 1908
Roy Staiger 1979
Tuck Stainback* 1942-45
Gerry Staley* 1955-56
Charley Stanceu* 1941, 1946
Andy Stankiewicz 1992-93
Fred Stanley 1973-80
Mike Stanley 1992-95, 1997
Mike Stanton 1997-2002, 2005
Dick Starr 1947-48
Dave Stegman 1982
Dutch Sterrett* 1912-13
Bud Stewart* 1948
Chris Stewart 2008
Lee Stine* 1938
Kelly Stinnett 2006
Snuffy Stirnweiss* 1943-50
Tim Stoddard 1986-88
Mel Stottlemyre 1964-74
Hal Stowe 1960
Darryl Strawberry 1995-99
Gabby Street* 1912
Marlin Stuart* 1954
Bill Stumpf* 1912-13
Tom Sturdivant* 1955-59
Johnny Sturm* 1941
Tanyon Sturtze 2004-06
Bill Sudakis 1974
Steve Sundra* 1936, 1938-40

Dale Sveum 1998
Ed Sweeney* 1908-15
Nick Swisher 2009-10
Ron Swoboda 1971-73

T (54)
Fred Talbot* 1966-69
Vito Tamulis* 1934-35
Frank Tanana 1993
Jesse Tannehill* 1903
Tony Tarasco 1999
Danny Tartabull 1992-95
Wade Taylor 1991
Zack Taylor* 1934
Mark Teixeira 2009-10
Frank Tepedino . . . 1967, 1969-72
Walt Terrell 1989
Ralph Terry 1956-57, 1959-64
Jay Tessmer 1998-00, 2002
Dick Tettelbach* 1955
Bob Tewksbury 1986-87
Marcus Thames . . . . . . .2002, '10
Ira Thomas* 1906-07
Lee Thomas 1961
Myles Thomas* 1926-29
Stan Thomas 1977
Gary Thomasson 1978
Homer Thompson* 1912
Kevin Thompson 2006-07
Ryan Thompson 2000
Tommy Thompson* 1912
Jack Thoney* 1904
Hank Thormahlen* 1917-20
Marv Throneberry* . . 1955, 1958-59
Mike Thurman 2002
Luis Tiant 1979-80
Dick Tidrow 1974-79
Bobby Tiefenauer* 1965
Eddie Tiemeyer* 1909
Ray Tift* 1907
Bob Tillman* 1967
Thad Tillotson 1967-68

Dan Tipple* 1915
Wayne Tolleson 1986-90
Brett Tomko 2009
Earl Torgeson* 1961
Rusty Torres 1971-72
Mike Torrez 1977
Cesar Tovar* 1976
Josh Towers 2009
Billy Traber 2008
Bubba Trammell 2003
Tom Tresh* 1961-69
Gus Triandos 1953-54
Steve Trout 1987
Virgil Trucks* 1958
Frank Truesdale* 1914
Bob Turley 1955-62
Chris Turner 2000
Jim Turner* 1942-45

U (4)
George Uhle* 1933-34
Tom Underwood* 1980-81
Bob Unglaub* 1904
Cecil Upshaw* 1974

V (20)
Elmer Valo* 1960
Russ Van Atta* 1933-35
Dazzy Vance* 1915, 1918
Joe Vance* 1937-38
John Vander Wal 2002
Bobby Vaughn* 1909
Hippo Vaughn* . . . 1908, 1910-12
Javier Vazquez . . . . .2004, '10
Bobby Veach* 1925
Randy Velarde . . . 1987-1995, 2001
Otto Velez 1973-76
Mike Vento 2005
Robin Ventura 2002-03
Jose Veras 2006-09
Joe Verbanic 1967-68, 1970
Frank Verdi* 1953

Yankees Serving Their Country

The following Yankees lost Major League service time for military service:

Rich Beck 1967
Norm Branch 1943-45
Bobby Brown 1952-54
Tommy Byrne 1944-45
Tommy Carroll 1958
Jerry Coleman 1952-53
Bill Dickey 1944-45
Joe DiMaggio 1943-45
Frank Fernandez .1967
Whitey Ford 1951-52
Joe Gordon 1944-45
Randy Gumpert 1943-45
Buddy Hassett 1943-45
Mike Hegan 1967
Rollie Hemsley 1945
Tommy Henrich 1943-45
Billy Johnson 1944-46
Jerry Kenney 1968
Tony Kubek 1962
Al Lyons 1945
Hank Majeski 1943-45
Billy Martin 1954-55
Tom Morgan 1952-53
Ross Moschitto 1966
Bobby Murcer 1967-68
Steve Peck 1942-45
Mel Queen 1945-46
Phil Rizzuto 1943-45
Araron Robinson .1944
Red Ruffing 1943-44
Marius Russo 1944-45
Ken Sears 1944-45
George Selkirk 1943-45
Ken Silvestri 1942-45
Charley Stanceu 1943-44
Johnny Sturm 1942-45
Jake Wade 1945
Roy Weatherly 1944-45
Bob Wiesler 1951-52
Butch Wensloff 1945-46

Phil Rizzuto is one of 40 Yankees that lost Major League service for military service.

Sammy Vick* 1917-20
Ron Villone 2006-07
Jose Vizcaino 2000
Luis Vizcaino 2007

W (96)

Jake Wade* 1946
Dick Wakefied* 1950
Jim Walewander 1990
Curt Walker* 1919
Dixie Walker* 1931, 1933-36
Mike Wallace 1974-75
Jimmy Walsh* 1914
Joe Walsh* 1910-11
Roxy Walters* 1915-18
Danny Walton 1971
Paul Waner* 1944-45
Chien-Ming Wang 2005-09
Jack Wanner* 1909
Pee Wee Wanninger* 1925
Aaron Ward* 1917-26
Gary Ward 1987-89
Joe Ward* 1909
Pete Ward 1970
Jack Warhop* 1908-15
George Washburn* 1941
Claudell Washington . 1986-88, '90
Gary Waslewski 1970-71
Allen Watson 1999-2000
Bob Watson 1980-82
Roy Weatherly* 1943, 1946
David Weathers 1996-97
Jeff Weaver 2002-03
Jim Weaver* 1931
Dave Wehrmeister 1981
Lefty Weinert* 1931
David Wells 1997-98, 2002-03
Ed Wells* 1929-32
Butch Wensloff* 1943, 1947
Julie Wera* 1927, 1929
Billy Werber* 1930, 1933
Dennis Werth 1979-81
Jake Westbrook 2000
John Wetteland 1995-96
Stefan Wever 1982
Steve Whitaker 1966-68
Gabe White 2003-04
Rondell White 2002
Roy White 1965-79
Wally Whitehurst 1996
George Whiteman* 1913
Mark Whiten 1997
Terry Whitfield 1974-76
Ed Whitson 1985-86
Kemp Wicker* 1936-38
Al Wickland* 1919
Bob Wickman 1992-96
Chris Widger 2002
Bob Wiesler 1951, 1954-55
Bill Wight* 1946-47
Ted Wilborn 1980
Ed Wilkinson* 1911
Bernie Williams 1991-2006
Bob Williams* 1911-13
Gerald Williams . 1992-96, 2001-02
Harry Williams* 1913-14
Jimmy Williams* 1903-07
Stan Williams 1963-64
Todd Williams 2001
Walt Williams 1974-75
Archie Wilson* 1951-52
Enrique Wilson 2001-04
George Wilson* 1956
Craig Wilson 2006

Kris Wilson 2006
Pete Wilson* 1908-09
Snake Wiltse* 1903
Gordie Windhorn 1959
Dave Winfield 1981-90
Randy Winn 2010
Jay Witasick 2001
Mickey Witek* 1949
Mike Witt 1990-91, 1993
Whitey Witt* 1922-25
Mark Wohlers 2001
Bill Wolfe* 1903-04
Harry Wolter* 1910-13
Harry Wolverton* 1912
Dooley Womack 1966-68
Tony Womack 2005
Kerry Wood 2010
Gene Woodling* 1949-54
Ron Woods 1969-71
Dick Woodson 1974
Hank Workman 1950
Chase Wright 2007
Jaret Wright 2005-06
Ken Wright 1974
Yats Wuestling* 1930
John Wyatt* 1968
Butch Wynegar 1982-86
Jimmy Wynn 1977

X (0)

Y (5)

Ed Yarnall 1999-2000
Joe Yeager* 1905-06
Jim York 1976
Curt Young 1992
Ralph Young* 1913

Z (8)

Tom Zachary* 1928-30
Jack Zalusky* 1903
George Zeber 1977-78
Rollie Zeider* 1913
Todd Zeile 2003
Guy Zinn* 1911-12
Bill Zuber* 1943-46
Paul Zuvella 1986-87

PASSINGS SINCE LAST PUBLICATION

NYY PLAYERS & COACHES

Oscar Azocar	Gil McDougald
Ryne Duren	Dale Roberts
Ken Holcombe	Jim Roland
Ralph Houk	Tom Underwood
Clyde King	Frank Verdi
Danny McDevitt	

YANKEES EXECUTIVES AND FAMILY

Stanley Kay
Dick Kraft
Shirley Martinez
Marion Merrill
Cora Rizzuto
Freddy "Sez" Schuman
Bill Shannon
Bob Sheppard
George M. Steinbrenner III
Christina-Taylor Green

All-Time Yankees Captains

1.	Hal Chase	1912
2.	Roger Peckinpaugh	1914-1921
3.	Babe Ruth	5/20/22-5/25/22
4.	Everett Scott	1922-1925
5.	Lou Gehrig	4/21/35-6/2/41
6.	Thurman Munson	4/17/76-8/2/79
7.	Graig Nettles	1/29/82-3/30/84
8.	Willie Randolph	3/4/86-10/2/88
9.	Ron Guidry	3/4/86-7/12/89
10.	Don Mattingly	2/28/91-1995
11.	**DEREK JETER**	6/3/03-PRESENT

Coaches Roster

Available records show that 115 men have served as a coach for the Yankees through the 2010 season.

*Deceased

A (2)

Neil Allen 2005
Joe Altobelli 1981-82, 1986

B (8)

Loren Babe* 1967
Vern Benson* 1965-66
Yogi Berra .... 1963, '76-83
Larry Bowa 2006-07
Clete Boyer* .... 1988, '92-94
Cloyd Boyer* 1975, 1977
Jimmy Burke* 1931-33
Brian Butterfield 1994-95

C (11)

Jose Cardenal 1996-99
Chris Chambliss ..... 1988, '96-2000
Tony Cloninger 1992-2001
Earle Combs* 1936-44
Mark Connor . 1984-85, '86-87, '90-93
Billy Connors .... 1989-90, '94-95, 2000
Nardi Contreras 1995
Pat Corrales 1989
John Corriden* 1947-48
Bobby Cox 1977
Frank Crosetti* 1946-68

D (6)

Tom Daly* 1914
Cot Deal* 1965
Gary Denbo 2001
Bill Dickey* .... 1949-57, '60
Rick Down 1993-95, 2002-03
Chuck Dressen* 1947-48

E (4)

Dave Eiland 2008-10
Lee Elia 1989
Sammy Ellis .... 1982-84, '86
Darrell Evans 1990

F (6)

Duke Farrell* .... 1909, '11, '15-17
Mike Ferraro .... 1979-82, '87-91
Art Fletcher* 1927-45
Whitey Ford .... 1964, '68, '74-75
Art Fowler* .... 1977-79, '83,88
Charlie Fox* 1989

G (4)

Joe Girardi 2005
Jimmy Gleeson* 1964
Ron Guidry 2006-07
Randy Gumpert* 1957

H (10)

Mike Harkey 2008-10
Jim Hegan* .... 1960-73, '79-80
Tommy Henrich* 1951
Marc Hill 1991
Doug Holmquist* 1984-85
Willie Horton 1985
Ralph Houk .... 1953-54, '58-60
Elston Howard* 1969-79
Frank Howard .... 1989, '91-93
Dick Howser* 1969-78

K (4)

Mick Kelleher 2009-10
Charlie Keller* 1957, 1959
Joe Kerrigan 2006-07
Clyde King* .... 1978, '81-82, '88

L (5)

Charlie Lau* 1979-81
Bob Lemon* 1976
Dale Long* 1963
Kevin Long 2007-10
Eddie Lopat* 1960

M (15)

Mickey Mantle* 1970
Harry Mathews* 1929
Don Mattingly 2004-07
Lee Mazzilli .... 2000-03, '06
Jerry McNertney 1984
Bobby Meacham 2008
Fred Merkle* 1925-26
Stump Merrill .... 1985, '87
Russ "Monk" Meyer* 1992
Gene Michael ..... 1976, '78, '84-86,
.... '88-89
George Mitterwald 1988
Bill Monbouquette 1985-86
Rich Monteleone 2002-04
Tom Morgan* 1979
Wally Moses* .... 1961-62, '66

N (4)

Ed Napoleon 1992-93
Graig Nettles 1991
Tom Nieto 2000-02
Johnny Neun* 1944-46

O (2)

Paddy O'Connor* 1918-19
Charlie O'Leary* 1921-30

P (4)

Tony Pena 2006-10
Joe Pepitone 1982
Cy Perkins* 1932-33
Lou Piniella 1984-85

R (3)

Willie Randolph 1994-2004
Red Rolfe* 1946
Frank Roth* 1921-22

S (13)

Johnny Sain* 1961-63
Germany Schaefer* 1916
Paul Schreiber* .... 1942, '45
John Schulte* 1934-48
Joe Sewell* 1934-35
Bob Shawkey* 1929
Glenn Sherlock 1995
Buck Showalter 1990-91
Luis Sojo 2004-05
Joe Sparks 1990
John Stearns 1989
Mel Stottlemyre 1996-2005
Champ Summers 1989-90

T (5)

Rob Thomson 2008-10
Jeff Torborg 1979-88
Earl Torgeson* 1961
Gary Tuck 1997-99, 2003-04
Jim Turner* .... 1949-59, '66-73

V (1)

Mickey Vernon* 1982

W (7)

Jerry Walker* 1981-82
Lee Walls* 1983
Jay Ward 1987
Roy White ... 1983-84, '86, 2004-05
Stan Williams .... 1980-82, '87-88
George Wiltse* 1925
Mel Wright* 1974-75

Z (1)

Don Zimmer .... 1983, '86, '96-03

Yankees by the Numbers

In 1929, the New York Yankees and Cleveland Indians became the first teams to make numbers a permanent part of the uniform. Other teams quickly adopted the idea and, by 1932, uniform numbers became standard for all teams. The Yankees' initial distribution of numbers was made according to the player's spot in the batting order. Therefore, in 1929, leadoff hitter Earle Combs wore No. 1; Mark Koenig No. 2; Babe Ruth No. 3; Lou Gehrig No. 4; Bob Meusel No. 5; Tony Lazzeri No. 6; Leo Durocher No. 7; Johnny Grabowski No. 8; Benny Bengough No. 9; and Bill Dickey No. 10 (Grabowski, Bengough and Dickey shared catching duties). After some exhaustive research, the Yankees' Media Relations staff compiled the following list of Yankees uniform numbers. The list represents uniform numbers worn by coaches (c), managers (m) and players who officially appeared in a regular season game. Yankees retired numbers are denoted in boldface text.

Yogi Berra (No. 8) congratulates Roger Maris on hitting his 61st home run on Oct. 1, 1961.

1

Earle Combs 1929-35
George Selkirk 1934
Roy Johnson 1936
Frank Crosetti 1937-44
Tuck Stainback 1944
Snuffy Stirnweiss 1945-50
Billy Martin 1951-57
Bobby Richardson 1958-66
Bobby Murcer 1969-74
Billy Martin (m) 1975-79,
. . . .'83, '85, '88

2

Mark Koenig 1929-30
Yats Wuestling 1930
Lyn Lary 1931-34
Red Rolfe 1931, 1934-42
Snuffy Stirnweiss 1943-44
Frank Crosetti 1945-46
Frank Crosetti (c) 1947-68
Jerry Kenney 1969-72

3

Babe Ruth 1929-34
George Selkirk 1935-42
Bud Metheny 1943-46
Eddie Bockman 1946
Roy Weatherly 1946
Allie Clark 1947
Frank Colman 1947
Cliff Mapes 1948

Matty Alou 1973
Sandy Alomar 1974-76
Paul Blair 1977-79
Darryl Jones 1979
Bobby Murcer 1979-83
Graig Nettles 1983
Tim Foli 1984
Dale Berra 1985-86
Wayne Tolleson 1986-90
Graig Nettles 1991
Mike Gallego 1992-94
Derek Jeter 1995-2010

4

Lou Gehrig 1929-39

5

Bob Meusel 1929
Tony Lazzeri 1930-31
Frank Crosetti 1932-36
Nolen Richardson 1935
Joe DiMaggio . . . 1937-42, '46-51
Nick Etten 1943-45

6

Tony Lazzeri 1929, 1934-37
Dusty Cooke 1930-31
Ben Chapman 1932-33
Joe Gordon . . . . 1938-43, '46
Don Savage 1944-45
Bobby Brown 1947-52
Mickey Mantle 1951
Andy Carey 1952-60
Deron Johnson 1960-61
Clete Boyer 1961-66
Charley Smith 1967-68
Roy White 1969-79
Brad Gulden 1980
Ken Griffey 1982
Roy White (c) . . . . . . 1983-84, '86
Mike Pagliarulo 1985
Rick Cerone 1987
Jack Clark 1988
Clete Boyer (c) 1988, 1992-94
Steve Sax 1989-91
Tony Fernandez 1995
Joe Torre (m) 1996-2007

7

Leo Durocher 1929
Ben Chapman . . . . . 1930-31,'34-36
Jack Saltzgaver 1932
Tony Lazzeri 1933
Jake Powell 1936-38
Tommy Henrich 1939-42
Roy Cullenbine 1942
Billy Johnson 1943
Oscar Grimes 1944-46
Bobby Brown 1946
Aaron Robinson 1946
Chuck Dressen (c) 1947-48
Cliff Mapes 1949-51
Bob Cerv 1951
Mickey Mantle 1951-68
Mickey Mantle (c) 1970

8

Johnny Grabowski 1929
Bill Dickey 1930-43
Johnny Lindell 1944-45
Aaron Robinson . . . . 1945, '47
Frank Colman 1946
Bill Dickey (m) 1946
Yogi Berra 1948-63
Yogi Berra (c) . . . . 1963, '76-83
Yogi Berra (m) . . . . . 1964, '84-85

9

Benny Bengough 1929
Bubbles Hargrave 1930
Cy Perkins 1931
Art Jorgens 1932-35
Joe Glenn 1933
Joe DiMaggio 1936
Myril Hoag 1937-38
Charlie Keller . . . . .1939-43, '45, '49
Ed Levy 1944
Tuck Stainback 1944
Hersh Martin 1944-45
Nick Etten 1946
Aaron Robinson 1946
George McQuinn 1947-48
Dick Wakefield 1950
Hank Workman 1950
Jim Brideweser 1951
Bobby Brown 1951
Hank Bauer 1952-59
Roger Maris 1960-66
Steve Whitaker 1968
Dick Simpson 1969
Ron Woods 1969-71
Graig Nettles 1973-82

10

Bill Dickey 1929
Benny Bengough 1930
Art Jorgens 1931
Tony Rensa 1933
George Pipgras 1932-33
Don Heffner 1934-37
Bill Knickerbocker 1938-40
Phil Rizzuto . . . . 1941-42, '46-56
Roy Weatherly 1943
Mike Garbark 1944-45
Tony Kubek 1958-65
Dick Howser 1967-68
Frank Fernandez 1969
Danny Cater 1970-71
Celerino Sanchez 1972-73
Chris Chambliss 1974-79
Rick Cerone 1980-84

11

Herb Pennock 1929
Ownie Carroll 1930
Waite Hoyt 1930
Lefty Gomez 1932-42
Tommy Byrne 1943
Rip Collins 1944
Joe Page 1945-50
Johnny Sain 1951-55
Jerry Lumpe 1956-59
Hector Lopez 1959-66
Bill Robinson 1967-69
Danny Walton 1971
Bernie Allen 1972-73
Fred Stanley 1973-80
Sandy Alomar 1974
Gene Michael (m) 1981-82
Jeff Torborg (c) 1983
Toby Harrah 1984
Billy Sample 1985
Gary Roenicke 1986
Lenn Sakata 1987
Don Slaught 1988-89
Rick Cerone 1990

Derek Jeter wears No. 2.

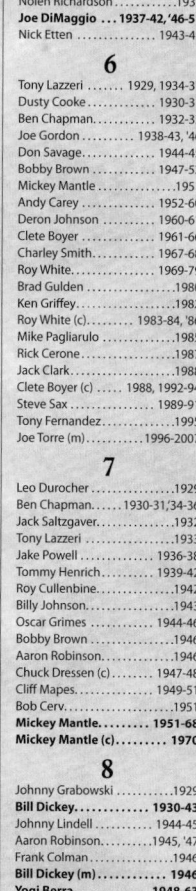

Buck Showalter (c) 1991
Buck Showalter (m) 1992-95
Dwight Gooden. 1996-97
Chuck Knoblauch 1998-2001
Chris Widger 2002
Erick Almonte. 2003
David Dellucci 2003
Curtis Pride 2003
Gary Sheffield. 2004-06
Doug Mientkiewicz 2007
Morgan Ensberg 2008
Brett Gardner 2008-10

12

Waite Hoyt. 1929
George Pipgras 1930-31
Herb Pennock. 1932-33
Jack Saltzgaver. 1934-37
Babe Dahlgren. 1938-40
Buddy Rosar 1941-42
Oscar Grimes 1943
Mike Milosevich. 1944
Joe Buzas 1945
Charlie Keller 1945-49
Vic Raschi 1946
Ralph Buxton 1949
Billy Martin 1950
Gil McDougald. 1951-60
Billy Gardner 1961-62
Mike Hegan. 1964
Phil Linz 1965
Ruben Amaro 1966-68
Billy Cowan 1969
Ron Blomberg 1969, 1971-77
Jim Spencer. 1978-81
Dave Revering 1981-82
Roy Smalley 1983-84
Ron Hassey 1985-86
Joel Skinner. 1986-88
Tom Brookens 1989
Alvaro Espinoza 1990
Jim Leyritz . . . . 1990-92, '99
Torey Lovullo 1991
Carlos Rodriguez. 1991
Wade Boggs 1993-97
Roger Clemens. 1999
Denny Neagle 2000
Clay Bellinger 2001
Alfonso Soriano 2002-03
Kenny Lofton 2004
Tony Womack 2005
Andy Phillips. 2006-07
Kevin Thompson 2007
Alberto Gonzalez 2008
Ivan Rodriguez. 2008
Cody Ransom 2009
Josh Towers 2009
Eduardo Nunez 2010

13

Spud Chandler. 1937
Lee Stine. 1938
Cliff Mapes. 1948
Curt Blefary 1970-71
Walt Williams 1974-75
Bobby Brown 1980-81
Keith Smith 1985
Mike Pagliarulo 1986-89
Mike Blowers 1989
Alvaro Espinoza 1990
Torey Lovullo 1991
Gerald Williams 1992
Jim Leyritz . . . . . .1993-96, '99-2000
Charlie Hayes 1997
Willie Banks. 1998
Mike Figga 1998-99
Jeff Manto 1999
Jose Vizcaino. 2000
Michael Coleman 2001
Lee Mazzilli (c) 2002
Antonio Osuna. 2003
Alex Rodriguez. 2004-10

14

George Pipgras 1929
Hank Johnson 1930-31
Ed Wells 1932
Russ Van Atta 1933-35
Bump Hadley 1936-40
Jerry Priddy 1941-42
Butch Wensloff. 1943
Monk Dubiel 1944-45
Bill Bevens 1946
Cuddles Marshall. 1946
Rugger Ardizoia. 1947
Ted Sepkowski 1947
Lonny Frey 1947-48
Jerry Coleman 1948
Gene Woodling 1949-54
Bill Skowron 1955-62
Harry Bright 1963-64
Pedro Ramos 1964-66
Jerry Kenney 1967
Bobby Cox 1968-69
Ron Swoboda 1971-73
Lou Piniella 1974-84
Lou Piniella (c) 1984-85
Lou Piniella (m) 1986-88
Mike Blowers 1991
Pat Kelly 1991-97
Hideki Irabu 1998-99
Wilson Delgado 2000
Luis Sojo. 2000
Joe Oliver. 2001
Enrique Wilson 2001-04
Robinson Cano 2005
Russ Johnson 2005

Spud Chandler wore No. 13 in 1937.

Andy Phillips. 2005
Miguel Cairo 2006
Kevin Thompson 2007
Matt DeSalvo 2007
Wilson Betemit. 2007-08
Angel Berroa 2009
Eric Hinske 2009
Curtis Granderson. 2010

15

Hank Johnson 1929
Art Jorgens 1929
Roy Sherid 1930-31
Red Ruffing . . . . 1932-42, '46
Hank Borowy 1943-45
Charlie Keller 1945
Tommy Henrich 1946-50
Tommy Henrich (c) 1951
Archie Wilson 1952
Joe Collins 1953-57
Jim Pisoni 1959-60
Jack Reed 1961
Tom Tresh 1961-69
Thurman Munson. 1969-79

16

Tom Zachary 1929-30
Herb Pennock. 1930-31
Gordon Rhodes 1932
Wilcy Moore 1932-33
Jimmy DeShong 1934-35
Monte Pearson. 1936-40
Johnny Lindell 1941
Tuck Stainback 1942-43
Joe Page 1944
Mel Queen 1944
Herb Crompton 1945
Frank Hiller 1946
Charley Stanceu. 1946
Bill Bevens 1946-47
Ernie Nevel 1950
Whitey Ford 1953-67
Whitey Ford (c) . .1964, '68, '74-75

17

Fred Heimach 1929
Ed Wells 1930-31
Hank Johnson 1932
Danny MacFayden 1932-34
Jumbo Brown 1935-36
Babe Dahlgren. 1937
Tommy Henrich 1938-39
Jake Powell 1939-40
Buster Mills 1940
Charley Stanceu. 1941
Ed Levy 1942
Bill Zuber 1943-46
Mel Queen 1946-47
Vic Raschi 1947-53

Enos Slaughter. 1954-59
Bobby Richardson. 1955-56
Elmer Valo 1960
Bob Cerv. 1960-62
Lee Thomas 1961
Bobby Murcer 1965-66
Tom Shopay 1967
Gene Michael 1968-74
Mickey Rivers 1976-79
Oscar Gamble. 1979-84
Vic Mata 1985
Mike Easler 1986-87
Paul Zuvella. 1987
Rafael Santana 1988
Bucky Dent (m) 1989
Claudell Washington 1990
Scott Lusader 1991
Pat Sheridan 1991
Andy Stankiewicz 1992
Spike Owen 1993
Luis Polonia 1994-95
Ruben Rivera 1995
Kenny Rogers 1996-97
Dale Sveum. 1998
Ricky Ledee 1999-2000
Dwight Gooden. 2000
Darren Bragg 2001
Gerald Williams 2001-02
Alex Arias 2002
John Flaherty 2003-05
Nick Green. 2006
Chris Basak 2007
Jeff Karstens 2007
Shelley Duncan 2007-08
Justin Christian 2008
Steven Jackson 2009
Kevin Cash. 2009
Jerry Hairston, Jr. 2009
Chad Moeller 2010
Lance Berkman 2010

18

Wilcy Moore 1929
Bill Henderson 1930
Lou McEvoy. 1930
Tom Zachary 1930
Red Ruffing 1931
Johnny Allen 1932-35
Art Jorgens 1936-39
Steve Peek 1941
Johnny Lindell 1942-43
Johnny Johnson 1944
Tuck Stainback. 1945
Karl Drews 1946
Randy Gumpert. 1946-48
Bob Porterfield. 1948-50
Fenton Mole 1949
Dave Madison 1950
Jack Kramer. 1951

Thurman Munson's No. 15 was retired in 1979.

Tino Martinez wore No. 24.

Russ Davis 1994-95
Tino Martinez ...... 1996-2001, '05
Ruben Sierra 2003-04
Sidney Ponson 2006
Robinson Cano 2007-10

25

Ben Paschal 1929
Jimmie Reese 1930
Sammy Byrd 1933-34
Jesse Hill 1935
Ted Kleinhans 1936
Kemp Wicker 1936-37
Joe Vance 1937-38
Wes Ferrell 1938-39
Marius Russo 1939
Steve Sundra 1940
Eddie Kearse 1942
Aaron Robinson 1943
Larry Rosenthal 1944
Al Gettel 1945-46
Ray Mack 1947
Butch Wensloff 1947
Hank Bauer 1948-51
Jackie Jensen 1952
Irv Noren 1952-56
Zeke Bella 1957
Norm Siebern 1958-59
Kent Hadley 1960
Dale Long 1960
Jesse Gonder 1961
Joe Pepitone 1962-69
Pete Ward 1970
Len Boehmer 1971
Johnny Callison 1972-73
Bobby Bonds 1975
Grant Jackson 1976
Willie Randolph 1976
George Zeber 1977-78
Brian Doyle 1978
Tommy John ...... 1979-82, '86-89
Stefan Wever 1982
Don Baylor 1983-85
Greg Cadaret 1989-92
Jim Abbott 1993-94
Scott Bankhead 1995
Ruben Sierra 1995-96
Cecil Fielder 1996
Ruben Sierra 1996
Joe Girardi 1996-99
Chris Turner 2000
Randy Velarde 2001
Jason Giambi 2002-08
Mark Teixeira 2009-10

26

Cedric Durst 1929
Sammy Byrd 1930
Jimmie Reese 1931
Joe Glenn 1932, 1935-38
George Uhle 1933-34
Johnny Broaca 1934
Buddy Rosar 1939-40
Ken Silvestri 1941
Ken Sears 1943
Steve Roser .... 1944, '46
Mike Milosevich 1945
Bill Drescher 1946
Karl Drews 1946
Marius Russo 1946
Don Johnson .... 1947, '50
Hugh Casey 1949
Tom Ferrick 1950-51
Ernie Nevel 1951
Art Schallock 1951
Gus Triandos 1953-54
Ryne Duren 1958-61
Tex Clevenger 1961-62
Dale Long 1962-63
Archie Moore 1964-65
John Kennedy 1967
John Miller 1966
Mike Ferraro 1968
Jimmie Hall 1969
Ron Klimkowski 1969
Frank Baker 1970-71
Fernando Gonzalez 1974
Rich Coggins 1975-76
Juan Bernhardt 1976
Cesar Tovar 1976
Domingo Ramos 1978

Tommy Byrne wore No. 28 from 1946-51 and again in 1954.

Juan Beniquez 1979
Johnny Oates 1980-81
Shane Rawley 1982-84
Neil Allen 1985
John Montefusco 1985-86
Joe Niekro 1985-86
Ivan DeJesus 1986
Bryan Little 1986
Paul Zuvella 1986
Rick Rhoden 1987-88
Stan Jefferson 1989
Steve Kiefer 1989
Jimmy Jones 1989-90
Steve Farr 1991-93
Daryl Boston 1994
Kevin Elster 1995
Darryl Strawberry 1995
Andy Fox 1996-97
Homer Bush 1997
Scott Pose 1997
Rey Sanchez 1997, 2005
Orlando Hernandez .... 1998-'02, '04
Mark Bellhorn 2005
Sal Fasano 2006
Koyie Hill 2006
Terrence Long 2006
Wil Nieves 2006-07
Jose Molina 2007-09
Nick Johnson 2010
Kevin Russo 2010
Greg Golson 2010
Austin Kearns 2010

27

Sammy Byrd 1929
Cedric Durst 1930
Joe Sewell 1931
Myril Hoag 1932
Dixie Walker 1933-36
Zack Taylor 1934
Blondy Ryan 1935
Spud Chandler 1939
Joe Gallagher 1939
Lee Grissom 1940
Buster Mills 1940
Frenchy Bordagaray 1941
Mike Chartak 1942
Rollie Hemsley 1943-44
Russ Derry 1945
Johnny Lindell 1946-50
Lew Burdette 1950
Jackie Jensen 1951
Tom Morgan 1951
Jim Brideweser 1952-53
Bobby Brown 1954
Marlin Stuart 1954
Woodie Held .... 1954, '57
Bobby Del Greco 1957-58
Johnny James 1958
Jesse Gonder 1960
Frank Leja 1960
Jack Reed 1962-63

Duke Carmel 1965
Dick Schofield 1966
Tom Shopay .... 1967, '69
Jim Lyttle 1970-71
Rich McKinney 1972
Elliott Maddox 1974-76
Marty Perez 1977
Dell Alston 1977-78
Jay Johnstone 1978-79
Brad Gulden 1979
Darryl Jones 1979
Bobby Murcer 1979
Paul Blair 1980
Aurelio Rodriguez 1980-81
Butch Wynegar 1982-86
Keith Hughes 1987
Mark Salas 1987
Neil Allen 1988
Mel Hall 1989-92
Bob Wickman 1993-96
Graeme Lloyd 1996-98
Tony Fossas 1999
Allen Watson 1999-2000
Rondell White 2002
Luis Sojo 2003
Todd Zeile 2003
Kevin Brown 2004-05
Kevin Reese 2006
Kevin Thompson 2006
Darrell Rasner 2007
Joe Girardi (m) 2008-09
Kevin Russo 2010
Colin Curtis 2010
Greg Golson 2010

28

Liz Funk 1929
Art Jorgens 1930
Myril Hoag 1931, 1934-36
Ivy Andrews 1932
Joe Glenn 1933
Babe Dahlgren 1937
Frank Makosky 1937
Atley Donald 1938-45
Spud Chandler 1944-45
Hank Majeski 1946
Tommy Byrne .... 1946-51, '54
Bill Wight 1947
Tom Morgan 1951-52, 1954-56
Charlie Keller 1952
Bill Renna 1953
Art Ditmar 1957-61
Bud Daley 1961-64
Gil Blanco 1965
Steve Whitaker 1966-67
Andy Kosco 1968
Thurman Munson 1969
Ron Hansen 1970-71
Sparky Lyle 1972-78
Mike Griffin 1979
Bob Watson 1980-82

John Mayberry 1982
Steve Balboni 1983
Bill Monbouquette (c) 1985
Rod Scurry 1986
Henry Cotto 1987
Jerry Royster 1987
Al Leiter 1988-89
Jesse Barfield 1989
Marcus Lawton 1989
Hensley Meulens 1989
Dale Mohorcic 1989
Hal Morris 1989
Dave Eiland .... 1989, '91
Brian Dorsett 1990
Alan Mills 1990
Charlie Hayes 1992
Andy Stankiewicz 1993
Scott Kamieniecki 1993-96
Ruben Rivera 1996
Chad Curtis 1997-99
David Justice 2000-01
John Vander Wal 2002
Karim Garcia 2003
Charles Gipson 2003
Chris Latham 2003
Esteban Loaiza 2004
Ruben Sierra 2005
Melky Cabrera 2006-08
Anthony Claggett 2009
Brett Tomko 2009
Shelley Duncan 2009
Joe Girardi (m) 2010

29

Bob Shawkey (c) 1929
Lou McEvoy 1930
Bob Shawkey (m) 1930
Sammy Byrd 1931
Art Fletcher (c) 1932-39
George Washburn 1941
Oscar Grimes 1943
Bill Bevens 1944
Bill Drescher 1945-46
Johnny Murphy 1946
Steve Souchock 1946
Charley Stanceu 1946
Johnny Lucadello 1947
Sherm Lollar 1947-48
Charlie Silvera 1949-56
Bobby Richardson 1957
Fritz Brickell 1958-59
Hal Stowe 1960
Duke Maas 1961
Earl Torgeson (c) 1961
Hal Brown 1962
Tom Metcalf 1963
Mike Jurewicz 1965
Bobby Tiefenauer 1965
Bill Henry 1966
Rocky Colavito 1968
Mike McCormick 1970
Jim Hardin 1971
Wade Blasingame 1972
Casey Cox 1973
Sam McDowell 1973
Tom Buskey 1973-74
Dick Woodson 1974
Catfish Hunter 1975-79
Dave Collins 1982
Bob Shirley 1983-87
Al Holland 1987
Paul Zuvella 1987
Randy Velarde 1987-88
Luis Aguayo 1988
Dave LaPoint 1989
Jesse Barfield 1989-92
Mike Humphreys 1993
Andy Stankiewicz 1993
Gerald Williams 1994-96
Ricky Bones 1996
Mike Stanton ...... 1997-2002, '05
Bubba Trammell 2003
Tony Clark 2004
Felix Escalona 2005
Tim Redding 2005
Octavio Dotel 2006
Kei Igawa 2007-08
Xavier Nady 2008
Cody Ransom 2008
Juan Miranda 2009
Francisco Cervelli 2009-10

30

Bots Nekola	1929
Gordon Rhodes	1929
Art Fletcher (c)	1930-31
Jimmy Burke (c)	1932
Cy Perkins (c)	1933
Joe Sewell (c)	1934-35
Earle Combs (c)	1936-39
Mike Chartak	1940
Norm Branch	1941-42
Jim Turner	1942-45
Bill Wight	1946
Dick Starr	1947
Eddie Lopat	1948-55
Rip Coleman	1955-56
Bobby Shantz	1957-60
Marshall Bridges	1962-63
Mel Stottlemyre	1964-74
Willie Randolph	1976-88
Bucky Dent (m)	1989
Willie Randolph (c)	1994-2004
Cory Lidle	2006
Matt Smith	2006
Scott Patterson	2008
David Robertson	2008-10

31

Roy Sherid	1929
Charles O'Leary (c)	1930
Jimmy Burke (c)	1931, '33
Cy Perkins (c)	1932
John Schulte (c)	1935-39
Art Fletcher (c)	1940-45
Red Rolfe (c)	1946
John Corriden (c)	1947-48
Jim Turner (c)	1949-59, '66-73
Johnny Sain (c)	1961-63
Jim Gleeson (c)	1964
Cot Deal (c)	1965
Mel Wright (c)	1974-75
Ed Figueroa	1976-80
Jeff Torborg (c)	1979
Dave Winfield	1981-90
Hensley Meulens	1990-91, '93
Mike Humphreys	1992
Bob Wickman	1992
Frank Tanana	1993
Xavier Hernandez	1994
Brian Boehringer	1995
Tim Raines	1996-98
Dan Naulty	1999
Brian Dorsett	1999
Ben Ford	2000
Glenallen Hill	2000
Lance Johnson	2000
Ed Yarnall	2000
Steve Karsay	2002-05
Jason Anderson	2005
Aaron Small	2005
Jose Veras	2006
Josh Phelps	2007
Edwar Ramirez	2007
Ian Kennedy	2008
Michael Dunn	2009
Javier Vazquez	2010

32

Art Jorgens	1929
Frank Barnes	1930
Ken Holloway	1930
Bill Karlon	1930
Dusty Cooke	1932
Eddie Phillips	1932
Tommy Henrich	1937
Steve Sundra	1938-39
Earle Combs (c)	1940-44
Johnny Neun (c)	1944-46
Johnny Neun (m)	1946
Ralph Houk	1947-52
Ralph Houk (c)	1953-54
Elston Howard	**1955-67**
Elston Howard (c)	**1969-79**

33

Charles O'Leary (c)	1929
Sam Gibson	1930
Jim Weaver	1931
Pete Appleton	1933

Charlie Devens	1933
Lee Stine	1938
John Schulte (c)	1940-48
Bill Dickey (c)	1949-57, '60
Randy Gumpert (c)	1957
Charlie Keller (c)	1957-59
Doc Medich	1974-75
Bob Lemon (c)	1976
Bobby Cox (c)	1977
Gene Michael (c)	1978
Mike Ferraro (c)	1979-82
Ken Griffey	1983-86
Tim Stoddard	1986
Claudell Washington	1986
Ron Kittle	1986-87
Jack Clark	1988
Steve Shields	1988
Bob Brower	1989
Scott Nielsen	1989
Eric Plunk	1989-91
Melido Perez	1992-95
Charlie Hayes	1996
David Wells	1997-98, 2002-03
Jose Canseco	2000
Ryan Thompson	2000
Alfonso Soriano	2000-01
Javier Vazquez	2004
Jaret Wright	2005
Kelly Stinnett	2006
Brian Bruney	2006-08
Nick Swisher	2009-10

34

Art Fletcher (m)	1929
Foster Edwards	1930
Lou McEvoy	1931
Ivy Andrews	1931-32
Frank Makosky	1937
Johnny Sturm	1941
Buddy Hassett	1942
Ed Bockman	1946
Ken Silvestri	1946-47
Bobo Newsom	1947
Jack Phillips	1948
Bob Cerv	1952
Harry Schaeffer	1952
Kal Segrist	1952
Tony Kubek	1957
Clete Boyer	1959-61
Bob Hale	1961
Phil Linz	1962-64
Mike Hegan	1966-67
Dick Howser (c)	1969-78
Lenny Randle	1979
Dick Howser (m)	1980
Dave LaRoche	1981-83
Roy Smalley	1982
Matt Keough	1983
Scott Bradley	1984-85
Mike Armstrong	1986
Doug Drabek	1986
Mike Ferraro (c)	1987-88
Bob Davidson	1989
Rich Dotson	1989
Don Schulze	1989
Walt Terrell	1989
Pascual Perez	1990-91
Mike Humphreys	1992
Jerry Nielsen	1992
Andy Cook	1993
Sterling Hitchcock	1993
Sam Militello	1993
Greg Harris	1994
Rob Murphy	1994
Bob MacDonald	1995
Mel Stottlemyre (c)	1996-2005
Jaret Wright	2006
Sean Henn	2007
Phil Hughes	2007
Damaso Marte	2008
A.J. Burnett	2009-10

35

Dixie Walker	1931
Spud Chandler	1937
Paul Schreiber (c)	1945
Aaron Robinson	1946
Yogi Berra	1947
Red Embree	1948
Mickey Witek	1949
Duane Pillette	1949-50

Joe Ostrowski	1950-52
Steve Kraly	1953
Johnny Schmitz	1953
Lou Berberet	1955
Ralph Houk (c)	1958-60
Ralph Houk (m)	1961-63, '66-73
Vern Benson (c)	1965-66
Don Gullett	1977-78
Bill Castro	1981
Roger Erickson	1982-83
Phil Niekro	1984-85
Bob Tewksbury	1986-87
Steve Trout	1987
Lee Guetterman	1988-92
Curt Young	1992
Andy Stankiewicz	1993
Paul Gibson	1993-1994
John Wetteland	1995-96
Hideki Irabu	1997
Clay Bellinger	1999-2000
Mike Mussina	2001-08

36

Mel Queen	1942
Bill Drescher	1945
Vic Raschi	1946
Jake Wade	1946
Al Lyons	1946-1947
Jack Phillips	1947-49
Dick Starr	1948
Johnny Mize	1949-53
Dave Madison	1950
Eddie Robinson	1954-56
Norm Siebern	1956
Harry Simpson	1957-58
Eddie Lopat (c)	1960
Wally Moses (c)	1961-62, '66
Loren Babe (c)	1967
Hal Lanier	1972
Pat Dobson	1973-75
Dock Ellis	1976-77
Stan Thomas	1977
Mike Torrez	1977
Rawley Eastwick	1978
Paul Lindblad	1978
Dave Rajsich	1978
Don Hood	1979
Paul Mirabella	1979
Jim Kaat	1979-80
Gaylord Perry	1980
Rick Reuschel	1981
Steve Balboni	1982
Mike Armstrong	1984-86
Al Holland	1986
Phil Lombardi	1986
Brad Arnsberg	1987
Jeff Moronko	1987
Rich Dotson	1988
Billy Connors (c)	1989-90, '94-95
Mike Humphreys	1991
Mike Witt	1991
Shawn Hillegas	1992
Dave Silvestri	1992
Russ Springer	1992
Gerald Williams	1993
David Cone	1995-2000
Bobby Estalella	2001
Nick Johnson	2002-03, '10
Tom Gordon	2004-05
Mike Myers	2006-07
Jim Brower	2007
Ian Kennedy	2007
Edwar Ramirez	2008-09

37

Herb Karpel	1946
Gus Niarhos	1946
Bucky Harris (m)	1947-48
Casey Stengel (m)	**1949-60**

38

Marius Russo	1939
Hank Borowy	1942
Yogi Berra	1946
Frank Hiller	1946
Mel Queen	1946
Karl Drews	1947
Gus Niarhos	1948-50
Johnny Hopp	1950-52
Loren Babe	1952-53
Willy Miranda	1953

Art Schallock	1953-55
Johnny Blanchard	1955, 1959-65
Doc Edwards	1965
Frank Fernandez	1967-68
Len Boehmer	1969
Steve Kline	1970-74
Cecil Upshaw	1974
Ken Brett	1976
Carlos May	1976-77
Jerry Narron	1979
Tom Underwood	1980-81
Barry Evans	1982
Curt Kaufman	1982
Dave Stegman	1982
Dave LaRoche	1983
Jose Rijo	1984
Ed Whitson	1985-86
Leo Hernandez	1986
Pat Clements	1987-88
Hal Morris	1988
Scott Nielsen	1988
Clay Parker	1989-90
Matt Nokes	1990-94
Josias Manzanillo	1995
Jeff Patterson	1995
Matt Howard	1996
Homer Bush	1997
Scott Pose	1997
Ricky Ledee	1998
Jason Grimsley	1999-2000
Randy Choate	2001-03
Drew Henson	2003
Brett Prinz	2003
Travis Lee	2004
Buddy Groom	2005
Ramiro Mendoza	2005
T.J. Beam	2006
Kris Wilson	2006
Chase Wright	2007
Chris Stewart	2008
Dan Giese	2008
Brian Bruney	2009
Ian Kennedy	2009
Marcus Thames	2010

39

Mike Chartak	1942
Rollie Hemsley	1942
Tommy Byrne	1946
Frank Hiller	1948-49
Wally Hood Jr.	1949
Loren Babe	1952
Harry Schaeffer	1952
Bob Wiesler	1954-55
Ted Gray	1955
George Wilson	1956
Darrell Johnson	1957
Jim Coates	1959-62
Steve Hamilton	1963-70
Gary Jones	1970-71
Rob Gardner	1971
Casey Cox	1972
Wayne Granger	1973
Jim Magnuson	1973
Larry Gura	1974-75
Gene Michael (c)	1976
Mickey Klutts	1977
Ron Davis	1979-81
Mike Morgan	1982
Ron Smalley Jr.	1982
Bert Campaneris	1983
Larry Milbourne	1983
Don Cooper	1985
Neil Allen	1985
Joe Niekro	1986-87
Pat Clements	1987
Roberto Kelly	1987-92
Mike Humphreys	1993
Mike Witt	1993
Donn Pall	1994
Dion James	1995-96
Brian Boehringer	1996
Paul Gibson	1996
Matt Luke	1996
Darryl Strawberry	1996-99
Mark Wohlers	2001
Ron Coomer	2002
Chris Hammond	2003
Andy Phillips	2004
Melky Cabrera	2005

Kevin Reese.....2005
Shawn Chacon.....2005-06
Craig Wilson.....2006
Chris Britton.....2007-08
Ross Ohlendorf.....2008
Richie Sexson.....2008
Anthony Claggett.....2009
Mark Melancon.....2009-10
Kerry Wood.....2010

40

Herb Karpel.....1946
Roy Weatherly.....1946
Cuddles Marshall.....1948
Charlie Silvera.....1948
Jackie Jensen.....1950-51
Bob Wiesler.....1951
Bobby Hogue.....1951-52
Johnny Schmitz.....1952
Ewell Blackwell.....1952-53
Tom Carroll.....1955-56
John Gabler.....1959-60
Jack Cullen.....1962
Lou Clinton.....1966-67
Bill Monbouquette.....1967-68
Lindy McDaniel.....1968-73
Rick Sawyer.....1974
Tippy Martinez.....1974-76
Fran Healy.....1976-78
Ron Davis.....1978
Bob Kammeyer.....1978
Larry McCall.....1978
Charlie Lau (c).....1979-81
Mickey Vernon (c).....1982
Don Zimmer (c).....1983, '86
Gene Michael (c).....1984-86
Clyde King (c).....1988
Steve Shields.....1988
Andy Hawkins.....1989-91
Scott Kamieniecki.....1991
Tony Cloninger (c).....1992-2001
Darren Holmes.....1998
Dan Miceli.....2003
Gabe White.....2003-04
C.J. Nitkowski.....2004
Chien-Ming Wang.....2005-09
Dustin Moseley.....2010

41

Frank Hiller.....1946
Steve Souchock.....1946, '48
Joe Collins.....1949-52
Bob Cerv.....1953-56
Marv Throneberry.....1955
Zeke Bella.....1957
Jake Gibbs.....1962-71
Frank Tepedino.....1972
Otto Velez.....1973
Duke Sims.....1974
Mike Wallace.....1974-75
Rick Sawyer.....1975
Cliff Johnson.....1977-79
George Scott.....1979
Jeff Torborg (c).....1980-83
Sammy Ellis (c).....1983-84, '86
Joe Cowley.....1984-85
Scott Nielsen.....1986
Charlie Hudson.....1987-88
Lance McCullers.....1989-90
Stump Merrill (m).....1990
Darrell Evans (c).....1990
Wade Taylor.....1991
Tim Burke.....1992
Russ Springer.....1992
Jake Gibbs (c).....1993
Sterling Hitchcock.....1994-95, '01-03
Jorge Posada.....1996
Brian Boehringer.....1996-97, 2001
Tony Cloninger (c).....1998
Denny Neagle.....2000
Mike Buddie.....1999
Ed Yarnall.....2000
Jorge DePaula.....2003
Miguel Cairo.....2004
Randy Johnson.....2005-06
Miguel Cairo.....2007
Jose Veras.....2007-09
Chad Gaudin.....2009-10
Ivan Nova.....2010

42

Bill Drescher.....1946
Vic Raschi.....1946
Butch Wensloff.....1947
Joe Collins.....1948
Bud Stewart.....1948
Jerry Coleman.....1949-57
Jesse Gonder.....1960
Pedro Gonzalez.....1963-65
Ray Barker.....1965-67
Charlie Spikes.....1972
Doc Medich.....1973
Ken Wright.....1974
Bob Oliver.....1975
Art Fowler (c).....1977-79, '83, '88
Tom Morgan (c).....1979
Stan Williams (c).....1980-82, '88
Clyde King (c).....1981
Clyde King (m).....1982
Jerry Walker (c).....1982
Jerry McNertney (c).....1984
Doug Holmquist (c).....1984-85
Stump Merrill (c).....1985-87
Billy Connors (c).....1989
Dave LaPoint.....1989-90
John Habyan.....1991-93
Domingo Jean.....1993
Mariano Rivera.....1995-2010

43

Frank Hiller.....1946
Vic Raschi.....1947
Art Schult.....1953
Deron Johnson.....1960
Roger Repoz.....1964-66
Mike Ferraro.....1966
Dale Roberts.....1967
Rob Gardner.....1970-72
Terry Ley.....1971
Jim Magnuson.....1973
Jim Ray Hart.....1973-74
Jim Deidel.....1974
Rudy May.....1974-76
Jim York.....1976
Ken Clay.....1978-79
Doug Bird.....1980-81
George Frazier.....1981-83
Jeff Torborg (c).....1984
Rich Bordi.....1985
Tim Stoddard.....1986-88
Lee Elia (c).....1989
Gene Michael (c).....1989
Jeff Robinson.....1990
Torey Lovullo.....1991
Jeff Johnson.....1991-93
Sam Militello.....1992
Paul Assenmacher.....1993
Bob Melvin.....1994
Nardi Contreras (c).....1995
Dave Silvestri.....1995
Jeff Nelson.....1996-2000, '03
Todd Greene.....2001
Christian Parker.....2001
Ted Lilly.....2002
Raul Mondesi.....2002-03
Jorge DePaula.....2004
Scott Proctor.....2005-07
Darrell Rasner.....2008
Damaso Marte.....2009-10

44

Bob Seeds.....1936
Frank Verdi.....1953
Dick Tettelbach.....1955
Gordie Windhorn.....1959
Ken Hunt.....1959-60
Jim Hegan (c).....1960-73
Bill Sudakis.....1974
Terry Whitfield.....1975-76
Reggie Jackson.....1977-81
Jeff Torborg (c).....1984-88
John Stearns (c).....1989
Mike Ferraro (c).....1990-91

45

Clint Courtney.....1951
Don Bollweg.....1953
Lou Skizas.....1956
Mark Freeman.....1959
Roland Sheldon.....1961-62, '64-65
Roger Repoz.....1965
Jack Cullen.....1965-66
John Miller.....1966
Steve Barber.....1967
Stan Bahnsen.....1968-71
Larry Gowell.....1972
Rich Hinton.....1972
Ed Herrmann.....1975
Jim Beattie.....1978-79
Rudy May.....1980-83
Dennis Rasmussen.....1984-87
Bill Gullickson.....1987
John Candelaria.....1988-89
Kevin Mmahat.....1989
Steve Balboni.....1990
Alan Mills.....1991
Rich Monteleone.....1991
Danny Tartabull.....1992-95
Andy Fox.....1995
Joe Girardi.....1996
Cecil Fielder.....1996-97
Chili Davis.....1998-99
Felix Jose.....2000
Ryan Thompson.....2000
Henry Rodriguez.....2001
Jay Witasick.....2001
Alberto Castillo.....2002
Ted Lilly.....2002
Jason Anderson.....2003
Armando Benitez.....2003
Felix Heredia.....2003-04
Carl Pavano.....2005, '07-08
Sergio Mitre.....2009-10

46

Frank Coleman.....1946
Charlie Silvera.....1948
Dave Madison.....1950
Bill Short.....1960
Frank Tepedino.....1969
Bobby Mitchell.....1970
Roger Hambright.....1971
Otto Velez.....1973
Rick Dempsey.....1973-76
Gene Locklear.....1976-77
Mike Heath.....1978
Don Hood.....1979
Joe Lefebvre.....1980
Gene Nelson.....1981
Joe Pepitone (c).....1982
Shane Rawley.....1982
Don Mattingly.....1982-83
Mike Pagliarulo.....1984
Henry Cotto.....1985-86
Juan DeJesus.....1986
Rich Bordi.....1987
Roberto Kelly.....1987
Jerry Royster.....1987
Hipolito Pena.....1988
Randy Velarde.....1988
Dallas Green (m).....1989
Stump Merrill (m).....1990
Joe Sparks (c).....1990
Frank Howard (c).....1991-93
Terry Mulholland.....1994
Donovan Osborne.....2004
Alan Embree.....2005
Darrell May.....2005
Scott Erickson.....2006
Aaron Guiel.....2006
Jose Veras.....2006
Andy Pettitte.....1995-2003, '07-10

47

Frank Colman.....1947
Eli Grba.....1959
Tom Sturdivant.....1955-59
Billy Shantz.....1960
Luis Arroyo.....1960-63
Bob Schmidt.....1965
Stan Bahnsen.....1966
Frank Tepedino.....1967
Fred Beene.....1972-74
Kerry Dineen.....1976
Larry Murray.....1976
Bob Lemon (m).....1978
Andy Messersmith.....1978
Jim Kaat.....1979
Jeff Torborg (c).....1979
Bruce Robinson.....1979-80
Dennis Sherrill.....1980
Curt Kaufman.....1982
Ray Fontenot.....1983-1984
Rod Scurry.....1985
Al Pulido.....1986
Juan Bonilla.....1987
Pete Filson.....1987
Alvaro Espinoza.....1988
Scott Nielsen.....1988
Pat Corrales (c).....1989
Champ Summers (c).....1989-90
Marc Hill (c).....1991
Lee Smith.....1993
Dave Silvestri.....1993-94
Dave Eiland.....1995
Rick Honeycutt.....1995
Billy Brewer.....1996
Dave Pavlas.....1996
Ruben Rivera.....1996
Ivan Cruz.....1997
Shane Spencer.....1998-2002
Erick Almonte.....2003
Jesse Orosco.....2003
Al Reyes.....2003
Brett Prinz.....2004
Felix Rodriguez.....2005
Ron Villone.....2006-07
Colter Bean.....2007
Chris Britton.....2008
Sidney Ponson.....2008
Freddy Guzman.....2009
Romulo Sanchez.....2010
Ivan Nova.....2010

48

Frank Colman.....1947
John Gabler.....1959
Elvio Jimenez.....1964
Pedro Ramos.....1964
Roy White.....1965-68
Cecil Perkins.....1967
Sam McDowell.....1973-74
Dave Kingman.....1977
Mike Torrez.....1977
Clyde King (c).....1978
Jim Hegan (c).....1979-80
Joe Altobelli (c).....1981-82, '86
Dale Murray.....1983-85
Willie Horton (c).....1985
Neil Allen.....1987
Gene Michael (c).....1988
George Mitterwald (c).....1988
Frank Howard (c).....1989
Buck Showalter (c).....1990
John Ramos.....1991
Russ Meyer (c).....1992
Rick Down (c).....1993-95
Don Zimmer (c).....1996-97
Chris Chambliss (c).....1998-2000
Randy Keisler.....2001
Robert Perez.....2001
Scott Seabol.....2001
Brandon Knight.....2002
Jay Tessmer.....2002
Fernando Seguignol.....2003
Paul Quantrill.....2004-05
Wayne Franklin.....2005
Kyle Farnsworth.....2006-08
Phil Coke.....2008-09
Boone Logan.....2010

49

Lou Berberet.....1954
Jim Bronstad.....1959
Bob Meyer.....1964
Stan Bahnsen.....1966
Charlie Sands.....1967
Loyd Colson.....1970
Kerry Dineen.....1975
Ron Guidry.... 1975-88, (c) 2006-07
Jeff Johnson.....1992

50

Ralph Houk.....1947
Bill Bryan.....1967
Bill Burbach.....1969-71
Alan Closter.....1971-72
Doc Medich.....1972
Dave Pagan.....1973
Duke Sims.....1973
Ken Clay.....1977

Roger Slagle 1979
Clyde King (c) 1981
Lynn McGlothen 1982
John Pacella 1982
Jay Howell 1983-84
Marty Bystrom 1985
Phil Lombardi 1986
Jay Ward (c) 1987
Chris Chambliss 1988
Chris Chambliss (c) 1996-97
Steve Balboni 1989
Oscar Azocar 1990
John Habyan 1990
Alan Mills 1991
Ed Napoleon (c) 1992-93
Robert Eenhoorn 1994-95
Don Zimmer (c) 1998-99
Todd Erdos 2000
Rich Monteleone (c) 2003-04
Matt Lawton 2005
Larry Bowa (c) 2006-07
Bobby Meacham (c) 2008
Mick Kelleher (c) 2009-10

51

George McQuinn 1947
Frank Leja 1954-55
Gordie Windhorn 1959
Pete Mikkelsen (m) 1964-65
Ralph Houk (m) 1966
Tony Solaita 1968
John Wyatt 1968
Ron Klimkowski 1969
Terry Whitfield 1974
Larry McCall 1977
Dom Scala (c) 1978-86
Cecilio Guante 1987-88
Chuck Cary 1989-91
Bernie Williams 1991-2006

52

Johnny Lucadello 1947
Ken Silvestri 1947
Jim Delsing 1949
Wally Hood Jr. 1949
Tom Morgan 1951
Jim Coates 1956
Bobby Murcer 1965
Fritz Peterson 1966
Joe Verbanic 1967-1970
Larry Murray 1974
Otto Velez 1975
Doyle Alexander ... 1976, '82-1983
Dave Rajsich 1978
Mike Griffin 1979-1981
Otis Nixon 1983
Mark Connor (c) ... 1984-87, '90-93
Juan Espino 1985
Orestes Destrade 1987
Dave Eiland 1988
Bob Geren 1988
Mike Ferraro (c) 1989
Charlie Fox (c) 1989
Mark Hutton ....1994, '96
David Weathers 1996-97
Joe Borowski 1997
Pete Incaviglia 1997
Danny Rios 1997
Mike Buddie 1998
Ed Yarnall 1999
Don Zimmer (c) 2000
Gary Denbo (c) 2001
Jose Contreras 2003-04
Joe Girardi 2005
Tony Pena (c) 2006
Luis Vizcaino 2007
Dave Eiland (c) 2008
CC Sabathia 2009-10

53

Bob Wiesler 1951
Bill Skowron 1954
Johnny Kucks 1955-59
Johnny James 1960-61
Ross Moschitto ......1965, '67
Dave Pagan 1974-76
Ken Holtzman 1976-78
Ron Davis 1978
Larry McCall 1978
Ray Burris 1979

Bob Kammeyer 1979
Tim Lollar 1980
Jerry Walker (c) 1981
Jay Howell 1982-83
Lee Walls (c) 1983
Marty Bystrom 1984
Neil Allen 1985
Orestes Destrade 1987
Bob Geren 1989-91
Glen Sherlock (c) .....1992, '94-95
Neal Heaton 1993
Mark Hutton 1993
Jose Cardenal (c) ... 1996-99
Alfonso Soriano 2000
Mike Thurman 2002
Don Zimmer (c) 2001
Lee Mazzilli (c) 2003
Luis Sojo (c) 2004-05
Larry Bowa (c) 2006
Bobby Abreu 2006-08
Melky Cabrera 2009
Juan Miranda 2010

54

Jim Delsing 1950
Andy Carey 1952
Thad Tillotson 1967-68
Ken Johnson 1969
Gary Waslewski 1970-71
Steve Blateric 1972
Jim Roland 1972
Jim Deidel 1974
Alex Johnson 1974
Dave Bergman 1977
Cecilio Guante 1977
Rich Gossage .... 1978-83, '89
Brian Fisher 1985-86
Jay Buhner 1987-98
Dale Mohorcic 1988-89
Tim Leary 1990-92
Sterling Hitchcock 1992
Bobby Munoz 1993
Jeff Reardon 1994
Joe Ausanio 1994-95
Jim Mecir 1996-97
Todd Erdos 1998-99
Lee Mazzilli (c) ... 2000-01, '06
Don Zimmer (c) 2002-03
Roy White (c) 2004-05
Kevin Long 2007-10

55

Bob Grim 1954-58
Zach Monroe 1958-59
Spud Murray (BP pitcher)
1961-69
Dave McDonald 1969
Paul Mirabella 1979
Roger Holt 1980
Andre Robertson 1981
Roy Smalley 1982
Stan Javier 1984
Vic Mata 1984
Juan Bonilla 1985
Rich Monteleone .....1990, '92-93
Brian Butterfield (c) ... 1994-95
Jorge Posada 1996
Wally Whitehurst 1996
Ramiro Mendoza 1997-2002
Hideki Matsui 2003-09

56

Jim Bouton 1962-68
John Cumberland 1968-70
Mike McCormick 1970
Dave Righetti 1979
Ted Wilborn 1980
Bill Castro 1981
Mike Patterson 1981-82
Andre Robertson 1982
Bert Campaneris 1983
Curt Brown 1984
Rex Hudler 1984-85
Al Leiter 1987
Brian Dorsett 1989
Mark Leiter 1990
Dave Silvestri 1992
Andy Cook 1993
Dave Pavlas 1995
Dale Polley 1996

Darrell Einertson 2000
Ted Lilly 2000
Juan Rivera 2001
Todd Williams 2001
Rick Down (c) 2002-03
Scott Proctor 2004
Tanyon Sturtze 2004-06
Tony Pena (c) 2007-10

57

Art Lopez 1965
Roy Staiger 1979
Clyde King (c) 1980
Tucker Ashford 1981
Bobby Ramos 1982
Juan Bonilla 1987
Bob Geren 1988
Hensley Meulens 1991-96
Ramiro Mendoza 1996
Joe Borowski 1998
Jeff Juden 1999
Jay Tessmer 1999-2000
Jake Westbrook 2000
Carlos Almanzar 2001
Erick Almonte 2001
Mark Wohlers 2001
Karim Garcia 2002
Drew Henson 2002
Juan Acevedo 2003
Michael Hernandez 2003
Jorge DePaula 2004
Alex Graman 2004
Brad Halsey 2004
Scott Proctor 2004
Neil Allen (c) 2005
Joe Kerrigan (c) 2006-07
Mike Harkey (c) 2008-10

58

Dooley Womack 1966-68
Bobby Brown 1979
Bruce Robinson 1979
Andy McGaffigan 1981
Dave Wehrmeister 1981
Sammy Ellis 1982
Juan Espino ....1982, '86
Mike O'Berry 1984
Bob Geren 1988
Hensley Meulens 1989
Dave Eiland 1990
Mike Jerzembeck 1998
Alfonso Soriano 1999
Randy Choate 2000
Randy Keisler 2001
Jorge DePaula 2005
Alex Graman 2005
Sean Henn 2005
Mike Vento 2005
Colter Bean 2005-06
T.J. Beam 2006
Jeff Karstens 2006-07
Darrell Rasner 2006
Dave Eiland (c) 2009-10

59

Damaso Garcia 1979
Steve Adkins 1990
Hensley Meulens 1992
Billy Brewer 1996
Ryan Bradley 1998
D'Angelo Jimenez 1999
Donzell McDonald 2001
Juan Rivera 2002-03
Rob Thomson (c) 2007-10

60

Hipolito Pena 1988
John Habyan 1990
Darrin Chapin 1991
J.T. Snow 1992
Tim McIntosh 1996
Homer Bush 1997
Mike Lowell 1998
Craig Dingman 2000
Brett Jodie 2001
Nick Johnson 2001
Brandon Knight 2002
Erick Almonte 2003
Brandon Claussen 2003
Felix Escalona 2004

Sam Marsonek 2004
Wil Nieves 2005-06
Ross Ohlendorf 2007
Kevin Russo 2010

61

Marshall Brant 1980
Jim Lewis 1982
Phil Lombardi 1987
John Habyan 1990
Jim Bruske 1998
Ted Lilly 2001
Brad Halsey 2004
Juan Padilla 2004
Jorge DePaula 2005
Darrell Rasner 2006
Matt DeSalvo 2007
Billy Traber 2008
Chan Ho Park 2010
Royce Ring 2010

62

Cloyd Boyer 1975
Brian Dayett 1983-84
Brad Arnsberg 1986
Hal Morris 1988
Steve Adkins 1990
Jorge Posada 1995
Willie Banks 1997
Jay Tessmer 1998
Brandon Knight 2001
Bubba Crosby 2004
Sean Henn 2006
Joba Chamberlain.... 2007-10

63

Mike Morgan 1982
Jim Walewander 1990
Mike Figga 1997
Danny Rios 1997
Randy Keisler 2000
Andy Cannizaro 2006
Alberto Gonzalez 2007
Jonathan Albaladejo ... 2008-10
Chris Britton 2008

64

Bill Fulton 1987
Steve Kiefer 1989
Bronson Sardinha 2007
Francisco Cervelli 2008
Romulo Sanchez 2010

65

Clyde King (c) 1981-82
Juan Espino 1983
Adrian Hernandez.... 2001-02
Phil Hughes 2007-10

66

Steve Balboni 1981-83
Jim Deshaies 1984
Juan Miranda 2008

67

Clay Christiansen 1984
Dale Mohoricic 1988

68

Dioner Navarro 2004

69

Alan Mills 1990

72

Juan Miranda 2009

77

Humberto Sanchez 2008

91

Alfredo Aceves........ 2008-10

99

Charlie Keller 1952
Brian Bruney 2009

Unknown: Roy Schalk (1932)

(c) denotes coach
(m) denotes manager

All-Time Opening Day Lineups

2010 at Baltimore
SS . . . . JETER
DH . . . . Johnson
1B . . . . TEIXEIRA
3B . . . . . RODRIGUEZ
2B . . . . CANO
C . . . . POSADA
CF . . . GRANDERSON
RF . . . . SWISHER
LF . . . . GARDNER
P . . . . SABATHIA

2009 at Baltimore
SS . . . . JETER
LF . . . . Damon
1B . . . . TEIXEIRA
DH . . . . Matsui
C . . . . POSADA
2B . . . . CANO
RF . . . . Nady
3B . . . . Ransom
CF . . . . GARDNER
P . . . . SABATHIA

2008 vs. Toronto
LF . . . . Damon
SS . . . . JETER
RF . . . . Abreu
3B . . . . . RODRIGUEZ
1B . . . . Giambi
2B . . . . CANO
C . . . . POSADA
DH . . . . Matsui
CF . . . . Cabrera
P . . . . Wang

2007 vs. Tampa Bay
CF . . . . Damon
SS . . . . JETER
RF . . . . Abreu
3B . . . . . RODRIGUEZ
DH . . . . Giambi
LF . . . . Matsui
C . . . . POSADA
2B . . . . CANO
1B . . . . Phelps
P . . . . Pavano

2006 at Oakland
CF . . . . Damon
SS . . . . JETER
RF . . . . Sheffield
3B . . . . RODRIGUEZ
1B . . . . Giambi
LF . . . . Matsui
C . . . . POSADA
DH . . . . Williams
2B . . . . CANO
P . . . . Johnson

2005 vs. Boston
SS . . . . JETER
3B . . . . RODRIGUEZ
RF . . . . Sheffield
DH . . . . Sierra
LF . . . . Matsui
C . . . . POSADA
1B . . . . Giambi
CF . . . . Williams
2B . . . . Womack
P . . . . Johnson

2004 at Tampa Bay
SS . . . . JETER
LF . . . . Matsui
3B . . . . RODRIGUEZ
1B . . . . Giambi
RF . . . . Sheffield
C . . . . POSADA
DH . . . . Sierra
2B . . . . Wilson
CF . . . . Lofton
P . . . . Mussina

2003 at Toronto
2B . . . . Soriano
SS . . . . JETER
1B . . . . Giambi
CF . . . . Williams
LF . . . . Matsui
C . . . . POSADA
3B . . . . Ventura
RF . . . . Mondesi
DH . . . . Johnson
P . . . . Clemens

2002 at Baltimore
2B . . . . Soriano
SS . . . . JETER
1B . . . . Giambi
CF . . . . Williams
3B . . . . Ventura
C . . . . POSADA
LF . . . . White
RF . . . . Spencer
DH . . . . Johnson
P . . . . Clemens

2001 vs. Kansas City
LF . . . . Knoblauch
2B . . . . Soriano
RF . . . . O'Neill
CF . . . . Williams
DH . . . . Justice
1B . . . . Martinez
C . . . . POSADA
SS . . . . Sojo
3B . . . . Brosius
P . . . . Clemens

2000 at Anaheim
2B . . . . Knoblauch
SS . . . . JETER
RF . . . . O'Neill
DH . . . . Williams
1B . . . . Martinez
CF . . . . Ledee
C . . . . POSADA
LF . . . . Spencer
3B . . . . Brosius
P . . . . . . Hernandez

1999 at Oakland
2B . . . . Knoblauch
SS . . . . JETER
RF . . . . O'Neill
CF . . . . Williams
1B . . . . Martinez
DH . . . . Davis
LF . . . . Ledee
3B . . . . Brosius
C . . . . Girardi
P . . . . Clemens

1998 at Anaheim
2B . . . . Knoblauch
SS . . . . JETER
RF . . . . O'Neill
CF . . . . Williams
1B . . . . Martinez
DH . . . . Davis
LF . . . . Curtis
3B . . . . Brosius
C . . . . Girardi
P . . . . Pettitte

1997 at Seattle
SS . . . . JETER
3B . . . . Boggs
CF . . . . Williams
DH . . . . Fielder
1B . . . . Martinez
RF . . . . O'Neill
LF . . . . . . Strawberry
2B . . . . Duncan
C . . . . Girardi
P . . . . Cone

1996 at Cleveland
3B . . . . Boggs
2B . . . . Duncan
RF . . . . O'Neill
DH . . . . Sierra
1B . . . . Martinez
CF . . . . . B. Williams
LF . . . . . G. Williams
C . . . . Girardi
SS . . . . JETER
P . . . . Cone

1995 vs. Texas
3B . . . . Boggs
DH . . . . Leyritz
LF . . . . O'Neill
RF . . . . Tartabull
1B . . . . Mattingly
C . . . . Stanley
CF . . . . Williams
SS . . . . Fernandez
2B . . . . Kelly
P . . . . Key

1994 vs. Texas
LF . . . . Polonia
3B . . . . Boggs
1B . . . . Mattingly
DH . . . . Tartabull
RF . . . . O'Neill
C . . . . Stanley
CF . . . . Williams
SS . . . . Gallego
2B . . . . Kelly
P . . . . Key

1993 at Cleveland
CF . . . . Williams
3B . . . . Boggs
1B . . . . Mattingly
RF . . . . Tartabull
LF . . . . O'Neill
C . . . . Nokes
DH . . . . Maas
SS . . . . Owen
2B . . . . Kelly
P . . . . Sanderson

1992 vs. Boston
SS . . . . Velarde
1B . . . . Mattingly
RF . . . . R. Kelly
LF . . . . Hall
DH . . . . Tartabull
C . . . . Nokes
RF . . . . Barfield
3B . . . . Hayes
2B . . . . P. Kelly
P . . . . Sanderson

1991 at Detroit
2B . . . . Sax
1B . . . . Mattingly
CF . . . . Kelly
DH . . . . Maas
LF . . . . Meulens
RF . . . . Barfield
C . . . . Leyritz
3B . . . . Blowers
SS . . . . Espinoza
P . . . . Leary

1990 vs. Cleveland
2B . . . . Sax
SS . . . . Espinoza
1B . . . . Mattingly
DH . . . . Winfield
LF . . . . Hall
RF . . . . Barfield
CF . . . . Kelly
C . . . . Geren
3B . . . . Blowers
P . . . . LaPoint

1989 at Minnesota
LF . . . . . . Henderson
2B . . . . Sax
DH . . . . . Brookens
1B . . . . Balboni
RF . . . . Ward
3B . . . . Pagliarulo
C . . . . Slaught
SS . . . . Espinoza
CF . . . . . . R. Kelly
P . . . . John

1988 vs. Minnesota
LF . . . . . . Henderson
2B . . . . . . Randolph
1B . . . . . . Mattingly
DH . . . . Ward
RF . . . . Winfield
CF . . . . Kelly
3B . . . . Pagliarulo
C . . . . Skinner
SS . . . . Santana
P . . . . Rhoden

1987 at Detroit
RF . . . . . . Henderson
2B . . . . . . Randolph
1B . . . . . . Mattingly
DH . . . . Ward
RF . . . . Winfield
LF . . . . Pasqua
3B . . . . Pagliarulo
C . . . . Skinner
SS . . . . Tolleson
P . . . . . . Rasmussen

1986 vs. Kansas City
CF . . . . . . Henderson
2B . . . . . . Randolph
1B . . . . . . Mattingly
RF . . . . Winfield
DH . . . . . Roenicke
LF . . . . Cotto
3B . . . . Berra
C . . . . Wynegar
SS . . . . . . Meacham
P . . . . Guidry

1985 at Boston
CF . . . . Moreno
2B . . . . . . Randolph
1B . . . . . . Mattingly
RF . . . . Winfield
DH . . . . Baylor
LF . . . . Griffey
3B . . . . Pagliarulo
C . . . . Wynegar
SS . . . . . . Meacham
P . . . . . . P. Niekro

1984 at Kansas City
CF . . . . Moreno
2B . . . . . . Randolph
LF . . . . Kemp
DH . . . . Baylor
RF . . . . Winfield
3B . . . . Harrah
1B . . . . Griffey
C . . . . Cerone
SS . . . . Foli
P . . . . Guidry

1983 at Seattle
2B . . . . . . Randolph
SS . . . . Smalley
LF . . . . . . Winfield
RF . . . . Kemp
DH . . . . Baylor
1B . . . . Griffey
3B . . . . Nettles
CF . . . . . Mumphrey
C . . . . Wynegar
P . . . . Guidry

1982 vs. Chicago
2B . . . . . . Randolph
CF . . . . . Mumphrey
RF . . . . Griffey
LF . . . . . . Winfield
1B . . . . . Revering
DH . . . . . . Watson
3B . . . . Nettles
C . . . . Cerone
SS . . . . Dent
P . . . . Guidry

1981 vs. Texas
2B . . . . . . Randolph
CF . . . . . Mumphrey
LF . . . . . . Winfield
1B . . . . . . Watson
RF . . . . . . Piniella
C . . . . Cerone
3B . . . . Nettles
DH . . . . Werth
SS . . . . Dent
P . . . . John

1980 at Texas
2B . . . . . . Randolph
CF . . . . Jones
1B . . . . . . Watson
RF . . . . . . Jackson
LF . . . . . . Piniella
DH . . . . . Soderholm
3B . . . . Nettles
C . . . . Cerone
SS . . . . Dent
P . . . . Guidry

1979 vs. Milwaukee
CF . . . . Rivers
2B . . . . . . Randolph
C . . . . Munson
DH . . . . . Johnson
LF . . . . . Chambliss
3B . . . . Nettles
LF . . . . White
RF . . . . Blair
SS . . . . Dent
P . . . . Guidry

1978 at Texas
2B . . . . . . Randolph
CF . . . . Rivers
DH . . . . . . Munson
RF . . . . . . Jackson
LF . . . . . . Piniella
C . . . . . . Johnson
1B . . . . . Chambliss
3B . . . . Nettles
SS . . . . Dent
P . . . . Guidry

1977 vs. Milwaukee
CF . . . . Rivers
LF . . . . White
C . . . . Munson
1B . . . . . Chambliss
RF . . . . . . Jackson
3B . . . . Nettles
DH . . . . Wynn
2B . . . . . . Randolph
SS . . . . Dent
P . . . . Hunter

1976 at Milwaukee
CF . . . . Rivers
LF . . . . White
DH . . . . . . Munson
1B . . . . . Chambliss
RF . . . . . . Gamble
3B . . . . Nettles
2B . . . . . . Randolph
C . . . . . . Dempsey
SS . . . . Mason
P . . . . Hunter

1975 at Cleveland
2B . . . . Alomar
LF . . . . Piniella
CF . . . . Bonds
RF . . . . . . Blomberg
3B . . . . Nettles
DH . . . . . Herrmann
1B . . . . . Chambliss
C . . . . Munson
SS . . . . Mason
P . . . . Medich

1974 vs. Cleveland
LF . . . . White
1B . . . . Hegan
C . . . . Munson
CF . . . . Murcer
RF . . . . . . Blomberg
3B . . . . Nettles
DH . . . . . . Sudakis
2B . . . . . . Michael
SS . . . . Mason
P . . . . Stottlemyre

1973 at Boston
2B . . . . Clarke
LF . . . . White
RF . . . . . . M. Alou
CF . . . . Murcer
3B . . . . Nettles
DH . . . . . . Blomberg
1B . . . . . . F. Alou
C . . . . Munson
SS . . . . . . Michael
P . . . . Stottlemyre

1972 at Baltimore
SS . . . . Kenney
3B . . . . . McKinney
CF . . . . Murcer
LF . . . . White
1B . . . . . Blomberg
RF . . . . . . Callison
C . . . . Munson
2B . . . . Allen
P . . . . Stottlemyre

1971 at Boston
2B . . . . Clarke
C . . . . Munson
LF . . . . White
CF . . . . Murcer
1B . . . . Cater
3B . . . . Lyttle
SS . . . . . . Michael
P . . . . . . Bahnsen

1970 vs. Boston
2B . . . . Clarke
C . . . . Munson
LF . . . . White
1B . . . . Ellis
3B . . . . Cater
CF . . . . Murcer
RF . . . . Blefary
SS . . . . . . Michael
P . . . . Stottlemyre

1969 at Washington
2B . . . . Clarke
C . . . . Kenney
3B . . . . Murcer
LF . . . . White
1B . . . . . . Pepitone
SS . . . . Tresh
RF . . . . . . Robinson
C . . . . Gibbs
P . . . . Stottlemyre

1968 vs. California
2B	Clark
3B	Ferraro
1B	Mantle
LF	Tresh
RF	Robinson
CF	Pepitone
C	Fernandez
SS	Michael
P	Stottlemyre

1967 at Washington
LF	Tresh
RF	Robinson
1B	Mantle
CF	Pepitone
C	Howard
3B	C. Smith
2B	Clarke
SS	Kennedy
P	Stottlemyre

1966 vs. Detroit
2B	Richardson
LF	Tresh
RF	Maris
CF	Mantle
3B	Boyer
1B	Pepitone
C	Howard
SS	Amaro
P	Ford

1965 at Minnesota
CF	Tresh
2B	Richardson
RF	Maris
LF	Mantle
C	Howard
1B	Pepitone
3B	Boyer
SS	Kubek
P	Bouton

1964 vs. Boston
SS	Linz
2B	Richardson
RF	Maris
CF	Mantle
LF	Tresh
1B	Pepitone
C	Howard
3B	Boyer
P	Ford

1963 at Kansas City
SS	Kubek
2B	Richardson
LF	Tresh
CF	Mantle
1B	Pepitone
C	Howard
RF	Lopez
3B	Boyer
P	Terry

1962 vs. Baltimore
2B	Richardson
SS	Tresh
RF	Maris
CF	Mantle
C	Howard
1B	Skowron
LF	Lopez
3B	Boyer
P	Ford

1961 vs. Minnesota
2B	Richardson
LF	Lopez
C	Berra
CF	Mantle
RF	Maris
1B	Skowron
SS	Kubek
3B	Boyer
P	Ford

1960 at Boston
RF	Maris
2B	Richardson
3B	McDougald
LF	Lopez
CF	Mantle
1B	Skowron
C	Howard
SS	Kubek
P	Coates

1959 vs. Boston
RF	Bauer
LF	Siebern
CF	Mantle
C	Berra
2B	McDougald
1B	Throneberry
3B	Carey
SS	Richardson
P	Turley

1958 at Boston
RF	Bauer
SS	McDougald
CF	Mantle
C	Berra
1B	Skowron
LF	Howard
3B	Carey
2B	Richardson
P	Larsen

1957 vs. Washington
RF	Bauer
2B	Martin
CF	Mantle
C	Berra
1B	Skowron
SS	McDougald
LF	Howard
3B	Carey
P	Ford

Singer Paul Simon throws out the ceremonial first pitch for the 1969 home opener.

1956 at Washington
RF	Bauer
SS	Lumpe
CF	Mantle
C	Berra
1B	Skowron
2B	Martin
LF	Howard
3B	Carey
P	Larsen

1955 vs. Washington
2B	McDougald
3B	Carey
CF	Mantle
C	Berra
1B	Skowron
RF	Bauer
LF	Cerv
SS	Rizzuto
P	Ford

1954 at Washington
RF	Bauer
1B	Collins
CF	Mantle
C	Berra
3B	McDougald
LF	Woodling
2B	Coleman
SS	Rizzuto
P	Ford

1953 vs. Philadelphia
SS	Rizzuto
1B	Collins
RF	Bauer
CF	Mantle
C	Berra
LF	Woodling
3B	McDougald
2B	Martin
P	Raschi

1952 at Philadelphia
SS	Rizzuto
CF	Jensen
RF	Mantle
3B	McDougald
LF	Bauer
1B	Mize
2B	Coleman
C	Silvera
P	Raschi

1951 vs. Boston
LF	Jensen
SS	Rizzuto
RF	Mantle
CF	DiMaggio
C	Berra
1B	Mize
3B	Johnson
2B	Coleman
P	Raschi

1950 at Boston
SS	Rizzuto
1B	Henrich
RF	Bauer
CF	DiMaggio
C	Berra
3B	Johnson
LF	Lindell
2B	Coleman
P	Reynolds

1949 vs. Washington
2B	Stirnweiss
SS	Rizzuto
CF	Woodling
RF	Henrich
LF	Bauer
3B	Brown
1B	Kryhoski
C	Niarhos
P	Lopat

1948 at Washington
2B	Stirnweiss
RF	Henrich
LF	Keller
RF	Henrich
1B	McQuinn
3B	Johnson
SS	Rizzuto
C	Niarhos
P	Reynolds

1947 vs. Philadelphia
SS	Rizzuto
2B	Stirnweiss
1B	McQuinn
LF	Keller
RF	Berra
CF	Lindell
3B	Johnson
C	Robinson
P	Chandler

1946 at Philadelphia
SS	Crosetti
3B	Stirnweiss
RF	Henrich
CF	DiMaggio
1B	Etten
LF	Lindell
C	Dickey
2B	Grimes
P	Chandler

1945 vs. Boston
2B	Stirnweiss
LF	Martin
RF	Derry
CF	Lindell
1B	Etten
SS	Buzas
3B	Savage
C	Garbark
P	Donald

1944 at Boston
2B	Stirnweiss
RF	Metheny
1B	Etten
CF	Lindell
3B	Savage
LF	Levy
SS	Grimes
C	Garbark
P	Borowy

1943 vs. Washington
SS	Stirnweiss
CF	Weatherly
LF	Keller
2B	Gordon
1B	Etten
3B	Johnson
C	Dickey
RF	Lindell
P	Bonham

1942 at Washington
3B	Priddy
SS	Rizzuto
RF	Henrich
CF	DiMaggio
LF	Keller
2B	Gordon
C	Dickey
1B	Levy
P	Ruffing

1941 at Washington
SS	Rizzuto
3B	Rolfe
RF	Henrich
CF	DiMaggio
LF	Keller
2B	Gordon
C	Dickey
1B	Sturm
P	Russo

1940 at Philadelphia
SS	Crosetti
3B	Rolfe
RF	Selkirk
LF	Keller
C	Dickey
2B	Gordon
CF	Henrich
1B	Dahlgren
P	Ruffing

1939 vs. Boston
SS	Crosetti
3B	Rolfe
LF	Powell
CF	DiMaggio
1B	Gehrig
C	Dickey
RF	Gallagher
2B	Gordon
P	Ruffing

1938 at Boston
SS	Crosetti
3B	Rolfe
LF	Selkirk
1B	Gehrig
C	Dickey
RF	Henrich
CF	Hoag
2B	Gordon
P	Ruffing

1937 vs. Washington
SS	Crosetti
3B	Rolfe
LF	Johnson
1B	Gehrig
C	Dickey
RF	Selkirk
2B	Lazzeri
CF	Hoag
P	Gomez

1936 at Washington
3B	Rolfe
LF	Johnson
RF	Selkirk
1B	Gehrig
C	Dickey
CF	Chapman
2B	Lazzeri
SS	Crosetti
P	Gomez

1935 vs. Boston
LF	Combs
3B	Rolfe
RF	Selkirk
1B	Gehrig
C	Dickey
CF	Chapman
2B	Lazzeri
SS	Crosetti
P	Gomez

1934 at Philadelphia
CF	Combs
SS	Rolfe
LF	Ruth
1B	Gehrig
RF	Chapman
3B	Lazzeri
C	Dickey
2B	Heffner
P	Gomez

1933 vs. Boston
CF	Combs
3B	Sewell
RF	Ruth
1B	Gehrig
LF	Chapman
2B	Lazzeri
C	Dickey
SS	Crosetti
P	Gomez

1932 at Philadelphia
CF . . . . Byrd
2B . . . . Saltzgaver
LF . . . . Ruth
1B . . . . Gehrig
RF . . . . Chapman
3B . . . . Crosetti
C . . . . Dickey
SS . . . . Lary
P . . . . Gomez

1931 vs. Boston
CF . . . . Combs
SS . . . . Lary
RF . . . . Ruth
1B . . . . Gehrig
3B . . . . Lazzeri
2B . . . . . . Chapman
LF . . . . Cooke
C . . . . Dickey
P . . . . Ruffing

1930 at Philadelphia
CF . . . . Combs
SS . . . . Koenig
LF . . . . Ruth
1B . . . . Gehrig
2B . . . . Lazzeri
RF . . . . Chapman
3B . . . . Chapman
C . . . . Dickey
P . . . . Pipgras

1929 vs. Boston
CF . . . . Combs
3B . . . . Koenig
RF . . . . Ruth
1B . . . . Gehrig
LF . . . . Meusel
2B . . . . Lazzeri
SS . . . . Durocher
C . . . . Grabowski
P . . . . Pipgras

1928 at Philadelphia
CF . . . . Combs
SS . . . . Koenig
LF . . . . Ruth
1B . . . . Gehrig
RF . . . . Meusel
3B . . . . Dugan
2B . . . . . . Durocher
C . . . . Collins
P . . . . Pennock

1927 vs. Philadelphia
CF . . . . Combs
SS . . . . Koenig
RF . . . . Ruth
1B . . . . Gehrig
LF . . . . Meusel
2B . . . . Lazzeri
3B . . . . Dugan
C . . . . Grabowski
P . . . . Hoyt

1926 at Boston
SS . . . . Koenig
CF . . . . Combs
1B . . . . Gehrig
LF . . . . Ruth
RF . . . . Meusel
2B . . . . Lazzeri
3B . . . . Dugan
C . . . . Collins
P . . . . Shawkey

1925 vs. Washington
RF . . . . Paschal
3B . . . . Dugan
CF . . . . Combs
LF . . . . Meusel
1B . . . . Pipp
2B . . . . A. Ward
SS . . . . Scott
C . . . . O'Neill
P . . . . Shocker

1924 at Boston
CF . . . . Witt
3B . . . . Dugan
LF . . . . Ruth
1B . . . . Pipp
RF . . . . Meusel
2B . . . . Ward
C . . . . Schang
SS . . . . Scott
P . . . . Shawkey

1923 vs. Boston
CF . . . . Witt
3B . . . . Dugan
RF . . . . Ruth
1B . . . . Pipp
LF . . . . Meusel
C . . . . Schang
2B . . . . Ward
SS . . . . Scott
P . . . . Shawkey

1922 at Washington
CF . . . . Witt
LF . . . . Fewster
3B . . . . Baker
RF . . . . . . McMillan
1B . . . . Pipp
2B . . . . Ward
SS . . . . Scott
C . . . . Schang
P . . . . Jones

1921 vs. Philadelphia
2B . . . . Fewster
SS . . . . . Peckinpaugh
LF . . . . Ruth
1B . . . . Pipp
RF . . . . Meusel
CF . . . . Bodie
3B . . . . Ward
C . . . . Schang
P . . . . Mays

1920 at Philadelphia
RF . . . . Gleich
SS . . . . . Peckinpaugh
1B . . . . Pipp
CF . . . . Ruth
LF . . . . Lewis
3B . . . . Meusel
2B . . . . Pratt
C . . . . Ruel
P . . . . Shawkey

1919 vs. Boston
RF . . . . Vick
SS . . . . . Peckinpaugh
1B . . . . Pipp
3B . . . . Baker
2B . . . . Pratt
CF . . . . Lewis
LF . . . . Bodie
C . . . . Hannah
P . . . . Mogridge

1918 at Washington
RF . . . . . . Gilhooley
CF . . . . Miller
2B . . . . Pratt
1B . . . . Pipp
3B . . . . Baker
LF . . . . Bodie
SS . . . . . Peckinpaugh
C . . . . Hannah
P . . . . Mogridge

1917 vs. Boston
RF . . . . . . Gilhooley
LF . . . . High
2B . . . . Maisel
1B . . . . Pipp
3B . . . . Baker
CF . . . . Magee
SS . . . . . Peckinpaugh
C . . . . . . Nunamaker
P . . . . Caldwell

1916 vs. Washington
CF . . . . Maisel
RF . . . . . . Gilhooley
LF . . . . Magee
3B . . . . Baker
2B . . . . Gedeon
1B . . . . Pipp
SS . . . . Peckinpaugh
C . . . . . . Nunamaker
P . . . . Caldwell

1915 at Washington
3B . . . . Maisel
LF . . . . High
CF . . . . Cree
1B . . . . Pipp
RF . . . . Cook
SS . . . . Peckinpaugh
2B . . . . Boone
C . . . . Sweeney
P . . . . Warhop

1914 vs. Philadelphia
3B . . . . Maisel
2B . . . . Hartzell
LF . . . . Walsh
1B . . . . Williams
CF . . . . Holden
RF . . . . Cook
SS . . . . Peckinpaugh
C . . . . Sweeney
P . . . . McHale

1913 at Washington
RF . . . . Daniels
CF . . . . Wolter
3B . . . . Hartzell
LF . . . . Cree
2B . . . . Chase
1B . . . . . . Sterrett
C . . . . Sweeney
SS . . . . Young
P . . . . . . McConnell

1912 vs. Boston
RF . . . . Wolter
CF . . . . Daniels
1B . . . . Chase
LF . . . . Cree
SS . . . . . . Hartzell
3B . . . . Dolan
2B . . . . . . Gardner
C . . . . Street
P . . . . . . Caldwell

1911 at Philadelphia
RF . . . . Wolter
CF . . . . . . Hemphill
1B . . . . Chase
3B . . . . Hartzell
2B . . . . . . Knight
LF . . . . Cree
SS . . . . . Johnson
C . . . . Blair
P . . . . . . Vaughn

1910 vs. Boston
CF . . . . . . Hemphill
RF . . . . Wolter
1B . . . . Chase
LF . . . . . . Engle
2B . . . . . . Gardner
SS . . . . . . Foster
3B . . . . . . Austin
C . . . . . . Sweeney
P . . . . . . Vaughn

1909 at Washington
CF . . . . . . Hemphill
RF . . . . . . Keeler
3B . . . . . . Elberfeld
LF . . . . . . Engle
1B . . . . . . Ward
2B . . . . . . Ball
SS . . . . . . Knight
C . . . . . . Kleinow
P . . . . . . Newton

1908 vs. Washington
2B . . . . Niles
RF . . . . Keeler
LF . . . . Stahl
SS . . . . . Elberfeld
1B . . . . Chase
CF . . . . . Hemphill
3B . . . . . Conroy
C . . . . . . Kleinow
P . . . . . . Doyle

1907 at Washington
CF . . . . . . Hoffman
RF . . . . . . Keeler
SS . . . . . Elberfeld
2B . . . . . Williams
3B . . . . . LaPorte
LF . . . . . Conroy
1B . . . . . Moriarty
C . . . . . Kleinow
P . . . . . . Orth

1906 vs. Boston
RF . . . . . Dougherty
RF . . . . . . Keeler
SS . . . . . Elberfeld
3B . . . . . LaPorte
2B . . . . Williams
CF . . . . . Conroy
1B . . . . . Chase
C . . . . . McGuire
P . . . . Chesbro

1905 at Washington
LF . . . . . Dougherty
RF . . . . . Keeler
SS . . . . Elberfeld
2B . . . . Williams
CF . . . . Anderson
3B . . . . Conroy
1B . . . . . Chase
C . . . . . Kleinow
P . . . . Chesbro

1904 vs. Boston
3B . . . . . . Conroy
CF . . . . Fultz
RF . . . . . . Keeler
SS . . . . . Elberfeld
LF . . . . . Anderson
2B . . . . Williams
1B . . . . . Ganzel
C . . . . . McGuire
P . . . . . Chesbro

1903 at Washington
LF . . . . . . Davis
RF . . . . . Keeler
CF . . . . . Fultz
2B . . . . Williams
1B . . . . . Ganzel
3B . . . . . Conroy
SS . . . . . Long
C . . . . . O'Connor
P . . . . Chesbro

Yankees Managers on Opening Day

MANAGER	Years	G	W	L	PCT.
Joe McCarthy*	1931-46	16	10	6	.625
Miller Huggins*	1918-29	12	9	3	.750
Casey Stengel*	1949-60	12	10	2	.833
Joe Torre*	1996-2007	12	7	5	.583
Ralph Houk	1961-63, '67-73	11	5	5	.500
Clark Griffith	1903-08	6	5	1	.833
Billy Martin	1976-78, '83, '88	5	2	3	.400
Buck Showalter*	1992-95	4	4	0	1.000
Yogi Berra	1964, '84-85	3	0	3	.000
Bill Donovan	1915-17	3	0	3	.000
Frank Chance	1913-14	2	1	1	.500
JOE GIRARDI*	**2008-10**	**3**	**1**	**2**	**.333**
Bucky Harris	1947-48	2	1	1	.500
Johnny Keane	1965-66	2	0	2	.000
Bob Lemon	1979, '82	2	0	2	.000
Lou Piniella*	1986-87	2	2	0	1.000
George Stallings+	1909-10	2	0	1	.000 (1 tie)
Bill Virdon*	1974-75	2	1	1	.500
Hal Chase	1911	1	1	0	1.000
Dallas Green*	1989	1	1	0	1.000
Bucky Dent	1990	1	1	0	1.000
Dick Howser	1980	1	0	1	.000
Stump Merrill	1991	1	0	1	.000
Gene Michael*	1981	1	1	0	1.000
Bob Shawkey	1930	1	0	1	.000
Harry Wolverton	1912	1	0	1	.000
Total		**108**	**62**	**45**	**.579 (1 tie)**

* Won Yankees managerial debut on Opening Day.
+ 1910 opener called due to darkness tied 4-4.

2010 Opening Day Roster

PITCHERS (12): RHP Alfredo Aceves, RHP A.J. Burnett, RHP Joba Chamberlain, RHP Phil Hughes, LHP Damaso Marte, RHP Sergio Mitre, RHP Chan Ho Park, LHP Andy Pettitte, RHP Mariano Rivera, RHP David Robertson, LHP CC Sabathia, RHP Javier Vazquez.

CATCHERS (2): Francisco Cervelli, Jorge Posada.

INFIELDERS (5): Robinson Cano, Derek Jeter, Ramiro Pena, Alex Rodriguez, Mark Teixeira.

OUTFIELDERS (5): Brett Gardner, Curtis Granderson, Nick Swisher, Marcus Thames, Randy Winn.

DESIGNATED HITTER (1): Nick Johnson

All-Time Opening Day Results

YEAR	OPPONENT	W/L	SCORE	WP	LP
2010	at Boston	L	9-7	Okajima	Park
2009	at Baltimore	L	10-5	Guthrie	Sabathia
2008	vs. Toronto	W	3-2	Wang	Halladay
2007	vs. Tampa Bay	W	9-5	Vizcaino	Stokes
2006	at Oakland	W	15-2	Johnson	Zito
2005	vs. Boston	W	9-2	Johnson	Wells
2004	at Tampa Bay*	W	8-3	Zambrano	Mussina
2003	at Toronto	W	8-4	Clemens	Halladay
2002	at Baltimore	L	10-3	Erickson	Clemens
2001	vs. Kansas City	W	7-3	Clemens	Suppan
2000	at Anaheim	W	3-2	Hernandez	Hill
1999	at Oakland	L	5-3 (8)	Matthews	Stanton
1998	at Anaheim	L	4-1	Finley	Pettitte
1997	at Seattle	L	4-2	Fassero	Cone
1996	at Cleveland	W	7-3	Cone	Martinez
1995	vs. Texas	W	8-6	Key	Rogers
1994	vs. Texas	W	5-3	Key	Brown
1993	at Cleveland	W	9-1	Key	Nagy
1992	vs. Boston	W	4-3	Sanderson	Clemens
1991	at Detroit	L	6-4	Gibson	Cadaret
1990	vs. Cleveland	W	6-4	Plunk	Orosco
1989	at Minnesota	W	4-2	John	Viola
1988	vs. Minnesota	W	8-0	Rhoden	Viola
1987	at Detroit	W	2-1 (10)	Righetti	Morris
1986	vs. Kansas City	W	4-2	Guidry	Black
1985	at Boston	L	9-2	Boyd	Niekro
1984	at Kansas City	L	4-2	Black	Guidry
1983	at Seattle	L	5-4	Clark	Erickson
1982	vs. Chicago (AL)	L	7-6 (12)	Hickey	Gossage
1981	vs. Texas	W	10-3	John	Matlack
1980	at Texas	L	1-0 (12)	Lyle	Underwood
1979	vs. Milwaukee	L	5-1	Caldwell	Guidry
1978	at Texas	L	2-1	Matlack	Gossage
1977	vs. Milwaukee	W	3-0	Hunter	Travers
1976	at Milwaukee	L	5-0	Slaton	Hunter
1975	at Cleveland	L	5-3	Perry	Medich
1974	vs. Cleveland	W	6-1	Stottlemyre	Perry
1973	at Boston	L	15-5	Tiant	Stottlemyre
1972	at Baltimore	L	3-1	Dobson	Stottlemyre
1971	at Boston	L	3-1	Culp	Bahnsen
1970	vs. Boston	L	4-3	Peters	Stottlemyre
1969	at Washington	W	8-4	Stottlemyre	Pascual
1968	vs. California	W	1-0	Stottlemyre	Brunet
1967	at Washington	W	8-0	Stottlemyre	Richert
1966	vs. Detroit	L	2-1	Lolich	Ford
1965	at Minnesota	L	5-4(11)	Fosnow	Ramos
1964	vs. Boston	L	4-3(11)	Radatz	Ford
1963	at Kansas City	W	8-2	Terry	Segui
1962	vs. Baltimore	W	7-6	Terry	Brown
1961	vs. Minnesota	L	6-0	Ramos	Ford
1960	at Boston	W	8-4	Coates	Brewer
1959	vs. Boston	W	3-2	Turley	Brewer
1958	at Boston	W	3-0	Larsen	Nixon
1957	vs. Washington	W	2-1	Ford	Stobbs
1956	at Washington	W	10-4	Larsen	Pascual
1955	vs. Washington	W	19-1	Ford	McDermott
1954	at Washington	L	5-3	Dixon	Reynolds
1953	vs. Philadelphia	L	5-0	Kellner	Raschi
1952	at Philadelphia	W	8-1	Raschi	Kellner
1951	vs. Boston	W	5-0	Raschi	Wight
1950	at Boston	W	15-10	Johnson	Masterson
1949	vs. Washington	W	3-2	Lopat	Hudson
1948	at Washington	W	12-4	Reynolds	Wynn
1947	vs. Philadelphia	L	6-1	Marchildon	Chandler
1946	at Philadelphia	W	5-0	Chandler	Christopher
1945	vs. Boston	W	8-4	Donald	Cecil
1944	at Boston	W	3-0	Borowy	Terry
1943	vs. Washington	W	5-4	Murphy	Haeffner
1942	at Washington	W	7-0	Ruffing	Hudson
1941	at Washington	W	3-0	Russo	Leonard
1940	at Philadelphia	L	2-1 (10)	Dean	Ruffing
1939	vs. Boston	W	2-0	Ruffing	Grove
1938	at Boston	L	8-4	Bagby	Ruffing
1937	vs. Washington	W	3-2	Weaver	Gomez
1936	at Washington	L	1-0	Newsom	Gomez
1935	vs. Boston	L	1-0	Ferrell	Gomez
1934	at Philadelphia	L	6-5	Cascarella	Smythe
1933	vs. Boston	W	4-3	Gomez	Andrews
1932	at Philadelphia	W	12-6	Gomez	Earnshaw
1931	vs. Boston	W	6-3	Ruffing	Moore
1930	at Philadelphia	L	6-2	Grove	Pipgras
1929	vs. Boston	W	7-3	Pipgras	Ruffing
1928	at Philadelphia	W	8-3	Pennock	Grove
1927	vs. Philadelphia	W	8-3	Hoyt	Grove
1926	at Boston	W	12-11	Shawkey	Ehmke
1925	vs. Washington	W	5-1	Shocker	Mogridge
1924	at Boston	W	2-1	Shawkey	Ehmke
1923	vs. Boston	W	4-1	Shawkey	Ehmke
1922	at Washington	L	6-5	Mogridge	Jones
1921	vs. Philadelphia	W	11-1	Mays	Perry
1920	at Philadelphia	L	3-1	Perry	Shawkey
1919	vs. Boston	L	10-0	Mays	Mogridge
1918	at Washington	W	6-3	Mogridge	Johnson
1917	vs. Boston	L	10-3	Ruth	Caldwell
1916	vs. Washington	L	3-2 (11)	Johnson	Caldwell
1915	at Washington	L	7-0	Johnson	Warhop
1914	vs. Philadelphia	W	8-2	McHale	Bush
1913	at Washington	L	2-1	Johnson	McConnell
1912	vs. Boston	L	5-3	Wood	Caldwell
1911	at Philadelphia	W	2-1	Vaughn	Bender
1910	vs. Boston	T	4-4 (14)	Game called because of darkness	
1909	at Washington	L	4-1	Smith	Newton
1908	vs. Philadelphia	W	1-0 (12)	Carter	Doyle
1907	at Washington	W	3-2	Orth	Hughes
1906	vs. Boston	W	2-1	Chesbro	Young
1905	vs. Washington	W	4-2	Chesbro	Patten
1904	vs. Boston	W	8-2	Chesbro	Young
1903	at Washington	L	3-1	Orth	Chesbro

*at Tokyo Dome, Yankees were visiting team

OPENING DAY HOME RUNS

The Yankees have hit 96 Opening Day home runs in franchise history by 58 different players. In 2010 at Boston, Jorge Posada and Curtis Granderson hit back-to-back homers, marking the first Yankees to go back-to-back on Opening Day since Dave Winfield and Steve Kemp in 1983 at Seattle. Joe Pepitone (pictured) was the last Yankee to homer twice on Opening Day.

MULTI-HOME RUN GAMES ON OPENING DAY (6)

Babe Ruth (2)	4/12/32	at Philadelphia
Sammy Byrd (2)	4/12/32	at Philadelphia
Russ Derry (2)	4/17/45	vs. Boston
Mickey Mantle (2)	4/17/56	at Washington
Roger Maris (2)	4/19/60	at Boston
Joe Pepitone (2)	4/9/63	at Kansas City

Home Opener Ceremonial First Pitches

New York Governor Al Smith throws out the ceremonial first pitch at Yankee Stadium's inaugural game on April 18, 1923.

2010 Bernie Williams
2009 Yogi Berra
2008 Reggie Jackson
2007 Melanie Lidle and Christopher Lidle, widow and son of Cory Lidle
2006 Yogi Berra
2005 Yogi Berra
2004 Yogi Berra, Whitey Ford, and Phil Rizzuto
2003 Yogi Berra and Whitey Ford
2002 Michael Bloomberg, New York City Mayor
2001 Mel Stottlemyre
2000 Yogi Berra
1999 Yogi Berra
1998 Joe DiMaggio
1997 Joe DiMaggio
1996 Joe DiMaggio
1995 Joe DiMaggio
1994 Joe DiMaggio
1993 Dean Smith, University of North Carolina Head Basketball Coach (representing North Carolina State University Head Basketball Coach Jim Valvano, who was too ill to attend)
1992 Joe DiMaggio
1991 General Colin Powell, Chairman, Joint Chiefs of Staff
1990 Bill Martin Jr.
1989 P.J. Carlesimo, Seton Hall University Head Basketball Coach
1988 Diane Munson, widow of Thurman Munson; and Arlene Howard, widow of Elston Howard
1987 Rachel Robinson, widow of Jackie Robinson
1986 Robert Merrill, Metropolitan Opera
1985 Mickey Mantle
1984 Scott Hamilton, U.S. Olympic Skater
1983 Joe DiMaggio
1982 Jimmy Esposito, Head Groundskeeper whose crew got the field in shape after a heavy snow storm
1981 Elston Howard Jr.
1980 Eric Heiden, Mike Eruzione, and Herb Brooks; 1980 U.S. Olympic Heroes
1979 Lucielle James, widow of World War II hero
1978 No first-pitch ceremony (Mickey Mantle and Roger Maris raised 1977 championship flag)
1977 Vince Polito, randomly selected fan
1976 Bob Shawkey, Yankees starting pitcher at opener of Yankee Stadium on 4/18/23
1975 Five children of slain "Good Samaritan" Frank J. Walker
1974 Ted Kennedy Jr., son of United States Senator Ted Kennedy
1973 Herb Bluestone, who attended opening of Yankee Stadium in 1923
1972 Jim Farley, former Postmaster General of the United States
1971 John Lindsay, New York City Mayor
1970 Whitney Young Jr., President of the National Urban League
1969 Paul Simon, singer/songwriter
1968 Marianne Moore, famed 81-year-old poet and baseball fan
1967 John Lindsay, New York City Mayor
1966 John Lindsay, New York City Mayor
1965 Rick O'Keefe, 7-year-old fan (he would later be a first-round draft pick of the Milwaukee Brewers in 1975)
1964 William Bracciodieta, Columbia University student and baseball player (second winner of Yogi Berra Scholarship Award)
1963 Joe DiMaggio
1962 Claire Ruth, widow of Babe Ruth
1961 James Lyons, Bronx Borough President (standing in for Mayor Robert Wagner, who was ill)
1960 Joe Cronin, Hall of Famer and President of the American League
1959 Will Harridge, recently-retired President of the American League
1958 James Lyons, Bronx Borough President
1957 Robert F. Wagner Jr., New York City Mayor

1956 Robert F. Wagner Jr., New York City Mayor
1955 Robert F. Wagner Jr., New York City Mayor
1954 James Lyons, Bronx Borough President
1953 Vincent Impellitteri, New York City Mayor
1952 Joe DiMaggio, who retired after the 1951 season
1951 Whitey Ford (in military service)
1950 Ed Barrow, former Yankees President
1949 Gary Simpson, student at St. Mary's Industrial School in Baltimore, Md. (which was attended by Babe Ruth, who passed away the previous season)…Ruth monument also unveiled.
1948 Thomas Dewey, New York Governor
1947 Sgt. Anthony Guzzetta, wounded World War II veteran
1946 Sgt. Hulon B. Whittington, Congressional Medal of Honor recipient
1945 Fiorello LaGuardia, New York City Mayor
1944 Fiorello LaGuardia, New York City Mayor
1943 Fiorello LaGuardia, New York City Mayor
1942 Fiorello LaGuardia, New York City Mayor
1941 Fiorello LaGuardia, New York City Mayor
1940 Fiorello LaGuardia, New York City Mayor
1939 Fiorello LaGuardia, New York City Mayor
1938 Newbold Morris, New York City Council President
1937 Fiorello LaGuardia, New York City Mayor
1936 Fiorello LaGuardia, New York City Mayor
1935 Fiorello LaGuardia, New York City Mayor
1934 Fiorello LaGuardia, New York City Mayor
1933 John O'Brien, New York City Mayor
1932 Jimmy Walker, New York City Mayor
1931 Jimmy Walker, New York City Mayor
1930 Jimmy Walker, New York City Mayor
1929 Joseph V. McKee, President of the New York City Board of Aldermen (substituting for Mayor Walker)
1928 Jimmy Walker, New York City Mayor

1927 Jimmy Walker, New York City Mayor
1926 Jimmy Walker, New York City Mayor
1925 Rear Admiral Charles P. Plunkett
1924 John F. Hylan, New York City Mayor
1923 Al Smith, New York Governor
1922 John F. Hylan, New York City Mayor
1921 John F. Hylan, New York City Mayor
1920 Lt. General Robert Bullard
1919 Robert Moran, President of the New York City Board of Aldermen
1918 Brigadier General William Mann
1917 Major General Leonard Wood
1916 Al Smith, Sheriff of New York
1915 John Mitchell, New York City Mayor
1914 Robert Wagner, New York Lieutenant Governor
1913 Bill Devery, co-owner
1912 Edward B. McCall, judge
1911 City Chamberlain Hyde
1910 Bill Devery, co-owner
1909 Tim Foley, Sheriff of New York
1908 George McClellan, New York City Mayor
1907 Diamond Jim Brady
1906 John M. Ward, former player
1905 Game was rained out (Congressman Tim Sullivan had thrown the first pitch)
1904 William Olcott, judge
1903 Ban Johnson, President of the American League

All-Time New York Yankees Managers

MANAGER	YEARS	WON	LOST	PCT	A. L. PENNANTS	WORLD CHAMPIONSHIPS
Joe McCarthy	1931-46	1460	867	.627	8	7
Casey Stengel	1949-60	1149	696	.623	10	7
Joe Torre	1996-2007	1173	767	.605	6	4
Miller Huggins	1918-29	1067	719	.597	6	3
Ralph Houk	1961-63, '66-73	944	806	.539	3	2
Billy Martin	1975-78, '79, '83, '85, '88	556	385	.591	2	1
Clark Griffith	1903-08	419	370	.531	0	0
Buck Showalter	1992-95	313	268	.539	0	0
Lou Piniella	1986-87, '88	224	193	.537	0	0
Bill Donovan	1915-17	220	239	.479	0	0
JOE GIRARDI	2008-10	287	199	.591	1	1
Yogi Berra	1964, '84-85	192	148	.565	1	0
Bucky Harris	1947-48	191	117	.620	1	1
George Stallings	1909-10	153	138	.526	0	0
Bill Virdon	1974-75	142	124	.534	0	0
Stump Merrill	1990-91	120	155	.436	0	0
Frank Chance	1913-14	117	168	.411	0	0
Dick Howser	1980	103	60	.632	0	0
Bob Lemon	1978-79, '81-82	99	73	.576	2	1
Gene Michael	1981, '82	92	76	.548	0	0
Bob Shawkey	1930	86	68	.558	0	0
Hal Chase	1910-11	85	78	.521	0	0
Johnny Keane	1965-66	81	101	.445	0	0
Bill Dickey	1946	57	48	.543	0	0
Dallas Green	1989	56	65	.463	0	0
Harry Wolverton	1912	50	102	.329	0	0
Bucky Dent	1989-90	36	53	.404	0	0
Clyde King	1982	29	33	.468	0	0
Norm Elberfeld	1908	27	71	.276	0	0
Roger Peckinpaugh	1914	10	10	.500	0	0
Johnny Neun	1946	8	6	.571	0	0
Art Fletcher	1929	6	5	.545	0	0
Totals	**1903-2010**	**9552**	**7208**	**.570**	**40**	**27**

New York Yankees General Managers

Harry Sparrow (1) 1/11/15-5/7/20
Ed Barrow (2) 10/28/20-2/20/45
Larry MacPhail 2/21/45-10/7/47
George Weiss 10/7/47-11/2/60
Roy Hamey 10/3/60-10/22/63
Ralph Houk 10/22/63-5/7/66
Dan Topping, Jr. (3) 5/7/66-10/12/66
Lee MacPhail 12/3/66-10/23/73
Gabe Paul (4) 11/1/73-12/31/77
Cedric Tallis (5) 1/1/78-10/31/79
Gene Michael 11/1/79-11/20/80
Cedric Tallis and Bill Bergesch (6) 11/21/80-7/1/83
Murray Cook 7/1/83-4/9/84
Clyde King 4/9/84-10/9/86
Woody Woodward 10/10/86-10/18/87
Lou Piniella 10/19/87-5/29/88
Bob Quinn 6/8/88-3/20/89
Syd Thrift (7) 3/21/89-8/29/89
Bob Quinn 8/29/89-10/13/89
Harding Peterson 10/18/89-8/19/90
Gene Michael 8/20/90-10/22/95
Bob Watson 10/23/95-2/2/98
Brian Cashman 2/3/98-present

(1) Held title of business manager.
(2) Formally held titles of Yankees Business Manager and Secretary until Jan. 17, 1939 when he was named president, but performed GM duties throughout.
(3) Served as acting GM and frequently consulted Ralph Houk.
(4) Did not have title of general manager during points of his tenure but performed GM duties.
(5) Al Rosen, who was team president, also performed baseball operations duties typical of a general manager during parts of his tenure from 3/27/78-7/19/79.
(6) Did not have title of general manager but together performed GM duties.
(7) Formally held title of "Senior Vice President of Baseball Operations" but performed the duties of a GM. Bob Quinn served as his assistant while maintaining the General Manager title he held previous to Thrift's arrival.

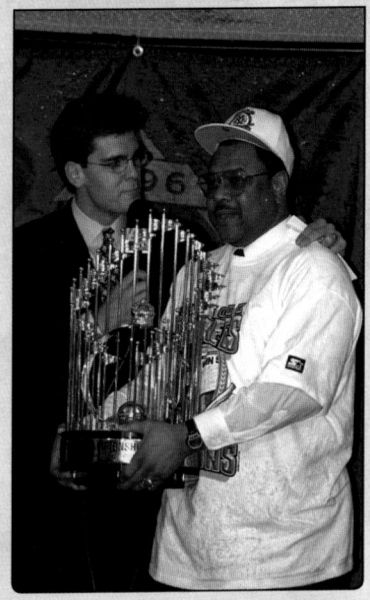

General Manger Bob Watson celebrates with the 1996 World Series trophy after the Yankees defeated Atlanta in Game 6 at Yankee Stadium.

Year-by-Year Results

Franchise History: 108 seasons, 49 playoff appearances (Won 27 World Series, Lost 13 World Series, Lost 3 ALCS, Lost 6 ALDS)
Division Winner (since start of Div. play in 1969): 16 times (incl. first-half win in 1981); **Wild Card:** 4 times (1995, '97, 2007, '10)

Year	Postseason	Position	GA/GB	Won	Lost	Pct.	Manager	Attendance	Stadium
1903		Fourth	-17.0	72	62	.537	Clark Griffith	211,808	Hilltop Park
1904		Second	-1.5	92	59	.609	Clark Griffith	438,919	Hilltop Park
1905		Sixth	-21.5	71	78	.477	Clark Griffith	309,100	Hilltop Park
1906		Second	-3.0	90	61	.596	Clark Griffith	434,700	Hilltop Park
1907		Fifth	-21.0	70	78	.473	Clark Griffith	350,020	Hilltop Park
1908		Eighth	-39.5	51	103	.331	Griffith-Kid Elberfeld	305,500	Hilltop Park
1909		Fifth	-23.5	74	77	.490	George Stallings	501,000	Hilltop Park
1910		Second	-14.5	88	63	.583	Stallings-Hal Chase	355,857	Hilltop Park
1911		Sixth	-25.5	76	76	.500	Hal Chase	302,444	Hilltop Park
1912		Eighth	-55.0	50	102	.329	Harry Wolverton	242,194	Hilltop Park
1913		Seventh	-38.0	57	94	.377	Frank Chance	357,551	Polo Grounds
1914		Sixth	-30.0	70	84	.455	Chance-Peckinpaugh	359,477	Polo Grounds
1915		Fifth	-32.5	69	83	.454	Bill Donovan	256,035	Polo Grounds
1916		Fourth	-11.0	80	74	.519	Bill Donovan	469,211	Polo Grounds
1917		Sixth	-28.5	71	82	.464	Bill Donovan	330,294	Polo Grounds
1918		Fourth	-13.5	60	63	.488	Miller Huggins	282,047	Polo Grounds
1919		Third	-7.5	80	59	.576	Miller Huggins	619,164	Polo Grounds
1920		Third	-3.0	95	59	.617	Miller Huggins	1,289,422	Polo Grounds
1921	Lost WS	First	+4.5	98	55	.641	Miller Huggins	1,230,696	Polo Grounds
1922	Lost WS	First	+1.0	94	60	.610	Miller Huggins	1,026,134	Polo Grounds
1923	Won WS	First	+16.0	98	54	.645	Miller Huggins	1,007,066	Orig. Yankee Stad.
1924		Second	-2.0	89	63	.586	Miller Huggins	1,053,533	Orig. Yankee Stad.
1925		Seventh	-28.5	69	85	.448	Miller Huggins	697,267	Orig. Yankee Stad.
1926	Lost WS	First	+3.0	91	63	.591	Miller Huggins	1,027,095	Orig. Yankee Stad.
1927	Won WS	First	+19.0	110	44	.714	Miller Huggins	1,164,015	Orig. Yankee Stad.
1928	Won WS	First	+2.5	101	53	.656	Miller Huggins	1,072,132	Orig. Yankee Stad.
1929		Second	-18.0	88	66	.571	Huggins-Art Fletcher	960,148	Orig. Yankee Stad.
1930		Third	-16.0	86	68	.558	Bob Shawkey	1,169,230	Orig. Yankee Stad.
1931		Second	-13.5	94	59	.614	Joe McCarthy	912,437	Orig. Yankee Stad.
1932	Won WS	First	+13.0	107	47	.695	Joe McCarthy	962,320	Orig. Yankee Stad.
1933		Second	-7.0	91	59	.607	Joe McCarthy	728,014	Orig. Yankee Stad.
1934		Second	-7.0	94	60	.610	Joe McCarthy	854,682	Orig. Yankee Stad.
1935		Second	-3.0	89	60	.597	Joe McCarthy	657,508	Orig. Yankee Stad.
1936	Won WS	First	+19.5	102	51	.667	Joe McCarthy	976,913	Orig. Yankee Stad.
1937	Won WS	First	+13.0	102	52	.662	Joe McCarthy	998,148	Orig. Yankee Stad.
1938	Won WS	First	+9.5	99	53	.651	Joe McCarthy	970,916	Orig. Yankee Stad.
1939	Won WS	First	+17.0	106	45	.702	Joe McCarthy	859,785	Orig. Yankee Stad.
1940		Third	-2.0	88	66	.571	Joe McCarthy	988,975	Orig. Yankee Stad.
1941	Won WS	First	+17.0	101	53	.656	Joe McCarthy	964,722	Orig. Yankee Stad.
1942	Lost WS	First	+9.0	103	51	.669	Joe McCarthy	988,251	Orig. Yankee Stad.
1943	Won WS	First	+13.5	98	56	.636	Joe McCarthy	645,006	Orig. Yankee Stad.
1944		Third	-6.0	83	71	.539	Joe McCarthy	789,995	Orig. Yankee Stad.
1945		Fourth	-6.5	81	71	.533	Joe McCarthy	881,846	Orig. Yankee Stad.
1946		Third	-17.0	87	67	.565	McCarthy-Dickey-Neun	2,265,512	Orig. Yankee Stad.
1947	Won WS	First	+12.0	97	57	.630	Bucky Harris	2,178,937	Orig. Yankee Stad.
1948		Third	-2.5	94	60	.610	Bucky Harris	2,373,901	Orig. Yankee Stad.
1949	Won WS	First	+1.0	97	57	.630	Casey Stengel	2,281,676	Orig. Yankee Stad.
1950	Won WS	First	+3.0	98	56	.636	Casey Stengel	2,081,380	Orig. Yankee Stad.
1951	Won WS	First	+5.0	98	56	.636	Casey Stengel	1,950,107	Orig. Yankee Stad.
1952	Won WS	First	+2.0	95	59	.617	Casey Stengel	1,629,665	Orig. Yankee Stad.
1953	Won WS	First	+8.5	99	52	.656	Casey Stengel	1,537,811	Orig. Yankee Stad.
1954		Second	-8.0	103	51	.669	Casey Stengel	1,475,171	Orig. Yankee Stad.
1955	Lost WS	First	+3.0	96	58	.623	Casey Stengel	1,490,138	Orig. Yankee Stad.
1956	Won WS	First	+9.0	97	57	.680	Casey Stengel	1,491,138	Orig. Yankee Stad.
1957	Lost WS	First	+8.0	98	56	.636	Casey Stengel	1,497,134	Orig. Yankee Stad.
1958	Won WS	First	+10.0	92	62	.597	Casey Stengel	1,428,438	Orig. Yankee Stad.
1959		Third	-15.0	79	75	.513	Casey Stengel	1,552,030	Orig. Yankee Stad.
1960	Lost WS	First	+8.0	97	57	.630	Casey Stengel	1,627,349	Orig. Yankee Stad.
1961	Won WS	First	+8.0	109	53	.673	Ralph Houk	1,747,725	Orig. Yankee Stad.
1962	Won WS	First	+5.0	96	66	.593	Ralph Houk	1,493,574	Orig. Yankee Stad.
1963	Lost WS	First	+10.5	104	57	.646	Ralph Houk	1,308,920	Orig. Yankee Stad.
1964	Lost WS	First	+1.0	99	63	.611	Yogi Berra	1,305,638	Orig. Yankee Stad.
1965		Sixth	-25.0	77	85	.475	Johnny Keane	1,213,552	Orig. Yankee Stad.
1966		Tenth	-26.5	70	89	.440	Keane-Houk	1,124,648	Orig. Yankee Stad.
1967		Ninth	-20.0	72	90	.444	Ralph Houk	1,259,514	Orig. Yankee Stad.
1968		Fifth	-20.0	83	79	.512	Ralph Houk	1,185,666	Orig. Yankee Stad.
1969		Fifth	-28.5	80	81	.497	Ralph Houk	1,067,996	Orig. Yankee Stad.
1970		Second	-15.0	93	69	.574	Ralph Houk	1,136,879	Orig. Yankee Stad.
1971		Fourth	-21.0	82	80	.506	Ralph Houk	1,070,771	Orig. Yankee Stad.
1972		Fourth	-6.5	79	76	.510	Ralph Houk	966,328	Orig. Yankee Stad.
1973		Fourth	-17.0	80	82	.494	Ralph Houk	1,262,103	Orig. Yankee Stad.

Year-by-Year Results

Year	Postseason	Position	GA/GB	Won	Lost	Pct.	Manager	Attendance	Stadium
1974		Second	-2.0	89	73	.549	Bill Virdon	1,273,075	Shea Stadium
1975		Third	-12.0	83	77	.519	Virdon-Billy Martin	1,288,048	Shea Stadium
1976	Lost WS	First	+10.5	97	62	.610	Billy Martin	2,012,434	Orig. Yankee Stad. (R)
1977	Won WS	First	+2.5	100	62	.617	Billy Martin	2,103,092	Orig. Yankee Stad. (R)
1978	Won WS	First	+1.0	100	63	.613	Martin-Bob Lemon	2,335,871	Orig. Yankee Stad. (R)
1979		Fourth	-13.5	89	71	.556	Lemon-Martin	2,537,765	Orig. Yankee Stad. (R)
1980	LostALCS	First	+3.0	103	59	.636	Dick Howser	2,627,417	Orig. Yankee Stad. (R)
1981	Lost WS	First	+2.0	34	22	.607	Gene Michael		Orig. Yankee Stad. (R)
		Sixth	-5.0	25	26	.490	Michael-Lemon	1,614,353	Orig. Yankee Stad. (R)
1982		Fifth	-16.0	79	83	.488	Lemon-Michael-C. King	2,041,219	Orig. Yankee Stad. (R)
1983		Third	-7.0	91	71	.562	Billy Martin	2,257,976	Orig. Yankee Stad. (R)
1984		Third	-17.0	87	75	.537	Yogi Berra	1,821,815	Orig. Yankee Stad. (R)
1985		Second	-2.0	97	64	.602	Berra-Martin	2,214,587	Orig. Yankee Stad. (R)
1986		Second	-5.5	90	72	.556	Lou Piniella	2,268,030	Orig. Yankee Stad. (R)
1987		Fourth	-9.0	89	73	.549	Lou Piniella	2,427,672	Orig. Yankee Stad. (R)
1988		Fifth	-3.5	85	76	.528	Martin-Piniella	2,633,701	Orig. Yankee Stad. (R)
1989		Fifth	-14.5	74	87	.460	Dallas Green-B. Dent	2,170,485	Orig. Yankee Stad. (R)
1990		Seventh	-21.0	67	95	.414	Dent-Stump Merrill	2,006,436	Orig. Yankee Stad. (R)
1991		Fifth	-21.0	71	91	.438	Stump Merrill	1,863,733	Orig. Yankee Stad. (R)
1992		Fourth	-20.0	76	86	.469	Buck Showalter	1,748,773	Orig. Yankee Stad. (R)
1993		Second	-7.0	88	74	.543	Buck Showalter	2,416,965	Orig. Yankee Stad. (R)
1994		First	+6.5	70	43	.619	Buck Showalter	1,675,556	Orig. Yankee Stad. (R)
1995	Lost ALDS	Second (WC)	-7.0	79	65	.549	Buck Showalter	1,705,263	Orig. Yankee Stad. (R)
1996	Won WS	First	+4.0	92	70	.568	Joe Torre	2,250,877	Orig. Yankee Stad. (R)
1997	Lost ALDS	Second (WC)	-2.0	96	66	593	Joe Torre	2,580,445	Orig. Yankee Stad. (R)
1998	Won WS	First	+22.0	114	48	.704	Joe Torre	2,919,046	Orig. Yankee Stad. (R)
1999	Won WS	First	+4.0	98	64	.605	Joe Torre	3,292,736	Orig. Yankee Stad. (R)
2000	Won WS	First	+2.5	87	74	.540	Joe Torre	3,227,657	Orig. Yankee Stad. (R)
2001	Lost WS	First	+13.5	95	65	.594	Joe Torre	3,264,777	Orig. Yankee Stad. (R)
2002	Lost ALDS	First	+10.5	103	58	.640	Joe Torre	3,461,644	Orig. Yankee Stad. (R)
2003	Lost WS	First	+6.0	101	61	.623	Joe Torre	3,465,585	Orig. Yankee Stad. (R)
2004	Lost ALCS	First	+3.0	101	61	.623	Joe Torre	3,775,292	Orig. Yankee Stad. (R)
2005	Lost ALDS	First	0.0	95	67	.586	Joe Torre	4,090,692	Orig. Yankee Stad. (R)
2006	Lost ALDS	First	+10.0	97	65	.599	Joe Torre	4,243,780	Orig. Yankee Stad. (R)
2007	Lost ALDS	Second (WC)	-2.0	94	68	.580	Joe Torre	4,271,083	Orig. Yankee Stad. (R)
2008		Third	-8.0	89	73	.549	Joe Girardi	4,298,543	Orig. Yankee Stad. (R)
2009	Won WS	First	+8.0	103	59	.636	Joe Girardi	3,719,358	Yankee Stadium
2010	Lost ALCS	Second (WC)	-1.0	95	67	.586	Joe Girardi	3,765,807	Yankee Stadium
Totals				**9,552**	**7,208**	**.570**		(R) Remodeled Orig. Yankee Stadium	

Yankees Silver Slugger Award Winners by Year

Award given since 1980

Year:	Player (Position)	Year:	Player (Position)	Year:	Player (Position)
1980:	Willie Randolph (2B)	1991:	None	2003:	JORGE POSADA (C)
1981:	Dave Winfield (OF)	1992:	None	2004:	Gary Sheffield (OF)
1982:	Dave Winfield (OF)	1993:	Mike Stanley (C),	2005:	ALEX RODRIGUEZ (3B),
1983:	Dave Winfield (OF),		Wade Boggs (3B)		Gary Sheffield (OF)
	Don Baylor (DH)	1994:	Wade Boggs (3B)	2006:	ROBINSON CANO (2B),
1984:	Dave Winfield (OF)	1995:	None		DEREK JETER (SS)
1985:	Don Mattingly (1B),	1996:	None	2007:	JORGE POSADA (C),
	Rickey Henderson (OF),	1997:	Tino Martinez (1B)		ALEX RODRIGUEZ (3B),
	Dave Winfield (OF),	1998:	None		DEREK JETER (SS)
	Don Baylor (DH)	1999:	None	2008:	ALEX RODRIGUEZ (3B),
1986:	Don Mattingly (1B)	2000:	JORGE POSADA (C)		DEREK JETER (SS)
1987:	Don Mattingly (1B)	2001:	JORGE POSADA (C)	2009:	MARK TEIXEIRA (1B),
1988:	None	2002:	JORGE POSADA (C),		DEREK JETER (SS)
1989:	None		Jason Giambi (1B),	2010:	ROBINSON CANO (2B)
1990:	None		Alfonso Soriano (2B),		
			Bernie Williams (OF)		

Yankees Silver Slugger Award Winners by Position

Position	Winner (Years)
Catcher	Mike Stanley (1993); JORGE POSADA (2000-03, '07)
First Base	Don Mattingly (1985-87); Tino Martinez (1997); Jason Giambi (2002); MARK TEIXEIRA (2009)
Second Base	Willie Randolph (1980); Alfonso Soriano (2002), ROBINSON CANO (2006, '10)
Third Base	Wade Boggs (1993-94), ALEX RODRIGUEZ (2005, '07-08)
Shortstop	DEREK JETER (2006-09)
Outfield	Dave Winfield (1981-85); Rickey Henderson (1985); Bernie Williams (2002), Gary Sheffield (2004-05)
Designated Hitter	Don Baylor (1983, '85)

Yankees Postseason Appearances

YEAR	SERIES	OPPONENT	W	L
1921	WS	Giants	3	5
1922*	WS	Giants	0	4 (1 tie)
1923	WS	Giants	4	2
1926	WS	Cardinals	3	4
1927	WS	Pirates	4	0
1928	WS	Cardinals	4	0
1932	WS	Cubs	4	0
1936	WS	Giants	4	2
1937	WS	Giants	4	1
1938	WS	Cubs	4	0
1939	WS	Reds	4	0
1941	WS	Dodgers	4	1
1942	WS	Cardinals	1	4
1943	WS	Cardinals	4	1
1947	WS	Dodgers	4	3
1949	WS	Dodgers	4	1
1950	WS	Phillies	4	0
1951	WS	Giants	4	2
1952	WS	Dodgers	4	3
1953	WS	Dodgers	4	2
1955	WS	Dodgers	3	4
1956	WS	Dodgers	4	3
1957	WS	Braves	3	4
1958	WS	Braves	4	3
1960	WS	Pirates	3	4
1961	WS	Reds	4	1
1962	WS	Giants	4	3
1963	WS	Dodgers	0	4
1964	WS	Cardinals	3	4
1976	LCS	Royals	3	2
	WS	Reds	0	4
1977	LCS	Royals	3	2
	WS	Dodgers	4	2
1978	LCS	Royals	3	1
	WS	Dodgers	4	2

YEAR	SERIES	OPPONENT	W	L
1980	LCS	Royals	0	3
1981	DS	Brewers	3	2
	LCS	Athletics	3	0
	WS	Dodgers	2	4
1995	DS	Mariners	2	3
1996	DS	Rangers	3	1
	LCS	Orioles	4	1
	WS	Atlanta	4	2
1997	DS	Indians	2	3
1998	DS	Rangers	3	0
	LCS	Indians	4	2
	WS	Padres	4	0
1999	DS	Rangers	3	0
	LCS	Red Sox	4	1
	WS	Braves	4	0
2000	DS	Athletics	3	2
	LCS	Mariners	4	2
	WS	Mets	4	1
2001	DS	Athletics	3	2
	LCS	Mariners	4	1
	WS	Diamondbacks	3	4
2002	DS	Angels	1	3
2003	DS	Twins	3	1
	LCS	Red Sox	4	3
	WS	Marlins	2	4
2004	DS	Twins	3	1
	LCS	Red Sox	3	4
2005	DS	Angels	2	3
2006	DS	Tigers	1	3
2007	DS	Indians	1	3
2009	DS	Twins	3	0
	LCS	Angels	4	2
	WS	Phillies	4	2
2010	DS	Twins	3	0
	LCS	Rangers	2	4

SERIES TOTALS

	W	L
ALDS (10-6 in series, 66 games)	39	27
ALCS (11-3 in series, 73 games)	45	28
World Series (27-13 in series, 225 games*)	134	90
All Postseason Games (48-22 in series, 364 games*)	218	145

*includes one 3-3, 10-inning tie in 1922 WS Game 2 vs. New York-NL

1921 American League Champion Yankees - The first pennant-winning team in franchise history

It wasn't until the 19th season in franchise history (after moving to New York from Baltimore prior to the 1903 season) that the Yankees won their first American League pennant, finishing 98-55, 4.5 games ahead of Cleveland. The club was led by Babe Ruth, who batted .378 (204-for-540) with 59 home runs and a career-high 171 RBI. Carl Mays (27-5), Waite Hoyt (19-13) and Bob Shawkey (18-12) fronted a pitching staff that allowed the fewest earned runs in the American League (579). In the World Series, the last of Baseball's three-year experiment with a nine-game format, the Yankees were defeated 5-games-to-3 by the Giants, with whom they shared the Polo Grounds. Hoyt, who lost Game 8, 1-0, on an unearned run in the first inning, went 2-1 (27.0IP) in three complete games. Injuries suffered by Ruth in Game 2 (cut arm while sliding, which later became infected) and Game 5 (wrenched knee) limited him to just one pinch-hitting plate appearance in the final three games of the Series.

Top Row: Jack Quinn, Tom Rodgers, Alex Ferguson, Elmer Miller, Mike McNally, Harry "Rip" Collins, Bill Piercy, Frank "Home Run" Baker, Harry Harper, Al DeVormer, Fred Hofmann, Bob Meusel, Bob "Braggo" Roth, Roger Peckinpaugh. **Middle Row:** Aaron Ward, Bill "Chick" Fewster, Wally Pipp, Bob Shawkey, Wally Schang, Babe Ruth, Carl Mays, Waite Hoyt, Nelson "Chicken" Hawks. **Seated:** Johnny Mitchell, Bennet (Mascot), Miller Huggins (manager), Charles O'Leary (coach), Frank Roth (coach).

Year-by-Year Team Hitting Statistics

YEAR	AVG	AB	R	H	HR	RBI	SB	BB	SO	E
1903	.249	4565	579	1136	18	474	160	332	465	264
1904	.259	5220	598	1354	27	499	163	312	548	275
1905	.248	4957	587	1228	23	480	200	360	537	293
1906	.264	5095	641	1345	17	528	192	331	--	272
1907	.249	5042	604	1257	15	497	206	304	--	334
1908	.236	5036	456	1187	13	372	230	288	--	337
1909	.248	4981	591	1234	16	473	187	407	--	330
1910	.248	5050	629	1252	20	492	289	464	--	285
1911	.272	5056	686	1375	25	577	270	493	--	328
1912	.259	5095	632	1320	18	502	247	463	--	382
1913	.237	4880	529	1157	8	430	203	534	617	293
1914	.229	4992	536	1144	12	416	251	577	711	238
1915	.233	4982	583	1162	31	459	198	570	668	217
1916	.246	5200	575	1277	35	492	179	516	632	225
1917	.239	5136	524	1226	27	445	136	496	535	219
1918	.257	4224	491	1085	20	406	88	367	370	161
1919	.267	4775	582	1275	45	499	101	386	479	193
1920	.280	5176	838	1448	115	747	64	539	626	194
1921	.300	5249	948	1576	134	861	89	588	567	222
1922	.287	5245	758	1504	95	674	62	497	532	157
1923	.291	5347	823	1554	105	770	69	521	516	144
1924	.289	5340	798	1516	98	734	69	478	420	156
1925	.275	5353	706	1471	110	638	67	470	482	160
1926	.289	5221	847	1508	121	794	79	642	580	210
1927	.307	5347	975	1644	158	908	90	635	605	195
1928	.296	5337	894	1578	133	817	51	562	544	194
1929	.295	5379	899	1587	142	828	51	554	518	178
1930	.309	5448	1062	1683	152	986	91	644	569	207
1931	.297	5608	1067	1667	155	990	139	748	554	169
1932	.286	5477	1002	1564	160	955	77	766	527	188
1933	.283	5274	927	1495	144	849	74	700	506	165
1934	.278	5368	842	1494	135	791	71	700	597	157
1935	.280	5214	818	1462	104	755	68	604	469	151
1936	.300	5591	1065	1676	182	995	76	700	594	163
1937	.283	5487	979	1554	174	922	60	709	607	170
1938	.274	5410	966	1480	174	917	91	749	616	169
1939	.287	5300	967	1521	166	903	72	701	543	126
1940	.259	5286	817	1371	155	757	59	648	606	152
1941	.269	5444	830	1464	151	774	51	616	565	165
1942	.269	5305	801	1429	108	744	69	591	556	142
1943	.256	5282	669	1350	100	635	46	624	562	160
1944	.264	5331	674	1410	96	631	91	523	627	156
1945	.259	5176	676	1343	93	639	64	618	567	175
1946	.248	5139	684	1275	136	649	48	627	706	150
1947	.271	5308	794	1439	115	746	27	610	581	109
1948	.278	5324	857	1480	139	806	24	623	478	120
1949	.269	5196	829	1396	115	759	58	731	539	138
1950	.282	5361	914	1511	159	863	41	687	463	119
1951	.269	5194	798	1395	140	741	78	605	547	144
1952	.267	5294	727	1411	129	672	52	566	652	127
1953	.273	5194	801	1420	139	762	34	656	644	126
1954	.268	5226	805	1400	133	747	34	650	632	126
1955	.260	5161	762	1342	175	722	55	609	658	128
1956	.270	5312	857	1433	190	788	51	615	755	136
1957	.268	5271	723	1412	145	682	49	562	709	123
1958	.268	5294	759	1418	164	715	48	537	822	128
1959	.260	5379	687	1397	153	651	45	457	828	131
1960	.260	5290	746	1377	193	699	37	537	818	129
1961	.263	5559	827	1461	240	781	28	543	785	124
1962	.267	5644	817	1509	199	791	42	584	842	131
1963	.252	5506	714	1387	188	666	42	434	808	110
1964	.253	5705	730	1442	162	688	54	520	976	109
1965	.235	5470	611	1286	149	576	35	489	951	137
1966	.235	5330	611	1254	162	569	49	485	817	142
1967	.225	5443	522	1225	100	473	63	532	1043	154
1968	.214	5310	536	1137	109	501	90	566	958	139
1969	.235	5308	562	1247	94	521	119	565	840	131
1970	.251	5492	680	1381	111	627	105	588	808	130
1971	.254	5413	648	1377	97	607	75	581	717	125
1972	.249	5168	557	1288	103	526	71	491	689	134
1973	.261	5492	641	1435	131	616	47	489	680	156
1974	.263	5524	671	1451	101	637	53	515	690	142

YEAR	AVG	AB	R	H	HR	RBI	SB	BB	SO	E
1975	.264	5415	681	1430	110	642	102	486	710	135
1976	.269	5555	730	1496	120	682	163	470	616	126
1977	.281	5605	831	1576	184	784	93	533	681	132
1978	.267	5583	735	1489	125	693	98	505	695	113
1979	.266	5421	734	1443	150	594	64	509	590	122
1980	.267	5553	820	1484	189	772	86	643	739	138
1981	.252	3529	421	889	100	403	46	391	434	72
1982	.256	5526	709	1417	161	666	69	590	719	128
1983	.273	5631	770	1535	153	728	84	533	686	139
1984	.276	5661	758	1560	130	725	62	534	673	142
1985	.267	5458	839	1458	176	793	155	620	771	126
1986	.271	5570	797	1512	188	745	139	645	911	127
1987	.262	5511	788	1445	196	749	105	604	949	102
1988	.263	5592	772	1469	148	713	146	588	935	134
1989	.269	5458	698	1470	130	657	137	502	831	122
1990	.241	5483	603	1322	147	561	119	427	1027	126
1991	.256	5541	674	1418	147	630	109	473	861	133
1992	.261	5593	733	1462	163	703	78	536	903	114
1993	.279	5615	821	1568	178	793	39	629	910	105
1994	.290	3986	670	1155	139	632	55	530	660	80
1995	.276	4947	749	1365	122	709	50	625	851	74
1996	.288	5628	871	1621	162	830	96	632	909	91
1997	.287	5710	891	1636	161	846	99	676	954	104
1998	.288	5643	965	1625	207	907	153	653	1025	98
1999	.282	5568	900	1568	193	855	104	718	978	111
2000	.277	5556	871	1541	205	833	99	631	1007	109
2001	.267	5577	804	1488	203	774	161	519	1035	109
2002	.275	5601	897	1540	223	857	100	640	1171	127
2003	.271	5605	877	1518	230	845	98	684	1042	114
2004	.268	5527	897	1483	242	863	84	670	982	99
2005	.276	5624	886	1552	229	847	84	637	989	95
2006	.285	5651	930	1608	210	902	139	649	1053	104
2007	.290	5717	968	1656	201	929	123	637	991	88
2008	.271	5572	789	1512	180	758	118	535	1015	83
2009	.283	5660	915	1604	244	881	111	663	1014	86
2010	.267	5567	859	1485	201	823	103	662	1136	69

Year-by-Year Team Pitching Statistics

YEAR	W-L	ERA	CG	SHO	SV	SO	BB
1903	72-62	3.08	111	7	2	463	245
1904	92-59	2.57	123	15	1	684	311
1905	71-78	2.93	88	10	9	642	396
1906	90-61	2.78	99	18	5	605	351
1907	70-78	3.03	93	9	7	511	428
1908	51-103	3.16	91	11	6	584	457
1909	74-77	2.68	94	16	14	597	422
1910	88-63	2.59	110	14	10	654	364
1911	76-76	3.54	91	5	9	667	406
1912	50-102	4.13	109	3	3	637	436
1913	57-94	3.27	78	7	6	530	455
1914	70-84	2.81	97	5	7	563	390
1915	69-83	3.09	100	11	2	559	517
1916	80-74	2.77	83	10	18	616	476
1917	71-82	2.66	87	9	7	571	427
1918	60-63	3.03	59	9	11	369	463
1919	80-59	2.78	85	14	7	500	433
1920	95-59	3.31	88	16	11	480	420
1921	98-55	3.79	92	7	15	481	470
1922	94-60	3.39	98	7	14	458	423
1923	98-54	3.66	102	9	10	506	491
1924	89-63	3.86	76	13	13	487	522
1925	69-85	4.33	80	8	13	492	505
1926	91-63	3.86	64	4	20	486	478
1927	110-44	3.20	82	11	20	431	409
1928	101-53	3.74	82	13	21	487	452
1929	88-66	4.17	64	12	18	484	485
1930	86-68	4.88	65	7	15	572	524
1931	94-59	4.20	78	4	17	686	543
1932	107-47	3.98	95	11	15	780	561
1933	91-59	4.36	70	8	22	711	612
1934	94-60	3.76	83	13	10	656	542
1935	89-60	3.60	76	12	13	594	516
1936	102-51	4.17	77	6	21	624	663
1937	102-52	3.65	82	15	21	652	506
1938	99-53	3.91	91	11	13	567	566
1939	106-45	3.31	87	13	26	565	567

Urban Shocker

YEAR	W-L	ERA	CG	SHO	SV	SO	BB
1940	88-66	3.89	76	10	14	559	511
1941	101-53	3.53	75	13	26	589	598
1942	103-51	2.91	88	18	17	558	431
1943	98-56	2.93	83	14	13	653	489
1944	83-71	3.39	78	9	13	529	532
1945	81-71	3.45	78	9	14	474	485
1946	87-67	3.13	68	17	17	653	552
1947	97-57	3.39	73	14	21	691	628
1948	94-60	3.75	62	16	24	654	641
1949	97-57	3.69	59	12	36	671	812
1950	98-56	4.15	66	12	31	712	708
1951	98-56	3.56	66	24	22	664	562
1952	95-59	3.14	72	17	27	666	581
1953	99-52	3.20	50	16	39	604	500
1954	103-51	3.26	51	16	37	655	552
1955	96-58	3.23	52	19	33	732	688
1956	97-57	3.63	50	10	35	732	652
1957	98-56	3.00	41	13	42	810	580
1958	92-62	3.22	53	21	33	796	557
1959	79-75	3.60	38	15	28	836	594
1960	97-57	3.52	38	16	42	712	609
1961	109-53	3.46	47	14	39	866	542
1962	96-66	3.70	33	10	42	838	499
1963	104-57	3.07	59	19	31	965	476
1964	99-63	3.15	46	18	45	989	504
1965	77-85	3.28	41	11	31	1001	511
1966	70-89	3.42	29	7	32	842	443
1967	72-90	3.24	37	16	27	898	480
1968	83-79	2.79	45	14	27	831	424
1969	80-81	3.23	53	13	20	801	522
1970	93-69	3.25	36	6	49	777	451
1971	82-80	3.45	67	15	12	707	423
1972	79-76	3.05	35	19	39	625	419
1973	80-82	3.34	47	16	39	708	457
1974	89-73	3.31	53	13	24	829	528
1975	83-77	3.29	70	11	20	809	502
1976	97-62	3.19	62	15	37	448	674
1977	100-62	3.61	52	16	34	758	486
1978	100-63	3.18	39	16	36	817	478
1979	89-71	3.83	43	10	37	731	455
1980	103-59	3.58	29	15	50	845	463
1981	59-48	2.90	16	13	30	606	287
1982	79-83	3.99	24	8	39	939	491
1983	91-71	3.86	47	12	32	892	455
1984	87-75	3.78	15	12	43	992	518
1985	97-64	3.69	25	9	49	907	518
1986	90-72	4.11	13	8	58	878	492
1987	89-73	4.36	19	10	47	900	542
1988	85-76	4.25	16	4	43	861	487
1989	74-87	4.50	15	9	44	787	521
1990	67-95	4.21	15	6	41	909	618
1991	71-91	4.42	3	11	37	936	506
1992	76-86	4.21	20	9	44	851	612
1993	88-74	4.35	11	13	38	899	552
1994	70-43	4.34	8	2	31	656	398
1995	79-65	4.56	18	5	35	908	535
1996	92-70	4.65	6	9	52	1139	610
1997	96-66	3.84	11	10	51	1165	532
1998	114-48	3.82	22	16	48	1080	466
1999	98-64	4.13	6	10	50	1111	581
2000	87-74	4.76	9	6	40	1040	577
2001	95-65	4.02	7	9	57	1266	465
2002	103-58	3.87	9	11	53	1135	403
2003	101-61	4.02	8	12	49	1119	375
2004	101-61	4.69	1	5	59	1058	445
2005	95-67	4.52	8	14	46	985	463
2006	97-65	4.41	5	8	43	1019	496
2007	94-68	4.49	1	5	34	1009	578
2008	89-73	4.28	1	11	42	1141	489
2009	103-59	4.26	3	8	51	1260	574
2010	95-67	4.06	3	8	39	1154	540

Bob Turley

Whitey Ford

Ron Guidry

Mike Mussina

Year-by-Year Hitting Leaders

	AVERAGE		RUNS		HITS		DOUBLES	
Year	Leader	Avg.	Leader	Runs	Leader	Hits	Leader	Doubles
1903	Keeler	.318	Keeler	98	Keeler	164	Williams	30
1904	Keeler	.343	Dougherty*	80	Keeler	185	Williams	31
1905	Keeler	.302	Keeler	81	Keeler	169	Williams	20
1906	Chase	.323	Keeler	96	Chase	193	Williams	25
1907	Chase	.287	Hoffman	81	Chase	143	Chase	23
1908	Hemphill	.297	Hemphill	62	Hemphill	150	Conroy	22
1909	LaPorte	.298	Demmitt	68	Engle	137	Engle	20
1910	Knight	.312	Daniels	68	Chase	151	Knight	25
1911	Cree	.348	Cree	90	Cree	181	Chase	33
1912	Paddock	.288	Daniels	72	Chase	143	Daniels	25
1913	Cree	.272	Hartzell	60	Cree	145	Cree	23
1914	Cook	.282	Maisel	78	Cook	133	Maisel	23
1915	Maisel	.281	Maisel	77	Maisel	149	Pipp	20
1916	Pipp	.263	Pipp	70	Pipp	143	Baker	23
1917	Baker	.282	Pipp	82	Baker	156	Pipp	29
1918	Baker	.306	Baker, Pratt	65	Baker	154	Baker	25
1919	Peckinpaugh	.305	Peckinpaugh	89	Baker	166	Pratt, Bodie	27
1920	Ruth	.376	Ruth*	158	Pratt	180	Meusel	40
1921	Ruth	.377	Ruth*	177	Ruth	204	Ruth	44
1922	Pipp	.329	Witt	98	Pipp	190	Pipp	32
1923	Ruth	.394	Ruth*	151	Ruth	205	Ruth	45
1924	Ruth*	.378	Ruth*	143	Ruth	200	Meusel	40
1925	Combs	.342	Combs	117	Combs	203	Combs	36
1926	Ruth	.372	Ruth*	139	Ruth	184	Gehrig	47
1927	Gehrig	.373	Ruth*	158	Combs*	231	Gehrig*	52
1928	Gehrig	.374	Ruth*	163	Gehrig	210	Gehrig*	47
1929	Lazzeri	.353	Gehrig	127	Combs	202	Lazzeri	37
1930	Gehrig	.379	Ruth	150	Gehrig	220	Gehrig	42
1931	Ruth	.373	Gehrig	163	Gehrig	211	Lary	36
1932	Gehrig	.349	Combs	143	Gehrig	208	Gehrig	42
1933	Gehrig	.334	Gehrig*	138	Gehrig	198	Gehrig	41
1934	Gehrig*	.363	Gehrig	128	Gehrig	210	Gehrig	40
1935	Gehrig	.329	Gehrig*	125	Rolfe	192	Chapman	38
1936	Dickey	.362	Gehrig*	167	DiMaggio	206	DiMaggio	44
1937	Gehrig	.351	DiMaggio*	151	DiMaggio	215	Gehrig	37
1938	DiMaggio	.324	Rolfe	132	Rolfe	196	Rolfe	36
1939	DiMaggio*	.381	Rolfe*	139	Rolfe*	213	Rolfe*	46
1940	DiMaggio*	.352	Gordon	112	DiMaggio	179	Gordon	32
1941	DiMaggio	.357	DiMaggio	122	DiMaggio	193	DiMaggio	43
1942	Gordon	.322	DiMaggio	123	DiMaggio	186	Henrich	30
1943	Johnson	.280	Keller	97	Johnson	166	Etten	35
1944	Stirnweiss	.319	Stirnweiss*	125	Stirnweiss*	205	Stirnweiss	35
1945	Stirnweiss*	.309	Stirnweiss*	107	Stirnweiss*	195	Stirnweiss	32
1946	DiMaggio	.290	Keller	98	Keller	148	Keller	29
1947	DiMaggio	.315	Henrich	109	DiMaggio	168	Henrich	35
1948	DiMaggio	.320	Henrich*	138	DiMaggio	190	Henrich	42
1949	Henrich	.287	Rizzuto	110	Rizzuto	169	Rizzuto	22
1950	Rizzuto	.324	Rizzuto	125	Rizzuto	200	Rizzuto	36
1951	McDougald	.306	Berra	92	Berra	161	McDougald	23
1952	Mantle	.311	Berra	97	Mantle	171	Mantle	37
1953	Bauer	.304	Mantle	105	McDougald	154	McDougald	27
1954	Noren	.319	Mantle*	128	Berra	179	Berra	28
1955	Mantle	.306	Mantle	121	Mantle	158	Mantle	25
1956	Mantle*	.353	Mantle*	132	Mantle	188	Berra	29
1957	Mantle	.365	Mantle*	121	Mantle	173	Mantle	28
1958	Mantle	.304	Mantle*	127	Mantle	158	Bauer, Skowron	22
1959	Richardson	.301	Mantle	104	Mantle	154	Berra, Kubek	25
1960	Skowron	.309	Mantle*	119	Skowron	166	Skowron	34
1961	Howard	.348	Maris*	132	Richardson	173	Kubek	38
1962	Mantle	.321	Richardson	99	Richardson*	209	Richardson	38
1963	Howard	.287	Tresh	91	Richardson	167	Tresh	28
1964	Howard	.313	Mantle	91	Richardson	181	Howard	27
1965	Tresh	.279	Tresh	94	Tresh	168	Tresh	29
1966	Mantle	.288	Pepitone	85	Richardson	153	Boyer	22
1967	Clarke	.272	Clarke	74	Clarke	160	Tresh	23
1968	White	.267	White	89	White	154	White	20
1969	White	.290	Clarke, Murcer	82	Clarke	183	White	30
1970	Munson	.302	White	109	White	180	White	30
1971	Murcer	.331	White	94	Murcer	175	Murcer	25
1972	Murcer	.292	Murcer*	102	Murcer	171	Murcer	30
1973	Murcer	.304	White	88	Murcer	187	Murcer, Munson	29
1974	Piniella	.305	Maddox	75	Murcer	166	Maddox, Piniella	26
1975	Munson	.318	Bonds	93	Munson	190	Chambliss	38
1976	Rivers	.312	White*	104	Chambliss	188	Chambliss	32
1977	Rivers	.326	Nettles	99	Rivers	184	Jackson	39
1978	Piniella	.314	Randolph	87	Munson	183	Piniella	34
1979	Piniella, Jackson	.297	Randolph	98	Randolph, Chambliss	155	Chambliss	27
1980	Watson	.307	Randolph	99	Jackson	154	Cerone	30
1981	Mumphrey	.307	Randolph	59	Winfield	114	Winfield	25
1982	Mumphrey	.300	Randolph	85	Randolph	155	Mumphrey, Winfield	24
1983	Baylor	.303	Winfield	99	Winfield	169	Baylor	33
1984	Mattingly*	.343	Winfield	106	Mattingly*	207	Mattingly*	44
1985	Mattingly	.324	Henderson*	146	Mattingly	211	Mattingly*	48
1986	Mattingly	.352	Henderson*	130	Mattingly*	238	Mattingly*	53
1987	Mattingly	.327	Randolph	96	Mattingly	186	Mattingly	38
1988	Winfield	.322	Henderson	118	Mattingly	186	Mattingly, Winfield	37
1989	Sax	.315	Sax	88	Sax	205	Sax	37
1990	R. Kelly	.285	R. Kelly	85	R. Kelly	183	R. Kelly	32
1991	Sax	.304	Sax	85	Sax	198	Sax	38
1992	Mattingly	.288	Mattingly	86	Mattingly	184	Mattingly	40
1993	O'Neill	.311	Mattingly	89	Boggs	169	O'Neill	34
1994	O'Neill*	.359	B. Williams	80	O'Neill	132	B. Williams	29
1995	Boggs	.324	B. Williams	93	B. Williams	173	Mattingly	32
1996	JETER	.314	B. Williams	108	JETER	183	O'Neill	35
1997	B. Williams	.328	JETER	116	JETER	190	O'Neill	42
1998	B. Williams*	.339	JETER*	127	JETER	203	O'Neill	40
1999	JETER	.349	JETER	134	JETER*	219	O'Neill	39
2000	JETER	.339	JETER	119	JETER	201	B. Williams, Martinez	37
2001	JETER	.311	JETER	110	JETER	191	B. Williams	38
2002	B. Williams	.333	Soriano*	128	Soriano*	209	Soriano	51
2003	JETER	.324	Soriano	114	Soriano	198	Matsui	42
2004	Matsui	.298	Sheffield	117	JETER	188	JETER	44
2005	RODRIGUEZ	.321	RODRIGUEZ*	124	JETER	202	Matsui	45
2006	JETER	.343	JETER	118	JETER	214	CANO	41
2007	POSADA	.338	RODRIGUEZ*	143	JETER	206	POSADA	42
2008	Damon	.303	RODRIGUEZ	104	Abreu	180	Abreu	39
2009	JETER	.334	Damon, JETER	107	JETER	212	CANO	48
2010	CANO	.319	TEIXEIRA*	113	CANO	200	CANO	41

Year-by-Year Hitting Leaders

Year	TRIPLES Leader	Triples	Year	HOME RUNS Leader	HR	Year	RBI Leader	RBI	Year	STOLEN BASES Leader	SB
1903	Williams, Conroy	12	1903	McFarland	5	1903	Williams	82	1903	Conroy	33
1904	Anderson, Conroy	12	1904	Dougherty, Ganzel	6	1904	Anderson	82	1904	Conroy	30
1905	Conroy	11	1905	Williams	6	1905	Williams	60	1905	Fultz	44
1906	Chase, Conroy	10	1906	Conroy	4	1906	Williams	77	1906	Hoffman	33
1907	Conroy, LaPorte, Williams	11	1907	Hoffman	5	1907	Chase	68	1907	Conroy	41
1908	Hemphill	9	1908	Niles	4	1908	Hemphill	44	1908	Hemphill	42
1909	Demmitt	12	1909	Chase, Demmitt	4	1909	Engle	71	1909	Austin	30
1910	Cree	16	1910	Wolter, Cree	4	1910	Chase	73	1910	Daniels	41
1911	Cree	22	1911	Wolter, Cree	4	1911	Hartzell	91	1911	Cree	48
1912	Hartzell, Daniels	11	1912	Zinn	6	1912	Chase	58	1912	Daniels	37
1913	Peckinpaugh	7	1913	Wolter, Sweeney	2	1913	Cree	63	1913	Daniels	28
1914	Maisel, Hartzell	9	1914	Peckinpaugh	3	1914	Peckinpaugh	51	1914	Maisel*	74
1915	Pipp	13	1915	L. Boone, Peckinpaugh	5	1915	Pipp	58	1915	Maisel	51
1916	Pipp	14	1916	Pipp*	12	1916	Pipp	99	1916	Magee	29
1917	Pipp	12	1917	Pipp*	9	1917	Pipp	72	1917	Maisel	29
1918	Pipp	9	1918	Baker	6	1918	Baker	68	1918	Bodie	8
1919	Pipp	10	1919	Baker	10	1919	Baker	78	1919	Pratt	22
1920	Pipp	14	1920	Ruth*	54	1920	Ruth*	136	1920	Ruth	14
1921	Ruth, Meusel	16	1921	Ruth*	59	1921	Ruth*	171	1921	Meusel, Pipp, Ruth	17
1922	Meusel	11	1922	Ruth	35	1922	Ruth	99	1922	Meusel	13
1923	Ruth	13	1923	Ruth*	41	1923	Ruth*	131	1923	Ruth	17
1924	Pipp*	19	1924	Ruth*	46	1924	Ruth	121	1924	Meusel	26
1925	Combs	13	1925	Meusel*	33	1925	Meusel*	138	1925	Paschal	14
1926	Gehrig*	20	1926	Ruth*	47	1926	Ruth*	150	1926	Meusel	16
1927	Combs*	23	1927	Ruth*	60	1927	Gehrig*	175	1927	Meusel	24
1928	Combs	21	1928	Ruth*	54	1928	Gehrig*	146	1928	Lazzeri	15
1929	Combs	15	1929	Ruth	46	1929	Ruth	154	1929	Combs, Lazzeri	11
1930	Combs*	22	1930	Ruth*	49	1930	Gehrig*	174	1930	Combs	16
1931	Gehrig	15	1931	Ruth*, Gehrig*	46	1931	Gehrig*	184	1931	Chapman*	61
1932	Lazzeri	16	1932	Ruth	41	1932	Gehrig	151	1932	Chapman*	38
1933	Combs	16	1933	Ruth	34	1933	Gehrig	139	1933	Chapman*	27
1934	Chapman	13	1934	Gehrig*	49	1934	Gehrig*	165	1934	Chapman	26
1935	Selkirk	12	1935	Gehrig	30	1935	Gehrig	119	1935	Chapman	17
1936	DiMaggio*, Rolfe*	15	1936	Gehrig*	49	1936	Gehrig	152	1936	Crosetti	13
1937	DiMaggio	15	1937	DiMaggio*	46	1937	DiMaggio	167	1937	Crosetti	13
1938	DiMaggio	13	1938	DiMaggio	32	1938	DiMaggio	140	1938	Crosetti*	27
1939	Rolfe	10	1939	DiMaggio	30	1939	DiMaggio	126	1939	Selkirk	12
1940	Keller	15	1940	DiMaggio	31	1940	DiMaggio	133	1940	Gordon	18
1941	DiMaggio	11	1941	Keller	33	1941	DiMaggio*	125	1941	Rizzuto	14
1942	DiMaggio	13	1942	Keller	26	1942	DiMaggio	114	1942	Rizzuto	22
1943	Lindell*	12	1943	Keller	31	1943	Etten	107	1943	Stirnweiss	11
1944	Stirnweiss, Lindell*	16	1944	Etten*	22	1944	Lindell	103	1944	Stirnweiss*	55
1945	Stirnweiss*	22	1945	Etten	18	1945	Etten*	111	1945	Stirnweiss*	33
1946	Keller	10	1946	Keller	30	1946	Keller	100	1946	Stirnweiss	18
1947	Henrich*	13	1947	DiMaggio	20	1947	DiMaggio	98	1947	Rizzuto	11
1948	Henrich*	14	1948	DiMaggio*	39	1948	DiMaggio*	155	1948	Rizzuto	6
1949	Rizzuto, Woodling	7	1949	Henrich	24	1949	Berra	91	1949	Rizzuto	18
1950	Bauer, DiMaggio	10	1950	DiMaggio	32	1950	Berra	124	1950	Rizzuto	12
1951	Woodling	8	1951	Berra	27	1951	Berra	88	1951	Rizzuto	18
1952	Rizzuto	10	1952	Berra	30	1952	Berra	98	1952	Rizzuto	17
1953	McDougald	7	1953	Berra	27	1953	Berra	108	1953	Mantle	8
1954	Mantle	12	1954	Mantle	27	1954	Berra	125	1954	Mantle, Carey	5
1955	Mantle*, Carey*	11	1955	Mantle*	37	1955	Berra	108	1955	Hunter	9
1956	Bauer	7	1956	Mantle*	52	1956	Mantle*	130	1956	Mantle	10
1957	Bauer*, McDougald*	9	1957	Mantle	34	1957	Mantle	94	1957	Mantle	16
1958	Bauer	6	1958	Mantle*	42	1958	Mantle	97	1958	Mantle	18
1959	McDougald	8	1959	Mantle	31	1959	Mantle	75	1959	Mantle	21
1960	Maris	7	1960	Mantle*	40	1960	Maris*	112	1960	Mantle	14
1961	Mantle, Kubek	6	1961	Maris*	61	1961	Maris*	141	1961	Mantle	12
1962	Skowron	6	1962	Maris	33	1962	Maris	100	1962	Richardson	11
1963	Howard, Richardson	6	1963	Howard	28	1963	Pepitone	89	1963	Richardson	15
1964	Tresh, Boyer	5	1964	Mantle	35	1964	Mantle	111	1964	Tresh	13
1965	Tresh, Boyer	6	1965	Tresh	26	1965	Tresh	74	1965	Richardson	7
1966	Boyer, Clarke, Tresh, Pepitone	4	1966	Pepitone	31	1966	Pepitone	83	1966	White	14
1967	Pepitone, Smith, Tresh, Whitaker	3	1967	Mantle	22	1967	Pepitone	64	1967	Clarke	21
1968	White, Robinson	7	1968	Mantle	18	1968	White	62	1968	Clarke, White	20
1969	Clarke	7	1969	Pepitone	27	1969	Murcer	82	1969	Clarke	33
1970	Kenney	7	1970	Murcer	23	1970	White	94	1970	Clarke, White	23
1971	Clarke, White	7	1971	Murcer	25	1971	Murcer	94	1971	Clarke	17
1972	Murcer	4	1972	Murcer	33	1972	Murcer	96	1972	White	23
1973	Munson	5	1973	Murcer, Nettles	22	1973	Murcer	95	1973	White	16
1974	White	8	1974	Nettles	22	1974	Murcer	88	1974	White	15
1975	White	5	1975	Bonds	32	1975	Munson	102	1975	Bonds	30
1976	Rivers	8	1976	Nettles*	32	1976	Munson	105	1976	Rivers	43
1977	Randolph	11	1977	Nettles	37	1977	Jackson	110	1977	Rivers	22
1978	Rivers	8	1978	Jackson, Nettles	27	1978	Jackson	97	1978	Randolph	36
1979	Randolph	13	1979	Jackson	29	1979	Jackson	89	1979	Randolph	33
1980	Randolph	7	1980	Jackson*	41	1980	Jackson	111	1980	Randolph	30
1981	Mumphrey	5	1981	Jackson, Nettles	15	1981	Winfield	68	1981	Randolph	14
1982	Mumphrey	10	1982	Winfield	37	1982	Winfield	106	1982	Randolph	16
1983	Winfield	8	1983	Winfield	32	1983	Winfield	116	1983	Baylor	17
1984	Moreno	6	1984	Baylor	27	1984	Winfield	100	1984	Moreno	20
1985	Winfield	6	1985	Mattingly	35	1985	Mattingly*	145	1985	Henderson*	80
1986	Henderson, Winfield	5	1986	Mattingly	31	1986	Mattingly	113	1986	Henderson*	87
1987	Henderson, Pagliarulo	3	1987	Pagliarulo	32	1987	Mattingly	115	1987	Henderson	41
1988	Washington	3	1988	Clark	27	1988	Winfield	107	1988	Henderson*	93
1989	R. Kelly, Sax, Slaught	3	1989	Mattingly	23	1989	Mattingly	113	1989	Sax	43
1990	R. Kelly	4	1990	Barfield	25	1990	Barfield	78	1990	Sax	43
1991	B.Williams, P. Kelly	6	1991	Nokes	24	1991	Hall	80	1991	R. Kelly	32
1992	Hall	3	1992	Tartabull	25	1992	Mattingly	86	1992	R. Kelly	28
1993	B. Williams	4	1993	Tartabull	31	1993	Tartabull	102	1993	P. Kelly	14
1994	Polonia	6	1994	O'Neill	21	1994	O'Neill	83	1994	Polonia	20
1995	B. Williams	9	1995	O'Neill	22	1995	O'Neill	96	1995	Polonia	10
1996	B. Williams	7	1996	B. Williams	29	1996	Martinez	117	1996	B. Williams	17
1997	JETER	7	1997	Martinez	44	1997	Martinez	141	1997	JETER	23
1998	JETER	8	1998	Martinez	28	1998	Martinez	123	1998	Knoblauch	31
1999	JETER	9	1999	Martinez	28	1999	B. Williams	115	1999	Knoblauch	28
2000	B. Williams	6	2000	B. Williams	30	2000	Martinez	121	2000	JETER	22
2001	JETER, Soriano, Knoblauch	3	2001	Martinez	34	2001	Martinez	113	2001	Soriano	43
2002	Soriano, Spencer	5	2002	Giambi	41	2002	Giambi	122	2002	Soriano*	41
2003	B. Williams, Wilson, Soriano	5	2003	Giambi	41	2003	Giambi	107	2003	Soriano	35
2004	Lofton	5	2004	RODRIGUEZ, Sheffield	36	2004	Sheffield	121	2004	RODRIGUEZ	28
2005	JETER	5	2005	RODRIGUEZ*	48	2005	RODRIGUEZ	130	2005	Womack	27
2006	Damon	5	2006	Giambi	37	2006	RODRIGUEZ	121	2006	JETER	34
2007	CABRERA	8	2007	RODRIGUEZ*	54	2007	RODRIGUEZ*	156	2007	Damon	27
2008	Damon	5	2008	Rodriguez	35	2008	RODRIGUEZ	103	2008	Damon	29
2009	GARDNER	6	2009	TEIXEIRA*	39	2009	TEIXEIRA*	122	2009	JETER	30
2010	GARDNER, GRANDERSON	7	2010	TEIXEIRA	33	2010	RODRIGUEZ	125	2010	GARDNER	47

* Tied or Led League

Year-by-Year Pitching Leaders

Year	STRIKEOUTS Leader	SO	INNINGS PITCHED Leader	IP	WINS Leader	Wins	ERA Leader	ERA
1903	Chesbro	147	Chesbro	323.0	Chesbro	21-15	Griffith	2.70
1904	Chesbro	239	Chesbro*	455.0	Chesbro*	41-12	Chesbro	1.82
1905	Chesbro	156	Orth	305.0	Chesbro	20-15	Chesbro	2.20
1906	Chesbro	152	Orth*	339.0	Orth*	27-17	Clarkson	2.32
1907	Doyle	94	Orth	249.0	Orth	14-21	Chesbro	2.53
1908	Chesbro	124	Chesbro	289.0	Chesbro	14-20	Chesbro	2.93
1909	Lake	117	Warhop	243.0	Lake	14-11	Lake	1.88
1910	Ford	209	Ford	300.0	Ford	26-6	Ford	1.65
1911	Ford	158	Ford	281.0	Ford	22-11	Ford	2.28
1912	Ford	112	Ford	292.0	Ford	13-21	McConnell	2.75
1913	Fisher	92	Fisher	246.0	Fisher, Ford	11-17, 11-18	Caldwell	2.43
1914	Keating	109	Warhop	217.0	Caldwell	17-9	Caldwell	1.94
1915	Caldwell	130	Caldwell	303.0	Caldwell	19-16	Fisher	2.10
1916	Shawkey	122	Shawkey	278.0	Shawkey	23-14	Cullop	2.05
1917	Caldwell	102	Shawkey	236.0	Shawkey	13-15	Shawkey	2.28
1918	Love	95	Mogridge	239.0	Mogridge	16-13	Mogridge	2.27
1919	Shawkey	123	Quinn	266.0	Shawkey	20-11	Mogridge	2.50
1920	Shawkey	126	Mays	312.0	Mays	26-11	Shawkey*	2.45
1921	Shawkey	126	Mays*	336.0	Mays*	27-9	Mays	3.04
1922	Shawkey	133	Shawkey	300.0	Bush	26-7	Shawkey	2.91
1923	Bush, Shawkey	125	Bush	275.0	Jones	21-8	Hoyt	3.01
1924	Shawkey	114	Pennock	286.0	Pennock	21-9	Pennock	2.83
1925	Jones	92	Pennock*	276.0	Pennock	16-17	Pennock	2.96
1926	Pennock	78	Pennock	266.0	Pennock	23-11	Shocker	3.38
1927	Hoyt	86	Pennock	256.0	Hoyt*	22-7	W. Moore*	2.28
1928	Pipgras	138	Pipgras	302.0	Pipgras*	24-13	Pennock	2.56
1929	Pipgras	125	Pipgras*	225.0	Pipgras	18-12	Sherid	3.49
1930	Ruffing	117	Pipgras	221.0	Pipgras, Ruffing	15-15, 15-5	Pipgras	4.11
1931	Gomez	150	Gomez	242.0	Gomez	21-9	Gomez	2.63
1932	Ruffing	190	Gomez	265.0	Gomez	24-7	Ruffing	3.09
1933	Gomez*	164	Gomez, Ruffing	235.0	Gomez	16-10	Gomez	3.18
1934	Gomez*	158	Gomez*	282.0	Gomez*	26-5	Gomez*	2.33
1935	Gomez	138	Gomez	246.0	Ruffing	16-11	Ruffing	3.12
1936	Pearson	118	Ruffing	271.0	Ruffing	20-12	Pearson	3.71
1937	Gomez*	194	Gomez*	278.0	Gomez*	21-11	Gomez*	2.33
1938	Gomez	129	Ruffing	247.0	Ruffing*	21-7	Ruffing	3.32
1939	Gomez	102	Ruffing	233.0	Ruffing	21-7	Ruffing	2.94
1940	Ruffing	97	Ruffing	226.0	Ruffing	15-12	Russo	3.29
1941	Russo	105	Russo	210.0	Ruffing, Gomez	15-6, 15-5	Russo	3.09
1942	Borowy	85	Bonham	226.0	Bonham	21-5	Bonham	2.27
1943	Chandler	134	Chandler	253.0	Chandler*	20-4	Chandler*	1.64
1944	Borowy	107	Borowy	253.0	Borowy	17-12	Borowy	2.63
1945	Bevens	76	Bevens	184.0	Bevens	13-9	Bonham	3.28
1946	Chandler	138	Chandler	257.0	Chandler	20-8	Chandler	2.10
1947	Reynolds	129	Reynolds	242.0	Reynolds	19-8	Shea	3.07
1948	Byrne	124	Reynolds	236.0	Raschi	19-8	Shea	3.41
1949	Reynolds	129	Raschi	275.0	Raschi	21-10	Lopat	3.27
1950	Reynolds	160	Raschi	257.0	Raschi	21-8	Lopat	3.47
1951	Raschi*	164	Raschi	258.0	Raschi, Lopat	21-10, 21-9	Lopat	2.91
1952	Reynolds*	160	Reynolds	244.0	Reynolds	20-8	Reynolds*	2.07
1953	Ford	110	Ford	207.0	Ford	18-6	Lopat*	2.43
1954	Ford	126	Ford	211.0	Grim	20-6	Ford	2.82
1955	Turley	210	Ford	254.0	Ford*	18-7	Ford*	2.62
1956	Ford	141	Ford	226.0	Ford	19-6	Ford*	2.47
1957	Turley	152	Sturdivant	202.0	Sturdivant	16-6	Shantz*	2.45
1958	Turley	168	Turley	245.0	Turley*	21-7	Ford*	2.01
1959	Ford	114	Ford	204.0	Ford	16-10	Ditmar	2.90
1960	Terry	92	Ditmar	200.0	Ditmar	15-9	Ditmar	3.06
1961	Ford	209	Ford*	283.0	Ford*	25-4	Stafford	2.68
1962	Terry	176	Terry*	299.0	Terry*	23-12	Ford	2.90
1963	Ford	189	Ford*	269.0	Ford*	24-7	Bouton	2.53
1964	Downing	217	Bouton	271.0	Bouton	18-13	Ford	2.13
1965	Downing	179	Stottlemyre*	291.0	Stottlemyre	20-9	Stottlemyre	2.63
1966	Downing	152	Stottlemyre	251.0	Stottlemyre, Peterson	12-20, 12-11	Peterson	3.31
1967	Downing	171	Stottlemyre	255.0	Stottlemyre	15-15	Downing	2.63
1968	Bahnsen	162	Stottlemyre	279.0	Stottlemyre	21-12	Bahnsen	2.06
1969	Peterson	150	Stottlemyre	303.0	Stottlemyre	20-14	Peterson	2.55
1970	Stottlemyre	127	Stottlemyre	271.0	Peterson	20-11	Peterson	2.91
1971	Peterson	139	Peterson	274.0	Stottlemyre	16-12	Stottlemyre	2.87
1972	Stottlemyre	110	Stottlemyre	260.0	Peterson	17-15	Kline	2.40
1973	Medich	145	Stottlemyre	273.0	Stottlemyre	16-16	Medich	2.95
1974	Dobson	157	Dobson	281.0	Dobson, Medich	19-15, 19-15	Dobson	3.07
1975	Hunter	177	Hunter*	328.0	Hunter*	23-14	Hunter	2.58
1976	Hunter	173	Figueroa	239.0	Figueroa	19-10	Figueroa	3.01
1977	Guidry	176	Figueroa	239.0	Guidry, Figueroa	16-7, 16-11	Guidry	2.82
1978	Guidry	248	John	274.0	Guidry*	25-3	Guidry*	1.74
1979	Guidry	201	John	276.0	John	21-9	Guidry	2.78
1980	Guidry	166	John	265.0	John	22-9	May*	2.46
1981	Guidry	104	May	148.0	Guidry	11-5	Righetti	2.05
1982	Righetti	163	Guidry	222.0	Guidry	14-8	John	3.69
1983	Righetti	169	Guidry	250.1	Guidry	21-9	Guidry	3.42
1984	Niekro	136	Niekro	215.2	Niekro	16-8	Niekro	3.09
1985	Guidry	143	Guidry	259.0	Guidry*	22-6	Guidry	3.27
1986	Guidry	140	Rasmussen	202.0	Rasmussen	18-6	Rasmussen	3.88
1987	Rhoden	107	John	187.2	Rhoden	16-10	Rhoden	3.86
1988	Candelaria	121	Candelaria	197.0	Candelaria	13-7	Rhoden	4.29
1989	Hawkins	98	Hawkins	208.1	Hawkins	15-15	Hawkins	4.80
1990	Leary	138	Leary	208.0	Guetterman	11-7	Leary	4.11
1991	Sanderson	130	Sanderson	208.0	Sanderson	16-10	Sanderson	3.81
1992	M. Perez	218	M. Perez	247.2	M. Perez	13-16	M. Perez	2.87
1993	Key	173	Key	236.2	Key	18-6	Key	3.00
1994	M. Perez	109	Key	168.0	Key*	17-4	Key	3.27
1995	McDowell	157	McDowell	217.2	McDowell	15-10	Cone	3.82
1996	Pettitte	162	Pettitte	221.0	Pettitte	21-8	Pettitte	3.87
1997	Cone	222	Pettitte	240.1	Pettitte	18-7	Cone	2.82
1998	Cone	209	Pettitte	216.1	Cone*	20-7	Wells	3.49
1999	Cone	177	O. Hernandez	214.1	O. Hernandez	17-9	Clemens	4.60
2000	Clemens	188	Pettitte	204.2	Pettitte	19-9	Clemens	3.70
2001	Mussina	214	Mussina	228.2	Clemens	20-3	Mussina	3.15
2002	Clemens	192	Mussina	215.2	Wells	19-7	Wells	3.75
2003	Mussina	195	Mussina	214.2	Pettitte	21-8	Mussina	3.40
2004	Vazquez	150	Vazquez	198.0	Lieber, Vazquez	14-8, 14-10	Lieber	4.33
2005	Johnson	211	Johnson	225.2	Johnson	17-8	Johnson	3.79
2006	Johnson, Mussina	172	Wang	218.0	Wang*	19-6	Mussina	3.51
2007	Pettitte	141	Pettitte	215.1	Wang	19-7	Wang	3.70
2008	Pettitte	158	Pettitte	204.0	Mussina	20-9	Mussina	3.37
2009	SABATHIA	197	SABATHIA	230.0	SABATHIA*	19-8	SABATHIA	3.37
2010	SABATHIA	197	SABATHIA	237.2	SABATHIA*	21-7	SABATHIA	3.18

* Tied or Led League

Year-by-Year Games Played Leaders

Year	CATCHER	FIRST BASE	SECOND BASE	THIRD BASE
	Leader.............C	Leader.............1B	Leader.............2B	Leader.............3B
1903	Beville...75	Ganzel...129	Williams...104	Conroy...123
1904	McGuire...97	Ganzel...118	Williams...146	Conroy...110
1905	Kleinow...83	Chase...122	Williams...129	Yeager...90
1906	Kleinow...95	Chase...150	Williams...139	LaPorte...114
1907	Kleinow...86	Chase...121	Williams...139	Moriarty...91
1908	Kleinow...89	Chase...98	Niles...85	Conroy...119
1909	Kleinow...77	Chase...118	LaPorte...83	Austin...111
1910	Sweeney...78	Chase...130	LaPorte...79	Austin...133
1911	Blair...84	Chase...124	Gardner...101	Hartzell...124
1912	Sweeney...108	Chase...121	Simmons...88	Hartzell...56
1913	Sweeney...112	Knight...50	Hartzell...81	Midkiff...76
1914	Sweeney...78	Mullen...93	Boone...90	Maisel...148
1915	Nunamaker...77	Pipp...134	Boone...134	Maisel...134
1916	Nunamaker...79	Pipp...148	Gedeon...122	Baker...96
1917	Nunamaker...91	Pipp...155	Maisel...116	Baker...146
1918	Hannah...88	Pipp...91	Pratt...126	Baker...126
1919	Ruel...81	Pipp...140	Pratt...154	Baker...141
1920	Ruel...80	Pipp...153	Pratt...154	Ward...114
1921	Schang...132	Pipp...153	Ward...123	Baker...83
1922	Schang...119	Pipp...152	Ward...152	Baker...60
1923	Schang...81	Pipp...144	Ward...152	Dugan...146
1924	Schang...106	Pipp...153	Ward...120	Dugan...148
1925	Bengough...94	Gehrig...114	Ward...113	Dugan...96
1926	Collins...100	Gehrig...155	Lazzeri...149	Dugan...122
1927	Collins...89	Gehrig...155	Lazzeri...113	Dugan...111
1928	Grabowski...75	Gehrig...154	Lazzeri...110	Dugan...91
1929	Dickey...127	Gehrig...154	Lazzeri...147	Robertson...77
1930	Dickey...101	Gehrig...153	Lazzeri...77	Chapman...91
1931	Dickey...125	Gehrig...155	Lazzeri...90	Sewell...121
1932	Dickey...108	Gehrig...155	Lazzeri...138	Sewell...122
1933	Dickey...127	Gehrig...152	Lazzeri...138	Sewell...131
1934	Dickey...104	Gehrig...153	Lazzeri...92	Saltzgaver...84
1935	Dickey...118	Gehrig...149	Lazzeri...118	Rolfe...136
1936	Dickey...107	Gehrig...155	Lazzeri...148	Rolfe...133
1937	Dickey...137	Gehrig...157	Lazzeri...126	Rolfe...154
1938	Dickey...126	Gehrig...157	Gordon...126	Rolfe...151
1939	Dickey...126	Dahlgren...144	Gordon...151	Rolfe...152
1940	Dickey...102	Dahlgren...155	Gordon...155	Rolfe...138
1941	Dickey...104	Sturm...124	Gordon...131	Rolfe...131
1942	Dickey...80	Hassett...132	Gordon...147	Crosetti...62
1943	Dickey...71	Etten...154	Gordon...152	Johnson...155
1944	Garback...85	Etten...154	Stirnweiss...154	Johnson...97
1945	Garback...59	Etten...152	Stirnweiss...152	Grimes...141
1946	Robinson...95	Etten...84	Gordon...108	Stirnweiss...79
1947	Robinson...74	McQuinn...142	Stirnweiss...141	Johnson...132
1948	Niarhos...82	McQuinn...90	Stirnweiss...141	Johnson...118
1949	Berra...109	Henrich...52	Coleman...122	Brown...86
1950	Berra...148	Collins...99	Coleman...152	Johnson...100
1951	Berra...141	Collins...114	Coleman...102	Brown...90
1952	Berra...140	Collins...119	Martin...107	McDougald...117
1953	Berra...133	Collins...113	Martin...146	McDougald...136
1954	Berra...149	Collins...117	McDougald...92	Carey...120
1955	Berra...145	Skowron...74	McDougald...126	Carey...135
1956	Berra...135	Skowron...120	Martin...105	Carey...131
1957	Berra...121	Skowron...115	Richardson...93	Carey...81
1958	Berra...88	Skowron...118	McDougald...115	Carey...99
1959	Berra...116	Skowron...72	Richardson...109	Lopez...76
1960	Howard...91	Skowron...142	Richardson...141	Boyer...99
1961	Howard...111	Skowron...149	Richardson...161	Boyer...141
1962	Howard...129	Skowron...135	Richardson...161	Boyer...157
1963	Howard...132	Pepitone...143	Richardson...150	Boyer...141
1964	Howard...146	Pepitone...155	Richardson...157	Boyer...123
1965	Howard...95	Pepitone...115	Richardson...158	Boyer...147
1966	Howard...100	Pepitone...119	Richardson...147	Boyer...85
1967	Gibbs...99	Mantle...131	Clarke...146	Smith...115
1968	Gibbs...121	Mantle...131	Clarke...139	Cox...132
1969	Gibbs...66	Pepitone...132	Clarke...156	Kenney...83
1970	Munson...125	Cater...131	Clarke...157	Kenney...135
1971	Munson...117	Cater...78	Clarke...156	Kenney...109
1972	Munson...132	Blomberg...95	Clarke...143	Sanchez...68
1973	Munson...142	F. Alou...67	Clarke...146	Nettles...157
1974	Munson...137	Chambliss...106	Alomar...147	Nettles...154
1975	Munson...130	Chambliss...147	Alomar...150	Nettles...157
1976	Munson...121	Chambliss...155	Randolph...124	Nettles...158
1977	Munson...136	Chambliss...157	Randolph...147	Nettles...156
1978	Munson...105	Chambliss...155	Randolph...134	Nettles...159
1979	Munson...88	Chambliss...134	Randolph...153	Nettles...144
1980	Cerone...147	Watson...104	Randolph...138	Nettles...88
1981	Cerone...69	Watson...50	Randolph...93	Nettles...97
1982	Cerone...89	Mayberry...64	Randolph...143	Nettles...122
1983	Wynegar...94	Griffey...100	Randolph...104	Nettles...129
1984	Wynegar...126	Mattingly...133	Randolph...142	Harrah...74
1985	Wynegar...96	Mattingly...159	Randolph...143	Pagliarulo...134
1986	Wynegar...57	Mattingly...160	Randolph...139	Pagliarulo...143
1987	Cerone...111	Mattingly...140	Randolph...119	Pagliarulo...147
1988	Slaught...94	Mattingly...143	Randolph...110	Pagliarulo...124
1989	Slaught...105	Mattingly...145	Sax...158	Pagliarulo...69
1990	Geren...107	Mattingly...89	Sax...154	Velarde...74
1991	Nokes...130	Mattingly...127	Sax...149	P. Kelly...80
1992	Nokes...111	Mattingly...143	P. Kelly...101	Hayes...139
1993	Stanley...122	Mattingly...130	P. Kelly...125	Boggs...134
1994	Stanley...72	Mattingly...97	P. Kelly...93	Boggs...93
1995	Stanley...107	Mattingly...125	P. Kelly...87	Boggs...117
1996	Girardi...110	Martinez...152	Duncan...98	Boggs...123
1997	Girardi...109	Martinez...147	Sojo...51	Hayes...89
1998	POSADA...85	Martinez...139	Knoblauch...149	Brosius...147
1999	POSADA...98	Martinez...151	Knoblauch...150	Brosius...130
2000	POSADA...106	Martinez...149	Knoblauch...82	Brosius...133
2001	POSADA...127	Martinez...146	Soriano...156	Brosius...130
2002	POSADA...131	Giambi...92	Soriano...154	Ventura...130
2003	POSADA...131	Giambi...85	Soriano...154	Ventura...76
2004	POSADA...126	Clark...64	Cairo...96	RODRIGUEZ...155
2005	POSADA...133	Martinez...122	CANO...131	RODRIGUEZ...161
2006	POSADA...134	Phillips...94	CANO...118	RODRIGUEZ...151
2007	POSADA...138	Mientkiewicz...70	CANO...159	RODRIGUEZ...154
2008	Molina...97	Giambi...113	CANO...159	RODRIGUEZ...131
2009	POSADA...100	TEIXEIRA...152	CANO...161	RODRIGUEZ...116
2010	CERVELLI...90	TEIXEIRA...149	CANO...158	RODRIGUEZ...124

Year-by-Year Games Played Leaders

Year	SHORTSTOP Leader	SS	Year	DESIGNATED HITTER Leader	DH	Year	OUTFIELD Leader	OF	Year	OUTFIELD Leader	OF	Year	OUTFIELD Leader	OF
1903	Elberfeld	90	1903			1903	Keeler	128	1903	Davis	102	1903	McFarland	103
1904	Elberfeld	122	1904			1904	Keeler	142	1904	Anderson	112	1904	Dougherty	106
1905	Elberfeld	108	1905			1905	Keeler	139	1905	Fultz	122	1905	Dougherty	108
1906	Elberfeld	98	1906			1906	Keeler	152	1906	Hoffman	98	1906	Conroy	97
1907	Elberfeld	118	1907			1907	Hoffman	135	1907	Keeler	107	1907	Conroy	100
1908	Ball	130	1908			1908	Hemphill	142	1908	Keeler	88	1908	Stahl	95
1909	Knight	78	1909			1909	Engle	134	1909	Demmitt	109	1909	Keeler	95
1910	Knight	123	1910			1910	Cree	134	1910	Wolter	130	1910	Hemphill	94
1911	Knight	82	1911			1911	Cree	137	1911	Daniels	120	1911	Wolter	113
1912	Martin	64	1912			1912	Daniels	131	1912	Zinn	106	1912	Hartzell	55
1913	Peckinpaugh	93	1913			1913	Cree	144	1913	Wolter	121	1913	Daniels	87
1914	Peckinpaugh	157	1914			1914	Hartzell	128	1914	Cook	126	1914	Cree	76
1915	Peckinpaugh	142	1915			1915	Cook	131	1915	High	117	1915	Hartzell	107
1916	Peckinpaugh	146	1916			1916	Magee	128	1916	High	109	1916	Gilhooley	57
1917	Peckinpaugh	148	1917			1917	Miller	112	1917	Hendry	107	1917	High	100
1918	Peckinpaugh	122	1918			1918	Gilhooley	111	1918	Bodie	90	1918	Miller	62
1919	Peckinpaugh	121	1919			1919	Lewis	141	1919	Bodie	134	1919	Bodie	98
1920	Peckinpaugh	137	1920			1920	Ruth	139	1920	Bodie	129	1920	Lewis	99
1921	Peckinpaugh	147	1921			1921	Ruth	152	1921	Meusel	147	1921	Miller	56
1922	Scott	154	1922			1922	Witt	138	1922	Meusel	121	1922	Ruth	110
1923	Scott	152	1923			1923	Ruth	148	1923	Witt	144	1923	Meusel	121
1924	Scott	153	1924			1924	Ruth	152	1924	Witt	143	1924	Meusel	143
1925	Wanninger	111	1925			1925	Combs	149	1925	Combs	150	1925	Ruth	98
1926	Koenig	141	1926			1926	Ruth	149	1926	Combs	145	1926	Meusel	107
1927	Koenig	122	1927			1927	Combs	152	1927	Ruth	151	1927	Meusel	131
1928	Koenig	125	1928			1928	Ruth	154	1928	Meusel	131	1928	Meusel	108
1929	Durocher	93	1929			1929	Combs	141	1929	Ruth	135	1929	Meusel	96
1930	Lary	113	1930			1930	Ruth	144	1930	Combs	137	1930	Rice	84
1931	Lary	155	1931			1931	Ruth	142	1931	Chapman	138	1931	Combs	129
1932	Crosetti	83	1932			1932	Chapman	149	1932	Ruth	132	1932	Combs	127
1933	Crosetti	133	1933			1933	Chapman	147	1933	Ruth	137	1933	Combs	104
1934	Crosetti	119	1934			1934	Chapman	149	1934	Ruth	111	1934	Byrd	104
1935	Crosetti	87	1935			1935	Chapman	138	1935	Selkirk	127	1935	Hill	94
1936	Crosetti	151	1936			1936	DiMaggio	138	1936	Selkirk	135	1936	Powell	84
1937	Crosetti	147	1937			1937	DiMaggio	150	1937	Hoag	99	1937	Powell	94
1938	Crosetti	157	1938			1938	DiMaggio	145	1938	Henrich	130	1938	Selkirk	95
1939	Crosetti	152	1939			1939	Selkirk	124	1939	DiMaggio	117	1939	Keller	105
1940	Crosetti	145	1940			1940	Keller	136	1940	DiMaggio	130	1940	Selkirk	111
1941	Rizzuto	128	1941			1941	Henrich	139	1941	DiMaggio	139	1941	Keller	137
1942	Rizzuto	144	1942			1942	DiMaggio	154	1942	Henrich	152	1942	Henrich	119
1943	Crosetti	90	1943			1943	Keller	141	1943	Lindell	122	1943	Metheny	85
1944	Milosevich	91	1944			1944	Lindell	149	1944	Metheny	132	1944	Martin	80
1945	Crosetti	126	1945			1945	Metheny	128	1945	Martin	102	1945	Stainback	83
1946	Rizzuto	125	1946			1946	Keller	149	1946	DiMaggio	131	1946	Henrich	111
1947	Rizzuto	151	1947			1947	DiMaggio	139	1947	Henrich	132	1947	Lindell	118
1948	Rizzuto	128	1948			1948	DiMaggio	152	1948	Henrich	102	1948	Lindell	79
1949	Rizzuto	152	1949			1949	Mapes	108	1949	Woodling	98	1949	Bauer	95
1950	Rizzuto	155	1950			1950	DiMaggio	137	1950	Woodling	118	1950	Bauer	110
1951	Rizzuto	144	1951			1951	Woodling	116	1951	DiMaggio	113	1951	Bauer	107
1952	Rizzuto	152	1952			1952	Mantle	141	1952	Bauer	139	1952	Woodling	118
1953	Rizzuto	133	1953			1953	Bauer	126	1953	Mantle	121	1953	Woodling	119
1954	Rizzuto	126	1954			1954	Mantle	145	1954	Noren	125	1954	Bauer	108
1955	Hunter	98	1955			1955	Mantle	145	1955	Bauer	133	1955	Noren	126
1956	McDougald	92	1956			1956	Bauer	146	1956	Mantle	144	1956	Howard	65
1957	McDougald	121	1957			1957	Mantle	139	1957	Bauer	135	1957	Howard	71
1958	Kubek	134	1958			1958	Mantle	150	1958	Siebern	133	1958	Bauer	123
1959	Kubek	67	1959			1959	Mantle	143	1959	Bauer	111	1959	Siebern	93
1960	Kubek	136	1960			1960	Mantle	150	1960	Maris	131	1960	Lopez	106
1961	Kubek	145	1961			1961	Maris	160	1961	Mantle	150	1961	Berra	87
1962	Tresh	111	1962			1962	Maris	154	1962	Mantle	117	1962	Lopez	84
1963	Kubek	132	1963			1963	Tresh	144	1963	Lopez	124	1963	Reed	89
1964	Kubek	99	1964			1964	Tresh	146	1964	Mantle	137	1964	Mantle	132
1965	Kubek	93	1965			1965	Tresh	154	1965	Mantle	108	1965	Moschitto	89
1966	Amaro	63	1966			1966	Mantle	97	1966	Maris	95	1966	Tresh	84
1967	Amaro	123	1967			1967	Pepitone	123	1967	Tresh	118	1967	Whitaker	114
1968	Tresh	119	1968			1968	White	154	1968	Robinson	98	1968	Kosco	95
1969	Michael	118	1969			1969	White	126	1969	Murcer	118	1969	Woods	67
1970	Michael	123	1970			1970	White	161	1970	Murcer	155	1970	Blefary	79
1971	Michael	136	1971			1971	White	145	1971	Murcer	143	1971	F. Alou	80
1972	Michael	121	1972			1972	White	155	1972	Murcer	151	1972	Callison	74
1973	Michael	128	1973	Hart	106	1973	White	162	1973	Murcer	160	1973	M. Alou	85
1974	Mason	152	1974	Blomberg	58	1974	Murcer	156	1974	Maddox	135	1974	Piniella	130
1975	Mason	93	1975	Herrmann	35	1975	White	135	1975	Bonds	129	1975	Maddox	55
1976	Stanley	110	1976	May	81	1976	White	156	1976	Rivers	136	1976	Gamble	104
1977	Dent	157	1977	May	55	1977	Rivers	136	1977	White	135	1977	Jackson	146
1978	Dent	123	1978	Johnson	39	1978	Rivers	138	1978	Jackson	104	1978	Piniella	103
1979	Dent	141	1979	Spencer	71	1979	Jackson	125	1979	Piniella	112	1979	Murcer	70
1980	Dent	141	1980	Soderholm	51	1980	Brown	131	1980	Piniella	104	1980	Jackson	94
1981	Dent	73	1981	Murcer	33	1981	Winfield	102	1981	Mumphrey	79	1981	Jackson	61
1982	Smalley	93	1982	Gamble	74	1982	Winfield	135	1982	Griffey	125	1982	Mumphrey	123
1983	Smalley	90	1983	Baylor	136	1983	Winfield	151	1983	Kemp	101	1983	Mumphrey	83
1984	Meacham	96	1984	Baylor	127	1984	Winfield	140	1984	Moreno	108	1984	Griffey	82
1985	Meacham	155	1985	Baylor	140	1985	Winfield	152	1985	Henderson	141	1985	Griffey	110
1986	Meacham, Tolleson	56	1986	Easler	129	1986	Henderson	146	1986	Winfield	145	1986	Pasqua	81
1987	Tolleson	118	1987	Kittle	49	1987	Winfield	145	1987	Ward	94	1987	Pasqua	74
1988	Santana	148	1988	Clark	112	1988	Winfield	149	1988	Henderson	136	1988	Washington	117
1989	Espinoza	146	1989	Balboni	68	1989	R. Kelly	137	1989	Barfield	129	1989	Hall	108
1990	Espinoza	150	1990	Balboni	72	1990	R. Kelly	160	1990	Barfield	151	1990	Azocar	57
1991	Espinoza	147	1991	Maas	109	1991	R. Kelly	125	1991	Hall	120	1991	B. Williams	85
1992	Stankiewicz	81	1992	Maas	62	1992	R. Kelly	146	1992	Hall	136	1992	Tartabull	69
1993	Owen	96	1993	Tartabull	88	1993	B. Williams	139	1993	O'Neill	138	1993	James	103
1994	Gallego	72	1994	Tartabull	78	1994	B. Williams	107	1994	O'Neill	99	1994	Polonia	84
1995	Fernandez	103	1995	Sierra	46	1995	B. Williams	144	1995	O'Neill	121	1995	G. Williams	92
1996	JETER	156	1996	Sierra	61	1996	O'Neill	146	1996	B. Williams	140	1996	G. Williams	117
1997	JETER	148	1997	Fielder	88	1997	O'Neill	145	1997	B. Williams	127	1997	Curtis	92
1998	JETER	148	1998	Strawberry	79	1998	O'Neill	148	1998	B. Williams	123	1998	Curtis	121
1999	JETER	158	1999	Davis	127	1999	B. Williams	153	1999	O'Neill	150	1999	Ledee	68
2000	JETER	148	2000	Spencer	33	2000	O'Neill	141	2000	B. Williams	136	2000	Justice	57
2001	JETER	150	2001	Justice	65	2001	B. Williams	144	2001	O'Neill	127	2001	Knoblauch	104
2002	JETER	156	2002	Giambi	63	2002	B. Williams	147	2002	Ron. White	105	2002	Mondesi	59
2003	JETER	118	2003	Giambi	69	2003	Matsui	156	2003	B. Williams	113	2003	Mondesi	95
2004	JETER	150	2004	Sierra	54	2004	Matsui	160	2004	Sheffield	136	2004	B. Williams	93
2005	JETER	157	2005	Giambi	59	2005	Matsui	143	2005	Sheffield	131	2005	B. Williams	112
2006	JETER	150	2006	Giambi	70	2006	Damon	131	2006	Cabrera	116	2006	B. Williams	91
2007	JETER	155	2007	Giambi	57	2007	Abreu	158	2007	Cabrera	131	2007	Matsui	112
2008	JETER	148	2008	Matsui	66	2008	Abreu	150	2008	Cabrera	117	2008	Damon	87
2009	JETER	150	2009	Matsui	118	2009	Damon	132	2009	SWISHER	130	2009	Cabrera	103
2010	JETER	151	2010	Thames	41	2010	GARDNER	146	2010	GRANDERSON	134	2010	SWISHER	134

Top 20 Career Batting Leaders

Special thanks to the *Elias Sports Bureau*

Games

1.	Mantle	2401
2.	**JETER**	**2295**
3.	Gehrig	2164
4.	Berra	2116
5.	Ruth	2084
6.	B. Williams	2076
7.	White	1881
8.	Dickey	1789
9.	Mattingly	1785
10.	DiMaggio	1736
11.	**POSADA**	**1714**
12.	Randolph	1694
13.	Crosetti	1683
14.	Rizzuto	1661
15.	Lazzeri	1659
16.	Nettles	1535
17.	Howard	1492
18.	Pipp	1488
19.	Combs	1456
20.	Munson	1423

At-Bats

1.	**JETER**	**9322**
2.	Mantle	8101
3.	Gehrig	8001
4.	B. Williams	7869
5.	Berra	7545
6.	Ruth	7215
7.	Mattingly	7003
8.	DiMaggio	6821
9.	White	6650
10.	Dickey	6304
11.	Randolph	6303
12.	Crosetti	6276
13.	Lazzeri	6096
14.	Rizzuto	5816
15.	Combs	5752
16.	**POSADA**	**5748**
17.	Pipp	5594
18.	Nettles	5519
19.	Richardson	5386
20.	Munson	5344

Runs

1.	Ruth	1959
2.	Gehrig	1888
3.	**JETER**	**1685**
4.	Mantle	1675
5.	DiMaggio	1390
6.	B. Williams	1366
7.	Combs	1186
8.	Berra	1176
9.	Randolph	1027
10.	Mattingly	1007
11.	Crosetti	1006
12.	White	964
13.	Lazzeri	952
14.	Rolfe	942
15.	Dickey	931
16.	Henrich	901
17.	Rizzuto	878
18.	**POSADA**	**866**
19.	Pipp	820
20.	Bauer	792

Hits

1.	**JETER**	**2926**
2.	Gehrig	2721
3.	Ruth	2518
4.	Mantle	2415
5.	B. Williams	2336
6.	DiMaggio	2214
7.	Mattingly	2153
8.	Berra	2148
9.	Dickey	1969
10.	Combs	1866
11.	White	1803
12.	Lazzeri	1784
13.	Randolph	1731
14.	Rizzuto	1588
15.	**POSADA**	**1583**
16.	Pipp	1577
17.	Meusel	1565
18.	Munson	1558
19.	Crosetti	1541
20.	Richardson	1432

Doubles

1.	Gehrig	534
2.	**JETER**	**468**
3.	B. Williams	449
4.	Mattingly	442
5.	Ruth	424
6.	DiMaggio	389
7.	**POSADA**	**365**
8.	Mantle	344
9.	Dickey	343
10.	Meusel	339
11.	Lazzeri	327
12.	Berra	321
13.	Combs	309
14.	O'Neill	304
15.	White	300
16.	Henrich	269
17.	Crosetti	260
18.	Pipp	259
	Randolph	259
20.	Rolfe	257

Triples

1.	Gehrig	163
2.	Combs	154
3.	DiMaggio	131
4.	Pipp	121
5.	Lazzeri	115
6.	Ruth	106
7.	J. Williams	87
8.	Meusel	86
9.	Henrich	73
10.	Dickey	72
	Mantle	72
12.	Keller	69
13.	Rolfe	67
14.	Stirnweiss	66
15.	Crosetti	65
16.	Chapman	64
17.	Cree	62
	Rizzuto	62
19.	**JETER**	**61**
20.	Conroy	59

Home Runs

1.	Ruth	659
2.	Mantle	536
3.	Gehrig	493
4.	DiMaggio	361
5.	Berra	358
6.	B. Williams	287
7.	**RODRIGUEZ**	**268**
8.	**POSADA**	**261**
9.	Nettles	250
10.	**JETER**	**234**
11.	Mattingly	222
12.	Giambi	209
13.	Winfield	205
14.	Maris	203
15.	Dickey	202
16.	Martinez	192
17.	O'Neill	185
18.	Keller	184
19.	Henrich	183
20.	Murcer	175

RBI (since 1920)

1.	Gehrig	1996
2.	Ruth	1976
3.	DiMaggio	1538
4.	Mantle	1509
5.	Berra	1430
6.	B. Williams	1257
7.	Dickey	1210
8.	Lazzeri	1160
9.	**JETER**	**1135**
10.	Mattingly	1099
11.	**POSADA**	**1021**
12.	Meusel	1013
13.	O'Neill	858
14.	**RODRIGUEZ**	**841**
15.	Nettles	834
16.	Winfield	818
17.	Henrich	795
18.	White	758
19.	Martinez	739
20.	Howard	732

Batting Average (min. 500g)

1.	Ruth	.349
2.	Gehrig	.340
3.	DiMaggio	.325
4.	Combs	.324
5.	**JETER**	**.314**
6.	Boggs	.313
7.	Dickey	.312
8.	Meusel	.311
9.	**CANO**	**.309**
10.	Mattingly	.307
11.	Chapman	.305
12.	O'Neill	.303
13.	Mantle	.298
14.	B. Williams	.297
15.	**RODRIGUEZ**	**.296**
16.	Schang	.296
17.	Piniella	.295
18.	Keeler	.294
19.	Skowron	.294
20.	Cree	.293

Stolen Bases

1.	Henderson	326
2.	**JETER**	**323**
3.	Randolph	251
4.	Chase	249
5.	White	232
6.	Conroy	185
7.	Chapman	184
8.	Maisel	183
9.	Mantle	153
10.	Clarke	151
	R. Kelly	151
12.	Rizzuto	149
13.	Lazzeri	147
	B. Williams	147
15.	Daniels	146
16.	Peckinpaugh	143
17.	Meusel	134
18.	Cree	132
19.	Stirnweiss	130
20.	**RODRIGUEZ**	**124**

Single-Season Leaders by Position*

*P	No.	Player	Year
BA	.374	Ruffing	1930
H	49	Mays	1921
HR	5	Ruffing	1936
RBI	22	Mays	1921
	22	Ruffing	1936, '41

C	No.	Player	Year
BA	.362	Dickey	1936
H	192	Berra	1950
HR	30	Berra	1952, '56
	30	POSADA	2003
RBI	133	Dickey	1937

1B	No.	Player	Year
BA	.379	Gehrig	1930
H	238	Mattingly	1986
HR	49	Gehrig	1934, '36
RBI	184	Gehrig	1931

2B	No.	Player	Year
BA	.354	Lazzeri	1929
H	209	Soriano	2002
HR	39	Soriano	2002
RBI	114	Lazzeri	1926

3B	No.	Player	Year
BA	.342	Boggs	1994
H	213	Rolfe	1939
HR	54	RODRIGUEZ	2007
RBI	156	RODRIGUEZ	2007

SS	No.	Player	Year
BA	.349	JETER	1999
H	219	JETER	1999
HR	24	JETER	1999
RBI	107	Lary	1931

OF	No.	Player	Year
BA	.394	Ruth	1923
H	231	Ruth	1927
HR	61	Maris	1961
RBI	171	Ruth	1921

*Played at least 75% of games at that position and had at least 3.1PA/team game (except pitchers - 50% at P; 100PA for BA)

Top 20 Career Pitching Leaders

Games Pitched

1.	**RIVERA**	**978**
2.	Righetti	522
3.	Ford, W.	498
4.	Stanton	456
5.	Ruffing	426
6.	Lyle	420
7.	Shawkey	415
8.	Pettitte	405
9.	Murphy	383
10.	Guidry	368
11.	Gomez	367
12.	Hoyt	365
13.	Stottlemyre	360
14.	Pennock	346
15.	Nelson	331
16.	Gossage	319
17.	Hamilton	311
18.	Reynolds	295
19.	Peterson	288
20.	Page	278
	Mendoza	278

Wins

1.	Ford, W.	236
2.	Ruffing	231
3.	Pettitte	203
4.	Gomez	189
5.	Guidry	170
6.	Shawkey	168
7.	Stottlemyre	164
8.	Pennock	162
9.	Hoyt	157
10.	Reynolds	131
11.	Chesbro	128
12.	Mussina	123
13.	Raschi	120
14.	Lopat	113
15.	Chandler	109
	Peterson	109
17.	Caldwell	95
18.	Murphy	93
	Pipgras	93
20.	John	91

Strikeouts

1.	Ford, W.	1957
2.	Pettitte	1823
3.	Guidry	1778
4.	Ruffing	1526
5.	Gomez	1468
6.	Mussina	1278
7.	Stottlemyre	1259
8.	Shawkey	1166
9.	**RIVERA**	**1051**
10.	Downing	1028
11.	Clemens	1014
12.	Reynolds	967
13.	Righetti	940
14.	Chesbro	913
15.	Turley	909
16.	Peterson	891
17.	Cone	888
18.	Raschi	832
19.	Caldwell	803
20.	Hoyt	709

Complete Games

1.	Ruffing	261
2.	Gomez	173
3.	Chesbro	168
4.	Pennock	164
	Shawkey	164
6.	Ford, W.	156
	Hoyt	156
8.	Stottlemyre	152
9.	Caldwell	150
10.	Chandler	109
11.	Warhop	105
12.	Orth	102
13.	Ford, R.	100
14.	Raschi	99
15.	Reynolds	96
16.	Guidry	95
17.	Bonham	91
	Lopat	91
	Mays	91
20.	Fisher	88

Games Started

1.	Ford, W.	438
2.	Pettitte	396
3.	Ruffing	391
4.	Stottlemyre	356
5.	Guidry	323
6.	Gomez	319
7.	Hoyt	276
8.	Shawkey	274
9.	Pennock	268
10.	Peterson	265
11.	Mussina	248
12.	Chesbro	227
13.	Reynolds	209
14.	Raschi	207
15.	John	203
16.	Lopat	202
17.	Caldwell	196
18.	Chandler	184
19.	Downing	175
	Turley	175

Win Pct. (min. 100 decisions)

1.	Chandler	.717
2.	Raschi	.706
3.	Ford, W.	.690
4.	Reynolds	.686
5.	Mays	.669
6.	Clemens	.664
7.	Lopat	.657
8.	Gomez	.652
9.	Guidry	.651
10.	Ruffing	.651
11.	Pettitte	.644
12.	Byrne	.643
	Pennock	.643
14.	Murphy	.637
15.	Mussina	.631
16.	Bush	.620
17.	Hoyt	.616
18.	Cone	.615
19.	Figueroa	.614
20.	Bonham	.612

Shutouts

1.	Ford, W.	45
2.	Stottlemyre	40
	Ruffing	40
4.	Gomez	28
5.	Reynolds	27
6.	Chandler	26
	Guidry	26
	Shawkey	26
9.	Raschi	24
10.	Turley	21
11.	Lopat	20
12.	Pennock	19
13.	Chesbro	18
	Peterson	18
15.	Bonham	17
	Caldwell	17
17.	Hoyt	15
18.	Orth	14
	Pipgras	14
	Terry	14

ERA (Since 1913, min. 800.0 IP)

1.	**RIVERA**	**2.23**
2.	Fisher	2.60
3.	Caldwell	2.70
4.	Bonham	2.73
5.	Mogridge	2.74
6.	Ford, W.	2.75
7.	Chandler	2.84
8.	Stottlemyre	2.97
9.	Peterson	3.10
10.	Bahnsen	3.11
11.	Righetti	3.11
12.	Shawkey	3.12
13.	May, R.	3.12
14.	Shocker	3.16
15.	Lopat	3.19
16.	Downing	3.23
17.	Mays	3.25
18.	Guidry	3.29
19.	Reynolds	3.31
20.	Gomez	3.34

Earned runs became an official AL statistic in 1913.

Innings

1.	Ford, W.	3171.0
2.	Ruffing	3168.0
3.	Stottlemyre	2662.0
4.	Pettitte	2535.2
5.	Gomez	2497.0
6.	Shawkey	2494.0
7.	Guidry	2393.0
8.	Hoyt	2274.0
9.	Pennock	2201.0
10.	Chesbro	1950.0
11.	Peterson	1856.0
12.	Caldwell	1713.0
13.	Reynolds	1700.0
14.	Mussina	1553.0
15.	Raschi	1538.0
16.	Lopat	1497.0
17.	Chandler	1485.0
18.	Warhop	1413.0
19.	Fisher	1386.0
20.	John	1366.0

Year-by-Year Save Leaders

Saves became an official statistic in 1969

Year	Pitcher	W	S	Year	Pitcher	W	S
1969	Aker	8	11	1990	Righetti	1	36
1970	McDaniel	9	29	1991	Farr	5	23
1971	McDaniel	5	4	1992	Farr	2	30
	Aker	4	4	1993	Farr	2	25
1972	Lyle	9	*35	1994	Howe	3	15
1973	Lyle	5	27	1995	Wetteland	1	31
1974	Lyle	9	15	1996	Wetteland	2	43
1975	Martinez	1	8	1997	RIVERA	6	43
1976	Lyle	7	23	1998	RIVERA	3	36
1977	Lyle	13	26	1999	RIVERA	4	*45
1978	Gossage	10	*27	2000	RIVERA	7	36
1979	Gossage	5	18	2001	RIVERA	4	*50
1980	Gossage	6	*33	2002	RIVERA	1	28
1981	Gossage	3	20	2003	RIVERA	5	40
1982	Gossage	4	30	2004	RIVERA	4	*53
1983	Gossage	13	22	2005	RIVERA	7	43
1984	Righetti	5	31	2006	RIVERA	5	34
1985	Righetti	12	29	2007	RIVERA	3	30
1986	Righetti	8	*46	2008	RIVERA	6	39
1987	Righetti	8	31	2009	RIVERA	3	44
1988	Righetti	5	25	2010	RIVERA	3	33
1989	Righetti	2	25		*Denotes League Leader		

Saves (Since 1969)

1.	**RIVERA**	**559**
2.	Righetti	224
3.	Gossage	151
4.	Lyle	141
5.	Farr	78
6.	Wetteland	74
7.	McDaniel	48
8.	Aker	31
	Howe	31
10.	Tidrow	23
11.	Davis	22
12.	Guetterman	21
13.	Fisher	20
14.	Mendoza	16
15.	Stanton	15
16.	Karsay	12
	Frazier	12
	Guante	12
19.	Stoddard	11
	Wickman	11

Top 10 Single-Season Leaders

BATTING

At-Bats
1. Soriano . . . . .696 . . .2002
2. Richardson . .692 . . .1962
3. Clarke . . . . . .686 . . .1970
4. Soriano . . . . .682 . . .2003
5. Richardson . .679 . . .1964
6. Mattingly . . .677 . . .1986
7. Richardson . .664 . . .1965
8. JETER . . . . . . 663 . . 2010
9. Richardson . .662 . . .1961
10. Crosetti . . . . .656 . . .1939

Runs Scored
1. Ruth . . . . .177 . . .1921
2. Gehrig . . . . .167 . . .1936
3. Ruth . . . . . . .163 . . .1928
   Gehrig . . . . .163 . . .1931
5. Ruth . . . . . . .158 . . .1920
   Ruth . . . . . . .158 . . .1927
7. Ruth . . . . . . .151 . . .1923
   DiMaggio . . .151 . . .1937
9. Ruth . . . . . . .150 . . .1930
10. Gehrig . . . . .149 . . .1927
    Ruth . . . . .149 . . .1931

Hits
1. Mattingly . . .238 . . .1986
2. Combs . . . . .231 . . .1927
3. Gehrig . . . . .220 . . .1930
4. JETER . . . . . . 219 . . 1999
5. Gehrig . . . . .218 . . .1927
6. DiMaggio . . .215 . . .1937
7. JETER . . . . . . 214 . . 2006
8. Rolfe . . . . . .213 . . .1939
9. JETER . . . . . . 212 . . 2009
10. Gehrig . . . . . .211 . . .1931
    Mattingly . . .211 . . .1985

Doubles
1. Mattingly . . .53 . . .1986
2. Gehrig . . . . .52 . . .1927
3. Soriano . . . .51 . . .2002
4. Mattingly . . .48 . . .1985
   CANO . . . . 48 . . 2009
6. Gehrig . . . . .47 . . .1926
   Meusel . . . . .47 . . .1927
   Gehrig . . . . .47 . . .1928
9. Rolfe . . . . . .46 . . .1939
10. Ruth . . . . . . .45 . . .1923
    Meusel . . . . .45 . . .1928
    Matsui . . . . .45 . . .2005

Triples
1. Combs 23 1927
2. Cree 22 1911
   Combs 22 1930
   Stirnweiss . .22 1945
5. Combs 21 1928
6. Gehrig 20 1926
7. Pipp 19 1924
8. Gehrig 18 1927
9. Gehrig 17 1930
10. 7 tied 16

Home Runs
1. Maris 61 1961
2. Ruth 60 1927
3. Ruth 59 1921
4. Ruth 54 1920
   Ruth 54 1928
   Mantle 54 1961
   RODRIGUEZ . . 54 . . 2007
8. Mantle 52 1956
9. Ruth 49 1930
   Gehrig 49 1934
   Gehrig 49 1936

Runs Batted In
1. Gehrig . . . . .184 . . .1931
2. Gehrig . . . . .175 . . .1927
3. Gehrig . . . . .174 . . .1930
4. Ruth . . . . . . .171 . . .1921
5. DiMaggio . . .167 . . .1937
6. Gehrig . . . . .165 . . .1934
7. Gehrig . . . . .164 . . .1927
8. Ruth . . . . . . .162 . . .1931
9. Gehrig . . . . .159 . . .1937
10. **RODRIGUEZ . . 156 . . .2007**

Total Bases
1. Ruth . . . . . . .457 . . .1921
2. Gehrig . . . . .447 . . .1927
3. Gehrig . . . . .419 . . .1930
4. DiMaggio . . .418 . . .1937
5. Ruth . . . . . . .417 . . .1927
6. Gehrig . . . . .410 . . .1931
7. Gehrig . . . . .409 . . .1934
8. Gehrig . . . . .403 . . .1936
9. Ruth . . . . . . .399 . . .1923
10. Ruth . . . . . . .391 . . .1924

Stolen Bases
1. Henderson . .93 1988
2. Henderson . .87 1986
3. Henderson . .80 1985
4. Maisel 74 1914
5. Chapman . . .61 1931
6. Stirnweiss . .55 1944
7. Maisel 51 1915
8. Cree 48 1911
9. **GARDNER . . 47 . . . 2010**
10. Fultz 44 1905

Walks
1. Ruth . . . . . . .170 . . .1923
2. Ruth . . . . . . .150 . . .1920
3. Mantle . . . . .146 . . .1957
4. Ruth . . . . . . .145 . . .1921
   Ruth . . . . . . .144 . . .1926
6. Ruth . . . . . . .142 . . .1924
7. Ruth . . . . . . .137 . . .1927
   Ruth . . . . . . .137 . . .1928
9. Ruth . . . . . . .136 . . .1930
10. Gehrig . . . . . .132 . . .1935

Strikeouts (Batter)
1. Soriano . . . . .157 . . .2002
2. Tartabull . . . .156 . . .1993
3. **POSADA . . . 151 . . 2000**
4. Barfield . . . .150 . . .1990
5. R. Kelly . . . .148 . . .1990
6. **POSADA . . . 143 . . 2002**
7. Clark . . . . . .141 . . .1988
8. Giambi . . . . . .140 . . .2003
9. **RODRIGUEZ . . 139 . . . 2005**
   RODRIGUEZ . . 139 . . . 2006
   SWISHER . . 139 . . 2010

Batting Avg. (min. 500 PA)
1. Ruth . . . . .394 . . .1923
2. DiMaggio . . .381 . .1939
3. Gehrig . . . . .379 . . .1930
4. Ruth . . . . . . .378 . .1924
5. Ruth . . . . . . .377 . .1921
6. Ruth . . . . . . .376 . .1920
7. Gehrig . . . . .374 . .1928
8. Gehrig . . . . .373 . .1927
9. Ruth . . . . . . .373 . .1931
10. Ruth . . . . . . .372 . .1926

Hitting Streaks
1. DiMaggio . . .56 1941
2. Chase 33 1907
3. Peckinpaugh . .29 . . .1919
   Combs 29 1931
   Gordon 29 1942
6. Ruth 26 1921
7. **JETER . . . . . . 25 . . 2006**
8. Mattingly . . .24 1986
9. DiMaggio . . .23 1940
10. DiMaggio . . .22 1937

PITCHING

Games Pitched
1. Quantrill 86 2004
2. Proctor 83 2006
3. Gordon 80 2004
4. Stanton 79 2002
   Gordon 79 2005
6. Karsay 78 2002
7. Nelson 77 1997
   Vizcaino 77 2007
9. Stanton 76 2001
10. Righetti . . . . .74 . . .1985
    Righetti . . . . .74 . . .1986
    RIVERA . . . . 74 . . . 2004

Complete Games
1. Chesbro 48 1904
2. Powell 38 1904
3. Orth 36 1906
4. Chesbro 33 1903
5. Caldwell 31 1915
6. R. Ford 30 1912
   Mays 30 1921
   Hunter 30 1975
9. R. Ford 29 1910
10. Orth 26 1905
    R. Ford 26 1911
    Mays 26 1920

Wins
1. Chesbro 41 1904
2. Orth 27 1906
   Mays 27 1921
4. R.Ford 26 1910
   Mays 26 1920
   Bush 26 1922
   Gomez 26 1934
8. W. Ford 25 1961
   Guidry 25 1978
10. 4 tied 24

Shutouts
1. Guidry 9 1978
2. R. Ford 8 1910
   W. Ford 8 1964
4. Reynolds 7 1951
   W. Ford 7 1958
   Stottlemyre . .7 . . .1971
   Stottlemyre . .7 . . .1972
   Hunter 7 1975
9. 14 tied 6

Strikeouts (Pitcher)
1. Guidry . . . . . .248 . . .1978
2. Chesbro . . . .239 . . .1904
3. Cone . . . . . .222 . . .1997
4. M. Perez . . . .218 . . .1992
5. Downing . . . .217 . . .1964
6. Mussina . . . .214 . . .2001
7. Clemens . . . .213 . . .2001
8. Johnson . . . .211 . . .2005
9. Turley . . . . . .210 . . .1955
10. R. Ford . . . . .209 . . .1910
    W. Ford . . . . . .209 . . .1961
    Cone . . . . .209 . . .1998

ERA (min. 1.0IP/per team game)
1. Chandler . . .1.64 . . .1943
2. Guidry . . . . .1.74 . . .1978
3. Caldwell . . . .1.94 . . .1914
4. W. Ford . . . . .2.01 . . .1958
5. Cullop . . . . . .2.05 . . .1916
6. Bahnsen . . . .2.06 . . .1968
7. Reynolds . . .2.07 . . .1952
8. Chandler . . .2.10 . . .1946
9. Fisher . . . . . .2.11 . . .1915
10. W. Ford . . . .2.13 . . .1964
Since earned runs became an
official AL statistic in 1913.

Saves
1. **RIVERA . . . . 53 . . . 2004**
2. **RIVERA . . . . 50 . . . 2001**
3. Righetti . . . . .46 . . .1986
4. **RIVERA . . . . 45 . . . 1999**
5. **RIVERA . . . . 44 . . . 2009**
6. Wetteland . .43 . . .1996
   RIVERA . . . . 43 . . . 1997
   RIVERA . . . . 43 . . . 2005
9. **RIVERA . . . . 40 . . . 2003**
10. **RIVERA . . . . 39 . . . 2008**

All-Time Club Records

KEY: ^-ML record (since 1900)   **-tied for ML record
+-AL record   #-tied for AL record

Single-Season Club Records

Most Wins

Season	114	1998
Home	65^	1961
Road	54	1939
Month	28	Aug. 1938
Consecutive	19	1947
Consecutive, home	18	1942
Consecutive, road	15	1953
Shutout	24	1951
1-0	6	1908, 1968

Fewest Wins

Season	50	1912
Home	27	1913
Road	19	1912

Most Losses

Season	103	1908
Home	47	1908, 1913
Road	58	1912
Month	24	July 1908
Consecutive	13	1913
Consecutive, home	17	1913
Consecutive, road	12	1908
Shutout	27	1914
1-0	9	1914

Fewest Losses

Season	44	1927
Home	15^	1932
Road	20+	1939

Miscellaneous

Most games	164**	1964, 1968
Fewest games	107	1981
Consecutive extra-inning games	4	1992 (5/19-23)
Longest 1-0 game won	15 inn	vs. PHI, 7/4/25, G1
Longest 1-0 game lost	14 inn	at BOS, 9/24/69
Most players used	51	2005, 2008
Fewest players used	25	1923, 1927
Most pitchers used	28	2005, 2007
Fewest pitchers used	8	1922, 1923

Longest Games in Club History
(Innings)

Inn.	Opponent	Date, Result
22	at Detroit	6/24/62, a 9-7 win
20	vs. Boston	8/29/67 (G2), a 4-3 win
19 (3x)	vs. Cleveland	5/24/18, a 3-2 loss
	vs. Detroit	8/23/68 (G2), a 3-3 tie
	vs. Minnesota	8/25/76, a 5-4 win
18 (6x)	vs. Chicago	6/25/1903, a 6-6 tie
	at Boston	9/5/27, a 12-11 loss
	at Chicago	8/21/33, a 3-3 tie
	vs. Boston	4/16/67, a 7-6 win
	at Washington	4/22/70, a 2-1 loss
	vs. Detroit	9/11/88, a 5-4 win
17	at Detroit	last on 6/1/2003, a 10-9 win
16	vs. Oakland	last on 8/9/02, a 3-2 loss

Single-Season Batting Records

Most at-bats	5717	2007
Most runs	1067^	1931
Fewest runs	459	1908
Most hits	1683	1930
Fewest hits	1136	1903
Batting avg (high)	.309	1930
Batting avg (low)	.214	1968
Most singles	1237	1988
Most doubles	327	2006
Most triples	110	1930
Most home runs	244	2009
Most home runs (home)	136	2009
Most home runs (road)	128	1961
Most home runs (month)	54	July 1940; Aug. 1998
Most inside-the-park HR	22	1904, '23
Consecutive games with a HR	25 (40 HR total)	1941
Grand slams	10	1987, 2010
Pinch hit home runs	10	1961
Total bases	2703	1936, 2009
Runs batted in	995^	1936
Most bases on balls	766	1932
Most hit by pitch	81	2003
Fewest hit by pitch	14	1969
Most stolen bases	289	1910
Fewest stolen bases	24	1948
Most caught stealing	82	1920
Fewest caught stealing	18	1961, 1964
Most strikeouts	1171	2002
Fewest strikeouts	420	1924
Highest on-base pct.	.384	1930
Lowest on-base pct.	.282	1908
Highest slugging pct.	.489	1927
Lowest slugging pct.	.287	1914
Most GIDP	153	1996
Fewest GIDP	91	1963
Most left on base	1258	1996
Fewest left on base	1010	1920
Double-digit HR hitters	10	1998
Most .300 hitters	6	1930/31/36 (min 300AB)
Most "walk-off" wins	17	1943

Single-Season Pitching Records

Lowest ERA (since 1913)	2.66	1917
Highest ERA (since 1913)	4.88	1930
Innings pitched	1506.2	1964
Complete games	123	1904
Fewest complete games	1	2004, 2007, 2008
Most shutouts	24	1951
Consecutive shutouts	4	1932
Consecutive shutout innings	40	5/10-16/1932
Fewest shutouts	2	1994
Most saves (since 1969)	59	2004
Fewest hits allowed	1143	1919
Most hits allowed	1566	1930
Fewest home runs allowed	13	1907
Most home runs allowed	182	2004
Fewest runs allowed	507	1942
Most runs allowed	898	1930
Fewest earned runs allowed	394	1904
Most earned runs allowed	753	2000
Fewest bases on balls	245^	1903
Most bases on balls	812	1949
Fewest strikeouts	431	1927
Most strikeouts	1266+	2001

Single-Season Fielding Records

Highest fielding pct.	.988	2010
Lowest fielding pct.	.939	1912
Fewest errors	69	2010
Most errors	386	1912
Most errorless games	107^	2010
Consecutive errorless games	18^	5/14-6/1/2009
Most putouts	4520^	1964
Fewest putouts	3993	1935
Most assists	2086	1904
Fewest assists	1487	2000
Most double plays	214	1956
Fewest double plays	81	1912
Consecutive games, DP turned	19 (27 DPs)	1992
Most passed balls	32	1913
Fewest passed balls	0^	1931
Most chances	6584	1916
Fewest chances	5551	1935

Single-Game/Inning Batting Records

Most runs

Game, 9 innings, home	22	7/26/31 vs. CWS (G2)
Game, 9 innings, road	25	5/24/36 at PHI
Game, both teams	33 (3x)	5/3/12 at PHI
		5/22/30 at PHI (G2)
		6/3/32 at PHI
Game, both teams, home	31	6/21/2005 vs. TB
Game, opponent, home	22 (2x)	8/31/2004 vs. CLE
		4/18/2009 vs. CLE
Game, opponent, road	24	7/29/28 at CLE
Shutout game	21	8/13/39 at PHI
Shutout game, opponent	22	8/31/2004 vs. CLE
Two consecutive games	40	15 in G2 on 5/23/36
		and 25 on 5/24/36 at CLE
Three consecutive games	52	
		12 in G1 on 5/23/36 at PHI
		15 in G2 on 5/23/36 at PHI
		and 25 on 5/24/36 at PHI
Consecutive games scoring 10 or more	5	6/12-17/30
Inning	14	7/6/20 at WAS (5th)
Start of game, no outs	8	4/24/60 vs. BAL
		9/25/90 vs. BAL
Largest margin of victory	23	5/24/36 at PHI (25-2)
Largest margin of victory, home	20	7/4/27 vs. WAS (21-1)
		7/24/99 vs. CLE (21-1 win)
Largest margin of defeat	22	8/31/04 vs. CLE (22-0)

Most hits

Game, 9 innings	30	9/28/23 at BOS
Game, 9 innings, both teams	45#	9/29/28 at DET
Consecutive, start of game	8**	9/25/90 vs. BAL
Most singles	22	8/12/53 at WAS
Most doubles	10	4/12/88 at TOR
		and 6/5/2003 at CIN
Most triples	5	5/1/34 at WAS
Most extra-base hits, game	12	6/5/2003 at CIN
Most extra-base hits, inning	7	5/3/51 vs. SLB

Most bases on balls

Game	16	6/23/15 at PHI
Game, vs. one pitcher	9 (11x)	last: Josh Beckett, 8/19/06 at BOS

Most strikeouts

Game, 9 inn.	17	8/11/10 at TEX and 9/10/99 vs. BOS (all vs. Pedro Martinez)
Game, extra inn.	17	9/30/01 at BAL (15 inn.)l

Most home runs

Game	8	6/28/39 at PHI (G1) 7/31/07 vs. CWS
Game, both teams	11	6/23/50 at DET (NYY-6 HR, DET-5 HR)
Game, vs. one pitcher	6	off Tommy Thomas, 6/27/36 at STL
Inning	4 (2x)	6/30/77 at TOR 6/21/2005 vs. TB
Inning, with 2 outs	3 (2x)	6/28/39 at PHI (3rd) 6/21/2005 vs. TB (8th)
Consecutive	3 (11x)	last on 5/20/2009 vs. BAL - SWISHER, CANO, Cabrera
Start of game	2 (5x)	4/27/55 vs. CWS, Bauer and Carey; 7/30/99 at BOS, Knoblauch and JETER; 4/6/2003 at TB, Soriano and Johnson; 6/28/2003 at NYM, Soriano and JETER; 9/23/2005 vs. TOR, Jeter and CANO
Most "walk-off" HR in a season	7	2009

Most grand slams

Game	2** (3x)	5/24/36 vs. PHI 6/29/87 at TOR 9/14/99 at TOR
Inning	1	(Many times)

Most stolen bases

Game	15^	9/28/11 vs. SLB
Game, both clubs	15#	NY 15, SLB 0, 9/28/11
Game, steals of home	3**	4/17/15 vs. PHI

Most GIDP

Game	5 (3x)	last on 9/27/68 at BOS

Most LOB

Game, 9 innings	20^	9/21/56 at BOS
Game, extra innings	23	9/5/27 at BOS (G1)

Single-Game/Inning Club Pitching Records

Most runs allowed

Game	24	7/29/28 at CLE (24-6)
Game, home	22 (2x)	
		8/31/2004 vs. CLE (22-0)
		4/18/2009 vs. CLE (22-4)
Inning	14	4/18/2009 vs. CLE (2nd)
Two consecutive games	33	9 on 7/28/28 at CLE and 24 on 7/29/28 at CLE

Most hits allowed

Game	28	9/29/28 at DET
Game, home	27	5/28/05 vs. BOS

Most home runs allowed

Game	7	7/4/2003 vs. BOS
Inning	4 (5x)	6/23/50 at DET 6/17/77 at BOS 5/2/92 vs. MIN 8/21/2005 at CWS 4/22/2007 at BOS

Most strikeouts

Game, 9 inn.	18	6/17/78 vs. CAL (all by Ron Guidry)
Game, extra inn.	19	4/19/01 at TOR (17 inn.) and 7/11/87 vs. CWS (15 inn.)

Most walks

Game	17	9/11/49 vs. WAS (G1, 9 inn.)
Inning	11	9/11/49 vs. WAS (3rd)

Most wild pitches

Most wild pitches, game	5	6/24/94 vs. CLE

KEY: ^–ML record (since 1900)   **–tied for ML record   +–AL record   #–tied for AL record

Single-Game Club Miscellaneous

Longest game, time	7:00	6/24/62 at DET (22 inn.)
Longest game, time, 9 innings	4:45^	8/18/06 at BOS
Largest deficit overcome	9 (4x)	last on 5/16/06 vs. TEX
Largest lead blown	9 (2x)	last on 7/28/31 vs. CWS

Single-Game/Inning Club Fielding Records

Most errors, game	10	6/12/1907 vs. DET
Most errors, inning (since 1969)	5	Stottlemyre, Clarke, Pepitone, Murcer (2) on 5/9/69 at OAK

Individual Single-Game/Inning Pitching Records

Runs allowed, game	13 (3x)	Jack Warhop, 7/31/11 vs. CWS
		Ray Caldwell, 10/3/13 at PHI
		Carl Mays, 7/17/23 at CLE
Hits allowed, game	21	Jack Quinn, 6/29/12 at BOS
HRs allowed, game	5 (5x)	Joe Ostrowski, 6/22/50 at CLE
		John Cumberland, 5/24/70 at CLE
		Ron Guidry, 9/17/85 at DET
		Jeff Weaver, 7/21/2002 vs. BOS
		David Wells, 7/4/2003 vs. BOS
HRs allowed, inning	4 (4x)	Catfish Hunter, 6/17/77 at BOS (1st)
		Scott Sanderson, 5/2/92 vs. MIN (5th)
		Randy Johnson, 8/21/2005 at CWS (4th)
		Chase Wright, 4/22/2007 at BOS (3rd), all consecutive tying ML record
Most strikeouts, game, LH	18	Ron Guidry, 6/17/78 vs. CAL
Most strikeouts, game, RH	16	David Cone, 6/23/97 at DET
Most strikeouts, inning	3	Many pitchers
Most strikeouts, relief	12	Jumbo Brown, 6/3/33 vs. PHI
Consecutive strikeouts	8	Ron Davis, 5/4/81 at CAL
Most bases on balls, game	13	Tommy Byrne, 6/8/49 at DET
Balks, game	#4	Vic Raschi, 5/3/50 vs. CWS

Individual Single-Game Batting Records

Most at-bats	**11	Bobby Richardson, 6/24/62 at DET (22 inn.)
Most runs	5 (16x)	last by Johnny Damon, 4/29/2006 vs. TB
Most hits	#6 (3x)	Myril Hoag (6-for-6), 6/6/34 at BOS
		Gerald Williams (6-for-8), 5/1/96 at BAL, 15 innings
		Johnny Damon (6-for-6), 6/7/08 vs. KC
Most singles	** 6	Myril Hoag, 6/6/34 at BOS
Most doubles	**4 (2x)	Johnny Lindell, 8/17/44 vs. CLE
		Jim Mason, 7/8/74 at TEX
Most triples	**3 (3x)	Hal Chase, 8/30/06 vs. WAS
		Earle Combs, 9/22/27 vs. DET
		Joe DiMaggio, 8/27/38 vs. CLE (G1)
Most home runs	**4	Lou Gehrig (consecutive), 6/3/32 at PHI
Most grand slams	**2	Tony Lazzeri, 5/24/36 at PHI
Most total bases	#16	Lou Gehrig, 6/3/32 at PHI
Most times reaching base safely (9-inning game)	+**7	Ben Chapman, 5/24/36 at PHI
Most RBI (game)	+11	Tony Lazzeri (2GS, solo HR, 2R-triple), 5/24/36 at PHI
Most RBI (inning)	+7	ALEX RODRIGUEZ, (Top 6th - GS, 3R-HR)10/4/09 at TB
Most sacrifice flies	**3 (2x)	Bob Meusel, 9/15/26 at CLE
		Don Mattingly, 5/3/86 vs. TEX
Most stolen bases	4 (18x)	last, Tony Womack, 5/15/2005 at OAK
Most caught stealing	3 (2x)	Fritz Maisel, 4/26/16 vs. BOS
		Lee Magee, 6/29/18 at PHI
Most walks	5 (7x)	last, MARK TEIXEIRA, 4/25/09 at BOS
Most strikeouts	**5 (6x)	Johnny Broaca, 6/25/34 vs. CWS
		Stan Bahnsen, 6/17/68 at CAL
		Bernie Williams, 8/1/91 vs. MIN
		Andy Phillips, 5/2/2005 at TB
		Melky Cabrera, 7/7/2007 vs. LAA
		MARK TEIXEIRA, 6/5/10 at TOR
Most grounded into DPs	3 (3x)	Eddie Robinson, 5/30/55 at WAS
		Jim Leyritz, 7/4/90 at KC
		Matt Nokes, 5/3/92 vs. MIN

KEY: ^–ML record (since 1900)   **–tied for ML record   +–AL record   #–tied for AL record

Individual Single-Season Pitching Records

Most wins, RHP	41+	Jack Chesbro, 1904
Most wins, LHP	26	Lefty Gomez, 1934
Most consecutive wins, RHP	16#	Roger Clemens, 2001
Most consecutive wins, LHP	14	Whitey Ford, 1961
Most shutouts	9	Ron Guidry, 1978
Most shutouts lost	7	Bill Zuber, 1945
Lowest ERA, RHP	1.64	Spud Chandler, 1943
Lowest ERA, LHP	1.74	Ron Guidry, 1978
Highest winning pct.	.893	Ron Guidry, 1978
Most losses, RHP	22	Joe Lake, 1908
Most losses, LHP	17	Herb Pennock, 1921
Consecutive losses, RHP	9 (2x)	Bill Hogg, 1908
		Thad Tillotson, 1967
Consecutive losses, LHP	11	George Mogridge, 1916
Most innings pitched, RHP	454.0	Jack Chesbro, 1904
Most innings pitched, LHP	286.0	Herb Pennock, 1924
Most consecutive scoreless IP	39.0	Al Orth, 6/29-7/21/1905
Most saves, RHP	53	MARIANO RIVERA, 2004
Most saves, LHP	46	Dave Righetti, 1986
Most games, RHP	86	Paul Quantrill, 2004
Most games, LHP	79	Mike Stanton, 2002
Most games started	51^	Jack Chesbro, 1904
Most complete games	48^	Jack Chesbro, 1904
Most strikeouts, RHP	239	Jack Chesbro, 1904
Most strikeouts, LHP	248	Ron Guidry, 1978
Most bases on balls, RHP	177	Bob Turley, 1955
Most bases on balls, LHP	179	Tommy Byrne, 1949
Most hits allowed	337	Jack Chesbro, 1904
Most runs allowed	165	Russ Ford, 1912
Most earned runs allowed	127	Sam Jones, 1925
Most home runs allowed, RHP	40	Ralph Terry, 1962
Most home runs allowed, LHP	32	Randy Johnson, 2005
Most hit batsmen	26	Jack Warhop, 1909
Most wild pitches	23	Tim Leary, 1990

Individual Single-Season Batting Records

Games	163	Hideki Matsui, 2003
Most at-bats	696	Alfonso Soriano, 2002
Highest batting average, RH	.381	Joe DiMaggio, 1939
Highest batting average, LH	.394	Babe Ruth, 1923
Highest batting average, SH	.365	Mickey Mantle, 1957
Most Hits, RH	219	DEREK JETER, 1999
Most Hits, LH	238	Don Mattingly, 1986
Most Hits, SH	204	Bernie Williams, 2002
Consecutive games hit safely	56^	Joe DiMaggio, 1941
Most runs	177^	Babe Ruth, 1921
Consecutive games, run scored	18^	Red Rolfe, 1939
Most singles	171	Steve Sax, 1989
Most doubles	53	Don Mattingly, 1986
Most triples	23	Earle Combs, 1927
Most home runs, RH	54	ALEX RODRIGUEZ, 2007
Most home runs, LH	61+	Roger Maris, 1961
Most home runs, SH	54^	Mickey Mantle, 1961
Most HR, home, LH (Polo Grounds)	32	Babe Ruth, 1921
Most HR, home, RH (Polo Grounds)	14	Bob Meusel, 1921
Most HR, home, LH (Orig. Yankee Stad.)	30	Lou Gehrig, 1934
		Roger Maris, 1961
Most HR, home, RH (Orig. Yankee Stad.)	26	A. RODRIGUEZ, 2005, '07
Most HR, home, LH (Yankee Stad.)	17	Johnny Damon, 2009
Most HR, home, RH (Yankee Stad.)	18	A. RODRIGUEZ, 2009
Most HR, home, SH (Yankee Stad.)	24	MARK TEIXEIRA, 2009
Most home runs, home, SH	27	Mickey Mantle, 1956
Most home runs, road, RH	28	A. RODRIGUEZ, 2007
Most home runs, road, LH	32#	Babe Ruth, 1927
Most home runs, road, SH	30	Mickey Mantle, 1961
Most home runs, month	17	Babe Ruth, Sept., 1927
Most home runs, rookie, RH	29	Joe DiMaggio, 1936
Most home runs, rookie, LH	21	Kevin Maas, 1990
Most home runs, rookie, SH	20	Tom Tresh, 1962
Most home runs, month	17	Babe Ruth, Sept. 1927
Consecutive games with HR	8**	Don Mattingly, 1987
Most grand slams	6**	Don Mattingly, 1987
Most RBI, RH	167	Joe DiMaggio, 1937

Most RBI, LH	184+	Lou Gehrig, 1931
Most RBI, SH	130	Mickey Mantle, 1956
Consecutive games with RBI	11	Babe Ruth, 1931
Most extra-base hits	119^	Babe Ruth, 1921
Most total bases	457^	Babe Ruth, 1921
Highest slugging pct.	.847^	Babe Ruth, 1920
Most strikeouts, RH	157	Alfonso Soriano, 2002
Most strikeouts, LH	133	Reggie Jackson, 1978
Most strikeouts, SH	151	JORGE POSADA, 2000
Most bases on balls, RH	119	Willie Randolph, 1980
Most bases on balls, LH	170+	Babe Ruth, 1923
Most bases on balls, SH	146	Mickey Mantle, 1957
Most sacrifice hits	42	Willie Keeler, 1905
Most sacrifice flies	17#	Roy White, 1971
Most stolen bases	93	Rickey Henderson, 1988
Most caught stealing	23	Ben Chapman, 1931
Most hit by pitch	24	Don Baylor, 1985
Most grounded into DP	30	Dave Winfield, 1983
Fewest grounded into DP	2 (2x)	Mickey Mantle, 1961
		Mickey Rivers, 1977

Note: Records in "fewest" categories are based on full seasons and do not include 1918, 1981 and 1994.

Yankees Rawlings Gold Glove Winners by Year
Award given since 1957

Year	NAME, POS	Year	NAME, POS
1957	Bobby Shantz, P	1985	Ron Guidry, P
1958	Bobby Shantz, P		Don Mattingly, 1B
	Norm Siebern, OF		Dave Winfield, OF
1959	Bobby Shantz, P	1986	Ron Guidry, P
1960	Bobby Shantz, P		Don Mattingly, 1B
	Roger Maris, OF	1987	Don Mattingly, 1B
1961	Bobby Richardson, 2B		Dave Winfield, OF
1962	Bobby Richardson, 2B	1988	Don Mattingly, 1B
	Mickey Mantle, OF	1989	Don Mattingly, 1B
1963	Elston Howard, C	1991	Don Mattingly, 1B
	Bobby Richardson, 2B	1992	Don Mattingly, 1B
1964	Elston Howard, C	1993	Don Mattingly, 1B
	Bobby Richardson, 2B	1994	Don Mattingly, 1B
1965	Joe Pepitone, 1B		Wade Boggs, 3B
	Bobby Richardson, 2B	1995	Wade Boggs, 3B
	Tom Tresh, OF	1997	Bernie Williams, OF
1966	Joe Pepitone, 1B	1998	Bernie Williams, OF
1969	Joe Pepitone, 1B	1999	Scott Brosius, 3B
1972	Bobby Murcer, OF		Bernie Williams, OF
1973	Thurman Munson, C	2000	Bernie Williams, OF
1974	Thurman Munson, C	2001	Mike Mussina, P
1975	Thurman Munson, C	2003	Mike Mussina, P
1977	Graig Nettles, 3B	2004	DEREK JETER, SS
1978	Chris Chambliss, 1B	2005	DEREK JETER, SS
	Graig Nettles, 3B	2006	DEREK JETER, SS
1982	Ron Guidry, P	2008	Mike Mussina, P
	Dave Winfield, OF	2009	DEREK JETER, SS
1983	Ron Guidry, P		MARK TEIXEIRA, 1B
	Dave Winfield, OF	2010	ROBINSON CANO, 2B
1984	Ron Guidry, P		DEREK JETER, SS
	Dave Winfield, OF		MARK TEIXEIRA, 1B

Yankees Rawlings Gold Glove Winners by Position

Pos.	Winner (Years)
P	Bobby Shantz (1957-60); Ron Guidry (1982-86); Mike Mussina (2001; '03, '08)
C	Elston Howard (1963-64); Thurman Munson (1973-75)
1B	Joe Pepitone (1965-66, '69); Chris Chambliss (1978); Don Mattingly (1985-89; '91-94); MARK TEIXEIRA (2009-10)
2B	Bobby Richardson (1961-65), ROBINSON CANO (2010)
3B	Graig Nettles (1977-78); Wade Boggs (1994-95); Scott Brosius (1999)
SS	DEREK JETER (2004-06; '09-10)
OF	Norm Siebern (1958); Roger Maris (1960); Mickey Mantle (1962); Tom Tresh (1965); Bobby Murcer (1972); Dave Winfield (1982-85, '87); Bernie Williams (1997-2002)

KEY: ^–ML record (since 1900)   **–tied for ML record   +–AL record   #–tied for AL record

Yankees 20-Game Winners

Year	Pitcher	W	L	Year	Pitcher	W	L	Year	Pitcher	W	L
1903	Jack Chesbro	21	15	1931	Lefty Gomez	21	9	1963	Whitey Ford	24	7
1904	Jack Chesbro	41	12	1932	Lefty Gomez	24	7		Jim Bouton	21	7
	Jack Powell	23	19	1934	Lefty Gomez	26	5	1965	Mel Stottlemyre	20	9
1906	Al Orth	27	17	1936	Red Ruffing	20	12	1968	Mel Stottlemyre	21	12
	Jack Chesbro	24	16	1937	Lefty Gomez	21	11	1969	Mel Stottlemyre	20	14
1910	Russell Ford	26	6		Red Ruffing	20	7	1970	Fritz Peterson	20	11
1911	Russell Ford	22	11	1938	Red Ruffing	21	7	1975	Catfish Hunter	23	14
1916	Bob Shawkey	24	14	1939	Red Ruffing	21	7	1978	Ron Guidry	25	3
1919	Bob Shawkey	20	11	1942	Ernie Bonham	21	5		Ed Figueroa	20	9
1920	Carl Mays	26	11	1943	Spud Chandler	20	4	1979	Tommy John	21	9
	Bob Shawkey	20	13	1946	Spud Chandler	20	8	1980	Tommy John	22	9
1921	Carl Mays	27	9	1949	Vic Raschi	21	10	1983	Ron Guidry	21	9
1922	Joe Bush	26	7	1950	Vic Raschi	21	8	1985	Ron Guidry	22	6
	Bob Shawkey	20	12	1951	Eddie Lopat	21	9	1996	Andy Pettitte	21	8
1923	Sad Sam Jones	21	8		Vic Raschi	21	10	1998	David Cone	20	7
1924	Herb Pennock	21	9	1952	Allie Reynolds	20	8	2001	Roger Clemens	20	3
1926	Herb Pennock	23	11	1954	Bob Grim	20	6	2003	Andy Pettitte	21	8
1927	Waite Hoyt	22	7	1958	Bob Turley	21	7	2008	Mike Mussina	20	9
1928	George Pipgras	24	13	1961	Whitey Ford	25	4	2010	CC SABATHIA	21	7
	Waite Hoyt	23	7	1962	Ralph Terry	23	12				

Mel Stottlemyre

Yankees Free Agent Signings

C. Hunter 12/31/74	D. Tartabull 1/6/92	J. Flaherty 12/15/03
D. Gullett 11/18/76	S. Owen 12/4/92	G. Sheffield 12/17/03
R. Jackson 11/29/76	S. Howe 12/8/92	M. Cairo 12/19/03
R. Gossage 11/22/77	J. Key 12/10/92	P. Quantrill 12/22/03
R. Eastwick 12/9/77	W. Boggs 12/15/92	T. Gordon 12/23/03
L. Tiant 11/13/78	L. Polonia 12/20/93	K. Lofton 12/23/03
T. John 11/22/78	D. Pall 1/18/94	T. Clark 1/13/04
R. May 11/8/79	S. Bankhead 11/1/94	T. Womack 12/21/04
B. Watson 11/8/79	T. Fernandez 12/14/94	C. Pavano 12/22/04
D. Winfield 12/15/80	W. Boggs 12/5/95	J. Wright 12/22/04
B. Castro 2/15/81	M. Duncan 12/11/95	T. Martinez 12/31/04
R. Guidry 12/15/81	D. Cone 12/21/95	R. Sanchez 2/16/05
D. Collins 12/23/81	K. Rogers 1/4/96	K. Stinnett 11/30/05
D. Baylor 12/1/82	D. Gooden 10/16/96	K. Farnsworth 12/2/05
S. Kemp 12/9/82	M. Stanton 12/11/96	M. Myers 12/15/05
B. Shirley 12/15/82	D. Wells 12/19/96	B. Williams 12/22/05
D. Murray 11/21/83	M. Whiten 1/9/97	J. Damon 12/23/05
P. Niekro 1/6/84	D. Sveum 11/25/97	O. Dotel 12/29/05
E. Whitson 12/27/84	C. Davis 12/10/97	M. Cairo 1/5/06
J. Niekro 1/8/86	D. Holmes 12/22/97	S. Ponson 7/14/06
P. Niekro 1/8/86	O. Hernandez 3/7/98	M. Mussina 11/27/06
B. Wynegar 1/8/86	S. Brosius 11/10/98	A. Pettitte 12/20/06
A. Holland 2/6/86	B. Williams 11/25/98	D. Mientkiewicz 1/5/07
T. John 5/2/86	M. Stanton 11/29/99	M. Cairo 1/26/07
R. Scurry 12/5/86	D. Cone 12/6/99	S. Patterson 11/20/07
C. Washington 12/11/86	A. Watson 12/7/99	J. POSADA 11/29/07
L. Sakata 12/16/86	P. O'Neill 11/16/00	J. Molina 12/3/07
G. Ward 12/24/86	J. Oliver 11/21/00	A. Pettitte 12/12/07
T. John 1/8/87	M. Mussina 11/30/00	A. RODRIGUEZ 12/13/07
W. Tolleson 1/8/87	L. Sojo 12/7/00	M. RIVERA 12/17/07
W. Randolph 1/8/87	H. Rodriguez 2/16/01	L. Hawkins 12/27/07
B. Shirley 1/28/87	S. Karsay 12/7/01	R. Sexson 7/18/08
R. Cerone 2/13/87	J. Giambi 12/13/01	C. SABATHIA 12/18/08
R. Guidry 5/1/87	Rond. White. 12/17/01	A. BURNETT 12/18/08
D. Righetti 12/23/87	S. Hitchcock 12/18/01	M. TEIXEIRA 1/6/09
J. Clark 1/6/88	A. Castillo 12/21/01	A. Pettitte 1/26/09
J. Candelaria 1/18/88	D. Wells 1/10/02	A. Pettitte 12/9/09
J. Cruz 2/25/88	R. Rivera 2/14/02	N. Johnson 12/23/09
S. Sax 11/23/88	B. Rivera 11/21/02	R. Winn 2/8/10
D. LaPoint 12/3/88	C. Latham 12/4/02	C.H. Park 2/28/10
A. Hawkins 12/8/88	R. Ventura 12/6/02	C. Gaudin 5/26/10
J. Quirk 12/20/88	C. Widger 12/7/02	D. JETER 12/7/10
R. Guidry 2/3/89	C. Hammond 12/12/02	M. RIVERA 12/14/10
T. John 2/13/89	T. Zeile 12/18/02	R. MARTIN 12/16/10
P. Perez 11/21/89	H. Matsui 12/19/02	P. FELICIANO 1/3/11
M. Hall 11/30/89	J. Contreras 12/24/02	R. SORIANO 1/18/11
R. Cerone 12/22/89	R. Clemens. 12/30/02	A. JONES 2/14/11
D. Garcia 12/22/89	E. Wilson 12/2/03	
T. Leary 11/19/90	F. Heredia 12/3/03	*Free agent signings through 2/15/11*
S. Farr 11/26/90	R. Sierra 12/8/03	

AL Most Valuable Players

YEAR	PLAYER	AGE	POS	G	AB	R	H	2B	3B	HR	RBI	BA	E
1923	Babe Ruth	28	OF	152	520	*151*	205	45	13	*41*†*	*130*	.394	11
1927	Lou Gehrig	23	1B	*155*†	584	149	218	*52*	18	47	*175*	.373	15
1936	Lou Gehrig	32	1B	*155†*	579	*167*	205	37	7	*49*	152	.354	9
1939	Joe DiMaggio	24	OF	120	462	108	176	32	6	30	126	*.381*	5
1941	Joe DiMaggio	26	OF	139	541	122	193	43	11	30	*125*	.357	9
1942	Joe Gordon	27	2B	147	538	88	173	29	4	18	103	.322	28
1947	Joe DiMaggio	32	OF	141	534	97	168	31	10	20	97	.315	1
1950	Phil Rizzuto	32	SS	155	617	125	200	36	7	7	66	.324	14
1951	Yogi Berra	25	C	141	547	92	161	19	4	27	88	.294	13
1954	Yogi Berra	28	C	151	584	88	179	28	6	22	125	.307	8
1955	Yogi Berra	29	C	147	541	84	147	20	3	27	108	.272	13
1956	Mickey Mantle	24	OF	150	533	*132*	188	22	5	*52*	*130*	*.353*	4
1957	Mickey Mantle	25	OF	144	474	*121*	173	28	6	34	94	.365	7
1960	Roger Maris	25	OF	136	499	98	141	18	7	39	112	.283	4
1961	Roger Maris	26	OF	161	590	*132*	159	16	4	*61*	*141†*	.269	9
1962	Mickey Mantle	30	OF	123	377	96	121	15	1	30	89	.321	5
1963	Elston Howard	34	C	135	487	75	140	21	6	28	85	.287	5
1976	Thurman Munson	28	C	152	616	79	186	27	1	17	105	.302	14
1985	Don Mattingly	23	1B	159	652	107	211	*48*	3	35	*145*	.324	7
2005	ALEX RODRIGUEZ	29	3B	*162*†	605	*124*	194	29	1	*48*	130	.321	12
2007	ALEX RODRIGUEZ	31	3B	158	583	*143*	183	31	0	*54*	*156*	.314	13

YEAR	PITCHER	AGE	POS	G	GS	IP	W	L	PCT.	SV	H	R	ER	SO	BB	ERA
1943	Spud Chandler	35	RHP	30	30	253.0	*20†*	4	*.833*	0	197	62	46	134	54	*1.64*

Cy Young Awards

YEAR	PITCHER	AGE	POS	G	GS	IP	W	L	PCT.	SV	H	R	ER	SO	BB	ERA
1958	Bob Turley	27	RHP	33	31	245.1	*21*	7	*.750*	1	178	82	81	168	*128*	2.97
1961	Whitey Ford	32	LHP	39	*39*	*283.0*	*25*	4	*.862*	0	242	108	101	209	92	3.21
1977	Sparky Lyle	32	LHP	72	0	137.0	13	5	.722	26	131	41	33	68	33	2.17
1978	Ron Guidry	27	LHP	35	35	273.2	*25*	3	*.893*	0	187	61	53	248	72	*1.74*
2001	Roger Clemens	38	RHP	33	33	220.1	20	3	*.870*	0	205	94	86	213	72	3.51

AL Rookie of the Year Awards

YEAR	PLAYER	AGE	POS	G	AB	R	H	2B	3B	HR	RBI	BA	E
1951	Gil McDougald	22	INF	131	402	72	123	23	4	14	63	.306	14
1957	Tony Kubek	21	INF-OF	127	431	56	128	21	3	3	39	.297	20
1962	Tom Tresh	24	INF-OF	157	622	94	178	26	5	20	93	.286	20
1970	Thurman Munson	22	C	132	453	59	137	25	4	6	53	.302	8
1996	DEREK JETER	21	SS	157	582	104	183	25	6	10	78	.314	22

YEAR	PITCHER	AGE	POS	G	GS	IP	W	L	PCT.	SV	H	R	ER	SO	BB	ERA
1954	Bob Grim	24	RHP	37	20	199.0	20	6	.769	0	175	78	72	108	85	3.26
1968	Stan Bahnsen	23	RHP	37	34	267.1	17	12	.586	0	216	72	61	162	68	2.05
1981	Dave Righetti	22	LHP	15	15	105.1	8	4	.667	0	75	25	24	89	38	2.05

AL Triple Crown Winners

YEAR	PLAYER	AGE	POS	G	AB	R	H	2B	3B	HR	RBI	BA
1934	Lou Gehrig	30	1B	*154*†	579	128	210	40	6	*49*	*165*	*.363*
1956	Mickey Mantle	24	OF	150	533	*132*	188	22	5	*52*	*130*	*.353*

AL Batting Champions

YEAR	PLAYER	AGE	POS	AVG.	G	AB	R	H	2B	3B	HR	RBI	E
1924	Babe Ruth	29	OF	.378	153	529	*143*	200	39	7	*46*	121	14
1934	Lou Gehrig	31	1B	*.363*	*154*†	579	128	210	40	6	*49*	*165*	8
1939	Joe DiMaggio	24	OF	.381	120	462	108	176	32	6	30	126	5
1940	Joe DiMaggio	25	OF	.352	132	508	93	179	28	9	31	133	8
1945	Snuffy Stirnweiss	26	2B	.309	152	632	107	195	32	*22*	10	64	29
1956	Mickey Mantle	24	OF	.353	150	533	*132*	188	22	5	*52*	*130*	4
1984	Don Mattingly	23	1B	.343	153	603	91	207	*44*	2	23	110	7
1994	Paul O'Neill	31	OF	.359	103	368	68	132	25	1	21	83	1
1998	Bernie Williams	29	OF	.339	128	499	101	169	30	5	26	97	3

KEY: *Italics – league leader*   *–Major League leader   †–Tied for AL or ML lead

AL Home Run Champions

YEAR	YANKEE	G	AB	HR
1916	Wally Pipp	151	545	12*¹
1917	Wally Pipp	155	587	9
1920	Babe Ruth	142	458	54*
1921	Babe Ruth	152	541	59*
1923	Babe Ruth	152	520	41*¹
1924	Babe Ruth	153	529	46*
1925	Bob Meusel	156	624	33
1926	Babe Ruth	152	495	47*
1927	Babe Ruth	151	540	60*
1928	Babe Ruth	154	536	54*
1929	Babe Ruth	135	499	46*
1930	Babe Ruth	145	518	49
1931	Babe Ruth	145	534	46*
	Lou Gehrig	155	619	46*
1934	Lou Gehrig	154	579	49*
1936	Lou Gehrig	155	579	49*
1937	Joe DiMaggio	151	621	46*
1944	Nick Etten	154	573	22
1948	Joe DiMaggio	153	594	39
1955	Mickey Mantle	147	517	37
1956	Mickey Mantle	150	533	52*
1958	Mickey Mantle	150	519	42
1960	Mickey Mantle	153	527	40
1961	Roger Maris	161	590	61*
1976	Graig Nettles	158	583	32
1980	Reggie Jackson	143	514	41ᵗ
2005	ALEX RODRIGUEZ	162	605	48
2007	ALEX RODRIGUEZ	158	583	54*
2009	MARK TEIXEIRA	156	609	39ᵀ

AL RBI Champions

YEAR	YANKEE	G	AB	RBI
1920	Babe Ruth	142	458	136
1921	Babe Ruth	152	541	171*
1923	Babe Ruth	152	520	131*
1925	Bob Meusel	156	624	138
1926	Babe Ruth	152	495	150*
1927	Lou Gehrig	155	584	175*
1928	Lou Gehrig	154	562	146*
1930	Lou Gehrig	154	581	174
1931	Lou Gehrig (AL RBI record)	155	619	184*
1934	Lou Gehrig	154	579	165*
1941	Joe DiMaggio	139	541	125*
1945	Nick Etten	152	565	111
1948	Joe DiMaggio	153	594	155*
1956	Mickey Mantle	150	533	130*
1960	Roger Maris	136	499	112
1961	Roger Maris	161	590	141ᵗ
1985	Don Mattingly	159	652	145*
2007	ALEX RODRIGUEZ	158	583	156*
2009	MARK TEIXEIRA	156	609	122

AL Runs Leaders

1920	Babe Ruth	158*
1921	Babe Ruth	177*
1923	Babe Ruth	151*
1924	Babe Ruth	143*
1926	Babe Ruth	139*
1927	Babe Ruth	158*
1928	Babe Ruth	163*
1931	Lou Gehrig	163*
1933	Lou Gehrig	138*
1935	Lou Gehrig	125
1936	Lou Gehrig	167*
1937	Joe DiMaggio	151*
1939	Red Rolfe	139*
1944	Snuffy Stirnweiss	125*
1945	Snuffy Stirnweiss	107
1948	Tommy Henrich	138*
1954	Mickey Mantle	128*
1956	Mickey Mantle	132*
1957	Mickey Mantle	121*
1958	Mickey Mantle	127*
1960	Mickey Mantle	119*
1961	Roger Maris	132*
1972	Bobby Murcer	102
1976	Roy White	104
1985	Rickey Henderson	146*
1986	Rickey Henderson	130*
1998	DEREK JETER	127
2002	Alfonso Soriano	128*
2005	ALEX RODRIGUEZ	124
2007	ALEX RODRIGUEZ	143*
2010	MARK TEIXEIRA	113

AL Hits Leaders

1927	Earl Combs	231
1931	Lou Gehrig	211
1939	Red Rolfe	213*
1944	Snuffy Stirnweiss	205*
1962	Bobby Richardson	209
1984	Don Mattingly	207
1986	Don Mattingly	238
1999	DEREK JETER	219
2002	Alfonso Soriano	209

AL Doubles Leaders

1927	Lou Gehrig	52*
1928	Lou Gehrig	47
1939	Red Rolfe	46
1984	Don Mattingly	44*
1985	Don Mattingly	48*
1986	Don Mattingly	53*

Lou Gehrig

Don Mattingly

KEY: * indicates Major League leader, ᵗ indicates tied for AL or ML lead

AL Triples Leaders

Year	Player	Value
1924	Wally Pipp	19
1926	Lou Gehrig	20
1927	Earl Combs	23*
1928	Earl Combs	21*
1930	Earl Combs	22
1934	Ben Chapman	13
1936	Joe DiMaggio	15*†
	Red Rolfe	15*†
1943	Johnny Lindell	12†
1944	Johnny Lindell	16†
	Snuffy Stirnweiss	16†
1945	Snuffy Stirnweiss	22*
1947	Tommy Henrich	13
1948	Tommy Henrich	14
1955	Andy Carey	11†
	Mickey Mantle	11†
1957	Hank Bauer	9†
	Gil McDougald	9†

AL Stolen Bases Leaders

1914	Fritz Maisel	74*
1931	Ben Chapman	61*
1932	Ben Chapman	38*
1933	Ben Chapman	27*
1938	Frank Crosetti	27*
1944	Snuffy Stirnweiss	44*
1945	Snuffy Stirnweiss	33*
1985	Rickey Henderson	80
1986	Rickey Henderson	87
1988	Rickey Henderson	93*
2002	Alfonso Soriano	41

200-Hit Seasons

AL leaders noted in *italics* / ML leaders noted with *

YEAR	YANKEE	AVG	AB	H
1921	Babe Ruth	.377	541	204
1923	Babe Ruth	.394	520	205
1924	Babe Ruth	.378	529	200
1925	Earle Combs	.342	593	203
1927	Earle Combs	.356	648*	*231*
1927	Lou Gehrig	.373	584	218
1928	Lou Gehrig	.374	562	210
1929	Earle Combs	.345	586	202
1930	Lou Gehrig	.379	581	220
1931	Lou Gehrig	.341	619	*211*
1932	Lou Gehrig	.349	596	208
1934	Lou Gehrig	*.363**	579	210
1936	Joe DiMaggio	.323	637	206
1936	Lou Gehrig	.354	579	205
1937	Joe DiMaggio	.346	621	215
1937	Lou Gehrig	.351	569	200
1939	Red Rolfe	.329	648	*213**
1944	Snuffy Stirnweiss	.319	643	*205**
1950	Phil Rizzuto	.324	617	200
1962	Bobby Richardson	.302	692	*209*
1984	Don Mattingly	.343	603	*207*
1985	Don Mattingly	.324	652	211
1986	Don Mattingly	.352	677	*238**
1989	Steve Sax	.315	651	205
1998	DEREK JETER	.324	626	203
1999	DEREK JETER	.349	627	*219**
1999	Bernie Williams	.342	591	202
2000	Derek Jeter	.339	593	201
2002	Alfonso Soriano	.300	*696**	*209**
2002	Bernie Williams	.333	612	204
2005	DEREK JETER	.309	654	202
2006	DEREK JETER	.343	623	214
2007	DEREK JETER	.322	639	206
2009	DEREK JETER	.334	634	212
2009	ROBINSON CANO	.320	637	204
2010	ROBINSON CANO	.319	626	200

AL Wins Leaders

1904	Jack Chesbro	(Modern Era Record) 41*
1906	Al Orth	27*†
1921	Carl Mays	27*†
1927	Waite Hoyt	22†
1928	George Pipgras	24†
1934	Lefty Gomez	26
1937	Lefty Gomez	21
1938	Red Ruffing	21
1943	Spud Chandler	20†
1955	Whitey Ford	18†
1958	Bob Turley	21
1961	Whitey Ford	25*
1962	Ralph Terry	23
1963	Whitey Ford	24
1975	Catfish Hunter	23*†
1978	Ron Guidry	25*
1985	Ron Guidry	22
1994	Jimmy Key	17†
1996	Andy Pettitte	21
1998	David Cone	20*†
2006	Chien-Ming Wang	19*†
2009	CC SABATHIA	19*†
2010	CC SABATHIA	21*†

AL Games Leaders

1904	Jack Chesbro	55*
1906	Jack Chesbro	49*
1918	George Mogridge	45*†
1921	Carl Mays	49*
1948	Joe Page	55
1949	Joe Page	60*
1961	Luis Arroyo	65*†
1977	Sparky Lyle	72
1994	Bob Wickman	53
2004	Paul Quantrill	86
2006	Scott Proctor	83

AL Innings Pitched Leaders

1904	Jack Chesbro	455.0*
1906	Al Orth	339.0
1921	Carl Mays	336.0*
1925	Herb Pennock	276.0
1928	George Pipgras	302.0
1934	Lefty Gomez	282.0
1961	Whitey Ford	283.0*
1962	Ralph Terry	299.0
1963	Whitey Ford	269.0
1965	Mel Stottlemyre	291.0
1975	Catfish Hunter	328.0*

AL Strikeouts Leaders

Year	Player	Value
1932	Red Ruffing	190
1933	Lefty Gomez	163
1934	Lefty Gomez	158
1937	Lefty Gomez	194*
1951	Vic Raschi	164*†
1952	Allie Reynolds	160
1964	Al Downing	217

AL ERA Leaders

1927	Waite Hoyt	2.64
1934	Lefty Gomez	2.33*
1937	Lefty Gomez	2.33
1943	Spud Chandler	1.64*
1947	Spud Chandler	2.46
1952	Allie Reynolds	2.07*
1953	Ed Lopat	2.43*
1956	Whitey Ford	2.47*
1957	Bobby Shantz	2.45*
1958	Whitey Ford	2.01*
1978	Ron Guidry	1.74*
1979	Ron Guidry	2.78*
1980	Rudy May	2.47*

KEY: * indicates Major League leader, † indicates tied for AL or ML lead

Home Run Feats (Regular Season)

Four HR, One Game (1x)
Lou Gehrig . . . . 6/3/32 at PHI

Three HR, One Game (26x by 18 players)
Tony Lazzeri . . . . 6/8/27 vs. CWS
  5/24/36 at PHI
Lou Gehrig. . . . . 6/23/27 at BOS
  5/4/29 at CWS
  5/22/30 at PHI
Babe Ruth . . . . .5/21/30 at PHI
Ben Chapman . . . . 7/9/32 vs. DET (G2)
Joe DiMaggio . . . . .6/13/37 at STL
  5/23/48 at CLE
  9/10/50 at WAS
Bill Dickey . . . . 7/26/39 vs. STL
Charlie Keller . . . . .7/28/40 at CWS
Johnny Mize . . . . 9/15/50 at DET
Mickey Mantle . . . . .5/13/55 vs. DET
Tom Tresh. . . . . 6/6/65 vs. CWS
Bobby Murcer. . . . . .6/24/70 vs. CLE
  7/13/73 vs. KC
Cliff Johnson . . . . 6/30/77 at TOR
Mike Stanley . . . . .8/10/95 vs. CLE
Paul O'Neill . . . . .8/31/95 vs. CAL
Darryl Strawberry . . . . . . .8/6/96 vs. CWS
Tino Martinez . . . . .4/2/97 at SEA
Tony Clark . . . . 8/28/04 at TOR
ALEX RODRIGUEZ . . . . . . 4/26/05 vs. LAA
MARK TEIXEIRA . . . . 5/8/10 at BOS
ALEX RODRIGUEZ . . . . . . .8/14/10 at KC

Also accomplished three times in World
Series play by Babe Ruth, 10/6/26 at
STL, and 10/9/28 at STL; by Reggie
Jackson, 10/18/77 vs. LAD).

HR, First Major League
Plate Appearance (3x)
John Miller. . . . . 9/11/66 at BOS
Marcus Thames . . . . 6/10/02 vs. ARI
Andy Phillips. . . . . 9/26/04 at BOS

HR, in First Two Major League Games (1x)
Joe Lefebvre . . . . 5/22/80 & 5/23/80

Two HR, One Inning (5x)
Joe DiMaggio . . . . .6/24/36 vs. CWS
Joe Pepitone. . . . . .5/23/62 vs. KC
Cliff Johnson. . . . . 6/30/77 at TOR
ALEX RODRIGUEZ . . . . . . .9/5/07 vs. SEA
ALEX RODRIGUEZ . . . . . . .10/4/09 at TB

HR, First Two Plate Appearances
(or At-Bats) with Yankees (1x)
Cody Ransom . . . . .8/7/08 vs. KC and
  8/22/08 at BAL

Four Consecutive HR (4x)
Lou Gehrig. . . . . 6/3/32 at PHI
John Blanchard 7/21-7/26/61
Mickey Mantle 7/4-7/6/62
Bobby Murcer*. . . . . .6/24/70 vs. CLE (DH)
* All but Murcer were consecutive PAs

Pinch-Hit HR in Consecutive ABs (4x)
Ray Caldwell 1915
Charlie Keller 1948
John Blanchard 1961
Ray Barker 1965

Most Walk-off HR as Yankee, Career
Mickey Mantle 12
Babe Ruth 11
Yogi Berra. 7
A. RODRIGUEZ, Nettles 6
DiMaggio, R. Jackson. 4
Gehrig, Dickey, Gordon, Keller, Henrich,
J. Collins, Tresh, Gamble, Chambliss,
Baylor, Hall, B. Williams, Giambi. 3

Switch-Hit HR, Single Game (46x)
Mickey Mantle . . . . 10 times
JORGE POSADA . . . . .8 times
*Bernie Williams . . . . .8 times
MARK TEIXEIRA, Roy White . . . . . .5 times
Tom Tresh, NICK SWISHER . . . . . . .3 times
Cabrera, T. Clark, Sierra, Smalley. . . . . .1 time
*Also twice in postseason play - on
10/6/95 at SEA; and 10/5/96 at TEX.

Switch-Hit HR by Teammates,
One Game
Bernie Williams and JORGE POSADA
each hit home runs from both sides of
the plate on 4/23/00 in a 10-7 win at
Toronto, the only time in Major League
history that two teammates have hit
switch-hit home runs in the same game.

Most Switch-hit HR by Teammates,
One Season
According to *Elias*, the 2009 season
marked the first time in Baseball
history a team had three different
players homer from both sides of the
plate in a single game within the same
season (Cabrera-1x, SWISHER-3x and
TEIXEIRA-3x).

Most Switch-hit HR,
One Player in a Season
According to the *Elias Sports Bureau*,
three AL players have hit three sets of
switch-hit homers in a single season:
MARK TEIXEIRA (2009 w/ NYY), NICK
SWISHER (2009 w/ NYY and 2007 w/
Oakland) and Tony Clark (1998 w/
Detroit).

Most Back-to-Back HR by
Teammates in a Single Season
1. Johnny Damon/M. TEIXEIRA 6 (2009)
2. Gary Sheffield/A. RODRIGUEZ . . . 5 (2005)
  Joe DiMaggio/Lou Gehrig 5 (1936)
  Babe Ruth/Lou Gehrig 5 (1927)

Most Yankees With At Least
25HR in the Same Season
5 2009
(CANO, MATSUI, RODRIGUEZ, SWISHER, TEIXEIRA)
4 2010
  (CANO, RODRIGUEZ, SWISHER, TEIXEIRA)
4 1938
(Bill Dickey, Joe DiMaggio, Lou Gehrig, Joe Gordon)

Extra Innings HR, Team in One Season
8 .1941,'62, 88
7 1957
6 . . . . .1955,'60,'80,'83, 2006
5 . . . . 1922,'59,'61,'84,'97, 2009
4 . . . . . 1935,'42,'43,'66,'72,'78 '91, 2010

Extra Innings HR, Player in Career
Babe Ruth, Mickey Mantle. 14
Yogi Berra. 9
Craig Nettles. .8
Tommy Henrich 7
Jason Giambi 6
Joe Gordon, Dave Winfield, JORGE POSADA,
ALEX RODRIGUEZ 5

Extra Innings HR, Player in Season
Gehrig (1935), Mantle (1959) 3
Many Players. .2

Most Leadoff HR, Career
Rickey Henderson, DEREK JETER 24
Alfonso Soriano 21
Hank Bauer 18
Chuck Knoblauch 15

Most Leadoff HR, Season
Alfonso Soriano . . . . (2003)13
Rickey Henderson . . . . (1986) 9
Chuck Knoblauch . . . . (1999) 8
Alfonso Soriano. . . . . (2002) 8
Rickey Henderson . . . . (1985) 7

Most Inside-the-Park HR
Career
Earle Combs 23
Season
Patsy Dougherty (1904) 6

Youngest to hit HR
Bobby Murcer. 9/14/65 (19y,117d)

Oldest to hit HR
Enos Slaughter. 7/19/59 (43y,83d)

LAST TIME IT HAPPENED:
Multi-HR Game by Two Yankees
in Same Game
RODRIGUEZ-2; Hinske-2. . . 7/11/09 at LAA

**Cody Ransom is the only player in
franchise history to hit home runs in
each of his first two plate appearances
as a Yankee.**

No-Hitters

Regular Season (10)

Year	Pitcher	Score
1917	*George Mogridge, at Boston, April 24	2-1
1923	Sad Sam Jones, at Philadelphia, September 4	2-0
1938	Monte Pearson, vs. Cleveland, August 27 (G2)	13-0
1951	Allie Reynolds, at Cleveland, July 12 (night)	1-0
	Allie Reynolds, vs. Boston, September 28 (G1)	8-0
1983	*Dave Righetti, vs. Boston, July 4	4-0
1993	*Jim Abbott, vs. Cleveland, September 4	4-0
1996	Dwight Gooden, at Seattle, May 14	2-0
1998	*+ David Wells, vs. Minnesota, May 17	4-0
1999	+ David Cone, vs. Montreal, July 18	6-0

Post Season (1)

Year	Pitcher	Score
1956	+Don Larsen, vs. Brooklyn, October 8	2-0
	(Game 5 of the World Series; remains the only no-hitter in World Series history)	

No-Hitters vs. Yankees (7)

Year	Pitcher	Score
1908	Cy Young, for Boston at New York, June 30	8-0
1916	Rube Foster, for Boston at Boston, June 21	2-0
1919	Ray Caldwell, for Cleveland at New York, September 10 (G1)	3-0
1946	Bob Feller, for Cleveland at New York, April 30	1-0
1952	Virgil Trucks, for Detroit at New York, August 25	1-0
1958	Hoyt Wilhelm, for Baltimore at Baltimore, September 20	1-0
2003	Six pitchers, for Houston at New York, June 11 (Oswalt, Munro, Saarloos, Lidge, Dotel, Wagner)	8-0

* Lefthanded pitcher   + Perfect Game

Don Larsen and Yogi Berra

David Cone's Perfect Game

On July 18, 1999, David Cone tossed the 15th perfect game in Baseball history (since 1901) on a day Don Larsen was on hand to throw out the game's ceremonial first pitch. It came only one season after David Wells accomplished the feat and gave the Yankees a record three perfect games in their history, including Don Larsen in the 1956 World Series. Prior to Wells' and Cone's feats, perfect games had only been pitched in consecutive seasons once (by Jim Bunning of the Phillies in 1964 and the Dodgers' Sandy Koufax in 1965) and never by pitchers from the same team. The original Yankee Stadium also became the only park to host as many as three perfect games (Dodger Stadium was the site of perfect games by Koufax in 1965 and Montreal's Dennis Martinez in 1991).

David Cone celebrates with Joe Girardi.

One-Hit Games

Mike Mussina

The most-recent Yankee to have a one-hit complete game was Ted Lilly on 4/27/02 in a 1-0 defeat at Seattle, becoming the first Yankee in franchise history to lose a one-hit CG in the regular season (allowed a walk, WP and RBI-single in 7th).

The Yankees' last one-hit complete-game win was by Mike Mussina on 9/2/01 at Boston in a 1-0 Yankees victory...he retired 26 consecutive batters before Carl Everett singled with two outs in the ninth...it was the first complete-game one-hit victory by a Yankee since Jimmy Key on 4/27/93 at California.'

The Yankees have had two postseason one-hit complete games...Roger Clemens still holds the all-time record for fewest hits allowed in an AL or NL Championship Series complete game with his one-hit, 15K performance in the Yankees' 5-0 ALCS Game 4 win at Seattle on 10/14/00...Bill Bevens famously lost his one-hit CG in Game 4 of the 1947 World Series vs. Brooklyn...he was one out from a no-hitter when pinch-hitter Cookie Lavagetto doubled in two runs to give the Dodgers a 3-2 victory...Bevens walked 10 batters and had one wild pitch on the day...the World Series marked the last games Bevens and Lavagetto ever played in the Majors.

Yankees with multiple complete-game one hitters are Whitey Ford (3), Bob Turley (3), Lefty Gomez (2), Rip Collins (2) and Vic Raschi (2), while Bill Bevens (see above paragraph) also threw a one-hit CG in the regular season.

One hitters by opponents against the Yankees: The Yankees were last held to 1H on 6/30/07 at Yankee Stadium by Oakland's Chad Gaudin and Rich Harden...the last starter to throw a one-hitter against the Yankees was Mike Maroth on 7/16/04 at Detroit...Joe Wood, Earl Hamilton and Nolan Ryan are the only pitchers with a pair of one-hitters against the Yankees, with both of Hamilton's coming in 1913...Hoyt Wilhelm, who no-hit the Yankees in 1958, also tossed a one-hitter against them in 1959.

Grand Slams

Grand slam notes from 2010: The Yankees hit 10 grand slams in 2010, tying the franchise record set in 1987...Jorge Posada hit grand slams in consecutive games on 6/12 and 6/13/10 vs. Houston, becoming the first Yankee to hit a grand slam in back-to-back games since Bill Dickey in 1937...Alex Rodriguez was one of three Major Leaguers to hit three grand slams in 2010.

Career Leaders

Gehrig	23
DiMaggio	13
Ruth	12
A. RODRIGUEZ, B. Williams	11
Berra, Mantle, POSADA	9
Dickey, Lazzeri	8
Keller, T. Martinez	7
Giambi, Mattingly, Stanley	6

Single-Season Leaders

Don Mattingly	6	1987
Tommy Henrich	4	1948
Lou Gehrig	4	1934
ALEX RODRIGUEZ	3	2007, '10
Ruben Sierra	3	2004
JORGE POSADA	3	2001
*Shane Spencer	3	1998
Mike Stanley	3	1993
Joe DiMaggio	3	1937
Lou Gehrig	3	1931
Babe Ruth	3	1931
Most in single season by an NYY rookie

Most Hit by Club, Season

10	1987, 2010
9	1998, 2003, '04
7	1940, '48, '80, '99, 2005, '08
6	1927, '29, '30-32, '35, '37, '62, 2000-02
5	1934, '36, '41, '42, '56, '65, '66, '78, '82, '93, '94

Most Allowed by Club, Season

9	2000
8	1995
7	2007, '08
6	1935, '59, '84, '90, '91, '98

Multiple Grand Slams in Same Game (3x)

Tony Lazzeri (2)	5/24/36 at PHI
Winfield/Mattingly	6/29/87 at TOR
B. Williams/O'Neill (consec. inn.)	9/14/99 at TOR

Grand Slams in Consecutive Games (4x)

JORGE POSADA	6/12-13/10 vs. HOU
Bill Dickey	8/3(G2)-4/37 vs. CWS
Babe Ruth	8/6/29 (G2) vs. WAS, 8/7/29 (G1) at PHI
Babe Ruth	9/27/27 vs. WAS, 9/29/27 vs. PHI

On June 12, 2008 at Oakland, Hideki Matsui became the only Yankee to hit a grand slam on his birthday.

Pinch-Hit Grand Slams (21x)

Berra, Murcer, Skowron, Strawberry....2
17 others.............................1
Last by Jorge Posada on 6/6/01 vs. BAL

Walkoff Grand Slams (8x)

Alex Rodriguez	4/7/07 vs. BAL (9th)
*Jason Giambi	5/17/02 vs. MIN (14th)
Mike Pagliarulo	5/8/87 vs. MIN (9th)
Ruppert Jones	8/12/80 vs. CWS (10th)
Joe Pepitone	4/17/69 (G1) vs. WAS (10th)
Charlie Keller	8/12/42 vs. BOS (9th)
Red Ruffing	4/14/33 vs. BOS (9th)
*Babe Ruth	9/25/25 vs. CWS (10th)
Hit when trailing by three runs.

Pitchers to Hit Grand Slam (4x)

Mel Stottlemyre	7/20/65 vs. BOS
Don Larsen	4/22/56 vs. BOS
Spud Chandler	7/26/40 at CWS
Red Ruffing	4/14/33 at PHI

Grand Slam Hit on Birthday (1x)

*Hideki Matsui..........6/12/08 at OAK
Accounted for all four runs in a 4-1 win.

LAST TIME IT HAPPENED
Extra-inning GS
Bobby Abreu......9/24/08 (10th) at TOR

Pinch-Hit Home Runs

2010 Notes: The Yankees hit two pinch-hit home runs in 2010 – one by Jorge Posada and one by Colin Curtis...Curtis' homer on 7/21 vs. Los Angeles-AL came after he entered the game with an 0-2 count when Brett Gardner was ejected...Curtis became the first Yankee to hit his first career home run as a pinch-hitter since Andy Phillips on 9/26/04 at Boston.

Other Pinch-hit HR Notes: In 1998, the Yankees hit two pinch-hit home runs, both ninth-inning grand slams by Darryl Strawberry (on 5/2 at Kansas City and 8/4 at Oakland, G2)...the Yankees franchise has 255 pinch-hit home runs, including 21 pinch-hit grand slams.

Career Leaders ....No.

Yogi Berra	9
Bob Cerv	8
Mickey Mantle, Bobby Murcer	7
Johnny Blanchard	6
Johnny Mize, J. POSADA, Moose Skowron	5

Season Leaders........No. .. Season

Johnny Blanchard	4	1961
Ken Phelps	3	1989
Dan Pasqua	3	1987
Bobby Murcer	3	1981
Ray Barker	3	1965
Bob Cerv	3	1961
Johnny Mize	3	1953
Tommy Henrich	3	1950

Club .... Season

10	1961
7	1953, '54, '60, '86
6	1959, '66, '79, '80, '87, '90
5	1955, '56, '62, '70, '85, 88, 94, 2004

Hitting for the Cycle

YANKEES TO HIT FOR THE CYCLE (15X BY 11 PLAYERS)

Bert Daniels (LF)	7/25/12 vs. Chicago
Bob Meusel (RF)	5/7/21 at Washington
Bob Meusel (RF)	7/3/22 at Philadelphia
Bob Meusel (RF)	7/26/28 at Detroit
*Tony Lazzeri (2B)	6/3/32 at Philadelphia
Lou Gehrig (1B)	6/25/34 vs. Chicago
Joe DiMaggio (CF)	7/9/37 vs. Washington
Lou Gehrig (1B)	8/1/37 vs. St. Louis
Buddy Rosar (C)	7/19/40 vs. Cleveland
Joe Gordon (2B)	9/8/40 at Boston
Joe DiMaggio (OF)	5/20/48 at Chicago
**Mickey Mantle (CF)	7/23/57 vs. Chicago
Bobby Murcer (CF)	8/29/72 vs. Texas (G1)
**Tony Fernandez (SS)	9/3/95 vs. Oakland
**Melky Cabrera (CF)	8/2/09 at Chicago-AL
* Natural Cycle, **Switch-hitter*

OPPONENTS TO HIT FOR THE CYCLE AGAINST THE YANKEES (9X BY 9 PLAYERS)

B.J. Upton (CF)	8/2/09 at Tampa
Travis Fryman (3B)	7/28/93 at Detroit
Jim Fregosi (SS)	7/28/64 at L.A. Angels
Doc Cramer (CF)	6/10/34 vs. Philadelphia
Mickey Cochrane (C)	8/2/33 vs. Philadelphia
Goose Goslin (LF)	8/28/24 vs. Washington
Frank Baker (3B)	7/3/11 vs. Philadelphia (G2)
**Otis Clymer (RF)	10/2/08 vs. Washington
Patsy Dougherty (LF)	7/29/03 at Boston
**Switch-hitter*	

Yankees All-Star Game Selections

Casey Stengel managed more All-Star teams (10) than anyone else.

1933....Chapman*, lf
..........Dickey, c
..........Gehrig*, 1b
..........Gomez†, p
..........Lazzeri, 2b
..........Ruth*, rf
1934....Chapman, of
..........Dickey*, c
..........Gehrig*, 1b
..........Gomez†, p
..........Ruffing, p
..........Ruth*, rf
1935....Chapman, of
..........Gehrig*, 1b
..........Gomez†, p
1936....Crosetti, ss
..........Dickey, c
..........DiMaggio*, rf
..........Gehrig*, 1b
..........Gomez, p
..........Pearson, p
..........Selkirk, of
..........McCarthy, mgr
1937....Dickey*, c
..........DiMaggio*, rf
..........Gehrig, 1b
..........Gomez†, p
..........Murphy, p
..........Rolfe*, 3b
..........McCarthy, mgr
1938....Dickey*, c
..........DiMaggio*, rf
..........Gehrig, 1b
..........Gomez†, p
..........Rolfe, 3b
..........Ruffing, p
..........McCarthy, mgr
1939....Crosetti, ss
..........Dickey*, c
..........DiMaggio*, cf
..........Gehrig, 1b
..........Gomez, p
..........Gordon*, 2b
..........Murphy, p
..........Ruffing, p
..........Selkirk*, lf
..........McCarthy, mgr
1940....Dickey*, c
..........DiMaggio*, cf
..........Gordon*, 2b
..........Keller*, rf
..........Pearson, p
..........Rolfe, 3b
..........Ruffing†, p
..........McCarthy, mgr
1941....Dickey*, c
..........DiMaggio*, cf
..........Gordon, 2b
..........Keller, of
..........Ruffing, p
..........Russo, p
1942....Bonham, p
..........Chandler†, p
..........Dickey, c
..........DiMaggio*, cf
..........Gordon*, 2b
..........Henrich*, rf
..........Rizzuto, ss
..........Rosar, c
..........Ruffing, p
..........McCarthy, mgr
1943....Bonham, p
..........Chandler, p
..........Dickey, c
..........Gordon, 2b
..........Keller, of

..........Lindell, of
..........McCarthy, mgr
1944....Borowy†, p
..........Hemsley, c
..........Page, p
..........McCarthy, mgr
1945....No game due
..........to World War II
..........travel restrictions
1946....Chandler, p
..........Dickey, c
..........DiMaggio*, cf
..........Gordon, 2b
..........Keller*, rf
..........Stirnweiss, 3b
1947....Chandler, p
..........DiMaggio*, cf
..........Henrich, of
..........Johnson, 3b
..........McQuinn*, 1b
..........Page, p
..........Robinson, c
..........Shea, p
..........Keller, of
1948....Berra, c
..........DiMaggio*, of
..........Henrich†, rf
..........McQuinn, 1b
..........Page, p
..........Raschi, p
..........Harris, mgr
1949....Berra, c
..........DiMaggio*, cf
..........Ford†, p
..........Henrich, of
..........Raschi, p
..........Reynolds, p
1950....Berra*, c
..........Byrne, p
..........Coleman, 2b
..........DiMaggio, of
..........Henrich, 1b
..........Raschi†, p
..........Reynolds, p
..........Rizzuto*, ss
..........Stengel, mgr
1951....Berra*, c
..........DiMaggio, of
..........Lopat, p
..........Rizzuto, ss
..........Stengel, mgr
1952....Bauer*, rf
..........Berra*, c
..........Mantle, of
..........Raschi†, p
..........Reynolds, p
..........Rizzuto, ss
..........McDougald, 2b
..........Stengel, mgr

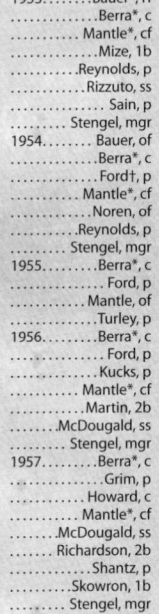

1953....Bauer*, rf
..........Berra*, c
..........Mantle, cf
..........Mize, 1b
..........Reynolds, p
..........Rizzuto, ss
..........Sain, p
..........Stengel, mgr
1954....Bauer, of
..........Berra*, c
..........Ford†, p
..........Mantle*, cf
..........Noren, of
..........Reynolds, p
..........Stengel, mgr
1955....Berra*, c
..........Ford, p
..........Mantle, of
..........Turley, p
1956....Berra*, c
..........Ford, p
..........Kucks, p
..........Mantle*, cf
..........Martin, 2b
..........McDougald, ss
..........Stengel, mgr
1957....Berra*, c
..........Grim, p
..........Howard, c
..........Mantle*, cf
..........McDougald, ss
..........Richardson, 2b
..........Shantz, p
..........Skowron, 1b
..........Stengel, mgr

1958....Berra, c
..........Duren, p
..........Ford, p
..........Howard, c
..........Kubek, inf
..........Mantle*, cf
..........McDougald, 2b
..........Skowron, 1b
..........Turley†, p
..........Stengel, mgr
1959....Berra3, c
..........Duren3, p
..........Ford1, p
..........Mantle3, of
..........McDougald3, ss
..........Richardson2, 2b
..........Skowron*3, 1b
..........Howard2, c
..........Kubek3, ss
..........Stengel, mgr
1960....Berra*3, c
..........Coates3, p
..........Ford†3, p
..........Howard3, c
..........Mantle*3, cf
..........Maris*3, rf
..........Skowron*3, 1b
1961....Arroyo2, p
..........Berra3, of
..........Ford3, p
..........Howard3, c
..........Kubek*3, ss
..........Mantle*3, cf
..........Maris*3, rf
..........Skowron2, 1b
1962....Berra2, c
..........Howard3, c
..........Mantle*3, rf
..........Maris*3, cf
..........Richardson3, 2b
..........Terry3, p
..........Tresh3, ss
..........Houk2, mgr
1963....Bouton, p
..........Howard, c
..........Mantle, of
..........Pepitone*, 1b
..........Richardson, 2b
..........Tresh, of
1964....Ford, p
..........Howard*, c
..........Mantle*, cf
..........Pepitone, 1b
..........Richardson, 2b

1965....Howard, c
..........Mantle, of
..........Pepitone, 1b
..........Richardson, 2b
..........Stottlemyre, p
1966....Richardson, 2b
..........Stottlemyre, p.
1967....Downing, p
..........Mantle, 1b
1968....Mantle, 1b
..........Stottlemyre, p
1969....Stottlemyre†, p
1970....Peterson, p
..........Stottlemyre, p
..........White, of
1971....Munson, c
..........Murcer*, of
1972....Murcer*, cf
1973....Lyle, p
..........Munson, c
..........Murcer*, lf
1974....Munson*, c
..........Murcer*, cf
1975....Bonds*, cf
..........Hunter, p
..........Munson*, c
..........Nettles, 3b
1976...Chambliss, 1b
..........Hunter, p
..........Lyle, p
..........Munson*, c
..........Randolph, 2b
..........Rivers, of
1977....Jackson*, lf
..........Lyle, p
..........Munson, c
..........Nettles, 3b
..........Randolph*, 2b
..........Martin, mgr
1978....Gossage, p
..........Guidry, p
..........Jackson*, of
..........Nettles, 3b
..........Martin, mgr
1979....Guidry, p
..........Jackson, of
..........John, p
..........Nettles, 3b
1980....Dent*, ss
..........Gossage, p
..........Jackson*, rf
..........John, p
..........Nettles*, 3b
..........Randolph*, 2b

* - Selected as starter   † - Started, but not elected   1 - On team for first game only
2 - On team for second game only   3 - On team for both games

Yankees All-Star Game Selections

1981......... Davis, p	1988.. Henderson*, cf	1998..... Brosius, 3b	......Soriano*, 2b	2008........ JETER*, ss
.... Dent*, ss	.... Mattingly, 1b	.... JETER, ss	...........Ventura, 3b	.............RIVERA, p
.... Gossage, p	.... Winfield*, rf	.... O'Neill, of	............Torre, mgr.	.... RODRIGUEZ*, 3b
.... Jackson*, rf	1989... Mattingly, 1b	.... Wells*, p	2003.... Clemens, p	2009....... JETER*, ss
.......Randolph*, 2b	.... Sax, 2b	.....B. Williams, of	.... Giambi, 1b	.............RIVERA, p
.... Winfield*, cf	1990........ Sax, 2b	1999....... Cone, p	...........Matsui*, cf	.... TEIXEIRA*, 1b
1982...... Gossage, p	1991... Sanderson, p	.... JETER, ss	.... POSADA*, c	2010...... CANO*, 2b
.... Guidry, p	1992..... R. Kelly, of	.... RIVERA, p	.... Soriano*, 2b	...... GIRARDI, mgr.
.... Winfield, of	1993..... Boggs*, 3b	.....B. Williams, of	2004.... Giambi*, lb	.... HUGHES, p
1983...... Guidry, p	.... Key, p	............Torre, mgr.	.... Gordon; p	.... JETER*, ss
.... Winfield*, rf	1994...... Boggs*, 3b	2000..... JETER†, ss	.... JETER*; ss	.... Pettitte, p
1984....... P. Niekro, p	.... Key*, p	.... POSADA, c	.... Matsui*, of	.............RIVERA, p
.... Mattingly, 1b	.... O'Neill, of	.... RIVERA, p	...........RIVERA, p	...... RODRIGUEZ, 3b
.... Winfield*, lf	1995...... Boggs*, 3b	.B. Williams*, of	.... RODRIGUEZ*; 3b	.... SABATHIA, p
1985.. Henderson*, cf	.... O'Neill, of	............Torre, mgr.	.... Sheffield, of	.... SWISHER#, of
.... Mattingly, 1b	.............Stanley, c	2001....Clemens†, p	.... VAZQUEZ, p	
.... Winfield*, rf	......Showalter, mgr.	.... JETER, ss	2005..RODRIGUEZ*, 3b	* - Selected as starter
1986...Henderson*, lf	1996...... Boggs*, 3b	.... Pettitte, P	...........RIVERA, p	† - Started, not elected
.... Mattingly, 1b	.... Pettitte, P	.... POSADA, c	.... Sheffield, of	# - Selected via MLB.com
.... Righetti, p	.... Wetteland, p	.... RIVERA, p	2006 . RODRIGUEZ*, 3b	Final Vote
.... Winfield*, rf	1997........ Cone, p	.... Stanton, p	.... JETER*, ss	1 - On team for first
1987.. Henderson*, cf	.... Martinez*, 1b	.....B. Williams, of	.... CANO, 2b	game only
........Mattingly*, 1b	.... O'Neill†, of	............Torre, mgr.	...........RIVERA, p	2 - On team for second
.......Randolph*, 2b	............RIVERA, p	2002..... Giambi*, 1b	2007....... JETER*, ss	game only
.........Righetti, p	.....B. Williams, of	.... JETER, ss	.... POSADA, c	3 - On team for both
.... Winfield*, rf	............Torre, mgr.	.... POSADA*; c	..... RODRIGUEZ*, 3b	games
		.... RIVERA, p		

Yankees All-Stars by Total Selections

Mickey Mantle 20	Red Rolfe 4	
Yogi Berra............... 18	Hank Bauer 3	
Joe DiMaggio 13	Ben Chapman 3	
Elston Howard 12	Ryne Duren 3	
Bill Dickey 11	Jason Giambi 3	
DEREK JETER 11	Sparky Lyle 3	
MARIANO RIVERA 11	Billy Martin .... 3 (2 as Mgr)	
Whitey Ford............. 10	Joe Page 3	
Casey Stengel (MGR) 10	Joe Pepitone 3	
Bobby Richardson........ 8	Andy Pettitte 3	
Dave Winfield........... 8	Tom Tresh 3	
Lou Gehrig............... 7	Ernie Bonham 2	
Lefty Gomez............. 7	**ROBINSON CANO** 2	
Joe McCarthy (MGR) 7	Roger Clemens............. 2	
Bill Skowron 7	Jim Coates 2	
Joe Gordon 6	David Cone 2	
Don Mattingly........... 6	Frank Crosetti 2	
Gil McDougald........... 6	Bucky Dent 2	
Thurman Munson........ 6	Ralph Houk (MGR) 2	
ALEX RODRIGUEZ 6	Catfish Hunter 2	
Red Ruffing 6	Tommy John 2	
Joe Torre (MGR) 6	Jimmy Key 2	
Tommy Henrich........... 5	Hideki Matsui 2	
Reggie Jackson 5	George McQuinn.......... 2	
Charlie Keller 5	John Murphy 2	
Roger Maris 5	Monte Pearson............ 2	
Graig Nettles............ 5	Dave Righetti 2	
JORGE POSADA 5	Babe Ruth 2	
Willie Randolph.......... 5	Steve Sax 2	
Allie Reynolds............ 5	George Selkirk 2	
Phil Rizzuto 5	Gary Sheffield............. 2	
Mel Stottelmyre.......... 5	Alfonso Soriano 2	
Bernie Williams 5	Ralph Terry 2	
Wade Boggs............. 4	Bob Turley 2	
Spud Chandler........... 4	Luis Arroyo 1	
Goose Gossage........... 4	Bobby Bonds 1	
Ron Guidry 4	Hank Borowy 1	
Rickey Henderson........ 4	Jim Bouton 1	
Tony Kubek 4	Scott Brosius 1	
Bobby Murcer........... 4	Tommy Byrne 1	
Paul O'Neill 4	Chris Chambliss 1	
Vic Raschi............... 4	Jerry Coleman 1	

Derek Jeter is the only Yankee to take home All-Star MVP honors, going 3-for-3 with 1 double and 2 RBI in the 2000 Midsummer Classic.

Ron Davis................. 1	Mickey Rivers 1
Al Downing................ 1	Aaron Robinson........... 1
JOE GIRARDI (MGR) 1	Buddy Rosar 1
Tom Gordon 1	Marius Russo.............. 1
Bob Grim................. 1	**CC SABATHIA** 1
Bucky Harris (MGR)........ 1	Johnny Sain............... 1
Rollie Hemsley............ 1	Scott Sanderson 1
PHIL HUGHES 1	Bobby Shantz............. 1
Billy Johnson............. 1	Spec Shea 1
Roberto Kelly 1	Buck Showalter (MGR)..... 1
Johnny Kucks 1	Mike Stanley.............. 1
Tony Lazzeri 1	Mike Stanton 1
Bob Lemon (MGR)......... 1	Snuffy Stirnweiss.......... 1
Johnny Lindell 1	**NICK SWISHER.** 1
Eddie Lopat............... 1	**MARK TEIXEIRA.** 1
Tino Martinez 1	Javier Vazquez 1
Johnny Mize 1	Robin Ventura 1
Phil Neikro 1	David Wells 1
Irving Noren 1	John Wetteland 1
Fritz Peterson 1	Roy White................ 1

Previous Yankee Stadium All-Star Games

The Yankees have hosted four All-Star Games, including the 2008 Midsummer Classic in Yankee Stadium's final season. The Stadium also hosted the All-Star Game in 1977 (48th), 1960 (29th) and 1939 (seventh). Only Cleveland's old Municipal Stadium hosted as many All-Star Games as Yankee Stadium. Overall, New York City has hosted eight MLB All-Star Games, the highest total in Major League history, with the Polo Grounds (1934 and 1942), Ebbets Field (1949) and Shea Stadium (1964) also serving as host sites. The 2008 game marked the first time the Midsummer Classic was held in the host team's final season at its ballpark.

Since the game originated in 1933, the Yankees have had the most All-Star players (116) and the highest total All-Star selections (364) of any Major League Baseball franchise. Mickey Mantle owns the most All-Star selections in club history, having been named to 20 All-Star teams (fourth-most all-time). Yankees pitcher Lefty Gomez is the only pitcher in All-Star Game history to earn three wins, having made five career All-Star starts. Joe DiMaggio (13-time All-Star) and Tom Tresh (three-time All-Star), own the distinction as the only Yankees rookies to start for the American League (1936 and 1962, respectively). Of the 80 All-Star Games, a Yankees Manager has skippered the American League team 29 times. Among Yankees on the roster as of Feb. 1, 2011, third baseman Alex Rodriguez leads the team with 13 career trips to the Midsummer Classic, followed by shortstop Derek Jeter and closer Mariano Rivera with 11 All-Star appearances apiece. Jeter holds the distinction as the only All-Star MVP in club history, taking home the honor in 2000 after going 3-for-3 with 1 double and 2RBI in the AL's 6-3 win at Atlanta's Turner Field. He became just the fourth shortstop to earn the award. Rodriguez led the Majors in All-Star balloting in 2007 and 2008.

Seventh All-Star Game
American League 3, National League 1
July 11, 1939, Yankee Stadium

Yankee Stadium was chosen to host the 1939 All-Star Game due to the World's Fair which was being held at Flushing-Meadows in Queens during the 1939 season. The Cubs' Gabby Hartnett managed the National League squad while Yankees skipper Joe McCarthy led the American League team, which featured 10 Yankees All-Stars, six of whom were starters. Yankees centerfielder Joe DiMaggio was 1-for-4 in the game, hitting a solo home run. Lou Gehrig, who announced his retirement in May of 1939, was an honorary member of the AL squad.

All-Star Team	1	2	3	4	5	6	7	8	9	R	H	E
National League	0	0	1	0	0	0	0	0	0	1	7	1
American League	0	0	0	2	1	0	0	0	x	3	6	1

Winning Pitcher: Tommy Bridges
Losing Pitcher: Bill Lee

48th All-Star Game
National League 7, American League 5
July 19, 1977, Yankee Stadium

Showcasing its renovation, Yankee Stadium hosted the All-Star Game on July 19, 1977, in a game dedicated to Jackie Robinson. With the Yankees defending their 1976 pennant, Billy Martin managed the AL team on his home field. The National League won its sixth consecutive All-Star Game, part of the Senior Circuit's 11-game win streak. Joe Morgan opened the game with a home run off Jim Palmer as the NL squad scored four first-inning runs. Yankees outfielder Reggie Jackson and second baseman Willie Randolph were AL starters. National League Manager Sparky Anderson described the game's final score by saying, "the only reason we're here is to kick the living hell out of those guys."

All-Star Team	1	2	3	4	5	6	7	8	9	R	H	E
National League	4	0	1	0	0	0	0	2	0	7	9	1
American League	0	0	0	0	2	1	0	2	0	5	8	0

Winning Pitcher: Don Sutton
Losing Pitcher: Jim Palmer

29th All-Star Game
National League 6, American League 0
July 13, 1960 (Game #2), Yankee Stadium

Yankee Stadium was the host site for baseball's second All-Star Game in three days in 1960. The National League completed the All-Star sweep with a 6-0 win, having won Game 1 on July 11 in Kansas City, marking the only year that both All-Star games were won by the same team. Yankees hurler Whitey Ford was the starting pitcher for the AL squad, while fellow Yankees Yogi Berra (catcher), Mickey Mantle (left field), Roger Maris (centerfield) and Bill Skowron (first base) all appeared in the starting lineup. The National League used six different pitchers to combine on the shutout effort and hit an All-Star record-tying four home runs, including one by Willie Mays. The 38,000 fans who attended the game witnessed Ted Williams in his final All-Star appearance.

All-Star Team	1	2	3	4	5	6	7	8	9	R	H	E
National League	0	2	1	0	0	0	1	0	2	6	10	0
American League	0	0	0	0	0	0	0	0	0	0	8	0

Winning Pitcher: Vern Law
Losing Pitcher: Whitey Ford

79th All-Star Game
American League 4, National League 3
July 15, 2008, Yankee Stadium

In the final Midsummer Classic at the original Yankee Stadium, the American League emerged with a 4-3 win in 15 innings as Texas' Michael Young brought home Minnesota's Justin Morneau with a "walk-off" sacrifice fly. The 4-hour, 50-minute contest was the longest All-Star Game time-wise and tied for the longest ASG in innings (also 1967 at Anaheim, 2-1 NL win). It was the AL's 12th straight All-Star Game victory and ensured American League homefield advantage in the World Series. SS Derek Jeter started and recorded the game's first hit in the first inning. RHP Mariano Rivera pitched 1.2 scoreless innings. Yankees Manager Joe Girardi joined the AL coaching staff as did Yankees Head Athletic Trainer Gene Monahan, who made his fourth All-Star Game appearance (also 1977, '86 and '92). Pregame ceremonies included 49 Hall of Famers, marking one of the largest gatherings of living baseball HOFers ever. The festivities were highlighted by Yankees Principal Owner/Chairperson George Steinbrenner, who delivered baseballs to the ceremonial first pitch participants (Reggie Jackson, Whitey Ford, Yogi Berra and Goose Gossage).

All-Star Team	1	2	3	4	5	6	7	8	9	10	11	12	13	14	15	R	H	E
National League	0	0	0	0	1	1	0	1	0	0	0	0	0	0	0	3	13	4
American League	0	0	0	0	0	0	2	1	0	0	0	0	0	0	1	4	14	1

Winning Pitcher: Scott Kazmir
Losing Pitcher: Brad Lidge

Yankees Postseason Summaries

1921 WORLD SERIES

Marked the Yankees' first ever World Series appearance in Baseball's last nine-game Fall Classic...Waite Hoyt went 2-1 despite not allowing an earned run in 27.0IP (18H, 11BB) over three starts...is tied with Christy Mathewson (1905) for the most IP without allowing an ER in a single World Series...lost, 1-0, in the Game 8 clincher, tossing a complete game and allowing an unearned run in the first inning...Carl Mays went 1-2 with a 1.73 ERA (26.0IP, 5ER) in his three starts, setting a still-standing record for most innings pitched in a single postseason without allowing a walk...Babe Ruth hit the first of his 15 career World Series home runs in a losing effort in Game 4.

New York Yankees (AL)	3
New York Giants (NL)	5

Babe Ruth hit the first of his 15 career World Series home runs in Game 4 of the 1921 World Series.

1922 WORLD SERIES

The Yankees went 0-4-1 against the Giants, marking just one of three times in 40 World Series appearances that the Yankees have been held without a win (were swept in 1963 vs. Los Angeles and 1976 vs. Cincinnati)...hit just .203 as a team...Game 2 marked the Yankees' only tie in 225 overall World Series games (134-90-1).

New York Yankees (AL)	0
New York Giants (NL)	4

1923 WORLD SERIES

Won the first World Series in franchise history in the inaugural season of the original Yankee Stadium...their Game 2 win snapped a nine-game World Series winless streak dating to 1921 (0-8-1)...scored five runs in the eighth inning of the Game 6 clincher to win, 6-4...Babe Ruth and Bob Meusel led the Yankees in HR (3) and RBI (8), respectively.

New York Giants (NL)	2
New York Yankees (AL)	4

1926 WORLD SERIES

The Series is most remembered for Game 7, which featured Pete Alexander's bases-loaded, seventh-inning strikeout of Tony Lazzeri, and Babe Ruth making the final out of the series attempting to steal second base with the Yankees down, 3-2, in the ninth...Ruth became the first player to hit 3HR in a single World Series game (Game 4 at St. Louis) and the first to hit 4HR over an entire World Series.

St. Louis Cardinals (NL)	4
New York Yankees (AL)	3

1927 WORLD SERIES

The Murderers' Row Yankees became the first AL team to sweep a World Series...Babe Ruth had a Series-high 7RBI and his 2HR were the only homers of the Series...Herb Pennock was perfect through his first 22 batters of Game 3 before a Pie Traynor single...Yankees completed the sweep on a ninth-inning wild pitch from Pirates pitcher Johnny Miljus in Game 4...marked the first of eight consecutive winning World Series appearances for the franchise (1927-28, 32, '36-39, '41).

New York Yankees (AL)	4
Pittsburgh Pirates (NL)	0

1928 WORLD SERIES

The Yankees' win marked their first back-to-back titles...was the sixth and last Series for manager Miller Huggins, who died during the 1929 season...used only three pitchers in the entire Series as each earned complete-game wins (Waite Hoyt in Games 1 and 4; George Pipgras in Game 2 and Tom Zachary in Game 3)...Lou Gehrig led the Yankees with 4HR and 9RBI...Babe Ruth tied his own record with 3HR in Game 4 at St. Louis.

St. Louis Cardinals (NL)	0
New York Yankees (AL)	4

1932 WORLD SERIES

The Yankees swept the Cubs to run their World Series winning streak to 12 games...was the first of Manager Joe McCarthy's eight Series appearances and seven titles with the club...Babe Ruth hit his "called shot" off Cubs pitcher Charlie Root in the fifth inning of Game 3...he and Gehrig each hit 2HR in the game...the Yankees outscored the Cubs 37-19 in the Series...Gehrig batted .529 (9-for-17) with 9R, 3HR and 8RBI...was Ruth's last World Series with the Yankees.

Chicago Cubs (NL)	0
New York Yankees (AL)	4

1936 WORLD SERIES

The Yankees' victory was the first of four consecutive titles...had their 12-game World Series winning streak snapped with a Game 1 loss...the Yankees' 18-4 Game 2 win still marks the most runs scored by one team in a World Series game...Bill Dickey and Tony Lazzeri (grand slam) each had 5RBI in the game...rookie Joe DiMaggio batted .346 (9-for-26) with 3RBI in the Series.

New York Yankees (AL)	4
New York Giants (NL)	2

1937 WORLD SERIES
The Yankees defeated the Giants for the second year in a row…Yankees pitchers posted a 2.45 ERA (44.0, 12ER) in the Series…Lefty Gomez recorded complete-game wins in Game 1 and in the Game 5 clincher…George Selkirk led the Yankees with 5R and 6RBI.

New York Giants (NL)	1
New York Yankees (AL)	4

1938 WORLD SERIES
The Yankees ran their all-time World Series mark vs. the Cubs to 8-0…became the first team to win three consecutive Series…middle infielders Joe Gordon and Frank Crosetti each drove in a team-high 6R in the series…used just four pitchers, who sported a 1.75 combined ERA (36.0IP, 7ER)…Red Ruffing recorded complete-game wins in Game 1 and 4, compiling a 1.50 ERA in the Series (18.0IP, 3ER).

New York Yankees (AL)	4
Chicago Cubs (NL)	0

1939 WORLD SERIES
The Yankees won the last of four consecutive World Series with their second straight sweep…were led by Charlie Keller, who batted .438 (7-for-16) with 8R, 3HR and 6RBI…the Yankees hit just .206 (27-for-131) as a team…Yankees pitching compiled a 1.22 ERA, holding the Reds to just four extra-base hits (0HR) in the Series…Game 4 was won in the 10th inning on Joe DiMaggio's single with Charlie Keller on first and Frank Crosetti on third…after the Cincinnati RF misplayed the ball, Keller successfully scored from first, crashing into Reds catcher Ernie Lombardi and dazing him long enough for DiMaggio to score as in a play since known as "Lombardi's Snooze."

Cincinnati Reds (NL)	0
New York Yankees (AL)	4

1941 WORLD SERIES
Marked the first World Series meeting between the Yankees and Dodgers…Game 4 featured the famous passed ball by Dodgers catcher Mickey Owen, which would have been the final out of the game and evened the Series at 2-2…the Yankees went on to score 4R with two out in the ninth to win, 7-4, at Ebbets Field…in the Game 5 clincher, Tiny Bonham tossed a complete game (1ER, 5H) and Tommy Henrich hit a solo homer…Joe Gordon (.500, 1HR, 5RBI) and Charlie Keller (.389, 5RBI) paced Yankees hitters…capped a run of 32 wins in 36 World Series games dating to 1927.

Brooklyn Dodgers (NL)	1
New York Yankees (AL)	4

1942 WORLD SERIES
The Yankees won Game 1 behind Red Ruffing but lost the next four games…marked the Yankees' first losing World Series since falling in seven games to the Cardinals in 1926…Joe DiMaggio went 7-for-21 (.333) and Phil Rizzuto went 8-for-21 (.381), while Charlie Keller led the Yankees with 2HR and 5RBI.

New York Yankees (AL)	1
St. Louis Cardinals (NL)	4

1943 WORLD SERIES
The Yankees reversed the prior year's result, winning in five games…Spud Chandler was dominant, allowing just 1ER over 18.0IP for complete-game wins in Games 1 and 5…Bill Dickey's two-run homer in the Game 5 clincher marked the only runs of the game…Yankees Joe DiMaggio, Tommy Henrich, Phil Rizzuto, George Selkirk, Red Ruffing and Buddy Hassett were all serving in the military and did not appear in the Series…marked the seventh and final World Series title in eight appearances under manager Joe McCarthy.

St. Louis Cardinals (NL)	1
New York Yankees (AL)	4

1947 WORLD SERIES
The Yankees were piloted by Bucky Harris in his only World Series managing the team…in Game 4, Yankees pitcher Bill Bevens lost both his no-hit bid and the game with two outs in the bottom of the ninth as pinch-hitter Cookie Lavagetto doubled home two runs for a 3-2 Brooklyn win…Spec Shea recorded two wins and Johnny Lindell batted .500 (9-for-18) with 7RBI.

Brooklyn Dodgers (NL)	3
New York Yankees (AL)	4

1949 WORLD SERIES
Marked the first of five straight World Series championships…was the first of 10 World Series appearances in a 12-year stretch under manager Casey Stengel (won seven)…Allie Reynolds allowed just 2H, winning Game 1, 1-0, over Don Newcombe on Tommy Henrich's leadoff homer in the bottom of the ninth…also pitched 3.1 scoreless innings to close out Game 4…Commissioner Happy Chandler ordered lights turned on during Game 5, marking the first time a World Series game was finished under electric light.

Brooklyn Dodgers (NL)	1
New York Yankees (AL)	4

Manager Casey Stengel led the Yankees to a record five-consecutive World Series titles from 1949-53.

1950 WORLD SERIES

Yankees pitchers allowed just 5R (3ER) all Series, tallying a 0.73 combined ERA in 37.0IP…each of the first three games were decided by one run, including a 1-0 victory behind Vic Raschi in Game 1 and a 2-1, 10-inning win behind Allie Reynolds in Game 2…Whitey Ford earned the first of his record 10 career World Series wins in the Game 4 clincher as Reynolds came out of the bullpen to strike out the final batter of the game with two runners on base.

New York Yankees (AL)	4
Philadelphia Phillies (NL)	0

1951 WORLD SERIES

The Yankees defeated the Giants in Joe DiMaggio's final World Series…Willie Mays and Mickey Mantle made their Series debuts, both in their rookie seasons…in Game 2, Mantle seriously injured his right knee after getting his cleat caught in a drainpipe, ending his Series…Ed Lopat allowed just 1ER in 18.0IP, notching wins in Games 2 and 5.

New York Giants (NL)	2
New York Yankees (AL)	4

1952 WORLD SERIES

Led by Mickey Mantle (.345, 5R, 2HR), Johnny Mize (.400, 3HR, 6RBI) and Gene Woodling (.348), the Yankees won in seven games…Allie Reynolds and Vic Raschi each recorded a pair of victories…in Game 7, second baseman Billy Martin made a running catch on a two-out, seventh-inning, based-loaded pop-up from Jackie Robinson to preserve the Yankees' lead.

New York Yankees (AL)	4
Brooklyn Dodgers (NL)	3

Billy Martin makes a game-saving catch on a two-out, seventh-inning, based-loaded pop-up from Jackie Robinson to preserve the win in Game 7 of the 1952 World Series.

1953 WORLD SERIES

The Yankees won their all-time record fifth consecutive title…Billy Martin batted .500 (12-for-24) with 2HR and 8RBI…still shares the all-time mark for hits in a six-game World Series…Mickey Mantle won Game 2 with a two-run homer in the eighth inning…added a grand slam in the Game 5 win…Martin drove in the winning run in the Game 6 clincher with a single in the bottom of the ninth.

Brooklyn Dodgers (NL)	2
New York Yankees (AL)	4

1955 WORLD SERIES

Marked the Yankees' first Series loss to the Dodgers after five successive wins (1941, '47, '49, '52, '53)…is the only time the Dodgers triumphed over the Yankees before relocating to Los Angeles in 1958…Brooklyn's Johnny Podres tossed an eight-hit, 2-0, shutout in the Game 7 clincher at Yankee Stadium…with two on and no out in the sixth, Yogi Berra's slicing line drive was famously caught by Brooklyn's Sandy Amoros, who then threw the ball back to the infield to double off Gil McDougald, preventing a potential rally.

New York Yankees (AL)	3
Brooklyn Dodgers (NL)	4

1956 WORLD SERIES

Lost the first two games in Brooklyn, then came back to win in seven…was highlighted by Don Larsen's Game 5 perfect game caught by Yogi Berra, the only no-hitter in postseason history…Larsen didn't know he was pitching until he got to the park that day…had lasted only 1.2 innings in his Game 2 start, (4R, 0ER, 1H, 4BB)…Berra led the Yankees with a .360 (9-for-25) batting average, 3HR and a then-record 10 RBI…the Yankees hit 12HR, the second-highest total in Series history (San Francisco 14HR in 2002).

New York Yankees (AL)	4
Brooklyn Dodgers (NL)	3

1957 WORLD SERIES

The Yankees dropped their second seven-game World Series in three years in their first-ever meeting against Milwaukee…the Braves' Lew Burdette won Games 2, 5 and 7, the latter two on seven-hit shutouts…second baseman Jerry Coleman batted .364 (8-for-22) with 2 doubles and 2RBI in a losing effort.

Milwaukee Braves (NL)	4
New York Yankees (AL)	3

1958 WORLD SERIES

The Yankees came back from two-games-to-none and three-games-to-one deficits to win in seven…after getting bombed for 4ER in just 0.1IP in his Game 2 start, Yankees pitcher Bob Turley tossed a five-hit shutout in Game 5, came on with two on and a one-run lead in the 10th inning to get the final out in Game 6, and earned the victory in Game 7 with 6.2 innings (1ER) in relief of Don Larsen…winning the title gave the Yankees a World Series championship over each of the eight modern NL teams (since 1900)…Hank Bauer batted .323 (10-for-31) with 4HR, making him just one of four Yankees in franchise history to hit four-or-more homers in a single Series (also Ruth 4HR in 1926; Gehrig 4HR in 1928; and Reggie Jackson 5HR in 1977)…was held hitless in Game 4, snapping an all-time Major League-best 17-game World Series hitting streak.

New York Yankees (AL)	4
Milwaukee Braves (NL)	3

Bobby Richardson [crossing home plate] drove in an all-time record 12 runs in the 1960 Fall Classic, becoming the only player to win World Series MVP honors on a losing team.

1963 WORLD SERIES

The Yankees were swept despite allowing just 12 overall runs, marking just one of two four-game Series exits in franchise history (also 1976 vs. Cincinnati)…scored just four runs and batted .171 over the four games, marking the third and four-lowest all-time totals, respectively, by any team in a World Series.

Los Angeles Dodgers (NL)	4
New York Yankees (AL)	0

1964 WORLD SERIES

The Yankees' seven-game loss marked Mickey Mantle's final World Series…batted .333 (8-for-24) with 3HR, giving him a record 18 World Series HR for his career…Jim Bouton won both of his starts, allowing just 3ER in 17.1IP…Bobby Richardson batted .406 (13-for-32), setting an all-time record for hits in a Series (since tied by Lou Brock in 1968 and Marty Barrett in 1986).

New York Yankees (AL)	3
St. Louis Cardinals (NL)	4

1960 WORLD SERIES

Despite outscoring Pittsburgh 55-27 and setting still-standing World Series marks for runs scored and team batting average (.338), the Yankees lost the decisive Game 7, 10-9, on Bill Mazeroski's ninth-inning "walk-off" homer off Ralph Terry…marked Casey Stengel's final game as Yankees manager…Bobby Richardson batted .367 (11-for-30) and recorded a still-standing record 12RBI, becoming the only player in Baseball history to win the World Series MVP Award on a losing team…Whitey Ford tossed complete game shutouts in Games 3 and 6, allowing just 11H and 2BB in 18.0 Series IP.

New York Yankees (AL)	3
Pittsburgh Pirates (NL)	4

1961 WORLD SERIES

With the Series tied 1-1, the Yankees won Game 3 on a game-tying solo homer by Johnny Blanchard in the eighth and Roger Maris' game-winning solo shot in the ninth…outscored Cincinnati 20-5 in the final two games…Manager Ralph Houk became the third Yankees skipper to win the World Series with the Yankees in his first season managing the club…Hector Lopez led the Yankees with 7RBI in just 9AB…Whitey Ford pitched 14.0 scoreless innings, notching wins in Games 1 and 4.

Cincinnati Reds (NL)	1
New York Yankees (AL)	4

1962 WORLD SERIES

The Yankees clinched a tight seven-game Series on a 1-0, four-hit, Game 7 shutout from Ralph Terry…scored their only run when Tony Kubek grounded into a fifth-inning double play…Terry allowed just 17H and 5ER in 25.0 Series IP, taking home the MVP Award…the teams combined for just 41 total runs in a Series that stretched over 13 days due to rainouts.

New York Yankees (AL)	4
San Francisco Giants (NL)	3

1976 CHAMPIONSHIP SERIES

Chris Chambliss batted .524 (11-for-21) with 2HR and 8RBI, including the Series-winning "walk-off" home run off the Royals' Mark Littell in Game 5.

Kansas City Royals (AL)	2
New York Yankees (AL)	3

1976 WORLD SERIES

Marked the Yankees' first World Series appearance after a 11-year drought…was the first Series appearance under the majority ownership of George M. Steinbrenner…also was the club's first Series following the 1974-75 remodeling of the original Yankee Stadium…was the second and last time the Yankees have been swept in a Series…Thurman Munson led the Yankees, batting .529 (9-for-17) with 2R and 2RBI.

New York Yankees (AL)	0
Cincinnati Reds (NL)	4

1977 CHAMPIONSHIP SERIES

Sparky Lyle appeared in four of the five games and recorded wins in relief in Game 4 (5.1IP, 2H, 0R, 0BB, 1K) and Game 5 (1.1IP, 1H, 0R, 1K)…Yankees scored 1R in the eighth and 3R in the ninth to win the Game 5 clincher, 5-3.

New York Yankees (AL)	3
Kansas City Royals (AL)	2

1977 WORLD SERIES

The Yankees snapped a 14-season championship drought, defeating the Dodgers in six games…in the Game 6 clincher, Reggie Jackson joined Babe Ruth (twice) as the only players to hit 3HR in a single World Series game…batted .450 (9-for-20) with 10R (tied for most all-time), 5HR (tied for most all-time) and 8RBI, taking home the Series MVP…Mike Torrez won both of his starts, tossing complete-game wins in Games 3 and 6.

Los Angeles Dodgers (NL)	2
New York Yankees (AL)	4

1978 CHAMPIONSHIP SERIES

Reggie Jackson led the Yankees in batting .462 (6-for-13), HR (2) and RBI (6)...Ron Guidry (8.0IP, 1ER) and Goose Gossage (1.0IP, 0ER) pitched the Yankees to a Game 4 win.

Kansas City Royals (AL)	1
New York Yankees (AL)	3

1978 WORLD SERIES

The Yankees defeated the Dodgers for the second consecutive year, 4-games-to-2...Series cemented Graig Nettles' reputation for defensive excellence...Bucky Dent won the MVP, batting .417 (10-for-24) with 7RBI...second baseman Brian Doyle, filling in for the injured Willie Randolph, batted .438 (7-for-16) with 4R...Catfish Hunter allowed just 2ER in 7.0IP in recording the win in the Game 6 clincher at Los Angeles.

New York Yankees (AL)	4
Los Angeles Dodgers (NL)	2

1980 CHAMPIONSHIP SERIES

The Yankees' scored just two runs in each game, marking the only time in franchise history the Yankees have been swept in the ALCS or ALDS.

Kansas City Royals (AL)	3
New York Yankees (AL)	0

1981 DIVISION SERIES

The Yankees almost squandered a two-games-to-none lead but defeated Milwaukee behind two wins from Dave Righetti (one as a starter, one as a reliever)...Oscar Gamble went 6-for-10 with 2HR and 4RBI.

Milwaukee Brewers (AL)	2
New York Yankees (AL)	3

1981 CHAMPIONSHIP SERIES

The Yankees outscored Oakland 20-4 in their only ALCS sweep in franchise history...Graig Nettles drove in three runs in each game, batting .500 (6-for-12) with 1HR.

New York Yankees (AL)	3
Oakland Athletics (AL)	0

1981 WORLD SERIES

After winning the first two games of the Series, the Yankees dropped the next four, falling to 8-3 in their World Series appearances vs. the Dodgers...pitcher George Frazier became the first pitcher to lose three games in a best-of-seven World Series...future GM Bob Watson led the club with 7RBI.

Los Angeles Dodgers (NL)	4
New York Yankees (AL)	2

1995 DIVISION SERIES

The Yankees snapped a 13-year playoff drought...Don Mattingly batted .417 (10-for-24) with 1HR and 6RBI in his only career postseason series...won the first two games at home before dropping three straight in Seattle...won Game 2, 7-5, on Jim Leyritz's 15th-inning "walk-off" homer in the longest postseason game in franchise history...after throwing 135 pitches in a Game 1 win, David Cone threw 147 pitches in a Game 5 no-decision.

New York Yankees (AL)	2
Seattle Mariners (AL)	3

1996 DIVISION SERIES

The Yankees bullpen recorded wins in Games 2, 3 and 4, allowing just 1ER in 19.2IP over the series.

Texas Rangers (AL)	1
New York Yankees (AL)	3

1996 CHAMPIONSHIP SERIES

Down, 4-3, going into the bottom of the eighth inning of Game 1, the Yankees tied the score on Derek Jeter's disputed home run to right field...Bernie Williams (9-for-19) batted .474 with 6R, 2HR and 6RBI, earning ALCS MVP honors.

Baltimore Orioles (AL)	1
New York Yankees (AL)	4

1996 WORLD SERIES

The Yankees snapped a 17-year World Championship drought, coming back from a two-games-to-none deficit...Manager Joe Torre won in his first year at the helm...club came back from a 6-0 deficit in Game 4, with Jim Leyritz knotting the score at 6-6 with a three-run, eighth inning homer...Andy Pettitte outdueled John Smoltz, 1-0, in Game 5...Jimmy Key defeated Greg Maddux in the Game 6 clincher...John Wetteland saved each of the Yankees' victories, earning MVP honors.

Atlanta Braves (NL)	2
New York Yankees (AL)	4

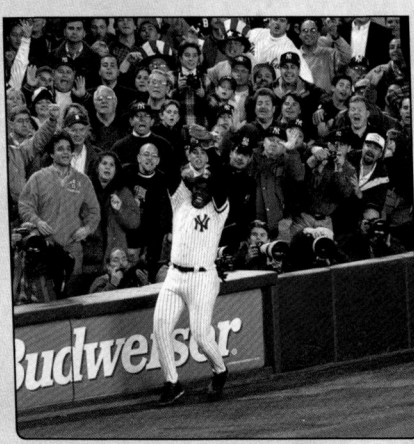

Third baseman Charlie Hayes catches the final out of the 1996 World Series.

1997 DIVISION SERIES

The Yankees' Game 1 win featured the first-ever back-to-back-to-back postseason homers (Tim Raines, Derek Jeter and Paul O'Neill)…O'Neill finished the series with a .421 batting average (8-for-19), 2HR and 7RBI, including a grand slam in Game 3…Mariano Rivera suffered a blown save in Game 4, on Sandy Alomar, Jr.'s eighth-inning solo home run…would not allow another run in his next 23 postseason appearances, spanning 33.1IP.

New York Yankees (AL)	2
Cleveland Indians (AL)	3

1998 DIVISION SERIES

The Yankees outscored Texas, 9-1, in the series, behind wins from David Wells, Andy Pettitte and David Cone…outfielder Shane Spencer recorded 4RBI in the series, including a three-run homer in Game 3.

New York Yankees (AL)	3
Texas Rangers (AL)	0

1998 CHAMPIONSHIP SERIES

The Yankees won the final three games of the series, taking the series in six…their Game 4 win featured 7.0 scoreless IP from starter Orlando Hernandez…David Wells earned series MVP honors with wins in Games 1 and 5.

Cleveland Indians (AL)	2
New York Yankees (AL)	4

Orlando Hernandez recorded the first of nine career post-season wins with the Yankees in Game 4 of the 1998 ALCS vs. Cleveland.

1998 WORLD SERIES

The Yankees swept the Padres to finish with a 125-50 overall record (including the postseason), setting the all-time mark for most wins in a season…trailing, 5-2, in Game 1 at Yankee Stadium, Chuck Knoblauch's three-run HR tied the game and Tino Martinez's grand slam put the Yankees ahead in the seventh…also came back from a 3-0 deficit after six innings in Game 3 with Series MVP Scott Brosius hitting a leadoff HR in the seventh and a three-run HR in the eighth…Mariano Rivera notched three saves, marking his highest total in a single World Series.

San Diego Padres (NL)	0
New York Yankees (AL)	4

Mariano Rivera [L] celebrates with Joe Girardi after the final out of the 1998 World Series.

1999 DIVISION SERIES

The Yankees defeated the Rangers in the ALDS for the third time in three attempts over a four-year stretch…outscored them 14-1 in the series…in Game 1, Orlando Hernandez limited Texas to 2H over 8.0 scoreless IP and Bernie Williams drove in six runs, which ties Bobby Richardson (1960 WS, Game 3) and Hideki Matsui (2009 WS, Game 6) for the most in a single postseason game franchise history.

Texas Rangers (AL)	0
New York Yankees (AL)	3

1999 CHAMPIONSHIP SERIES

The Yankees won their first-ever postseason meeting vs. Boston…Bernie Williams won Game 1 with a 10th-inning walk-off home run…the club had a 12-game postseason winning streak snapped in a Game 3 loss…Derek Jeter led the Yankees with a .350 (7-for-20) batting average.

Boston Red Sox (AL)	1
New York Yankees (AL)	4

1999 WORLD SERIES

The Yankees recorded their second straight World Series sweep… Orlando Hernandez allowed just 1R on 1H in 7.0IP (10K) in Game 1…David Cone followed with 7.0 scoreless innings on 1H in Game 2…Chad Curtis hit a 10th-inning walk-off homer in Game 3…the Game 4 win extended the Yankees' World Series winning streak to 12 games.

Atlanta Braves (NL)	0
New York Yankees (AL)	4

2000 DIVISION SERIES

Dropped Game 1 of a postseason series for the first time since the 1996 World Series, snapping a winning streak of seven such games…also lost Game 4 at Yankee Stadium, snapping their postseason winning streak at 10 games…Andy Pettitte and Mariano Rivera shut out the A's, 4-0, in Game 2…the Yankees scored 6R in the first inning of the deciding Game 5 in Oakland to provide the margin of victory in a 7-5 win.

New York Yankees (AL)	3
Oakland Athletics (AL)	2

2000 CHAMPIONSHIP SERIES

The Yankees scored 19 of their 31 total runs in the series in the seventh-inning-or-later, including three come-from-behind victories...MVP David Justice hit 2HR and had a series-best 8RBI...Bernie Williams hit .435 (10-for-23)...Roger Clemens struck out 15 batters while tossing a 1H, 2BB complete-game shutout in Game 4 at Seattle.

Seattle Mariners (AL)	2
New York Yankees (AL)	4

2000 WORLD SERIES

Marked the first "Subway Series" since the Yankees-Dodgers matchup in 1956...the Yankees were victorious in Games 1 and 5 in their last at-bat, winning on a 12th-inning single from Jose Vizcaino and a ninth-inning Luis Sojo single, respectively...Derek Jeter was named Series MVP, batting .409 (9-for-22) with 6R and 2 solo HR, including one on the first pitch of Game 4.

New York Mets (NL)	1
New York Yankees (AL)	4

2001 DIVISION SERIES

The postseason began less than a month after the attacks of 9/11...after losing Games 1 and 2, the Yankees won three straight...were held to just two hits in Game 3 at Oakland but won, 1-0, behind Mike Mussina (7.0IP), Mariano Rivera (2.0IP) and Jorge Posada's fifth-inning solo home run...the game also featured Derek Jeter's famous "Flip Play," which nailed Jeremy Giambi at the plate in the seventh.

New York Yankees (AL)	3
Oakland Athletics (AL)	2

Derek Jeter [R] makes his famous "Flip Play" relay throw to Jorge Posada in Game 3 of the 2001 ALDS at Oakland.

2001 CHAMPIONSHIP SERIES

The Yankees defeated a Seattle club that won an AL-record 116 games during the regular season...Andy Pettitte was named Series MVP, going 2-0 with a 2.51 ERA...Game 4 ended on Alfonso Soriano's two-run walk-off homer in the ninth...Bernie Williams homered in three consecutive games (Games 3-5).

New York Yankees (AL)	4
Seattle Mariners (AL)	1

2001 WORLD SERIES

All games were won by the home team in one of the most thrilling World Series of all time...President George W. Bush threw out the ceremonial first pitch prior Game 3 at Yankee Stadium...the Yankees came back from two-run deficits with two outs in the ninth vs. Arizona's Byung-Hyun Kim in both Games 4 and 5...Tino Martinez tied Game 4 with a two-run home run and Derek Jeter earned the nickname, "Mr. November," with a solo HR to win it in the 10th...Scott Brosius hit a two-run homer to tie Game 5 before Alfonso Soriano won the game with an RBI-single in the 12th...despite taking a 2-1 lead on a Soriano solo homer in the eighth inning of Game 7, the Yankees lost the Series after allowing two runs in the ninth.

New York Yankees (AL)	3
Arizona Diamondbacks (NL)	4

Tino Martinez sets the stage for an improbable Yankees comeback with a game-tying, two-out, two-run, ninth-inning home run in Game 4 of the 2001 World Series.

2002 DIVISION SERIES

The Yankees had their Division Series winning streak snapped at four, losing their first DS since 1997 vs. Cleveland...Derek Jeter batted .500 (8-for-16) with 2HR and 3RBI.

Anaheim Angels (AL)	3
New York Yankees (AL)	1

2003 DIVISION SERIES

The Yankees held Minnesota to just six runs in four games, including one run in each of Games 2, 3 and 4...Derek Jeter batted .429 (6-for-14) with 1HR.

Minnesota Twins (AL)	1
New York Yankees (AL)	3

2003 CHAMPIONSHIP SERIES

Defined by the final game, the Series was won on Aaron Boone's first pitch leadoff home run off Tim Wakefield in the bottom of the 11th inning of Game 7...in the contest, the Yankees came back from a 5-2 deficit heading into the bottom of the eighth...Mike Mussina made his first-ever relief appearance, getting a strikeout and double play with two on and no outs in the fourth to keep the Yankees in the game...tossed 3.0 scoreless IP on two days' rest...Jason Giambi hit solo homers in the fifth and seventh...the Yankees scored three runs in the eighth off Pedro Martinez to tie the game, 5-5...Mariano Rivera tossed 3.0 scoreless innings, pitching the ninth, 10th and 11th, to earn the win.

Boston Red Sox (AL)	3
New York Yankees (AL)	4

2003 WORLD SERIES

The Yankees outscored Florida, 21-17, in defeat...Andy Pettitte allowed just 3R (1ER) in 15.2IP over two starts, including a win in Game 2 and a loss in the decisive Game 6...Bernie Williams batted .400 (10-for-25) with 5R, 2HR and 5RBI.

Florida Marlins (NL)	4
New York Yankees (AL)	2

2004 DIVISION SERIES

The Yankees defeated Minnesota in the ALDS for the second straight season...won Game 2 scoring twice in the 12th inning and Game 4 with one run in the 11th...Alex Rodriguez batted .421 (8-for-19) with 1HR and 3RBI.

Minnesota Twins (AL)	1
New York Yankees (AL)	3

2004 CHAMPIONSHIP SERIES

The Yankees lost their first-ever postseason series after being up 3-games-to-0...scored 19 runs in their Game 3 win, marking the most ever by one team in an ALCS game...Hideki Matsui batted .412 (14-for-34) with 6 doubles, 1 triple, 2HR and 10RBI in the series, establishing the all-time mark for extra-base hits in a postseason series and ALCS marks for hits, total bases and doubles.

Boston Red Sox (AL)	4
New York Yankees (AL)	3

2005 DIVISION SERIES

Mariano Rivera saved both of the Yankees' victories... Derek Jeter tied for the team lead in both RBI (5) and runs scored (4).

New York Yankees (AL)	2
Los Angeles Angels of Anaheim (AL)	3

2006 DIVISION SERIES

Chien-Ming Wang recorded his first career postseason win in Game 1...Derek Jeter (8-for-16) and Jorge Posada (7-for-14) combined for 15 of the team's 33 overall hits.

Detroit Tigers (AL)	3
New York Yankees (AL)	1

2007 DIVISION SERIES

The Yankees were outhit, .315 to .228, in the series...the Yankees' 2-1, 11-inning loss in Game 2 featured the unusual postseason debut of Joba Chamberlain, who allowed the go-ahead run in the eighth on 2BB, 2WP and 1HP while "midges" descended on the pitcher's mound.

New York Yankees (AL)	1
Cleveland Indians (AL)	3

2009 DIVISION SERIES

The Yankees recorded their third all time ALDS sweep (also 1998-99 vs. Texas) and fourth "best-of-five" series sweep (also 1981 ALCS vs. Oakland)...came back from deficits in all three games...out-homered the Twins, 6-0...Yankees starters allowed just 3ER and three extra-base hits in 19.0IP with a 1.42 ERA...Alex Rodriguez batted a team-high .455 (5-for-11) with 2HR and 6RBI.

Minnesota Twins (AL)	0
New York Yankees (AL)	3

2009 CHAMPIONSHIP SERIES

The Yankees won their 40th AL pennant...hit 8HR and drew 38BB over the six games, while holding the Majors' second-highest scoring team to an average of 3.2R/G...won Game 2 in 13 innings on a throwing error by Maicer Izturis...CC Sabathia earned ALCS MVP honors, going 2-0 with a 1.13 ERA (16.0IP, 2ER) in two starts...Alex Rodriguez batted a team-high .429 (9-for-21) with 6R, 3HR, 6RBI and 8BB.

Los Angeles Angels (AL)	2
New York Yankees (AL)	4

2009 WORLD SERIES

The Yankees won their 27th World Championship and first since 2000...Hideki Matsui (.615 avg., 3HR, 8RBI) was the unanimous World Series MVP, marking the first time a Japanese player earned the honor...had 6RBI (single, double, HR) in the Game 6 clincher, tying Bobby Richardson's single-game World Series record (1960 Game 3)...Andy Pettitte became the third-oldest pitcher to win a World Series clinching game (behind Burleigh Grimes-1931 and Eddie Plank-1913) and the first pitcher in baseball history to start and win all three clinching games of a single postseason (DS, CS, WS).

Philadelphia Phillies (NL)	2
New York Yankees (AL)	4

Andy Pettitte, Jorge Posada, Derek Jeter and Mariano Rivera admire the 2009 World Series Trophy following Game 6 at Yankee Stadium.

2010 DIVISION SERIES

The Yankees swept Minnesota for the second straight year in the ALDS...marked their first ALDS series win after qualifying for the postseason as a Wild Card...outscored the Twins 17-7 in the series...10 different Yankees drove in at least one run...Yankees relievers combined to allow just 1ER in 7.0IP...Phil Hughes won Game 3 with 7.0 shutout IP (4H, 1BB) in his first career postseason start).

Minnesota Twins (AL)	0
New York Yankees (AL)	3

2010 CHAMPIONSHIP SERIES

The Yankees lost a postseason series to Texas for the first time after wins in the ALDS in 1996, '98 and '99...were outscored 38-19 in the series and outhit 63-38...their 8-0 loss in Game 3 marked the worst postseason shutout loss in franchise history...Robinson Cano batted .348 (8-for-23) with 4HR and 5RBI...Curtis Granderson reached base safely in 13 of his 25PA (.520).

New York Yankees (AL)	2
Texas Rangers (AL)	4

Postseason Honors

ALCS MVP

YEAR	PLAYER	AGE	POS	G	AB	R	H	2B	3B	HR	RBI	BA
1981	Graig Nettles	37	3B	3	12	2	6	2	0	1	9	.500
1996	Bernie Williams	28	CF	5	19	6	9	3	0	2	6	.474
2000	David Justice	34	LF	6	26	4	6	2	0	2	8	.231

YEAR	PITCHER	AGE	POS	G	GS	IP	W	L	SV	H	R	ER	SO	BB	ERA
1998	David Wells	35	LHP	2	2	15.2	2	0	0	12	5	5	18	2	2.87
1999	Orlando Hernandez	30	RHP	2	2	15.0	1	0	0	12	4	3	13	6	1.80
2001	Andy Pettitte	29	LHP	2	2	14.1	2	0	0	11	4	4	8	2	2.51
2003	Mariano Rivera	33	RHP	4	0	8.0	1	0	2	5	1	1	6	0	1.13
2009	CC Sabathia	29	LHP	2	2	16.0	2	0	0	9	2	2	12	3	1.13

World Series MVP

YEAR	PLAYER	AGE	POS	G	AB	R	H	2B	3B	HR	RBI	BA
1960	Bobby Richardson	25	2B	7	30	8	11	2	2	1	12	.367
1977	Reggie Jackson	31	RF	6	20	10	9	1	0	5	8	.450
1978	Bucky Dent	26	SS	6	24	3	10	1	0	0	7	.417
1998	Scott Brosius	32	3B	4	17	3	8	0	0	2	6	.471
2000	Derek Jeter	26	SS	5	22	6	9	2	1	2	2	.409
2009	Hideki Matsui	35	DH	6	13	3	8	1	0	3	8	.615

YEAR	PITCHER	AGE	POS	G	GS	IP	W	L	SV	H	R	ER	SO	BB	ERA
1956	Don Larsen	27	RHP	2	2	10.2	1	0	0	1	4	0	7	4	0.00
1958	Bob Turley	28	RHP	4	2	16.1	2	1	1	10	5	5	13	7	2.76
1961	Whitey Ford	32	LHP	2	2	14.0	2	0	0	6	0	0	7	1	0.00
1962	Ralph Terry	26	RHP	3	3	25.0	2	1	0	17	5	5	16	2	1.80
1996	John Wetteland	30	RHP	5	0	4.1	0	0	4	4	1	1	6	1	2.08
1999	Mariano Rivera	29	RHP	3	0	4.2	1	0	2	3	0	0	3	1	0.00

Yankees All-Time Postseason Leaders

BATTING

Games Played
1. DEREK JETER 147
2. Bernie Williams 121
3. JORGE POSADA 120
4. MARIANO RIVERA 94
5. Tino Martinez .... .81

At-Bats
1. DEREK JETER 599
2. Bernie Williams 465
3. JORGE POSADA 402
4. Tino Martinez 287
5. Paul O'Neill 270

Runs
1. DEREK JETER 101
2. Bernie Williams 83
3. JORGE POSADA 49
4. Mickey Mantle 42
5. Yogi Berra .... .41

Hits
1. **DEREK JETER 185**
2. Bernie Williams 128
3. JORGE POSADA 97
4. Paul O'Neill 76
5. Yogi Berra 71

Doubles
1. DEREK JETER 30
2. Bernie Williams 29
3. JORGE POSADA 23
4. Mickey Mantle................. .15
5. Tino Martinez, Paul O'Neill....... 14

Triples
1. DEREK JETER, Bill Johnson 4
3. Bauer, B. Brown, CANO, Gehrig,
   B. Martin, Meusel 3

Home Runs
1. Bernie Williams 22
2. DEREK JETER 20
3. Mickey Mantle 18
4. Babe Ruth 15
5. Yogi Berra, Reggie Jackson 12

RBI
1. Bernie Williams 80
2. DEREK JETER 57
3. JORGE POSADA................. 42
3. Mickey Mantle 40
T5. Yogi Berra, Hideki Matsui 39

Batting Average (min. 75PA)
1. Lou Gehrig .... .361
2. Thurman Munson .... .357
3. Babe Ruth .... .347
4. Billy Martin .... .333
5. Reggie Jackson................. .328

Slugging Percentage (min. 75PA)
1. Babe Ruth .... .788
2. Lou Gehrig .... .731
3. Reggie Jackson................. .672
4. Charlie Keller .... .611
5. Billy Martin .... .566

PITCHING

Games
1. MARIANO RIVERA................ 90
2. Jeff Nelson 44
3. Andy Pettitte 38
4. Mike Stanton 31
5. Whitey Ford 22

Games Started
1. Andy Pettitte 38
2. Whitey Ford 22
3. Roger Clemens 18
4. Mike Mussina 15
5. Orlando Hernandez 14

Innings Pitched
1. Andy Pettitte 237.2
2. Whitey Ford 146.0
3. MARIANO RIVERA.............139.2
4. Roger Clemens 102.1
5. Orlando Hernandez 102.0

Wins
1. Andy Pettitte 18
2. Whitey Ford 10
3. Orlando Hernandez 9
4. MARIANO RIVERA...............8
5. Clemens, Reynolds, Ruffing, Wells. . .7

Strikeouts
1. Andy Pettitte 157
2. MARIANO RIVERA 109
3. Orlando Hernandez 101
4. Roger Clemens 99
5. Whitey Ford 94

ERA (min. 40.0IP)
1. MARIANO RIVERA.............. .0.71
2. Waite Hoyt 1.62
3. Herb Pennock 2.06
4. Vic Raschi 2.24
5. Ed Lopat.......................2.60

Saves (official stat since 1969)
1. MARIANO RIVERA 42
2. Goose Gossage.................7
   John Wetteland 7
4. Ken Clay, Sparky Lyle,
   Ramiro Mendoza 1

YANKEES
BASEBALL

318FT

WATCH IT ON AMERICA'S #1
REGIONAL SPORTS NETWORK

YES

yesnetwork.com

Yankee STADIUM

The New York Yankees began a new chapter in their storied history with the opening of Yankee Stadium in 2009. Located directly across the street from the site of the original, the new Stadium's architecture is a celebration of the spirit and tradition of the franchise. While firmly rooted in the past, the Stadium has a vision toward the future, incorporating the best in technology and state-of-the-art guest services.

All of the Stadium's modern amenities exist within the framework of classic elements of the original, most notably the instantly recognizable frieze that again circles the grandstand. Among the countless fan-friendly elements, massive video boards give Yankees fans more information than ever before, and concessions have been placed on concourses that allow for continuous viewing of the game.

Yankee Stadium, as a living museum, has been designed to set the standard—much like the team has done with its 27 World Championships.

The current Yankee Stadium [L] and the original Yankee Stadium in 2008.

THE STADIUM SITE

The Yankees are proud to play in the Bronx, which is home to approximately 1.4 million residents and is one of the five boroughs that make up New York City.

The Stadium sits on former parkland from Macombs Dam Park and Mullaly Park, with the Stadium grounds bounded by Jerome Avenue to the west, River Avenue to the east, and 161st Street to the south. The northern edge of the site is located between 162nd Street and 164th Street. In a nod to tradition, the footprint of the original Stadium has been replicated in the new Stadium.

Yankee Stadium is the fourth permanent home of the New York Yankees, following Hilltop Park (1903-12), the Polo Grounds (1913-22), and the original Yankee Stadium (1923-73, '76-2008). The Yankees also played two full seasons at Shea Stadium (1974-75) in Queens when the original Stadium underwent remodeling.

Gate 4 at Yankee Stadium

HOMAGE TO THE ORIGINAL STADIUM

The current Yankee Stadium evokes the spirit of the original, while restoring many of the lost treasures from before the renovations of 1974-75.

The signature frieze once again outlines the top of the Stadium bowl. As in the past, it is attached to a roof that extends into the Stadium, covering the top rows of the Grandstand.

Monument Park has been relocated to its original position in center field, albeit behind the fence, unlike before the renovation when the monuments were on the playing field. All plaques, monuments and tribute displays for the 16 Yankees who have had their numbers retired are on display for fans, who may visit Monument Park prior to all home games.

On the Main Level, near Gate 6, the Yankees Museum presented by Bank of America—a museum within a museum—tells the story of baseball and the Yankees franchise through various displays of artifacts and memorabilia. Items include a "Ball Wall" with hundreds of signed baseballs from Yankees greats, Thurman Munson's locker from the original Yankee Stadium and a replica of a locker from the Yankees clubhouse in the current Stadium. On game days, fans are welcome in the museum from the time the gates open until one hour after the game ends. On non-game days, visitors can enjoy the museum as part of Yankee Stadium tours.

Babe Ruth Plaza, located on the south side of the Stadium in between Gates 4 and 6, honors the man proverbially credited with building the original House that Ruth Built. Through a series of storyboards displayed on light posts, the Babe's life story is recounted throughout the plaza.

Statue of Yogi Berra in the New York Yankees Museum

INNOVATIVE ARCHITECTURE AND MODERN AMENITIES

One of the goals in building Yankee Stadium was to bring fans closer to the action in a facility more attuned to modern needs and expectations. The new building is 63 percent larger than the original Stadium with about 500,000 square feet of additional space.

Improved sight lines, wider concourses and the installation of nearly 1,400 high-definition video monitors throughout the Stadium all ensure guests won't miss a minute of on-field action while in their seats or at concession stands.

In addition to the live game broadcast, these centrally controlled Internet protocol monitors can also provide up-to-the-moment news, scores, weather, traffic information and safety updates.

The Great Hall is a 31,000-square-foot space located between the Stadium's exterior wall and the interior of the Stadium. Spanning from Gate 4 to Gate 6, it is covered overhead but has massive open-air archways, which help support the Yankees' "green initiative." It is home to large banners bearing the images of past Yankees greats from Babe Ruth and Lou Gehrig to more modern stars such as Don Mattingly and Paul O'Neill. A 24-foot-high-by-36-foot-wide 10mm true high-definition video board and a 5-foot-by-383-foot LED ribbon board immediately greet guests who enter through this portion of the Stadium.

The audio/visual experience at Yankee Stadium is highlighted by a 59-foot-high-by-101-foot-long 16mm true high-definition centerfield video board, which is flanked by two smaller video boards that display day-of-game lineups and out-of-town scores. Additionally, the entire length of the Terrace Level is spanned by a 3-foot-high, 1,279-foot long full-color LED ribbon board. A distributed sound system optimizes speaker placement for audio quality vastly superior to that in the original Stadium. The entire Stadium is built with a future-proof infrastructure designed by Cisco Systems that is easily adaptable to new technologies.

A 7,000-square-foot state-of-the-art banquet and conference center is designed to meet the needs of guests who wish to host business functions in the ballpark.

The Great Hall stretches from Gate 4 to Gate 6.

URBAN PLANNING

Babe Ruth Plaza facilitates pedestrian movement outside Yankee Stadium

The site for Yankee Stadium was in part selected for its proximity to mass transit. Like the original Stadium, it is served at the 161st Street/Yankee Stadium subway stop by the No. 4, B and D trains.

Metro-North offers train service to Yankee Stadium from anywhere in its service territory. For more information, call the MTA at (212) 532-4900 or visit www.mta.info.

As in previous years, Yankee Stadium is accessible by ferry service (800-53-FERRY) and New York City Transit bus lines (718-330-1234).

Pedestrian access points are located at Yankee Stadium's four gates: Gate 2 on Jerome Avenue and 164th Street; Gate 4 at Jerome Avenue and 161st Street; Gate 6 at River Avenue and 161st Street and Gate 8 at River Avenue, south of 164th Street.

RETAIL & FOOD OPTIONS

Traditional baseball fare at Yankee Stadium

There are three distinct retail stores in Yankee Stadium—the 5,825-square-foot Home Plate Team Store in the Great Hall near Gate 4, which houses the largest selection of Yankees merchandise and memorabilia; the New Era Team Store on the Main Level, which sells caps and other Yankees merchandise; and the Great Hall Team Store at Gate 6, which sells various items and is open year-round.

Yankee Stadium is home to two premier dining establishments. The iconic Hard Rock Cafe is open year-round and houses music memorabilia and Yankees-related pieces in a 7,000 square-foot restaurant at Gate 6, and NYY Steak, located above the Hard Rock Cafe, offers an upscale dining experience.

More casual fare can be found at a New York-themed food court located on the third-base side of the Field Level concourse.

Membership restaurants include the Audi Yankees Club on the H&R Block Suite Level and the Mohegan Sun Sports Bar above Monument Park in center field.

DISABLED SERVICES

Yankee Stadium strives to provide an accessible environment for all of its guests. Wheelchair accessible and aisle transfer seats are available at various price points and locations, and include the Yankees' Premium Offerings seat locations.

There are two dedicated open-captioning video boards for guests who are deaf or have hearing impairments: one in left field, just below Section 233B, and one in right field, just below Section 206. Captioning is also provided on the right-center field televisions, the high-definition video board in the Great Hall, high-definition video monitors throughout Yankee Stadium and on the video board in the New York Yankees Museum presented by Bank of America.

The Yankees extend their appreciation to those who participated in periodic outreach meetings led by United Spinal Association, which helped build a Stadium that Acting U.S. Attorney for the Southern District of New York Lev Dassin called, "a model of accessibility to people with disabilities."

BRONX INCENTIVES

Yankee Stadium is one of the premier building projects to take place in the Bronx in the last 50 years. The hard work and dedication of engineers, architects and construction professionals in building and designing the Stadium makes the facility one of the most impressive and fan-friendly venues in Major League Baseball. Equally important was the project's dedication to support local community groups, institutions and residents as the Yankees remain devoted to the long-term development of the Bronx.

Building a new state-of-the-art facility required an army of talented and experienced professionals. As part of the Yankees' commitment to ensure that the Stadium project creates economic opportunities in the Bronx, the Yankees made a concerted effort to recruit a wide range of vendors and employees from the local community. Of the 190 contracts awarded, 63 were allotted to Bronx-based businesses (accounting for over 33 percent of the contracts and resulting in $133 million in contracts to Bronx-based businesses). The Yankees also stayed committed to hiring at least 25 percent of the total workforce from Bronx residents, again providing incentive to the surrounding community.

Yankee Stadium Firsts

Starting Lineups for Opening Game
4/16/09 vs. Cleveland

YANKEES:	INDIANS:
Derek Jeter-SS	Grady Sizemore-CF
Johnny Damon-LF	Mark DeRosa-3B
Mark Teixeira-1B	Victor Martinez-1B
Nick Swisher-RF	Jhonny Peralta-SS
Jorge Posada-C	Shin-Soo Choo-DH
Robinson Cano-2B	Ben Francisco-RF
Hideki Matsui-DH	Kelly Shoppach-C
Cody Ransom-3B	Tony Graffanino-2B
Brett Gardner-CF	Trevor Crowe-LF
CC Sabathia-P	Cliff Lee-P

BATTING
First Out: Cleveland's Grady Sizemore, first-inning ground out to first base on 4/16/09
Hit: Johnny Damon first-inning single to center on 4/16/09 vs. Cleveland
Home Run: Jorge Posada, solo, fifth-inning, to center off Cliff Lee on 4/16/09 vs. Cleveland
Run Scored: Cleveland's Ben Francisco in the fourth inning on 4/16/09
RBI: Cleveland's Kelly Shoppach in the fourth inning on 4/16/09
Stolen Base: Johnny Damon in the first inning on 4/17/09 vs. Cleveland

PITCHING
Pitch (Result): CC Sabathia to Cleveland's Grady Sizemore in the first inning on 4/16/09 (ball)
Win: Cleveland's Cliff Lee on 4/16/09 (10-2 Cleveland victory)
Save: Mariano Rivera on 4/17/09 vs. Cleveland
Strikeout: CC Sabathia on 4/16/09 vs. Cleveland (Victor Martinez, swinging, first inning)

GAMES
Exhibition Game: April 3, 2009 vs. Chicago Cubs (7-4 Yankees victory)
Regular Season Game: April 16, 2009 vs. Cleveland (10-2 Indians victory)

OTHER
Star-Spangled Banner Performer: Kelly Clarkson
God Bless America Singer: Ronan Tynan
Ceremonial First Pitch: 4/16/09 vs. Cleveland, Yogi Berra

YANKEE STADIUM TIMELINE

JUNE 15, 2005 – The Yankees announce plans for a new Yankee Stadium to be constructed on parkland north of 161st Street – adjacent to the original Stadium's longtime site.

AUGUST 16, 2006 – The Yankees break ground for Yankee Stadium at a ceremony featuring George M. Steinbrenner, New York Governor George Pataki, New York City Mayor Michael Bloomberg, Bronx Borough President Adolfo Carrion and Commissioner Bud Selig.

OCTOBER 2006 – The first concrete is poured.

DECEMBER 2007 – The first piece of frieze is put in place.

DECEMBER 2007 – The Stadium is considered 50 percent completed.

JANUARY 14-15, 2008 – Limestone Panels containing "YANKEE STADIUM" gold lettering are installed above Gate 4.

MARCH 29, 2008 – Eagle medallions inspired by those on the 1923 Stadium are lifted into place above Gate 4.

APRIL 2008 – Frieze installation is completed.

MAY 1, 2008 – A "topping off" ceremony is held to commemorate the completion of Yankee Stadium's steel structure.

MAY 2008 – The foul poles are installed, along with the first seats.

JUNE 18, 2008 – The Yankees hold their first press conference at the new Yankee Stadium, announcing a long-term agreement with Seminole Hard Rock Entertainment to open a Hard Rock Cafe near Gate 6. In addition, the Yankees introduce the newly-branded NYY Steak, a prime steakhouse to be located in Yankee Stadium.

SEPTEMBER 19, 2008 – The massive, blue, backlit "YANKEE STADIUM" lettering above Gate 4 is hoisted and installed.

OCTOBER 15, 2008 – The first sections of sod are laid.

OCTOBER 2008 – Lighting in the interior bowl is tested for the first time.

NOVEMBER 8, 2008 – Yankees executives and former players, including Scott Brosius, David Cone, Paul O' Neill and Jeff Nelson, along with 60 local Bronx high school youth groups remove home plate, the pitcher's rubber and pails of dirt from the original Stadium and install them in the new Yankee Stadium. The participating Bronx youth groups—Youth Force 2020, led by Turner Construction Company, and the ACE Mentor Program at Yankee Stadium, guided by Tishman Speyer—took part in Yankees-sponsored after-school programs relating to the construction and engineering of the new Yankee Stadium.

JANUARY 23, 2009 – The front office moves in, bringing World Series trophies from 1977 and 2000 to the new building.

FEBRUARY 2009 – Plaques and monuments are placed in the new Monument Park.

APRIL 3-4, 2009 – The first exhibition games are played vs. the Chicago Cubs.

APRIL 16, 2009 – The home opener is played vs. the Cleveland Indians.

Yankee Stadium by the Numbers

THE STRUCTURE

Location: In the Bronx, bounded by 164th St. (north); 161st St. (south); Jerome Ave. (west); River Ave. (east)

Mailing address: Yankee Stadium, One East 161st Street, Bronx, NY 10451

Switchboard phone number: (718) 293-4300

Architect: Populous (formerly HOK Sport)

Construction: Turner Construction

Developer: Tishman Speyer

Square footage: approximately 1.3 million square feet

Distance around the building: 4,755 linear feet

Size of entire site: 634,335 square feet or 14.56 acres

Number of gates: Four (Gates 2, 4, 6 and 8)

Height at highest point: The top of the frieze is 134 feet, 7 inches above Field Level.

Internet bandwidth: 135 megabits

Light bulbs (number of): 20,000

Main centerfield video board size: 59-feet-by-101-feet

Ribbon board ringing the Terrace Level: 3-feet-by-1,279-feet

Great Hall size: 31,000 square feet

Great Hall LED ribbon board: 5-feet-by-383-feet

Great Hall high-definition video board: 24-feet-by-36-feet

Number of player flags in the Great Hall: 10 double-sided

Seating Capacity: 50,291

FIELD

Surface: Kentucky bluegrass grown at DeLea Sod Farms in Pilesgrove, N.J.

Acreage: 3.14 acres, including the bullpens

Dimensions: LF 318'; LC 399'; CF 408'; RC 385'; RF 314'

Outfield walls height: From left-field foul pole, wall is 8-feet, 6-inches high until the Yankees bullpen, where it gradually descends to 8 feet at the right-field foul pole.

Distance from the plate to the backstop: 52 feet, 4 inches

Yankees bullpen size: averages approximately 82 feet wide by 32 feet deep

Opponents bullpen size: averages approximately 85 feet wide by 30 feet deep

Distance of batter's eye glass to home plate: 432 feet away and 19 feet off the ground

Height of Bleachers Café above the field: 37 feet

Infield foundation: Sand-based

Feet below street level: approximately 8 feet on average

Drainage pipe length: 14,000 linear feet

Irrigation pipe: 17,100 linear feet

Irrigation heads: 116

Distance from first base or third base to the nearest spectator: 43 feet

Concourse (average width): 32 feet

Foul poles height: 90 feet

MATERIALS

Concrete: approximately 45,000 cubic yards

Excavation: approximately 363,000 cubic yards

Rebar: approximately 4,000 tons

Structural steel: approximately 11,800 tons in over 30,000 pieces

Piles driven: 1,675 piles averaging 80 feet long

Stone: Indiana Limestone and Deer Isle Granite

Frieze: approximately 1,400 feet long with 300 tons of structural steel

Doors: 1,300

Gallons of paint: 15,000

Length of electrical wire: 946 miles (*The distance from Yankee Stadium to George M. Steinbrenner Field in Tampa is approximately 1,012 miles*)

Length of Ethernet cable (CAT 6A): 227 miles

Power required to turn on sports lighting: 3,500 KVA

Power required to turn on video board: 2,000 KVA

IN THE BUILDING

Ticket windows: 26 Total, including 19 by Gate 4, four by the Bleachers and three in-Stadium

Concessions (fixed): 25

Concessions (moveable): more than 100

Total concessions points of sale: approximately 444

Retail locations (fixed): approximately 10

Retail locations (moveable): approximately 46

Total retail points of sale: 86

Width of seats: 19 inches to 24 inches

Width of aisles: 4 feet

Legroom in front of seats: 33 inches to 39 inches

Number of elevators: 16 (two each at Gates 2, 4, 6 and 8 and eight in the Great Hall)

Stairways: 30

Pedestrian ramps: 2 (at Gates 2 and 6)

Video monitors: approximately 1,400 flat-panel, high-definition monitors

Cup holders: approximately 45,000

Toilet fixtures: approximately 878

Men's fixtures ratio in non-premium seating: approximately 1 fixture per 78 men (based on 50% male / 50% female attendance)

Women's fixtures ratio in non-premium seating: approximately 1 fixture per 75 women (based on 50% male / 50% female attendance)

Family bathrooms: 12

Yankees clubhouse dressing area: 3,344 square feet

Visitors clubhouse dressing area: 1,496 square feet

Other Events at the Current Yankee Stadium

College Football

Notre Dame-27, Army-3 **11/20/10**
The first football game at the current Yankee Stadium marked the 50th all-time meeting between the two teams. Pregame festivities included a parachute jump from the Army's Black Daggers, followed by the national anthem sung by actor Patrick Wilson. Heisman Trophy winners Johnny Lujack of Notre Dame and Pete Dawkins of Army served as honorary captains, joining Yankees Managing General Partner Hal Steinbrenner for the coin toss. The crowd of 54,251 was the largest ever at the current Yankee Stadium.

New Era Pinstripe Bowl **12/30/10**
Syracuse-36, Kansas State-34
The inaugural New Era Pinstripe Bowl marked the second-ever college football bowl game in the Bronx (also Gotham Bowl in 1962). Following an exciting week of events throughout New York City during the week leading up the game, Syracuse and Kansas State played an instant classic that was decided by one play – a failed two-point conversion by the Wildcats with just over one minute left in regulation.

The inaugural New Era Pinstripe Bowl was played Dec. 30, 2010.

Concerts

JAY-Z/Eminem Concerts **9/13-14/10**
Yankee Stadium played host to its first-ever concerts, featuring Grammy Award winners JAY-Z and Eminem in a two-night affair. The sold-out shows featured crowds of 45,434 and 46,272, respectively. The concerts marked the second half of a home-and-home series of shows for New York City-native JAY-Z and Eminem, who was raised in the Detroit metropolitan area, as the pair also performed at Detroit's Comerica Park on September 2-3, 2010. Guest performers over the two nights at Yankee Stadium included Beyoncé, Mary J. Blige, Dr. Dre, 50 Cent, Kanye West and Coldplay lead singer Chris Martin.

JAY-Z/Eminem Concert

Boxing

Press Conference to Announce **9/10/09**
Manny Pacquiao-Miguel Cotto Fight
Yankee Stadium played host to a press conference to announce the boxing match between Miguel Cotto and Manny Pacquiao, which took place on November 14, 2009, at the MGM Grand Garden in Las Vegas. The free event took place on the field just beyond first base.

As the main event in Yankee Stadium's first boxing card, Miguel Cotto fought Yuri Foreman on June 5, 2010.

Miguel Cotto TKO (9th Rd.) Yuri Foreman **6/5/10**
Boxing returned to the Bronx for the first time in 34 years with "Stadium Slugfest," as Miguel Cotto and Yuri Foreman squared off in the Yankee Stadium outfield on June 5, 2010 in the main event. In front of a crowd of 20,272, Cotto recorded a ninth-round technical knockout after landing a left-hand hook to the body to win the WBA Super Welterweight title. Foreman slipped in the seventh round and appeared to twist his knee. In a bizarre turn, the fight was temporarily halted in the eighth, when a towel was thrown in the ring from Foreman's corner. But referee Arthur Mercante felt Foreman was fit enough to fight through it and allowed the bout to continue.

Other Performers and Events

Joel and Victoria Osteen – "A Night of Hope" **4/25/09**
In the first non-baseball event at the current Yankee Stadium, 34,195 people were on hand for a celebration of faith.

NYU Graduation **5/13/09**
Commencement address was given by Secretary of State Hillary Rodham Clinton.

Victoria Secret Model Search **10/3/09**
Yankee Stadium was the home for an open casting call to select Runway Angels to walk in the 2009 Victoria's Secret Fashion Show. Five finalists were selected from the nearly 3,000 entrants that tried out at Yankee Stadium.

Damon Runyon 5K Charity Run/Walk **11/15/09**
More than 2,500 participants including cancer patients and survivors, family, friends, supporters and Damon Runyon scientists ran or walked the Yankee Stadium concourses, warning track and playing field. Proceeds went to support young scientists funded by the Damon Runyon Cancer Research Foundation.

PepsiCo Global Investor Relations Meeting **3/22-23/10**
PepsiCo, the second-largest food and beverage company in the world, hosted 300 senior executives and investors at the two-day event, which included discussions regarding the company's long-term vision and strategies.

NYU Graduation **5/12/10**
Commencement address was given by award-winning actor and NYU alumnus Alec Baldwin.

CBS Radio Expo **6/26/10**
An all-day expo featuring radio personalities and celebrities as well as live entertainment in the Yankee Stadium Great Hall.

Damon Runyon 5K Charity Run/Walk **8/15/10**

PSAL Football Championship **12/7/10**
Ft. Hamilton H.S.-8, Abraham Lincoln H.S.-6

Winter Wonderland **12/17/10**
Yankee Stadium transformed into the North Pole for the 2010 Bronx Winter Wonderland event. Approximately 5,000 children from the Bronx were treated to a holiday extravaganza in Yankee Stadium's Great Hall, complete with Christmas decorations, festive holiday music and complimentary food and beverages. Santa set up his workshop in the Great Hall, handing out a toy to each child in attendance. The Yankees purchased $25,000 in toys, and Mattel donated 2,000 toys.

Attendance Records

Yankees All-Time Attendance Records (Regular Season)

Largest Single-Season Home Attendance (2008).. 4,298,543
Largest Single-Season Road Attendance (2004)... 3,308,666
Largest Single-Season Combined Home-Road Attendance (2006) 7,325,051
Largest Crowd in Baseball History (Exhibition Game for Roy Campanella - NYY vs. LAD, at the L.A. Coliseum, 5/7/1959) ... 93,103
Most Consecutive Seasons with 4 Million Attendance in Baseball History: 4 (2005-2008)

2010 Regular Season Attendance

HOME

Largest Night Game Attendance (vs. Boston, 8/6/10)... 49,555*
Largest Day Game Attendance (vs. Boston, 8/7/10).. 49,716

ROAD

Largest Night Game Attendance (at Los Angeles-NL, 6/25-27/10)................................... 56,000
Largest Day Game Attendance (at Los Angeles-AL, 4/24/10)....................................... 43,390

OVERALL

Yankees Home Attendance (81 games, 81 dates).................................... 3,765,807 (46,491 avg.)
Yankees Road Attendance (81 games, 81 dates)................................... 2,830,138 (34,940 avg.)
Yankees Total Attendance (162 games, 162 dates).. 6,595,945
Largest Single-Game Home Attendance at the current Yankee Stadium (ALDS Game 3 vs. Minnesota, 10/9/10).......... 50,840
*Largest Regular Season Single-Game Home Attendance at the current Yankee Stadium

Remodeled Original Yankee Stadium 1976-2008 (Regular Season)

Largest Single-Game Home Attendance, Day (vs. Oakland, 4/10/1998, Opening Day)..................... 56,717
Largest Single-Game Home Attendance, Night (vs. N.Y. Mets, 6/17/1997)............................. 56,253
Largest Day Doubleheader Home Attendance (vs. Detroit, 10/4/1980) 55,410
Largest Twi-Night Doubleheader Attendance (vs. Baltimore, 9/10/1983) 55,605
Largest Weekday/Day/Non-Opening Day Crowd (vs. N.Y. Mets, Wed., 6/18/1997)....................... 56,278
Largest Opening Day Home Attendance (vs. Oakland, 4/10/1998)..................................... 56,717
Largest Old-Timers' Day Attendance (vs. Chicago-AL, 7/25/1998).................................... 55,642
Largest Home Series Attendance, three-game series (vs. N.Y. Mets, 6/4-6/1999).................... 168,404
Largest Home Series Attendance, all series (vs. Boston, 9/16-17/2006, 4 games, 2 day-night DH)....... 220,481
Largest Single-Season Home Attendance (2008)... 4,298,543

	Top 10 Crowds at Remodeled Yankee Stadium (1976-2008)*				Top 10 Regular Season Crowds at Remodeled Yankee Stadium (1976-2008)		
1.	vs. Texas	10/7/99, ALDS Game 2	57,485	1.	vs. Oakland	4/10/98, Opening Day	56,717
2.	vs. Cleveland	9/30/97, ALDS Game 1	57,398	2.	vs. Oakland	4/11/97, Opening Day	56,710
3.	vs. Texas	9/29/98, ALDS Game 1	57,362	3.	vs. Texas	4/4/94, Opening Day	56,706
4.	vs. Texas	9/30/98, ALDS Game 2	57,360	4.	vs. Kansas City	4/12/93, Opening Day	56,704
	vs. Cleveland	10/2/97, ALDS Game 2	57,360	5.	vs. Detroit	4/9/99, Opening Day	56,583
6.	vs. Texas	10/1/96, ALDS Game 1	57,205	6.	vs. Boston	4/7/92, Opening Day	56,572
7.	vs. Boston	10/13/99, ALCS Game 1	57,181	7.	vs. Kansas City	4/9/96, Opening Day	56,329
8.	vs. Boston	10/14/99, ALCS Game 2	57,180	8.	vs. N.Y. Mets	6/6/99	56,294
9.	vs. Seattle	10/3/95, ALDS Game 1	57,178	9.	vs. N.Y. Mets	6/18/97	56,278
10.	vs. Texas	10/2/96, ALDS Game 2	57,156	10.	vs. N.Y. Mets	6/17/97	56,253

*All postseason games

Pre-Remodeled Original Yankee Stadium, 1923-1973 (Regular Season)

Please note: Official Attendance Records are not available prior to 1938.

Largest Single-Game Home Attendance, Day (vs. Boston, 9/26/1948) 69,755*
Largest Single-Game Home Attendance, Night (vs. Boston, 5/26/1947)............................. 74,747
Largest Doubleheader Home Attendance (vs. Boston, 5/30/1938)................................... 81,841
Largest Opening Day Home Attendance (vs. Washington, 4/19/1946)............................... 54,826*
Largest Old-Timers' Day Attendance (vs. Boston, 8/9/1958)....................................... 67,916
Largest Home Series Attendance, all series (vs. Cleveland 6/11-13, 4 games, DH on 6/12)............. 186,151
Largest Single-Season Total Attendance (1948) 2,373,901
According to published reports, the Stadium's first Opening Day (vs. Boston, 4/18/23) had an estimated attendance of 74,200.

Home Ballparks

TOTAL ATTENDANCE

Hilltop Park (1903-12, 10 seasons, 168th St. & Broadway, Manhattan).............................. 3,451,542
Polo Grounds (1913-22, 10 seasons, 157th St. & 8th Avenue, Manhattan) 6,220,031
Pre-Remodeled Original Yankee Stadium (1923-73, 51 seasons, 161st St. & River Avenue, Bronx) 64,333,705
Shea Stadium (1974-75, 2 seasons, 126th St. & Roosevelt Avenue, Queens).......................... 2,561,123
Remodeled Original Yankee Stadium (1976-2008, 33 seasons, 161st St. & River Avenue, Bronx).......... 87,625,300*
Yankee Stadium (2009-10, 2 seasons, One East 161st St., Bronx, NY)................................ 7,485,163
TOTAL 171,676,864
Game vs. Anaheim on 4/15/1998 was played at Shea Stadium when Yankee Stadium was closed by the City of New York after an expansion joint fell on 4/13/1998.

New York Yankees
YANKEE STADIUM

Yankee Stadium Map

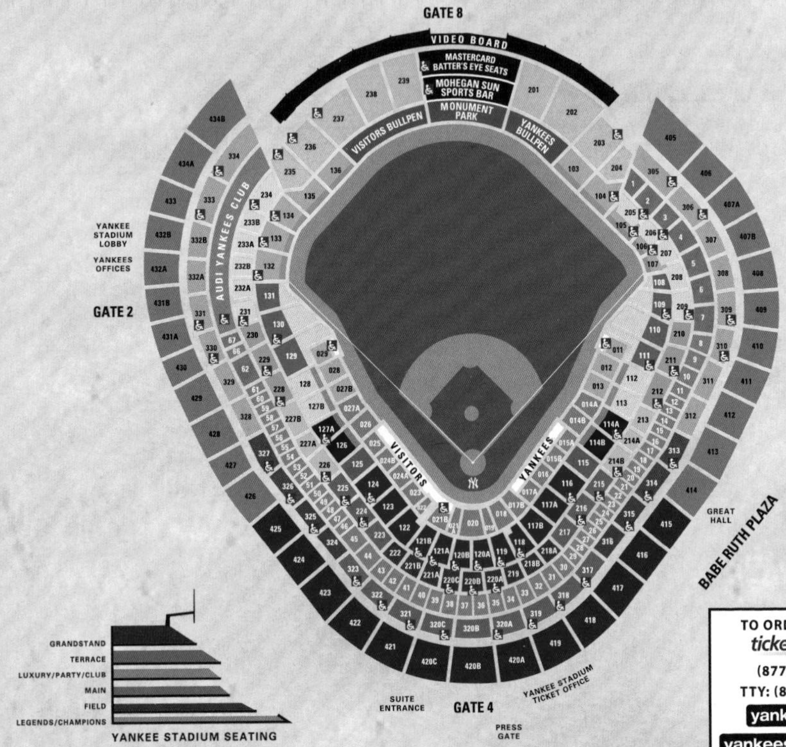

GATE 8

VIDEO BOARD

MASTERCARD & BATTER'S EYE SEATS

MOHEGAN SUN SPORTS BAR

MONUMENT PARK

VISITORS BULLPEN

YANKEES BULLPEN

VISITORS

YANKEES

AUDI YANKEES CLUB

YANKEE STADIUM LOBBY

YANKEES OFFICES

GATE 2

GATE 6

NYY

Hard Rock

YANKEES TEAM STORE

GREAT HALL PLAZA

BABE RUTH PLAZA

MasterCard

Preferred by

YANKEE STADIUM SEATING

GRANDSTAND
TERRACE
LUXURY/PARTY/CLUB
MAIN
FIELD
LEGENDS/CHAMPIONS

SUITE ENTRANCE

GATE 4

YANKEE STADIUM TICKET OFFICE

PRESS GATE

TO ORDER TICKETS:
ticketmaster
(877) 469-9849
TTY: (800) 943-4327
yankees.com
yankeesbeisbol.com

ALCOHOL-FREE SEATING
Sections 407A and 433

ATMs presented by Bank of America
Great Hall: Adjacent to the Guest
Services Booth near Gate 6
Field Level: Sections 127B-128
Main Level: Sections 214A and 222
Terrace/Grandstand Level: Sections
313, 320C and 330-331
Bleachers: Section 239

AUDI YANKEES CLUB
H&R Block Suite Level

BUDWEISER HALL OF FAME LOUNGE
H&R Block Suite Level

ELEVATORS
Yankee Stadium's 16 public elevators
are located in the Great Hall and
throughout Yankee Stadium.

ESCALATORS
Escalators are located near
Gates 4 and 6.

FAMILY RESTROOMS
Field Level: Sections 106, 124 and 130
Delta SKY360° Suite: Section 221B
Main Level: Sections 219, 227A and 234
Terrace/Grandstand Level: Sections 311, 316,
327 and 333
Bleachers: Section 201

FIRST AID
Field Level: Section 128
Main Level: Section 221
Terrace/Grandstand Level: Section 320C

GREAT HALL
The Great Hall is located along Babe Ruth Plaza
between the exterior wall and the interior of
Yankee Stadium between
Gates 4 and 6.

GUEST SERVICES BOOTHS/KIOSKS
Great Hall: Near Gate 6
Field Level: Section 128
Guest Services kiosks are located in and around
Yankee Stadium to assist guests.

H&R BLOCK SUITE LOUNGE   H&R BLOCK
H&R Block Suite Level

MALIBU ROOFTOP DECK
Terrace/Grandstand Level:
Adjacent to Section 310

MERCHANDISE STORES
Yankees Team Store-Home Plate:
Great Hall, near Gate 4
Yankees Team Store-Great Hall:
Gate 6
Yankees Women's Team Store: 5TH & OCEAN
Section 114A
New Era Team Store: NEW ERA
Main Level, behind home plate
Monument Park Store:
Field Level, behind centerfield

YANKEES-STEINER
COLLECTIBLES STORE
Field Level: Section 114B

MOHEGAN SUN   Mohegan Sun
SPORTS BAR
Center field above Monument Park

RAMPS
Adjacent to Gates 2 and 6

Tommy Bahama's BAR
Great Hall, near Gate 4

NOTICE: All persons specifically consent to and are subject to metal detector and physical pat-down inspections prior to entry. Any person or property that could affect the safety of Yankee Stadium occupants/property shall be denied entry.

WARNING: During all batting practices, fielding practices, warm-ups and the course of the game and postseason game experience, hard hit baseballs and bats and fragments thereof may be thrown or hit into the stands, concourses and concessions areas. For everyone's safety, please stay alert and be aware of your surroundings. Any guest who is concerned with his or her seat location should contact any guest services representative for an alternate seat location.

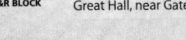

SEATING CATEGORY	FULL SEASON PRICE	41-GAME/ 20-GAME/ PARTIAL SEASON PRICE	ADVANCE PRICE	GAME-DAY PRICE
FIELD MVP*	$260	$275	$325	$325
FIELD	$235	$250	$275	$300
FIELD	$225	N/A	$250	$275
FIELD**	$175	N/A	$235	$250
FIELD	$150	N/A	$200	$225
FIELD	$110	N/A	$125	$150
FIELD	$100	N/A	$125	$150
FIELD	$80	$90	$95	$100
FIELD	$75	$85	$95	$100
MAIN	$125	N/A	$150	$175
MAIN	$110	N/A	$125	$150
MAIN	$80	N/A	$90	$95
MAIN	$65	$70	$75	$80
MAIN	$50	$55	$57	$60
TERRACE†	$65	$75	$80	$85
TERRACE††	$55	$65	$70	$75
TERRACE††	$40	$45	$48	$50
GRANDSTAND	$25	$25	$29	$30
GRANDSTAND	$20	$20	$22	$23
BLEACHERS§	$15/$5§§	$15/$5§§	$15/$5§§	$15/$5§§
MASTERCARD BATTER'S EYE SEATS	N/A	N/A	$125	$135
MOHEGAN SUN SPORTS BAR	N/A	N/A	$95	$100
AUDI YANKEES CLUB	N/A	N/A	$160‡	$175‡

LEGENDS SUITE	
CHAMPIONS SUITE	For more information on full- and partial-season Yankees Premium plans, please visit yankees.com, call (212) YANKEES or e-mail premium@yankees.com.
DELTA SKY360° SUITE	
LUXURY SUITES	
PARTY CITY PARTY SUITES/ CLUB SUITE (62)	
JIM BEAM SUITE‡‡	

* Wheelchair accessible seating in Sections 116 and 124 is $235 for Full Season price, $250 for 41-Game/20-Game/Partial Season price, $275 for advance price and $300 for game-day price.

** Wheelchair accessible seating in Sections 114A and 127A is $110 for Full Season price, $125 for advance price and $150 for game-day price.

† Wheelchair accessible seating in Sections 315, 317-319, 321-323 and 325 is $25 for Full Season and 41-Game/20-Game/Partial Season price, $29 for advance price and $30 for game-day price.

† † Wheelchair accessible seating in Sections 305, 306, 309, 310, 313, 314, 326, 327, 330, 331, 333 and 334 is $20 for Full Season and 41-Game/20-Game/Partial Season price, $22 for advance price and $23 for game-day price.

§ Wheelchair accessible seating in the Bleachers is $5 for Full Season, 41-Game/20-Game/Partial Season, advance and game-day price.

§§ Designated seats in Sections 201 and 239 are considered obstructed and are sold for $5.

‡ Included in the price is a $65 charge for food and nonalcoholic beverages.

‡ ‡ Wheelchair accessible seating in the Jim Beam Suite is located in Sections 320A and 320C.

The game-day ticket price is effective as of 12:01 a.m. on the day the game initially is scheduled to be played.

Be advised that the Yankees reserve the right to take appropriate action against individuals who fraudulently obtain wheelchair accessible and companion seats, including, without limitation, ejection and legal action.

The term "premium games" is defined as the Opening Day game, the Old-Timers' Day game and all home games played against the Boston Red Sox and New York Mets.

Getting to Yankee Stadium

Yankee Stadium, One East 161st Street, Bronx, NY 10451
Yankee Stadium is accessible from the Major Deegan Expressway. (Interstate 87) at the following exits:

 Northbound I-87: Exit 3 (Grand Concourse and E. 138th St.), Exit 4 (E. 149th St.) and Exit 5 (E. 161st St.)

Southbound I-87: Exit 6 (E. 153rd St. and River Ave.) and Exit 5 (E. 161st St.)

BY CAR

For directions from points other than those listed below, as well as parking locations surrounding Yankee Stadium, visit yankees.com.

MANHATTAN

From East Side: FDR Drive north to Exit 18 (Willis Ave. Bridge). Cross bridge. Follow signs for Major Deegan (I-87) north.

From West Side: Henry Hudson Pkwy. (Route 9A) north to Exit 14. Follow Cross Bronx Expy. (I-95 north) to Major Deegan (I-87) south.

BROOKLYN/QUEENS

Brooklyn-Queens Expy.: Take BQE (I-278) east to RFK Bridge (formerly Triboro Bridge). Cross bridge. Follow signs for Bronx and Major Deegan (I-87) north.

LONG ISLAND

From Throgs Neck or Whitestone Bridge:

• **Option 1:** Follow signs for I-95 south, which becomes westbound Cross Bronx Expy. Proceed to Major Deegan (I-87) south.

• **Option 2:** Follow signs for westbound Bruckner Expy. (I-278). From Bruckner, take exit for Major Deegan (I-87) north.

From RFK Bridge (formerly Triboro Bridge): Once over bridge, follow signs for Bronx and Major Deegan (I-87) north.

WESTCHESTER

From Bronx River Pkwy. or Hutchinson River Pkwy.: Take Cross County Pkwy. west to I-87 south, which becomes Major Deegan.

NEW JERSEY/GEORGE WASHINGTON BRIDGE

• **Option 1:** Take eastbound Cross Bronx Expy. (I-95 north). Exit for Major Deegan (I-87).

• **Option 2:** Take eastbound Cross Bronx Expy. (I-95 north). Use Exit 2A (Jerome Avenue). Make right off exit and continue on Jerome Avenue to Yankee Stadium.

• **Option 3:** Take Exit 2 (Harlem River Drive). Once on Harlem River Drive south, take Exit 23 toward W. 155th St. At first light, turn left onto W. 155th St. Cross Macombs Dam Bridge. Yankee Stadium is ahead.

CONNECTICUT

From Merritt Pkwy.: Merritt Pkwy. becomes Hutchinson River Pkwy. Proceed to westbound Cross County Pkwy., then to I-87 south, which becomes Major Deegan.

Guests and employees are encouraged to utilize public transportation in order to reduce CO_2 emissions and reliance on foreign oil.

BY SUBWAY

The Yankee Stadium subway stop is on E. 161st St. and River Ave. The No. 4 train and B and D trains make stops there. For more information, call (718) 330-1234 or visit www.mta.info.

BY TRAIN

Metro-North offers train service to Yankee Stadium from anywhere in its service territory. For more information, call the MTA at (212) 532-4900 or visit www.mta.info.

BY BUS

The Bx6 and Bx13 buses stop at 161st St. and River Ave. The Bx1 and Bx2 buses stop at 161st St. and the Grand Concourse — a short walk from Yankee Stadium. For information, call (718) 330-1234 or visit www.mta.info.

BY FERRY

For information, call (800) 53-FERRY or visit www.nywaterway.com.

History of Original Yankee Stadium

One year after changing the course of Baseball history with the purchase of Babe Ruth from the Boston Red Sox, the Yankees made another acquisition that would forever alter the way the game was watched.

On February 5, 1921, the Yankees issued a press release announcing the purchase of 10 acres of property in the west Bronx. The land, purchased from the estate of William Waldorf Astor for $675,000, sat directly across the Harlem River from the Manhattan-situated Polo Grounds, which the Yankees had been unhappily sharing with their landlord, the New York Giants of the National League, since 1913.

The relationship between the clubs crumbled after the 1920 season when the Yankees' attendance—boosted by their new slugging sensation—doubled to almost 1.3 million, approximately 25 percent more than that of the Giants. In 1921, the Giants asked the Yankees to vacate the Polo Grounds as soon as possible. With their departure from the Polo Grounds now inevitable, Yankees co-owners Jacob Ruppert and Tillinghast l'Hommedieu Huston set out to build a spectacular ballpark of their own, Baseball's first triple-decked structure. With an advertised capacity of 70,000, it would also be the first to be labeled a "stadium."

Original plans by the architect—the Osborn Engineering Company of Cleveland, Ohio—had the Stadium triple-decked and roofed all the way around. An early press release, in fact, described the Yankees' new home as a field enclosed with towering embattlements rendering the events inside "impenetrable to all human eyes, save those of aviators." But the initial grand design was quickly scaled back with the triple-decked grandstand not reaching either foul pole. Contrary to the owners'

wishes, the action would be visible from the elevated trains that passed by the outfield, as well as from the buildings that would spring up across River Avenue. Fortunately, a purely decorative element survived the project's early downsizing and would become the park's most recognizable feature. A 15-foot-high copper frieze would adorn the front of the roof, which covered much of the Stadium's third deck. It would give Yankee Stadium a stately dignity that no park has possessed—either before or since.

The new stadium would favor left-handed power with the right-field foul pole only 295 feet from home plate (though the right-field fence would shoot out to 429 feet in right-center). The left-field pole measured only 281 feet from the plate, but right-handed hitters would be neutralized by a 395-foot left field and a whopping 460 feet to left-center. The new stadium would also be patron-friendly, boasting an unheard of "eight toilet rooms for men and as many for women scattered throughout the stands and bleachers." (After the Stadium was remodeled 50 years later, it included more than 50 restrooms.) The club's executive offices would be moved from Midtown Manhattan and relocated between the main and mezzanine decks with an electric elevator connecting them with the main entrance.

The construction contract was awarded to New York's White Construction Company on May 5, 1922, with the edict that the job be completed "at a definite price" of $2.5 million by Opening Day 1923. Incredibly, it was. In only 284 working days, Yankee Stadium was ready for its inaugural game on April 18, 1923 vs. the Boston Red Sox.

An announced crowd of 74,200 fans packed Yankee Stadium while thousands more milled around outside after the fire department finally ordered the gates closed. Before the game began, John Philip Sousa and the Seventh Regiment Band led both clubs to the flagpole in deep center field, where the American flag and the Yankees' 1922 pennant were raised. Appropriately, Ruth christened his new home with a three-run homer to cap a four-run third inning as the Yankees coasted to a 4-1 win over the Boston Red Sox.

Because it was widely recognized that Ruth's tremendous drawing power made the new stadium possible, *New York Evening Telegram* sportswriter Fred Lieb dubbed it "The House That Ruth Built." Later that season, the Stadium

Yankee Stadium in the 1920s

hosted the first of 37 World Series, as the Yankees won their first World Championship, defeating their former landlord, the Giants. Of course, as the original Stadium became the stage for a staggering 26 world titles, it would also become known as "The Home of Champions."

In its early years, when wooden bleachers surrounded the outfield, a grass slope rose toward the outfield walls from foul pole to foul pole. Outfielders, especially Ruth in right, routinely backed up the small hill to pull down fly balls. Advertising signs lined the tops of the bleachers except in right-center, where a lone manually operated wooden scoreboard was large enough to record 12 innings for games played by every club in the two major leagues. Over the years, the board would be replaced by more modern models. The Yankees, in fact, would unveil Baseball's first electronic message board in 1959.

By 1928, the Stadium was ready for its first major face-lift. The triple-decked grandstand in left field was extended beyond the foul pole and several rows of box seats were removed in order to extend the left-field foul pole distance to 301 feet. The right-field grandstand was extended in 1937, allowing for "upper-deck" home runs in both directions. With the grandstand expansion, the remaining wooden bleachers were replaced with a concrete structure, and the distance to center field dropped from 490 feet to a still-distant 461 feet.

The original manual scoreboard

In 1932, the Yankees began their tradition of commemorating their heroes with monuments and plaques when they dedicated a monument to Manager Miller Huggins, who had died suddenly during the 1929 season. Five more monuments were added (one each for Lou Gehrig, Ruth, Mickey Mantle and Joe DiMaggio and one to honor the victims and heroes of the terrorists attacks of September 11, 2001) along with numerous plaques. For years, existing monuments were in the field of play in deep center field, and outfielders occasionally had to work around them to retrieve baseballs hit to that part of the park.

Except for the addition of lights in 1946, the look of Yankee Stadium remained relatively the same until the winter of 1966-67. Then, under the direction of the Yankees' new owner, CBS, the 44-year-old facility received a $1.5 million modernization, most of which was spent on 90 tons of paint. The brown concrete exterior was painted white as was the timeworn greenish copper frieze. Also, all of the grandstand seats went from green to blue, a color scheme that would be retained when the Stadium was completely remodeled after the 1973 season.

On August 8, 1972, after years of debate about the future of the aging ballpark, the Yankees signed a 30-year lease with the City of New York, which called for Yankee Stadium to be completely modernized in time for the 1976 season. After completing the Stadium's 50th-anniversary in 1973, the Yankees moved to Shea Stadium for two seasons while the majority of Yankee Stadium was torn down and rebuilt.

The most striking change of the modernization was the removal of the numerous obstructive steel columns that supported the second and third decks, as well as the roof. By "cantilevering" the upper decks and lowering the playing field while increasing the slope of the lower stands, sight lines for fans were dramatically improved. Capacity was reduced from 65,010 in 1973 to 54,028 upon reopening as wider plastic seats replaced wooden seats.

Of course, with the removal of the original roof, the Stadium almost lost its most-recognizable feature: the copper frieze. However, an innovative design concept included an exact replica of the frieze atop the new 560-foot-long scoreboard wall, which stretched across the rear of the bleachers. The board also included Baseball's first "telescreen," which could provide instant replays of the action by employing a then-incredible "nine shades of gray."

Yankee Stadium's exterior changed dramatically, as three escalator towers were added, one at each of the Stadium's three entrances. With seven additional

The original Yankee Stadium, shown during construction, was completed in only 284 working days.

rows of seats added to the upper deck, the already grand Stadium received an even more majestic look. A 138-foot Louisville Slugger-shaped smokestack, commonly called "The Bat," was added outside the Stadium near the home-plate entrance.

The renovated Stadium also saw the mammoth fence distances in left and center field greatly reduced as "Death Valley" in left-center was brought in from 457 feet to 430 feet, and straightaway center field was slimmed from 463 feet to 417 feet. Subsequent alterations prior to the 1985 and 1988 seasons brought fences in to the configuration that is now replicated in the current Yankee Stadium.

The remodeled original Yankee Stadium reopened on April 15, 1976—with the Yankees topping Minnesota, 11-4. Like its predecessor and successor, it hosted the World Series in its inaugural season. In fact, the remodeled Stadium hosted the Fall Classic in its first three seasons, as the Yankees followed their 1976 Series loss to Cincinnati by winning back-to-back World Series titles in 1977 and 1978 over the Dodgers.

As one of the world's most prestigious addresses, the original Yankee Stadium was also the home for scores of other sports, entertainment and cultural events. While the Yankees were on the road or in the offseason, the Stadium opened its gates to college and pro football, soccer, political assemblies, religious conventions, concerts and even the circus.

Boxing immediately found a home at Yankee Stadium with Benny Leonard winning a 15-round decision over Lou Tendler for the lightweight title just three months after the gates opened on July 23, 1923. When Muhammad Ali stopped Ken Norton on September 28, 1976, it marked the 30th championship fight at the Stadium. All previous title bouts had taken place between 1923 and 1959–perhaps none more memorable than the June 22, 1938, heavyweight championship match between Joe Louis and Germany's Max Schmeling. After suffering a knockout loss in the initial non-title encounter at the Stadium two years earlier, Louis—now the heavyweight champ—avenged his defeat with a stunning first-round KO in the rematch.

Football also became an immediate fixture at Yankee Stadium with the 1923 Army-Navy game inaugurating a rich history of collegiate and professional football matchups. On November 12, 1928, with Notre Dame and Army locked in a scoreless game at halftime, the legendary Knute Rockne made his famous "Win One for the Gipper" pep talk, and the Fighting Irish went on to defeat the Cadets, 12-6.

The New York football Giants also called Yankee

Stadium home from 1956 through 1973 and on December 28, 1958, played in what is widely recognized as "The Greatest Game Ever Played." With the NFL championship at stake, a crowd of 64,185 watched the Baltimore Colts tie the game, 17-17, on a Steve Myrha field goal with seven seconds left. Eight minutes into professional football's first-ever "sudden-death" overtime period, the Colts' Alan Ameche crashed into the end zone from the 1-yard line, ending a contest that would help establish pro football as a major sport.

The Stadium was also an important stop for religious conventions, especially those of the Jehovah's Witnesses. In 1950, the group began holding conventions at the Stadium, including one that drew 123,707 people on August 8, 1958—the largest single-day event in Stadium history. On October 4, 1965—with the Yankees out of the World Series for only the third time in 17 years—the Stadium held the first-ever Papal Mass in the United States as Pope Paul VI celebrated Mass before a crowd in excess of 80,000. Pope John Paul II also celebrated Mass at the original Yankee Stadium on October 2, 1979, during his tour of the United States.

On August 16, 2006, a groundbreaking ceremony was held for a new Yankee Stadium to be ready for the 2009 season. The location chosen for the new building was the north side of 161st Street and River Avenue in the Bronx, directly across the street from the site of the original.

As part of its final season in 2008, Yankee Stadium hosted a third papal visit on April 20 from Pope Benedict XVI, NYU's commencement ceremony on May 14 (believed to be the first ever college commencement in Stadium history) and a 15-inning 4-3 AL victory in the 2008 All-Star Game on July 15 (the fourth at Yankee Stadium, joining Midsummer Classics in 1939, 1960-Game 2, and 1977).

The building took its final bow on September 21, when the Yankees played the last game in Stadium history. Gates opened at 1:00 p.m., allowing approximately 13,000 fans the opportunity to visit Monument Park and walk around the warning track. With a national Sunday night audience watching on television, all-time Yankees greats, along with the evening's starting lineup, took their positions in the field before Julia Ruth Stevens, daughter of Babe Ruth, tossed out the ceremonial first pitch. Fittingly, the game ended in a Yankees victory, this one over the Baltimore Orioles, 7-3. After the final out, the club assembled by the pitcher's mound at the side of captain Derek Jeter. Over the PA, he thanked the crowd for their years of support, while reminding everyone of the new memories soon to be made. *

I n the bottom of the seventh inning of the Yankees' final home game on September 21, 2008, a taped valedictory was given on the Yankee Stadium video board by longtime public address announcer Bob Sheppard, who was unable to say goodbye in person as he continued to recover at home from an illness that had kept him away from the Stadium for the entire season. His appearance on screen brought a reverential hush to the crowd as everyone recognized they were about to hear the most perfect of all couplings perhaps for the last time—Bob Sheppard's voice reverberating in the original Yankee Stadium. He said the following:

"Farewell, old Yankee Stadium, farewell.
What a wonderful story you can tell.
DiMaggio, Mantle, Gehrig and Ruth,
A baseball cathedral in truth."

Original Yankee Stadium Information

Original Yankee Stadium Dimensions

Field	Distances/Dates	Distances/Dates	Distances/Dates	Distances/Dates	Distances/Dates
Left Field Foul Pole:	281 Ft. (1923-27)	301 Ft. (1928-73)	312 Ft. (1976-84)	312 Ft. (1985-87)	318 Ft. (1988-2008)
Left Field:	395 Ft. (1923-27)	402 Ft. (1928-73)	387 Ft. (1976-84)	379 Ft. (1985-87)	NA
Left-center Field:	460 Ft. (1923-36)	457 Ft. (1937-73)	430 Ft. (1976-84)	411 Ft. (1985-87)	399 Ft. (1988-2008)
Center Field:*	461 Ft. (1937-66)	463 Ft. (1967-73)	417 Ft. (1976-84)	410 Ft. (1985-87)	408 Ft. (1988-2008)
Right-center Field:	429 Ft. (1923-36)	407 Ft. (1937-73)	385 Ft. (1976-84)	385 Ft. (1985-87)	385 Ft. (1988-2008)
Right Field:	370 Ft. (1923-36)	344 Ft. (1937-73)	353 Ft. (1976-84)	353 Ft. (1985-87)	NA
Right-field Foul Pole:	295 Ft. (1923-38)	296 Ft. (1939-73)	310 Ft. (1976-84)	310 Ft. (1985-87)	314 Ft. (1988-2008)

* 490 Ft. (1923-36)

Original Yankee Stadium Firsts and Lasts

FIRSTS

Game: April 18, 1923 (4-1 win over Boston Red Sox)
Ceremonial First Pitch: N.Y. Governor Al Smith
Pitch: Bob Shawkey (ball)
Victory: April 18, 1923 (4-1 over Boston)
Loss: April 22, 1923 (4-3 to Washington)
Batter: Boston's Chick Fewster (grounded to short)
Yankee Batter: Whitey Witt
Hit: Boston's George Burns (April 18, 2nd-inning single)
Yankee Hit: Aaron Ward (April 18, 3rd-inning single)
Run: Bob Shawkey (April 18, on Joe Dugan's single in 3rd)
Home Run: Babe Ruth (April 18, three-run homer in 3rd)
Error: Babe Ruth (April 18, dropped fly ball in 5th)

PRE-REMODELING LASTS

Game: September 30, 1973 (8-5 loss to Detroit Tigers)
Attendance: 32,969
Batter: Mike Hegan (flied out to CF)
Home Run: Duke Sims (September 30 off Detroit's Fred Holdsworth)
Pitch: Detroit's John Hiller
Victory: September 29, 1973 (3-0 over Detroit Tigers)
NYY Winning Pitcher: Doc Medich (September 29, 3-0 CG over Detroit)

REMODELED YANKEE STADIUM LASTS

Game: September 21, 2008 (7-3 win over Baltimore)
Ceremonial First Pitch: Julia Ruth Stevens (daughter of Babe Ruth)
Pitch: Mariano Rivera to Baltimore's Brian Roberts
Batter: Baltimore's Brian Roberts (9th-inning ground out to first base)
Yankees Batter: Derek Jeter (8th-inning ground out to third base)
Hit: Jason Giambi (7th-inning single to left on Sept. 21, 2008)
Run: Brett Gardner (7th-inning on Sept. 21, 2008)
Home Run: Jose Molina (4th-inning, two-run homer to left off Chris Waters on Sept. 21, 2008)
Error: Baltimore's Brandon Fahey (misplayed grounder in 7th on Sept. 21, 2008)
Winning Pitcher: Andy Pettitte on Sept. 21, 2008 vs. Baltimore (7-3 Yankees victory)
Strikeout: Joba Chamberlain (Baltimore's Aubrey Huff on Sept. 21, 2008 in the 7th inning)
Star-Spangled Banner Performer: United States Army Field Band
God Bless America Singer: Ronan Tynan
Final Two Songs Played over PA: "Good Night Sweetheart" played by organist Ed Alstrom in memory of Eddie Layton, followed by "New York, New York" sung by Frank Sinatra

ORIGINAL YANKEE STADIUM LEADERS (1923-2008)

Most Career Games
1 Mickey Mantle 1,213
2 Lou Gehrig 1,080
3 Yogi Berra 1,068
4 Bernie Williams 1,039
5 Derek Jeter 1,004

Most Career Hits
1 Derek Jeter 1,274
2 Lou Gehrig 1,269
3 Mickey Mantle 1,211
4 Bernie Williams 1,123
5 Joe DiMaggio 1,060

Most Career Home Runs
1 Mickey Mantle 266
2 Babe Ruth 259
3 Lou Gehrig 251
4 Yogi Berra 210
5 Joe DiMaggio 148

Most Career RBI
1 Lou Gehrig 949
2 Babe Ruth 777
3 Mickey Mantle 744
4 Yogi Berra 727
5 Joe DiMaggio 720

Most Career Wins
1 Red Ruffing 126
2 Whitey Ford 120
3 Lefty Gomez 112
4 Ron Guidry 99
5 Andy Pettitte 94

Best Career ERA (500+ innings)
1 Fritz Peterson 2.52
2 Whitey Ford 2.57
3 Mariano Rivera 2.61
4 Spud Chandler 2.62
5 Stan Bahnsen 2.65

Most Career Strikeouts
1 Ron Guidry 969
2 Andy Pettitte 816
3 Whitey Ford 748
4 Roger Clemens 710
5 Mike Mussina 701

Most Career Saves (since 1969)
1 Mariano Rivera 230
2 Dave Righetti 111
3 Goose Gossage 70
4 Sparky Lyle 63
5 Steve Farr 45

Most Career Managerial Wins
1 Joe McCarthy 809
2 Joe Torre 614
3 Casey Stengel 604
4 Ralph Houk 550
5 Miller Huggins 339

The Yankees posted an all-time regular season record of 4,133-2,430-17 at the original Yankee Stadium.

Negro Leagues at Original Yankee Stadium

Satchel Paige warming up at Yankee Stadium on August 2, 1942

For almost 20 years in the 1930s and '40s, Yankee Stadium was a regular home to Negro Leagues baseball. During that time the greatest black stars of the day drew thousands of fans to watch players prohibited from playing in the Major Leagues at the time. Almost every Negro Leagues player of note over that two-decade stretch played at Yankee Stadium, including Hall of Famers Leroy "Satchel" Paige, John Henry "Pop" Lloyd, "Cool Papa" Bell, Oscar Charleston, Buck Leonard, Hilton Smith and Josh Gibson, who hit some of the longest home runs in the Stadium's history.

Yankee Stadium opened to black baseball on July 5, 1930, when Yankees owner Jacob Ruppert donated the free use of the facility to the New York Lincoln Giants and Baltimore Black Sox for a benefit doubleheader to raise money for the Brotherhood of Sleeping Car Porters, one of America's most prominent black unions. The games raised approximately $3,500 and included the appearance of Bill "Bojangles" Robinson who entertained the crowd along with the 369th Hell Fighters marching band.

Black baseball games at Yankee Stadium usually took place on Sundays when the Yankees played on the road. Sometimes a pair of teams would play a doubleheader, while at other times four-team doubleheaders were scheduled in order to maximize attendance and profits. Bands often performed and celebrities such as Joe Louis and New York City Mayor Fiorello La Guardia were common. Track races and other pregame contests also delighted fans.

In 1931, Lloyd organized an All-Star team of black players named the "Harlem Stars," which played several games at Yankee Stadium. Eventually, that team became the New York Black Yankees of the Negro National League. The club went on to use Yankee Stadium for a portion of their home schedule between 1936 and 1947, often wearing the used

uniforms of the Major League Yankees. In the spring of 1941, Paige, black baseball's greatest pitcher, briefly joined the Black Yankees, pitching and winning his only game in a New York uniform at Yankee Stadium.

Yankee Stadium also served as the venue for black baseball All-Star games and championship contests. One of the most memorable Negro Leagues All-Star games took place on August 27, 1939, when the Negro National League defeated the Negro American League, 10-2, with the help of Gibson's bases-clearing triple.

Ruppert's death in 1939 did not put a stop to black baseball at the Stadium. In fact, the Yankees sponsored a Jacob Ruppert Memorial Cup tournament among Negro National League teams. Ten doubleheaders were held at Yankee Stadium that summer to determine a winner, and on September 24, 1939, the Baltimore Elite Giants were crowned champs in Ruppert's name.

In October 1946, Yankee Stadium was home to two noteworthy exhibition games between an African-American All-Star team managed by Paige and an American League All-Star team led by future Hall of Famer Bob Feller. Cleveland Indians pitcher Bob Lemon hit a home run to win the first game for the AL but Paige out-pitched Feller in the second game to earn a split.

When Jackie Robinson finally broke the color barrier with the Brooklyn Dodgers in 1947, it was a watershed moment in the history of civil rights in the United States. But it did precipitate the decline and eventual extinction of the Negro Leagues.

Black baseball's relationship with the New York Yankees came to a close on August 20, 1961, as stars of the Negro American League gathered for its All-Star Game at Yankee Stadium. Paige, reportedly 55 years old at the time, pitched three scoreless innings and claimed the game's Most Valuable Player honors. ♈

Dressed in their Homewood Grays uniforms, Hall of Famers Josh Gibson [L] and Buck Leonard [R] join Sam Bankhead [C] at Yankee Stadium in 1939.

Other Events at Original Yankee Stadium

Championship Fights

(unless otherwise noted)

DATE	WINNER/LOSER
7/23/23	Leonard dec Tendler
6/26/24	Greb dec Moore
5/30/25	Berlenbach dec McTigue
9/11/25	Berlenbach KO Slattery
9/21/25	Walker dec Shade
6/10/26	Berlenbach dec Stribling
7/21/27	Dempsey KO Sharkey
	(first $1 million non-title fight)
7/26/28	Tunney KO Heeney
7/18/29	Loughran dec Braddock
6/12/30	Schmeling DQ (foul) Sharkey
7/17/30	Singer KO Mandell
8/30/37	Louis dec Farr
6/22/38	Louis KO Schmeling
6/28/39	Louis KO Galento
8/22/39	Ambers dec Armstrong
6/20/40	Louis KO Godoy
6/19/46	Louis KO Conn
9/18/46	Louis KO Mauriello
9/27/46	Zale KO Graziano
6/25/48	Louis KO Walcott
9/23/48	Williams KO Flores
8/10/49	Charles KO Lesnevich
9/8/50	Saddler KO Pep
9/27/50	Charles dec Louis
6/25/52	Maxim KO Robinson
6/17/54	Marciano dec Charles
9/17/54	Marciano KO Charles
9/21/55	Marciano KO Moore
9/23/57	Basilio dec Robinson
6/26/59	Johansson KO Patterson
9/28/76	Ali dec Norton

Professional Football

1926	New York Yankees (AFL)
1927-28	New York Yankees (NFL)
1936-37	New York Yankees (AFL)
1940	New York Yankees (AFL)
1946-49	New York Yankees (AAFC)
1950-51	New York Yanks (NFL)
1956-73	New York Giants (NFL); all-time regular season record at Yankee Stadium, 66-49-6. All-time postseason record at Yankee Stadium, 2-2.
1976	New York Jets (NFL) exhibition games

Notable Games:

12/30/56	New York Giants 47 - Chicago Bears 7; NFL Championship Game, Giants win third title in team history.
12/28/58	Baltimore Colts 23 - New York Giants 17 (OT); "The Greatest Game Ever Played," NFL Championship Game, first OT game in NFL history.
12/30/62	Green Bay Packers 16 - New York Giants 7; NFL Championship Game
12/10/72	Miami Dolphins 23 - New York Giants 13; Dolphins improve to 13-0 en route to perfect 17-0 season.

College Football

1923-46	Fordham vs. NYU series
1923-48	NYU uses Stadium as a secondary home field
1925-46	Army vs. Notre Dame at the Stadium (also played in 1969)
1930-31	Army vs. Navy played at the Stadium
1968-'73; '76-87	Grambling played 18 times

Notable Games:

11/12/28	Notre Dame 12 - Army 6, scoreless at halftime, Knute Rockne gives his famous "win one for the Gipper" speech in the locker room
11/9/46	Notre Dame 0 - Army 0 in battle featuring four Heisman Trophy winners (Doc Blanchard-1945, Glenn Davis-1946, Johnny Lujack-1947 and Leon Hart-1949)
12/15/62	Gotham Bowl, Nebraska 36 - Miami 34

Notable Team Records in Yankee Stadium Games:

Army	17-17-4 in 38 games
Fordham	13-5-1 in 19 games
Notre Dame	15-6-3 in 24 games
NYU	52-40-4 in 96 games

Soccer

6/28/31	Exhibition: Glasgow Celtic 4, New York Yankees 1 (of the American Soccer League)
9/16/34	Charity match: Jewish All-Stars 3 - Irish All-Stars 0
9/27/36	Macabees of Palestine 6 - NY State All-Stars 0
11/8/36	ASL All-Stars 4 - Macabees of Palestine 1
5/4/47	Hapoel of Palestine 2 - U.S. All-Stars 0 (61,000 tickets sold)
1952	American Soccer League games
6/15/52	Tottenham Hotspur 7 - Manchester United 1
6/8/53	International Soccer Friendly: England 6 - United States 3
6/14/53	Liverpool 1 - Young Boys Club of Switzerland 1
4/29/56	Israel Olympic Team 2 - ASL All-Stars 1
9/5/66	Santos 4 - Inter Milan 1
1967	New York Skyliners a.k.a. Cerro of Uruguay (United Soccer Association)
1967-68	New York Generals (NPSL)
8/26/67	Inter Milan 1 - Santos 0
10/15/67	Israel National Team 3 - ASL All-Stars 1
6/21/68	Santos 4 - Napoli 2
7/12/68	New York Generals 5 - Santos 3
8/21/68	Real Madrid 4 - New York Generals 1
9/1/68	Santos 1 - Benfica 1
5/30/69	Barcelona 3 - Juventus 2
6/27/69	Inter Milan 2 (PK win) - Sparta Prague 2 A.C. Milan 4 - Panathinaikos 0
6/29/69	A.C. Milan 6 - Inter Milan 4
1971, 1976	New York Cosmos (NASL), including Pele
5/28/76	USA Bicentennial Cup, England 3 - Italy 2, Att: 40,650

Other Performers and Events

7/20/57	Rev. Billy Graham preaches.
12/7/57	Cardinal Spellman celebrates Mass.
8/8/58	A Jehovah's Witnesses convention draws a single-day Stadium record 123,707 people.
10/4/65	Pope Paul VI celebrates Mass.
10/2/79	Pope John Paul II celebrates Mass.
5/1/86	Cardinal O'Connor officiates at World Youth Assembly.
6/21/90	Nelson Mandela welcomed with a huge celebration.
6/22/90	Billy Joel performs first of two dates in succession.
8/29/92	U2 performs first of two dates in succession.
6/10/94	Pink Floyd performs first of two dates in succession.
6/25/94	Closing ceremonies for the 1994 Unity Games.
4/25/99	Paul Simon sings "Mrs. Robinson" while standing in center field on the day Joe DiMaggio's Monument is dedicated.
9/23/01	"A Prayer for America" service held for those lost on September 11, 2001.
3/10/06	Baseball reporter Ed Lucas marries Allison Pheifle in the first on-field wedding in Stadium history.
4/20/08	Pope Benedict XVI celebrates Mass.
5/14/08	New York University holds commencement.

Previous Homes of the Yankees

Hilltop Park

American League Park (commonly known as Hilltop Park) was the Yankees' first home. Hastily constructed in just six weeks on one of the highest points in Upper Manhattan, the all-wooden ballpark sat on a block bounded by Broadway, 165th Street, Fort Washington Avenue and 168th Street, in close proximity to the New York Giants' 155th Street home, the Polo Grounds. The first game at Hilltop Park was played on April 30, 1903—a 6-2 win over Washington, started by Hall of Famer Jack Chesbro.

The ballpark had a covered grandstand ringing the infield from first base to third base and uncovered bleachers running up the foul lines. There was seating for approximately 15,000 people, but as was the case in many ballparks of that time, it could accommodate overflow crowds both in the outfield and along foul ground in the infield, occasionally bringing capacity up toward 25,000.

Hilltop Park (above/below) served as the Yankees' first home. It was built in just six weeks and was located near Broadway and 168th Street in Upper Manhattan.

When a fire ravaged the Polo Grounds on April 14, 1911, the Yankees allowed the Giants to play their home games at Hilltop Park until the Polo Grounds could be rebuilt. From April 15 through May 30, the Giants put together a 20-8 record at their temporary home.

The Yankees were successful in their 10 years at Hilltop Park, compiling a 398-342 all-time record there. The club's final game at the structure came on October 5, 1912—an 8-6 win vs. Washington. After the Yankees' lease at Hilltop Park expired at the end of the season, they decided to leave the rickety ballpark to become renters at the Polo Grounds, where the Giants became their landlords. The move, unthinkable years earlier, was facilitated by the Yankees' post-fire hospitality.

In 1914, Hilltop Park was torn down. Currently, its former location is the site of Columbia-Presbyterian Medical Center.

Polo Grounds

The Yankees called the Polo Grounds home from 1913 through 1922, sharing the park with the New York Giants. Located on West 157th Street and Eighth Avenue in Upper Manhattan, the Polo Grounds was overlooked by a promontory called Coogan's Bluff to the west. To the east was the Harlem River—on the other side of which Yankee Stadium was built in 1923.

The Polo Grounds was constructed with straight sides, and the outfield fences by the foul poles ran parallel to each other and away from home plate. The foul poles in left and right were approximately 277 and 258 feet away from the plate, respectively, while left-center, center and right fields were all in the range of 445-483 feet away from home.

The Yankees compiled a 416-338 all-time regular season record at the uniquely-shaped facility, winning the first two pennants in franchise history while tenants in 1921 and 1922.

The Polo Grounds, located on West 157th Street and Eighth Avenue in Upper Manhattan, served as the home of the Yankees from 1913-22.

The club lost both of those World Series to the NL Champion Giants—5 games to 3 in 1921 and 4 games to none with one tie in 1922—in Fall Classics played entirely at the Polo Grounds.

The American Leaguers were welcome tenants as long as they remained less popular than the Giants. But with Babe Ruth's arrival in 1920 and the team's subsequent success, the dynamic quickly changed. After the Yankees started outdrawing the Giants in their own park in 1920 and 1921, the National Leaguers asked the Pinstripers to vacate to a new facility as soon as possible. The 1922 season marked their final season in Manhattan before their April 18, 1923, Yankee Stadium debut in the Bronx.

The Polo Grounds remained home to the Giants until they moved to San Francisco in 1958. It stood empty until 1962 when the Mets arrived to play two seasons there before moving into Shea Stadium. In 1964, the Polo Grounds was demolished. Apartment buildings called the Polo Grounds Towers occupy the site today.

Monument Park

Since 1932, the New York Yankees have honored their all-time greats with the dedication of monuments and plaques in Yankee Stadium. The tradition continues in the current Stadium in Monument Park, located behind the outfield fence in centerfield.

The first monument was dedicated on May 30, 1932, to the memory of Miller Huggins, who died suddenly in 1929. The diminutive manager guided the Yankees to six American League pennants and three World Championships in his 11-plus seasons.

The first plaque was placed on the center-field wall in April 1940, a tribute to Jacob Ruppert, the former owner who built Yankee Stadium and brought the tradition of winning to the Yankees.

Two additional monuments followed: in 1941 for Lou Gehrig and in 1949 for Babe Ruth. Later plaques were placed in center field for General Manager Ed Barrow (1954) and two great Yankees center fielders, Joe DiMaggio and Mickey Mantle (1969). After his death, Mantle's plaque was removed and replaced

Monument Park is located just behind the centerfield fence and is accessible to all fans.

by a fourth monument on August 25, 1996. On April 25, 1999, DiMaggio—who passed away less than two months earlier—was honored with the Stadium's fifth monument. (The two plaques which previously honored DiMaggio and Mantle were donated by the Yankees to the Yogi Berra Museum and Learning Center in Montclair, N.J.).

Originally, the monuments and plaques were part of the playing field. The monuments and Stadium flagpole were located in straight-away center field on the warning track approximately 10 feet in front of the wall. Sometimes long hits and fly balls forced fielders to go behind the monuments to retrieve the baseball.

One tradition of Yankee Stadium before it was remodeled was to allow fans to exit through the center-field gates via the warning track, where they could pause and reflect on the achievements of these honored legends. After Yankee Stadium was remodeled in 1974 and 1975, the monuments and plaques were relocated to an area off the field between the Yankees' and visitors' bullpens.

In 1976, two more plaques were added to memorialize managers Joe McCarthy and Casey Stengel. In the 1980s, [pla]ques were dedicated to [Yank]es greats Thurman

Munson (1980), Elston Howard and Roger Maris (1984), Phil Rizzuto (1985), Billy Martin (1986), Whitey Ford and Lefty Gomez (1987), Yogi Berra and Bill Dickey (1988), and Allie Reynolds (1989). The Yankee also dedicated two plaques to non-uniformed Yankees legends: the "Voice of the Yankees," Mel Allen (1998); and the "Voice of Yankee Stadium," public-address announcer Bob Sheppard (2000). Yankees greats Don Mattingly (1997), Reggie Jackson (2002), Ron Guidry (2003) and Red Ruffing (2004) are the most recent Bombers to be honored with plaques in Monument Park.

Plaques commemorating the visits of Pope Paul VI in 1965 and Pope John Paul II in 1979 were dedicated by the Knights of Columbus, and a plaque commemorating the visit of the New York Yankees' interlocking "NY" insignia was added to the park in 2001. The most recent plaque was dedicated in 2008 following the visit of Pope Benedict XVI.

In 1985, after the left-center-field fence of the original Stadium was moved in, the Yankees were able to open Monument Park for up-close fan viewing.

By 1988, long lines and increased fan interest caused the Yankees to move the fence in further and expand the area. A special walkway was added with an exhibit honoring those Yankees who have had their uniform numbers retired.

In a pregame ceremony on Sept. 11, 2002, the Yankees dedicated a monument in remembrance of the victims and heroes of the 9/11 tragedy. It was the sixth monument dedicated in Yankee Stadium and the first to non-Yankees personnel.

During the 2010 season, a monument was erected in honor of Yankees Principal Owner George M Steinbrenner, III, who passed away on July 13, 2010. During a special pregame ceremony on Sept. 20, 2010, the entire Yankees team joined the Steinbrenner family and Yankees alumni in unveiling the monument.

In all, there are seven monuments (for four Yankees players, one manager, one owner and one to commemorate the tragedy of 9/11) and 24 plaques (for 14 players, two managers, one owner, one executive, one PA announcer, one broadcaster, three Papal visit commemorations and one noting the history of the NY logo). ⚑

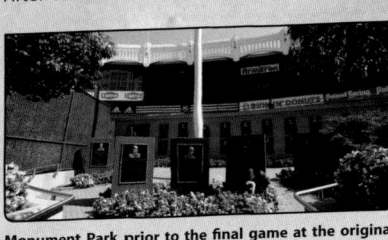

Monument Park prior to the final game at the original Yankee Stadium on September 21, 2008.

Monument Park Monuments

(In order of dedication)

MILLER JAMES HUGGINS
MANAGER OF NEW YORK YANKEES, 1918-1929
PENNANT WINNERS, 1921-22-23...1926-27-28
WORLD CHAMPIONS, 1923, 1927 AND 1928

AS A TRIBUTE TO A SPLENDID CHARACTER
WHO MADE PRICELESS CONTRIBUTION TO BASEBALL
AND ON THIS FIELD BROUGHT GLORY TO THE
NEW YORK CLUB OF THE AMERICAN LEAGUE

THIS MEMORIAL IS ERECTED BY
COL. JACOB RUPPERT
AND
BASEBALL WRITERS OF NEW YORK

MAY 30, 1932

HENRY LOUIS GEHRIG
JUNE 19TH 1903 - JUNE 2ND 1941
A MAN, A GENTLEMAN
AND
A GREAT BALL PLAYER
WHOSE AMAZING RECORD
OF 2130 CONSECUTIVE GAMES
SHOULD STAND FOR ALL TIME.

THIS MEMORIAL IS A TRIBUTE
FROM THE
YANKEE PLAYERS
TO THEIR BELOVED CAPTAIN AND TEAM MATE

JULY THE FOURTH
1941

(Dedication ceremony held July 6, 1941)

GEORGE HERMAN "BABE" RUTH
1895 - 1948
A GREAT BALL PLAYER
A GREAT MAN
A GREAT AMERICAN

ERECTED BY
THE YANKEES
AND
THE NEW YORK BASEBALL WRITERS

APRIL 19, 1949

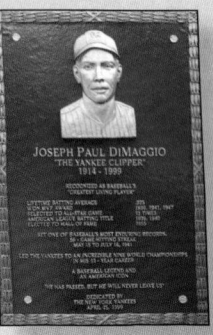

MICKEY MANTLE
"A GREAT TEAMMATE"
1931-1995
536 HOME RUNS

WINNER OF TRIPLE CROWN	1956
MOST WORLD SERIES HOMERS	18
SELECTED TO THE ALL STAR GAME	20 TIMES
WON MVP AWARD	1956, 1957 + 1962
ELECTED TO HALL OF FAME	1974

A MAGNIFICENT YANKEE
WHO LEFT A LEGACY OF
UNEQUALED COURAGE

DEDICATED BY
THE NEW YORK YANKEES
AUGUST 25, 1996

JOSEPH PAUL DIMAGGIO
"THE YANKEE CLIPPER"
1914 - 1999
RECOGNIZED AS BASEBALL'S
"GREATEST LIVING PLAYER"

LIFETIME BATTING AVERAGE	.325
WON MVP AWARD	1939, 1941, 1947
SELECTED TO ALL-STAR GAME	13 TIMES
AMERICAN LEAGUE BATTING TITLE	1939, 1940
ELECTED TO HALL OF FAME	1955

SET ONE OF BASEBALL'S MOST ENDURING RECORDS,
56-GAME HITTING STREAK
MAY 15 TO JULY 16, 1941

LED THE YANKEES TO AN INCREDIBLE NINE WORLD
CHAMPIONSHIPS
IN HIS 13-YEAR CAREER

A BASEBALL LEGEND AND
AN AMERICAN ICON
"HE HAS PASSED, BUT HE WILL NEVER LEAVE US"

DEDICATED BY
THE NEW YORK YANKEES,
APRIL 25, 1999

SEPTEMBER 11, 2001 TRIBUTE
We Remember
On September 11, 2001, despicable acts of terrorism were
perpetrated on our country.

In tribute to the eternal spirit of the innocent victims of these
crimes and to the selfless courage shown by both public
servants and private citizens, we dedicate this plaque.

These valiant souls, with unfettered resolve,
exemplify the true
character of this great nation. Their unity and resilience
during this time of distress defined American heroism for
future generations.

Dedicated by the New York Yankees
September 11, 2002

GEORGE M. STEINBRENNER III
July 4, 1930 – July 13, 2010
New York Yankees Principal Owner
"The Boss"
1973 - 2010

Purchased the New York Yankees on January 3, 1973.
A true visionary who changed the game of baseball forever,
he was considered the most influential owner in all of sports.
In his 37 years as Principal Owner, the Yankees posted a
Major League-best .566 winning percentage,
while winning 11 American League pennants and seven World Series titles,
becoming the most recognizable sports brand in the world.

A devoted sportsman, he was Vice President of the
United States Olympic Committee, a member of the
Baseball Hall of Fame's Board of Directors and a member
of the NCAA Foundation Board of Trustees.
A great philanthropist whose charitable efforts were
mostly performed without fanfare, he followed a personal
motto of the greatest form of charity is anonymity.

Dedicated by the New York Yankees
September 20, 2010

Monument Park Plaques
(In order of dedication)

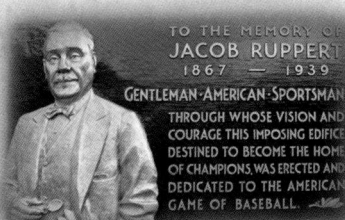

JACOB RUPPERT
TO THE MEMORY OF
JACOB RUPPERT
1867-1939
GENTLEMAN - AMERICAN - SPORTSMAN
THROUGH WHOSE VISION AND
COURAGE THIS IMPOSING EDIFICE,
DESTINED TO BECOME THE HOME
OF CHAMPIONS, WAS ERECTED AND
DEDICATED TO THE AMERICAN
GAME OF BASEBALL.

EDWARD GRANT BARROW
1868-1953
MOULDER OF A TRADITION OF VICTORY
UNDER WHOSE GUIDANCE THE YANKEES WON
FOURTEEN AMERICAN LEAGUE PENNANTS AND
TEN WORLD CHAMPIONSHIPS AND BROUGHT
TO THIS FIELD SOME OF THE GREATEST
BASEBALL STARS OF ALL TIME
THIS MEMORIAL IS A TRIBUTE FROM THOSE
WHO SEEK TO CARRY ON HIS GREAT WORKS
ERECTED APRIL 15, 1954

POPE PAUL VI
IN COMMEMORATION
OF THE SOLEMN MASS
FOR PEACE OFFERED
BY HIS
HOLINESS POPE PAUL VI
OCTOBER 4, 1965
HERE IN YANKEE STADIUM
GIFT OF
KNIGHTS OF COLUMBUS

JOSEPH VINCENT McCARTHY
MANAGER
NEW YORK YANKEES
1931-1946
ONE OF BASEBALL'S MOST BELOVED
AND RESPECTED LEADERS
LED YANKEES TO 8 PENNANTS AND
7 WORLD CHAMPIONSHIPS INCLUDING
4 CONSECUTIVE 1936-1939, COMPILING
A .627 WINNING PERCENTAGE

ERECTED BY
NEW YORK YANKEES
APRIL 21, 1976

CHARLES DILLON "CASEY" STENGEL

1890-1975

BRIGHTENED BASEBALL FOR OVER 50 YEARS

WITH SPIRIT OF ETERNAL YOUTH
YANKEE MANAGER 1949-1960 WINNING
10 PENNANTS AND 7 WORLD CHAMPIONSHIPS
INCLUDING A RECORD 5 CONSECUTIVE
1949-1953

ERECTED BY
NEW YORK YANKEES
JULY 30, 1976

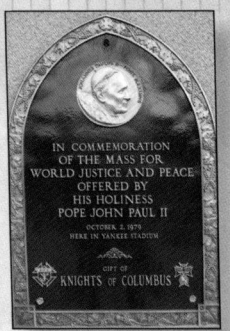

POPE JOHN PAUL II

IN COMMEMORATION
OF THE MASS FOR
WORLD JUSTICE AND PEACE
OFFERED BY
HIS HOLINESS
POPE JOHN PAUL II
OCTOBER 2, 1979
HERE IN YANKEE STADIUM
GIFT OF
KNIGHTS OF COLUMBUS

THURMAN MUNSON

NEW YORK YANKEES
JUNE 7, 1947-AUGUST 2, 1979
YANKEE CAPTAIN

"OUR CAPTAIN AND LEADER HAS NOT
LEFT US-
TODAY, TOMORROW, THIS YEAR, NEXT...
OUR ENDEAVORS WILL REFLECT OUR
LOVE AND ADMIRATION FOR HIM."

ERECTED BY
THE NEW YORK YANKEES
SEPTEMBER 20, 1980

ELSTON GENE HOWARD

1929-1980

"A MAN OF GREAT GENTLENESS AND DIGNITY"
ONE OF ALL-TIME YANKEE GREATS
AMERICAN LEAGUE MVP IN 1963
WINNER OF TWO GOLD GLOVES
A FITTING LEADER TO BE FIRST BLACK PLAYER
TO WEAR THE YANKEE UNIFORM
"IF INDEED, HUMILITY IS A TRADEMARK
OF MANY GREAT MEN-ELSTON HOWARD WAS
ONE OF THE TRULY GREAT YANKEES"

ERECTED BY
NEW YORK YANKEES
JUNE 21, 1984

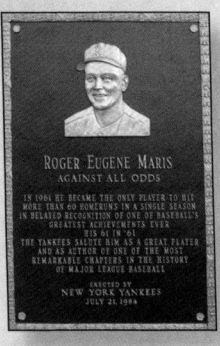

ROGER EUGENE MARIS

AGAINST ALL ODDS

IN 1961 HE BECAME THE ONLY PLAYER TO HIT
MORE THAN 60 HOMERUNS IN A SINGLE SEASON
IN BELATED RECOGNITION OF ONE OF BASEBALL'S
GREATEST ACHIEVEMENTS EVER
HIS 61 IN '61
THE YANKEES SALUTE HIM AS A GREAT PLAYER
AND AS AUTHOR OF ONE OF THE MOST
REMARKABLE CHAPTERS IN THE HISTORY
OF MAJOR LEAGUE BASEBALL

ERECTED BY
NEW YORK YANKEES
JULY 21, 1984

PHILIP FRANCIS RIZZUTO

"A MAN'S SIZE IS MEASURED BY HIS HEART"
SCOOTER SPARKED YANKEES TO 10
PENNANTS AND 8 WORLD CHAMPIONSHIPS
1950 AMERICAN LEAGUE MVP
1950 MAJOR LEAGUE PLAYER OF THE YEAR
MVP OF WORLD SERIES IN 1951
HAS ENJOYED TWO OUTSTANDING CAREERS
ALL-TIME YANKEE SHORTSTOP
ONE OF GREAT YANKEE BROADCASTERS
"HOLY COW"

ERECTED BY
NEW YORK YANKEES
AUGUST 4, 1985

ALFRED MANUEL
"BILLY" MARTIN
CASEY'S BOY

A YANKEE FOREVER
A MAN WHO KNEW ONLY ONE WAY TO PLAY-TO WIN
AS A PLAYER FOR CASEY STENGEL HE THRIVED ON
PRESSURE, DELIVERING THE KEY PLAY OR HIT.
MVP OF 1953 WORLD SERIES, SETTING RECORD FOR
MOST HITS IN SIX-GAME SERIES WITH 12.
LATER AS MANAGER HE BECAME
ONE OF THE GREATEST YANKEE MANAGERS.

ERECTED BY
NEW YORK YANKEES
AUGUST 10, 1986

EDWARD "WHITEY" FORD
"CHAIRMAN OF THE BOARD"
NEW YORK YANKEES 1950, 1953-67

LED YANKEES TO 11 PENNANTS AND SIX WORLD
CHAMPIONSHIPS LEADS ALL YANKEE PITCHERS
IN GAMES, INNINGS, WINS, STRIKEOUTS AND
SHUTOUTS CY YOUNG AWARD WINNER IN 1961
HOLDS MANY WORLD SERIES RECORDS INCLUDING
33 2/3 CONSECUTIVE SCORELESS INNINGS

ERECTED BY
NEW YORK YANKEES
AUGUST 2, 1987

VERNON "LEFTY" GOMEZ
NEW YORK YANKEES 1930-42

KNOWN FOR HIS EXCELLENT WIT AS HE
WAS FAST WITH A QUIP AND A PITCH
SET WORLD SERIES RECORD WITH
SIX VICTORES AND NO DEFEATS
HAD FOUR 20-WIN SEASONS, LEADING
YANKEES TO SEVEN PENNANTS AND
SIX WORLD CHAMPIONSHIPS

ERECTED BY
NEW YORK YANKEES
AUGUST 2, 1987

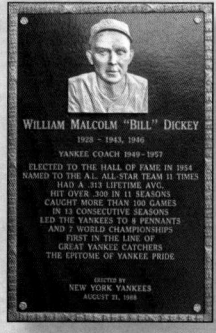

WILLIAM MALCOLM
"BILL" DICKEY
1928-1943, 1946
YANKEE COACH 1949-1957

ELECTED TO THE HALL OF FAME IN 1954
NAMED TO THE A.L. ALL-STAR TEAM 11 TIMES
HAD A .313 LIFETIME AVG.
HIT OVER .300 IN 11 SEASONS
CAUGHT MORE THAN 100 GAMES
IN 13 CONSECUTIVE SEASONS
LED THE YANKEES TO 8 PENNANTS
AND 7 WORLD CHAMPIONSHIPS
FIRST IN THE LINE OF
GREAT YANKEE CATCHERS
THE EPITOME OF YANKEE PRIDE

ERECTED BY
NEW YORK YANKEES
AUGUST 21, 1988

LAWRENCE PETER "YOGI" BERRA

1946-1963
YANKEE MANAGER 1964, 1984-1985

ELECTED TO THE HALL OF FAME IN 1972
"IT AIN'T OVER 'TIL IT'S OVER"
THREE TIME MVP 1951-54-55
SELECTED TO THE A.L. ALL-STAR TEAM
15 CONSECUTIVE YEARS
HIT MOST HOME RUNS
BY A YANKEE CATCHER
OUTSTANDING CLUTCH HITTER
AND WORLD SERIES PERFORMER
LED YANKEES TO 14 PENNANTS
AND 10 WORLD CHAMPIONSHIPS
A LEGENDARY YANKEE

ERECTED BY
NEW YORK YANKEES
AUGUST 21, 1988

ALLIE PIERCE REYNOLDS

"SUPERCHIEF"

NEW YORK YANKEES 1947-1954
ONE OF THE YANKEES' GREATEST
RIGHT-HANDED PITCHERS
HURLED TWO NO-HITTERS IN 1951
STARRED ON FIVE STRAIGHT
WORLD CHAMPIONS 1949-1953
FIVE-TIME ALL-STAR
.686 YANKEE WINNING PERCENTAGE

ERECTED BY
NEW YORK YANKEES
AUGUST 26, 1989

DONALD ARTHUR MATTINGLY

"DONNIE BASEBALL"
1982-1995

AMERICAN LEAGUE BATTING CHAMPION	1984
AMERICAN LEAGUE MVP (145 RBI)	1985
NINE-TIME GOLD GLOVE WINNER	
SIX-TIME AMERICAN LEAGUE ALL-STAR	
SET RECORDS FOR MOST GRAND SLAMS IN A SEASON (6)	1987
MAJOR LEAGUE RECORD FOR MOST HOME RUNS IN	1987
SEVEN CONSECUTIVE GAMES (9) AND EIGHT	
CONSECUTIVE GAMES (10)	
10TH PLAYER IN TEAM HISTORY TO BE NAMED CAPTAIN	1991

A HUMBLE MAN OF GRACE AND DIGNITY.
A CAPTAIN WHO LED BY EXAMPLE.
PROUD OF THE PINSTRIPE TRADITION
AND DEDICATED TO THE PURSUIT OF EXCELLENCE,
A YANKEE FOREVER

DEDICATED BY
THE NEW YORK YANKEES
AUGUST 31, 1997

MEL ALLEN

"THE VOICE OF THE YANKEES"
1939-1964

WITH HIS WARM PERSONALITY AND SIGNATURE GREETING
"HELLO THERE, EVERYBODY," HE SHAPED BASEBALL
BROADCASTING BY CHARISMATICALLY BRINGING THE
EXCITEMENT AND DRAMA OF YANKEES BASEBALL TO
GENERATIONS OF FANS. HE MADE PET PHRASES SUCH
AS "GOING, GOING, GONE" A PART OF OUR LANGUAGE
AND CULTURE.

A YANKEE INSTITUTION, A NATIONAL TREASURE.

"HOW ABOUT THAT?"

DEDICATED BY
THE NEW YORK YANKEES
JULY 25, 1998

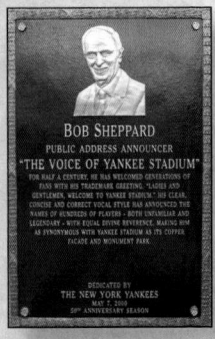

BOB SHEPPARD

PUBLIC ADDRESS ANNOUNCER
"THE VOICE OF YANKEE STADIUM"

FOR HALF A CENTURY, HE HAS WELCOMED GENERATIONS OF
FANS WITH HIS TRADEMARK GREETING, "LADIES AND
GENTLEMEN, WELCOME TO YANKEE STADIUM." HIS CLEAR,
CONCISE AND CORRECT VOCAL STYLE HAS ANNOUNCED THE
NAMES OF HUNDREDS OF PLAYERS - BOTH UNFAMILIAR AND
LEGENDARY - WITH EQUAL DIVINE REVERENCE, MAKING HIM
AS SYNONYMOUS WITH YANKEE STADIUM AS ITS COPPER
FACADE AND MONUMENT PARK.

DEDICATED BY
THE NEW YORK YANKEES
MAY 7, 2000
50TH ANNIVERSARY SEASON

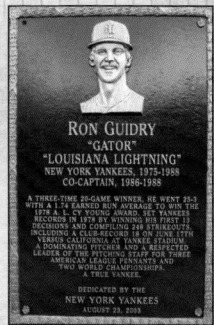

REGGIE JACKSON

"MR. OCTOBER"
NEW YORK YANKEES
1977-1981

ONE OF THE MOST COLORFUL AND EXCITING PLAYERS OF HIS ERA

A PROLIFIC POWER HITTER WHO THRIVED IN PRESSURE SITUATIONS

IN FIVE YEARS IN PINSTRIPES, HELPED LEAD THE YANKEES TO
FOUR DIVISION TITLES, THREE AMERICAN LEAGUE PENNANTS
AND TWO WORLD CHAMPIONSHIPS

AT HIS BEST IN OCTOBER, BELTED FOUR HOME RUNS ON FOUR
CONSECUTIVE SWINGS IN THE 1977 WORLD SERIES—INCLUDING
THREE IN GAME SIX AT YANKEE STADIUM

INDUCTED INTO THE BASEBALL HALL OF FAME IN 1993

DEDICATED BY
THE NEW YORK YANKEES
JULY 6, 2002

RON GUIDRY

"GATOR"
"LOUISIANA LIGHTNING"
NEW YORK YANKEES, 1975-1988
CO-CAPTAIN, 1986-1988

A THREE-TIME 20-GAME WINNER, HE WENT 25-3
WITH A 1.74 EARNED RUN AVERAGE TO WIN THE
1978 A.L. CY YOUNG AWARD. SET YANKEES
RECORDS IN 1978 BY WINNING HIS FIRST 13
DECISIONS AND COMPILING 248 STRIKEOUTS,
INCLUDING A CLUB-RECORD 18 ON JUNE 17TH
VERSUS CALIFORNIA AT YANKEE STADIUM.
A DOMINATING PITCHER AND A RESPECTED
LEADER OF THE PITCHING STAFF FOR THREE
AMERICAN LEAGUE PENNANTS AND
TWO WORLD CHAMPIONSHIPS.
A TRUE YANKEE.

DEDICATED BY
THE NEW YORK YANKEES
AUGUST 23, 2003

CHARLES HERBERT
"RED" RUFFING

New York Yankees
1930-1942
1945-1946
U.S. ARMY AIR DIVISION
1943-1945

THE YANKEES' ALL-TIME LEADER IN WINS BY A
RIGHT-HANDED PITCHER WITH 231. THE ONLY
PITCHER IN FRANCHISE HISTORY TO COMPILE
FOUR CONSECUTIVE 20-WIN SEASONS, FROM 1936-1939,
WHEN HE LED THE YANKEES TO FOUR STRAIGHT WORLD
CHAMPIONSHIPS. A DURABLE PITCHER, HE HOLDS THE YANKEES'
RECORD FOR MOST COMPLETE GAMES WITH 261. ONE OF
THE GREATEST HITTING PITCHERS OF ALL TIME, HE BATTED .300
OR BETTER IN EIGHT SEASONS.
INDUCTED INTO THE BASEBALL HALL OF FAME IN 1967

DEDICATED BY
THE NEW YORK YANKEES
JULY 10, 2004

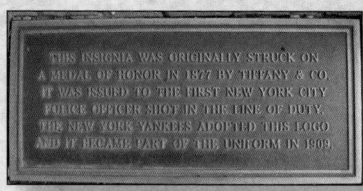

NEW YORK YANKEES INSIGNIA

THIS INSIGNIA WAS ORIGINALLY STRUCK ON
A MEDAL OF HONOR IN 1877 BY TIFFANY & CO.
IT WAS ISSUED TO THE FIRST NEW YORK CITY
POLICE OFFICER SHOT IN THE LINE OF DUTY.
THE NEW YORK YANKEES ADOPTED THIS LOGO
AND IT BECAME PART OF THE UNIFORM IN 1909.

POPE BENEDICT XVI

IN COMMEMORATION
OF THE
SOLEMN PONTIFICAL MASS
MARKING THE BICENTENNIAL
OF THE
ARCHDIOCESE OF NEW YORK
OFFERED BY
HIS HOLINESS
POPE BENEDICT XVI
APRIL 20, 2008
HERE IN YANKEE STADIUM
GIFT OF
KNIGHTS OF COLUMBUS

ANGEL MULKAY, MD
Holy Name Medical Center
Cardiologist

Stephen Angeli, MD
Holy Name Medical Center
Cardiologist

Our team approach
to healing hearts
is saving lives.

Our cardiologists understand heart disease and the importance of finding it early. They're using technology that's ahead of the curve—including cardiac PET/CT stress testing and CT angiography that can capture detailed images of your heart in just five seconds. And if a blockage is diagnosed, they can remove it at a moment's notice in our state-of-the-art catheterization lab. When your heart is at risk, trust the team who can heal it.

To make an appointment with a Holy Name cardiologist, call 877-HOLY-NAME (465-9626).

Know the signs of a heart attack

Chest discomfort—Pain commonly occurs in the center of the chest and lasts more than a few minutes, or goes away and comes back. It can feel like an uncomfortable pressure, squeezing, fullness or pain.

Discomfort in other areas of the upper body—Symptoms can include pain or discomfort in one or both arms, the back, neck, jaw or stomach.

Shortness of breath with or without chest discomfort.

Other signs—Breaking out in a cold sweat, nausea or lightheadedness may also be signs of a heart attack.

Gender matters—As with men, women's most common heart attack symptom is chest pain or discomfort. **But** women are somewhat more likely than men to experience some of the other common symptoms, particularly shortness of breath, nausea/vomiting, and back or jaw pain.

Know the signs of a stroke

Act F.A.S.T.

Face—Ask the person to smile. Does one side of the face droop?

Arms—Ask the person to raise both arms. Does one arm drift downward?

Speech—Ask the person to repeat a simple sentence. Are the words slurred? Can he/she repeat the sentence correctly?

Time—If the person shows any of these symptoms, time is important. Call 911 or get to the hospital fast. Brain cells are dying.

HEALTH GRADES®
THE HEALTHCARE QUALITY EXPERTS®

Holy Name Medical Center
Cardiovascular Services

member
NewYork-Presbyterian
Healthcare System
affiliate: Columbia University College of Physicians and Surgeons

Healing begins here. • www.holyname.org • 718 Teaneck Road • Teaneck, NJ 07666

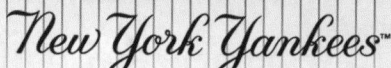

PLAYER DEVELOPMENT

RHP **DAVID PHELPS** was named the
organization's 2010 "Pitcher of the Year,"
going 10-2 with a 2.50 ERA and 141K in
26 combined games (25 starts) with
Trenton and Scranton/WB.

YANKEES

2011 Player Development & Scouting Directory

EXECUTIVE

Mark Newman . . . . Senior Vice President, Baseball Operations
Billy Connors . . . . Vice President, Player Personnel

PLAYER DEVELOPMENT

Pat Roessler . . . . Director of Player Development
Eric Schmitt . . . . Assistant Director, Baseball Operations

PROFESSIONAL SCOUTING

Billy Eppler . . . . Senior Director, Pro Personnel
Will Kuntz . . . . Assistant, Pro Scouting
Ron Brand . . . . Professional Scout (Plano, Tex.)
Joe Caro . . . . Professional Scout (Tampa, Fla.)
Jay Darnell . . . . Professional Scout (San Diego, Calif.)
Gary Denbo . . . . Professional Scout (Tampa, Fla.)
Bill Emslie . . . . Professional Scout (Tampa, Fla.)
Dan Freed . . . . Professional Scout (Lexington, Ill.)
Jalal Leach . . . . Professional Scout (Sacramento, Calif.)
Bill Livesey . . . . Professional Scout (St. Petersburg, Fla.)
Bill Mele . . . . Professional Scout (Boston, Mass.)
Tim Naehring . . . . Professional Scout (Cincinnati, Ohio)
Greg Orr . . . . Professional Scout (Sacramento, Calif.)
Josh Paul . . . . Professional Scout (Tampa, Fla.)
Kevin Reese . . . . Professional Scout (Sterling, Va.)
Rick Williams . . . . Professional Scout (Tampa, Fla.)
Tom Wilson . . . . Professional Scout (Lake Havasu, Ariz.)
Bob Miske . . . . Part-time Professional Scout (Amherst, N.Y.)

AMATEUR SCOUTING

Damon Oppenheimer . . . . Vice President, Amateur Scouting
John Kremer . . . . Assistant Director, Amateur Scouting
Kendall Carter . . . . National Crosschecker
Brian Barber . . . . National Crosschecker
Tim Kelly . . . . National Crosschecker
Mark Batchko . . . . South Texas, Kansas
Steve Boros . . . . South Texas, Kansas
Andy Cannizaro . . . . Louisiana, Mississippi
Jeff Deardorff . . . . Central and South Florida (excluding Miami/Ft. Lauderdale)
Mike Gibbons . . . . Central Canada, Indiana, Kentucky, Michigan, Ohio, W. Virginia
Matt Hyde . . . . Conn., Maine, Mass., New Hampshire, N.Y. State, Penn., Rhode Island, Vermont, Quebec
Dave Keith . . . . Southern California (Orange County)
Steve Kmetko . . . . Arizona, Colorado, New Mexico, Utah, El Paso (Tex.)
Steve Lemke . . . . Illinois, Iowa, Kansas, Minn., Missouri, Nebraska, N. Dakota, S. Dakota, Wisconsin
Scott Lovekamp . . . . Maryland, North Carolina, Virginia, Washington D.C.
Carlos Marti . . . . Miami (Fla.), Puerto Rico
Tim McIntosh . . . . Northern California, Northern Nevada (Reno)
Darryl Monroe . . . . Georgia, S. Carolina
Jeff Patterson . . . . Inland Empire (Calif.), Las Vegas
Cesar Presbott . . . . Delaware, New Jersey, New York City
D.J. Svihlik . . . . Alabama, Tennessee, Florida Panhandle
Mike Thurman . . . . Alaska, Idaho, Montana, Oregon, Washington, Wyoming, British Columbia
Dennis Twombley . . . . California (North L.A. to Fresno), Hawaii

INTERNATIONAL SCOUTING

Pat McMahon . . . . Coordinator of International Player Development
Donny Rowland . . . . Director, International Scouting
Dennis Woody . . . . International Crosschecker
Alex Cotto . . . . Assistant Director, International Operations
Joel Lithgow . . . . Director, Latin Baseball Academy
Aniuska Sanchez . . . . Manager, Latin Baseball Academy
Victor Mata . . . . International Scouting Supervisor, Dominican Republic
Ricardo Finol . . . . International Scouting Supervisor, Venezuela
Argenis Paulino . . . . Scouting Development Coach (Dominican Republic)
Jonnathan Saturria . . . . Scouting Development Coach (Dominican Republic)
Angel Ovalles . . . . Dominican Republic
Juan Rosario . . . . Dominican Republic
Jose Sabino . . . . Dominican Republic
Raymond Sanchez . . . . Dominican Republic
Alan Atacho . . . . Venezuela
Darwin Bracho . . . . Venezuela
Jose Gavidia . . . . Venezuela
Cesar Suarez . . . . Venezuela
Chairon Isenia . . . . Curacao
Carlos Levy . . . . Panama
Edgar Rodriguez . . . . Nicaragua
Luis Sierra . . . . Colombia
Lee Sigmen . . . . Mexico
Jason Lee . . . . Korea
Ken Su . . . . Pacific Rim
John Wadsworth . . . . Australia
Doug Skiles . . . . Europe

Player Development Staff

NARDI CONTRERAS - PITCHING COORDINATOR
BORN: 9/19/51 in Tampa, Fla. • **RESIDES:** Lutz, Fla.

COACHING CAREER: Enters his seventh season as the Yankees' pitching coordinator…will be his 41st year in professional baseball and his 29th as a coach…prior to rejoining the Yankees organization in 2005, served as the pitching coach for the rookie-level Princeton Devil Rays in the 2004 season after spending seven years as a Major League pitching coach with the Chicago White Sox (1998-2002), Seattle Mariners (1997) and Yankees (1995)…began his coaching career in the White Sox organization in 1982 and made stops within the minor league systems of the Atlanta Braves, Montreal Expos, Yankees and Arizona Diamondbacks before being promoted to the Yankees' Major League squad in 1995…**PLAYING CAREER:** Pitched for 13 seasons in the minor leagues, compiling a 69-72 career record and 3.86 ERA…appeared in eight Major League games with the White Sox in 1980 (0-0, 5.93 ERA)…**PERSONAL:** Graduated from Tampa Catholic High School in 1969, where he was named the "Most Valuable Athlete"…later graduated from Hillsborough Community College.

JAMES ROWSON - HITTING COORDINATOR
BORN: 9/12/76 in Mount Vernon, N.Y. • **RESIDES:** Spring Hill, Fla.

COACHING CAREER: Begins his fourth season as the Yankees' hitting coordinator…will be his sixth season in the organization also spending two seasons (2006-07) as the hitting coach at Single-A Tampa…previously served four seasons in the Angels organization as the hitting coach at Single-A Rancho Cucamonga (2004-05), Single-A Cedar Rapids (2003) and rookie-level Provo (2002)…**PLAYING CAREER:** Originally drafted by the Seattle Mariners out of Mount St. Michael High School in the Bronx …played minor league ball with the Mariners, Yankees and White Sox…**PERSONAL:** Is married to Maria with two daughters, Katiria and Kiana.

TORRE TYSON - DEFENSIVE COORDINATOR
BORN: 12/31/75 in Tampa, Fla. • **RESIDES:** Columbia, Mo.

COACHING CAREER: Begins his first season as defensive coordinator…spent the 2010 season as manager of Single-A Tampa, where he led the Yankees to their second consecutive FSL title…served the prior three years (2007-09) as Single-A Charleston's skipper, leaving as the RiverDogs' all-time winningest manager with 232 career victories…had served the two previous seasons as Charleston's hitting coach (2005-06)…was selected as a coach for the South Atlantic League's All-Star game in 2008 and '09, and joined the Yankees' Major League staff in September 2008…is his eighth season as a professional instructor/coach, having also worked as a coach with short-season Single-A Staten Island in 2004…**PLAYING CAREER:** Began his professional baseball career in 1998 when he signed with the Boston Red Sox as a non-drafted free agent…after spending almost two seasons in the Boston farm system, joined the Yankees in 2000 and spent time with Single-A Greensboro, Single-A Tampa and Double-A Norwich…**PERSONAL:** He and his wife, Jennifer, have a son, Tagger, and a daughter, Taryn…graduated from John Burroughs High School (Mo.) in 1994…played baseball at the University of Missouri…is the son of former Major League infielder Mike Tyson.

JACK HUBBARD - OUTFIELD INSTRUCTOR
BORN: 10/4/50 in Chestertown, Md. • **RESIDES:** Trinity, Fla.

COACHING CAREER: Returns for a seventh season as outfield instructor in the Yankees organization…previously served as the first base coach for the Triple-A Columbus Clippers in 2004…was a scouting supervisor for the state of Florida…a former Physical Education teacher, he spent more than 10 years as a minor league instructor and coach, special assignment scout, professional scout, and director of player development…worked in various capacities with several teams including the St. Louis Cardinals, Toronto Blue Jays and Chicago White Sox…**PERSONAL:** Is a graduate of the University of Baltimore with a bachelor of science degree in marketing.

JULIO MOSQUERA - CATCHING COORDINATOR
BORN: 1/29/72 in Panama City, Panama • **RESIDES:** Tarpon Springs, Fla.

COACHING CAREER: Enters his sixth season as the catching coordinator with the Yankees…joined the Yankees player development staff in 2005 after playing professionally for 15 years…**PLAYING CAREER:** Signed by the Toronto Blue Jays as a non-drafted free agent in 1991 and played parts of 15 seasons within the minor league systems of the Blue Jays, Tampa Bay Devil Rays, Yankees, Texas Rangers, Seattle Mariners and Milwaukee Brewers…made his Major League debut on 8/17/96 with Toronto and appeared in 12 career Major League games across three seasons (1996, '97, 2005)…**PERSONAL:** Lives with wife, Jennifer, and their two children, Dayana and Julio, Jr. in Tarpon Springs, Fla.

MARK LITTLEFIELD - HEAD ATHLETIC TRAINER
BORN: 11/27/67 in Portland, Maine • **RESIDES:** Tampa, Fla.

Begins his 20th season in the Yankees organization, his 18th as head athletic trainer…served as trainer for the Single-A Oneonta Yankees in 1991-92…graduated from Portland High School (Maine) in 1986…earned a bachelor of science degree from the University of South Carolina in physical education/athletic training…joined the Yankees as a minor league athletic trainer in 1991…married to his wife, Cara, and has a son, R.J., and daughter, Alexis.

MIKE WICKLAND - STRENGTH AND CONDITIONING COORDINATOR
BORN: 7/24/77 in Bridgeport, W.V. • **RESIDES:** Tampa, Fla.

Enters his fourth season as the Yankees' strength and conditioning coordinator with the player development staff…is his tenth consecutive season in the organization, having served for six seasons as the head trainer at Single-A Tampa (2002-07) and spending a season as the trainer with Single-A Greensboro in 2001…graduated from the University of North Carolina at Greensboro with a bachelor's degree in exercise and sports science in 1999…was an athletic trainer at UNC-Greensboro during his four years there.

Additional Player Development Staff

JAVIER ALVIDREZ - ASSISTANT STRENGTH & CONDITIONING COORDINATOR
BORN: 7/14/75 in El Paso, Tex. • RESIDES: El Paso, Tex.
Returns for his fourth season in the Yankees' player development staff as the assistant strength and conditioning coordinator...served for seven seasons (2000-06) as a trainer in the Oakland organization, including the last three at Double-A Midland of the Texas League...graduated from New Mexico State University.

DAVID HAYS - PLAYER DEVELOPMENT EQUIPMENT MANAGER
BORN: 2/21/49 in Herrin, Ill. • RESIDES: Lutz, Fla.
Enters his 23rd season as the Yankees' player development equipment manager and clubhouse supervisor...prior to joining the Yankees, taught in the Southwestern (Ill.) school system for 14 years and also coached baseball and basketball...was a member of the 1989 Eastern League Diamond Diplomacy team that toured the Soviet Union...graduated from Southern Illinois University with a bachelor of arts degree in education...married (Lissa) with two sons, Christopher and Michael.

CHRIS ROOT - PLAYER DEVELOPMENT CLUBHOUSE MANAGER
BORN: 5/22/69 in Cleveland, Ohio • RESIDES: Tampa, Fla.
Enters his ninth season in the Yankees organization and his seventh consecutive season as the Yankees' player development clubhouse manager in Tampa...previously worked in the Boston Red Sox system...prior to joining the Tampa staff, served as the clubhouse manager for the Eastern League's Trenton Thunder...graduated from High Point University with a bachelor of arts degree in Sports Management...married (Adina).

Yankees Roots

Entering spring training*, there were 28 players on opposing teams' active 40-man rosters that came through the Yankees' system (either drafted or originally signed as a non-drafted free agent by the Yankees).

Manny Acosta (New York-NL) . . . . Signed by the Yankees as a non-drafted free agent on January 6, 1998
John Axford (Milwaukee) . . . . Signed by the Yankees as a non-drafted free agent on August 11, 2006
Justin Berg (Chicago-NL) . . . . Selected by the Yankees in the 43rd round of the 2003 First-Year Player Draft
Melky Cabrera (Kansas City) . . . . Signed by the Yankees as a non-drafted free agent on November 13, 2001
Randy Choate (Florida) . . . . Selected by the Yankees in the fifth round of the 1997 First-Year Player Draft
Tyler Clippard (Washington) . . . . Selected by the Yankees in the ninth round of the 2003 First-Year Player Draft
Phil Coke (Detroit) . . . . Selected by the Yankees in the 26th round of the 2002 First-Year Player Draft
Jose Contreras (Philadelphia) . . . . Signed by the Yankees as a non-draft free agent on February 5, 2003
Dane De La Rosa (Tampa Bay) . . . . Selected by the Yankees in the 24th round of the 2002 First-Year Player Draft
Shelley Duncan (Cleveland) . . . . Selected by the Yankees in the second round of the 2001 First-Year Player Draft
Mike Dunn (Florida) . . . . Selected by the Yankees in the 33rd round of the 2004 First-Year Player Draft
Eric Hacker (Minnesota) . . . . Selected by the Yankees in the 23rd round of the 2002 First-Year Player Draft
Austin Jackson (Detroit) . . . . Selected by the Yankees in the eighth round of the 2005 First-Year Player Draft
Jeff Karstens (Pittsburgh) . . . . Selected by the Yankees in the 19th round of the 2003 First-Year Player Draft
Ian Kennedy (Arizona) . . . . Selected by the Yankees in the first round (21st overall) of the 2006 First-Year Player Draft
George Kontos (San Diego) . . . . Selected by the Yankees in the fifth round of the 2006 First-Year Player Draft
Zach Kroenke (Arizona) . . . . Selected by the Yankees in the fifth round of the 2005 First-Year Player Draft
Wilton Lopez (Houston) . . . . Signed by the Yankees as a non-drafted free agent on April 30, 2002
Jeff Marquez (Chicago-AL) . . . . Selected by the Yankees in Comp. Rd-A (41st overall) of the 2004 First-Year Player Draft
Hideki Matsui (Oakland) . . . . Signed by the Yankees as a free agent on January 14, 2003
Zach McAllister (Cleveland) . . . . Selected by the Yankees in the third round of the 2006 First-Year Player Draft
Dan McCutchen (Pittsburgh) . . . . Selected by the Yankees in the 13th round of the 2006 First-Year Player Draft
Mark Melancon (Houston) . . . . Selected in the ninth round in the 2006 First-Year Player Draft
Juan Miranda (Arizona) . . . . Signed by the Yankees as a non-drafted free agent on December 22, 2006
Carlos Monasterios (Los Angeles-NL) . . . . Signed by the Yankees as a non-drafted free agent on September 19, 2004
Dioner Navarro (Los Angeles-NL) . . . . Signed by the Yankees as a non-drafted free agent on August 21, 2000
Jimmy Paredes (Houston) . . . . Signed by the Yankees as a non-drafted free agent on July 2, 2006
Lance Pendleton (Houston) . . . . Selected in the fourth round of the 2005 First-Year Player Draft
Juan Rivera (Los Angeles-AL) . . . . Signed by the Yankees as a non-drafted free agent on April 12, 1996
Alfonso Soriano (Chicago-NL) . . . . Signed by the Yankees as a non-drafted free agent (Japan) on September 29, 1998
Jose Tabata (Pittsburgh) . . . . Signed by the Yankees as a non-drafted free agent on August 12, 2004
Chein-Ming Wang (Washington) . . . . Signed by the Yankees as a non-draft free agent on May 5, 2000

Rosters as of 1/21/11

Yankees Around the Globe

As the game of Baseball continues to grow on a global scale, "America's Pastime" has become infused with talent from all four corners of the world.

The New York Yankees, as one of the most recognized brands in the world, are dedicated to making meaningful and lasting footprints throughout the international Baseball community.

Just under 28 percent of players on Major League rosters on Opening Day 2010 were born outside the United States. For the Yankees, the total was 36.0 percent, with nine of the Yankees' 25 players on the team's Opening Day roster having been born in a foreign country. Among American League clubs, only the Rangers and Angels (10 each) had more foreign-born players on their Opening Day roster. The Yankees' 2010 Major League Opening Day roster was composed of players from six different nations outside the United States (Dominican Republic, South Korea, Mexico, Panama, Puerto Rico and Venezuela), tying for the second-most among all Major League clubs.

The Yankees' brand transcends international borders as fans show their pride around the globe.

Signing and developing exceptional talent from around the globe has become a trademark of the Yankees organization. Some of the club's acquisitions include the American League's all-time saves leader and Panama native Mariano Rivera, five-time All-Star Jorge Posada of Puerto Rico, two-time All-Star Hideki Matsui from Japan, 2006 Cy Young Award runner-up Chien-Ming Wang from Taiwan and All-Star Robinson Cano of the Dominican Republic.

At the minor league level, the organization has signed two Chinese minor leaguers, two players from the Israel Baseball League, and procured top minor league talent from Australia, Brazil, Canada, Colombia, Mexico, Nicaragua and Taiwan. In addition, the Yankees field two Dominican Summer League teams and operate a state-of-the-art Latin Baseball Academy in the Dominican Republic.

The Latin Béisbol Academy

For the vast majority of the Yankees' Latin American prospects, the Latin Béisbol Academy is the starting point for their professional careers.

Constructed in Boca Chica, Dominican Republic, the Yankees built their academy from scratch, allowing player development personnel to manage every detail of the project, from the trainer's room to the clubhouses to the classrooms. The end result is a four-building, four-field complex with the capacity to house up to 110 players. There is also a small apartment building for coaches and instructors. The academy, which officially opened in June 2005 and was completed in the spring of 2006, has a campus feel to it that is not lost on the ballplayers, many of whom are spending time away from their families for the first time.

Previously, the Yankees had leased a variety of facilities in Latin America for scouting and player development use, but it became apparent that it was necessary to find and develop their own facility.

"We've never had as many fields or batting cages," said Mark Newman, Yankees Senior Vice President of Baseball Operations, at the time the academy opened. "We've never had this level of control over player nutrition or this kind of strength and conditioning facility. All of these things enhance our player development efforts. Already, we've seen the physical, mental, emotional and fundamental maturation of players at a more rapid rate, and we should see it to a greater degree in the future."

As a dedicated investor in Latin American talent, the Yankees make every effort to enhance the instruction the players receive off the field. The complex is staffed with educators who teach American customs and provide one-on-one tutoring sessions. To further these goals, the Yankees created a partnership with Iberoamerican University (UNIBE) in Santo Domingo, a private institution that brings a group of 12 college professors to the academy. The professors teach everything from basic Spanish to three different levels of English, in addition to leading lectures on subjects such as conflict resolution and financial literacy.

The Yankees also arrange for past and present Major League stars, such as Mariano Rivera, Robinson Cano and Reggie Jackson, to be guest lecturers for the prospects. In November 2007, Yankees Manager Joe Girardi visited the Béisbol Academy and spoke to the coaching staff and 55 Latin players, including eight players from the 2006 and 2007 drafts. He also dined with the Yankees' senior Latin staff and watched a Dominican Instructional League game.

> **"The Latin Béisbol Academy was built to instruct, enhance and further develop the inherent skills in young, aspiring baseball players from all parts of Central and South America."**
>
> ~ **Yankees Chief International Officer, Executive Vice President Felix Lopez**

The players and staff are also active in local community events as well, hosting annual instructional clinics in the Dominican Republic, Nicaragua and Venezuela. In addition, the Yankees' Latin complex has hosted several R.B.I. (Reviving

Baseball in the Inner City) tournament games and joined the Yankees organization in the 2007 donation of $65,000 in food and cash to hurricane damaged areas in the D.R. and Nicaragua. The Yankees have also adopted an orphanage in the Dominican town of La Romana, supplying it with food, money and clothing. In July 2010, Dominican Summer League players delivered gifts to ailing children at a local hospital in Santo Domingo. The Latin Beisbol Academy also played host to a fundraiser game against the Dominican National Police Department to raise money for local charities throughout the D.R.

The Yankees field two Dominican Summer League teams and have reached the playoffs in four of the last six years (2005-07, '09), taking home back-to-back titles in 2005 and 2006. With the hard work and dedication of the Yankees Player Development staff, the organization looks forward to the future, when these young players can be a part of a World Championship in the Bronx.

Partners in Japan

During the 2002 season, the Yankees entered into a working agreement with the Yomiuri Giants, winners of 21 Japan Series Championships. Pursuant to the agreement, the teams consented to share baseball information, ideas and strategies. Also in 2002, the Yankees pursued and signed three-time Central League MVP Hideki Matsui. A nine-time Japanese League All-Star and three-time home run champion, Matsui became the first bonafide power hitter to make the transition from Japan to the Major Leagues.

In 2004, the Yankees traveled to Tokyo to open the regular season against the Tampa Bay Devil Rays. The historic trip marked the 70th anniversary of Babe Ruth and Lou Gehrig's 1934 All-Star tour of Japan. It also recognized the anniversary of the founding of the Yomiuri Giants franchise, Japan's oldest professional baseball team. The two-game series was just the second-ever Major League season opener to take place in Japan. At the time, the two games were the highest-rated televised Major League games in Japan's history.

Korean Baseball Commissioner Young Koo You threw out the ceremonial first pitch prior to the Yankees-Blue Jays game on July 2, 2010.

Yankees Teach in Taiwan

In January 2009, the Yankees joined the Chinese Taipei Baseball Association under the auspices of Major League Baseball in holding a clinic for high school pitchers, catchers and coaches at the National Taiwan Sport University's Taoyuan Campus in Taipei, Taiwan. It marked the Yankees' first-ever large-scale outreach in Taiwan and represented the club's initiative in cultivating baseball talent and increasing brand recognition in Asia and the greater international community. The five-day clinic focused on pitching and catching fundamentals and philosophy.

Yankees and Chinese Baseball Association
Reach Memorandum of Understanding

The New York Yankees and the Chinese Baseball Association (CBA) held a press conference in Beijing, China, on January 29, 2007, to announce a Memorandum of Understanding that for the first time formalized a strategic alliance between a Major League Baseball club and the Chinese Baseball Association. During the Yankees' 2009 World Series trophy tour, club officials met with the CBA in Beijing to further the cooperation agreement between the two entities.

The agreement, subject to Major League Baseball's rules, regulations and agreements pertaining to the People's Republic of China, states that the Yankees will provide the CBA with guidance in training baseball players, including sending coaches, player development staff, scouting and training personnel to China to assist the CBA. The partnership also allows the CBA to send staff to the Yankees' facilities in the United States in furtherance of those goals.

During their 2007 trip, the Yankees were represented in Beijing by team President Randy Levine, Senior Vice President and General Manager Brian Cashman, Vice President and Assistant General Manager Jean Afterman, and Vice President of Corporate Sales and Sponsorship Michael Tusiani. Beijing Womei Advertising Company Limited and Sportscorp China, headed by President and Managing Director Marc Ganis and Managing Director Kenneth Huang, coordinated the meetings and were instrumental in the Yankees' involvement in China.

Yankees Team President Randy Levine and General Manager Brian Cashman established a working agreement with the Chinese Baseball Association on Jan. 29, 2007.

"This agreement marks another milestone in Baseball's international evolution," Levine said. "We are excited to begin working alongside our friends in the Chinese Baseball Association, and they will receive our full support throughout this exciting process. The Yankees brand is recognized around the world, and this unprecedented opportunity allows us to further integrate the Yankees name and our proud history of success into Baseball's global landscape."

"It is a great honor to be a part of this unique and exciting opportunity," Cashman said. "Throughout China's history it's easy to see their passion for sports and their determination to excel in all athletic fields. With that belief in excellence, we are proud to begin work with the Chinese Baseball Association, and we will provide all of our available tools and resources to help develop and cultivate their baseball program from the ground up."

The CBA was represented by Chairman Hu Jianguo, Secretary General Shen Wei and Deputy Secretary General Tian Yuan.

On June 16, 2007, the Yankees announced the signings of C Zhenwang Zhang and LHP Kai Liu to minor league contracts, marking the first-ever acquisition by a Major League organization of Chinese baseball players. Both players were members of the Chinese National team that competed in the 2008 Olympics in Beijing.

Yankees Championship Trophy Tour of the Dominican Republic, Japan and China

Following their 2009 championship season, the Yankees embarked on a world tour with their 2009 World Series Trophy, traveling to the Dominican Republic and Asia.

Led by Chief International Officer and Executive Vice President Felix M. Lopez, Jr., a Yankees contingent took the championship trophy to the Dominican Republic for a three-day tour from Jan. 7-9, 2010. On the first night, the Yankees and the trophy went to the National Palace for a ceremony with Dominican Republic President Dr. Leonel Fernández. Lopez was joined by bench coach Tony Pena, and players Robinson Cano, Damaso Marte, Francisco Cervelli and Edwar Ramirez as well as by several Yankees minor leaguers. The next day, the Yankees visited the U.S. Embassy and the National Police Headquarters. That evening prior to the Dominican Winter League playoff game between the Licey Tigers and Escogido Lions at Quisqueya Stadium in Santo Domingo, Lopez threw out the ceremonial first pitch, and the Yankees displayed the trophy for fans in attendance. In their final day in the D.R., the Yankees placed the trophy on display for residents of the

The Yankees' 2009 championship trophy (left) visited the MLB Café in Tokyo, Japan, on Feb. 1, 2010. It was displayed alongside the Yomiuri Giants' 2009 Championship trophy (right) in the first-ever instance of the two titles being side-by-side.

town of Casa de Campo. In the evening, Lopez tossed the ceremonial first pitch at a game between La Romano and Escogido, and the Yankees again displayed the trophy for fans.

Three weeks later, a Yankees delegation including Team President Randy Levine, Senior Vice President and General Manager Brian Cashman, Vice President and Assistant General Manager Jean Afterman and Senior Vice President of Corporate Sales and Sponsorships Michael Tusiani, took the trophy on a six-day tour to Tokyo, Beijing and Hong Kong from Jan. 31 through Feb. 5, 2010.

The contingent was met by fans and media at Tokyo's Narita Airport, marking this first-ever occasion of a Yankees World Series trophy being brought to Asia. The next day, another historic moment took place at the MLB Café in Tokyo as the trophy was displayed alongside the Yomiuri Giants' 2009 Japan Series championship trophy in the first-ever instance of the two titles being side-by-side. Following a press event, the trophies then remained on display throughout the evening.

From there, the trophy traveled to China, where fans in Beijing and Hong Kong had their first opportunity to gaze at Major League Baseball's grandest prize. The trophy tour in China was organized by QSL Sports, which has been active in the promotion of Baseball in the People's Republic of China (PRC) and operates the China Youth Baseball League together with the Chinese Baseball Association. The events in China were hosted by QSL Sports, New World Department Stores (one of the largest owners and operators of department stores in China), and K11, the "World's First Art Mall," which integrates elements of art, culture and nature, while elevating the shopping experience.

On Feb. 3, 2010, Yankees officials met with the CBA in Beijing to further the cooperation agreement between the two entities, after which the groups held a joint press conference at the Kunlun Hotel. Later that evening, the championship trophy made its first public appearance in

Chinese youth players were on hand to see the trophy during a press conference with the Chinese Baseball Association on Feb. 3, 2010.

China at the New World Department Store, which included traditional Chinese performances and ceremonies. Joining the Yankees delegation were CBA officials, New World representatives and the Beijing Yankees youth baseball team, which is part of MLB's "Play Ball" youth baseball program in China.

Hong Kong marked the final stop on the Asian tour, with a Feb. 5, 2010, event at the Hyatt Regency hotel adjacent to the recently-opened K11 Mall. The next morning, the trophy was introduced to players and fans during the opening ceremony for Phoenix Cup 2010, Hong Kong's International Women's Baseball Tournament.

The Yankees thank their partner Delta Air Lines for ensuring the safe transportation of the World Series trophy and appreciate the efforts of Sportscorp China, led by president Marc Ganis.

The Yankees received a warm greeting from their Hong Kong fans on Feb. 4, 2010, when they became the first Major League team to step foot in the Chinese city.

From January 19-28, 2011, Yankees **OF Curtis Granderson** toured New Zealand as part of Major League Baseball's Ambassador program. While in the country, he held clinics and was on hand for the BCO Under-16 tournament, which determines which nation will represent the Oceania region at the Under-16 International Baseball Federation World Championships. The trip marked Granderson's fourth journey abroad as an MLB Ambassador, including stops in Europe, South Africa and China.

New York Yankees 2010 First-Year Player Draft

RD	SEL	PLAYER	POS	HT	WT	B	T	DOB	SCHOOL (STATE)
1	#32	**Cito Culver**	SS	6'0"	172	S	R	8/26/92	**Irondequoit HS (N.Y.)**
2	#82	**Angelo Gumbs**	SS	6'3"	175	R	R	10/13/92	**Torrance HS (Calif.)**
3	#112	**Robert Segedin**	3B	6'3"	220	R	R	11/10/88	**Tulane University**
4	#145	**Mason Williams**	CF	6'0"	150	L	R	8/21/91	**West Orange HS (Fla.)**
5	#175	**Thomas Kahnle**	RHP	6'1"	220	R	R	8/7/89	**Lynn University**
6	#205	**Gabe Encinas**	RHP	6'3"	195	R	R	12/21/91	**St. Paul HS (Calif.)**
7	#235	**Taylor Anderson**	CF	6'0"	170	L	R	12/3/91	**Woodlawn School (La.)**
8	#265	**Kyle Roller**	1B	6'1"	235	L	R	3/27/88	**East Carolina University**
9	#295	Taylor Morton	RHP	6'3"	194	R	R	12/18/91	Bartlett HS (Tenn.)
10	#325	**Benjamin Gamel**	CF	5'10"	180	L	L	5/17/92	**Bishop Kenny HS (Fla.)**
11	#355	**Zachary Varce**	RHP	6'0"	195	R	R	12/14/88	**University of Portland (Ore.)**
12	#385	**Daniel Burawa**	RHP	6'3"	190	R	R	12/30/88	**St. John's University**
13	#415	**Christopher Austin**	C	6'2"	200	R	R	9/6/91	**Heritage HS (Ga.)**
14	#445	Travis Dean	RHP	6'5"	175	R	R	5/3/91	Newton South HS (Mass.)
15	#475	**Chase Whitley**	RHP	6'4"	220	R	R	6/14/89	**Troy University**
16	#505	**Evan Rutckyj**	LHP	6'5"	213	R	L	1/31/92	**St. Joseph's HS (Windsor, Ontario)**
17	#535	**Preston Claiborne**	RHP	6'3"	230	R	R	1/21/88	**Tulane University**
18	#565	Kevin Jacob	RHP	6'6"	225	R	R	3/26/89	Georgie Tech
19	#595	Kevin Jordan	CF	6'0"	192	L	R	11/14/91	Northside HS (Ga.)
20	#625	**Michael Ferraro**	LF	6'2"	200	L	L	5/31/88	**University of San Diego**
21	#655	**Dustin Hobbs**	RHP	6'2"	200	R	R	8/18/89	**Yavapai College**
22	#685	Trevor Johnson	LHP	6'3"	190	L	L	7/29/88	College of the Desert
23	#715	**Shane Brown**	C	5'11"	197	R	R	1/11/88	**Central Florida**
24	#745	**Conor Mullee**	RHP	6'3"	185	R	R	2/25/88	**St. Peter's College (N.J.)**
25	#775	Casey Stevenson	2B	6'3"	200	L	R	5/18/88	University of Calif. - Irvine
26	#805	Richard James Hively	RHP	6'2"	205	R	R	11/27/88	Santa Ana College (Calif.)
27	#835	Martin Viramontes	RHP	6'5"	190	R	R	7/12/89	Loyola Marymount University
28	#865	Josh Dezse	RHP	6'4"	205	R	R	6/18/92	Olentangy Liberty HS (Ohio)
29	#895	Stewart Ijames	LF	6'1"	200	R	R	8/21/88	Louisville University
30	#925	**Zachary Nuding**	RHP	6'4"	250	R	R	3/29/90	**Weatherford College**
31	#955	**James Gipson**	RHP	6'1"	180	R	R	9/15/88	**Florida Atlantic University**
32	#985	**Kramer Sneed**	LHP	6'3"	185	L	L	10/7/88	**Barton College**
33	#1015	Michael Hachadorian	RHP	6'5"	215	R	R	5/3/90	San Diego Mesa College
34	#1045	William Kish	RHP	6'3"	170	L	R	11/29/91	Germantown Academy (Pa.)
35	#1075	**William Oliver**	RHP	6'2"	180	R	R	7/4/87	**Palomar College**
36	#1105	**Nick McCoy**	C	5'10"	180	R	R	3/2/87	**University of San Diego**
37	#1135	Cameron Hobson	LHP	6'0"	200	L	L	4/10/89	University of Dayton
38	#1165	James Ramsay	CF	6'0"	170	L	L	3/2/92	Brandon HS (Fla.)
39	#1195	Jaycob Brugman	OF	5'11"	170	L	L	1/18/92	Desert Vista HS (Ariz.)
40	#1225	Michael Gerber	CF	6'2"	175	L	L	7/8/92	Neuqua Valley HS (Ill.)
41	#1255	Tymothy Pearson	CF	6'2"	205	R	R	10/30/90	Columbia Basin CC (Ore.)
42	#1285	Michael O'Neill	CF	6'0"	175	R	R	6/12/92	Olentangy Liberty HS (Ohio)
43	#1315	Kyle Hunter	LHP	6'3"	185	L	L	6/18/89	Kansas State University
44	#1345	David Middendorf	LHP	6'3"	225	R	L	1/23/89	Northern Kentucky University
45	#1375	Tyler Johnson	OF	6'0"	185	R	R	5/20/89	Penn State University
46	#1405	**Nathan Forer**	RHP	6'1"	172	R	R	6/6/88	**Southern Ill. Univ. - Carbondale**
47	#1435	**Frederick Lewis**	LHP	6'2"	210	L	L	12/16/86	**Tennessee Wesleyan College**
48	#1465	Alex Brown	RHP	6'1"	165	R	R	10/8/91	Amphitheater HS (Ariz.)
49	#1495	Will Arthur	OF	6'2"	180	L	R	4/4/92	Abbotsford Sec. School (B.C.)
50	#1525	James Rice	C	6'3"	190	R	R	5/8/89	Western Kentucky University

Bold=Signed

New York Yankees No. 1 Draft Choices

Year	Round	Pick	Name	Pos	School/Hometown	w/NYY in Majors
2010	1	32	Cito Culver	SS	Irondequoit HS (N.Y.)	-
2009	1	29	Slade Heathcott	OF	Texas HS (TX)	-
2008	1	28	Gerritt Cole	RHP	Orange Lutheran HS (CA)	Did not sign
2007	1	30	Andrew Brackman	RHP	North Carolina St.	-
2006	1	21	Ian Kennedy	RHP	University of Southern California	2007-2009
2005	1	17	Carl (C.J.) Henry	SS	Putnam City HS (OK)	-
2004	1	23	Phil Hughes	RHP	Foothill HS (CA)	2007-present
2003	1	27	Eric Duncan	3B	Seton Hall Prep (NJ)	-
2002	2	71	Brandon Weeden	RHP	Santa Fe HS (NM)	-
2001	1	23	John-Ford Griffin	OF	Florida State University	-
	1	34	Bronson K. Sardinha	INF	Kamehameha HS (HI)	2007
	1	42	Jon S. Skaggs	RHP	Rice University	-
2000	1	28	David Parrish	C	University of Michigan	-
1999	1	27	David Walling	RHP	University of Arkansas	-
1998	1	24	Andrew Brown	OF	Richmond H.S. (Ind)	-
	1	43	Mark Prior	RHP	University H.S. (S.D.)	Did not sign
1997	1	24	Tyrell Godwin	OF	East Bladen H.S. (NC)	-
	1	40	Ryan Bradley	RHP	Arizona State University	1998
1996	1	20	Eric Milton	LHP	University of Maryland	-
1995	1	27	Shea Morenz	RF	University of Texas	-
1994	1	24	Brian Buchanan	OF	University of Virginia	-
1993	1	13	Matt Drews	RHP	Sarasota H.S. (FL)	-
1992	1	6	Derek Jeter	SS	Kalamazoo Cent. H.S. (MI)	1995-present
1991	1	1	Brien Taylor	LHP	East Carteret H.S. (NC)	-
1990	1	10	Carl Everett	OF	Hillsborough H.S. (FL)	-
1989	2	42	Andy Fox	3B	Christian Bros. H.S. (CA)	1995-97
1988	4	105	Todd Malone	LHP	Casa Robles H.S. (CA)	-
1987	3	81	Bill DaCosta	RHP	New York Tech	-
1986	2	25	Rich Scheid	LHP	Seton Hall University (NJ)	-
1985	1	27	Rick Balabon	RHP	Berwyn, PA	-
1984	1	22	Jeff Pries	RHP	U.C.L.A.	-
1983	4	13	Mitch Lyden	C	Beaverton, OR	-
1982	2	8	Tim Birtsas	LHP	Michigan St. University	-
	2	22	Bo Jackson	SS	Bessemer, AL	-
1981	2	26	John Elway	OF	Stanford University	-
1980	3	22	Billy Cannon	SS	Baton Rouge, LA	-
1979	2	25	Todd Demeter	INF	Oklahoma City, OK	-
1978	1	18	Rex Hudler	SS	Fresno, CA	1984-85
	1	24	Matt Winters	OF	Williamsville, NY	-
	1	26	Brian Ryder	RHP	Shrewsbury, MA	-
1977	1	23	Steve Taylor	RHP	University of Delaware	-
1976	1	16	Pat Tabler	OF	Cincinnati, OH	-
1975	1	19	James McDonald	1B	Los Angeles, CA	-
1974	1	12	Dennis Sherrill	SS	Miami, FL	1978, '80
1973	1	13	Doug Heinold	RHP	Victoria, TX	-
1972	1	14	Scott McGregor	LHP	El Segundo, CA	-
1971	1	19	Terry Whitfield	OF	Blythe, CA	1974-76
1970	1	12	Dave Cheadle	LHP	Ashevill, NC	-
1969	1	11	Charlie Spikes	OF	Bogalusa, LA	1972
1968	1	4	Thurman Munson	C	Kent State University	1969-79
1967	1	1	Ron Blomberg	1B	Atlanta, GA	1969, '71-77
1966	1	10	Jim Lyttle	OF	Florida St. University	1969-71
1965	1	19	Bill Burbach	RHP	Dickeyville, WI	1969-71

Yankees from the Start

Twenty-one players on the Yankees active 40-man roster entering the 2011 season were either drafted or originally signed as a non-drafted free agent by the Yankees (as of Feb. 8).

Andrew Brackman	Selected in the first round (30th overall) of the 2007 First-Year Player Draft
Robinson Cano	Signed as a non-drafted free agent on January 5, 2001
Francisco Cervelli	Signed as a non-drafted free agent on March 1, 2003
Reegie Corona	Signed by the Yankees as a non-drafted free agent on July 2, 2003
Joba Chamberlain	Selected in Compensation Round A (41st overall) of the 2006 First-Year Player Draft
Wlkin De La Rosa	Signed as a non-drafted free agent on November 15, 2001
Christian Garcia	Selected in the third round of the 2004 First-Year Player Draft
Brett Gardner	Selected in the third round of the 2005 First-Year Player Draft
Phil Hughes	Selected in the first round (23rd overall) of the 2004 First-Year Player Draft
Derek Jeter	Selected in the first round (sixth overall) of the 1992 First-Year Player Draft
Nick Johnson	Selected in the third round of the 1996 First-Year Player Draft
Mark Melancon	Selected in the ninth round of the 2006 First-Year Player Draft
Juan Miranda	Signed as a non-drafted free agent on December 22, 2006
Hector Noesi	Signed by the Yankees as a non-drafted free agent on December 3, 2004
Ivan Nova	Signed as a non-drafted free agent on July 15, 2004
Eduardo Nunez	Signed by the Yankees as a non-drafted free agent on February 25, 2004
Ramiro Pena	Signed as a non-drafted free agent on February 18, 2005
Andy Pettitte	Selected in the 22nd round of the 1990 First-Year Player Draft
Jorge Posada	Selected in the 24th round of the 1990 First-Year Player Draft
David Robertson	Selected in the 17th round of the 2006 First-Year Player Draft
Mariano Rivera	Signed as a non-drafted free agent on February 17, 1990
Kevin Russo	Selected in the 20th round of the 2006 First-Year Player Draft

GEORGIAN COURT UNIVERSITY

Where saying, "You run kick serve swing break catch shoot block jump attack spike check hit assist charge pass defend hook pitch swish dribble shield steal stuff tackle set trap dig roll ace vault toss field draft save **like a girl!" is no insult.**

**Renowned Women's College
Coeducational University College
8 NCAA Division II women's sports**

**800.458.8422, ext. 2700
www.georgian.edu
www.gculions.com
Lakewood, New Jersey**

Organizational Summary

AAA	Scranton/Wilkes-Barre Yankees	International League	87-56 (.608)
AA	Trenton Thunder	Eastern League	83-59 (.585)
A	Tampa Yankees	Florida State League	78-57 (.578)
A	Charleston RiverDogs	South Atlantic League	65-74 (.468)
Short-A	Staten Island Yankees	New York-Penn League	34-40 (.459)
R	GCL Yankees	Gulf Coast League	24-32 (.429)

WINNING BASEBALL: Yankees affiliates combined for a 443-389 (.532) record in 2010, finishing the regular season with the third-best winning percentage among American League organizations…in fact, Yankees farm clubs have combined for a winning record in each of the last 21 seasons (1990-2010).

CHAMPS AGAIN: The Single-A Tampa Yankees (78-57) won their second consecutive Florida State League championship in 2010 and fifth in franchise history, marking the first time that a FSL team has won back-to-back league titles since the Lakeland Flying Tigers from 1975-76…the **Triple-A Scranton/Wilkes-Barre Yankees** (83-56) won their fifth straight International League North Division title and fourth consecutive as an affiliate of the New York Yankees, extending their record for most consecutive division championships in league history…the **Double-A Trenton Thunder** went 83-59, winning the Eastern League's North Division title for the third time in the last four years.

CREAM OF THE CROP: INF Brandon Laird (EL) and **OF Melky Mesa** (FSL) were each named Player of the Year in their respective leagues…marked the second straight year that the Yankees had two players awarded with the honor after Shelley Duncan (IL) and Austin Romine (FSL) accomplished the feat in 2009…Laird was also named to the *Sporting News* 2010 All-Minor League team…**C Jesus Montero** made the IL's midseason and postseason All-Star squad…entered the 2010 season tabbed by *Baseball America* as the Yankees' top prospect and the fifth-best prospect in all of Baseball (top catcher).

2010 DRAFT SUMMARY: With their first-round pick (32nd selection) in the 2010 First-Year Player Draft, the Yankees selected **INF Cito Culver** out of Irondequoit High School (N.Y.)…was ranked as the third best prospect from the state of New York…was also a three-time all-county selection as well as an Under Armour All-American…the Yankees drafted a total of 21 pitchers, four catchers, five infielders and 13 outfielders…the Yankees signed 26 of their draft picks, including each of the top eight and 19 of the top 24.

DSL YANKEES: The Dominican Summer League Yankees 1 completed the 2010 season with a 44-27 record, finishing second in the Boca Chica South Division…the Dominican Summer League Yankees 2 finished 28-44, ranking eighth in the Boca Chica North Division…**RHPs Cristofer Cabrera** and **Deivi Mojica** and **OF Yeicok Calderon**, of the DSL Yankees 1, and **INF Rafael Polo**, of the DSL Yankees 2, were each selected to the DSL All-Star team…Cabrera went 3-1 with a 0.51 ERA in eight starts, allowing just 2ER in 35.0IP…in 13G/2GS, Mojica was 8-2 with a 2.00 ERA, limiting opposing batters to a .193 (36-for-187) batting average…Calderon hit .339 (83-for-245), leading the DSL in extra-base hits (30), slugging percentage (.551) and total bases (135), ranking second in HRs and hits, third in on-base percentage (.439) and ninth in batting average…Polo batted .323 (80-for-248) with 17 doubles, nine triples and 30RBI in 63G…ranked second in extra-base hits (27) and triples, third in total bases (118), fifth in hits and slugging percentage (.476) and ninth in average.

ORGANIZATIONAL LEADERS

Batting Average

Robert Lyerly	CHA	.312
Jesus Montero	SWB	.289
Eduardo Nunez	SWB	.289
Justin Christian	SWB	.289
Marcos Vechionacci	TRE	.283

HR

Brandon Laird	SWB	.25
Jesus Montero	SWB	.21
Melky Mesa	TAM	.19
Jorge Vazquez	SWB	.18
Juan Miranda	SWB	.15

RBI

Brandon Laird	SWB	102
Daniel Brewer	TRE	84
Bradley Suttle	TAM	.80
Jesus Montero	SWB	.75
Melky Mesa	TAM	.74

SB

Raymond Kruml	TAM	.42
Jimmy Paredes	CHA	.36
Melky Mesa	TAM	.31
Jose Pirela	TAM	.30
Daniel Brewer	TRE	.29

ERA

Michael O'Brien	STA	2.08
Graham Stoneburner	TAM	2.41
David Phelps	SWB	2.50
Adam Warren	TRE	2.59
Ivan Nova	SWB	2.86

Wins

Hector Noesi	SWB	14
D.J. Mitchell	SWB	13
Ivan Nova	SWB	12
Lance Pendleton	SWB	12
2 others tied		11

Strikeouts

Hector Noesi	SWB	153
David Phelps	SWB	141
Graham Stoneburner	TAM	137
Lance Pendleton	SWB	133
2 others tied		126

Saves

Jonathan Albaladejo	SWB	.43
Jonathan Ortiz	TAM	.21
Ryan Pope	TRE	.17
Chase Whitley	TAM	.15
Ryan Flannery	TAM	.14

The Tampa Yankees captured their second straight Florida State League Championship in 2010.

Scranton/Wilkes-Barre Yankees (AAA)

AFFILIATE SINCE 2007
International League – PNC Field
Office Address: 235 Montage Mountain Road, Moosic, PA 18507
Telephone: (570) 969-2255. **Fax:** (570) 963-6564
Website: www.swbyankees.com
Executive Vice President and General Manager: Jeremy Ruby
Director of Broadcasting and Media Relations: Mike Vander Woude
2010 record, finish: 87-56, First in North Division

DAVE MILEY – MANAGER
BORN: 4/3/62 in Tampa, Fla. • **RESIDES:** Covington, Ky.
COACHING CAREER: Returns for his sixth season as the Yankees' Triple-A Manager...has guided the SWB Yankees to the IL North Division title in each of the last four seasons, compiling an IL-best 340-231 (.595) combined mark over the stretch...earned his 1,500th career win in 2010 and helped guide the SWB Yankees to the second-best record in the IL...recorded the league's best record in 2007 and '08, winning the league title in 2008 and finishing as runner-up in 2009...named 2007 IL "Manager of the Year"...owns 24 seasons of minor league managerial experience with a record of 1,524-1,145 (.571), including 17 winning seasons...ranks fifth among active minor league managers in wins...joined the Yankees organization in 2006 after spending 26 seasons with Cincinnati as a player, coach and manager...took over as manager of the Reds on 7/28/03, replacing Bob Boone...was named *Baseball America's* NL "Manager of the Year" for the first half of the 2004 season...also spent time on the Major League staff in 1993 as bench coach...served as the organization's assistant minor league field coordinator in 1994...spent three-plus seasons as manager at Triple-A Louisville from 2000-03, where he established franchise records for wins (296) and games managed (541)...in 2001, guided Louisville to its first IL championship...also had managerial assignments with Indianapolis (1996-99), Chattanooga (1992, '95), Nashville (1992), Charleston (1991), Cedar Rapids (1989-90) and Greensboro (1988)...coached at Vermont in 1997...began his coaching career in 1986, splitting the season at Single-A Tampa and Single-A Sarasota...**PLAYING CAREER:** Signed with the Reds in 1980 as a catcher and played in seven minor league seasons (1980-86)...in 403 minor league games, hit .238 with 16HR, 172RBI and 13SB...**PERSONAL:** Attended Chamberlain High School in Tampa, Fla., where he played football and baseball...was a second-team all-conference defensive end.

CODY MILEY SCHOLARSHIP FUND: In 2008, a scholarship fund was established for Cody Miley, the 17-year-old son of Scranton/Wilkes-Barre Manager Dave Miley, who was killed in a car accident in August of that year...the Cody Miley Memorial Art Scholarship Fund is awarded each year to a deserving and needy student from Chamberlain High School in Tampa.

SCOTT ALDRED – PITCHING COACH
BORN: 6/12/68 in Flint, Mich. • **RESIDES:** Fenton, Mich.
COACHING CAREER: Begins his third season as pitching coach with Scranton/Wilkes-Barre...guided a staff that earned a league-high four IL "Pitcher of the Week" Awards in 2010...SWB pitchers led the IL in ERA (3.32) and shutouts (16) in 2009...is his sixth year as a coach, after spending the prior two seasons (2007-08) as pitching coach with Double-A Trenton and one season (2006) at Single-A Charleston in the same role...his 2007 staff had a 3.18 ERA, second-lowest among all full-season minor league clubs and struck out 1,159 batters, second-most among all Double-A clubs...**PLAYING CAREER:** Originally drafted by the Detroit Tigers in 1987...appeared in 229 games over an 11-year Major League career, posting a 20-39 record with a 6.02 ERA with six different teams (Detroit, 1990-92, '96; Colorado, 1993; Montreal, 1993; Minnesota, 1996-97; Tampa Bay, 1998-99 and Philadephia, 1999-2000)...**PERSONAL:** Married to Stacy with three daughters: Lindsey, Courtney and Kiley.

BUTCH WYNEGAR – HITTING COACH
BORN: 3/14/56 in York, Pa. • **RESIDES:** Longwood, Fla.
COACHING CAREER: Enters his fifth season with the Yankees organization as hitting coach at Triple-A Scranton/Wilkes-Barre...In 2010, SWB hitters ranked second in the IL in average (.277) and OBP (.353)...under his guidance in 2007, SWB led the IL in runs scored...spent his previous four years as the hitting coach for Milwaukee...under his direction, the Brewers established a franchise record with 327 doubles in 2005...prior to joining the Brewers, served as a coach in the Texas organization from 1995-2002...spent part of the 1999 season as the Rangers' Major League bullpen coach...**PLAYING CAREER:** Played 13 Major League seasons with Minnesota (1976-82), the Yankees (1982-86) and California (1987-88)...was named the 1976 *Sporting News* "AL Rookie of the Year" and became the youngest player at the time to appear in an All-Star Game (20 yrs, 212 days)...while with the Yankees, caught Dave Righetti's no-hitter on 7/4/83 and Phil Niekro's 300th career win on 10/1/85...**PERSONAL:** Full name is Harold Delano Wynegar, Jr...married (Debbie) with one son (Mark)...graduated from Red Lion High School in York, Penn.

FRANK MENECHINO – COACH
BORN: 1/7/1971 in Staten Island, NY • **RESIDES:** Staten Island, NY.
COACHING CAREER: Begins his first season as coach with Scranton/Wilkes-Barre after serving as hitting coach for Double-A Trenton in 2009 and 2010 in his first carer coaching assignment...**PLAYING CAREER:** Played in 450 Major League games over parts of seven seasons with Oakland (1999-2004) and Toronto (2004-05), batting .240 with 58 doubles, 36HR and 149RBI...was originally drafted by Chicago-AL in the 45th round of the 1993 First-Year Player Draft, was a minor league Rule 5 selection by Oakland in 1997...the infielder also spent time in the Cincinnati (2006), Yankees (2006), Colorado (2007) and San Diego (2007) organizations...played for Team Italy in the 2006 World Baseball Classic and played in the Italian Baseball League in 2008...**PERSONAL:** Graduated from Wagner High School in Staten Island...played ball at the University of Alabama.

DARREN LONDON – TRAINER
BORN: 12/26/66 in Sherman Station, Maine • **RESIDES:** Hilliard, Ohio
Enters his 22nd consecutive season in the Yankees organization, 19th with the Triple-A affiliate...was honored as the 2006 IL "Athletic Trainer of the Year," as selected by the Professional Baseball Athletic Trainers Society (PBATS)...began his career in 1989 with Single-A Prince William where he worked for two seasons...was named trainer at Single-A Ft. Lauderdale in 1991 and moved to Double-A Albany in 1992...**PERSONAL:** Graduated from the University of Maine-Orono, where he earned a BS in physical education with a coaching minor.

LEE TRESSEL – STRENGTH AND CONDITIONING COACH
BORN: 5/6/81 in Cleveland, Ohio • **RESIDES:** Tampa, Fla.
Returns for his third season as SWB's strength and conditioning coach...served as the assistant strength and conditioning coordinator at the Yankees' minor league complex in Tampa, Fla. in 2007 before joining Double-A Trenton's staff in 2008...served for three seasons (2004-06) as an assistant in the Yankees' baseball operations department under General Manager Brian Cashman...graduated from Baldwin Wallace College in Berea, Ohio, in 2003 with a degree in sports management and business.

2010 Scranton/Wilkes-Barre Yankees (AAA)

BATTERS	AVG	G	AB	R	H	2B	3B	HR	RBI	BB	SO	SB	CS	OBP	SLG	E
Bruntlett, Eric	.265	70	253	35	67	14	0	9	38	16	59	4	0	.316	.427	7
Christian, Justin	.242	16	66	9	16	0	0	0	4	8	9	2	0	.324	.242	0
#Corona, Reegie	.238	105	387	46	92	20	5	5	31	36	58	14	1	.306	.354	4
*Curtis, Colin	.289	66	239	28	69	24	0	5	27	21	38	1	2	.358	.452	0
*Cusick, Matthew	.265	29	83	11	22	6	0	0	9	10	7	0	0	.337	.337	5
Golson, Greg	.263	116	415	51	109	23	5	10	40	25	99	17	4	.313	.414	5
Gonzalez, Edwar	.154	4	13	1	2	0	0	0	0	1	5	0	0	.214	.154	0
Gorecki, Reid	.253	78	281	45	71	18	5	3	30	32	67	12	3	.332	.384	5
*Granderson, Curtis	.250	5	16	0	4	0	0	0	2	2	2	0	0	.333	.250	0
Hammock, Robby	.180	22	61	6	11	2	0	0	4	11	13	0	1	.306	.213	1
Huffman, Chad	.274	104	368	48	101	20	0	10	45	40	81	0	2	.353	.410	3
Laird, Brandon	.246	31	122	13	30	6	0	2	12	4	27	0	0	.268	.344	2
*Miranda, Juan	.285	80	295	52	84	15	1	15	43	33	71	1	0	.371	.495	4
Moeller, Chad	.230	28	87	8	20	6	0	1	9	6	15	0	0	.302	.333	1
Montero, Jesus	.289	123	453	66	131	34	3	21	75	46	91	0	0	.353	.517	6
Natale, Jeff	.182	14	22	3	4	1	0	0	6	3	1	0	0	.286	.227	1
Nunez, Eduardo	.289	118	464	55	134	25	4	4	50	32	60	23	5	.340	.381	14
Pilittere, P.J.	.357	22	56	6	20	4	0	1	5	5	13	0	1	.419	.482	1
Rivera, Rene	.250	19	68	3	17	3	0	2	11	1	17	0	0	.257	.382	0
Russo, Kevin	.259	81	332	41	86	16	2	1	24	28	65	9	4	.333	.328	9
*Snyder, Justin	.333	2	6	0	2	0	0	0	1	0	0	0	0	.333	.333	0
Thames, Marcus	.200	4	15	0	3	0	0	1	0	1	0	0	0	.200	.200	0
*Tracy, Chad	.324	18	68	14	22	5	0	6	18	4	6	0	0	.356	.662	1
Vazquez, Jorge	.270	76	293	47	79	21	0	18	62	17	95	0	0	.313	.526	6
*Weber, Jon	.258	47	163	18	42	7	2	0	11	18	25	0	2	.333	.325	2
Winfree, David	.264	52	201	24	53	16	0	5	33	9	32	0	0	.301	.418	3
Team Total	**.267**	**143**	**4827**	**630**	**1291**	**286**	**26**	**118**	**591**	**408**	**957**	**83**	**25**	**.330**	**.411**	**93**

PITCHERS	W-L	ERA	G	GS	CG	SHO	SV	IP	H	R	ER	HR	HB	BB	SO	WP
Aceves, Alfredo	0-0	7.36	3	2	0	0	0	3.2	4	4	3	0	2	5	4	0
Albaladejo, Jonathan	4-2	1.42	57	0	0	0	43	63.1	38	10	10	3	2	18	82	6
Duff, Grant	0-0	6.00	4	0	0	0	0	6.0	8	4	4	0	0	2	6	0
Hirsh, Jason	9-7	3.90	26	19	0	0	0	122.1	102	55	53	17	8	39	95	1
*Igawa, Kei	3-4	4.32	22	10	0	0	0	77.0	81	37	37	9	0	23	68	2
Kontos, George	0-1	10.12	2	0	0	0	0	2.2	5	3	3	1	0	1	2	0
*Logan, Boone	0-1	2.11	14	0	0	0	0	21.1	18	5	5	1	2	4	23	1
McAllister, Zach	8-10	5.09	24	24	1	0	0	132.2	165	82	75	20	6	38	88	7
Melancon, Mark	6-1	3.67	40	0	0	0	6	56.1	63	24	23	5	3	31	58	7
Mitchell, D.J.	2-0	3.57	3	3	0	0	0	17.2	19	7	7	0	0	7	16	2
Mitre, Sergio	0-1	7.04	2	2	0	0	0	7.2	9	6	6	1	1	2	7	1
Moseley, Dustin	4-4	4.21	12	12	0	0	0	72.2	83	40	34	6	4	18	55	4
Noesi, Hector	1-1	4.82	3	3	1	0	0	18.2	23	10	10	1	1	4	14	1
Norton, Tim	0-0	0.00	1	0	0	0	0	1.0	1	0	0	0	0	1	0	0
Nova, Ivan	12-3	2.86	23	23	0	0	0	145.0	135	50	46	10	2	48	115	4
Park, Chan Ho	0-0	0.00	1	1	0	0	0	1.0	1	0	0	0	0	0	2	1
Pendleton, Lance	2-1	4.24	6	5	0	0	0	34.0	29	17	16	6	0	12	22	1
Phelps, David	4-2	3.07	12	11	0	0	0	70.1	76	31	24	4	1	13	57	1
Redding, Tim	7-4	2.46	13	12	1	0	0	84.0	68	24	23	2	2	17	62	2
*Ring, Royce	2-1	1.93	52	0	0	0	2	42.0	35	12	9	2	5	11	39	2
Sanchez, Romulo	10-8	3.97	31	14	0	0	0	104.1	88	50	46	8	1	59	96	6
Sanit, Amaury	3-2	7.75	21	1	0	0	0	33.2	47	29	29	7	0	15	22	5
Schmidt, Josh	1-0	7.20	2	0	0	0	0	5.0	6	4	4	0	1	2	3	0
Segovia, Zack	3-2	4.19	44	0	0	0	4	62.1	68	32	29	6	2	14	51	5
Van Benschoten, John	2-0	2.31	6	1	0	0	1	11.2	13	3	3	1	0	6	8	1
Whelan, Kevin	2-1	6.30	17	0	0	0	1	20.0	19	15	14	2	1	10	22	3
Wordekemper, Eric	2-0	3.13	24	0	0	0	1	31.2	31	11	11	2	0	9	29	2
Team Total	**87-56**	**3.78**	**143**	**143**	**3**	**7**	**58**	**1248.0**	**1235**	**565**	**524**	**114**	**44**	**409**	**1046**	**65**

KEY: *- Lefthanded hitter/pitcher, # - switch hitter

Trenton Thunder (AA)

AFFILIATE SINCE 2003
Eastern League – Mercer County Waterfront Park
Office Address: One Thunder Rd., Trenton, NJ 08611
Telephone: (609) 394-3300. **Fax:** (609) 394-9666
Website: www.trentonthunder.com
General Manager, Chief Operating Officer: Will Smith
Director of Public Relations: Bill Cook
2010 record, finish: 83-59, First in Eastern Division

TONY FRANKLIN - MANAGER

BORN: 6/9/50 in Portland, Maine • **RESIDES:** Los Angeles, Calif.

COACHING CAREER: Returns for his fifth season as Manager of the Thunder…led Trenton to the best record in the Eastern League (83-59) in 2010 and the team's third appearance in the EL Championship Series in the last four years…joined Ozzie Smith's staff as a coach at the 2009 All-Star Futures Game…led Trenton to back-to-back league championships in 2007 and '08 in his first two seasons with the team…were the franchise's first titles in its 14-year history…also compiled the EL's best regular season record each of the two seasons…owns a 925-830 (.527) career managerial record over 15 seasons…also managed in the Arizona Fall League in 2007 (Peoria Javelinas)…prior to joining the Yankees organization in 2007, spent most of the previous 11 years as the minor league infield instructor for the San Diego Padres…his managerial career began with the White Sox organization at Single-A Geneva of the NY-Penn League from 1982-85…managed at rookie-level Wytheville (1986) before taking over the helm of the Single-A Sarasota White Sox from 1987-89…served as manager for Double-A Birmingham from 1990-91, guiding the Barons to the 1991 SL Championship Series…led Single-A South Bend to the Midwest League title in 1993…also served as the interim manager with Triple-A Las Vegas in 2000…**PERSONAL:** Married to Haiba with three children: Derrick, Wayne and Shelby…was honored by San Diego in 1997 with the Jack Krol Award for Outstanding Minor League Instruction in the Padres organization…was honored at the 11th Annual Black Executive Awards on 2/26/09 in Trenton…managed former Heisman Trophy winner Bo Jackson for four rehab games while with Birmingham in 1991.

TOMMY PHELPS – PITCHING COACH

BORN: 3/7/74 in Seoul, S. Korea • **RESIDES:** Valrico, Fla.

COACHING CAREER: Begins his third season with the Thunder after serving as the Yankees' minor league rehabilitation coach in 2008…**PLAYING CAREER:** Pitched for 14 seasons from 1993-2006 in the Montreal (1993-99), Detroit (2000-01), Florida (2002-04), Milwaukee (2005) and Yankees (2006) organizations…appeared in 75 combined Major League games (11 starts) with the Marlins and Brewers, posting a 4-5 record with one save and a 4.34 ERA…went 2-3 with a 4.00 ERA in 27 games (seven starts) for the 2003 World Series champion Marlins…the right-hander pitched in 330 career minor league games (199 starts), going 84-72 with five saves and a 4.14 ERA…**PERSONAL:** Full name is Thomas Allen Phelps…graduated from Robinson High School in Tampa, Fla. in 1992.

JULIUS MATOS – HITTING COACH

BORN: 12/12/74 in New York, N.Y. • **RESIDES:** New Port Richey, Fla.

COACHING CAREER: Returns to Trenton as a coach, reuniting with the team he made his coaching debut with in 2008…spent the past two seasons (2009-10) as the hitting coach for Single-A Tampa…**PLAYING CAREER:** Had a 13-year professional playing career in the Cleveland (1994-95), Arizona (1998-99), San Diego (2000-02, '06), Kansas City (2003), Toronto (2004, '05) and Montreal (2004) organizations…also played in the Independent Northern League with Thunder Bay in 1995 and Sioux City in 1996…saw Major League action with the Padres in 2002 and the Royals in 2003, combining to bat .244 (59-for-242) with 4 doubles, 4HR and 26RBI in 104 games…was originally selected by Cleveland in the 16th round of the 1994 First-Year Player Draft.

JUSTIN POPE – COACH

BORN: 11/8/79 in West Palm Beach, Fla. • **RESIDES:** Lake Worth, Fla.

COACHING CAREER: Enters his first season as a coach with Trenton after making his coaching debut with short-season Single-A Staten Island in 2010, guiding a staff that issued the fewest walks in the NYPL (204)…**PLAYING CAREER:** Originally selected by St. Louis in the first round (28th overall) of the 2001 First-Year Player Draft…played for eight seasons in the minors, going 38-34 with a 3.24 ERA in 66 games (6GS)…was acquired by the Yankees in 2003 as part of the trade that sent LHP Sterling Hitchcock to the Cardinals, making stops in Single-A, Double-A and Triple-A with the Yankees…pitched his final season in 2008 with Double-A Reading in the Phillies organization…**PERSONAL:** Played baseball at the University of Central Florida where he was named First-Team All-American.

TIM LENTYCH - TRAINER

BORN: 9/3/78 in South Bend, Ind. • **RESIDES:** Tampa, Fla.

Begins his fourth season as the Thunder's trainer and his eighth year in the Yankees organization…named the 2009 "Athletic Trainer of the Year" in the EL…spent three seasons as the trainer with Single-A Charleston from 2005-07 after making his pro debut as the trainer for short-season Single-A Staten Island in 2004…earned his bachelor's degree in applied sciences and technology with a concentration in athletic training from Ball State University in 2001 and a master's degree from the University of Tennessee in 2004…previously worked as an athletic training intern with the Baltimore Orioles in 2001.

KAZ MANABE - STRENGTH AND CONDITIONING COACH

BORN: 9/13/72 in Iwakuni, Japan • **RESIDES:** Iwakuni, Japan

Enters his first season as strength and conditioning coach with Trenton and third in the Yankees organization, after previously serving in the same role the prior two seasons with Single-A Charleston…spent the 2008 season as strength and conditioning coach with Single-A Beloit in the Twins organization…following his graduation from Hiroshima University in Japan, Manabe worked as a personal trainer before coming to California State University, Northridge to earn his Masters degree in Kinesiology.

2010 Trenton Thunder (AA)

BATTERS	AVG	G	AB	R	H	2B	3B	HR	RBI	BB	SO	SB	CS	OBP	SLG	E
Adams, David	.309	39	152	31	47	15	3	3	32	18	31	5	2	.393	.507	0
Baker, Ryan J.	.000	3	3	0	0	0	0	0	0	0	1	0	0	.000	.000	0
#Berkman, Lance	.250	2	8	1	2	0	0	0	0	1	3	0	0	.333	.250	0
Brewer, Daniel	.270	136	508	83	137	34	3	10	84	53	117	29	10	.346	.407	2
Christian, Justin	.297	87	343	65	102	21	6	9	51	40	47	20	5	.374	.472	1
*Cusick, Matthew	.234	59	201	17	47	7	3	3	26	22	31	3	1	.310	.343	1
Gil, Jose	.236	31	106	19	25	6	1	5	25	9	23	0	0	.305	.453	3
Gonzalez, Edwar	.235	74	243	37	57	8	4	6	35	28	59	4	2	.333	.374	1
Gorecki, Reid	.257	29	105	10	27	7	0	2	15	13	20	8	3	.347	.381	0
*Grote, Taylor	.000	1	1	0	0	0	0	0	0	0	1	0	0	.500	.000	0
*Joseph, Corban	.216	31	111	11	24	6	4	0	13	15	33	1	0	.305	.342	7
*Krum, Austin	.229	120	459	77	105	17	1	5	44	64	86	16	7	.328	.303	3
Laird, Brandon	.291	107	409	73	119	22	2	23	90	38	84	2	2	.355	.523	20
*Mahoney, Kevin	.267	6	15	2	4	1	0	0	1	5	6	0	0	.476	.333	2
Nunez, Luis	.241	131	449	60	108	24	5	8	44	25	70	7	10	.284	.370	14
Rivera, Rene	.319	25	94	13	30	10	0	5	17	7	17	0	0	.369	.585	1
Romine, Austin	.268	115	455	61	122	31	4	10	69	37	94	2	0	.324	.402	5
*Rye, Jack	.212	15	52	5	11	3	1	1	7	6	9	1	0	.293	.365	1
*Smith, Kevin	.168	41	131	9	22	6	0	0	5	17	49	0	0	.273	.214	3
*Snyder, Justin	.245	90	261	56	64	13	2	3	27	49	44	2	1	.365	.345	12
*Sublett, Damon	.214	35	112	14	24	4	1	2	14	22	37	1	1	.343	.321	2
Vazquez, Jorge	.390	10	41	4	16	4	0	0	6	1	8	0	0	.405	.488	1
#Vechionacci, Marcos	.283	114	406	56	115	17	3	11	55	40	111	6	2	.350	.421	8
Team Total	**.259**	**142**	**4665**	**704**	**1208**	**256**	**39**	**106**	**660**	**511**	**981**	**107**	**46**	**.337**	**.399**	**97**

PITCHERS	W-L	ERA	G	GS	CG	SHO	SV	IP	H	R	ER	HR	HB	BB	SO	WP
Aceves, Alfredo	0-0	5.63	4	3	0	0	0	8.0	10	5	5	1	0	1	7	0
Arbiso, Cory	5-5	4.38	32	11	0	0	0	84.1	100	46	41	9	1	22	49	6
*Arias, Wilkins	4-3	3.65	57	0	0	0	0	61.2	61	27	25	5	2	30	70	6
*Banuelos, Manuel	0-1	3.52	3	3	0	0	0	15.1	15	8	6	2	0	8	17	1
Betances, Dellin	0-0	3.77	3	3	0	0	0	14.1	10	7	6	3	1	3	20	3
*Bleich, Jeremy	3-2	4.79	8	8	0	0	0	41.1	35	22	22	2	3	28	26	3
Brackman, Andrew	5-7	3.01	15	14	0	0	0	80.2	77	38	27	3	7	30	70	6
Bush, Paul	0-2	15.00	3	0	0	0	0	3.0	3	5	5	1	1	4	1	0
Castillo, Noel	3-2	6.27	17	0	0	0	0	18.2	12	15	13	4	1	16	20	3
Cox, J.B.	3-0	4.28	26	0	0	0	0	33.2	34	18	16	1	2	12	23	3
*De La Rosa, Wilkin	2-4	5.33	36	8	0	0	0	72.2	82	51	43	7	3	41	56	3
Duff, Grant	1-4	2.84	28	0	0	0	8	31.2	30	16	10	4	0	16	38	3
Garcia, Christian	1-0	0.00	1	1	0	0	0	5.2	2	0	0	0	1	1	3	0
Kontos, George	0-2	3.38	17	0	0	0	0	32.0	30	13	12	2	0	11	28	0
Mitchell, D.J.	11-4	4.06	23	22	0	0	0	133.0	128	69	60	11	6	57	96	12
Noesi, Hector	8-4	3.10	17	16	2	1	0	98.2	90	37	34	7	2	18	86	5
Norton, Tim	1-0	0.90	6	0	0	0	1	10.0	4	1	1	0	0	3	15	0
Olbrychowski, Adam	0-0	2.08	2	0	0	0	0	4.1	4	1	1	0	0	1	4	1
Pendleton, Lance	10-4	3.43	23	22	0	0	0	120.2	95	50	46	9	4	45	111	4
Phelps, David	6-0	2.04	14	14	0	0	0	88.1	63	21	20	2	2	23	84	2
Pope, Ryan	4-6	4.20	46	7	0	0	17	94.1	88	48	44	10	7	31	85	7
Schmidt, Josh	3-3	2.67	47	0	0	0	0	60.2	41	18	18	3	4	28	71	0
Snyder, Justin	0-0	0.00	1	0	0	0	0	1.0	1	0	0	0	0	1	0	0
Van Benschoten, John	2-0	0.00	3	0	0	0	0	6.0	4	1	0	0	1	4	4	0
Venditte, Pat	1-1	9.00	2	0	0	0	0	2.0	4	2	2	0	0	1	4	0
Warren, Adam	4-2	3.15	10	10	0	0	0	54.1	49	26	19	2	3	16	59	4
Whelan, Kevin	3-3	5.83	24	0	0	0	3	29.1	20	19	19	1	1	21	40	5
Wordekemper, Eric	3-0	2.88	23	0	0	0	8	34.1	26	12	11	5	1	8	35	5
Team Total	**83-59**	**3.66**	**142**	**142**	**2**	**12**	**41**	**1240.0**	**1118**	**576**	**504**	**94**	**53**	**480**	**1125**	**82**

KEY: *- Lefthanded hitter/pitcher, # - switch hitter

Tampa Yankees (A)

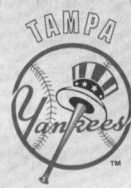

AFFILIATE SINCE 1994
Florida State League – George M. Steinbrenner Field
Office Address: One Steinbrenner Dr., Tampa, FL 33614
Telephone: (813) 875-7753. **Fax:** (813) 673-3174
Web Site: www.steinbrennerfield.com
General Manager: Vance Smith
2010 record, finish: Florida State League Champions
  36-32, Second in North Division (1st Half)
  42-25, First in North Division (2nd Half)

LUIS SOJO – MANAGER
BORN: 1/3/66 in Caracas, Venezuela • **RESIDES:** Lutz, Fla.
COACHING CAREER: Returns for his fifth season as Tampa's Manager, after having previously served in the role from 2006-09…led Tampa to the 2009 Florida State League Championship and was named by *Baseball America* as the "Best Managerial Prospect" in the FSL…was selected as a coach on the FSL postseason All-Star team in 2007…prior to joining Tampa, was a coach for the Yankees at the Major League level for two seasons (2004-05)…spent the second half of the 2003 season as a special instructor before returning to action as an active player…made his managerial debut with the Double-A Norwich Navigators in 2002 and led the team to the Eastern League Championship…**PLAYING CAREER:** A versatile infielder, played parts of seven seasons with the Yankees (1996-2001, 2003) and contributed to four World Championships (1996, 1998, 1999 and 2000)…was originally signed by the Toronto Blue Jays as a non-drafted free agent in 1986 and spent parts of 13 seasons with five Major League clubs (Toronto, 1990 and 1993; California, 1991-92; Seattle, 1994-96; Pittsburgh, 2000; and the Yankees)…batted .400 with 1RBI in 10 postseason games in 1996, including .600 vs. Atlanta in the World Series…hit a career-high .307 in his first full season with the Yankees in 1997…tied for second on the team with 9RBI in 15 postseason games in 2000, including driving in the World Series-clinching run with a ninth-inning single in Game 5 vs. the Mets at Shea Stadium…won four Venezuelan Winter League batting crowns in his career and on 12/18/06, recorded the 1,000th hit in his Venezuelan career…joined an elite group of players to reach the 1,000-hit plateau in both the Majors and the Venezuelan Winter League…**PERSONAL:** Married to Zuleima and has two children, LesLuis and Luis.

JEFF WARE – PITCHING COACH
BORN: 11/11/70 in Norfolk, Va. • **RESIDES:** Palm Harbor, Fla.
COACHING CAREER: Enters his first season as pitching coach with Tampa, having served the same role with Single-A Charleston from 2008-10 and with short-season Single-A Staten Island in 2007…his 2008 staff ranked second in the SAL in ERA (3.41), strikeouts (1,123) and shutouts (12)…spent the 2006 season as the pitching coach for the North Shore Spirit in the Can-Am League, guiding the Spirit pitching staff to a league-best 58 wins and a 2.78 combined ERA…**PLAYING CAREER:** Selected by the Toronto Blue Jays in the first round of the 1991 First-Year Player Draft (35th overall), made stops in the Milwaukee Brewers, Anaheim Angels, Chicago White Sox and Blue Jays organizations…appeared in 18 Major League games with the Blue Jays over two seasons (1995-96), going 3-6 with a 7.47 ERA…was a member of Team USA in the Pan-American Games, winning a bronze medal in 1991…**PERSONAL:** Went 22-9 in three seasons at Old Dominion University in Virginia…graduate of First Colonial High School in Virginia Beach.

JUSTIN TURNER – HITTING COACH
BORN: 12/19/79 in Indianapolis, Ind. • **RESIDES:** Lake Wales, Fla.
COACHING CAREER: Enters his first season as a coach with Tampa after making his coaching debut with Single-A Charleston in 2010…**PLAYING CAREER:** Originally selected by the Angels in the eighth round of the 2001 First-Year Player Draft, the former infielder played four seasons of affiliated minor league ball in the Angels (2001-04) and Red Sox (2004) farm systems…also pitched for one season with Sioux City in the independent Nothern League…**PERSONAL:** Played ball at Warner Robbins College in Florida.

MARIO GARZA – COACH
BORN: 5/26/81 in Shreveport, La. • **RESIDES:** Tampa, Fla.
COACHING CAREER: Makes his professional coaching debut with Tampa in 2011…previously assisted hitters and catchers at Melbourne Central Catholic High School (Fla.)…**PLAYING CAREER:** Was originally selected by the Astros in the 25th round of the 2003 First-Year Player Draft…played four seasons in Houston's minor league system from 2003-06, batting .253 with 58 doubles, 41HR, 176RBI and 11SB in 285 career minor league games…finished his playing career with the Washington Wildthings of the independent Frontier League in 2007.

SCOTT DiFRANCESCO – TRAINER
BORN: 10/8/84 in Hanover, N.H. • **RESIDES:** Thetford, Vt.
Enters his first season as Tampa's trainer after previously serving in the same role with Single-A Charleston the prior three seasons… completed an internship with Mark Littlefield at the Yankees Tampa complex during the 2006 Gulf Coast League season…graduated from Ball State University with a Bachelor of Science in athletic training…was also the head manager for the Ball State men's basketball team.

JAY SIGNORELLI – STRENGTH AND CONDITIONING COACH
BORN: 5/27/78 in Bradenton, Fla. • **RESIDES:** Nashville, Tenn.
Enters his fourth season as strength and conditioning coordinator with Single-A Tampa…spent prior two seasons in the Diamondbacks system at short-season Single-A Yakima in 2007 and Single-A Lancaster in 2006…prior to his work with Major League organizations, worked at the International Performance Institute at the IMG Academy as well as Velocity Sports Performance…graduated from Tennessee Wesleyan with a bachelors degree in exercise science…was a pitcher in college, also playing at Manatee Community College and Florida Southern…was selected by the Yankees in the 32nd round 1998 First-Year Player Draft but did not sign…is a member of the National Strength and Conditioning Association…he and his wife, Julia, have a son, Brody.

2010 Tampa Yankees (A)

BATTERS	AVG	G	AB	R	H	2B	3B	HR	RBI	BB	SO	SB	CS	OBP	SLG	E
Abeita, Mitch	.273	77	256	33	70	15	1	1	26	42	60	0	0	.375	.352	6
#Almonte, Abraham	.263	15	57	9	15	3	1	0	3	6	16	5	3	.333	.351	1
#Almonte, Zoilo	.261	63	238	26	62	10	3	3	26	23	65	8	1	.322	.366	1
Baker, Ryan J.	.086	15	35	6	3	0	0	0	2	7	15	0	0	.250	.086	0
#Feliz, Anderson	.280	10	25	6	7	1	0	1	4	3	9	2	0	.357	.440	1
*Flores, Ramon	.250	8	28	0	7	0	0	0	2	0	5	0	0	.250	.250	0
Gil, Jose	.255	40	141	17	36	4	0	5	19	11	31	4	0	.316	.390	1
#Ibarra, Walter	.301	72	246	28	74	12	1	1	14	15	46	15	7	.348	.370	10
*Joseph, Corban	.302	98	381	52	115	27	3	6	52	43	74	5	8	.378	.436	13
#Kruml, Raymond	.271	66	291	44	79	14	2	1	21	21	63	30	6	.325	.344	3
#Leslie, Myron	.262	80	260	40	68	14	1	6	39	30	53	8	0	.339	.392	8
*Lockwood, Trent	.257	86	292	37	75	17	0	4	37	35	67	4	0	.334	.356	8
*Mahoney, Kevin	.400	3	5	0	2	2	0	0	1	1	2	0	0	.500	.800	0
Maruszak, Addison	.284	68	243	32	69	16	0	1	34	11	40	3	2	.312	.362	10
*Medchill, Neil	.178	51	180	17	32	5	1	3	21	18	70	3	2	.260	.267	0
Mesa, Melky	.260	121	446	81	116	21	9	19	74	44	129	31	9	.338	.475	4
*Pena, Henry	.000	2	3	0	0	0	0	0	0	0	2	0	0	.000	.000	0
Pirela, Jose	.252	130	497	68	125	15	13	5	61	57	87	30	7	.329	.364	30
*Rye, Jack	.274	92	332	49	91	22	3	6	45	34	41	7	1	.342	.413	3
*Santana, Francisco	.135	23	74	3	10	4	1	0	8	1	23	1	0	.145	.216	0
#Suttle, Bradley	.272	133	514	61	140	33	4	10	80	53	136	12	2	.340	.411	15
Team Total	**.263**	**135**	**4544**	**609**	**1196**	**235**	**43**	**72**	**569**	**455**	**1034**	**166**	**48**	**.333**	**.381**	**125**

PITCHERS	W-L	ERA	G	GS	CG	SHO	SV	IP	H	R	ER	HR	HB	BB	SO	WP
*Banuelos, Manuel	0-3	2.23	10	10	0	0	0	44.1	38	16	11	1	1	14	62	2
Bartleski, Philip	3-3	4.54	37	0	0	0	3	69.1	82	41	35	8	3	17	57	4
Betances, Dellin	8-1	1.77	14	14	0	0	0	71.0	43	18	14	1	3	19	88	3
Black, Sean	1-0	1.59	2	2	0	0	0	11.1	9	2	2	0	2	1	12	0
Braboy, Brandon	0-0	3.57	11	2	0	0	1	22.2	31	11	9	0	1	4	17	4
Brackman, Andrew	5-4	5.10	12	12	0	0	0	60.0	67	38	34	5	5	9	56	6
Castillo, Noel	2-2	2.28	16	0	0	0	0	27.2	18	8	7	2	3	13	36	5
Claiborne, Preston	0-1	3.68	5	0	0	0	0	7.1	7	3	3	1	1	4	6	1
Cox, J.B.	0-1	8.59	5	0	0	0	0	7.1	14	11	7	1	1	2	4	1
Flannery, Ryan	1-0	2.25	2	0	0	0	0	4.0	2	1	1	0	0	0	6	0
Forer, Nathan	0-0	9.39	6	0	0	0	0	7.2	16	8	8	0	0	4	5	0
*Hall, Shaeffer	9-5	3.91	15	14	0	0	0	69.0	81	38	30	7	0	10	57	1
Heredia, Jairo	0-6	6.93	6	6	0	0	0	24.2	37	28	19	2	4	11	14	1
Heyer, Craig	8-4	3.52	26	12	1	0	0	92.0	92	42	36	1	5	6	66	3
Kapala, Daniel	1-6	4.53	12	11	0	0	0	57.2	61	33	29	2	7	30	26	6
Kontos, George	0-1	2.61	5	2	0	0	0	10.1	7	3	3	0	0	3	8	0
*Lare, Trenton	1-2	4.00	42	1	0	0	0	74.1	95	46	33	6	1	19	73	4
Leslie, Myron	0-0	9.00	1	0	0	0	0	1.0	3	1	1	0	0	0	0	0
*Marcano, Juan	1-0	0.00	3	0	0	0	0	5.0	1	0	0	0	0	3	8	0
Marshall, Brett	0-0	4.50	1	1	0	0	0	4.0	5	3	2	0	0	0	6	0
Marte, Ronny	1-0	2.93	15	0	0	0	0	15.1	16	9	5	0	0	8	11	2
Mitre, Sergio	0-0	0.00	1	0	0	0	0	1.0	0	0	0	0	0	0	1	0
Noesi, Hector	5-2	2.72	8	8	0	0	0	43.0	35	14	13	3	2	6	53	5
Norton, Tim	0-0	1.69	12	0	0	0	2	21.1	16	7	4	2	0	3	32	2
Olbrychowski, Adam	3-2	4.02	30	1	0	0	1	62.2	59	33	28	1	4	27	52	6
Ortiz, Jonathan	7-1	2.47	46	0	0	0	21	54.2	41	17	15	4	0	11	62	1
*Romanski, Josh	0-1	4.50	3	3	0	0	0	12.0	15	6	6	2	0	4	12	1
Rulon, Brad	1-0	2.50	11	0	0	0	0	18.0	18	8	5	1	0	6	16	3
Sanit, Amaury	0-0	1.80	3	0	0	0	0	5.0	0	1	1	0	0	2	6	0
Stoneburner, Graham	8-5	2.53	19	19	1	0	0	103.0	80	35	29	4	8	24	93	4
Van Benschoten, John	2-1	4.50	12	2	0	0	0	26.0	30	14	13	4	1	8	24	0
Venditte, Pat	4-1	1.73	41	0	0	0	6	72.2	49	17	14	2	2	14	85	0
Warren, Adam	7-5	2.22	15	15	1	1	0	81.0	72	23	20	2	6	17	67	0
Whitley, Chase	0-0	3.00	2	0	0	0	0	3.0	1	1	1	1	0	6	6	0
Team Total	**78-57**	**3.30**	**135**	**135**	**3**	**19**	**34**	**1189.1**	**1141**	**536**	**436**	**63**	**60**	**299**	**1127**	**65**

KEY: *- Lefthanded hitter/pitcher, # - switch hitter

Charleston RiverDogs (A)

AFFILIATE SINCE 2005
South Atlantic League – Joseph P. Riley, Jr. Ballpark
Office Address: 360 Fishburne Street, Charleston, SC 29403
Telephone: (843) 723-7241. **Fax:** (843) 723-2641
Web site: www.riverdogs.com
Executive Vice President & General Manager: Dave Echols
Media Contact: Danny Reed
2010 record, finish: 31-38, Fifth in Southern Division (1st Half)
34-36, Fifth in Southern Division (2nd Half)

AARON LEDESMA – MANAGER
BORN: 9/12/1976 in Union City, Calif. • **RESIDES:** Spring Hill, Fla.

COACHING CAREER: Begins his first managerial assignment with the RiverDogs in 2011…will mark his fourth season as a professional coach in the Yankees organization, after serving as a coach with Single-A Tampa in 2008 and Triple-A Scranton/Wilkes-Barre from 2009-10…helped SWB record the IL's second-best fielding percentage in 2009 (.980)…**PLAYING CAREER:** Originally drafted by the New York Mets in the second round of the 1990 First-Year Player Draft…batted .296 with 38 doubles, 4 triples, 2HR and 76RBI in 284 career Major League games over parts of five seasons with the Mets, Baltimore, Tampa Bay and Colorado…**PERSONAL:** Graduated from James Logan (Calif.) HS where he hit .488 as a senior…earned Junior College All-American honors at Chabot College in 1990…is married to Kersten with a son, Samuel.

CARLOS CHANTRES – PITCHING COACH
BORN: 4/1/76 in Miami, Fla. • **RESIDES:** Miami, Fla.

COACHING CAREER: Enters his first season as pitching coach for the RiverDogs and sixth season in the Yankees organization after serving in the same role with the GCL Yankees from 2007-10 and short-season Single-A Staten Island in 2006…his staff led all rookie-level teams with a 2.72 ERA in 2007 with a GCL-best 42-17 regular season record and a league-low .228 opponents batting average…**PLAYING CAREER:** Played parts of 11 professional seasons in the systems of the Chicago White Sox, Tampa Bay Devil Rays, St. Louis Cardinals and Philadelphia Phillies, going 80-88 with a 4.01 ERA in 291 games (233 starts)…**PERSONAL:** Is married to Melisa with two daughters, Nina and Lia…selected in the 12th round of the 1994 First-Year Player Draft by the Chicago White Sox out of Christopher Columbus High School in Miami, Fla.

GREG COLBRUNN – HITTING COACH
BORN: 7/26/69 in Fontana, Calif. • **RESIDES:** Mt. Pleasant, S.C.

COACHING CAREER: Begins his fifth season with Charleston, fourth as the RiverDogs' hitting coach…managed the club in 2010…guided the 2008 RiverDogs to the SAL's second-highest average (.256) and second-most runs scored (705)…**PLAYING CAREER:** Selected by the Montreal Expos in the sixth round of the 1987 First-Year Player Draft…played in 992 Major League games over 13 seasons for the Expos (1992-93), Florida Marlins (1994-96), Minnesota Twins (1997), Atlanta Braves (1997, '98), Colorado Rockies (1998), Arizona Diamondbacks (1998-2002, '04) and Seattle Mariners (2003)…was a member of the Diamondbacks' World Series Championship squad in 2001…**PERSONAL:** With wife, Erika and daughters, Danielle and Kelsey Paige, makes home in nearby Mount Pleasant, S.C…graduated in 1987 from Fontana High School (Calif.), earning All-State honors in baseball and All-Conference honors in football…turned down a baseball scholarship to Stanford in order to sign with Montreal.

VICTOR VALENCIA – COACH
BORN: 5/30/77 in Maracay, Venezuela • **RESIDES:** Maracay, Venezuela

COACHING CAREER: Enters his fourth season of coaching after making his debut with short-season Single-A Staten Island in 2008…**PLAYING CAREER:** Was signed by the Yankees as a non-drafted free agent in 1993 and played 10 seasons of minor league baseball in the Yankees (1995-2000), Cincinnati (2001), Texas (2002), Cleveland (2003-04) and Toronto (2004) systems…the catcher combined for a .224 career average with 120 doubles, 114HR and 395RBI in 885 games…named the "best defensive catcher" in the Eastern League by *Baseball America* following the 1999 season…played with Newark in the independent Atlantic League in 2006.

LEE MEYER – TRAINER
BORN: 12/27/83 in Marinette, Wisc. • **RESIDES:** Pound, Wisc.

Begins his second season in the Yankees organization, after serving in the same role with short-season Single-A Staten Island in 2010…received his undergraduate degree in Athletic Training from the University of Wisconsin–Stevens Point in May 2008, while also holding a minor in Spanish…is currently working towards his Master's Degree in Sports Management at Minnesota State University, Mankato…previously worked as an Athletic Training Intern with the Colorado Rockies and Pittsburgh Pirates as well as the NFL's Indianapolis Colts.

MIKE KICIA – STRENGTH AND CONDITIONING COACH
BORN: 11/21/85 in Fuquay-Varina, N.C. • **RESIDES:** Fuquay-Varina, N.C.

Begins his first season with Charleston and in the Yankees organization…spent the 2009 and 2010 season in the same role with Single-A Greensboro in the Marlins organization…earned his Bachelor of Science degree in Kinesiology from the University of Lethbridge in 2005 and a second Bachelor of Science degree in Exercise Science from Mount Olive College in 2008.

2010 Charleston RiverDogs (A)

BATTERS	AVG	G	AB	R	H	2B	3B	HR	RBI	BB	SO	SB	CS	OBP	SLG	E
#Almonte, Zoilo	.278	58	227	33	63	13	2	10	35	21	65	7	6	.341	.485	3
#Arcia, Francisco	.314	17	51	2	16	4	0	0	3	7	8	1	0	.397	.392	2
Castro, Kelvin	.224	123	437	55	98	20	5	2	39	30	96	15	11	.274	.307	37
*Flores, Ramon	.250	14	48	3	12	3	0	0	2	3	15	1	0	.294	.313	0
*Grote, Taylor	.278	28	90	11	25	7	0	2	9	16	30	1	2	.383	.422	0
*Heathcott, Slade	.258	76	298	48	77	16	3	2	30	42	101	15	10	.359	.352	7
Higashioka, Kyle	.225	90	320	35	72	18	0	6	24	31	64	0	2	.303	.338	6
*Kruml, Raymond	.261	51	184	21	48	9	1	0	11	7	35	12	2	.297	.321	0
#Landoni, Emerson	.280	84	261	39	73	13	1	3	32	21	44	13	8	.330	.372	17
*Lassiter, Garrison	.102	27	88	2	9	1	0	0	4	14	36	1	1	.223	.114	5
Liccien, Jhorge	.200	2	5	0	1	0	0	0	0	1	2	0	0	.333	.200	0
*Lyerly, Robert	.312	131	503	72	157	36	4	9	71	34	129	9	7	.352	.425	33
*Mack, Deangelo	.252	116	424	52	107	20	5	12	56	46	99	5	5	.333	.408	8
*Mahoney, Kevin	.298	26	84	15	25	8	0	2	7	13	25	1	1	.404	.464	1
*Medchill, Neil	.215	65	237	29	51	10	1	9	32	23	84	5	4	.295	.380	2
*Milo, Justin	.231	16	52	8	12	0	0	0	4	11	15	3	1	.359	.231	1
Murphy, JR	.255	87	330	46	84	15	2	7	54	36	64	4	5	.327	.376	11
Murton, Luke	.282	106	397	48	112	32	2	12	55	39	71	2	0	.361	.463	4
#Paredes, Jimmy	.282	99	404	59	114	24	6	5	48	18	82	36	10	.312	.408	36
Rabago, Hector	.160	40	119	7	19	3	0	3	16	9	29	0	0	.239	.261	13
*Santana, Francisco	.257	34	101	16	26	5	2	2	15	5	22	2	1	.292	.406	1
Toussen, Jose	.000	2	3	1	0	0	0	0	0	0	0	0	0	.000	.000	0
Team Total	**.258**	**139**	**4663**	**602**	**1201**	**257**	**30**	**84**	**547**	**427**	**1116**	**133**	**78**	**.324**	**.380**	**203**

PITCHERS	W-L	ERA	G	GS	CG	SHO	SV	IP	H	R	ER	HR	HB	BB	SO	WP
Acosta, Ryan	5-4	3.50	42	0	0	0	1	61.2	61	31	24	0	3	23	46	8
Barreda, Manuel	1-0	0.00	6	0	0	0	0	7.1	8	0	0	0	1	5	7	0
Black, Sean	7-8	3.88	23	22	1	1	0	116.0	118	75	50	6	10	40	92	9
Flannery, Ryan	7-6	2.26	45	0	0	0	14	79.2	61	25	20	2	4	14	70	4
Gil, Francisco	1-3	1.25	28	0	0	0	9	36.0	32	10	5	0	2	12	27	3
Gipson, Mike	0-2	7.88	3	2	0	0	0	8.0	11	7	7	1	2	3	6	0
Greene, Shane	0-2	4.58	4	4	0	0	0	19.2	14	10	10	1	5	8	22	1
*Hall, Shaeffer	2-2	1.85	10	10	0	0	0	68.0	52	19	14	1	2	11	46	0
Heredia, Jairo	4-2	3.45	20	9	0	0	0	70.1	74	34	27	4	2	19	65	2
Marquez, Dickson	0-5	10.62	15	0	0	0	1	20.1	30	25	24	1	2	12	10	1
Marshall, Brett	4-2	2.50	13	13	1	1	0	72.0	52	26	20	2	1	22	56	5
Marte, Ronny	2-3	3.13	35	2	0	0	4	54.2	67	30	19	4	3	15	36	10
Martinez, Richard	1-0	3.60	1	1	0	0	0	5.0	5	2	2	0	0	2	4	0
Perez, Kelvin	5-5	3.18	30	13	0	0	0	104.2	93	53	37	6	5	36	80	14
*Quintana, Jose	0-1	4.70	5	3	0	0	0	15.1	11	10	8	1	1	10	12	0
Ramirez, Jose A.	6-5	3.60	22	21	0	0	0	115.0	106	56	46	3	9	42	105	20
Rodriguez, Wilton	0-1	7.71	1	1	0	0	0	4.2	4	4	4	0	0	4	3	0
*Romanski, Josh	8-4	3.16	15	15	0	0	0	88.1	84	39	31	8	4	17	73	4
*Rondon, Francisco	1-2	7.71	10	0	0	0	1	11.2	12	10	10	3	1	7	16	2
Shive, Andrew	1-1	3.38	6	0	0	0	0	8.0	4	7	3	0	1	8	4	3
Solbach, Michael	4-6	3.90	30	15	0	0	0	99.1	109	47	43	4	5	23	95	11
Stoneburner, Graham	1-3	2.08	7	7	0	0	0	39.0	27	11	9	2	1	10	44	1
Tatis, Gabriel	2-3	4.14	37	0	0	0	0	58.2	56	38	27	2	11	18	49	12
Watkins, Benjamin	3-4	3.88	35	1	0	0	0	58.0	59	28	25	3	3	16	34	4
Team Total	**65-74**	**3.43**	**139**	**139**	**2**	**12**	**30**	**1221.1**	**1150**	**597**	**465**	**54**	**78**	**377**	**1002**	**114**

KEY: *- Lefthanded hitter/pitcher, # - switch hitter

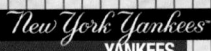

Staten Island Yankees (Short-Season A)

AFFILIATE SINCE 1999
New York-Penn League – Richmond County Bank Ballpark at St. George
Office Address: 75 Richmond Terrace, Staten Island, NY 10301
Telephone: (718) 720-9265. **Fax:** (718) 273-5763
Website: www.siyanks.com
Executive VP, General Manager: Jane M. Rogers
Media Contact: John McCutchan
2010 record, finish: 34-40, tied for third in the McNamara Division

TOM SLATER – MANAGER
BORN: 4/6/68 in Charlottesville, Va. • **RESIDES:** Auburn, Ala.

COACHING CAREER: Enters his first season as manager of Staten Island after serving in the same role with the GCL Yankees the prior two seasons…led GCL to a first-place finish in the North Division in 2009 in his pro coaching debut…spent his previous four seasons (2005-08) as the head coach at Auburn University, going 115-113 and seeing 15 of his players drafted by Major League clubs over the four-year span…was his second stint with the Tigers, having served as an assistant coach there from 1995-2000…prior to taking over as head coach at Auburn, spent one season (2004) as an assistant coach at the University of Florida under Pat McMahon and three years (2001-03) as the head coach at Virginia Military Institute, earning Southern Conference "Coach of the Year" in 2003…began his coaching career in 1991 as an assistant coach at St. Christopher's School in Richmond, Va., then served as an assistant at Marshall in 1992 and VMI from 1993-94…was the hitting coach and third base coach for the 2006 USA National Team that won the gold medal…**PERSONAL:** With wife Beth, has two children, Julia and Jack…graduated from VMI in 1990 where he was a four-year starter, ending his career ranked in the top five in RBI, total bases, runs scored and doubles…was part of the 1988 Southern Conference Northern Division championship team.

DANNY BORRELL – PITCHING COACH
BORN: 1/24/79 in Landsdale, Penn. • **RESIDES:** Wichita, Kan.

COACHING CAREER: Enters his first season as pitching coach with Staten Island after having spent the prior two seasons as a rehabilitation pitching coach in the GCL…**PLAYING CAREER:** Selected by the Yankees in the second round of the 2000 First-Year Player Draft, played nine minor league seasons with the Yankees (2000-06) and Oakland (2007-08)…the left-hander compiled a career record of 39-35 with a 3.49 ERA in 138 games (130 starts)…split the 2008 season between the Athletics' Double-A Midland and Triple-A Sacramento squads, before landing on the disabled list in June for the remainder of the season with a left elbow strain…**PERSONAL:** Pitched at Wake Forest.

TY HAWKINS – HITTING COACH
BORN: 11/8/67 in Point Pleasant, N.J. • **RESIDES:** Brielle, N.J.

COACHING CAREER: Returns for his sixth consecutive season as the hitting coach in Staten Island…led the Yankees to the second-best batting average in the NYPL in three of the last four seasons, and an NYPL-most 52HR in 2009…guided the 2006 Staten Island offense to a league-best .267 average and 365R en route to the club's second consecutive NY-Penn League Championship…also fulfilled coaching duties with Double-A Trenton (2005), Single-A Tampa (2004), Single-A Battle Creek (2003), Single-A Greensboro (2002) and the Gulf Coast Yankees (1999-2001)…before joining the Yankees organization, coached at Vanderbilt University and the University of Illinois…**PLAYING CAREER:** Played baseball at Old Dominion University, helping his team advance to the NCAA Regionals in 1990…graduated with a Bachelor of Science degree from ODU in that year as well…**PERSONAL:** Married to Jennifer with two children, Brier and Ty Bayley.

DANILO VALIENTE – COACH
BORN: 1/13/66 in Havana, Cuba. • **RESIDES:** Tampa, Fla.

COACHING CAREER: Enters his first season as a coach with Staten Island after coaching the prior two seasons with the GCL Yankees…is his fifth season in the Yankees organization, serving as a coach with Single-A Tampa from 2007-08…**PERSONAL:** A native of Cuba, Valiente managed and coached for 15 seasons with the Cuban professional team, Industriales…also served as a third base coach and hitting instructor with the Cuban National team…also served as a coach with Cuba's mid-superior league where future Major Leaguers Jose Contreras, Orlando Hernandez and Kendry Morales played for him…won the league championship in 1997.

JORGE VARGAS – TRAINER
BORN: 5/11/81 in Mayaguez, P.R. • **RESIDES:** West Nyack, N.Y.

Begins his first season in the Yankees organization…spent the prior two seasons as a trainer in the Rays organization…graduated from Seton Hall University in May 2007 with a Master of Science in athletic training…earned his undergraduate degree in physical education from the University of Puerto Rico at Mayaguez, where he played four years of baseball.

Organizational Accomplishments

The Yankees are one of only two organizations whose minor-league affiliates have posted a winning record in each season since 1990 (also the Cleveland Indians)…the Yankees were named the "Organization of the Year" in 1998 by *Baseball America* and in 1999 by *USA Today*.

2010 Staten Island Yankees (Short-Season A)

BATTERS	AVG	G	AB	R	H	2B	3B	HR	RBI	BB	SO	SB	CS	OBP	SLG	E
#Arcia, Francisco	.224	25	98	13	22	4	0	2	14	5	13	1	0	.267	.327	5
Brown, Isaiah	.218	24	78	7	17	5	1	1	5	10	26	4	1	.307	.346	3
Brown, Shane	.234	60	209	30	49	7	0	2	25	37	28	2	4	.375	.297	6
#Culver, Cito	.186	15	43	2	8	1	0	0	0	8	10	1	1	.340	.209	6
De Leon, Kelvin	.236	69	259	33	61	12	1	6	37	17	80	5	1	.288	.359	6
*Duran, Kelvin	.172	18	58	4	10	3	0	0	4	2	31	2	2	.213	.224	1
Farnham, Jeffrey	.227	36	110	15	25	5	0	0	11	13	19	4	1	.331	.273	5
*Ferraro, Michael	.204	43	152	14	31	10	0	1	13	5	47	1	1	.252	.289	4
*Lassiter, Garrison	.285	39	123	10	35	3	1	0	10	19	29	1	3	.389	.325	3
*Mahoney, Kevin	.276	38	134	18	37	5	2	6	22	18	35	4	1	.384	.478	4
McCoy, Nick	.237	20	59	5	14	4	0	0	7	9	16	1	0	.366	.305	2
Mojica, Jose	.241	53	187	16	45	10	0	0	12	11	20	2	1	.284	.294	19
*Parache, Luis	.235	45	149	17	35	9	1	3	20	10	20	4	2	.284	.369	9
*Roller, Kyle	.272	67	246	36	67	11	3	5	31	31	65	3	2	.367	.402	5
Sanchez, Gary	.278	16	54	8	15	2	0	2	7	3	16	1	1	.333	.426	1
Segedin, Rob	.243	20	70	13	17	6	1	1	7	7	7	0	1	.321	.400	3
*Sosa, Eduardo	.256	47	180	31	46	13	3	2	15	24	48	15	6	.353	.394	2
*Stevenson, Casey	.217	52	198	18	43	8	0	6	23	10	35	0	2	.266	.348	5
Urena, Carlos	.182	6	22	0	4	2	0	0	3	0	5	0	0	.182	.273	1
Team Total	**.239**	**74**	**2429**	**290**	**581**	**120**	**13**	**37**	**266**	**239**	**550**	**51**	**30**	**.320**	**.345**	**101**

PITCHERS	W-L	ERA	G	GS	CG	SHO	SV	IP	H	R	ER	HR	HB	BB	SO	WP
Barreda, Manuel	0-0	4.76	7	0	0	0	0	17.0	14	9	9	0	3	11	18	1
*Brooks, Gavin	0-0	0.00	1	0	0	0	0	0.1	1	0	0	0	0	0	0	0
Burawa, Daniel	0-0	7.71	6	0	0	0	0	7.0	8	7	6	0	0	7	10	1
Claiborne, Preston	1-2	2.28	19	0	0	0	2	23.2	20	9	6	0	0	8	30	2
Cotton, Bryant	1-1	6.20	14	0	0	0	0	20.1	24	15	14	1	0	6	23	1
*Elam, Sam	0-1	8.68	4	2	0	0	0	9.1	9	13	9	2	3	15	9	4
Farnham, Jeffrey	0-0	0.00	1	0	0	0	0	2.0	1	0	0	0	0	4	2	0
Forer, Nathan	0-0	1.99	16	0	0	0	0	22.2	19	7	5	2	1	7	14	0
Gipson, Mike	3-1	4.42	12	6	0	0	0	38.2	37	21	19	4	2	11	50	6
Greene, Shane	2-6	4.59	10	10	0	0	0	49.0	57	28	25	1	7	21	44	3
Hobbs, Dustin	0-2	9.00	2	2	0	0	0	9.0	11	10	9	0	1	7	5	1
*Jernstad, Matthew	2-2	3.32	14	3	0	0	0	43.1	38	18	16	3	3	11	44	1
Kahnle, Thomas	0-0	0.56	11	0	0	0	3	16.0	3	1	1	0	3	5	25	2
*Lewis, Fred	1-0	2.45	5	0	0	0	0	3.2	3	2	1	0	0	5	3	0
Mahoney, Kevin	0-1	13.50	1	0	0	0	0	2.0	6	4	3	1	0	2	1	1
Martinez, Richard	4-1	1.69	16	2	0	0	0	32.0	22	9	6	1	0	16	34	4
Mitchell, Bryan	0-1	6.75	1	1	0	0	0	4.0	7	4	3	0	2	1	3	1
O'Brien, Michael	6-2	2.08	11	11	0	0	0	60.2	49	19	14	1	1	18	38	5
Oliver, William	0-0	5.06	4	0	0	0	0	5.1	6	4	3	0	0	4	7	3
Recchia, Michael	0-1	4.93	22	0	0	0	1	34.2	30	22	19	1	1	12	30	5
Rodriguez, Wilton	1-3	4.39	6	4	0	0	0	26.2	38	22	13	0	1	7	17	2
Shive, Andrew	0-1	5.17	10	0	0	0	0	15.2	17	10	9	0	2	12	10	2
*Sneed, Kramer	1-3	4.09	8	7	0	0	0	33.0	35	20	15	3	2	7	42	2
*Turley, Nik	4-4	4.38	12	12	1	0	0	61.2	57	36	30	0	2	29	47	4
Varce, Zachary	4-6	4.54	15	14	0	0	0	71.1	75	42	36	4	1	17	74	5
Whitley, Chase	4-2	1.31	28	0	0	0	15	34.1	18	8	5	0	1	15	44	2
Team Total	**34-40**	**3.86**	**74**	**74**	**1**	**6**	**21**	**643.1**	**605**	**340**	**276**	**24**	**36**	**258**	**624**	**58**

KEY: *- Lefthanded hitter/pitcher, # - switch hitter

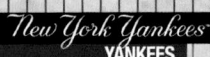
Gulf Coast Yankees (Rookie)

AFFILIATE SINCE 1990
Gulf Coast League – Yankees Complex
Office Address: 3102 N. Himes Ave, Tampa, FL 33607
Telephone: (813) 875-7569. **Fax:** (813) 873-2302
General Manager: Eric Schmitt
2010 record, finish: 24-32, Sixth place, North Division

CARLOS MENDOZA – MANAGER
BORN: 11/27/79 in Barquisimeto, Venezuela • **RESIDES:** Barquisimeto, Venezuela

COACHING CAREER: Enters his first season as GCL manager after coaching with short-season Single-A Staten Island in 2009 and Single-A Charleston in 2010...**PLAYING CAREER:** Originally signed by San Francisco as a non-drafted free agent in 1996, played 13 seasons of minor league baseball as a utility infielder in the Giants and Yankees organizations as well as three years for the Independant Pensacola Pelicans...the switch-hitter owned a .232 average with 97 doubles, 15 triples, 19HR and 200RBI in 705 career minor league games...also had two brief Major League appearances, with the Mets in 1997 and the Rockies in 2000, appearing in 28 combined games.

JOSE ROSADO – PITCHING COACH
BORN: 11/9/74 in Jersey City, N.J. • **RESIDES:** Dorado, P.R.

COACHING CAREER: Will be making his professional coaching debut in 2011...**PLAYING CAREER:** Was originally selected in the 12th round of the 1994 First-Year Player Draft by the Royals...in five seasons with Kansas City, went 37-45 with 4.27 ERA in 125 career games at the Major League level...**PERSONAL:** Attended Galveston Junior College (TX)...was named MVP of the National Junior College World Series in 1994, recording two wins and one save.

GREG PAVLICK – PITCHING COACH
BORN: 3/10/50 in Washington, D.C. • **RESIDES:** Tierra Verde, Fla.

COACHING CAREER: Begins his first season as pitching coach for the GCL Yankees after spending nine consecutive seasons as the pitching coach for Single-A Tampa...served in the same capacity for the Triple-A Columbus Clippers in 2001...guided a 2008 staff that led the FSL in shutouts (13) and ranked second in strikeouts (996) and third in ERA (3.53)...in 2004, helped lead the Tampa pitching staff to the Florida State League Championship...prior to joining the coaching ranks in 2001, spent four years as the roving pitching instructor for the Yankees organization from 1997-2000...before joining the Yankees, spent 26 seasons in the New York Mets organization...began his coaching career in 1977 as a pitching instructor for Single-A Tidewater...coached for the Mets at the Major League level from 1985-86, 1988-91 and again from 1994-96...**PLAYING CAREER:** Was the Mets' second pick in the secondary phase of the January 1971 free-agent draft...in 1971, tied for the Appalachian League lead in victories and ranked sixth in ERA and was named to the league's All-Star team...in 1973, finished eighth in the California League in ERA...won a career-high nine games for Triple-A Victoria of the Texas League in 1976...**PERSONAL:** Graduated from Thomas Edison High School in Alexandria, Va. in 1968...attended the University of North Carolina.

JOHN RODRIGUEZ – HITTING COACH
BORN: 1/20/78 in New York, N.Y. • **RESIDES:** New York, N.Y.

COACHING CAREER: Will be making his professional coaching debut in 2011...**PLAYING CAREER:** Played in 158 career Major Legaue games from 2005-06 with St. Louis, batting .298 with 7HR and 43RBI...was originally signed as a non-drafted free agent by the Yankees in 1997 after attending a tryout at Yankee Stadium...batted .270 with 205 doubles, 36 triples, 158HR and 597RBI in 1,077 career minor league games in the Yankees, Mets, Rays, Cardinals and Indians organizations...**PERSONAL:** Graduated from Louis D. Brandeis (N.Y.) High School in Manhattan.

BRIAN BAISLEY - COACH
BORN: 12/19/82 in Tampa, Fla. • **RESIDES:** Tampa, Fla.

COACHING CAREER: Will be making his professional coaching debut in 2011...**PLAYING CAREER:** Was originally selected by the Yankees in the 24th round of the 2006 First-Year Player Draft...hit .299 with 47 doubles, 17HR and 116RBI in 201 career minor league games over four seasons in the Yankees system...**PERSONAL:** Played baseball at the University of South Florida and was named to the *Tampa Tribune* and *St. Petersburg Times* All-County teams as a junior and senior and was an All-Sunshine Athletic Conference selection as a senior...twin brother, Jeff, is a third baseman in the Oakland Athletics system and older brother, Brad, was a former second-round selection by the Phillies in the 1998 First-Year Player Draft.

GREG SPRATT – TRAINER
BORN: 7/8/65 in Lexington, Ky. • **RESIDES:** Plant City, Fla.

Returns for his fifth consecutive season as the athletic trainer for the Yankees' Gulf Coast squad after rejoining the Yankees organization in 2007...previously served with the Yankees for parts of 16 seasons beginning in 1990...was selected Eastern League "Trainer of the Year" in 1995...began with Oneonta in 1990 and moved to Greensboro in 1991, where he was the All-Star trainer for the Northern Division squad...was voted "Trainer of the Year" in 1992 by the Professional Baseball Athletic Trainers Society...earned a bachelor's degree from the University of Louisville...was the trainer for the National Champion Louisville Cardinals and the U.S. Pan American basketball team in 1986...received a master's degree in sports medicine from Ohio University.

2010 Gulf Coast Yankees (Rookie)

BATTERS	AVG	G	AB	R	H	2B	3B	HR	RBI	BB	SO	SB	CS	OBP	SLG	E
Alcantara, Jorge	.229	10	35	2	8	3	0	0	2	0	10	0	1	.229	.314	4
Aron, Nathan	.240	9	25	5	6	1	0	0	2	5	8	0	0	.394	.280	0
Austin, Tyler	.000	2	2	0	0	0	0	0	0	0	1	0	0	.500	.000	0
#Culver, Cito	.269	41	160	21	43	7	1	2	18	13	41	6	3	.320	.363	13
*Duran, Kelvin	.221	35	136	18	30	5	0	2	10	17	35	10	4	.303	.301	2
#Feliz, Anderson	.273	47	198	33	54	9	6	4	27	15	44	11	7	.324	.439	12
*Flores, Ramon	.329	43	158	33	52	10	4	2	22	28	22	4	1	.436	.481	9
*Gamel, Benjamin	.280	7	25	3	7	1	0	0	0	3	8	1	2	.357	.320	1
*Golsan, Judd	.188	35	101	9	19	4	0	0	9	8	35	9	3	.261	.228	2
Gumbs, Angelo	.192	7	26	1	5	1	0	0	0	1	3	3	0	.222	.231	3
Hammock, Robby	.500	4	12	4	6	2	0	2	4	1	1	1	0	.538	1.167	0
Kuo, Fu-Lin	.243	42	136	21	33	4	0	4	23	15	34	0	0	.329	.360	16
Liccien, Jhorge	.215	27	79	9	17	5	1	1	14	7	22	0	1	.279	.342	7
Maruszak, Addison	.375	2	8	1	3	1	0	0	2	0	0	0	0	.375	.500	0
Moronta, Eladio	.107	9	28	1	3	0	0	0	3	2	10	1	1	.188	.107	1
Nunez, Reymond	.222	27	108	10	24	4	1	3	20	5	30	1	0	.263	.361	6
*Pena, Henry	.302	26	86	12	26	7	1	3	7	14	25	3	0	.406	.512	1
Perkins, Kyle	.083	13	24	1	2	0	0	0	1	6	9	0	0	.258	.083	2
Rosario, Jose	.245	36	110	22	27	4	1	2	7	8	22	6	0	.320	.355	14
Sanchez, Gary	.353	31	119	25	42	11	0	6	36	11	28	1	1	.419	.597	7
Segedin, Rob	.250	2	8	3	2	0	0	1	3	0	1	0	0	.333	.625	1
*Sublett, Damon	.158	5	19	3	3	0	0	1	3	3	3	0	1	.273	.316	0
Taveras, Damian	.252	31	107	14	27	5	0	2	14	10	30	2	0	.336	.355	7
Toussen, Jose	.277	45	148	24	41	4	0	1	15	11	20	9	1	.333	.324	9
*Williams, Mason	.222	5	18	0	4	0	0	0	0	1	4	1	2	.263	.222	0
Team Total	**.258**	**56**	**1876**	**275**	**484**	**88**	**15**	**36**	**242**	**184**	**446**	**69**	**28**	**.332**	**.378**	**132**

PITCHERS	W-L	ERA	G	GS	CG	SHO	SV	IP	H	R	ER	HR	HB	BB	SO	WP
Arias, Justo	2-2	5.40	14	0	0	0	0	26.2	37	19	16	2	2	4	27	1
*Banuelos, Manuel	0-0	1.80	2	2	0	0	0	5.0	1	1	1	0	0	3	6	1
Checo, Mariel	0-1	5.92	10	2	0	0	0	24.1	26	21	16	4	1	11	24	7
*DeLuca, Evan	1-3	9.35	9	6	0	0	0	26.0	37	36	27	4	7	24	30	4
*Iam, Sam	0-0	4.26	10	0	0	0	0	12.2	8	9	6	0	4	15	15	3
Garce, Harold	2-0	2.79	12	0	0	0	1	19.1	13	7	6	0	1	13	9	2
Garcia, Charlyn	0-0	10.29	7	0	0	0	0	7.0	15	8	8	0	2	1	4	1
Gerritse, Brett	2-2	3.82	9	2	0	0	1	35.1	39	20	15	3	2	12	27	2
Hobbs, Dustin	3-1	2.30	7	7	0	0	0	27.1	23	10	7	0	2	7	33	1
Isabel, George	0-0	18.00	2	0	0	0	0	2.0	5	4	4	1	0	1	3	3
*Johnson, Trevor	0-2	9.00	7	0	0	0	0	7.0	9	9	7	1	0	5	2	3
*Lewis, Fred	0-1	2.25	9	0	0	0	0	12.0	9	4	3	0	1	11	15	0
*Marcano, Juan	1-1	1.05	6	3	0	0	1	25.2	15	3	3	0	0	2	21	0
Marshall, Brett	0-0	2.25	2	1	0	0	0	8.0	6	5	2	0	1	4	8	0
Marte, Joel	0-2	3.43	18	0	0	0	2	21.0	25	13	8	0	3	7	25	2
Mitchell, Bryan	2-1	3.67	10	9	0	0	0	41.2	28	24	17	2	3	22	36	5
Mitre, Sergio	0-1	1.80	2	2	0	0	0	5.0	2	1	1	0	0	0	8	0
Mullee, Conor	2-1	1.64	14	0	0	0	1	22.0	19	9	4	0	1	6	20	1
Nuding, Zachary	0-1	4.50	1	1	0	0	0	2.0	4	2	1	0	0	1	2	0
Oliver, William	2-0	4.38	8	0	0	0	1	12.1	12	9	6	2	2	4	10	0
*Quintana, Jose	3-1	2.31	15	0	0	0	1	23.1	14	11	6	0	3	8	32	1
Reyes, Yobanny	0-1	21.21	4	0	0	0	0	4.2	11	11	11	0	1	3	4	2
Richardson, Matthew	1-4	5.00	11	9	0	0	0	45.0	38	36	25	1	5	29	36	5
Rodriguez, Wilton	0-3	4.05	6	4	0	0	0	20.0	16	13	9	2	0	9	21	2
*Rutckyj, Evan	0-0	0.00	1	0	0	0	0	1.0	0	0	0	0	0	0	0	0
Sanit, Amaury	0-0	2.70	3	3	0	0	0	6.2	4	2	2	0	1	0	10	0
*Sneed, Kramer	0-0	2.70	4	0	0	0	0	6.2	3	3	2	0	0	3	9	0
*Tapia, Erick	2-1	1.15	9	0	0	0	0	15.2	7	3	2	1	1	5	14	0
Triplet, David	0-0	0.00	2	0	0	0	0	2.0	0	0	0	0	0	0	2	0
*Turley, Nik	0-2	0.84	3	2	0	0	0	10.2	11	7	1	0	0	2	9	0
Van Benschoten, John	1-1	1.29	4	3	0	0	0	7.0	5	1	1	1	0	2	8	0
Team Total	**24-32**	**4.03**	**56**	**56**	**0**	**1**	**8**	**485.0**	**442**	**301**	**217**	**24**	**42**	**214**	**470**	**46**

KEY: *- Lefthanded hitter/pitcher, # - switch hitter

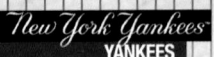

Dominican Summer League Yankees

The Latin Béisbol Academy • One Yankee Way • Boca Chica, Dominican Republic

PAT McMAHON – COORDINATOR OF INTERNATIONAL PLAYER DEVELOPMENT
BORN: 5/28/53 in Lakawanna, N.Y. • **RESIDES:** Jacksonville, Fla.

COACHING CAREER: Begins his second season as Coordinator of International Player Development in his fourth season with the Yankees organization…prior to joining the Yankees in 2007, served for seven seasons (2001-07) as the Head Coach with the University of Florida where he earned the Collegiate Baseball Foundation's "National Coach of the Year" and Southeastern Conference "Coach of the Year" Awards in 2005 after guiding the Gators to a second-place finish in the College World Series…owns a career coaching record of 555-287-1 with Old Dominion (1990-94), Mississippi State (1997-2000) and Florida…also managed the 2001 USA Baseball team that played in tournaments in the United States, Japan and Taiwan…**PERSONAL:** Married (Cheri) with daughter Logan and son J. Wells…is one of eight siblings.

JOEL LITHGOW – LATIN AMERICAN ACADEMY DIRECTOR
BORN: 12/4/78 in Santo Domingo, D.R. • **RESIDES:** Santo Domingo, D.R.

Enters his second full season as the Operations Director of the DSL Yankees Latin Beisbol Academy…as director, supervises the Yankees' entire Dominican baseball development program…responsibilities include overseeing scouting, player signings and ensuring proper maintenance of all baseball-related facilities…also aids in coordinating community events, such as skill-building baseball clinics, in the Dominican…prior to joining the Yankees organization, worked as an attorney in the Department of Investigations for Major League Baseball in the Dominican Republic…he is a graduate of the Pontifica Universidad Catolica Madre y Maestra.

RAUL DOMINGUEZ – MANAGER, DSL 1
BORN: 7/25/81 in Panama City, Panama • **RESIDES:** Panama City, Panama

COACHING CAREER: Enters his first season as Manager of the DSL 1 team after spending the prior two seasons as Manager of the DSL 2 team…guided the DSL 2 team to a first place finish in the Boca Chica Division in 2009…began his coaching career in 2008 with the DSL 2 squad after spending 2007 as the Yankees' tryout scout in the Dominican Republic…**PLAYING CAREER:** Signed by the Yankees as a non-drafted free agent in 2001, he played four minor league seasons as an outfielder with the DSL and GCL clubs.

WILFRIDO CORDOVA – PITCHING COACH, DSL 1
BORN: 8/11/57 in Panama City, Panama • **RESIDES:** Panama City, Panama

COACHING CAREER: Begins his 11th season as a pitching coach with the Yankees player development system in the Dominican Republic…has served as an instructor within the Yankees organization since 1991…**PLAYING CAREER:** Played five professional seasons in the Pittsburgh Pirates organization from 1981-85…was signed by the Pirates as a non-drafted free agent on 4/2/81…also played one year of professional baseball in Mexico…**PERSONAL:** Married to Magdalena with five children: Maira, Marleen, Keyla, Wilfredo and Maria…played high school baseball in Panama City and won MVP honors as an amateur.

ROY GOMEZ – HITTING COACH, DSL 1
BORN: 1/7/85 in Santo Domingo, D.R. • **RESIDES:** Santo Domingo, D.R.

COACHING CAREER: Enters his first season as hitting coach for the DSL 1 team, after serving in the same role the prior two seasons with the DSL 2 squad…**PLAYING CAREER:** Played for five years in the Yankees organization with the Tampa, Staten Island, Gulf Coast League and Dominican Summer League Yankees after being signed as a non-drafted free agent on 11/26/03…compiled a .271 batting average with 40 doubles, 9HR and 99RBI in 259 combined games.

TEURIS OLIVARES – COACH, DSL 1
BORN: 12/15/78 in San Francisco de Macoris, D.R. • **RESIDES:** San Francisco de Macoris, D.R.

COACHING CAREER: Will make his coaching debut in 2011…**PLAYING CAREER:** Was originally signed as a free agent by the Yankees in 1995…over nine seasons in the Yankees system, batted .250 with 101 doubles, 27 triples, 40HR and 270RBI in 669 career minor league games.

ANTONIO GARCIA – TRAINER, DSL 1
BORN: 7/20/69 in Maracaibo, Venezuela • **RESIDES:** Maracaibo, Venezuela

Enters his sixth season with the Yankees Player Development System…prior to joining the Yankees, served for six years as a trainer in the Dominican Republic for the Texas Rangers organization.

CARLOS MENDEZ MOTA – MANAGER, DSL 2
BORN: 1/10/67 in San Cristobal, D.R. • **RESIDES:** Haina, D.R.

COACHING CAREER: Enters his 10th season as a coach or manager in the Yankees player development system…prior to joining the Yankees in 2002, served as a coach in the Arizona Diamondbacks system from 2000-01…began his career in player development with the St. Paul Saints of the independent Northern League as a player/coach…**PLAYING CAREER:** Played for 12 seasons in the minor leagues as a catcher…was signed by Cleveland as a non-drafted free agent in 1986 and played in the Indians system through the 1989 season…played four seasons in independent leagues from 1996-1999…**PERSONAL:** Married (Runalina Medina) with two children: Carlos and Dahiana…played baseball at San Marcos High School in Haina.

JOSE DURAN – PITCHING COACH, DSL 2
BORN: 5/19/64 in Santo Domingo, D.R. • **RESIDES:** Santo Domingo, D.R.

COACHING CAREER: Enters his eighth season as a coach in the Yankees organization…has served as a professional pitching coach since he made his coaching debut with the Florida Marlins in 1994…prior to joining the Yankees, spent two years as a special instructor with the Cincinnati Reds and parts of two seasons with the Los Angeles Dodgers organization…**PLAYING CAREER:** Played professionally in the Los Angeles Dodgers system from 1984-88…**PERSONAL:** Married (Sandra Garcia) with four children: Darwin, Alexandra, Erika and Alby…graduated from San Francisco de Asis High School in Santo Domingo.

CAONABO COSME – HITTING COACH, DSL 2
BORN: 3/18/79 in La Vega, D.R. • **RESIDES:** La Vega, D.R.

COACHING CAREER: Will make his coaching debut in 2011…**PLAYING CAREER:** Was originally signed by the Athletics as a minor league free agent in 1995…over parts of 13 minor league seasons with the A's, Cardinals, Yankees, Reds and Tigers organizations, hit .257 with 239 doubles, 58HR and 478RBI in 1,192 career minor league games.

SONDER ENCARNACION – COACH, DSL 2
BORN: 4/28/77 in San Cristobal, D.R. • **RESIDES:** San Cristobal, D.R.

Enters his seventh season of coaching in the Yankees system with the Dominican Summer League entries…the former infielder signed with Seattle in 1995 and played three seasons for the Mariners' Dominican Summer League team.

LUIS MORILLO – TRAINER, DSL 2
BORN: 1/13/78 in Azua, D.R. • **RESIDES:** Santo Domingo, D.R.

Enters his third season as a trainer in the Yankees player development system…began his professional training career with the Nationals organization, where he worked for three years before joining the Yankees…**PLAYING CAREER:** Was originally signed as a minor league free agent by the Blue Jays in 1996…in three seasons in the Toronto system, hit .262 with eight extra-base hits and 13RBI in 51 games.

RAUDO BAEZ – CLUBHOUSE/EQUIPMENT MANAGER
BORN: 4/5/70 in San Cristobal, D.R. • **RESIDES:** Palenque, D.R.

Enters his 10th season with the Yankees player development system in the Dominican Republic…**PERSONAL:** Married (Jovanna) with one son, Raudy…graduated from Padre Borbon High School in Palenque.

Tony Dimel - Head Groundskeeper
Pat Maturine - Assistant Head Groundskeeper
Jose Guillen - Assistant Equipment Manager
Ambiorix Osuna - Assistant Clubhouse Attendant
Luis Rojas - Strength and Conditioning Coach

U.S. MILITARY ALL-STAR BASEBALL TEAM VISITS YANKEES' LATIN BÉISBOL ACADEMY IN THE DOMINICAN REPUBLIC

On April 24, 2008, the U.S. Military Baseball Team paid a visit to the Yankees' Latin Béisbol Academy in Boca Chica, Dominican Republic to join Yankees players for a workout as part of their Armed Forces'"Baseball Diplomacy" program in conjunction with the United States Embassy, the Dominican Armed Forces and National Police Sporting Club, and the Dominican Baseball Federation. Following the training session, coaches from the academy joined U.S. military players at Ensanche Luperon, in Santo Domingo, to give a baseball clinic to local children. In return, the Yankees sent coaches and scouts to participate in a clinic on April 26, 2008 at the Olympic Center, also in Santo Domingo.

Minor League Players, Non-Roster Invitees

ABEITA, Mitch – C
HT: 5-10; **WT:** 195; **B:** R; **T:** R; **BORN:** 4/7/86 in Oakcliff, Tex.; **RESIDES:** Duncanville, Tex.; **COLLEGE:** University of Nebraska; **OBTAINED:** Selected by the Yankees in the 19th round of the 2008 First-Year Player Draft; **M.L. SVC:** 0.000; **CAREER NOTES: 2010:** Spent the entire season with Single-A Tampa and batted .273 (70-for-256) with 15 doubles, 1HR and 26RBI in 77 games with the Yankees...named to the FSL's mid-season All-Star team...led all Tampa batters with a .400 batting average (4-for-10) in four games during the postseason...committed just six errors in 665 total chances...**2009:** Batted .225 with 12 doubles, 4HR and 32RBI in 74 games with Single-A Charleston...threw out 28-of-109 base runners attempting to steal (25.7%)...**2008:** Made his professional debut, batting .250 with 10 doubles, 1HR and 19RBI in 53 games with short-season Single-A Staten Island...ranked fourth among catchers in the NYPL with a 40.7% caught-stealing rate (22-for-54)...hit .167 (1-for-6) with 1HR in two postseason games...**PERSONAL:** Last name is pronounced "Uh-bay-tuh"...attended the University of Nebraska where he majored in sociology...batted .337 with 45R, 7 doubles, 10HR and 49RBI in 56 games during his senior year, recording more walks (43) than strikeouts (29)...earned an All-Big 12 honorable mention in 2007...was named to the Big 12 Commissioner's Honor Roll in Fall 2007...also attended North Central Texas College in Duncanville, Tex.

ACOSTA, Ryan – RHP
HT: 6-1; **WT:** 184; **B:** R; **T:** R; **BORN:** 11/4/88 in Lubbock, Tex.; **RESIDES:** Portales, N.M.; **OBTAINED:** Signed by the Yankees as a free agent on 8/21/09; **M.L. SVC:** 0.000; **CAREER NOTES: 2010:** Spent the entire season with Single-A Charleston where he went 5-4 with a 3.50 ERA, allowing 24ER in 61.2IP out of the bullpen...**2009:** Was released during spring training and signed a minor league contract with Kansas City before being released two weeks later on 5/6...signed with the Yankees on 8/21 and pitched in one game with the GCL Yankees, tossing 1.0 scoreless inning...**2008:** Combined to go 1-1 with a 4.42 ERA in 11 games (eight starts) with Single Peoria and Rookie-level Mesa...missed the final two months of the season with right elbow tendinitis...**2007:** Split his first professional season with Mesa and Single-A Boise, going 0-2 with a 3.00 ERA in six combined games (four starts)...**PERSONAL:** His father, Oscar, played in the Phillies farm system for three years and was a coach with the Cubs (2000-01) and Rangers (2002), was a minor league manager with the Yankees...was originally selected by the Cubs in the 12th round of the 2007 First-Year Player Draft out of Clearwater Central Catholic HS where he was named an Under Armour-All American and Rawlings All-American.

ADAMS, David – INF
HT: 6-1; **WT:** 202; **B:** R; **T:** R; **BORN:** 5/15/87 in Margate, Fla.; **RESIDES:** Margate, Fla.; **COLLEGE:** University of Virginia; **OBTAINED:** Selected by the Yankees in the third round of the 2008 First-Year Player Draft; **M.L. SVC:** 0.000; **CAREER NOTES: 2010:** With Double-A Trenton, batted .309 (47-for-152) with 15 doubles, three triples, 3HR and 32RBI in 39 games before having his season cut short with a right ankle injury on 5/23...had the ankle scoped on 8/2 to remove three small bone chips...rated by *Baseball America* as having the "Best Strikezone Discipline" among Yankees farmhands, following the season...**2009:** Combined to hit .286 with 69R, 40 doubles, 8 triples, 7HR and 75RBI in 132 games with Single-A Charleston and Single-A Tampa...tied for third among all Yankees minor leaguers in RBI...began the season with Charleston, batting .290 with 23 doubles and 34RBI in 67 games...tied for second on the team in doubles...was promoted to Tampa on 6/25, where he batted .281 with 17 doubles, 6 triples, 7HR and 41RBI in 65 games...ranked second on the team in triples and tied for third in RBI...**2008:** Made his professional debut, batting .257 with 45R, 19 doubles, 4HR and 31RBI in 67 games with short-season Single-A Staten Island...batted .333 (3-for-9) with 1RBI in two postseason games...**PERSONAL:** Full name is David Lee Adams...attended the University of Virginia where he batted .286 with 48R, 11 doubles, 6HR and 51RBI in 61 games his junior year...successfully stole a base in 16-of-19 attempts (84.2%)...was a career .325 batter in college, scoring 150 runs with 30 doubles, 16HR and 143RBI in 183 games...was named the 2008 Third-Team Louisville Slugger Preseason All-America squad and the Wallace Award Watch List...was also named co-team captain...finished his junior season with 84 hits, tied for sixth-most in school history for a single season...was one of *Baseball America's* Top 30 prospects (No. 27) from the Cape Cod League in 2007 after hitting .302 for Falmouth...led the league in doubles (14), ranked second in hits (51) and triples (3) and placed ninth in batting average...was named Second Team *Baseball America* Freshman All-American, a Louisville Slugger Freshman All-American and earned a spot on *Baseball America's* Fab 50 list for top freshman in 2006...attended Grandview Prep (Fla.) where he played for his father, Dale, and was a four-year letter-winner in baseball...was named team captain and MVP in his senior year...was rated the No. 19 prospect by *Baseball America* in 2005...named a scholar athlete each year from 2002-05...also lettered three years in football...was drafted by the Tigers in the 21st round of the 2005 First-Year Player Draft but chose to attend college.

AGRAMONTE, Kenedy – RHP
HT: 5-9; **WT:** 157; **B:** R; **T:** R; **BORN:** 12/4/90 in Haina, D.R.; **RESIDES:** Haina, D.R.; **OBTAINED:** Signed as a minor league free agent on 3/25/10; **M.L. SVC:** 0.000; **CAREER NOTES: 2010:** Made his professional debut with the DSL Yankees 1, and went 1-1 with a 2.61 ERA in 13 appearances (12 starts)...led the team in strikeouts (80)...struck out 13 batters on 7/3 in 6.0IP.

ALCANTARA, Jorge – INF
HT: 6-1; **WT:** 183; **B:** R; **T:** R; **BORN:** 8/9/91 in Cristo Rey, D.R.; **RESIDES:** Cristo Rey, D.R.; **OBTAINED:** Signed by the Yankees as a non-drafted free agent on 7/11/09; **M.L. SVC:** 0.000; **CAREER NOTES: 2010:** Started the season with the DSL Yankees 1, batting .331 (49-for-148) with 8 doubles, 5 triples, 4HR and 23RBI in 44 games...had a 10-game hitting streak from 6/9-19, batting .535 (15-for-28) with 3 doubles, 2 triples, 1HR and 5RBI...was transferred to the GCL Yankees on 8/4, where he batted .229 (8-for-35) with 3 doubles and 2RBI in 10 games...**2009:** Made his professional debut with the DSL Yankees 1, batting .250 with 11R, 2 doubles, 1HR and 9RBI in 22 games...appeared in games at 3B and SS.

ALLEN, Scott - RHP
HT: 6-1; **WT:** 170; **B:** R; **T:** R; **BORN:** 7/3/91 in Lyman, Calif.; **RESIDES:** Apopka, Fla.; **OBTAINED:** Acquired by the Yankees from the Arizona Diamondbacks in exchange for 1B Juan Miranda on 11/18/10; **M.L. SVC:** 0.000; **CAREER NOTES: 2010:** Went 4-4 with a 4.73 ERA (78.0IP, 41ER) in 16 starts with the South Bend Silver Hawks in the Arizona minor league system...allowed 3ER or less in 10 of his 16 starts...**2009:** Made his professional debut with the Missoula Osprey and appeared in 12 games out of the bullpen, going 1-0 with a 0.51 ERA, allowing just 1ER in 17.2IP.

ALMONTE, Abraham – OF

HT: 5-9; **WT:** 200; **B:** S; **T:** R; **BORN:** 6/27/89 in Santo Domingo, D.R.; **RESIDES:** Santo Domingo, D.R.; **OBTAINED:** Signed by the Yankees as a non-drafted free agent on 7/2/05; **M.L. SVC:** 0.000; **CAREER NOTES: 2010:** Was limited to 17 games with Single-A Tampa, batting .263 (15-for-57) with 3 doubles, 1 triple and 3RBI before undergoing sugery for a right labrum tear…**2009:** Batted .280 (123-for-440) with 14 doubles, 10 triples, 5HR and 56RBI in 115 games with Single-A Charleston, establishing career highs in hits, triples and RBI…recorded a career-high 26-game hitting streak from 8/6-9/4, batting .405 (45-for-111) with 12 extra-base hits (six doubles, three triples, 3HR) over the stretch…was the longest hitting streak recorded in the South Atlantic League in 2009…**2008:** Hit .228 with 61R, 20 doubles, 7 triples, 8HR and 46RBI in 115 games with Single-A Charleston…led the team and ranked second among Yankees farmhands with 29SB…began the season with a seven-game hitting streak, batting .400 (12-for-30) over the span…was placed on the disabled list from 5/9-29 with a left hamstring strain…was named to the South Atlantic League midseason All-Star team…appeared in three games for the Leones del Escogido of the Dominican Baseball League following the season…**2007:** Batted .288 with 29R and 16RBI in 49 games with the GCL Yankees…led the team in runs, walks (21) and stolen bases (8)…fashioned a nine-game hitting streak from 7/31-8/11…**2006:** Made his professional debut in 2006, batting .254 in 63 games played with the Yankees' Dominican Summer League 1 squad (25 games at 2B)…led the league in stolen bases (36), ranked fourth in home runs (8) and ranked fifth among all Dominican Summer League players with 51 runs scored.

ALMONTE, Zoilo – OF

HT: 6-0; **WT:** 205; **B:** S; **T:** R; **BORN:** 6/10/89 in Santo Domingo, D.R.; **RESIDES:** Santo Domingo, D.R.; **OBTAINED:** Signed by the Yankees as a non-drafted free agent on 7/2/05; **M.L. SVC:** 0.000; **CAREER NOTES: 2010:** Combined to hit .269 (125-for-465) with 23 doubles, 5 triples, 13HR and 61RBI in 121 games with Single-A Charleston and Single-A Tampa…began the season with Charleston where he hit .278 (63-for-227) with 13 doubles, 2 triples, 10HR and 35RBI in 58 games with the RiverDogs, earning a spot on the SAL's midseason All-Star team…was promoted to Single-A Tampa on 6/24 where he batted .261 (62-for-238) with 10 doubles, 3 triples, 3HR and 26RBI in 63 games…played in six games during the postseason with Tampa, batting .208 (5-for-24) with three doubles and 2RBI…**2009:** Played the entire season at short-season Single-A Staten Island and hit .274 with 20 doubles, 7HR and 39RBI in 69 games…tied for third in the New York-Penn League in doubles, ranked fourth in AB (259) and tied for fourth in extra-base hits (28)…was named to the league's midseason All-Star team…hit .333 (8-for-24) with a team-high five extra-base hits and 5RBI during the NYPL playoffs…**2008:** Batted .239 with 7 doubles, 5HR and 20RBI in 57 games with the GCL Yankees, leading the club in homers…played in the second-most games in the GCL…grounded into eight double plays, tied for most in the league…hit .486 (18-for-37) when leading off an inning…**2007:** Batted .268 with 25R, 11 doubles and 24RBI in 50 games with the GCL Yankees…**2006:** Made his professional debut with the Yankees DSL 1 squad, batting .219 in 53 games played…hit the Yankees' only grand slam of the season on 8/23 vs. the Diamondbacks.

ANDERSON, Brian – RHP   NON-ROSTER INVITEE

HT: 6-2; **WT:** 220; **B:** R; **T:** R; **BORN:** 3/11/82 in Tucson, Ariz.; **RESIDES:** Tucson, Ariz.; **COLLEGE:** University of Arizona; **OBTAINED:** Signed by the Yankees as a minor league free agent on 12/1/10; **M.L. SVC:** 3.053; **CAREER NOTES:** Originally drafted by Chicago-AL in the first round (15th overall pick) of the 2003 First-Year Player Draft…converted to pitcher following the 2009 season, having spent the first seven seasons (2003-09) of his professional career as an outfielder in the Chicago White Sox and Boston Red Sox organizations…has appeared in 355 Major League games as a position player, batting .227 (181-for-799) with 108R, 47 doubles, 22HR and 80RBI…**2010:** Saw his first action as a pitcher, combining to make 14 appearances (four starts) with the ASL Royals, Single-A Burlington and Triple-A Omaha (0-0, 2.08 ERA) of the Kansas City Royals organization…**2009:** Split the season in the Red Sox and White Sox organizations, combining to hit .243 (49-for-202) with 9 doubles, 4HR and 18RBI in 86 games with Chicago and Boston at the Major League level…**2008:** Spent the season with Chicago-AL and batted .232 (42-for-181) with 13 doubles, 8HR and 26RBI in 109 games with the White Sox…over a seven-game stretch from 4/19-26, hit .462 (12-for-34) with 2 doubles and 4RBI…**2007:** Began the season with the White Sox, batting .118 (2-for-17) in 13 games with Chicago-AL…was transferred to Triple-A Charlotte on 4/29 where he hit .255 (51-for-200) with eight doubles, two triples, 8HR and 31RBI in 57 games…**2006:** Played the entire season with the White Sox and batted .225 (82-for-365) with 23 doubles, 8HR and 33RBI in 134 games…enjoyed his best month of the year in July when he hit .313 (20-for-64) with 1HR and 7RBI in 22 games…**2005:** Entered the season rated as the No. 1 prospect in the White Sox system by *Baseball America*…began the season with Triple-A Charlotte and hit .295 (132-for-448) with 24 doubles, 3 triples, 16HR and 57RBI in 118 games…played in 13 games with Chicago-AL and hit .176 (6-for-34) to close out the season…recorded his first career Major League hit on 8/16 vs. the Twins, singling off Brad Radke…followed that up ten days later by hitting his first and second career Major League home runs off Seattle's Felix Hernandez on 8/26…**2004:** Combined to hit .313 (131-for-419) with 31 doubles, 7 triples, 12HR and 73RBI in 117 games with Single-A Winston-Salem and Double-A Birmingham…was named to the Carolina League midseason All-Star team…**2003:** Made his professional debut, batting .388 (19-for-49) with 2HR and 13RBI in 13 games with the Great Falls White Sox…**PERSONAL:** Full name is Brian Nikola Anderson…attended Canyon Del Oro High in Tucson, Ariz., where he was named 5A State "Player of the Year" by the Arizona Baseball Coaches Association in 2000…played baseball at the University of Arizona…was named to the 2003 *Baseball America* and *USA Today* Second-Team All-America squads in 2003 following his junior season…created TeamAnderson in 2008, a mentoring program benefitting residents of Mercy Home for Boys and Girls in Chicago.

ANDERSON, Jake – OF

HT: 6-0; **WT:** 158; **B:** L; **T:** R; **BORN:** 12/3/91 in Baton Rouge, La.; **RESIDES:** Baton Rouge, La.; **OBTAINED:** Selected by the Yankees in the seventh round of the 2010 First-Year Player Draft; **M.L. SVC:** 0.000; **CAREER NOTES: 2010:** Missed the season after undergoing elbow surgery on 7/9…**PERSONAL:** Full Name is Taylor Jake Anderson…graduated from Woodlawn HS in Baton Rouge (La.).

ANGELINI, Carmen – INF

HT: 6-1; **WT:** 182; **B:** R; **T:** R; **BORN:** 9/22/88 in Lake Charles, La.; **RESIDES:** Lake Charles, La.; **OBTAINED:** Selected by the Yankees in the 10th round of the 2007 First-Year Player Draft; **M.L. SVC:** 0.000; **CAREER NOTES: 2010:** Missed the entire season rehabbing a right hip injury…**2009:** Split the season with Single-A Charleston and short-season Single-A Staten Island, batting .193 with 10 doubles, 4HR and 22RBI…**2008:** Batted .236 with 14 doubles, 4HR and 46RBI in 134 games with Single-A Charleston…**2007:** Made his professional debut, playing in one game for the GCL Yankees and going 0-for-1 as a pinch-hitter…**PERSONAL:** Was selected out of A.M. Barbe High School (La.)…hit .433 with 58R, 14 doubles, 8 triples, 6HR and 52RBI in 40 games during his senior year, setting a school record in triples…also stole 38 bases in 42 attempts (90.5%).

AQUINO, Daury – RHP

HT: 6-1; **WT:** 179; **B:** R; **T:** R; **BORN:** 4/4/91 in San Cristobal, D.R.; **RESIDES:** San Cristobal, D.R.; **OBTAINED:** Signed as a minor league free agent on 4/1/10; **M.L. SVC:** 0.000; **CAREER NOTES: 2010:** Missed the season, serving a suspension for violating the Minor League Drug Prevention and Treatment Program.

AQUINO, Melvin – INF

HT: 5-11; **WT:** 160; **B:** R; **T:** R; **BORN:** 7/14/92 in Santo Domingo, D.R.; **RESIDES:** Santo Domingo, D.R.; **OBTAINED:** Signed as a minor league free agent on 4/1/10; **M.L. SVC:** 0.000; **CAREER NOTES: 2010:** Made his professional debut with DSL Yankees 2, batting .263 (40-for-152) with 8 doubles, 5HR and 27RBI in 49 games…hit all 5HR off left-handed pitchers.

ARBISO, Cory – RHP

HT: 6-2; **WT:** 210; **B:** R; **T:** R; **BORN:** 4/21/86 in LaMirada, Calif.; **RESIDES:** LaMirada, Calif.; **COLLEGE:** Cal State Fullerton; **OBTAINED:** Selected by the Yankees in the 22nd round of the 2008 First-Year Player Draft; **M.L. SVC:** 0.000; **CAREER NOTES: 2010:** Spent the season with Double-A Trenton where he went 5-5 with a 4.38 ERA (84.1IP, 41ER) in 32 games (11 starts)…was 2-0 with a 2.06 ERA (35.0IP, 8ER) in 21 games as a reliever, and 3-5 with a 6.02 ERA (49.1IP, 33ER) in 11 starts…**2009:** Combined at three levels (Single-A Charleston, Single-A Staten Island and Triple-A Scranton/Wilkes-Barre) to go 4-8 with a 4.64 ERA in 33 appearances (12 starts)…**2008:** Made his professional debut, going 0-2 with a 4.18 ERA in eight appearances (seven starts) with short-season Single-A Staten Island…was placed on the disabled list from 7/2-8/10 with a sprained left ankle…made one postseason relief appearance with Staten Island, tossing 1.2 scoreless innings (2H, 1BB, 1K)…**PERSONAL:** Full name is Cory Edward Arbiso…has a twin brother, Casey…attended California State University at Fullerton, going 12-3 with a 4.46 ERA in 16 starts during his senior year, leading the team in wins.

ARCIA, Francisco – C

HT: 5-11; **WT:** 197; **B:** S; **T:** R; **BORN:** 9/14/89 Maiquetia, Venezuela; **RESIDES:** Catia La Mar, Venezuela; **OBTAINED:** Signed by the Yankees as a non-drafted free agent on 7/2/06; **M.L. SVC:** 0.000; **CAREER NOTES: 2010:** Started the season with Single-A Charleston, batting .314 (16-for-51) with 4 doubles and 3RBI in 17 games…transferred to short-season Single-A Staten Island on 5/16, and batted .224 (22-for-98) with 4 doubles, 2HR and 14RBI in 25 games over the remainder of the season…**2009:** Played his second straight season with the GCL Yankees, hitting .247 and catching 12-of-37 stolen base attempts (32.4%)…**2008:** Hit .128 with 1HR in 22 games with the GCL Yankees…**2007:** Batted .269 with 26R and 21RBI in 47 games with the DSL Yankees 2.

ARIAS, Gian – INF

HT: 5-11; **WT:** 179; **B:** S; **T:** R; **BORN:** 10/6/91 in Santo Domingo, D.R.; **RESIDES:** Santo Domingo, D.R.; **OBTAINED:** Signed by the Yankees as a non-drafted free agent on 7/2/08; **M.L. SVC:** 0.000; **CAREER NOTES: 2010:** Appeared in 58 games with the DSL Yankees 2, batting .256 (53-for-207) with 9 doubles, 1 triple, 2HR and 2RBI…was transferred to the DSL Yankees 1 on 8/17 and appeared in four games (.385, 5-for-13, 1 HR, 2RBI)…**2009:** Made his professional debut with DSL Yankees 2, batting .227 with 47R, 7 doubles, 2 triples and 26RBI in 62 games…drew a team-high 48BB.

ARIAS, Wilkins – LHP

HT: 6-1; **WT:** 168; **B:** L; **T:** L; **BORN:** 11/4/80 in San Cristobal, D.R.; **RESIDES:** San Cristobal, D.R.; **OBTAINED:** Signed by the Yankees as a non-drafted free agent on 6/7/05; **M.L. SVC:** 0.000; **CAREER NOTES: 2010:** Played the entire season with Double-A Trenton and went 4-3 with a 3.65 ERA (61.2IP, 25ER) in 57 appearances out of the bullpen…following the season, made 17 relief appearances with the Estrellas de Oriente of the Dominican Winter League and went 3-0 with a 3.21 ERA, striking out 19 batters and allowing 5ER in 14.0IP…**2009:** Spent the season with Double-A Trenton, going 5-4 with a 3.65 ERA in 48 appearances (two starts)…held left-handed batters to a .183 (20-for-109) batting average with 1HR…following the season, pitched for the Aguilas Cibaenas of the Dominican Winter League, going 2-1 with one save and a 4.76 ERA in 26 relief outings…**2008:** Appeared in 40 combined games with Single-A Tampa and Trenton, going 4-0 with a 3.34 ERA…surrendered just 2HR in 62.0IP…threw more than 1.0 inning in 23 of his 40 outings…limited lefthanders to a .141 average (9-for-64, 0HR)…collected his first save since 2006 on 5/13 vs. Lakeland (1.0IP, 2H)…allowed just 3ER over his final 14 appearances (22.1IP, 1.21 ERA) with Tampa before being promoted on 7/27 for his first Double-A action…did not allow a run in the month of June (8G, 13.0IP)…**2007:** Was 6-3 with a 4.59 ERA in 41 relief appearances with Single-A Tampa…**2006:** Went 9-6 with a 3.01 ERA in 31 games (22 starts) with Single-A Charleston, leading the staff in wins…finished the season tied for sixth among all South Atlantic League pitchers in ERA…was named SAL "Pitcher of the Week" on 8/21…finished the season with a 28.0-consecutive-inning scoreless streak…his 3.01 ERA also ranked eighth among all Yankees minor leaguers…**2005:** In his first professional season, posted a 3-3 record with a 1.40 ERA in 11 games (seven starts) with the Yankees' Dominican Summer League 1 squad.

ARON, Nathan – OF

HT: 6-1; **WT:** 205; **B:** R; **T:** R; **BORN:** 5/15/91 in Melbourne, Australia; **RESIDES:** Dingley Village, Australia; **OBTAINED:** Signed by the Yankees as a non-drafted free agent on 1/17/08; **M.L. SVC:** 0.000; **CAREER NOTES: 2010:** Appeared in nine games for the GCL Yankees, batting .240 (6-for-25) with 1 double and 2RBI…following the season, played with the Melbourne Aces in the Australian Baseball League where he hit .316 (6-for-19) with 2 doubles, 1HR and 6RBI in nine games…**PERSONAL:** Was signed at the age of 16 after being spotted during the under-18 national championship in Canberra, Australia, where he was teammates with fellow signee Kyle Perkins.

AUSTIN, Tyler – C

HT: 6-1; **WT:** 219; **B:** R; **T:** R; **BORN:** 9/6/91 in Conyers, Ga.; **RESIDES:** Conyers, Ga.; **OBTAINED:** Selected by the Yankees in the 13th round of the 2010 First-Year Player Draft; **M.L. SVC:** 0.000; **CAREER NOTES: 2010:** Appeared in two games with the GCL Yankees before his season came to end after fracturing his left hand on 8/4…**PERSONAL:** Full name is Christopher Tyler Austin…graduated from Heritage High School (Ga.).

AYALA, Luis – RHP

HT: 6-2; **WT:** 190; **B:** R; **T:** R; **BORN:** 1/12/78 in Los Mochis, Mexico; **RESIDES:** Santa Monica; Calif.; **OBTAINED:** Signed by the Yankees as a minor league free agent on 2/10/11; **M.L. SVC:** 6.121; **CAREER NOTES:** In 377 games over parts of six seasons with Montreal (2003-04), Washington (2005-08), New York-NL (2008), Minnesota (2009) and Florida (2009), owns a 29-39 career record with 18 saves and a 3.67 ERA (390.1IP, 159ER)…since 2003, is tied for fifth in the National League in wins as a reliever with 28, behind Ryan Madson (35), Guillermo Mota (31), Chad Qualls (30) and Scott Linebrink (29)…represented Mexico in the inaugural World Baseball Classic in 2006 and made three relief appearances, allowing 1ER in 1.1IP (6.75 ERA)…**2010:** Combined at the Triple-A level with three organizations (Los Angeles-NL, Colorado and Arizona) to go 2-10 with a 6.42 ERA (47.2IP, 34ER) and four saves in 36 relief appearances…following the season, combined to go 2-0 with a 2.27 ERA (35.2IP, 9ER) and 12 saves in 33 games with the Yaquis de Obregon and Aguilas de Mexicali of the Mexican Pacific League…made four relief appearances in the Caribbean World Series for Mexico, and earned two saves, not allowing a run in 5.0IP (2H, 1K, 2BB)…**2009:** Combined to go 1-5 with a 5.63 ERA (40.0IP, 25ER) and four saves in 38 relief appearances with Minnesota and Florida…began the season with the Twins and went 1-2 with a 4.18 ERA (32.1IP, 15ER) with three saves in 28 appearances out of the bullpen…was released and placed on waivers in June and claimed by the Marlins in July…with Florida, went 0-3 with a 11.74 ERA (7.2IP, 10ER) and one save in 10 relief appearances…**2008:** Went 2-10 with a 5.71 ERA (75.2IP, 48ER) and nine saves in 81 combined appearances with Washington and New York-NL…began the season with Washington and went 1-8 with a 5.77 ERA (57.2IP, 37ER) in 62 relief appearances…was traded to New York-NL on 8/17 in exchange for a player to be named later (INF Anderson Hernandez) and made 19 relief appearances with the Mets, going 1-2 with nine saves and a 5.50 ERA (18.0IP, 11ER)…did not allow a run in 13 of those 19 appearances and finished the season tied for fifth among all NL relievers in games…**2007:** Began the season on the 15-day disabled list, recovering from "Tommy John" surgery performed on his right elbow…was reinstated from the D.L. on 6/20 and went 2-2 with one save and a 3.19 ERA (42.1IP, 15ER) in 44 appearances with Washington…earned the win in the final Major League game at RFK Stadium on 9/23 vs. Philadelphia…**2006:** Missed the entire season recovering from "Tommy John" surgery performed on his right elbow on 3/30 by Dr. Lewis Yocum and Nationals team orthopedist Dr. Ben Shaffer…**2005:** Spent the entire season with Washington, going 8-7 with a 2.66 ERA (71.0IP, 21ER) and one save in 68 relief appearances…held the opposition scoreless in 53 of his 68 appearances and tied for first in wins among NL relievers…**2004:** Went 6-12 with seven saves and a 2.69 ERA (90.1IP, 27ER) in 81 appearances with the Expos, establishing career highs in games, innings pitched, strikeouts (63) and ERA…led all Montreal relievers in appearances, ranking eighth in the NL…pitched in every series of the season, except two (6/11-13 at Seattle and 8/27-8/29 vs. San Diego)…recorded his first ML hit on 4/9 off the Mets' David Weathers at Hiram Bithorn Stadium in San Juan, P.R…**2003:** In 65 relief appearances with the Expos, went 10-3 with five saves and a 2.92 ERA (71.0IP, 23ER)…led all NL rookies in wins and ranked fourth in appearances…recorded his first Major League win on 4/19 vs. the Reds at Hiram Bithorn Stadium, striking out one batter in 1.1IP in relief…allowed just five of his 30 inherited runners to score (16.7%)…**2002:** Began the season with the Saraperos de Saltillo of the Mexican Summer League and went 3-5 with a 1.68 ERA (53.2IP, 10ER) and 23 saves in 49 relief appearances…had his contract purchased by Triple-A Ottawa on 8/18 where he made six relief outings (0-0, 3.52 ERA)…was signed by Arizona as a minor league free agent following the season, then selected by Montreal in the Rule 5 Draft on 12/16…**2001:** Began the season with Single-A Salem of the Rockies organization and made 13 relief appearances, going 0-1 with seven saves and a 4.05 ERA (13.1IP, 6ER)…had his contract purchased by Saltillo of the Mexican League in May where he went 1-2 with 21 saves and a 2.03 ERA (40.0IP, 9ER) in 33 relief appearances…**2000:** Was loaned by Colorado to Saltillo and was 5-3 with 25 saves and a 2.76 ERA, allowing 20ER in 65.1IP in relief…recorded saves in each of his last 10 appearances of the season…**1999:** Went 7-3 with a 1.71 ERA (79.0IP, 15ER), establishing a Mexican Summer League record with 41 saves…**1998:** Spent the entire season with Saltillo and was 7-8 with seven saves and a 5.62 ERA, allowing 52ER in 83.1IP in 47G (four starts)…**1997:** Made his professional debut with Saltillo and went 7-5 with a 4.62 ERA (62.1IP, 32ER) in 37G (2 starts)…**PERSONAL:** Is married to Dayasi Cerrano with one son, Luis Jr.

BAKER, Ryan – C

HT: 5-8; **WT:** 195; **B:** R; **T:** R; **BORN:** 11/9/84 in Portland, Maine; **RESIDES:** Portland, Maine; **M.L. SVC:** 0.000; **OBTAINED:** Signed by the Yankees as a non-drafted free agent on 6/12/08; **CAREER NOTES:** 2010: Hit .079 (3-for-38) in 18 combined games with Single-A Tampa and Double-A Trenton…**2009:** Combined to bat .200 with 1 double, 2HR and 6RBI in 18 games with short-season Single-A Staten Island and Double-A Trenton…began the season with Staten Island, batting .241 with 1 double, 2HR and 6RBI in 10 games…hit his first career HR and recorded his first professional RBI on 7/15 at Mahoning Valley…five of his six RBI on the season came on 7/22 vs. Jamestown…in eight games with Trenton, batted .125 with 2BB…was placed on the disabled list on 8/27 with a right ankle contusion, where he remained for the rest of the season…**2008:** Made his professional debut, combining to bat .100 (2-for-20) in 12 games with the GCL Yankees and Single-A Tampa.

BANUELOS, Manuel – LHP

HT: 5-11; **WT:** 195; **B:** L; **T:** L; **BORN:** 3/13/91 in Monterrey, Mexico; **RESIDES:** Durango, Mexico; **OBTAINED:** Signed by the Yankees as a non-drafted free agent on 3/30/08; **M.L. SVC:** 0.000; **CAREER NOTES:** 2010: Combined to go 0-4 with a 2.51 ERA (64.2IP, 18ER) in 15 starts with the GCL Yankees, Single-A Tampa and Double-A Trenton…spent the majority of the year with Tampa, where he went 0-3 with a 2.23 ERA (44.1IP, 11ER), recording 62K over 10 starts…fanned a career-high 11 batters on 8/6 vs. St. Lucie…owned a 1.64 ERA over a nine-start stretch from 7/1-8/12, recording 56K and allowing just 7ER in 38.1IP…following the season, made seven starts with the Phoenix Desert Dogs of the Arizona Fall League, going 0-2 with a 3.60 ERA, allowing 10ER in 25.0IP…started in the 2010 AFL Rising Stars Game, allowing 1R in 2.0IP (2K)…named by Baseball America as the Yankees' fourth-best prospect and top left-hander…**2009:** Went 9-5 with a 2.67 ERA in 25 games (19 starts) with Single-A Charleston…began the season as a starter and allowed 2ER or less in 14 of his 19 starts…moved to the bullpen in August where he went 1-0 with a 1.64 ERA (11.0IP, 2ER) in six relief appearances with the RiverDogs…was transferred to Single-A Tampa on 9/14 and made one appearance out of the bullpen, recording 2K in 1.0IP…was selected to the World Team in the 2009 Futures Game during All-Star Weekend at St. Louis' Busch Stadium, but did not pitch…**2008:** Made his professional debut, going 4-1 with a 2.57 ERA in 12 appearances (three starts) with the GCL Yankees.

BARREDA, Manuel – RHP

HT: 5-9; **WT:** 200; **B:** R; **T:** R; **BORN:** 10/8/88 in Sahuarita, Ariz.; **RESIDES:** Amado, Ariz.; **OBTAINED:** Selected by the Yankees in the 12th round of the 2007 First-Year Player Draft; **M.L. SVC:** 0.000; **CAREER NOTES:** 2010: Combined at short-season Single-A Staten Island and Single-A Charleston to go 1-0 with a 3.23 ERA (24.1IP, 9ER) and 25K over 13 relief appearances…opened year with the SI Yankees, posting a 4.76 ERA with no decisions…made final six appearances with the RiverDogs, tossing 7.1 scoreless IP with 7K…**2009:** Opened the season with the GCL Yankees and went 0-1 with a 1.93 ERA in 14 relief appearances, 13 of which were scoreless…his .123 opponents batting average was second-lowest among GCL relievers…promoted to Single-A Charleston on 9/2 and appeared in two games, allowing 4ER in 2.2IP…**2008:** Appeared in six games (two starts) with the GCL Yankees, recording one save and a 2.65 ERA…had season cut short after undergoing season-ending elbow surgery on 7/28…**2007:** Made his professional debut, going 5-0 with a 3.00 ERA in 11 games (three starts) with the GCL Yankees…tossed a season-high 6.1 scoreless innings in relief in 8/7 win at the GCL Tigers (2H, 1BB, 5K)…recorded at least 2K in each of his 11 appearances…**PERSONAL:** Attended Sahuarita High School (Ariz.) before being drafted by the Yankees.

BARTLESKI, Philip – RHP

HT: 6-6; **WT:** 253; **B:** R; **T:** R; **BORN:** 4/22/83 in Lynchburg, Va.; **RESIDES:** Charlottesville, Va.; **COLLEGE:** Oklahoma City University; **OBTAINED:** Signed by the Yankees as a non-drafted free agent on 5/23/07; **M.L. SVC:** 0.000; **CAREER NOTES: 2010:** Spent the season with Single-A Tampa where he went 3-3 with a 4.54 ERA, allowing 35ER in 69.1IP...enjoyed his best success during daytime contests, where he was 2-0 with a 1.02 ERA (17.2IP, 2ER) in eight relief appearances, holding the opposition to a .190 (12-for-63) batting average...**2009:** Combined to go 4-2 with a 3.38 ERA in 21 relief appearances with the GCL Yankees, Single-A Staten Island, Single-A Tampa and Double-A Trenton...spent the majority of the season with Tampa, going 4-1 with a 2.86 ERA in 16 appearances out of the bullpen, holding the opposition without an earned run in 13 of the 16 outings...opponents combined to hit just .225 (32-for-142) off of him during the year...**2008:** Made 29 relief appearances with Single-A Tampa, going 2-1 with one save and a 1.64 ERA...opponents batted just .179 (34-for-190, 2HR)...allowed runs in only five outings...threw a season-high 3.0IP five times, including four straight appearances from 6/1-17...**2007:** Made his professional debut, going 1-1 with a 4.03 ERA in 13 appearances with short-season Single-A Staten Island...was placed on the D.L. from 8/30-9/16 with a right elbow strain.

BATISTA, Gean – RHP

HT: 6-4; **WT:** 175; **B:** R; **T:** R; **BORN:** 10/27/91 in Santo Domingo, D.R.; **RESIDES:** Santo Domingo, D.R.; **OBTAINED:** Signed as a minor league free agent on 7/1/10; **M.L. SVC:** 0.000; **CAREER NOTES: 2010:** Made his professional debut with the DSL Yankees 2, going 1-0 with a 3.45 ERA in 11 games...recorded 11K in 15.2IP.

BAUTISTA, Rony – LHP

HT: 6-7; **WT:** 200; **B:** L; **T:** L; **BORN:** 9/17/91 in San Juan, D.R.; **RESIDES:** San Juan, D.R.; **OBTAINED:** Signed by the Yankees as a non-drafted free agent on 11/4/09; **M.L. SVC:** 0.000; **CAREER NOTES:** Will be making his professional debut in 2011.

BEARD, Edwin – OF

HT: 6-3; **WT:** 190; **B:** R; **T:** R; **BORN:** 8/31/89 in Moca, D.R.; **RESIDES:** Moca, D.R.; **OBTAINED:** Signed by the Yankees as a non-drafted free agent on 7/2/07; **M.L. SVC:** 0.000; **CAREER NOTES: 2010:** Appeared in 36 games with the DSL Yankees 1, batting .250 (29-for-116) with 7 doubles, 1HR and 11RBI...**2009:** Appeared in a career-high 55 games with the DSL Yankees 1 and batted .290 (63-for-217) with 9 doubles, 2HR and 26 RBI...hit .331 (56-for-169) against right-handed pitching with nine doubles and 2HR...**2008:** Made his professional debut with the DSL Yankees 1, batting .211 with 1HR and 1RBI in 19 games.

BELLIARD, Ronnie – INF   NON-ROSTER INVITEE

HT: 5-9; **WT:** 211; **B:** R; **T:** R; **BORN:** 4/7/75 in the Bronx, N.Y.; **RESIDES:** Miami; Fla.; **OBTAINED:** Signed by the Yankees as a minor league free agent on 2/10/11; **M.L. SVC:** 11.149; **CAREER NOTES:** In 1,484 games over parts of 13 seasons with Milwaukee (1998-2002), Colorado (2003), Cleveland (2004-06), St. Louis (2006), Washington (2007-09) and Los Angeles-NL (2009-10), owns a .273 (1,377-for-5,045) career batting average with 328 doubles, 114HR and 601RBI...among active second basemen, ranks fourth in doubles, fifth in home runs and RBI and sixth in games played...was a member of the 2006 World Champion St. Louis Cardinals and represented the Dominican Republic in the inaugural World Baseball Classic during the same year...was voted to the AL All-Star team in 2004, while with Cleveland...**2010:** Played in 82 games with the Dodgers and hit .216 (35-for-162) with 10 doubles, 2HR and 19RBI...committed just three errors in 36 total chances combined at the first, second and third-base positions...**2009:** Batted .277 (73-for-264) with 10HR and 39RBI in 110 combined games with the Dodgers and Nationals...was acquired by Los Angeles-NL from Washington on 8/30 in exchange for RHP Luis Garcia and a player to be named later (LHP Victor Garate)...with the Dodgers, hit .351 (27-for-77) with 7 doubles, 5HR and 17RBI in 24 games, starting in 19 of those appearances...became the fourth Dodger in team history to homer in his first plate appearance when he accomplished the feat on 8/31 off Arizona's Doug Davis...started all eight postseason games at second base, hitting .300 (9-for-30) overall, including a .316 (6-for-19) batting average in the NLCS vs. Philadelphia...following the season, appeared in 15 games with the Tigres del Licey of the Dominican Winter League and hit .160 (8-for-50) with 3RBI...**2008:** Played in 96 games with Washington and hit .287 (85-for-296) with 11HR, 37BB and 46RBI, establishing career-highs in both slugging (.473) and on-base percentage (.372)...was placed on the 15-day disabled list from 5/16-6/10 with a left calf strain, missing 23 games...led the Nationals in batting average (.353) and on-base percentage (.423) in 40 games after being reinstated from the D.L....established a single-month, career-best .391 (36-for-92) batting average in 26 games during August, including a .429 on-base percentage...returned to the DL on 9/4 with a right-groin strain, ending his season...played in 18 games with Licey following the season, and hit .333 (22-for-66) with 4HR and 16RBI...**2007:** Batted .290 (148-for-511) with 35 doubles, 11HR and 58RBI in 147 games with Washington...ranked second among all National League second basemen with a .989 fielding percentage, recording just six errors in 569 total chances...was one of five Major Leaguers at the position to hit 30 or more doubles that season...recorded 12 assists at second base on 4/18 vs. Philadelphia, becoming the first Major League second baseman to notch 12 or more assists in a single-game since San Diego's Mark Loretta recorded 13 on 5/7/2003...following the season, batted .195 (16-for-82) with 3 doubles and 9RBI in 22 games with Licey...**2006:** Combined to hit .272 (148-for-544) with 30 doubles, 13HR and 67RBI in 147 games with Cleveland and St. Louis...was acquired by the Cardinals from the Indians on 7/30 in exchange for INF Hector Luna...in 54 games with St. Louis, batted .237 (46-for-194) with 5HR and 23RBI after beginning the season hitting .291 (102-for-350) with 8HR and 44RBI in 93 games with Cleveland...while with the Indians, established a career-best 14-game hitting streak from 6/25-7/9, batting .321 (18-for-56) with 4HR and 10RBI over the stretch...made his postseason debut with the Cardinals, starting in 14 of St. Louis' 16 games, hitting .240 (12-for-50) with 4RBI and 2SB for the eventual World Series Champion...prior to the season, represented the Dominican Republic in the inaugural World Baseball Classic and hit .429 (3-for-7) in five games...**2005:** Played in 145 games with Cleveland and batted .284 (152-for-536) with 36 doubles, a career-high 17HR and 78RBI...hit his first career grand slam on 8/25 off Tampa Bay's Travis Harper...following the season, played for the Dominican Republic during the Caribbean World Series and hit .304 (7-for-23) in six games...**2004:** In his first season with the Indians, batted .282 (169-for-599) with a career-best 48 doubles, 12HR and 70RBI in 152 games...led the team in games, hits and doubles, recording the most doubles by an Indian in a single season since Albert Belle posted 52 in 1995...hit .304 (103-339) with 5HR and 37RBI during the first half of the year, earning a spot on the AL All-Star team...**2003:** In 116 games with the Rockies, hit .277 (124-for-447) with 31 doubles, 8HR and 50RBI...became the franchise's first non-roster invitee ever to start on Opening Day...collected a career-high 8RBI on

9/23 vs. Arizona, matching Colorado's single-game franchise record and marking the most RBI by a leadoff hitter since Detroit's Jim Northrup accomplished the feat on 7/11/73 vs. Texas…went a perfect 5-for-5 on 5/29 vs. the Angels, establishing a career-high for hits in a single game…**2002:** Played in 104 games with Milwaukee and hit .211 (61-for-289) with 3HR and 26RBI…was 6-for-23 (.261) as a pinch-hitter, including his first career pinch-hit home run off Cincinnati's Gabe White on 7/5…**2001:** Batted .264 (96-for-364) with 30 doubles, 11HR and 36RBI in 101 games with the Brewers…recorded his first career multi-homer game on 7/25 vs. the Dodgers and the first ever stolen base in Miller Park history on 4/6 vs. the Reds…had his season cut short after being placed on the disabled list with a high right ankle sprain on 8/10…**2000:** Made his first career Opening Day roster, hitting .263 (150-for-571) with 30 doubles, a franchise-record 9 triples, 8HR and 54RBI in 152 games with Milwaukee…recorded 83R and 82BB, establishing career-highs in both categories…**1999:** Hit a career-high .295 (135-for-457) with 29 doubles, 4 triples, 8HR and 58RBI in 124 games with the Brewers after being recalled from Triple-A Louisville on 5/11…earned the organization's "Rookie of the Year" award, leading all NL rookies in batting average, walks (67) and on-base percentage (.379), ranking second in doubles, third in slugging percentage (.429), fourth in hits and sixth in RBI…**1998:** Spent the majority of the year with Triple-A Louisville and earned International League All-Star honors, batting .321 (163-for-507) with 36 doubles, seven triples, 14HR and 73RBI in 133 games…was recalled by Milwaukee on 9/12 and made his ML debut on 9/12 as a pinch-runner…recorded his first big league hit on 9/16 of the Reds' Gabe White…**1997:** Hit .282 (125-for-443) with 35 doubles, 4HR and 55RBI in 118 games with Triple-A Tucson…recorded a 22-game hitting streak from 7/27-8/21, batting .347 during the stretch…**1996:** Was a Texas League All-Star with Double-A El Paso, batting .279 (116-for-416) with 20 doubles, 8 triples, 3HR and 57RBI in 109…tied for fourth in the TL with a career-high .297 (137-for-461) with 28 doubles, 13HR and 76RBI…ranked second in the club in hits and tied for second in RBI…**1994:** Made his professional debut, batting .294 (42-for-143) with 7 doubles, 3 triples and 27RBI in 39 games with the AZL Brewers…**PERSONAL:** Is a1994 graduate of Central High School in Miami, Fla.…is married to Candida, with two children, Rachel and Ronnie, Jr.

BELLO, Hector – LHP

HT: 6-1; **WT:** 175; **B:** L; **T:** L; **BORN:** 5/19/91 in San Cristobal, D.R.; **RESIDES:** San Cristobal, D.R.; **OBTAINED:** Signed as a minor league free agent on 6/28/10; **M.L. SVC:** 0.000; **CAREER NOTES: 2010:** Made his professional debut with the DSL Yankees 2, going 0-2 with a 13.06 ERA in 12 games.

BELLO, Yoely – LHP

HT: 6-2; **WT:** 150; **B:** L; **T:** L; **BORN:** 12/16/90 in Valverde Mao, D.R.; **RESIDES:** Valverde Mao, D.R.; **OBTAINED:** Signed as a minor league free agent on 3/20/10; **M.L. SVC:** 0.000; **CAREER NOTES: 2010:** Made his professional debut with the DSL Yankees 1, and went 1-1 with one save and a 3.25 ERA in 15 games…collected 42K in 36.0IP, ranking third on the team in strikeouts.

BERIGUETE, Victor – RHP

HT: 6-1; **WT:** 185; **B:** R; **T:** R; **BORN:** 11/6/88 in Santo Domingo, D.R.; **RESIDES:** Santo Domingo, D.R.; **OBTAINED:** Signed by the Yankees as a non-drafted free agent on 11/2/07; **M.L. SVC:** 0.000; **CAREER NOTES: 2010:** In 13 appearances (two starts), went 2-0 with two saves and a 1.49 ERA with the DSL Yankees 1…**2009:** Went 2-3 with a 3.56 ERA in a team-high-tying 11 starts with the DSL Yankees 1, issuing just 10BB in 43.0IP…held opponents to a .217 batting average…**2008:** Made his professional debut with the DSL Yankees 2, posting a 2-1 record with a 4.50 ERA in 10 games (nine starts).

BERNIER, Doug – INF   NON-ROSTER INVITEE

HT: 6-0; **WT:** 185; **B:** S; **T:** R; **BORN:** 6/24/80 in Santa Maria, Calif.; **RESIDES:** Palm Beach Gardens, Fla.; **COLLEGE:** Oral Roberts; **OBTAINED:** Signed by the Yankees as a free agent on 12/14/10; **M.L. SVC:** 0.008; **CAREER NOTES:** Owns a career .238 (576-for-2,420) minor league batting average with 101 doubles, 12 triples, 20HR and 239RBI in 809 games…**2010:** Hit .240 (48-for-200) with 14 doubles, 1HR and 15RBI in 69 games with the Triple-A Indianapolis Indians, reaching base safely in 10 of his last 12 games played…**2009:** Played in 79 games with Triple-A Scranton/Wilkes-Barre in his first stint with the Yankees organization and hit .181 (41-for-227) with 9 doubles, 2 triples and 20RBI…batted .326 (14-for-43) with 20RBI with runners in scoring position…**2008:** Saw his first Major League action after being added to the Colorado roster on 6/17 from Triple-A Colorado Springs…appeared in two games, making his lone start on 6/19 vs. Cleveland, starting at 2B and going 0-for-4…appeared in 110 games with Colorado Springs, batting .255 with 10 doubles, 4 triples, 9HR and 42RBI and setting career highs in triples, homers and RBI…had 10HR total entering the season…collected his first career multi-homer game on 6/2 vs. Sacramento and hit first career grand slam on 8/16 at Salt Lake…appeared in games at all four infield positions as well as one game in RF, combining for a .986 fielding percentage (7E, 504TC), with all the errors coming at shortstop where he saw the majority of his playing time…**2007:** Played entire season with Triple-A Colorado Springs, starting at least five games at each infield position…batted a career-high .310 with 15 doubles, 2HR and 27RBI, leading the Sky Sox with a .396 on-base percentage…batted .276 (21-for-76) vs. left-handed pitchers and .329 (46-for-140) vs. righties…**2006:** Hit .280 with 16 doubles, 1HR and 27RBI in 87 games with Double-A Tulsa…led the team with a .380 average (27-for-71) in the month of July…recorded 20 multi-hit games…**2005:** In his first Double-A action, batted .203 with 14 doubles, 3HR and 39RBI in a career-high 117 games with Tulsa…batted .302 (26-for-86) through the first 27 games of the season before dropping to a .173 clip (49-for-283) over the final three months of the season…played the majority of his games at shortstop (113G), leading all Texas League shortstops with a .974 fielding percentage (14E, 557TC)…**2004:** Appeared in 102 games with Single-A Visalia, batting .272 with 13 doubles, 3HR and 24RBI…played 58 games at SS and 39 games at 3B…made an emergency relief appearance on 7/3 vs. Modesto, allowing a solo home run in 1.0IP…**2003:** Hit just .201 with Single-A Visalia with 5 doubles and 21RBI…stole a career-high 12 bases…drew 64 walks (fifth-most in Cal League), while striking out only 63 times…**2002:** Made professional debut with short-season Single-A Tri-City, batting .197 with 5 doubles, 1HR and 24RBI in 64 games…led the Northwest League with 58 walks…hit first career homer on 7/8/02 at Everett…made an emergency relief appearance on 7/24 at Salem-Kaiser (0.1IP, 1H)…**PERSONAL:** Full name is Douglas Howell Bernier…was originally signed by Colorado as a non-drafted free agent in June 2002…carried a .332 career average at Oral Roberts and was a first-team All Mid-Continent Conference selection as a senior in 2002.

BLACK, Sean – RHP

HT: 6-3; **WT:** 211; **B:** R; **T:** R; **BORN:** 4/23/88 in Mt. Laurel, N.J.; **RESIDES:** South Orange, N.J.; **COLLEGE:** Seton Hall; **OBTAINED:** Selected by the Yankees in the seventh round of the 2009 First-Year Player Draft; **M.L. SVC:** 0.000; **CAREER NOTES: 2010:** Went a combined 8-8 with a 3.68 ERA (127.1IP, 52ER) in 25 games (24 starts) with Single-A Charleston and Single-A Tampa…spent the majority of the season with Charleston where he was 7-8 with a 3.88 ERA, allowing 50ER in 116.0IP…was promoted to Tampa on 8/23 where he made two starts, going 1-0 with a 1.59 ERA and allowing just 2ER in 11.1IP…**2009:** Went 6-0 with a 1.62 ERA in 10 starts with short-season Single-A Staten Island in his first professional action…ERA for the team lead in wins…named NYPL "Pitcher of the Week" for the period of 8/10-17, going 2-0 and allowing only 2ER in 11.0IP over two starts…included was 6.0 innings of no-hit ball on 8/13 vs. Auburn (2BB, 8K)…**PERSONAL:** Attended Seton Hall University where as a junior in 2009 was named the school's "Junior Male Athlete of the Year" and was a member of the All-New Jersey College Baseball Association First Team and All-Big East Second Team…was drafted by Washington in 2006 but chose to attend college.

BLEICH, Jeremy – LHP

HT: 6-1; **WT:** 200; **B:** L; **T:** L; **BORN:** 6/18/87 in Metairie, La.; **RESIDES:** Metairie, La.; **COLLEGE:** Stanford University; **OBTAINED:** Selected by the Yankees in Compensation Round A (44th overall) of the 2008 First-Year Player Draft.; **M.L. SVC:** 0.000; **CAREER NOTES: 2010:** Made eight starts with Double-A Trenton, going 3-2 with a 4.79 ERA (41.1IP, 22ER) in eight starts, before landing on the disabled list with a left shoulder strain…underwent season-ending surgery to repair a torn left labrum…**2009:** Entered the season ranked as the Yankees' ninth-best prospect by *Baseball America*…combined to go 9-10 with a 4.86 ERA in 27 starts with Single-A Tampa and Double-A Trenton…ranked fifth among all Yankees minor leaguers with 116K…began the season with Tampa, going 6-4 with a 3.40 ERA in 14 starts…won his final three decisions with Tampa, holding his opponents to 1ER in 18.1IP (15H, 2R, 3BB, 13K)…was promoted to Trenton on 6/30, going 3-6 with a 6.65 ERA in 13 starts…**2008:** Made his professional debut with short-season Single-A Staten Island, making one start and allowing 2H and 2ER in 3.0IP (4K, 1HR)…made one postseason relief appearance for Staten Island, tossing 4.0 scoreless innings (2H, 4K)…pitched for the Waikiki BeachBoys in the Hawaiian Winter Baseball League following the season, going 3-2 with a 1.77 ERA in seven starts (35.2IP, 29H, 10R, 7ER, 12BB, 33K, 1HR)…**PERSONAL:** Full name is Jeremy Michael Bleich…attended Stanford University, where he went 3-3 with a 2.09 ERA during his junior year in 2008, allowing just 11ER in 47.1IP and leading the team in ERA (min. 5G)…missed eight weeks of the season (March through mid-May) with a strained ligament in his left elbow…started the opening game of the 2008 College World Series vs. Florida State, recording a no-decision despite allowing 1ER while striking out a season-high seven batters in 5.0IP…his sixth-inning leadoff HR allowed to FSU's Dennis Quinn on his 89th and final pitch of the game snapped a 25.2-inning stretch without allowing an earned run…faced fellow Yankees-draftee Jack Rye in the game, with Rye going 0-for-3 with 1K…earned Cape Cod League All-Star honors while playing for the Wareham Gatemen in 2006…was on the U.S.A. Junior National Team in 2005.

BRABOY, Brandon – RHP

HT: 5-11; **WT:** 195; **B:** R; **T:** R; **BORN:** 10/31/85 in Kevil, Ky.; **RESIDES:** Kevil, Ky.; **COLLEGE:** University of Indianapolis; **OBTAINED:** Selected by the Yankees in the 18th round of the 2008 First-Year Player Draft; **M.L. SVC:** 0.000; **CAREER NOTES: 2010:** Appeared in 11 games (two starts) with Single-A Tampa and did not record a decision, allowing 9ER in 22.2IP (3.57 ERA)…went on the disabled list from 4/22-5/7 with a right forearm strain…returned to the D.L. again on 5/27 with a strained right hip…**2009:** Went 4-5 with a 3.97 ERA in 33 games (nine starts) with Single-A Charleston…went 2-3 as a reliever with one save and a 4.01 ERA (49.1IP, 22ER) in 24 appearances out of the bullpen…shifted to the starting rotation in July and made nine consecutive starts to end the campaign, going 2-2 with a 3.92 ERA (43.2IP, 19ER)…threw 5.0IP or more in five of his nine starts…**2008:** Made his professional debut with short-season Single-A Staten Island, going 2-1 with a 3.21 ERA in 10 starts…was named the New York-Penn League's "Pitcher of the Week" for the period of 7/21-27, going 1-0 with a 0.00 ERA in two starts (11.0IP, 5H, 1R, 0ER, 3BB, 10K)…was placed on the disabled list on 8/7 for the remainder of the season with right shoulder tendinitis…**PERSONAL:** Attended the University of Indianapolis, going 8-3 with a 3.61 ERA and four complete games in 14 appearances (13 starts) during his junior year…named All-Region and team MVP in baseball and basketball as a senior at Heath (Ky.) High School.

BREWER, Daniel – OF   NON-ROSTER INVITEE

HT: 5-11; **WT:** 195; **B:** R; **T:** R; **BORN:** 7/19/87 in Brookfield, Ill.; **RESIDES:** Batavia, Ill.; **COLLEGE:** Bradley University; **OBTAINED:** Selected by the Yankees in the eighth round of the 2008 First-Year Player Draft; **M.L. SVC:** 0.000; **CAREER NOTES: 2010:** Spent the entire season with Double-A Trenton and batted .270 (137-for-508) with 34 doubles, 3 triples, 10HR, 84RBI and 29SB in 136 games…recorded the second-most RBI among all Yankees minor league hitters and the fifth most stolen bases…in seven postseason games, hit a team-high .400 (10-for-25) with one double, 1HR, 4RBI and 2SB…**2009:** Combined to hit .306 with 70R, 25 doubles, 6HR and 54RBI in 117 games with Single-A Charleston and Single-A Tampa…tied for third among all Yankees minor leaguers in batting average and ranked fifth in stolen bases (22)…began the season with Charleston, batting .323 with 38R, 18 doubles, 2HR and 25RBI in 58 games…was promoted to Tampa on 6/25 and hit .290 with 32R, 7 doubles, 4HR and 29RBI in 59 games…**2008:** Made his professional debut, batting .296 with 29R, 19 doubles, 3HR and 40RBI in 66 games with short-season Single-A Staten Island…tied for fourth among Yankees minor leaguers in batting average…hit .381 (43-for-113) with 12 doubles and 17RBI in 31 road games…batted .571 (4-for-7) with 1 double and 9RBI with the bases loaded…hit .111 (1-for-9) with 2RBI in two postseason games…**PERSONAL:** Attended Bradley University where he majored in business with an emphasis in marketing…was named to the Brooks Wallace Award Preseason Watch List prior to his junior year and batted .341 (63-for-185) with 51R, 15 doubles, 6HR and 36RBI in 53 games…was named First-Team All-MVC as an outfielder, becoming the fourth Brave since 1973 to earn the honor…became the first player in school history with at least 20 career homers and 40 stolen bases…was a career .333 (197-for-592) batter with 142R, 47 doubles, 21HR and 101RBI in 163 games at Bradley, tying for fourth all-time with nine triples and ranking seventh in runs, doubles and stolen bases (47), while placing ninth in total bases (325)…was a Cape Cod League All-Star in 2007…attended Lyons Township High School where he played football and baseball for four seasons and wrestled for three years…was a three-time all-conference performer in baseball, batting .460 with 13HR and 57RBI during his senior year.

BRITO, Sandy – OF

HT: 6-3; **WT:** 170; **B:** S; **T:** R; **BORN:** 6/9/93 in Santo Domingo, D.R.; **RESIDES:** Santo Domingo, D.R.; **OBTAINED:** Signed as a minor league free agent on 4/23/10; **M.L. SVC:** 0.000; **CAREER NOTES: 2010:** Made his professional debut with the DSL Yankees 2, batting .199 (35-for-176) with 8 doubles, 6 triples, 3HR and 22RBI in 57 games.

BROOKS, Gavin – LHP

HT: 6-3; **WT:** 220; **B:** L; **T:** L; **BORN:** 10/27/87 in Vista, Calif.; **RESIDES:** Los Angeles, Calif.; **COLLEGE:** UCLA; **OBTAINED:** Selected by the Yankees in the ninth round of the 2009 First-Year Player Draft; **M.L. SVC:** 0.000; **CAREER NOTES: 2010:** Spent the season on the disabled list, undergoing shoulder surgery in June…**2009:** Made 30 appearances in relief for short-season Single-A Staten Island in his first professional season, going 5-1 with a 0.62 ERA…struck out 48 batters in 43.1IP and held opponents scoreless in 25 of his outings…did not allow an earned run over his first 12 appearances (14.2IP, 10H, 3R, 11BB, 18K)…ranked fourth in the NYPL in appearances…made five postseason appearances for the NYPL champs, going 1-1 with a 1.29 ERA (7.0IP, 1ER)…**PERSONAL:** Drafted out of UCLA where he recorded a team-high eight saves as a Junior and earned All-Pac 10 honorable mention…graduated from Rancho Buena Vista HS (Calif.), earning AFLAC All-American honors in 2005 as a junior and the school's "Male Athlete of the Year" as a senior in 2006.

BROWN, Breland – OF

HT: 5-9; **WT:** 200; **B:** R; **T:** R; **BORN:** 12/12/84 in Marrero, La.; **RESIDES:** Harvey, La.; **OBTAINED:** Signed as a minor league free agent on 10/5/10; **M.L. SVC:** 0.000; **CAREER NOTES: 2010:** Was released from Giants organization on 3/25 and signed with the Yankees…will make his professional debut in 2011.

BROWN, Isaiah – OF

HT: 6-0; **WT:** 171; **B:** R; **T:** R; **BORN:** 10/16/89 in Phoenix, Ariz.; **RESIDES:** Glendale, Ariz.; **COLLEGE:** Paradise Valley CC; **OBTAINED:** Selected by the Yankees in the 43rd round of the 2009 First-Year Player Draft; **M.L. SVC:** 0.000; **CAREER NOTES: 2010:** Hit .218 (17-for-78) with 5 doubles, 1 triple, 1HR and 5RBI in 24 games with short-season Single-A Staten Island…**2009:** Played in 20 games with the GCL Yankees in his first professional season, batting .167.

BROWN, Shane – OF

HT: 5-10; **WT:** 187; **B:** R; **T:** R; **BORN:** 1/11/88 in Roanoke, Va.; **RESIDES:** Winter Park, Fla.; **COLLEGE:** University of Central Florida; **OBTAINED:** Selected by the Yankees in the 23rd round of the 2010 First-Year Player Draft; **M.L. SVC:** 0.000; **CAREER NOTES: 2010:** Made his professional debut with the short-season Single-A Staten Island Yankees, hitting .234 (49-for-209) with 7 doubles, 2HR and 25RBI in 60 games…ranked third on the team in RBI…**PERSONAL:** Selected as a 2010 *Louisville Slugger/Collegiate Baseball* and *Ping!Baseball* All-American at University of Central Florida…also named to the 2010 All-Conference USA First Team…finished college career with a .363 batting average, the sixth-highest in UCF history…ranked 18th in the nation in batting average, while also ranking fourth in OBP.

BURAWA, Daniel – RHP

HT: 6-2; **WT:** 200; **B:** R; **T:** R; **BORN:** 12/30/88 in Riverhead, N.Y.; **RESIDES:** Rocky Point, N.Y.; **COLLEGE:** St. John's University; **OBTAINED:** Selected by the Yankees in the 12th round of the 2010 First-Year Player Draft; **M.L. SVC:** 0.000; **CAREER NOTES: 2010:** Made his professional debut with short-season Single-A Staten Island, making seven relief appearances (0-0, 7.71 ERA)…held the opposition without an earned run in four of his seven outings…**PERSONAL:** Full name is Daniel James Burawa…graduated from Rocky Point High School (N.Y.) where he was a two-time all-league selection and earned all-county and all-Long Island honors as a senior…tossed two no-hitters in high school…attended Suffolk County CC his freshman year before transferring to St. John's.

CABRERA, Cristofer – RHP

HT: 6-0; **WT:** 180; **B:** R; **T:** R; **BORN:** 12/25/92 in Altamira, Puerto Plata, D.R.; **RESIDES:** Altamira, Puerto Plata, D.R.; **OBTAINED:** Signed by the Yankees as a non-drafted free agent on 7/2/09; **M.L. SVC:** 0.000; **CAREER NOTES: 2010:** Made his professional debut with the DSL Yankees 1, and went 3-1 with a 0.51 ERA (35.0IP, 2ER) in eight starts…held opponents scoreless in six of his eight starts, allowing just a .129 batting average (15-for-116).

CALDERON, Yeicok – OF

HT: 6-1; **WT:** 220; **B:** L; **T:** L; **BORN:** 12/23/91 in La Romana, D.R.; **RESIDES:** La Romana, D.R.; **OBTAINED:** Signed by the Yankees as a non-drafted free agent on 7/2/08; **M.L. SVC:** 0.000; **CAREER NOTES: 2010:** Appeared in 69 games with the DSL Yankees 1, batting .339 (83-for-245) with 16 doubles, 6 triples, 8HR and 44RBI…led the DSL in slugging (.551), total bases (135) and extra-base hits (30), ranked second in hits and HR, third in OBP (.439) and fifth in average…led the team in doubles, triples, HR, average, OBP and slugging (.551)…had 24 multi-hit games…hit for the cycle on 8/7 vs. the DSL Giants (4-for-7)…named to DSL midseason All-Star team…**2009:** Made his professional debut with the DSL Yankees 1, batting .321 with 38R, 5 doubles, 2 triples, 3HR, 27RBI and 9SB…ranked eighth in the league in batting average…hit safely in 10 straight games from 7/6-16, batting .526 (20-for-38) with 13R and 8BB over the stretch.

CAMILO, Gustavo – RHP

HT: 5-10; **WT:** 156; **B:** R; **T:** R; **BORN:** 1/2/92 in Santo Domingo, D.R.; **RESIDES:** Santo Domingo, D.R.; **OBTAINED:** Signed as a minor league free agent on 6/4/10; **M.L. SVC:** 0.000; **CAREER NOTES: 2010:** Made his professional debut with the DSL Yankees 1, and went 2-0 with one save and a 4.58 ERA in 11 relief appearances.

CARLYLE, Buddy – RHP   NON-ROSTER INVITEE

HT: 6-3; **WT:** 210; **B:** L; **T:** R; **BORN:** 12/21/77 in Omaha, Neb.; **RESIDES:** Tyrone, Ga.; **OBTAINED:** Signed by the Yankees as a minor league free agent on 12/7/10; **M.L. SVC:** 3.047; **CAREER NOTES:** In 104 career Major League appearances (27 starts) with San Diego (1999-2000), Los Angeles-NL (2005) and Atlanta (2007-09), is 11-11 with a 5.61 ERA (245.2IP, 153ER)…was originally selected by Cincinnati in the second round of the 1996 First-Year Player Draft…**2010:** Spent the season pitching for the Hokkaido Nippon Ham Fighters of Japan's Pacific League, going 0-3 with a 4.88 ERA in seven appearances (27.2IP, 35H, 18R, 15ER, 11BB, 14K, 2HR)…**2009:** Made 16 relief appearances with Atlanta, going 0-1 with an 8.86 ERA, allowing 21ER in 21.1IP out of the bullpen for the Braves…combined to go 3-1 with a 1.56 ERA (17.1IP, 3ER) with Triple-A Gwinnett and Single-A Rome…**2008:** Played the majority of the season with Atlanta, going 2-0 with a 3.59 ERA (62.2IP, 25ER) in a career-high 45 relief appearances…held opponents scoreless in 18 of his final 22 outings of the year, allowing just 9ER in 30.0IP (2.70 ERA)…four of his six outings of 3.0IP or more were scoreless (19.1IP)…made two appearances out of the bullpen for Richmond and did not record a decision, allowing 6ER in 7.2IP (7.04 ERA)…**2007:** Appeared in 22 games (20 starts) for the Braves and went 8-7 with a 5.21 ERA (107.0IP, 62ER)…earned his second career win with a seven-inning, one-hit performance on 6/5 in game one

of a doubleheader vs. the Marlins…following the game, was transferred to Richmond, where he went 5-2 with a 2.59 ERA (48.2IP, 14ER)…tied for first on the club in wins and ranked second in the IL, earning league Pitcher of the Week honors from 4/30-5/7…**2006**: Played his first season in the Marlins organization and went 3-1 with a 1.93 ERA (28.0IP, 6ER) in 13 games (2 starts) with Triple-A Albuquerque prior to having his contract purchased by the LG Twins in Seoul, Korea, on 5/18…**2005**: In 31 combined games (7 starts) with the Dodgers, Triple-A Las Vegas and the GCL Dodgers, went 1-2 with two saves and a 5.54 ERA (65.0IP, 40ER)…began the season on the Dodgers' Opening Day roster and made nine appearances, going 0-0 with an 8.18 ERA before being outrighted on 5/6…was placed on the disabled list on 6/12 to have his appendix removed…did not allow an earned run in 13 appearances following his DL stint…**2004**: In his first stint with the Yankees organization, went 4-0 with a 0.72 ERA (37.1IP, 3ER) in eight games (five starts) with Double-A Trenton before being promoted to Triple-A Columbus on 6/15…while with the Clippers, went 8-5 with a 4.05 ERA in 19 games (18 starts), allowing 48ER in 106.2IP…had his best month of the year in June, where he went 2-0 with a 1.83 ERA for Columbus…**2003**: Spent the majority of the season with Double-A Wichita of the Royals organization and went 3-2 with a 1.98 ERA (27.1IP, 6ER) in 15 appearances out of the bullpen…began the year with Triple-A Omaha and went 0-1 with a 5.40 ERA, allowing 3ER in 5.0IP over two relief appearances…**2002**: Pitched for the Hanshin Tigers of the Japanese League and went 0-2 with a 7.53 ERA in three starts…**2001**: Went 7-10 with a 3.87 ERA in 28 games (26 starts) with Hanshin…recorded 111K in 153.1IP…**2000**: Spent the majority of the season with Triple-A Las Vegas and went 8-6 with a 4.29 ERA in 27 starts…made four relief appearances with the Padres and allowed 7ER in 3.0IP (21.00 ERA)…**1999**: Played the majority of the year with Las Vegas and went 11-8 with a 4.89 ERA (160.0IP, 87ER) in 25 starts…made seven relief appearances with the Padres and went 1-3 with a 5.97 ERA, allowing 25ER in 37.2IP…**1998**: Went 0-1 with a 5.40 ERA in one start with Double-A Chattanooga before being traded from the Reds to the Padres on 4/8 in exchange for RHP Marc Koon…went 14-6 with a 3.38 ERA in 27 starts with Double-A Mobile, matching his career-high in wins…**1997**: Made 23 starts with Single-A Charleston and went 14-5 with a 2.77 ERA, allowing 44ER in 143.0IP…**1996**: Made his professional debut, appearing in 10 games (nine starts) with Single-A Princeton, going 2-4 with a 4.66 ERA (46.1IP, 24ER)…**PERSONAL**: Married (Jessica) with one son (Carter) and one daughter (Kennedy)…full name is Earl Carlyle.

CASTELLON, Alfredo – C

HT: 6-2; **WT:** 155; **B:** L; **T:** R; **BORN:** 6/4/92 in Cartagena, Colombia; **RESIDES:** Cartagena, Colombia; **OBTAINED:** Signed as a minor league free agent on 7/1/10; **M.L. SVC:** 0.000; **CAREER NOTES: 2010:** Made his professional debut with the DSL Yankees 2, batting .232 (16-for-69) with 5 doubles and 10RBI in 22 games.

CASTILLO, Ali – INF

HT: 5-10; **WT:** 165; **B:** R; **T:** R; **BORN:** 6/19/89 in Maracaibo, Venezuela; **RESIDES:** Maracaibo, Venezuela; **OBTAINED:** Signed by the Yankees as a non-drafted free agent on 10/10/07; **M.L. SVC:** 0.000; **CAREER NOTES: 2010:** Split season between both DSL teams, batting .333 (48-for-144) with 7 doubles, 4 triples, 1HR and 28RBI…**2009:** Batted .319 with 40R, 13 doubles, 9 triples, 1HR, 27RBI and 10SB in 52 games…drew 24BB with only 14K…was caught stealing just once…ranked fifth in the league in slugging (.503) and 10th in average, and tied for the team lead in triples…had the fifth-most PA/K (15.14)…led all DSL third basemen with a .955 fielding percentage (9E, 198TC)…**2008:** In his professional debut, hit .288 with 10 doubles, 4 triples and 36RBI in 68 games for the DSL Yankees 1…fashioned a 15-game hitting streak from 7/22-8/9, batting .369 (24-for-65) with 11R, 3 doubles and 11RBI over the stretch.

CASTILLO, Noel – RHP

HT: 6-0; **WT:** 182; **B:** R; **T:** R; **BORN:** 10/05/83 in San Pedro de Macoris, D.R.; **RESIDES:** San Pedro de Macoris, D.R.; **OBTAINED:** Signed by the Yankees as a non-drafted free agent on 9/16/04; **M.L. SVC:** 0.000; **CAREER NOTES: 2010:** Combined to go 5-4 with a 3.88 ERA (46.1IP, 20ER) in 33 appearances out of the bullpen with Single-A Tampa and Double-A Trenton…finished the year with Tampa and went 2-2 with a 2.28 ERA, recording 36K and allowing 7ER in 27.2IP in relief…recorded 30 of his 36 strikouts with Tampa over his last 20.1IP…**2009:** Combined to go 3-2 with a 3.92 ERA in 37 appearances (two starts) with Single-A Tampa and Double-A Trenton…began the season with Tampa, going 3-2 with a 2.91 ERA in 31 appearances (two starts)…combined to toss 6.0 scoreless innings in his only two starts on 8/11 at Daytona and 8/18 (Game 2) vs. Daytona (4H, 2BB, 4K)…appeared in six games with Trenton from 4/25-5/13, allowing 10ER in 8.0IP (11.25 ERA) without recording a decision…following the season, pitched in three game for the Estrellas de Oriente of the Dominican Winter League…**2008:** Combined to go 8-8 with a 3.79 ERA in 26 appearances (22 starts) with Single-A Charleston and Single-A Tampa…ranked fourth among Yankees minor league pitchers in strikeouts (126)…struck out a season-high eight batters three times (4/5 at Rome, 5/18 vs. Asheville and 6/8 at Savannah)…was placed on the disabled list from 7/18-26 with a right oblique muscle strain…tossed a rain-shortened complete-game on 8/14 at Delmarva and recorded the loss, for his first career CG (5.2IP, 10H, 4ER, 1BB, 6K)…was promoted to Tampa on 8/30 and made the start that day at Fort Myers, allowing 6H and 1ER in 6.0IP (2BB, 7K)…**2007:** Was 6-3 with two saves and a 1.88 ERA in 13G (seven starts) with the GCL Yankees…ranked eighth in the minors, fourth in the GCL and led all Yankees minor league pitchers in ERA…did not allow a run in back-to-back starts on 8/3 and 8/9 (11.0IP)…struck out at least one batter in each of his 13 appearances and allowed only one home run during the season…**2006:** Made 14 appearances (10 starts) for the Yankees' Dominican Summer League 1 team, posting a 3-1 record with a 2.67 ERA…held opposing hitters to a .202 batting average and limited right-handed batters to just .188…**2005:** In first professional season, posted a 2-0 record with a 0.69 ERA in four games with the Yankees' Dominican Summer League 1 squad.

CASTRO, Kelvin – INF

HT: 6-2; **WT:** 190; **B:** R; **T:** R; **BORN:** 12/14/87 in San Pedro, D.R.; **RESIDES:** San Pedro, D.R.; **OBTAINED:** Signed by the Yankees as a non-drafted free agent on 1/28/06; **M.L. SVC:** 0.000; **CAREER NOTES: 2010:** Played the entire season with Single-A Charleston and hit .224 (98-for-437) with 20 doubles, 3 triples, 2HR and 39RBI in 123 games…recorded a career-high 15SB, tying for the second-most on the RiverDogs…**2009:** Spent the entire season with short-season Single-A Staten Island, batting .212 with a career-high 11 doubles, 5 triples, 2HR and 27RBI…**2008:** Was limited to 15 combined games with the GCL Yankees and Staten Island after beginning the season on the disabled list with a strained muscle in his back…**2007:** Batted .277 with 25R, 10 doubles and 22RBI in 49 games for the GCL Yankees…**2006:** Made professional debut with the DSL Yankees 2, batting .183 in 65 games at shortstop…among DSL shortstops, led the league in games, total chances (353), putouts (108), assists (214) and double plays (35).

CHAVEZ, Eric – INF

NON-ROSTER INVITEE

HT: 6-1; **WT:** 211; **B:** L; **T:** R; **BORN:** 12/7/77 in Los Angeles, Calif.; **RESIDES:** Paradise Valley, Ariz.; **OBTAINED:** Signed by the Yankees as a minor league free agent on 2/10/11; **M.L. SVC:** 12.020; **CAREER NOTES:** Originally selected by Oakland in the first round (10th overall pick) of the 1996 First-Year Player Draft…owns a .267 (1276-for-4783) career average with 282 doubles, 230HR and 787RBI in 1,320 games over 13 seasons with the Athletics…leaves the A's organization ranking among the franchise's top 10 in nearly every offensive category: second in doubles (282) and extra base hits (532), third in total bases (2,288), fourth in runs (730), home runs (230), RBI (787), games (1,320), at bats (4,783) and strikeouts (922), fifth in hits (1,276) and seventh in walks (565) and slugging percentage (.478)…won six consecutive AL Gold Glove awards at third base from 2001-06, tied with Buddy Bell for the second-most awards by an American Leaguer at the position behind Brooks Robinson (16)…set an Oakland record for fielding percentage by a third baseman with a .987 mark in 2006…was named to the 2002 *Sporting News* AL All-Star team and received the AL Silver Slugger award for third basemen…was named 1998 "Minor League Player of the Year" by *Baseball America* and received the J.G. Taylor Spink Award as the Topps "Minor League Player of the Year"…**2010:** Limited to just 33 games (.234, 1HR, 10RBI) after landing on the disabled list on 5/22 with neck spasms, marking his fourth straight season with a stint on the D.L…had a one-game rehab assignment with the Arizona Rookie League Athletics on 8/23 (1-for-3) but would not play again for the remainder of the season…made his 11th Opening Day start on 4/5 vs. Seattle, tying Jimmy Dykes for second most in Athletics franchise history…**2009:** Had season-ending surgery for the third consecutive season, appearing in just eight games (.100, 3-for-30, 1RBI) before having microdiscectomy surgery on his back on 6/23…procedure was performed by Dr. Robert Watkins in Los Angeles and it was his fifth surgery since September 2007, second on his back (also 10/9/07)…appeared in just 11 games during Spring Training as he continued rehabbing from shoulder surgery…was placed on the 15-day disabled list on 5/22 with neck spasms, before being reinstated on 5/29…did not make the A's season opening trip to Japan and had his streak of consecutive Opening Day starts snapped at an Oakland-record tying nine…was transferred to the 60-day DL on 4/24…played from 5/29-7/1 before going back on the disabled list with a right shoulder inflammation…had season-ending surgery to repair the labrum in his right shoulder on 8/13…**2007:** Was limited to 90 games, missing the final two months of the season on the disabled list…hit .240 (82-for-341) with 21 doubles, 15HR and 46RBI…hit his second career "walk-off" home run in the A's 5-4 win over Boston on 6/4, a solo HR with two outs in the 11th inning off Kyle Snyder…was placed on the 15-day disabled list on 8/3 (retro. to 7/27) with lower back spasms and had three surgeries over a 10-week span to repair a torn labrum on his right shoulder (9/5), microdiscectomy surgery on his back (10/9) and a left shoulder debridement (11/16)…**2006:** Batted .241 (117-for-485) with 24 doubles, 22HR and 72RBI in 137 games…won his sixth consecutive AL Gold Glove award at third base…led the Majors and set an Oakland record by a third baseman with a .987 fielding pct…was the fourth-best fielding percentage by a third baseman in AL history and was second best by an Athletic to Hank Majeski's .988 with Philadelphia in 1947…set what was then an Oakland record for consecutive errorless games by a third baseman with a 65-game streak from 5/1-8/4…hit 10HR in his first 25G and just 12HR over his final 112G…hit his 200th career HR on 5/2 at Los Angeles-AL, a three-run HR off John Lackey in the first inning…started all seven of the A's postseason games at third base and hit .217 with 2HR with 3RBI…**2005:** Led the A's in nearly every offensive category, including a career-high 160 games…tied for fourth in the AL in sacrifice flies, ranked sixth in strikeouts and was tied for eighth in doubles (40) and games played…won his fifth consecutive AL Gold Glove award at third base…led or tied for the team lead in home runs for the fourth consecutive season to become the first Athletic to accomplish the feat since Norm Siebern led the Kansas City A's from 1960-63…joined Jimmie Foxx (1929-35) as the only two players in franchise history with six consecutive seasons of 25 or more home runs…was named AL "Player of the Week" for the second time in his career on 6/5…singled off Scot Shields in the eighth inning on 8/31 at Los Angeles-AL for the 1000th hit of his career in his 1000th career game…**2004:** Batted .276 (131-for-475) with 20 doubles, 20HR and 77RBI in 125 games…led the AL with 95BB, tied for fifth in on-base percentage (.397) and ranked eighth in pitches/PA (4.05)…won his fourth consecutive AL Gold Glove Award at third base…agreed to terms on a six-year contract extension ith a club option for 2011 on 3/18…was hit by a Damaso Marte pitch in the 11th inning on 6/1 vs. Chicago-AL, breaking a bone in his right hand and causing him to miss 33 games through 7/9…**2003:** Appeared in 154 games, leading the A's in average (.282), home runs (29), multi-hit games (46) and extra-base hits (73)…led AL third basemen in RBI and tied for the lead in home runs…won his third consecutive AL Gold Glove award at third base…homered in three straight games at Seattle, 4/15-17, and again from 6/24-26 at Texas…went 1-for-22 in the ALDS against Boston, starting the series 0-for-17…**2002:** Named to the *Sporting News* AL All-Star team and received the AL Silver Slugger award and the AL Gold Glove Award at third base…batted .275 (161-for-585) with 31 doubles, a career-high 34HR and 109RBI in 153 games…tied for seventh in the AL in home runs and was ninth in RBI…hit his first career Opening Day HR on 4/1 vs. Texas…made his professional debut in the outfield on 5/7 vs. Boston in LF…earned AL "Player of the Week" honors on 8/25…hit his 100th career HR on 8/20 at Cleveland off Jake Westbrook…hit .381 in the Division Series against Minnesota and had a team-leading 5RBI, including his first career postseason home run, a three-run HR off Joe Mays in the first inning of Game 2…hit safely in all five games…played in the 2002 All-Star Series in Japan following the season and hit .294 with 1HR and 3RBI in 7G…**2001:** Hit .288 (159-for-552) with 43 doubles, 32HR and 114RBI in 151 games, setting career highs in average, doubles, RBI and stolen bases (8)…broke Sal Bando's A's franchise record for homers and RBI by a third baseman…also won the AL Gold Glove Award after leading the league third basemen with a .972 fielding percentage, 433 total chances and 321 assists…had his first career multi-HR game on 4/26 at Chicago-AL…hit his first career "walk-off" HR on 6/20 vs. Seattle, a two-out, three-run homer in the 6-4 A's win…reached base safely via hit or walk in each of his final 31 regular season games…named AL September "Player of the Month" (.370, 8HR, 26RBI)…hit .143 in five starts at third base in the ALDS loss vs. the Yankees…**2000:** Hit .277 (139-for-501) with 23 doubles, 26HR and 86RBI in 153 games…had a career high 15-game hitting streak from 5/27-6/18…hit for the cycle on 6/21 vs. Baltimore, the first cycle in Coliseum history by any player…at the age of 22 years, 197 days, became the eighth youngest player in Major League history to hit for the cycle…had an inside the park home run on 8/8 at Yankee Stadium…hit .333 in the ALDS loss vs. the Yankees…**1999:** Was the A's Opening Day starter at third base at the age of 21 years, 119 days, the A's youngest Opening Day starter since Rickey Henderson in 1980…batted .247 (88-for-356) with 21 doubles, 13HR and 50RBI in 115 games…hit his first ML home run on 5/15 vs. Minnesota off LaTroy Hawkins…went on the D.L. from 8/21-9/18 with torn plantar fascia in his right foot…**1998:** Named "Minor League Player of the Year" by *Baseball America* and also received the J.G. Taylor Spink Award as the Topps "Minor League Player of the Year," after combining to hit .327 (173-for-529) with 33HR and 126RBI in 135 games at Double-A Huntsville and Triple-A Edmonton…collected the third-most RBI and extra-base hits (79) among all minor leaguers…made his Major League debut with Oakland as a September callup, batting .311 (14-for-45)…was recalled on 9/8 and made his ML debut that night as a pinch-hitter (struck out) vs. Baltimore…made his first start the next day at 3B vs. Baltimore, recording his first hit with a second-inning single off Juan Guzman…was named to the Southern League Postseason All-Star Team as well as the Topps Double-A All-Star Team…played for Peoria in the Arizona Fall League and hit .311 with 1HR and 8RBI in 11 games…**1997:** Hit .271 (141-for-520) with 30 doubles, 18HR and 100RBI in 134 games with Single-A Visalia in his first pro season…earned a spot on the Cal League Postseason All-Star roster and was rated as the best defensive third baseman in the Cal League by *Baseball America*…**PERSONAL:** Full name is Eric Cesar Chavez…graduated from Mount Carmel High School in 1996 where he was a two-time *Baseball America* High School All-America selection…supports former A's pitcher Dave Stewart's Ante Up for Autism event…donates tickets to local fire and police stations each season…served as a member of the Oakland Action Team, a national youth volunteer initiative administered by Major League Baseball.

CHECO, Mariel – RHP

HT: 6-2; **WT:** 210; **B:** R; **T:** R; **BORN:** 10/16/89 in New York, N.Y.; **RESIDES:** New York, N.Y.; **OBTAINED:** Selected by the Yankees in the 41st round of the 2009 First-Year Player Draft; **M.L. SVC:** 0.000; **CAREER NOTES: 2010:** Went 0-1 in 10 games (two starts) with a 5.92 ERA and recorded 24K in 24.1IP with the GCL Yankees…**2009:** Made his professional debut, going 1-1 with an 8.40 ERA in 10 appearances out of the bullpen with the GCL Yankees…recorded 14K in 15.0IP.

CLAIBORNE, Preston – RHP

HT: 6-2; **WT:** 225; **B:** R; **T:** R; **BORN:** 1/21/88 in Dallas, Tex.; **RESIDES:** Carrollton, Tex.; **OBTAINED:** Selected by the Yankees in the 17th round of the 2010 First-Year Player Draft; **M.L. SVC:** 0.000; **CAREER NOTES: 2010:** Made his professional debut, combining to go 1-3 with a 2.61 ERA (31.0IP, 9ER) in 24 relief appearances with short-season Single-A Staten Island and Single-A Tampa…began the season with Staten Island, and went 1-2 with a 2.28 ERA, recording 30K and allowing 6ER in 23.2IP in relief…was named to the NYPL American League All-Star team, prior to being promoted to Tampa on 8/23…made two postseason relief appearances with the Yankees, going 0-1 with a 2.25 ERA (4.0IP, 1ER).

COA, Rainiero – C

HT: 5-10; **WT:** 170; **B:** L; **T:** R; **BORN:** 1/2/93 in Puerto Ordaz; Venezuela; **RESIDES:** Puerto Ordaz; Venezuela; **OBTAINED:** Signed as a minor league free agent on 4/30/10; **M.L. SVC:** 0.000; **CAREER NOTES: 2010:** Made his professional debut with the DSL Yankees 2 and hit .255 (39-for-153) with 7 doubles and 18 RBI in 49 games.

COLON, Bartolo – RHP   NON-ROSTER INVITEE

HT: 5-11; **WT:** 267; **B:** R; **T:** R; **BORN:** 5/24/73 in Altamira, D.R.; **RESIDES:** Puerto Plata; D.R.; **OBTAINED:** Signed by the Yankees as a minor league free agent on 2/10/11; **M.L. SVC:** 12.061; **CAREER NOTES:** Has appeared in 328 career games (325 starts) over parts of 13 seasons with Cleveland (1997-2002), Montreal (2002), Chicago-AL (2003,'09) Los Angeles-AL (2004-07) and Boston (2008)…owns a 153-103 career record with a 4.10 ERA (2076.2IP, 945ER)…was voted to the AL All-Star team and was named the league's Cy Young Award winner in 2005, after going 21-8 with a 3.48 ERA in 33 starts with the Angels…from 1998-2005, was the only Major League pitcher to win at least 14 games in each season, ranking second among all big-league hurlers in wins (135) and starts (261), fifth in complete games (29) and innings pitched (1,725.2), sixth in quality starts (158) and seventh in strikeouts (1,369) during the stretch…is one of two pitchers in Major League history to win at least 10 games in both the AL and NL during the same season, when he went 10-4 with both Cleveland and Montreal in 2002 (also Hank Borowy, 1945)…has recorded 31 career complete games and eight shutouts and has struck out 10 or more batters in a game 17 times (15 during the regular season and two during the postseason)…**2010:** Following the Major League season, made seven starts for the Aguilas Cibaenas of the Dominican Winter League and went 2-1 with a 1.93 ERA (37.1IP, 8ER), recording 28K with just 6BB…held opponents to a .167 (5-for-30) batting average with runners in scoring position…**2009:** Spent the majority of the season with the White Sox, going 3-6 with a 4.19 ERA (62.1IP, 29ER) in 12 starts before being released on 9/16…allowed 3ER or less in eight of his 12 outings…went on the disabled list on 6/8 with left knee inflammation…was reinstated from the D.L on 7/23 after going 1-2 with a 3.32 ERA in three combined rehab starts with Triple-A Charlotte and Single-A Kannapolis (19.0IP, 7ER, 17H, 5BB, 9K)…returned to the disabled list on 7/23 with right elbow inflammation…following the season, made one start with the Aguilas Cibaenas of the DWL and recorded a loss (0.2IP, 4H, 5ER, 1BB)…**2008:** In his lone season in the Boston organization, began the year on Triple-A Pawtucket's disabled list, recovering from a strained left oblique…reinstated on 5/10 and made nine starts with Pawtucket, going 3-1 with a 2.27 ERA (31.2IP, 8ER)…was signed to a Major League contract by the Red Sox and selected from Pawtucket on 5/21 and went 4-2 with a 3.92 ERA (39.0IP, 17ER) in seven starts at the Major League level…was placed on the disabled list on 6/17 with a lower back strain and made only one more start the remainder of the season on 9/13 vs. Toronto, allowing 2ER in 6.0IP in a no-decision (7H, 5R, 1BB, 1K)…**2007:** In his final season in the Angels organization, began the season on the disabled list, recovering from a strained right Lattisimus Dorsi muscle…made three combined rehab starts with Triple-A Salt Lake and Single-A Rancho Cucamonga in the Angels organization, going 2-0 with a 1.08 ERA (16.2IP, 2ER), before being recalled on 4/21…appeared in 19 games (18 starts) with Los Angeles-AL, going 6-8 with a 6.34 ERA (99.1IP, 70ER), winning his first five decisions for the first time in his career…recorded his 1,500th career strikeout (Chris Duncan) on 6/8 at St. Louis and made his 300th career start on 6/24 vs. Pittsburgh…was placed on the disabled list on 7/24 with a strained right elbow…was recalled by the Angels on 9/9 and made his third career relief appearance on 9/29 at Oakland (1.0IP, 2K) and first since he made two appearances out of the bullpen with the Indians in 1997…**2006:** Went 1-5 with a 5.11 ERA (56.1IP, 32ER) in 10 starts with the Angels…was placed on the 15-day disabled list on 4/16 with inflammation in his right shoulder…made three rehab starts with Triple-A Salt Lake and Single-A Rancho Cucamonga, combining to go 0-1 with a 4.60 ERA (15.2IP, 8ER) before being returned from rehab and reinstated on 6/17…returned to the D.L. on 7/30 with a partial tear in his right rotator cuff and missed the remainder of the season…prior to the season, pitched for the Dominican Republic in the inaugural World Baseball Classic and went 1-0 with a 0.64 ERA (14.0IP, 1ER) in three starts…**2005:** Won the AL Cy Young Award after going 21-8 with a 3.48 ERA (222.2IP, 86ER) and two complete games in 33 starts with the Angels…became the second Angels pitcher to garner the honor (also Dean Chance in 1964) and was also named the *Sporting News'* "AL Pitcher of the Year" and the Players Choice "AL Pitcher of the Year"…ranked first in the league in wins, fourth in winning percentage (.714), seventh in innings pitched, eighth in ERA and tied for eighth in strikeouts (157)…his 21 victories tied for third most in club history (also Nolan Ryan in 1973) and marked the first time that an Angels pitcher won at least 20-games since 1974…was named the AL "Pitcher of the Month" for August after going 5-0 with a 1.72 ERA during the month, his third career such award…was named to the AL All-Star team and threw 1.0 inning in relief (1H) in the American League's 7-5 victory…**2004:** Went 18-12 with a 5.01 ERA (208.1IP, 116ER), matching his career-high with 34 starts (third time) in his first season with the Angels…became the first pitcher since Bobo Newsom in 1938 (20-16, 5.08 ERA) to win at least 18 games with a 5.00 ERA or higher…led the Angels in wins and starts, tying for third in the league in each category…**2003:** In his first season with the White Sox, went 15-13 with a 3.87 ERA (242.0IP, 104ER) with nine complete games and 173K in 34 starts…his nine complete games tied for the Major League lead and were the most by a Sox pitcher since Jack McDowell threw 10 in 1993…ranked second in the league in innings pitched, tied for fifth in starts and ranked seventh in strikeouts…tossed four complete games in a six-game span from 9/2-28, including three straight from 9/2-13…earned his 100th career victory on 9/7 at Kansas City and earned American League "Pitcher of the Week" honors for the third time in his career for the period from 9/8-14…**2002:** Split the season between Cleveland and Montreal, combining to go 20-8 with a 2.93 ERA (233.1IP, 76ER), eight complete games, three shutouts and 149K in 33 starts…tied Arizona's Randy Johnson for the Major League-lead in complete games, tied for third in shutouts, tied for fifth in wins, ranked sixth in innings pitched and seventh in ERA…was traded by Cleveland to the Expos on 6/27 with RHP Tim Drew and cash in exchange for INFs Lee Stevens and Brandon Phillips, LHP Cliff Lee and OF Grady Sizemore…**2001:** Went 14-12 with a 4.09 ERA (222.1IP, 101ER) and 201K in a career-high 34 starts with the Indians…became the first Indians pitcher since Gaylord Perry (1972-74) to record at least 200K in back-to-back seasons…was suspended for seven games by MLB after throwing over the head of Houston's Scott Servais on 7/17…the suspension was later reduced to six games and was served from 7/28 to 8/2…**2000:** Made 30 starts with the Indians, going 15-8 with a 3.88 ERA (188.0IP, 81ER) and a career-high 212K…threw a career-best 20 consecutive scoreless innings from 9/13-28…**1999:** Went 18-5 with a 3.95 ERA (205.0IP, 90ER) and 161K in 32 starts with Cleveland…won five straight starts from 8/9-30 and was 8-1 with a 2.75 ERA (68.2IP, 21ER) over his last 10 starts of the season…**1998:** In his first full season at the Major League level, was 14-9 with a 3.71 ERA (204.0IP, 84ER) in 31 starts…struck out a career-high 14 batters in a complete game at Toronto on 5/29…**1997:** Made his Major League debut, spending five separate stints with the Indians and going 4-7 with a 5.65 ERA (94.0IP, 59ER)…**1996:** Entered the seasons tabbed by *Baseball America* as the No. 1 pitching prospect in Cleveland's organization…combined at Triple-A Buffalo and Double-A Canton-Akron to go 2-2 with a 2.57 ERA (77.0IP, 22ER) in 21 games (12 starts)…**1995:** Played the entire season at Single-A Kinston and was named the Carolina League "Pitcher of the Year" after going 13-3 with a 1.96 ERA (128.2IP, 28ER) and 152K in 21 starts…held opponents to a .202 (91-for-451) batting average…**1994:** Spent the entire year with Single-A Burlington and went 7-4 with a 3.14 ERA (66.0IP, 23ER) in 12 starts, ranking second in the Appalachian League in wins and third in strikeouts (84)…**1993:** Made his professional debut, going 6-1 with a 2.59 ERA (66.0IP, 19ER) in 1G (10 starts) with the DSL Indians…**PERSONAL:** Is married to Rosanna with three children, Bartolo, Emilio and Wilder…in 2005, donated $50,000 to the American Red Cross to benefit Hurricane Katrina victims and has provided funds for the construction of an amateur baseball stadium in his hometown of Altamira, D.R.…his brother Jose previously was a pitcher in the Indians system.

COTHAM, Caleb – RHP

HT: 6-1; **WT:** 200; **B:** R; **T:** R; **BORN:** 11/6/87 in Mt. Juliet, Tenn.; **RESIDES:** Mt. Juliet, Tenn.; **COLLEGE:** Vanderbilt University; **OBTAINED:** Selected by the Yankees in the fifth round of the 2009 First-Year Player Draft; **M.L. SVC:** 0.000; **CAREER NOTES: 2010:** Missed the season recovering from knee surgery on 3/31…**2009:** Made three combined starts with the GCL Yankees and short-season Single-A Staten Island, going 0-1 with a 3.38 ERA and 13K in 8.0IP…**PERSONAL:** Was a two-year captain of the Mt. Juliet High School baseball team…was also his high school junior class president and a member of the National Junior Honor Society.

COTTON, Bryant – RHP

HT: 6-2; **WT:** 200; **B:** R; **T:** R; **BORN:** 2/15/88 in Arnold, Mo.; **RESIDES:** Arnold, Mo.; **COLLEGE:** St. Louis University; **OBTAINED:** Signed as a minor league free agent on 6/16/10; **M.L. SVC:** 0.000; **CAREER NOTES: 2010:** Made his professional debut with short-season Single-A Staten Island Yankees, going 1-1 in 14 relief appearances with a 6.20 ERA…collected 23K in 20.1IP.

COTTS, Neal – LHP   NON-ROSTER INVITEE

HT: 6-3; **WT:** 200; **B:** L; **T:** L; **BORN:** 3/25/80 in Lebanon, Ill.; **RESIDES:** Chicago, Ill.; **COLLEGE:** Illinois State; **OBTAINED:** Signed by the Yankees as a minor league free agent on 11/19/10; **M.L. SVC:** 4.081; **CAREER NOTES:** Owns a 10-12 record with a 4.62 ERA (256.1IP, 132ER) in 284 appearances (five starts) over seven Major League seasons with the White Sox (2003-06) and Cubs (2007-09)…was originally selected by Oakland in the second round of the 2001 First-Year Player Draft…**2010:** Missed the entire season recovering from "Tommy John" surgery performed in July 2009…**2009:** Went 0-2 with a 7.36 ERA (11.0IP, 9ER) in 19 appearances out of the bullpen with the Cubs…made 12 relief appearances with Triple-A Iowa, going 1-1 with a 2.84 ERA, allowing 4ER in 12.2IP…**2008:** Began the season with Iowa and went 2-0 with a 2.00 ERA, recording 33K and allowing 6ER in 27.IP in relief…was promoted to the Cubs on 5/29 where he went 0-2 with a 4.29 ERA (35.2IP, 17ER)…**2007:** Started the year with the Cubs and went 0-1 with a 4.86 ERA, allowing 9ER in 16.2IP…recorded 11 consecutive scoreless outings from 4/2-5/6 (10.2IP)…was transferred to Iowa on 5/20 and went 2-2 with a 4.83 ERA (50.1IP, 27ER) in 24 games (six starts)…struck out a season-high six batters over 4.1IP on 6/17 vs. Memphis…Iowa posted a 16-8 record in games in which Cotts made an appearance…**2006:** Spent the entire season with the White Sox and went 1-2 with a 5.17 ERA (54.0IP, 31ER), in 70 appearances out of the bullpen, ranking eighth on the White Sox' all-time single-season appearances list by a left-handed pitcher…earned his first Major League save on 4/30 at Los Angeles-AL…**2005:** Played the entire season with the White Sox, making 69 relief appearances and going 4-0 with a 1.94 ERA (60.1IP, 13ER)…among all American League relievers, ranked first in HR/innings pitched (0.15), third in opponents batting average against (.179), hits/9.0IP (5.67) and ERA, fourth in opponents slugging percentage (.241) and tied for 11th in games pitched…limited right-handed batters to a .155 (17-for-110) batting average and left-handed hitters to a .206 (21-for-102) mark…earned the victory in each of his four decisions and posted 13 holds, holding opponents scoreless in 58 of his 69 outings…compiled a 1.58 ERA over his last 57.0IP of the season (10ER)…made 23 consecutive appearances without allowing an earned run from 7/15-9/6 (18.1IP)…went 1-0 and did not allow an earned run in six postseason appearances (2.1IP), stranding all seven inherited runners, including five in the World Series…**2004:** Played the entire season with the White Sox, appearing in 56 games (1 start) and going 4-4 with a 5.65 ERA, allowing 41ER in 65.1IP…his 56 appearances ranked third on the team and were tied for fourth among A.L. rookies…earned his first Major League victory on 6/18 at Montreal, throwing 1.1 scoreless innings in relief…**2003:** Spent the majority of the season with Double-A Birmingham, going 9-7 with a 2.16 ERA (108.1IP, 26ER) in 21 starts…was named the Southern League "Pitcher of the Month" for April after recording 41K and going 4-0 with a 0.98 ERA (27.2IP, 3ER)…made his Major League debut on 8/12 at Los Angeles-AL and earned his first big-league victory in his home debut on 8/22 vs. Texas, allowing 1ER on 5H in 5.0IP…ended the year ranked by *Baseball America* as the number three prospect in the White Sox organization and as having the best changeup in the system…**2002:** Played the entire season with Single-A Modesto of the Athletics organization, and went 12-6 with a 4.12 ERA (137.2IP, 63ER)…ranked second in the California League in strikeouts (178) and tied for third in wins…won eight of his last 10 decisions, striking out 106 batters in 82.0IP…**2001:** Made his professional debut and combined to go 4-2 with a 2.73 ERA (66.0IP, 20ER) in 16 games (14 starts) with Single-A Vancouver and Single-A Visalia…**PERSONAL:** Was the starting pitcher for the United States in the All-Star Futures Game on 7/13/03 at U.S. Cellular Field, allowing 1ER in 1.0IP (1K)…attended Illinois State University, where he earned First-Team All-Missouri Valley Conference and ABCA All-Midwest Region Team honors…graduated from Lebanon HS (Ill.) in 1998.

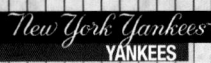

COX, J.B. – RHP

HT: 6-3; **WT:** 205; **B:** L; **T:** R; **BORN:** 5/13/84 in Bay City, Tex.; **RESIDES:** Austin, Tex.; **COLLEGE:** University of Texas; **OBTAINED:** Selected in the second round of the 2005 First-Year Player Draft; **M.L. SVC:** 0.000; **CAREER NOTES: 2010:** Combined to go 3-1 with a 5.05 ERA (41.0IP, 23ER) in 31 relief appearances with Single-A Tampa and Double-A Trenton…spent the majority of the season with Trenton, where he went 3-0 with a 4.28 ERA (33.2IP, 16ER)…while with the Thunder, held left-handed batters to a .127 (8-for-63) batting average…**2009:** Combined to go 0-3 with a 7.30 ERA in 17 appearances (one start) with Triple-A Scranton/Wilkes-Barre and Double-A Trenton…made his first start on 5/25 with Scranton/WB, recording the loss after allowing 6H and 5ER in 2.1IP (2BB)…was placed on the disabled list on 5/27 with right shoulder inflammation…reinstated from the D.L. on 6/12 and transferred to Trenton, where he made five relief appearances, going 0-2 with an 8.31 ERA before being placed on the disabled list for a second time on 6/26 with right shoulder inflammation and missing the remainder of the season…**2008:** Combined at three levels (Single-A Tampa, Double-A Trenton and Triple-A Scranton/Wilkes-Barre) to go 5-4 with a 4.07 ERA in 39 relief appearances…held right-handers to a .198 average (18-for-91, 2HR)…joined Scranton/WB on 5/13 and did not allow a run in his first nine outings (10.1IP)…**2007:** Spent the season on the disabled list after having right elbow surgery on 3/27…entered the 2007 season ranked as the eighth-best prospect in the Yankees organization by *Baseball America* and as having the "best slider" among all Yankees farmhands…**2006:** Posted a 6-2 record with a 1.75 ERA and three saves in 41 relief appearances for Double-A Trenton…did not allow a run in 15 consecutive appearances from 6/8-7/23 (22.0IP)…was selected to be a member of Team USA at the COPABE Olympic Qualifying Tournament in Cuba in August…appeared in three games for Team USA and allowed one run in 5.2IP with one walk and six strikeouts to help lead the US to a first-place finish and automatic berth in the 2008 Olympics in Berlin…**2005:** In first professional season, went 1-2 with a 2.60 ERA in 16 games for the Single-A Tampa Yankees…held opposing hitters to a .206 batting average…**PERSONAL:** Full name is James Brent Cox…played baseball at the University of Texas and helped guide the Longhorns to the National Championship in 2005, leading the club with a 1.72 ERA and 19 saves in 42 appearances…following the season, was named to the 2005 College World Series All-Tournament Team…was honored as the first-ever winner of the National Collegiate Baseball Writers' Association (NCBWA) "Stopper of the Year" Award, given to the top relief pitcher in collegiate baseball…was a 2005 first-team All-Big 12 selection and second-team All-American after tying the UT record with 19 saves in a single season…previously named to the 2004 Big-12 All-Conference Team, ranking third with a 2.12 ERA in 37 appearance…also named to the Big-12 All-Conference Team in 2003.

CRUZ, Dawerd – RHP

HT: 6-1; **WT:** 185; **B:** R; **T:** R; **BORN:** 12/7/88 in San Pedro de Macoris, D.R.; **RESIDES:** San Pedro de Macoris, D.R.; **OBTAINED:** Signed by the Yankees as a non-drafted free agent on 12/12/07; **M.L. SVC:** 0.000; **CAREER NOTES: 2010:** Went 4-2 in 14 games (12 starts) with a 2.69 ERA with the DSL Yankees 1…**2009:** Went 6-2 with one save and a 3.48 ERA in 16 games (one start) with the DSL Yankees 2…tied for the team lead in wins…**2008:** In his professional debut with the DSL Yankees 2, went 1-0 with a 4.11 ERA in 11 appearances out of the bullpen.

CULVER, Cito – INF

HT: 6-0; **WT:** 190; **B:** S; **T:** R; **BORN:** 8/26/92 in Rochester, N.Y.; **RESIDES:** Wesley Chapel, Fla.; **OBTAINED:** Selected by the Yankees in the first round (32nd overall) of the 2010 First-Year Player Draft; **M.L. SVC:** 0.000; **CAREER NOTES: 2010:** Signed on 6/18 and made his professional debut with the GCL Yankees on 6/25, batting .269 (43-for-160) with 7 doubles, 1 triple, 2HR and 18RBI in 41 games…was transferred to short-season Single-A Staten Island on 8/19, where he hit .186 (8-for-43) with 1 double in 15 games…**PERSONAL:** First name is Christopher…graduated from Irondequoit High School in Rochester, New York…batted .561 (37-for-66) with 10 doubles, 5 triples, 9HR, 38RBI and 20BB in 22 regular season games as a high school senior…had a .933 fielding percentage and committed just eight errors in each of the last three seasons…was a three-time all-county selection and an Under Armour All-American…in the summer of 2009 played on the Yankees' Area Code team…*Baseball America* rated him as the third-best prospect out of the state of New York.

CUSTODIO, Claudio – INF

HT: 5-10; **WT:** 150; **B:** R; **T:** R; **BORN:** 10/30/90 in Sabana Grande de Boya, D.R.; **RESIDES:** San Cristobal, D.R.; **OBTAINED:** Signed as a minor league free agent on 4/24/10; **M.L. SVC:** 0.000; **CAREER NOTES: 2010:** Made his professional debut with the DSL Yankees 1 on 5/29…appeared in 61 games and batted .217 (44-for-203) with 9 doubles, 3 triples, 5HR and 36RBI…ranked second on the team in stolen bases (14) and third in RBI and HR.

DE LA CRUZ, Joel – RHP

HT: 6-1; **WT:** 210; **B:** S; **T:** R; **BORN:** 6/9/89 in Haina, D.R.; **RESIDES:** Santo Domingo, D.R.; **OBTAINED:** Signed as a minor league free agent on 3/19/06; **M.L. SVC:** 0.000; **CAREER NOTES: 2010:** With the DSL Yankees 1, went 1-0 with a 0.00 ERA in two relief appearances…was transferred to the DSL Yankees 2 on 7/17, where he was 0-1 with two saves and a 7.11 ERA in seven games…**2009:** Went 0-4 with a 7.27 ERA with the DSL Nationals…was released on 7/23…**2008:** Signed with the DSL Nationals on 2/5, did not play…**2007:** Was placed on the 60-day DL with the AZL Brewers, did not play…**2006:** Signed as a minor league free agent on 3/19 with the AZL Brewers, went 0-0 with a 0.00 ERA and 3.0IP in two appearances.

DE LA ROSA, Elio – INF

HT: 6-0; **WT:** 185; **B:** R; **T:** R; **BORN:** 4/18/91 in Bani, D.R.; **RESIDES:** Bani, D.R.; **OBTAINED:** Signed by the Yankees as a non-drafted free agent on 7/2/07; **M.L. SVC:** 0.000; **CAREER NOTES: 2010:** Started the season with the DSL Yankees 2, batting .262 (33-for-126) with 7 doubles, 1 triple, 4HR and 27RBI in 36 games…was transferred to the DSL Yankees 1 on 7/17, batting .264 (28-for-106) with 7 doubles, 1 triple, 2HR and 19 RBI for the final 30 contests of the year…tied for tops in the DSL in RBI (46)…**2009:** Batted .226 with 9 doubles, 1 triple, 4HR and 21RBI in 53 games with the DSL Yankees 2…**2008:** In his professional debut, batted .134 with 3 doubles and 12 RBI in 32 games with the DSL Yankees 2.

DE LA ROSA, Maikol – LHP

HT: 6-2; **WT:** 190; **B:** L; **T:** L; **BORN:** 11/25/90 in Santo Domingo, D.R.; **RESIDES:** Santo Domingo, D.R.; **OBTAINED:** Signed as a minor league free agent on 3/19/10; **M.L. SVC:** 0.000; **CAREER NOTES: 2010:** Made his professional debut with the DSL Yankees 2, going 1-1 with a 6.75 ERA in 11 relief appearances (16.0IP).

DE LA ROSA, Roberto – RHP

HT: 6-1; **WT:** 180; **B:** R; **T:** R; **BORN:** 3/27/93 in El Seybo, D.R.; **RESIDES:** El Seybo, D.R.; **OBTAINED:** Signed as a minor league free agent on 9/21/10; **M.L. SVC:** 0.000; **CAREER NOTES:** Will make his professional debut in 2011.

DE LEON, Kelvin – OF

HT: 6-2; **WT:** 210; **B:** R; **T:** R; **BORN:** 10/29/90 in Boca Chica, D.R.; **RESIDES:** Boca Chica, D.R.; **OBTAINED:** Signed by the Yankees as a non-drafted free agent on 7/2/07; **M.L. SVC:** 0.000; **CAREER NOTES: 2010:** Appeared in a career-high 69 games with short-season Single-A Staten Island, batting .236 (61-for-259) with 12 doubles, 1 triple 6HR and 37RBI…led the team in HR, RBI and AB, and ranked second in doubles…**2009:** Batted .269 with 13 doubles, 7HR and 31RBI in 56 games with the GCL Yankees…led the team in HR and RBI and ranked third in the GCL in homers…following the season, named by *Baseball America* as the second-best prospect in the GCL in 2009…**2008:** In his first professional season, batted .289 with 9HR and 43RBI in 63 games with the DSL Yankees 2…recorded 27 extra-base hits in 235AB (16 doubles, 2 triples, 9HR)…did not go more than two consecutive games without recording at least 1H until going hitless over the last three games of the season.

DE LEON, Nestor – LHP

HT: 6-2; **WT:** 200; **B:** R; **T:** R; **BORN:** 6/22/89 in Azua, D.R.; **RESIDES:** Azua, D.R.; **OBTAINED:** Signed by the Yankees as a non-drafted free agent on 6/6/09; **M.L. SVC:** 0.000; **CAREER NOTES: 2010:** Completed a 50-game suspension from the 2009 season for violating the Minor League Drug Prevention and Treatment Program, was reinstated on 7/31…went 1-1 with two saves and a 3.18 ERA in eight relief appearances.

DELGADO, Johansel – RHP

HT: 5-11; **WT:** 150; **B:** R; **T:** R; **BORN:** 12/3/90 in Santo Domingo, D.R.; **RESIDES:** Santo Domingo, D.R.; **OBTAINED:** Signed as a minor league free agent on 5/27/10; **M.L. SVC:** 0.000; **CAREER NOTES: 2010:** Made his professional debut with the DSL Yankees 2…went 3-1 with one save and a 3.86 ERA in 19 game appearances.

DELUCA, Evan – LHP

HT: 6-1; **WT:** 202; **B:** L; **T:** L; **BORN:** 3/9/91 in Whitehouse Station, N.J.; **RESIDES:** Whitehouse Station, N.J.; **OBTAINED:** Selected by the Yankees in the 44th round of the 2009 First-Year Player Draft; **M.L. SVC:** 0.000; **CAREER NOTES: 2010:** Made his professional debut with short-season Single-A Staten Island, and went 1-3 with a 9.35 ERA in nine appearances (six starts)…recorded 30K in 26.0IP…**PERSONAL:** Graduated from Immaculata High School.

DE OLEO, Eduardo – C

HT: 5-10; **WT:** 180; **B:** R; **T:** R; **BORN:** 1/25/93 in San Juan de la Maguana, D.R.; **RESIDES:** San Juan de la Maguana, D.R.; **OBTAINED:** Signed as a minor league free agent on 9/20/10; **M.L. SVC:** 0.000; **CAREER NOTES:** Will make his professional debut in 2011.

DE PAULA, Rafael – RHP

HT: 6-2; **WT:** 210; **B:** R; **T:** R; **BORN:** 3/24/91 in La Victoria, D.R.; **RESIDES:** La Victoria, D.R.; **OBTAINED:** Signed as a minor league free agent on 11/18/10; **M.L. SVC:** 0.000; **CAREER NOTES:** Will make his professional debut in 2011.

DUFF, Grant – RHP

HT: 6-6; **WT:** 240; **B:** R; **T:** R; **BORN:** 12/19/82 in Milton, Fla.; **RESIDES:** Mammoth Lakes, Calif.; **COLLEGE:** College of the Sequoias (Calif.); **OBTAINED:** Selected by the Yankees in the 31st round of the 2004 First-Year Player Draft; **M.L. SVC:** 0.000; **CAREER NOTES: 2010:** Combined to go 1-4 with a 3.35 ERA (37.2IP, 14ER) and 44K in 32 appearances out of the bullpen with Double-A Trenton and Triple-A Scranton/Wilkes-Barre…went on the disabled list on 6/30 with right elbow inflammation, missing the remainder of the season…**2009:** Combined to go 4-3 with two saves and a 3.52 ERA in 45 appearances (one start) with Single-A Tampa and Double-A Trenton (71.2IP, 28ER)…began the season with Tampa, before being promoted to Trenton on 7/8, where he went 4-2 with one save and a 3.22 ERA in 21 relief appearances (36.1IP, 13ER)…following the season, pitched for the Surprise Rafters of the Arizona Fall League, earning two saves without recording a decision in 10 relief appearances (2.89 ERA, 9.1IP, 7H, 3ER)…**2008:** Went 3-6 with two saves and a 4.30 ERA in 30 appearances (eight starts) with Single-A Tampa…struck out a season-high six batters on 6/9 at St. Lucie, while tossing a season-high 6.1 innings on 6/19 at Lakeland…recorded a career-high five straight losing decisions from 5/10-7/6…was placed on the disabled list from 8/21 through the remainder of the season with a left knee strain…**2007:** Was 14-8 with a 3.82 ERA in 27 starts with Single-A Charleston…tied for fourth in the South Atlantic League in starts and tied for fifth with a career-high and team-high 14 wins…tied for second among all Yankees minor leaguers in wins and ranked third in strikeouts…had two career-high four-game winning streaks (4/22-5/9 and 6/16-7/8)…recorded at least 1K in 26 of his 27 appearances…was placed on the D.L. from 7/30-8/8 with a right thigh contusion…**2006:** Ranked third among all Yankees' minor-league pitchers with a 1.97 combined ERA, posting a 5-4 record in 14 games with the Gulf Coast League Yankees and short-season Single-A Staten Island…spent majority of season with the Gulf Coast Yankees, posting a 5-1 record with a 1.14 ERA in 11 games (eight starts)…led all Gulf Coast League pitchers in ERA and strikeouts (59) and ranked second in the league in wins…made three starts with Class-A Staten Island and went 0-3 with a 5.25 ERA…**2005:** In his first professional season, went 0-1 with a 6.48 ERA in four games (two starts) with the Gulf Coast Yankees…appeared in only four games before being placed on the disabled list with a fractured right foot…**PERSONAL:** Was selected by the Yankees in the 30th round of the 2003 First-Year Player Draft but elected to attend the College of the Sequoias in Visalia, Calif., where he graduated from in May 2005.

DURAN, Francisco – C

HT: 6-2; **WT:** 185; **B:** R; **T:** R; **BORN:** 10/3/91 in San Francisco de Aci, Venezuela; **RESIDES:** San Francisco de Aci, Venezuela; **OBTAINED:** Signed by the Yankees as a non-drafted free agent on 2/13/09; **M.L. SVC:** 0.000; **CAREER NOTES: 2010:** Hit .221 (27-for-122) with 9 doubles, 1 triple, 1HR and 15RBI in 48 games with the DSL 2...**2009:** Made his professional debut with the DSL Yankees 1 and batted .250 (39-for-156) with 5 doubles, 2 triples and 23RBI in 40 games.

DURAN, Juan C. – RHP

HT: 6-1; **WT:** 200; **B:** R; **T:** R; **BORN:** 8/26/92 in Barquisimeto, Venezuela; **RESIDES:** Barquisimeto, Venezuela; **OBTAINED:** Signed as a minor league free agent on 10/26/10; **M.L. SVC:** 0.000; **CAREER NOTES:** Will make his professional debut in 2011.

DURAN, Kelvin – OF

HT: 5-10; **WT:** 172; **B:** L; **T:** L; **BORN:** 11/10/90 in Santo Domingo, D.R.; **RESIDES:** Sabana Perdida, D.R.; **OBTAINED:** Signed by the Yankees as a non-drafted free agent on 4/17/08; **M.L. SVC:** 0.000; **CAREER NOTES: 2010:** Started the season with the GCL Yankees, batting .221 (30-for-136) with 5 doubles, 2HR and 10RBI in 35 games...was transferred to short-season Single-A Staten Island on 8/13 for 18 games, where he hit .172 (10-for-58) with 3 triples and 4RBI...**2009:** Hit .302 with 59R, 9 doubles, 12 triples, 3HR and 39RBI in 62 games with the DSL Yankees 2...led the DSL in triples, tied for third in runs scored and tied for fourth in total bases (121)...**2008:** Made his professional debut, hitting .278 with 10R, 2 triples and 5RBI in nine games with the DSL Yankees 1.

ELAM, Sam – LHP

HT: 6-3; **WT:** 247; **B:** L; **T:** L; **BORN:** 6/16/87 in Mesquite, Tex.; **RESIDES:** Mesquite, Tex.; **COLLEGE:** Notre Dame ; **OBTAINED:** Selected by the Yankees in the eighth round of the 2009 First-Year Player Draft; **M.L. SVC:** 0.000; **CAREER NOTES: 2010:** Started the season with short-season Single-A Staten Island, going 0-1 with a 8.68 ERA in four appearances (two starts)...was transferred to the GCL Yankees on 7/12, posting a 4.26 ERA with no decisions in 10 relief appearances...recorded 15K in 12.2IP out of the bullpen...**2009:** Split his first professional season between short-season Single-A Staten Island and the GCL Yankees, combining to go 0-2 with a 12.38 ERA...**PERSONAL:** Graduated from Poteet HS (Ind.)...was drafted by the Rockies in the 23rd round in 2008 but returned to college.

ENCINAS, Gabriel – RHP

HT: 6-3; **WT:** 195; **B:** R; **T:** R; **BORN:** 12/21/91 in Whitter, Calif.; **RESIDES:** Whitter, Calif.; **OBTAINED:** Selected by the Yankees in the sixth round of the 2010 First-Year Player Draft; **M.L. SVC:** 0.000; **CAREER NOTES: 2010:** Will make his professional debut in 2011...**PERSONAL:** Graduated from Saint Paul High School (Calif.).

EVARTS, Steve – LHP

HT: 6-3; **WT:** 200; **B:** L; **T:** L; **BORN:** 10/13/87 in Pordenone, Italy; **RESIDES:** Tampa, Fla.; **OBTAINED:** Signed by the Yankees as a free agent on 12/13/10; **M.L. SVC:** 0.000; **CAREER NOTES: 2010:** Will make his debut in the Yankees minor league system in 2011...**2009:** Was released from the Braves organization on 6/23...**2008:** Was limited to three starts (2-0, 1.50) with Single-A Rome before undergoing season ending "Tommy John" surgery 6/28...**2007:** Went 4-0 with a 1.95 ERA in seven starts...Did not allow a run in his first three contests, including his only relief appearance on 7/19 (2.0 IP, 1 H, 2 K)...averaged nearly nine strikeouts for every walk...following the season was named by *Baseball America* as the ninth-best prospect in the Appalachian League...**2006:** Named GCL July "Pitcher of the Month" by the Braves organization.

FARNHAM, Jeffrey – C

HT: 6-1; **WT:** 190; **B:** R; **T:** R; **BORN:** 8/30/87 in Las Vegas, Nev.; **RESIDES:** Las Vegas, Nev.; **COLLEGE:** New Mexico State University; **OBTAINED:** Selected by the Yankees in the 27th round of the 2009 First-Year Player Draft; **M.L. SVC:** 0.000; **CAREER NOTES: 2010:** Played the entire season with short-season Single-A Staten Island, batting .227 (25-for-110) with 5 doubles and 11RBI in 36 games...caught 33.0% (11-of-33) of potential basestealers...also appeared in 10G at 1B and made an emergency relief appearance on 7/12 vs. Batavia, tossing 2.0 scoreless IP...**2009:** Opened the season in the Gulf Coast League, playing in five games before being promoted to Single-A Charleston on 7/23...batted .323 with 13R, 6 doubles, 1HR and 10RBI in 20 games with the RiverDogs...threw out 11-of-34 (32.4%) potential base stealers with Charleston...**PERSONAL:** Graduated from Faith Lutheran High School (Nev.) where he was a member of the State Championship team in 2003, '04 and '05...was a first-team All-State catcher in 2004 and 2005...played two seasons at Allen Hancock Junior College before transferring to New Mexico State where he earned All-Western State Conference honors as a sophomore.

FELIZ, Anderson – INF

HT: 6-0; **WT:** 175; **B:** S; **T:** R; **BORN:** 5/11/92 in Santo Domingo, D.R.; **RESIDES:** Boca Chica, D.R.; **OBTAINED:** Signed by the Yankees as a non-drafted free agent on 7/2/08; **M.L. SVC:** 0.000; **CAREER NOTES: 2010:** Batted .273 (61-for-123) with 10 doubles, 6 triples, 5HR and 31RBI in 57 combined games between the GCL Yankees and Single-A Tampa...spent the majority of the season in the GCL (.273, 54-for-198), appearing in a team-high 47 games before his promotion on 8/20...ranked second in the GCL in triples (6), fourth in AB and tied for fourth in total bases (87)...**2009:** Made his professional debut and hit .254 with 5 doubles, 3 triples, 1HR and 16RBI in 40 games with the DSL Yankees 2.

FERRARO, Mike – OF

HT: 6-1; **WT:** 205; **B:** L; **T:** L; **BORN:** 5/31/88 in Irvine, Calif.; **RESIDES:** Irvine, Calif.; **COLLEGE:** University of San Diego; **OBTAINED:** Selected by the Yankees in the 20th round of the 2010 First-Year Player Draft; **M.L. SVC:** 0.000; **CAREER NOTES: 2010:** Hit .204 (31-for-152) with 10 doubles, 1HR and 13RBI in 43 games with short-season Single-A Staten Island...appeared at all three outfield positions...**PERSONAL:** Played at Orange Coast Community College for two years before transferring to San Diego...led the league in hits (62) as a freshman.

FLANNERY, Ryan – RHP

HT: 6-2; **WT:** 245; **B:** R; **T:** R; **BORN:** 1/6/86 in Carlstadt, N.J.; **RESIDES:** Carlstadt, N.J.; **OBTAINED:** Selected by the Yankees in the 47th round of the 2008 First-Year Player Draft; **M.L. SVC:** 0.000; **CAREER NOTES: 2010:** Combined to go 8-6 with a 2.26 ERA (83.2IP, 21ER) in 47 games out of the bullpen with Single-A Charleston and Single-A Tampa...was promoted to Tampa on 9/1, after going 7-6 with 14 saves and a 2.26 ERA in 45 appearances with Charleston, recording 70K and walking just 14 batters in 79.2IP...made one postseason appearance for Tampa, tossing 2.0 scoreless innings (2K, 1HP)...**2009:** Combined to go 4-2 with six saves and a 2.40 ERA in 40 appearances with Single-A Charleston and short-season Single-A Staten Island...held opponents without an earned run in 34 of his 40 outings...led the New York-Penn League in appearances...**2008:** Made his professional debut, going 2-1 with a 0.86 ERA in 15 games with the GCL Yankees...ranked fifth in the GCL with seven saves...allowed runs in just two of his 15 appearances out of the bullpen...held opponents to a .164 batting average (12-for-73).

FLORES, Ramon – OF

HT: 5-11; **WT:** 190; **B:** L; **T:** L; **BORN:** 3/26/92 in Barinas, Venezuela; **RESIDES:** Barinas, Venezuela; **OBTAINED:** Signed by the Yankees as a non-drafted free agent on 7/4/08; **M.L. SVC:** 0.000; **CAREER NOTES: 2010:** Played at three different levels (GCL, Single-A Tampa and Single-A Charleston)...combined to hit .303 (71-for-234)...**2009:** Made his professional debut and combined to hit .208 with five doubles, four triples and 19RBI in 62 combined games with the DSL Yankees 2 and the GCL Yankees...began the season in the DSL before being transferred to the GCL on 6/12, where he batted .196 with five doubles and 14RBI in 51 games.

FORER, Nathan – RHP

HT: 6-1; **WT:** 172; **B:** R; **T:** R; **BORN:** 6/6/88 in Ontario, Canada; **RESIDES:** Ontario, Canada; **COLLEGE:** Southern Illinois University; **OBTAINED:** Selected by the Yankees in the 46th round of the 2010 First-Year Player Draft; **M.L. SVC:** 0.000; **CAREER NOTES: 2010:** Combined at short-season Single-A Staten Island and Single-A Tampa to go 0-0 with a 3.86 ERA (30.1IP, 13R) in 22 relief appearances in his first professional action...began the season with the SI Yankees, allowing just 5ER in 22.2IP over 16 relief outings...held lefthanders to a .133 (4-for-30) average with SI...did not allow a run or run over his first five outings (7.1IP)...**PERSONAL:** Full name is Nathan Leigh Forer...was a second-team All-Missouri Valley Conference selection and *ESPN The Magazine* Academic All-District V first team as a senior...pitched for two years at Kaskaskia College, earning Academic All-American honors and All-Star honors before transferring to S. Illinois...graduated from Mayfield Secondary School where was named team MVP his junior and senior seasons.

FULGENCIO, Edwin – OF

HT: 6-2; **WT:** 190; **B:** R; **T:** R; **BORN:** 7/22/91 in Santo Domingo, D.R.; **RESIDES:** Santo Domingo, D.R.; **OBTAINED:** Signed by the Yankees as a non-drafted free agent on 10/18/08; **M.L. SVC:** 0.000; **CAREER NOTES: 2010:** Started the season with the DSL Yankees 1, batting .152 (7-for-48) with 2 doubles, 2HR and 5RBI in 16 games...was transferred to DSL Yankees 2 on 7/17, batting .222 (6-for-27) with 1 double, 1HR and 3RBI in 9 games...**2009:** Made his professional debut with the DSL Yankees 1 and hit .172 with 4HR and 17RBI in 53 games...15 of his 31H went for extra-bases (9 doubles, 2 triples, 4HR).

GAMEL, Benjamin – OF

HT: 5-10; **WT:** 170; **B:** L; **T:** L; **BORN:** 5/17/92 in Neptune Beach, Fla.; **RESIDES:** Neptune Beach, Fla.; **OBTAINED:** Selected by the Yankees in the 10th round of the 2010 First-Year Player Draft; **M.L. SVC:** 0.000; **CAREER NOTES: 2010:** Made his professional debut with the GCL Yankees on 8/19...appeared in seven games and hit .280 (7-for-25) with 1 double...**PERSONAL:** Graduated from Bishop Kenny (Fla.) High School in 2010.

GARCIA, Freddy – RHP   NON-ROSTER INVITEE

HT: 6-4; **WT:** 250; **B:** R; **T:** R; **BORN:** 10/6/76 in Caracas, Venezuela; **RESIDES:** Miami, Fla.; **OBTAINED:** Signed by the Yankees as a minor league free agent on 2/10/11; **M.L. SVC:** 10.060; **CAREER NOTES:** In 303 games (302 starts) over parts of 12 seasons with Seattle (1999-2004), Chicago-AL (2004-06, '09-10), Philadelphia (2007) and Detroit (2008), owns a 133-87 career record with a 4.13 ERA (1929.2IP, 885ER)...among all Venezuelan-born pitchers, ranks first in innings pitched, is tied for first in wins (also Johan Santana) and ranks third in strikeouts (1,390)...since 2001, owns the fourth-most wins in the American League among active right-handed pitchers (106), trailing Tim Wakefield (108), John Lackey (116) and Roy Halladay (135)...has made two All-Star Game appearances, earning the win in the 2000 Midsummer classic in Seattle, tossing 1.0 scoreless inning in relief...pitched for Venezuela in the inaugural World Baseball Classic in 2006, going 1-0 with a 1.23 ERA (7.1IP, 1ER) and 11K in two starts...was voted Mariners "co-Pitcher of the Year" in 2001 by the Seattle chapter of the BBWAA...finished second to Kansas City's Carlos Beltran in the 1999 AL "Rookie of the Year Award" voting...is 6-2 with a 3.11 ERA in nine career postseason starts, tied for the fourth-most playoff starts among active AL pitchers...was originally signed by the Astros as a non-drafted free agent on 10/21/93...**2010:** Went 12-6 with a 4.64 ERA (157.0IP, 81ER) in 28 starts with the White Sox, making more appearances than he did the prior three seasons combined (23) and marking his most outings in a season since 2006 (33)...held opponents to 3ER or less in 20 of his outings and lost consecutive starts just once (4/10 vs. Minnesota and 4/15 at Toronto)...**2009:** Began the year as a spring training non-roster invitee with the Mets, but was released on 4/28 after making two starts at Triple-A Norfolk...was signed by the White Sox as a minor league free agent on 6/8 and made nine starts for Chicago-AL, going 3-4 with a 4.34 ERA (56.0IP, 27ER)...held right-handed batters to a .196 (20-for-102) batting average...following the season, made one appearance with the Navegantes del Magallanes of the Venezuelan Winter League, allowing 1ER in 3.1IP in relief (2R, 3H, 3K)...**2008:** Missed the majority of the season rehabbing from right-shoulder surgery...signed with Detroit as a minor league free agent on 8/14 and made three starts for the Tigers, going 1-1 with a 4.20 ERA (15.0IP, 7ER)...following the season, made two starts with Magallanes and did not record a decision, combining to allow 4ER in 7.0IP (9H, 1BB, 5K)...**2007:** In his lone season with Philadelphia, began the season on the disabled list with right biceps tendinitis...was reinstated on 4/16 and made 11 starts for the Phillies, going 1-5 with a 5.90 ERA (58.0IP, 38ER)...was placed back on the disabled list on 6/9 for the remainder of the year after having right-shoulder surgery...**2006:** Went 17-9 with a 4.53 ERA (216.1IP, 109ER) in 33 starts with the White Sox, recording a career-low 48BB...became one of four pitchers to register at least 10 wins, 30 starts and 200.0IP each season from 2001-06, joining Mark Buehrle, Livan Hernandez and Barry Zito...became the first pitcher since Toronto's Dave Stieb in 1988 to allow just 1H over 8.0IP in two consecutive outings (9/13 and 9/19)...was 4-0 with a 2.10 ERA (30.0IP, 7ER) in Interleague play and 12-3 with a 3.87 ERA (118.2IP, 51ER) vs. clubs with a winning record...earned his 100th career victory on 4/10 at Detroit, allowing 3ER in 6.0IP (5H, 2BB, 5K, 1HR)...**2005:** In his first full season with the White Sox, went 14-8 with a 3.87 ERA (228.0IP, 98ER) in 33 starts, recording his fifth consecutive 10-win season and fourth consecutive 200.0IP campaign...tossed a "one-hitter" in a 1-0 loss at Minnesota on 8/23, losing the no-hit bid after a Jacque Jones leadoff home run in the eighth inning...won six

consecutive decisions over an 11-start stretch from 5/20-7/15, going 6-0 with a 2.99 ERA (78.1IP, 26ER)…recorded a season-high 10K in his victory at Colorado on 6/6 and his 1,000th career strikeout in his win vs. Tampa Bay on 7/5 (Jorge Cantu)…went 3-0 with a 2.14 ERA (21.0IP, 5ER) in three postseason starts for the World Champion White Sox…all three victories came on the road, the first time a pitcher accomplished that feat since John Smoltz with the Braves in 1996…**2004:** Combined to go 13-11 with a 3.81 ERA (210.0IP, 89ER) in 31 starts with Seattle and Chicago-AL…began the season with the Mariners and went 4-7 with a 3.20 ERA (107.0IP, 38ER) in 15 starts before being traded to the White Sox, along with catcher Ben Davis, on 6/27 in exchange for catcher Miguel Olivo and minor-leaguers Michael Morse and Jeremy Reed…made 16 starts with the White Sox, going 9-4 with a 4.46 ERA (103.0IP, 51ER)…was 9-0 with a with a 2.43 ERA during day games, became one of seven Major League pitchers since 1971 to post a 9-0 record or better during such contests…**2003:** Went 12-14 with a 4.51 ERA (201.1IP, 101ER) in 33 starts with the Mariners…made his third consecutive Opening Day start, becoming the first pitcher in franchise history to do so since Randy Johnson from 1992-95…named the AL "Pitcher of the Month" for June after going 5-0 with a 2.05 ERA (44.0IP, 10ER)…allowed only 2ER over his last four starts of the season, going 1-1 with a 0.67 ERA (27.0IP)…**2002:** Tied a career high with 34 starts, going 16-10 with a 4.39 ERA (223.2IP, 109ER)…tied for second in the AL in starts, ranked fifth in strikeouts (181) and eighth in innings pitched (223.2)…joined Randy Johnson as the only pitchers in Mariners history to record three seasons of at least 16 wins…was named to his second consecutive All-Star game after going 11-5 with a 3.44 ERA during the first half…**2001:** Established a career-high in wins, going 18-6 with a 3.05 ERA in 34 starts…led the AL in ERA, innings pitched (238.2) and opponents batting average (.225), tied for second in shutouts (three), tied for third in games started, tied for fifth in wins, winning percentage (.750), complete games (four) and tied for ninth in strikeouts (163)…became the first Mariners pitcher to lead the league in IP and the second to lead the AL in ERA (Randy Johnson – 1995)…was named to the All-Star game and earned the win in the, tossing 1.0 scoreless inning in relief…became the first Mariners pitcher since Randy Johnson accomplished the feat in 1998, to throw back-to-back complete-game shutouts on 7/1 at Anaheim and 7/6 at Los Angeles-NL…went 1-2 with a 3.79 ERA (19.0IP, 8ER) in three postseason starts with the Mariners…**2000:** Appeared in 21 games (20 starts) with Seattle and went 9-5 with a 3.91 ERA (124.1IP, 54ER)…missed the majority of the first of half of the season, going on the disabled list on 4/22 with a stress fracture in his right tibia…was reinstated on 7/7 and made his first career relief appearance on 8/18 at Cleveland, tossing 3.0 scoreless innings out of the bullpen (1H, 1BB, 2K)…**1999:** Went 17-8 with a 4.07 ERA (201.1IP, 91ER) in 33 starts with the Mariners…finished second in the AL Rookie of the Year voting behind Kansas City's Carlos Beltran…led all regular rookies in wins, ERA, starts, strikeouts (170), winning percentage (.680) and opponents batting average against (.263)…his 17 wins tied the franchise rookie record shared by Mark Langston and Dave Fleming…recorded his first career shutout on 8/24 vs. Detroit, striking out a career-high 12 batters…**1998:** Combined to go 10-8 with a 3.35 ERA (166.1IP, 62ER) and 158K in 25 starts between Triple-A New Orleans of the Astros organization and Double-A Jackson and Triple-A Tacoma of the Astros organization…was traded, with INF Carlos Guillen and a player to be named later (John Halama,) to Seattle for Randy Johnson on 7/31…**1997:** Went 10-8 with a 2.56 ERA (179.0IP, 51ER) in 27 starts with Single-A Kissimmee, ranking second in the Florida State League in innings pitched, and fifth in ERA and complete games (5)…**1996:** Made 13 starts for Single-A Quad City and went 5-4 with a 3.12 ERA (60.2IP, 21ER)…went on the disabled list from 6/29-7/31 with a sprained right shoulder and from 8/16-rest of the season with a sprained right elbow…**1995:** Went 6-3 with a 4.47 ERA (58.1IP, 29ER) in 11 starts with the GCL Astros, leading the team in wins…**1994:** Pitched for San Pedro de Macoris of the Dominican Summer League, going 4-6 with a 5.29 ERA (85.0IP, 50ER)…**PERSONAL:** Is married to Glendys and has two children, Sophia and Anthony.

GARCIA, Samuel – RHP

HT: 6-0; **WT:** 180; **B:** R; **T:** R; **BORN:** 3/4/93 in Bonao, D.R.; **RESIDES:** Bonao, D.R.; **OBTAINED:** Signed as a minor league free agent on 1/15/10; **M.L. SVC:** 0.000; **CAREER NOTES: 2010:** Made his professional debut with the DSL Yankees 2, going 0-5 with a 7.66 ERA in eight games (seven starts)…recorded 26K in 22.1IP.

GERRITSE, Brett – RHP

HT: 6-3; **WT:** 225; **B:** R; **T:** R; **BORN:** 3/4/91 in Cypress, Calif.; **RESIDES:** Cypress, Calif.; **OBTAINED:** Selected by the Yankees in the 12th round of the 2009 First-Year Player Draft; **M.L. SVC:** 0.000; **CAREER NOTES: 2010:** Went 2-2 with one save and a 3.82 ERA in nine appearances (two starts) with the GCL Yankees…**2009:** Made his professional debut, going 0-1 with a 3.93 ERA in six games (five starts) with the GCL Yankees…**PERSONAL:** Graduated from Pacifica (Calif.) High School.

GIL, Francisco Daniel – RHP

HT: 6-3; **WT:** 240; **B:** R; **T:** R; **BORN:** 4/24/89 in Agua Prieta, Mexico; **RESIDES:** Agua Prieta, Mexico; **OBTAINED:** Signed by the Yankees as a non-drafted free agent on 12/15/00; **M.L. SVC:** 0.000; **CAREER NOTES: 2010:** Spent the entire season with Single-A Charleston where he went 1-3 with a 1.25 ERA, allowing 5ER in 36.0IP out of the bullpen…led all RiverDogs relievers in ERA and did not allow an earned run in 23 of his 28 relief appearances…following the season, appeared in four games for the Naranjeros de Hermosillo of the Mexican Pacific League yielding a 10.50 ERA with no decisions in relief (6.0IP, 7ER)…**2009:** Missed the entire season, recovering from "Tommy John" surgery…**2008:** Underwent surgery on his right elbow on 5/8 and missed the remainder of the season…**2007:** Went 2-1 with a 6.00 ERA in five games (one start) with the GCL Yankees…struck out 12 batters while walking just four in 15.0IP…was placed on the disabled list on 8/24 with a right knee sprain, ending his season…**2006:** Posted a 1-2 record with a 3.26 ERA in nine games (seven starts) with the Yankees DSL 1 squad…allowed only 27 hits in 30.1IP.

GIL, Jose – C   NON-ROSTER INVITEE

HT: 6-0; **WT:** 205; **B:** S; **T:** R; **BORN:** 9/4/86 in Barcelona, Venezuela; **RESIDES:** Barcelona, Venezuela; **OBTAINED:** Signed by the Yankees as a non-drafted free agent on 7/2/03; **M.L. SVC:** 0.000; **CAREER NOTES: 2010:** Combined to hit .247 (61-for-247) with 10 doubles, 10HR and 44RBI in 71 games with Single-A Tampa and Double-A Trenton…played the final 40 games of the season with Tampa where he batted .255 (36-for-141) with 5HR and 19RBI…appeared in two postseason games with the Tampa Yankees and recorded 4H in 8AB (.500), including 1 triple and 3RBI…following the season, appeared in 25 games with the Caribes de Anzoategui of the Venezuelan Winter League and hit .247 (19-for-77) with 6 doubles, 2HR and 12RBI…**2009:** Batted .205 with six doubles, 2HR and 12RBI in 41 combined games with Double-A Trenton and Single-A Tampa…combined to catch 35.4% of potential base stealers (17-of-48)…**2008:** Batted .243 with 17 doubles, 1HR and 25RBI in 73 games with Single-A Tampa, matching his career high in doubles…caught 39.7 percent of potential basestealers (25-of-63)…**2007:** Combined to hit .234 with 40R, 21 doubles, 12HR and 50RBI in 100 games with Single-A Charleston and short-season Single-A Staten Island…caught 33.7 percent of potential base stealers (29-of-86), third-best caught stealing rate in the New York-Penn League…**2006:** Combined to bat .229 with 2HR and 21RBI in 56 games with Single-A Charleston and Staten Island…**2005:** Batted .279 with 11 doubles, one home run and 20RBI in 41 games with the Gulf Coast Yankees…batted .301 (22-for-73) in 22 road games and posted a .294 (15-for-51) average with runners in scoring position…helped lead the Yankees to the GCL Championship for the second straight season…**2004:** In first professional season, batted .223 in 45 games with the Yankees DSL 2 squad.

GIPSON, James – RHP

HT: 6-1; **WT:** 195; **B:** R; **T:** R; **BORN:** 9/15/88 in Boynton Beach, Fla.; **RESIDES:** Lake Worth, Fla.; **COLLEGE:** Florida Atlantic University; **OBTAINED:** Selected by the Yankees in the 31st round of the 2010 First-Year Player Draft; **M.L. SVC:** 0.000; **CAREER NOTES: 2010:** Made his professional debut with short-season Single-A Staten Island, going 3-1 with a 4.42 ERA in 12 games (six starts)…recorded 50K in 38.2IP, ranking second on the team in strikeouts…was promoted to Single-A Charleston on 8/23, where he went 0-2 with a 7.88 ERA in three appearances (two starts)…**PERSONAL:** Full name is James Michael Gipson…in his junior year at Florida Atlantic University appeared in 16 games and went 8-2 with a 3.20 ERA, recorded 46ER, 43BB and 96K in 112.0IP…graduated from Palm Beach Central High School in Florida.

GOLSAN, Judd – OF

HT: 6-0; **WT:** 178; **B:** L; **T:** R; **BORN:** 12/6/90 in Birmingham, Ala.; **RESIDES:** Birmingham, Ala.; **OBTAINED:** Selected by the Yankees in the 31st round of the 2009 First-Year Player Draft; **M.L. SVC:** 0.000; **CAREER NOTES: 2010:** Appeared in 35 games with the GCL Yankees, batting .188 (19-for-101) with 4 doubles and 9RBI…**2009:** Made his professional debut and batted .224 with three doubles and five RBI in 39 games with the GCL Yankees.

GOMEZ, Jhoan – INF

HT: 6-0; **WT:** 175; **B:** R; **T:** R; **BORN:** 2/14/93 in Mao, D.R.; **RESIDES:** Mao, D.R.; **OBTAINED:** Signed as a minor league free agent on 10/4/10; **M.L. SVC:** 0.000; **CAREER NOTES:** Will make his professional debut in 2011.

GONZALEZ, Felipe – RHP

HT: 6-2; **WT:** 165; **B:** R; **T:** R; **BORN:** 8/15/91 in Guadalupe, Mexico.; **RESIDES:** Guadalupe, Mexico; **OBTAINED:** Signed as a non-drafted free agent on 2/16/08; **M.L. SVC:** 0.000; **CAREER NOTES: 2010:** Went 4-2 with a 3.38 ERA in 13 starts…led the team in starts, wins and innings pitched (56.0), and ranked second in strikeouts (49)…**2009:** Made two relief appearances for the DSL Yankees 2 and went 0-1, not allowing an earned run in 1.0IP…**2008:** Made his professional debut with the DSL Yankees 1, going 2-1 with a 8.79 ERA in seven relief appearances.

GONZALEZ, Malduino – C

HT: 5-11; **WT:** 215; **B:** R; **T:** R; **BORN:** 3/7/91 in Maracaibo, Venezuela; **RESIDES:** Maracaibo, Venezuela; **OBTAINED:** Signed as a minor league free agent on 5/12/10; **M.L. SVC:** 0.000; **CAREER NOTES: 2010:** Made his professional debut with the DSL Yankees 1, going 1-for-13 (.077) in 12 games.

GREENE, Shane – RHP

HT: 6-3; **WT:** 197; **B:** R; **T:** R; **BORN:** 11/17/88 in Clermont, Fla.; **RESIDES:** Clermont, Fla.; **COLLEGE:** Daytona State College; **OBTAINED:** Selected by the Yankees in the 15th round of the 2009 First-Year Player Draft; **M.L. SVC:** 0.000; **CAREER NOTES: 2010:** Made 14 combined starts with short-season Single-A Staten Island and Single-A Charleston, going 2-8 with a 4.58 ERA (68.2IP, 35ER) and 66K…in his final start of the season, tossed 6.0 scoreless, two-hit innings…**2009:** Made 13 appearances with the GCL Yankees in first professional season, going 1-2 with a 5.87 ERA and 20K in 23.0IP.

GROTE, Taylor David – OF

HT: 6-1; **WT:** 200; **B:** L; **T:** R; **BORN:** 12/5/88 in The Woodlands, Tex.; **RESIDES:** The Woodlands, Tex.; **OBTAINED:** Selected by the Yankees in the eighth round of the 2007 First-Year Player Draft; **M.L. SVC:** 0.000; **CAREER NOTES: 2010:** Combined to hit .275 (25-for-91) with 7 doubles, 2HR and 9RBI in 29 games with Single-A Charleston and Double-A Trenton…in 29 games as the designated hitter with the RiverDogs, batted .345 (10-for-29) with 2 doubles, 1HR and 3RBI…**2009:** With Single-A Charleston, hit .232 with 22 doubles, 4HR and 42RBI…hit safely in 12 of his first 13 games of the season…**2008:** Batted .223 with 6 doubles, 3HR and 20RBI in 56 games with short-season Single-A Staten Island…ranked fourth in the NYPL with 73K…**2007:** Appeared in only one game with the Gulf Coast Yankees in his professional debut, going 0-for-1 with 1BB on 8/24.

GUMBS, Angelo – INF/OF

HT: 5-11; **WT:** 195; **B:** R; **T:** R; **BORN:** 10/13/92 in Torrance, Calif.; **RESIDES:** Torrance, Calif.; **OBTAINED:** Selected by the Yankees in the second round of the 2010 First-Year Player Draft; **M.L. SVC:** 0.000; **CAREER NOTES: 2010:** Made his professional debut with the GCL Yankees, batting .192 (5-for-26) with 1 double in seven games…**PERSONAL:** Graduated from Torrance High School (Calif.)…his favorite number is 21 in honor of Roberto Clemente…played at MLB's Urban Youth Academy in Compton.

GUZMAN, Miguel – INF

HT: 5-11; **WT:** 167; **B:** S; **T:** R; **BORN:** 7/18/90 in Paya Bani, D.R.; **RESIDES:** Paya Bani, D.R.; **OBTAINED:** Signed by the Yankees as a non-drafted free agent on 5/7/09; **M.L. SVC:** 0.000; **CAREER NOTES: 2010:** Hit .185 (10-for-32) with 2RBI in 32 games with the DSL Yankees 1…**2009:** Made his professional debut, batting .250 with 2 doubles and 5RBI in 15 games with the DSL Yankees 1…recorded 4SB in five attempts.

HALL, Shaeffer – LHP

HT: 6-0; **WT:** 203; **B:** R; **T:** L; **BORN:** 10/2/87 in Independence, Mo.; **RESIDES:** Lee's Summit, Mo.; **COLLEGE:** Kansas; **OBTAINED:** Selected by the Yankees in the 25th round of the 2009 First-Year Player Draft; **M.L. SVC:** 0.000; **CAREER NOTES: 2010:** Combined to go 11-7 with a 2.89 ERA (137.0IP, 44ER) in 25 games (24 starts) with Single-A Charleston and Single-A Tampa…began the season with Charleston, where he went 2-2 with a 1.85 ERA, allowing just 14ER in 68.0IP…was promoted to Tampa on 5/28 and went 9-5 with a 3.91 ERA (69.0IP, 30ER) in 15 games (14 starts), allowing 3ER or less in nine of his 14 starts with the Tampa Yankees…**2009:** Made two starts with short-season Single-A Staten Island, striking out 11 batters in 9.2IP…**PERSONAL:** Full name is William Shaeffer Hall…graduated from Lee's Summit West HS (MO), earning the 2006 *Kansas City Star* "All-Metro Player of the Year" award and First Team All-State by the Missouri Sportswriters and Missouri Coaches…was selected by Texas in the 28th round of the 2006 First-Year Player Draft and Cleveland in the 23rd round in 2007…attended Jefferson College before transferring to Kansas.

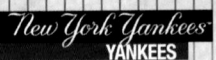

HEATHCOTT, Slade – OF

HT: 6-0; **WT:** 197; **B:** L; **T:** L; **BORN:** 9/28/90 in Texarkana, Tex.; **RESIDES:** Texarkana, Tex.; **OBTAINED:** Selected by the Yankees in the first round (29th overall) of the 2009 First-Year Player Draft; **M.L. SVC:** 0.000; **CAREER NOTES:** 2010: Appeared in 76 games with Single-A Charleston, batting .258 (77-for-298) with 16 doubles, 3 triples, 2HR and 30RBI in his first full season…hit .321 (36-for-112) with runners on base…following the season was named as the ninth-best prospect and the "Best Defensive Outfielder" in the Yankees organization by *Baseball America*…**2009:** Appeared in three games with the GCL Yankees, going 1-for-10…named the Yankees' fourth-best prospect by *Baseball America* following the season…**PERSONAL:** Full name is Zachary Heathcott…graduated from Texas High School where he was a third-team All-State selection and named first-team All-District as a senior…was an AFLAC All-American selection as a left-handed pitcher in 2008, while also playing outfield at various events, including the Perfect Game National Showcase and the Area Code Games…ranked as the 72nd-best prospect (18th-best high school position player) in the draft by *Baseball America* and rated by the publication as the 10th-best prospect in the state of Texas in 2009.

HEREDIA, Jairo – RHP

HT: 6-1; **WT:** 170; **B:** R; **T:** R; **BORN:** 10/8/89 in Santo Domingo, D.R.; **RESIDES:** Santo Domingo, D.R.; **OBTAINED:** Signed by the Yankees as a non-drafted free agent on 7/2/06; **M.L. SVC:** 0.000; **CAREER NOTES:** 2010: Combined to go 4-8 with a 4.36 ERA (95.0IP, 46ER) in 26 games (15 starts) with Single-A Charleston and Single-A Tampa…spent the majority of the season with Charleston, where he went 4-2 with a 3.45 ERA, allowing 27ER in 70.1IP…recorded 23K and allowed just 3ER over his last 22.1IP of the year (1.21 ERA)…was 1-0 with a 1.54 ERA (23.1IP, 4ER) as a reliever with the RiverDogs, and 3-2 with a 4.40 ERA (47.0IP, 23ER) in nine starts with the team…**2009:** Went 3-3 with a 3.99 ERA in 10 combined starts with the GCL Yankees, Single-A Charleston and Single-A Tampa…was placed on the disabled list on 4/9 with right shoulder inflammation…did not record a decision in two rehab starts with the GCL Yankees, allowing 3H and 1ER in 5.0IP (2R, 2BB, 5K)…reinstated from the DL on 7/21 and made four starts with Charleston, going 1-1 with a 2.37 ERA…was transferred to Tampa on 8/17 where he went 2-2 with a 6.91 ERA in four starts…named the Florida State League "Pitcher of the Week" on 8/24 after earning two wins and combining to allow just 1ER in 12.0IP over two starts (14H, 4BB, 5K)…**2008:** Went 6-7 with a 3.25 ERA in 21 starts with Single-A Charleston…was placed on the disabled list from 4/21-5/23 with right elbow tendinitis…tossed a career-high 7.0 innings on 6/30 vs. Savannah…was named the SAL's "Pitcher of the Week" for the period of 6/30-7/6, going 2-0 with a 0.00 ERA in two starts, allowing just 5H and striking out 11 batters in 13.1IP (2R, 2BB)…struck out a career-high-tying eight batters in 5.1IP on 7/27 vs. Hickory…allowed just 1HR over his final 11 starts of the season (60.0IP) after giving up 6HR over his first 10 starts (52.1IP)…**2007:** Made his professional debut with the GCL Yankees, going 2-2 with a 2.72 ERA in 11 games (six starts)…led the GCL staff with 52 strikeouts, while walking just 11 batters in 46.1IP…recorded a career-high 8K in back-to-back starts on 7/10 and 7/18.

HEREDIA, Juan – LHP

HT: 6-3; **WT:** 160; **B:** L; **T:** L; **BORN:** 1/20/89 in San Pedro de Macoris, D.R.; **RESIDES:** San Pedro de Macoris, D.R.; **OBTAINED:** Signed by the Yankees as a non-drafted free agent on 4/18/08; **M.L. SVC:** 0.000; **CAREER NOTES:** 2010: Went 0-2 with a 5.40 ERA in six games (five starts) with the DSL Yankees 2…**2009:** Allowed just 3R/2ER in 13 starts (57.0IP) with the DSL Yankees 2, posting a 0.32 ERA…fell just shy of qualifying for the league's lowest ERA…did not allow a run until his seventh start of the season, opening the year with 27.0 consecutive scoreless innings…limited opponents to a .179 batting average (34-for-190), holding the opposition to 3H or less in eight starts…**2008:** Made his professional debut, posting a record of 5-3 with a 3.35 ERA in 15 games (six starts) with the DSL Yankees 2…recorded at least 6K in six of his 15 appearances, including three straight outings from 7/4-15.

HEYER, Craig – RHP

HT: 6-2; **WT:** 200; **B:** R; **T:** R; **BORN:** 11/15/85 in Scottsdale, Ariz.; **RESIDES:** Scottsdale, Ariz.; **COLLEGE:** University of Nevada-Las Vegas; **OBTAINED:** Selected by the Yankees in the 22nd round of the 2007 First-Year Player Draft; **M.L. SVC:** 0.000; **CAREER NOTES:** 2010: Spent the season with Single-A Tampa where he went 8-4 with a 3.52 ERA, allowing 36ER in 92.0IP…began season in the bullpen, going 3-1 with a 1.26 ERA (28.2IP, 4ER) as a reliever…allowed just 1ER over his first nine outings (18.1IP)…entered the starting rotation on 5/20 and went 5-3 with a 4.55 ERA (63.1IP, 32ER) as a starter…following the season, made seven appearances (three starts) for the Phoenix Desert Dogs, of the Arizona Fall League, and went 1-2 with a 2.50 ERA, allowing 5ER in 18.0IP…**2009:** Spent the season with Single-A Tampa, going 4-3 with one save and a 3.11 ERA in 30 appearances (six starts)…held left-handed batters to a .231 (34-for-147, 1HR) batting average, while right handers hit .302 (39-for-129, 0HR)…made all of his starts over his final seven appearances of the season (7/13-8/12)…was placed on the disabled list on 8/21 with a right hand fracture, missing the remainder of the season…**2008:** Went 7-1 with one save and a 2.08 ERA in 41 appearances (one start) with Single-A Charleston…tossed a season-high 3.2 innings on 6/23 vs. Rome…made his only start of the season on 8/12 at Delmarva, allowing 5H and 2ER in 3.0IP (3K)…recorded his first professional loss on 8/26 vs. Savannah after winning his first 12 career decisions (five in 2007 and first seven in 2008)…**2007:** Made his professional debut with short-season Single-A Staten Island, going 5-0 with a 3.20 ERA in 17 games (one start)…recorded the win in three consecutive relief appearances from 7/31-8/7, allowing 1ER in 11.1IP…**PERSONAL:** Attended the Community College of Southern Nevada before transferring to UNLV in 2006…earned all-state honors in 2003 and 2004 at Coronado (Ariz.) High School.

HIGASHIOKA, Kyle – C ## NON-ROSTER INVITEE

HT: 6-0; **WT:** 205; **B:** R; **T:** R; **BORN:** 4/20/90 in Huntington Beach, Calif.; **RESIDES:** Huntington Beach, Calif.; **OBTAINED:** Selected by the Yankees in the seventh round of the 2008 First-Year Player Draft; **M.L. SVC:** 0.000; **CAREER NOTES:** 2010: Played the entire season with Single-A Charleston and batted .225 (72-for-320) with 18 doubles, 6HR and 24RBI in 90 games…hit .192 (41-for-213) prior to the All-Star break, compared to .290 (31-for-107) in the second half…committed just six errors in 479 total chances, catching 27-of-83 potential base stealers (32.5%)…**2009:** Batted .253 with 11 doubles, 2HR and 32RBI in 60 games with short-season Single-A Staten Island…led all league catchers in games (57), chances (497) and putouts (451) and ranked fifth in caught stealing percentage (25.3, 19-for-75)…**2008:** Made his professional debut, appearing in 18 games with the GCL Yankees and making 14 starts behind the plate…hit .261 with 1 double, 1HR and 3RBI…**PERSONAL:** Graduated from Edison (Calif.) High School where he batted .382 with 7HR and 31RBI in his senior season and earned All-County honors…was selected as the starting catcher for the 2008 Orange County All-Star South team…was the 2006 All-Sunset League "Rookie of the Year."

HOBBS, Dustin – RHP

HT: 6-2; **WT:** 200; **B:** R; **T:** R; **BORN:** 8/18/89 in Las Vegas, Nev.; **RESIDES:** Las Vegas, Nev.; **COLLEGE:** Yavapai Junior College; **OBTAINED:** Selected by the Yankees in the 21st round of the 2010 First-Year Player Draft; **M.L. SVC:** 0.000; **CAREER NOTES: 2010:** Started the season with the GCL Yankees and went 3-1 with a 2.30 ERA in seven starts, recording 33K in 27.1IP…was transferred to short-season Single-A Staten Island on 8/25, where he went 0-2 in two starts with a 9.00 ERA…**PERSONAL:** As a sophomore at Yavapai Junior College went 12-3 with a 3.05 ERA…recorded 29ER, 85K, 44BB in 85.2IP…was an All-State pitcher at Arbor View High School in Las Vegas, Nevada.

HORNE, Alan – RHP

HT: 6-2; **WT:** 195; **B:** R; **T:** R; **BORN:** 1/05/83 in Marianna, Fla.; **RESIDES:** Marianna, Fla.; **COLLEGE:** University of Florida; **OBTAINED:** Selected by the Yankees in the 11th round of the 2005 First-Year Player Draft; **M.L. SVC:** 0.000; **CAREER NOTES: 2010:** Missed the entire season rehabbing a torn right rotator cuff…**2009:** Began the season on the disabled list to continue rehabbing his shoulder injury from 2008…was reinstated from the D.L. on 4/30 and assigned to Trenton where he went 0-3 with an 11.15 ERA in five appearances (four starts)…was placed on the disabled list for a second time from 5/13-6/2 with a left hamstring strain…made two appearances (one start) with the Thunder before being placed back on the D.L. for a third stint on 6/8 with a left hamstring strain…began a rehab assignment with the GCL Yankees on 7/23, going 4-0 with a 2.86 ERA in six appearances (five starts)…was reinstated from the disabled list on 8/25 and assigned to Charleston where he went 0-1 with a 5.50 ERA in three starts…**2008:** Combined to go 2-4 with an 8.77 ERA in 11 starts with Triple-A Scranton/Wilkes-Barre and Single-A Tampa…began the season with Scranton/WB, going 2-3 with a 5.63 ERA in eight starts (32.0IP, 20ER)…was placed on the disabled list twice with Scranton/WB (4/11-6/8 with a right biceps strain and 7/2-28 with a cracked fingernail)…was transferred to Tampa on 7/31 where he went 0-1 with a 23.14 ERA in three starts (7.0IP, 18ER)…made two D.L. stints while with Tampa (8/4-17 with a right shoulder strain and 8/23-9/17 with right shoulder inflammation)…**2007:** Went 12-4 with a 3.11 ERA in 27 starts for Double-A Trenton…was named Eastern League "Pitcher of the Year" after leading the league in ERA, strikeouts (165) and a .750 winning percentage while ranking fourth in innings pitched (153.1)…ranked first among all Yankees farmhands in strikeouts and fourth in ERA…was named to the Eastern League midseason All-Star team and was selected as the EL's top right-handed starter on the postseason All-Star squad…had six or more strikeouts in 21 of his 27 starts…from 6/13-7/31, recorded a career-high five game winning streak, tossing 51.2 innings and allowing 11ER, while striking out 49 batters during the nine-game span…following the season, was ranked by *Baseball America* as the Yankees' fifth-best prospect…**2006:** Made professional debut with Single-A Tampa, posting a 6-9 record with a 4.84 ERA…ranked third in the Florida State League with 122K and 61BB…ranked fourth among all Yankees minor-league pitchers in strikeouts…**PERSONAL:** Full name is William Alan Horne…led the 2005 University of Florida team with 10 wins and 108K…helped lead the Gators to the finals of the College World Series…previously played at Chipola Junior College in 2004 and was selected in the 30th round of the 2004 draft by the Anaheim Angels (did not sign)…played baseball at Ole Miss in 2002 and 2003 before undergoing "Tommy John" surgery on his right elbow in 2003…was ranked No. 6 on *Baseball America's* list of the nation's top 50 sophomores prior to the 2003 season and also rated as the SEC's No. 2 prospect for the 2004 Major League Baseball Draft…also listed as one of the top players to watch in the SEC by *Collegiate Baseball*…earned honorable mention Freshman All-America honors from *Collegiate Baseball* in 2002…helped lead Marianna (Fla.) High School to four consecutive appearances in the state 3A Final Four, including a state title his junior year…was originally drafted in the first round by the Cleveland Indians with the 27th overall pick in the 2001 First-Year Player Draft but did not sign…was a Louisville Slugger "National Player of the Year" finalist and a three-time all-state honoree.

IBARRA, Walter – INF

HT: 5-11; **WT:** 175; **B:** S; **T:** R; **BORN:** 11/1/87 in Los Mochis Sinola, Mexico; **RESIDES:** Monterrey, Mexico; **OBTAINED:** Signed by the Yankees as a non-drafted free agent on 8/23/05; **M.L. SVC:** 0.000; **CAREER NOTES: 2010:** Played the entire season with Single-A Tampa and hit .301 (74-for-246) with 12 doubles, 1HR and 14 RBI in 72 games…endured three stints on the disabled list with a right hamstring strain (5/1-11), a cut on his left hand (5/18-6/7) and left shoulder inflammation (8/20-end of the season)…hit .378 (31-for-82) over the first two months…following the season, appeared in 56 games with the Naranjeros de Hermosillo of the Mexican Pacific League and batted .303 (47-for-155) with eight doubles, one triple, 1HR and 14RBI…during his winter league stint, hit .323 (30-for-93) off right-handed pitching and .324 (12-for-37) with runners in scoring position…**2009:** Hit .262 (69-for-263) with 10 doubles, one triple and 19RBI in 86 combined games with Single-A Charleston and Single-A Tampa…following the season, appeared in 34 games with the Naranjeros de Hermosillo of the Mexican Winter League and hit .250 (16-for-64) with one double and 4RBI…**2008:** Combined to bat .224 with 28R, 12 doubles, 4HR and 24RBI in 57 games with Single-A Charleston, short-season Single-A Staten Island and Double-A Trenton…began the season with Charleston, batting .198 in 27 games before being transferred to Staten Island on 6/27…in 12 games with Staten Island, batted .224…was promoted to Trenton on 7/12 where he hit .268…missed time from 8/7-12 to be with his wife for the birth of their child…sprained his left ankle on 8/24 vs. Reading and was placed on the disabled list the following day…remained on the D.L. through the end of the season…played for the Naranjeros de Hermosillo of the Mexican Pacific League following the season…**2007:** Split time between the GCL Yankees and Single-A Tampa…in 16 games with GCL, hit .205 (8-for-39) with 6R and 4RBI…batted .179 (5-for-28) with 5R and 1 double in 10 games for Tampa…**2006:** Made professional debut with the Gulf Coast Yankees, batting .264 in 24 games played (19 at SS, five at 2B).

IGAWA, Kei – LHP

HT: 6-1; **WT:** 212; **B:** L; **T:** L; **BORN:** 7/13/79 in Ibaraki, Japan; **RESIDES:** Ibaraki, Japan; **OBTAINED:** Signed through the MLB/Japanese posting system on 12/27/06…signed a five-year contract that runs through 2011; **M.L. SVC:** 0.095; **CAREER NOTES:** Owns the record for most career wins in Scranton/WB history with 32 victories…**2010:** Went 3-4 with a 4.32 ERA (77.0IP, 37ER) in 22 games (10 starts) with Triple-A Scranton/Wilkes-Barre…made one postseason start and recorded a no-decision, striking out six batters and allowing just 4H in 7.0 scoreless innings (4H, 1BB)…struck out a season-high 10 batters, despite recording the loss, on 8/28 vs. Buffalo…allowed 3ER or less in 10 of his 11 starts…**2009:** Went 10-8 with a 4.15 ERA in 26 starts for Triple-A Scranton/Wilkes-Barre, leading the team in both wins and games started and ranking fourth among all Yankees minor leaguers in wins…owned a 7-3 record with a 2.72 ERA (76.0IP, 23ER) in 13 home starts, compared to a 3-5 mark with a 5.71 ERA in 13 starts on the road (69.1IP, 44ER)…struck out a season-high eight batters twice (6/16 vs. Toledo and 7/16 vs. Gwinnett)…made two postseason appearances (one start) for the International League runner-ups, going 0-2 with a 10.29 ERA (7.0IP, 8ER)…**2008:** Was 0-1 with a 13.50 ERA in two games (one start) over two stints with the Yankees (5/9-15; 6/27-28)…recalled from Triple-A Scranton/Wilkes-Barre and started on 5/9 at Detroit, making

his only start of the season and recording the loss in a 6-5 Tigers victory (3.0IP, 6ER, 11H)…recalled a second time from Scranton/WB prior to Game 2 of a split-stadium doubleheader on 6/27 vs. the Mets…made his only relief appearance of the season in the 9-0 Yankees victory at Shea Stadium (1.0IP, 2H)…was optioned back to Scranton/WB the following day…earned Scranton/WB's "Pitcher of the Year" Award, appearing in 26 games (24 starts) and going 14-6 with a 3.45 ERA…led the team in wins, starts, innings pitched (156.1IP) and strikeouts (117)…tied for second in the International League in wins and ranked fourth in ERA…made two starts in the IL playoffs, going 1-0 with a 1.35 ERA for the IL champions…**2007:** Was 2-3 with a 6.25 ERA in 14 games (12 starts) over three stints with the Yankees (4/2-5/7; 6/22-7/27; 9/9-9/30)…made Opening Day roster and started on 4/7 vs. Baltimore in his Major League debut, allowing 7ER in 5.0IP and recording a no-decision in a 10-7 Yankees victory…earned his first Major League win on 4/18 vs. Cleveland in his third career start (6.0IP, 5H, 2ER, 1BB, 5K)…was optioned to Single-A Tampa on 5/7 after going 2-1 with a 7.63 ERA in six games (5GS) with the Yankees…went 1-1 in two starts at Tampa, allowing 7H and 2ER in 9.0IP…was transferred to Triple-A Scranton/Wilkes-Barre on 5/29…overall with Scranton/WB, was 5-4 with a 3.69 ERA (68.1IP, 68H, 30R, 28ER, 15BB, 71K, 10HR) in 11 starts…in his only minor league postseason start, recorded a no-decision in Scranton/Wilkes-Barre's 6-4 Game 2 victory on 9/6 in the first round of the International League playoffs at Richmond (5.0IP, 6H, 2ER, 2BB, 4K)…received the 2007 James P. Dawson Award for "Most Outstanding Rookie in Spring Training" from the New York chapter of the BBWAA on 3/31 at Steinbrenner Field (formerly Legends Field)…in six Grapefruit League starts, posted a 2-0 record with a 3.13 ERA and a team-high 22 strikeouts…**JAPANESE PLAYING CAREER:** Played with the Hanshin Tigers of the Central League from 1998-2006…was selected to the Central League All-Star Team in three consecutive seasons from 2001-03…led the Central League in strikeouts in 2002, 2004 and 2006…in 2003, helped lead Hanshin to the pennant with a league-leading 20 victories and a 2.80 ERA…was named the Central League's "Most Valuable Player" and was honored as the co-winner of the prestigious Sawamura Award, given to the top pitcher in Japanese baseball each year…was also named to the Best Nine following the season, recognizing the top player at each of the nine baseball positions in the Japan League…tossed a no-hitter on 10/4/04 at Hiroshima in a 1-0 Hanshin victory…won at least 13 games in five consecutive seasons (2002-06)…played in the 2006 Major League Baseball Japan All-Star Series…made one start for the Japanese All-Stars vs. the U.S. Major League All-Star Team on 11/7, allowing 2ER—including a David Wright home run—in 6.0IP (5H, 6BB, 4K)…was posted by the Hanshin Tigers on 11/16…on 11/29, the New York Yankees posted the highest bid and gained exclusive negotiating rights for a 30-day window…**PERSONAL:** Name is pronounced "KAY Ee-GAH-wah"…was originally selected by the Hanshin Tigers out of Mito Shogyo High School…enjoys playing shogi (Japanese chess)…according to the *Elias Sports Bureau*, was the 39th Japanese-born player in Major League history, the 26th Japanese-born pitcher and just the eighth to debut as a starter.

ISABEL, George – RHP

HT: 6-5; **WT:** 222; **B:** R; **T:** R; **BORN:** 9/9/89 in New York City, N.Y.; **RESIDES:** Manhattan, N.Y.; **OBTAINED:** Signed as a minor league free agent on 8/13/10; **M.L. SVC:** 0.000; **CAREER NOTES: 2010:** Started the season with the DSL Yankees 1, going 2-2 with a 1.38 ERA with 16K in 13.0IP…transferred to the GCL Yankees, where he made two appearances (0-0, 18.00 ERA).

JAVIER, Jose – INF

HT: 5-10; **WT:** 160; **B:** R; **RT:** R; **BORN:** 9/16/92 in Puerto Plata, D.R.; **RESIDES:** Puerto Plata, D.R.; **OBTAINED:** Signed as a minor league free agent on 4/1/10; **M.L. SVC:** 0.000; **CAREER NOTES: 2010:** Hit .181 (29-for-160) with 4 doubles, 2 triples and 12RBIs in 55 games with the DSL Yankees 2.

JIMENEZ, Warlin – RHP

HT: 6-0; **WT:** 165; **B:** R; **T:** R; **BORN:** 10/26/88 in Baharona, D.R.; **RESIDES:** Boca Chica, D.R.; **OBTAINED:** Signed by the Yankees as a non-drafted free agent on 11/21/07; **M.L. SVC:** 0.000; **CAREER NOTES: 2010:** Went 1-0 with a 3.38 ERA in four games (two starts) with the DSL Yankees 1, striking out 11 batters in 8.0IP…**2009:** Posted a 2-1 record with a 2.51 ERA in nine games (six starts) with the DSL Yankees 1…worked to a 1.16 ERA (23.1IP, 3ER) as a starter, allowing just 1ER over his final four starts of the year (20.0IP, 17H, 5R, 1ER, 3BB, 19K, 1HR)…**2008:** In his professional debut, went 2-2 with a 4.50 ERA in 12 games (five starts) with the DSL Yankees 1…was 2-0 with a 3.80 ERA and recorded 11K in 21.1IP as a reliever.

JOHNSON, Cody – OF

HT: 6-4; **WT:** 240; **B:** L; **T:** R; **BORN:** 8/18/88 in Panama City, Fla.; **RESIDES:** Southport, Fla.; **OBTAINED:** Acquired by the Yankees from Atlanta in exchange for cash considerations on 11/19/10; **M.L. SVC:** 0.000; **CAREER NOTES: 2010:** Combined to hit .212 (73-for-344) with 10 doubles, 18HR and 60RBI in 106 games with the GCL Braves, Double-A Mississippi Braves and Single-A Myrtle Beach Pelicans…was named to the Southern League's mid-season All-Star team…**2009:** In 128 games with Mississippi and Myrtle Beach, combined to hit .239 (106-for-444) with 18 doubles, a career-high 32HR and 87RBI, earning a post on both the mid-season and postseason Carolina League All-Star squad…**2008:** Played in 127 games with the Rome Braves and batted .252 (118-for-468) with a career-high 26 doubles and 26HR and 89RBI…**2007:** Batted .305 (74-for-243) with 18 doubles, five triples, 17HR and 57RBI in 63 games with the Danville Braves…was named an Appalachian League post-season All-Star and was the APP Player of the Week on 8/27/07…following the season, was named to *Baseball America's* Rookie All-Star team and was honored as the MLB.com Offensive Player of the Year…**2006:** Made his professional debut with the GCL Braves and batted .184 (21-for-114) with six doubles and 16RBI in 32 games…**PERSONAL:** Full name is John Cody Johnson…originally selected by the Braves in the first round (24th overall pick) of the 2006 First-year Player Draft…graduated from Crawford Moseley (Fla.) HS and atended Florida State University.

JOHNSON, Trevor – LHP

HT: 6-1; **WT:** 164; **B:** L; **T:** L; **BORN:** 8/13/90 in Lake Elsinore, Calif.; **RESIDES:** Lake Elsinore, Calif; **COLLEGE:** Palm Desert Junior College; **OBTAINED:** Selected by the Yankees in the 22nd round of the 2010 First Year Player Draft; **M.L. SVC:** 0.000; **CAREER NOTES: 2010:** Made his professional debut with the GCL Yankees, going 0-2 with a 9.00 ERA (7.0IP, 7ER) in seven relief appearances.

JOSEPH, Corban – INF

HT: 6-0; **WT:** 180; **B:** L; **T:** R; **BORN:** 10/28/88 in Franklin, Tenn.; **RESIDES:** Franklin, Tenn.; **OBTAINED:** Selected by the Yankees in the fourth round of the 2008 First-Year Player Draft; **M.L. SVC:** 0.000; **CAREER NOTES: 2010:** Combined to bat .283 (139-for-492) with 33 doubles, 7 triples, 6HR and 65RBI in 129 games with Single-A Tampa and Double-A Trenton…began the season with Tampa where he was named to the FSL midseason All-Star team…prior to his promotion to Trenton on 8/2, led all Tampa batters in average (.302), hits (115), doubles (27) and on-base percentage (.378)…with the Thunder, hit .216 (24-for-111) with 6 doubles, 4 triples and 13RBI in 31 games…**2009:** Batted .300 with 29 extra-base hits (17 doubles, 8 triples, 4HR) and 57RBI in 100 games with Single-A Charleston…ranked fifth in the SAL in average…began the season by recording a hit in 12 consecutive contests from 5/11-5/23, batting .308 (16-for-52) with 4 doubles and 1 triple over the stretch…was named the South Atlantic League's "Player of the Month" in July after hitting .410 (43-for-105) during the month with 13 multi-hit games…was selected to the SAL's postseason All-Star team as the league's top third baseman…**2008:** Made his professional debut, batting .277 with 25R, 15 doubles, 2HR and 18RBI in 49 games with the GCL Yankees…led team in doubles, tying for third-most in the GCL, and runs…reached base safely in a team-high 18 straight games from 7/11 through the end of the season…**PERSONAL:** Batted .510 with 15HR and 58RBI in his senior season at Franklin (Tenn.) High School and was named Midstate "Player of the Year"…his brother, Caleb, was drafted in 2008 by Baltimore.

KAHNLE, Tommy – RHP

HT: 6-1; **WT:** 228; **B:** R; **T:** R; **BORN:** 8/7/89 in Latham, N.Y.; **RESIDES:** Latham, N.Y.; **COLLEGE:** Lynn University; **OBTAINED:** Selected by the Yankees in the fifth round of the 2010 First-Year Player Draft; **M.L. SVC:** 0.000; **CAREER NOTES: 2010:** Made 11 relief appearances with short-season Single-A Staten Island, allowing just 3H and 1ER with 25K in 16.0IP (0.56 ERA, .061 opponents average)…**PERSONAL:** Became the highest drafted player from Division II Lynn University…led the team in ERA, strikeouts and opponents average as a sophomore in 2010 and tossed the third no-hitter in the school's history on 3/13/10…was part of the school's NCAA Division II Championship team in 2009, tossing 12.2 scoreless IP in the postseason as a freshman…graduated from Shaker High School (N.Y.) where he also lettered in basketball and football.

KRUM, Austin – OF

NON-ROSTER INVITEE

HT: 5-10; **WT:** 195; **B:** L; **T:** L; **BORN:** 1/19/86 in Highlands Ranch, Colo.; **RESIDES:** McGregor, Tex.; **COLLEGE:** Dallas Baptist University; **OBTAINED:** Selected by the Yankees in the ninth round of the 2007 First-Year Player Draft; **M.L. SVC:** 0.000; **CAREER NOTES: 2010:** Played the entire season with Double-A Trenton and batted .229 (105-for-459) with 17 doubles, 1 triple, 5HR, 44RBI and 16SB in 120 games…appeared in seven games for the Thunder during the 2010 playoffs and hit .296 (8-for-27) with three doubles, 2RBI and 3SB, leading all EL postseason players in both doubles and stolen bases…**2009:** Combined to bat .249 with 75R, 21 doubles, 8 triples, 2HR and 38RBI in 130 games with Single-A Tampa and Double-A Trenton…began the season with Tampa, hitting .272 with 32R, 7 doubles and 14RBI in 53 games…was promoted to Trenton on 6/16, where he hit .234 with 43R, 14 doubles, 2HR and 24RBI in 77 games…**2008:** Batted .272 with 74R, 21 doubles, 6 triples, 8HR and 67RBI in 131 games with Single-A Charleston…ranked third on the team in RBI and stolen bases (12)…hit .339 (20-for-59) with 4 doubles, 2 triples and 1HR with RISP and two outs, driving in 28 runs…recorded an 11-game hitting streak from 7/28-8/7, batting .500 (19-for-38) with 2 doubles, 1 triple, 3HR and 9RBI…**2007:** Made his professional debut with short-season Single-A Staten Island, batting .238 with 32R, 14 doubles, 4 triples, 1HR and 22RBI in 60 games…recorded a career-high nine-game hitting streak from 8/29-9/5, batting .543 (19-for-35) with 5R, 4 doubles, 1 triple, 1HR and 10RBI during the stretch…In those nine games, recorded three-hits five times, including in each of the first four games of the streak…**PERSONAL:** Was a two-year starter at Dallas Baptist University (.356, 22 doubles, 18HR, 78RBI, and 38SB in 45 attempts)…led team in average in 2006 and hits in 2007…was invited to try out for the 2006 USA Baseball team.

KRUML, Ray – OF

HT: 5-11; **WT:** 185; **B:** L; **T:** R; **BORN:** 8/5/85 in Lisle, Ill.; **RESIDES:** Lisle, Ill.; **COLLEGE:** University of South Alabama; **OBTAINED:** Selected by the Yankees in the 11th round of the 2008 First-Year Player Draft; **M.L. SVC:** 0.000; **CAREER NOTES: 2010:** Combined to hit .267 (127-for-475) with 23 doubles, 3 triples, 1HR and 32 RBI in 117 games with Single-A Charleston and Single-A Tampa…began the season with the RiverDogs, where he hit .261 (48-for-184) with 9 doubles and 11RBI in 51 games…was promoted to Tampa on 6/24 and batted .271 (79-for-291) with 14 doubles, 2 triples, 1HR and 21RBI in 66 games…**2009:** Hit .246 with 15 doubles, 4 triples, 2HR and 35RBI in 100 games with Single-A Charleston…stole 23 bases in 28 attempts…**2008:** Made his professional debut with short-season Single-A Staten Island, batting .294 with 42R, 15 doubles and 24RBI in 65 games…batted .286 (2-for-7) with 2R, 2BB and 1SB in two postseason games…**PERSONAL:** Attended the University of South Alabama, earning second-team All-Sun Belt Conference honors during his senior year…batted .350 with 68R, 21 doubles, 8HR and 45RBI in 57 games as a senior, leading the team in batting average and successfully stealing a base in 31 of his 36 attempts (86.1%)…also attended Indian Hills Community College where he lettered in both of his two seasons there…went to St. Francis High School (Ill.) where he was named an all-conference, all-city, all-area, all-state and the conference "Player of the Year" in baseball during his senior year…batted .420 during his team's regional championship season in 2003…was also all-conference and all-city selection in football…was selected in the 35th round of the 2005 First-Year Player Draft by Arizona but did not sign.

KUO, Fu-Lin – INF

HT: 6-0; **WT:** 195; **B:** R; **T:** R; **BORN:** 1/57/91 in Tainan City, Taiwan; **RESIDES:** Tainan City, Taiwan; **OBTAINED:** Signed by the Yankees as a free agent on 12/1/09; **M.L. SVC:** 0.000; **CAREER NOTES: 2010:** Made his professional debut with the GCL Yankees…in 42 games batted .243 (33-for-136) with 4 doubles, 4HR and 23RBI…led all GCL third basemen with 16E…**PERSONAL:** Graduated from Nan-Ying High School in Tainan City…was a member of the 2008 IBAF Taiwanese youth national team.

LANDONI, Emerson Jose – INF

HT: 5-11; **WT:** 180; **B:** S; **T:** R; **BORN:** 2/19/89 in Maracay, Venezuela; **RESIDES:** El Tigrito, Venezuela; **OBTAINED:** Signed by the Yankees as a free agent on 10/18/07; **M.L. SVC:** 0.000; **CAREER NOTES: 2010:** With Single-A Charleston, batted .280 (73-for-261) with 13 doubles, 3HR and 32RBI in 84 games…hit .321 (25-for-78) with 8 doubles, 2HR and 14RBI off left-handed pitching…**2009:** Played at three different levels, combining to bat .217 with 1 double, 1 triple and 12RBI…**2008:** Hit .310 (31-for-100) with 15R, 1HR and 8RBI in 36 games with the GCL Yankees…hit his first home run on 8/11 at the GCL Phillies…signed by Florida as a non-drafted free agent on 12/1/05 and played with their Venezuela Summer League team in 2006, appearing in games at 2B, 3B and SS…did not play in 2007 after he was released by the Marlins on 5/18/07.

LARE, Trent – LHP

HT: 6-3; **WT:** 238; **B:** L; **T:** L; **BORN:** 8/29/84 in Edgerton, Kan.; **RESIDES:** Edgerton, Kan.; **COLLEGE:** Emporia State University; **OBTAINED:** Signed by the Yankees as a minor league free agent on 6/18/09; **M.L. SVC:** 0.000; **CAREER NOTES:** **2010:** Played the entire season with Single-A Tampa and went 1-2 with a 4.00 ERA, recording 73K and allowing 33ER in 74.1IP over 42 games (1 start)…lone start came on 5/21 vs. Palm Beach, tossing 4.0 scoreless innings (3H, 1K) in the no-decision…**2009:** Combined to go 5-5 with a 2.19 ERA in 14 appearances (13 starts) with short-season Single-A Staten Island, Single-A Charleston and Single-A Tampa…struck out 75 batters while walking just 10…began the season with Staten Island, going 3-2 with a 1.07 ERA in six starts…did not allow an earned run in four of those six outings…was transferred to Single-A Charleston on 7/21 and went 2-3 with a 2.76 ERA in seven starts…tossed a season-high 7.2IP on 8/24 at Augusta (4H, 1R, 0ER, 1BB, 8K)…was transferred to Tampa on 8/31, allowing 2ER in 2.0IP in one relief appearance (9.00 ERA)…**2008:** Pitched for the Kalamazoo Kings of the independent Frontier League, going 8-5 with a 4.13 ERA in 21 appearances (19 starts)…**2007:** Went 5-4 with a 3.17 ERA in 12 games (11 starts) for the independent Kalamazoo Kings…**PERSONAL:** Full name is Trenton Lare…graduated Emporia State University where he went 9-3 with a 3.00 ERA in 13 starts (78.0IP, 26ER), earning second team All-MIAA recognition as a senior…was also named to the All-Central Region's Second Team…led the team with 74K…prior to ESU, attended Coffeyville Community College and Oklahoma State University.

LASSITER, Garrison Lane – INF

HT: 6-1; **WT:** 200; **B:** L; **T:** R; **BORN:** 12/22/89 in High Point, N.C.; **RESIDES:** Tampa, Fla.; **OBTAINED:** Selected by the Yankees in the 27th Round of the 2008 First-year Player Draft; **M.L. SVC:** 0.000; **CAREER NOTES:** **2010:** Split the season between Single-A Charleston and short-season Single-A Staten Island, batting .209 (44-for-211)…**2009:** Spent the season with Single-A Charleston, batting .260 with 12 doubles, 1 triple, 2HR and 29RBI in 74 games…was on the disabled list from 5/6-6/8 with a right shoulder strain…played in one rehab game with the GCL Yankees…**2008:** Made his professional debut with the GCL Yankees, batting .261 with 6H and 2RBI in six games.

LEONORA, Ericson – OF

HT: 5-11; **WT:** 174; **B:** R; **T:** R; **BORN:** 8/25/92 in Punto Fijo, Venezuela; **RESIDES:** Punto Fijo, Venezuela; **OBTAINED:** Signed by the Yankees as a non-drafted free agent on 8/25/08; **M.L. SVC:** 0.000; **CAREER NOTES:** **2010:** Appeared in a career high 68 games for the DSL Yankees 1, batting .272 (67-for-246) with 8 doubles, 2 triples, 2HR and 27RBI…hit .429 (21-for-49) against left-handed pitching with 4 doubles, 1 triple and 5RBI…**2009:** Made his professional debut and batted .286 with 25 extra-base hits (12 doubles, nine triples, 4HR) and 39RBI in 61 games with the DSL Yankees 1…recorded a career-high 12-game hitting streak from 7/9–24, hitting .393 (22-for-56) with three doubles, two triples and 1HR over the stretch.

LESLIE, Myron – INF

HT: 6-3; **WT:** 240; **B:** S; **T:** R; **BORN:** 5/2/82 in Panama City, Fla.; **RESIDES:** Tampa, Fla.; **OBTAINED:** Signed by the Yankees as minor league free agent on 3/2/10; **M.L. SVC:** 0.000; **CAREER NOTES:** **2010:** Played in 80 games with Single-A Tampa and batted .262 (68-for-260) with 14 doubles, 6HR and 39RBI…**2009:** Hit .272 (86-for-316) with 10 doubles, three triples, 18HR and 75RBI with the New Jersey Jackals of the Independent League…**2008:** Batted .248 (91-for-367) with 18 doubles, 10HR and 43RBI in 108 games with the Midland RockHounds of the Oakland Athletics organization…**2007:** Played in 108 games with Midland and hit .288 (111-for-386) with 28 doubles, 5HR and 47RBI…**2006:** In 136 games with the Stockton Ports of the A's system, hit .273 (140-for-513) with 17HR, and a career-high 100RBI…**2005:** Played in 131 games with the Kane County Cougars in the Oakland system, hitting .275 (130-for-472) with a career-high 32 doubles, 15HR and 68RBI, earning a spot on the Midwest League's mid-season All-Star squad…**2004:** Made his professional debut and batted .245 (67-for-273) with 12 doubles and 28RBI in 73 games with the Vancouver Canadians of the A's system…**PERSONAL:** Was originally selected by the Oakland Athletics in the eighth round of the 2004 First-Year Player Draft..

LEWIS, Fred – LHP

HT: 6-1; **WT:** 204; **B:** L; **T:** L; **BORN:** 12/16/86 in Gainesville, Fla.; **RESIDES:** Hawthorne, Fla.; **COLLEGE:** Tennessee Wesleyan College; **OBTAINED:** Selected by the Yankees in the 47th round of the 2010 First-Year Player Draft; **M.L. SVC:** 0.000; **CAREER NOTES:** **2010:** Made his professional debut with short-season Single-A Staten Island, and went 1-0 with a 2.45 ERA in five appearances…transferred to the GCL Yankees on 7/15, where he went 0-1 with a 2.25 ERA in nine appearances, recording 15K in 12.0IP.

LICCIEN, Jhorge Ramon – C

HT: 5-11; **WT:** 188; **B:** R; **T:** R; **BORN:** 10/10/90 in Tucupita, Venezuela; **RESIDES:** Barrana del Orinoco, Venezuela; **OBTAINED:** Signed as a non-drafted free agent on 7/2/07; **M.L. SVC:** 0.000; **CAREER NOTES:** **2010:** Started the season with the GCL Yankees, and batted .215 (17-for-79) with 5 doubles, 1 triple, 1HR and 14RBI in 27 games…made final two apearances with Single-A Charleston (.200, 1-for-5)…**2009:** Appeared in 29 games with the DSL Yankees 2 and hit .100 with 7BB…**2008:** Batted .274 with 3HR and 22RBI in 56 games in his professional debut with the DSL Yankees 2…recorded an 11-game hitting streak from 7/1-18…committed just one error in 46 appearances at catcher.

LOPEZ, Daniel Jhonfary – OF

HT: 6-2; **WT:** 175; **B:** R; **T:** R; **BORN:** 1/17/92 in Santiago, D.R.; **RESIDES:** Santiago, D.R.; **OBTAINED:** Signed by the Yankees as a non-drafted free agent on 7/13/09; **M.L. SVC:** 0.000; **CAREER NOTES:** **2010:** Appeared in 70 games with the DSL Yankees 2, batting .293 (79-for-270) with 10 doubles, 6 triples, 1HR, 33RBI and 17SB…led the team in games, runs (40) and stolen bases…**2009:** Made his professional debut, batting .259 (14-for-54) with 2 doubles, 2 triples and 7RBI in 18 games with the DSL Yankees 2.

LOPEZ, Jerison – INF

HT: 5-11; **WT:** 177; **B:** R; **T:** R; **BORN:** 8/24/91 in San Pedro de Macoris, D.R.; **RESIDES:** San Pedro de Macoris, D.R.; **OBTAINED:** Signed by the Yankees as a non-drafted free agent on 4/22/09; **M.L. SVC:** 0.000; **CAREER NOTES:** **2010:** Hit .243 (28-for-115) with 25R, 8 doubles and 10RBI in 45 games with the DSL Yankees 1…struck out only 17 times…appeared in games at 1B, 2B, 3B, OF and C…**2009:** Made his professional debut, hitting .238 with 8 doubles, 3 triples, 3HR and 33 RBI in 58 games with the DSL Yankees 1…recorded 15 multi-hit games.

LOPEZ, Jose – C

HT: 5-10; **WT:** 178; **B:** R; **T:** R; **BORN:** 8/13/91 in San Francisco, Zulia, Venezuela; **RESIDES:** San Francisco, Zulia, Venezuela; **OBTAINED:** Signed by the Yankees as a non-drafted free agent on 4/14/10; **M.L. SVC:** 0.000; **CAREER NOTES:** **2010:** Appeared in 16 games with the DSL Yankees 2, batting .214 (6-for-28)…caught 7-of-19 potential base stealers (36.8%).

LYERLY, Robert – INF

HT: 6-1; **WT:** 200; **B:** L; **T:** R; **BORN:** 7/23/87 in Indian Trail, N.C.; **RESIDES:** Indian Trail, N.C.; **COLLEGE:** UNC-Charlotte; **OBTAINED:** Selected by the Yankees in the sixth round of the 2009 First-Year Player Draft; **M.L. SVC:** 0.000; **CAREER NOTES: 2010:** Played the entire season with Single-A Charleston, batting .312 (157-for-503) with 36 doubles, 7HR and 71RBI in 131 games…finished third in the South Atlantic League in both batting average and hits and was the lone RiverDogs player to be named to the SAL postseason All-Star team…hit .324 (122-for-377) with 25 doubles, 5HR and 56RBI off left-right handed pitching and .333 (49-for-147) with 62RBI with runners in scoring position…**2009:** Made his professional debut with the short-season Single-A Staten Island Yankees, batting .268 with 8 doubles and 7RBI and appearing in games at 1B (two) and 3B (18).

MACK, DeAngelo – OF

HT: 5-8; **WT:** 190; **B:** L; **T:** L; **BORN:** 11/19/86 in West Columbia, S.C.; **RESIDES:** West Columbia, S.C.; **COLLEGE:** University of South Carolina; **OBTAINED:** Selected by the Yankees in the 13th round of the 2009 First-Year Player Draft **M.L. SVC:** 0.000; **CAREER NOTES: 2010:** Appeared in 116 games with Single-A Charleston, batting .252 (107-for-424) with 20 doubles, 5 triples, 12HR and 56RBI…led the team in HR…**2009:** Made his professional debut with short-season Single-A Staten Island, batting .306 with 19 doubles, 4 triples, 7HR and 41RBI in 66 games…ranked second in the NYPL in extra-base hits (30), tied for third in total bases (119), placed fifth in slugging (.513) and sixth in average and was a member of the midseason All-Star team…**PERSONAL:** Selected as a Second-Team All-SEC in 2009 at USC…graduated from Airport HS (S.C.) where he was an All-State selection his junior and senior seasons.

MADRIGAL, Warner Antonio – RHP   NON-ROSTER INVITEE

HT: 6-1; **WT:** 235; **B:** R; **T:** R; **BORN:** 3/1/84 in San Pedro de Macoris, D.R.; **RESIDES:** San Pedro de Macoris, D.R.; **OBTAINED:** Signed as a minor league free agent on 2/10/11; **M.L. SVC:** 0.164; **CAREER NOTES:** Has made 44 career Major League appearances (one start)–all with the Texas Rangers–going 0-2 with a 6.10 ERA…originally signed with the Angels as an un-drafted free agent on 7/21/01 as an outfielder…hit .272 (300-for-1102) with 63 doubles, 34HR and 158RBI in six seasons before converting to pitcher during the 2006 season…**2010:** Combined at Double-A Frisco and Triple-A Oklahoma City to go 5-2 with three saves and a 3.73 ERA (50.2IP, 21ER)…struck out 42 batters with only 14BB and held opponents to a .215 (41-for-191) batting average…opened the season on the 15-day disabled list with right forearm inflammation and was transferred to the 60-day D.L. on 4/8…following an eight-game rehab stint with Frisco, spent the rest of the season with Oklahoma City appearing in 27 games in relief…following the season, made two relief appearances with the Toros del Este in the Dominican Winter League…was limited to one spring training appearance, experiencing forearm soreness…underwent MRI on 3/15 that was negative…**2009:** Appeared in 13 games over five stints (4/4-14; 5/16-6/2; 6/14-16; 7/30-8/1 and 9/1-10/4) with the Rangers, posting a 9.95 ERA with no decisions…made his first Opening Day roster…spent remainder of the season with Triple-A Oklahoma, going 0-2 with 17 saves and a 2.57 ERA in 42 appearances…led the team in saves and ranked second in games…**2008:** Saw his first Major League action, going 0-2 with a 4.75 ERA in 31 appearances (one start)…recalled from triple-A Oklahoma City on 6/28 and made his Major League debut in 7/2 loss at the original Yankee Stadium, allowing 6ER in 0.1IP…marked the third time in club history a reliever allowed six-or-more runs in a ML debut…had a 3.28 ERA (13 ER/35.2 IP) over his final 30 games following debut…made only start in a bullpen-by-committee effort in 7/9 win vs. Los Angeles-AL, allowing 1ER in 3.0IP…recorded only ML save on 9/9 at Seattle…**2007:** Went 5-4 with 20 saves and a 2.07 ERA in 54 appearances, striking out 75 batters in 61.0IP…ranked among the Midwest League leaders in games (3rd, 54), games finished (3rd, 40), and saves (4th, 20) at Single-A Cedar Rapids in first full season on the mound and final season in Angels organization…held opponents to a .202 batting average, third lowest among MWL relievers, while his 11.07 K/9.0IP ratio was second highest for in the league…following the season, did not allow an earned run in 3.2 IP over 6 relief appearances for Escogido in Dominican Winter League…**2006:** Began year as outfielder with Cedar Rapids, but started conversion to pitching less than 2 months into the season…played final game as a position player on 5/5 at Quad Cities…was transferred to the AZL Angels on 6/13, where he went 2-1 with a 3.75 ERA in his first action on the mound…tossed 1.0 scoreless inning in his pitching debut on 7/20 at AZL Mariners…**2005:** Hit .247 (100-for-405) with 21 doubles, 15HR and 53RBI in 111 games at Cedar Rapids…**2004:** Was limited to 26 games with Cedar Rapids, missing nearly 4 months after suffering a stress fracture of the hamate bone in left hand on 4/8…remained on the disabled list until 8/6…**2003:** Hit .369 (103-for-279) with 28 doubles, 9HR and 51RBI over 70 games for short-season Single-A Provo…led the Pioneer League in hits (103), total bases (162), slugging (.581), runs (75), extra-base hits (39), and doubles (28)…**2002:** Batted .229 (32-for-140) in 42 games for Dominican Summer League Angels…**2001:** Made his professional debut with the DSL Angels, batting .181 (13-for-72) in 22 games.

MAHONEY, Kevin – INF

HT: 6-0; **WT:** 211; **B:** L; **T:** R; **BORN:** 5/11/87 in Miller Place, N.Y.; **RESIDES:** Coram, N.Y.; **COLLEGE:** Canisius College; **OBTAINED:** Selected by the Yankees in the 23rd round of the 2009 First-Year Player Draft; **M.L. SVC:** 0.000; **CAREER NOTES: 2010:** Combined to hit .286 (68-for-238) with 16 doubles, 2 triples, 8HR and 31RBI in 73 games with short season Single-A Staten Island, Single-A Charleston, Single-A Tampa and Double-A Trenton…spent the majority of the season with Staten Island, batting .276 (37-for-134) with 6HR and 22RBI…was promoted to Charleston on 8/2 where he hit .298 (25-for-84) with 8 doubles, 2HR and 7RBI, reaching base safely in 19 of his 26 games played with the RiverDogs…**2009:** Made his professional debut with the GCL Yankees, batting .226 with 17 doubles, 6HR and 30RBI in 57 games…played the second-most games in the GCL, tied for second in the league in doubles, tied for fourth in extra-base hits (24)…led all league third basemen with a .954 fielding percentage (8E, 173TC)…hit a grand slam on 8/3 at the GCL Phillies…**PERSONAL:** While at Canisius, selected as the 2009 MAAC "Player of the Year," 2008 Rawlings "Coastal Plains Offensive Player of the Year"…left as the school's all-time career leader in runs (202), hits (317) and RBI (130)…lettered in football, basketball and baseball at Miller Place High School…named All-State, All-County and league MVP as a senior in 2005.

MARSHALL, Brett – RHP

HT: 5-11; **WT:** 191; **B:** R; **T:** R; **BORN:** 3/22/90 in Highlands, Tex.; **RESIDES:** Highlands, Tex.; **OBTAINED:** Selected by the Yankees in the sixth round of the 2008 First-Year Player Draft; **M.L. SVC:** 0.000; **CAREER NOTES: 2010:** Combined to go 4-2 with a 2.57 ERA (84.0IP, 24ER) in 36 games (35 starts) with Single-A Charleston, Single-A Charleston and Single-A Tampa…spent the majority of the year with Charleston, where he was 4-2 with a 2.50 ERA, making 13 starts and allowing 20ER in 72.0IP…made one postseason start for Tampa (Game 2 of the Championship round) and earned the victory, striking out five batters and allowing 2ER in 6.0IP (3H)…**2009:** Went 3-6 with a 5.56 ERA in 17 starts with Single-A Charleston…held lefthanders to a .231 batting average…season was cut short on 7/17 when he was placed on disabled list for the remainder of the season with right elbow tendinitis…**2008:** Made his professional debut with the GCL Yankees, holding opponents to only one unearned run and two hits in three starts (6.0IP)…**PERSONAL:** Graduated from Ross Sterling (Tex.) High School…named the 2008 All-Greater Houston "Player of the Year" by the *Houston Chronicle*…went 10-2 with a 2.27 ERA and 116 strikeouts as a senior…also served as the cleanup hitter, batting .440 with 10HR and 49RBI…signed a letter of intent at Rice University…has a brother (Chris) who serves in the Army.

MARTE, Joel – RHP

HT: 5-10; **WT:** 212; **B:** R; **T:** R; **BORN:** 1/18/88 in Santiago, D.R.; **RESIDES:** Santiago, D.R.; **OBTAINED:** Signed by the Yankees as a non-drafted free agent on 6/1/07; **M.L. SVC:** 0.000; **CAREER NOTES: 2010:** Made 18 appearances with the GCL Yankees, going 0-2 with two saves and a 3.43 ERA…**2009:** Made 20 relief appearances with the DSL Yankees 2, going 4-2 with a 3.89 ERA…recorded 43K in 39.1IP and threw 2.0IP or more in nine of his 20 outings…**2008:** Appeared in 15 games (nine starts) with the DSL Yankees 1, going 1-4 with a 3.02 ERA…allowed 2ER or less in eight of his nine starts…**2007:** Made his professional debut with the DSL Yankees 1, going 5-2 with a 4.04 ERA in 14 appearances (six starts)…struck out 58 batters in only 49.0IP, including a career-high 8K in 7/28 win vs. the DSL Blue Jays (4.0IP).

MARTE, Ronny – RHP

HT: 6-1; **WT:** 173; **B:** R; **T:** R; **BORN:** 2/26/86 in Las Guaras, D.R.; **RESIDES:** San Pedro de Macoris, D.R.; **OBTAINED:** Signed by the Yankees as a non-drafted free agent on 7/22/04; **M.L. SVC:** 0.000; **CAREER NOTES: 2010:** Combined to go 3-3 with a 3.09 ERA (70.0IP, 24ER) in 44 games (two starts) with Single-A Charleston and Single-A Tampa…spent the majority of the year with Charleston, going 2-3 with a 3.13 ERA in 35 games (two starts), and allowing 19ER in 54.2IP…compiled eight consecutive outings without allowing an ER from 4/21-5/10 (10.0IP)…**2009:** Opened the season with Single-A Tampa, making two relief appearances before being transferred to short-season Staten Island for the remainder of the season…ranked third in the New York-Penn League in appearances (31), converting seven of 10 save opportunities…**2008:** Combined to go 4-2 with one save and a 3.53 ERA in 18 appearances (two starts) with the GCL Yankees and Tampa…began the season with the GCL Yankees, going 3-1 with one save and a 2.60 ERA in 14 appearances (one start), striking out 26 batters in 27.2IP (5BB)…recorded his first professional save on 7/11 at the GCL Braves…made four appearances with Tampa (one start), going 1-1 with a 6.75 ERA…**2007:** Went 2-1 with a 4.14 ERA in 12 appearances (eight starts) with the DSL Yankees 1…tossed a season-high 6.2 innings in 8/20 (Game 2) win vs. the DSL Reds, allowing 3H (4K)…**2006:** Made 18 relief appearances for the DSL Yankees 1 and posted a 3-1 record with a 3.34 ERA…**2005:** In sophomore campaign, posted a 2-1 record with a 4.22 ERA in 10 games with the Yankees' Dominican Summer League 1 squad…**2004:** Made professional debut with the DSL Yankees 2, posting an 0-6 record with an 8.63 ERA.

MARTINEZ , Daniel – LHP

HT: 6-3; **WT:** 190; **B:** L; **T:** L; **BORN:** 6/4/90 in Maracay, Venezuela; **RESIDES:** Turmero, Venezuela; **OBTAINED:** Signed by the Yankees as a minor league free agent on 11/18/10; **M.L. SVC:** 0.000; **CAREER NOTES: 2010:** With the VSL Reds went 0-0 with a 4.32 ERA in 16.2IP over eight appearances (two starts)…was released by Cincinnati on 7/14…signed with the Yankees on 11/18 and will make his debut in the Yankees minor league system in 2011…**2009:** Finished the season 2-4 with a 4.21 ERA in 18 games with 36.1IP…recorded one save in two opportunities…**2008:** With the DSL Reds went 3-1 with a 2.00 ERA in 16 appearances (five starts) with 45.0IP…**2007:** Signed a first year minor league contract with the VSL Reds, went 0-3 with a 5.53 ERA in 14 games (13 starts).

MARTINEZ, Richard Jesus – RHP

HT: 6-0; **WT:** 220; **B:** R; **T:** R; **BORN:** 7/19/88 in Turmero, Venezuela; **RESIDES:** Turmero, Venezuela; **OBTAINED:** Signed by the Yankees as a non-drafted free agent on 11/18/05; **M.L. SVC:** 0.000; **CAREER NOTES: 2010:** Made 16 appearances (two starts) with short-season Single-A Staten Island, going 4-1 with a 1.69 ERA and 34K in 32.0IP…held opponents to a .191 average (22-for-151), with right-handers batting .160 (12-for-75, 1HR)…final two outings came as a starter, tossing 9.0 combined scoreless IP…**2009:** Missed the season after undergoing an appendectomy on 6/22…**2008:** Was 0-3 with a 4.50 ERA in six relief appearances for the GCL Yankees…**2007:** Was 2-3 with a 4.67 ERA in 13 appearances (eight starts) with the DSL Yankees 1…tossed 3.2 hitless innings in his first appearance of the season on 6/6 at the DSL Diamondbacks (4BB, 4K)…**2006:** Made professional debut with the DSL Yankees 1, going 3-4 with a 4.72 ERA in 14 games (nine starts).

MARTINI, Renzo – INF

HT: 6-1; **WT:** 190; **B:** R; **T:** R; **BORN:** 8/25/92 in Valera, Venezuela; **RESIDES:** Valera, Venezuela; **OBTAINED:** Signed as a minor league free agent on 8/16/10; **M.L. SVC:** 0.000; **CAREER NOTES:** Will make his professional debut in 2011.

MARUSZAK, Addison – INF

HT: 6-1; **WT:** 190; **B:** R; **T:** R; **BORN:** 12/21/86 in Pinellas Park, Fla.; **RESIDES:** Pinellas Park, Fla.; **COLLEGE:** University of South Florida; **OBTAINED:** Selected by the Yankees in the 17th round of the 2008 First-Year Player Draft; **M.L. SVC:** 0.000; **CAREER NOTES: 2010:** Played in 70 combined games with the GCL Yankees and Single-Tampa, batting .287 (72-for-251) with 17 doubles, 1HR and 36RBI…spent the majority of the season with Tampa, hitting .284 (69-for-243) with 16 doubles, 1HR and 34RBI in 68 games…missed time on the disabled list from 6/17-8/4 after spraining his right ankle…**2009:** Combined to hit .232 with 5 doubles, 1 triple, 2HR and 24RBI in 88 games with Single-A Tampa and Single-A Charleston…**2008:** Made his professional debut, batting .317 with 30R, 9 doubles, 6HR and 25RBI in 44 games with short-season Single-A Staten Island…hit safely in 34 of his 44 games, never going more than two consecutive games without a hit…was named to the New York-Penn League midseason All-Star team…hit .341 (14-for-41, 6HR) off right-handed pitching and .310 (39-for-126, 0HR) off lefties…was placed on the disabled list from 6/27-7/9 with a sprained right knee and again from 8/19-9/5 with a right hip contusion…recorded a 10-game hitting streak from 8/1-11, batting .405 (17-for-42) with 11R, 2 doubles, 2 triples, 1HR and 6RBI…hit .556 (5-for-9) with 1 double and 3RBI in two postseason games…**PERSONAL:** Full name is Addison John Maruszak…attended the University of South Florida where he majored in pre-business administration…hit .364 with 55R, 12 doubles, 6HR and 32RBI in 58 games during his junior year, ranking second on the team in batting average (33BB, 20K)…played for the Bourne Braves of the Cape Cod League in 2007, batting .278 with 14R, 1HR, 17RBI and 4SB…was named Big East "Rookie of the Year" and a Louisville Slugger Freshman All-American in 2006…attended St. Petersburg Catholic High School where he was a four-year letter-winner…was named team captain during his senior year…graduated sixth in his class.

MATEO, Andres – RHP

HT: 5-11; **WT:** 200; **B:** R; **T:** R; **BORN:** 4/24/91 in Santo Domingo, D.R.; **RESIDES:** Santo Domingo, D.R.; **OBTAINED:** Signed as a minor league free agent on 7/1/10; **M.L. SVC:** 0.000; **CAREER NOTES: 2010:** Made his professional debut with the DSL Yankees 2, going 1-1 with a 15.88 ERA in seven relief appearances.

MATOS, Guillermo – INF
HT: 6-2; **WT:** 210; **B:** R; **T:** R; **BORN:** 10/26/91 in Santo Domingo, D.R.; **RESIDES:** Santo Domingo, D.R.; **OBTAINED:** Signed as a minor league free agent on 3/20/10; **M.L. SVC:** 0.000; **CAREER NOTES: 2010:** Made his professional debut with the DSL Yankees 2, batting .143 (14-for-98) with 5 doubles, 2HR and 6RBI in 31 games.

MATOS, Juan – RHP
HT: 6-2; **WT:** 190; **B:** R; **T:** R; **BORN:** 10/6/93 in Santo Domingo, D.R.; **RESIDES:** Santo Domingo, D.R.; **OBTAINED:** Signed as a minor league free agent on 9/16/10; **M.L. SVC:** 0.000; **CAREER NOTES:** Will make his professional debut in 2011.

MCCOY, Nick – C
HT: 5-9; **WT:** 170; **B:** R; **T:** R; **BORN:** 3/2/87 in San Diego, Calif.; **RESIDES:** San Diego, Calif.; **COLLEGE:** University of San Diego; **OBTAINED:** Selected by the Yankees in the 36th round of the 2010 First-Year Player Draft; **M.L. SVC:** 0.000; **CAREER NOTES: 2010:** Made his professional debut with short-season Single-A Staten Island, batting .237 (14-for-59) with 4 doubles and 7RBI in 20 games…**PERSONAL:** Graduated from Westview High School in San Diego, California…finished his senior year at the University of San Diego hitting .315 (58-for-184) with 9 doubles, 4HR and 35RBI in 54 games.

MEDCHILL, Neil – OF
HT: 6-3; **WT:** 210; **B:** L; **T:** R; **BORN:** 6/25/87 in Oxford, Mich.; **RESIDES:** Henderson, Nev.; **COLLEGE:** Oklahoma State University; **OBTAINED:** Selected by the Yankees in the 11th round of the 2009 First-Year Player Draft; **M.L. SVC:** 0.000; **CAREER NOTES: 2010:** Combined to hit .199 (83-for-417) with 15 doubles, 2 triples, 12HR and 53RBI in 116 games with Single-A Charleston and Single-A Tampa…closed out the season with Charleston, where he batted .215 (51-for-237) with 9HR and 32 RBI in 65 games…**2009:** Made his professional debut, hitting .278 with 13 doubles, 14HR and 41RBI in 62 games with short-season Single-A Staten Island…finished the season ranked first in the New York-Penn League in HR and slugging (.551) and third in extra-base hits (29)…awarded the NYPL "Player of the Week" on 7/20 and was named to the league's midseason All-Star team…**PERSONAL:** Attended Chandler-Gilbert Community College for two years before transferring to OSU, and was a National Junior College All-American as a freshman, becoming the first baseball to earn the honor in the school's history…was previously drafted by the Los Angeles Angels in 2005 (30th round) and New York Mets in 2008 (33rd round)…graduated from Lake Orion High School (MI) where he played baseball and basketball and earned first-team all-state as a senior.

MEDO, Yheraldy – INF
HT: 6-1; **WT:** 200; **B:** R; **T:** R; **BORN:** 7/8/91 in San Pedro de Macoris, D.R.; **RESIDES:** San Pedro de Macoris, D.R.; **OBTAINED:** Signed as a minor league free agent on 12/8/10; **M.L. SVC:** 0.000; **CAREER NOTES:** Will make his professional debut in 2011.

MEJIA, Edison – RHP
HT: 6-1; **WT:** 185; **B:** R; **T:** R; **BORN:** 7/2/90 in Bienvenido, D.R.; **RESIDES:** Bienvenido, D.R.; **OBTAINED:** Signed by the Yankees as a non-drafted free agent on 6/18/08; **M.L. SVC:** 0.000; **CAREER NOTES: 2010:** With the DSL Yankees 1, went 3-2 with a 2.96 ERA in 12 games (four starts)…**2009:** Went 0-3 with a 4.50 ERA in 12 games (eight starts) with the DSL Yankees 2…**2008:** In his professional debut, went 1-1 with a 2.90 ERA in 10 games (five starts) with the DSL Yankees 1.

MERCEDES, Melvin – RHP
HT: 6-3; **WT:** 170; **B:** R; **T:** R; **BORN:** 8/28/89 in Municipio Mata Palacio, D.R.; **RESIDES:** Municipio Mata Palacio, D.R.; **OBTAINED:** Signed as a minor league free agent on 1/27/10; **M.L. SVC:** 0.000; **CAREER NOTES: 2010:** Made his professional debut with the DSL Yankees 2, going 1-5 with one save and a 3.05 ERA in 15 games (11 starts)…ranked third on the team in strikeouts (43).

MITCHELL, Bryan – RHP
HT: 6-2; **WT:** 193; **B:** L; **T:** R; **BORN:** 4/19/91 in Pensacola, Fla.; **RESIDES:** Pensacola, Fla.; **OBTAINED:** Selected by the Yankees in the 16th round of the 2009 First-Year Player Draft; **M.L. SVC:** 0.000; **CAREER NOTES: 2010:** Made his professional debut with the GCL Yankees, and went 2-1 with a 3.67 ERA in 10 appearances (nine starts)…recorded 36K in 41.2IP…was transferred to short-season Single-A Staten Island on 9/1 for one appearance, taking the loss.

MITCHELL, D.J. – RHP   NON-ROSTER INVITEE
HT: 6-0; **WT:** 160; **B:** R; **T:** R; **BORN:** 5/13/87 in Winston-Salem, N.C.; **RESIDES:** Rural Hall, N.C.; **COLLEGE:** Clemson University; **OBTAINED:** Selected by the Yankees in the 10th round of the 2008 First-Year Player Draft; **M.L. SVC:** 0.000; **CAREER NOTES: 2010:** Began the season with Double-A Trenton where he went 11-4 with a 4.06 ERA (133.0IP, 60ER) in 23 games (22 starts), holding batters to a .183 (26-for-142) average with runners in scoring position…was one of two Thunder pitchers named to the midseason All-Star team…was promoted to Triple-A Scranton/Wilkes-Barre on 8/23, where he made three starts, going 2-0 with a 3.57 ERA (17.2IP, 7ER)…made one start for Scranton/WB during the postseason and recorded a no-decision, allowing 3ER on 8H in 5.0IP (4R, 2BB, 4K, 1HR)…**2009:** Made his professional debut, combining to go 12-7 with a 2.63 ERA in 25 appearances (24 starts) for Single-A Charleston and Single-A Tampa…ranked second among all Yankees minor leaguers in strikeouts (125), tied for second in wins and ranked fourth in ERA…began the season with Charleston, going 4-1 with a 1.95 ERA in six starts…won each of his first four decisions from 4/10-5/1…was transferred to Tampa on 5/13 where he remained for the rest of the season, going 8-6 with a 2.87 ERA in 19 appearances (18 starts)…tossed his first career complete game on 6/18 vs. Palm Beach, taking the loss after allowing 7H and 5ER in 7.0IP (2BB, 7K)…**2008:** Was placed on the 60-day disabled list on 8/19 with a right oblique muscle strain before appearing in a game…**PERSONAL:** Full name is William Douglas Mitchell, Jr…attended Clemson University where he went 6-5 with a 3.47 ERA in 20 appearances (14 starts) while leading all team starters in ERA and tying for the team-lead in games started (98.2IP, 97H, 49R, 38ER, 40BB, 106K, 5HR) in 2008…made the transition from position player to pitcher during the 2007 season…played for the Bourne Braves of the Cape Cod League in 2007, going 1-2 with a 1.47 ERA in eight starts (49.0IP, 36H, 8ER, 23BB, 58K)…appeared in *Sports Illustrated*'s "Faces in the Crowd" edition on 9/3/07 for leading the Cape Cod League in strikeouts…attended North Forsyth Senior High School (N.C.) where he was a three-time all-conference pick…also lettered four times in baseball and twice in basketball.

MOJICA, Deivi – RHP

HT: 6-1; **WT:** 165; **B:** R; **T:** R; **BORN:** 1/19/90 in San Cristobal, D.R.; **RESIDES:** San Cristobal, D.R.; **OBTAINED:** Signed by the Yankees as a non-drafted free agent on 6/19/08; **M.L. SVC:** 0.000; **CAREER NOTES: 2010:** With the DSL Yankees 1, went 8-2 with a 2.00 ERA in 13 games (two starts)…led the team in wins, tying for second in the DSL…**2009:** Went 2-4 with a 3.17 ERA in 14 games (11 starts) with the DSL Yankees 2, striking out 64 batters in 59.2IP…held the opposition to 3ER or less in each of his starts…**2008:** In his professional debut with the DSL Yankees 1, was 1-4 with a 5.45 ERA in 12 games (six starts).

MOJICA, Jose – INF

HT: 6-0; **WT:** 172; **B:** R; **T:** R; **BORN:** 12/26/88 in Bani, D.R.; **RESIDES:** Bani, D.R.; **OBTAINED:** Signed by the Yankees as a non-drafted free agent on 7/2/07; **M.L. SVC:** 0.000; **CAREER NOTES: 2010:** Batted .241 (45-for-187) with 10 doubles and 12RBI in 53 games with short-season Single-A Staten Island…**2009:** Made his professional debut, batting .278 with 18R, 11 doubles, 2 triples, 1HR and 22RBI in 55 games with the GCL Yankees.

MOJICA, Miguel – OF

HT: 6-2; **WT:** 180; **B:** R; **T:** R; **BORN:** 8/23/92 in San Pedro de Macoris, D.R.; **RESIDES:** San Pedro de Macoris, D.R.; **OBTAINED:** Signed as a minor league free agent on 9/21/10; **M.L. SVC:** 0.000; **CAREER NOTES:** Will make his professional debut in 2011.

MOLINA, Gustavo – C   NON-ROSTER INVITEE

HT: 6-1; **WT:** 245; **B:** R; **T:** R; **BORN:** 2/24/82 in La Guaira, Venezuela; **RESIDES:** La Guaira, Venezuela; **OBTAINED:** Signed by the Yankees as a minor league free agent on 12/18/10; **M.L. SVC:** 0.132; **CAREER NOTES:** Has played in 23 career Major League games with Chicago-AL (2007), Baltimore (2007), New York-NL (2008) and Boston (2010), making 11 starts at catcher…owns a career .122 (5-for-41) batting average at the Major League level…was originally signed by Chicago-AL as a non-drafted free agent on 1/3/00…**2010:** Spent the majority of the year with Triple-A Pawtucket, batting .241 (27-for-112) with 8HR and 18RBI in 35 games…also played in four games with the Red Sox, going 1-for-7 (.143)…**2009:** Did not play at the Major League level for the first time since 2006, appearing in 72 games with Triple-A Syracuse of the Nationals organization…batted .209 (44-for-211) with 2HR and 24RBI with the Chiefs and threw out 24-of-59 attempted base stealers (41%)…following the season, played in 31 games with the Navegantes del Magallanes of the Venezuelan Winter League, hitting .170 (9-for-53) with 2HR and 8RBI…**2008:** Appeared in two games with The Mets, but spent the majority of the year with Triple-A New Orleans, batting .206 (47-for-228) with 7HR and 27RBI in 74 games…hit .167 (8-for-48) with 3HR and 6RBI in 23 games with the Navegantes of the VWL, following the season…**2007:** Made his Major League debut, combining to play in 17 games with the White Sox and Orioles, batting .111 (3-for-27)…did not make an error in 56 total chances at the Major League level…split the rest of the year with Double-A Bowie (Orioles) and Triple-A Charlotte (White Sox), combining to bat .264 (57-for-216) with eight doubles, 2HR and 15RBI in 65 games…**2006:** Split the season with Double-A Birmingham and Triple-A Charlotte, combining to set minor league career highs in games (113) and at-bats (374)…ranked second in the Southern League, throwing out 44% (37-of-84) potential base stealers…**2005:** Played in 109 games with Single-A Winston-Salem and batted .261 (90-for-345), posting single-season career-highs in runs (38), hits, doubles (20), home runs (11), total bases (145) and walks (47)…**2004:** Combined to hit .214 (39-for-182) with 7HR and 31RBI in 62 games with Winston-Salem and Single-A Kannapolis…**2003:** Played in 96 games with Kannapolis and batted .229 (72-for-315), playing every position in the field but pitcher…**2002:** In 94 games with Kannapolis, hit .226 (70-for-310) with 13 doubles, one triple, 2HR and 34RBI, recording a career-high 7SB…**2001:** Played in 46 games, 40 at the catcher position, with the Bristol Sox and hit .283 (47-for-166) with nine doubles, 2HR and 24RBI…**2000:** Made his professional debut, playing in 31 games with the AZL White Sox, hitting .243 (28-for-115) with 10 doubles and 22RBI…tied for third on the team in doubles…**PERSONAL:** Married (Carla Gutierrez) with one daughter, Andrea Victoria.

MONTERO, Jesus Alejandro – C   NON-ROSTER INVITEE

HT: 6-3; **WT:** 235; **B:** R; **T:** R; **BORN:** 11/28/89 in Guacara, Venezuela; **RESIDES:** Guacara, Venezuela; **OBTAINED:** Signed by the Yankees as a non-drafted free agent on 10/17/06; **M.L. SVC:** 0.000; **CAREER NOTES:** Enters the 2011 season ranked by *Baseball America* as the Yankees' top prospect and the fifth-best prospect in all of Baseball (top catcher)…was also tabbed by the publication as the organization's "Best Hitter for Average" and "Best Power Hitter"…also named the organization's top prospect by *The Sporting News*…**2010:** Spent the entire season with Triple-A Scranton/Wilkes-Barre, where he hit .289 (131-for-453) with 34 doubles, 3 triples, 21HR and 75RBI in 123 games…among all Yankees minor league hitters in 2010, tied for second in batting average, ranked second in home runs and ranked fourth in RBI…led the team in home runs and RBI and ranked third in the IL in extra-base hits (58), tied for third in doubles and ranked fifth in both slugging percentage (.517) and total bases (234)…was named to the league's midseason and postseason All-Star teams…was also named the July Topps "Player of the Month" after hitting .342 (26-for-76) with 7 doubles, 5HR, 15RBI and 18R in 23 games during the month…caught 30-of-129 (23.3%) of potential base stealers and led all IL catchers in games (109), total chances (785), putouts (703) and assists (76)…**2009:** Combined to bat .337 (117-for-347) with 45R, 25 doubles, 17HR and 70RBI in 92 games with Single-A Tampa and Double-A Trenton, ranking fourth among all Yankees minor leaguers in home runs…was named to the midseason All-Star teams with both Tampa and Trenton…began the season with Tampa, batting .356 with 8HR and 37RBI in 48 games…was promoted to Trenton on 6/3 where he hit .317 with 9HR and 33RBI in 44 games…homered in four straight games from 6/28-7/2, including 2HR on 6/30 at Erie…appeared for the World Team in the 2009 Futures Game during All-Star Weekend at St. Louis' Busch Stadium on 7/12…was removed defensively in the third inning on 8/1 at Altoona after being hit by a pitch while behind the plate, fracturing his middle finger…was placed on the disabled list on 8/2 through the end of the season with the injury…**2008:** Hit .326 with 86R, 34 doubles, 17HR and 87RBI in 132 games with Single-A Charleston…owned the eighth-most hits (171) among all minor leaguers and most among any catcher in 2008…led the Yankees organization in batting average, runs, hits and RBI, while ranking fourth in home runs…was named the seventh-best prospect in the South Atlantic League by *Baseball America*…led the SAL and ranked third among all Single-A batters in hits and led all SAL catchers with a .993 fielding percentage (4E, 588TC)…was selected to the midseason All-Star team and the South Atlantic League's postseason All-Star team as the league's top catcher…went 1-for-2 and caught the final four innings in the All-Star Futures Game at Yankee Stadium, playing for the World Team…participated in the SAL All-Star Home Run Derby, totaling 11 homers for a second-place finish…hit .360 (95-for-264) with 49R, 15 doubles, 8HR and 39RBI in 64 road games…recorded a career-high 15-game hitting streak from 7/29-8/13, batting .414 (24-for-58) with 5 doubles, 4HR and 11RBI…attended spring training with the Yankees as a non-roster invitee, hitting a solo-homer in his only at-bat…was named by *Baseball America* as the second-best prospect in the Yankees' system following the season, as well as the organization's "Best Power Hitter"…**2007:** Made his professional debut with the GCL Yankees, batting .280 with 3HR and 19RBI in 33 games…was rated the Yankees' top catching prospect (sixth overall) and the organization's "Best Power Hitter" by *Baseball America*…committed just 1E in 182TC as catcher…went 2-for-5 on 8/31 at the GCL Dodgers, with a game-tying home run to lead the Yankees in the decisive Game 3 win in the GCL Championship.

MORONTA, Eladio – OF

HT: 5-11; **WT:** 175; **B:** R; **T:** R; **BORN:** 12/16/88 in Azua, D.R.; **RESIDES:** Azua, D.R.; **OBTAINED:** Signed by the Yankees as a non-drafted free agent on 11/17/09; **M.L. SVC:** 0.000; **CAREER NOTES: 2010:** Made his professional debut with the DSL Yankees 2…batted .286 (26-for-91) with 5 doubles, 2 triples, 1HR and 5RBI in 26 games…was transferred to the DSL Yankees 1 on 7/17, batting .301 (22-for-73) with 2 doubles, 2HR and 11RBI in 19 games…had an 11-game hit streak from 7/28-8/7, batting .386 (17-for-44) with 3 doubles, 2HR and 7RBI…was transferred to the GCL Yankees on 8/13, where he hit .107 (3-for-28) with 3RBI in nine games.

MORTON, Taylor – RHP

HT: 6-2; **WT:** 195; **B:** R; **T:** R; **BORN:** 12/18/91 in Bartlett, Tenn.; **RESIDES:** Bartlett, Tenn.; **OBTAINED:** Selected by the Yankees in the ninth round of the 2010 First-Year Player Draft; **M.L. SVC:** 0.000; **CAREER NOTES: 2010:** Will make his professional debut in 2011…**PERSONAL:** Graduated from Bartlett High School in Tennessee.

MULLEE, Conor – RHP

HT: 6-3; **WT:** 185; **B:** R; **T:** R; **BORN:** 2/25/88 in Ashburn, Va.; **RESIDES:** Ashburn, Va.; **COLLEGE:** St. Peters College (N.J.); **OBTAINED:** Selected by the Yankees in the 24th round of the 2010 First-Year Player Draft; **M.L. SVC:** 0.000; **CAREER NOTES: 2010:** Saw his first professional action with the GCL Yankees, going 2-1 with one save and a 1.64 ERA in 14 relief appearances…struck out 20 batters in 22.0IP…allowed just 1ER over his final nine outings (15.0IP)…**PERSONAL:** Played four seasons at St. Peters, appearing in all 205 games the team played during his time there…left as the school's all-time leader in games played (205), games started (205), at-bats (743), hits (216), doubles (55), RBIs (141) and total bases (331), ranked second in runs scored (130) and tied for third in home runs (16)…graduated from Broad Run High School (Va.) where he played infield.

MURPHY, J.R. – C

HT: 5-11; **WT:** 195; **B:** S; **T:** R; **BORN:** 5/13/91 in Bradenton, Fla.; **RESIDES:** Bradenton, Fla.; **OBTAINED:** Selected by the Yankees in the second round of the 2009 First-Year Player Draft; **M.L. SVC:** 0.000; **CAREER NOTES: 2010:** Appeared in 87 games with Single-A Charleston (53 starts at C), batting .255 (84-for-330) with 46R, 15 doubles, 2 triples, 7HR, 54RBI and 36BB…caught 20-of-88 (22.7%) potential basestealers…went 3-for-6 with a grand slam, three-run homer and 9RBI in 8/13 win at Hickory, marking his first career multi-homer game and falling 1RBI shy of the SAL single-game record …**2009:** Played in nine games with the GCL Yankees in his professional debut, hitting safely in eight of the contests…following the season, was selected as the Yankees' eighth-best prospect by *Baseball America* and their best "pure hitter" from the draft…also tabbed as the organization's sixth-best prospect by *Baseball Digest*…**PERSONAL:** John Murphy…attended the Pendleton Academy in Bradenton, Fla…Rated by *Baseball America* as fifth-best catcher among the 2009 draft class and as having the second-best "strike-zone judgment" among high school players.

MURTON, Luke – INF

HT: 6-4; **WT:** 225; **B:** R; **T:** R; **BORN:** 5/21/86 in McDonough, Ga.; **RESIDES:** McDonough, Ga.; **COLLEGE:** Georgia Tech; **OBTAINED:** Selected by the Yankees in the 19th round of the 2009 First-Year Player Draft; **M.L. SVC:** 0.000; **CAREER NOTES: 2010:** Spent the entire season with Single-A Charleston, batting .282 (112-for-397) with 32 doubles, 12HR and 55RBI…was named the SAL's "Player of the Week" for the period of 5/24-5/30 and ended the season reaching base safely in 15 of his last 16 games played…was one of three Charleston players named to the league's midseason All-Star team…**2009:** Played his first professional season with the short-season Single-A Staten Island Yankees, batting .295 with 45R, 17 doubles, 8HR and 35RBI in 69 games…made 68 starts at 1B, recording the most total chances (683), putouts (613) and assists (61) and tying for the most errors (9) among NYPL first basemen…tied for second in the league in home runs…**PERSONAL:** Is the brother of Major Leaguer Matt Murton…graduated from Eagle's Landing High School (GA), earning Henry County "Player of the Year" honors as a senior…selected by the Yankees in the 40th round of the 2007 First-Year Player Draft but returned to school.

NORGUERA, Freddy – INF

HT: 5-9; **WT:** 160; **B:** R; **T:** R; **BORN:** 1/10/91 in Valencia, Venezuela; **RESIDES:** Valencia, Venezuela; **OBTAINED:** Signed as a minor league free agent on 11/18/10; **M.L. SVC:** 0.000; **CAREER NOTES:** Will make his professional debut in 2011.

NORTON, Timothy – RHP

HT: 6-4; **WT:** 230; **B:** R; **T:** R; **BORN:** 5/23/83 in Franklin, Mass.; **RESIDES:** Franklin, Mass.; **COLLEGE:** University of Connecticut; **OBTAINED:** Selected in the seventh round of the 2006 First-Year Player Draft; **M.L. SVC:** 0.000; **CAREER NOTES: 2010:** Combined to go 1-0 with a 1.39 ERA (32.1IP, 5ER) in 19 appearances out of the bullpen with Single-A Tampa, Double-A Trenton and Triple-A Scranton/Wilkes-Barre before having his season cut short on 7/23 with a strained back…**2009:** Went 2-1 with a 2.75 ERA in 23 appearances out of the bullpen with Single-A Tampa…did not allow an earned run in 18 of his 23 relief appearances…tossed at least 2.0 innings in 11 outings…recorded 30K and held right-handed hitters to a .195 batting average…was placed on the DL on 8/5 with right shoulder inflammation for the remainder of the season…**2008:** Missed the season on the disabled list, recovering from rotator cuff surgery…**2007:** Was limited to five starts with Single-A Charleston, going 1-3 with a 3.71 ERA…was placed on the disabled list on 4/27 through the end of the season with a right shoulder strain…underwent surgery on his right rotator cuff on 5/10…**2006:** Made 15 starts for short-season Single-A Staten Island, posting a 3-3 record with a 2.60 ERA and 83K in 72.2IP…led all NY-Penn League pitchers with his 15 starts and ranked second in the league in strikeouts…was named the NY-Penn League "Pitcher of the Week" for the week of 9/4…helped lead the Yankees to their second consecutive NY-Penn League Championship…**PERSONAL:** Drafted by the Yankees out of the University of Connecticut, where he was a 2006 Pre-Season All-Big East selection and led the Huskies with a 2.04 ERA…recorded 226 career strikeouts at UConn, ranking second on the Connecticut all-time list…following the season was named All-Big East First Team and All-New England First Team.

NUDING, Zachary – RHP

HT: 6-4; **WT:** 260; **B:** R; **T:** R; **BORN:** 3/29/90 in Fort Worth, Tex.; **RESIDES:** Fort Worth, Tex.; **COLLEGE:** Weatherford College; **OBTAINED:** Selected by the Yankees in the 30th round of the 2010 First-Year Player Draft; **M.L. SVC:** 0.000; **CAREER NOTES: 2010:** Made one start with the GCL Yankees, allowing 2R (1ER) in 2.0IP and taking the loss (4H, 1BB, 2K)…**PERSONAL:** Pitched in the Texas Collegiate League and was named to *Baseball America's* top 10 summer league prospects…selected by Pittsburgh in the 2009 draft (37th round), but chose to return to school

NUNEZ, Julian – RHP

HT: 6-7; **WT:** 190; **B:** R; **T:** R; **BORN:** 7/11/89 in La Vega, D.R.; **RESIDES:** La Vega, D.R.; **OBTAINED:** Signed as a minor league free agent on 9/16/10; **M.L. SVC:** 0.000; **CAREER NOTES:** Will make his professional debut in 2011.

NUNEZ, Luis – INF

HT: 5-10; **WT:** 185; **B:** R; **T:** R; **BORN:** 11/21/86 in Maracaibo, Venezuela; **RESIDES:** Maracaibo, Venezuela; **OBTAINED:** Signed by the Yankees as a non-drafted free agent on 11/12/03; **M.L. SVC:** 0.000; **CAREER NOTES: 2010:** Played the entire season with Double-Trenton and hit .241 (108-for-449) with 24 doubles, 5 triples, 8HR and 44RBI in 131 games…following the season, played in 15 games with the Aguilas del Zulia, of the Venezuelan Winter League, and recorded 13H in 36AB (.361) with 6RBI…**2009:** Combined to hit .276 with 34R, 12 doubles, 3 triples, 3HR and 27RBI in 74 games with Single-A Tampa and Triple-A Scranton/Wilkes-Barre…began the season with Tampa, batting .304 with 23R, 10 doubles, 3HR and 23RBI in 49 games…made one relief outing—the first pitching appearance of his career—in 8/29 loss vs. Brevard County, tossing a scoreless ninth inning in the 9-2 loss (1.0IP, 2BB)…also appeared for Scranton/WB, hitting .214 with 11R, 2 doubles and 4RBI in 25 games…following the season, played for the Aguilas del Zulia of the Venezuelan Winter League, batting .289 (13-for-45) with 2R, 3 doubles and 7RBI in 15 games…**2008:** Batted .280 with 17 doubles, 3HR and 40RBI in 110 games with Single-A Tampa…appeared in games at 1B, 2B, 3B, SS, LF and DH…collected a career-high five hits on 8/10 at Clearwater…hit his first career grand slam on 8/31 at Fort Myers…hit .346 (37-for-107) with 20RBI in August, including a .407 mark (33-for-81) over his final 20 games…promoted to Triple-A Scranton/Wilkes-Barre from 6/14-19, appearing in three games and going 3-for-9 (.333)…played with Zulia in the Venezuelan Winter League…**2007:** Combined to hit .235 (71-for-302) with 17 doubles, 2HR and 27RBI in 89 games with short-season Single-A Staten Island, Single-A Charleston and Single-A Tampa…**2006:** Played in 16 games and batted .279 with Single-A Tampa before being placed on the disabled list on 6/11 with a strained right hamstring, missing the remainder of the season…**2005:** Batted .230 in 42 games with the Gulf Coast League Yankees…helped lead the Yankees to the GCL Championship…**2004:** Made his professional debut with the DSL Yankees 1, posting a .249 batting average with 7 doubles and 33 RBI in 63 games.

NUNEZ, Reymond – INF

HT: 6-4; **WT:** 247; **B:** R; **T:** R; **BORN:** 9/25/90 in Santo Domingo, D.R.; **RESIDES:** Santo Domingo, D.R.; **OBTAINED:** Signed by the Yankees as a non-drafted free agent on 11/21/07; **M.L. SVC:** 0.000; **CAREER NOTES: 2010:** Appeared in 27 games with the GCL Yankees, batting .222 (24-for-108) with 4 doubles, 1 triple, 3HR and 20RBI…was placed on the disabled list on 8/19 with a hamstring injury…**2009:** Hit .296 with 12 doubles, 1 triple and 10HR in 59 games with the DSL Yankees 2…recorded a career-high 13-game hitting streak from 7/1-17, batting .455 (25-for-55) with 4HR and 23RBI over the stretch…**2008:** Made his professional debut with the DSL Yankees 2, batting .230 with 8 doubles, 2HR and 41RBI in 65 games.

O'BRIEN, Michael – RHP

HT: 5-11; **WT:** 188; **B:** R; **T:** R; **BORN:** 3/3/90 in Salem, Va.; **RESIDES:** Roanoke, Va.; **OBTAINED:** Selected by the Yankees in the ninth round of the 2008 First-Year Player Draft; **M.L. SVC:** 0.000; **CAREER NOTES: 2010:** Made 11 starts with short-season Single-A Staten Island, going 6-2 with a 2.08 ERA in 11 starts…led the staff in wins and was named to the midseason All-Star team…ranked third in the NYPL in ERA, allowing 2ER or less in nine of his 11 starts, and fifth in opponents average (.228)…**2009:** Spent his second straight season with the GCL Yankees, going 2-4 with a 5.09 ERA in 11 games (eight starts)…**2008:** Made his professional debut with the GCL Yankees, going 1-0 with a 5.00 ERA in six games (two starts)…**PERSONAL:** Michael Todd O'Brien…graduated from Hidden Valley (Va.) High School…named the 2008 Timesland "Player of the Year," after going 11-1 with a 0.69 ERA and 142 strikeouts in 81.0IP as a senior…also named the Virginia High School Coaches Association's "Player of the Year."…has been diagnosed as a Type 1 diabetic…hosts baseball clinics in Roanoke in the offseason…bypassed a scholarship offer from Winthrop.

OKAMOTO, Naoya – LHP

HT: 5-10; **WT:** 185; **B:** L; **T:** L; **BORN:** 7/28/83 in Yokohama, Japan; **RESIDES:** Okayama, Japan; **OBTAINED:** Signed by the Yankees as a minor league free agent on 8/20/10; **M.L. SVC:** 0.000; **CAREER NOTES: 2010:** Did not pitch during the regular season, seeing his first action with the Guerreros de Oaxaca and Piratas de Campeche of the Mexican Winter League…combined to go 1-2 with a 3.57 ERA (17.2IP, 7ER) in 21 relief appearances.

OLIBERTO, Mikeson – OF

HT: 5-10; **WT:** 164; **B:** R; **T:** R; **BORN:** 8/23/90 in La Romana, D.R.; **RESIDES:** La Romana, D.R.; **OBTAINED:** Signed as a minor league free agent on 7/1/10; **M.L. SVC:** 0.000; **CAREER NOTES: 2010:** Made his professional debut with the DSL Yankees 2, and batted .287 (43-for-150) with 8 doubles, 2 triples, 6HR and 31RBI in 40 games.

OLIVER, William – RHP

HT: 6-1; **WT:** 205; **B:** R; **T:** R; **BORN:** 7/4/87 in Escondido, Calif.; **RESIDES:** Escondido, Calif.; **COLLEGE:** Palomar College; **OBTAINED:** Selected by the Yankees in the 35th round of the 2010 First-Year Player Draft; **M.L. SVC:** 0.000; **CAREER NOTES: 2010:** Made his professional debut with the GCL Yankees, going 2-0 with a 4.38 ERA in eight relief appearances…recorded one save and 10K in 12.1IP…transferred to short-season Single-A Staten Island on 8/25 and went 0-0 in four appearances with a 5.06 ERA.

OROZCO, Jamiel – INF

HT: 5-11; **WT:** 156; **B:** R; **T:** R; **BORN:** 1/29/93 in Santo Domingo, D.R.; **RESIDES:** Santo Domingo, D.R.; **OBTAINED:** Signed by the Yankees as a non-drafted free agent on 11/4/09; **M.L. SVC:** 0.000; **CAREER NOTES:** Made his professional debut with the DSL Yankees 2, hitting .267 (55-for-206) with 9 doubles, 2 triples and 15RBI…recorded a 10-game hit streak from 6/12-7/1, batting .489 (15-for-31) with 3 doubles.

PARRAZ, Jordan – OF

HT: 6-3; **WT:** 215; **B:** R; **T:** R; **BORN:** 10/8/84 in Henderson, Nev.; **RESIDES:** Manhattan Beach, Calif.; **COLLEGE:** Southern Nevada Community College; **OBTAINED:** Claimed off waivers by the Yankees from the Boston Red Sox on 12/17/10; **M.L. SVC:** 0.000; **CAREER NOTES: 2010:** Played the entire season with Triple-A Omaha, batting .266 (115-for-432) with 58R, 27 doubles, 11HR and 61RBI in 123 games…posted a .255 (102-for-400) batting average with 11HR in his starts in RF, and hit .406 (13-for-32) as a DH…was hit by a pitch 19 times, leading all Triple-A batters…went 5-for-6 with 4 doubles, 1HR and 4RBI in 5/18 win at Las Vegas…hit safely in 19 of 22 games from 6/14-7/10…following the season, played with La Guaira in the Venezuelan Winter League, batting .306 (22-for-72) in 25 games…was claimed off waivers by the Red Sox from the Royals on 11/24/10, then claimed off waivers by the Yankees from the Red Sox on 12/17/10…**2009:** In his first season in the Kansas City organization, combined at three levels (Double-A Northwest Arkansas, rookie-level Idaho Falls and Triple-A Omaha) to hit .348 (101-for-290) with 26 doubles, 8HR and 52RBI in 81 games… opened the season at Northwest Arkansas where he hit .417 (30-for-72) with RISP and .423 (11-for-26) with RISP and two outs, and walked 29 times with only 25K…named the Texas League's June "Player of the Month" and earned a spot on the midseason All-Star team…was placed on the disabled list on 7/9 with a strained right hamstring…had a brief rehab stint with Idaho Falls before returning to action with Omaha…appeared in 13 games with Omaha before returning to the D.L. on 8/13 with strained left hamstring, missing the remainder of the season…following the season, was tabbed by *Baseball America* as having the "Best Outfield Arm" in the Royals organization…was added to the team's 40-man roster on 11/20/09…**2008:** Earned postseason All-Star team honors with Single-A Salem, hitting .289 (123-for-425) with 82R, 31 doubles, 6HR, 42RBI and 21SB in 114 games, setting career highs in runs and doubles…ranked third in the Carolina League in on-base percentage (.399) and fourth in runs…hit his first career grand slam on 7/1 vs. Winston-Salem…following the season, played with North Shore of the Hawaiian Winter League before being traded to the Royals on 12/11 as the player to be named later in exchange for LHP Tyler Lumsden…**2007:** Named his team's MVP for the second straight year, batting .281 (130-for-462) with 28 doubles, 14HR, 76RBI and 33SB with Single-A Lexington…in his first year at the full-season level, led the team in games, runs, hits, doubles, RBI and stolen bases…hit for the cycle on 7/26 vs. Lakewood, going 4-for-6 with 3R and 3RBI…**2006:** Hit .336 (85-for-253) with 46R, 18 doubles, 6HR, 38RBI and 23SB in 70 games with short-season-Single-A Tri-City, earning team MVP honors…led the New York-Penn League in average, on-base pct. (.421) and slugging pct. (.494), ranked second in runs and stolen bases, tied for second in hits, tied for third in doubles, ranked fourth in total bases (125) and tied for fourth in extra-base hits (26)…**2005:** Appeared in 71 games with Tri-City, batting .262 (74-for-282) with 11 doubles, 5HR and 35RBI…was 17-for-20 in stolen base attempts, leading the team in steals…**2004:** Made his professional debut, batting .244 (44-for-180) with 6 doubles, 5 triples, 4HR and 21RBI in 53 games with rookie-level Greenville…ranked second in the Appalachian League in triples…**PERSONAL:** Graduated from Green Valley High School (Nev.), winning the state championship in 2001 and '03…was selected by the Philadelphia Phillies in the sixth round of the 2003 First-Year Player Draft, but did not sign…his brother, Zeke, was drafted by Oakland in 2005 and played two seasons of minor league baseball in the Athletics system…signed by Doug Deutsch (Astros).

PENA, Henry – OF

HT: 6-0; **WT:** 180; **B:** L; **T:** R; **BORN:** 10/26/90 in Bani, D.R.; **RESIDES:** Bani, D.R.; **OBTAINED:** Signed by the Yankees as a non-drafted free agent on 7/2/07; **M.L. SVC:** 0.000; **CAREER NOTES: 2010:** Saw the majority of action with the GCL Yankees, hitting .302 (26-for-86) with 12R, 7 doubles, 3HR and 7RBI in 26 games…was promoted to Single-A Tampa on 7/14 for one game (0-for-3)…landed on the disabled list on 8/16 after undergoing knee surgery…**2009:** In 57 games with the DSL Yankees 1, batted .315 with 23 extra-base hits (15 doubles, four triples, 4HR) and 36RBI…recorded a career-high 4H in back-to-back games from 8/4–8/5, going 8-for-9 with 2 doubles and 6RBI in the two contests…**2008:** Made his professional debut, hitting .167 with 14 doubles, 1HR and 17RBI in 51 games with the DSL Yankees 2.

PENA, Jose – RHP

HT: 6-0; **WT:** 160; **B:** R; **T:** R; **BORN:** 3/22/91 in Guayubin, D.R.; **RESIDES:** Guayubin, D.R.; **OBTAINED:** Signed by the Yankees as a non-drafted free agent on 7/11/09; **M.L. SVC:** 0.000; **CAREER NOTES: 2010:** In 14 games (13 starts) with the DSL Yankees 1, went 6-2 with a 2.64 ERA…ranked second on the team in wins, innings pitched (61.1) and strikeouts (63)…**2009:** Made his professional debut with the DSL Yankees 2 and went 2-0 with a 1.42 ERA in five relief appearances, striking out 11 batters in 12.2IP…threw 2.0IP or more in each of his five outings.

PEREZ, Elvin – RHP

HT: 6-4; **WT:** 193; **B:** R; **T:** R; **BORN:** 8/3/90 in San Francisco de Macoris, D.R.; **RESIDES:** San Francisco de Macoris, D.R.; **OBTAINED:** Signed as a minor league free agent on 6/4/10; **M.L. SVC:** 0.000; **CAREER NOTES: 2010:** Made his professional debut with the DSL Yankees 1, and went 0-4 with a 1.91 ERA in 33.0IP in 14 games (six starts).

PEREZ, Kelvin – RHP

HT: 6-1; **WT:** 152; **B:** R; **T:** R; **BORN:** 10/10/85 in Manoguallavo, D.R.; **RESIDES:** Manoguallavo, D.R.; **OBTAINED:** Signed by the Yankees as a non-drafted free agent on 3/16/05; **M.L. SVC:** 0.000; **CAREER NOTES: 2010:** Spent the entire season with Single-A Charleston where he went 5-5 with a 3.18 ERA (104.2IP, 37ER) in 30 games (13 starts)…was 2-1 with a 2.08 ERA (30.1IP, 7ER) as a reliever and 3-4 with a 3.63 ERA (74.1IP, 30ER) as a starter…allowed only 4ER over his final 22.2IP (1.59 ERA)…**2009:** Went 5-2 with a 2.01 ERA in 15 combined games (two starts) with the GCL Yankees and short-season Single-A Staten Island…started and won his lone postseason game, tossing 5.0 scoreless innings to clinch the first round of the NYPL playoffs…**2008:** Opened the season on the disabled list, recovering from right elbow surgery performed on 8/17/07…began year on a rehab assignment with the GCL Yankees, going 0-2 with a 4.08 ERA in eight games (one start) before being promoted to Single-A Tampa for his final appearance of the season…**2007:** Joined the GCL Yankees, going 5-3 with a 2.84 ERA in 11 games (five starts), striking out 32 with nine walks…was 3-1 with a 1.77 ERA in six relief appearances and 2-2 with a 4.08 ERA in his five starts…held opponents scoreless in five consecutive outings from 6/26-7/17, going 4-0 and holding opponents to a .153 average (19.0IP, 10H, 2BB, 14K)…struck out a career-high seven batters in a 5.0-inning start on 8/11 vs. the GCL Phillies to earn the win…**2006:** Made 14 appearances (nine starts) with the Yankees DSL 1 squad, posting a 7-2 record with a 3.18 ERA and 52K in 51.0IP…held opponents to a .205 batting average…helped lead the squad to their second consecutive Dominican Summer League championship…**2005:** In first professional season, posted a 1-3 record with a 5.42 ERA in 12 games (five starts) for the Yankees' DSL 2 squad.

PERKINS, Kyle – C

HT: 6-0; **WT:** 175; **B:** R; **T:** R; **BORN:** 6/28/89 in Canberra, Australia; **RESIDES:** Macquarie, Australia; **OBTAINED:** Signed by the Yankees as a free agent on 1/26/08; **M.L. SVC:** 0.000; **CAREER NOTES: 2010:** Started the year with the Canberra Cavalry in the Australian Baseball League, going hitless in 8AB in five games…was transferred to the GCL Yankees on 6/17, and batted .083 (2-for-24) in 13 games…**PERSONAL:** Was signed at the age of 16 after being spotted during the under-18 national championship in Canberra, Australia, where he was teammates with fellow signee Nathan Aron.

PEROZO, Junior – RHP

HT: 6-2; **WT:** 155; **B:** R; **T:** R; **BORN:** 8/9/91 in Ciudad Ojeda, Venezuela; **RESIDES:** Ciudad Ojeda, Venezuela; **OBTAINED:** Signed as a non-drafted free agent on 1/28/10; **M.L. SVC:** 0.000; **CAREER NOTES: 2010:** Made his professional debut with the DSL Yankees 2, going 2-2 with a 2.26 ERA in 13 game appearances (seven starts)…recorded 41K in 51.2IP.

PHELPS, David – RHP   NON-ROSTER INVITEE

HT: 6-2; **WT:** 185; **B:** R; **T:** R; **BORN:** 10/9/86 in St. Louis, Mo.; **RESIDES:** Hazelwood, Mo.; **COLLEGE:** Notre Dame; **OBTAINED:** Selected by the Yankees in the 14th round of the 2008 First-Year Player Draft; **M.L. SVC:** 0.000; **CAREER NOTES: 2010:** Named the organization's minor league "Pitcher of the Year"…began the season with Double-A Trenton where he went 6-0 with a 2.04 ERA, allowing only 20ER in 88.1IP…at the time of his promotion, led the league in strikeouts (84) and ranked second in ERA…was named to the EL All-Star squad, but did not appear due to his promotion to Triple-A Scranton/Wilkes-Barre on 7/2…with Scranton/WB, went 4-2 with a 3.07 ERA (70.1IP, 24ER) in 12 games (11 starts)…made one postseason start and recorded a no-decision, allowing 3ER on 5H in 6.0IP (4BB, 4K, 1HR)…tabbed by *Baseball America* as having the organization's "Best Slider"…**2009:** Combined to go 13-4 with a 2.38 ERA in 26 starts with Single-A Charleston and Single-A Tampa…ranked third among all Yankees minor leaguers in ERA and strikeouts (122)…was promoted to Tampa on 7/21, going 3-1 with a 1.17 ERA in seven starts…allowed 1ER in the first inning of his first start with Tampa on 7/24 and then held opponents scoreless over the next 18.1 innings before allowing 1ER in the second inning of his fourth start on 8/9…**2008:** Made his professional debut, going 8-2 with a 2.72 ERA in 15 starts with short-season Single-A Staten Island (72.2IP, 67H, 28R, 22ER, 18BB, 52K, 4HR)…tied for second in the New York-Penn League in wins and ranked fourth in the league in ERA, earning a spot on the league's midseason All-Star roster…tied for fourth among Yankees farmhands in ERA…went 6-0 with a 2.75 ERA in eight road starts…won each of his final six decisions of the season over his last nine starts…made one postseason start for Staten Island, going 0-1 with a 33.75 ERA (1.1IP, 5H, 8R, 5ER, 2BB, 1K)…**PERSONAL:** Full name is David Edward Phelps…attended the University of Notre Dame where he majored in political science and computer applications…went 5-5 with a 4.65 ERA in his junior year in 2008, allowing 102H and 48ER while leading the team in games started (14), innings pitched (93.0) and strikeouts (75)…was named to the 2008 Preseason Watch List for the Brooks Wallace national "Player of the Year" award, as well as earning pre-season First Team All-Big East honors in 2007 and '08…became the second Notre Dame pitcher in school history to strike out at least 100 batters (102) and record an ERA under 2.00 (1.88) in the same season in 2007 (also Aaron Heilman)…attended Hazelwood West High School (Mo.) where he went 14-4 with a 2.96 ERA in 27 appearances (17 starts), striking out 172 batters in 109.2IP…was named a top prospect in Missouri among 2005 prep seniors by *Baseball America* after setting a school record with a 30.0-inning scoreless stretch that season…was a team captain, all-conference and all-metro performer in 2004 and '05.

PINA, Julio – C

HT: 5-9; **WT:** 190; **B:** R; **T:** R; **BORN:** 6/18/1991 in La Romana, D.R.; **RESIDES:** La Romana, D.R.; **OBTAINED:** Signed as a non-drafted free agent on 10/7/10; **M.L. SVC:** 0.000; **CAREER NOTES:** Will make his professional debut in 2011.

PIRELA, Jose Manuel – INF

HT: 5-11; **WT:** 210; **B:** R; **T:** R; **BORN:** 11/21/89 in Valera, Venezuela; **RESIDES:** Bobures, Venezuela; **OBTAINED:** Signed by the Yankees as a non-drafted free agent on 7/2/06; **M.L. SVC:** 0.000; **CAREER NOTES: 2010:** Played the entire season with Single-A Tampa and batted .252 (125-for-497) with 15 doubles, 13 triples, 5HR, 61RBI and 30SB…tied for first in the FSL in triples and tied for second on the team in stolen bases…played in six postseason games for the FSL champion Tampa Yankees, and hit .208 (5-for-24) with one double, 2RBI and 3SB…following the season, appeared in 23 games for the Phoenix Desert Dogs of the Arizona Fall League, batting .180 (16-for-89) with 3 doubles, 1HR, 5RBI and 2SB…following the season, made 29 appearances with the Aguilas del Zulia, of the Venezuelan Winter League, where he hit .333 (34-for-102) with 2 triples, 3HR and 14RBI…**2009:** Hit .295 with 23 extra-base hits (23 doubles, 6 triples) and 46RBI in 97 games with Single-A Charleston…recorded multiple hits in six of seven games from 7/23–8/1, batting .516 (16-for-31) with two doubles, one triple and 4RBI over the stretch…**2008:** Appeared in 35 games with the GCL Yankees, batting .234 with 4 doubles, 1 triple and 10RBI…**2007:** Made his professional debut with the DSL Yankees 1, batting .273 with 7 doubles, 3 triples, 4HR, 29RBI and 15SB in 65 games…ranked second on the team in stolen bases and third in runs (44).

POLANCO, Jose – OF

HT: 6-1; **WT:** 190; **B:** R; **T:** R; **BORN:** 5/22/91 in Puerto Plata, D.R.; **RESIDES:** Puerto Plata, D.R.; **OBTAINED:** Signed as a minor league free agent on 10/7/10; **M.L. SVC:** 0.000; **CAREER NOTES:** Will make his professional debut in 2011.

POLANCO, Reynaldo – RHP

HT: 6-2; **WT:** 180; **B:** R; **T:** R; **BORN:** 5/20/93 in Puerto Plata, D.R.; **RESIDES:** Puerto Plata, D.R.; **OBTAINED:** Signed as a minor league free agent on 5/17/10; **M.L. SVC:** 0.000; **CAREER NOTES: 2010:** Made his professional debut with the DSL Yankees 2, and went 0-6 with a 7.67 ERA in 11 appearances (10 starts).

POLO, Rafael – INF

HT: 6-2; **WT:** 165; **B:** R; **T:** R; **BORN:** 4/2/93 in Bani, D.R.; **RESIDES:** Bani, D.R.; **OBTAINED:** Signed as a minor league free agent on 4/1/10; **M.L. SVC:** 0.000; **CAREER NOTES: 2010:** Made his professional debut with the DSL Yankees 2, batting .323 (80-for-248) with 17 doubles, 9 triples, 1HR and 30RBI in 63 games…led the team in triples and ranked second in games and batting average…ranked second in the DSL in extra-base hits (27) and triples (9), third in total bases (118), fifth in hits and slugging (.476) and ninth in average…named to the DSL midseason All-Star team.

PRIOR, MARK—RHP

NON-ROSTER INVITEE

HT: 6-5; **WT:** 230; **B:** R; **T:** R; **BORN:** 9/7/80 in San Diego, Calif.; **RESIDES:** Chicago, Ill.; **COLLEGE:** University of Southern California; **OBTAINED:** Signed by the Yankees as a free agent on 12/15/10; **M.L. SVC:** 6.131; **CAREER NOTES:** Owns a 42-29 career record with a 3.51 ERA (657.0IP, 582H, 277R, 256ER, 223BB, 757K, 77HR) in 106 Major League starts over parts of five seasons with the Cubs (2002-06)…has struck out at least 10 batters in 21 career starts…was named to the NL All-Star team and placed third in NL Cy Young Award voting in 2003…in three career postseason starts—all coming in the 2003 ALDS and ALCS—owns a 2-1 record with a 2.31 ERA (23.1IP, 6ER)…**2010:** Missed the beginning of the season rehabbing from shoulder surgeries performed in 2007 and '08…in August, signed with the Orange County Flyers of the independent Golden Baseball League…did not allow an earned run in nine relief appearances (11.0IP, 5H, 1R, 0ER, 5BB, 22K)…signed with Triple-A Oklahoma City—a Texas Rangers affiliate—on 9/4, tossing 1.0 scoreless inning in relief (2H, 1BB, 2K)…**2009:** Signed a minor league contract with San Diego on 1/18…missed the season rehabbing from shoulder surgeries performed in 2007 and '08…was released by the Padres on 8/1…**2008:** Signed with the Padres…began the season on the 60-day disabled list with a right shoulder strain…underwent right shoulder surgery in June, missing the remainder of the season…**2007:** Underwent arthroscopic surgery on his right shoulder in April, missing the entire season…signed a one-year contract with Chicago-NL on 2/15…**2006:** Was 1-6 with a 7.21 ERA` (43.2IP, 35ER) in nine starts with the Cubs…began the year on the 15-day disabled list on 3/27 with a subscapularis strain…was transferred to the 60-day D.L. on 5/26…was reinstated from the D.L. and made his season debut in 6/18 loss vs. Detroit, allowing 7ER and a career-high-tying 4HR in 3.2IP (7H, 8R, 1BB, 1HP, 2K)…was placed back on the disabled list from 7/5-21 with a strained left oblique…made his final start of the season—and his most recent Major League outing—on 8/10 at Milwaukee, allowing 5ER in 3.0IP to record the loss…was placed on the 15-day D.L. the following day with right shoulder tendinitis, where he stayed for the remainder of the season…**2005:** Went 11-7 with a 3.67 ERA (166.2IP, 68ER) in 27 starts with the Cubs…led the NL with 10.2K/9.0IP (166.2IP, 188K)…ranked fifth in the league with a .227 opponents batting average and ninth in strikeouts…allowed more than 3ER in a start just three times (5/1 at Houston-8ER, 7/7 at Atlanta-6ER and 8/4 at Philadelphia-6ER)…began the season on the 15-day disabled list with right elbow inflammation until 4/12…allowed just 2ER in 19.0IP over his first three starts of the season from 4/13-25…was hit by a line drive off the bat of the Rockies' Brad Hawpe in 5/27 win vs. Colorado, fracturing his right elbow…was placed on the 15-day D.L. from 5/28-6/26 with the injury…in his first start following the injury, retired 18-of-19 batters faced (Pablo Ozuna third-inning single) in 6.0 shutout innings…**2004:** Went 6-4 with a 4.02 ERA (118.2IP, 53ER) in 21 starts with the Cubs…began the season on the 15-day disabled list with right Achilles tendinitis…was transferred to the 60-day D.L. on 5/7 and reinstated on 6/4…made three combined rehab starts with Single-A Lansing and Triple-A Iowa, going 1-0 with a 2.13 ERA (12.2IP, 3ER)…struck out his first five batters faced on 6/14 at Houston, earning his first win of the season (5.0IP, 0ER)…missed one start in July after being removed in the second inning of 7/15 win vs. Milwaukee with discomfort in the posterior area of his right elbow…in September, went 2-0 with a 2.17 ERA (37.1IP, 9ER) in five starts…struck out a career-high-tying 16 batters in his final start of the season in 9/30 loss vs. Cincinnati (9.0IP, 3H, 1ER, 1BB, 1HR)…**2003:** Went 18-6 with a 2.43 ERA (211.1IP, 57ER) in 30 starts, establishing career highs in wins, starts, innings pitched and strikeouts (245)…placed third in the NL Cy Young Award voting, the highest finish for a Cubs pitcher since Greg Maddux won the award in 1992…tied for second in the NL in wins, ranked second in strikeouts and third in ERA…led the league in road ERA (2.08) and ranked fifth in home ERA (2.85)…recorded 4.9K/BB (245K, 50BB), the second-best strikeout-to-walk ratio in the NL, trailing only Arizona's Curt Schilling (6.1K/BB)…hit his first Major League home run—a third-inning solo-HR off the Rockies' Nelson Cruz—and went 2-for-4 with 4RBI in 4/25 win at Colorado…struck out a career-high-tying 16 batters in 6/26 loss vs. Milwaukee (8.0IP, 4H, 2ER, 0BB), tied for the second-highest single-game strikeout total in Cubs history…was placed on the 15-day disabled list from 7/12-8/4 with a right shoulder contusion suffered in a second-inning collision with the Braves' Marcus Giles on 7/11 vs. Atlanta…was named to the NL All-Star team, but did not pitch due to the right shoulder injury…was the youngest Cubs player to go to an All-Star Game since Greg Maddux in 1988…went 10-1 with a 1.52 ERA (82.2IP, 14ER) in 11 starts after being reinstated from the D.L. (67H, 16BB, 95K)…was named the NL "Pitcher of the Month" in August (5-0, 0.69 ERA) and September (5-1, 2.27 ERA), becoming the first Cubs pitcher to win a monthly award since Mike Morgan in May 1992…in just Rick Reuschel (June and July 1977) as the only Cubs pitchers ever to win the award in back-to-back months…won a career-high seven consecutive starts from 8/5-9/6, becoming the first pitcher to have a seven-game winning streak since Kevin Tapani from 8/4-9/15/98…was named NL "Pitcher of the Week" for the period ending 9/21…went 2-1 with a 2.31 ERA (23.1IP, 6ER) in three postseason starts, including a complete game win vs. Atlanta in ALDS Game 3 (9.0IP, 2H, 1ER, 4BB, 7K)…**2002:** Saw his first Major League action, going 6-6 with a 3.32 ERA (116.2IP, 43) in 19 starts with 147K…began his professional career with Double-A West Tenn, going 4-1 with a 2.60 ERA (34.2IP, 10ER) in six starts…won the Southern League's "Pitcher of the Week" in each of the first two weeks of the season…struck out 15 batters in 4/27 win at Chattanooga (8.0IP), setting a West Tenn single-game record…was promoted to Triple-A Iowa on 5/4, going 1-1 with a 1.65 ERA (16.1IP, 3ER) in three starts…made his Triple-A debut on 5/7 vs. Tucson, earning the win after striking out 10 batters in 7.2IP…also hit a pair of solo home runs off Tucson's Horacio Estrada in the contest…was recalled from Iowa on 5/22 and made his Major League debut that night vs. Pittsburgh, allowing 4H and 2ER in 6.0IP to earn the win (2BB, 10K, 1HR)…marked the most strikeouts for a Cubs pitcher in his Major League debut since divisional play began in 1969 (first strikeout was Brian Giles in the first inning)…recorded three double-digit strikeout games in his first five Major League starts (5/22 vs. Pittsburgh-10K, 6/7 at Seattle-11K and 6/12 at Houston-10K), becoming the first pitcher to accomplish the feat since the Dodgers' Fernando Valenzuela in 1981…recorded his first Major League hit in 6/1 loss vs. Houston—a two-run double off Roy Oswalt…over his final seven starts of the season (7/30-8/31), struck out 61 batters in 43.2IP (8BB)…placed on the disabled list from 9/2-17 with a strained left hamstring suffered while running the bases in 8/31 loss vs. St. Louis…**PERSONAL:** Full name is Mark William Prior…married to Heather…his father, Jerry, played football at Vanderbilt University…his sister, Millie, played tennis at the University of San Diego, while his brother, Jerry III, was a tennis player at Villanova University…graduated from University of San Diego High School in 1998, earning all-America honors after going 10-5 with a 0.93 ERA as a senior…was also named the San Diego County "Player of the Year" by the *San Diego Union-Tribune*…in 1999, was selected to the *Baseball America* second-team all-summer team…pitched for the USA National Team in 1999 and 2000, recording wins over Japan and Cuba during the Haarlem (The Netherlands) Tournament during the summer of 2000…was originally selected by the Yankees in Compensation Round A (43rd pick overall) of the 1998 First-Year Player Draft, but instead chose to attend Vanderbilt University…spent his freshman year at Vanderbilt—earning *Baseball America* freshman second-team all-America honors—before transferring to the University of Southern California, where he received a business degree in 2004…pitched for USC for two seasons…as a sophomore in 2000, earned Pac-10 honorable mention honors after going 10-7 with a 3.56 ERA in 23 games (19 starts) for the Trojans…in 2001, earned numerous all-America selections and won seven national "Player of the Year" awards—including "Player of the Year" nods from the American Baseball Coaches' Association, *Baseball America*, *Collegiate Baseball* and *The Sporting News*—after going 15-1 with a 1.69 ERA, six complete games and three shutouts during his junior year while leading the Trojans to the College World Series (138.2IP, 18BB, 5HR, 202K, .201 opp. BA)…also in 2001, won the Golden Spikes Award, the Rotary Smith Award and the Dick Howser Trophy (National Collegiate Baseball Writers' Association)…was a 2002 finalist for the 72nd annual Amateur Athletic Union (AAU) James E. Sullivan Memorial Award, recognizing the top amateur athlete in the nation…was just the fourth baseball player to be a finalist for the award…in 2005, was named to USA Baseball's board of directors…was selected by the Cubs in the first round (second pick overall) of the 2001 First-Year Player Draft.

QUINTANA, Jose – LHP
HT: 6-1; **WT:** 215; **B:** R; **T:** L; **BORN:** 1/24/89 in Arjona, Colombia; **RESIDES:** Barranquilla, Colombia.; **OBTAINED:** Signed by the Yankees as a free agent on 3/10/08; **M.L. SVC:** 0.000; **CAREER NOTES: 2010:** Appeared in 20 combined games (three starts) with the GCL Yankees and Single-A Charleston, going 3-2 with one save and a 3.26 ERA (38.2IP, 14ER)…struck out 44 batters with only 18BB, holding opponents to a .178 batting average (25-for-140)…worked exclusively in relief with GCL, going 3-1 with one save and a 2.31 ERA (23.1IP, 6ER)…made single-A debut following 8/19 promotion to Charleston…**2009:** Went 2-1 with a 2.32 ERA in 14 games with the DSL Yankees 2…led all DSL Yankees pitchers with 80K (in 50.1IP)…struck out six or more batters in eight of his 11 starts…**2008:** Posted a record of 3-2 with a 1.96 ERA in 15 games (12 starts) with the DSL Yankees 2…recorded a career-high 10K in an 8/2 no-decision vs. the DSL Twins (5.1IP, 2H, 1HB, 1WP)…**2007:** Did not pitch during the regular season…**2006:** Was 0-1 with an 8.44 ERA in 3G with the VSL Mets.

RABAGO, Hector – C/INF
HT: 5-10; **WT:** 190; **B:** R; **T:** R; **BORN:** 8/24/88 in Riverside, Calif.; **RESIDES:** Riverside, Calif.; **COLLEGE:** University of Southern California; **OBTAINED:** Selected by the Yankees in the 18th round of the 2009 First-Year Player Draft; **M.L. SVC:** 0.000; **CAREER NOTES: 2010:** Played the entire year with Single-A Charleston, batting .160 (19-for-40) with 3HR and 16RBI in 40 games…recorded 3H on 5/22 and 7/25, tying a single-game career-high…**2009:** Played entire season with short-season Single-A Staten Island, appearing in games at catcher, second base, third base and shortstop…**PERSONAL:** Named the *Los Angeles Times'*"Player of the Year" for the Inland Empire area as a junior in 2005…played infield and pitched with USC.

RAMIREZ, Jose Altagracia – RHP
HT: 6-3; **WT:** 185; **B:** R; **T:** R; **BORN:** 1/21/90 in Yaguate, D.R.; **RESIDES:** Yaguate, D.R.; **OBTAINED:** Signed by the Yankees as a free agent on 6/10/07; **M.L. SVC:** 0.000; **CAREER NOTES: 2010:** Spent the entire season with Single-A Charleston and went 6-5 with a 3.60 ERA in 22 games (21 starts), allowing 46ER in 115.0IP…recorded 105K and held opposing batters to a .223 batting average (33-for-148) with runners in scoring position…held opponents to 3ER or less in all but four of his 21 starts…tabbed by *Baseball America* as having the organization's "Best Changeup"…**2009:** Earned milb.com's "Short-Season Starting Pitcher of the Year" award…went 6-0 with a 1.48 ERA in 11 games (10 starts) with the GCL Yankees…was promoted to Single-A Tampa on 9/5 where he made one relief appearance, tossing 3.0 scoreless innings…tied for third in the GCL in wins and ranked eighth in ERA and strikeouts (53)…had the lowest opponents average (.159) and allowed the fewest baserunners per 9.0IP (7.23) among GCL starters…**2008:** In his first professional season, posted an 0-3 record and 4.15 ERA in 12 games (10 starts) for the Dominican Summer League Yankees 2…tossed a season-high 5.0 innings in 8/9 win vs. the DSL Reds (6H, 3ER, 1BB, 2K, 1HR).

RAMOS, Abraham – INF
HT: 5-10; **WT:** 150; **B:** R; **T:** R; **BORN:** 8/3/92 in Santiago-Ixcuintla, Mexico; **RESIDES:** Santiago-Ixcuintla, Mexico; **OBTAINED:** Signed by the Yankees as a non-drafted free agent on 9/8/08; **M.L. SVC:** 0.000; **CAREER NOTES: 2010:** With the DSL Yankees 2, batted .267 (16-for-60) with 4 doubles and 8RBI in 21 games…**2009:** Made his professional debut with the DSL Yankees 1 and hit .182 (8-for-44) with 2RBI and 1SB…three of his eight hits went for extra bases (3 doubles).

RECCHIA, Michael – RHP
HT: 6-0; **WT:** 225; **B:** R; **T:** R; **BORN:** 4/2/89 in Crestwood, Ill.; **RESIDES:** Crestwood, Ill.; **COLLEGE:** Eastern Illinois; **OBTAINED:** Signed by the Yankees as a non-drafted free agent on 6/16/10; **M.L. SVC:** 0.000; **CAREER NOTES: 2010:** Made 22 relief appearances with short-season Single-A Staten Island (second-most on the team), going 0-1 with one save and a 4.93 ERA (34.2IP, 19ER)…lefthanders batted just .214 (12-for-56).

REYES, Derbin – RHP
HT: 5-10; **WT:** 170; **B:** R; **T:** R; **BORN:** 3/12/87 in Barahona, D.R.; **RESIDES:** Barahona, D.R.; **OBTAINED:** Signed as a minor league free agent on 7/1/10; **M.L. SVC:** 0.000; **CAREER NOTES: 2010:** In his professional debut with the DSL Yankees 2, went 2-2 with a 7.71 ERA in 13 games (one start).

REYES, Yobanny – RHP
HT: 5-10; **WT:** 197; **B:** R; **T:** R; **BORN:** 11/29/88 in Villa Gonzalez, Venezuela; **RESIDES:** Santiago, D.R.; **OBTAINED:** Signed by the Yankees as a non-drafted free agent on 2/25/06; **M.L. SVC:** 0.000; **CAREER NOTES: 2010:** Appeared in four games with the GCL Yankees (0-1, 21.21 ERA)…**2009:** Appeared in 11 games (one start) with the DSL Yankees 2, going 2-1 with a 3.54 ERA in 20.1IP…held right-handed batters to a .200 batting average (11-for-55)…**2008:** Made his professional debut with the DSL Yankees 2, going 2-0 with a 5.64 ERA in 14 games…recorded his first career save on 7/17 vs. the DSL Cubs 1, allowing 1H in 2.0IP (1K, 1HB).

RICHARDSON, Matthew – RHP
HT: 6-2; **WT:** 200; **B:** R; **T:** R; **BORN:** 5/28/90 in Lake Mary, Fla.; **RESIDES:** Lake Mary, Fla.; **OBTAINED:** Selected by the Yankees in the 15th round of the 2008 First-year Player Draft; **M.L. SVC:** 0.000; **CAREER NOTES: 2010:** Appeared in 11 games (nine starts) with the GCL Yankees, going 1-4 with a 5.00 ERA in 45.0IP…**2009:** Split the season between the GCL Yankees and short-season Single-A Staten Island, going 3-3 with a 3.96 ERA in 14 games (13 starts)…did not allow a run over three straight starts from 6/29-7/10 with the GCL Yankees (16.0IP, 10H, 1BB, 14K, 1HP)…**2008:** Made his professional debut, going 0-1 with a 3.86 ERA in six appearances (four starts) with the GCL Yankees…recorded 17K in 14.0IP.

RINCON, Angel – RHP
HT: 6-1; **WT:** 180; **B:** R; **T:** R; **BORN:** 9/26/92 in La Romana, D.R.; **RESIDES:** La Romana, D.R.; **OBTAINED:** Signed as a minor league free agent on 1/26/10; **M.L. SVC:** 0.000; **CAREER NOTES:** 2010: Made his professional debut with the DSL Yankees 1, and did not record a decision in two games (one start) with a 4.50 ERA...served a 50-game suspension beginning 6/4 for violating the Minor League Drug Prevention and Treatment Program.

RIVERA, Eduardo – RHP
HT: 6-5; **WT:** 190; **B:** R; **T:** R; **BORN:** 9/24/92 in La Romana, D.R.; **RESIDES:** La Romana, D.R.; **OBTAINED:** Signed as a minor league free agent on 9/21/10; **M.L. SVC:** 0.000; **CAREER NOTES:** Will make his professional debut in 2011.

RODINO, Manuel Alfonso – RHP
HT: 6-3; **WT:** 190; **B:** R; **T:** R; **BORN:** 3/7/90 in Santa Barbara de Zulia, Venezuela; **RESIDES:** Santa Barbara de Zulia, Venezuela; **OBTAINED:** Signed by the Yankees as a non-drafted free agent on 12/4/07; **M.L. SVC:** 0.000; **CAREER NOTES:** 2010: Appeared in 12 games out of the bullpen for the DSL Yankees 2, going 1-0 with a 1.59 ERA...led the team in saves, converting five out of seven opportunities...2009: Appeared in 18 games in relief for the DSL Yankees 2, going 6-1 with a 3.94 ERA...tied for the team lead in wins...11 of the outings were at least 2.0IP...2008: Made his professional debut with the DSL Yankees 1, going 2-1 with a 6.00 ERA in 18 games (two starts).

RODRIGUEZ, Edwin – RHP
HT: 6-0; **WT:** 150; **B:** R; **T:** R; **BORN:** 5/16/90 in Puerto Plata, D.R.; **RESIDES:** Puerto Plata, D.R.; **OBTAINED:** Signed as a minor league free agent on 5/26/10; **M.L. SVC:** 0.000; **CAREER NOTES:** 2010: Made his professional debut with the DSL Yankees 2, going 2-4 with one save and a 3.48 ERA in 16 games (six starts)...led the team in strikeouts (53).

RODRIGUEZ, Johel – RHP
HT: 6-0; **WT:** 195; **B:** R; **T:** R; **BORN:** 1/13/91 in San Cristobal, D.R.; **RESIDES:** San Cristobal, D.R.; **OBTAINED:** Signed as a minor league free agent on 6/28/10; **M.L. SVC:** 0.000; **CAREER NOTES:** 2010: Went 1-0 with a 4.82 ERA in 11 relief appearances in his professional debut with the DSL Yankees 2.

RODRIGUEZ, Ramon – RHP
HT: 6-1; **WT:** 170; **B:** R; **T:** R; **BORN:** 7/23/91 in Callejon Los Cocos, D.R.; **RESIDES:** Callejon Los Cocos, D.R.; **OBTAINED:** Signed by the Yankees as a non-drafted free agent on 6/6/09; **M.L. SVC:** 0.000; **CAREER NOTES:** 2009: Made his professional debut, going 2-2 with a 6.31 ERA in 15 games with the DSL Yankees 1.

RODRIGUEZ, Wilton – RHP
HT: 5-11; **WT:** 210; **B:** R; **T:** R; **BORN:** 11/6/90 in Haina, D.R.; **RESIDES:** Haina, D.R.; **OBTAINED:** Signed by the Yankees as a non-drafted free agent on 6/19/08; **M.L. SVC:** 0.000; **CAREER NOTES:** 2010: Played at three different levels (rookie GCL, short-season Single-A Staten Island and Single-A Charleston), combining to go 1-7 with a 4.56 ERA (51.1IP, 26ER) in 13 games (nine starts)...2009: Spent the majority of the season with the GCL Yankees, going 0-1 with a 3.32 ERA in eight games (two starts), striking out 18 batters in 19.0IP...was promoted to Single-A Charleston on 9/3 and made two start with the RiverDogs (1-0, 6.75 ERA), winning his Single-A debut on 9/3 vs. Savannah...2008: Made his professional debut, going 0-2 with a 6.75 ERA in 10 games (five starts) with the DSL Yankees 1.

ROLLER, Kyle – 1B/DH
HT: 6-1; **WT:** 250; **B:** L; **T:** R; **BORN:** 3/27/88 in Rockingham, N.C.; **RESIDES:** Rockingham, N.C.; **COLLEGE:** East Carolina University; **OBTAINED:** Selected by the Yankees in the eighth round of the 2010 First-Year Player Draft; **M.L. SVC:** 0.000; **CAREER NOTES:** 2010: Appeared at 1B and DH for short-season Single-A Staten Island, batting .272 (67-for-246) with 11 doubles, 3 triples, 5HR, 31RBI and 31BB in 67G...led team in hits and total bases (99)...PERSONAL: Was a two-year starter at ECU...earned 2010 preseason All-American honors from *Collegiate Baseball*...ranked third in the nation with a school-record 61BB in 2010 and 14th with a .529 OBP...was a 2009 First Team All-American by *ABCA/Rawlings* and first team All-Conference USA...was selected by Oakland in 47th round of the 2009 draft, but chose to return to school...played in the Cape Cod League following 2008 and 2009 season, earning league MVP honors in '09.

ROMANSKI, Josh – LHP
HT: 5-11; **WT:** 180; **B:** L; **T:** R; **BORN:** 10/18/86 in Corona, Calif.; **RESIDES:** Corona, Calif.; **COLLEGE:** University of San Diego; **OBTAINED:** Signed by the Yankees as a minor league free agent on 4/14/10; **M.L. SVC:** 0.000; **CAREER NOTES:** 2010: Combined to go 8-5 with a 3.32 ERA (100.1IP, 37ER) in 18 starts with Single-A Charleston and Single-A Tampa...began the season with the RiverDogs and went 8-4 with a 3.16 ERA, allowing 31ER in 88.1IP over 15 starts...was promoted to Tampa on 8/24 and went on to make one start for the Yankees during the postseason and earned the win, allowing just 2ER in 6.0IP (4H, 5K, 2HR)...2009: Did not play after undergoing left elbow surgery on 6/21...2008: Made his professional debut and made four starts at DH with the Helena Brewers in the Milwaukee minor league system and batted .333 (5-for-15) with three doubles in four games...PERSONAL: Was originally selected by the Milwaukee Brewers in the fourth round of the 2008 First-Year Player Draft.

ROMERO, Wilmer – OF
HT: 6-1; **WT:** 185; **B:** R; **T:** R; **BORN:** 12/19/93 in Santo Domingo, D.R.; **RESIDES:** Santo Domingo, D.R.; **OBTAINED:** Signed as a minor league free agent on 10/25/10; **M.L. SVC:** 0.000; **CAREER NOTES:** Will make his professional debut in 2011.

ROMINE, Austin – C

NON-ROSTER INVITEE

HT: 6-0; **WT:** 220; **B:** R; **T:** R; **BORN:** 11/22/88 in Lake Forest, Calif.; **RESIDES:** Lake Forest, Calif.; **OBTAINED:** Selected by the Yankees in the second round of the 2007 First-Year Player Draft; **M.L. SVC:** 0.000; **CAREER NOTES:** Enters the 2011 season ranked as the sixth-best prospect in the Yankees organization and the "Best Defensive Catcher" by *Baseball America*…**2010:** Spent the entire season with Double-A Trenton where he batted .268 (122-for-455) with 31 doubles, 10HR and 69RBI in 115 games…hit .319 (37-for-116) with 11 doubles, 4HR and 11RBI off left-handed pitching and was named to the EL's midseason All-Star team…recorded just 5 errors in 853 total chances, catching 22.7% of potential base stealers (25-of-110)…led all EL catchers in games (99), chances (853) and putouts (787)…following the season, appeared in 16 games with the Phoenix Desert Dogs of the Arizona Fall League, and batted .279 (17-for-61) with three doubles and 7RBI, earning a spot on the Rising Star team…**2009:** Was named the Yankees "Minor League Player of the Year" and Topps Florida State League "Player of the Year," batting .276 with 28 doubles, 13HR and 72RBI in 118 games for Single-A Tampa…tied his career high in hits (122) and established career highs in doubles and RBI…led the team in hits and doubles, tied for the team lead in homers, and ranked second in games played, runs scored and RBI…ranked fourth in the league in RBI and tied for fourth in both doubles and extra-base hits (44)…did not go more than three straight games without recording a hit and went hitless in three straight contests just once (both games of a doubleheader on 4/15 and 4/16)…was named to the midseason and postseason FSL All-Star teams…following the season, played in four games for the Surprise Rafters of the Arizona Fall League, batting .400 (6-for-15) with 2R and 2RBI…named by *Baseball America* as the Yankees' second-best prospect…**2008:** Batted .300 with 66R, 24 doubles, 10HR and 49RBI in 104 games with Single-A Charleston…ranked second on the team and third among Yankees minor leaguers in batting average…recorded 35 multi-hit games, including 12 games with at least 3H and four contests with four hits…batted .517 (15-for-29) with six multi-hit contests from 4/12-20…was placed on the D.L. from 4/23-5/22 with a right groin strain…played for the Waikiki BeachBoys in the Hawaii Winter Baseball League after the season, hitting .208 (11-for-53) with 8R, 4 doubles and 4RBI in 17 games…was named by *Baseball America* as the fourth-best prospect in the Yankees organization following the season…attended spring training as a non-roster invitee, but did not appear in a game…**2007:** Made his professional debut, appearing in one game–the season finale–with the GCL Yankees, going 1-for-2 with 1RBI as the DH…doubled in his first at-bat…after signing, reported to the Dominican Republic to take part in an instructional league…**PERSONAL:** Full name is Austin Allen Romine…rated by *Baseball America* as having the third-best arm strength among high school catchers in the 2007 draft…is the son of former Major League outfielder Kevin Romine (Boston, 1985-91) and his brother, Andrew, was the Los Angeles Angels' fifth-round pick in the 2007 draft.

RONDON, Francisco – LHP

HT: 6-0; **WT:** 160; **B:** L; **T:** L; **BORN:** 4/19/88 in Santo Domingo, D.R.; **RESIDES:** Santo Domingo, D.R.; **OBTAINED:** Signed as a non-drafted free agent on 2/25/06; **M.L. SVC:** 0.000; **CAREER NOTES: 2010:** Started the season with Single-A Charleston, and went 1-2 with one save and a 7.71 ERA in 10 appearances (16K in 11.2IP)…was placed on the disabled list on 5/1 with left elbow inflammation…**2009:** Made 11 starts with short-season Single-A Staten Island, going 3-2 with a 2.32 ERA…was named to the NYPL midseason All-Star team…**2008:** Appeared in nine games (four starts) with the GCL Yankees, going 2-1 with a 3.22 ERA…recorded 34K in 36.1IP…**2007:** Went 4-1 with a 3.65 ERA in 13 appearances (eight starts) with the DSL Yankees 1 team…all four wins came as a reliever, pitching to a 1.42 ERA out of the bullpen and holding opponents to a .194 batting average…was 0-1 with a 5.33 ERA in his eight starts with a .263 opponents average…all of his relief appearances were 3.0-or-more innings…**2006:** Made his professional debut with the Yankees' DSL 2 team, posting a 1-3 record with a 3.09 ERA…held opponents to a .195 batting average.

ROSARIO, Jose – INF

HT: 5-11; **WT:** 170; **B:** R; **T:** R; **BORN:** 11/29/91 in Villa Mella, D.R.; **RESIDES:** Villa Mella, D.R.; **OBTAINED:** Signed by the Yankees as a non-drafted free agent on 6/30/09; **M.L. SVC:** 0.000; **CAREER NOTES: 2010:** Appeared in 36 games for the GCL Yankees, batting .245 (27-for-110) with 4 doubles, 1 triple, 2HR and 7RBI…**2009:** Made his professional debut, hitting .253 (19-for-75) with 4 doubles and 6RBI in 23 games with the DSL Yankees 1.

ROSARIO, Maximo – OF

HT: 6-3; **WT:** 180; **B:** R; **T:** R; **BORN:** 11/2/90 in San Pedro de Macoris, D.R.; **RESIDES:** San Pedro de Macoris, D.R.; **OBTAINED:** Signed as a minor league free agent on 5/14/09; **M.L. SVC:** 0.000; **CAREER NOTES:** Will make his professional debut in 2011.

RUTCKYJ, Evan – LHP

HT: 6-5; **WT:** 205; **B:** R; **T:** L; **BORN:** 1/31/92 in Windsor, Canada; **RESIDES:** Clearwater, Fla.; **OBTAINED:** Selected by the Yankees in the 16th round of the 2010 First-Year Player Draft; **M.L. SVC:** 0.000; **CAREER NOTES: 2010:** Made his professional debut with the GCL Yankees, tossing 1.0 scoreless inning in his only outing…**PERSONAL:** Last name is pronounced ROOT-ski…graduated from St. Joseph's Catholic High School in Windsor, Canada…was a 2009 Under Armour High School All-American…played on the 2009 Canadian Junior National Team.

RYE, Jack – OF

HT: 6-0; **WT:** 217; **B:** L; **T:** L; **BORN:** 3/8/86 in Irvine, Calif.; **RESIDES:** South Miami, Fla.; **COLLEGE:** Florida State University; **OBTAINED:** Selected by the Yankees in the 13th round of the 2008 First-Year Player Draft; **M.L. SVC:** 0.000; **CAREER NOTES: 2010:** Combined to bat .266 (102-for-384) with 25 doubles, 4 triples, 7HR and 52RBI in 107 games with Single-A Tampa and Double-A Trenton…spent the majority of the season with Tampa, where he batted .274 (91-for-332) with 3 triples, 6HR and 45RBI in 92 games…appeared in six postseason games with Tampa and hit .280 (7-for-25) with 1HR and 4RBI…**2009:** Combined to bat .241 with 31R, 14 doubles, 1HR and 21RBI in 78 games with Single-A Tampa and Double-A Trenton…began the season with Tampa, batting .256 with 31R, 13 doubles, 1HR and 21RBI in 75 games…hit his only home run of the season on 6/22 at Clearwater…recorded a season-high four hits on 8/16 at Clearwater and 9/2 vs. Dunedin…**2008:** Made his professional debut with short-season Single-A Staten Island, batting .276 with 26R, 10 doubles, 2HR and 17RBI in 49 games…recorded a career high in hits on 8/14 at State College, going 4-for-5 with 3R, 2 doubles and 1RBI…ended the season with an eight-game hitting streak, including six multi-hit contests, to raise his average from .236 to .276 (14-for-30, .467 during the stretch)…went hitless in his only postseason game with Staten Island (0-for-4)…**PERSONAL:** Attended Florida State University, where he was named baseball team captain during his senior year…left FSU ranked fifth in school history in hits (312), seventh in walks (162) and tied for 10th in doubles (57)…recorded more walks than strikeouts in each of his four seasons, totaling 162BB and 107K…batted .371 with 48R, 15 doubles, 7HR and 52RBI as the team's primary No. 4 hitter in 2008, ranking sixth in the ACC in OBP (.478), seventh in walks (47) and eighth in batting average…was named to the 2006 and 2008 All-ACC Academic Team and was a four-time member of the ACC Academic Honor Roll…majored in real estate…attended Woodbridge High School (Calif.)…hit over .400 all four years en route to being named first team all-league four times and second team All-Southern California once…won the "Big Stick Award" in the Mickey Mantle World Series…hobbies include surfing and snowboarding.

SAAVEDRA, John – RHP
HT: 6-2; **WT:** 180; **B:** R; **T:** R; **BORN:** 2/2/89 in Ciudad Bolivar, Venezuela; **RESIDES:** Ciudad Bolivar, Venezuela; **OBTAINED:** Signed as a minor league free agent on 6/13/10; **M.L. SVC:** 0.000; **CAREER NOTES: 2010:** Made his professional debut with the DSL Yankees 2…went 2-1 with a 4.36 ERA in 14 games (three starts), recording 38K in 33.0IP.

SANCHEZ, Gary – C
HT: 6-2; **WT:** 217; **B:** R; **T:** R; **BORN:** 12/2/92 in Santo Domingo, D.R.; **RESIDES:** Santo Domingo, D.R.; **OBTAINED:** Signed by the Yankees as a non-drafted free agent on 7/2/09; **M.L. SVC:** 0.000; **CAREER NOTES: 2010:** In his first professional season, combined at GCL and short-season Single-A Staten Island to bat .329 (57-for-173) with 33R, 13 doubles, 8HR and 43RBI in 47 games…spent the majority of season with the GCL Yankees, hitting .353 (42-for-119) with 11 doubles, 6HR and 36RBI in 31 games…hit safely in each of his first 10 games (.459, 17-for-37)…hit a grand slam in his second pro AB on 6/21 vs. the GCL Pirates…promoted to Staten Island on 8/19, where he hit .278 (15-for-54) with 2HR and 7RBI in 16 games over the remainder of the season…following the season, was named to the Topps Short-Season/Rookie All-Star Team and tabbed by *Baseball America* as the second-best prospect in the Yankees organization.

SANCHEZ, Josias – OF
HT: 6-3; **WT:** 190; **B:** R; **T:** R; **BORN:** 12/29/87 in San Pedro de Macoris, D.R.; **RESIDES:** San Pedro de Macoris, D.R.; **OBTAINED:** Signed as a minor league free agent on 9/29/08; **M.L. SVC:** 0.000; **CAREER NOTES: 2010:** Will make his professional debut in 2011.

SANIT, Amaury – RHP
HT: 5-9; **WT:** 205; **B:** R; **T:** R; **BORN:** 7/4/79 in Havana, Cuba; **RESIDES:** San Jose, Costa Rica; **OBTAINED:** Signed by the Yankees as a non-drafted free agent on 8/9/08; **M.L. SVC:** 0.000; **CAREER NOTES: 2010:** Combined to go 3-2 with a 6.35 ERA (45.1IP, 32ER) in 27 games (four starts) with the GCL Yankees, Single-A Tampa and Triple-A Scranton/Wilkes-Barre…spent the majority of the year with Scranton/WB where he appeared in 21 games (one start), going 3-2 with a 7.75 ERA (33.2IP, 29ER)…appeared in two games during the postseason and went 0-1, allowing a combined 3ER on 4H in 1.2IP out of the bullpen (1HR, 1HBP)…following the season, made five starts with the Aguilas del Zulia of the Venezuelan Winter League, where he went 2-2 with a 2.96 ERA (24.1IP, 8ER)…**2009:** Combined to go 1-5 with 10 saves and a 3.16 ERA in 44 relief appearances with Single-A Tampa, Double-A Trenton and Triple-A Scranton/Wilkes-Barre…began the season with Tampa, making four scoreless relief appearances (6.0IP) before being transferred to Trenton on 4/25…went 1-2 with a 2.95 ERA in 21 relief appearances with the Thunder, converting 10 of his 12 save opportunities…was promoted to Scranton/WB on 7/8 and went 0-3 with a 4.13 ERA in 19 relief appearances…made two relief appearances for the International League runner-ups, allowing 4H and 2ER in 3.0IP (6.00 ERA) without recording a decision…following the season, made six relief appearances for the Indios de Mayaguez of the Puerto Rican Winter League, going 1-0 with one save and an 8.31 ERA (4.1IP, 9H, 4ER)…**2008:** Made his professional debut with the DSL Yankees, recording one save without allowing a run in two relief appearances (0.00 ERA, 2.0IP, 1H, 2K)…pitched for the Tigres del Licey in the Dominican Baseball League following the season, recording a 5.19 ERA in seven relief appearances.

SANTANA, Francisco – OF
HT: 5-10; **WT:** 190; **B:** L; **T:** L; **BORN:** 6/18/88 in Higuey, D.R.; **RESIDES:** Higuey, D.R.; **OBTAINED:** Signed by the Yankees as a non-drafted free agent on 6/15/06; **M.L. SVC:** 0.000; **CAREER NOTES: 2010:** Started the season with Single-A Tampa, hitting .137 (10-for-73) with 4 doubles, 1 triple and 8RBI…was transferred to Single-A Charleston on 6/24 and batted .257 (26-for-101) with 5 doubles, 2 triples, 2HR and 15RBI in 34 games…**2009:** Played the season at short-season Single-A Staten Island, batting .236 with 6 doubles, 1 triple, 1HR and 10RBI in 40 games in CF…was transferred to Double-A Trenton from 8/12-29, going hitless in 7AB over five games…**2008:** Batted .307 with 10 doubles, 8 triples, 6HR and 38RBI in 52 games with the DSL Yankees 1…tied for third in the DSL in triples…**2007:** Hit .264 with 11 doubles, 7 triples, 3HR and 25RBI for the DSL Yankees 2…tied for second in the league in triples…was 4-for-10 (.400) with 9RBI with the bases loaded…drove in a career-high 5R on 7/11 vs. the DSL Blue Jays 2, going 4-for-5 with 1 double and 1 triple…**2006:** In his first professional season, batted a combined .118 in 31 games with both of the Yankees' Dominican Summer League teams.

SANTANA, Gabriel – RHP
HT: 6-2; **WT:** 170; **B:** R; **T:** R; **BORN:** 11/9/89 in Santo Domingo, D.R.; **RESIDES:** Santo Domingo, D.R.; **OBTAINED:** Signed by the Yankees as a non-drafted free agent on 8/1/09; **M.L. SVC:** 0.000; **CAREER NOTES: 2010:** Went 0-1 with a 8.31 ERA in nine appearances with the DSL Yankees 1…was transferred to the DSL Yankees 2 on 7/17 and went 0-0 with a 6.75 ERA in six appearances…**2009:** Made his professional debut with the DSL Yankees 1 and did not record a decision, allowing 5ER in 1.2 IP in two relief appearances (27.00 ERA).

SANTANA, Ravel – OF
HT: 6-2; **WT:** 175; **B:** R; **T:** R; **BORN:** 5/1/92 in San Pedro de Macoris, D.R.; **RESIDES:** San Pedro de Macoris, D.R.; **OBTAINED:** Signed by the Yankees as a non-drafted free agent on 11/17/08; **M.L. SVC:** 0.000; **CAREER NOTES: 2010:** Appeared in a team-high 63 games for the DSL Yankees 2 and batted .322 (64-for-199) with 10 doubles, 1 triple, 10HR and 38RBI…led the DSL in HR, ranked second in on-base percentage (.440) and slugging percentage (.533) and 10th in average…**2009:** Made his professional debut, hitting a combined .234 (39-for-167) with 8 doubles, 1 triple and 5HR in 50 games with both DSL entries.

SCHMIDT, Josh – RHP

HT: 6-2; **WT:** 182; **B:** R; **T:** R; **BORN:** 11/14/82 in Sierra Madre, Calif.; **RESIDES:** Sierra Madre, Calif.; **COLLEGE:** University of the Pacific; **OBTAINED:** Selected by the Yankees in the 15th round of the 2005 First-Year Player Draft; **M.L. SVC:** 0.000; **CAREER NOTES:** **2010:** Combined to go 4-3 with a 3.02 ERA (65.2IP, 22ER) in 49 relief appearances with Double-A Trenton and Triple-A Scranton/Wilkes-Barre…spent the majority of the year with Trenton where he went 3-3 with a 2.67 ERA, striking out 71 batters and allowing 18ER in 60.2IP out of the bullpen…was selected to the Eastern League's midseason All-Star team…made four relief appearances during the postseason with Trenton, going 1-0, striking out seven batters and allowing 1ER on just 2H in 4.2IP (2BB, 1HR)…following the season, appeared in 14 games (13 starts) with the Aguilas del Zulia of the Venezuelan Winter League, going 5-3 with a 2.79 ERA (71.0IP, 22ER)…ranked first in the VWL in strikeouts (69), third in innnings pitched (71.0) and seventh in ERA (2.79)…**2009:** Went 8-4 with a 1.61 ERA in 46 appearances (five starts) for Double-A Trenton…as a starter, went 1-0 and allowed only 4ER in 21.0IP (1.71 ERA)…was 7-4 as a reliever, recording 77K in 41 appearances out of the bullpen…34 of his 46 appearances were scoreless, including 32 of his 41 relief outings…was named to the mid-season All-Star team…made his first career start on 6/1 vs. Bowie (5.0IP, 2H, 0ER, 1BB, 3K), recording the win in his longest outing since a 3.2-inning relief appearance on 8/5/06 w/ Tampa vs. Palm Beach…also marked the longest outing of his career, later matched on 9/2 at Portland…following the season, pitched for the Aguilas del Zulia in the Venezuelan Winter League…**2008:** Made 38 combined relief appearances with Single-A Tampa and Double-A Trenton, going 1-3 with 16 saves and a 2.57 ERA…ranked third in the organization in saves…struck out 49 batters in 49.0IP and held opponents to a .233 batting average (41-for-176)…began season at Trenton before being transferred to Tampa on 5/20 for the remainder of the season…allowed only 1ER over his final 10 games (12.1IP)…**2007:** Went 6-1 with three saves and a 2.79 ERA in 39 relief appearances with Single-A Tampa, leading Yankees relievers in wins, strikeouts (92) and opponents average (.214)…ranked second overall among FSL relievers, averaging 12.24 K/9.0IP and third in opponents average…held opponents to a .214 batting average, including a .196 mark against right-handers…was 2-0 with a 4.40 ERA prior to the All-Star break and 4-1 with a 1.46 ERA after the break…did not allow a run over his final seven outings (11.1IP) and allowed only 1ER over his final 11 appearances of the season (18.0IP)…**2006:** Appeared in 39 games with the Tampa Yankees, posting a 4-4 record with one save and a 4.24 ERA…**2005:** Made professional debut with the short-season Single-A Staten Island Yankees, posting a 5-1 record with a 0.27 ERA and 47 strikeouts in 26 games (33.0IP, 1ER)…was named the NY-Penn League Rolaids "Relief Man of the Year"…ranked second among all NYPL pitchers with 13 saves and third in games pitched (26)…**PERSONAL:** Graduated from the University of the Pacific in Stockton, Calif. with a degree in communications…led the Tigers pitching staff in his senior season, posting a 6-4 record with a 1.79 ERA in a school-record 36 appearances out of the bullpen…also established a school record with 11 saves during the season…transferred to Pacific in 2003 after two years at Citrus College in Glendora, Calif…helped lead his team to the Western States Conference (WSC) title in 2003…and was named to the All-WSC Second Team…graduated from La Salle High School in Pasadena, Calif. in 2001 and led the Lancers to the state playoffs during each of his final three years there.

SEGEDIN, Robert – RHP

HT: 6-2; **WT:** 220; **B:** R; **T:** R; **BORN:** 11/10/88 in Old Tappan, N.J.; **RESIDES:** Palm Beach, Fla.; **COLLEGE:** Tulane University; **OBTAINED:** Selected by the Yankees in the third round of the 2010 First-Year Player Draft; **M.L. SVC:** 0.000; **CAREER NOTES:** **2010:** In his first professional season, combined at GCL and short-season Single-A Staten Island to bat .243 (19-for-78) with 6 doubles, 2HR and 8RBI in 22 games…played majority of season with SI Yankees, hitting .243 (17-for-70) with 6 doubles, 1HR and 7RBI in 20 games…recorded a .940 fielding percentage at 3B (3E, 50TC)…**PERSONAL:** Named the 2010 "Hitter of the Year" by the Louisiana Sports Writers Association as a redshirt sophomore at Tulane…earned First Team All-Conference USA in 2009…played in all 62 games as a freshman in 2007, earning a spot on the Conference USA All-Freshman Team…played high school baseball at Northern Valley in New Jersey, graduating Magna Cum Laude.

SISCO, Andy – LHP   NON-ROSTER INVITEE

HT: 6-10; **WT:** 270; **B:** L; **T:** L; **BORN:** 1/13/83 in Steamboat Springs, Col.; **RESIDES:** Covington, Wash.; **OBTAINED:** Signed by the Yankees as a minor league free agent on 12/3/10; **M.L. SVC:** 3.057; **CAREER NOTES:** In 151 career Major League outings with Kansas City (2005-06) and Chicago-AL (2007), has gone 3-9 with one save and a 5.18 ERA (147.2IP, 85ER)…was originally drafted by Chicago-AL in the second round of the 2001 First-Year Player Draft…**2010:** Made 48 relief outings for Double-A Richmond, going 4-4 with one save and a 4.32 ERA (66.2IP, 32ER)…following the season, made 15 starts with the Aguilas de Mexicali of the Mexican Pacific League and went 6-5 with a 4.04 ERA, recording 85K and allowing 35ER in 78.0IP…in six good starts with the Aguilas, went 4-1 with a 1.15 ERA (31.1IP, 4ER), holding opposing batters to a .162 (17-for-105) batting average…ranked first among all Mexican winter ball players in strikeouts and third in opponents batting average (.225)…**2008-09:** Did not play in either season, recovering from "Tommy John" surgery performed on 4/7/08…**2007:** Began the season with Chicago-AL and went 0-1 with 8.36 ERA (14.0IP, 13ER) in 19 appearances out of the bullpen with the White Sox…was transferred to Triple-A Charlotte on 5/27 where he appeared in 23 games (15 starts), going 3-6 with a 4.35 ERA (78.2IP, 38ER)…went 0-2 with a 3.48 ERA (10.1IP, 4ER) as a reliever and 3-4 with a 4.48 ERA (68.1IP, 34ER) as a starter…**2006:** Began the season with Kansas City and went 1-3 with a 7.10 ERA (58.1IP, 46ER) in 65 games out of the bullpen with the Royals…was transferred to Triple-A Omaha on 7/27 and made three relief appearances, allowing 1ER in 4.2IP (1.93 ERA)…**2005:** Spent the entire season at the Major League level with Kansas City and went 2-5 with a 3.11 ERA in 67 relief appearances, recording 76K and allowing 26ER in 75.1IP…**2004:** Was 4-10 with a 4.21 ERA (126.0IP, 59ER) in 26 games (25 starts) with Single-A Daytona…**2003:** Made 19 starts with Single-A Lansing, going 6-8 with a 3.54 ERA, recording 99K and allowing 37ER in 94.0IP…allowed 3ER or less in 16 of his 19 starts and 2ER or less in 12 of his 19 outings…**2002:** Went 7-2 with a 2.43 ERA (77.2IP, 21ER) in 14 starts with short-season Single-A Boise…**2001:** Made his professional debut with the AZL Cubs and went 1-0 with a 5.24 ERA (34.1IP, 20ER) in 10 games (seven starts)…**PERSONAL:** Attended Eastlake HS in Sammamish, Wash. before being drafted by the White Sox in 2001.

SNEED, Kramer – LHP

HT: 6-3; **WT:** 195; **B:** L; **T:** L; **BORN:** 10/7/88 in Winterville, N.C.; **RESIDES:** Winterville, N.C.; **COLLEGE:** Barton College; **OBTAINED:** Selected by the Yankees in the 32nd round of the 2010 First-Year Player Draft; **M.L. SVC:** 0.000; **CAREER NOTES:** **2010:** Combined at GCL and short-season Single-A Staten Island to go 1-3 with a 3.86 ERA in 12 appearances (seven starts), striking out 51 batters in 39.2IP…began year at GCL, making four relief outings (6.2IP, 3H, 3R, 2ER, 3BB, 9K)…promoted to Staten Island on 7/30 where he appeared in eight games, making seven starts (1-3, 33.0IP, 35H, 20R, 15ER, 7BB, 42K)…**PERSONAL:** Was named to the 2010 All-Conference Carolina Team…became first Barton player drafted since 1995…earned All-State honors twice at Greenville Christian Academy (N.C.).

SNYDER, Justin – INF

HT: 5-9; **WT:** 205; **B:** L; **T:** R; **BORN:** 4/8/86 in El Cajon, Calif.; **RESIDES:** El Cajon, Calif.; **COLLEGE:** University of San Diego; **OBTAINED:** Selected by the Yankees in the 21st round of the 2007 First-Year Player Draft; **M.L. SVC:** 0.000; **CAREER NOTES: 2010:** Appeared in two games with Triple-A Scranton/Wilkes-Barre, but played the majority of the season with Double-A Trenton, batting .245 (64-for-261) with 13 doubles, 2 triples, 3HR and 27RBI in 90 games with the Thunder…played in seven postseason games with Trenton, going 9-for-31 (.290) with 2 doubles and 1RBI…**2009:** Spent the season with Double-A Trenton, batting .195 with 25R, 9 doubles, 3HR and 29RBI in 94 games…made just nine errors after making 27E the previous season…**2008:** Batted .288 with 33 doubles, 7HR and 59RBI in 132 games with Single-A Tampa…led the team with 68BB, ranking third in the South Atlantic League…named to the midseason All-Star Team…led all SAL second basemen in games (124), total chances (634), putouts (216), assists (393) and double plays (77)…also saw time at 1B, 3B, SS, CF and DH…collected 12H in 17AB over a four-game stretch from 7/18-21…**2007:** Made his professional debut with short-season Single-A Staten Island, batting .335 with 20 doubles, 1 triple, 5HR and 40RBI in 73 games…saw time at 2B, SS, CF and DH…led the New York-Penn League in runs (68), hits (87) and on-base percentage (.459), ranked second in walks (58), tied for third with a team-high 20 doubles and fifth with a team-high .335 average…scored at least one run in each of his first six games and 23 of his first 28 games (27R total)…compiled a 10-game hitting streak from 7/9-20 with seven multi-hit games during the span (.488, 20-for-41, 2HR, 12RBI)…on 8/6 vs. Hudson Valley, hit a two-out, two-run "walk-off" home run in the bottom of the ninth inning…started at 3B in the NYPL All-Star Game on 8/14 in Fishkill…named the starting shortstop on *Baseball America's* Short-Season All-Star Team…**PERSONAL:** Full name is Justin Richard Snyder…played three seasons at University of San Diego, batting .326 with 44 doubles, 11HR, 100RBI, 112BB and 86K in his college career…led the Toreros in batting (.352) and doubles (21) in 2007, recording the second-most hits (89) and doubles in a single-season in school history…lettered in baseball and football at El Capitan (Calif.) High School…won back-to-back baseball conference championships as a junior and senior, garnering prep All-American honors in senior season.

SOLBACH, Michael – RHP

HT: 6-3; **WT:** 200; **B:** R; **T:** R; **BORN:** 7/31/85 in Woodbridge, Va.; **RESIDES:** Aldie, Va.; **COLLEGE:** Liberty University; **OBTAINED:** Signed by the Yankees as a free-agent on 8/8/07; **M.L. SVC:** 0.000; **CAREER NOTES: 2010:** Spent the entire season with Single-A Charleston where he went 4-6 with a 3.90 ERA in 30 games (15 starts), allowing 43ER in 99.1IP…recorded 95K on the season and at least 1K in 29 of his 30 outings, including a single-game season high of eight on both 5/14 and 8/27…earned SAL "Player of the Week" honors (8/16-22)…**2009:** Went 2-3 with a 3.92 ERA in 24 games (two starts) with short-season Single-A Staten Island…allowed just 1ER in each of his two starts…earned his first save in his only chance of the season on 7/18 vs. State College, tossing 1.0 scoreless innings…**2008:** Made his professional debut, combining to go 1-2 with a 1.29 ERA in five appearances (one start) with the GCL Yankees and Single-A Tampa…opened the season on the disabled list with a right elbow strain…made four scoreless relief rehab appearances at the GCL Yankees before being activated and assigned to Tampa on 8/29…made one start with Tampa, allowing 1ER in 2.0IP…**PERSONAL:** Full name is Michael Thomas Solbach…played baseball for three years at Liberty University, going 22-10 with a 4.03 ERA…tied for fifth-most career wins in school history…originally selected by the Arizona Diamondbacks in the 19th round of the 2007 First-Year Player Draft but his contract was voided…was also selected by the Diamondbacks in the 48th round of the 2006 First-Year Player Draft.

SOSA, Eduardo Jose – OF

HT: 6-0; **WT:** 180; **B:** L; **T:** L; **BORN:** 3/14/91 in Bolivar, Venezuela; **RESIDES:** Bolivar, Venezuela; **OBTAINED:** Signed by the Yankees as a non-drafted free agent on 7/2/07; **M.L. SVC:** 0.000; **CAREER NOTES: 2010:** Appeared in 47 games with short-season Single-A Staten Island, batting .256 (46-for-180) with 13 doubles, 3 triples, 2HR and 15RBI…led the team in doubles, triples and stolen bases (15)…from 6/30-7/10 had a 10-game hit streak (.426, 20-for-47 with 5 doubles, 1HR, 5RBI and 6SB)…**2009:** Hit .200 with 2HR and 14RBI in 49 games with the GCL Yankees…**2008:** In his first professional season, hit .315 with 18 doubles, 4HR and 37RBI in 63 games with the DSL Yankees 2…finished the season tied for third in the DSL with 80H…recorded at least 1H in 25 of his first 27G (.358, 39-for-109)…batted .319 (68-for-213) against right-handed pitchers, including 25 extra-base hits (17 doubles, five triples, 3HR).

SOTO, Dubeny – RHP

HT: 5-11; **WT:** 185; **B:** R; **T:** R; **BORN:** 10/30/88 in La Victoria, Estado Aragua, Venezuela; **RESIDES:** La Victoria, Estado Aragua, Venezuela; **OBTAINED:** Signed as a minor league free agent on 1/28/10; **M.L. SVC:** 0.000; **CAREER NOTES: 2010:** Made his professional debut with the DSL Yankees 2…went 1-2 with one save and a 4.15 ERA in 12 games (one start)…transferred to DSL Yankees 1 on 7/17, went 0-1 with a 3.60 ERA in seven games (two starts).

STEVENSON, Casey – INF

HT: 6-3; **WT:** 185; **B:** L; **T:** R; **BORN:** 5/18/88 in Saugus, Calif.; **RESIDES:** Saugus, Calif.; **COLLEGE:** University of California – Irvine; **OBTAINED:** Selected by the Yankees in the 25th round of the 2010 First-Year Player Draft; **M.L. SVC:** 0.000; **CAREER NOTES: 2010:** Made his professional debut with short-season Single-A Staten Island, and batted .217 (43-for-198) with 8 doubles, 6HR and 23RBI in 52 games…**PERSONAL:** Finished his senior year at the University of California–Irvine batting .324 (77-for-238) with 16 doubles, 4 triples, 4HR and 41RBI in 60 games…in 2009 was an All-Big West Conference second-team honoree and a member of the Irvine Regional All-Tournament team.

STONEBURNER, Graham – RHP

HT: 6-0; **WT:** 203; **B:** R; **T:** R; **BORN:** 9/29/87 in Richmond, Va.; **RESIDES:** Richmond, Va.; **COLLEGE:** Clemson University; **OBTAINED:** Selected by the Yankees in the 14th round of the 2009 First-Year Player Draft; **M.L. SVC:** 0.000; **CAREER NOTES: 2010:** In his first extended professional season, combined to go 9-8 with a 2.41 ERA (142.0IP, 32ER) in 26 starts with Single-Charleston and Single-A Tampa…prior to his promotion to Tampa on 5/12, made seven starts with the RiverDogs, going 1-3 with a 2.08 ERA (103.0IP, 29ER)…retired 20 consecutive batters in Charleston's 12-inning, 4-3 loss to Rome on 4/24…recorded 11K, including seven in-a-row, in the team's 2-0 victory over Lakewood on 5/5…the 11K marked the first time that a Charleston hurler fanned 10 or more batters since Dellin Betances recorded 12K on 8/16/08…**2009:** Made just one relief appearance with short-season Single-A Staten Island, tossing 1.0 scoreless inning and striking out two.

SUBLETT, Damon – OF

HT: 6-1; **WT:** 207; **B:** L; **T:** R; **BORN:** 9/22/85 in Wichita, Kan.; **RESIDES:** Wichita, Kan.; **COLLEGE:** Wichita State University; **OBTAINED:** Selected by the Yankees in the seventh round of the 2007 First-Year Player Draft; **M.L. SVC:** 0.000; **CAREER NOTES: 2010:** With Double-A Trenton, hit .214 (24-for-112) with 2HR and 14RBI in 35 games…missed over three months of action (4/26-8/3) on the disabled list with a sprained right thumb ligament…**2009:** Spent the season with Single-A Tampa, batting .270 with 68R, 24 doubles, 11 triples, 4HR and 41RBI in 114 games…led the team in triples, ranked second in doubles, tied for third in RBI and ranked third in hits (107)…switched positions from second base to the outfield on 6/16, seeing time in center field and left field…made just two errors as an outfielder (both coming in Game 2 of a doubleheader on 7/10 vs. Daytona), while making 9E as an infielder…**2008:** Was limited to 42 games with Single-A Tampa, batting .263 with 22R, 6 doubles, 2HR and 11RBI before being placed on the disabled list on 5/30 for the remainder of the season with a sprained left ankle…played for the Waikiki BeachBoys in the Hawaii Winter Baseball League following the season, batting .253 (19-for-75) with 15R, 6 doubles, 2HR and 18RBI in 20 games…**2007:** Made his professional debut with short-season Single-A Staten Island, batting .326 with 19 doubles, 3 triples, 8HR, 5RBI and 10SB in 68 games at 2B and DH…led the New York-Penn League in RBI and sacrifice flies (9), ranked second in slugging percentage (.531), tied for third in extra-base hits (30), fourth in walks (43) and on-base percentage (.426) and fifth in total bases (127)…his average ranked sixth in the league and led all minor league second baseman…led the team with 8HR…played in 65 games at 2B and was involved in 40 double plays, both ranking second among league second basemen…batted .280 (49-for-175) in prior to the All-Star break then hit at a .453 clip following the break (29-for-64)…batted from the third spot in the lineup the entire season and was a .379 hitter when leading off an inning (11-for-29, 3 doubles, 7BB)…was 4-for-7 (.571) with the bases loaded, including his first career grand slam on 7/17 at Mahoning Valley…hit safely in a season-high 10 straight games from 7/3-17…played ball with the Harwich Mariners of the Cape Cod League in the summer of 2006 and was invited to play in the Team USA trials…**PERSONAL:** Full name is Damon Alexander Sublett…studied psychology at Wichita State…played on the baseball team for three seasons, appearing primarily at 2B but also pitching in relief…as a sophomore in 2006, was named the Joe Carter Missouri Valley Conference "Player of the Year" and a semi-finalist for the Dick Howser Trophy after leading the conference in batting average (.394) and ranking third in home runs (10)…was named MVC "Freshman of the Year" in 2005 and first team Freshman All-American…was an All-State selection in 2002 and 2004 with Northwest (Kan.) High School.

SUTTLE, Bradley – INF   NON-ROSTER INVITEE

HT: 6-2; **WT:** 205; **B:** S; **T:** R; **BORN:** 1/24/86 in Boerne, Tex.; **RESIDES:** Boerne, Tex.; **COLLEGE:** University of Texas; **OBTAINED:** Selected by the Yankees in the fourth round of the 2007 First-Year Player Draft; **M.L. SVC:** 0.000; **CAREER NOTES: 2010:** Played the entire season with Single-A Tampa and batted .272 (140-for-514) with 33 doubles, 4 triples, 10HR and 80RBI in 133 games with the Yankees…led all FSL third basemen with a .951 fielding percentage and ranked second in RBI, fourth in hits and fifth in doubles…played in six games during Tampa's run to the FSL Championship and batted .304 (7-for-23) with 3HR, 9RBI and 2SB, ranking first among all league postseason batters in HR and RBI, tying for second in stolen bases and ranking fourth in average…named to the FSL postseason All-Star team…**2009:** Missed the entire season on the disabled list rehabbing from shoulder surgery performed on 9/30/08…**2008:** Batted .271 with 63R, 23 doubles, 11HR and 44RBI in 96 games with Single-A Charleston…was placed on the disabled list from 4/13-24 with a left hip flexor strain…appeared in four games (going 2-for-12) before being placed back on the disabled list until 6/1 with the same injury…following the season, was named the South Atlantic League's "Best Defensive Third Baseman" in *Baseball America's* Best Tools Survey, as well as the publication's 10th-best prospect in the organization and the Yankees'"Best Hitter for Average"…**2007:** Appeared in three games with the GCL Yankees, batting .125 (1-for-8) with 1RBI in his first professional action…entered the 2007 draft ranked as the 34th-best prospect and fifth-best third baseman by *Baseball America* as well as the top pure hitter in college…**PERSONAL:** Played two seasons at the University of Texas, earning All-American honors in 2007 as well as first team All-Big 12 and a spot on the COSIDA Academic All-American team…was the Longhorns' 2007 co-MVP after ranking second on the squad in batting average (.359), hits (84), home runs (12) and RBI (68)…also named an ABCA/Rawlings All-American second team…entered the year one of the top 50 players on the Dick Howser watch list…was named to the 2006 Freshman All-American first team.

TAMAREZ, Christopher – INF

HT: 6-2; **WT:** 170; **B:** R; **T:** R; **BORN:** 10/25/93 in Sabana Palenque, D.R.; **RESIDES:** San Cristobal, D.R.; **OBTAINED:** Signed as a minor league free agent on 8/17/10; **M.L. SVC:** 0.000; **CAREER NOTES:** Will make his professional debut in 2011.

TATIS, Gabriel – RHP

HT: 5-11; **WT:** 195; **B:** R; **T:** R; **BORN:** 5/18/85 in Santo Domingo, D.R.; **RESIDES:** Santo Domingo, D.R.; **OBTAINED:** Signed by the Yankees as a non-drafted free agent on 2/21/06; **M.L. SVC:** 0.000; **CAREER NOTES: 2010:** Pitched the entire season with Single-A Charleston, going 2-3 with a 4.14 ERA (58.2IP, 27ER) in 37 relief appearances…held opponents scoreless in nine of his first 11 outings…**2009:** Went 5-2 with a 4.25 ERA in 21 combined relief appearances between GCL Yankees and Single-A Charleston…opened the season with the GCL squad, allowing 1ER in six relief appearances before being promoted to Charleston on 7/15 where he made 15 relief outings (3-2, 5.68 ERA)…allowed just 1ER over his final four appearances (9.0IP)…**2008:** Appeared in 11 games out of the bullpen with the GCL Yankees and went 1-2 with a 3.71 ERA in 17.0IP…**2007:** Combined at both DSL teams to go 2-1 with a 2.53 ERA in 20 relief appearances…did not allow a home run in 32.0IP…**2006:** In first professional season, posted an 0-2 record and 6.00 ERA in eight games (three starts) for the DSL Yankees 2.

TAVERAS, Damian – INF/C

HT: 6-1; **WT:** 215; **B:** R; **T:** R; **BORN:** 11/28/89 in Santo Domingo, D.R.; **RESIDES:** Santo Domingo, D.R.; **OBTAINED:** Signed by the Yankees as a non-drafted free agent on 7/29/06; **M.L. SVC:** 0.000; **CAREER NOTES: 2010:** Appeared in nine games for the DSL Yankees 1, batting .270 (10-for-37) with 1HR and 4RBI…transferred to the GCL Yankees on 6/15, where he appeared in 31 games and hit .252 (27-for-107) with 5 doubles, 2HR and 14RBI…**2009:** Batted .396 with 13 doubles, 2HR and 22RBI in 30 games with the DSL Yankees 1…hit safely in 25 of his 30 contests…**2008:** Batted .229 with 24R and 19RBI in 43 games with the DSL Yankees 1…recorded 12 extra-base hits (9 doubles, 2 triples and 1HR)…**2007:** Made his professional debut with the DSL Yankees 2, hitting .207 with 22R and 16RBI in 55 games.

TEJEDA, Isaias – C

HT: 6-0; **WT:** 195; **B:** R; **T:** R; **BORN:** 10/28/91 in Santo Domingo, D.R.; **RESIDES:** Santo Domingo, D.R.; **OBTAINED:** Signed by the Yankees as a non-drafted free agent on 9/3/09; **M.L. SVC:** 0.000; **CAREER NOTES: 2010:** Appeared in 58 games for the DSL Yankees 1, hitting .255 (56-for-220) with 16 doubles, 3HR and 33RBI.

TOLENTINO, Israel – RHP
HT: 6-4; **WT:** 190; **B:** R; **T:** R; **BORN:** 1/11/88 in Monte Plata, D.R.; **RESIDES:** Monte Plata, D.R.; **OBTAINED:** Signed by the Yankees as a non-drafted free agent on 11/2/07; **M.L. SVC:** 0.000; **CAREER NOTES: 2010:** Served a 50-game suspension at the start of the season for violating the Minor League Drug Prevention and Treatment Program…made three appearances with the DSL Yankees 1 (0-0 with, 8.00 ERA, 9.0IP, 11H, 8ER, 7BB, 7K)…**2009:** Made 13 appearances (11 starts) with the DSL Yankees 1 and went 1-2 with a 4.76 ERA in 45.1P…recorded a career-high 6K twice, on 6/27 at the DSL Rangers 1 and on 8/6 at the DSL Mets…**2008:** Made his professional debut with the DSL Yankees 2, going 0-0 with a 13.50 ERA in six games…did not allow more than 1H in five of his six relief appearances.

TOUSSEN, Jose – INF
HT: 6-0; **WT:** 180; **B:** R; **T:** R; **BORN:** 11/13/89 in El Ceybo, D.R.; **RESIDES:** La Romana, D.R.; **OBTAINED:** Signed by the Yankees as a non-drafted free agent on 7/2/06; **M.L. SVC:** 0.000; **CAREER NOTES: 2010:** Played the majority of the season with the GCL Yankees, batting .277 (41-for-148) with 24R, 4 doubles, 1HR and 15RBI…was 9-for-10 in stolen base attempts…appeared in games at 2B, 3B, SS, LF, CF and RF…promoted to Single-A Charleston for the final week of the season, appearing in two games (0-for-3)…**2009:** Played the entire season with the GCL Yankees, hitting .223 with 12 doubles, 1 triple, 2HR and 15RBI and leading the league with 58 games played…**2008:** Batted .269 with 41R, 12 doubles and 23RBI in 65 games with the DSL Yankee's 2…recorded the most putouts (123) among all league shortstops…**2007:** Batted .235 with 12 doubles, 4 triples, 3HR and 31RBI in 62 games with the DSL Yankees 2 in his professional debut…was 3-for-5 in his first pro game on 7/2 at the DSL Giants…hit a grand slam on 7/16 vs. the DSL Giants.

TRIPLET, David – RHP
HT: 5-11; **WT:** 185; **B:** R; **T:** R; **BORN:** 1/28/87 in Atlanta, Ga.; **RESIDES:** Austell, Ga,; **OBTAINED:** Signed as a minor league free agent on 8/16/10; **M.L. SVC:** 0.000; **CAREER NOTES: 2010:** Appeared in two games for the GCL Yankees, tossing 2.0 scoreless innings.

TURLEY, Nik – LHP
HT: 6-4; **WT:** 230; **B:** L; **T:** L; **BORN:** 9/11/89 in La Canada, Calif.; **RESIDES:** La Canada, Calif.; **OBTAINED:** Selected by the Yankees in the 50th round of the 2008 First-Year Player Draft; **M.L. SVC:** 0.000; **CAREER NOTES: 2010:** Went 4-2 with a 3.86 ERA (72.1IP, 31ER) in 15 games (14 starts) with the GCL Yankees and short-season Single-A Staten Island…opened the season with the GCL Yankees, allowing 1ER in 10.2IP before being promoted to Staten Island on 7/5…made final 12 starts of the season with the SI Yanks…credited with first career complete game in final outing on 9/2 at Hudson Valley, recording the loss in the first game of a doubleheader (6.0IP)…**2009:** Pitched for the second straight season with the GCL Yankees, going 2-3 with a 2.82 ERA in 11 games (10 starts)…**2008:** Made his professional debut with the GCL Yankees, going 2-1 with a 1.13 ERA in four games (one start)…**PERSONAL:** Graduated from Harvard-Westlake (Calif.) High School and had signed a letter of intent with Brigham Young University.

VALERA, Jackson – INF/C
HT: 6-1; **WT:** 210; **B:** R; **T:** R; **BORN:** 4/8/92 in Valencia, Venezuela; **RESIDES:** Valencia, Venezuela; **OBTAINED:** Signed by the Yankees as a non-drafted free agent on 7/4/08; **M.L. SVC:** 0.000; **CAREER NOTES: 2010:** With the DSL Yankees 1, batted .269 (18-for-67) with 4 doubles and 14 RBI…**2009:** Made his professional debut and hit .217 with 7 doubles, 2HR and 23RBI in 53 games with the DSL Yankees 2.

VARCE, Zachary – RHP
HT: 5-11; **WT:** 180; **B:** R; **T:** R; **BORN:** 12/14/88 in Seattle, Wash.; **RESIDES:** Seattle, Wash.; **COLLEGE:** University of Portland; **OBTAINED:** Selected by the Yankees in the 11th round of the 2010 First-Year Player Draft; **M.L. SVC:** 0.000; **CAREER NOTES: 2010:** Made his professional debut with short-season Single-A Staten Island, going 4-6 with a 4.54 ERA in 15 games (14 starts)…led team in starts and innings pitched…led the New York-Penn League with 74K and a 9.34 K/9.0IP average…allowed 1ER over a three-start stretch from 8/15-26 (17.0IP), going 3-0…**PERSONAL:** Began college career at Portland as closer and converted to No. 1 start in 2010…collected 111K in the 2010 regular season, the 18th-most in the nation…named first-team All-Metro as a junior at West Seattle HS…was a member of the Seattle Mariners Fall Scout Team in 2006.

VARGAS, Cesar – RHP
HT: 6-1; **WT:** 160; **B:** R; **T:** R; **BORN:** 12/30/91 in Puebla, Mexico; **RESIDES:** Puebla, Mexico; **OBTAINED:** Signed by the Yankees as a non-drafted free agent on 2/9/09; **M.L. SVC:** 0.000; **CAREER NOTES: 2010:** Went 2-2 with two saves and a 2.06 ERA in 14 games (two starts) in 39.1IP with the DSL Yankees 2…tossed at least 2.0 innings in each relief appearance…**2009:** In his professional debut, made 16 relief appearances with the DSL Yankees 1, going 2-1 with three saves and a 3.50 ERA.

VAZQUEZ, Jorge – INF   **NON-ROSTER INVITEE**
HT: 5-11; **WT:** 150; **B:** R; **T:** R; **BORN:** 3/15/82 in Culiacan, Mexico; **RESIDES:** Culiacan, Mexico; **OBTAINED:** Signed by the Yankees as a free agent on 12/7/08; **M.L. SVC:** 0.000; **CAREER NOTES: 2010:** Combined to hit .284 (95-for-334) with 25 doubles, 18HR and 68RBI in 86 games with Double-A Trenton and Triple-A Scranton/Wilkes-Barre…recorded a season-high 12-game hitting streak from 6/19-7/1, batting .314 (16-for-51) with 8R, 6 doubles, 2HR and 8RBI over the stretch…ranked fourth among all Yankees minor league hitters in HR…following the season, appeared in 36 games with the Tomateros de Culiacan of the Mexican Pacific League, and hit .346 (46-for-133) with 10 doubles, 10HR and 30RBI…earned series MVP honors in leading Mexico to the 2011 Caribbean World Series championship, batting .310 (9-for-29) with 2 HR and 6 RBI in 6 games…**2009:** Made his Double-A debut, batting .329 with 13HR and 56RBI in 57 games for Trenton…hit .352 (57-for-162) with 12 of his 13HR off right-handed pitching…went 2-for-4 with 1HR and a season-high-tying 4RBI (also 5/6 at Bowie and 5/8 vs. Binghamton) in his first game on 4/23 at New Britain…was placed on the disabled list from 7/17 for the remainder of the season with a left wrist sprain…following the season, played for the Tomateros de Culiacan…played for Mexico in the World Baseball Classic prior to the season, batting .294 (5-for-17) with 5R, 1 double, 1HR and 5RBI in five games (4GS at DH)…**PERSONAL:** Was a 10-year veteran of the Mexican League, recording at least a .300 average and 15HR in each of his final five seasons there (2004-08)…led the league in slugging percentage (.796) and ranked second in homers (33) in 2005…also led the league in slugging (.739) in 2006…was a member of the 2000 and '01 Mexican League championship teams…**2008:** Played for the Tigres de Quintana Roo of the Mexican League, batting .339 with 30R, 7 doubles, 18HR and 59RBI in 56 games…hit safely in 17 straight games from 5/18-6/11, batting .431 (31-for-72) with 1 double, 10HR and 25RBI during the stretch, including a career-high 3HR and 5RBI on 6/7 at Saltillo…recorded a hit in 25-of-26 games from 5/18-7/2 (Game 1), going 43-for-109 (.394) over the span…played for the Tomateros de Culiacan of the Mexican Pacific League, following the season, leading the league in slugging percentage (.636), ranking second in batting average (.348), homers (15) and extra-base hits (.27), placing third in on-base percentage (.416) and ranking fifth in RBI (46).

VENDITTE, Pat – SP

HT: 6-0; **WT:** 197; **B:** R; **T:** S; **BORN:** 6/30/85 in Omaha, Neb.; **RESIDES:** Omaha, Neb.; **COLLEGE:** Creighton University; **OBTAINED:** Selected by the Yankees in the 20th round of the 2008 First-Year Player Draft; **M.L. SVC:** 0.000; **CAREER NOTES: 2010:** Combined to go 5-2 with six saves, a 1.93 ERA (74.2IP, 16ER) and 85K in 43 relief appearances with Single-A Tampa and Double-A Trenton...spent the majority of the season with Tampa, where he went 4-1 with a 1.73 ERA, recording 85K and allowing 14ER in 72.IP...allowed the fewest baserunners/9.0IP in the Florida State League (8.05), ranked second with a .187 opponents average and fourth with a 10.53 K/9.0IP ratio...surrendered just 1ER combined over June and July (29.2IP, 16H, 3R, 1HR, 4BB, 37K), including 15.2 scoreless IP in eight June outings...was promoted to Trenton on 9/1 and made two relief appearances, going 1-1, allowing 2ER in 2.0IP...made four appearances in relief for the Thunder during the postseason and did not allow a run in 2.2 scoreless innings (4K, 2BB)...**2009:** Combined to go 4-2 with 22 saves and a 1.87 ERA (67.1IP 14ER) in 49 relief appearances with Single-A Charleston and Single-A Tampa...recorded 87K and allowed just 11BB...led the RiverDogs with 20 saves and was named to the South Atlantic League's midseason All-Star team before being promoted to Tampa on 6/27...went 2-0 with two saves and a 2.21 ERA with Tampa...made five postseason relief appearances for the Florida State League champions, going 1-0 with a 1.69 ERA (5.1IP, 1ER)...appeared in seven games for the Aguilas del Zulia of the Venezuelan Winter League and went 1-0 with a 4.82 ERA (9.1IP, 11H, 6R, 5ER, 3BB, 7K, 2HR)...**2008:** Went 1-0 with a 0.83 ERA in 30 relief appearances with short-season Single-A Staten Island, converting each of his 23 save opportunities...led the league in saves and ranked second in appearances...owned the most saves among all short-season relievers...ranked second among all Yankees farmhands in saves...was named to the New York-Penn League midseason All-Star team...held opponents to a .117 batting average, with left-handers batting .089 (4-for-45, 1HR) and righties hitting .136 (9-for-66, 1HR)...allowed an earned run in just two of his outings (7/12 at Tri-City – 1ER and 7/21 vs. Brooklyn – 2ER)...held opponents hitless in 21 of his 30 appearances...did not allow an earned run over his final 17 regular season appearances (19.1IP)...made one postseason relief appearance, tossing 1.0 scoreless inning (1H)...was named MiLB's "Best Short-Season Reliever of the Year" at the close of the season...**PERSONAL:** Full name is Patrick Michael Venditte...is the only ambidextrous pitcher in professional baseball...uses a six-finger glove with two thumb holes...is a natural right-hander, but has thrown with both arms since the age of three...caused the Professional Baseball Umpire Corporation (PBUC) to create a new rule regarding ambidextrous pitchers on 7/2/08, that stated that a "pitcher must visually indicate to the umpire, batter and runner(s) which way he will begin pitching to the batter"...attended Creighton University where he majored in marketing...went 9-3 with seven saves and a 3.34 ERA in 37 appearances (one start) during his senior year in 2008...led the team in wins, innings pitched, saves, strikeouts and opponents batting average (.207)...was named second-team preseason All-American by the NCBWA and *Collegiate Baseball* in 2008 and was selected to the Brooks Wallace Watch List...earned All-America honors from *Baseball America* and *Collegiate Baseball* in 2007...was also named the MVC Tournament Most Outstanding Player and Collegiate Baseball's national "Player of the Week" after leading Creighton to its first-ever tournament title...attended Central High School (Neb.) where he was named All-Nebraska second team, team MVP and a *Lincoln Journal Star* Academic All-Star during his senior year...lettered twice in baseball...was previously drafted by the Yankees in the 45th round of the 2007 First-Year Player Draft, but chose to finish his senior year of college.

VINAS, Leonel – RHP

HT: 5-10; **WT:** 165; **B:** R; **T:** R; **BORN:** 8/27/91 in Santo Domingo, D.R.; **RESIDES:** Freeport, N.Y.; **OBTAINED:** Signed as a minor league free agent on 12/14/10; **M.L. SVC:** 0.000; **CAREER NOTES: 2010:** Will make his professional debut in 2011...**PERSONAL:** Was a member of Hank's Yanks, a youth baseball team sponsored by Yankees General Partner/Co-Chairperson Hank Steinbrenner.

WARREN, Adam – RHP   NON-ROSTER INVITEE

HT: 6-2; **WT:** 215; **B:** R; **T:** R; **BORN:** 8/25/87 in Birmingham, Ala.; **RESIDES:** New Bern, N.C.; **COLLEGE:** University of North Carolina; **OBTAINED:** Selected by the Yankees in the fourth round of the 2009 First-Year Player Draft; **M.L. SVC:** 0.000; **CAREER NOTES: 2010:** Combined to go 11-7 with a 2.59 ERA (135.1IP, 39ER) in 25 starts with Single-A Tampa and Double-A Trenton...allowed 3R or less in 19 of his outings and was the starting pitcher for four shutouts...began the season with Tampa where he went 7-5 with a 2.22 ERA, allowing 20ER in 81.0IP...was named to the FSL midseason All-Star team...went 4-2 with a 3.15 ERA (54.1IP, 19ER), after being promoted to Trenton on 7/16...was named Eastern League "Pitcher of the Week" for the week ending on 8/22, after recording a franchise-record 15K and allowing only 2H in seven shutout innings in the Thunder's 3-0 victory vs. Bowie on 8/18...**2009:** Made his professional debut, going 4-2 with a 1.43 ERA (56.2IP, 9ER) in 12 starts with short-season Single-A Staten Island...allowed 1ER or less in 10 of his 12 starts...earned NYPL "Pitcher of the Week" honors twice and was named to the NYPL midseason All-Star team...made two starts in the playoffs for the NYPL Champions, going 1-0 with a 1.69 ERA...led all postseason pitchers with 15K and tied for the league lead in innings pitched (10.2)...**PERSONAL:** Graduated from North Carolina with a degree in business administration...went 32-4 with a 3.42 ERA and 240K in 65 games (49 starts) in his collegiate career...left school with the second-most wins by a Tar Heel and tied with Scott Bankhead for the school's highest winning percentage (.889)...won his first 19 games at UNC, marking the longest since Bankhead won 20 straight from 1983-84...graduated fifth in his class from New Bern High School (N.C.) where he earned all-state honors as a junior in 2004 and was selected as the *New Bern Sun Journal* "Baseball Player of the Year."

WATKINS, Benjamin – RHP

HT: 6-2; **WT:** 215; **B:** R; **T:** R; **BORN:** 3/11/87 in Johnstown, Penn.; **RESIDES:** Johnstown, Penn.; **COLLEGE:** University of Pittsburgh-Johnstown; **OBTAINED:** Selected by the Yankees in the 40th round of the 2009 First-Year Player Draft; **M.L. SVC:** 0.000; **CAREER NOTES: 2010:** Spent the entire season with Single-A Charleston, where he went 3-4 with a 3.88 ERA in 35 games (one start), allowing 25ER in 58.0IP...made his only start of the year in his last outing on 9/4 and did not allow a run 3.0IP (1H, 1BB, 3K)...**2009:** Went 5-0 with a 2.47 ERA in 25 games (two starts) with short-season Single-A Staten Island in his first professional season...held opponents to a .210 batting average, including a .167 mark vs. right-handers...made back-to-back starts (8/26 and 8/31) and did not allow an earned run in either outing (10.0IP, 4H, 1R, 1BB, 9K)...tossed 5.0 scoreless innings of relief and earned the win in the SI Yankees' championship-clinching game on 9/16 vs. Mahoning Valley...**PERSONAL:** Selected as the 2008-09 Atlantic Region Male Scholar-Athlete of the Year, *ESPN The Magazine* Academic All-American and West Virginia Intercollegiate Athletic Conference Male Scholar-Athlete in 2009...also named WVIAC "Pitcher of the Year" after leading Division II and setting a WVIAC record with a 0.84 ERA in 2009.

WHELAN, Kevin – RHP

HT: 5-11; **WT:** 205; **B:** R; **T:** R; **BORN:** 1/8/84 in Kerrville, Tex.; **RESIDES:** Kerrville, Tex.; **OBTAINED:** Acquired by the Yankees from the Detroit Tigers on 11/10/06 along with RHPs Humberto Sanchez and Anthony Claggett in exchange for OF Gary Sheffield; **M.L. SVC:** 0.000; **CAREER NOTES: 2010:** Went a combined 5-4 with a 6.02 ERA (49.1IP, 33ER) with Double-A Trenton and Triple-A Scranton/Wilkes-Barre…began and ended the season with Scranton/WB where he was 2-1 with a 6.30 ERA, allowing 14ER in 20.0IP…in two postseason appearances, was 1-0 with 0.00 ERA, striking out three batters in 2.1 scoreless innings out of the bullpen…went 3-3 with a 5.83 ERA with the Thunder, recording 40K in 29.1IP (19ER)…**2009:** Combined to go 4-0 with three saves and a 2.67 ERA in 44 relief appearances (67.1IP, 20ER) with Double-A Trenton and Triple-A Scranton/Wilkes-Barre, allowing just 1HR…began the season with Trenton, going 4-0 with two saves and a 2.63 ERA in 30 relief outings…was promoted to Scranton/WB on 7/21 where he had one save and a 2.84 ERA in 14 relief appearances without recording a decision…made two postseason appearances out of the bullpen for the International League runner-ups, earning one save and tossing 2.2 scoreless innings (1H, 4BB, 6K)…**2008:** Posted a 1-0 record with two saves and a 4.50 ERA in 24 combined appearances between Single-A Tampa and Double-A Trenton…struck out 46 batters in 38.0IP…opened the season on the disabled list with a right forearm strain (4/3-5/13)…missed four games (6/9-12) for the birth of his child…also missed another month from 6/24-7/30 with a right elbow strain…held left-handed batters to a .098 batting average (5-for-51, 0HR)…made two postseason appearances for the Eastern League champions, allowing 4ER in 2.1IP…pitched with the Peoria Javelinas in the Arizona Fall League, holding opponents scoreless in nine of his 11 outings…**2007:** Combined at Single-A Tampa and Double-A Trenton to go 6-2 with a 2.62 ERA in 38 appearances (eight starts) in his first season with the Yankees organization…overall, held opponents to a .162 batting average with right-handers batting just .133 off him…began season with Trenton, was transferred to Tampa on 6/11, then returned to Trenton on 7/23…appeared in a starting role for the first time with Tampa, making seven starts (2-0, 1.93 ERA, 12BB, 28K) and holding opponents scoreless four times…was named Florida State League "Pitcher of the Week" for the period ending 7/8 (1-0, 10.0IP, 2H, 0ER, 3BB, 8K)…began the season with five straight scoreless outings, converting on all three save opportunities (9.0IP, 5H, 4BB, 11K)…following the season, appeared in three games with the Peoria Javelinas of the Arizona Fall League (0-0, 12.00 ERA)…**2006:** Ranked third among all Detroit Tigers' minor-league pitchers with 27 saves in 2006, going 4-1 with a 2.67 ERA in 51 games for the Single-A Lakeland Tigers…limited opposing hitters to a .178 batting average (33-for-185) and held right-handed hitters to a .158 average (18-for-114)…ranked second among all Florida State League pitchers with 46 games finished, ranked third in the league in saves and ranked fourth with 51 games pitched…**2005:** Selected as the Tigers Minor League "Pitcher of the Month" for August after posting a 0.84 ERA (10.2IP, 1ER), nine saves and 20 strikeouts in 11 appearances for short-season Single-A West Michigan…named the 10th-best prospect in the Tigers organization and 18th-best prospect in the New York-Penn League following the season by *Baseball America*…selected to the publication's all-star squad for players drafted out of college…**PERSONAL:** Pitched for three seasons at Texas A&M…compiled a 4-1 record with four saves and a 2.90 ERA (40K) in 19 games in 2005…also saw time at catcher in 2004 as a sophomore…finished 0-2 with a 4.15 ERA in 10 games as a pitcher and hit .233 (10-for-43) with 1HR and 4RBI behind the plate…tabbed as a 2004 Second-Team Summer All-American by *Baseball America* after earning Cape Cod League All-Star honors for Wareham, finishing 2-2 with a 0.42 ERA, 11 saves and 31K in 18 games…named the 10th-best prospect overall in the Cape Cod League by *Baseball America*…batted .245 with 1HR and 6RBI as a freshman catcher…named the eighth-best prospect in the Jayhawk League during the summer by *Baseball America* after pitching for Liberal High School.

WHITLEY, Chase Coleman – RHP

HT: 6-3; **WT:** 213; **B:** R; **T:** R; **BORN:** 6/14/89 in Ranburne, Ala.; **RESIDES:** Ranburne, Ala.; **COLLEGE:** Troy University; **OBTAINED:** Selected by the Yankees in the 15th round of the 2010 First-Year Player Draft; **M.L. SVC:** 0.000; **CAREER NOTES: 2010:** Made his professional debut, combining to go 4-2 with 15 saves, a 1.45 ERA and 50K in 37.1IP over 30 appearances with short-season Single-A Staten Island and Single-A Tampa…began the season with Staten Island where he was 4-2 with a 1.31 ERA and 15 saves in 34.1IP in relief…prior to his promotion to Tampa on 9/1, led all Staten Island relievers with 44K and tied for second in the NYPL in saves, earning him a spot on the All-Star team…finished the season ranked second in games and tied for second in saves in the NYPL, while recording the third-lowest opponents average (.157) among league relievers…in three relief appearances with Tampa during the postseason, recorded 5K and allowed 2H in 3.1 scoreless innings…**PERSONAL:** Attended Southern Union Community College before transferring to Troy…as a junior at Ranburne High School (Ala.), earned All-District, All-Area and All-State honors.

WILLIAMS, Mason – OF

HT: 6-1; **WT:** 155; **B:** L; **T:** R; **BORN:** 8/21/91 in Winter Garden, Fla.; **RESIDES:** Winter Garden, Fla.; **OBTAINED:** Selected by the Yankees in the fourth round of the 2010 First-Year Player Draft; **M.L. SVC:** 0.000; **CAREER NOTES: 2010:** Made his professional debut with the GCL Yankees, appearing in five games and batting .222 (4-for-18)…named the "Fastest Baserunner" in the Yankees organization by *Baseball America*…**PERSONAL:** Graduated West Orange High School (Fla.).

WORDEKEMPER, Eric – RHP

NON-ROSTER INVITEE

HT: 6-1; **WT:** 215; **B:** R; **T:** R; **BORN:** 8/8/83 in Storm Lake, Iowa; **RESIDES:** Storm Lake, Iowa; **COLLEGE:** Creighton University; **OBTAINED:** Selected by the Yankees in the 46th round of the 2005 First-Year Player Draft; **M.L. SVC:** 0.000; **CAREER NOTES: 2010:** Went a combined 5-0 with nine saves and a 3.00 ERA (66.0IP, 22ER) in 47 appearances out of the bullpen with Double-A Trenton and Triple-A Scranton/Wilkes-Barre…made two relief appearances for Scranton/WB during the postseason, and went 0-1 with a 2.25 ERA (4.0IP, 1ER)…following the season, appeared in 21 games for the Tomateros de Culiacan of the Mexican Pacific League and did not record a decision, recording 19K in 19.1IP in relief (19ER)…**2009:** Combined to go 3-2 with a 3.38 ERA in 38 relief appearances with Double-A Trenton and Triple-A Scranton/Wilkes-Barre…began the season with Trenton, going 1-2 with a 3.00 ERA in 28 relief outings…held right-handed batters to a .171 (14-for-82, 0HR) batting average, while left-handers hit .243 (17-for-70, 3HR)…went 2-0 with a 4.32 ERA in 10 relief appearances with Scranton/WB…went 0-1 with a 3.86 ERA in two postseason relief appearances for the International League runner-ups, allowing 3H and 1ER in 2.1IP (2K)…following the season, earned one save while pitching for the Aguilas del Zulia of the Venezuelan Winter League, making five appearances (one start) and allowing 12H and 9ER in 8.1IP (9.72 ERA, 10R, 5BB, 3K)…**2008:** Appeared in 33 games (one start) for Double-A Trenton, going 3-2 with six saves and a 3.93 ERA…landed on the disabled list from 7/29-8/14 with a muscle strain in his left ribcage…had not allowed an earned run in seven July appearances prior to the injury (12.1IP)…was activated and assigned to Single-A Tampa where he made two relief appearances, allowing four runs (2ER) in 1.2IP…**2007:** Was 2-0 with 33 saves and a 0.57 ERA in 43 relief appearances for Single-A Tampa, leading the team in ERA, saves and games…was named the Florida State League's "Most Valuable Pitcher" after leading the league in saves and earned a spot on the league's mid- and postseason All-Star teams as well as the Topps Class-A All-Star team…appeared in one game with Double-A Trenton on 9/2, throwing a scoreless inning to earn the save…appeared in one postseason game with Trenton, throwing a scoreless inning in the Thunder's Division Series win at Portland on 9/8…his organization-high 34 combined saves were the fifth-most in the minors…allowed an earned run in just three of his 44 appearances in 2007, finishing the season with 28 consecutive outings without allowing an earned run (from 5/31 on)…with Tampa, struck out 34 batters with only 11 walks and held opponents to a .223 batting average, converting 33-of-35 save opportunities…did not allow a home run all season…following the season, pitched with the Peoria Javelinas of the Arizona Fall League, going 1-0 with one save and a 2.89 ERA…**2006:** With Single-A Charleston, posted a 4-3 record with a 1.81 ERA…appeared in one game with Triple-A Columbus on 9/3 at Toledo, retiring all six batters faced (2K)…**2005:** Made professional debut with the Gulf Coast Yankees, going 2-0 with a 2.12 ERA in nine games (five starts)…was promoted to short-season Single-A Staten Island on 8/28 and made two starts, going 0-2 with a 4.50 ERA…**PERSONAL:** Played baseball at Creighton University before being drafted by the Yankees in 2005…was given All-MVC Conference Honorable Mention following the 2004 season…graduated from St. Mary's HS in Storm Lake, Iowa, where he participated in four years of baseball and three years of basketball and track…won the Bob Feller Award as a senior for "Pitcher of the Year" in Iowa after going 11-2 with three saves and 180K with just 14BB in 83.0IP…was named to the all-conference team all four seasons…chosen as a first-team all-state player his junior and senior seasons and a second-team selection as a sophomore and freshman…voted the team MVP his sophomore through senior seasons and named the area "Athlete of the Year" his junior year.

ZHANG, Zhenwang – C

HT: 6-1; **WT**: 170; **B**: R; **T**: R; **BORN**: 3/1/88 in Tianjin, China; **RESIDES**: Tianjin, China; **OBTAINED**: Signed by the Yankees as a non-drafted free agent on 6/16/07; **M.L. SVC**: 0.000; **CAREER NOTES**: Appeared in three games for Team China in the 2009 World Baseball Classic and went hitless in 6AB…along with LHP Kai Liu, were the first members of Chinese Baseball to sign with a Major League team in accordance with the Yankees and Chinese Baseball Association's Memorandum of Understanding signed in January 2007…along with Liu, was introduced at a press conference at Yankee Stadium on 7/6/07 and then reported to the Yankees complex in Tampa.

Yankee Stadium Earns Top Honors

In an August 10, 2009, pregame ceremony, the American Academy of Hospitality Sciences recognized Yankee Stadium with its highest honor, the "Six Star Diamond Award," which is bestowed on superlative establishments that are deemed to be of pinnacle quality.

Additionally, Legends Hospitality Management, LLC, received the academy's "Five Star Award" for providing a commitment of consistent excellence in cuisine, products and services to its guests. The newly formed Stadium concessionaire and hospitality company is the first such organization to be recognized as award-winning by the academy.

New York Yankees™

MEDIA

Yankees Manager **JOE GIRARDI** addresses
media during spring training at George M.
Steinbrenner Field in Tampa, Fla.

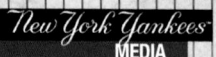

Media Services at Yankee Stadium

Media Relations Department
Yankee Stadium • One East 161st Street • Bronx, NY 10451
Switchboard: (718) 293-4300
Media Relations: (718) 579-4460
Fax: (718) 293-8414
E-mail: media@yankees.com, credentials@yankees.com
Web site: www.yankees.com, www.yankeesbeisbol.com

Jason Zillo – Director, Communications and Media Relations
Jason Latimer – Assistant Director, Media Relations & Player Relations
Michael Margolis – Asst. Director, Baseball Information & Public Communications
Lauren Moran – Coordinator, Baseball Information
Kenny Leandry – Coordinator, Media Relations and Publicity
Alexandra Trochanowski – Assistant, Media Relations and Publicity
Germania-Dolores Hernandez – Administrative Assistant

Media Services for Yankees Games
The New York Yankees Media Relations staff welcomes you to Yankee Stadium. Please see below for helpful information and guidelines for the 2011 season. Contact us with any questions or concerns you may have. We look forward to working with you.

ADMISSION TO STADIUM/CREDENTIAL PICK-UP: All media must enter Yankee Stadium via the Press Gate, adjacent to Gate 4. The Press Gate opens five hours prior to game time. BBWAA cards, MLB-issued passes or credentials issued by the New York Yankees are necessary for admittance. NO OTHER CREDENTIAL WILL BE HONORED. All bags are subject to search upon entry. Photo ID will be required.

ADMISSION TO FIELD AND DUGOUTS: On game days, the field and dugouts can be accessed from the Service Level (000) via the Field Access Tunnel (located on the outfield side of the Visitors Clubhouse) or through either team's clubhouse when open to the media during regular clubhouse hours. Take the press elevator or stairs from the Press Gate or Main Press Box down to the Service Level and follow the interior concourse to the right for the Yankees Clubhouse or to the left for the Field Access Tunnel and Visitors Clubhouse. Please note that the field is closed to media at the conclusion of the visiting team's batting practice.

CLUBHOUSES: The Yankees Clubhouse is open to those with BBWAA cards, MLB-issued passes or applicable credentials issued by the New York Yankees. NO OTHER CREDENTIAL WILL BE HONORED. The Clubhouse is open from three and a half hours prior to the game until one hour before game time. At times, certain additional restrictions may be imposed. Private corridors inside the clubhouse, including the trainer's room, player's lounge, weight room, etc. are CLOSED TO MEDIA AT ALL TIMES. Visiting clubhouse is governed by the visiting club.

CREDENTIAL QUESTIONS: Please direct questions to Alexandra Trochanowski in the Yankees Media Relations office at credentials@yankees.com or (718) 579-4460.

DAILY CREDENTIALS: All requests for 2011 single-game regular season media credentials for games played at Yankee Stadium may be made online at https://credentials.mlb.com. The online application is the only acceptable method for requesting single-game regular season media credentials for games played at Yankee Stadium. Applications must be completed by a Sports Editor or Sports Director and require at least 24 hours notice.

ELEVATOR TO PRESS BOX: The Field Level entrance is directly behind the Press Gate between Gate 4 and the Great Hall. A staircase adjacent to the press elevator also provides route to the Service, Field and Press Box Levels. Entrance on the Service Level is near the Legends Suite Club on the first base side.

FIELD: All media, with BBWAA cards or applicable credentials issued by the New York Yankees, are permitted on the field in designated areas during pre-game practice. For Safety Purposes, All Media Must Leave The Field Once The Batting Cage Is Removed. Dugouts Are To Be Cleared One-Half Hour Prior To All Games. Please Display Passes At All Times.

INTERNET: Wireless internet is available throughout all working media areas. Please see a Yankees Media Relations representative for login instructions.

INTERVIEW REQUESTS: To schedule interviews requiring special arrangements, please e-mail your request to media@yankees.com.

MEDIA GUIDES: Please see a member of the Yankees Media Relations department.

NO AUTOGRAPHS: ANY MEMBER OF THE MEDIA REQUESTING AUTOGRAPHS WHILE CREDENTIALED WILL HAVE THEIR CREDENTIAL REVOKED.

Departamento de Medios de Comunicacion
Yankee Stadium • One East 161st Street • Bronx, NY 10451
Centralita de Teléfonos: (718) 293-4300
Medios de Prensa: (718) 579-4460 • **Fax:** (718) 293-8414
Correo Electrónico: media@yankees.com, credentials@yankees.com
Página de Internet: www.yankees.com, www.yankeesbeisbol.com

Jason Zillo – Director, Communiciónes y Relaciones de Prensa
Jason Latimer – Subdirector, Relaciones de Prensa y del Equipo
Michael Margolis – Subdirector, Información sobre el Béisbol y Comunicaciones
Lauren Moran – Coordinadora, Información sobre el Béisbol
Kenny Leandry – Coordinador, Relaciones de Prensa y Publicidad
Alexandra Trochanowski – Asistente, Relaciones de Prensa y Publicidad
Germania- Dolores Hernandez – Asistente de Administración

Servicios a los medios de comunicación durante la temporada
El departamento de medios de comunicacion de los Yankees de Nueva York quisiera darle la bienvenida al Yankee Stadium. Por favor vea abajo las pautas para la temporada del 2011. Por favor comuníquese con nuestra oficina para cualquier pregunta o preocupación que usted pueda tener. Deseamos tener el placer de trabajar con ustedes este año.

ADMISIÓN AL ESTADIO/ ENTREGA DE CREDENCIALES: Todos los medios deben de entrar por la entrada de la prensa (Press Gate), adyacente a la entrada número 4 del estadio (Gate 4). La entrada de la prensa (Press Gate) abre cinco horas antes del inicio del juego. Las tarjetas BBWAA, los pases distribuidos por MLB o las credenciales repartidas por los Yankees de Nueva York son necesarios para entrar. NO SE HONRARÁ NINGUNO OTRO CREDENCIAL. Todas las bolsas están sujetas a ser revisadas a la entrada. Identificación de foto será requerida.

ENTRADA AL TERRENO Y LAS TRINCHERAS: Durante los juegos en casa, las entradas al terreno y a las trincheras son accesibles por el tunel (ubicado en el Service Level (000) al lado del clubhouse del equipo visitante con acceso al campo largo del terreno) o por medio al clubhouse de los equipos durante las horas designadas a los medios de comunicacion. Tome el ascensor o escalera por la entrada de la prensa o desde el palco principal de prensa al Service Level y siga el corredor interior hacia la derecha en direction al Yankees Clubhouse o el tunel a la izquierda en direction al Clubhouse de los Visitantes con acceso al campo largo del terreno. Por favor tome encuenta que el terreno cierra para los medios de comunicacion a la conclusion de la practica del equipo visitante.

CLUBHOUSES: El clubhouse de los Yankees es accesible por aquellos que tengan las tarjetas BBWAA, los pases distribuidos por MLB o las credenciales repartidas por los Yankees de Nueva York. NO SE HONRARÁ NINGUNA OTRA CREDENCIAL. El Clubhouse abre tres horas y media antes del juego y cierra una hora antes del inicio del juego. Ocasionalmente, ciertas restricciones adicionales seran aplicadas. CORREDORES PRIVADOS DENTRO DEL CLUBHOUSE, INCLUYENDO EL CUARTO DEL ENTRENADOR, EL SALÓN DE LOS JUGADORES Y EL GIMNASIO ESTÁN SIEMPRE CERRADOS PARA LA PRENSA. El clubhouse de los visitantes es gobernado por el equipo visitante.

PREGUNTAS SOBRE CREDENCIALES: Por favor de dirigir cualquier pregunta a Alexandra Trochanowski o a Germania-Dolores Hernandez, del departamento de medios de comunicacion de los Yankees, vía correo electrónico a credentials@yankees.com o al número de teléfono (718) 579-4460.

CREDENCIALES POR JUEGO INDIVIDUAL: Solicitudes de credenciales por juego individual en el Yankee Stadium deben ser sometidas vía la página web de *Major League Baseball (MLB)* en https://credentials.mlb.com. La solicitud vía el internet es el único método aceptable para el pedido de credenciales para juegos individuales durante la temporada 2011. Dichos pedidos solo pueden ser hechos por un director o editor de deportes y deben ser recibidas con un mínimo de 24-horas de aviso.

ASCENSOR AL PALCO DE PRENSA: La entrada Field Level está ubicada directamente detrás de la entrada de la prensa (Press Gate), entre la entrada número 4 (Gate 4) del estadio y el Great Hall. Una escalera al lado del elevador de la prensa también provee ruta a los niveles Service, Field y Press Box. La entrada en el Service Level está cerca del Legends Suite Club, que está localizado por la parte de la primera base del estadio.

EL TERRENO: Toda la prensa con tarjetas BBWAA o con credenciales con terreno asignado distribuidos por los Yankees de Nueva York, son permitidos en el terreno en áreas designadas durante la práctica de bateo. CON PROPOSITOS DE SEGURIDAD, TODA LA PRENSA DEBE IRSE DEL TERRENO UNA VEZ QUE LA JAULA DE BATEO ES RETIRADA DEL TERRENO. LAS TRINCHERAS DEBEN SER DESALOJADAS MEDIA HORA ANTES DE CADA JUEGO. POR FAVOR MANTENGAN SUS CREDENCIALES VISIBLES EN TODOS MOMENTO.

INTERNET: El internet inalámbrico está disponible en todas las areas de trabajo para los medios. Por favor comunicárselo a un representante del departamento de prensa de los Yankees de Nueva York para que lo atienda.

SOLICITUD PARA ENTREVISTAS: Entrevistas que requieran arreglos especiales. Envíelo por escrito vía correo electrónico a media@yankees.com.

GUIAS DE PRENSA: Por favor comunicárselo a un representante del departamento de prensa de los Yankees de Nueva York para que lo atienda.

NO AUTOGRAFOS: TODOS LOS MIENBROS DE MEDIOS DE COMUNICACIÓN QUE SOLICITE UN AUTOGRAFO Y HAYA ADQUIRIDO ADMISION VIA UN CREDENCIAL, ESTE SE LE SERA REVOCADO.

NOTAS, RECORDS, ETC.: Las notas de prensa y estadísticas están disponible a petición en la sesión principal y en el salón laborar de la prensa antes del juego. Hojas de jugadas por jugadas y las notas post- juego están disponible en la sesión principal de la prensa al final del juego.

NOTES, RECORDS, ETC.: Press notes and statistics are available upon request in the press box and press conference room prior to games. Postgame box scores and notes are available in the press box after games.

PARKING: Media are encouraged to park in the Ruppert Plaza Garage, located on the corner of Jerome Ave. and the Macombs Dam Bridge ramp, directly across the street from the Press Gate. The garage will open six hours prior to the start of the game and remain open at least three hours after the last pitch.

PHOTO REQUESTS: Please e-mail media@yankees.com.

PHOTOGRAPHERS: Photographers will not be permitted on the field during games and have no access to the clubhouse. All photographers work from assigned locations. NO ROVING PHOTO PASSES WILL BE ISSUED.

PREGAME AND POSTGAME TV INTERVIEWS: Available upon request whenever possible. Please notify a Yankees Media Relations representative so assistance can be provided.

PRESS BOX: Take the press elevator or stairs to Main Level. Doors open by the TV and radio booths. The press box, working press room and media dining room will be to your left. Please sit in assigned seats. If no seat is assigned, please ask a Yankees Media Relations representative for assistance.

PRESS CONFERENCE ROOM: Take the press elevator or stairs down to the Service Level. The Press Conference Room is on the first base side, opposite the Yankees clubhouse.

PRESS DINING: Sheppard's Place is open to those with BBWAA cards, MLB-issued passes or applicable credentials issued by the New York Yankees. Entrance is through the Press Box, behind the working press box. Meals are served starting 2 hours and 30 minutes prior to game time and will remain available through the sixth inning.

TELEPHONE ASSISTANCE: For assistance with ordered telephone lines, please call a Yankee Global Technology representative at 646-977-TECH.

TELEVISION CREWS: Crews are not permitted on field during games. LIVE TRANSMISSION IS NOT PERMITTED DURING GAMES FOR NON-RIGHTSHOLDERS. NO ROVING TV CREW PASSES WILL BE ISSUED.

WORKING PRESS ROOMS: Both Print and Audio Workrooms are located behind the working press box. The Photographers workroom is on the Service Level across from the Visitors' clubhouse on the third base side.

Roving in the stands and concourses is prohibited. Likewise, field access during the game is limited to the first and third base photo boxes.

ESTACIONAMIENTO: Los medios de prensa deben de estacionarse en el garaje *Ruppert Plaza*, localizado en la esquina de la avenida Jerome y el *Macombs Dam Bridge*, al otro lado de la entrada número 4 del estadio. El garaje estará abierto seis horas antes del principio del juego y hasta tres horas después del último lanzamiento.

SOLICITUD PARA FOTOGRAFIAS: Por favor envíe un correo electrónico a media@yankees.com.

FOTOGRAFIAS: Fotógrafos no serán permitidos al terreno durante juegos y no tienen admisión al clubhouse. Fotógrafos laboran en puntos asignados. NO SE LE OTORGARA ADMISION A FOTOGRAFOS PARA VAGAR.

ENTREVISTAS TELEVISIVAS PRE Y POST-JUEGO: SE PUEDEN OBTERNER CON SOLICITUD PREVIA CUANDO SEA POSIBLE. Por favor comunicárselo a un representante del departamento de prensa de los Yankees de Nueva York para que lo atienda.

PALCO PRINCIPAL DE PRENSA: Tome el ascensor de prensa o las escaleras hacia el Main Level. Las puertas del ascensor abren cerca de las salas de televisión y radio. El palco principal de la prensa y el comedor están localizados a la izquierda del ascensor. Por favor tomen los asientos asignados. Si no se le asigno un asiento, por favor pregunte a un representante del departamento de prensa de los Yankees.

SALA DE CONFERENCIAS DE PRENSA: Tome el elevador de prensa o las escaleras hacia abajo para el Service Level. Tome una derecha el salón laborar de prensa se encuentra al mismo lado de la primera base, y al otro lado del clubhouse de los Yankees.

COMEDOR DE PRENSA: El comedor de prensa está abierto para aquellos con tarjetas de admisión del BBWAA, pases de admisión de las grandes ligas o los credenciales con comedor asignado por los New York Yankees. La entrada está localizada en el palco de prensa, detrás del espacio laborar de la prensa. Las comidas serán servidas dos horas y medias antes del juego y se mantendrá disponible hasta la sexta entrada.

ASISTENCIA TELEFONICA: Asistencia para ordenar lineas telefónicas, por favor llame a un representante de Yankees Global Technology a 646-977-TECH.

EQUIPO DE TRABAJADORES DE TELEVISION: Ningún miembro del equipo tendrá admisión al terreno durante el juego. TRAMISION EN VIVO NO SERA PERMITIDA DURANTE LOS JUEGOS A NINGUNA PERSONA QE NO TENGA DERECHOS RESERVADOS. NO SE LE OBTORGARAN PASES PARA VAGAR A NINGUN MIEMBRO DEL EQUIPO DE TELEVISION.

SALA LABORAR DE PRENSA: Las salas laborares de la prensa escritas y de la prensa audiovisual están localizadas detrás de la sesión principal de la prensa. El salón laborar de los fotógrafos esta en el Service Level al cruzar el CLUBHOUSE de los visitantes en el lado de la tercera base.

VAGAR POR LAS ALCOVAS Y LOS PASILLO ES PROIVIDO. AL IGUAL, ACESO AL TERRENO DURANTE EL JUEGO ES LIMITADO A LAS SECIONES FOTOGRAFICAS DE PRIMERA Y TERCERA BASE.

Useful New York Telephone Numbers

AIRLINES		TAXI COMPANIES	AUTO RENTALS
Air Canada.... (888) 247-2262	American ... (800) 433-7300	City Ride...... (718) 706-6666	Avis .... (800) 331-1212
Continental... (800) 523-3273	Delta .... (800) 221-1212	Coast to Coast (718) 439-3810	Budget ..... (800) 527-0700
USAir....... (800) 428-4322	United...... (800) 241-6522	Flyte Time .. (888) 880-5466	Hertz .... (800) 654-3131
Jet Blue....... (800) 538-2583			

HOTELS

Grand Hyatt	42nd St. at Grand Central bet. Lex and Park	(212) 883-1234
Hilton	650 Terrace Ave, Hasbrouck Hts., NJ	(201) 288-6100
Hilton New York and Towers	Ave. of Americas/6th Ave. bet. 53rd and 54th	(212) 586-7000
Hotel Edison	228 W. 47th St. bet. Broadway and 8th Ave.	(212) 840-5000
Marriott Marquis	1535 Broadway	(212) 398-1900
Park Central	870 7th Ave. bet. 55th and 56th	(212) 247-8000
Sheraton New York	811 7th Ave. at 53rd St.	(212) 581-1000
Sheraton–Manhattan	790 7th Ave. at 51st St.	(212) 581-3300
Waldorf Astoria	301 Park Ave.	(212) 355-3000

RESTAURANTS

Artisanal	2 Park Avenue	(212) 725-8585
Aureole	34 E. 62st St. between Madison and Park Ave.	(212) 319-1660
Ben Benson's	123 W. 52nd St. between 6th and 7th Ave.	(212) 581-8888
Carmine's	200 W. 44th St. between Broadway and 8th Ave.	(212) 221-3800
Elaine's	1703 2nd Ave. between 88th and 89th St.	(212) 534-8103
Gallagher's Steak House	228 W. 52nd St. between Broadway and 8th Ave.	(212) 245-5336
Hard Rock Cafe.	Yankee Stadium	(646) 977-8888
Il Fornaio	132A Mulberry St. between Grand and Hester St.	(212) 226-8306
Il Vagabondo	351 E. 62nd St. between 1st and 2nd Ave.	(212) 832-9221
Mesa Grill	102 Fifth Ave. between 15th and 16th St.	(212) 807-7400
Mickey Mantle's	42 Central Park South between 5th and 6th Ave.	(212) 688-7777
Monte's	97 MacDougal St.	(212) 228-9194
NYY Steak	Yankee Stadium	(646) 977-8325
Palm	837 Second Ave. between 44th and 45th St.	(212) 687-2953
Peter Luger Steak House	178 Broadway, Brooklyn	(718) 387-7400
TAO	42 E. 58th Street	(212) 888-2288
Union Square Café	21 E. 16th St. bet. Union Square West and 5th Ave.	(212) 243-4020
Yolanda's Restaurant	292 E. 149th St., Bronx	(718) 993-2709

Yankees Broadcasters

Michael Kay

Now in his 10th season as the play-by-play announcer for the YES Network and WWOR-TV, Michael Kay immerses himself in all things New York in order to provide his listeners and viewers with original opinions and the most exclusive, up-to-the-minute Yankees information. Additionally, Kay is the host of YES' CenterStage series, hosts his own radio talk show on ESPN 1050 AM in New York and is a frequent contributor to ESPN's Emmy Award-winning *Sports Reporters*. In 2008, he handled play-by-play duties for ESPN Radio Network's coverage of the AL Division Series.

A 21-time Emmy Award nominee and three-time Emmy winner, Kay signed a multi-year extension with the YES Network in 2008 to remain as the club's lead play-by-play voice as well as host on a variety of YES Network programs.

Before joining the YES Network, Kay worked at the MSG Network from 1989-2001 as a Yankees reporter. In 1992, he added the assignment of Knicks locker room reporter to his responsibilities and continued in that role through the 1998-99 season.

In addition to his television work, Kay also worked as a Yankees analyst on WABC Radio from 1992-2002. Kay was a winner with Bob Goldscholl (WBBR) for "Best Sports Reporter" at the 2000 New York Metro Achievement in Radio Awards. After the Yankees' World Series victories in 1996, 1998, 2000 and 2009, Kay and John Sterling were asked by New York City's Mayor to host the post-parade victory celebration at City Hall.

In 1998, Kay also began co-hosting *Sports Talk with John Sterling and Michael Kay*, an MSG-produced nightly sports radio call-in show which aired on WABC Radio during the winter months. During the baseball season, Kay and Sterling hosted *Yankee Talk* which aired 90 minutes prior to all weekend Yankees games.

Shortly after graduating from Fordham University in 1982 with a B.A. in Communications, the Bronx, N.Y., native became one of the hot sports reporters in New York City with a style that combined great reporting skills with quality writing. While at Fordham, he honed his skills working for the school newspaper and radio station, working at Sports Phone and as the public address announcer for the New York Pro Summer Basketball League. In 1982, Kay landed a job as a general assignment writer for the *New York Post*. Two years later he began covering college basketball (1984-85) and then the New Jersey Nets, whom he covered for two seasons before becoming the newspaper's general basketball writer. In 1987, he moved to baseball where he served as his paper's Yankees beat reporter. While he was in that position, he got his first television job with MSG Network as host of the "Hot Stove League" segment of MSG's Sports Night. Kay moved from the *Post* to the *New York Daily News* in 1989, where he covered the Yankees until 1992, when he made the jump to radio. With the move, he became the first newspaper reporter in any sport to make the jump into the broadcast booth full-time, performing both play-by-play and analysis.

Kay was given the Dick Young Award for Excellence in Sports Media by the New York Pro Baseball Scouts in 1995. He was also a part of the Yankees/MSG Production team that was nominated for New York Emmy Awards for six consecutive years. In 1998, he was on the MSG team that won for "Outstanding Live Sports Coverage–Series". In 1996 and '97, he was a member of the MSG team that won New York Emmys for "Outstanding Live Sports Coverage–Single Program" for Dwight Gooden's no-hitter and "The Battle for New York: Yankees vs. Mets".

Kay resides in Hartsdale, N.Y., and is active with the Alzheimer's Association in memory of his mother, Rose, who passed away from the disease in 2006. For the past three years, Kay has joined Joe Girardi for the "Remember When, Remember Now" banquet at the Grand Central Oyster Bar to benefit Girardi's Catch 25 Foundation and Alzheimer's research. He and his wife, Jodi, were married in February.

Ken Singleton

Former Major Leaguer Ken Singleton enters his 10th season as a game analyst and announcer for YES Network broadcasts of the New York Yankees. Known on the diamond as a consistent power hitter, Singleton has proven to be equally as reliable since joining the radio and television broadcast booths.

Prior to joining YES, Singleton divided his time calling play-by-play and providing commentary at the MSG Network. In 1998, he was part of MSG's production team that won four New York Emmys for its Yankees coverage.

Singleton joined the MSG Network in 1997 from The Sports Network (TSN), where he served as analyst for the Montreal Expos from 1985-96. From 1991-96, he also called play-by-play and served as analyst for CIQ Radio, the Expos' flagship radio network. In 1996 and '97, he was named by FOX Sports as a lead analyst for Saturday afternoon baseball broadcasts. In 1997 and '98, he worked as an analyst for Major League Baseball International.

Singleton enjoyed a 15-year Major League career with the New York Mets, Montreal Expos and Baltimore Orioles, batting .282 with 317 doubles and 246HR. He is one of only 10 players in Baseball history to hit 35 or more home runs in a season as a switch-hitter. He also ranks among the all-time leaders in most Baltimore offensive categories, including homers, RBI and total bases. During his career, Singleton was named to the American League All-Star team in 1977, '79, and '81. He was named Most Valuable Oriole in 1975, '77, and '79 and was a member of the Orioles' 1983 World Championship team. In 1982, he was the recipient of Major League Baseball's Roberto Clemente Award, honoring him for his contributions both on and off the field.

A native New Yorker, Singleton played both baseball and basketball in high school, and also played baseball in the Bronx Federation League at Macombs Dam Park on the current site of Yankee Stadium. After getting a basketball scholarship to Hofstra University and playing baseball as well for one year, Singleton was drafted by the Mets in 1967.

He enjoys golf and reading historical novels and lives with his wife Suzanne in Sparks, Md. He also has three sons and a daughter.

Bill Boland
Senior Producer

John Moore
Director

Bob Lorenz
Studio Anchor

Nancy Newman
Studio Host

Chris Shearn
Studio Host

Yankees Broadcasters

Jack Curry

Jack Curry joined the YES Network in 2010 as studio analyst, reporter and program contributor, following a 20-year career covering the Yankees for the *New York Times*. In addition, he contributes as a columnist on YESNetwork.com

During his career with the *Times*, Curry authored more than 4,500 articles, covering 18 World Series, 11 All-Star Games and two World Baseball Classics. The New Jersey native also was nominated for a Pulitzer Prize in 1999, and won multiple *Times* Publisher Awards.

Curry's television experience extends back to 1991, when he began contributing to Madison Square Garden Network's Yankees pre-game show and weekly baseball magazine show. He also co-wrote a book with Derek Jeter entitled *Life You Imagine: Life Lessons for Achieving Your Dreams*, which was a *New York Times* best-seller.

A 1986 graduate of Fordham University, Curry resides with his wife, Pamela, in New Jersey.

John Flaherty

Former Yankees catcher John Flaherty enters his sixth season as a field reporter, studio analyst and game analyst for YES Network telecasts in 2011.

Drafted by Boston in 1988, Flaherty progressed through the Red Sox farm system before joining their Major League squad in 1992. He played 14 seasons in the Majors with Boston (1992-93), Detroit (1994-96), San Diego (1996-97), Tampa Bay (1998-2002) and the Yankees (2003-05), compiling a .252 average with 80 HR in 1,047 games.

Flaherty brought his knowledge of the game and his veteran style of leadership to the Yankees clubhouse when he signed as a free agent in 2003. He played in 134 games with the Yankees across three seasons, and will be long remembered for his dramatic pinch-hit, "walk-off" single that defeated the Boston Red Sox in the 13th inning of a 5-4 victory on June 1, 2004, in the contest that featured Derek Jeter's famous dive in the third base stands.

Flaherty is a New York City native and a graduate of George Washington University. On May 15, 2009, he was awarded an honorary Doctorate of Humane Letters from St. Thomas Aquinas College in Sparkill, N.Y.

Kimberly Jones

Kimberly Jones returns for her seventh season as a Yankees pregame and postgame clubhouse reporter. She is also a contributor to YES Network's *This Week in Football* and *Yankees Hot Stove* shows, as well as occasionally hosting talk shows on WFAN-AM 660 in New York.

Jones previously spent four-and-a-half years at the *Star-Ledger* (Newark, N.J.), where she covered the New York Giants for three seasons and was the NFL columnist for one. For the 2005 NFL season, she continued to contribute as the *Star-Ledger's* Sunday NFL notes columnist and also appeared as an NFL contributor on *Out of Bounds* on CN8, The Comcast Network.

Prior to moving to New Jersey, Jones worked at the *Central Daily Times* (State College, Pa.), where she was the beat writer for Penn State football and men's basketball.

A native of Dallastown, Pa., Jones graduated from Penn State with a B.A. in Journalism and an M.S. in Exercise and Sport Science. Following graduation, she completed an internship in the communications department of the Big Ten Conference in suburban Chicago.

Al Leiter

Entering his sixth year with the YES Network, former Yankees pitcher Al Leiter serves as color commentator, providing viewers with insight gained from his 19 years as a player in the Major Leagues. Prior to signing with YES, Leiter had worked as a postseason game analyst for FOX Sports and ESPN.

Originally drafted by the Yankees in 1984, Leiter played parts of 19 professional seasons with the Yankees (1987-89, 2005), Toronto Blue Jays (1989-95), Florida Marlins (1996-97, 2005) and New York Mets (1998-2004). A two-time All-Star (1996, 2000), he was a part of two world championship teams (Toronto in 1993 and Florida in 1997) and became the first pitcher in history to record a victory against all 30 Major League teams. On May 11, 1996, Leiter tossed the first no-hitter in Marlins history in an 11-0 win vs. Colorado.

A native of Bayville, N.J., Leiter has been nearly as busy off the field as he was on it. Since 1996, he has donated more than $1.5 million to various charities in the New York area and South Florida. In 2000, he was honored by Major League Baseball with the Roberto Clemente Award for his contributions to the community and in 2002, he was appointed to the board of directors of the Twin Towers Fund in New York City. He was named the March of Dimes "Sportsman of the Year" in 2003 and the John V. Mara "Sportsman of the Year" in 2004 by the Catholic Youth Organization. With his wife, Lori, he created "Leiter's Landing," a charitable organization committed to the betterment of youth through education, health care and social and community service. Leiter has also been the recipient of numerous other awards and honors as a result of his charity work, including the 2008 "Breakthrough Spirit Award" at the Children's Cancer and Blood Foundation gala in New York City.

Paul O'Neill

Paul O'Neill returns for his 10th consecutive season in broadcast television in 2011, serving as a game analyst for the YES Network.

The five-time All-Star outfielder played 17 years in the Majors, spending his final nine seasons in pinstripes. He appeared in six World Series, winning five titles, including four with the Yankees (1996, '98-2000).

Affectionately known as a "warrior" to most Yankees followers, O'Neill began his Major League career in 1985 with the Cincinnati Reds and earned the first of his five World Series championships in 1990. He joined the Yankees in 1993 after eight great seasons with the Reds, and in 1994 claimed the American League batting title with a .359 average. From July 1995 to May 1997, he played in 235 consecutive games in right field without making an error. In 2001, at the age of 38, O'Neill became the oldest player in Major League history to steal 20 bases and hit 20 home runs in the same season.

He lives in his native Cincinnati with his wife, Nevalee, and their three children: Andrew, Aaron and Alexandra. He was named the "Father of the Year" in June 2008 by the National Father's Day Council at its 67th Annual Father of the Year dinner in New York.

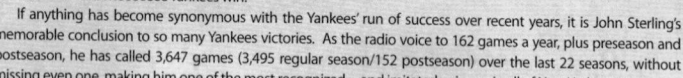

Yankees Broadcasters

WCBS
NEWSRADIO
880

John Sterling

"Yankees win! Theeeeeee Yankees win!"

If anything has become synonymous with the Yankees' run of success over recent years, it is John Sterling's memorable conclusion to so many Yankees victories. As the radio voice to 162 games a year, plus preseason and postseason, he has called 3,647 games (3,495 regular season/152 postseason) over the last 22 seasons, without missing even one, making him one of the most recognized—and imitated voices—in all of New York sports.

Sterling joined the Yankees broadcast team in 1989 from Atlanta's TBS and WSB Radio, where he called Hawks basketball (1981-89) and Braves games (1982-87). It marked a return to the town where he first achieved fame, hosting a talk show on WMCA from 1971-78, and calling the Nets (1975-80, and as a fill-in, in 1997) and Islanders (1975-78) for WMCA ,WVNJ, WWOR-TV and SportsChannel.

Sterling also previously broadcasted Morgan State Football (eight years) and Washington Bullets basketball in 1981. In addition to his seven years at WMCA and a year at WSB in Atlanta, he has also hosted talk shows on WFAN and WABC in New York. He has not missed a broadcast since the fall of 1981.

As the host of the YES Network's acclaimed *Yankeeography* series, Sterling has won a total of nine Emmy Awards since 2003. He has also been honored by the New Jersey Sportswriters Association with its Radio-TV Excellence Award (1999), and was the winner of the 2001 Whitney Radio Jimmy Cannon Award. In addition, his call of a Jason Giambi home run on WCBS radio in 2002 was voted the "Best Baseball Call" of the year in a poll conducted by MLB.com. In 2002, Sterling was also honored by the NY Air Awards for being a part of the best play-by-play team on radio.

When he's not in the booth, Sterling serves as a master of on-field ceremonies for major Yankees events, and is well known for his emcee work at City Hall (with his former radio partner Michael Kay) at "Key to the City" ceremonies following Yankees World Series victories.

Sterling enjoys attending Broadway shows and boasts an extensive knowledge of the lyrics to many American pop standards. In 2007, he embarked on his own Broadway venture in a cabaret show titled "Baseball and Broadway" in which he both served as emcee and sang alongside broadway talent.

For the past 18 years, he has been a spokesman for the Leukemia Society of America. He enjoys reading, movies and swimming. He lives in Bergen County, N.J., and is the proud father of four children: daughter Abigail and triplets, Veronica, Bradford and Derek.

Suzyn Waldman

Award-winning journalist Suzyn Waldman begins her 25th season either covering or broadcasting the New York Yankees. She joined John Sterling in the radio booth in 2005 as the Yankees' color commentator on WCBS-AM radio, becoming the first woman to hold a full-time position as a Major League broadcaster.

Waldman has spent more than two decades overcoming all the obstacles that go along with being a female sports broadcaster and has risen to the top of her profession. In 2006, she became a permanent part of the "Women in Baseball" exhibit at the Hall of Fame in Cooperstown, and in 2009, her World Series Game 6 scorecard was added to the Hall of Fame's collection, commemorating her being the first female broadcaster to call game action in the World Series.

In 1987, Waldman became the first female voice heard on WFAN-AM in New York, the first all-sports radio station in the country. She was a mainstay on that station for almost 15 years, creating the job of the radio beat reporter, covering both the New York Yankees and New York Knicks. Her news-breaking reports, exclusive interviews and always original and controversial opinions won her countless journalism awards. Her accolades include the "International Radio Award" for her live and emotional reporting from the upper deck of Candlestick Park during the 1989 San Francisco earthquake, the 1996 "NY Sportscaster of the Year" Award from the National Sportscasters & Sportswriters and the 1999 "Star Award" for radio from the American Women in Radio and TV. Waldman became a popular talk show host at WFAN and co-hosted the coveted midday slot until leaving WFAN in 2002 to join the YES Network.

The word "first" invariably precedes the name of Suzyn Waldman in every facet of her television and radio career. The first woman to work on a nationally-televised baseball broadcast, Waldman added another first, being the first woman to provide play-by-play for a Major League team, when she started broadcasting New York Yankees games for WPIX, MSG Network and WNYW/FOX5 in the mid 1990s. The first woman ever to host an NBA pre-and post-game show, Suzyn worked in that capacity for the New York Knicks on WFAN, provided play-by-play for the WNBA on Lifetime TV and was an analyst on St. John's basketball games for MSG and WFAN.

She has been honored by countless organizations, including the Thurman Munson Foundation, the March of Dimes, B'nai B'rith, the Jimmy Fund of Boston and the US Federal Women's Program. In 2006, she received the first Women's Global Health Award from the Albert Einstein College of Medicine at the United Nations. She is a tireless motivational speaker at schools and cancer centers around the country, encouraging young women to pursue their dreams despite any pitfalls they may encounter.

Waldman's life and accomplishments have been the subject of hundreds of magazine and newspaper articles, and chapters in children's and motivational books. She has been profiled on the *Today Show*, *CBS Evening News with Dan Rather*, ABC's *20/20* and NBC's *Dateline*.

A native Bostonian with a degree in Economics from Boston's prestigious Simmons College, Suzyn spent 15 years on the Broadway Musical Stage and performed in countless night clubs around the world. She is proudest of her two years starring opposite Richard Kiley in *Man of La Mancha*. She lives in Westchester with her German Shepherds, Gatsby and A.J.

Carlos Silva

Carlos Silva, a native of Caracas, Venezuela, enters his sixth season producing and engineering Yankees games for WCBS Radio 880 AM (Spanish and English). The 2011 season will mark his 11th year working on Yankees radio broadcasts and his 22nd overall season in baseball. Silva has also worked for ESPN Radio, Phillies Spanish radio as well the NBA's Orlando Magic and New Jersey Nets. He is also responsible for the translations and recording of Spanish broadcast spots throughout the season.

In the offseason, he resides in Tampa, Fla., with his wife, Teresa, and his children Leslie , Kimberly and Matthew .

Yankees en Español

For the 15th consecutive season, the Yankees – in conjunction with WCBS radio – will provide Spanish radio and SAP (second audio programming) for game broadcasts.

Beto Villa

Beto Villa, a native of Caracas, Venezuela, has been broadcasting the Yankees since the beginning of the club's Spanish radio network in 1997, becoming one of the most recognized voices in baseball. The 2011 season will mark Villa's 15th as the "Spanish voice of the New York Yankees." His famous home run call: "*¡La bola va atrás, se va, se va, se va, se vaaaaaaaaaa…se fue de cuadrangular…jonrón de…!*" has made him very popular in the tri-state area and around the world.

Beto provides Spanish listeners with thorough and thoughtful Yankees coverage. He treasures his pages and pages of statistics of Latin American ballplayers, which he uses during his radiocasts. After beginning his career in 1981, he has had the opportunity to broadcast both the Major League World Series and the Caribbean World Series. He is currently a Senior Editor of Latinobaseball.com, a Web site covering Latin American players in the Majors and Winter Leagues. Beto has a daughter, Margarita.

Francisco Rivera

Since 1995, Francisco Rivera has been involved in baseball as a color commentator and play-by-play announcer, including six years in the Yankees' broadcast booth. A native of Morovis, Puerto Rico, he covered the Philadelphia Phillies for "Radio Tropical" from 1995 to 1998 and worked the American League Championship Series in 2003 and 2004 for ESPN. Rivera received his Bachelors Degree in Spanish Literature from Rutgers University and graduated from the Cambridge University-affiliated Miguel Angel Torres School of Communications in Manhattan in 1978. He was one of the pioneers of the talk show *WADO Deportivo* where he worked until 2003, and began his communications career covering NBA basketball for WADO.

Felix DeJesus

Felix DeJesus, a native New Yorker, enters his sixth season as a back-up commentator for the New York Yankees. He also serves as a Yankees correspondent for WCBS, writes for *Listin Diario* and is one of the co-hosts of *El Mundo de Las Grandes Ligas*, an internet show on MLB Radio.

DeJesus has been involved with the Hispanic market since 1993 when he became the color commentator for the NHL's Florida Panthers. He has worked in all areas of broadcasting, television, radio and the Internet. From 1998 to 2004, he covered Major League Baseball on television for XTRA Innings in New York. He covered the Caribbean World Series in 2002 for New York's Radio Unica 1660 AM and served as one of the play-by-play voices for the international broadcast of the 2007 Caribbean Series. He has also worked for FOX Sports, ESPN International and CNN. In 1999, he became the first announcer to broadcast in SAP for NBC News. DeJesus has also served the last five years as the Spanish language translator for Showtime Championship Boxing.

DeJesus graduated from Fordham University in 1988 with a degree in Economics and currently resides in the tri-state area. He and his wife, Melissa, have three children, Christopher, Brendan and Giselle.

BATTING PRACTICE SCHEDULE AT YANKEE STADIUM				
Start Time	1:05 p.m.	4:05 p.m.	7:05 p.m.	8:05 p.m.
Yankees Hit	10:40-11:40	1:40-2:40	4:40-5:40	5:40-6:40
Visitors Hit	11:40-12:40	2:40-3:20	5:40-6:20	6:40-7:20
Yankees Infield	12:20-12:30	3:20-3:30	6:20-6:30	7:20-7:30
Visitors Infield	12:30-12:40	3:30-3:40	6:30-6:40	7:30-7:40

New York Yankees Broadcast Teams - Radio & TV

(Rightsholders in parentheses)

1939 (WABC) Arch McDonald, Garnett Marks and Mel Allen
1940 (WABC) Mel Allen and J. C. Flippen
1941 No games broadcast
1942 (WOR) Mel Allen and Connie Desmond
1943 No games broadcast
1944 (WINS) Don Dunphy and Bill Slater
1945 (WINS) Bill Slater and Al Helfer
1946 (WINS) Mel Allen and Russ Hodges
1947 (WINS) Mel Allen and Russ Hodges
1948 (WINS) Mel Allen and Russ Hodges
1949 (WINS radio, Dumont TV) Mel Allen and Curt Gowdy
1950 (WINS radio, Dumont TV) Mel Allen and Curt Gowdy
1951 (WINS radio, WPIX TV) Mel Allen and Art Gleeson
1952 (WINS radio, WPIX TV) Mel Allen, Art Gleeson and Bill Crowley
1953 (WINS radio, WPIX TV) Mel Allen, Jim Woods and Joe E. Brown
1954 (WINS radio, WPIX TV) Mel Allen, Jim Woods and Red Barber
1955 (WINS radio, WPIX TV) Mel Allen, Jim Woods and Red Barber
1956 (WINS radio, WPIX TV) Mel Allen, Jim Woods and Red Barber
1957 (WINS radio, WPIX TV) Mel Allen, Red Barber and Phil Rizzuto
1958 (WMGM radio, WPIX TV) Mel Allen, Red Barber and Phil Rizzuto
1959 (WMGM radio, WPIX TV) Mel Allen, Red Barber and Phil Rizzuto
1960 (WMGM radio, WPIX TV) Mel Allen, Red Barber and Phil Rizzuto
1961 (WCBS radio, WPIX TV) Mel Allen, Red Barber and Phil Rizzuto
1962 (WCBS radio, WPIX TV) Mel Allen, Red Barber and Phil Rizzuto
1963 (WCBS radio, WPIX TV) Mel Allen, Red Barber, Phil Rizzuto and Jerry Coleman
1964 (WCBS radio, WPIX TV) Mel Allen, Red Barber, Phil Rizzuto and Jerry Coleman
1965 (WCBS radio, WPIX TV) Red Barber, Phil Rizzuto, Jerry Coleman and Joe Garagiola
1966 (WCBS radio, WPIX TV) Red Barber, Phil Rizzuto, Joe Garagiola and Jerry Coleman
1967 (WHN radio, WPIX TV) Phil Rizzuto, Jerry Coleman and Joe Garagiola
1968 (WHN radio, WPIX TV) Phil Rizzuto, Jerry Coleman and Frank Messer
1969 (WHN radio, WPIX TV) Phil Rizzuto, Jerry Coleman, Frank Messer and Whitey Ford
1970 (WHN radio, WPIX TV) Phil Rizzuto, Frank Messer, Whitey Ford and Bob Gamere
1971 (WMCA radio, WPIX TV) Phil Rizzuto, Frank Messer, Bill White and Whitey Ford
1972 (WMCA radio, WPIX TV) Phil Rizzuto, Frank Messer and Bill White
1973 (WMCA radio, WPIX TV) Phil Rizzuto, Frank Messer and Bill White
1974 (WMCA radio, WPIX TV) Phil Rizzuto, Frank Messer and Bill White
1975 (WMCA radio, WPIX TV) Phil Rizzuto, Frank Messer, Bill White and Dom Valentino
1976 (WMCA radio, WPIX TV) Phil Rizzuto, Frank Messer and Bill White
1977 (WMCA radio, WPIX TV) Phil Rizzuto, Frank Messer and Bill White
1978 (WINS radio, WPIX TV) Phil Rizzuto, Frank Messer, Bill White, Mel Allen and Fran Healy
1979 (WINS radio, WPIX TV, Sports Channel) Phil Rizzuto, Frank Messer, Bill White, Mel Allen and Fran Healy
1980 (WINS radio, WPIX TV, Sports Channel) Phil Rizzuto, Frank Messer, Bill White, Mel Allen and Fran Healy
1981 (WABC radio, WPIX TV, Sports Channel) Phil Rizzuto, Frank Messer, Bill White, Mel Allen and Fran Healy
1982 (WABC radio, WPIX TV, Sports Channel) Phil Rizzuto, Frank Messer, Bill White, Mel Allen and John Gordon
1983 (WABC radio, WPIX TV, Sports Channel) Mel Allen, Phil Rizzuto, Frank Messer, Bill White and John Gordon
1984 (WABC radio, WPIX TV, Sports Channel) Mel Allen, Phil Rizzuto, Frank Messer, Bill White and John Gordon
1985 (WABC radio, WPIX TV, Sports Channel) Phil Rizzuto, Bill White, Frank Messer, Mel Allen, Mickey Mantle, John Gordon and Spencer Ross
1986 (WABC radio, WPIX TV, Sports Channel) Phil Rizzuto, Bill White, Jim Kaat, Billy Martin, Mel Allen, Mickey Mantle, John Gordon, Spencer Ross and Bobby Murcer
1987 (WABC radio, WPIX TV, Sports Channel) Phil Rizzuto, Bill White, Billy Martin, Ken "Hawk" Harrelson, Bobby Murcer, Mickey Mantle, Spencer Ross, Hank Greenwald and Tommy Hutton
1988 (WABC radio, WPIX TV, Sports Channel) Phil Rizzuto, Bill White, Ken "Hawk" Harrelson, Hank Greenwald, Bobby Murcer, Mickey Mantle, Ed Randall and Tommy Hutton
1989 (WABC radio, WPIX TV, MSG NETWORK) Phil Rizzuto, George Grande, Tom Seaver, Tommy Hutton, Bobby Murcer, Lou Piniella, Greg Gumbel, Michael Kay, John Sterling and Jay Johnstone
1990 (WABC radio, WPIX TV, MSG NETWORK) Phil Rizzuto, George Grande, Tom Seaver, Dewayne Staats, Tony Kubek, Al Trautwig, Michael Kay, John Sterling and Jay Johnstone

1967 Yankees broadcast team (from left): Jerry Coleman, Phil Rizzuto and Joe Garagiola

1991 (WABC radio, WPIX TV, MSG NETWORK) Phil Rizzuto, Bobby Murcer, Tom Seaver, Dewayne Staats, Tony Kubek, Al Trautwig, Michael Kay, John Sterling and Joe Angel
1992 (WABC radio, WPIX TV, MSG NETWORK) Phil Rizzuto, Bobby Murcer, Tom Seaver, Dewayne Staats, Tony Kubek, Al Trautwig, John Sterling and Michael Kay
1993 (WABC radio, WPIX TV, MSG NETWORK) Phil Rizzuto, Bobby Murcer, Tom Seaver, Dewayne Staats, Tony Kubek, Al Trautwig, John Sterling and Michael Kay
1994 (WABC radio, WPIX TV, MSG NETWORK) Phil Rizzuto, Dewayne Staats, Tony Kubek, Al Trautwig, John Sterling and Michael Kay
1995 (WABC radio, WPIX TV, MSG NETWORK) Phil Rizzuto, Bobby Murcer, Paul Olden, Dave Cohen, Jim Kaat, Al Trautwig, Steve Palermo, John Sterling and Michael Kay
1996 (WABC radio, WPIX TV, MSG NETWORK) Phil Rizzuto, Bobby Murcer, Rick Cerone, Paul Olden, Dave Cohen, Jim Kaat, Al Trautwig, Steve Palermo, John Sterling and Michael Kay
1997 (WABC radio, WPIX TV, MSG NETWORK) Jim Kaat, Ken Singleton, Bobby Murcer, Al Trautwig, Michael Kay, Rick Cerone, Steve Palermo, Suzyn Waldman, John Sterling and Michael Kay
1998 (WABC radio, WPIX TV, MSG NETWORK) Bobby Murcer, Jim Kaat, Ken Singleton, Bobby Murcer, Al Trautwig, Tommy John, Suzyn Waldman, John Sterling and Michael Kay
1999 (WABC radio, WNYW TV, MSG NETWORK) Tim McCarver, Bobby Murcer, Jim Kaat, Ken Singleton, Al Trautwig, Suzyn Waldman, John Sterling and Michael Kay
2000 (WABC radio, WNYW TV, MSG Network) Tim McCarver, Bobby Murcer, Jim Kaat, Ken Singleton, Al Trautwig, Suzyn Waldman, John Sterling and Michael Kay
2001 (WABC radio, WNYW TV, MSG NETWORK) Tim McCarver, Bobby Murcer, Jim Kaat, Ken Singleton, Al Trautwig, Suzyn Waldman, John Sterling and Michael Kay
2002 (WCBS radio, WCBS TV, YES NETWORK) Fred Hickman, Jim Kaat, Michael Kay, Bobby Murcer, Paul O'Neill, Ken Singleton, Suzyn Waldman, Charley Steiner and John Sterling
2003 (WCBS radio, WCBS TV, YES NETWORK) Fred Hickman, Jim Kaat, Michael Kay, Bobby Murcer, Paul O'Neill, Ken Singleton, Suzyn Waldman, Charley Steiner and John Sterling
2004 (WCBS radio, WCBS TV, YES NETWORK) Joe Girardi, Fred Hickman, Jim Kaat, Michael Kay, Bobby Murcer, Paul O'Neill, Ken Singleton, Suzyn Waldman, Charley Steiner and John Sterling
2005 (WCBS radio, WWOR TV, YES NETWORK) Jim Kaat, Michael Kay, Bobby Murcer, Paul O'Neill, Ken Singleton, Suzyn Waldman and John Sterling
2006 (WCBS radio, WWOR TV, YES NETWORK) Kimberly Jones, David Justice, Jim Kaat, Michael Kay, Bobby Murcer, Paul O'Neill, Ken Singleton, Suzyn Waldman and John Sterling
2007 (WCBS radio, WWOR TV, YES NETWORK) Michael Kay, Ken Singleton, Bobby Murcer, David Justice, Joe Girardi, John Flaherty, Kimberly Jones, Paul O'Neill, Al Leiter , Suzyn Waldman and John Sterling
2008 (WCBS radio, WWOR TV, YES NETWORK) Michael Kay, Ken Singleton, Bobby Murcer, David Cone, John Flaherty, Kimberly Jones, Paul O'Neill, Al Leiter, Suzyn Waldman and John Sterling
2009 (WCBS radio, WWOR TV, YES NETWORK) Michael Kay, Ken Singleton, David Cone, John Flaherty, Kimberly Jones, Paul O'Neill, Al Leiter, Suzyn Waldman and John Sterling
2010 (WCBS radio, WWOR TV, YES NETWORK) Michael Kay, Ken Singleton, John Flaherty, Kimberly Jones, Paul O'Neill, Al Leiter, Suzyn Waldman and John Sterling
2011 (WCBS radio, WWOR TV, YES NETWORK) Michael Kay, Ken Singleton, Jack Curry, John Flaherty, Kimberly Jones, Paul O'Neill, Al Leiter, Suzyn Waldman and John Sterling

Bring the Best of the Indoors...*Outdoors!*

Bring home theater-quality viewing to your backyard with Model 5510HD,
a 55-inch full-HD 1080p 120Hz LCD TV - Photo Credit: CentralCoastAV.com

SunBriteTV. *All-Weather Outdoor LCD HD TV*

New! *Model 4630HD is a 46-inch full-HD 1080P LCD TV designed with
an ASA outdoor-rated plastic resin exterior and integrated speakers.*

www.sunbritetv.com
866.357.8688

With SunBriteTV, you can now watch your favorite sport in the comfort of your own back yard. Worried about the weather? Relax! These TVs are designed for permanent outdoor installation. That means they withstand rain, dust, insects and extreme temperature ranges from -24° up to +122° F.

Concerned about durability? No reason! SunBriteTV's all-weather outdoor TVs have the longest history of proven product durability and reliability. They have been time-tested in backyards across America since 2004.

And, with 22-, 32,- 46- and 55-inch HD LCD screen sizes and a full complement of all-weather mounting solutions, you'll find the perfect fit for your balcony, patio, gazebo and/or outdoor room!

George M. Steinbrenner Field

This year marks the 16th season the Yankees will play their spring training games at George M. Steinbrenner Field in Tampa, Fla. The complex has also served as the home of the Single-A Tampa Yankees of the Florida State League since it opened in 1996. The field's dimensions are an exact replica of Yankee Stadium in the Bronx, measuring 318 feet down the left line, 408 feet to center field and 314 feet down the right field line. In 2008, the addition of the *Tampa Tribune* Deck in right field expanded the Stadium's capacity to 11,076, making it the largest spring training facility in the Grapefruit League.

Fans will also notice another link to the Bronx with replicas of the Yankees' retired numbers placards from Yankee Stadium greeting them as they enter the complex.

Originally opened in 1996 as Legends Field, the complex was renamed in honor of the late Yankees' Principal Owner and Chairman prior to the Yankees' March 27, 2008, spring training game against the Pittsburgh Pirates. On February 14, 2008, Hal and Hank Steinbrenner announced that the New York Yankees would rename the facility George M. Steinbrenner Field. The name change followed two unanimous resolutions recommending and supporting the change from the Hillsborough County Commission and the Tampa City Council.

"I am humbled and flattered to have this outstanding and totally unexpected honor conferred on me,"

said George M. Steinbrenner at the time the resolution was passed. "I extend my thanks to the Tampa City Council and to the Hillsborough County Commissioners for passing resolutions suggesting and recommending the change. I also thank my family for supporting the renaming of the stadium and for everything they have done for so many years that helped bring about this great day "

The resolution passed by the Tampa City Council on February 7, 2008, cited Mr. Steinbrenner's many charitable donations on behalf of youth activities, hospitals and the arts. The resolution passed by the Board of the Hillsborough County Commissioners on February 6, 2008, recognized Mr. Steinbrenner's numerous extraordinary contributions to the area.

STADIUM CAPACITY

Total Seating	11,076
Rooms To Go Luxury Suites	13 suites, 290 seats
Field Box Seats	161
Bright House Networks Dugout Club	104
Tampa Tribune Deck	539
Reserved Seats	9,982
FIRST GAME:	3/1/96 vs. Cleveland
LARGEST CROWD:	11,120 – 3/18/10 vs. Tampa Bay

STADIUM DIMENSIONS*

Left Field foul line	318 feet
Center Field	408 feet
Right Field foul line	314 feet

* Identical to Yankee Stadium

Spring Training Records Since 1962

Year	Record	Year	Record	Year	Record
1962	17-10	1979	7-18	1996	16-15
1963	12-17-1	1980	10-8-1	1997	20-11
1964	12-16	1981	13-13-1	1998	15-12
1965	12-18	1982	9-16	1999	14-19
1966	17-11	1983	16-8	2000	13-20
1967	13-17	1984	10-16	2001	9-20
1968	14-14-1	1985	15-12	2002	20-14
1969	16-9	1986	17-11	2003	15-13
1970	18-9	1987	14-15	2004	13-9
1971	8-23	1988	22-10	2005	14-15
1972	11-15-1	1989	16-15	2006	15-16
1973	18-11	1990	5-9	2007	14-13-3
1974	14-14-1	1991	19-12	2008	14-12-2
1975	14-17	1992	17-14	2009	24-10-1
1976	10-7	1993	20-12	2010	13-15-1
1977	11-13	1994	12-15-1		
1978	10-13	1995	11-18/4-8		

2011 Yankees Spring Training Schedule

Day/date	Opponent	Site	Time	TV/RADIO
Sat., Feb. 26	**Philadelphia**	**GMS Field**	**1:05 p.m.**	**YES/WCBS**
Sun., Feb 27	Philadelphia	at Clearwater	1:05 p.m.	YES
Mon., Feb. 28	Detroit	at Lakeland	1:05 p.m.	
Tue., Mar. 1	Pittsburgh	at Bradenton	1:05 p.m.	
Wed., Mar. 2	**Houston**	**GMS Field**	**1:05 p.m.**	**YES**
Thur., Mar. 3	Tampa Bay	at Port Charlotte	1:05 p.m.	
Fri., Mar. 4	**Boston**	**GMS Field**	**7:05 p.m.**	**YES/WCBS**
Sat., Mar. 5	**Washington**	**GMS Field**	**1:05 p.m.**	**WCBS**
Sun., Mar. 6	Houston	at Kissimmee	1:05 p.m.	
Mon., Mar. 7	**Philadelphia (ss)**	**GMS Field**	**1:05 p.m.**	**YES**
	Baltimore (ss)	at Sarasota	7:05 p.m.	
Tue., Mar. 8	Atlanta	at Lake Buena Vista	1:05 p.m.	YES
Wed., Mar. 9	**Pittsburgh**	**GMS Field**	**7:05 p.m.**	
Thur., Mar. 10	Philadelphia	at Clearwater	1:05 p.m.	
Fri., Mar. 11	**Atlanta (ss)**	**GMS Field**	**1:05 p.m.**	**YES**
	Toronto (ss)	at Dunedin	1:05 p.m.	
Sat., Mar. 12	Washington	at Viera	1:05 p.m.	
Sun., Mar. 13	**Minnesota**	**GMS Field**	**1:05 p.m.**	**YES/WCBS**
Mon., Mar. 14	Boston	at Ft. Myers	7:05 p.m.	
Tue., Mar. 15	Off Day			
Wed., Mar. 16	**Baltimore**	**GMS Field**	**7:05 p.m.**	**YES/WCBS**
Thur., Mar. 17	**Tampa Bay**	**GMS Field**	**7:05 p.m.**	
Fri., Mar. 18	Toronto	at Dunedin	1:05 p.m.	
Sat., Mar. 19	**Toronto**	**GMS Field**	**1:05 p.m.**	**YES/WCBS**
Sun., Mar. 20	Philadelphia	at Clearwater	1:05 p.m.	WCBS
Mon., Mar. 21	Tampa Bay	at Port Charlotte	7:05 p.m.	
Tue., Mar. 22	Baltimore	at Sarasota	1:05 p.m.	YES
Wed., Mar. 23	**Toronto**	**GMS Field**	**7:05 p.m.**	
Thur., Mar. 24	Off Day			
Fri., Mar. 25	**Houston**	**GMS Field**	**7:05 p.m.**	
Sat., Mar. 26	**Pittsburgh**	**GMS Field**	**1:05 p.m.**	**YES/WCBS**
Sun., Mar. 27	Minnesota	at Ft. Myers	1:05 p.m.	
Mon., Mar. 28	**Tampa Bay**	**GMS Field**	**7:05 p.m.**	**YES**
Tue., Mar. 29	**Detroit**	**GMS Field**	**1:05 p.m.**	**YES**

Bold=Home Games ss=Split Squad *All Times Eastern and Subject to Change*

Frank Hiller pitches to Tommy Henrich during 1949 Spring Training in San Juan, Puerto Rico.

2010 SPRING TRAINING ATTENDANCE
Home Attendance at GMS Field in Tampa, FL (14 dates, 10,540 average)............147,557
Road Attendance (15 dates/8,377 average) 125,659
Overall Attendance (29 dates/9,421 average)...273,216

SPRING TRAINING HOME ATTENDANCE SINCE 1996	
1996	173,247
1997	172,092
1998	149,496
1999	164,015
2000	153,385
2001	173,107
2002	172,544
2003	162,890
2004	122,374
2005	152,640
2006	152,024
2007	154,590
2008	139,496
2009	168,905
2010	147,557

Yankees All-Time Spring Training Sites

Year	Location
1903-04	Atlanta, GA
1905	Montgomery, AL
1906	Birmingham, AL
1907-08	Atlanta, GA
1909	Macon, GA
1910-11	Athens, GA
1912	Atlanta, GA
1913	Hamilton, Bermuda
1914	Houston, TX
1915	Savannah, GA
1916-18	Macon, GA
1919-20	Jacksonville, FL
1921	Shreveport, LA
1922-24	New Orleans, LA
1925-42	St. Petersburg, FL
1943	Asbury Park, NJ
1944-45	Atlantic City, NJ
1946-50	St. Petersburg, FL
1951	Phoenix, AZ
1952-61	St. Petersburg, FL
1962-95	Ft. Lauderdale, FL
1996-present	Tampa, FL

2011 New York Yankees Schedule

MARCH/APRIL

2011 PRELIMINARY SCHEDULE IS EFFECTIVE AS OF FEBRUARY 2011;
OPPONENTS, GAME DATES, AND CLUB ROSTERS
AND LINEUPS ARE SUBJECT TO CHANGE.

JULY

MAY

AUGUST

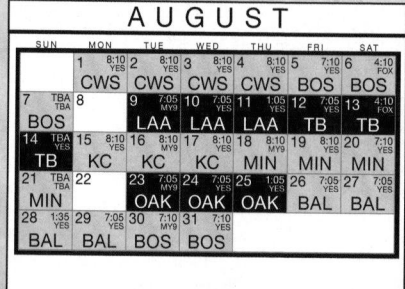

JUNE

OLD-TIMERS' DAY IS JUNE 26.
CEREMONIES BEGIN AT 11:15 A.M. ON THE YES NETWORK

SEPTEMBER

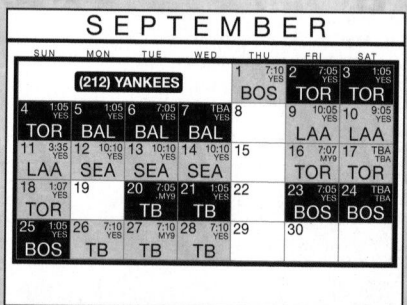

 HOME 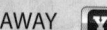 AWAY

ALL GAMES ARE EASTERN TIME

FOR YANKEES TICKET INFORMATION, PLEASE VISIT YANKEES.COM OR CALL (212) YANKEES

Game times listed as TBA are subject to determination by Major League Baseball and its television partners.

All seat locations are subject to availability.

Time, opponent, date and team rosters and lineups, including the Yankees' roster and lineup, are subject to change.

Tickets may not be used by the ticket holder/licensee or anyone else other than the Yankees for advertising, promotion or other commercial purposes, including, without limitation, contests, auctions, sweepstakes and giveaways.

NOTICE: All persons specifically consent to and are subject to metal detector and physical pat-down inspections prior to entry. Any person or property that could affect the safety of Yankee Stadium occupants/property shall be denied entry.

WARNING: During all batting practices, fielding practices, warm-ups and the course of the game and postseason game experience, hard hit baseballs and bats and fragments thereof may be thrown or hit into the stands, concourses and concessions areas. For everyone's safety, please stay alert and be aware of your surroundings. Any guest who is concerned with his or her seat location should contact any guest services representative for an alternate seat location.

Be advised that the Yankees reserve the right to take appropriate action against individuals who fraudulently obtain wheelchair accessible and companion seats, including, without limitation, ejection and legal action.

Distribution of promotional items is for fans in attendance only, while supplies last. Promotion dates, items and distribution are subject to change and/or cancellation.